Thinking About
PSYCHOLOGY
The Science of Mind and Behavior

Fourth Edition

Thinking About
PSYCHOLOGY
The Science of Mind and Behavior

Fourth Edition

Charles T. Blair-Broeker
Hawkeye Community College, Iowa

Randal M. Ernst
Nebraska Wesleyan University, Nebraska

Special Consultant
David G. Myers
Hope College, Michigan

SAKIstyle/BLOOMimage/Getty Images

 bedford, freeman & worth
high school publishers

Boston | New York

Bedford, Freeman & Worth
High School Publishers

Senior Vice President, Content Strategy: Charles Linsmeier
Vice President and General Manager, High School: Paul Altier
Senior Program Director, High School: Ann Heath
Senior Developmental Editor: Heidi Bamatter
Editorial Assistant: Carla Duval
Media Editor: Kim Morté
Senior Media Project Manager: Jodi Isman
Senior Marketing Manager: Janie Pierce-Bratcher
Marketing Assistant: Kelly Noll
Director, Content Management Enhancement: Tracey Kuehn
Senior Managing Editor: Lisa Kinne
Senior Project Manager: Matt Gervais, Lumina Datamatics, Inc.
Senior Content Project Manager: Won McIntosh
Senior Workflow Project Manager: Jennifer Wetzel
Production Supervisor: Brianna Lester
Senior Photo Editor: Sheena Goldstein
Photo Researcher: Julie Tesser
Director of Design, Content Management: Diana Blume
Design Services Manager: Natasha Wolfe
Cover Designer: John Callahan
Interior Designer: Patrice Sheridan
Art Manager: Matthew McAdams
Illustrations: Monika Suteski, Jesse Ewing, David Chen
Composition: Lumina Datamatics, Inc.
Printing and Binding: Transcontinental Printing
Cover Photo: SAKIstyle/BLOOMimage/Getty Images
Design Image/Icon: COOL STUFF/Shutterstock, VooDoo13/Shutterstock, Oksana Telesheva/Shutterstock, VectorPlotnikoff/Shutterstock, iperion/Shutterstock

Library of Congress Control Number: 2018963848

ISBN-13: 978-1-4641-8654-7
ISBN-10: 1-4641-8654-5

Printed in Canada
2 3 4 5 6 7   24 23 22 21 20 19

BFW/Worth Publishers
One New York Plaza
Suite 4600
New York, NY 10004-1562
highschool.bfwpub.com/thinkingaboutpsychology4e

*To the dedicated community of high school
psychology teachers who continuously strive to
teach well, nourish their students, and spark interest in
the fascinating and important science of psychology.*

Charlie

*To Dr. Teresa Wanser-Ernst, affectionately appreciative
of your encouragement, expertise, support and
love throughout the course of this project.*

Randy

ABOUT THE AUTHORS 🐾🐾🐾🐾🐾🐾🐾🐾🐾🐾🐾🐾🐾🐾

Charles Blair-Broeker taught at Cedar Falls (Iowa) High School for 36 years and now teaches part-time at Hawkeye Community College. Charlie has been involved in a number of American Psychological Association (APA) initiatives, serving as a member of the task force that authored the *National Standards for High School Psychology Curricula*, as the first elected chair of the Executive Board of Teachers of Psychology in Secondary Schools (TOPSS), as coeditor of the fourth volume of the *Activities Handbook for the Teaching of Psychology*, and as a member of the Steering Committees for the 2017 Summit on High School Psychology, the 2008 National Conference on Undergraduate Education in Psychology, and the 1999 National Forum on Psychology Partnerships. He has been a Test Developer, Question Leader, Rubric Master, Table Leader, or Reader for Advanced Placement Psychology since the test was first administered in 1992. He has given scores of presentations about the teaching of psychology across the nation. Among his teaching awards are the Grinnell College Outstanding College Teacher Award, the University of Iowa Distinguished Teaching Award, and the APA Division 2 Teaching Excellence Award. The TOPSS Charles T. Blair-Broeker Excellence in Teaching Award was named after him in 2014, the same year he received an APA Presidential Citation for "exemplary efforts to promote high-quality instruction of and professionalism in teaching high school psychology." He has been married for 40 joyous years to Lynn. Together, they keep up on the adventures of their kids Carl (married to Liz) and Eric (married to Brittany and father of Marin). Charlie plays pickleball most mornings with far more passion than precision.

Randy Ernst has been part of the high school psychology scene for over 30 years and is thankful to all who provided him opportunities along the way. In 2017, American Psychological Association (APA) President Antonio Puente awarded Randy a Presidential Citation for "pioneering leadership of modern day pedagogy of psychology." This honor was bestowed on Randy at the 2017 APA Summit on High School Psychology Education, an event Randy cochaired. The APA's Teachers of Psychology of Secondary Schools (TOPSS), which Randy helped found, recently honored him by establishing the Randal M. Ernst Lecture, given each year at the APA national convention. After serving on the initial AP® Psychology test development committee, Randy was the first high school teacher invited to be a Question Leader (and Exam Leader) at the AP® psychology Reading. He has cowritten articles published in numerous journals including *American Psychologist, Teaching of Psychology*, and *The Oxford Review of Education*. Randy has long been a proponent of flourishing and coined the phrase "Positive Education" while preparing a presentation on teaching well-being with Marty Seligman for the Australian Department of Education. Randy has worked for years as a resilience trainer with the University of Pennsylvania and as a cultural proficiency trainer with the Lincoln public schools, which named Randy its Multicultural Educator of the Year in 2016. Additional honors include the NAACP's Service to Children award, Nebraska's Social Studies Educator of the Year award, and Time-Warner's Crystal Apple National Teacher Award. His picture hangs in Broken Bow High School's Distinguished Alumni hall of fame. The APA and the University of Nebraska have also recognized Randy for excellence in teaching. Randy's bachelor's and master's degrees are from Nebraska Wesleyan University, and his doctorate is from the University of Nebraska. He is the proud father of Emily, Meredith, and Jocelyn.

... and special consultant

Hope College Public Relations

David Myers received his B.A. in chemistry from Whitworth University and his psychology Ph.D. from the University of Iowa. He has spent his career at Hope College in Michigan, where he has taught dozens of introductory psychology sections. Hope College students have invited him to be their commencement speaker and voted him outstanding professor.

David Myers has chaired his city's Human Relations Commission, helped found a thriving assistance center for families in poverty, and spoken worldwide to hundreds of college, community, and professional groups. He has also spoken to many high school groups, including AP® psychology conferences, an AP® psychology reading, Teachers of Psychology in Secondary Schools, the National Council for Social Studies Psychology Community, and the 2017 APA Summit on High School Psychology Education. David is the author of many textbooks on psychology, including the market leading, *Myers' Psychology for the AP® Course*. He has twice offered AP® psychology workshops in China, and he served on the APA's working group that created the 2010 revision of the *National Standards for High School Psychology Curricula*.

Content Advisors and Supplements Team

Creating this book is a team effort. Like so many human achievements, it is the product of a collective intelligence. For this edition, we were fortunate to collaborate closely with an expert Content Advisory Board throughout the development process. The Content Advisory Board understands the needs of the psychology teacher and student. They provided helpful direction on how to make the content relevant, engaging, and appropriate for a high school classroom. Board members provided sage guidance on key content, organizational and pedagogical issues, and ensured that assessments adequately test student understanding on core materials. We extend gratitude and admiration to each of these talented educators for their enduring contributions to the teaching of psychology.

Elizabeth (Liz) Yost Hammer
Xavier University of Louisiana
Teacher's Edition, Teacher's Resource Materials

Dr. Liz Yost Hammer is the director of the Center for the Advancement of Teaching and Faculty Development and a Kellogg Professor in Teaching at Xavier University of Louisiana. A social psychologist by training, she regularly teaches introductory psychology, research methods, health psychology, and human sexuality. Her research interests focus on the scholarship of teaching and learning, and she has contributed chapters to several books intended to enhance teaching preparation. In addition, she is a co-author of the textbook *Psychology Applied to Modern Life,* now in its twelfth edition. She is a past president of Psi Chi and a past treasurer of the Society for the Teaching of Psychology. She joined the AP® psychology Reading in 1998 and served as Chief Reader from 2012 to 2016.

Nancy Fenton
Adlai E. Stevenson High School, IL
Content Advisor

Nancy Fenton has taught high school psychology since 2004. She has served as a Reader and Table Leader at the AP® psychology Reading and as a College Board® consultant since 2014. She teaches AP® psychology at Adlai E. Stevenson High School and online for the Center for Talent Development at Northwestern University. Nancy was awarded the 2013 APA TOPSS Excellence in Teaching Award for dynamic teaching and commitment to the advancement of psychology, and has presented at regional and national conferences for AP® psychology teachers. Nancy is the co-author of the review book *AP® Psychology All Access,* co-author of the blog *Books for Psychology Class,* and co-author of the iScore5™ Psych app.

Amy Fineburg
Jefferson County Schools, AL
Accuracy Checker

An award-winning teacher, Dr. Amy Fineburg chaired the TOPSS Committee, served as a Reader and then Table Leader at the AP® psychology Reading, chaired the APA working group that created the 2010 *National Standards for High School Psychology Curricula,* and co-chaired the Steering Committee for the APA Summit for High School Psychology Education. She wrote the 2003 edition of the *Teacher's Guide for AP® Psychology.* She has contributed articles to AP® Central and is a frequent workshop presenter and consultant for AP® Coordinators for the College Board®. She has been an adjunct instructor in psychology at Samford University and in educational psychology for the University of Alabama. She is the Advanced Programs Specialist for Jefferson County Schools leading AP®, dual enrollment, and virtual learning programs for Alabama's second-largest school district.

Stephen Foley
The Linsly School, WV
Content Advisor, Labs

Stephen Foley has taught AP® psychology since 2013 and became involved with the AP® psychology exam as a Reader in 2018. In the summers, Stephen teaches cognitive psychology at The Johns Hopkins Center for Talented Youth. Stephen contributed to the American Psychological Association's 2017 Summit on High School Psychology Education on the *National Standards for High School Psychology Curricula* Strand, and he currently serves on the APA's *National Standards* Working Group.

Stephanie Franks
Springboro High School, OH
Content Advisor, Life Matters

Stephanie Franks has been teaching since 2005, currently teaching AP® Psychology and serving as Springboro High School's Social Studies Department Chair. She was selected to participate in the 2017 APA Summit on High School Education in Ogden, Utah, and has remained an active member of Strand 4, Assessment. She is an AP® Reader, the co-chair of the Ohio Psychology Teaching Conference, and a member of the EPIC steering committee for the University of Wisconsin–Green Bay. In 2016 she was selected as the Project Excellence Award Recipient for Warren County for her commitment to education.

Kent Korek
Germantown High School, WI
Lecture Slides

Kent Korek has taught psychology since 1978 and AP® psychology since its inception in 1992. Beginning in 2005, Kent has been invited annually to serve as a Reader or Table Leader for the AP® psychology Reading. Endorsed as a College Board® consultant in 2004, he has conducted numerous one-day workshops and week-long AP® summer institutes in the United States and Canada. Kent served on the AP® Psychology Development Committee from 2010 to 2014 and continues to write questions for the AP® psychology exam. Kent participated in the 2017 APA Summit on High School Psychology Education as part of the Technology and Online Learning Strand. He has been awarded the Herb Kohl Fellowship, recognizing teaching excellence and innovation in the State of Wisconsin.

Daria Schaffeld
Prospect High School, IL
Content Advisor

Daria Schaffeld, MA, has been teaching AP® Psychology, Psychology 1, and Psychology 2 at Prospect High School since the fall of 1996. She has dedicated her tenure to creating innovative and powerful lessons for her students as well as nurturing several student teachers. In November 2004, Daria assumed leadership of the National Council of the Social Studies Psychology Community and advocates for psychological science on the national stage. She presents each year at NCSS and at Chi-TOPSS. Daria was on the Steering Committee for the APA Summit For High School Psychology Education and was awarded the APA TOPSS Charles T. Blair-Broeker Excellence in Teaching Award in 2017.

Sejal Schullo
Glenbrook South High School, IL
Content Advisor

Sejal Schullo has been teaching AP® psychology since 2002. She has been a regular presenter at the National Council for the Social Studies annual conference and is assistant chair for the National Council for the Social Studies Psychology Community. She also participated in the 2017 APA Summit on High School Psychology Education and helped create resources needed for the teaching of psychology.

BRIEF CONTENTS

CONTENTS

READ THE TEXT and use the features to help grasp the big ideas.

Thinking About Psychology — Module 1

Welcome to the wonderful world of psychological science! We are Charlie and Randy, and we wrote this book to serve as the guide for your introductory tour of a fascinating field that attempts to understand the behaviors, thoughts, and emotions of people and animals. The book is an extension of our many years in the high school classroom, and our goal is to provide you, your classmates, and your teacher with the information you need to:

- master the sometimes surprising conclusions of psychology;
- learn how the scientific method is used to study behavior and thinking; and
- develop critical thinking skills that will enable you to evaluate claims about psychological issues you encounter in the media.

If you have a cell phone, you probably have it set to notify you through pushes or notifications when someone sends you a message or posts something to social media. Many also set their phones to notify them of breaking news. Here's a sample of the headlines from just one 24-hour news cycle:

"Advances in Depression Treatment Announced"
"More Single Parents as Divorce Rates Climb"
"Opioid Drug Overdoses Addressed by Review Panel"
"Foreign Nuclear Weapon Arsenal Considered Threat"
"Sexual Harassment Case Sent to Jury"
"Water Poisoning Said to Impair Brain Functioning"
"Supremacist Group Promotes Violence"
"School Shooting Stuns Community"
"Senator Calls Charges Fake News"

1

What is psychology all about? **Module 1** offers context for what to expect in this life-relevant course and explains the themes that connect the content. It also reviews the main subfields of psychology, called Domains, that provide the organization for the text.

DOMAIN 3

Development and Learning

Module 12
Prenatal and
Childhood Development
Module 13
Adolescence
Module 14
Adulthood and Aging
Module 15
Language Development

Module 16
Classical
Conditioning
Module 17
Operant Conditioning
Module 18
Observational Learning

Each Domain is divided into **short modules** to make it easy to read and study.

Prenatal and Childhood Development — Module 12

Whether learning to talk or learning how to put your toys away, growing up is not exactly child's play.

You are a genetic and environmental marvel. It only took you about 9 months to grow from the size of the dot on this i to a full-size (more or less) newborn baby. From the moment the egg from your mother and the sperm cell from your father united until the minute you were born, the cells that became you progressed through a delicate, predictable, and fantastic sequence of events. This sequence is virtually the same for all of us.

You are physically different than you were 5 or 6 years ago. If you compare your sixth-grade photo to a current one, you might even find the differences startling. These physical changes are obvious because you can see them, but you also differ in ways that are not so obvious. You think differently than you did in elementary school, and your emotions are more developed. Psychologists interested in these kinds of changes research *developmental psychology*, which studies physical, cognitive, emotional, and social changes from womb to tomb.

In this module (and in the next two as well), we will explore three fundamental issues in developmental psychology:

1. Continuity and stages—Is development a gradual, continuous process, like an elevator going up? Or is it a series of distinctly different stages, like the steps of a staircase?

2. Stability and change—Will the person you think of as the real you still be there in 2060, or will that person change dramatically as you move through adulthood?

3. Nature and nurture—How much of our development is a result of genetics (our nature), and how much is a result of environment (the nurturing we receive)?

Let's search for answers to these questions as we take a look at prenatal and childhood development.

177

Learning Goals

12-1 Describe how humans grow from single cells into newborns.

12-2 Explain how genes and early experiences affect infant and child development.

12-3 Describe Jean Piaget's theory of cognitive development, and explain how children think at specific cognitive stages.

12-4 Identify the probable effects of attachment types and parenting styles.

12-5 Explain the three major issues developmental psychologists debate regarding infant and child development.

Meet the author who will be "talking to you" in each module by looking at the **caricature** and reading a quick personal **snapshot** of what's to come in the module.

Scan the **Learning Goals** for an overview of the critical concepts you will be tackling in the module. Focus on mastering these skills.

Cognitive Development in Infancy and Childhood

12-3 How does Jean Piaget's theory of cognitive development describe how children think at specific cognitive stages?

JEAN PIAGET [PEE-AH-ZHAY] (1896–1980) Pioneer in the study of developmental psychology who introduced a stage theory of cognitive development that led to a better understanding of children's thought processes.

Few people have had a greater impact on **developmental psychology** than Swiss psychologist **Jean Piaget** (pronounced pee-ah-zHAY). In 1920, Piaget was working on intelligence tests to determine the age at which children were likely to answer questions correctly. However, Piaget became interested in the *incorrect* responses children gave, cleverly realizing there was a lot to learn from wrong answers. Children at a given age were making remarkably similar mistakes.

Over the next 50 years, Piaget[20] advanced the belief that the way children think and solve problems depends on their stage of cognitive development. **Cognition** refers to all mental activities associated with thinking, knowing, and remembering. Children know less than you and I know, but they also think *differently*. Trying to explain to a 3-year-old how you exchange pretend money for property will get you nowhere, but an 8-year-old can understand that Boardwalk costs $400 when you're playing Monopoly. Given your more advanced reasoning skills, that same 8-year-old will not stand much of a chance against you if you're playing a game of strategy.

Piaget wrote that all people, even infants, regularly face and adapt to environmental challenges. We do so by developing **schemas** (sometimes called *schemes*), which are concepts or mental frameworks that organize and interpret information. As a toddler, for example, your schema for getting food may have been to pull on the pant leg of the nearest adult or to start crying. By now, you have countless schemas, from how to start the car to which remote you need to which buttons you push to switch from Netflix to the Food Network. How did you develop all of these helpful mental plans? Piaget's answer would be that you used two different experiences:

developmental psychology A subfield of psychology that studies physical, cognitive, and social change throughout the life span.

cognition All mental processes associated with thinking, knowing, and remembering.

schemas Concepts or mental frameworks that organize and interpret information.

Learn the vocabulary. Watch for the purple **Key Term** boxes, which define each boldface term, and read the **Key Figure** biographies for a brief introduction to the most important psychologists and theorists discussed in the text. The key terms and key figures are repeated in the Summary and Assessment section at the end of the module and in the Glossary/Glosario at the end of the book.

KEY TERMS AND KEY PEOPLE

zygote, p. 178
genes, p. 178
embryo, p. 178
fetus, p. 178
teratogens, p. 179
fetal alcohol syndrome (FAS), p. 179
rooting reflex, p. 179
temperament, p. 179
maturation, p. 181
developmental psychology, p. 183

cognition, p. 183
schemas, p. 183
assimilation, p. 184
accommodation, p. 184
sensorimotor stage, p. 185
object permanence, p. 185
preoperational stage, p. 186
conservation, p. 186
egocentrism, p. 186
concrete operational stage, p. 186

formal operational stage, p. 187
stranger anxiety, p. 188
attachment, p. 189
critical period, p. 190
imprinting, p. 190
authoritarian parenting, p. 191
permissive parenting, p. 192
authoritative parenting, p. 192
Jean Piaget [pee-ah-ZHAY] (1896–1980), p. 183
Konrad Lorenz (1903–1989), p. 190

Focus on each **Learning Goal** question as you read the module. They are repeated at point of use to make it easier to study and review.

Classical Conditioning Processes

16-3 What are the two basic processes in classical conditioning?

Now that you understand the four main components of classical conditioning, you need to know a little more about two basic processes in this type of learning: acquisition and extinction.

Remember:
● **Unconditioned** means automatic and reflexive
● **Conditioned** means learned
● A **stimulus** is something presented to the learner
● A **response** is something the learner does

Find the **Margin Notes** for reminders of especially critical concepts and for questions and answers posed throughout the text and in figure legends.

phoneme In language, the smallest distinctive sound unit.

morpheme In language, the smallest unit that carries meaning.

 Fun with language: How do you pronounce *ghoti*? (Turn the page after making your best guess.)

The most basic building block is the **phoneme,** the smallest distinctive unit of sound in a language. Make the sound represented by the letter *k*—that's a phoneme. So is the sound represented by the letter *b*, and the sound from the combination *th*. Each of our vowels has several phonemes (the sound of the *a* in *shape* is different from the sound of the *a* in *hat*). Hundreds of phonemes, including clicking sounds and tones, have been identified. The English language has about 40; the number of phonemes in other languages ranges from 20 to over 80. Notice that phonemes represent *spoken* sounds, not written symbols. (We will have more to say about written symbols later.)

As a young baby, you could produce all the phonemes of all the languages in the world—but only for a short time. The basic rule here is use 'em or lose 'em. By the time you reached your first birthday, you lost your remarkable ability to babble in multiple languages and instead settled into using the phonemes of

EXAMINE THE FIGURES and graphs.
The art is developed to support the words and to help you learn...

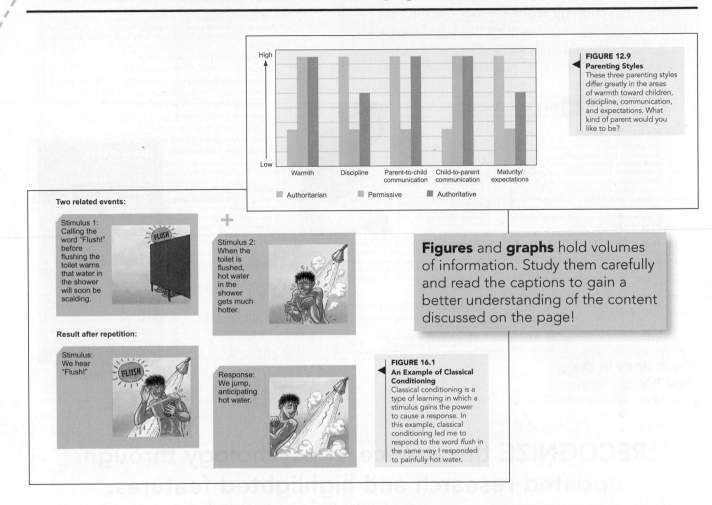

FIGURE 12.9
Parenting Styles
These three parenting styles differ greatly in the areas of warmth toward children, discipline, communication, and expectations. What kind of parent would you like to be?

High / Low

Warmth | Discipline | Parent-to-child communication | Child-to-parent communication | Maturity/expectations

Authoritarian | Permissive | Authoritative

Two related events:

Stimulus 1: Calling the word "Flush!" before flushing the toilet warns that water in the shower will soon be scalding.

Stimulus 2: When the toilet is flushed, hot water in the shower gets much hotter.

Result after repetition:

Stimulus: We hear "Flush!"

Response: We jump, anticipating hot water.

FIGURE 16.1
An Example of Classical Conditioning
Classical conditioning is a type of learning in which a stimulus gains the power to cause a response. In this example, classical conditioning led me to respond to the word *flush* in the same way I responded to painfully hot water.

Figures and **graphs** hold volumes of information. Study them carefully and read the captions to gain a better understanding of the content discussed on the page!

See the **photos** for visual context of the topics on the page. Photos are great resources to see psychology at work in the real world!

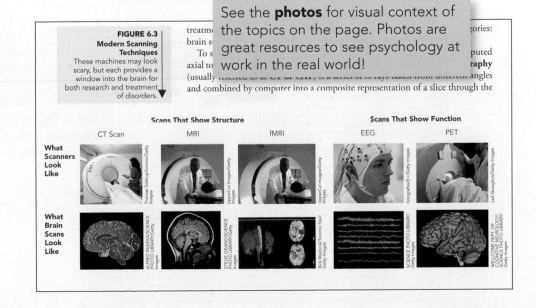

FIGURE 6.3
Modern Scanning Techniques
These machines may look scary, but each provides a window into the brain for both research and treatment of disorders.

treatme... ...gories: brain s...

To s... ...puted axial to... ...raphy (usually referred to as CT or CAT) is a series of X-rays taken from different angles and combined by computer into a composite representation of a slice through the

Scans That Show Structure

CT Scan | MRI | fMRI

Scans That Show Function

EEG | PET

What Scanners Look Like

What Brain Scans Look Like

CONNECT the text material with your everyday life!

Be your best! Pick up tips on how to live and work at your optimal performance level by finding the **Positive Psychology Icons** throughout the text. This icon highlights content for this significant and fascinating area of psychology.

Adolescence, Optimism, and Positive Psychology

Erik Erikson teaches us that optimism is an important characteristic of adolescent identity. But how do you measure optimism? And does optimism really provide benefits? According to research done by positive psychologists, optimism truly is an important ingredient for happy, productive lives. Before we take a look at some of the benefits of optimism, answer this brief survey to see how you measure up on optimism.

Life Orientation Test: How Optimistic Are You?

Respond to each statement using the following scale:

0—strongly disagree; 1—disagree; 2—neutral; 3—agree; 4—strongly agree

1. In uncertain times, I usually expect the best.
2. If something can go wrong for me, it will.
3. I'm always optimistic about my future.
4. I hardly ever expect things to go my way.
5. I rarely count on good things happening to me.
6. Overall, I expect more good things to ...

To score yourself, first reverse the numb... 2, 4, and 5. That is, for each of these item... to 0 (a 2 remains a 2). Leave the number... unchanged. Then add up the numbers in f... Scores range from 0 to 24, with higher sc... average (mean) score is between 14 and 15...

If you scored 15 or above on the test... Among college students, those who are mo... loneliness, stress, and depression.[38] They a...

PSYCHOLOGY IN THE REAL WORLD

Motion Perception

Our ability to perceive motion is just as critical for survival as is our ability to perceive depth. In many ways, motion perception is the more complex task. To perceive motion accurately, you must interpret a large number of variables rapidly. Not only does the object move, but so does your body. Swing your head from side to side and you will see a great deal of motion—motion that you correctly conclude is a result of head movement rather than object movement.

Sometimes, however, our conclusions are wrong, and we perceive motion when there is none. These mistakes are not all bad. We rely on this illusion of movement to make movies move. When we watch a film, we are able to see motion from a rapidly projected (24 images per second) series of slightly ... *stroboscopic* ... ur advantage if ... as the one that ... le of an appar- ... non, which cre- ... fixed lights are ... ay construction

FIGURE 8.8
Movement That Isn't Movemen...
Stroboscopic Motion
Each of these figures differs only ... on either side of it. This is the firs... stroboscopic motion: Project each ... after the other in order, and the r... appear to dance.

A stadium scoreboard at the University of Northern Iowa, located in my town, is programmed to display a panther, the team mascot, leaping across the display area. The action seems so real that it's easy to forget that all you're looking at is a bunch of tiny lights blinking on and off.

THINK ABOUT . . . Psychology in the Real World

1. What are stroboscopic motion and the phi phenomenon?
2. Why do designers incorporate the phi phenomenon into lighted signs?

Apply psychological research to your everyday world by diving into the **Psychology in the Real World** boxes.

Ever wonder why you do the things you do? Read the **Life Matters** margin tips to think critically about psychology's function in your day-to-day life.

LIFE MATTERS

Lack of sleep affects our emotional memories. In a study conducted by Walker at the University of California (2006), participants who were deprived of sleep were at least twice as likely to remember negative words as they were to remember positive or neutral words. Participants who rested typically had no difference between their memories of positive, negative or neutral words. Not sleeping enough can literally make you perceive your world as being more negative.

RECOGNIZE the science of psychology through updated research and highlighted features.

THINKING LIKE A PSYCHOLOGICAL SCIENTIST

What Ever Happened to Little Albert?

Research by Hall Beck and Sharman Levinson in 2009 shed new light on one of the longstanding mysteries of American psychology[2]—what ever happened to Little Albert, the 11-month-old boy in Watson and Rayner's experiments? In establishing how widespread curiosity about Little Albert has been, Hall and Levinson even cite a previous edition of this book, where we speculated that Little Albert might still be alive, an old man with a lingering fear of rats. We are used to thinking of experimental research done in the here and now, but Beck and Levinson demonstrated that research techniques can also be used to deepen our understanding of the history of psychology.

Beck and Levinson approached the Little Albert mystery by gathering information from a wide variety of sources. They looked for clues about the identity of Little Albert in Watson and Rayner's published articles, expense reports, letters, and films they made of their research. They also scoured journals to learn what had been uncovered by others interested in the puzzle. In order to better understand a date discrepancy, they surveyed librarians to verify when the journal publishing the Little Albert study was actually received. They hoped to find evidence of Albert by examining the patient records of the hospital home at Johns Hopkins University, where they knew he lived, but the records had all been destroyed. Instead they sought out data from the 1920 national census and state birth certificates. They identified three babies who fit their criteria for possibly being Little Albert.

▲ **Behaviorism**
John Watson and Rosalie Rayner set out to prove that all behavior was the result of environmental factors by classically conditioning a fear of rats and other small, furry animals in an 11-month-old boy known as Little Albert.

All this digging led these researchers to believe that Albert was really Douglas Merritte, the child of Arvilla Irons, born on March 9, 1919. From this, they used the Internet to locate Gary Irons, Douglas's half-brother. He was able to provide a photograph of young Douglas. Experts compared the photograph with stills of Little Albert made by Watson during the original research and concluded that the photos could be of the same child. They decided, "...the available evidence strongly supports the hypothesis that Douglas Merritte is Little Albert."

So, what happened to this "Albert"? Sadly, 6-year-old Douglas Merritte died in 1925 of a brain disorder called hydrocephalus. (His mother lived until 1988.) Beck and

Psychology is a science! Learn how scientific methods are applied to topics in psychology by reading the **Thinking Like a Psychological Scientist** boxes.

TEST YOURSELF to assess what you know and what you need to review further.

PSYCHOLOGY IN THE REAL WORLD

Groupthink

Groupthink seems to have played a role in several national fiascos and tragedies. Groupthink may have contributed to the 1986 explosion of the U.S. space shuttle *Challenger*, which killed seven crew members, including social studies teacher Christa McAuliffe.[53] The National Aeronautics and Space Administration (NASA) management team had tremendous confidence in their ability to launch *Challenger* into space, but they had been frustrated by numerous delays of this high-profile launch. Just before the launch was to take place, engineers voiced their opposition, citing concerns that rocket seals would not hold in the below-freezing weather. The management team demanded proof, and they did not pass on the engineers' concerns to the NASA executive in charge of the launch. The executive, thinking everybody had approved the mission, gave the order to launch, and *Challenger* flew into the history books as a space disaster. The managers, who agreed to overlook the engineers' weather-related concerns, had given in to the lure of groupthink.

As you can see, resisting groupthink is sometimes vitally important. But *how* do you resist it? Irving Janis has three suggestions for group leaders:

1. Assign people to identify problems.
2. Be open to, and welcome, various opinions.
3. Invite experts to critique plans in various stages of development.[54]

When it comes to making important decisions, there is strength in numbers—but only if you carefully consider your reasons for casting your vote with the majority.

THINK ABOUT . . . Psychology in the Real World

1. How can you avoid groupthink when trying to guide a group of your friends to a decision?
2. Apply groupthink to a time you and a group of others made a bad decision.
3. Think of and explain a time when students or adults at your school made a decision that appeared to be a result of groupthink. What was the outcome of that decision?

> Challenge yourself to **Think About** the ideas presented in each high-interest box by contemplating the answers to the open-ended questions posed at the end.

> Stop at the end of each Learning Goal to test yourself with the **Make it Stick!** questions. These quick questions test your knowledge of the material you've just read and will help you to identify areas you've mastered and those you need to review.

MAKE IT STICK!

1. What does this textbook call the enhancement of a group's already-existing attitudes through discussion within the group?
   a. group polarization   c. groupthink
   b. social loafing   d. deindividuation
2. You're assigned to a group project with three friends. You and one of the others end up doing most of the work. What phenomenon explains the lack of work by the other two members in the group?
3. Statements such as "Let's all get along" and "Don't rock the boat" could lead a group of people to dismiss the critical thinking necessary to make a decision. This is called _____.
4. True or False: The loss of self-awareness and the loss of self-restraint are both characteristic of social loafing.

the written word as easily. We learn to speak without conscious effort as young children, yet we must go to school and work to master reading and writing. Even spoken language becomes more difficult after about age 10—when a critical developmental window seems to slam shut. In rare, tragic cases in which a child has been raised in isolation through the first decade of life, language development does not proceed normally. After this window of opportunity closes, those of us who easily developed a first language must struggle to learn a second one. Knowing this, linguists often argue that it makes more sense to introduce foreign languages in preschool than in middle or high school. Your introductory psychology course barely scratches the surface when it comes to the wonders of human language, but one thing is certain: The course could not exist without it. The very fact that you can read about and discuss language proves its importance—which extends to every aspect of human interaction.

Beyond the Critical Period We can learn language, and even more than one language, as a natural, automatic process when we are children because we are born with a predisposition to learn language. But there seems to be a catch—if we haven't learned language by the time we reach high school, the window of easy learning seems to slam shut and we have to work hard to master grammar and vocabulary. We should be offering foreign language in preschool!

MAKE IT STICK!

1. A young child usually enters the one-word stage at about
   a. 6 months of age.   c. 18 months of age.
   b. 12 months of age.   d. 24 months of age.
2. True or false? Babies babble using only the phonemes of their native language.
3. _____ is the spontaneous production of phonemes by babies.

Module 15 Summary and Assessment

Language Development

15-1 What are the building blocks of language?

- The basic building block of language is the phoneme, the smallest distinctive unit of sound in a spoken language.
- A morpheme is a single phoneme or a combination of phonemes and is the smallest unit that carries meaning in a language.
- Grammar is a system of rules that govern how we can combine phonemes, morphemes, and words to produce meaningful communication.

15-2 What is the evidence for each of the competing theories of language acquisition?

- Noam Chomsky believes that our brains are wired to process vocabulary and rules of grammar virtually

without effort. Evidence for this is that all languages have complicated rules that young children are able to master.

- B. F. Skinner stated that we learn our language through association (linking certain sounds with certain objects), imitation (modeling how we see others speak), and rewards (hugs, smiles, and so on). The fact that we speak the language we hear at home is evidence of this theory.

15-3 What are the stages of language development?

- Language develops through a series of stages: babbling, the one-word stage, and the two-word stage.

Summative Assessment

1. Which of the following represents a single phoneme?
   a. The sound you make when you pronounce *bat*
   b. The sound you make when you pronounce *eat*
   c. The sound you make when you pronounce *shh*
   d. The sound you make when you pronounce *ten*
2. Young babies have the ability to produce
   a. all phonemes humans are capable of producing.
   b. only the phonemes of the language(s) spoken in their homes.
   c. only the phonemes of the language(s) spoken in their homes and other phonemes from similar languages.
   d. only the phonemes that are modeled for them by caregivers.
3. A morpheme
   a. always communicates meaning.
   b. determines the order of words in a sentence.
   c. is not likely to be produced by a baby after the babbling stage.
   d. represents a particular speech sound.
4. Noam Chomsky believes that
   a. learning language depends primarily on being reinforced for using words correctly.
   b. learning language involves making associations between words and objects.
   c. learning language gets easier as children get older.
   d. the brains of children are predisposed to make it easy to learn language.
5. Which language acquisition theorist best explains the fact that children grow up speaking the language of their parents instead of a foreign language?
   a. Chomsky
   b. Skinner
   c. Both Chomsky and Skinner provide good explanations for this.
   d. Neither Chomsky nor Skinner provides a good explanation for this.
6. Washoe, the chimpanzee,
   a. was able to learn only a few signs despite years of effort by her trainers.
   b. learned to use several thousand signs appropriately, but could not use them as flexibly and creatively as human children.
   c. learned thousands of symbols and used American Sign Language as effectively as human children.
   d. was able to teach dozens of signs to another chimpanzee.
7. The first language stage is the _____ stage.
   a. phoneme
   b. morpheme
   c. babbling
   d. one-word
8. Children enter the two-word stage of language when they are about
   a. 6 months old.
   b. 1 year old.
   c. 2 years old.
   d. 3 years old.
9. A person learns, on average, more than _____ words a day throughout childhood.
   a. 3
   b. 8
   c. 13
   d. 20
10. Which of the following is an example of overgeneralization?
    a. A child says, "Look at the three deers in the back yard."
    b. A child points at the family dog and says, "Meow, meow."
    c. A child points at her mother and says, "Daddy!"
    d. A child says, "My friend and I has two balls."

KEY TERMS AND KEY PEOPLE

language, p. 229	morpheme, p. 230	Noam Chomsky (1928–), p. 232
phoneme, p. 230	grammar, p. 231	B. F. Skinner (1904–1990), p. 232

> Answer the 10 multiple-choice **Summative Assessment** questions at the end of every module to test your cumulative knowledge of the module's content. Answers appear in **Appendix B** at the end of the book.

READ, STUDY, AND PRACTICE
when and where you want.

Access everything you need for this course online. Our **digital platform** includes all of the resources you need in one convenient place.

The interactive, mobile-ready **e-book** allows you to read and reference the text online or to download it to read when an Internet connection is not available.

Thinking About
PSYCHOLOGY
The Science of Mind and Behavior

Fourth Edition

Charles T. Blair-Broeker • Randal M. Ernst

Alexey Boldin/Shutterstock; SAKIstyle/BLOOMimage/Getty Images

LearningCurve
Adaptive quizzing offers individualized question sets and feedback. Test yourself and get extra practice on areas of confusion without stressing about grades.

← Back to Study Plan   Score: 46/600   Question Value: 15 points

Shaping is a method used by Skinner to:

○ decrease an undesirable behavior.

○ condition taste aversions in rats.

○ explain how classical conditioning works.

○ guide an organism to exhibit a complex behavior using successive approximations.

Need help on this question?

[📄 Read the ebook page on this topic (no penalty)]   [Get a hint (fewer points)]   [Show answer (no points)]

Thinking About Psychology

Welcome to the wonderful world of psychological science! We are Charlie and Randy, and we wrote this book to serve as the guide for your introductory tour of a fascinating field that attempts to understand the behaviors, thoughts, and emotions of people and animals. The book is an extension of our many years in the high school classroom, and our goal is to provide you, your classmates, and your teacher with the information you need to:

- master the sometimes surprising conclusions of psychology;
- learn how the scientific method is used to study behavior and thinking; and
- develop critical thinking skills that will enable you to evaluate claims about psychological issues you encounter in the media.

If you have a cell phone, you probably have it set to notify you through pushes or notifications when someone sends you a message or posts something to social media. Many also set their phones to notify them of breaking news. Here's a sample of the headlines from just one 24-hour news cycle:

"Advances in Depression Treatment Announced"

"More Single Parents as Divorce Rates Climb"

"Opioid Drug Overdoses Addressed by Review Panel"

"Foreign Nuclear Weapon Arsenal Considered Threat"

"Sexual Harassment Case Sent to Jury"

"Water Poisoning Said to Impair Brain Functioning"

"Supremacist Group Promotes Violence"

"School Shooting Stuns Community"

"Senator Calls Charges Fake News"

Notice anything tying these headlines together? First, all seem to focus on some kind of *problem*. Second, and more interesting to psychology students and teachers, all of these particular problems involve *humans* and *behaviors*. How to deal with depression, single parenting, divorce, drug abuse, aggression, harassment, and bigotry will not be found in your calculus, world language, or contemporary literature courses. This is why we proudly say: Welcome to the most important high school class you'll ever take.

By the time you turn in your final psychology exam, we want your headline for this course to be "Psychological Science Helps Students Flourish." Having a new understanding of how your mind, brain, environment, and culture drive your behavior and the behavior of others will provide you with a greater understanding, and perhaps appreciation, of the world around you.

So, it's time to start thinking about psychology. We'll do this by following the overarching psychological themes and domains identified by psychology teachers and professors (all of whom were once psychology students like you) from around the world.

Psychology's Themes

Most of your teachers probably have themes for their classes. The themes for chemistry might include atomic bonds and chemical reactions. Economics themes might cover scarcity and incentives. Here are psychology's themes:

1. *Psychology courses promote scientific attitudes and skills.*
   The skills in this first theme promote critical thinking and problem solving. In this course, you will learn how to think like a scientist, ponder what valid research looks like, and learn how to address everyday issues using a scientific approach. Scientists know how to separate fact from fiction. Using the knowledge you gain from this class, you'll learn how to do that as well.

2. *The people advancing our understanding of psychology come from all walks of life.*
   People of all ethnicities, religious backgrounds or religions, and geographic regions contribute to our understanding of psychology. The people who conduct the research that contributes to psychological knowledge, whether it's Barbara Fredrickson explaining emotions, Martin Seligman explaining strengths, or Angela Duckworth discussing grit, represent our world well. Their success is determined by accomplishment, not by their background.

3. *Diversity and a multicultural perspective is important to understanding psychology.*
   How are you similar and how are you different from your classmates? To generate answers to that question, we would want to use multiple perspectives (biological, social, historical) to determine areas of similarity and difference. But hold on! What if your class consists of all girls? Can we say that the same similarities and differences would exist in an all-boys school? Or what if your classroom lacks ethnic diversity? The point is, to understand a diverse world, we need to study a great diversity of people. Psychology wants to understand all people, not just people of one race or gender identification. You'll see that diversity represented as your read these modules.

4. *Scientific knowledge evolves rapidly as new discoveries are made every day.*
   The American Psychological Association currently publishes almost 90 journals to communicate research findings. Other psychological organizations publish dozens more. Each article adds to the accumulated knowledge and helps us better understand people and become better problem solvers.

5. *Psychologists study humans and animals.*
   Animals from insects to mammals are interesting in their own right, and we can often learn more about humans by studying the ways that animals think and behave.

6. *There are ethical standards for conducting research.*
   Sometimes it is obvious when experiments should not be used, because they violate the rights of the people, or animals, being experimented on. For example, you can't conduct an experiment on the effects of brain surgery if the surgery would lead to the death of most of the participants. This experiment would be ethically inappropriate even if you thought the potential knowledge it would lead to would be useful. What about less obvious scenarios, like whether or not your social media posts can be collected and analyzed by researchers? Debates about what is ethically appropriate for research have occurred through most of psychology's history and are still occurring today. We will discuss this critically important issue several times in the pages that follow.

7. *The different modules in this book are interconnected.*
   Perhaps you've taken a biology class where you've studied the various human biological systems. You studied the nervous system, the digestive system, the immune system, the circulatory system, among others as separate units; but it's obvious that each of these systems connects with and influences the others. The same is true in psychology. What you learn about child development will connect with what you learn about personality. What you learn about the brain will connect with what you learn about psychological disorders. All of the modules in *Thinking About Psychology* are very much interrelated. The more you understand about one aspect of thinking and behavior, the more you will understand about the others!

8. *There are ways to relate psychological knowledge to everyday life.*
   All of the subjects you study in school have applications in real life, but perhaps none have as many connections as psychology. By the time you finish this course, you will be able to apply psychological knowledge to virtually every story that comes across your news feed. Almost everything is psychology!

9. *There are numerous careers available to those who study psychology.*
   Your image of psychology may be one of a therapist treating a patient who is lying on a couch. While it's true that some psychologists do work like this, this image only represents a small percentage of them. There are many other psychologists who engage in therapy or counseling and make no use of a couch—or the theories that led to the use of the couch in first place. Many others apply psychology in entirely different areas—to help athletes function to the best of their ability, for example, or to design controls that are easy to operate and minimize the possibility of sometimes catastrophic mistakes. Still others spend their careers conducting research rather than trying to solve problems. These researchers are fascinated with learning about what makes us tick; in other words finding out why we think, feel, and behave the

way we do. The American Psychological Association has divisional groups for professionals in over 50 different specialty areas ranging from peace psychology to the psychology of masculinity and femininity. You will learn about some of these career possibilities in the course.

10. *Psychological science and knowledge help address a wide array of issues, from individual to global levels.*

By now you should be getting the idea that psychology is an extraordinarily broad field. Not only does it operate across lots of topics, it also operates on multiple levels. Do you have a personal problem you need help with? Do you want to lose weight or become a more effective studier? Psychology can help. Psychology can also help couples who are trying to improve their marriage and families who are trying to communicate more effectively with each other. Psychology can help a school deal with bullying or a business deal with harassment. This scales all the way up to communities (what is the best way to maintain positive relationships between the police and citizens?), societal institutions (how can military combat soldiers protect themselves from post-traumatic stress disorder?), and international relations (how can two countries that have been battlefield enemies learn to trust one another in peace?). Psychologists are actively working to address these problems and many, many more.

11. *Valid evidence is required to support beliefs about psychological phenomena.*

One of the things you will learn in psychology is that common sense is not always a good way to make decisions. Perhaps common sense tells us that rereading material several times for an upcoming test is an effective studying strategy. The problem is that a lot of available evidence indicates that simply reading and rereading is a relatively ineffective way to study. Common sense also tells us that the memories of an eyewitness to a crime are usually accurate because the witness's memory recorded the crime. However, the evidence tells us that memories—even vivid memories of a frightening crime—are likely to be constructed of both true and false details. For issues about which people disagree, psychology can often play a critical role in determining what is true and what is not.

Pause just for a moment to think about psychology's themes. What key words do you remember? Words such as science, evidence, ethics, knowledge, and diversity help give you an idea of what's at the core of psychological science. All of these terms are also important to psychology's seven domains.

Psychology's Domains
Scientific Inquiry Domain

- Perspectives in Psychological Science
- Research Methods, Measurement, and Statistics

The modules in the Scientific Inquiry Domain help lay the foundation for understanding psychology. In module 2, we define psychology, discuss its history, and explain the perspectives psychologist use to understand the mind and behavior. In modules 3 and 4, we introduce research strategies, how to design an experiment, and how to find meaning in the results generated by experiments.

Klaus Vedfelt/Getty Images

Biopsychology Domain

- Biological Bases of Behavior
- Sensation and Perception
- Consciousness

The modules in the Biopsychology Domain put biology in the spotlight. No, this isn't a biology course, but without biology there are no thoughts or behaviors. Without biology, you'd never feel anxiety about a test, enjoy the taste of your favorite beverage, or move to the beat of your favorite song. You'll also learn more about why sleep is important and how psychoactive drugs impact your mind and behavior.

Development and Learning Domain

- Life Span Development
- Learning
- Language Development

The modules in the Development and Learning Domain explore three different periods of development (childhood, adolescence, and adulthood), focusing on the three fundamental issues in developmental psychology to help us gain insight into how we grow up. For instance, is our development a product of our environment or is it more related to our genetic makeup? This Domain also addresses how we learn and how language develops.

Sociocultural Context Domain

- Social Interactions
- Sociocultural Diversity

The modules in the Sociocultural Domain show that we may very well act like different people in different situations. We'll explore how the situation you're in, the upbringing you've had, your culture, and your gender identity can affect your behavior. After reading these modules, you'll have a better understanding of attitudes, conformity, and membership in a group. Special attention is given to cultural roles in determining who you are and how you think.

Cognition Domain

- Memory
- Thinking
- Intelligence

The modules in the Cognition Domain address memory, memory failure, how our thought processes work, and intelligence (along with intelligence testing). How do we solve problems? Why do we forget some events while remembering others? How do we conceptualize our world? What do we mean when we speak of intelligence and can we really measure it? These are just a few of the high-interest questions addressed in these modules.

Antonio Guillem/Shutterstock.com

Individual Variations Domain

- Motivation
- Emotion
- Personality
- Psychological Disorders

The seven modules in the Individual Variations Domain celebrate the differences that make us all unique. Why do you express emotion differently than your friends? What truly defines the pain and variety of psychological disorders that touch so many lives? How come some students do better than others in the classroom? Each one of us exudes individuality. In these modules, we explore the factors that make YOU who you are.

VGstockstudio/Shutterstock

Applications of Psychological Science Domain

- Treatment of Psychological Disorders
- Health
- Vocational Applications

The final Domain, the Applications of Psychological Science, explores the science behind the psychological and biomedical therapies that clinical psychologists use to help people get back on their feet. The last two modules examine the link between stress and illness, and how certain behaviors and thoughts can improve health and wellness. Are there ways to help decrease the chance that hard times will get the better of us? According to psychological science, the answer is yes.

So what are we waiting for? Let's get started! The next module will provide important background information that will help you understand what *thinking about psychology* really means.

Scientific Inquiry

Klaus Vedfelt/Getty Images

Module 2

History and Perspectives in Psychological Science

This psychograph would never be used by today's psychologists, but it illustrates psychology's interesting history.

An unusually large group of students collects in the hallway during the 5-minute break between class periods. Some stand on tiptoe, craning their necks from side to side, trying to gain a better view of the two students shouting at each other 10 feet from my classroom door. Cell phones are out, held high, filming the altercation. The tardy bell rings, but nobody leaves for class.

The crowd swells in number, making it nearly impossible to identify who is at the center of this argument. An assistant principal intervenes, and the escalating shouting match ends as quickly as it started. Both students are escorted to the office to sort things out.

Fortunately, these disruptions are very rare where I teach, but talk of the dispute, which started as an insult over what someone was wearing, buzzes from desk to desk. As a way to bring my students back from the almost-fight, we begin class by discussing some questions that psychologists might pose about the incident we just witnessed:

- Are some of us born more aggressive than others?
- How are levels of aggression affected by the presence of peers?
- What are the biological influences on aggression?
- What motivates some people to settle their differences physically, while others are more likely to talk them out?
- Are young adults more likely than middle-aged adults to take part in physical confrontations?
- How could this situation have been avoided or defused?

- Why were students more likely to film this altercation with their phones than to break it up or intervene?
- Why do some groups get along better than others?

In fact, psychologists try to find the answers to all kinds of interesting questions, such as these:

- Why does writing down the good things that happen in our lives help us deal with the challenges we face?
- Why do we have to sleep?
- What is the best way to help a 19-year-old soldier cope with the trauma experienced during battle?
- How do people's race or ethnicity affect the way they are treated by others?

After you finish this course, you should be able to answer these and many other interesting questions about the human mind and human behavior.

Getting Along—The Math Behind Groups That Thrive

One interesting question psychologists explore is how people work best in groups. One day, if you haven't already, you'll participate in a committee or group that meets regularly in your high school, the college you attend, or your community. Whether you're involved in a student council, youth group, or Spanish club, group members must get along to agree upon and accomplish goals. Some groups get along well and get a lot done, but others get bogged down. Psychologists have asked, What's the difference between productive and nonproductive groups or committees?

It turns out that there is an emotional recipe for healthy, productive groups. The number of positive experiences during meetings (compared to negative experiences) has a HUGE impact on a group's productivity. Psychologists have found that productive groups usually have at least three positive interactions for every negative one. This doesn't mean that there shouldn't be debates on topics that need resolving, but you should keep this 3-to-1 ratio in mind when you are working with others on a committee or a project.

Research shows that groups, committees, or student councils with positivity–negativity ratios worse than 3 to 1 rarely get much done and are almost never considered successful by its group members. If you think the positivity–negativity ratio of a group you belong to is worse than 3 to 1, what should you do? Research suggests that you should

- promote undivided focus as each group member speaks. (Outlaw texting during meetings!)
- express support, encouragement, or appreciation during and after a group member's presentation.
- ask questions that explore a speaker's viewpoint instead of saying things like, "That will never work."
- minimize sarcasm.
- discourage nonverbal behaviors (like eye rolling and smirking) during meetings.

The 3-to-1 ratio idea is likely to spill over into other aspects of your life. Interestingly, unsuccessful business teams, failed relationships, and even feelings of depression are also characterized by very few positive interactions and lots of negative interactions with others. Learning to integrate these suggestions can help you build better group experiences and more positive relationships in other areas of your life. Studying psychology can make navigating life easier!

The Definition of Psychology

🐾 **2-1** What is psychology, and what kinds of topics do
🐾 psychologists study?

Psychology is the scientific study of behavior and mental processes. Before going any further, let's make sure we understand the three parts of this definition: Scientific study, behavior, and mental processes.

When we say that psychology is a *scientific study,* we mean that psychologists rely on scientific research methods in their attempts to unravel answers to questions such as, Why do some people offer help when others do not? Psychologists systematically collect research data and use statistical formulas to analyze the results. Scientific research methods are an essential key to unlocking psychology's secrets.

The last two parts of our definition, *behavior* and *mental processes,* establish the incredibly broad range of interesting topics that psychologists study. Any directly observable thing you do, from laughing to turning the pages of this book, is a behavior that psychologists could study. But psychologists also study the things we cannot observe directly—our mental processes, which include all our thoughts and emotions.

Are some people simply born more aggressive than others? To find out, psychologists might study children in a day care by watching for aggressive behaviors at early ages. Psychologists might also study the parts of the brain that are most active during aggressive behavior to try to determine what chemicals affect the brain. Psychologists who are less biologically inclined might examine a person's home life in search of the origins of aggressive acts. Interestingly, psychologists also study people who witness aggressive behavior, trying to understand why some people offer help and try to stop the aggression, while others do not.

Psychologists who do research on such topics do so with various goals in mind. Some conduct **basic research,** which is done to increase the scientific knowledge base of psychology. Others conduct **applied research,** which is intended to solve

psychology Scientific study of behavior and mental processes.

"So, how do you want to play this? Nature, nurture, or a bit of both?"

basic research Pure science that aims to increase the scientific knowledge base.

applied research Scientific study that aims to solve practical problems.

What Makes You Smile? Psychologists use scientific methods to study topics such as happiness, love, and friendship.

practical problems. Basic research on aggressive behavior might aim to find out more about the biological influences on aggression. Applied research on helping behaviors might aim to reduce apathy in bystanders who witness aggressive behavior. Knowing more about the biology of aggression would add to our knowledge of aggression but wouldn't solve any problems. That makes it basic research. Research aimed at figuring out how to reduce apathy is applied research.

Fascinating subjects such as aggression against others, helping others, gratitude, and the development of children as they grow into adolescents and young adults are examined in this textbook. The psychologists studying these concepts chose one of the many careers (see Appendix A: Careers in Psychology) available to those who decide to pursue psychology as an occupation.

MAKE IT STICK!

1. Which of the following best matches the definition of psychology?

   a. Scientific research about why we act and think in the ways we do
   b. The study of people
   c. Thinking about human behaviors
   d. Investigations of the human psyche and why we think the things we think

2. What is the primary tool psychologists use to answer questions about behavior and thinking?

   a. Insight
   b. The unconscious mind
   c. Dream analysis
   d. The scientific method

3. Dr. Schullo conducts research on cell phones, attempting to find out what would make them easier to use. What kind of research is Dr. Schullo conducting?

   a. Applied research   c. Behavioral processes
   b. Basic research   d. Mental processes

4. Psychology is a scientific study. This means that psychology relies on which of the following to answer questions about behavior and mental processes?

   a. Scientific research methods
   b. Best-guess hunches
   c. Observation only
   d. Applied research methods only

Modern Psychology's Roots

2-2 How did the study of psychology as a science get started?

We humans have probably been curious about ourselves and the world around us for as long as we have been around, yet the history of modern psychology represents less than 150 years of work. As a science, psychology is relatively new.

Understanding what psychologists used to think about the mind and human behavior helps us understand current beliefs about psychology. Thus, we will start with the first experimental psychologist, Wilhelm Wundt.

Wilhelm Wundt and the Beginning of Psychology as a Science

Psychology's earliest pioneers shared a keen interest in understanding mental processes and later, behavior. One of these early pioneers was German physiologist **Wilhelm Wundt** (pronounced VOONT). As a youngster, Wundt had trouble concentrating in school. He often got bad grades and had to repeat his first year

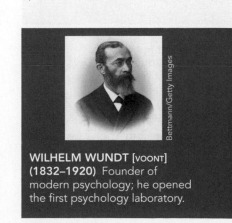

WILHELM WUNDT [VOONT] **(1832–1920)** Founder of modern psychology; he opened the first psychology laboratory.

of high school. Fortunately, the future founder of psychology buckled down and eventually graduated from medical school. But Wundt didn't want to practice medicine; he wanted to understand human consciousness. So, he began conducting experiments that tested how perceptions, sensations, and feelings related to human behavior. Wundt was given laboratory space in 1879, which is now recognized as the birth year of psychology.

Wundt's attempts to understand human consciousness used a process called *introspection*. Students trained in the introspection method were taught to describe their own conscious experiences in a step-by-step way. For instance, Wundt would create some kind of sound (like banging a gong) and ask all his students to explain what they heard first, how the sound changed after first hearing it, and how it ended. Wundt used their detailed descriptions as a foundation for understanding consciousness. Trying to figure out the mind's basic elements was generally at the heart of Wundt's research.

Wundt is considered the founder of modern psychology because he was the first to use experimental methods to study consciousness. For example, in one study, participants were told to press a button as soon as they saw a light come on. This was called Task 1. The time it took them to respond was recorded. Next, participants were told that either a red or a green light would come on. Their instructions were to press the left-hand button if the light was green and the right-hand button if the light was red. This was called Task 2. Again, the time to respond was recorded. Task 1 required only perception of a light before responding, but Task 2 required perception of the light, a decision about which color was shown, and a second decision about whether to push the left button or the right button. The time needed to respond to Task 2 was longer than that for Task 1, and Wundt believed the time difference between tasks measured the speed of mental processes. No one had used experimental methods such as these to study consciousness before Wundt.

structuralism Theory that the structure of conscious experience could be understood by analyzing the basic elements of thoughts and sensations.

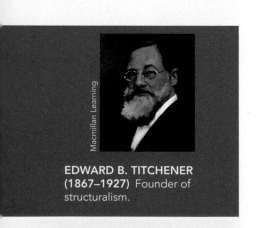

EDWARD B. TITCHENER (1867–1927) Founder of structuralism.

Gestalt [gih-SHTALT] psychology Psychological perspective that emphasized our tendency to integrate pieces of information into meaningful wholes.

functionalism Theory that emphasized the functions of consciousness or the ways consciousness helps people adapt to their environment.

Edward B. Titchener and Structuralism

One of Wundt's students, **Edward B. Titchener,** introduced **structuralism,** the first major school of thought in psychology. Just as a chemist tries to understand the different elements in chemical compounds, structuralists tried to understand the *structure* of conscious experience by analyzing the intensity, clarity, and quality of its basic parts. For example, picture a blade of grass. A structuralist might have lingered over the intensity of the green color of the blade of grass, the clarity of its texture, and the roughly rectangular shape of the blade. For Titchener and his students, successful descriptions of such basic elements were the building blocks of consciousness. Unlike Wundt, Titchener did not want to use something invisible (such as mental processes) to explain consciousness. Instead, Titchener steered psychology toward a descriptive science, one that he could see.

Ultimately, structuralism did not produce many followers and died out. One reason for this was that in practice, it didn't prove to be very reliable. You see, since psychology is a science, the results from psychological research must be reliable meaning the methods used to study something get roughly the same results. Titchener's students often described the same object differently; hence, they produced unreliable data. Perhaps the greatest contribution structuralism made to psychology is that it provided a theory for others to disprove, giving rise to other schools of thought in psychology.

Gestalt Psychology

Gestalt (a German word that means *configuration* and is pronounced gih-SHTALT) **psychology** was a perspective that emphasized our tendency to integrate pieces of information into meaningful wholes. Gestalt psychologists suggested that adding together the individual elements of an experience created something new and different—that *the whole is different from the sum of its parts* (see **Figure 2.1**). For example, think of the notes to your favorite song. Individually, each note means little, but put them together and you have a great tune. Combining the elements, then, creates something that did not exist before. Most prominent Gestalt psychologists were persecuted by Nazis in the 1930s and fled to the United States as immigrants in search of safety. This slowed their research, but their work resurfaced in new psychological theories later in the century.

drxy/iStock/Getty Images

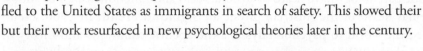

FIGURE 2.1
The Gestalt of Sound
In Gestalt theory, the whole (in this case, the collective notes of a song) is different from the individual parts (that is, the notes).

William James and Functionalism

Another psychologist who disagreed with the structuralist approach was **William James.** James, the first American psychologist, once noted that the first psychology lecture he ever heard was his own. He went on to write the first psychology textbook, published in 1890, which influenced thousands of students over the next several decades. For James, psychology needed to study the *functions* of consciousness, or the ways consciousness helps people adapt to their environment, a view that became known as **functionalism.** James was influenced by Charles Darwin's theory of evolution and believed that mental processes evolved over time. James also thought that we developed useful habits—such as washing our hands before eating or brushing our teeth after a meal—because they help us function more effectively in our daily lives. That is, washing our hands keeps us from eating germs and becoming sick, and brushing our teeth keeps them from rotting and falling out. James's idea was that consciousness helped us adapt to and function in our surroundings, and he thought that understanding this idea should be the goal of psychology.

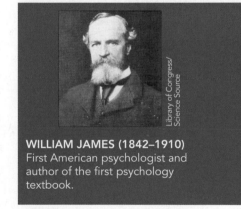

Library of Congress/ Science Source

WILLIAM JAMES (1842–1910)
First American psychologist and author of the first psychology textbook.

MAKE IT STICK!

1. Wilhelm Wundt is considered the founder of psychology as a science because

   a. it was decided that clinical psychology should become a medical field.

   b. he conducted important research on the unconscious mind.

   c. he established the first experimental psychology laboratory.

   d. he won the Nobel Prize for science.

2. Which research question would have been most interesting to the Gestalt psychologists?

   a. Why do we perceive objects in specific groups?

   b. Can introspection be used to describe thought accurately?

   c. What is the structure of conscious experience?

   d. How is our personality expressed in our dreams?

3. According to this textbook, who wrote that mental processes *evolve* over time?

   a. Wundt (introspection)

   b. Titchener (structuralism)

   c. James (functionalism)

   d. A Gestalt psychologist

4. Which of the following is associated with the notion that the whole is different from the sum of its parts?

   a. Functionalism   c. Structuralism

   b. Gestalt   d. Introspection

5. Who wrote the first psychology textbook?

   a. James   c. Titchener

   b. Wundt   d. None of them

Psychology in the Twentieth Century

🐾🐾 **2-3** In what ways did twentieth-century psychologists change how psychology was studied?

As the 1900s began, the science of psychology was heading in new directions. The most influential figure of this time was a man whose name you have likely heard associated with psychology, Sigmund Freud.

Sigmund Freud and Psychoanalysis

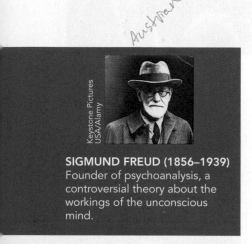

SIGMUND FREUD (1856–1939) Founder of psychoanalysis, a controversial theory about the workings of the unconscious mind.

psychoanalysis Freud's theory of personality; also, a therapeutic technique that attempts to provide insight into thoughts and actions by exposing and interpreting the underlying unconscious motives and conflicts.

Few outside psychology have heard of structuralism and functionalism, but almost everyone has heard of the Austrian physician **Sigmund Freud.** In 1900, Freud introduced the world to **psychoanalysis,** a therapeutic technique and theory of personality that attributes our thoughts and actions to unconscious motives and conflict.

The stereotypical image of a therapist comes from pop culture notions surrounding Freud, whom countless cartoons have poked fun at over the years. Freud's approach to psychology differed from structuralism and functionalism in two key ways:

1. Psychoanalysis focused on abnormal behavior, which Freud attributed to unconscious drives and conflicts, often stemming from childhood. For instance, Freud thought that a conflict experienced in childhood, such as a difficult time in potty training, could reappear for that person as an obsession for order and cleanliness later in life.

2. Psychoanalysis relied on personal observation and reflection instead of controlled laboratory experimentation as its means of discovery. While Freud claimed his work was scientific, it really wasn't because he relied on self-reported reflections rather than scientific methods to gather information.

Freud died in 1939, and many of his ideas have since been disproved. However, elements of Freud's original theory are still part of pop culture. A Freudian slip, for example, is a misstatement reflective of something you'd *like* to say. For instance, during an interview, a member of the president's cabinet referred to her boss as my husband and not the president. She corrected herself, but did this mistake indicate a longing for a closer relationship? News anchors were quick to label the error as a Freudian slip, implying it's what she wished for. The term *anal retentive* comes from one of Freud's developmental stages and refers to someone who is excessively neat, clean, and compulsive (stuck in the "anal stage," where we supposedly come to terms with bodily functions). Freud's greater legacy, however, was his novel approach to understanding behavior, and some of these ideas have been incorporated into *psychodynamic theory,* which is a modernized version of Freud's original theories (and is discussed in more detail later in this module). Psychologists influenced by psychodynamic theory still assume, as Freud did, that our unconscious thoughts, inner conflicts, and childhood experiences significantly affect our personality and behaviors.

"I'm right there in the room, and no one even acknowledges me."

behaviorism The theory that psychology should only study observable behaviors, not mental processes.

Pavlov's dogs

Ivan Pavlov, John Watson, and Behaviorism

In 1906, the classic studies on animal learning of Russian physiologist **Ivan Pavlov** fueled a move in psychology toward an interest in *observable* behaviors and away from the self-examination of inner ideas and experiences. Pavlov's emphasis on things we can see (rather than mental processes) quickly caught on in the United States. Consider the following, which appeared in *Psychological Review* 7 years after Pavlov first published his work and struck a nerve in the world of psychology: "Psychology as the behaviorist views it is a purely objective experimental branch of natural science. Its theoretical goal is the prediction and control of human behavior.[1]" It can be argued that the words in this article sent the study of mental processes into hibernation for the next 40 years.

John B. Watson, the author of this article that encouraged psychologists to dismiss the study of consciousness, considered structuralism and functionalism failures, given his belief that the methods of these perspectives were unscientific. He wanted psychology to move in a more experimental direction, and to that end he launched **behaviorism,** the theory that psychology should only study observable behaviors, not mental processes. Watson's work made psychology more objective and scientific in its methods, although most behaviorists today recognize the significance of studying both mental processes and behaviors.

Watson's behaviorism was the most dominant school of thought in psychology in the twentieth century, and he promoted the study of learned reflexes originally developed by Pavlov. This method included precise experimental observations of human reactions to various stimuli. His most famous study paired the presentation of a furry white object to an infant along with the presentation of a loud noise. The loud noise frightened the infant, but pairing a furry white object with the loud noise also led the child to fear furry white objects. Later, the sight of something like a white rabbit would lead to uncontrollable crying by the infant.

In the years since, this school of thought has been modified somewhat by other behaviorists, such as **B. F. Skinner.** Today, behaviorism focuses on learning through rewards and observation, and studies that include frightening small children would neither be approved by a research review panel nor be conducted by any ethical psychologist.

Abraham Maslow, Carl Rogers, and Humanistic Psychology

Behaviorism and psychoanalysis maintained their hold on the field into the 1960s, when a third force began to influence psychology.[2] **Humanistic psychology,** led by **Abraham Maslow** and **Carl Rogers,** rejected the idea that humans are controlled by a series of rewards and reinforcements. Instead, they emphasized *conscious experience* as the proper focus of psychology. They also believed that humans have free will in their decision making and that healthy people strive to reach their full potential. Furthermore, humanistic psychologists did not believe that humans could be reduced to various parts and pieces. That is, an entire human—the whole person—is different from the sum of all the parts (brain, neurons, emotions, and so on). Does this remind you of an older school of thought? *Yes,* the humanistic psychologists were influenced by the Gestalt psychologists who preceded them.

IVAN PAVLOV (1849–1936)
Russian physiologist and learning theorist famous for the discovery of classical conditioning, in which learning occurs through association.

JOHN B. WATSON (1878–1958)
Founder of behaviorism, the theory that psychology should restrict its efforts to studying observable behaviors, not mental processes.

▲ **Animal Behavior**
Ivan Pavlov studied animal (dogs) behavior to gain insight into how we learn.

humanistic psychology A perspective that focuses on the study of conscious experience, the individual's freedom to choose, and the individual's capacity for personal growth.

B. F. SKINNER (1904–1990)
American behavioral psychologist who developed the fundamental principles and techniques of operant conditioning and devised ways to apply them in the real world.

ABRAHAM MASLOW (1908– 1970) Humanistic psychologist who proposed the *hierarchy of needs*, with *self-actualization* as one of the ultimate psychological needs.

CARL ROGERS (1902–1987)
Humanistic psychologist who developed *client-centered therapy* and stressed the importance of acceptance, genuineness, and empathy in fostering human growth.

JEAN PIAGET [pee-ah-ZHAY] **(1896–1980)** Pioneer in the study of developmental psychology who introduced a stage theory of cognitive development that led to a better understanding of children's thought processes.

Humanistic psychology showed great promise early in its existence, but many believe its subsequent decline resulted from the lack of scientific research to back up its proposals.[3] The idea of striving to reach one's potential, proposed by Maslow 40 years ago, has been picked up by the *positive psychologists* of the twenty-first century, as you will see later in this module.

Jean Piaget and Child Development

Swiss biologist and psychologist **Jean Piaget** (pronounced pee-ah-ZHAY) was another pioneer; he is best known for his work on how children develop their thinking abilities. His early work focused on biology, but after he moved to France in the 1920s, his interest turned to psychology. When he began teaching in a school known for administering intelligence tests, Piaget noticed an interesting phenomenon: Students of a certain age consistently made mistakes on the tests that older children did not make. This led Piaget to believe that younger children thought differently than older children. Piaget published more than 60 books over the next 50 years that most often dealt with how thinking develops in children.

MAKE IT STICK!

1. Sigmund Freud's theories differed from all other early psychological theories because of his emphasis on

   a. the effect of the unconscious mind on our thinking and behavior.
   b. our conscious experience and perception of the world around us.
   c. introspection as a form of gathering data about thinking.
   d. experimental research and gathering data on observable behaviors.

2. What was Watson's primary complaint about early psychological theories?

   a. Early theories emphasized human actions instead of the basic thinking behind them.
   b. Early theories addressed thinking instead of observable behaviors.
   c. Early theories were based on experimental methods instead of introspection.
   d. Early theories were too closely tied to William James's work.

3. Which of the following would most likely be said by a behaviorist?

   a. We should only study observable behaviors.
   b. We should only study mental processes.
   c. We should only study drives and conflicts.
   d. We should only study conscious experiences.

4. Which of the following, considered by some to be the third force in psychology, would most likely be associated with the idea that humans have free will in their decision making?

   a. Behaviorism
   b. Psychoanalysis
   c. Development
   d. Humanism

5. Striving to reach one's potential is a field of study picked up by which of the following kinds of psychologists?

   a. Humanistic
   b. Psychoanalytic
   c. Positive
   d. Developmental

Psychology's American Groundbreakers

2-4 How did psychology's groundbreakers move psychology forward and help advance gender and race equality?

Like other academic fields, early psychology lacked the ethnic and gender diversity it has today. Although it is difficult to imagine by today's standards, women and minority students were often discouraged from attending colleges and universities at the time of and for decades after psychology's birth. If this seems shocking, remember, for example, that women were not allowed to vote in the United States until 1920. The spirit of the times in North America and in Europe (where psychology flourished) favored the advancement of white men at the expense of nonwhite men and all women. These racial and gender barriers meant white males dominated psychology (and all sciences) because others rarely had the opportunity to gain the education, knowledge, and training necessary to become a psychologist. Several groundbreakers in psychology excelled in, and in spite of, this hostile cultural climate (see **Figure 2.2**).

G. Stanley Hall was a student of Wundt's who achieved a number of psychological firsts. Hall was the first American to receive a doctoral degree (Ph.D.) in psychology. He also opened the first psychology laboratory in the United States (at Johns Hopkins University), and he was the first president of the American Psychological Association (APA), elected in 1892.

Working with William James, Mary Whiton Calkins had to overcome discrimination and prejudice against women to become the first woman to complete the requirements for a Ph.D. in psychology, in 1895. Harvard at that time did not admit women and so would not award her a degree. Years later, Harvard offered to give her a degree from Radcliffe College (established by Harvard to educate women). Calkins refused the offer, stating that she had completed her work at Harvard, not Radcliffe. Calkins was elected president of the APA in 1905.

Margaret Floy Washburn was Edward B. Titchener's first graduate student at Cornell University, and she was the first woman to receive a Ph.D. in psychology. In 1908, Washburn wrote the first textbook on comparative psychology, which examined animal behavior.

Francis Cecil Sumner, in 1920, became the first African American to receive a Ph.D. in psychology. Sumner wrote many articles on racial prejudice, education for African Americans, and nature–nurture issues. Sumner also established the psychology department at Howard University.

Inez Beverly Prosser, the first African American woman to earn an Ed.D. in psychology, completed the requirements in 1933 at the University of Cincinnati. She studied the development of African American children in segregated and integrated schools.

Kenneth Clark and **Mamie Phipps Clark** were educational psychologists whose research was presented as evidence to the U.S. Supreme Court during the landmark court case on desegregating schools, *Brown v. Board of Education*. The Clarks (both students of Francis Sumner) helped show that internalized racism was a product of the stigmas attached to "separate but equal" schools for white children and black children. For instance, black children attending a segregated school (where they were apart from white children) often viewed *white* as good and pretty and *black* as bad and ugly. The Supreme Court listened to the Clarks' findings and mentioned them when ruling in 1954 that segregated schools were unconstitutional. Kenneth Clark was also the first African American to be president of the APA.

American Psychological = APA Association [handwritten annotation]

KENNETH CLARK (1914–2005) AND MAMIE PHIPPS CLARK (1917–1983) Researchers whose work was used in the *Brown v. Board of Education* case that overturned segregation in schools.

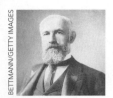

G. Stanley Hall
(1844–1924)

Alfred Binet
(1857–1911)

Karen Horney
(1885–1952)

Albert Bandura
(1925–   )

Martin Seligman
(1942–   )

1879 Wilhelm Wundt opens the first psychology laboratory in Leipzig, Germany.

1890 William James publishes the first psychology textbook, *Principles of Psychology*.

1892 G. Stanley Hall founds the American Psychological Association (APA). E. B. Titchener introduces structuralism.

1900 Sigmund Freud publishes his psychoanalytic views in *The Interpretation of Dreams*.

1905 Mary Whiton Calkins becomes the first woman to be president of the APA. Alfred Binet develops the first intelligence test.

1906 Ivan Pavlov publishes his results on learning by association.

1908 Margaret Floy Washburn becomes the first woman to receive a doctoral degree (Ph.D.) in psychology.

1913 John B. Watson publishes "Psychology as the Behaviorist Views It."

1920 Francis Cecil Sumner becomes the first African-American to earn a doctoral degree in psychology.

1926 Jean Piaget publishes *The Language and Thought of the Child*.

1933 Inez Beverly Prosser becomes the first African-American woman to earn a doctoral degree in psychology.

1938 B. F. Skinner promotes behaviorism, publishing *The Behavior of Organisms*.

1939 Kenneth Clark and Mamie Phipps Clark begin work that will be cited by the U.S. Supreme Court 1954 decision ending racial segregation in public schools.

1945 Karen Horney challenges the male bias in Freud's psychoanalytic theory and proposes a social-cultural approach.

1950 Erik Erikson publishes *Childhood and Society*, outlining stages of psychosocial development.

1954 Abraham Maslow presents the humanistic perspective. Gordon Allport publishes *The Nature of Prejudice*.

1961 Albert Bandura stresses the importance of imitation in learning, proposing a social-learning theory.

1969 John Berry calls attention to the importance of cross-cultural research in psychology.

1974 Eleanor Maccoby and Carol Jacklin publish *The Psychology of Sex Differences*.

1981 Roger Sperry receives a Nobel Prize for research on split-brain patients.

1998 Martin Seligman's APA presidential address launches the positive psychology movement.

2002 Daniel Kahneman receives a Nobel Prize for research on decision making.

2007 Barbara Fredrickson advances a new broaden-and-build theory on emotions.

2012 The American Psychiatric Association issues official position statements supporting the civil rights of gender-nonconforming individuals.

2013 President Barack Obama announces the BRAIN initiative to map the activity of every neuron in the human brain.

2014 Psychologist John O'Keefe is awarded the Nobel Prize for his work on brain networks and memory.

2015 The American Psychological Association bars psychologists from participating in interrogations at sites violating international law.

2017 First-ever High School Psychology Summit on how to best teach psychology held in Ogden, Utah. (Both of your authors spoke at the summit.)

Mary Whiton
Calkins
(1863–1930)

Francis Cecil
Sumner
(1895–1954)

Mamie Phipps
Clark
(1917–1983)

Daniel Kahneman
(1934–   )

John O'Keefe
(1939–   )

FIGURE 2.2
Psychology's
Groundbreakers

There is ample evidence to show that psychology supports and promotes the importance of diversity more than ever. In 2017, over two-thirds of all psychology doctorates were awarded to women. Half of the APA presidents elected this century have been women, and the 2017 APA president was born in Cuba.[4] Worldwide, psychology is growing rapidly. In 1977, China had no psychology department in any of its universities. Less than 30 years later, there were over 200.[5] But although roughly 33 percent of the U.S. population consists of nonwhites, the proportion of minority students in graduate programs is far from one in three. This gap will continue to close as university psychology departments across the country work to recruit the best and brightest students from all backgrounds. To meet the demands of our increasingly multicultural and ethnically diverse population, psychology will need to continue evolving.

MAKE IT STICK!

1. Kenneth and Mamie Phipps Clark's work, which showed that African American children attending a segregated school often viewed *white* as _good/pretty_, was used in the *Brown v. Board of Education* case that overturned _segregation_

2. An example of how psychology has been a progressive science is that even though universities like Harvard University did not allow women to enroll in 1905, Mary Whiton Calkins was elected president of the _APA_ that same year.

3. Today, about what percentage of psychology doctorates are awarded to women?
   a. 25 percent
   b. 10 percent
   c. 50 percent
   d. 65 percent

4. Who of the following opened the first psychology lab in the United States?
   a. Alfred Binet
   b. G. Stanley Hall
   c. Albert Bandura
   d. Mamie Phipps Clark

5. Which of the following likely contributed to the fact that no woman received a doctorate in psychology until about 30 years after the first man received a doctorate?
   a. At the time, many universities did not admit women.
   b. Prejudicial attitudes toward women were prevalent.
   c. Psychology, like all sciences at the time, was dominated by men.
   d. All of the answers are correct.

Six Psychological Perspectives

 2-5 How do six psychological theories explain thinking and behavior?

We can explain behavior from many viewpoints, or perspectives. *Psychological perspectives, schools of thought,* and *psychological approaches* are all synonyms for the ways in which psychologists classify collections of ideas. Put another way, the psychologist who believes in a particular collection of ideas is said to view behavior from that particular perspective. For instance, a behaviorist views psychology from a behavioral perspective.

Psychology has seen many perspectives come and go. We have already noted the emergence of psychoanalysis, behaviorism, and humanistic psychology. The other three discussed here are the cognitive perspective, the biological perspective, and the social-cultural perspective (see **Figure 2.3**).

To understand these six perspectives, let's apply each to the same real-life possibility: whether or not a person helps a stranger pick up a spilled sack of groceries when given the opportunity. Why do some people help when others don't? Each of the six perspectives has an explanation.

Psychologists who are psychoanalysts work from the *psychodynamic perspective,* a school of thought that focuses on how behavior springs from unconscious drives and conflicts. A psychologist influenced by the psychodynamic perspective might suggest that a person does *not* help the stranger pick up the groceries because she has an unresolved childhood conflict about her father always yelling at her to pick up her toys. The assumption is that there is a conflict, from long ago, that needs to be resolved. The psychologist assumes that until it is resolved, the conflict will affect behavior.

Psychologists who are behaviorists work from the *behavioral perspective,* a school of thought that focuses on how we learn observable responses. As we learned

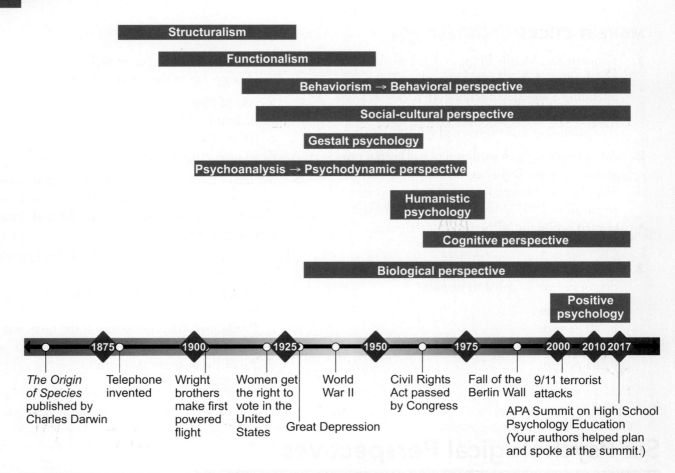

FIGURE 2.3
Historical Development of Psychology's Main Schools of Thought
This figure shows the periods in which each psychological perspective has had its most profound influence on psychology's development. (Adapted from Schultz & Schultz, 2016.)

cognitive perspective School of thought that focuses on how people think—how we take in, process, store, and retrieve information.

biological perspective School of thought that focuses on the physical structures and substances underlying a particular behavior, thought, or emotion.

social-cultural perspective School of thought that focuses on how thinking or behavior changes in different situations or as a result of cultural influences.

earlier, behaviorists believe we learn certain responses through rewards, punishments, and observation. So, they might suggest that a person helps the stranger pick up the spilled sack of groceries because that person has observed someone being rewarded for helpful behavior in the past. Learning that rewards come to those who help others fosters helping behavior.

Psychologists who are humanistic therapists work from the *humanistic perspective,* a school of thought that focuses on how healthy people strive to reach their full potential. A humanistic psychologist might suggest that a person who has met his own basic needs (hunger, thirst, shelter) would be able to reach out socially and help another person in need.

Structuralism, functionalism, and Gestalt psychology are the forerunners of the **cognitive perspective,** a school of thought that focuses on how people think—how they take in, process, store, and retrieve information. Remembering something you've learned, for example, is a cognitive activity. From the cognitive perspective, helping a stranger could be a function of how we think about or interpret a situation. We may choose to help the stranger who spills a bag of groceries because we *think* it will make us look good to others. However, if we think helping will cause us to look silly, then we may well leave the stranger to pick up the groceries alone.

The **biological perspective** is a school of thought that focuses on physical structures and substances underlying a particular behavior, thought, or emotion. Biological psychologists might remind us that levels of a naturally occurring feel-good chemical found in the brain could affect whether we help the stranger or not. Those lacking normal amounts of this brain chemical might be feeling down and may not feel up to helping the stranger pick up the spilled groceries.

The **social-cultural perspective** is a school of thought that focuses on how thinking or behavior changes in different situations or as a result of cultural influences. Social-cultural psychologists might tell us that a person is more likely to help the stranger if that person is with some close-knit family members and 50 feet from his front door, less likely if he is alone in a crowded big-city grocery store he has never been to before.

As you can see, no one perspective lays claim to having all the answers to the question, What makes us tick? But look at these six perspectives collectively (see **Table 2.1**). Can you see why most psychologists today subscribe to more than one perspective? These six perspectives complement one another, and psychologists draw from them all in their attempts to understand behavior and mental processes. Sometimes they even look beyond these six—to developments on psychology's horizon—in their efforts to understand human behavior.

TABLE 2.1 Six Perspectives in Psychology

Perspective	Why Do We Help?
• **Cognitive**	
How we process information	Our individual interpretations of an event affect how we respond.
• **Biological**	
How our biological structures and substances underlie a given behavior, thought, or emotion	Our brain chemistry controls the emotions and thoughts that eventually produce helping behavior.
• **Social-Cultural**	
How thinking and behavior change depending on the situation or as a result of cultural influences	If we come from a cultural background that values helping, we're more likely to help. We're also more likely to help if we are in a comfortable situation, such as with a good friend, than if we are in a large, unfamiliar crowd.
• **Behavioral**	
How we learn through rewards, punishments, and observation	If we have witnessed or been rewarded for helping behavior in the past, we are more likely to help later.
• **Humanistic**	
How healthy people strive to reach their full potential	If our needs for nourishment and safety have been met, we are more likely to feel we can reach out and help others.
• **Psychodynamic**	
How we are affected by unconscious drives and conflicts	Unresolved inner conflicts can affect whether or not we help others.

MAKE IT STICK!

1. A psychologist from which psychological perspective would be most likely to agree that thinking and behavior are caused by combinations of hormone and neurotransmitter activity in the brain?

   a. Biological   c. Cognitive
   b. Social-cultural   d. Behavioral

2. A psychologist from which psychological perspective would be most likely to agree that people act in the ways they do because of rewards and punishments?

   a. Behavioral   c. Biological
   b. Cognitive   d. Social-cultural

3. A psychologist from which of the following perspectives would most likely focus her research on what people think?

   a. Social-cultural   c. Biological
   b. Cognitive   d. Behavioral

4. Which of the following books would most likely contain information about unresolved unconscious conflicts?

   a. *Humanistic Psychology and You*
   b. *Thinking About Cognitive Psychology*
   c. *Psychodynamic Psychology for Dummies*
   d. *The Adventures of Biological Psychology*

Psychology in the Twenty-First Century

 2-6 What are the basic ideas behind three of psychology's developing areas?

Psychology continues to grow. Three particularly strong developing areas in psychology are behavior genetics, evolutionary psychology, and positive psychology.

behavior genetics The school of thought that focuses on how much our genes and our environment influence our individual differences.

Those studying **behavior genetics** focus on how much our genes and environment influence our individual differences. Does this sound like a combination of biology and behaviorism? You bet. Apply the behavior genetics perspective to the helping example. A psychologist interested in behavior genetics might ask two questions: Is there a helpfulness trait? If so, is it triggered by growing up in a family that promotes and values helping those in need? If the answer to both questions is *Yes,* and if you possess the helping trait and the helpful family, then you'll be bending down to help that stranger pick up the oranges and the loaf of bread. From the perspective of behavior genetics, helping behavior is the product of learning *and* inherited genetic traits.

Some psychologists study behaviors that helped our ancestors survive. These psychologists hope to gain insight into behavior by using the **evolutionary perspective.** This approach combines biological, psychological, and social aspects of human behavior. Is it possible to explain helping from the perspective of evolutionary psychology? Well, helping may have been a behavior generally seen as favorable, and helping could have occurred in the past because helping behavior made us more desirable to others. Those who were well liked in the community had good odds for surviving and successfully producing offspring.

evolutionary psychology School of thought that focuses on the principles of natural selection to study the roots of behavior and mental processes.

positive psychology A movement in psychology that focuses on the study of optimal human functioning and the factors that allow individuals and communities to thrive.

Humanistic psychology is the forerunner of **positive psychology,** which became a force after Martin Seligman's 1998 APA presidential address on the positive psychology movement. Positive psychology shares with humanistic psychology a focus on wellness and on healthy people reaching their full potential, but it differs in one crucial way: Positive psychology is firmly grounded in psychological science, thereby avoiding humanistic psychology's lack of scientific research to support its theoretical foundations. Schools focusing on increased well-being (for example, teaching students how to express gratitude and how to be more resilient) in their curriculum have shown increases in achievement and attendance and decreases in the number of students experiencing symptoms of depression.[6, 7, 8]

MAKE IT STICK!

1. Which psychological perspective is most directly interested in factors such as wellness and human thriving?

   a. The psychodynamic perspective
   b. Behavior genetics
   c. Positive psychology
   d. The evolutionary perspective

2. Which psychological perspective is most directly interested in how genes and experiences combine to form personalities?

   a. Behavior genetics
   b. The humanistic perspective
   c. The psychodynamic perspective
   d. Positive psychology

MAKE IT STICK! (continued)

3. Which psychological perspective is most directly interested in how the behavior of our ancestors helped them to survive?

   a. The humanistic perspective
   b. The evolutionary perspective
   c. Behavior genetics
   d. Positive psychology

4. Which type of psychologist would say, We should study what it means to flourish and how to promote well-being?

   a. Positive psychologist
   b. Behavioral psychologist
   c. Cognitive psychologist
   d. Biological psychologist

Module 2 Summary and Assessment
History and Perspectives in Psychological Science

 2-1 What is psychology, and what kinds of topics do psychologists study?

- Psychology is the scientific study of behavior and mental processes.
- Psychologists rely on scientific research methods to answer questions.
- Any observable behavior or mental process can be studied by psychologists, with a focus on either basic or applied research.

 2-2 How did the study of psychology as a science get started?

- Wilhelm Wundt is considered the founder of modern psychology because he established a lab and used experimental methods to study consciousness.
- Edward B. Titchener introduced structuralism, the theory that the structure of conscious experience could be understood by analyzing the basic elements of thoughts and sensations.
- Gestalt psychology emphasized our tendency to integrate pieces of information into meaningful wholes.
- William James introduced functionalism, the theory that explored the ways consciousness helps people adapt to their environment.

2-3 In what ways did twentieth-century psychologists change how psychology was studied?

- Sigmund Freud introduced psychoanalysis, a theory of personality and therapeutic technique that attributes our thoughts and actions to unconscious motives and conflicts. Freud's new approach to understanding behavior and some of the ideas that developed from it have been incorporated into psychodynamic theory, which is a modernized version of Freud's original theories.
- Ivan Pavlov fostered interest in studying observable behavior by reporting how animals learn in certain situations.
- John B. Watson introduced behaviorism, the theory that psychology should only study observable behaviors, not mental processes. Behaviorism was the most dominant school of thought in psychology during the twentieth century and was later adapted and expanded by other behaviorists such as B. F. Skinner.
- Humanists such as Abraham Maslow and Carl Rogers emphasized conscious experience as the proper focus of psychology. They believed that humans have free will and that healthy people strive to reach their full potential.
- Jean Piaget's pioneering research in developmental psychology focused on how children develop their thinking abilities.

 2-4 How did psychology's groundbreakers move psychology forward and help advance gender and race equality?

- G. Stanley Hall was the first American to receive a doctoral degree (Ph.D.) in psychology. He opened the first psychology laboratory in the United States and was the first American Psychological Association (APA) president.

- Mary Whiton Calkins was the first woman to qualify for a Ph.D. in psychology and was elected president of the APA in 1905.

- Margaret Floy Washburn was the first woman to receive a Ph.D. in psychology.

- Francis Cecil Sumner was the first African American to receive a Ph.D. in psychology.

- Inez Beverly Prosser was the first African American woman to earn an Ed.D. in psychology.

- Kenneth Clark and Mamie Phipps Clark were educational psychologists whose research was used during the *Brown v. Board of Education* Supreme Court case.

- Psychology values the diversity of perspectives people from different backgrounds bring to the research and application of science.

 2-5 How do six psychological theories explain thinking and behavior?

- Psychological perspectives describe the ways in which psychologists view thinking and behavior. Many historical theories were forerunners to one or more modern perspectives.

- Psychological perspectives include the psychodynamic, behavioral, humanistic, cognitive, biological, and social-cultural perspectives.

- Psychodynamic psychologists focus on how our behavior springs from unconscious drives and conflicts.

- Behavioral psychologists believe we learn responses through rewards, punishments, and observation.

- Humanistic psychologists focus on how healthy people strive to reach their full potential.

- The cognitive perspective focuses on how people think—how they take in, process, store, and retrieve information.

- The biological perspective focuses on physical structures and substances underlying a particular behavior, thought, or emotion.

- The social-cultural perspective focuses on how thinking or behavior changes in different situations or as a result of cultural influences.

 2-6 What are the basic ideas behind three of psychology's developing areas?

- Behavior genetics focuses on how much our genes and environment influence our individual differences (a combination of biology and behaviorism).

- Evolutionary psychology focuses on behaviors that helped our ancestors survive and combines biological, psychological, and social theories of human behavior.

- Positive psychology focuses on the study of optimal human functioning and the factors that allow individuals and communities to thrive.

Summative Assessment

1. What do we call research intended to increase the scientific knowledge base?

   a. Basic research   c. Behavioral research

   b. Mental research   d. Applied research

2. Which theory attempts to understand conscious experience by analyzing the basic elements of thoughts?

   a. Functionalism   c. Structuralism

   b. Gestalt   d. Psychoanalysis

3. What do psychoanalysts call a misstatement reflective of something you'd like to say?

   a. Observable error   c. Pavlovian mistake

   b. Freudian slip   d. Behavioral bobble

4. Which kind of psychology focuses on the study of conscious experience and the individual's capacity for personal growth?

   a. Behavioral   c. Functionalist

   b. Psychoanalytic   d. Humanistic

5. Which of the following psychologists is most closely associated with client-centered therapy?

   a. Carl Rogers   c. John Watson

   b. Abraham Maslow   d. Jean Piaget

6. Which of the following psychologists presented research on internalized racism, helping the Supreme Court end legalized racial segregation?

   a. Kenneth and Mamie Clark

   b. Danial and Louise Kahneman

   c. Martin and Mandy Seligman

   d. Mary Calkins and Margaret Washburn

7. Which psychological school of thought focuses on how people think?

   a. Social-cultural

   b. Cognitive

   c. Biological

   d. Behavioral

8. Elliott helps his little sister because he has learned that rewards come to those who help. Which of the following perspectives is illustrated in this scenario?

   a. Psychodynamic
   b. Cognitive
   c. Behavioral
   d. Biological

9. Research from which of the following areas has shown that student achievement increases when students are taught how to be more resilient?

   a. Positive psychology
   b. Evolutionary psychology

   c. Behavioral genetics
   d. Structural cognition

10. Which of the following questions would most likely be asked by an evolutionary psychologist?

    a. What did Freud have to say about personality?
    b. How does a behaviorist explain learning?
    c. Who opened the first psychology laboratory?
    d. How does a certain behavior help us survive?

KEY TERMS AND KEY PEOPLE

psychology, p. 10

basic research, p. 10

applied research, p. 10

structuralism, p. 12

Gestalt [gih-SHTALT] psychology, p. 13

functionalism, p. 13

psychoanalysis, p. 14

behaviorism, p. 15

humanistic psychology, p. 15

cognitive perspective, p. 20

biological perspective, p. 20

social-cultural perspective, p. 20

behavior genetics, p. 22

evolutionary psychology, p. 22

positive psychology, p. 22

Wilhelm Wundt [VOONT] (1832–1920), p. 11

Edward B. Titchener (1867–1927), p. 12

William James (1842–1910), p. 13

Sigmund Freud (1856–1939), p. 14

Ivan Pavlov (1849–1936), p. 15

John B. Watson (1878–1958), p. 15

B. F. Skinner (1904–1990), p. 15

Abraham Maslow (1908–1970), p. 15

Carl Rogers (1902–1987), p. 15

Jean Piaget [pee-ah-ZHAY] (1896–1980), p. 16

Kenneth Clark (1914–2005) and Mamie Phipps Clark (1917–1983), p. 17

Module 3 | Research Strategies

Learning Goals

3-1 Identify the advantage research has over other ways of knowing things.

3-2 Describe ways that bias can influence research.

3-3 Explain why psychological scientists use case studies.

3-4 Explain why you can't conclude that a correlation represents a cause-and-effect relationship.

3-5 Explain why we should be cautious about data from surveys.

3-6 Describe why longitudinal and cross-sectional studies are used.

3-7 Explain how experiments are designed and why this makes experiments the most powerful research technique.

3-8 Describe the ethical guidelines that protect human and animal research participants.

scientific method A method of learning about the world through the application of critical thinking and tools such as observation, experimentation, and statistical analysis.

Psychological scientists use a variety of tools, methods, and research subjects to learn about behavior and mental processes.

How do you know what you know? You can know something because a friend told you or because you read it. You can also know something because it "seems obvious"—in other words, through common sense. These and many other ways of knowing may be right. But they may also be wrong. Psychologists use the **scientific method,** a method of learning about the world through the application of critical thinking and tools such as observation, experimentation, and statistical analysis. Psychologists rely on the scientific method because it is more likely than other methods to answer certain kinds of questions correctly. In this module, we explore some research tools available to scientists seeking knowledge. It is because psychologists use these tools that psychology is considered a science.

Tempura/E+/Getty Images
Gorodenkoff/Shutterstock
Tom M Johnson/Getty Images

The Scientific Method at Work
What do these individuals have in common? They are researchers who rely on the scientific method to learn about their chosen area of study. By using the tools of science and critical thinking, they can help us understand how the world operates.

Why Is Research Important?

 3-1 What advantage does research have over other ways of knowing things?

Many students sign up for their first psychology class hoping to cover the stuff associated with psychology that they've seen on TV and the Internet. How do I analyze my dreams? What makes me (and others) tick? Does my friend have an eating disorder? Too often, the "answers" we find in the media are more myth than reality. Psychological scientists use research tools and critical thinking to find correct answers to these questions.

Even if you don't believe you're interested in research, give it a chance. Do you like solving problems and figuring out the answers to puzzles? If so, research should be right up your alley. Research is not just a series of experiments and it doesn't always involve fancy lab equipment. It's a set of methods, a way of asking questions about the world and drawing logical, supported conclusions. These are important life skills for everyone. Headlines trumpet the latest findings about caffeine, and news anchors are forever introducing segments on new ways to treat depression and on how the brain works. If you don't know enough about research to decide when conclusions are reasonable and when they are not, you leave yourself at the mercy of the media. (See **Figure 3.1** for an example of how the media might bombard us with contradictory claims.) We surely won't all conduct research, but we will all be called on to evaluate its relevance. Just as modern civilization requires people to be computer literate to function well, it requires people to be research literate to make informed decisions.

In this module, we will see how psychologists conduct research by considering an example. Suppose your school is about to institute a new policy banning the use of earbuds and earphones to listen to music in study halls. How might we predict the effect of this new policy?

One way is to use common sense. Perhaps the common sense of school administrators told them that students can concentrate better if they are not distracted by music. But wait! *Your* common sense might lead you to the opposite conclusion. Maybe you feel that the music allows you to block out distracting noises and focus more effectively on your homework. That's the trouble with common sense; too often, it can lead you to whatever conclusion you want (see **Table 3.1**). Scientific methods that psychologists use can help you evaluate the competing hunches.

▲ **FIGURE 3.1**
How Do You Know What to Believe?
Critical thinking and knowledge of research help us evaluate competing claims.

Charles Blair-Broeker

▲ **Listen Up!**
Does listening to your earbuds affect studying? Science can provide answers to questions like this.

TABLE 3.1   The Limits of Common Sense

Common sense leaves us unsure of the truth, but research helps us apply principles appropriately in different situations.

Common sense says . . .

Opposites attract	but	Birds of a feather flock together
Out of sight, out of mind	but	Absence makes the heart grow fonder
Nothing ventured, nothing gained	but	A penny saved is a penny earned

MAKE IT STICK!

1. One advantage of the scientific method over other ways of understanding the world is that

   a. the scientific method can answer any question.

   b. the scientific method leads to more reliable, reproducible answers.

   c. people are more likely to agree with scientific answers than other kinds of answers.

   d. scientific answers are more likely to fit with our common sense.

2. Briefly describe why it is important for all people to have an understanding of the scientific method. *It's professional*

3. True or false? We should be skeptical of all claims made in the media.

   debatable

Observation and Bias

3-2 What are some ways that bias can influence research?

Charles Blair-Broeker

The simplest scientific technique is *observation*. In our example, you might watch students using earbuds and compare them with students not using earbuds. Which students look more focused and more intent on their work?

Observation, however, presents a problem: the potential for bias. The most common bias on the part of the researcher is called **confirmation bias,** a tendency to search for information that agrees with a preconception. As you might imagine, researchers try to avoid bias as they would the plague. In our example, you and an administrator might observe the same students listening to music while studying and come to opposite conclusions. You want the research to demonstrate that music is helpful, so you may be especially sensitive to behaviors that support this conclusion. An administrator may miss the behaviors you notice and may instead pay closer attention to actions that seem to indicate music is distracting. Both you and the administrator are being influenced by your biases.

Confirmation Bias
Some students are studying and some aren't. Both the administrator and student tend to notice examples that support their own points of view.

There are many ways to reduce confirmation bias, and the best method depends on the particular study. In our example, we might try to make the observations more *objective* (that is, less biased) by finding ways to rely less on the observer's opinion. For example, we could compare the grades of students who listen to music while studying with the grades of students who don't. Or perhaps we could have the observers count specific behaviors, like how many times in a 10-minute period students look away from their work or how many pages students read in 10 minutes. If you're thinking these methods could have flaws as well (just because students are turning pages does not mean they are learning anything), congratulations! You're using **critical thinking.** Psychologists use critical thinking to examine assumptions, uncover hidden values, evaluate evidence, and assess conclusions.

confirmation bias The tendency to focus on information that supports preconceptions.

critical thinking Thinking that does not blindly accept arguments and conclusions.

The point is that there is no perfect way to eliminate bias. The goal of psychological research is to minimize bias and maximize the probability of obtaining a reliable, meaningful conclusion.

Charles Blair-Broeker

act different when observed

Researchers must also watch for **participant bias,** a tendency for research participants to behave in a certain way because they know they are being observed or because they want to please the researcher. For example, the students might study harder because the administrator is in the room, which might lead the administrator to conclude that they are studying more effectively because they are not distracted by music. To minimize participant bias, psychologists often use **naturalistic observation,** observing and recording behaviors without manipulating or controlling the situation. To avoid influencing participants' behavior simply because of their presence, observers in a lab setting may use hidden cameras or one-way mirrors. Now, researchers have begun to observe by mining "big data"; that is, what we search for on Google and what we tweet, among other Internet sources, can provide important clues about what the public is thinking and feeling.

▲ **Naturalistic Observation**
Under which circumstances do you think the principal's observations are more accurate? Naturalistic observation requires that the behavior not be unduly influenced by the observer. Can you see that this might sometimes produce ethical concerns?

participant bias A tendency for research participants to behave in a certain way because they know they are being observed or they believe they know what the researcher wants.

naturalistic observation Observing and recording behavior in naturally occurring situations without manipulating or controlling the situation.

MAKE IT STICK!

1. _Confirmation_ bias exists when researchers only look for information that supports their point of view.

2. One way to minimize participant bias is to use ___Naturalistic___ observation to collect data.

3. True or false? Critical thinking means finding ways to criticize someone's position. *False*

Case Studies

 3-3 Why do psychologists use case studies?

In the previous section, we looked at observation and bias. Now we turn our attention to a specific technique that relies on observational skills. Researchers who study single individuals in depth in the hope of revealing universal principles are using the **case study** method. Keep in mind that the case study method is prone to bias, and it may not be possible to extend the results of one case study to other people or situations. For example, an in-depth study of just one earbud-using

case study A research technique in which one person is studied in depth in the hope of revealing universal principles.

student in study hall could provide some very unrepresentative results because that particular student could naturally be exceptionally focused or distractible.

Sometimes, however, a case study is all that is ethically possible. Child abuse, for example, is often researched with case studies. Obviously, it would be unethical for researchers to abuse a sample of children, so they must wait until authorities discover a case of abuse and then attempt to study the effects of that abuse. "Genie" was the subject of just such a study. She was discovered in California in 1970, a 13-year-old victim who had spent her life in such isolation that she had not even learned to speak. Since 1970, psychologists have intensively studied Genie's behavior and progress to learn about the development of language and social skills. Researchers who study cases such as Genie's hope to glean important knowledge from these tragic situations that can help explain general truths about human development and behavior.

Because no two cases of abuse are exactly alike, there is always some doubt about the conclusions of any one case study. But as similar case studies accumulate, researchers gain increasing confidence in the accuracy of their conclusions.

MAKE IT STICK!

1. A researcher would use a _____ to learn about a unique situation, such as a child growing up in a household in which four languages are spoken.

2. Why must researchers be cautious about the results of a case study?

Correlation

 3-4 Why is it impossible to conclude cause-and-effect relationships from correlational data?

correlational study A research project strategy that investigates the degree to which two variables are related to each other.

Another technique available to researchers is to collect and examine correlational data. Is there a relationship between diet and health? Between communication style and divorce? Between training techniques and success at the Olympics? To answer these kinds of questions, researchers use a **correlational study,** a research project designed to discover the degree to which two variables are related to each other. In the question about use of earbuds during studying, there are two variables:

1. Whether or not a student listens to music

2. Effectiveness of studying

If effectiveness of studying increases when students listen to music and decreases when students do not, then we can say that the two variables are *positively correlated.* That is, the two variables increase (or decrease) together. But if effectiveness of studying decreases when students listen and increases when they do not, then the variables are *negatively correlated*—one variable increases while the other decreases (see **Figure 3.2**).

Remember, the discovery of a correlation *does not prove that a cause-and-effect relationship exists.* Results from correlational studies can tell us that two variables are related, but not *why* they are related. Suppose a researcher discovered a negative correlation between TV watching and grade point average (GPA): Students who watched more television had lower GPAs. Based on this correlation alone, can we conclude that TV watching *causes* grades to suffer? The answer is *no.* It is indeed

LIFE MATTERS

When you see headlines that make claims such as "Science proves…" or makes statements, like "Cell Phones Cause Depression," what keywords should you look for to determine if these are correlational studies? "Prove" and "cause" have specific meanings in science - that the results were obtained using experimental methods, not correlational.

Perfect positive correlation

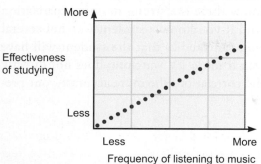

Perfect negative correlation

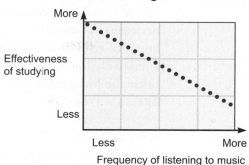

Moderate positive correlation

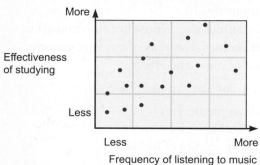

Moderate negative correlation

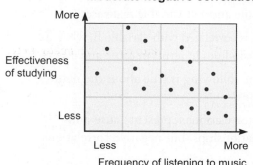

▲ **FIGURE 3.2**
Positive and Negative Correlations
Correlations can be easily visualized with these scatterplots. Each red dot represents one student. Dots that are higher on the plot indicate more effective studying. Dots that are farther right indicate more time listening to music.

The two top graphs show what perfect positive and negative correlations would look like for listening to music and effectiveness of studying. In the positive correlation, as music use increases, so does effectiveness of studying. In the negative correlation, effectiveness of studying decreases as music use increases. Actual data would surely look more like one of the two bottom graphs, which show moderate positive and negative correlations.

FIGURE 3.3
Correlation Is Not Causation
The discovery of a negative correlation between TV watching and grade point average (GPA) would not provide any information about what caused the correlation. Here are three equally plausible explanations.

possible that watching television causes one's grades to decline, but there are other possible explanations as well. It may be that having low grades causes one to watch more TV. There could even be some other variable—say, low intelligence—that could cause both a lot of TV watching and low grades. Correlation does not tell us which of these explanations is correct (see **Figure 3.3**).

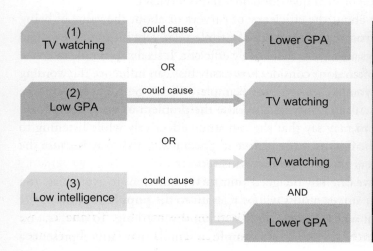

JUICE/ILI/Juice Images/Alamy

Correlations cannot establish cause-and-effect relationships, but they are useful for making predictions. If you know there is a strong negative correlation between TV watching and grades, and if you know a student watches several hours of television each day, then you can predict that the student will have a relatively low GPA. This is true even if more TV watching does not directly cause the low grades. The stronger the correlation, the more accurate your prediction will be.

MAKE IT STICK!

1. A _____ correlation exists when one variable increases while another variable decreases.

2. If variable A is correlated with variable B, what are the three possibilities in terms of cause and effect?

3. Which of the following is true about the nature of correlations?

   a. Positive correlations represent cause-and-effect relationships, but negative correlations do not.
   b. Negative correlations represent cause-and-effect relationships, but positive correlations do not.

   c. All correlations represent cause-and-effect relationships.
   d. Correlations may represent cause-and-effect relationships, but alone they don't provide proof of cause and effect.

4. What are correlations useful for?

   a. Making predictions
   b. Eliminating bias
   c. In-depth studies of individuals
   d. Establishing cause and effect

Surveys

 3-5 Why should we be cautious when applying data obtained from surveys?

survey method A research technique that questions a sample of people to collect information about their attitudes or behaviors.

How do researchers go about collecting data to establish a correlation? One way is to use the **survey method,** a research technique that questions a sample of people to collect information about their attitudes or behaviors. In the music example, you might have students fill out a short questionnaire about the effect of earbud use in study hall. Surveys allow researchers to collect large amounts of data efficiently through the use of such questionnaires and interviews.

There is no doubt about the efficiency of surveys or about the value of being able to collect data from large numbers of people relatively inexpensively. The problem is that surveys are almost seductively efficient. It seems so simple to create a survey that people often don't consider how easily bias can influence the wording of the questions. Do you like flowers?, for example, will not get the same response as, Do you like horticulture? Surveys also raise the problem of *social desirability.* For example, a student may say that she can study effectively while listening to music even though she doesn't really believe it. She answers that way because she thinks that's how others would want her to answer.

population The entire group of people about whom you would like to know something.

random sample A sample that fairly represents a population because each member of the population has an equal chance of being included.

But assume you have carefully designed your survey questions to avoid bias. You still must be sure your survey results will be relevant to the **population,** the entire group of people about which you would like to know something. To do this, you must draw an adequately sized **random sample,** a sample that fairly represents a population because each member of the population has an equal chance of being included (see **Figure 3.4**).

If the population you wish to study is the students in study halls at your school, you could, for example, draw a random sample by selecting every tenth name from a list of students registered for study halls. But is this number adequate? Researchers answer that question with mathematical formulas, but in general, larger samples are better—if they are random. If the sample is not random, it might have a larger percentage of good (or bad, or sick, or sassy) students than the whole study hall population does. This makes the sample biased and therefore not a good way to draw conclusions about the study hall population.

FIGURE 3.4
Sample and Population
The larger jar contains a population—in this case, a mixture of two colors of marbles. You can efficiently learn the percentage of each color in this larger group of marbles by randomly removing a sample (represented by the marbles in the smaller jar) and counting the two colors.

MAKE IT STICK!

1. What is the most important caution you would give to a researcher interested in using a survey?

2. To be useful, a survey must be administered to a _____ sample pulled from a larger representative _____.

3. True or false? In a random sample, each member of the population has an equal chance of being included.

Longitudinal and Cross-Sectional Studies

 3-6 Why do psychologists conduct longitudinal and cross-sectional studies?

How much do you think you will change in the next 20 years? Will you have the same personality traits, for example? Be interested in the same things you are now? Longitudinal and cross-sectional studies are techniques of particular use to developmental psychologists, who study how individuals change throughout the life span. **Longitudinal studies** follow the same group of individuals over a long time. In the 1920s, psychologist Lewis Terman began a famous longitudinal study of a group of highly intelligent California children. He, and later other researchers, studied these individuals for 70 years to discover what happens to bright children as they grow up. The researchers learned that in general, these gifted people had successful careers.[1] Longitudinal studies provide a rich source of data as time passes, but they are quite expensive and difficult to conduct. As a result, they tend to be pretty rare. Imagine the challenges of keeping track of a group of study hall students throughout their lifetime to determine the long-term effects of listening to (or not listening to) music with earbuds.

It is more common to conduct **cross-sectional studies,** which compare people of different ages at one time. A psychologist interested in how memory changes over the life span could gather a random sample of people from different age

longitudinal study A research technique that follows the same group of individuals over a long period.

cross-sectional study A research technique that compares individuals from different age groups at one time.

groups and administer a memory test to all of them. Cross-sectional studies are more efficient than longitudinal studies, but they have their own problems. If the test showed that the older groups had less memory ability than the younger groups, that *could* mean that memory declines as people age. But this difference could also be explained by other factors, such as changes over time in the educational system or the introduction of computers (or earbuds).

MAKE IT STICK!

1. _____ studies compare individuals from different age groups at one time.

2. Why are more cross-sectional studies conducted than longitudinal studies?

Experiments

 3-7 Why are experiments the most powerful research technique of all, and what factors contribute to the design of an experiment?

> **experiment** A research method in which the researcher manipulates and controls certain variables to observe the effect on other variables.

Observation, case studies, correlational studies, surveys, longitudinal studies, and cross-sectional studies are all important research techniques. Psychologists often use these different techniques in combination—for example, by using naturalistic observations to do a case study or by conducting surveys to establish correlations. But for establishing *cause and effect,* there is only one game in town, and researchers prefer it above all others. The **experiment** is the *only* method that allows us to draw conclusions about cause-and-effect relationships. Because experiments require researchers to control the things that can change—the variables—in a study, the chances of isolating the variable causing a particular effect are much greater.

Let's design an experiment to find out if banning listening to music in study halls would affect grades.

Hypotheses and Operational Definitions

> **hypothesis** A testable prediction about the outcome of research.
>
> **operational definition** An explanation of the exact procedures used to make a variable specific and measurable for research purposes.

In designing our experiment, the first thing we do is generate a **hypothesis**—a testable prediction about the outcome of research. Researchers often start with general expectations (Music influences concentration in study halls), but then put their variables in a more specific form that allows them to be precisely measured. In the language of research, they provide **operational definitions** of the variables—explanations of the exact procedures used to define research variables. One way to operationalize our hypothesis is to put it in this form: *Students assigned to listen to music each day in study hall will have higher average grades at the end of the term than students banned from listening to music.* We could operationalize the hypothesis in many other ways. We could say, *Students who are banned from listening to music each day in study hall will read fewer pages each day than students who are not banned from listening to music,* or *Students who use earbuds each day in study hall will have fewer conversations with other students in study hall than students who are not allowed to use earbuds.* Each of these versions has slightly different implications. Researchers must settle on the one operational definition that they believe does the best job of accurately reflecting the general hypothesis.

This is an important point even if you never conduct an experiment of your own. When you are evaluating research done by others, you should consider whether the operational definitions are appropriate or inappropriate. For example, every year *U.S. News and World Report* publishes rankings of the best colleges and universities in the United States. But how do the researchers operationalize *best?* The material that accompanies the rankings tells you they use a complex formula that considers factors like first-year retention rate, financial support for students, and undergraduate reputation. If you don't agree with the weightings in the formula (maybe you're much more concerned about financial support than they are or much less concerned with reputation), then you shouldn't put much faith in the rankings.

Operational Definitions and Positive Psychology

Positive psychologists have research problems similar to those faced by all scientists. One of them is to develop adequate operational definitions. Like many things, this is often more difficult than it appears.

For example, positive psychologists are interested in happiness. They recognize that it's not exactly the opposite of, or even the absence of, depression. So, what is it? And more important, how do you measure it for research purposes? There are many ideas about how to do this, and none of them are perfect.

- Perhaps you could measure happiness with some physiological measure. Wouldn't it be nice if it were as easy to measure happiness as it is to measure blood pressure or cholesterol level? *Yes,* it would be nice, but so far we haven't been able to discover a direct physiological measure.

- Maybe you could measure happiness using observation. One way to do this would be to look for evidence that a person is smiling. However, people don't always agree about what a smile is—another problem with the operational definition! Smiles aren't always genuine, either, and it's also possible to be happy without smiling (or to smile without being happy).

- Another way to measure happiness would be to administer surveys, and survey results, in fact, are often used as the operational definition of happiness. One such survey is the Satisfaction With Life Scale, seen in **Figure 3.5**.[2] Why don't you give it a try!

Directions: Below are five statements with which you may agree or disagree. Using the 1–7 scale below, indicate your agreement with each item by placing the appropriate number in the line preceding that item. Please be open and honest in your responding.

1 = strongly disagree
2 = disagree
3 = slightly disagree
4 = neither agree nor disagree
5 = slightly agree
6 = agree
7 = strongly agree

_____ 1. In most ways my life is close to my ideal.
_____ 2. The conditions of my life are excellent.
_____ 3. I am satisfied with my life.
_____ 4. So far I have gotten the important things I want in life.
_____ 5. If I could live my life over, I would change almost nothing.

Source: Diener et al. (1985).

FIGURE 3.5
Satisfaction With Life Scale

Scores on this Satisfaction With Life Scale can range from 5 to 35, with scores above 20 generally indicating satisfaction with life. Does your overall score seem accurate? Does it match your impression of what it means to be happy? If so, that means you believe that scores on this survey are a good operational definition of happiness.

Independent and Dependent Variables

Back to our experiment. Let's assume we have agreed on this hypothesis: *Students assigned to listen to music each day in study hall will have higher average grades at the end of the term than students banned from listening.* To discuss this hypothesis, you should know a little more about how variables are labeled. Trying to discuss experiments without knowing the different names for variables is like trying to discuss skateboarding without knowing the names of the tricks. It may be possible to describe a kickflip backside tailslide without knowing the phrase, but it sure is difficult.

You already know that the purpose of an experiment is to establish a cause-and-effect relationship (in our case, finding out whether listening to music causes student grades to go up). Every hypothesis for an experiment reflects this cause-and-effect pattern, and when you read a hypothesis, you should be able to identify two variables, the independent variable and the dependent variable:

- The variable that should cause something to happen is the **independent variable (IV).**
- The variable that should show the effect (or the outcome) of changing the IV is the **dependent variable (DV).**

Whenever you think about an experiment, a good first step is to identify the IV and the DV. If you are unable to figure this out, you will almost certainly not understand the point of the experiment.

So, what is the IV—the cause variable—for our example? In our hypothesis, the variable that we predict will make a difference—our IV—is the presence or absence of music. The DV, or the variable that shows the effect, is the participants' average end-of-term grades.

Groups, Random Assignment, and Confounding Variables

To make the independent variable vary (take on different values), researchers set up groups of participants. Typical experiments have at least two groups: an experimental group and a control group (sometimes referred to as the experimental and control conditions). In the **experimental group,** the participants are exposed to the treatment (the IV). In the **control group,** the participants are not exposed to the treatment (the IV). Control group participants function as a comparison for the experimental group participants. In our example, the experimental group will comprise all students assigned to listen to music, and the control group will comprise all students who are not allowed to listen. These two groups will permit us to compare the effect of music on two groups of similar students.

The number of participants assigned to each group depends on some complicated statistical factors, but usually there are at least 20 participants per group. Therefore, we need to select 40 students for the experiment. We need to draw these students randomly from the entire population of 400 study hall students (for example, by selecting every tenth name from a complete list of study hall

independent variable (IV) The variable that the researcher will actively manipulate and, if the hypothesis is correct, that will cause a change in the dependent variable.

dependent variable (DV) The variable that should show the effect of the independent variable.

experimental group The participants in an experiment who are exposed to the independent variable.

control group The participants in an experiment who are not exposed to the independent variable.

students). If the selection is not random, the sample may be biased, and we would not be able to apply the results to the whole study hall population.

Now comes one of the most important steps: How do we decide which 20 students in the pool of participants should be in the experimental group and which 20 should be in the control group? An absolutely critical feature of experimental design is that the participants are placed in groups by **random assignment.** Because chance alone determines group assignment, we can assume individual differences among participants (for example, how well they sleep or how smart they are) will be equally distributed between the two groups. You could use a computer program to do the random assignment or a low-tech method like drawing names out of a hat. **Figure 3.6** summarizes the various components of our design.

Individual differences among participants like health, attitude, and sleep quality are the largest category of a special kind of variable known as **confounding variables** (from a Latin word that means *to confuse*). These are variables other than the IV that could produce a change in the DV. To draw cause-and-effect conclusions from an experiment, researchers must adequately control for confounding variables. To see how this works, imagine for a moment that we didn't randomly assign the students to groups and those in the experimental group (the ones who listen to music) are also healthier than the students in the control group (those banned from music). If the experimental group does have higher average grades at the end of the term, how would we know what caused this? The cause could have been the IV—music—but it could also have been that a higher level of health in the experimental group allowed them to study more effectively. We really don't know because the health variable *confounds* the music variable.

We have to be careful about how we set up the two groups so that we can eliminate confounding variables that could influence our experimental group's performance. Potential confounding variables include the amount of sleep participants get, the number of personal problems they're experiencing, and the quality of the

random assignment A procedure for creating groups that allows the researcher to control for individual differences among research participants.

confounding variable In an experiment, a variable other than the independent variable that could produce a change in the dependent variable.

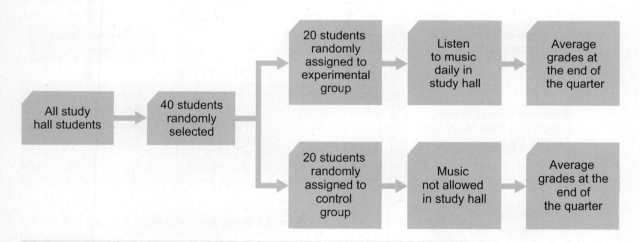

▲ **FIGURE 3.6**
Experimental Design
The hypothesis is that students who are assigned to listen to music in study hall will have higher average grades at the end of the term than students banned from listening to music. To create different levels of the IV, the presence or absence of music, 40 randomly sampled students will be randomly assigned to an experimental group that listens to music and a control group that does not. Later we will determine the effect of this manipulation by measuring the DV, average grades at the end of the term, for each group. The hypothesis leads us to predict that the experimental group will have higher average grades.

teachers they have. This is why random assignment of participants to groups is so critical: It enables the researcher to assume that these potentially confounding factors will balance almost evenly across the two groups, just as 40 coin flips will usually balance fairly evenly between heads and tails. (Go ahead. Try it!) Without random assignment, there is a much greater likelihood that a confounding variable will bias the results of the research. You have to randomly assign participants to groups to conduct a true experiment and identify the cause-and-effect relationship between the IV and the DV.

Control for Other Confounding Variables

In addition to controlling for individual differences, a good experimental design must control for two other types of confounding variables: environmental differences and expectation effects (see **Figure 3.7**). It is relatively easy to control for environmental differences. In our music example, you would want to make sure that all participants were in a study hall with the same temperature, lighting, and noise conditions.

Researchers must take special care, however, to control for expectation effects. They begin by making sure that participants are not aware of the hypothesis of the experiment. If participants were aware, then their expectations could influence the outcome. In our example, students in the experimental group might do better because their knowledge of the hypothesis led them to expect better grades and raised their confidence when taking tests. To control for expectation effects, experimenters often use a *blind* (or masked)

FIGURE 3.7
The Challenge of Confounding Variables
Experimenters use a variety of techniques to minimize the disruptive effects of confounding variables. There are two challenges involved: anticipating what the confounding variables will be, and then deciding on the best method of dealing with each of them.

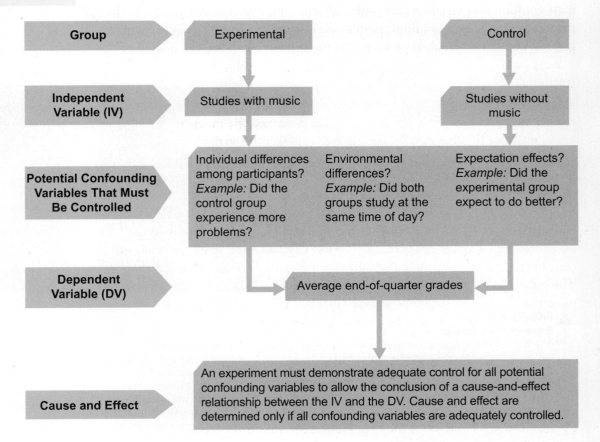

procedure, which means that they do not tell participants what the hypothesis is until after the data are collected. Sometimes researchers use a **double-blind procedure,** in which neither the data collectors nor the research participants know the expected outcome of the experiment. Using a double-blind procedure is particularly important when the researchers collecting data are asked to make judgments about the dependent variable (for example, judging whether or not students are studying effectively). Without the double-blind procedure, researchers might be inclined to see what they expected to see and not see what they didn't expect. After the experiment, of course, the research participants are told the hypothesis.

If a drug is the independent variable, researchers deal with expectation effects by using a **placebo,** an inactive pill that has no known effect. Imagine that you want to test the effectiveness of a new drug that may enhance memory. To set up this experiment, you would form an experimental group and a control group to manipulate whether participants would receive the drug, the IV. You would measure the effect of the drug by comparing the two groups' performance on, say, a memory task, the DV. However, if the experimental group receives a pill and the control group does not, you will not be able to successfully interpret better performance by the experimental group. Why? Because our expectations have a profound and well-documented effect on our responses. People receiving a pill of any sort will expect to experience change, and they will work harder to achieve the expected results. Given this extra effort, you would not know whether the drug caused the enhanced memory in the experimental group or whether the expectations created by taking that drug enhanced people's memory.[3] You could control for this, however, by giving a placebo pill, containing no active substances, to the control group. Now, because all participants in both groups receive a pill and neither group knows whether the pill contains active or inactive substances, you can be sure that the expectations produced by taking a pill did not account for any improvement in memory.

Let's return to our music example and review what we've accomplished so far. We are conducting an experiment to test this hypothesis: *Students assigned to listen to music each day in study hall will have higher average grades at the end of the term than students banned from listening.* We have identified the independent variable as the presence or absence of music and are studying this variable by establishing an experimental group that does listen to music and a control group that doesn't. We have randomly selected the participants for the experiment from the entire study hall population, so we can be sure that the sample is not biased and the results will apply to all study hall students. We then randomly assigned the participants to the two groups to control for any individual differences among them, and we controlled for other confounding variables by making sure the environmental conditions and expectation effects for the two groups are as similar as possible. The only thing we want to differ between the two groups is the IV—whether or not students listen to music—because we want to be able to conclude that there is a cause-and-effect relationship between listening to music and having higher end-of-term grades.

Data Analysis

Now we run the experiment and collect the data. Then we analyze the numbers, using statistics, to find out if the hypothesis is supported.

double-blind procedure A research procedure in which both the data collectors and the research participants do not know the expected outcome of the experiment.

placebo An inactive substance or condition used to control for confounding variables.

Let's say the average end-of-term grade for the experimental group is a B and for the control group is a C. Is this enough of a difference to conclude that there is a cause-and-effect relationship between listening to music (or not) and grades? *Maybe.* But what if the difference was between a B and a B minus? How different must the values of the dependent variable be for the two groups? Perhaps you've heard the phrase *statistically significant.* Most researchers have agreed that we can consider a result statistically significant if the possibility that the difference between groups would occur by chance alone is no more than 5 percent. To determine this likelihood, statistical formulas consider three questions:

1. How big is the difference *between* the groups?

2. How similar are the results *within* each group?

3. How many participants are in each group?

If we find a big difference *between* two large groups of students and small variations in results *within* each group (for example, mostly As and Bs in one group and mostly Cs and Ds in the other), we can be confident that the results are statistically significant.

The steps of the experimental method are summarized for you in **Table 3.2**.

TABLE 3.2   The Experimental Method Step by Step

1. Develop the *hypothesis.*
2. Create *operational definitions* for the *independent variable (IV) and dependent variable (DV).*
3. *Randomly select* a sample of participants from the population.
4. *Randomly assign* the participants to the *experimental and control groups.*
5. Expose the experimental group, but not the control group, to the IV. If necessary, use a *placebo* with the control group to balance expectations.
6. Control for other *confounding variables* by using a *doubleblind procedure* and treating both groups the same except for exposure to the IV.
7. Learn the effect of the IV by measuring the DV for both groups.
8. Use *statistical analysis* to discover whether the difference in the DV between the two groups is likely to have been caused by the manipulation of the IV.

Replication

There is one other safeguard required for an experiment. Researchers must be able to **replicate** the results—that is, repeat an experiment to see whether the results can be reliably reproduced. Unless a study can be replicated, the results are likely to be a fluke occurrence. If an experimental result can be obtained only once, we must conclude that it was caused by some chance variable and not by the independent variable. This means there is no apparent cause-and-effect relationship between the IV and the DV. In our study hall experiment, replication studies might involve repeating the experiment at different schools or under slightly different conditions. Replication helps us know that the results apply in a variety of situations, and it depends on having clear operational definitions for all our variables. It is no accident that our topic in this module is *research*—not search. Researchers have to demonstrate their findings again and again and again!

replicate To repeat the essence of a research study to see whether the results can be reliably reproduced.

MAKE IT STICK!

1. Why are placebos used in some experiments?

   a. They provide a way for the dependent variable to vary.

   b. They allow for statistical analysis of results.

   c. They are necessary for observational studies.

   d. They help control for some confounding variables.

2. Explain why random assignment is a critical feature of experimental design.

3. Which of the following is the best operational definition of learning in an experiment designed to identify techniques to help students learn math formulas?

   a. Students' scores in other courses

   b. Students' scores on a test over math formulas

   c. The quality of the teacher

   d. The number of minutes the teacher spends instructing students about the formulas

4. For the hypothesis *students who sleep more than 8 hours on school nights will have higher GPAs than students who sleep less than 8 hours on school nights*, what is the independent variable?

   a. The amount of sleep

   b. Students who sleep less than 8 hours

   c. GPA

   d. The night of the week

5. Repeating an experiment to see whether the results can be reliably reproduced is called _____.

Research Ethics

 3-8 What ethical guidelines are in place to protect the rights of human research participants and animal research subjects?

Is it ethical (morally proper) to force people to participate in research if they don't want to? According to current standards, *no*. Is it ethical to tell people that an experiment is about one's ability to solve math problems when it is really about how one behaves under stress? Current ethical standards allow researchers to deceive participants (as long as they clear up the deception at the end of the project), so this answer is *yes*. There are ethical considerations with all research, especially when the participants are humans. These ethical issues extend well beyond the methodological issues we have been discussing so far. For moral reasons, many hypotheses cannot be tested experimentally, even though we could design sound experiments that would provide good answers. For example, suppose your hypothesis is that children who are disciplined by being whipped with a belt will not behave as well as children disciplined without physical punishment. This experiment would be quite simple to set up. The IV would be exposure to whippings, and the DV would be some measure of behavior, such as number of broken rules. You would then choose a sample of participants and randomly assign them to two groups. Those in the experimental group would be whipped by their parents, and those in the control group would be disciplined by their parents in other ways. Here we have a straightforward experimental design, but it would be unethical to conduct this experiment. You would be exposing your experimental group participants to a procedure that you believe would harm them.

Human Research

Most research takes place on university campuses, where ethics committees screen all research proposals in advance. The committee checks that the research will comply with the strict ethical guidelines for research with human participants set by the American Psychological Association. There are four basic principles:

- *Informed consent.* Researchers must inform potential participants in advance about the general nature of the research and any potential risks involved. Participants must understand that they have a right to refuse to participate or to withdraw at any time. To hide specific details of the research is permissible if the general nature and potential risks are accurately portrayed.

- *The right to be protected from harm and discomfort.* Researchers may conduct studies that involve harm and discomfort only under certain circumstances and only with the participants' informed consent.

- *The right to confidentiality.* Researchers must never release data about individual participants, and members of the research team may not gossip or spread information about the participants.

- *The right to debriefing.* Participants must receive a full explanation of the research when their involvement is done. This is especially important if the research has included deception about specific details of the procedure.

Animal Research

The four ethical principles discussed here help protect the rights of human research participants, but what about animals? We sometimes hear media reports of research that seems to subject animals to unwarranted cruelty, pain, and suffering. Why are animals used in research? What is done to protect them?

Psychologists use animals in research for several reasons:

- Many psychologists are simply interested in how animals behave. It is a fascinating and legitimate field of study.

- There are biological and behavioral similarities between animals and humans. Therefore, by studying animals, we can learn things that apply to humans.

- Because many species of animals develop more rapidly and therefore have shorter life spans than humans do, we can study genetic effects over generations much more rapidly in animals than in humans.

- It is often possible to exercise more control over experiments with animals than over those with humans. For example, researchers can observe animals 24 hours a day and control their diet completely. Humans usually will not agree to such conditions.

- Procedures that are not ethical to perform on humans may be considered acceptable when performed on animals. My sister-in-law once had a job in a medical laboratory, where she performed surgery on unclaimed dogs that had been slated to be killed at a local animal shelter. She tied off an artery and created heart attacks in these dogs so that researchers could run controlled tests of experimental drugs designed for human heart attack patients. Is it right to place the needs of humans above those of animals? It's a difficult question, but we live in a society where some animals (cows and chickens) are raised for food and others (rats and insects) are exterminated to reduce the threat of disease. Since it has given rise to so many valuable findings, supporters of animal research argue that it's permissible to use or even kill animals for the good of humans.

So, what is done to protect animals from abuses? Federal legislation has been passed to protect animals used in research. This legislation, which has the support of the vast majority of researchers,[4] says that animals must have clean housing, adequate ventilation, and appropriate food, and that they must be otherwise well cared for.

Just as every marathon runner is also an athlete and every pianist is also a musician, every psychologist is also a scientist. This means psychologists use a particular set of research strategies to learn about behavior and mental processes. All the factual information you will read in this book was gathered using these research methods. Your knowledge of these methods will deepen your understanding of psychology and help prepare you to think critically in a world where research can (and should) drive many decisions. Now, what will you say when your school administrators announce that new study hall music policy?

Ethics of Animal Research
Despite stories about the abuse of animals in the cosmetics industry, there are many regulations to protect the animals used by psychological researchers. In fact, many psychologists choose to study animals because they care about the animals and what they can teach us.

MAKE IT STICK!

1. _____ occurs when a research participant knows the general nature of the research and agrees to participate.

2. _____ is when a participant receives a full explanation at the conclusion of the research.

3. Explain one reason why psychologists use animals in research.

Module 3 Summary and Assessment
Research Strategies

3-1 What advantage does research have over other ways of knowing things?

- Well-designed research produces data-supported conclusions.
- Research is better than common sense at providing reliable, logical answers to questions.

3-2 What are some ways that bias can influence research?

- Bias is any influence that unfairly increases the possibility that we will reach a particular conclusion.
- Research can be negatively influenced by a researcher's confirmation bias and by participant bias.

3-3 Why do psychologists use case studies?

- Case studies collect in-depth information on a single person or situation. However, researchers cannot know from the case study alone if the conclusions are true for other people or situations.

 3-4 Why is it impossible to conclude cause-and-effect relationships from correlational data?

- A correlational study tells us the extent to which two variables are related. If the variables change in the same direction, then it's a positive correlation; if the variables change in opposite directions, then it's a negative correlation. Correlations do not establish that there is a cause-and-effect relationship between the two variables. We do not know if one of the two variables caused the change or even if a third variable caused the change in each of the correlated variables.

 3-5 Why should we be cautious when applying data obtained from surveys?

- Surveys are an efficient way to collect information about people's attitudes or behaviors by asking questions on a questionnaire or in an interview. Researchers must be careful to construct unbiased questions and to use a random sample to draw adequate conclusions about their populations.

 3-6 Why do psychologists conduct longitudinal and cross-sectional studies?

- These techniques allow psychologists to study how individuals change across the life span. Longitudinal studies follow the same group for many years. Cross-sectional studies compare people of different ages at one time.

 3-7 Why are experiments the most powerful research technique of all, and what factors contribute to the design of an experiment?

- Only experiments can establish cause-and-effect relationships. They do this by generating a hypothesis with operationalized independent and dependent variables, by randomly selecting participants and randomly assigning them to the experimental and control groups to control for confounding variables, and by controlling for other confounding variables relating to expectations and environmental differences.

- Data from experiments must be analyzed to reveal statistically significant conclusions.

- It must be possible to replicate experimental results before a cause-and-effect relationship can be concluded.

 3-8 What ethical guidelines are in place to protect the rights of human research participants and animal research subjects?

- Ethical guidelines for research require that human participants have the rights of informed consent, protection from harm, confidentiality, and debriefing.

- Federal guidelines protect the health and safety of animals used in research.

Summative Assessment

1. A tendency to focus on information that supports what I already believe to be true is called
   a. critical thinking.
   b. participant bias.
   c. a confounding variable.
   d. confirmation bias.

2. Which of the following is naturalistic observation?
   a. A principal comes in to the classroom to evaluate a teacher.
   b. A marketing researcher sits outside of a busy store at the mall and notes what percentage of the people leaving the store are carrying bags or packages.
   c. A coach times potential team members to see how fast they can run 100 meters.
   d. A father supervises as his son picks up his toys.

3. If there is a positive correlation between having a high income and having a successful marriage, what can we conclude about cause and effect?

   a. Having a high income leads to a successful marriage.
   b. Having a successful marriage leads to a high income.
   c. Some other factor leads to both a successful marriage and a high income.
   d. Nothing.

4. The best sample to use for learning the opinions of the students in a high school is

   a. the first 50 students to walk through the door one morning.
   b. all of the students in the high school.
   c. 50 names drawn from a box containing the names of all the students.
   d. the 50 students with the highest GPAs.

5. A research technique that compares individuals from different age groups at one time is known as

   a. an experiment.
   b. a correlational study.
   c. a cross-sectional study.
   d. a longitudinal study.

6. If I am interested in the effect of exercise on health, which of the following could I use for the operational definition of the DV?

   a. The age of the participants in the study
   b. The number of days each week that the participants go to the gym
   c. The people in the group that does not go to the gym
   d. The number of days the participants call in sick

7. A researcher sets up an experiment where one group of students studies an hour each evening and another group studies 30 minutes each evening to see if this has an effect on test scores. The researcher is concerned that how smart the students are might be a confounding variable. How should the researcher control for this?

   a. By using a large sample of students
   b. By randomly assigning the students to the two groups
   c. By giving students an IQ test to find out how smart they are
   d. By using a double-blind procedure

8. In an experiment designed to determine if taking a nap each afternoon leads to fewer dinnertime arguments, what would be true of the control group?

   a. They are the participants who would not nap in the afternoon.
   b. They are the participants who would nap in the afternoon.
   c. They are the participants who had more arguments at dinner.
   d. They are the participants who had fewer arguments at dinner.

9. Statistical significance means

   a. an experiment has been replicated.
   b. an experiment is likely to produce changes in the way people live their lives.
   c. the results of an experiment were probably not caused by chance.
   d. the experiment used a double-blind procedure.

10. Which of the following ethical principles requires the researcher to divulge any deception that may have occurred?

    a. The right to be protected from harm and discomfort
    b. The right to confidentiality
    c. Informed consent
    d. Debriefing

KEY TERMS

scientific method, p. 26
confirmation bias, p. 28
critical thinking, p. 28
participant bias, p. 29
naturalistic observation, p. 29
case study, p. 29
correlational study, p. 30
survey method, p. 32

population, p. 32
random sample, p. 32
longitudinal study, p. 33
cross-sectional study, p. 33
experiment, p. 34
hypothesis, p. 34
operational definition, p. 34
independent variable (IV), p. 36

dependent variable (DV), p. 36
experimental group, p. 36
control group, p. 36
random assignment, p. 37
confounding variable, p. 37
double-blind procedure, p. 39
placebo, p. 39
replicate, p. 40

Module 4

Psychology's Statistics

Learning Goals

4-1 Explain why a frequency distribution is more useful than a random list of scores.

4-2 Describe three measures of the central tendency.

4-3 Describe two measures of variation.

4-4 Identify the important characteristics of a normal distribution.

4-5 Describe two comparative statistics.

4-6 Explain what the correlation coefficient indicates about the relationship between two variables.

4-7 Explain what is meant when research is described as statistically significant.

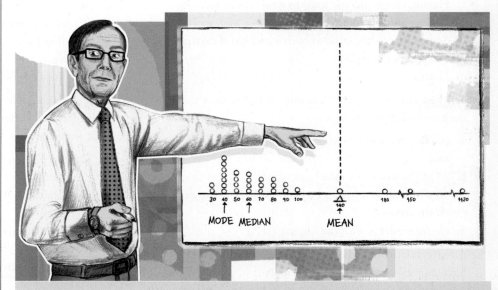

Psychologists use statistics to make numbers more meaningful and useful.

Statistics are more a matter of attitude than numbers. Many people (not *you*, of course) have a negative view of statistics and convince themselves that this is a topic beyond comprehension. Maybe it's the word—*statistics* is hard to pronounce! The concepts themselves are really not so hard. Lots of people enjoy the subject, and there is no denying its usefulness. Think of trying to participate in a fantasy sports league, or a real sports league for that matter, without the presence of statistical data—numbers—to guide your decisions or to determine winners and losers. Think of all the advertisers that try to sway consumers with statistics they say prove their product is best. A lack of understanding of statistics puts you at a serious disadvantage because statistical information is all around us. Television, newspapers, magazines, and the Internet are all full of statistical data. Some people do use statistics accurately and appropriately, but others use statistics inappropriately because of lack of knowledge or in an effort to deliberately mislead. To think critically about all the information bombarding you, you'll need to sort the good stuff from the bad. Educated people need statistical literacy as much as computer literacy.

Statistics may seem difficult at first simply because this is a new way of looking at things. Riding a bike or driving a car seems hard the first time you try, too. Think of the first time you went bowling, the first time you picked up a musical instrument, or the first time you attempted a new computer game. These were all significant challenges the first time around. If you're like most people, you're willing to work hard to learn something, despite the initial difficulty, if you believe in an activity's value. And statistics does have value—your efforts to understand will arm you with tools that will help you think critically about lots of choices you'll be making in life. So, stick around and take our guided tour of this important area.

Before we begin, take note of this key concept: *The purpose of statistics is to make numbers more meaningful.* If a friend told you she got 27 questions right on

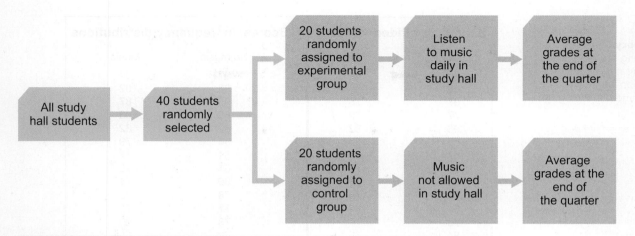

▲ **FIGURE 4.1**
Design for Music Experiment
The purpose of this experiment, fully explained in Module 3, is to determine whether or not students who listen to music during study hall will have higher grades.

her history test, how meaningful would that be? Wouldn't you also need to know how many items were on the test? If she got 27 right out of 30, that's great, but if she got 27 out of 100 . . . Well, you get the picture. And isn't it also important to know how other students did? Even if she did score 27 out of 30, that may have been the lowest score in the class on a very easy test. Or 27 out of 100 could be a good score if it was the highest score in the class on an exceptionally diffi-cult test. Statistics are an important extension of critical thinking. They provide a method for organizing information so that we can understand what a number really means.

To illustrate the statistics we discuss, we'll rely on an example we used in Module 3 to demonstrate research strategies: How would banning the use of music affect student learning in study halls? To find out, we designed an imaginary experi-ment with two groups (see **Figure 4.1**). The experimental group contained stu-dents assigned to listen to music while in study hall; the control group contained students who were not allowed to listen to music while there. We decided to mea-sure the effect of listening to music (our independent variable) by examining the two groups' average end-of-term grades (our dependent variable). We settled on a hypothesis that the experimental group, students who listened to music, would have higher grades at the end of the term than the control group, students who did not listen to music.

Daniel Bendjy / istockphoto

▲ **Statistical Literacy**
People in modern society need to understand statistics well enough to make informed decisions about data presented in the media. The number of runs scored by a baseball player could be influenced by his batting average, the number of bases he steals, or his position in the batting order, among other things.

Frequency Distributions

 4-1 What can we learn from frequency distributions?

A **frequency distribution** is, quite simply, a list of scores ordered from highest to lowest. **Figure 4.2** shows some possible data from the hypothetical experiment, before and after being made into an ordered list. Do you notice how much more useful these numbers are after we arrange them in a frequency distribution from highest to lowest? At a glance, you can tell the high score for each group and the low score for each group.

frequency distribution A list of scores ordered from highest to lowest.

FIGURE 4.2
Frequency Distributions
Putting scores in order creates a frequency distribution and makes the raw data more meaningful.

Scores, in random order		Scores, in frequency distributions	
No music	Music	No music	Music
80	64	97	94
58	83	93	92
97	75	93	87
77	72	89	83
93	92	89	82
69	68	84	79
67	87	84	77
89	79	84	75
93	94	80	74
78	74	78	72
84	82	77	71
73	77	73	69
84	68	69	68
84	71	67	68
89	69	58	64

FIGURE 4.3
Bar Graphs
Data from a frequency distribution can easily be converted to a bar graph.

The information from the frequency distribution can be easily presented as a graph, like the bar graphs in **Figure 4.3**. By viewing our scores this way, we can discover the meaning behind the numbers even more easily because we can see at a glance how the scores cluster and what the most common scores are.

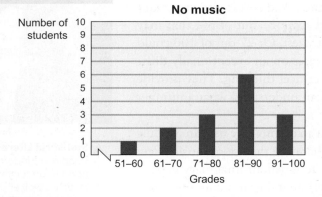

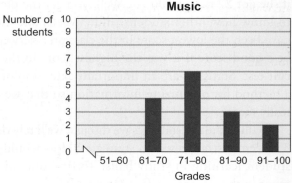

MAKE IT STICK!

1. Which of the following is an example of a frequency distribution?

   a. A baseball team roster, organized by jersey number

   b. An alphabetized grocery list

   c. A list of the number of points scored by a basketball team in each game of the season, in order from highest to lowest

   d. A list of ingredients and amounts in a chocolate chip cookie recipe

2. What is the advantage of creating a frequency distribution?

Measures of Central Tendency

 4-2 What are three measures of central tendency?

The next thing we need to know about a frequency distribution is where its center—the "normal" score—is located. We call this the *central tendency*. For the study hall research, we have two groups—one that listens to music and one that does not—and you just learned how to create a frequency distribution for each.

If the center of one frequency distribution is higher than the center of the other, this may help us decide whether the hypothesis is correct. It seems as though there should be some easy and reliable way to determine the center. However, it isn't quite that simple. There are three methods—*mode, mean,* and *median*—and each is appropriate only in certain situations.

Mode

The **mode** is the most frequently occurring score or scores in a distribution. Using the sample data from our frequency distributions, we can see that the mode for the music group is 68 and the mode for the no-music group is 84 because these are the numbers that appear most often in the two lists (see **Figure 4.4**). Modes are not the ideal source of information—at least for our purposes here. It's possible for the most common score (the mode) to *not* be near the center of the distribution. For example, I once gave a test to my students on which almost everyone did either very well or very poorly; the most frequent scores did not represent the center of the distribution. The mode is most useful when the data can only be put into distinct groups. For example, if you were categorizing people as male or female—by assigning males the number 1 and females the number 2—it would not make any sense to say that the average sex for the group was 1.5. When the numbers represent distinct groups, the mode is the only appropriate way to establish central tendency. Here's another example: If a high school had 100 sophomores, 200 juniors, and 150 seniors, the mode would be juniors, the group with the largest number. In finding the center of this distribution, the best you can do is use the mode and say that the most common student is a junior.

	No music	Music
Mode (Most common)	84	68
Mean (Average)	$\frac{1215}{15} = 81$	$\frac{1155}{15} = 77$
Median (Middle score)	84	75

mode The most frequently occurring score or scores in a distribution.

FIGURE 4.4
The Three Measures of Central Tendency
The three primary methods of finding the center of a distribution of scores are the mode, mean, and median. Each has its own strengths and weaknesses.

Mean

The most familiar measure of central tendency is the **mean,** the mathematical *average* of a distribution. As you know, we compute averages by adding all the scores and dividing by the total number of scores. The means for the two groups in the music study are presented in Figure 4.4—81 for the no-music group and 77 for the music group. Under most circumstances, the mean is the statistic of choice for central tendency.

Sometimes, however, the mean can mislead us. This occurs when a few scores are either extremely high or extremely low. It's not a good idea to use the mean, for example, to report the central tendency for housing costs in a community because most communities have a few very valuable homes. When you calculate a mean, these few expensive homes will affect the mean much more than each of the moderately priced homes will. As a result, housing will appear to be more expensive than it really is. Or, if a very rich person walked into a restaurant and you calculated the mean net worth of the people in the restaurant, you might find that the mean net worth was over a million dollars, even though the rich person was the only rich person in the building. Misleading, right? Under circumstances where there are a few extremely high or low scores, the median is a better representation of the center.

mean The mathematical average of a distribution, obtained by adding the scores and then dividing by the number of scores.

Median

median The middle score in a ranked distribution; half the scores are above it, and half are below it.

The third measure of central tendency is the **median,** the middle score in a ranked distribution; half of the scores are above the median and half are below. To remember this, just think of the median of a rural interstate highway, usually a strip of grass running down the center of the highway between the two sets of lanes. An extreme score in the top or bottom half of the distribution will have no greater effect than any other score. Figure 4.4 also shows the median for the students who listen to music (75) and students who don't (84).

When the mean, median, and mode are all the same, it's easy to identify central tendency. The three measures of central tendency can, however, be vastly different. **Figure 4.5** shows what can happen when a distribution, in this case for family income, is distorted, or **skewed**—not evenly distributed around the mean. In a skewed distribution, there is an unusual number of high scores or low scores.

skewed Distorted; not evenly distributed around the mean.

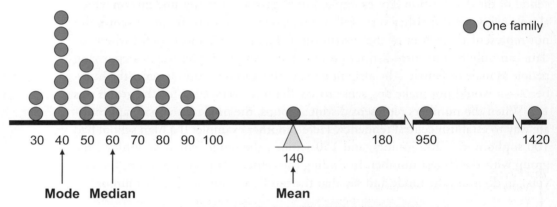

Income per family in thousands of dollars

▲ **FIGURE 4.5**
Central Tendency in a Skewed Distribution
This diagram shows the three measures of central tendency for a distribution of incomes skewed by a few families with very high incomes. Notice that, under these circumstances, the mean (which, as the average, balances the distribution) produces a result that is far above what most people would consider the center of this distribution. In cases like this, the median is probably a better representation of central tendency because it is less influenced by skew.

MAKE IT STICK!

1. The _____ is the average of a set of numbers.

2. The median is generally a better representation of the center of a distribution when the distribution is distorted, or _____, by some unusually high or low scores.

3. Which of the following is the best measure of central tendency if the data can only be put into distinct groups (like which state a person is born in)?
   a. mean   c. mode
   b. median   d. skew

Measures of Variation

 4-3 How do we determine the variation of a distribution of scores?

It is important to have a sense of where the center of a distribution falls. To truly understand the meaning of the numbers, however, we need to add another piece of the puzzle. Two distributions can have the same center and still be different. Consider a school Cs-Only Club that was open only to people who got a grade of C in every class they took. The mode for this club's grades would be a C. The mean and median grades would also be a C. But can you now imagine a situation in which *all* students in a school were invited to join an Everybody's Welcome Club and the mode, mean, and median for the grades would still be a C? The B students would balance the D students, and the A students would balance the failing students. The students in the Cs-Only Club are packed together at the same point on the grade distribution. The students in the Everybody's Welcome Club are spread throughout the distribution. These differences are represented in **Figure 4.6**. In this section, we examine ways to measure how spread out scores are.

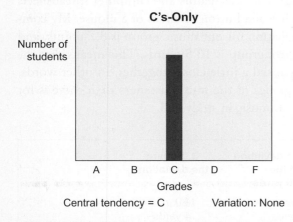

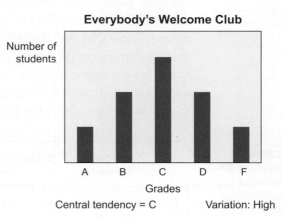

▲ FIGURE 4.6
Variation Makes a Difference
Both of these bar graphs represent distributions of students in which the measures of central tendency are C grades. It's clear, however, that the distributions are different. For the Cs-Only Club, there is no variation; for the Everybody's Welcome Club, there is high variation. Measures of variation allow us to understand such differences.

Range

The simplest measure of variation is the **range,** or the difference between the highest and the lowest scores in a distribution. The range is a simple, often helpful, indicator of how much variation there is in a distribution. It's nice to know, for example, that the range of grades for the music group was 30 (from a high of 94 to a low of 64 points) and that the range for the no-music group was 39 (97 to 58). The only problem with this measure is that a range considers only two scores: the highest and the lowest. Let's assume for a minute that the student who got a 58 in the no-music group missed a lot of school because of illness. This already marginal student's grade might easily have dropped to a 38 because of the absences. A change in this one student's grade could add 20 points to the range! A better statistic would consider *every* score, not just the two extremes. That's where the standard deviation comes in.

range The difference between the highest and lowest scores in a distribution.

Standard Deviation

Standard deviation is a statistic that tells us how much scores vary around the mean score of a distribution. The higher the standard deviation, the more spread out the scores are; the smaller the standard deviation, the more closely the scores are packed near the mean. In fact, if a distribution had a standard deviation of zero, it would signify that *every* score was the mean score—there would be no variation at all! This would happen in the Cs-Only Club. The standard deviation would be zero because every grade would be the average grade of C. The Everybody's

standard deviation A computed measure of how much scores vary around the mean score of a distribution.

Welcome Club would have a higher standard deviation because its members have a variety of grades.

Figure 4.7 shows an example of how the standard deviation is calculated for a small set of scores (in this case, punting distances for a football player). The important thing to understand here is the meaning behind the statistic. When you compute the standard deviation, you are coming up with a number that represents how far the scores spread from the mean. If there were two punters on my team who both have a mean of 40 yards, the punter with the smaller standard deviation is the one who is most consistent.

Calculating the standard deviation by hand would be tedious if you have more than just a few scores. Thank goodness for calculators and computer spreadsheets that will do the job with a few pushes of a button or clicks of a mouse. My computer tells me that the standard deviation for our music group is 8.7 points, and the standard deviation for the control group is 10.5 points. This means that the scores for the music listeners are packed a little closer together. In other words, there is less variation among the grades of the music listeners than there is for those who weren't allowed to listen to music in study hall.

FIGURE 4.7
Calculating Standard Deviation ▶
Here is how to calculate the standard deviation of a small set of scores.

1. Calculate the mean	2. Determine deviation from the mean (40 yards)	3. Square the deviations
36 yards	–4 yards	16 yards^2
38 yards	–2 yards	4 yards^2
41 yards	+1 yard	1 yard^2
<u>45</u> yards	+5 yards	<u>25</u> yards^2
Mean = $\frac{160}{4}$ = 40 yards		46 yards^2 = Sum of (deviations)^2

4. Take the square root of the mean of column 3

$$\text{Standard deviation} = \sqrt{\frac{\text{Sum of (deviations)}^2}{\text{Number of punts}}} = \sqrt{\frac{46 \text{ yards}^2}{4}} = 3.4 \text{ yards}$$

Steps in Calculating the Standard Deviation

1. Calculate the mean.
2. Determine how far each score (punt distances, in this example) deviates (differs) from the average.
3. Square the deviation scores and add them together. Note that you cannot just average the deviations without squaring them because the sum of the deviation scores will always be zero.
4. Take the square root of the average of the squared deviation scores. This step brings you back to the original units—yards rather than yards squared.

LIFE MATTERS

When selecting your quarterback for Fantasy Football, you have to decide between Carson Wentz and Dak Prescott, but their total points from the previous season were similar. How would the standard deviation help you to draft the best quarterback?

MAKE IT STICK!

1. The standard deviation is a good way to get a sense of the _____ of a distribution of scores.

   a. consistency
   b. center
   c. accuracy
   d. reasonableness

2. Two measures of variation are the standard deviation and the _____.

3. Two friends have played the same video game for years. They have the same mean score, but Hassan has a higher standard deviation than Alex. Given this, which of the following is correct?

   a. Alex is a better player than Hassan.
   b. Hassan is a better player than Alex.
   c. Alex is a more consistent player than Hassan.
   d. Hassan is a more consistent player than Alex.

Normal Distribution

4-4 What are the important characteristics of a normal distribution?

Much psychological data can be represented in a graph called a **normal distribution,** a frequency distribution shaped like a symmetrical bell. In a normal distribution, most scores fall near the mean with fewer scores at the extremes. A normal distribution, like the one in **Figure 4.8**, is not skewed; its left and right sides are mirror images of each other. Furthermore, the high point of a normal distribution is in the center. This high point represents all three measures of central tendency: the mode, the mean, and the median. Many collections of data produce a normal distribution. In intelligence test scores, for example, most people pile up at or near the middle of the distribution. The farther you move above or below the mean, the fewer people are represented. This distinctive pileup produces the bell shape of the normal distribution.

Data distributed in a bell-shaped curve illustrate some useful principles. Let's take a look at scores on intelligence tests. Scores on the Wechsler intelligence tests (the most widely used family of tests) produce a mean score of 100 points and a standard deviation of 15 points. This means that a person with a score of 115 is one standard deviation above average on this test. A person with a score of 80 falls about 1.33 standard deviations below average. There are some remarkable consistencies about normally distributed data. The most important things to remember, illustrated in Figure 4.8, are these:

- Approximately 68 percent of the population will fall within one standard deviation of the average. In the case of the Wechsler test scores, this means that 68 percent of the population scores between 85 (one standard deviation below average) and 115 (one standard deviation above average). In other words, roughly two-thirds of any normal population falls in this range.

- If you move one more standard deviation on both sides of the mean, you have now accounted for about 96 percent of any normal population. In other words, about 24 out of 25 people fall within two standard deviations of the mean. For the Wechsler test scores, this represents the spread from a score of 70 (two standard deviations below average) to a score of 130 (two standard deviations above average).

- By the time you've gone one more standard deviation, you've included darn near everyone. Slightly more than 99.7 percent of any normal population falls within

normal distribution A frequency distribution that is shaped like a symmetrical bell.

Erika Larsen/Redux

Marilyn vos Savant
Marilyn vos Savant, who writes a Sunday column for *Parade* magazine, was once listed by the Guinness Book of World Records as the person with the highest intelligence test score. Guinness no longer maintains this category because the scores are not reliable enough to determine a single "winner." Her score was reported to be over 220. There is controversy about her score, but if true, this would put her over eight standard deviations above average, astonishing when you realize that only 0.3 percent of the population is more than three standard deviations away from average!

FIGURE 4.8
A Normal Distribution or Bell-Shaped Curve
Intelligence test scores form a normal distribution with a mean of 100 points and a standard deviation of 15 points. The percentage figures shown are true for any normal distribution, not just for intelligence scores.

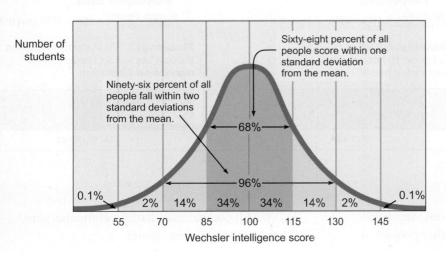

Number of students

Sixty-eight percent of all people score within one standard deviation from the mean.

Ninety-six percent of all people fall within two standard deviations from the mean.

68%

96%

0.1%   2%   14%   34%   34%   14%   2%   0.1%

55   70   85   100   115   130   145

Wechsler intelligence score

three standard deviations of the mean. For the Wechsler test scores, this is the range from a score of 55 to a score of 145. Statistically, then, it is very unusual for people to have Wechsler test scores below 55 or above 145. No matter what is being tested, in a normal distribution, it is unusual for any individual to exceed three standard deviations from the mean in either direction.

MAKE IT STICK!

1. If you know that scores on an exam in a class are normally distributed, then you know that about _____ of the class scored within one standard deviation of the average score on the exam.

   a. 96 percent   c. 50 percent
   b. 99.7 percent   d. 68 percent

2. Over _____ percent of all scores fall within three standard deviations of the mean.

3. Which of the following is the most common score on the Wechsler intelligence tests?

   a. 90   c. 105
   b. 100   d. 115

Comparative Statistics

 4-5 What is the difference between percentage and percentile rank?

percentage A comparative statistic that compares a score to a perfect score of 100 points.

percentile rank A comparative statistic that compares a score to other scores in an imaginary group of 100 individuals.

The two major *comparative statistics* are percentage and percentile rank. **Percentage,** as you probably know, compares a score to a perfect score of 100 points. If a student scores 83 percent on a test, for example, that student would have had 83 right on a test with 100 questions.

The **percentile rank** compares one score with other scores in an imaginary group of 100 individuals. Percentile rank tells you where a particular score stands in that group and how many people had equal or lower scores. If our student scores at the 83rd percentile, it means that score would have equaled or exceeded the score of 83 of every 100 people who took the test. **Figure 4.9** shows an example of how percentages and percentile ranks are calculated.

FIGURE 4.9
Calculating Percentage Scores and Percentile Ranks
These two common comparative statistics have similar names and are calculated with similar formulas, but they have different meanings.

Assume Jack gets 160 points on a 200-point test. His score is good enough to top 27 students out of his class of 36 students.

Percentage	**Percentile rank**
$\frac{160\ correct}{200\ possible} \times 100 = 80\%$	$\frac{27\ students\ beaten}{36\ total\ students} \times 100 = 75th\ percentile$
Meaning: If the test had been 100 points, Jack would have had 80 right.	**Meaning:** If 100 students had taken the test, Jack would have scored higher than 75 of them.

80 right	20 wrong		Below Jack's score	Above Jack's score
100 points			100 students	

MAKE IT STICK!

1. Which comparative statistic compares your score to the performance of other people?

2. Which comparative statistic compares your score to the perfect score?

Correlation Coefficient

4-6 What does the correlation coefficient indicate about the relationship between variables?

Another highly useful statistic is the **correlation coefficient,** a statistical measure of the strength of the relationship between two variables. Variables can be related in two ways—positively or negatively. If both variables increase (or decrease) together, there is a *positive correlation.* An example of a positive correlation is the one between a weight-lifting conditioning program and strength: Lift more, grow stronger. *Negative correlations* involve two variables that change in opposite directions—one variable increases as the other decreases. There is a negative correlation between practicing a song on the guitar and making mistakes playing that song: Practice more, make fewer mistakes.

The calculation of a correlation coefficient is quite complicated, and we won't go through it here. What's important to remember is that the number produced by the calculation has a value that always falls between −1.00 and +1.00. When $r = -1.00$ (the letter r stands for correlation coefficient), we have a perfect negative correlation. Every time one variable increases by a certain amount, the other variable would decrease by an equally certain amount. **Figure 4.10a** shows a perfect negative correlation (−1.00).

If $r = +1.00$, we are looking at a perfect positive correlation between two variables. Every time one variable increases by a certain amount, the other variable also increases by an equally certain amount. Similarly, every time one variable decreases by a certain amount, the other variable decreases by an equally certain amount (see Figure 4.10b).

If $r = 0.00$, there is no correlation whatsoever between two variables. Examples of this seem quite silly, like the relationship between practicing your song on the guitar and the temperature in Mexico City, or the relationship between the Los Angeles Lakers' basketball scores and the number of late arrivals into London's Heathrow Airport. When the first variable changes, we know nothing about what the second variable will do. When graphed, no relationship is apparent, as you can see in Figure 4.10c.

correlation coefficient A statistical measure of the strength of the relationship between two variables.

Positive Correlation
In a positive correlation, both variables increase (or decrease) together. The more this person trains, the stronger she will become.

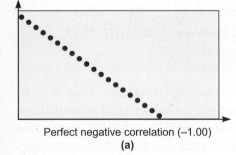
Perfect negative correlation (−1.00)
(a)

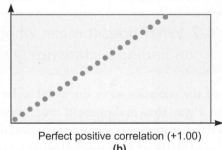
Perfect positive correlation (+1.00)
(b)

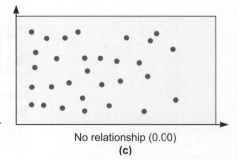
No relationship (0.00)
(c)

FIGURE 4.10
Correlations
These scatterplots allow us to visualize correlations. Each dot plots the score on two variables for one measurement (for example, a dot might indicate one person's height and weight). Graph (a) displays a perfect negative correlation ($r = -1.00$). Each time the variable represented on the vertical axis increases by a certain amount, the variable on the horizontal axis decreases by an equally certain amount. Graph (b) shows a perfect positive correlation ($r = +1.00$); the variables represented on the two axes increase in exact proportion. In graph (c), there is no correlation ($r = 0.00$). The random dots show that the two variables are not related.

We've now illustrated three situations: a perfect negative correlation, a perfect positive correlation, and no correlation at all. As you might imagine, the real world is rarely so neat and tidy. Positive correlations are usually less than $r = +1.00$, and negative correlations don't often reach $r = -1.00$. **Figure 4.11** shows you what a graph, called a *scatterplot,* would look like in a more realistic positive correlation between two variables—height and temperament.

FIGURE 4.11
Scatterplot of a Moderately Positive Correlation
These sample data show that taller people are somewhat more likely to be emotionally reactive than shorter people.

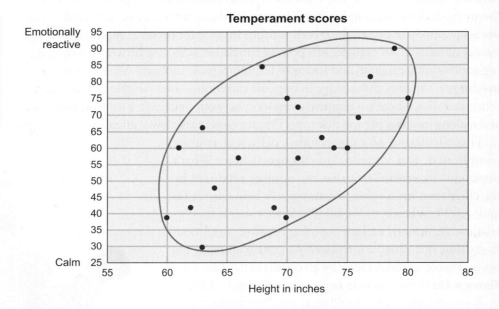

MAKE IT STICK!

1. What does it mean to say that the correlation coefficient is about 0.00?

2. Which of the following pairs of variables is likely to have an r value between 0.00 and -1.00?

    a. height and IQ scores
    b. studying and GPA

    c. standard deviation and measures of central tendency
    d. smoking and life span

3. Identify a variable you think might negatively correlate with GPA. Explain your answer.

Statistical Inference

 4-7 What does it mean when a researcher reports that a finding is statistically significant?

Most of the statistics we've discussed so far are *descriptive statistics.* They describe data in a way that makes them more meaningful. Another kind of statistics— **inferential statistics**—lets us make decisions or reach conclusions about data. Inferential statistics give psychologists guidelines for deciding whether data support hypotheses. Because inferential statistics are more complicated than descriptive statistics to calculate and interpret, we provide only a general discussion here.

Let's return, one last time, to our music example. (Will you miss it?) Assume we've collected grade data from the two groups: the experimental group, whose members did listen to music, and the control group, whose members did not. Recall Figure 4.4, which presents the measures of central tendency we calculated.

inferential statistics Statistics that can be used to make a decision or reach a conclusion about data.

You can see that the music group did not perform quite as well as the no-music group. By the end of the experiment, there was a 4-point difference between the means of the two groups (81 for the no-music group and 77 for the music group). The key question is whether this difference is **statistically significant,** a statistical statement of how likely it is that a result occurred by chance alone. In other words, does the 4-point difference represent a real difference, one that would be reflected in real-world conditions? Or is it simply the result of chance—a matter of luck that can be accounted for by some difference between our two groups (say, in study skills) despite our efforts to make them the same by using random assignment? We will never know with 100 percent certainty, but we can know how likely it is that this difference is statistically significant.

Most psychologists are willing to accept up to a 5 percent likelihood that an experiment's results did not occur by chance. This means being at least 95 percent sure that a difference in results is because of the manipulation of the *independent variable,* which in this case was whether or not students listened to music, and not some other unknown variable. A series of calculations with our results in the imaginary music experiment would tell us that with our 4-point difference we can be about 40 percent sure that the earbuds caused the difference in scores. So, this is not even close to a statistically significant result. For the difference to be statistically significant, the two groups would have to be more clearly separated, with a larger difference or less overlap between them.

There are a number of factors involved in inferential statistics. Here are the three most important:

- *The difference between the two groups' means.* If the means are far apart, the result is more likely to be statistically significant.

- *The number of participants in each group.* If each group has only a few people, the results are not as likely to be statistically significant as they would be if each group has a large number of randomly assigned people in it.

- *The standard deviations of the two groups.* If the scores of both groups are mostly packed close to the means, the means don't need to be separated by as much to produce a statistically significant result. If the scores are widely spread (represented by high standard deviations), the two groups are likely to overlap quite a bit. Many participants will score in the same overlap range no matter which group they are assigned to, and the result is not likely to be statistically significant. This is illustrated in **Figure 4.12**.

There is much to know about statistics, and much of it is beyond the scope of an introductory psychology course. This module has been just a brief introduction. Each formula is a logical application of accepted procedures that can be organized in a series of straightforward steps. The main point to remember is that we use statistics to make research results meaningful. The more you know about statistics, the better equipped you will be to critically evaluate information. Whether it's sports league player stats or advertisers' product claims, making sense of statistics in the world around you is a lifelong valuable skill.

statistical significance A statistical statement of how likely it is that a result occurred by chance alone.

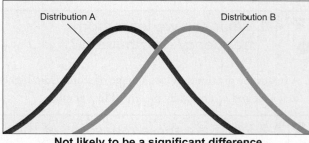
Not likely to be a significant difference

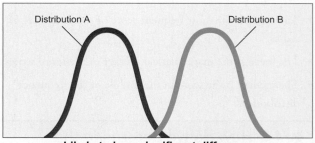
Likely to be a significant difference

FIGURE 4.12
Statistical Significance
A research result is statistically significant when it is unlikely that the result occurred by chance. Furthermore, when two distributions show little overlap, the difference between them is more likely to be statistically significant.

MAKE IT STICK!

1. Statistically significant results are not likely to be caused by _____.

2. Which of the following factors has the most influence on whether a result is statistically significant?

   a. The experience of the researcher
   b. The difference between the two groups' means
   c. The accuracy of the measurements
   d. Whether the results have been placed in a frequency distribution

3. Which of the following would most likely be true for a statistically significant result?

   a. On a 100-point scale, the mean of one group is 15 points higher than the mean of the other group.
   b. The groups each have 5 participants.
   c. On a 100-point scale, each group has a standard deviation of over 30 points.
   d. On a 100-point scale, each group has a standard deviation of over 50 points.

Module 4 Summary and Assessment
Psychology's Statistics

 4-1 What can we learn from frequency distributions?

- A frequency distribution lists a range of scores from highest to lowest and can be easily presented in a graph.

 4-2 What are three measures of the central tendency?

- The mode is the most frequent score or scores in a set of scores.
- The mean is the mathematical average of the set of scores.
- The median is the score in the middle of the frequency distribution.

 4-3 How do we determine the variation of a distribution of scores?

- Two ways of looking at the variation of a set of scores are to examine the range (the difference between the highest and the lowest scores) and to examine the standard deviation (how the scores are distributed around the mean).

 4-4 What are the important characteristics of a normal distribution?

- A graph of a normal distribution is shaped like a symmetrical bell, with most scores falling near the mean and fewer scores at the extremes.
- Of the scores, 68 percent are within one standard deviation of the mean, 96 percent are within two standard deviations, and 99.7 percent are within three standard deviations.

 4-5 What is the difference between percentage and percentile rank?

- Percentage refers to a comparison between a score and a perfect score of 100 points (for example, dividing the number of points earned on an exam by the number of possible points produces the percentage).
- Percentile rank explains where a score falls in an imaginary group of 100 individuals (for example, if your percentile rank on a test is 80, you scored at or better than 80 percent of the people who took the exam).

4-6 What does the correlation coefficient indicate about the relationship between variables?

- A correlation coefficient is a number (represented by r) between -1.00 and $+1.00$ that indicates the strength of a statistical relationship between two variables.

- Positive correlations indicate that as one variable increases, it is likely that the other variable will increase.

- Negative correlations indicate that as one variable increases, it is likely that the other variable will decrease.

4-7 What does it mean when a researcher reports that a finding is statistically significant?

- Statistical significance indicates that a research finding is most likely the result of the variable the researcher is studying, not random chance.

Summative Assessment

1. The overall purpose of statistics is to
   a. make numbers meaningful.
   b. identify the center of a distribution of numbers.
   c. determine statistical significance.
   d. discover how two variables are related.

2. Bar graphs are most closely related to
   a. correlation coefficients.
   b. statistical significance.
   c. standard deviations.
   d. frequency distributions.

3. When a distribution of data is skewed, the best measure of central tendency is the
   a. range.   c. median.
   b. standard deviation.   d. mean.

4. A limitation of the range is that it
   a. is too difficult to calculate.
   b. cannot be used as a measure of variation.
   c. considers only two pieces of data.
   d. may provide a false indication of statistical significance.

5. A statistic that always gets larger as data become less consistent is the
   a. percentile.   c. standard deviation.
   b. mean.   d. median.

6. Scores that are three standard deviations above the mean are
   a. an indication of statistical significance.
   b. an indication of positive correlation.
   c. rare.
   d. much more common than scores that are three standard deviations below the mean.

7. A student who scores at the 50th percentile on a test has scored at the
   a. mean.   c. mode.
   b. median.   d. standard deviation.

8. A scatterplot is a visual representation of
   a. a correlation.
   b. a standard deviation.
   c. percentage scores.
   d. statistical significance.

9. Which of the following can never be a correlation coefficient?
   a. $r = -1.00$ c. $r = +0.85$
   b. $r = -0.01$ d. $r = +2.00$

10. Which of the following does not contribute to statistical significance?
   a. the difference between the two groups' means
   b. the number of participants
   c. the standard deviations of the two groups
   d. the correlation coefficients of the two groups

KEY TERMS

frequency distribution, p. 47

mode, p. 49

mean, p. 49

median, p. 50

skewed, p. 50

range, p. 51

standard deviation, p. 51

normal distribution, p. 53

percentage, p. 54

percentile rank, p. 54

correlation coefficient, p. 55

inferential statistics, p. 56

statistical significance, p. 57

DOMAIN 2

Biopsychology

Westend61/Getty Images

The Nervous System and the Endocrine System

Have you ever heard of the fight-or-flight response? In a threatening situation, your body instantly prepares you to either fight off the threat or flee to safety. This response is produced by the nervous system and the endocrine system, our topics in this module.

Your body is an incredible organization of biological systems, each with its own important functions. Your skeletal system supports your body. Your digestive system extracts nutrients from food. Your immune system wards off disease. Your respiratory system allows you to take in oxygen and rid your cells of carbon dioxide. But the biological systems that psychologists focus on are the nervous system and the endocrine (hormonal) system. These two biological systems enable communication and information processing within our bodies. Without them, you wouldn't know when you place your hand on a hot stove, nor would you be able to take a video on Snapchat.

Neurons: The Building Blocks of the Nervous System

 5-1 What are the parts of a neuron, and what do they do?

The nervous system is your body's electrochemical communication system. Through it, your brain tells your body parts to move, your face to express emotion, and your internal organs to go about their business. Your nervous system, in partnership with your sensory systems, also gathers information so that your brain can respond appropriately to stubbed toes, fire alarms, and the smell of popcorn. Like every other system in your body, your nervous system is built of cells. Looking at those cells is a good starting point for understanding the whole system.

Juice Images/Alamy

▲ **The Computer and the Brain**
Both have amazing capabilities and get their power from millions of switches (electronic bits in the computer, neurons in the brain) that can be either on or off.

LIFE MATTERS

Metacognition is thinking about your thinking, and like any muscle, it improves with practice. Metacognition can allow you to confidently realize what topics you need to study more and what you've already mastered. How comfortable do you feel teaching the structure and function of neurons to another student? Can you correctly answer the Make It Stick questions that follow?

Your brain, spinal cord, and nerves are formed from *billions* of **neurons,** the highly specialized and unique nerve cells of the nervous system (and an even larger number of supporting glial cells). A neuron exists only to perform three tasks:

1. To receive information (in the form of chemical transmissions) from the other neurons that feed into it

2. To pass this information down its length as an electrochemical pulse (or, in some cases, to block its passage)

3. To move the information on to the next neurons in line

Every behavior, thought, and emotion you've ever experienced depends on the neuron's remarkable ability to process information in these three ways.

The wonder of it all is that neurons are actually quite limited in function—their main capability is simply transmitting an impulse, or firing. In some ways, the guts of computers operate similarly. A computer's central processor controls many digital switches that can be either on or off (1s and 0s). All of a computer's extraordinary capabilities—its communication functions, elaborate games, number crunching, mind-dazzling graphics, and sound—are ultimately accomplished by setting switches in the proper on-or-off pattern.

Neurons work in a similar way: They can either fire (that is, send an impulse down their length) or not. That's it. The beautiful colors you see in a sunset, the intense emotions you experience during your first crush, the memory of your first day of kindergarten, the taste of pepperoni pizza, and the thrill you feel when riding a roller coaster all emerge from a certain sequence of neurons either firing or not firing.

Neurons, like trees and dogs, come in a tremendous variety of shapes and sizes, but all neurons have similar structure. Take a minute now to look at **Figure 5.1**, which shows these structures in a *motor neuron,* a nerve cell that carries messages to muscles and glands. In this discussion, we examine the neuron's parts by following the order in which information travels—from the dendrites to the soma to the axon and then to the axon terminals.

FIGURE 5.1
A Typical Motor Neuron
Information travels from left to right in this neuron. Messages are received at the dendrites, travel through the soma and down the axon, and arrive at the axon terminals.

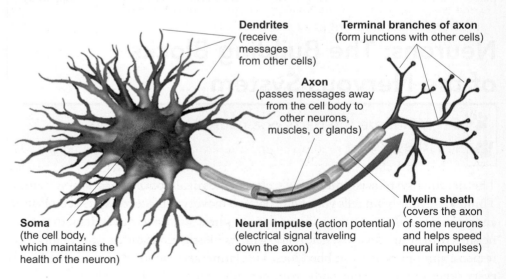

Dendrites (receive messages from other cells)

Terminal branches of axon (form junctions with other cells)

Axon (passes messages away from the cell body to other neurons, muscles, or glands)

Soma (the cell body, which maintains the health of the neuron)

Neural impulse (action potential) (electrical signal traveling down the axon)

Myelin sheath (covers the axon of some neurons and helps speed neural impulses)

Dendrites are the branching extensions of a neuron that listen for incoming information and conduct impulses toward the cell body. Dendrites look like branches, and in fact the word *dendrite* comes from the Greek word for *tree*. From the dendrites, the information moves to the soma, the cell body of a neuron. The soma contains the cell nucleus and other parts that keep the cell healthy and functioning properly. From there, information travels along the **axon,** the extension of a neuron through which neural impulses are sent. The neuron's purpose is to move information from point A to point B, and the axon creates distance between these points. Axons of neurons in the brain may be very short, because information doesn't have to travel far between the cells. But in some neurons in the leg, axons extend more than a meter in length, making these the giant redwoods of the nervous system, the longest cells in your body! Longer axons are covered by a *myelin sheath* that protects the axon and speeds up the transmission of information. Finally, the information reaches the **axon terminals,** the end point of a neuron, where neurotransmitters (discussed soon) are stored. As you will see, axon terminals are the points of departure for information as it makes its way to the dendrites of the next neurons in the sequence.

> **neuron** A nerve cell; the basic building block of the nervous system.
>
> **dendrite** The branching extensions of a neuron that receive information and conduct impulses toward the cell body (soma).
>
> **axon** The extension of a neuron through which neural impulses are sent.
>
> **axon terminal** The end point of a neuron, where neurotransmitters are stored.

MAKE IT STICK!

1. What is the general function of neurons?

   a. Neurons receive, carry, and pass on information to other neurons.

   b. Neurons rebuild our chemical, electrical, and hormonal systems after stress.

   c. Neurons control conscious behaviors.

   d. Neurons produce hormones to carry messages to endocrine glands.

2. The axons of some neurons are coated with a _____ sheath.

3. The axon terminals

   a. receive information.

   b. contain the cell nucleus and other parts that keep the cell healthy.

   c. are coated with myelin.

   d. store and release neurotransmitters.

4. The long extension of a neuron is the _____.

How Neurons Communicate

Now we're ready to look more closely at what happens when a neuron fires. This involves changes both within a neuron and between neurons.

The Neural Impulse

 5-2 How does a neuron fire?

When a neuron fires, it creates a neural impulse called an **action potential**. This brief electrical charge works its way from the dendrites to the axon terminals, much as a bite of swallowed food makes its way from your mouth to your stomach. This action potential represents the *on* condition of the neuron. Each action potential is followed by a brief recharging phase known as the refractory period, when a neuron, after firing, cannot generate another action potential. After the refractory period, the neuron is capable of another action potential when it is

> **action potential** A neural impulse; a brief electrical charge that travels down the axon of a neuron.

TABLE 5.1 Three Phases of Communication Within a Neuron

Action potential

The neural impulse created when a neuron fires. The impulse travels from the dendrites down the axon to the axon terminals.

Refractory period

The brief instant when a new action potential cannot be generated because the neuron is recharging after the previous action potential.

Resting potential

The state of a neuron when it is charged but waiting for the next action potential to be generated.

---

resting potential The state of a neuron when it is at rest and capable of generating an action potential.

all-or-none principle The principle stating that if a neuron fires, then it always fires at the same intensity; all action potentials have the same strength.

---

stimulated. When the cell is recharged, at rest, and capable of generating another action potential, a **resting potential** exists. **Table 5.1** illustrates these steps.

An interesting fact about how a neuron fires is called the **all-or-none principle,** which takes its name from the fact that a neuron always fires with the same intensity. All action potentials are the same strength. It doesn't matter if there is strong stimulation or weak stimulation at the cell's dendrites. As long as there is enough energy to trigger the neuron, it will fire with the same intensity.

One of the best analogies to a neuron and how it fires is, perhaps unfortunately, a toilet. Stop for a moment and think of how a toilet is similar to a neuron. Here are some similarities (perhaps you will be able to think of more):

- Like a neuron, a toilet has an action potential. When you flush, an "impulse" is sent down the sewer pipe.

- Like a neuron, a toilet has a refractory period. There is a short delay after flushing when the toilet cannot be flushed again because the tank is being refilled.

- Like a neuron, a toilet has a resting potential. The toilet is charged when there is water in the tank and it is capable of being flushed again.

- Like a neuron, a toilet operates on the all-or-none principle—it always flushes with the same intensity, no matter how much force you apply to the handle (as long as you provide enough force to trigger the mechanism).

Communication Between Neurons

 5-3 What is the role of neurotransmitters in communication between neurons?

So far, we have been discussing how information passes down the length of a single neuron. But how do messages travel from one neuron to the next? Amazingly, this happens without any two neurons actually coming in contact with each other! At every place where an axon terminal of one neuron and the dendrite of an adjacent neuron meet (and there may be thousands and thousands of such places on any single neuron), there is a tiny, fluid-filled gap called a **synapse** that action potentials cannot jump. Chemical messengers known as **neurotransmitters** travel across the synapse to carry the information from one neuron to the next. It is the neurotransmitter that influences whether the next neuron will generate an action potential (by firing) or not. When an action potential works its way to the end of a neuron, it causes the release of neurotransmitters from the axon terminals. The neurotransmitter molecules, which have a distinctive chemical shape, rapidly cross the synapse and fit into receptor sites on the dendrite of the next neuron (see **Figure 5.2**). Remember that it is this tiny "text message," repeated trillions of times among billions of neurons, that somehow accounts for all human experience.

The neurotransmitters can come to rest only in receptor sites designed to fit their shape, just as a key can open only certain locks. Once in the receptor site, neurotransmitters can serve two broad functions. Under some circumstances, neurotransmitters have an **excitatory effect,** which makes it more likely that the receiving neuron will generate its own action potential (fire). Other times, neurotransmitters have an **inhibitory effect,** which makes it less likely that the receiving neuron will generate an action potential. The excitatory role is like a green light. It shouts, Just do it! The inhibitory role is like a red light. Its message is, Just say no!

There are dozens of neurotransmitters, although so far researchers have not learned the specific functions of all of them. Different neurotransmitters serve different functions, depending not only on the type of receptor site each locks into but also on the place where they are released in the brain (see Thinking Like a Psychological Scientist: Neurotransmitters and Drugs).

synapse [SIN-aps] The tiny, fluid-filled gap between the axon terminal of one neuron and the dendrite of another.

neurotransmitter A chemical messenger that travels across the synapse from one neuron to the next and influences whether a neuron will generate an action potential.

excitatory effect A neurotransmitter effect that makes it more likely that the receiving neuron will generate an action potential, or fire.

inhibitory effect A neurotransmitter effect that makes it less likely that a receiving neuron will generate an action potential, or fire.

The Neural Chain

The neural chain describes the path information follows as it is processed by the nervous system. To understand it, consider the example of playing your favorite radio station on your sound system. What is necessary for this task? First, the radio station must broadcast the music over radio waves. Second,

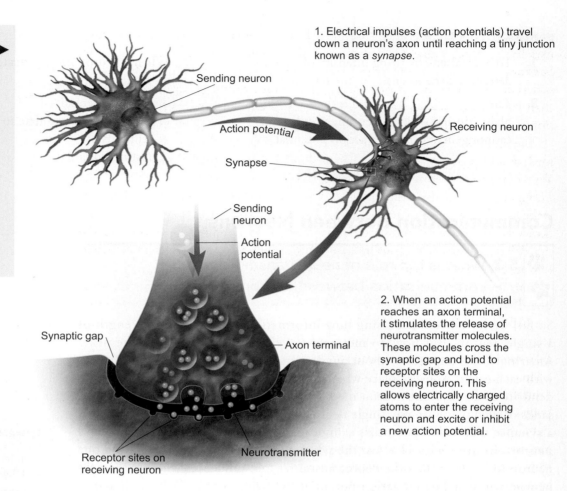

FIGURE 5.2 Communication Between Neurons The action potential triggers the release of a neurotransmitter from the axon terminals of the sending neuron. The neurotransmitter crosses the synapse and locks into receptor sites located on the dendrites of the receiving neuron.

1. Electrical impulses (action potentials) travel down a neuron's axon until reaching a tiny junction known as a *synapse*.

Sending neuron

Action potential

Receiving neuron

Synapse

Sending neuron

Action potential

2. When an action potential reaches an axon terminal, it stimulates the release of neurotransmitter molecules. These molecules cross the synaptic gap and bind to receptor sites on the receiving neuron. This allows electrically charged atoms to enter the receiving neuron and excite or inhibit a new action potential.

Synaptic gap

Axon terminal

Receptor sites on receiving neuron

Neurotransmitter

receptor cells Specialized cells in every sensory system of the body that can turn other kinds of energy into action potentials (neural impulses) that the brain can process.

your system's antenna has to pick up the radio waves and send them as an electronic message along a wire to the radio receiver. The receiver must process this information by tuning to the proper frequency and then filtering and amplifying it. Then the electronic information is sent to the speakers, again along a wire. Finally, the speakers vibrate to create the sound of a new song. The stereo goes through this process of receiving, processing, and outputting information continuously.

Your nervous system also specializes in receiving and processing information, and it contains functional components similar to those that make up your sound system. First, you need to gather information from your environment. Your "antennae" are **receptor cells,** specialized cells in the sensory systems of the body. These amazing receptor cells can turn other kinds of energy into action potentials (impulses) your brain can understand. Your eyes, for example, have receptor cells that take light energy and turn it into nerve impulses. Your ears have receptor cells that process sound energy, and elsewhere in your body, other receptor cells process smells, tastes, and touches into nerve impulses. Without these receptor cells, your brain would be helpless. By itself, your brain cannot detect light, sound, or smell. Just as you need your sound system to turn radio waves into something meaningful (music), your brain needs your senses and their receptor cells to gather and transform information into a form your brain can understand.

The sense organs are not actually located in the brain, so your nervous system must literally move the information your receptor cells pull in. This movement occurs as trillions of neurotransmitter molecules pass messages among billions of these kinds of neurons—from your fingertips, your eyeballs, your ears, your nose, and your mouth to the proper area of the brain for processing. Just as a sound system uses wires to move information, your body uses living wires known as nerves, which are bundles of individual neurons. **Sensory nerves** carry information from the sense receptors to the brain and spinal cord. Without sensory nerves, your brain would be no more effective than your radio receiver would be if somebody cut the wire bringing information from the antenna.

The brain, like a radio receiver, is the real powerhouse of the system. The brain must process a constant barrage of sensory data flowing in from the sensory nerves. Your brain receives information about what you see, hear, taste, smell, and feel throughout your body (although most of it is ignored as probably insignificant). It is the brain's responsibility to deal with all of the information and make appropriate decisions, just as your sound system properly filters and amplifies an incoming radio signal. The billions of neurons in your brain and spinal cord that process information are called **interneurons**.

Your brain determines when action is necessary to deal with incoming information. If your brain detects a ball moving toward your head, you need to either catch the ball or duck to avoid being hit. If your brain detects a question asked by your teacher, you need to decide on an appropriate answer and say it. If your brain detects that you're overheating, you need to begin sweating. The point is that while the brain can *determine* a course of action on its own (such as speaking or sweating), it cannot actually *do* these things. To trigger actions, the brain must get word to the body's muscles and glands, just as your sound system must convey the processed signal from the receiver to its speakers. Your sound system uses more wires for this purpose. Similarly, your nervous system uses *motor nerves* to carry information away from your brain and spinal cord to your muscles and glands so that they can take action. Without motor nerves, your brain could not accomplish anything. (Your sound system wouldn't be much good without speakers, would it?)

Figure 5.3 shows a neural chain so basic that the initial action is determined by the spinal cord without the involvement of the brain. In this case, the response to the heat from the flame is a *simple reflex*. To react quickly to a dangerous situation, an interneuron in the spinal cord sends the command to withdraw the finger even before other interneurons relay the information to your brain.

sensory nerves Nerves that carry information from the sense receptors to the spinal cord and brain.

interneurons Nerve cells in the brain and spinal cord responsible for processing information.

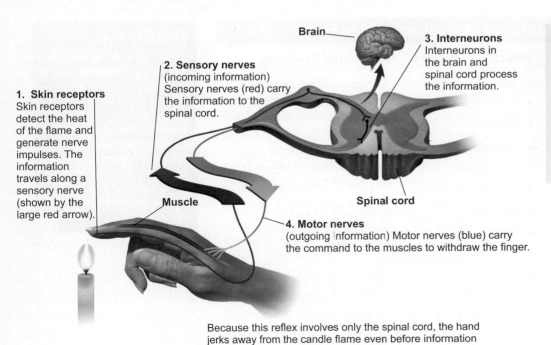

1. Skin receptors
Skin receptors detect the heat of the flame and generate nerve impulses. The information travels along a sensory nerve (shown by the large red arrow).

2. Sensory nerves (incoming information) Sensory nerves (red) carry the information to the spinal cord.

Brain

3. Interneurons
Interneurons in the brain and spinal cord process the information.

Muscle

Spinal cord

4. Motor nerves
(outgoing information) Motor nerves (blue) carry the command to the muscles to withdraw the finger.

FIGURE 5.3
A Neural Chain
When you burn your finger, a neural chain is activated. Receptor cells, sensory nerves, interneurons, motor nerves, and muscles all work together to minimize the damage from the flame.

Because this reflex involves only the spinal cord, the hand jerks away from the candle flame even before information about the event has reached the brain.

THINKING LIKE A PSYCHOLOGICAL SCIENTIST

Neurotransmitters and Drugs

The synapse is where it's at when it comes to the effects of many drugs. Let's take a look at the roles of three key neurotransmitters (see **Table 5.2**) and see what happens when outside chemicals are added to the mix.

One neurotransmitter, *acetylcholine (ACh)*, triggers muscle contraction and affects both learning and memory. (Alzheimer's disease is associated with low levels of ACh.) ACh is present in every synapse of motor nerves. Certain drugs can disrupt the normal effects of ACh, however. Some South American Indians use such a drug, a poison called curare, to coat the tips of the darts they use in their blowguns. When these darts strike an animal, the result is paralysis. Why? Because the curare molecules fill the receptor sites on dendrites that normally receive ACh, but the curare molecules do not stimulate an action potential in the receiving neuron the way ACh would. This means that ACh is blocked from doing its job, and movement ceases. Substances such as curare that block the effects of a neurotransmitter are called **antagonists**.

Black widow spider venom also interacts with ACh, but not in the same way curare does. The venom fills the ACh receptor sites, but its chemical structure is so similar to ACh's that it mimics ACh's effect on the receiving neuron. So, now two substances, ACh and spider venom, are doing the same thing. The result is excessive and uncontrollable movement in the form of convulsions. The spider venom is called an **agonist**, a drug that boosts the effect of a neurotransmitter. **Figure 5.4** illustrates how antagonists and agonists interact with neurotransmitters.

Another neurotransmitter with interesting effects is *dopamine*, which influences learning, attention, and emotions associated with pleasure. Schizophrenia, a serious illness that disrupts a person's sense of reality, is associated with high levels of dopamine. Drugs commonly prescribed for schizophrenia alleviate some of the symptoms by blocking the action of dopamine at the synapse. These drugs are dopamine antagonists.

Another disorder, depression, may be associated with low levels of the neurotransmitter *serotonin*, which affects hunger, sleep, arousal, and mood. Some medications, the most famous of which is Prozac (fluoxetine), work to reduce depression by enhancing the availability of serotonin at the synapse. Prozac, therefore, is a serotonin agonist.

Prescribed medications are not the only substances that exert their effects at the synapse. All mind-altering chemicals, ranging from caffeine to cocaine, operate by influencing neurotransmission. A single drug, such as alcohol, might influence several neurotransmitters in different ways depending on the synapse it enters. Research on neurotransmitters is always in progress and brings fascinating and important results.

TABLE 5.2   Examples of Neurotransmitter Functions

Neurotransmitter	Affected Functions	Associated Problems
Acetylcholine (ACh)	• Muscle action • Learning • Memory	ACh-producing neurons have deteriorated in people with Alzheimer's disease.
Dopamine	• Learning • Attention • Emotion	Excess dopamine activity is associated with schizophrenia.
Serotonin	• Hunger • Sleep • Arousal • Mood	Low levels of serotonin may be associated with depression.

LIFE MATTERS

While higher levels of dopamine are associated with schizophrenia, an underabundance is associated with Parkinson's disease. What do you think could be potential side effects of an antipsychotic medication, such as Haldol or thorazine, in that it acts as an antagonist of dopamine?

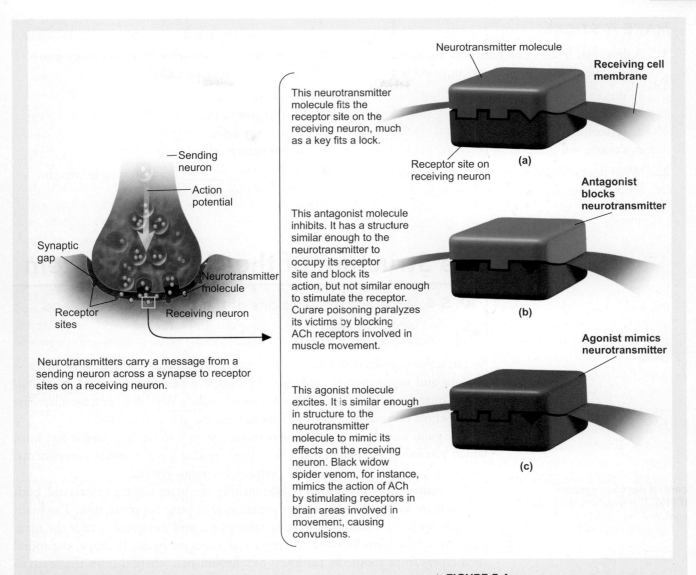

Neurotransmitters carry a message from a sending neuron across a synapse to receptor sites on a receiving neuron.

This neurotransmitter molecule fits the receptor site on the receiving neuron, much as a key fits a lock.

This antagonist molecule inhibits. It has a structure similar enough to the neurotransmitter to occupy its receptor site and block its action, but not similar enough to stimulate the receptor. Curare poisoning paralyzes its victims by blocking ACh receptors involved in muscle movement.

This agonist molecule excites. It is similar enough in structure to the neurotransmitter molecule to mimic its effects on the receiving neuron. Black widow spider venom, for instance, mimics the action of ACh by stimulating receptors in brain areas involved in movement, causing convulsions.

FIGURE 5.4
Antagonists and Agonists
When a drug *blocks* the effect of a neurotransmitter, it's called an antagonist. When a drug *boosts* the effect of a neurotransmitter, it's called an agonist.

THINK ABOUT . . . Psychological Science

1. What is one function of acetylcholine, one function of dopamine, and one function of serotonin?

2. What is the difference between an agonist drug and an antagonist drug?

3. A researcher discovers that disease X is associated with high levels of neurotransmitter A. If the researcher wanted to identify a drug effective against disease X, should she look for an agonist or an antagonist? Explain your answer.

antagonist A drug that blocks the effect of a neurotransmitter.

agonist A drug that boosts the effect of a neurotransmitter.

MAKE IT STICK!

1. A drug that treats symptoms of depression and affects the sleep cycle probably interacts with

   a. dopamine.
   b. acetylcholine.
   c. serotonin.
   d. curare.

2. What does it mean to say that a neurotransmitter can excite or inhibit neural impulses?

3. Cells that can turn other kinds of energy into action potentials are called

   a. interneurons.
   b. receptor cells.
   c. sensory cells.
   d. excitatory cells.

4. A(n) _____ is a drug that boosts the effect of a neurotransmitter.

The Structure of the Nervous System

 5-4 What are the divisions of the nervous system, and what do they do?

So far, we've examined the nervous system by zooming in on its smaller pieces—sensory and motor nerves made up of bundles of neurons that send their neurotransmitters to one another. Now it's time to take a step back for a broader view of the whole nervous system in which these smaller pieces function.

One good way to understand the nervous system is to study its major divisions, which you can see in **Figure 5.5**. The nervous system has two major components: the central nervous system and the peripheral nervous system.

The **central nervous system (CNS)** includes the brain and the spinal cord, both of which are so important that they are encased in bone for protection. The brain is where most information processing takes place, and the spinal cord is the main pathway information follows as it enters and leaves the brain. In shape, the spinal cord tapers from about the thickness of a broomstick where it joins the brain to

central nervous system (CNS) The brain and the spinal cord.

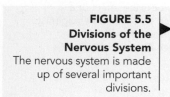

FIGURE 5.5 Divisions of the Nervous System The nervous system is made up of several important divisions.

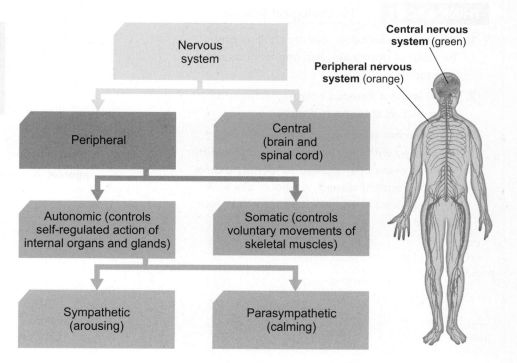

the diameter of a pencil lead at the base of the back. The interneurons that make up the CNS are responsible for processing information.

The **peripheral nervous system (PNS)** contains all sensory nerves and motor nerves that connect the brain and the spinal cord to the rest of the body. The word *peripheral* means *outer region*. (Perhaps you've heard of peripheral vision, which refers to your ability to see things on the outer regions of your visual field.) The PNS divides into two subsystems—the somatic nervous system and the autonomic nervous system:

- The **somatic nervous system** is the division of the peripheral nervous system that controls the body's skeletal muscles. It contains the motor nerves you use to activate muscles voluntarily and the sensory nerves you use to gather information about what's going on in your body and the outer world. You develop the idea to walk across a room using your central nervous system, but you rely on your somatic nervous system to carry the CNS's commands to the muscles of your legs and to get feedback about what your legs are actually doing.

- The **autonomic nervous system** is the division of the peripheral nervous system that controls the glands and muscles of the internal organs. The word *autonomic* means self-governing in the sense that you don't need conscious thought to activate it. This system monitors the automatic functions of your body, things like breathing, blood pressure, and digestive processes.

The autonomic nervous system has two subdivisions—a sympathetic division and a parasympathetic division (see **Figure 5.6**). These two divisions work together in a masterful example of checks and balances—it's not just our government that

peripheral nervous system (PNS) The sensory and motor nerves that connect the brain and the spinal cord to the rest of the body.

somatic nervous system The division of the peripheral nervous system that controls the body's skeletal muscles.

autonomic [aw-tuh-NAHM-ik] nervous system The division of the peripheral nervous system that controls the glands and muscles of the internal organs; its subdivisions are the sympathetic (arousing) division and the parasympathetic (calming) division.

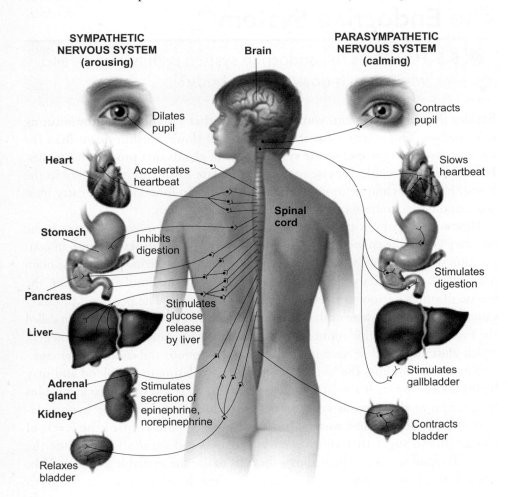

SYMPATHETIC NERVOUS SYSTEM (arousing)

PARASYMPATHETIC NERVOUS SYSTEM (calming)

Brain

Dilates pupil

Contracts pupil

Heart

Accelerates heartbeat

Slows heartbeat

Spinal cord

Stomach

Inhibits digestion

Stimulates digestion

Pancreas

Stimulates glucose release by liver

Liver

Stimulates gallbladder

Adrenal gland

Stimulates secretion of epinephrine, norepinephrine

Kidney

Contracts bladder

Relaxes bladder

FIGURE 5.6
The Sympathetic and Parasympathetic Divisions of the Autonomic Nervous System
The sympathetic division arouses us and expends energy. The parasympathetic division calms us and conserves energy.

sympathetic division The part of the autonomic nervous system that arouses the body to deal with perceived threats.

parasympathetic division The part of the autonomic nervous system that calms the body.

relies on this principle! The **sympathetic division** is the part of the autonomic nervous system that arouses the body to deal with perceived threats. It controls a number of responses collectively referred to as the *fight-or-flight response*. If you hear footsteps closing in behind you late at night on a deserted sidewalk, if a teacher announces a pop quiz at the beginning of class, or if you're about to make a nervous phone call to ask somebody out on a date, then your sympathetic nervous system will kick in.

The **parasympathetic division** is the part of the autonomic nervous system that calms the body. The sympathetic division may send your blood pressure higher when you are caught coming in after your curfew; your parasympathetic division brings your blood pressure back down to normal when your explanation of car trouble is fortunately accepted. This is referred to as the *rest-and-digest response*.

MAKE IT STICK!

1. The fight-or-flight response is triggered by the _____ division of the autonomic nervous system.

2. The peripheral nervous system divides into the autonomic nervous system and the _____ nervous system.

3. Which of the following responses is produced by the sympathetic nervous system?
   a. Heart rate increases.
   b. The pupils of the eyes get smaller.
   c. Digestion slows down.
   d. Glucose is not released by the liver.

The Endocrine System

 5-5 How does the endocrine system communicate, and what does it do within the body?

endocrine [EN-duh-krin] system One of the body's two communication systems; a set of glands that produce hormones, chemical messengers that circulate in the blood.

hormone A chemical messenger produced by the endocrine glands and circulated in the blood.

pituitary gland The endocrine system's master gland; in conjunction with an adjacent brain area, controls the other endocrine glands.

Besides the nervous system, your body has another system for communicating information. This system, slower to awaken and slower to shut down than the nervous system, is the **endocrine system,** a set of glands that produce hormones. **Hormones** are chemical messengers that circulate throughout the body in the blood. Hormones and neurotransmitters are similar in function: Both carry messages, and both communicate by locking into receptor sites.

Figure 5.7 illustrates the major endocrine glands. The most important is the pituitary gland, the endocrine system's master gland. The **pituitary gland,** in conjunction with an adjacent brain area, controls the other endocrine glands. The brain may call on the pituitary gland to release hormones that stimulate or inhibit the release of other hormones from other endocrine glands. The pea-sized pituitary gland is located at the base of the brain, and it connects to a part of the brain called the *hypothalamus*. At this connection, the tissue is part glandular and part neural, which illustrates the close relationship between the nervous and endocrine systems.

The brain monitors the levels of hormones circulating in the blood and may be influenced by their levels. Hunger, for example, is a response to a complex interaction of the nervous system and the endocrine system. The hypothalamus and pituitary gland work together to monitor and control the levels of *glucose* (blood sugar that your cells use for fuel) and *insulin* (a hormone the pancreas gland secretes, which allows the cells to use the available glucose). This, along with a host of other factors, determines how hungry you are at any given

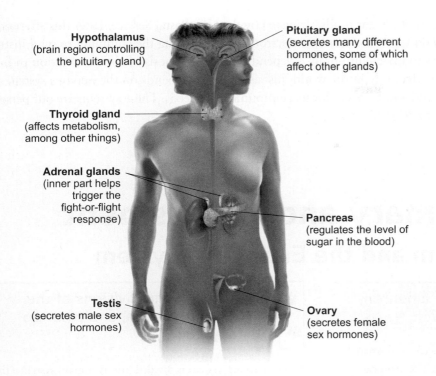

Hypothalamus
(brain region controlling
the pituitary gland)

Pituitary gland
(secretes many different
hormones, some of which
affect other glands)

Thyroid gland
(affects metabolism,
among other things)

Adrenal glands
(inner part helps
trigger the
fight-or-flight
response)

Pancreas
(regulates the level of
sugar in the blood)

Testis
(secretes male sex
hormones)

Ovary
(secretes female
sex hormones)

FIGURE 5.7
Major Glands of the Endocrine System
Endocrine glands secrete hormones into the bloodstream. The hormones can influence how we feel and behave.

moment. The important pituitary gland also releases hormones related to physical growth and pregnancy.

Other endocrine glands include the thyroid, the adrenals, and the sex glands (or gonads). The *thyroid gland,* located in the neck, helps regulate energy level. The *adrenal glands,* which perch atop the kidneys, release *epinephrine* and *norepinephrine* (also called *adrenaline* and *noradrenaline*). These substances enhance strength and endurance in emergency situations. The sex glands—*ovaries* in females and *testes* in males—release hormones that influence emotion, physical development, and reproduction. The primary male hormone is *testosterone* and the primary female hormones are *estrogens,* but both males and females have all of these hormones present in their systems.

MAKE IT STICK!

1. The body's two communications systems are the nervous system and the _____ system.

2. Which of the following is the master gland?

   a. The testes
   b. The pituitary gland
   c. The thyroid gland
   d. The adrenal glands

I'm seated at my desk right now, working on a computer that will process e-mail, connect to the Internet, display the photos I've taken with my phone, and play music on iTunes with a click of the mouse. It does this through a cable modem. The modem is also the source of the TV programming I can access with the remote control sitting next to the cell phone I used to talk to my son, 90 miles away, a few minutes ago. Also on the desk is a stack of requests from various organizations for funds, delivered by the U.S. Postal Service. Later this afternoon I will donate some money—electronically—by using the computer to send instructions to my credit union. I depend on these methods of communication to function effectively in the world, just as my body depends on the nervous system and the endocrine system for its communication needs. These systems are our personal information highways.

Module 5 Summary and Assessment
The Nervous System and the Endocrine System

5-1 What are the parts of a neuron, and what do they do?

- Neurons are made of dendrites, which receive information and pass it along to the cell body (soma). The axon carries this information to the axon terminals, which release neurotransmitters into the synapse, carrying information to the next neuron.

5-2 How does a neuron fire?

- Within the cell, a small electrical charge (an action potential) travels down the axon.

5-3 What is the role of neurotransmitters in communication between neurons?

- The neurotransmitters released from axon terminals into the synapse can either excite the next neuron to fire or inhibit it from firing.

5-4 What are the divisions of the nervous system, and what do they do?

- The nervous system is divided into two main systems: the central nervous system (CNS) and the peripheral nervous system (PNS).
- The PNS is divided into the somatic (which controls skeletal muscles) and autonomic (which controls glands and internal organs) nervous systems.
- The autonomic nervous system is divided into the sympathetic division, which speeds the body up, and the parasympathetic division, which slows it down.

5-5 How does the endocrine system communicate, and what does it do within the body?

- The endocrine system is a set of glands that communicate chemically using hormones.
- These glands use hormones to influence many functions within the body, including hunger, energy levels, strength, endurance, and physical development.

Summative Assessment

1. Which of the following is NOT a task accomplished by neurons?
   a. Neurons receive information from other neurons.
   b. Neurons carry information down their length.
   c. Neurons manufacture and release hormones.
   d. Neurons communicate with each other across small gaps.

2. Which of the following is a function of myelin?
   a. Myelin keeps neurons from overheating.
   b. Myelin allows information to travel down the axon more quickly.
   c. Myelin slows down action potentials.
   d. Myelin fills the synapse.

3. The all-or-none principle means that

   a. all the neurons in a region fire together.
   b. the action potential occurs at all parts of a neuron at the same time.
   c. neurons and endocrine glands work together to produce the body's response.
   d. a neuron always fires at the same intensity.

4. The function of neurotransmitters is to carry information across the

   a. axon.
   b. myelin sheath.
   c. soma.
   d. synapse.

5. What is the correct order for the neural chain?

   a. receptor, sensory neuron, interneuron, motor neuron
   b. receptor, motor neuron, interneuron, sensory neuron
   c. receptor, interneuron, sensory neuron, motor neuron
   d. receptor, interneuron, motor neuron, sensory neuron

6. Antidepressant medications like Prozac serve as an
   _____ for _____.

   a. agonist; serotonin
   b. antagonist; serotonin
   c. agonist; dopamine
   d. antagonist; dopamine

7. Which of the following cells are part of the central nervous system?

   a. Motor neurons
   b. Sensory neurons
   c. Receptor cells
   d. Interneurons

8. What is the neurotransmitter that allows for muscle action?

   a. Dopamine
   b. Prozac
   c. Acetylcholine
   d. Serotonin

9. Your heart rate gradually returns to normal after you are startled by a noise at night. Which part of the nervous system does NOT play a role in this calming?

   a. Central nervous system
   b. Somatic nervous system
   c. Autonomic nervous system
   d. Parasympathetic nervous system

10. The pituitary gland controls other endocrine glands by

   a. generating action potentials.
   b. releasing hormones into the bloodstream.
   c. releasing hormones into the synapse.
   d. generating neurotransmitters.

KEY TERMS

neuron, p. 62

dendrite, p. 63

axon, p. 63

axon terminal, p. 63

action potential, p. 63

resting potential, p. 64

all-or-none principle, p. 64

synapse [SIN-aps], p. 65

neurotransmitter, p. 65

excitatory effect, p. 65

inhibitory effect, p. 65

receptor cells, p. 66

sensory nerves, p. 67

interneurons, p. 67

antagonist, p. 68

agonist, p. 68

central nervous system (CNS), p. 70

peripheral nervous system (PNS), p. 71

somatic nervous system, p. 71

autonomic [aw-tuh-NAHM-ik] nervous system, p. 71

sympathetic division, p. 72

parasympathetic division, p. 72

endocrine [EN-duh-krin] system, p. 72

hormone, p. 72

pituitary gland, p. 72

Module 6 | The Brain

Learning Goals

6-1 Describe the tools available to psychological scientists for studying the brain.

6-2 Describe the functions of each of the lower-level brain structures.

6-3 Identify the regions of the cerebral cortex and describe the functions of each region.

6-4 Compare the functional differences between the left hemisphere and the right hemisphere of the brain.

The human brain is perhaps the most fascinating, complicated, and powerful structure in the universe.

A Universe of Brains

One indication of our endless fascination with brains is the number of objects that use the shape of a human brain to attract attention. My students have brought me several dozen toys, advertisements, and cards that use the human brain. When do you suppose they'll bring me a hot air balloon?

What is the most amazing thing in the universe? The answer is a matter of opinion, no doubt, but surely one of the leading candidates must be the brain. Think about it—oops, I guess that's already impossible without your brain! All art, music, and literature ever created began in a brain. The world's great (and not-so-great) architecture started in a brain. The principles of democracy, mathematics, and science began in a brain. You name it: If humans (or other animals) were behind it, the brain is what allowed it to happen. A brain can even think of itself in an effort to understand itself. Your liver can't do that.

The brain's complexity is, well, mind-boggling, but our discussion is limited to the basics. Vocabulary is the key. If you can master the words (most of which would already make perfect sense if you spoke Greek and Latin!), you will be well on your way to understanding your brain.

The brains of most animals and all mammals share certain similarities (see **Figure 6.1**). Most animal brains, for example, have similar components because they share certain functions, such as digestion and respiration. The more complex the organism, the more complex and highly developed its brain. Complex organisms share basic components with less complex life forms. These parts of the brain developed first and tend to be in the inside, lower regions of the brain. The more complex parts of the brain that control uniquely human functions—things like language and sense of humor—are layered around and on top of the lower, more basic regions of the brain. In isolation, no one part of the brain would be capable of anything, but functioning together, the parts of

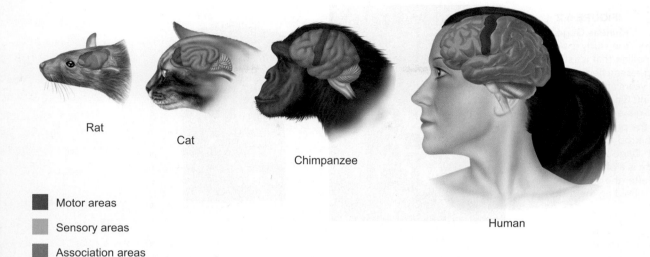

Rat

Cat

Chimpanzee

Human

- ■ Motor areas
- ■ Sensory areas
- ■ Association areas

▲ **FIGURE 6.1**
Brain Similarities in Different Mammals
Every mammal has a brain that can engage in similar functions, such as the ones noted here. The core areas of mammal brains are even more similar than the outer surfaces depicted here.

the brain form an integrated whole with remarkable abilities. We will begin our discussion with the lower structures of the brain and then progress to those complex structures that truly make humans special. But first, let's take a look at how psychological scientists study the brain.

Studying the Brain

 6-1 What tools are available to psychological scientists for studying the brain?

Case Studies

In a **case study,** one person is studied in depth in the hope of revealing useful information. One of the most famous case studies in the history of psychology is that of Phineas Gage. A young man in his twenties, Gage was working for the railroad in 1848 when he suffered a devastating brain injury. An explosion blew a pointed, 4-foot-long rod through Gage's cheek, just behind his eye, and straight out through the top of his skull (see **Figure 6.2**). Despite severe damage to his frontal lobe, Gage survived. In fact, he never even lost consciousness! The disruptive changes in his personality, however, have fascinated people ever since. Because the injury damaged the frontal lobe, where the judgment and the ability to make good decisions are located, Gage went from being a responsible worker to an unreliable, irritable, dishonest man who could not hold his previous job. Gage was, in the words of a friend, "no longer Gage," but over time he recovered enough to hold down jobs.[1]

Gage's injury and the annals of many other brain injuries over the years have allowed psychologists to speculate on the functions of the parts of the brain destroyed by the accidents. Each unfortunate injury allows psychologists to add another piece to the puzzle of how the brain operates.

Case studies have always been an important way to study the brain, but they are limited in the kind of information they provide because accidents are haphazard. And because case studies are based

case study A research technique in which one person is studied in depth in the hope of revealing universal principles.

Homer Simpson
Maybe a case study of Homer Simpson would reveal the source (and solution) of his problem!

Kurt Vinion/Getty Images

FIGURE 6.2
Phineas Gage
This case study is so compelling that it's still being researched more than 150 years after Gage's accident. On the left is a computer-generated image showing the probable path of the rod that passed through Gage's brain. On the right is a photograph taken after the accident. Gage is holding the rod.

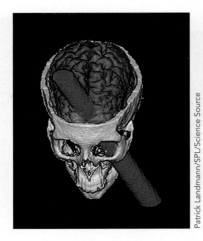

Patrick Landmann/SPL/Science Source

SCIENCE SOURCE/Science Source

on a sample size of one, it is difficult to generalize the findings to other cases. How do we know everyone would respond as Gage did to similar circumstances? Only experiments allow us to draw solid cause-and-effect conclusions. From a scientific point of view, our conclusions would be more sound if we could systematically damage specific brain regions in experiments on humans. You are probably already considering the ethical difficulties with this—at the least, it would be difficult to secure volunteers! So, given the ethical limits to gathering experimental evidence on the brain, case studies can provide important but somewhat limited information. Luckily, ever-improving technology gives us another line of evidence.

computed axial tomography (CT or CAT) A series of X-ray photographs taken from different angles and combined by computer into a composite representation of a slice through the body.

Scanning Techniques

With remarkable technological advances, various scanning techniques provide a window through which researchers can study healthy, functioning brains in living people. These techniques have revolutionized brain research and the diagnosis and treatment of brain problems. Brain scans provide information in two categories: brain structure and brain function (see **Figure 6.3**).

To study brain *structure,* researchers mostly use two kinds of scans: computed axial tomography and magnetic resonance imaging. **Computed axial tomography** (usually referred to as **CT or CAT**) is a series of X-rays taken from different angles and combined by computer into a composite representation of a slice through the

FIGURE 6.3
Modern Scanning Techniques
These machines may look scary, but each provides a window into the brain for both research and treatment of disorders. ▼

Scans That Show Structure			Scans That Show Function	
CT Scan	MRI	fMRI	EEG	PET

What Scanners Look Like

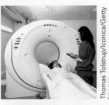

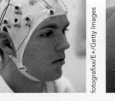

Thomas Tolstrup/Iconica/Getty Images

UpperCut Images/Getty Images

UpperCut Images/Getty Images

fotografixx/E+/Getty Images

Leif Skoogfors/Getty Images

What Brain Scans Look Like

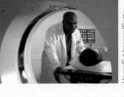
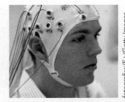
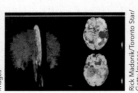
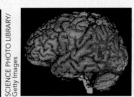

ALFRED PASIEKA/SCIENCE PHOTO LIBRARY/Getty Images

STEVIE GRAND/SCIENCE PHOTO LIBRARY/Getty Images

Rick Madonik/Toronto Star/Getty Images

SCIENCE PHOTO LIBRARY/Getty Images

WELLCOME DEPT. OF COGNITIVE NEUROLOGY/SCIENCE PHOTO LIBRARY/Getty Images

body. **Magnetic resonance imaging (MRI)** uses magnetic fields and radio waves to produce computer-generated images that distinguish among different types of soft tissue. This allows us to see different structures within the brain. These scans are ideal for examining what the specific parts of the brain (and other parts of the body as well) actually look like. For example, CT scans and MRI images can find a tumor or locate brain damage following a stroke. They are also being used to help find the cause of headaches, fainting spells, seizures, and other signs and symptoms that may indicate a neurological problem.

To study brain *function,* researchers mostly use the electroencephalogram, the positron emission tomography scan, and a variation of magnetic resonance imaging called **functional MRI (fMRI)**. These three types of scans allow researchers to see what the brain is doing at a given point in time. An **electroencephalogram (EEG)** is an amplified recording of the waves of electrical activity that sweep across the brain's surface. These electrical waves are measured by electrodes placed on the scalp. EEGs are often the tool of choice for diagnosing sleep disorders and seizure disorders. A **positron emission tomography (PET) scan** is a visual display of brain activity. Researchers inject a radioactive form of glucose (blood sugar) into a person, and the PET scan detects where it goes in the brain while the person performs a given task. PET and fMRI scans track the flow of blood to help identify which parts of the brain are active during a particular task. Such scans illustrate, for example, that the occipital lobes are responsible for visual processing and that facial recognition occurs in the temporal lobes.

The functional scanning techniques show that the brain never turns off. The entire brain is active 24 hours a day, 7 days a week—even when you're sleeping. There is a bit of a mystery surrounding the widespread notion that you only use 10 percent of your brain, but there is no mystery about whether the 10 percent idea is correct or incorrect. Researchers have demonstrated repeatedly that it's 100 percent wrong!

Phineas Gage remains famous for his tragic contribution to psychological knowledge. We are fortunate that new scanning techniques have made it possible to learn more about the brain with less human suffering. Consider what new windows to the brain will open up during your lifetime! Perhaps you will help develop one of them.

magnetic resonance imaging (MRI) and functional magnetic resonance imaging (fMRI) Techniques using magnetic fields and radio waves to produce computer-generated images that distinguish among substances; this allows us to see structures within the brain (MRI) and track blood flow to determine what parts of the brain are more active (fMRI).

electroencephalogram (EEG) An amplified recording of the waves of electrical activity that sweep across the brain's surface; these waves, measured by electrodes placed on the scalp, are helpful in evaluating brain function.

positron emission tomography (PET) scan A visual display of brain activity.

The Positive Neuroscience Project

> While considerable research in neuroscience has focused on disease, dysfunction, and the harmful effects of stress and trauma, very little is known about the neural mechanisms of human flourishing. Creating this network of future leaders in positive neuroscience will change that.[2]
>
> —Martin Seligman

These words were part of a multimillion dollar grant proposal that launched the Positive Neuroscience Project at the University of Pennsylvania's Positive Psychology Center. The purpose of the project was to fund research to determine the many ways the brain can enable and contribute to human flourishing.

In 2016, the book *Positive Neuroscience* summarized the substantial progress made in 13 different topics because the research supported by the project. These topics are organized into three major areas:

1. Social bonds. How does the brain contribute to positive relationships among people?

2. Altruism. How does the brain produce unselfish regard for the welfare of others?

3. Resilience and creativity. How does the brain promote musical and other kinds of creativity? How can the brain overcome negative emotions and situations?

Researchers are confident that neuroscience will ultimately help people become stronger emotionally, generate exceptional skills, find greater purpose in their lives, and make better decisions. Does this seem unrealistically optimistic to you? Consider that some people excel in all of these areas and that ultimately their success depends on what their brains are doing. The more we learn about neuroscience and positive outcomes, the better prepared we will be to produce these positive outcomes in all people.

MAKE IT STICK!

1. The in-depth examination of the results of Phineas Gage's brain injury is an example of a(n) _____.

2. Which of the following tools is most likely to be used by a researcher who needs to measure activity levels in the brain?

    a. EEG   c. CT

    b. MRI   d. PET

3. The brain waves that sweep across the surface of the brain can be measured with an _____.

4. Which two tools can identify blood flow in the brain?

    a. MRI and fMRI   c. CT and MRI

    b. fMRI and PET   d. PET and MRI

Lower-Level Brain Structures

 6-2 What kinds of behaviors and thoughts are controlled by the innermost parts of our brain, the lower-level brain structures?

The innermost structures of your brain are similar to the brains of all mammals. They are at the core because they evolved first. The newer regions are layered on top, much as paint builds up on the walls of older houses. In this section, we examine some of the innermost structures, called lower-level brain structures. They include the brainstem, the thalamus, the cerebellum, and the limbic system.

The Brainstem

brainstem The oldest part and central core of the brain; it begins where the spinal cord swells as it enters the skull and is responsible for automatic survival functions.

medulla [muh-DUL-uh] Located at the base of the brainstem, it controls basic life-support functions like heartbeat and breathing.

reticular formation A nerve network in the brainstem that plays an important role in controlling wakefulness and arousal.

No structural point marks where the brain and the spinal cord meet. You can either think of the brain as a rose that has blossomed on top of a stem or think of the spinal cord as a tail that extends down from the brain. Your choice! In an evolutionary sense, the **brainstem** is the oldest part and central core of the brain. It begins where the spinal cord swells as it enters the skull (see **Figure 6.4**).

Located at the base of the brainstem, the **medulla** controls basic life-support functions such as heartbeat, breathing, circulation, and swallowing. Don't hurt yours—damage in this region would almost certainly lead to death.

Another part of the brainstem is the **reticular formation,** a nerve network that plays an important role in controlling wakefulness and arousal. The reticular formation follows the back of the spinal cord as it rises into the brain. Damage to this region would cause a coma.

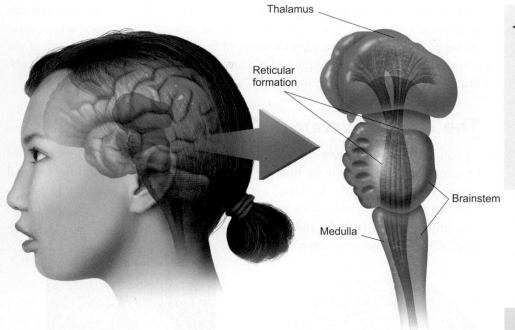

Thalamus

Reticular formation

Medulla

Brainstem

FIGURE 6.4
The Brainstem and the Thalamus
The brainstem is a swelling at the top of the spinal cord. The medulla and reticular formation support fundamental processes like breathing and wakefulness. The thalamus, perched on top, routes sensory information to the proper regions of the brain.

The Thalamus

The **thalamus,** Greek for inner chamber, is located at the top of the brainstem in the middle of the brain. The thalamus is the brain's sensory intersection, and it directs messages to the sensory receiving areas in the cortex. Imagine a major intersection of interstate highways. The various ramps, exits, and bridges make sure each car and truck end up pointed in the right direction. Such is the role of the thalamus. The incoming fibers of all your senses (except smell) funnel into the thalamus, which then distributes the sensory information to the proper regions of the brain for processing.

The Cerebellum

The **cerebellum,** Latin for little brain (and it does look a bit like an extra mini-brain), is attached to the rear of the brainstem. In conjunction with other brain regions, your cerebellum controls voluntary movements and balance (see **Figure 6.5**). Research has shown that the cerebellum plays a role in governing emotions, hearing, and touch.[3] The cerebellum also controls memories for knowing how to use your

thalamus [THAL-uh-muss] The brain's sensory switchboard, located on top of the brainstem; it directs messages to the sensory receiving areas in the cortex.

cerebellum [sehr-uh-BELL-um] The "little brain" attached to the rear of the brainstem; it helps coordinate voluntary movements and balance.

Ever notice how easily smell triggers memories? Smell information bypasses the thalamus and is routed directly to memory and emotion centers in the brain. This may be why the smell of your grandparents' house or a hospital ward can unleash a flood of emotions, sometimes positive and sometimes negative.

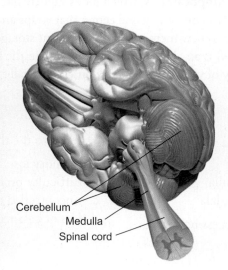

Cerebellum
Medulla
Spinal cord

FIGURE 6.5
The Cerebellum
The cerebellum is obvious as it juts out from the bottom rear of the brain. Its primary role is coordination and balance. Mike Trout would be unable to make contact with a baseball if his cerebellum weren't working properly.

limbic system A ring of structures at the border of the brainstem and cerebral cortex; it helps regulate important functions such as memory, fear, aggression, hunger, and thirst, and it includes the hypothalamus, the hippocampus, and the amygdala.

hypothalamus [hi-po-THAL-uh-muss] A neural structure lying below the thalamus; it helps regulate many of the body's maintenance activities, such as eating, drinking, and body temperature, and is linked to emotion.

body for things like walking or playing the guitar. The cerebellum makes it possible to smoothly engage in tasks such as running or writing. If your cerebellum were damaged, you could still decide to move your feet, but you would lose much of the coordination and balance required for dancing well. You could move your hands, but you would lose the dexterity required to play the guitar.

The Limbic System

As you can see from **Figure 6.6**, the **limbic system** (Latin for *border*), is a ring of structures at the border of the brainstem (the older core regions) and the cerebral cortex (the more recently developed surface regions). The limbic system helps regulate important functions such as memory, fear, aggression, hunger, and thirst. The limbic system includes the hypothalamus, the hippocampus, and the amygdala, as well as other structures.

FIGURE 6.6
The Limbic System
(a) The limbic system is a ring of structures (including the hippocampus, amygdala, and hypothalamus) surrounding the thalamus and forming a border between the brainstem (the older core regions) and the cerebral cortex (the more recently developed surface regions).
(b) The hypothalamus is tiny, but it plays a huge role in regulating responses ranging from thirst to pleasure. The hypothalamus is the green-colored region in this MRI brain scan.

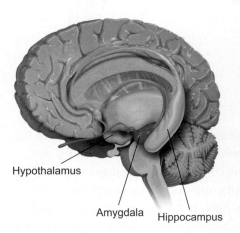

Hypothalamus

Amygdala   Hippocampus

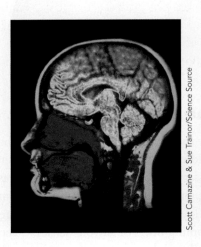

Scott Camazine & Sue Trainor/Science Source

Of the many structures in the limbic system, perhaps the most important is the **hypothalamus,** a neural structure lying beneath the front of the thalamus (*hypo* means *beneath*). The hypothalamus helps regulate many of your body's maintenance functions, including hunger and thirst, the fight-or-flight reaction to stress, and body temperature. The hypothalamus also plays a large role in the experience of emotion, pleasure, and sexual function. Cell for cell, it would be hard to identify a more crucial brain part.

Two other vital structures in the limbic system are the hippocampus and the amygdala. The **hippocampus,** which looks vaguely like a seahorse (you guessed it—*hippo* is Greek for *horse*), is a neural center that wraps around the back of the thalamus and helps process new memories for permanent storage. The **amygdala** (from the Greek for *almond*) is an almond-shaped structure in the limbic system. The amygdala controls many of your emotional responses, especially emotions like fear and anger.

hippocampus A neural center located in the limbic system that wraps around the back of the thalamus; it helps process new memories for permanent storage.

amygdala [uh-MIG-duh-la] An almond-shaped neural cluster in the limbic system that controls emotional responses, such as fear and anger.

MAKE IT STICK!

1. Damage to the brain's _____ would be life-threatening.

   a. hippocampus   c. medulla
   b. cerebellum   d. amygdala

2. The brain's _____ helps process new memories.

3. Damage to the thalamus would result in

   a. memory loss.
   b. difficulty processing sensory information.
   c. uncontrolled emotion.
   d. loss of balance.

The Cerebral Cortex

 6-3 What are the regions of the outer surface of the brain, the cerebral cortex, and what are the functions of these regions?

Close your eyes and conjure up an image of a brain. What did you see? Probably not the lower-level structures we have been discussing, right? More likely, you thought of the brain's wrinkled outer surface—the **cerebral cortex** (see **Figure 6.7**), an intricate fabric of interconnected neurons that make up the body's ultimate control and information-processing center. The cerebral cortex covers the brain's lower-level structures, just as a glove covers your hand. The word *cortex* is Latin for *bark*, an appropriate name given the tree bark–like appearance of the brain's outer surface. The wrinkles of the cerebral cortex allow more brain tissue to be packed into a confined space, like a sleeping bag into its stuff sack. Thanks to this efficient use of space, an estimated 20 billion to 23 billion neurons with 300 trillion connections among them can exist in a layer of brain tissue only one-eighth of an inch thick.[4] Even more amazing, there are several times as many *glial cells* sharing this space with the neurons. These glial cells assist and support the neurons, much as paramedics assist and support the work of physicians.[5]

cerebral [seh-REE-bruhl] cortex The intricate fabric of interconnected neurons that form the body's ultimate control and information-processing center.

longitudinal fissure The long crevice that divides the cerebral cortex into the left and right hemispheres.

Major Divisions of the Cortex

The most dramatic feature of the cortex is the **longitudinal fissure,** the crevice that divides the cerebral cortex into two halves called *hemispheres* (see Figure 6.7). If you were to poke your pencil down this fissure (not that you should try this,

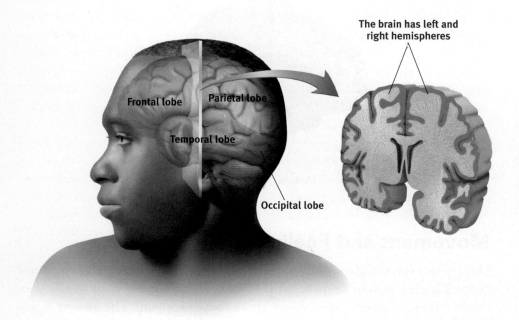

▲ **FIGURE 6.7**
Basic Landmarks of the Cerebral Cortex
The cerebral cortex is the wrinkled outer surface of the brain. It is divided by fissures into two hemispheres and four major lobes.

corpus callosum [KOR-pus kah-LOW-sum] The large band of neural tissue that connects the two brain hemispheres and allows them to communicate with each other.

frontal lobes The portion of the cerebral cortex lying just behind the forehead that is involved in planning and judgment; it includes the motor cortex.

parietal [puh-RYE-uh-tuhl] lobes The portion of the cerebral cortex lying at the top of the head and toward the rear; it includes the somatosensory cortex and general association areas used for processing information.

occipital [ahk-SIP-uh-tuhl] lobes The portion of the cerebral cortex lying at the back of the head; it includes the primary visual processing areas of the brain.

temporal lobes The portion of the cerebral cortex lying roughly above the ears; it includes the auditory (hearing) areas of the brain.

mind you), you would eventually meet resistance at the **corpus callosum,** a large band of neural tissue that connects the two brain hemispheres and allows them to communicate with each other. The corpus callosum is clearly visible in **Figure 6.8**.

If you look back at Figure 6.7 (and use your imagination), you may note that the brain resembles a side view of a boxing glove. If you make your way around the boxing glove, you can see that additional fissures—a lateral fissure and a central fissure—create major divisions of tissue on each side. These divisions create four brain lobes—frontal, parietal, occipital, and temporal (see Figure 6.7). Lying just behind the forehead, the **frontal lobes** (left hemisphere and right hemisphere) enable your most advanced cognitive (thinking) abilities, such as judgment and planning. The frontal lobes' rational abilities literally lie atop, and connect with, the more primitive limbic region where the roots of emotion are found. This means that both emotion and reason are going to influence the decisions you make. The frontal lobes include the motor cortex (discussed later).

Behind the frontal lobes, at the top of the head and toward the rear, are the **parietal lobes.** The parietal lobes include the somatosensory cortex (discussed later), but they are largely designated as *association areas*—regions that make up most of the cerebral cortex and are available for the general processing of information, including much mathematical reasoning and integration of memory. At the rear of the cerebral cortex are the **occipital lobes,** the primary visual processing areas of the brain. You may not have eyes in the back of your head, but you do see with the back of your brain. Finally, the thumb region of the boxing glove, lying roughly above the ears, holds the **temporal lobes,** which include the auditory (sound) processing areas of the brain.

FIGURE 6.8 The Corpus Callosum The corpus callosum is clearly visible in this photograph of a brain, made by cutting straight down through the longitudinal fissure. You can also see other structures we have discussed: the thalamus, the medulla, and the cerebellum.

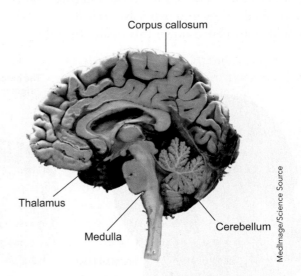

Corpus callosum

Thalamus

Medulla

Cerebellum

MedImage/Science Source

Movement and Feeling

Have you ever wondered how your brain tells your body parts to move? What happens in your brain to let you walk, raise your hand, or wiggle your ears? Is there a specific spot where these things happen? The answer is *yes*. The **motor cortex** is a strip of tissue on the rear edge of the frontal lobes that controls voluntary movements of your body parts (see **Figure 6.9**). Different points on the motor cortex control different parts of your body, but they do so in a curious cross-wired pattern. Thus, the motor cortex in your right hemisphere takes care of movement on the *left* side of your body, and the motor cortex in your left hemisphere controls movement on the *right* side of your body.

motor cortex A strip of brain tissue at the rear of the frontal lobes that controls voluntary movements.

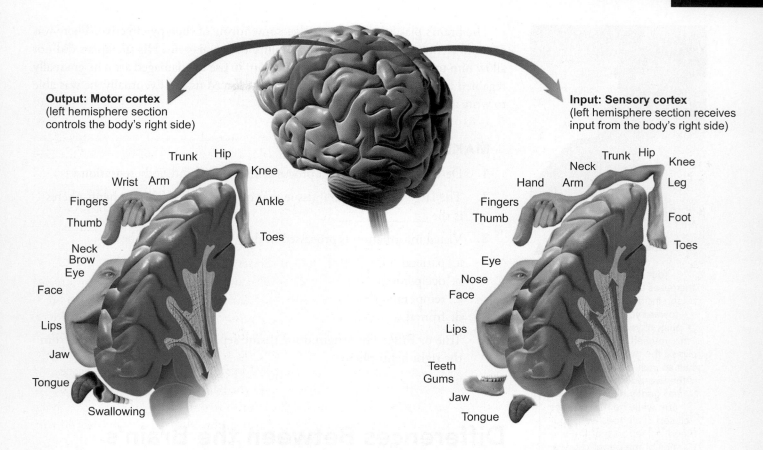

Output: Motor cortex
(left hemisphere section
controls the body's right side)

Input: Sensory cortex
(left hemisphere section receives
input from the body's right side)

Another odd thing about the motor cortex is that the bigger parts of your body don't have the largest amount of brain area. Instead, the parts of the body that are capable of more intricate movements (like the hands and the face) demand more brain tissue than body parts for which intricate movement is not possible (like the arm and the ankle). If you were to draw a body along the motor cortex so that the body parts were proportionate to the amount of brain tissue, you would have a distorted drawing indeed, like the one in Figure 6.9.

Just behind the motor cortex, a similar strip of tissue stretches along the front edge of the parietal lobes. This is the **somatosensory cortex,** a brain area that registers and processes body sensations. This term sounds more difficult than it really is. If you remember that *soma* is Greek for *body*, you'll remember that this strip of cortex is where your body senses register. For example, when you feel a tickle under your nose or the pain of a stubbed toe, your brain will register that stimulation in the somatosensory cortex. As you can see in Figure 6.9, the somatosensory cortex allots more brain tissue to parts of your body that are more sensitive to touch (like your fingertips) than to those that are less sensitive (like your arms).

Brain Plasticity

The brain has an extraordinary ability to compensate for damage or injury. While damage to the brain is always serious, under some circumstances, especially in young people, the cerebral cortex can actually reprogram itself to compensate for a problem. For example, if a tumor in one brain hemisphere starts to disrupt language ability, language function may transfer to the other hemisphere.[6] This remarkable ability is called **plasticity**.

> **FIGURE 6.9**
> **The Motor Cortex and the Somatosensory Cortex**
> On both sides of the central fissure, two strips of brain tissue handle information flowing from your senses to your body parts. The motor cortex is part of the frontal lobes, and the somatosensory cortex is part of the parietal lobes. The figure drawn on the expanded version of each strip roughly represents the amount of brain tissue devoted to particular body parts.

somatosensory cortex A strip of brain tissue at the front of the parietal lobes that registers and processes body sensations.

plasticity The brain's ability to change, especially during childhood, by reorganizing after damage or experience.

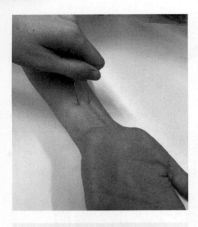

The brain's plasticity is what makes some forms of therapy effective. There was a stroke victim who lost much of the ability to use his arm. His therapists did not allow him to use his good arm. By forcing him to use the damaged arm, he gradually regained function as his brain adjusted to the forced usage. Eventually, he was able to write and play tennis with the arm.[7]

When Does One Point Become Two? Your sensitivity to touch increases as you move down the inside of your forearm toward your wrist and the palm of your hand. To test this yourself, unfold a paper clip so the two tips are about half an inch apart. Then drag the two-pointed clip slowly and gently down a friend's arm while he has his eyes closed. If all goes well, your friend will report that the two tips of the paper clip feel like one point when they are higher on his arm. The two tips will begin to feel like two points lower on the arm as you approach the wrist again. This happens because the wrist and hand have more brain tissue on the somatosensory cortex, and thus more sensitivity, than does the upper arm.

> **MAKE IT STICK!**
>
> 1. Describe where the brain processes movement and body sensations.
>
> 2. The large band of neural tissue that connects the two brain hemispheres is the _____.
>
> 3. Visual information is processed in the _____ lobes.
>   a. parietal
>   b. occipital
>   c. temporal
>   d. frontal
>
> 4. True or False? The longitudinal fissure separates the left hemisphere from the right hemisphere.

Differences Between the Brain's Two Hemispheres

 6-4 Are the left hemisphere and the right hemisphere responsible for different thoughts and behaviors?

Have you ever heard people speak of the right brain and the left brain or even describe someone as being left-brained or right-brained? Like many popular ideas, this pop psychology notion is partly right and partly wrong. In truth, you have only one brain, not two. Yes, your single brain *is* divided into two hemispheres, and some functions differ significantly between the two halves. But the two sides of your brain are allies, not enemies. They communicate constantly via the corpus callosum, and to accomplish most tasks, you must use both the right side and the left side of your brain.

Language and Spatial Abilities

Language is the best example of a clear-cut difference between the functions of your brain's two hemispheres. In most people, language functions are located primarily in the left hemisphere. A small percentage of the population seems to be wired for language in the right hemisphere, but nobody is quite sure why.

Two particularly important language regions of the left hemisphere are Broca's area and Wernicke's area (see **Figure 6.10**):

*   **Broca's area,** located in the left frontal lobe, directs the muscle movements involved in *expressive language* (speech). Damage to Broca's area, which often happens to victims of strokes, results in difficulty with spoken language. The stroke victim can form ideas but cannot turn those ideas into coherent speech.

Broca's area A brain area of the left frontal lobe that directs the muscle movements involved in speech.

- **Wernicke's area,** located in the left temporal lobe, is involved with *receptive language* (your ability to understand what someone else says). Damage to Wernicke's area might leave a person able to hear words but unable to comprehend the meaning of sentences created with the words. She would be able to recognize the individual parts of a computer (monitor, mouse, keyboard, and so on) but not understand that these parts together constitute a computer.

The right hemisphere, however, is not just a bystander. It houses most of your brain's *spatial* abilities. The word spatial relates to your ability to perceive or organize things in a given space, such as judging distance, understanding geometric objects, or packing a car's trunk efficiently. The right hemisphere also provides the insight to help us make connections among words. What word goes with *painting, ring,* and *nail*? Our right hemisphere finds the answer: *finger.* For a small handful of people with a surgically severed corpus callosum, however, the differing roles of the two hemispheres are much more dramatic.

The Split Brain

What would happen if the two halves of your brain were separated? Could you still function as a normal person? Why would anyone even consider such a dramatic procedure?

The last question is the easiest to answer. In the 1960s, scientists were working on ways to treat severe epilepsy, a brain disorder in which a person may have uncontrollable seizures. In an attempt to prevent these seizures from spreading from one side of the brain to the other, surgeons performed a split-brain operation, in which they cut the corpus callosum. The operation was successful—seizures no longer plagued the patients whose brains were split—but there were side effects.

Cutting the corpus callosum prevents the two hemispheres of the brain from communicating with each other. Surprisingly, neuropsychologists Roger Sperry and Michael Gazzaniga found that the surgery left patients' personality and intellect unchanged.[8, 9] However, it altered perception—and corresponding behaviors—in some interesting ways. To understand why these changes occurred, we need to take a closer look at the roles of the two hemispheres.

As you can see in **Figure 6.11**, we normally route visual information efficiently from the eyes to the brain. The important thing is that information from your left visual field (the area to the left of your nose) falls on the right side of the retina at the back of each of your two eyes. In an intact brain, this design includes distributing the information across the corpus callosum so that the visual information is available to both hemispheres.

So, what happens when the information is *not* shared between the two hemispheres? In cleverly designed experiments, Gazzaniga and Sperry asked split-brain patients to focus on a spot at the center of a screen while images were projected to either the left or the right visual field.[10] The results demonstrated some interesting gaps in perception among people whose corpus callosum had been severed. Here are two examples:

1. When the picture of an item was projected to the *left visual field,* the patient was unable to identify the object verbally. Why? Because information from the left visual field is processed in the right hemisphere, but the speech center is located in the left hemisphere. There is no way to move the information from the right to the left hemisphere if the corpus callosum has been cut.

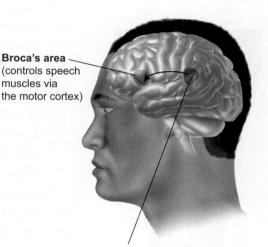

Broca's area
(controls speech
muscles via
the motor cortex)

Wernicke's area
(interprets auditory information)

▲ **FIGURE 6.10**
Broca's Area and Wernicke's Area
These two language areas are found only in the left hemisphere in most people.

Wernicke's [VER-nik-ees] area A brain area of the left temporal lobe involved in language comprehension and expression.

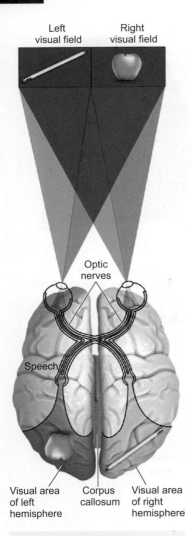

Left visual field   Right visual field

Optic nerves

Speech

Visual area of left hemisphere   Corpus callosum   Visual area of right hemisphere

FIGURE 6.11
The Flow of Visual Information
Both eyes receive information from both visual fields, but all information from the left visual field ends up in the right hemisphere. The right visual field is processed in the left hemisphere. When the corpus callosum is cut, the two hemispheres cannot share information.

FIGURE 6.12
Wonders of the Split Brain
This split-brain patient *says* she sees only the word ART because the speech center can receive information only from the left hemisphere, which processes the right visual field. Her left hand *points* to HE because it's controlled by the right hemisphere. The right hemisphere can process information only from the left visual field.

2. Look at the situation in **Figure 6.12**. In this case, the split-brain patient focuses on the dot while the *HE* is projected to the left visual field and *ART* is projected to the right visual field. The results are perfectly predictable, based on our understanding of the way the brain is organized. The patient will respond, *ART,* when asked what was seen, but to her own surprise will point to the word *HE* when asked to use her left hand to identify what she saw. What would the person do if asked to use her right hand to select the word she saw? That's right—she would point to *ART.* And, of course, a person with an intact corpus callosum would see the whole word, *HEART.*

These results are pretty strange—a bizarre but literal case of the left hand not knowing what the right hand is doing. Why, then, did the researchers conclude that the side effects of the surgery were minimal? Remember that to find these results, Sperry and Gazzaniga set up a procedure that required participants to focus on a dot at the center of the visual field. In real life, split-brain patients would be constantly moving their heads and eyes from side to side. Both visual fields would continually detect significant amounts of information and would make that information available to both brain hemispheres, despite the severed corpus callosum.

This is not to say the split-brain procedure has no lingering aftereffects. People who have had this surgery know that the left and right sides of the body seem at times to be under the command of different masters (because they are). When there is a conflict between the two hemispheres, the left brain usually tries to make

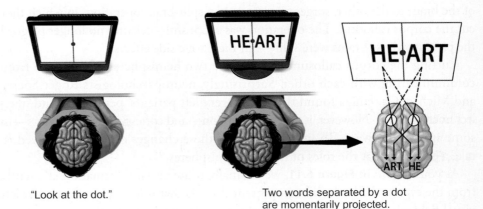

"Look at the dot."

Two words separated by a dot are momentarily projected.

"What word did you see?"   or

"Point with your left hand to the word you saw."

sense of it all. Thus, if the right hemisphere of the brain implements a behavior, like walking, the left hemisphere will try to explain the reason (I'm going to get a Coke). It must be unnerving to have a brain at odds with itself, but these strange events would not significantly reduce a person's ability to function, and they usually would not be obvious to other people.

This historic attempt to control epileptic seizures yielded important information about the role of the brain's two hemispheres. The information has since been verified with modern brain-scanning techniques that were not available in the 1960s. Maybe the most important lesson of this research relates to the vital communication that travels between the hemispheres via the corpus callosum. Our left and right hemispheres form one integrated brain. A recent book on the great myths of popular psychology reminds us that those trying to sell us products to develop one side of the brain or the other are more interested in our bank accounts than in science.[11]

> **LIFE MATTERS**
>
> How well can you explain what would happen with a split-brain procedure? Before moving on, try to internally describe how you would communicate that you saw a dog in your left visual field and a cat in your right, if your corpus callosum was severed.

MAKE IT STICK!

1. One method of examining differences between the two hemispheres is to study patients

    a. with a split corpus callosum.
    b. who were born with no brainstem.
    c. who developed both a left and a right frontal lobe.
    d. with a limbic system that includes both a hippocampus and an amygdala.

2. _____ area controls expressive speech and _____ area controls receptive speech.

3. True or false: Split-brain research proved effective in controlling epilepsy, but it did not reveal much about the functioning of the brain's two hemispheres.

Module 6 Summary and Assessment
The Brain

 6-1 What tools are available to psychological scientists for studying the brain?

- Case studies of brain injuries were the only method available before more current technological advances.

- Brain-scanning techniques can reveal a range of information about brain structure and function.

  - CT and MRI scans provide detailed images of brain structures.

  - EEGs reveal brain waves, an indication of brain activity levels.

  - PET and fMRI scans can provide information about activity levels of different regions of the brain.

 6-2 What kinds of behaviors and thoughts are controlled by the innermost parts of our brain, the lower-level brain structures?

- The innermost parts of our brain, the lower-level brain structures, control basic life-support functions, such as breathing, wakefulness, muscle coordination, and routing sensory messages.

- The limbic system is key to our emotional experiences and memory system.

- The four lobes of the cerebral cortex perform many functions, but the primary ones can be summarized as follows: The (left and right) frontal lobes control judgment and planning, the parietal lobes control general processing of information, the temporal lobes process auditory signals, and the occipital lobes process visual signals.

- Two of the most important specialized cortexes of the cerebral cortex are the motor cortex and the somatosensory cortex.

- Two regions in the left hemisphere, Broca's and Wernicke's areas, coordinate to allow speech.

- The right hemisphere seems to be more responsible for some spatial reasoning and word association tasks.

Summative Assessment

1. Case studies are of somewhat limited value because

   a. the findings might not apply to other cases.

   b. they can cost too much money.

   c. they may take too long to complete.

   d. they can provide information about brain structure but not brain function.

2. To locate a tumor in the brain, it would be best to use a(n)

   a. case study.   c. fMRI.

   b. EEG.   d. CT.

3. The reticular formation is part of the

   a. limbic system.

   b. cerebral cortex.

   c. somatosensory cortex.

   d. brainstem.

4. Damage to the amygdala would most likely have a negative impact on

   a. memory.

   b. speech.

   c. regulation of emotion.

   d. basic life functions.

5. All of the following are parts of the limbic system *except* the

   a. hippocampus.

   b. reticular formation.

   c. hypothalamus.

   d. amygdala.

6. The longitudinal fissure separates

   a. Broca's area from Wernicke's area.

   b. the cerebral cortex from the limbic system.

   c. the left hemisphere from the right hemisphere.

   d. the motor cortex from the somatosensory cortex.

7. Information from the ears is processed in the _____ lobes.

   a. temporal   c. parietal

   b. frontal   d. occipital

8. Brain plasticity refers to the

   a. ability of the brain to change to respond to damage.

   b. way the brain wrinkles to fit into the skull.

   c. difference in functions between the left hemisphere and the right hemisphere.

   d. method the thalamus uses to route sensory information to the proper area of the brain.

9. The somatosensory cortex can

   a. activate your left arm.

   b. sense very quiet sounds.

   c. understand the speech of others.

   d. allow you to feel a bug crawling up your leg.

10. Albert was unable to form words correctly following his stroke. The stroke probably damaged

   a. the corpus callosum.

   b. Broca's area.

   c. the somatosensory cortex.

   d. Wernicke's area.

KEY TERMS

Sensation

sensation The process by which sensory systems (eyes, ears, and other sensory organs) and the nervous system receive stimuli from our environment.

bottom-up processing Information processing that analyzes the raw stimuli entering through the many sensory systems.

perception The process of organizing and interpreting incoming sensory information.

top-down processing Information processing that draws on expectations and experiences to interpret incoming sensory information.

Ah, the thrill of a roller coaster is created by a wild combination of sensory experiences. Keep your eyes peeled as you read about vision and your other senses.

Stop for a moment to consider the amazing volume of information you're gathering right now. Begin by checking out the visual richness of your present environment. What kinds of shapes are present? Are people or things moving? How many colors can you detect? And vision is just one of your sensory systems. What sounds are you listening to? Is there music on? Are there mechanical sounds from the heating or air conditioning systems? Voices? What can you feel? The texture of your clothing? Pressure from the chair you're sitting on? And what can you taste or smell? This awareness of the world around you is **sensation.** Your nervous system sorts through all this incoming sensory information by using **bottom-up processing,** a form of information processing that analyzes the raw stimuli entering through your many sensory systems.

The analysis of sensory information that takes place during bottom-up processing is part of **perception,** the process of organizing and interpreting incoming sensory information. *Sensation* allows you to know that an object is a red sphere; that it has a cool, hard surface; and that it fits comfortably in your hand. The object has a particular aroma when you smell it and a crunch when you bite into it. When chewed, it produces a taste both sweet and tart. Analysis of this bottom-up stream of data leads to the *perception* that you're eating an apple.

Perception is influenced by **top-down processing,** information processing that draws on our experiences and expectations to interpret incoming sensations. Do you expect caramel-covered apples to taste great? I do, but I approach them with far more caution than most people because a friend of mine once tricked me into biting into a caramel-covered onion. It looked (and crunched) just like a caramel-covered apple, but it sure didn't taste like one! My perception of caramel-covered apples as a potential prank is an example of top-down processing produced by my experiences. For another example of top-down processing, see **Figure 7.1**.

Sensation and perception are two sides of the same coin. They can't be separated because these processes blend together in our everyday experiences. In an effort to keep the information simple and organized, however, we consider sensation in this module and save perception for the next. We begin with some basic principles of sensation and then turn our attention to the various sensory systems we use. I hope you find it as *sensational* as I do!

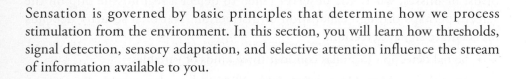

Izzy's volleyball game is a blowout.

Her school's down 15 to 3.

▲**FIGURE 7.1**
Sensation and Perception
Read these sentences carefully and you will note some odd things about them. The marks you interpreted as the word *is* in the top line are exactly the same marks you interpreted as *15* in the phone number. Can you find other examples of the same marks being interpreted two ways? Here is where sensation and perception come together. Sensation involves moving the image from the book to your brain, a bottom-up process of gathering environmental information through the senses. Perception involves knowing what to make of the individual marks in the sentence. This top-down interpretation relies on your experiences with, and expectations about, language. Did you find the other examples? The same mark represents *h* and *b*, and the same mark represents *d* and *l*.

Basic Principles

 7-1 What's a possible real-life application of thresholds, signal detection, sensory adaptation, and selective attention?

Sensation is governed by basic principles that determine how we process stimulation from the environment. In this section, you will learn how thresholds, signal detection, sensory adaptation, and selective attention influence the stream of information available to you.

Thresholds

A *threshold* is an edge, a boundary. One of the thresholds that interests psychologists is the **absolute threshold,** the minimum amount of stimulation needed to detect a particular stimulus. For example, the dimmest visible star in the sky would be right at the absolute threshold for vision because it is just barely bright enough for you to see. Likewise, the least amount of basil you can taste in the spaghetti sauce would be at the absolute threshold for taste. Humans

absolute threshold The minimum amount of stimulation needed to detect a particular stimulus.

Making a Living on the Just Noticeable Difference
People who have an unusual ability to detect very small differences between stimuli can often make high salaries doing so. This perfume tester in Paris can identify subtle aromas that will make perfumes more pleasing.

difference threshold (just noticeable difference) The minimum amount of difference needed to detect that two stimuli are not the same.

signal detection theory A theory that predicts how and when we detect the presence of a faint stimulus (signal) amid background stimulation (noise).

LIFE MATTERS
How many times have you checked your cell phone for a message after feeling a vibration, only to discover that no one messaged you? This false alarm is so common that 80% of college students have experienced it. Phantom cell phone buzzing suggests that our cell phones play an important role in our everyday social lives. In fact, there is a correlation between high phantom buzzing experiences and cell phone dependency.

have absolute thresholds that are low enough to detect most significant events that occur in our environment. According to one estimate, a person with normal vision in total darkness can detect the light of a single candle 30 miles away![1] If your hearing had a lower absolute threshold, you might constantly be distracted by the sound of blood pulsing near your ears. We have sensitive senses. (For more on what this might mean, see Thinking Like a Psychological Scientist: Can Subliminal Messages Improve Your Memory?)

Another type of threshold is the difference threshold, also called the just noticeable difference. As you might expect, the **difference threshold** represents an edge, too—this time, the minimum difference to detect that two stimuli are not the same. How much does the volume have to increase before you can tell that the music playing from your stereo has become louder? How much do the laces on your hiking boots need to be loosened so that they feel slightly less tight? How much does the room have to cool down before you realize there's a problem with the heating system? These are examples of the difference threshold—the smallest detectable change in a stimulus.

Signal Detection Theory

Is that image on the airport security monitor a phone, or is it an explosive device? Is that shadow on the X-ray harmless scar tissue, or is it a life-threatening tumor just beginning to grow? Is that smell the usual musty odor coming from the utility room, or is there a gas leak in the water heater? Knowing that thresholds can have profound life-or-death implications, researchers have devised sophisticated mathematical formulas to understand how we detect these faint signals. **Signal detection theory** predicts how and when we detect the presence of a faint stimulus (signal) amid background stimulation (noise). Signal detection depends on the stimulus, the environment, and the person doing the detecting. It grew out of the Cold War in the 1950s and 1960s as a way of improving our ability to detect incoming nuclear warheads in time to respond appropriately. The idea was for the person monitoring the radar to score hits—to recognize missiles on a radar screen for what they were and, equally important, to avoid mistakes. These mistakes were either false alarms, where the missile later turned out to be a commercial aircraft or a flock of birds, or misses, where the observer failed to detect a real missile blip on the screen, perhaps through exhaustion or distraction. National security depends on accurate signal detection.

- Signal detection formulas consider three kinds of variables:
- *Stimulus variables*—How bright is the blip on the radar screen?
- *Environmental variables*—How much distracting noise is there in the room with the radar equipment?
- *Person variables*—Is the operator properly trained and motivated?

Signal detection theory is now used in a variety of nonmilitary applications, ranging from understanding how physicians can more accurately detect tumors in time for successful treatment to improving air traffic controllers' ability to track aircraft and identify planes flying dangerously close to one another. Airport security personnel are periodically tested on their ability to detect significant stimuli by the addition of images of guns and knives to luggage X-rays. The system congratulates the screener when the dangerous images are successfully detected.[2]

What happens when you detect a stimulus continuously? That brings us to sensory adaptation.

The Image Bank/Getty Images/Getty Images

> **Signal Detection Theory**
> Signal detection theory helps us understand how quickly we can notice and correctly interpret a blip on a radar screen. The researcher would consider the nature of the screen itself (How bright are the blips?), the surrounding environment (How much noise, or distraction, is there?), and the person doing the detecting. (Is he trained, motivated, healthy, and alert?)

THINKING LIKE A PSYCHOLOGICAL SCIENTIST

Can Subliminal Messages Improve Your Memory?

Perhaps you've heard about subliminal messages. A Google search on the term turns up over half a million hits. One website near the top of the list promises subliminal programs that will improve your memory, make you rich, cause you to lose weight, and develop an extroverted personality, among the over 200 programs available at special sale prices. Each inserts messages, played at a frequency you cannot consciously perceive, into the sound of ocean surf. There are personal testimonials speaking to the success of the programs. And if you don't find this particular company to your liking, there are dozens of others ready to collect your money.

Can this really be? Is it possible to utilize these subliminal—the word means *below threshold*—messages to learn foreign languages, become more confident in relationships, and improve your athletic performance? Unfortunately, as with so many other things that seem too good to be true, the research doesn't support the claims.

It *is* true that you can be influenced by a stimulus you are unaware of. In one experiment, participants were shown a brief image of an emotionally positive scene (like kittens) or an emotionally troubling scene (like a dead body) so quickly that the scene registered only as a flash of light. These subliminal messages were enough to influence the participants' perceptions of how nice a person looked when asked to rate a photo right after exposure to the emotionally charged flash.[3]

These fleeting subliminal influences, however, are a far cry from the claims of the marketing companies. To test these claims, one study had college students listen to subliminal tapes that were supposed to improve their memory or enhance their self-esteem. While students believed the tapes were effective, the researchers did not discover any real changes.[4] Studies do not show the kinds of large, lasting effects that would be necessary for us to conclude that subliminal programs work. Alas, if you want to improve your memory, you're probably going to have to work at it.

THINK ABOUT . . . Psychological Science

1. What are subliminal messages?

2. What did Greenwald and his associates discover when they tested subliminal message tapes that were supposed to improve memory and enhance self-esteem?

3. Why do you think so many people believe in subliminal messages?

Sensory Adaptation

Living organisms must constantly adapt to meet the demands of their environment. This means we pay more attention to new stimuli, which are most likely to be significant. If nothing has changed in your visual field, you are probably OK. But if you sense movement off to one side, you'd best pay attention. That moving object could be an out-of-control car or something falling off a shelf; in either case, you're at risk.

Our adaptive nature means we filter out the unchanging aspects of our environments, a process known as **sensory adaptation**. When stimulation is constant and unchanging, you eventually fail to respond because you usually don't need to. One example of sensory adaptation occurs when you dive into a swimming pool filled with cold water. At first, the water seems frigid, but if you stay in for a while you'll eventually get used to it. In other words, you'll adapt to the constant stimulation of the cold water. You can also adapt to hot water, of course, or an odor, or the feel of an article of clothing, or a constant noise like the hum from an air conditioner. I even adapted once to the feel and sight of my eyeglasses. I had been wearing them so long that, in a sense, they "disappeared." I spent several minutes looking for them before my wife started laughing and pointed out they were right on my face where they usually are.

Selective Attention

Hundreds of millions of stimuli are competing for your attention right now. Every page of this textbook is a stimulus, as are every paragraph, sentence, word, syllable, letter, and part of a letter. Every sound within your hearing range is a stimulus, as is every taste in your mouth. (Is a hint of the flavor from your last meal still there?) Because you live in such a sensory-rich environment, you must select certain stimuli to attend to and ignore the rest. Focusing conscious awareness on a particular stimulus to the exclusion of others is **selective attention**.

A good example of selective attention can be seen in E. G. Boring's famous old woman–young woman drawing (see **Figure 7.2**). You can look at the drawing and see the old woman, *or* you can see the young woman. With practice, you can switch back and forth quickly, but you can focus your attention on only one of these faces at a time.

Sensory Adaptation: What Smell?
Inside the bucket is raw garbage that is to be fed to earthworms as part of a recycling demonstration. Notice that the young visitors have not yet adapted to the smell of garbage and so are holding their noses against the stench. The recyclers, on the other hand, have adapted to the smell and have probably filtered it out completely.

sensory adaptation
Diminished sensitivity to constant and unchanging stimulation.

selective attention Focusing conscious awareness on a particular stimulus to the exclusion of others.

FIGURE 7.2
Selective Attention: What Do You See?
You can perceive this famous drawing in one of two ways: as an old woman (with thin lips, a big nose, and her chin tucked down against her chest) or as a young woman (looking back over her right shoulder and wearing a black necklace, with her jawline and left ear clearly visible). You can attend to one or the other, and even learn to switch back and forth quickly, but you can't see both at once. What do you see in photo (b)?

(a)

(b)

Selective attention to a small number of stimuli lets you function in a busy, noisy world. Right now, you are effectively blocking out a variety of stimuli in your environment—the feel of the clothes you are wearing, the temperature of the air around you, the noises outside the room you are in, and so on. It is why you can focus on a movie while others are talking in the theater. Perhaps you have had the experience of being so caught up in a book or a conversation that you missed somebody walking into the room or saying something to you. Perhaps you can also identify times when you were trying to study and were too easily distracted by stimuli in your environment. Selective attention (or lack of it) plays an important role in our lives.

MAKE IT STICK!

1. While watching an exciting soccer game, Nadia didn't hear Ed calling her name. Which factor explains her failure to respond to Ed?

    a. Selective attention
    b. Difference threshold
    c. Just noticeable difference
    d. Sensory adaptation

2. What is the difference between an absolute threshold and a just noticeable difference?

3. Charlie did not notice the wonderful aroma of baking bread in the kitchen until he left for a minute to take out the garbage. The reason he did not notice until he left and returned is that sensory _____ had occurred.

The Visual System

If you asked several of your friends, who were born with normal vision, which of the basic senses they'd least like to lose, chances are the most common answer would be vision. Just the thought of losing this fundamental connection to the world is enough to help us appreciate the wonder of our ability to see. In this section, you will see how it all works.

The Nature of Light

 7-2 What is light, and what is the nature of light waves?

No light? No sight! Even nocturnal creatures depend on the low level of light available to their eyes at night. Light enters the eye as waves of *electromagnetic energy* (see **Figure 7.3**). The visible spectrum is the tiny part of the electromagnetic spectrum that produces the light (and colors) humans can see. Electromagnetic energy ranges all the way from gamma waves, with very short wavelengths, to long-wave radio waves.

Two characteristics of electromagnetic light waves determine what we see in the visual spectrum. The length of the light wave determines the light's color, or *hue* (see **Figure 7.4a, b**). Have you ever learned the memory trick ROY G BIV for remembering the colors of the rainbow in order (red, orange, yellow, green, blue, indigo, and violet)? These colors are produced as the wavelength of light shortens—red light, with a distance between peaks of about 700 billionths of a meter, has almost twice the wavelength of violet light, with a distance of about 400 billionths of a meter.

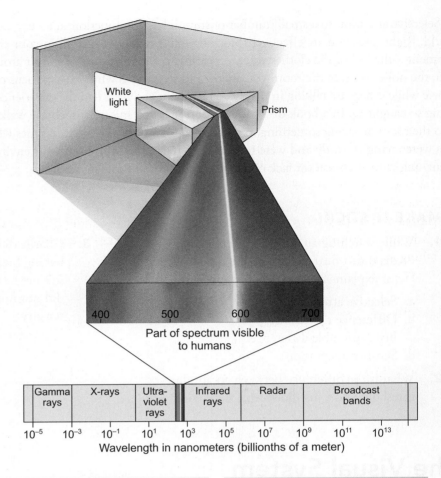

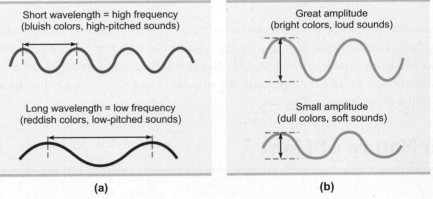

The second characteristic of waves—the *amplitude,* or height, of the wave—determines brightness (see Figure 7.4b). Taller waves of the same wavelength produce brighter levels of the same color.

MAKE IT STICK!

1. Light is a form of _____ energy.

2. As Rebecca looks at a light, its wavelength changes. Rebecca experiences this as

   a. a change in the hue of the light.
   b. a flickering effect.
   c. movement of the light from one spot to another.
   d. a change in the brightness of the light.

The Structure of the Visual System

7-3 How do the structures and receptor cells in the eye work together to detect light waves and change them into neural impulses?

Let's trace the path of a single light ray as it enters the eye. As we take our little trip along the visual pathway, follow along on **Figure 7.5**. The light first strikes the **cornea,** the clear, curved bulge on the front of the eye that bends light rays to begin focusing them. You can see the cornea move under the eyelid when someone looks back and forth with eyes closed. The cornea also protects the eye because it is rich in nerve endings, which you know if you've ever had the misfortune of scratching it.

cornea The clear, curved bulge on the front of the eye that bends light rays to begin focusing them.

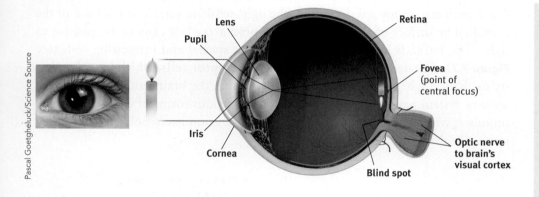

Pascal Goetgheluck/Science Source

FIGURE 7.5
The Eye
When you view an object, light rays travel through the cornea, the pupil, and the lens at the front of the eye. These structures work together to focus the image on the retina at the back of the eye. The retinal image is upside down and reversed, but your brain, of course, makes sure that you perceive the world in its correct orientation.

Because the cornea is clear, we can see a disk of colored tissue behind it, the part of the eye we're describing when we talk about the color of someone's eyes. This is the **iris,** a ring of muscle tissue that forms the colored portion of the eye and regulates the size of the pupil. The adjustable black opening in the center of the iris is the **pupil,** which controls the amount of light that enters the eye. The pupil appears to be black because no light is emitted *from* the eye. It's similar to looking at the opening of a dark cave.

The iris and pupil work together to regulate the amount of light that enters the eye. When exposed to bright light, the iris expands inward, making the pupil smaller and letting less light enter the eye. When exposed to dim light, the iris draws back and the pupil enlarges to admit more light. You can actually watch this process if you wake up in the night and stumble your way to the bathroom mirror. Turn on the light, and you will see the pupil shrink before (and within!) your eyes. It is rapidly working to restrict the incoming light that you find too bright.

Continuing our journey along the visual pathway, we next encounter the **lens,** a transparent structure behind the pupil that changes shape to focus images on the retina. Some of us have lenses that do not focus the light effectively; as a result, we are nearsighted or farsighted (see **Figure 7.6a, b, c**). Luckily, help is available in the form of glasses, contact lenses, or laser surgeries that actually reshape the surface of the cornea. These wonderful inventions correct our vision (I, for one, would be lost without them) by helping the lens effectively focus light reflected from the objects we are viewing.

iris A ring of muscle tissue that forms the colored portion of the eye and regulates the size of the pupil.

pupil The adjustable opening in the center of the iris, which controls the amount of light entering the eye.

lens A transparent structure behind the pupil in the eye that changes shape to focus images on the retina.

Do you believe in the "evil eye?" X-ray vision? Perhaps because of these popular ideas, roughly half of U.S. adults believe that vision— even normal, everyday vision— involves energy being sent out from the eye rather than being received by it.[17] After reading this section, we hope you will clearly see this notion as another myth disproved by psychological science.

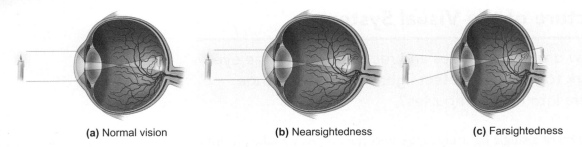

(a) Normal vision **(b)** Nearsightedness **(c)** Farsightedness

▲ **FIGURE 7.6**
Nearsightedness and Farsightedness
(a) With normal vision, the lens focuses the light rays into an image on the retina. The result is a clear, focused image. (b) In a nearsighted person's eye, the lens causes light rays from distant objects to converge in front of the retina, which blurs the image. (c) If a person is farsighted, the lens causes light rays from close objects to converge behind the retina. Corrective lenses, either in eyeglasses or as contact lenses, help the eye's own lens focus the image correctly on the retina. Laser eye surgery accomplishes the same goal by carefully reshaping the cornea so that it sharply focuses the image.

retina The light-sensitive surface at the back of the eyeball.

receptor cells Specialized cells in every sensory system of the body that can turn other kinds of energy into action potentials (neural impulses) that the brain can process.

Until this point in our journey, the structures in the eye have been moving visual information toward the **retina,** the light-sensitive surface at the back of the eyeball. The surface of the retina, like the pixel array in a camera, is sensitive to light. The retina is made up of three layers of special and interesting cells (see **Figure 7.7**). The deepest layer is composed of **receptor cells,** which have the ability to change light energy into nerve impulses that the brain can interpret. Every sensory system has receptor cells that convert various forms of energy into such impulses; without these cells, the brain would be completely isolated from information in the outside world.

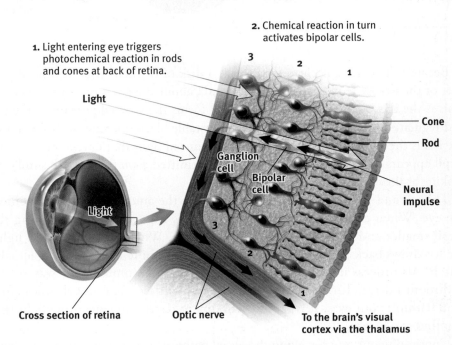

FIGURE 7.7
The Retina
Light rays filter to the innermost layer of the retina before the rods and cones convert the visual information to neural impulses. The information then travels through the retina's middle layer (made of bipolar cells) and outer layer (made of ganglion cells). The long axon fibers from the ganglion cells come together to form the optic nerve, which exits the eye at the blind spot and carries the information to the brain for further processing.

1. Light entering eye triggers photochemical reaction in rods and cones at back of retina.
2. Chemical reaction in turn activates bipolar cells.
3. Bipolar cells then activate the ganglion cells, the axons of which converge to form the optic nerve. This nerve transmits information to the visual cortex (via the thalamus) in the brain.

rods Visual receptor cells located in the retina that can detect only black, white, and gray.

Your visual system has two different types of receptor cells, rods and cones, to change light energy into nerve impulses that the brain can interpret (see **Table 7.1**). **Rods** can detect only black, white, and shades of gray. Also, rods have a lower absolute threshold than cones do. So, under dim light conditions, only

TABLE 7.1 Receptors in the Human Eye: Rod-Shaped Rods and Cone-Shaped Cones

	Cones	Rods	
Number	6 million	120 million	
Location in retina	Center	Periphery	
Sensitivity in dim light	Low	High	
Color sensitivity	High	Low	
Detail sensitivity	High	Low	

Omikron/Science Source

rods respond and you see the world in shades of gray. The less numerous **cones** detect sharp details and colors, but color becomes apparent only if there is enough light. The detail-oriented cones cluster at the center of the retina; this spot, known as the *fovea,* is the area where your vision is best.

The rods and cones feed their information into the middle layer of retinal cells, the *bipolar cells.* The bipolar cells in turn pass that information to the *ganglion cells,* which form the final layer in the retina. The axons of the ganglion cells come together to form the **optic nerve,** which carries information from your eyes to your brain's occipital lobes, where extensive visual processing occurs. We tend to think that we see with our eyes, but it is our brain that must process the information that the eyes deliver. Where the optic nerve exits the eye, we have a **blind spot** because no rods or cones can occupy that point on the retina. **Figure 7.8** will help you identify your own blind spot.

cones Visual receptor cells located in the retina that can detect sharp details and color.

optic nerve The nerve that carries visual information from the eye to the occipital lobes of the brain.

blind spot The point at which the optic nerve travels through the retina to exit the eye; the lack of rods and cones at this point creates a small blind spot.

FIGURE 7.8
A Blind Spot Detector
A blind spot exists where the optic nerve exits through the retina, because there are no rods or cones at this point. To find your blind spot, close your right eye and look at the boy. Maintain your focus on the boy and slowly adjust the distance of the book from your eyes until the cookie disappears. Under normal circumstances, you are unaware of your blind spot because one eye sees what the other does not. Even with one eye closed, you're not aware of the gap because your brain fills in the missing information by making an assumption about what belongs in the void. This assumption is another example of top-down processing.

MAKE IT STICK!

1. The two eye structures that focus light are the _____ and the _____.

2. Which of the following structures of the eye is designed to detect only certain wavelengths of light?

   a. pupil   c. lens
   b. cornea   d. cones

3. The receptor cells for vision are called _____ and _____.

Color Vision

  7-4 How do the trichromatic theory and opponent-process theory contribute to our understanding of color vision?

Our visual system is so good at detecting minor variations in color that we can detect *a million* separate hues.[5] The richness this ability adds to our visual world is apparent in the array of color chips available at the paint store and the variety of lipstick colors at the cosmetics counter.

Color, as we know, is a function of the cones. According to a theory first proposed in the nineteenth century and based on the work of Hermann von Helmholtz and Thomas Young, cones are sensitive to three wavelengths of light, which produce red, green, and blue. According to this **trichromatic (three-color) theory,** these three colors combine to create a million color combinations. The trichromatic system is similar to the design used to enable color on TV screens, video projectors, and computer monitors. These screens produce different intensities of red, green, and blue, and all the colors you see on the screen are mixtures of these three basic colors. The cones in the retina operate the same way.

If you've studied art, you may have learned that the primary colors are red, blue, and yellow and wonder why cones aren't tuned to these three colors. You'll find the answer in **Figure 7.9**. Painting produces color by a *subtractive* process: Each paint pigment subtracts—absorbs or soaks up—different wavelengths of light. Red paint, for example, absorbs all wavelengths except red, which is reflected back to the eye. If you mix red, blue, and yellow paint together, you end up with black; together, those three pigments subtract all wavelengths of light.

Vision, however, operates on an *additive* process, with each wavelength of light adding a new color to the mix. If you mix red, green, and blue lights, you end up with white, not black. Those three lights are primary because they produce white light, which combines all wavelengths.

Color-blind people generally lack one of the three types of cones. A more accurate term is *color deficient* because people with this condition are not blind to color but are just limited in the number of colors they can see. Usually they

trichromatic theory A theory of color vision that says cones are sensitive to red, green, or blue light—the three colors that combine to create millions of color combinations.

FIGURE 7.9
What Are the Primary Colors? ▶
That depends on whether you're mixing paints or lights. Mixing paints is a subtractive process—each new pigment soaks up another wavelength of reflected light. All wavelengths are subtracted with a mixture of red, blue, and yellow (the result is black), so they are primary. Mixing colored lights is an additive process—each new color adds another wavelength. In this case, the fewest colors that can be mixed to produce white light (representing all wavelengths) are red, green, and blue, so they are primary for this additive process.

Subtractive color mixing

Additive color mixing

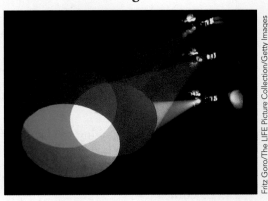

Fritz Goro/The LIFE Picture Collection/Getty Images

lack either the red cones or the green cones and have trouble telling the difference between the two.[6] This inherited condition is more common among males than females. Many times, the person with the color deficiency does not even realize a problem exists.

There are some things trichromatic theory does not explain. One of the most fascinating is why we see color afterimages. If you have normal color vision, try this for yourself with **Figure 7.10** by turning the odd green, black, and yellow American flag into the more familiar red, white, and blue version of the Stars and Stripes. Ewald Hering proposed an **opponent-process theory** of color to explain such images. Hering's theory argues that color is processed in opponent pairs (red–green, yellow–blue, and black–white). Light that stimulates one half of the pair inhibits or blocks the other half. For example, stimulation that turns *on* a green-processing neuron ensures that a red-processing neuron will be *off*.[7] Thus, you can see red *or* green at any one spot at a given time but not both simultaneously. Many color pairs combine easily (red and blue, for example, combine to form violet), but there is no greenish-red color.

When you stared at the flag in Figure 7.10, you did so long enough to fatigue your green-detection neurons. Then, when you looked at the white space, your red-detection neurons, which were not tired, produced a red aftereffect that lasted until the green cells recovered.

So, we have two entirely different theories of color vision: the Young-Helmholtz trichromatic theory and the Hering opponent-process theory. Which one is right? *Both* are. Substantial experimental evidence indicates that both systems function to let you see color, and we have no reason to suspect that the existence of one makes the other impossible. Color is clearly important to us.

Luis Santos/Shutterstock

Stop on Red, Go on Blue? Isn't it interesting that traffic lights use red and green—the two colors most likely to be confused by a person with color vision deficiencies—as the means of conveying the important information of whether to stop or proceed? If you check, you'll notice that newer traffic signals now have a lot of blue in the green light; now it's more of a teal light. This slight change helps people with color-deficient vision tell the difference between stop and go. It also helps, of course, that red and green occupy different positions in the box that houses the lights.

FIGURE 7.10
Color Afterimages
Look at the center dot of the flag for about a minute; then shift your gaze to the dot beside it. An afterimage will develop, but it will be in red, white, and blue. The opponent-process theory of color vision can explain this, but the trichromatic theory cannot.

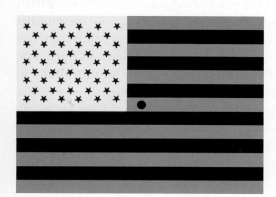

MAKE IT STICK!

1. Why is *color deficient* generally a more accurate term than *color blind* to describe people who have trouble seeing the world in normal color?

2. Reversed-color afterimage effects can be explained with the _____ theory of color vision.

3. The trichromatic theory of color visions says that

    a. color is processed as light travels through the three layers of the lens.
    b. rods, cones, and bipolar cells all play a role in color vision.
    c. three different kinds of cones detect three different colors.
    d. there are three color reversals in color afterimage drawings.

opponent-process theory
A theory of color vision that says color is processed by cones organized in opponent pairs (red–green, yellow–blue, and black–white); light that stimulates one half of the pair inhibits the other half.

Hearing

7-5 What are the structures of the ear? How do they work to detect sound waves and change them into neural impulses?

Silence may be golden, but sound enriches our experience of the world. In this section, we explore what sound is and how we process it into a form we can understand.

The Nature of Sound

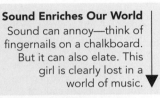

Sound Enriches Our World
Sound can annoy—think of fingernails on a chalkboard. But it can also elate. This girl is clearly lost in a world of music. ▼

pitch A sound's highness or lowness, which depends on the frequency of the sound wave.

Light enters the eye as waves of electromagnetic energy. Sound comes in waves, too (see Figure 7.4), but in this case the waves are produced by vibration. Sound *is* vibration. You can feel your vocal cords vibrate if you touch your neck while singing or talking. Musical instruments all produce vibrations—of strings in the case of guitars and pianos, of reeds in the case of saxophones, of drum skins in the case of kettledrums. But you won't hear any of these sounds unless the vibration is carried from its source to your ear. Typically, the vibration travels in pulses of air molecules. But other substances can carry sound waves, too, such as the bones of our skull transmitting the sound of a fast-beating heart to our ears or the water in a pool transmitting the sound of music to the ears of synchronized swimmers. In the case of light, the length of the wave produces hue, and the amplitude (height) of the wave produces brightness. For sound, the length of the wave (frequency) determines **pitch,** the sound's highness or lowness. Pitch is expressed as *hertz (Hz)*—the number of sound waves that reach the ear per second. Hertz represents the frequency of a sound wave and determines the pitch of a sound. Middle C on the piano, for instance, represents a sound of 256 Hz. Normal human hearing allows us to hear deep, rumbling bass sounds as low as 20 Hz or high-pitched whistles of 20,000 Hz, although as you get older you gradually lose your ability to hear higher-pitched sounds. This is why the so-called mosquito or teen buzz ringtone (you can find examples on the internet if you have not listened to it) can be heard by most teenagers but not by most adults. This sound is a little above 17,000 Hz.

The height, or amplitude, of the sound wave determines *loudness,* which is usually measured in *decibels (dB),* named after Alexander Graham Bell. The absolute threshold for hearing is 0 dB. You can see a rough approximation of the decibel level of some common sounds in **Figure 7.11**. Notice that any prolonged sound exceeding 85 dB can produce hearing loss. Sound at the 85 dB level is not painful, and many people play music through headphones at volume levels above 85 dB. This is not a good idea. The hearing loss will not be noticeable on a day-to-day basis, but exposure to any loud, prolonged noise (including good music!) will produce gradual, irreversible hearing loss. Many aging rockers from the 1960s—including Pete Townshend of The Who and Stephen Stills of Crosby, Stills, and Nash—are now dealing with hearing loss caused by exposure to loud amps at countless concerts. Listen up, music fans, and turn down the volume on your speakers and earbuds.

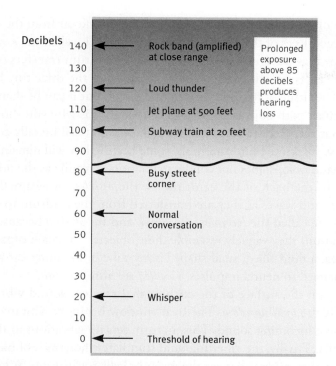

Decibels

140	Rock band (amplified) at close range
130	
120	Loud thunder
110	Jet plane at 500 feet
100	Subway train at 20 feet
90	
80	Busy street corner
70	
60	Normal conversation
50	
40	
30	
20	Whisper
10	
0	Threshold of hearing

Prolonged exposure above 85 decibels produces hearing loss

FIGURE 7.11
How Loud Is Loud?
The loudness of sound is measured in decibel (dB) units. Every 10 dB increase represents a *tenfold* increase in loudness (a 20 dB increase is 100 times louder, and a 30 dB increase is 1000 times louder). Prolonged exposure to sounds of 85 dB or more can cause hearing loss.

The Structure of the Auditory System

When your best friend shouts your name across the cafeteria at school, what happens? First, the vocal cord vibrations that constitute the sound must travel through the air from your friend's mouth to your ear. When the sound waves reach your ear, they are funneled by the tissue of your outer ear and travel down the *auditory canal,* the opening through which sound waves travel as they move into the ear for processing (see **Figure 7.12**). At the end of the auditory canal, the sound waves

FIGURE 7.12
The Amazing Journey of a Sound
Sound waves must travel through air, tissue, bone, and fluid before the receptor cells for hearing, the hair cells in the cochlea, generate nerve impulses that the brain can interpret. Use this diagram to follow the path of sound as you read about its journey in the text.

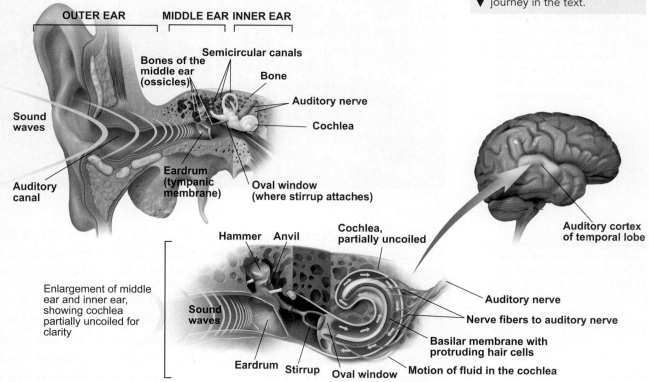

reach a piece of tissue that seals the inner workings of the ear from the dirt, Q-tips, and small Lego pieces of the outside world. This tissue is called the *eardrum* (more formally known as the *tympanic membrane*). The eardrum transfers sound vibration from the air (your friend shouting your name) to the three tiny bones of the middle ear. The tissue of the eardrum is quite tough, but it can be damaged, either by direct contact with objects inserted in the ear (this is why you shouldn't insert objects in your ear) or by exceptionally loud noises that can literally cause the eardrum to burst. When the eardrum heals, some hearing loss will remain because the scar tissue that develops does not conduct vibration as readily as the original tissue.

Attached to the back of the eardrum are the *ossicles,* three small bones that amplify the sound waves as they are transferred from the eardrum to the cochlea. These bones are called the *hammer,* the *anvil,* and the *stirrup* because (if you use your imagination) they vaguely resemble these objects. The main organ of hearing is the **cochlea,** a fluid-filled, snail-shaped bony tube in the inner ear where sound waves are changed to neural impulses. *Cochlea* is Latin for *snail.*

The point on the surface of the cochlea that receives sound vibrations from the ossicles is the *oval window.* The oval window begins to vibrate at the same frequency as an incoming sound. This, in turn, sets up vibrations in the fluid that fills the cochlea. Finally, the vibrating fluid stimulates thousands of **hair cells,** tiny projections in the cochlea that are the receptor cells for hearing. When vibration causes the tips of these hair cells to move even the width of an atom, the vibrations cause the hair cells to generate neural impulses that your brain can process.[8] But prolonged exposure to loud noise will damage these vitally important cells. The two photos in **Figure 7.13** show hair cells before and after such damage.

cochlea [KOHK-lee-uh] The major organ of hearing; a snail-shaped, bony, fluid-filled structure in the inner ear where sound waves are changed to neural impulses.

hair cells The receptor cells for hearing; these are located in the cochlea and are responsible for changing sound vibrations into neural impulses.

FIGURE 7.13
Warning: Rock Concerts Can Be Dangerous to Your Guinea Pig (and You) These scanning electron micrographs of the inner ear hair cells of a guinea pig (a) before and (b) after exposure to 24 hours of loud noise (comparable to that of a loud rock concert) testify to noise's destructive effects.

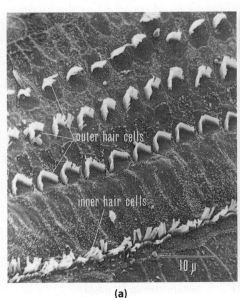
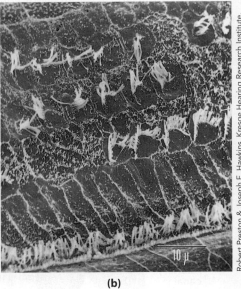

(a) (b)

Robert Preston & Joseph E. Hawkins, Kresge Hearing Research Institute, University of Michigan

auditory nerve The nerve that carries sound information from the ears to the temporal lobes of the brain.

The neural impulses are collected by fibers that attach to the base of each hair cell. These fibers join to form the **auditory nerve,** which exits the cochlea and carries sound information to the temporal lobes of the brain, where auditory processing occurs.

Sound Localization

If you are a hearing person, close your eyes for a moment and listen to the sounds around you. Do you have any difficulty knowing where a particular sound is coming from—whether it's behind you or in front, to your left or to your right?

Localizing sounds is something we are good at, and it's important that we are. Sounds often signify important environmental events, including the presence of danger. We'd *better* be able to locate the source quickly. How do we do it?

We rely on two important cues to locate sound sources (see **Figure 7.14**). Step one is to determine which ear hears the sound first. Sound traveling through air moves about 750 miles per hour. That's fast, but there is still a detectable time lag before sound reaches the farther ear.[9, 10] In step two, we determine which ear hears the louder, more intense sound. By the time a sound moves around to the ear farther from the source, the sound is muted enough for your brain to be aware of the difference.

Locating the source of sounds is only one of many determinations your brain makes without any conscious effort on your part.

FIGURE 7.14
How Do You Know Where a Sound Is Coming From? When a sound originates from your right, as in this figure, it reaches your right ear slightly faster and slightly louder than it reaches your left ear. Your brain calculates the differences to locate the source of the sound. Sometimes it is difficult to tell if a sound is coming from directly ahead of you or directly behind you because sounds in this plane reach both ears at the same time and with equal intensity.

MAKE IT STICK!

1. Which two structures can be most easily damaged by loud sounds?

   a. the oval window and the auditory nerve
   b. the auditory canal and the stirrup
   c. the tympanic membrane and the hair cells
   d. the hammer and the anvil

2. The snail-shaped organ of hearing is the _____.

3. The amplitude of sound waves determines

   a. loudness.   c. pitch.
   b. Hertz value.   d. sound localization.

Other Senses

 7-6 How are tastes, smells, and touch sensations processed?

We have spent considerable time on vision and hearing, which no doubt are vital senses. They also are the best-understood sensory systems and the ones that first come to mind when the topic of sensation comes up. But think about what life would be like with no ability to taste or smell. Without the ability to savor the taste and smell of food, would you still be willing to put effort into preparing meals and eating them? And what would life be like with no sense of touch? You would lose not only good touch, like the satisfaction of a hug or kiss from someone you care about deeply, but also the ability to detect pain. This loss may sound like an improvement, but it wouldn't be. Pain is one of the most effective mechanisms we have to protect ourselves from environmental dangers. Without pain, we wouldn't realize that we had placed our hand on a red-hot stove burner until we smelled our flesh burning—far too late to minimize the seriousness of the injury. Finally, what about your sense of balance and your ability to judge the position of your body parts? Walking would be incredibly difficult if you didn't have a sense of what your legs were doing at each step (excuse the pun) of the process.

Let's take a brief look at some of our remaining senses.

Taste

Taste is a chemical sense. You have receptor cells on the surface of the tongue (and, to a lesser degree, elsewhere in the mouth) that respond to the chemical structure of the foods you eat. These receptor cells can detect five tastes. We have known about salty, sweet, sour, and bitter for a long time.[11] Most recently, researchers discovered a fifth taste receptor for the savory, meaty, cheesy taste called *umami*.[12] It's possible there are other tastes still waiting to be discovered. Newborn babies have a natural attraction to salty and sweet tastes, a biological predisposition that ensures that they will seek mother's milk (which is sweet) and salt (which is necessary for survival). Babies also have natural dislikes—of sour and bitter tastes—which protect them from substances that are more likely to be poisonous.

Taste receptor cells can be damaged by heat, as you no doubt know if you've ever burned your mouth on hot food you couldn't wait to eat. Tobacco smoke also harms these cells. Fortunately, taste cells do replace themselves within a few days. An added benefit of kicking the cigarette habit is that food starts to taste better as the taste cells regenerate.

One interesting fact about taste is that we don't all have the same sensitivity to taste. About a quarter of the population, dubbed supertasters by researcher **Linda Bartoshuk** and her colleagues,[13] have an abundance of taste receptors that allow them to experience tastes, especially bitter tastes, more intensely than most of us do. Bartoshuk theorizes that these individuals were the poison detectors of ancient civilization. If they avoided a food, it was likely to be dangerous and others would avoid it as well. Even today, supertasters, with their enhanced sensitivity to alcohol's bitter taste, are less likely to become dependent on alcohol than are those who don't share this trait.

Another quarter of the population are nontasters. They do taste, of course, but with much less intensity than people with more taste cells. These individuals tend to do well in times of food scarcity because they are willing to eat anything, no matter how bad it tastes. In times of plenty, this tendency can be dangerous, but it just might allow survival in famine. Most of us, about half the population, fall in the middle as medium tasters.

Smell

Smell, like taste, is a chemical sense. Molecules given off by many substances circulate in the air (see **Figure 7.15**). When these molecules reach the upper nasal passages, *olfactory cells* that project from the brain can process these smells. In some ways, smell is more complicated than taste. By triggering various combinations of receptors on the olfactory cells, over a trillion odors can potentially be detected.[14]

Taste and smell interact to produce flavor. Perhaps you've noticed that flavor is greatly diminished when you have a head cold with lots of congestion. Odors that normally travel up to the nasal passages from the back of the throat are blocked when you have a head cold, and you are left with taste alone. Try plugging your nose and closing your lips tightly the next time you eat a fruit-flavored jelly bean or Starburst candy. You can detect sour (from the citrus) and sweet (from the sugar), but you cannot tell the flavor (cherry, lemon, and so on). As soon as you unplug your nose, however, the flavor becomes instantly apparent! Actually, flavor

Bob Krist/Getty Images

Flavor, a Sensory Interaction
We often speak of taste when we really mean flavor. Taste can detect only sweet, sour, salty, bitter, and umami. The flavors shown here on these sumptuous plates also involve their smell, texture, temperature, and appearance.

Courtesy University of Florida Health

LINDA BARTOSHUK (1938–)
Renowned researcher on the role of genetics and the treatment of disorders in the chemical senses of taste and smell.

LIFE MATTERS
Unlike our other senses, our sense of smell travels through the limbic system, where our memories are processed and emotions are regulated. It's no wonder why a simple whiff of an ex's cologne or perfume can instantly bring you back to a memory of your first kiss or to the heartache you felt when you were dumped.

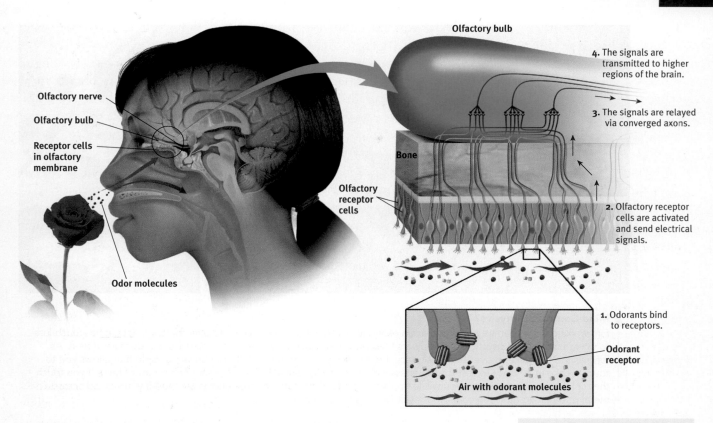

Olfactory bulb

4. The signals are transmitted to higher regions of the brain.

Olfactory nerve

Olfactory bulb

3. The signals are relayed via converged axons.

Receptor cells in olfactory membrane

Bone

2. Olfactory receptor cells are activated and send electrical signals.

Olfactory receptor cells

Odor molecules

1. Odorants bind to receptors.

Odorant receptor

Air with odorant molecules

▲ **FIGURE 7.15**
The Sense of Smell
We are sometimes advised to stop and smell the roses. This is not as easy as it seems!

is an interaction of more than just taste and smell. Appearance is important (how much appeal would blue milk have?), which is why fine restaurants spend so much effort on the visual presentation of their food. Feel or texture is also important (imagine soggy potato chips!), as is temperature (how does a steaming-hot cup of Coca-Cola sound?).

Touch

Touch is your physical connection with the outside world. Your skin is embedded with receptors that respond to various kinds of stimulation. The basic skin senses are pain, warmth, cold, and pressure. Your experience of other skin sensations flows from various combinations of these four basic skin senses. An itch, for example, results from gentle stimulation of pain receptors, hot from simultaneous stimulation of warm and cold (see **Figure 7.16**), and wetness from simultaneous stimulation of cold and pressure.

To explain pain, researchers Ronald Melzack and Patrick Wall have proposed a gate-control theory.[15] According to this gate-control theory, pain messages from the body travel on one set of nerve fibers in the spinal cord, while other kinds of sensory information travel on another set of fibers. The fibers carrying pain messages contain pain gates, which are open when we experience pain. Under some conditions, the nonpain fibers can actually close the pain gates.[16] This is why other touch sensations (rubbing the area that hurts or icing it, for example) can partially block the sensation of pain.

These incoming pain messages involve bottom-up processing. But pain also involves top-down processing. That is, your brain significantly affects whether and how you perceive pain. Athletes in competition may not be fully aware of a painful injury until after their competition is completed. Their level of focus blocks the pain messages from conscious awareness. You've witnessed another example of the top-down processing of pain if you've ever been taking care of a toddler who

Cold water   **Warm water**

HOT!

▲ **FIGURE 7.16**
When Is Hot Not?
When cold and warm receptors are stimulated at the same time, the result is an eerie sensation of hot.

Wally Santana/AP Images

Wally Santana/AP Images

▲ **Mind Control or Physics?**
Fire walking is sometimes presented as an example of mental discipline, or mind over matter. In fact, it has much less to do with supposed psychological powers than with basic physics. Burning coals are poor conductors of heat. As long as the firewalker moves at a brisk pace, he is unlikely to burn himself. It's the same principle that allows you to touch a cake in an oven to test for doneness without burning yourself. Cake is a poor conductor of heat. If you touch the metal cake pan, however, you will learn that it conducts heat much more effectively! And if you walked across a metal grid placed atop the coals, the result would be severe burns.

stumbled and scraped a knee. If you point to the reddened knee and say, "Look!" you'll probably initiate tears and crying. But if you distract the child by handing her a new toy to play with, chances are there will be no crying.

Body Senses

When people speak of the five senses, they are referring to sight, hearing, taste, smell, and touch, but two additional body senses are critically important to our functioning—the kinesthetic sense and the vestibular sense.

Your **kinesthetic sense** is the system that senses the position and movement of your individual body parts. It relies on receptor cells located throughout your muscles and joints. I experienced a disruption of this sense when I had surgery to repair a tendon in the pinky finger of my right hand. I was fully conscious during the surgery, and the anesthetic was administered by an injection in my armpit—which sounds worse than it was—while I held my hand behind my head. I temporarily lost all sensation in my arm after this injection. The odd thing was that I felt totally dissociated from that arm. After the injection, my arm was stretched straight out to my side for the operation, but my brain remembered it as being in the last place it had provided kinesthetic information. In other words, it felt like my hand was still behind my head even though I could see that my arm

kinesthetic sense The system for sensing the position and movement of individual body parts.

A Balancing Act ▶
Your ability to balance results from the vestibular sense that gets its information from the semicircular canals in the inner ear. Gymnasts like Simone Biles use this system to stay oriented no matter what position the body is in.

Ian MacNicol/Getty Images

was straight. A more common disruption of the kinesthetic sense happens when your leg falls asleep. This occurs when you've held your leg in the same position for so long that the nerve temporarily stops transmitting kinesthetic information. It is almost impossible to walk smoothly until the link is reestablished.

A second body sense, the **vestibular sense,** is the system for sensing body orientation and balance. The vestibular sense is located in your inner ear, and it relies on the fluid-filled semicircular canals perched on top of the cochlea, which are visible in Figure 7.12. The easiest way to disrupt your vestibular sense is to spin in circles until you become dizzy. After you stop spinning, the fluid in the vestibular system continues to spin, much as water continues to swirl in a beaker after you've stopped moving the container. You won't know which way is up until the fluid settles down.

> **vestibular sense** The system for sensing body orientation and balance, which is located in the semicircular canals of the inner ear.

MAKE IT STICK!

1. How are taste and smell different from the other senses?
   a. Taste and smell have higher difference thresholds than other senses.
   b. Taste and smell rely on chemical stimuli rather than some other form of energy.
   c. Taste and smell are the only senses that are part of the vestibular system.
   d. Taste and smell are top-down rather than bottom-up senses.

2. The _____ theory of pain describes how pain information travels up and down the spinal cord.

3. The _____ sense is located in the inner ear.

> **LIFE MATTERS**
> Have you ever gotten motion sickness from hilly backroads while riding in a bus or car? The nausea, dizziness and vomiting experienced with motion sickness are caused by the repeated movement of the vehicle, which overstimulates the semicircular canals in your inner ears.

Your senses are your windows to the world, sources of the raw information you need to guide your thoughts and behaviors. Now that you know a little about how they operate, surely you'll agree that they're *sensational*!

Module 7 Summary and Assessment
Sensation

7-1 What's a possible real-life application of thresholds, signal detection, sensory adaptation, and selective attention?

- A difference threshold allows us to tell that the heating system needs to be repaired because the room is very gradually becoming cooler than it was.

- Signal detection theory helps us know under what circumstances we will be able to successfully tell that there is a gas leak from the water heater.

- Sensory adaptation is useful because it helps us grow accustomed to and filter out an annoying constant hum from an air conditioner.

- Selective attention makes it possible to focus on a movie despite being able to hear the conversations of other people in the theater.

7-2 What is light, and what is the nature of light waves?

- Light is waves of electromagnetic radiation within the visible spectrum.

- The length of a light wave determines the hue, or color, of the light. The amplitude of the wave determines the brightness of the light.

 7-3 How do the structures and receptor cells in the eye work together to detect light waves and change them into neural impulses?

- Light passes through the protective covering of the cornea, passes through the pupil (the hole in the center of the iris), is focused by the lens, and is projected on the receptor cells on the retina.

- The receptor cells (rods and cones) turn the electromagnetic light energy into nerve impulses that can be processed by the brain.

 7-4 How do the trichromatic theory and opponent-process theory contribute to our understanding of color vision?

- The trichromatic theory explains color vision as a combination of firings of different kinds of receptor cells for color in the retina (cones).

- The opponent-process theory explains that color vision is produced because cones in the retina are paired in opposition, with one member of the pair firing in response to a color and its opposing cone not firing.

 7-5 What are the structures of the ear? How do they work to detect sound waves and change them into neural impulses?

- The structures in ears collect sound waves and transform them into neural impulses sent to the brain, producing a perception of sound.

- Sound waves move the eardrum, ossicles, and fluid inside the cochlea. Fluid inside the cochlea moves receptor cells, which creates neural signals that are transmitted to the brain through the auditory nerve.

7-6 How are tastes, smells, and touch sensations processed?

- Receptor cells in the nose and tongue absorb chemicals and transmit neural signals to the brain, producing the chemical senses of taste and smell.

- Receptor cells in the skin for pain, warmth, cold, and pressure detect stimuli and transmit signals to the brain.

Summative Assessment

1. Juan tends to interpret current events the same way as his father. This indicates
   a. top-down processing.
   b. bottom-up processing.
   c. absolute threshold.
   d. difference threshold.

2. Marin hears the music played by the ice cream truck when it is still several blocks away from her house. Her ability to relate to the faint sound relates to
   a. sensory adaptation.
   b. difference threshold.
   c. just noticeable difference.
   d. absolute threshold.

3. The size of the pupil is regulated by the
   a. iris.
   b. retina.
   c. ganglion cells.
   d. cornea.

4. The optic nerve leaves the eye at the
   a. fovea.
   b. cornea.
   c. blind spot.
   d. iris.

5. Prolonged exposure to loud noise is most likely to damage the
   a. cochlea.
   b. ossicles.
   c. hair cells.
   d. tympanic membrane.

6. We are able to localize sounds because

   a. the tympanic membrane is a slightly different shape in each ear.
   b. the cochlea is a slightly different shape in each ear.
   c. sound in the closer ear is higher pitched than sound in the more distant ear.
   d. sound reaches the closer ear faster than it reaches the more distant ear.

7. We have taste receptors for

   a. peppermint.
   b. umami.
   c. fruit flavors.
   d. spice.

8. Smell is dependent on

   a. olfactory cells.
   b. hair cells.
   c. ganglion cells.
   d. gate cells.

9. The gate-control theory of pain says that pain perception depends on

   a. bottom-up processing only.
   b. top-down processing only.
   c. both bottom-up and top-down processing.
   d. neither bottom-up nor top-down processing.

10. The kinesthetic sense can help you determine

   a. whether or not food is likely to be poisonous.
   b. the direction sound is coming from.
   c. which direction is up.
   d. the position of your feet when walking.

KEY TERMS AND KEY PEOPLE

sensation, p. 92

bottom-up processing, p. 92

perception, p. 92

top-down processing, p. 92

absolute threshold, p. 93

difference threshold, p. 94

signal detection theory, p. 94

sensory adaptation, p. 96

selective attention, p. 96

cornea, p. 99

iris, p. 99

pupil, p. 99

lens, p. 99

retina, p. 100

receptor cells, p. 100

rods, p. 100

cones, p. 101

optic nerve, p. 101

blind spot, p. 101

trichromatic theory, p. 102

opponent-process theory, p. 103

pitch, p. 104

cochlea [KOHK-lee-uh], p. 106

hair cells, p. 106

auditory nerve, p. 106

kinesthetic sense, p. 110

vestibular sense, p. 111

Linda Bartoshuk (1938–), p. 108

Perception

Learning Goals

8-1 Explain how Gestalt figure–ground and grouping principles affect the perception of what we see.

8-2 Describe the binocular and monocular cues that allow us to judge distance.

8-3 Explain the impact of constancy on visual perception.

8-4 Explain how our expectations affect what we perceive.

8-5 Explain the connection between principles of perception and optical illusions.

perception The process of organizing and interpreting incoming sensory information.

gestalt The whole, or the organizational patterns that we tend to perceive; the Gestalt psychologists emphasized that the whole is greater than the sum of its parts.

The Ames room illusion, which you will read about in this module, can make Randy appear to be taller than me, when he's actually several inches shorter!

Have you ever tasted one of your parents' favorite foods and found it disgusting? Or felt that a friend's playful shove was rude or even painful? Or disagreed with the popular opinion about how funny a new meme is? We are all exposed to the same audio, motion, and color sensations—indeed, to the same wavelengths of light and sound, the same physical touches and movements, and the same chemical tastes and smells. But our **perception** of these things can be different from the perception of others.

In Module 7, Sensation, we discuss how processing incoming stimulation (sensation) is known as bottom-up processing. In this module, Perception, we consider top-down processing, the influence that our experiences and expectations have on our perceptions as we organize and interpret incoming sensory information. Two people can look at the same situation and perceive it differently, so it is important to understand what influences perception. As author Anais Nin once said, "We don't see things as they are; we see them as we are."

Gestalt Organizational Principles

 8-1 How do Gestalt principles affect our perception of what we see?

Perception was important to the Gestalt psychologists in nineteenth-century Germany. They offered an alternative to the more common approach of breaking down conscious experience into its most fundamental components. The Gestalt psychologists felt that by breaking experiences into their basic parts, something important is lost—the **gestalt** (or whole), the organizational patterns that we tend to perceive. The Gestalt psychologists emphasized that the whole is greater than the sum of its parts.

When I was in high school, my biology teacher used an example to make the point that the whole is greater than the sum of its parts. He led us through an exercise in which we calculated the value of a human being. We reduced an imaginary human to the appropriate quantities of the elements found on the periodic table—hydrogen, oxygen, carbon, calcium, iron, and so on—and calculated the cost of each quantity. By adding up the various elements, we determined the cost of the elements that composed the human body. The surprising conclusion was that each of us was worth only a few dollars!

This simple biology exercise was a great lesson in how much we miss if we spend too much time breaking things down into ever-smaller pieces (see **Figure 8.1**). The Gestalt psychologists knew this when they urged their colleagues to look at the whole—the entirety, the gestalt. Furthermore, they believed that this was the way human perception occurs. We don't focus on discrete, individual stimuli in our environment; rather, we group them into more meaningful units.[1] Let's look at the way we use figure–ground relationships and grouping principles—of similarity, proximity, closure, and continuity—to better understand the world around us.

FIGURE 8.1
A Gestalt
The German Gestalt psychologists of the nineteenth century believed that the whole is greater than the sum of its parts. The parts of this figure are abstract red shapes (think of sliced pieces of pie) on a white background. Yet because of the way those parts are arranged, we perceive much more. The red shapes become circles cut by white lines, and the white lines produce a cube. Even the cube is subject to various interpretations. You can make the tiny X in the center seem to be on either the front edge of the cube or the back (but not both at the same time). You can make the cube seem to appear in front of a background with red circles or behind a white screen with holes cut out of it. (Research from Bradley et al., 1976.)

Figure–Ground Relationships

Gestalt psychologists pointed out that we naturally organize our environment into **figure–ground** relationships. We organize the visual field into objects (the figures) that stand out from their surroundings (the ground). In most photographs and visual scenes, you can easily pick out the *figure*. It will be some object that draws your attention, and it probably will be nearer the center of the visual field than the edge. It may be moving, and it will often be fairly large and colorful. The *ground* consists of the surrounding aspects that we commonly call the background. For example, in a photo of a jet flying across the sky, the airplane is the figure and the sky is the

figure–ground The organization of the visual field into objects (figures) that stand out from their surroundings (ground).

ground. In a sports photo, the swimmer touching the wall at the end of the race is the figure, and the other swimmers, the lane markers, the side of the pool, and the water itself are the ground. Sometimes the relationship between figure and ground is more ambiguous, as in **Figure 8.2**, which shows a reversible figure.

FIGURE 8.2
What Do You See?
If black is the figure, you see firefighters hurrying down the stairs. If black is the ground and white is the figure, you see arrows instead.

The tendency to perceive figure and ground is not exclusively visual. We strive to identify the figure in other contexts as well, such as the predominant taste, perhaps tuna, in a casserole or the melody of a song.

Principles of Grouping

grouping The perceptual tendency to organize stimuli into understandable units.

The Gestalt psychologists also believed people are predisposed to organize stimuli by **grouping** them into understandable units. Several principles guide the way we group stimuli—similarity, proximity, closure, and continuity (see **Figure 8.3**):

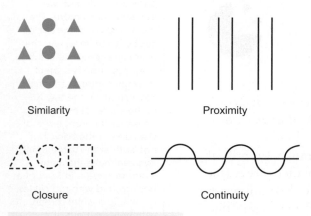

Similarity

Proximity

Closure

Continuity

FIGURE 8.3
Gestalt Grouping Principles
Similarity leads us to see two groups of triangles and one group of circles. Proximity leads us to see three groups of two lines each. Closure leads us to see intact shapes where there are none. Continuity leads us to see one long wavy line and one straight one, rather than four half-circles. Our brains are programmed to group objects to help us make sense of the world around us.

- *Similarity*—Perhaps the most basic principle of grouping is similarity. We place items that look similar in the same group. This is easy to see in team contests: All the players wearing blue shirts are from the University of Michigan; all those wearing red shirts represent the University of Wisconsin.

- *Proximity*—Proximity comes from the word *approximate*, which means "close." If objects are close together, we place them in the same group. Not only do the Michigan Wolverines basketball players wear the same uniform, they also share the same bench. It is partially because they are near one another, in proximity, that we put them in the same group.

- *Closure*—Our brain's tendency to look for the whole, not the parts, drives us to fill any gaps in a perceptual field. Look at **Figure 8.4**. When you follow the directions to make the object disappear, you will notice that the horizontal line appears to continue right through the area—there is no longer a gap in the line! Your brain doesn't like gaps, so it assumes this one doesn't belong there and fills the space for you. The principle of closure also allows you to perceive the cube shown earlier in Figure 8.1. The cube is in your head, not on the paper.

- *Continuity*—Once an object appears to move in a particular direction, your brain assumes that the movement continues unchanged. When highways require you to turn, for example, you can easily lose your way unless you really pay attention to the signs. We tend to assume the highway continues in the direction we've been moving.

FIGURE 8.4
Closure and the Blind Spot
Close your right eye, look at the boy, and slowly adjust the distance between your eye and the page until the cookie disappears (about a foot). When the cookie disappears, the two line segments will appear to join into one continuous line as your brain strives to create a gestalt.

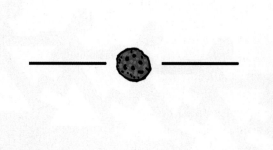

Depth Perception

 8-2 How can we see in three dimensions?

Driving a car depends on figure–ground (being able to identify a train approaching a crossing, for example) and grouping (identifying a space large enough for a safe merge on the freeway, for example). Now consider how more difficult (impossible, really) driving would be if you couldn't use **depth perception** to judge distance. You rely on your ability to perceive depth in parking, determining when it's safe to pull out onto a busy street, and deciding if you can safely pass another car. And it's not just driving that requires depth perception. Sports would also be impossible: Depth perception guides you when you position your hands to catch a ball, time a volleyball spike, and shoot accurate free throws. And think of the little things like plugging the power cord into your phone, tossing wadded-up paper into a recycling container, and placing clean dishes on a shelf. All these actions and many more depend on depth perception.

Is this vital human skill a product of nature or nurture? Eleanor Gibson and Richard Walk explored this question using a device called the **visual cliff,** laboratory equipment for testing depth perception in infants and young animals (see **Figure 8.5**). The visual cliff ensures the infant's safety while allowing researchers to determine whether an infant perceives depth. Gibson and Walk's research indicates that even young infants just barely able to crawl are reluctant to move past the edge of what appears to be a drop-off, so depth perception might be, to some extent, inborn.[2] Research with other species supports this nature view: Depth perception exists even for animals mobile at birth. But research also supports the nurture view. By the time children can crawl, they have already had a lot of interaction with the environment, so their reluctance to venture over the edge of a cliff may be learned. For example, 5-month-old babies do not use a toy's shadow to help determine how far away it is, but 7-month-olds do.[3] Depth perception improves as children experience increased interaction with the environment.[4] As is almost always the case, both nature and nurture are important.

depth perception The ability to see in three dimensions and to judge distance.

visual cliff A laboratory device for testing depth perception in infants and young animals.

FIGURE 8.5
The Visual Cliff
This device can safely test infants for the ability to perceive depth. Infants are reluctant to crawl onto the glass protecting them from the drop-off, even when their primary caregivers coax them to do so.

Radius Images/Alamy

The View-Master: A Binocular Depth Toy
This classic childhood toy produces an enhanced sense of depth by exaggerating the effect produced by retinal disparity. A separate image is projected to each of the child's two eyes. These images were taken by two cameras placed a couple of feet apart.

binocular cues Depth cues that require the use of both eyes.

FIGURE 8.6
The Binocular Finger Sausage
To see a bizarre illusion created by binocular vision, point your two index fingers together about 5 inches in front of your eyes with a half-inch gap between their tips. Look beyond them and you will see a finger sausage. By adjusting the distance separating your fingers or the distance between your fingers and your eyes, you can make the sausage grow and shrink. When you tire of it, simply close one eye. Without binocular vision, there can be no sausage. When you alternately close one eye and then the other, the gap between your fingers jumps from side to side. It's your brain's attempt to combine these two views that creates the sausage in the first place.

Given our anatomy, it's amazing that we even have these impressive abilities to perceive depth. The retina is a two-dimensional surface, yet we use it to determine height, width, *and* depth. Working together, your eyes and brain use a number of tricks to create that third dimension. Some depth cues are known as **binocular cues,** requiring the use of both eyes. Other depth cues are **monocular cues**—requiring only the use of a single eye.

Binocular Depth Cues

Do you remember playing with a View-Master® toy when you were young? To use this toy, you insert a round card containing pictures into a viewer and look through the eyepieces. What you see is an image with astounding depth. How does this seemingly simple toy create these complex images? The trick is that the toy's design relies on the binocular depth cue known as **retinal disparity,** which results from the slightly different images that fall on the retina of your left eye and the retina of your right eye. Let's see how this works.

If you look closely at the card containing the View-Master pictures, you will see that it seems to contain two identical pictures for each scene. But these images differ slightly because they were taken by two side-by-side cameras, with slightly different vantage points. The View-Master projects the image taken by the left camera only to your left eye and the image from the right camera only to your right eye. Your brain uses the different views to calculate distance and add depth to the scene.

Your brain does this easily because it uses the same technique all the time in real life. The two cameras are your two eyes. Because they are separated by a few inches in your head, your eyes receive slightly different views of any given scene. You can demonstrate this for yourself by creating the finger sausage described in **Figure 8.6**. This sausage appears to jump back and forth precisely because each of your eyes has its own distinct vantage point. View-Masters exaggerate the effects of retinal disparity because the two cameras that took the

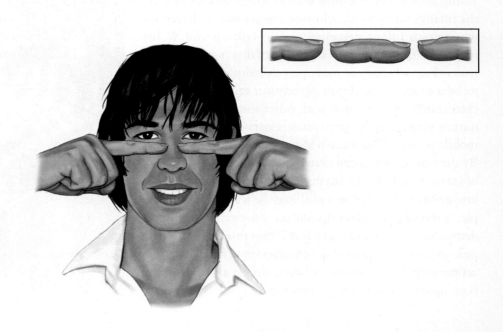

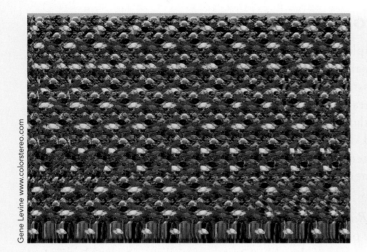

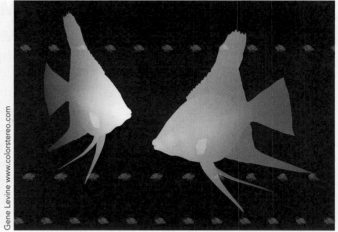

Gene Levine www.colorstereo.com

Gene Levine www.colorstereo.com

▲ **FIGURE 8.7**
Random Dot Stereogram
The ability to see an intriguing image in the stereogram to the left depends on retinal disparity. To make the repeating pattern of three-dimensional fish appear (the image on the right shows a portion of what you are looking for), you must trick your eyes into thinking the paper is either twice as far, or half as far, from your eyes than it really is. Try relaxing your eyes so they slowly swing outward. When you are at the proper depth, the dots projected to your right eye will align with the dots projected to your left eye to form the three-dimensional image. The dots that create the fish are among the other dots and become apparent only when your eyes line them up properly. If you have trouble, it simply means your eyes are difficult to trick; they want to focus at the proper depth.

photos were separated by more than the couple of inches separating your eyes. For another example of an image that relies on retinal disparity, try your luck at **Figure 8.7**. (Don't give up if you don't immediately see it.) Once you're able to produce the three-dimensional image, close or cover one eye. The effect will end, showing that this image was a creation of your two eyes interacting with your brain.

Retinal disparity is most effective when you are viewing items close to you. The farther away the object is, the less difference the placement of your eyes makes. The finger sausage jumps more when you hold your hands about 6 inches in front of your face than it does when you hold your arms farther away. Try it and you'll see.

The second binocular cue, **convergence**, translates tension in the eye muscles when the eyes track inward to focus on objects close to the viewer. If you were able to draw a line from each eye to a distant object, those lines would be nearly parallel. To maintain your focus on that object as it moved closer to you, your eyes would both have to swing inward. This movement puts tension on the muscles that control your eyeballs, and your brain notices that tension. The more tension required to keep both eyes aimed at the object, the closer the object must be. To feel this, focus on your finger with your arm fully extended. At this point, there is not much tension. However, as you continue to focus and slowly draw your finger closer to your nose, your eyes will cross. The closer your finger gets, the stronger the tension will be.

As you can see, convergence, like relative disparity, predicts depth most effectively at relatively short distances. Depth perception at longer distances relies mostly on the monocular cues, the next topic.

monocular cues Depth cues that require the use of only one eye.

retinal disparity A binocular depth cue resulting from slightly different images produced by the retina of the left eye and the retina of the right eye.

convergence A binocular depth cue related to the tension in the eye muscles when the eyes track inward to focus on objects close to the viewer.

Convergence
As the red knob is moved closer to the girl, she must cross her eyes to stay focused on it. This produces tension in the muscles surrounding her eyes, which helps her to know how far away the red knob is.

AMELIE-BENOIST/BSIP/Corbis Documentary/Getty Images

Charity Beck/The New York Times/Redux

Relative Size
The broadcasters in the foreground appear larger than the more distant fans and players.

Monocular Depth Cues

People who have lost vision in one eye cannot use retinal disparity or convergence cues. But they can calculate depth accurately using the monocular cues, which continue to operate even if when using just one eye. Artists use monocular cues to build a sense of depth into their paintings and drawings. Using them, a painter can trick our two-dimensional retinas into seeing three dimensions on a two-dimensional canvas. There are quite a number of these cues. We discuss seven of them:

1. *Relative size*—One of our best monocular depth cues is the perceived size of an object. If an object of known size appears large, it is probably close, and if the object appears small, it is probably distant. Passenger jets passing over your home at 35,000 feet appear so tiny it's hard to believe they hold full-size people inside. But you know the plane's real size, and the fact that it appears small is one of the main ways you know it is far away. That same plane flying only 20 feet over your home would appear frighteningly large.

   Don't underestimate how important monocular cues like relative size are. If you are driving a car, someone walking in the distance appears small. However, if that someone *is* small—a child—you might mistakenly believe the person is farther away than is actually the case. Tragic accidents can result from such misperceptions.[5]

2. *Relative motion*—Perceived slowness indicates that an object is distant. If a passenger jet passed 20 feet over your house, it not only would appear large but also would appear to be moving exceptionally fast. A plane flying high overhead seems to just barely crawl across the sky, even though you know it is moving several hundred miles an hour.

3. *Interposition*—This cue is so obvious that unless you think about it, you may fail to realize its significance: Closer objects partially obstruct the view of more distant objects. You know a tree is in front of a house because it blocks your view of part of the house. If the tree were more distant than the house, the house would block your view of the tree. If you're thinking, Well, duh, be impressed that your brain uses even simple information to assess depth.

4. *Relative height*—Distant objects appear higher in your field of vision than close objects do. This is why trees on the far side of a lake will appear to be above the lake, which is closer to you.

5. *Texture gradient*—Distant objects usually have a smoother texture than nearby objects. A park that appears to have a smooth carpet of green grass from a distance shows more and more texture as you move closer to it. When you reach the park, you can see individual blades of grass and weeds (and perhaps bugs, twigs, and wads of discarded chewing gum). The Black Hills in South Dakota appear uniformly black because of the dark green color of the fir trees.

Interposition
You know the number 7 horse is closer to you than the other horses because the number 7 horse partially blocks the view of the other horses.

Mitch Wojnarowicz/The Image Works

You can't see the individual trees (or boulders or streams) until you draw close.

6. *Relative clarity*—Distant objects are less clear than nearby objects. This monocular cue mostly functions outdoors, where distant objects have a bluish, hazy appearance because of the moisture and dust in the air. Smog can exaggerate your perception of depth, causing landmarks to appear farther away than they really are in a city beset by moist, dusty air. In the dry, clear American Southwest, however, distances appear compressed. You may drive over a hill and view mountains that seem close enough to reach for a lunchtime picnic. In reality, you may be lucky to get there by suppertime!

7. *Linear perspective*—Parallel lines seem to draw together in the distance. If you stand on a straight section of highway and look down the road, the shoulders of the road will seem to come ever closer to each other until they eventually merge at a point on the horizon.

Considered together, monocular cues like these seven—relative size, relative motion, interposition, relative height, texture gradient, relative clarity, and linear perspective—and the binocular cues of retinal disparity and convergence provide a powerful arsenal of tools to help us perceive depth. Look before you leap is good advice partially because distance cues allow you to determine how far away your landing spot is (see also Psychology in the Real World: Motion Perception).

Texture Gradient
Individual trees are visible in the foreground, but in the distance the trees look smooth and dark, giving the Black Hills their name.

Relative Clarity
The distant mountains look blue and hazy because of dust and moisture in the atmosphere.

Linear Perspective
The lights leading the way to this runway seem to come together in the distance.

PSYCHOLOGY IN THE REAL WORLD

Motion Perception

Our ability to perceive motion is just as critical for survival as is our ability to perceive depth. In many ways, motion perception is the more complex task. To perceive motion accurately, you must interpret a large number of variables rapidly. Not only does the object move, but so does your body. Swing your head from side to side and you will see a great deal of motion—motion that you correctly conclude is a result of head movement rather than object movement.

Sometimes, however, our conclusions are wrong, and we perceive motion when there is none. These mistakes are not all bad. We rely on this illusion of movement to make movies *move*. When we watch a film, we are able to see motion from a rapidly projected (24 images per second) series of slightly varying still images. This illusion is called *stroboscopic motion*, an outcome you've used to your advantage if you've ever created a flip movie, such as the one that we've begun in **Figure 8.8**.

A second and equally handy example of an apparent motion effect is the *phi phenomenon*, which creates the illusion of movement when fixed lights are turned on and off in sequence. Highway construction sites often use the phi phenomenon to make the arrows on signs appear to move, directing motorists to merge into a smaller number of lanes. Computerized marquee signs and even strings of holiday lights also use this illusion, as do sports scoreboards.

FIGURE 8.8
Movement That Isn't Movement—Courtesy of Stroboscopic Motion
Each of these figures differs only slightly from the ones on either side of it. This is the first step to creating stroboscopic motion: Project each figure rapidly one after the other in order, and the resulting figure would appear to dance.

A stadium scoreboard at the University of Northern Iowa, located in my town, is programmed to display a panther, the team mascot, leaping across the display area. The action seems so real that it's easy to forget that all you're looking at is a bunch of tiny lights blinking on and off.

THINK ABOUT . . . Psychology in the Real World

1. What are stroboscopic motion and the phi phenomenon?

2. Why do designers incorporate the phi phenomenon into lighted signs?

3. Activity: Shoot a video that illustrates two examples of the phi phenomenon in your town. If you don't have the ability to shoot video, find two examples of the phi phenomenon on the Internet.

MAKE IT STICK!

1. Briefly describe how three monocular depth cues operate.

2. When do people develop depth perception?
   a. At about age 4, when they start to develop perceptual sets
   b. At birth or in early infancy
   c. When the visual cortex of the brain develops during early adolescence
   d. When they are capable of developing gestalts

3. _____ depth cues rely on the use of one eye; _____ depth cues rely on the use of both eyes.

Perceptual Constancy

8-3 What happens to our visual perception of an object if the lighting, the distance to the object, or the viewing angle changes?

One amazing quality of human perception is **perceptual constancy,** perceiving the size, shape, and lightness of an object as unchanging even as the image of the object on the retina of the eye changes. The world would be a frightening place if we did not have perceptual constancy. It is comforting to have a deep understanding that things remain the same despite changes in the distance, angle of view, or level of lighting of an object. There are three major kinds of perceptual constancy: size constancy, shape constancy, and lightness constancy.

perceptual constancy
Perceiving the size, shape, and lightness of an object as unchanging even as the image of the object on the retina of the eye changes.

Size Constancy

Recall from our discussion of depth perception that an object's size is one of the best cues we have in judging the distance of an object. This relationship between size and distance is one of the most fundamental in depth perception: Objects that appear big are close, and objects that appear small are distant. What happens, however, when an object approaches you? Consider a friend walking toward you from the end of the street. Because your friend is some distance away, she appears quite small. But then, as she approaches, her image on your eyes grows larger and larger. Is she becoming bigger? Of course not! She is moving closer. That's the point of *size constancy:* We expect size to remain constant. Our knowledge of the world leads us to conclude that when the apparent size of an object changes, the actual size is not changing at all. What's changing is the distance.

You can use the flag demonstration in Figure 7.10 in module 7 to explore this size–distance relationship. If you follow the instructions and watch for an afterimage to appear in the white square in your book, you will find that the image is quite small (about the same size as the weirdly colored version of the green, black, and yellow flag). If you try the exercise again and watch for an afterimage on a wall across the room, the size of the image will be strikingly different. This time, you will see a large flag because the wall is farther away than the page in your book. Because the actual image on your retina is exactly the same size in both cases (it was produced by looking at the same stimulus in your book), your brain *concludes the image on the wall must have been produced by a bigger flag.* Only if the flag itself were larger could the retinal image be the same. Your brain has confused size and distance cues. Other examples of illusions based on a misperception of size and distance cues appear in **Figure 8.9**.

Consider how frightful the world would be without size constancy. As someone drew closer to you, you would have to stop and wonder whether that person was morphing into a giant before your eyes! Size constancy spares us such thoughts and allows us to be comfortable in our knowledge that the objects around us are not changing.

(a)   (b)

FIGURE 8.9
Size–Distance Relationships
Sometimes size and distance cues make it hard to perceive accurately. (a) The monocular depth cues of relative height and linear perspective force us to see the dog on top as more distant. We therefore think that this dog must be bigger to produce the same size image at our eyes. But each dog is the same size. (b) This illustration of the Ponzo illusion works the same way as the dogs. Depth cues force us to see the top bar as more distant, and this assumption leads us to distort our interpretation of size. The bars are actually the same size.

Shape Constancy

Shape constancy assures us that an object's shape has not changed even though our angle of view indicates it may have done so. As **Figure 8.10** illustrates, a closed door viewed straight on appears rectangular, which, of course, it is. But if someone begins to open the door, that rectangle will look like a trapezoid. Despite the changed appearance, you have no doubts about the shape of the door. You instantly realize that it's the viewing angle that has changed and not the door itself.

FIGURE 8.11
Lightness Constancy
In this astonishing illusion, the squares A and B are actually the exact same shade of gray. You can photocopy the figure and cut out the two squares to prove it to yourself. It's the surrounding context that forces us to perceive the two squares so differently.

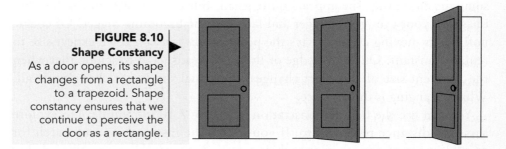

FIGURE 8.10
Shape Constancy
As a door opens, its shape changes from a rectangle to a trapezoid. Shape constancy ensures that we continue to perceive the door as a rectangle.

We automatically correct for changing angles in a number of different situations. The next time you are sitting to the side when your teacher uses the projector, note that the image becomes a trapezoid. Your brain will automatically correct for the distorted angle, and you will perceive the projected images as though you were viewing the objects straight on. Shape constancy lets you make these automatic corrections.

Lightness Constancy

The third type of constancy, *lightness constancy,* gives us the ability to see an object as having a constant level of lightness no matter how the lighting conditions change (see **Figure 8.11**). If you look at a sheet of printer paper in bright sunlight, it appears blazingly white; view the same sheet in a dimly lit room, and it appears gray. Has the paper changed? Of course not. We know that the white paper stays constant no matter what the lighting conditions are. We can make this adjustment even if we are outside, reading a page that is half in sunlight and half in shade. Without lightness constancy, this experience would be quite bizarre.

MAKE IT STICK!

1. Why *wouldn't* you perceive an opening rectangular door magically turning into a trapezoid?

   a. Size constancy
   b. Shape constancy
   c. Lightness constancy
   d. Distance constancy

2. Without size constancy, we would think objects become _____ the farther they are from us.

3. True or false? Shape constancy relates to our memory of basic shapes (square, circle, etc.).

Perceptual Set

 8-4 How do our expectations affect what we perceive?

Have you ever stopped to consider just how important your expectations are in any given situation? What happens in a class if you expect a teacher to be boring? If your favorite band is giving a concert and you expect it to be wonderful, how much does that influence your perception of the concert? If you've grown to like a particular TV show, do your expectations that the show will be good affect how you react to tonight's episode?

Expectations such as these produce **perceptual set,** a mental predisposition to perceive something one way and not another. Perceptual set is perhaps the clearest example yet of top-down processing, and this mind-set can profoundly affect our view of the world. Look, for example, at **Figure 8.12**. You can predispose a person toward seeing either a young woman's face or an elderly woman's face in the middle photo by showing either the left or the right picture first.[6] If you show the unambiguous (clear) younger woman's face first, the person will be more likely to see the younger woman in the ambiguous center drawing. If you show the older woman's face first, the person will be more likely to see the older woman's face in the center drawing.

This power of suggestion produced by perceptual set influences us in many ways. Six times as many preschool-age children think french fries taste

perceptual set A mental predisposition to perceive something one way and not another.

W.E. Hill

FIGURE 8.12
Perceptual Set
Cover the side pictures and ask a few friends what they see in the center. You can influence them to see the young woman by first having them glance briefly at the picture on the left. Similarly, a glance at the picture on the right will drive them toward interpreting the center picture as an old woman.

better when they are served in a McDonald's bag than in a plain white bag.[7] Perceptual set may also account for multiple false reports of unidentified flying objects, for example after people hear a report of one such false incident. The first report creates a perceptual set that influences what other people perceive. (Also see Thinking Like a Psychological Scientist: Extrasensory Perception). Perceptual set also accounts for reports of subliminal messages in the media. When I was a college student in the 1960s, my friends and I whiled away many hours spinning Beatles records backward on our turntables (this was long before the days of iPhones and Spotify). We were listening for messages about band member Paul McCartney, who was inaccurately rumored to be dead. We were finding them, too. Once you've determined that the recording *might* say, Paul is dead, it is almost impossible *not* to hear the message in the weird sounds produced when you play recorded music backward. We hear the message we expect to hear. If we'd started with the perceptual set that the ambiguous segments would say, Dolls eat bread, that is what we would have forever heard.

Perceptual set is often guided by *schemas,* concepts or mental frameworks that help us organize and interpret information about the world. One of our strongest schemas is for faces. We are so driven to perceive faces that we tend to see them everywhere (see **Figure 8.13**).

FIGURE 8.13
Schemas
We have such a strong schema for faces that we tend to see them everywhere, as in the case with the photo on the left. And when a schema is violated, as in the photo on the right that appears to be a two-headed giraffe (it's not really!), we might be amused or disturbed.

Kjell B. Sandved/Science Source

Westend61/Getty Images

THINKING LIKE A PSYCHOLOGICAL SCIENTIST

Extrasensory Perception

You've seen the stories about **extrasensory perception (ESP)**, the controversial claim that perception can occur apart from sensory input. Perhaps you've talked to people who believe they've had an ESP experience. Perhaps you think you have had one yourself. These beliefs are widespread, with several surveys showing that around half of all Americans believe in ESP. [8–11]

Belief in ESP sustains a billion-dollar industry.[12] Infomercials by psychics are a staple for late-night and cable TV broadcasters, and advertisements by psychics fill the back pages of countless magazines and *National Enquirer*–type newspapers in print and online. Some police departments have even called on psychics to help locate missing persons and attempt to solve other difficult crimes.

Some psychologists, including groups working at five British universities, investigate claims of ESP.[13] Skeptical scientists, however, are much more likely than the general public to assume the claims are false. This doesn't mean scientists are somehow mean or cynical, only that they require proof before accepting a claim.

What accounts for this difference between public opinion and scientific opinion? The answer is that we often misinterpret *correlations*, which are statements of how two events are related. Consider this strange coincidence: I'm thinking about my friend and he suddenly calls. I'm likely to notice that these two events—my thoughts and the phone call—occurred together, be impressed with the timing, and perhaps assume that I have a psychic ability. But the fact that these two events were correlated does *not* mean that my thoughts caused my friend to call. What I'm failing to notice are the times I think of my friend and he doesn't call and the times he calls when I haven't been thinking about him. These instances are much less likely to stand out in my memory because they seem much more ordinary. Similarly, you may be impressed when you dream about an event that occurs the next day.

That's impressive, but when you consider how often your dreams do not become reality the next day, this single event seems more likely to be a simple, ordinary coincidence.

If such events were not mere coincidences, shouldn't those who claim to have psychic abilities be able to exercise their powers more reliably? In 26 years of tracking annual psychic forecasts, the psychics had no success in predicting the coming year's most important events.[14] Why are they unable to provide adequate warnings before floods or tornadoes? Why is it impossible for them to locate missing persons? And, most telling, why are these people with ESP always on television asking for our credit card numbers instead of picking the winning lottery numbers and living off the proceeds?

THINK ABOUT . . . Psychological Science

1. What is extrasensory perception?
2. What are some reasons that so many people believe in ESP despite a lack of scientific evidence?
3. Lab activity: How would you design an experiment to discover whether or not some aspect of ESP was real?

extrasensory perception (ESP) The controversial claim that perception can occur apart from sensory input.

MAKE IT STICK!

1. Which of the following is an example of perceptual set?
   a. Seeing a violent image in a blurry photograph because your friend told you it was a photo of a big fight
   b. Seeing circles on a page in one group and triangles in another
   c. Seeing movement in a movie even though you know you're watching a series of rapidly projected still images
   d. Seeing an airplane as high up in the sky because it appears to be tiny

2. We are likely to see faces in many objects because humans have a strong _____ for faces.

Illusions

 8-5 How can the principles of perception explain illusions?

Perceptual illusions fascinate almost everyone. We are usually superb at decoding the nuances of the world around us. But sometimes—most often under fairly elaborate conditions—we are tricked into misinterpreting sensory stimuli. Psychologists study illusions because they provide clues about how our sensory and perceptual systems work. In this section, we look at several illusions. In each case, some basic perceptual principles help create the illusions. As you consider each illusion, see if you can link it to one or more of the principles you've read about in this module.

Müller-Lyer Illusion

This famous puzzle, the Müller-Lyer illusion, has been around since the late 1800s. You will see the illusion if you compare line segment AB with line segment BC in **Figure 8.14**. Does one appear longer? To most people the lines seem about the same, but if you measure them, you will see that AB is quite a bit longer. There are different explanations for this illusion, as there are for most illusion puzzles. One possibility, illustrated in **Figure 8.15**, is that we have learned to interpret arrowheads at the ends of a line as an indication of distance, which leads to a misapplication of size–distance relationships.

> **LIFE MATTERS**
>
> One of the most powerful truths of illusions, such as the Müller-Lyer illusion, is that our perception of something directly in front of our face can be wrong. No matter how long we look at the two lines, one still looks bigger than the other. What can this tell us about how we perceive the rest of our world?

FIGURE 8.14
The Müller-Lyer Illusion ▶
Which line appears longer—segment AB or segment BC?

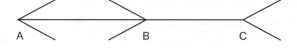

▲ **FIGURE 8.15**
Why Do We See the Müller-Lyer Illusion?
One suggested explanation (Gregory, 1968) is that we use the arrows at the ends of the lines to help judge distance and thus length.

Ames Room Illusion

In the next famous illusion, the Ames room, two people seem to change size as they switch positions in the room. A person who appears small on one side of the room is suddenly huge on the other side. Turn the page to see **Figure 8.18**, which reveals the secret. The room is distorted. When we view the room from the perspective of the peephole (as the camera did), however, we assume it is a standard, rectangular room. (Why wouldn't it be?) This is why we perceive the person who is closer as being larger. Our minds don't let us see that person as closer because that would defy what we have learned about the structure of normal rooms.

Richard T. Nowitz/Science Source

Gestalt Closure Illusion

Do you see the light-red ring in **Figure 8.16**? Well, it isn't there. If you look at a section of the ring that falls between the black objects and cover up the black lines, you will see that the area is just as red as the rest of the page. We perceive the light-red ring because of the Gestalt grouping principles. Our brains try to find closure for all those gaps in the black lines by seeing a ring that connects them.

Light Illusions

The two illusions in **Figure 8.17** depend on shadow and light. In Figure 8.17a there appears to be a ripple. Even though this pattern is printed on flat paper, it is difficult to interpret it as a flat drawing. The ridges change quite impressively if you turn the book upside down: The area of the drawing that had represented a valley now represents a hill. This reversal happens because we assume that light normally comes from above.[15] You can see a similar light-and-shadow effect in Figure 8.17b. The smaller circle in the upper right appears to bulge out from the background. The smaller circle at the lower left appears to dip in. This happens because we perceive the light source to be coming from above. If you turn the diagram upside down, the bulge and the dip reverse themselves, conforming to our assumption that a light is coming from above.

FIGURE 8.16
An Illusion Based on the Gestalt Principle of Closure
When is a red ring not really there? When the Gestalt principle of closure causes you to perceive it filling in the gaps in the black lines. Try covering up the black lines on both sides of a gap and you'll see that there is only one shade of red in this figure.

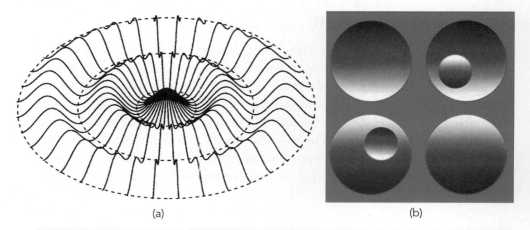

(a)   (b)

▲ **FIGURE 8.17**
Two Illusions Based on Our Assumptions About Light
Both image (a) and image (b) look different if you turn the book upside down. We always assume that light shines down from above.

FIGURE 8.18
Distorted Size
This view of the specially designed Ames room explains the puzzle shown earlier of incredibly shrinking and growing girls. It violates our expectations for how a room should be constructed, and we're tricked into thinking the size of the girls has changed, rather than the dimensions and angles of the room. ▶

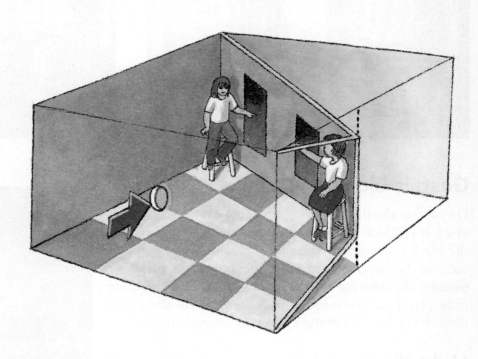

MAKE IT STICK!

1. The _____ illusion causes us to misjudge the length of lines.

2. The distorted _____ room causes the viewer to misjudge size and distance.

3. True or false? Illusions can help us understand how perception works.

Perception is the road we follow to make sense of the world. The constant stream of sensory input that bombards us is meaningless unless we can interpret it properly. We accomplish this so effortlessly that we are usually aware only of our rare mistakes. Perceptive, aren't we?

Module 8 Summary and Assessment

Perception

 8-1 How do Gestalt principles affect our perception of what we see?

- In figure–ground relationships, we perceive a central focus (figure) of an image in the foreground against a background (ground).

- We group objects because they are similar (similarity), because they are close to one another (proximity), because they help form a complete image (closure), or because they are part of a continuous pattern (continuity).

 8-2 How can we see in three dimensions?

- Two of the most important depth perception cues, retinal disparity and convergence, are possible because we have two eyes (binocular cues).

- Other depth perception cues, including relative size, relative motion, interposition, relative height, texture gradient, relative clarity, and linear perspective, can be seen with one eye (monocular cues).

 8-3 What happens to our visual perception of an object if the lighting, the distance to the object, or the viewing angle changes?

- We perceive the characteristics of objects as constant (perceptual constancy) even though their apparent size, shape, and brightness change in different lighting conditions, at different distances, and with different angles of viewing.

 8-4 How do our expectations affect what we perceive?

- Perceptual sets, our predispositions about what we expect to see, change how we organize sensations into perceptions. In general, we perceive what we expect to perceive.

 8-5 How can the principles of perception explain illusions?

- Many illusions rely on the principles of perception—including Gestalt principles, perceptual sets, and ambiguous size–distance cues—to trick us into misperceiving sensory stimuli.

Summative Assessment

1. A gestalt is best defined as a(n)

   a. expectation.
   b. whole.
   c. background.
   d. monocular depth cue.

2. Which of the following would probably be considered a figure in a painting of a woodland scene?

   a. A squirrel perched in a tree at the side of the painting
   b. A fern growing at the base of a small boulder
   c. A cloud drifting across the sky
   d. A large bear in the foreground catching a salmon out of the river

3. A group of four friends always eats lunch at the same table in the school cafeteria. Someone entering the cafeteria is likely to recognize them as a group because of

   a. continuity.
   b. similarity.
   c. closure.
   d. proximity.

4. The purpose of the visual cliff is to determine if a child

   a. is using binocular depth cues.
   b. is using monocular depth cues.
   c. can perceive depth.
   d. experiences size constancy.

5. The View-Master toy relies on _____ to produce an exaggerated sense of depth.

a. disparity
b. convergence
c. interposition
d. relative motion

6. Martha can tell the tree is closer than the house because her view of the house is partially blocked by the tree. This is called

a. relative height.
b. interposition.
c. convergence.
d. linear perspective.

7. The phi phenomenon relates to

a. an optical illusion based on size constancy.
b. the illusion of motion when fixed lights are turned on and off in sequence.
c. perceived movement when a series of still photos is projected rapidly.
d. an optical illusion based on lightness constancy.

8. Which of the following is an example of shape constancy?

a. A series of changing shapes is perceived as motion.
b. If we expect the shape of an object to change over time, we actually perceive it as changing in the way we expect.
c. The shape of an object provides a cue as to how distant the object is.
d. A door that casts the image of a trapezoid when it's partially open is perceived as rectangular.

9. We often see faces in objects partially because we have a(n) _____ for faces.

a. shape constancy
b. schema
c. illusion
d. interposition

10. the Müller-Lyer illusion relates to

a. the length of lines.
b. the shape of faces.
c. the distance of objects.
d. the color of objects.

KEY TERMS

perception, p. 114

gestalt, p. 114

figure–ground, p. 115

grouping, p. 116

depth perception, p. 117

visual cliff, p. 117

binocular cues, p. 118

monocular cues, p. 118

retinal disparity, p. 118

convergence, p. 119

perceptual constancy, p. 123

perceptual set, p. 125

extrasensory perception (ESP), p. 126

Sleep, Dreams, and Body Rhythms

We spend about one-third of our lives in bed, but how much is known about sleep and dreaming? It turns out we know quite a bit, and some of what we know will likely surprise you.

Learning Goals

9-1 Explain what psychologists mean by consciousness.

9-2 Identify different body rhythms, and explain how they affect us.

9-3 Describe what happens to your body when you don't get enough sleep.

9-4 Describe the benefits of sleeping.

9-5 Explain the stages we go through when we sleep.

9-6 Explain why REM sleep is described as paradoxical.

9-7 Describe the four modern explanations for why we dream.

9-8 Define sleep disorders, and describe how they interfere with our sleep cycles.

Consciousness

 9-1 What do psychologists mean by consciousness?

Has this ever happened to you? You're watching a movie with friends or family late at night, and no matter how hard you fight it, you simply cannot keep your eyes open. Or perhaps you've waged a similar struggle while reading a textbook (but definitely not your psychology text). You fight it, but soon you nod off—sleep wins again.

You don't stand much of a chance in the tiredness battle; virtually every night, sleep wins. And when you do stay up later than you should, the effects are often obvious. The day a 10-page paper is due, I can easily spot those students who, having waited until the last minute, spent most of the previous night at a keyboard. Fighting the nods (heads bobbing downward), they suddenly jerk upright after a brief trip to never-never land.

To nod off is to temporarily lose waking **consciousness,** or awareness of yourself and your environment. Once a person is in sleep's grasp, consciousness ceases as certain parts of the brain's cortex stop sending messages that would otherwise keep you awake.[1] Depriving yourself of sleep alters your body's natural rhythms, making it difficult to maintain normal waking consciousness. Indeed, your body has several naturally occurring rhythms that affect wakefulness and sleep.

consciousness
Awareness of yourself and your environment.

Antonio Guillem Fernández/Alamy stock Photo

Bored Senseless or Sleep Deprived? This student has clearly lost any struggle to stay awake.

pseudoscientific claim Any assertion that appears scientific but is not based on science.

biological rhythms Periodic physiological fluctuations.

circadian [ser-KAY-dee-un] rhythms Biological rhythms (for example, of temperature and wakefulness) that occur approximately every 24 hours.

ultradian [ul-TRAY-dee-un] rhythms Biological rhythms that occur more than once each day.

LIFE MATTERS

Lack of sleep affects our emotional memories. In a study conducted by Walker at the University of California (2006), participants who were deprived of sleep were at least twice as likely to remember negative words as they were to remember positive or neutral words. Participants who rested typically had no difference between their memories of positive, negative or neutral words. Not sleeping enough can literally make you perceive your world as being more negative.

MAKE IT STICK!

1.   Awareness of yourself and your environment is called _____.

2.   True or false? Your body has one naturally occurring rhythm that affects sleep.

Body Rhythms

 9-2 What are body rhythms, and how do they affect us?

An e-mail's subject line, Reliably Predict Your Mood for Free, once caught my eye. Closer investigation showed the predictions were anything but reliable—and certainly not free. This advertisement pitched something called a biorhythm chart, which was a good example of a **pseudoscientific claim**—an assertion that attempts to appear scientific but is not really based on science. The e-mail guaranteed that after I typed in the time and date of my birth, the chart could accurately predict my good and bad days, my illnesses and accidents, and even the best days for me to gamble. (Gullibility level was not predicted.)

Researchers have found that pseudoscientific biorhythm charts are useless.[2] Your body does, however, have real **biological rhythms**—periodic physiological fluctuations—that affect such things as body temperature, blood pressure, and the effectiveness of medicines. These biological rhythms fall into three main categories:

1.   **Circadian (ser-KAY-dee-un) rhythms** are biological rhythms that occur approximately once every 24 hours (*circa* and *dies* in Latin mean *about* and *day*, respectively). The sleep–wake cycle is an example of a circadian rhythm. Your body temperature, which drops at night, is another example of a circadian rhythm.

2.   **Ultradian (ul-TRAY-dee-un) rhythms** are biological rhythms that occur more than once a day. The most studied ultradian rhythm is the way we cycle through various stages of sleep each night. (You'll read more about these sleep stages shortly.)

3.   **Infradian (in-FRAY-dee-un) rhythms** are biological rhythms that occur once a month or once a season. Examples include a woman's monthly menstrual cycle and a bear's winter hibernation (one season).

We are aware of some of these biological rhythms as we cycle through them, but most run on autopilot, rarely generating a thought. An understanding of your body's natural rhythms may help you get more out of your day—and night.

MAKE IT STICK!

1.   The migration of monarch butterflies from the U.S. to Mexico that occurs every year is an example of a(n)

    a.   ultradian rhythm.   c.   infradian rhythm.
    b.   circadian rhythm.   d.   pseudoscientific rhythm.

2.   Biological rhythms (for example, of temperature and wakefulness) that occur approximately every 24 hours are called _____ rhythms.

Sleep and Sleep Deficit

 9-3 What happens to your body when you don't get enough sleep?

Live to be 90, and you will have spent about 30 years of your life in bed with your eyes closed. Ironically, few of us know much about what happens when we're asleep. Like most adults, I get around 8 hours of sleep per night. Most students your age get below-average sleep, and that's not good. Look at the research on sleep deprivation:

- Lack of sleep makes it more difficult for your body to fight illness.

- Sleep deprivation increases levels of the stress hormone cortisol, and that makes it harder for you to learn and remember things.

- Sleep deprivation increases appetite and eating, leading to weight gain.

- Sleep debt also contributes to high blood pressure, irritability, and premature aging.

With the evidence mounting against late nights, you'd think that a movement toward turning lights out earlier would gain momentum. *Wrong.* Many studies find that teenagers are getting almost 2 hours less sleep now than they did 70 years ago, before the days of cell phones, social media, and Netflix. Four out of five students are "dangerously sleep deprived," according to sleep researcher **William Dement**.[3] Dement states, "The brain keeps an accurate count of sleep debt," which helps explain why many high school students sleep effortlessly until noon on weekends if allowed. He matter-of-factly adds that given the damage a lack of rest inflicts on your brain, a large sleep debt "makes you stupid." Research also shows that losing an hour of sleep can make us more accident prone (See **Figure 9.1**). Are you getting the sleep you need? To find out, answer the questions in Psychology in the Real World: Are You Sleep Deprived? Most teens need 9 hours of sleep each

infradian [in-FRAY-dee-un] rhythms Biological rhythms that occur once a month or once a season.

A More Likely Cause of Accidents
Lack of sleep is a greater cause of accidental death than drunk driving for truck drivers (National Transportation Safety Board, 1995).

WILLIAM DEMENT (1928–) Sleep researcher who coined the term *rapid eye movement (REM)*.

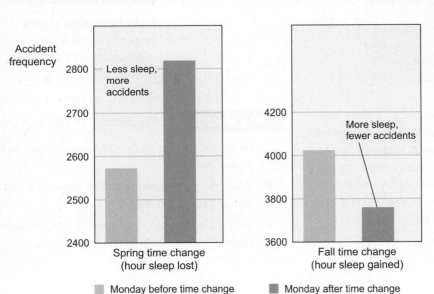

FIGURE 9.1
Spring Forward, Fall Back?
Compare the frequency of accidents on the Mondays before and after we lose an hour to daylight saving time in the spring. In the fall, the opposite trend appears. (Data from National Transportation Safety Board, 1995.)

PSYCHOLOGY IN THE REAL WORLD

Are You Sleep Deprived?

Cornell University psychologist James Maas reports that most college students suffer the consequences of sleeping less than they should. To see if you are headed toward being in that group, answer the following true–false questions:

True	False	
_____	_____	1. I often need an alarm clock in order to wake up at the appropriate time.
_____	_____	2. It's often a struggle for me to get out of bed in the morning.
_____	_____	3. Weekday mornings I often hit the snooze bar several times.
_____	_____	4. I often feel tired and stressed out during the week.
_____	_____	5. I often feel moody and irritable; little things upset me.
_____	_____	6. I often have trouble concentrating and remembering.
_____	_____	7. I often feel slow with critical thinking, problem solving, and being creative.
_____	_____	8. I need caffeine to get going in the morning or make it through the afternoon.
_____	_____	9. I often wake up craving junk food, sugars, and carbohydrates.

True	False	
_____	_____	10. I often fall asleep watching TV.
_____	_____	11. I often fall asleep in boring meetings or lectures or in warm rooms.
_____	_____	12. I often fall asleep after heavy meals.
_____	_____	13. I often fall asleep while relaxing after dinner.
_____	_____	14. I often fall asleep within 5 minutes of getting into bed.
_____	_____	15. I often feel drowsy while driving.
_____	_____	16. I often sleep extra hours on the weekends.
_____	_____	17. I often need a nap to get through the day.
_____	_____	18. I have dark circles around my eyes.
_____	_____	19. I fall asleep easily when watching a movie.
_____	_____	20. I rely on energy drinks or over-the-counter medications to keep me awake.

If you answered *true* to four or more items, consider yourself seriously sleep deprived. To determine your sleep needs, Maas recommends that you "go to bed 15 minutes earlier than usual every night for the next week—and continue this practice by adding 15 more minutes each week—until you awaken without an alarm clock and feel alert all day.[4]"

Source: Maas Robbins Alertness Questionnaire [MRAQ] adapted with permission from Maas & Robbins, 2010.

THINK ABOUT . . . Psychology in the Real World

1. How many times did you answer "True" to the above items?

2. What do your answers to the above items say about you as a sleeper?

3. What advice would you give to a friend who is seriously sleep deprived?

night, and 80 percent of all teens in the United States wish they slept more on school nights.[5] If you need an alarm to interrupt the sleep your body still wants, you're not getting enough.

MAKE IT STICK!

1. True or false? Sleep deprivation can lead to increased appetite and obesity.

2. True or false? Looking older than you really are can be a result of not sleeping enough.

3. Sleep deprivation increases the hormone called _____, which can hinder memory.

Why We Sleep

 9-4 How do we benefit from sleeping?

What causes us to sleep? Good question! Truth is, we still have no complete answer to the question of why we sleep. But scientists have gathered some partial answers by looking at the brain and nervous system.

The control center for the 24-hour rhythm of waking and sleeping appears to be the brain's hypothalamus (see **Figure 9.2**). You have a regulator in your hypothalamus that monitors changes in light and dark. Perceiving key changes in light level, your hypothalamus sends messages to parts of your brain and body, initiating the changes that will cause consciousness to fade and put you to sleep.[6] These physiological changes often involve the increase or decrease of hormones (chemical messengers) in your bloodstream.

One such hormone, **melatonin,** helps regulate the sleep–wake cycle.[7] Wake up in the morning and turn on the light or open the curtains, and the melatonin levels that built up while you slept will start to drop. Your melatonin levels will continue to drop until the next time you turn out the lights, close your eyes, and go to sleep. Some people with insomnia respond favorably to medically controlled amounts of melatonin supplements.

So, we know something about *how* we go to sleep, but *why* do we need to sleep? Why can't we simply stay up, day after day, doing the things we want to do? Two possible reasons revolve around the concepts of preservation and restoration.

If you've ever walked through your home in the dark without turning on lights and crashed into something, you can understand how sleep might help keep us safe. Such nighttime crashes must have been even more common for our ancestors, who lived in caves and on cliffs. Traveling or hunting at night (well before the invention of the flashlight!) was treacherous, and perhaps those who attempted it did not survive long enough to reproduce and pass along their genes. Sleep provides *protection* from nighttime's dangers, at least for daytime mammals like us who don't see well in the dark. The sleep cycles of other animals have adapted in different ways, depending on such factors as ability to hide and the need for nourishment.[8] Bats, for example, sleep 20 hours a day. Cats sleep twice as much as humans, but elephants drift off for only 3 to 4 hours. The adaptation theory suggests that we sleep at times of the night or day that maximize our safety and survival.

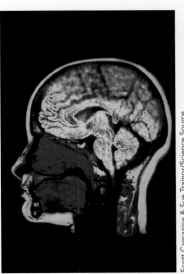

Scott Camazine & Sue Trainor/Science Source

▲ **FIGURE 9.2**
Sleep Command Center
The hypothalamus, colored green in this MRI brain scan photograph, sends messages to other parts of the brain saying, Time to sleep.

melatonin Hormone that helps regulate daily biological rhythms.

Another prominent theory suggests that sleep is restorative, allowing us to recuperate from the everyday wear and tear we put ourselves through. While sleeping, we undergo a rebuilding process as tissues are renewed, memories are consolidated, and things learned on the previous day are reorganized.

Getting your sleep also helps you be creative. After struggling with a problem, insightful solutions are more likely found by those who have slept on it than those who stayed awake.[9] Sleep helps you connect the dots between different pieces of unusual information.[10] In essence, sleep helps you be smart.

> **MAKE IT STICK!**
>
> **1.** True or false? Sleeping on it might actually help you solve a problem you'd been working on the night before.
>
> **2.** What is the name of the hormone that regulates daily biological rhythms such as the sleep-wake cycle?
>
> **3.** Which sleep theory would say we sleep at night because it's safer?

Sleep Stages, REM Sleep, and Dreaming

Many people think of sleep and dreaming as virtually identical processes. In fact, your brain, your voluntary muscles, and your eyes are doing very different things while dreaming compared to their actions during the basic stages of sleep.

Stages of Sleep

 9-5 What stages do we go through when we sleep?

The sleep–wake cycle itself is circadian, but we also have a 90-minute *ultradian* rhythm cycling throughout our night's sleep. During the 90-minute ultradian cycle, two types of sleep occur in a series of regular, repeating stages. How do we know this? Because sleep researchers have measured the brain waves, eye movements, and muscle tension of sleeping people. The challenges in gathering sleep data are twofold:

1. The person whom you're studying must be asleep.

2. The person must also agree to have a bunch of electrodes attached to his or her head (see **Figure 9.3**). The electrodes, which are connected to an **electroencephalograph (EEG),** are collecting brain wave measurements (not delivering shocks!), so the procedure is painless.

Fortunately, thousands of volunteers have agreed to sleep under observation with electrodes on. Would you volunteer to be a participant in a sleep study? For a few minutes, let's suppose you would. Here's what would happen.

As you relax, drifting from wakefulness to sleep, your brain waves cycle more and more slowly. You might yawn, which speeds up heart rate in an attempt to move you toward alertness, but it's a losing battle.[11] As you nod off for the benefit of science, you will cycle through three stages of relatively quiet sleep, all referred

electroencephalograph (EEG) Machine that amplifies and records waves of electrical activity as they sweep across the brain's surface; electrodes placed on the scalp measure these waves.

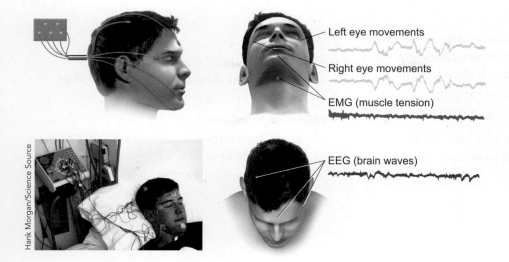

Left eye movements

Right eye movements

EMG (muscle tension)

EEG (brain waves)

FIGURE 9.3
Measuring Sleep
Sleep researchers use electrodes to measure brain waves (using an electroencephalograph, or EEG), eye movements, and muscle tension (using an electromyograph, or EMG) while we sleep. They can use the changes in these measurements to label the different stages of sleep and dreaming.

to as stages of *non–rapid eye movement sleep*, before you go into a more active dreaming state (see **Figure 9.4**). You will not be able to tell the exact moment you enter *NREM 1* (or non–rapid eye movement stage 1), but a sleep researcher, noticing your slowed breathing and irregular brain waves, could accurately point to these first moments of sleep, which rarely last longer than 5 minutes (see **Figure 9.5**). It would be easy to awaken you from this stage, and if the sleep researcher did, you'd probably insist you had not been sleeping.

But let's imagine that the researcher did not awaken you. As you exit NREM 1, your brain waves cycle more slowly and you slide into the deeper sleep of *NREM 2*. The first time you enter NREM 2, your stay lasts 20 minutes. Over the course of the night, you will spend up to half of your entire time asleep in this stage.

About 30 minutes after you fall asleep, your brain waves begin to slow way down as you drop into *NREM 3*. This is a stage called *slow-wave sleep*. Your brain waves slow to less than 1 cycle per second in NREM 3, compared with the 15 or so cycles per second you experienced just after you closed your eyes. The first time you travel through this ultradian cycle, the rejuvenating sleep of NREM 3 will last about 30 minutes.

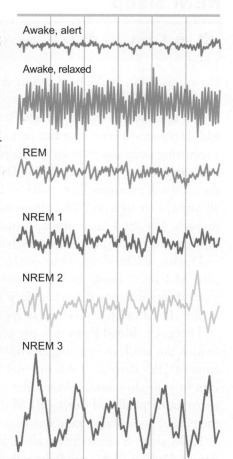

Awake, alert

Awake, relaxed

REM

NREM 1

NREM 2

NREM 3

6 sec

FIGURE 9.4
Brain Waves and Sleep Stages
Brain waves slow as we cycle into the deeper stages of sleep.

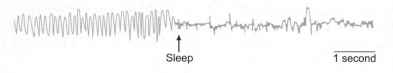

Sleep

1 second

FIGURE 9.5
Entering the Land of Nod
You wouldn't be able to say precisely when you fell asleep last night, but a sleep researcher charting your brain waves could pinpoint the time accurately. (Data from Dement, 1999.)

REM Sleep

 9-6 Why is REM sleep described as paradoxical?

Up to this point, you've been cycling down through the three stages of *non–rapid eye movement sleep,* or NREM sleep. After you reach NREM 3, your brain waves will begin to pick up a little speed and strength. You will move back up through NREM 2 and 1, and then you will enter your first period of rapid eye movement sleep, or **REM sleep,** a recurring sleep stage during which your eyes move rapidly under your closed lids and you dream vividly. Your initial REM period will not last long, and after it ends, the cycle will start again from NREM 1. This 90-minute ultradian rhythm continues all night, although NREM 3 drops out of the cycle after the second or third time through. The last 4 hours of sleep, assuming you get the 8 to 9 hours you're supposed to, are pretty much spent alternating between NREM 2 and REM (see **Figure 9.6**).

During REM sleep, your brain patterns most closely resemble those of NREM 1 sleep. Looks can be deceiving, however, because REM sleep is actually quite different from the other sleep stages. During REM, your eyes dart about under closed eyelids, your pulse speeds up, and your breathing becomes faster and irregular. Blood flows into the genitals at a rate faster than it can be removed (which can result in morning erections in males that are unrelated to actual dream content). But despite all this internal activity, the electrode measuring muscle tension in your chin would show a flat line on the EEG because you are, in essence, temporarily paralyzed during REM sleep—your brainstem blocks messages from the part of your brain that controls movement.

REM sleep is sometimes called *paradoxical* sleep because of its contrasting nature. During REM, you have active brain waves, you are processing input from your environment (for example, you might incorporate external noises into your dreaming), and you can be awakened more easily than at any other sleep stage. Yet you are still definitely asleep.

What's going on in our brains to produce all that internal activity? We're dreaming. More than 80 percent of people awakened during REM sleep report that the wake-up call interrupted a dream. REM sleep consumes about 25 percent of your nightly sleep, which means that you spend 100 minutes each night dreaming, whether you remember a second of it or not. This holds true for everyone. We *all* dream every night of our lives.

rapid eye movement (REM) sleep Recurring sleep stage during which vivid dreams commonly occur.

LIFE MATTERS

Napping is one of our favorite pastimes, but in order to get the best bang for your buck, what amount of time is the most beneficial? According to Sleep.Org, a 90-minute nap is best, because you actually can complete a full sleep cycle. If you don't have 90 minutes to spare, 20 minutes will do.

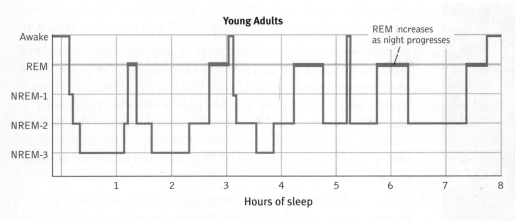

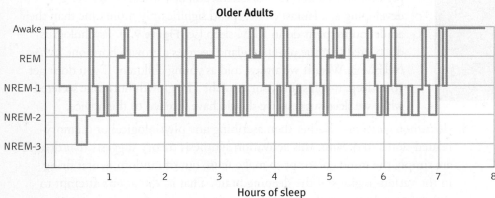

FIGURE 9.6
A Good Night's Sleep
We cycle through sleep stages all night. Young adults get restorative, deep sleep the first half of the night, then end up cycling through REM and Stage 2. As we age, we get less deep sleep, and wake up more often (Data from Kamel & Gammak, 2006; Neubauer, 1999).

MAKE IT STICK!

1. When you fall asleep,

   a. you immediately begin to dream.

   b. your brain stops sending messages that keep you awake.

   c. your brain stops sending messages that keep you asleep.

   d. your body enters a paralyzed state.

2. What kind of rhythm is NREM/REM cycle?

   a. ultradian   c. paradoxical

   b. circadian   d. pseudoscientific

3. True or false? REM brain waves cannot be measured on an electroencephalograph (EEG) like those of the other stages.

Why Do We Dream?

9-7 What are the four modern explanations for why we dream?

There are several theories of why we dream. Sigmund Freud created psychology's earliest dream theory. In his book *The Interpretation of Dreams*, published more than a century ago, Freud wrote that dreams were the key to understanding things that trouble us. He also believed that dreams were expressions of wish fulfillment and erotic wishes.[12] Sleep has remained an important subject of psychological study ever since. Modern theories of dreaming offer at least four more plausible

▲ **The Meaning of Dreams?**
Marc Chagall's painting *I and the Village* captures what a dream can look like to the dreamer: colorful, confusing, and possibly filled with meaning.

explanations—information processing, physiological function, activation synthesis, and cognitive development (all summarized in **Table 9.1**):

1. *Information processing*—Dreams serve an important memory-related function by sifting through the day's experiences and tying up loose ends. In other words, think of your brain as a computer that loses its Internet connection when it first goes to sleep but then comes back online during REM sleep to sort through some of the previous day's activities. Research shows that REM sleep facilitates memory storage, and the amount of REM sleep increases following stressful times.[13, 14]

2. *Physiological function*—Neural activity during REM sleep provides periodic stimulation for our brains. Infants, whose brains are developing at a fantastic rate, spend significantly more time than their adult counterparts do in REM sleep (see **Figure 9.7**). Psychologists discovered that the pituitary gland secretes a growth hormone *during* NREM 3. Weren't we always told as young children, If you don't get your sleep, it will stunt your growth? The growth hormone secreted while we sleep suggests we should have listened to this advice.

3. *Activation synthesis*—Rather than ascribing any physiological or memory-related status to dreams, this activation synthesis theory suggests that dreams are simply the mind's attempt to make sense out of random neural firing in the various regions of the sleeping brain. That is, the brain's attempt to interpret random neural activity during sleep is what causes a dream.

4. *Cognitive development*—Dreams also reflect what we've learned and what we know.[15] That is, the dreams of a third-grader are far less dynamic and active and tell less of a story than those of a 20-year-old. If we've never heard of a Native American sweat lodge or the ceremonies that take place inside such a lodge, we're not going to dream about them (see Table 9.1).

We are not the only animals who experience REM sleep. We don't know whether other animals are having dreams, but nearly all animals, from sheep to walruses, show measurable REM periods while hooked up to an EEG during sleep. (Just how do they keep electrodes on walruses?) Such evidence suggests a biological *need*

TABLE 9.1	**Dream Theories**	
Theory	**Explanation**	**Critical Considerations**
Information processing	Dreams help us sort out the day's events.	But why do we sometimes dream about things we have not experienced?
Physiological function	Regular brain stimulation from REM sleep may help develop and preserve neural pathways.	This may be true, but it does not explain why we experience meaningful dreams.
Activation synthesis	REM sleep triggers neural activity that evokes random visual memories, which our sleeping brain weaves into stories.	The individual's brain is weaving the stories, which still tells us something about the dreamer.
Cognitive development	Dream content reflects dreamers' cognitive development—their knowledge and understanding.	This theory does not address the neuroscience of dreams.

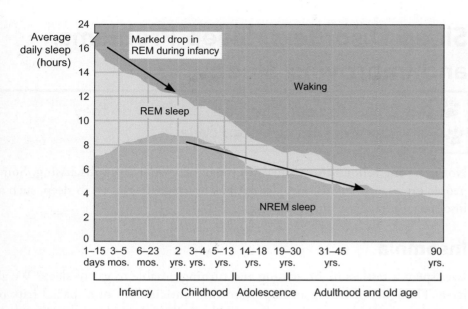

FIGURE 9.7
Sleep and Age
Sleep patterns change
as we grow older. (From
Snyder & Snyder, 1972.)

Cat Nap
The cat in NREM sleep (left)
is sleeping comfortably. On
entering REM sleep, the
cat's brain stops sending
the signals to the muscles
that let the cat hold its
head off the floor.

for REM sleep. We do know that people don't feel rested unless their sleep has contained REM periods. Also, when finally allowed to sleep after a period of sleep deprivation, we tend to dive straight into REM sleep rather than following the normal cycle. Furthermore, REM does not occur in fish, whose behavior (unlike mammals') is governed more by instinct and less by learning, supporting the information-processing model of why we dream. The truth behind dreams, once discovered, will surely encompass both psychological and biological explanations.

MAKE IT STICK!

1. Which of the following dream theories is considered a modern explanation of dreams?

   a. Symbolic interpretations of repressed memories
   b. Freudian dream analysis
   c. Random neural firing
   d. Precognition and clairvoyance

2. Which of the following theories would most likely explain dreaming as the mind's attempt to make sense of random neural firing in the brain?

   a. Activation synthesis
   b. Information processing

   c. Cognitive development
   d. Freudian dream analysis

3. Which of the following theories would most likely explain dreaming as simply a part of the maturational process?

   a. Cognitive development
   b. Information processing
   c. Activation synthesis
   d. Freudian dream analysis

Sleep Disorders, Sleep Problems, and Improving Sleep

 9-8 What are sleep disorders, and how do they interfere with our sleep cycles?

Not everyone follows the normal sleep patterns we've been discussing. Some people experience serious sleep disruptions or problems related to sleep, such as insomnia, sleep apnea, and narcolepsy.

Insomnia

insomnia Recurring problems in falling asleep or staying asleep.

sleep apnea Sleep disorder characterized by temporary cessations of breathing during sleep and consequent momentary reawakenings.

Ever spent a restless night, tossing and turning, unable to get to sleep? We all have. Thoughts of taking an important test, anticipation of a special trip, or distress over someone we love all carry the potential to block the sleep we'd like to have. Happily, difficulty in getting to sleep is rare for most of us. Those less fortunate have **insomnia,** recurring problems in falling asleep or staying asleep. For those with insomnia, getting to sleep or remaining asleep can be a real nightmare.

Oral medications for insomnia may actually worsen the problem. Sleeping pills, with sales increasing over 60 percent since the start of this century, can be addictive, and they inhibit or suppress REM sleep, leaving the sleep-hungry person feeling even worse than before.[16] And people who drink booze to help them sleep? Tell them not to! Alcohol keeps the drinker from getting into REM sleep, leading to next-day crankiness and all kinds of other problems associated with REM deprivation. Drinking before sleeping is a bad idea.

Stanley Coren's research sheds some interesting light on insomnia. Coren asked insomnia sufferers to estimate how long it took to get to sleep. He found that those who had trouble sleeping estimated that it took them twice as long to get to sleep as it actually did. Furthermore, they dramatically miscalculated the amount of time they slept, estimating they'd slept half the time they actually had. Perhaps we should keep this research in mind the next time we think we haven't slept much the night before. It's a lot easier to remember, and exaggerate, the times during the night when we were awake than the times we were asleep.

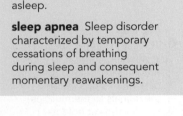

Actually, my species is not nocturnal: I'm just a teenager . . .

Sleep Apnea

Losing one night's sleep may not cause significant damage, but **sleep apnea**—a disorder characterized by repeated awakenings throughout the night as a result of not being able to breathe—can leave you exhausted. A person with sleep apnea is a loud snorer who stops breathing at the peak of a heavy, inhaled snore, and whose breathing may cease for as long as a minute. The only way the person can breathe again is to briefly awaken, which may happen more than 400 times a night. Apnea (meaning *with no breath*) sufferers experience dreadful sleepiness even after a full night's sleep, but they may be unaware they are having such poor-quality sleep.

Millions of Americans suffer from sleep apnea. The most common treatment involves use of a continuous positive airway pressure (CPAP) machine, which helps the person breathe during the night.

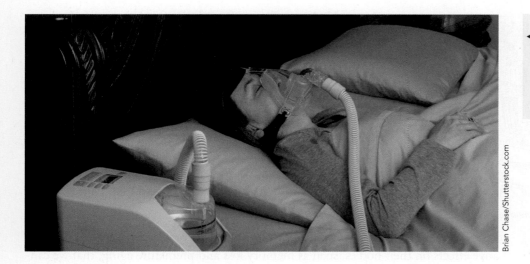

> **Sleeping Aid** Those with sleep apnea can turn to this continuous positive airway pressure, or CPAP, machine (and others like it) to help them get the sleep they need.

Narcolepsy

Can you imagine what it would be like to suddenly fall asleep because something made you laugh, cry, or feel infuriated? Such is the life of a person with **narcolepsy** (*narco* meaning *numbness, lepsy* meaning *seizure*), a sleep disorder characterized by uncontrollable sleep attacks. Narcolepsy is a rare disease (striking 1 in 2000 people) that runs in families. Those with narcolepsy experience sleep attacks when their nervous systems become aroused, often from a strong emotion.[17] When an attack occurs, they fall immediately into REM sleep, often at a dangerous time. Imagine being cut off in traffic, becoming angry at the other driver, and then instantly lapsing into sleep? That would simply be terrible #badtiming.

In recent years, researchers have isolated a narcolepsy-causing gene in dogs and have linked narcolepsy to the absence of the neurotransmitter hypocretin.[18, 19] Both of these developments raise hope for the development of a lasting treatment that would, in essence, cure narcolepsy. Until then, physicians will continue to treat narcolepsy with a form of REM-inhibiting stimulant. If you don't have narcolepsy now, chances are you never will; the onset of this disorder accompanies puberty.

narcolepsy Sleep disorder characterized by uncontrollable sleep attacks; the sufferer may lapse directly into REM sleep, often at inopportune times.

NREM Sleep Arousal Disorders

NREM sleep arousal disorders tend to occur when the brain is partially in NREM and partially awake. Most are treatable and do not have some kind of underlying condition. Examples include

- **Somnambulism,** or sleepwalking. Is it dangerous to awaken a sleepwalker? *No,* but it is pretty hard to awaken someone who is walking around with brain waves revving at 1 cycle per second. Is the sleepwalker acting out a dream? Again, *no.* Remember, most dreams occur during REM sleep, and during that type of sleep, we lose our ability to move around.

- **Night terrors** are characterized by every indication of being terrified. Night terrors most often afflict children, who look like they are awake and terrified even though they are sound asleep. The child rarely has any memory of the event when told about it in the morning. Night terrors are different from nightmares, which are dreams (so they occur during REM

somnambulism Sleepwalking, which usually starts in the deeper stages of NREM sleep; the sleepwalker can walk and talk and is able to see but rarely has any memory of the event.

night terrors Sleep-related problem characterized by high arousal and an appearance of being terrified; unlike nightmares, they occur during NREM 3 sleep, occur within 2 or 3 hours of falling asleep, and are seldom remembered.

"Wait! Don't! It can be dangerous to wake them!"

Danger?
Although it may be difficult, awakening this sleepwalker would definitely be the right decision.

sleep). Night terrors occur within a few hours of falling asleep, during NREM 3 sleep.

- *Bruxism* is teeth grinding that sounds as though two bricks are being rubbed together. Adults with this problem often wear some kind of tooth guard to keep from wearing away enamel.

- *Enuresis* is bed wetting.

- *Myoclonus* is a sudden jerking of a body part that occurs in NREM 1 or 2. Everyone experiences myoclonus now and then, but acute cases can result in daytime sleepiness, similar to the sleepiness accompanying sleep apnea.

Some people appear to get by on as few as 4 hours of sleep per night. However, most of these brief sleepers experience negative effects on their bodies, such as memory loss and premature aging, that we cannot immediately see. So, when you're tired and it's time to sleep, pay attention to your body. Ignore that last text message, resist the urge to check your Instagram account, and give in to the gentle tyrant that is your need for sleep.

Improving Sleep

Do you have trouble falling asleep? Do you often wake up during the night? If so, don't sweat it. There are several steps you can take to improve the quality of your sleep while reducing the anxiety you might experience when sleep does not come easily. Consider the following:

- Stop using your cell phone at least 2 hours before turning off the lights. Looking at your phone stimulates your brain and makes it harder for you to sleep. Research shows that the more you use your phone around bedtime, the longer it takes you to fall asleep. Shutting off your phone is likely the number one thing you should do if you are having trouble getting to sleep.

- Do not consume caffeinated beverages or foods after 3:00 P.M. Skip that soda with dinner, and turn away from late-night chocolate snacks.

- Exercise daily, but avoid late-night exercise.

- Drink milk, which aids in the production of a chemical (serotonin) in your body that promotes sleep.

- Dim the lights at night, and relax before bedtime.

- Accept that as a human being, you experience stress. Conflict during the day might naturally lead to a crummy night's sleep.

- Get up at the same time every morning. Sleeping late on weekends can make it difficult to get to sleep on Sunday night, leaving you extra tired on Monday morning. Naps can have the same effect: You may not be able to fall asleep at your normal bedtime.

- Avoid nighttime activities that rile you up. Angry text messages, action-packed video games, or emotional arguments right before attempting to sleep are not good ideas.

- Try not to worry when you can't get to sleep. Remember that it's normal to take 15 minutes or more to fall asleep at night. Besides, sleeping poorly for one night won't cause any great harm, and often you'll be able to sleep better the following night.

MAKE IT STICK!

1. A friend tells you her father is obese and snores loudly at night. Which of the following sleep disorders might you discuss with your friend?

   a. Enuresis
   b. Sleep apnea
   c. Narcolepsy
   d. Bruxism

2. Recurring problems in falling asleep or staying asleep are characteristic of what sleep disorder or problem?

   a. Insomnia
   b. Sleep apnea
   c. Bruxism
   d. Somnambulism

3. What do we call a sudden sleep attack?

   a. Night Terrors
   b. Sleep apnea
   c. Narcolepsy
   d. Somnambulism

4. Sleepwalking is also called

   a. enuresis.
   b. somnambulism.
   c. myoclonus.
   d. bruxism.

Module 9 Summary and Assessment

Sleep, Dreams, and Body Rhythms

 9-1 What do psychologists mean by consciousness?

- Consciousness is the degree to which we are aware of our environment and ourselves.

 9-2 What are body rhythms, and how do they affect us?

- We go through three types of body rhythms that occur in regular cycles—circadian, ultradian, and infradian—and that affect our consciousness and physiological processes.

 9-3 What happens to your body when you don't get enough sleep?

- Sleep deprivation causes physiological changes that can dramatically affect our moods, health, and ability to perform physically and mentally.

 9-4 How do we benefit from sleeping?

- Sleep helps restore our body physically and protect us from nighttime hazards.

 9-5 What stages do we go through when we sleep?

- We cycle through three stages of non–rapid eye movement (NREM) sleep every night.

- The stages of sleep describe different levels of brain activity, measured by brain waves.

 9-6 Why is REM sleep described as paradoxical?

- The REM stage of sleep is sometimes called paradoxical because of its contrasting nature. During REM, we have active brain waves, we can process input from our environment, and we can be awakened more easily than at any other sleep stage.

 9-7 What are the four modern explanations for why we dream?

- The four modern explanations of dreams focus on how dreams may be related to information processing, physiological function, activation synthesis, and cognitive development.

 9-8 What are sleep disorders, and how do they interfere with our sleep cycles?

- Sleep disorders interfere with our sleep cycles and can affect us mentally and physically during our waking life.

- Insomnia is the most common sleep disorder, but it is treatable.

- Apnea and narcolepsy (less common) are two serious sleep disorders.

Summative Assessment

1. Your sleep–wake cycle is an example of what kind of rhythm?
   a. circadian
   b. ultradian
   c. biorhythm
   d. developmental

2. What's another word for awareness of self and your environment?
   a. biorhythm
   b. REM
   c. consciousness
   d. NREM

3. Which of the following represents the deepest level of sleep?
   a. NREM 2
   b. NREM 3
   c. NREM 1
   d. REM

4. Gaining weight and premature aging are both linked to which of the following?
   a. sleep deficit
   b. sleepwalking
   c. sleep apnea
   d. sleep enhancement

5. Which of the following is a hormone that helps regulate the sleep–wake cycle?
   a. REM
   b. bruxism
   c. NREM
   d. melatonin

6. Which of the following dream theories maintains that dreams reflect knowledge and understanding?
   a. activation synthesis
   b. information processing
   c. wish fulfillment
   d. cognitive development

7. During REM sleep, your brain is active and you can process input from your environment. For this reason, REM sleep is also referred to as
   a. NREM 2 sleep.
   b. paradoxical sleep.
   c. EEG sleep.
   d. melatonin overload sleep.

8. Which of following sleep disorders is characterized by waking up many times during the night?
   a. narcolepsy
   b. enuresis
   c. sleep apnea
   d. bruxism

9. Which of the following is likely to increase your quality of sleep?
   a. running a couple miles after 11:00 p.m.
   b. playing a video game like *Call of Duty* before going to bed
   c. avoiding late-night chocolate bars
   d. keeping all the lights on until right before you try to sleep

10. Which of the following theories would most likely explain dreams as a sorting out of the day's events?
    a. physiological function
    b. activation synthesis
    c. cognitive development
    d. information processing

KEY TERMS AND KEY PEOPLE

consciousness, p. 133

pseudoscientific claim, p. 134

biological rhythms, p. 134

circadian [ser-KAY-dee-un] rhythms, p. 134

ultradian [ul-TRAY-dee-un] rhythms, p. 134

infradian [in-FRAY-dee-un] rhythms, p. 134

melatonin, p. 137

electroencephalograph (EEG), p. 138

rapid eye movement (REM) sleep, p. 140

insomnia, p. 144

sleep apnea, p. 144

narcolepsy, p. 145

somnambulism, p. 145

night terrors, p. 145

William Dement (1928–), p. 135

Psychoactive Drugs

Many people drink coffee in the morning to get going. The chemical in coffee that achieves this effect is actually a psychoactive drug. Surprised? Let's take a close look at psychoactive drugs and how they affect us.

What Are Psychoactive Drugs?

 10-1 What are psychoactive drugs, and what is dependence?

Most adults and young adults in this country regularly take **psychoactive drugs,** chemical substances that alter mood, behavior, or perceptions. Surprised? If so, perhaps you don't associate the phrase *psychoactive drug* with the three most commonly used psychoactive substances: caffeine, alcohol, and nicotine. These everyday chemical substances are drugs; as such, they can induce an altered state of consciousness. They also can lead to **dependence**—a state of physiological or psychological need (or combined need) to take more of a drug after continued use. Notice that we say *dependence,* not *addiction.* While the World Health Organization reports that over 90 million people suffer from drug and alcohol dependence,[1] the concept of addiction has lost much of its meaning. Addicted to an app on your phone? Addicted to pizza? Addicted to Twitter? True addictions seriously disrupt a person's ability to function in everyday life. Gambling and Internet use (online games and social networking) can fit this description, but few other behaviors do.[2] For the purposes of this module, we use the term *dependence* instead of *addiction* to discuss psychoactive drugs.

When users are deprived of a drug they are dependent on, they have **withdrawal** (usually discomfort and distress) symptoms. You may experience withdrawal if you normally drink a few cans of caffeinated cola daily and then go on a weekend

psychoactive drug Chemical substance that alters perceptions, mood, or behavior.

dependence State of physiological or psychological need (or combined need) to take more of a drug after continued use.

withdrawal Discomfort and distress that follow when a person who is dependent on a drug discontinues the use of that drug.

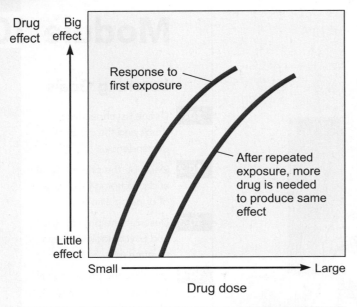

Drug effect

Big effect

Response to first exposure

After repeated exposure, more drug is needed to produce same effect

Little effect

Small ——————→ Large

Drug dose

FIGURE 10.1
Tolerance

The initial effect of a psychoactive drug is not the same as the effect that occurs with repeated use. As the user's body develops tolerance to the drug, increasing amounts are usually needed to achieve the same effect.

tolerance Reduced responsiveness to a drug, prompting the user to take larger doses to achieve the same pleasurable effects previously obtained by smaller doses.

camping trip where no soda is available. If you experience grogginess, develop a headache, and miss your cola, you are demonstrating caffeine dependence.

Withdrawal symptoms often resemble the opposite of a psychoactive drug's intended effect. For a heroin user, this means that the brief, drug-induced episodes of euphoria, relaxation, and slowed breathing will give way to prolonged depression, restlessness, and abnormally rapid breathing after the drug wears off.[3] Withdrawal is even worse in those with a long history of drug use. Regular drug use usually leads to **tolerance,** a reduced response to the drug, which prompts the user to take larger doses to achieve the same pleasurable effects previously obtained by smaller doses (see **Figure 10.1**). So, for example, a new drinker may get a buzz from one beer, but after drinking regularly over several weeks, the person will develop a tolerance for alcohol and may require two or three beers to achieve that same feeling. With this increased intake, the person's body must struggle to clean out the increased toxins and cope with the rising blood alcohol level. You'll read more about the effects of alcohol next.

We will study five kinds of psychoactive drugs: depressants (primarily alcohol), stimulants, hallucinogens, opioids, and marijuana. Most discussions of drugs and their effects use these five categories, but keep in mind the drug-taker's *expectations* and *mood* can cause some drugs to jump outside the boundaries of any one classification. For example, alcohol is a depressant, but it can have a wildly stimulating effect on a drinker who expects to feel stimulated, such as an excited fan celebrating a World Series championship.

Take Me Out to the Ball Game
You wouldn't know it by watching these fans, but alcohol is a central nervous system depressant. Another effect? Lowered inhibitions.

LAURA RAUCH/AP Images

MAKE IT STICK!

1. Anyone who experiences cravings for a drug and withdrawal symptoms without the drug can be said to be _____ that drug.

   a. resistant to
   b. dependent on
   c. tolerant of
   d. tired of

2. What is the relationship between tolerance and withdrawal?

   a. Withdrawal refers to the negative effects of drug use, and tolerance refers to the positive effects.
   b. Drug users may need to take increasing dosages of a drug (withdrawal) to avoid negative side effects of stopping drug use (tolerance).

   c. Repeated use of a drug will usually produce withdrawal effects and can lead to tolerance.
   d. Physical side effects of repeated drug use (tolerance) can be avoided if users go through long periods without using the drug (withdrawal).

3. A substance that alters mood and perception is likely

   a. psychoactive.
   b. illegal.
   c. inactive.
   d. intolerant.

Alcohol: A Depressant

 10-2 What are the physiological and psychological effects of drinking alcohol?

Depressants are drugs that slow body functions. Alcohol, one of many depressants, is the second most used psychoactive drug in the world (caffeine is the first). Like any depressant, alcohol slows thinking and impairs physical activity. Alcohol is unique among depressants in that its use is largely recreational: People drink to unwind, for the taste, or to increase sociability at a party. Those desires can quickly lead to dependence.

Alcoholic beverages vary widely in the amount of alcohol they contain. Beer is usually about 5 percent alcohol, wine is between 10 and 14 percent, and the hard stuff like whiskey, vodka, and tequila comes in at a whopping 40 percent or more. One 12-ounce can of beer has about the same effect as a 4-ounce glass of wine or a 1-ounce shot of hard liquor (see **Figure 10.2**). A 150-pound man needs about an hour to break down (metabolize) the alcohol from one beer. If he drinks more than one beer per hour, his *blood alcohol content (BAC)* quickly increases.

Alcohol affects women and men differently. A man and a woman who both weigh the same and drink the same amount of alcohol will have different amounts of alcohol in their bloodstreams an hour later for at least three reasons:[4]

- Men typically have 50 percent more of an enzyme responsible for breaking down alcohol. Men rid themselves of alcohol faster.

- Pound for pound, men have more blood in their vascular systems than women. Alcohol is diluted more in men.

- A higher percentage of body fat in women tends to concentrate more alcohol in blood plasma than in men, which raises BAC in women.

depressants Drugs (such as alcohol and sedatives) that reduce neural activity and slow body functions.

FIGURE 10.2
What Do We Mean by *One Drink*?
One 12-ounce bottle of beer has about the same amount of alcohol as a 4-ounce glass of wine or a 1-ounce shot of whiskey.

Louis DeLuca/Tribune News Service/Newscom

In all states, a BAC of 0.08 percent is legal intoxication (though Utah is 0.05 as of December 2018). However, a person may not necessarily be able to drive safely with a lower BAC. Behavioral impairment can begin at 0.01. For this reason, truck drivers are not allowed to drive at 0.04, and pilots should test no higher than 0.02 after going 24 hours without a drink. Even at this low BAC level, the time it takes to react increases, as does the likelihood of accidents.

But if alcohol depresses the nervous system, why do so many people report feeling enlivened or stimulated after drinking small amounts? I mean, how do we explain the following?

- René is normally quiet but talks a mile a minute after drinking a bottle of hard lemonade.

- Nick is usually mild mannered but becomes aggressive after downing a couple of beers.

- Juanita is a penny pincher but leaves the server a huge tip after an evening of martinis at a bar.

The answer lies in the brain area most affected by alcohol. Alcohol tends to shut down the parts of your brain responsible for controlling inhibitions and making judgments. So, poor decisions and unfiltered behaviors are typical in those under the influence of alcohol. This helps explain another example of alcohol-induced bad judgment: Most drinkers, even after scoring at or above 0.08 on a Breathalyzer test, judge themselves capable of driving home from the bar.[5, 6] It also may help explain the fights, sexual harassment, and risky sexual behavior (such as unprotected sexual intercourse) that often go hand in hand with drinking.[7] Alcohol intoxication dramatically increases the probability that we will act out the inappropriate or dangerous urges we keep in check while sober.

simonkr/ E+/Getty Images

TABLE 10.1 Do You Have an Alcohol Problem?

If you can answer Yes to even one of these questions, consider seeking advice about your use of alcohol.

1. Has someone close to you sometimes expressed concern about your drinking?
2. When faced with a problem, do you often turn to alcohol for relief?
3. Are you sometimes unable to meet home or work responsibilities because of drinking?
4. Have you ever required medical attention as a result of drinking?
5. Have you ever experienced a blackout—a total loss of memory while still awake—when drinking?
6. Have you ever come into conflict with the law in connection with your drinking?
7. Have you often failed to keep the promises you have made to yourself about controlling or cutting out your drinking?

Source: National Institute on Alcohol Abuse and Alcoholism

Alcohol also impairs memory. I remember a former college classmate who, when questioned on Saturday morning after a night of drinking, couldn't remember what he'd done, where he'd been, and whom he'd been with the night before. He vigorously denied statements I had heard him make just 12 hours earlier. My classmate lost these Friday night memories partly because alcohol suppresses the processing of recent events into long-term memory. Finally, alcohol suppresses dream sleep, which further disrupts memory storage.

Half of all beer, wine, and liquor consumed in this country is swallowed by only 10 percent of the population. Many of those included in that 10 percent are alcohol dependent. If you suspect that a family member or friend is dependent on alcohol, you might ask that person to read the questions distributed by the National Institute on Alcohol Abuse and Alcoholism (see **Table 10.1**). Answering *yes* to any of the questions indicates an alcohol problem of some sort. Answering *yes* to several of the questions may indicate alcoholism.

The recreational use of alcohol often gets out of hand, leading to dependence, health problems, accidental injuries, or death. No other drug has generated more problems, concern, or controversy than alcohol has in this country. For evidence, look no further than our Constitution, where 2 of the 27 Amendments deal with alcohol.

Alcoholism kills over 100,000 U.S. citizens every year. Professional medicine can detoxify and delay relapse, but most people dependent on alcohol treated only by modern medical science eventually relapse.[8]

It is difficult to calculate the success rate of interventions such as Alcoholics Anonymous (AA), but a 50-year project by George Vaillant provides evidence that AA works where medical science fails. According to Vaillant, AA contrasts with modern medical science in that its attempted "cure" is relapse prevention. AA uses four factors to prevent relapse:

1. External supervision
2. Ritualized dependency on a competing behavior
3. New love relationships
4. Deepened spirituality

Vaillant points out that except for external supervision, these factors depend on *positive emotions*. Let's take a closer look at the last three.

Ritualized dependency on a competing behavior. You can't easily give up a habit without having something you enjoy to replace it. Bad habits give way to substitutes, not simply prohibition. AA meetings focus only on enjoyable, positive emotions. Loving suggestions replace criticism.

New love relationships. People dealing with alcoholism need to bond with people they have not hurt. Giving and receiving compassion and love aids recovery and decreases relapse. AA home groups become deeply trusted, nonjudgmental family units.

Spirituality. AA is not about religion at all. But spirituality (one of the 24 character strengths identified by Peterson and Seligman[9]) is a common feature in recovery from drug dependency. Vaillant writes, "Inspirational, altruistic group membership and a faith in a power greater than 'me' is important to recovery from addiction."

Other studies[10] have shown that those recovering from alcoholism who attend AA regularly are much more likely to avoid relapse than those who only receive professional treatment. Vaillant believes this is because AA depends on positive emotions and being around other people and not simply compliance with treatment. To quote Vaillant, "Other people matter."

MAKE IT STICK!

1. Which cognitive activity is most dramatically affected by alcohol use?

   a. Encoding memories
   b. Visual perception
   c. Problem solving
   d. Nonverbal communication

2. Although alcohol is a(n) _____, some people report feeling stimulated after drinking because alcohol _____.

   a. hallucinogen; raises blood pressure
   b. depressant; lowers inhibitions

   c. amphetamine; excites neural activity
   d. psychoactive drug; acts as a stimulant on the nervous system

3. The top 10 percent of all drinkers consume about _____ of all alcohol in the U.S.

   a. 10 percent   c. 50 percent
   b. 25 percent   d. 90 percent

4. True or false? Inspirational, altruistic group membership and a faith in a power greater than 'me' is important to recovery from addiction.

Stimulants

 10-3 What are the physiological and psychological effects of stimulants?

We have noted that alcohol is a depressant, since it reduces neural activity and slows body functions. Next, we review **stimulants,** drugs that excite neural activity and speed up body functions. This category includes caffeine, nicotine, cocaine, and amphetamines. And one of those—caffeine—is the most widely used psychoactive drug in the world.

Caffeine

Caffeine is the stimulant found in coffee, tea, cocoa, and soda, as well as the primary stimulant in energy drinks. As many as 80 percent of the adults in this

stimulants Drugs (such as caffeine, nicotine, and the more powerful amphetamines and cocaine) that excite neural activity and speed up body functions.

caffeine Stimulant found in coffee, chocolate, tea, and some soft drinks.

country consume some form of it daily.[11] Many choose coffee as their caffeine delivery system. Coffee causes bad breath, stains your teeth, looks like motor oil, keeps you from sleeping, and tastes awful the first several times you drink it. Even after becoming hooked, many coffee drinkers require cream and sugar to force it down. So, why do millions reach for a cup to start their morning? Caffeine rewards the user with a sense of increased energy, mental alertness, and forced wakefulness, which prompts continued use regardless of taste. An 8-ounce cup of brewed coffee can contain 150 milligrams of caffeine, while lattes and cappuccinos usually contain about half of that. Sodas can have anywhere from 30 to 70 milligrams of caffeine, which is still a pretty good jolt.[12] And to put it in perspective, most energy drinks contain 500 milligrams of caffeine. With tiredness sent packing with any of these drinks, it's not surprising caffeine dependency can settle in quickly.

Unfortunately, as with so many psychoactive drugs, regular caffeine use produces tolerance as well as dependence. One cup of coffee no longer provides the artificial lift, so the caffeine drinker pours another cup (or buys another caffeinated soda). And then another. If you take in 200 or more milligrams of caffeine per day, you will probably experience withdrawal symptoms on a day you go without. Caffeine withdrawal includes headache, agitation, and tiredness, and the intensity of the withdrawal is tied directly to the normal daily amount of caffeine ingested. When the coffee pot runs dry, even mild-mannered tempers end on a short fuse.

I greatly underestimated the power of caffeine dependence early in my teaching career. It was my turn to start the 100-cup coffeemaker in the teachers' lounge by 7:00 A.M., and I simply forgot to do it. You've never seen so many adults become cranky so quickly, as withdrawal set in with no drinkable caffeine ready to go before teaching that first class. At lunch that day, a caffeine-deprived teacher jokingly suggested I be arrested for disorderly conduct. Harsh, but I got the message, and I never forgot again.

Although researchers have not found long-term damaging effects from small daily doses of caffeine (the equivalent of two small cups of coffee), you would be wise to avoid becoming dependent upon caffeine. Getting the sleep you need is infinitely better for your body (and attitude) than artificially stimulating a sleep-deprived brain.

Nicotine

Nicotine, the stimulant found in tobacco, ranks up there with alcohol and caffeine in the most used drug category. The stimulating effects of nicotine are similar to those of caffeine, but nicotine often enters the body in a cloud of thick, deadly smoke from a cigarette. Nicotine is extremely addictive and does not stay long in the body. For a nicotine-dependent smoker, this means lighting up frequently to sustain the effect. The statistics on smoking are bone-chilling:[13]

- In the U.S., 6000 teenagers will light up for the first time today.
- Of these, 3000 will develop a smoking habit and 1000 will die from smoking-related diseases.
- A full 37,000 nonsmokers will die this year from heart disease contracted by inhaling secondhand smoke.

"No I don't take any drugs, but I do have a $50 a day latte habit."

▲ **Excess Espresso**
Many adults have a caffeine dependency.

▲ **Drug Dependence?**
Caffeine dependence may occur with as little as two small cups of coffee (200 milligrams) per day. A single 8-ounce cup of coffee from Starbucks can contain 175 milligrams of caffeine.

nicotine Stimulant found in tobacco.

Smoker's Lung
The lung on the left was a healthy, normal lung. The lung on the right belonged to a smoker. We can't always see the damage smoking causes.

- Another 4000 nonsmokers will contract lung disease from secondhand smoke this year.
- Worldwide, the World Health Organization reports that close to 1 billion will likely die of tobacco use this century.[14]

Nearly 450,000 smokers will die in the U.S. this year alone because of their tobacco use. The good news about smoking, if that's possible, is that we've seen a 90 percent decline in the number of adults who smoke or chew tobacco (also a deadly habit) over the past 40 years,[15] and 81 percent of smokers want to quit.[16] Nicotine replacement therapies, where nicotine comes into the body through chewing gum, nasal sprays, or patches worn on the skin, have helped thousands kick the tobacco habit.

E-cigarettes, officially known as electronic nicotine delivery systems (ENDS), have become a popular alternative to smoking actual cigarettes in recent years. Vaporized nicotine replaces the smoke with e-cigarettes. The U.S. Surgeon General has noted a huge increase (over 900 percent) in the number of teens who have taken up vaping as an alternative to smoking tobacco. Unfortunately, research suggests that inhaling nicotine vapors poses its own health risks. One recent study showed that vaping can trigger immune system responses that result in inflammatory lung diseases such as bronchitis and cystic fibrosis. E-cigarettes were not available to the public until 2004, so the long-term effects are not known at this time. Your best bet, of course, is to steer clear of both cigarettes and e-cigarettes.

Cocaine

cocaine Stimulant derived from the leaves of the coca plant.

For centuries, some South American people have chewed the leaves of the coca plant for medicinal and religious purposes, as well as to increase endurance. It wasn't until the 1850s that scientists identified, purified, and named the active ingredient—**cocaine,** a stimulant derived from the leaves of the coca plant.[17] In the 1880s, Americans used cocaine as a surgical anesthetic, among other medical uses.

Sigmund Freud prescribed cocaine in the early 1900s as a treatment for depression and chronic fatigue. He reversed his stance after discovering cocaine's horrible side effects, which include dependence, tolerance, and depression after you quit taking it.

Like Freud, Coca-Cola initially endorsed cocaine. During the late 1800s, the company started adding about 60 milligrams of the active ingredient from the coca plant to every serving. A long-running Coke advertising campaign used to identify the sweet soda as "the real thing." Well, from 1896 to 1904, Coke was indeed the real thing. The company later changed the formula, replacing cocaine with caffeine.

Coca Leaves
Cocaine is extracted from leaves like these.

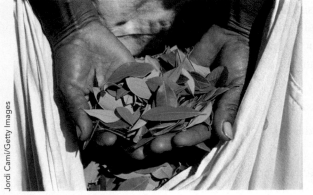

During the opioid epidemic in 1910, President William Howard Taft labeled cocaine public enemy number one; and soon after that, the drug was banned. Cocaine made a regrettable comeback in the late 1970s, with the introduction of inexpensive cocaine crystals called *crack.*

Cocaine and crack cocaine produce a strong euphoric effect but an even stronger crash. The user is instantly dependent, craving more cocaine to temporarily overcome the crash. All this places considerable strain on the cardiovascular system, which in some cases leads to instant death. Crack and cocaine users also can experience frightening feelings of paranoia and suspicion.

Amphetamines

I grew up hearing about **amphetamines** called *speed* or *uppers,* words that still characterize amphetamines' stimulating effects. What I didn't grow up hearing about was the cheaper and more dangerous amphetamine derivative, *methamphetamine* (also called *meth, crystal meth,* and *crank*).

Amphetamines' effects include restlessness, high blood pressure, insomnia, agitation, loss of appetite, and a state of hyperalertness. As with most stimulants, tolerance builds quickly, and to get high, longtime amphetamine abusers have been known to take doses 10 times the amount that would be lethal for a first-time user.[18]

Methamphetamine is more potent than regular amphetamines. And crystal meth, or ice (there's actually no end of nicknames for this drug), is to methamphetamine as crack is to cocaine. A major difference is that ice stays in your system much longer than crack cocaine. Drug researcher Robert Julien[19] warns of methamphetamine's dangers by using the following analogy: When referring to fast runners who help improve a team's chances of victory, football, soccer, and track coaches often use the colorful figure of speech *speed kills*. But for high doses of methamphetamine, *speed kills* is not merely a figure of speech.

> **amphetamines** Drugs that stimulate neural activity, speeding up body functions.
>
> **ecstasy** Also called MDMA, a hallucinogenic stimulant that produces lowered inhibitions, pleasant feelings, and greater acceptance of others.

Ecstasy

The hallucinogenic stimulant **ecstasy** (the street name for MDMA, or methylenedioxymethamphetamine) produces lowered inhibitions, pleasant feelings, and greater acceptance of others. Ecstasy was first manufactured more than 80 years ago, but this amphetamine derivative experienced a rebirth of sorts in the late 1990s. It is closely associated with rave-type dances, where hundreds of partygoers pack in shoulder to shoulder and dance to techno music for most of the night. The stimulating effects of the drug enable dancers to maintain the frenzied pace longer than they normally could.

The drug is seductive because it is relatively inexpensive, but its physiological and mental costs can be extremely high. Even moderate users may experience *permanent* brain damage, losing memory, concentration, and verbal reasoning skills.[20]

> **Dance Till You Drop?**
> The long-term consequences of taking ecstasy include permanent brain damage and memory loss.

Leelu Morris/Getty Images

MAKE IT STICK!

1. Two of the most commonly used stimulants in cultures around the world are

    a. beer and wine.
    b. marijuana and hashish.
    c. cocaine and tobacco.
    d. nicotine and caffeine.

2. A person who usually buys one coffee drink on the way to work in the morning but then starts feeling tired and sluggish unless she drinks another one after lunch is experiencing

    a. tolerance to caffeine.
    b. depression from lack of stimulant.
    c. cravings for amphetamines.
    d. lowered inhibitions.

3. Research shows that about 6000 teenagers in the U.S. will smoke their first cigarette today. About how many of these teens will die of smoking-related diseases?

    a. 1000   c. 100
    b. 500   d. 50

Hallucinogens

 10-4 What are the physiological and psychological effects of hallucinogens?

hallucinogens Psychedelic (mind-manifesting) drugs, such as LSD, that distort perceptions and evoke sensory images in the absence of sensory input.

LSD (lysergic acid diethylamide) Powerful hallucinogenic drug; also known as acid.

Hallucinogens—sometimes called *psychedelics*—are drugs that distort perceptions and evoke sensory images in the absence of corresponding sensory input. The most commonly used hallucinogens were first made in a laboratory. Most labs producing these drugs today are illegal. Let's take a closer look at one hallucinogen, LSD.

LSD

Weird Science
Albert Hoffman, a chemist, discovered and was the first to ingest LSD. ▼

VIRGINIA/ullstein bild via Getty Images

LSD (lysergic acid diethylamide) is a powerful hallucinogenic drug that is sometimes called *acid*. The first LSD experience by a human was an accident. Albert Hoffman, a Swiss chemist who first synthesized LSD in 1938, accidentally ingested the drug in April 1943 and found himself "seized by a peculiar sensation of vertigo and restlessness. Objects, as well as the shape of my associates in the laboratory, appeared to undergo optical changes."[21] Hoffman's experience is similar to that of those who have taken an acid trip, where visual distortions, detachment from reality, and panic are common. Acid trips vary from person to person. Some people experience a mildly pleasant or unpleasant reaction; others have nightmarish or deadly experiences. Panic-stricken LSD users, unable to detect the difference between reality and fabrication, can be dangerous not only to themselves but also to others.

Consciousness-altering LSD is made in the laboratory, but other hallucinogens are found in nature. *Mescaline* (from the peyote cactus) and *psilocybin* (from certain mushrooms) both produce perceptual disruption of time and space. Some states allow the use of these drugs for centuries-old religious ceremonies, but all states outlaw them for recreational use.

MAKE IT STICK!

1. The main difference between hallucinogens and the other drug categories is

   a. withdrawal effects are not produced by long-term use of hallucinogens, but they are associated with stimulant and depressant use.

   b. stimulants and depressants do not produce tolerance, but hallucinogens do.

   c. hallucinogen users experience withdrawal effects immediately after using the drug for the first time.

   d. hallucinogens interfere with perceptions of sensations instead of speeding up or slowing down the nervous system.

2. The primary hallucinogen discussed in the text was developed

   a. to help treat stimulant addictions.

   b. in a chemistry laboratory.

   c. to protect stimulant users from withdrawal effects.

   d. for deliberate use.

3. LSD has been around for about how long?

   a. 80 years or so

   b. Since about the 1960s

   c. Centuries

   d. Nobody really knows.

Opioids

 10-5 What are the physiological and psychological effects of opioids?

Opioids in the form of prescription painkillers have been in the news a lot lately, and not for good reasons. The opioids classification includes drugs prescribed to kill pain (for instance, oxycodone, hydrocodone, codeine, and morphine, heroin, and synthetic opioids such as fentanyl).[22]

Whether taken in prescription pill form or injected with a needle, opioids work by attaching to receptors in the brain and reducing the perception of pain. It is estimated that over 250 million prescriptions for pain-killing opioid pills were written in 2015. Overuse results in the feeling of euphoria—and near-instant addiction. Four out of five heroin users report that they got their start by using prescription pain-killing pills such as Oxycontin and Vicodin.[23] Clearly, opioids are very addictive.

Fentanyl is a synthetic opioid that is anywhere from 50 to 100 times stronger than morphine. An accidental overdose of this drug is what killed singer–songwriter Prince in 2016.[24]

MAKE IT STICK!

1. Which of the following is a synthetic opioid?
   a. Fentanyl
   b. Heroin
   c. Morphine
   d. Codeine
2. True or false? Fentanyl is stronger than morphine.
3. True or false? Opioids are very addictive.

Marijuana

 10-6 What are the physiological and psychological effects of marijuana?

Marijuana was used to make rope as far back as 8000 B.C. It was used for medical purposes in China in 5000 B.C. and for religious purposes in India in 2000 B.C. It comes from the *cannabis sativa*, or hemp, plant and is called *ganja, sinsemilla, pot, hash, Mary Jane, dope, weed, bhang,* and many more names. Most often, it's called **marijuana**—the leaves, stems, and flowers from the hemp plant. When smoked, marijuana lowers inhibitions and produces feelings of relaxation and mild euphoria.

Marijuana doesn't fit neatly into any of the categories we've discussed thus far for several reasons:

- Its behavioral effects can be similar to those of low doses of alcohol, but different in that high doses do not suppress breathing and are not lethal.

- Compared with LSD, it produces only mild hallucinogenic experiences.

- Its chemical structure does not resemble that of hallucinogens.

marijuana Leaves, stems, resin, and flowers from the hemp plant; when smoked, lowers inhibitions and produces feelings of relaxation and mild euphoria.

For these reasons, we've given marijuana its own category in this module.

Marijuana's active ingredient, *delta-9-tetrahydrocannabinol (THC)*, was isolated in 1964. When smoked or ingested as an edible, THC heightens sensitivity to tastes, smells, and sounds. THC can stay in a regular user's body for months, producing a kind of reverse tolerance effect. That is, the user can take smaller subsequent doses to induce the high feeling once again because of the amounts of THC already stored in the body. Withdrawal is unpleasant and occurs within 48 hours of nonuse. Symptoms include depression, insomnia, nausea, cramping, and irritability.

As with most psychoactive drugs, marijuana's temporary pleasures come at a long-term cost:

- Frequent marijuana users are at higher risk to experience depression and possibly schizophrenia.[25]
- Pot smoke is much harder on your lungs than cigarette smoke.[26]
- Brain cell loss accelerates with large doses.[27]
- Memory is still impaired long after marijuana's effect has worn off.[28]
- Marijuana seems to suppress the immune system, making it harder for your body to fight off disease and infection.[29]

There is evidence suggesting THC counteracts the nausea accompanying cancer's chemotherapy treatments, seizures from epilepsy, and the terrible side effects of AIDS. Because of these and other findings, more than half of all states have passed laws allowing marijuana to be administered under a physician's supervision for medical conditions. Also, states including California, Colorado, Nevada, Massachusetts, and Oregon have legalized recreational marijuana use for adults. With tax rates set at around 20 percent, the state of Colorado raised over $200 million in tax revenue from the sale of marijuana in 2017. Attitudes toward marijuana use appear to be changing in these and others states as well.

MAKE IT STICK!

1. Which of the following most accurately describes some long-term effects of marijuana use?

   a. Lung damage, brain cell loss, and memory impairment
   b. Increased tolerance to the drug because the active ingredient does not stay in the body long
   c. Heart damage and repeated perceptual distortions
   d. Restlessness, high blood pressure, loss of appetite, and hyperalertness

2. True or false? THC, when ingested by regular users, lowers sensitivity to tastes and smells, and only stays in the user's body for a week.

3. The legalization of marijuana sales to adults in some states is evidence of

   a. a lowering of tolerance to THC.
   b. the decreased strength of THC in marijuana.
   c. increasing pressure to pass laws that criminalize marijuana use.
   d. changing attitudes toward marijuana.

Prevention

 10-7 What factors help prevent the use of dangerous psychoactive drugs?

Consider these questions:

1. Is it true that the more educated you are, the less likely you are to abuse illegal drugs?

2. Is hopelessness related to dependence?

3. Is genetics a factor in the development of dependence?

4. Are your peers' attitudes toward drugs important?

An Ounce of Prevention
One of the best ways to avoid drinking and smoking is to hang out with friends who don't smoke or drink.

The answer to all of these questions is *yes*.

1. *Education is related to drug use.* Only 6 percent of people with a 4-year college degree smoke cigarettes. Roughly 15 percent of U.S. college dropouts smoke cigarettes, as do a whopping 42 percent of high school dropouts.[30]

2. *Hope matters.* Those who believe their life is meaningless are more likely to take drugs.[31]

3. *Genetics plays a role.* Geneticists have, for example, found a gene occurring more often among alcohol-dependent people than among others.[32]

4. *Peers count.* If the friends you hang out with *never* light up or drink alcohol, there is a good chance you won't either.

If a person is already dependent on some psychoactive substance, effective treatment is essential. However, prevention—never getting started—is even more important. There are three vital sides to prevention's triangle:

1. A clear understanding of the painful, long-term costs of psychoactive drug use, despite pleasurable, short-term rewards (see **Table 10.2**)

2. Positive environments that increase self-esteem and foster determination in teens

3. Associating with peers who are adept at saying *no* or willing to learn how to refuse

TABLE 10.2   A Guide to Selected Psychoactive Drugs

Drug	Type	Pleasurable Effects	Adverse Effects
Alcohol	Depressant	Initial high followed by relaxation and disinhibition	Depression, memory loss, organ damage, and impaired reactions
Heroin	Depressant	Rush of euphoria and relief from pain	Depressed physiology and agonizing withdrawal
Caffeine	Stimulant	Increased alertness and wakefulness	Anxiety, restlessness, and insomnia in high doses; uncomfortable withdrawal
Methamphetamine	Stimulant	Euphoria, alertness, and energy	Irritability, insomnia, hypertension, and seizures
Cocaine	Stimulant	Rush of euphoria, confidence, and energy	Cardiovascular stress, suspiciousness, and depressive crash
Nicotine	Stimulant	Arousal and relaxation; sense of well- being	Heart disease and cancer
Ecstasy (MDMA)	Stimulant and mild hallucinogen	Euphoria and disinhibition	Brain damage, depression, and fatigue
Marijuana	Mild hallucinogen	Enhanced sensation, relief of pain, distortion of time, and relaxation	Disrupted memory and lung damage from smoke

Drug use among high school seniors dropped steadily from 1979 to 1992, but as **Figure 10.3** indicates, marijuana use rose for several years after that.[33] However, peer groups who disapprove, an understanding of the physiological and psychological costs of drug use, and positive self-regard could help renew a downward trend. The long-term biological and psychological effects of drugs like marijuana clearly indicate that use, and the temporary impairment that comes with it, are not worth the risk.

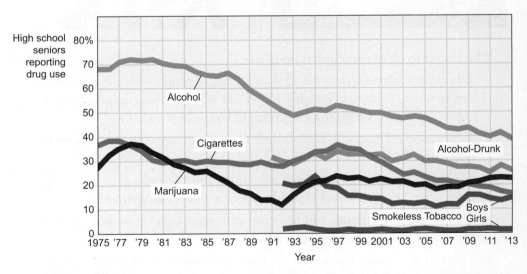

FIGURE 10.3
Self-Reports of Drug Use Among High School Seniors
Reported use of alcohol, marijuana, and cocaine declined among high school seniors from 1979 to 1992. Marijuana use partially rebounded after 1992, with drug paraphernalia becoming easier to purchase in local stores. Since then, however, it has joined alcohol and cocaine use in declining or holding steady. (Data from Johnston et al., 2009.)

MAKE IT STICK!

1. True or false? Research indicates that feelings of hopelessness are unrelated to predicting whether a person will become a drug user.

2. True or false? If the friends you hang out with *never* smoke cigarettes, the chances you'll smoke are very slim.

Module 10 Summary and Assessment

Psychoactive Drugs

 10-1 What are psychoactive drugs, and what is dependence?

- Psychoactive drugs are chemical substances that alter mood, behavior, or perceptions.

- Drug dependence is a state of physiological or psychological need to take more of a drug after continued use.

 10-2 What are the physiological and psychological effects of drinking alcohol?

- Alcohol is a depressant, so its main effects are to reduce neural activity and slow body functions. Alcohol slows the parts of the brain responsible for controlling inhibitions and making judgments.

- Alcohol is the most commonly used depressant and is the second most used psychoactive drug. Most people use alcohol responsibly, but recreational use of alcohol can get out of hand, leading to dependence, health problems, accidental injuries, or death.

 10-3 What are the physiological and psychological effects of stimulants?

- Stimulants excite neural activity and speed up body functions.

- Caffeine is used by more than 80 percent of adults, and regular use produces both tolerance and dependence.

- Nicotine produces effects similar to those of caffeine, but is more addictive.

- Cocaine is a powerful stimulant derived from the leaves of the coca plant. Dependency occurs instantly after the first use, and its users crave more cocaine to temporarily overcome withdrawal symptoms.

- Amphetamines cause restlessness, high blood pressure, insomnia, agitation, loss of appetite, and a state of hyper-alertness. Tolerance builds quickly, and longtime amphetamine abusers may take doses 10 times the amount that would be lethal for a first-time user.

- Ecstasy is a hallucinogenic stimulant that produces lowered inhibitions, pleasant feelings, and greater acceptance of others. Repeated use may result in brain damage, possibly affecting memory, concentration, and reasoning skills.

 10-4 What are the physiological and psychological effects of hallucinogens?

- Hallucinogens cause changes in how we perceive the world. Different hallucinogens produce different kinds of distortions of reality. Some people may experience mild or moderate hallucinations that they report as pleasant, but some hallucinations can be disturbing and even harmful.

- Repeated use of any hallucinogen can affect cognitive abilities, including memory, concentration, and communication skills.

 10-5 What are the physiological and psychological effects of opioids?

- Opioids reduce the brain's perception of pain.

- Opioids are highly addictive and can be ingested legally through prescription pills and illegally through heroin use.

 10-6 What are the physiological and psychological effects of marijuana?

- Marijuana lowers inhibitions and produces feelings of relaxation and mild euphoria.

- Marijuana doesn't fit well into the other categories of psychoactive drugs.

- Marijuana's active ingredient, delta-9-tetrahydrocannabinol (THC), heightens sensitivity to tastes, smells, and sounds. Repeated use can result in a reverse tolerance effect because THC remains in the body for months. Regular use can damage the lungs, accelerate brain cell loss, impair memory, and suppress the immune system.

- Withdrawal symptoms can include depression, insomnia, nausea, cramping, and irritability.

 10-7 What factors help prevent the use of dangerous psychoactive drugs?

- Risk factors for damaging drug use include dropping out of school, feelings of hopelessness, genetic history of drug use, and peers who use drugs.

- An understanding of the harmful long-term effects of drugs, a positive environment, and non-drug-using peers help prevent young people from starting drug use.

Summative Assessment

1. Which of the following has been shown to help prevent people from starting drug use?

   a. Hanging out with people who smoke a lot

   b. An oppressive environment

   c. Understanding the long-term effects of drugs

   d. Dropping out of school

2. What is one of the common threads running through several factors that prevent alcoholism relapse?

   a. Spirituality

   b. Supervision

   c. Compliance

   d. Positive emotion

3. Which of the following is true about alcohol?

   a. Alcohol impairs memory.

   b. Alcohol helps you dream.

   c. Chemically speaking, women break down alcohol faster than men.

   d. Alcohol enhances one's ability to make decisions.

4. Moderate use of _____ can cause permanent brain damage.

   a. nicotine

   b. caffeine

   c. ecstasy

   d. tobacco

5. Which of the following is primarily a stimulant?

   a. Alcohol

   b. Cocaine

   c. Marijuana

   d. LSD

6. Which of the following would most likely be classified as a hallucinogen?

   a. Nicotine

   b. LSD

   c. Alcohol

   d. Amphetamines

7. The drug known as *crystal meth* is classified as a(n)

   a. hallucinogen.

   b. opioid.

   c. depressant.

   d. stimulant.

8. About how long does it take cocaine users to develop a sense of dependency on the drug?

   a. About a month

   b. Never

   c. Almost no time

   d. About a week

9. What do we call a state of physiological or psychological need to take a drug after continued use?

   a. Dependence

   b. Cognition

   c. Stimulation

   d. Depression

10. About how many people on Earth will die of tobacco use in this century?

    a. about 1 million

    b. about 1 billion

    c. about 10 million

    d. about 100 million

KEY TERMS

psychoactive drug, p. 149

dependence, p. 149

withdrawal, p. 149

tolerance, p. 150

depressants, p. 151

stimulants, p. 154

caffeine, p. 154

nicotine, p. 155

cocaine, p. 156

amphetamines, p. 157

ecstasy, p. 157

hallucinogens, p. 158

lysergic acid diethylamide (LSD), p. 158

marijuana, p. 159

Hypnosis and Other States of Consciousness

Relax . . . you are getting verrrry sleeeepy. Is a swinging watch necessary for hypnosis? If not, what does produce this remarkable state of consciousness? Let's get comfortable and learn about hypnosis, relaxation, and meditation.

Learning Goals

11-1 Identify the relationship between dual processing and differing states of consciousness.

11-2 Debate whether hypnosis is really a different state of consciousness.

11-3 Describe the power of hypnotic suggestions.

11-4 Evaluate the claims of different applications of hypnosis, such as whether hypnosis can improve our memory or our physical state.

11-5 Describe the benefits of relaxation and meditation.

States of Consciousness

 11-1 How does dual processing help explain differing states of consciousness?

What are you doing right now? Yes, I know you're reading, but what else is going on? I bet you're breathing. You're also pumping blood, maintaining a sense of balance, controlling the temperature of your body, listening to sounds in your environment, blinking occasionally to keep the surface of your eyes clean and moist, digesting the remnants of your last meal, and literally hundreds of other things. Pretty amazing, isn't it?

The nature of **consciousness** is to process information on two tracks. A tiny amount of information is on the conscious (or explicit) track. This is the limited amount of information that you are aware of at any given point in time; it is the information appearing on your mental screen. A far larger amount of information is dealt with on an unconscious (also called implicit) track— that is, without awareness. Your brain is continually monitoring and adjusting behind the scenes to free up your awareness for the things you want to focus on. It's much like when an executive hires an administrative assistant to take care of the numerous routine tasks that must be accomplished in the course of the day. This enables the executive to turn her attention to a limited number of high-priority tasks, confident that the mundane but necessary work is being

consciousness
Awareness of yourself and your environment.

FIGURE 11.1 ▲
Change Blindness
Imagine yourself in the position of the white-haired gentleman. The man with the map in the left image has just asked you, a stranger, for directions. As you are talking, two rude workers (actually confederates of the researcher) carrying a door walk right between you and the man who needs directions. As the door passes between you, the man with the map quickly changes places with the second door carrier. Would you notice the change? Two out of three people in this experiment did not!

dual processing The principle that information is often processed on separate conscious and unconscious tracks at the same time.

taken care of. This ability to process information both consciously and unconsciously at the same time is called **dual processing**.

One fascinating result of this dual processing is *change blindness,* our failure to notice changes in our environment because the conscious awareness track of our mind is so narrow. Would you notice if a stranger you were giving directions to suddenly changed into a different stranger?[1] Remarkably, two-thirds did not when put into this situation (see **Figure 11.1**). The narrow conscious track of the mind is occupied with providing the directions, so the change in the environment, if it is noticed at all, registers only in the unconscious mind.

In this module, we'll explore some of the more interesting variations of consciousness. Hypnosis may or may not involve a form of dual processing—research has yet to provide a definite answer. Then we'll look at relaxation and meditation, both methods of using our conscious awareness of self to improve our lives.

MAKE IT STICK!

1. True or false? Dual processing allows us to consciously think about two different things at the same time.

2. An example of information that we process unconsciously is _____.

3. The explicit track of the mind is

   a. unconscious
   b. dual
   c. blind
   d. conscious

Hypnosis

 11-2 Is hypnosis really a different state of consciousness?

Ever been hypnotized? For several years, my school's post prom party has featured an entertainer who uses hypnosis as part of his act. Students always return to class on the following Monday tired but full of questions about what they've seen and, in some cases, what they've experienced. Let's look at how psychology can help us understand what happens during hypnosis.

Geoff Moore/REX/Shutterstock

Equally Reliable?
Stage hypnotists such as the one who suggested these students were on the beach in need of sunscreen fascinate their audiences with many of the same techniques researchers examine in the laboratory.

What Is Hypnosis?

Hypnosis is a social interaction in which a hypnotist makes suggestions about perceptions, feelings, thoughts, or behaviors and the person experiencing hypnosis follows those suggestions. For example, a hypnotist might suggest that a young man is at a funny movie, and he begins to laugh heartily. Or a hypnotist might suggest that a woman's arm was filling with helium and her arm would rise in the air. Researchers, therapists, and entertainers—and most of the rest of us—are interested in why these suggestions seem to have such power over people. As you will see, there is plenty of evidence that hypnotic effects are real—they are not simply a matter of a hoax or faking it—but there is disagreement about what causes these effects. Psychological scientists have proposed two key explanations: social influence theory and divided consciousness theory.

Social Influence Theory As evidence, supporters of social influence theory note that no special physical condition marks hypnosis as anything other than normal consciousness—the natural state of awareness we experience when we're fully awake and alert.[2, 3] Our social environment can indeed have a huge effect on our behavior and experiences. One day this year, I was feeling fine until my wife said my voice sounded scratchy and asked if my throat hurt. All of a sudden, I started to feel as though I was becoming ill. I never did get sick, so it was apparently only my wife's suggestive question that made me feel less than 100 percent.

Peer pressure, one of the many forms of social influence, can lead people to behave in ways they wouldn't normally. A mob mentality, for example, may lead otherwise law-abiding sports fans to engage in destructive behavior while "celebrating" a big win. Social influence is also apparent in religious cults. A charismatic leader may seem to cast a spell on followers, who then behave in ways they would have had difficulty imagining before the cult experience.

Is hypnosis governed by similar social pressures? Certainly the hypnotist's status and authority increase the likelihood that people will be influenced by suggestions. And hypnotized people often want to appear cooperative, which increases their suggestibility. Keep in mind that neither the hypnotist nor the person hypnotized is necessarily faking it—both may believe strongly in the powers of hypnosis.

hypnosis Social interaction in which a hypnotist makes suggestions about perceptions, feelings, thoughts, or behaviors and those suggestions are followed.

social influence theory
Theory that powerful social influences can produce a state of hypnosis.

divided consciousness theory Theory that during hypnosis our consciousness splits so that one aspect of consciousness is not aware of the role other parts are playing.

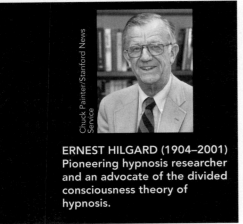

ERNEST HILGARD (1904–2001)
Pioneering hypnosis researcher and an advocate of the divided consciousness theory of hypnosis.

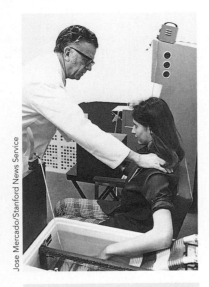

Hypnosis as Divided Consciousness ▲
Ernest Hilgard has demonstrated that some part of the consciousness of hypnotized people, like this young woman, remains aware of pain (caused here by ice water) even though such participants behave as though pain does not exist. Hilgard called the part that remained aware the hidden observer.

In fact, the stronger their beliefs, the more likely they are to experience results—real results. The strongest support for the **social influence theory** is that behaviors produced with hypnosis can often be produced in other ways. You may hypnotize me into believing I have a suggested illness, but I might also acquire this belief by reading a list of symptoms or by seeing a program on television. I might even succumb to an offhand comment like the one made by my wife.

Divided Consciousness Theory Some psychologists who oppose social influence theory believe hypnosis is a state of **divided consciousness**, that our consciousness splits so that one aspect of consciousness is not aware of the role other parts are playing. We are all capable of dividing our consciousness to some extent. When I go out for a long run, for example, I sometimes get so caught up in thinking about things that a mile goes by unnoticed. Some tiny part of my consciousness continues to monitor traffic, curbs I might trip over, and the route so that the rest of my mind can spin free on other topics.

Ernest Hilgard argued that hypnosis is a more dramatic form of this divided consciousness.[4, 5] He stumbled on this idea while demonstrating hypnosis to his class at Stanford University one day. He used a suggestion to produce deafness in a hypnotized student and then challenged the class to prove that the young man was not deaf. Class members tried the sorts of things you probably would, such as sneaking up behind the young man and making loud noises and insulting him in hopes of getting a response. Nothing worked until one student asked if there was a part of the hypnotized person that was still listening. Hilgard was skeptical, but he asked the student to raise his finger if some part of him could still hear. Up went the finger. The odd thing is that even the person did not know why he had raised his finger until it was explained to him after the demonstration. The part that could hear, which Hilgard called the *hidden observer,* was so effectively divided from the rest of his consciousness that even the person was unaware of it.

The key difference between the two explanations of hypnosis is this: Social influence theory says that hypnosis is a result of *external* social variables. Divided consciousness theory says that hypnosis is the result of an exaggerated division of *internal* consciousness. It's possible, of course, that both positions may be partially correct. Hypnosis is complex enough that several variables may be interacting to produce the effects.[6]

By now you may be wondering just how someone enters into this complex state of being hypnotized. Let's consider some of the techniques used.

MAKE IT STICK!

1. True or false? Social influence theory views hypnosis as an altered state of consciousness.

2. A difference between the two theories of hypnosis is that social influence theory sees hypnosis as governed by _____ forces and divided consciousness theory sees hypnosis as governed by _____ forces.

   a. external; internal   c. suggestive; biological
   b. cognitive; behavioral   d. natural; supernatural

3. Ernest Hilgard hypnotized a student and suggested he was deaf. Although the student behaved as though he were deaf in interactions with the class, he raised his finger when asked if he could still hear. This is evidence for _____ theory.

Hypnosis Techniques

 11-3 How powerful are hypnotic suggestions?

Have you seen hypnosis depicted in cartoons? Perhaps the hypnotist was swinging a pocket watch on a chain back and forth (like I am at the beginning of this module) or using a spiraling disc. The zombie-like hypnotized person muttered, "Yes, master," and lurched forward with outstretched arms to do the hypnotist's bidding. As you may have guessed, the reality of hypnotic induction is far different. Inducing hypnosis requires nothing more than the hypnotist's voice and is so easily accomplished that the Federal Communication Commission set up rules preventing the procedure from being broadcast on television. A hypnotist performing on TV could hypnotize people at home in their living rooms. Stage hypnotists do experience this problem. They frequently find that some members of the audience become as deeply hypnotized as the volunteers on stage.

There is nothing magical or mystical in the process—the "secret" is a calm, rhythmic tone in the hypnotist's voice, which becomes a focal point for the person's attention. The hypnotist begins by giving easy, logical suggestions: Your eyes are getting tired. You feel very relaxed. Most people find the state of hypnosis to be relaxing, so these suggestions are particularly easy to follow. Continuing to focus the person's attention, the hypnotist then gradually moves on to more difficult tasks.

Hypnosis is sometimes falsely characterized as a deep sleep. During hypnosis, people sometimes do physically slump in their chairs. However, it is possible to talk, move, and open your eyes while hypnotized.

Certain tests help determine in advance who may be a good candidate for hypnosis. The Stanford Hypnotic Susceptibility Scale, in which people respond to a series of suggestions (for example, that your hands are glued together and you cannot separate them), is one such test. This test indicates that most people are moderately hypnotizable. About 10 percent are poor candidates, about 10 percent are highly hypnotizable, and the rest fall in the middle (see **Figure 11.2**). The higher you score on this scale, the more easily you can be hypnotized and the more easily you will respond to suggestions. In general, those who are imaginative and prone to fantasy are better suited for hypnosis.[7]

Puffy, red, tired eyes? Heavy eyelids? Getting heavier? Heavier. Completely relaxed now. On the count of 10, you will awaken fresh, invigorated and ready to support our following sponsors . . .

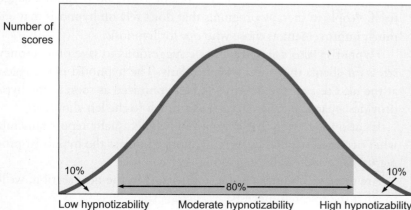

FIGURE 11.2
Stanford Hypnotic Susceptibility Scale
Can everyone be hypnotized? People differ in how susceptible they are to hypnosis. About one-tenth of all people are excellent candidates for hypnosis, and an equal number are difficult to hypnotize. Most people are moderately susceptible to hypnosis.

Hypnotizability also depends on the circumstances of the session. It is more difficult to achieve hypnosis in front of an audience than in a one-on-one private office session. Less susceptible individuals who do not become hypnotized on stage may respond differently in an office setting.

Hypnotic Suggestions   The key technique in hypnosis is making suggestions that the hypnotized person follows. These suggestions can influence a variety of behaviors, sensations, thoughts, and emotions.[8] This means that hypnotized people can be made to flap their arms like birds, hallucinate the smell of roses, believe that it's midnight in the middle of the day, or be angry about something that supposedly happened at school. The hypnotist creates a new and interesting reality. Sometimes the results are entertaining, which explains the popularity of stage hypnotists like the one who performs at my school's post prom party.

How powerful are these suggestions? Could they lead you to do something against your will? Could an evildoer hypnotize you to commit crimes on her behalf? The answers to these questions are complicated. In one study,[9] hypnotized people dipped their hands into what they were told was acid and then threw the "acid" into the face of another person. Proof that hypnosis could be used to do evil deeds, right? Not necessarily. There are other explanations for this behavior. Perhaps the hypnotized participants knew that because they were involved in an experiment they wouldn't be asked to do something truly harmful. Or perhaps our natural tendency to obey an authority figure could by itself produce these results. When nonhypnotized people were asked to engage in the same acid-throwing behavior, they were just as likely as the hypnotized people to do so. This seems to indicate that hypnosis alone does not cause the behavior. Hypnosis *can* lead people to do things they otherwise wouldn't, but so can powerful suggestions of any kind.

Posthypnotic Suggestions   Some hypnotic instructions, called **posthypnotic suggestions,** are carried out by the individual *after* the hypnosis session has ended. Entertainers may, for example, make a posthypnotic suggestion that a person bark like a dog on a prearranged signal after returning to the audience. Therapists also use this technique to help clients lose weight or with some other objective. The hypnotist may plant a posthypnotic suggestion that certain high-calorie foods will taste terrible, like rancid meat. Research indicates that people with low hypnotic susceptibility benefit just as much from posthypnotic suggestions as do those with high hypnotic susceptibility.[10] This finding suggests that the therapist's attention may be as important as the posthypnotic suggestion itself. People in therapy programs that don't rely on hypnosis may show as much improvement as those who opt for hypnosis.

Hypnotists also use posthypnotic suggestions to save time, money, and stress for clients they meet with regularly. The hypnotist may suggest that at the next session the person will be hypnotized as soon as the hypnotist provides a particular signal, such as a touch to the left shoulder.

It's also interesting that hypnotized people usually report remembering what occurred while they were hypnotized unless the hypnotist produces *posthypnotic amnesia* by suggesting they will not.

Are these techniques reliable and useful? In the next section, we'll turn to what the research suggests.

posthypnotic suggestion
Hypnotic suggestion that the person will carry out after the hypnosis session has ended.

Courtesy of Kim Whitton

A Magical Cure? ▲
Many people turn to hypnosis for help to stop smoking or lose weight. How effective are these programs? It turns out that people enrolled in programs that don't use hypnosis fare just as well.

MAKE IT STICK!

1. Briefly describe three suggestions that might be acted upon under the influence of hypnosis.

2. While hypnotized, Kristi is told she will stand on one foot when she hears the word *flamingo*. After hypnosis, Kristi does stand on one foot when the hypnotist says *flamingo*. This is an example of

   a. divided consciousness.   c. posthypnotic suggestion.
   b. social influence theory.   d. posthypnotic amnesia.

3. True or false? Hypnosis is very similar to deep sleep.

Applications of Hypnosis

 11-4 Can hypnosis improve our memory or our physical state?

Memory and pain control are the two bookends of hypnosis. On the one side, researchers are skeptical of claims that hypnosis can enhance memory because the data does not support the claim. On the other side, data does support claims that hypnosis can help control pain. As you might imagine, other claims tend to fall somewhere in the middle of this bookshelf.

Hypnosis and Memory Many people believe that hypnosis is a good way to retrieve lost memories. The idea is that if memories can somehow be lost, hypnosis may provide a way to retrieve them from the subconscious (a proposed storehouse for ideas and memories you cannot easily access) or wherever else they may be hiding. This idea has appeared in the media so often that most college students agree that a person can accurately recall events from childhood while under hypnosis.[11] Some police departments have even used hypnosis to try to uncover details witnesses may have lost.

There *have* been instances when individuals recovered seemingly lost memories during hypnosis sessions. For example, Ed Ray, a bus driver who had been kidnapped and held captive with 26 children in 1976, was able, when hypnotized, to remember enough of the kidnappers' license plate to lead to an arrest.

However, we need to be cautious about generalizing from these specific cases. First, they are quite rare. Second, we cannot be sure that hypnosis was the reason for the retrieval—maybe the memory would have come back anyway. The most substantial problem is that hypnosis is a state of suggestibility. In an effort to please the hypnotist, the hypnotized person may inadvertently manufacture *untrue* details and then later be unable to distinguish the real from the unreal. This happens even without hypnosis because your brain stores memories in pieces, much like a jigsaw puzzle. (See modules 24 and 25 to learn more about memory.) When you try to retrieve a memory, your brain may not be able to locate all the pieces, and then it fills in the holes with plausible events that could have occurred. When this happens, psychologists say that you have constructed a false memory. Hypnosis increases the likelihood of constructing false memories and may give people a false sense of confidence in the accuracy of these "retrieved" memories.[12] Many courts now recognize the significant problems associated with using "hypnotically refreshed" memories and have banned testimony from witnesses who have been hypnotized.[13, 14, 15]

patrickheagney/Getty Images

Hypnosis and Memory ▲
The use of hypnosis to retrieve memories is controversial. Will this police hypnotist help the witness accurately recall the details of a crime or instead inadvertently suggest details that the witness will later be unable to distinguish from reality?

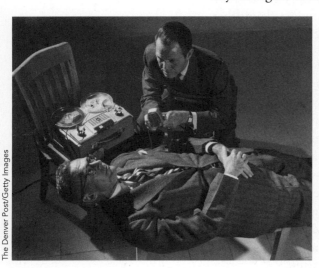

The Denver Post/Getty Images

Age Regression? ▲
The case of Bridey Murphy took hypnotic age regression to a new level in the 1950s. Murphy is a young Irish woman who "appeared" when a hypnotist regressed Virginia Tighe to a time before her birth, and Tighe began giving details of nineteenth-century life in Ireland. Is this evidence for reincarnation? Hardly. Investigators discovered that one of Tighe's childhood neighbors in Wisconsin was Bridey Murphy Corkell, who proved to be the source of much of the information Tighe reported when later hypnotized.

Other Hypnosis Claims Hypnosis has been used in a variety of therapeutic settings in which people have experienced relief with problems ranging from headaches to warts.[16] (See Psychology in the Real World: Hypnosis and Pain Control.) The problem is that we have no way of knowing for sure that hypnosis caused these improvements. Many studies have shown that people who receive treatment of *any* kind (even sugar pills) tend to show more improvement than those who receive no treatment, thanks to the power of our positive expectations. This is called the **placebo** effect. Hypnosis may function as a type of placebo—producing an effect simply because people expect it to do so. For example, in the study in which hypnosis proved beneficial in getting rid of warts, a control group given positive suggestions *without* hypnosis showed similar improvement.[17]

Researchers are particularly skeptical of two types of claims for the power of hypnosis: feats of strength and age regression. A favorite trick of those who believe feats of strength can be achieved through hypnosis is to have someone stand on an individual who stretches rigid and plank-like between two chairs. The problem is that this feat is also possible without hypnosis. *Age regression* under hypnosis is an attempt to turn back the clock to an earlier time in a person's life. Psychologists consider this feat equally unreliable. Hypnotically enhanced memories are not dependable. The hypnotist's suggestions could lead a person to unknowingly (but falsely) manufacture the regression to some earlier time. This happened in one study that tried to demonstrate how participants could be regressed to the day of their fourth birthday party, at which point they could remember the day of the week with great accuracy.[18] A follow-up analysis revealed that typical 4-year-olds don't even know what day of the week it is. The hypnotist in this case was actually communicating the correct answer to his participants by asking the days of the week in order (Is it Monday? Is it Tuesday?[19]). Because the hypnotist knew the correct answer, he may have inadvertently signaled that answer to the participants with slight changes in the inflection of his voice. In any case, hypnotic age regression could not have led the individuals to the correct answer because, as 4-year-olds, they wouldn't have known it.

Hypnosis remains one of the more fascinating topics studied by psychologists. Researchers may disagree on the best theory for explaining hypnosis, but they agree on one thing: We can be influenced by suggestions. With that in mind, please now think the following thoughts to yourself: Things are going quite well today. I'm enjoying my psychology class. The time I spend studying will be effective and productive!

MAKE IT STICK!

1. True or false? Hypnosis is a reliable method for recovering lost memories.

2. The most supported use of hypnosis in medicine is for the control of _____.

3. Expectations can sometimes produce real results. This is called the _____ effect.

PSYCHOLOGY IN THE REAL WORLD

Hypnosis and Pain Control

For a clear success story about the use of hypnosis, look no further than pain control. Here, there is solid evidence that hypnosis works. Holding your arm in ice water for 30 seconds or so generally produces intense discomfort. If you don't believe it, fill your sink with ice water and try it! Hypnotized people, however, report little pain under the same circumstances.[20, 21] Apparently, they are able to separate themselves from the pain they are experiencing, much as an injured athlete may be able to set aside feelings of pain until after the competition ends.

These pain management strategies have been applied to several real-life settings. For example, some dentists use light hypnosis to help their nervous patients relax and deal more effectively with discomfort. Hypnosis has also helped relieve chronic pain associated with arthritis, migraine headaches, and cancer.[22, 23] These techniques may allow people to avoid painkilling drugs, which often have unwanted side effects such as dependence and the loss of mental sharpness.

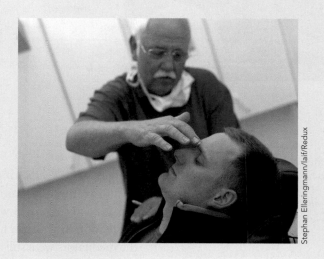
Stephan Elleringmann/laif/Redux

▲ **Hypnotic Experience**
Some dentists use hypnosis to help patients deal with anxiety and discomfort during dental procedures.

THINK ABOUT . . . Psychology in the Real World

1. What is an advantage of using hypnosis rather than drugs to control chronic pain?

2. How can the social influence theory explain the effectiveness of hypnosis to control pain?

3. How can the divided consciousness theory explain the effectiveness of hypnosis to control pain?

Relaxation and Meditation

 11-5 What are some benefits of relaxation and meditation?

Can we use conscious control of our bodies and our thoughts to improve our lives? The answer is *yes. Relaxation*, a state of calm, occurs when physical measures like muscle tension, breathing, blood pressure, and heart rate decline. One way of achieving this is through using meditation to control one's thoughts. These simple methods, such as focusing on breathing or a particular sound or image, require no equipment, no technology, and no medicine yet can relieve headaches, high blood pressure, anxiety, and sleep difficulties.[24, 25] In our busy lives, however, we often fail to take advantage of these timeless techniques to enhance well-being.

Sometimes, however, using these techniques can be the difference between life and death. One experiment studied driven, middle-aged males who had survived heart attacks. All of them learned about medications, diet, and exercise, but only some were encouraged to slow down, relax, smile, enjoy life, and renew their religious faith. Did these life-style changes make a difference? Indeed, as you can see in **Figure 11.3**, only half as many of the life-style change group experienced repeat heart attacks.[26]

Meditation techniques that provide an opportunity to control one's thoughts and body can be a powerful pathway for positive change. Given their years of meditation experience, it is perhaps not surprising that Buddhist monks demonstrate beneficial

placebo An inactive substance or condition used to control for confounding variables.

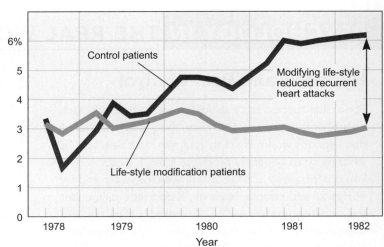

Percentage of patients with recurrent heart attacks (cumulative average)

Control patients

Modifying life-style reduced recurrent heart attacks

Life-style modification patients

1978   1979   1980   1981   1982

Year

FIGURE 11.3
Relaxation and Heart Attacks
Men who survived heart attacks were much less likely to have a second heart attack if they had been taught life-style changes, including relaxation (Data from Friedman & Ulmer, 1984).

changes while meditating. However, one study showed that some of these changes—including improved immune and brain function—were also apparent in people who had been given only 8 weeks of instruction in meditation.[27] Another study provided meditation instruction to some elderly patients but not to others. After 3 years, all of the meditators were still alive, but a quarter of the control group had died.[28]

And now it's time to take a deep breath, relax, and marvel at all your mind can accomplish—both consciously and unconsciously.

MAKE IT STICK!

1. _____ is a state of calm produced when physical measures like breathing rate decline.

2. True or false? Relaxation has proven beneficial for headaches and high blood pressure but not for sleep difficulties.

Module 11 Summary and Assessment

Hypnosis and Other States of Consciousness

11-1 How does dual processing help explain differing states of consciousness?

- It is the nature of consciousness to process information on two tracks.

- Dual processing can result in change blindness and may be related to hypnosis.

11-2 Is hypnosis really a different state of consciousness?

- Hypnosis is a social interaction in which a hypnotist makes suggestions about perception, feelings, thoughts, or behaviors, and the person experiencing hypnosis follows those suggestions.

- Social influence theory argues that powerful social influences can produce a state of hypnosis.

- Divided consciousness theory states that our consciousness splits during hypnosis so that one aspect of consciousness is not aware of the role other parts are playing.

11-3 How powerful are hypnotic suggestions?

- Hypnosis can lead people to follow many kinds of suggestions (even actions they otherwise wouldn't perform), but so can powerful suggestions of any kind.

11-4 Can hypnosis improve our memory or our physical state?

- In some cases, hypnosis has helped people retrieve memories, but hypnotized people may inadvertently manufacture untrue details or false memories.

- Hypnosis has been used in a variety of therapeutic settings to treat various medical problems, but it is difficult to separate the effects of hypnosis from a placebo effect.

- Research does not support claims for the power of hypnosis to increase strength or for age regression (remembering events from much earlier in a person's life).

Summative Assessment

1. Awareness of self and the environment is called
   a. hypnosis.
   b. consciousness.
   c. dual processing.
   d. meditation.

2. An example of dual processing is
   a. walking and chewing gum at the same time.
   b. driving and texting at the same time.
   c. regulating heart rate and breathing at the same time.
   d. having a conversation and maintaining a sense of balance at the same time.

3. Hypnosis is
   a. an effective way to recover lost memories.
   b. probably not real because there are no data to support that it really happens.
   c. a social interaction where suggestions are made and followed.
   d. not effective as a means of controlling pain.

4. Social influence theory argues that hypnosis is produced by
   a. mostly internal variables.
   b. mostly external variables.
   c. both internal and external variables.
   d. neither internal nor external variables.

5. The idea that consciousness can split and that segments may or may not be aware of the other segments is called
   a. divided consciousness theory.
   b. the placebo effect.
   c. dual processing.
   d. social influence theory.

6. The Federal Communication Commission has rules prohibiting showing the induction of hypnosis on television because
   a. many people believe hypnosis is immoral or evil.

 11-5 What are some benefits of relaxation and meditation?

- Relaxation and meditation can lead to a wide variety of physical and psychological benefits, perhaps even including a longer life span.

   b. many people believe hypnosis is fake.
   c. it is too easy for people watching to become hypnotized.
   d. data regarding the effects of hypnosis are controversial.

7. Which of the following is true regarding hypnotic susceptibility?
   a. Very few people can really be hypnotized.
   b. Most people are moderately hypnotizable.
   c. Almost everyone can be deeply hypnotized.
   d. Hypnotizability varies depending on variables like hunger.

8. One common use of posthypnotic suggestions is to
   a. get people to experience itching or other skin sensations.
   b. manipulate people's emotions.
   c. produce hypnotic age regression.
   d. rehypnotize people quickly and easily.

9. Psychological scientists believe that hypnosis
   a. should not be used to retrieve lost memories.
   b. is effective for retrieving lost memories from childhood but not for memories established after 10 years of age.
   c. is effective for retrieving lost memories established after 10 years of age but not for memories established during childhood.
   d. is not perfect for recovering lost memories but is good enough to use as evidence in courts of law.

10. The placebo effect refers to the impact of
    a. dual processing.
    b. expectations.
    c. the biological effects of sugar.
    d. divided consciousness.

KEY TERMS AND KEY PEOPLE

consciousness, p. 165

dual processing, p. 166

hypnosis, p. 167

social influence theory, p. 168

divided consciousness theory, p. 168

posthypnotic suggestion, p. 170

placebo, p. 172

Ernest Hilgard (1904–2001), p. 168

DOMAIN 3

Development and Learning

mimagephotos/Deposit Photos

Prenatal and Childhood Development

Whether learning to talk or learning how to put your toys away, growing up is not exactly child's play.

You are a genetic and environmental marvel. It only took you about 9 months to grow from the size of the dot on this *i* to a full-size (more or less) newborn baby. From the moment the egg from your mother and the sperm cell from your father united until the minute you were born, the cells that became you progressed through a delicate, predictable, and fantastic sequence of events. This sequence is virtually the same for all of us.

You are physically different than you were 5 or 6 years ago. If you compare your sixth-grade photo to a current one, you might even find the differences startling. These physical changes are obvious because you can see them, but you also differ in ways that are not so obvious. You think differently than you did in elementary school, and your emotions are more developed. Psychologists interested in these kinds of changes research *developmental psychology*, which studies physical, cognitive, emotional, and social changes from womb to tomb.

In this module (and in the next two as well), we will explore three fundamental issues in developmental psychology:

1. Continuity and stages—Is development a gradual, continuous process, like an elevator going up? Or is it a series of distinctly different stages, like the steps of a staircase?

2. Stability and change—Will the person you think of as the real you still be there in 2060, or will that person change dramatically as you move through adulthood?

3. Nature and nurture—How much of our development is a result of genetics (our nature), and how much is a result of environment (the nurturing we receive)?

Let's search for answers to these questions as we take a look at prenatal and childhood development.

KidStock/Blend Images/Getty Images

zygote A fertilized egg.

genes The biochemical units of heredity that make up chromosomes.

embryo A developing human organism from about 2 weeks after fertilization through the end of the eighth week.

fetus A developing human organism from 9 weeks after conception to birth.

FIGURE 12.1
Nine Weeks After Conception
At 9 weeks, the developing organism becomes a fetus and is unmistakably human in form. Facial features, hands, and feet are visible at this time. ▼

The Beginnings of Life

🐾🐾 12-1 How do humans grow from single cells into newborns?

If you are a young woman, you were born with all the egg cells you'll ever have, although they were immature when you were just a baby. Only about 1 of every 5000 egg cells will mature and be released from an ovary. If you are a young man, you did not begin producing sperm cells until you reached puberty, but you'll keep producing them until you die. Although the rate slows with age, males produce about 2 million sperm cells in the 30 minutes it takes to eat lunch, a rate of about 1000 per second.

Prenatal Development

Prenatal literally means *before (pre-) birth (-natal).* The prenatal stage of development starts at conception and ends at birth.

A newly fertilized egg is called a **zygote.** Less than half of all zygotes make it past the first 14 days after being fertilized.[1,2] Luckily, you and I survived that risky period. A lot happens during those 2 weeks. First, the single-cell zygote begins to divide into identical cells; one cell becomes two, and two cells become four. In the first week, after dividing about seven times, the cells start to *differentiate,* to specialize in function. For example, some cells start to develop into a brain, and others start to develop into lungs or a heart. **Genes**—the biochemical units of heredity—direct this process.

Around the tenth day, the zygote attaches to the mother's uterine wall, where it will stay for about 37 weeks. But when the developing human organism passes the 14-day milestone, it is no longer known as a *zygote;* it is now an **embryo,** the developing human organism from about 2 weeks after fertilization through the end of the eighth week (see **Figure 12.1**). The embryo has a noticeable heartbeat and red blood cells produced by its own liver. Most of the body's major organs will have formed by the end of the embryonic stage.

At 9 weeks, the developing organism enters the fetal period. A **fetus** is the developing human organism from 9 weeks after conception to birth. It is unmistakably human in form. Fetuses born prematurely at the end of 22 weeks have organs that are developed enough to provide a chance at survival.[3]

But let's not hurry things. While still in the mother's body, the fetus receives oxygen and nutrients from the *placenta,* a cushion of cells that also screens out some

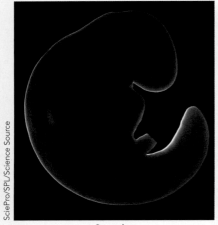

SciePro/SPL/Science Source

3 weeks

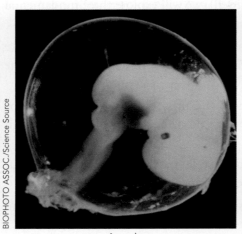

BIOPHOTO ASSOC./Science Source

4 weeks

DEA / L. RICCIARINI/Getty Images

9 weeks

substances that could harm the fetus. Unfortunately, the placenta is not a perfect screen, and some viruses, toxins, and drugs do slip through. **Teratogens** are substances that cross the placental barrier and prevent the fetus from developing normally.

Teratogens take many forms. Radiation, toxic chemicals in the water or air, or viruses like Zika can harm a fetus, as can some prescription and over-the-counter drugs. Other teratogens include nicotine, alcohol, and the viruses associated with sexually transmitted infections (STIs). Women who smoke during pregnancy increase the risk of abnormal fetal heartbeat, premature birth and its related complications, and miscarriage.[4] The effects of alcohol on a fetus can be even more dramatic. There is no known safe quantity of alcohol to consume while pregnant, and even moderate drinking can damage a fetus's brain.[5] Children whose mother drinks heavily during pregnancy may be born with **fetal alcohol syndrome (FAS).** The cognitive abnormalities that appear in children whose mother consumed large amounts of alcohol while pregnant can result in lifelong struggles. Physical symptoms of FAS may include a small, misproportioned head and unusual facial features. Mothers may also transmit STIs to their unborn children. Pregnant women with STIs are more likely than other women to have babies with mental disabilities and blindness.[6]

As frightening as teratogens are, most fetuses survive their 9 months in the womb and enter the world as healthy newborns.

The Newborn

If left to fend for themselves shortly after birth, infants would not survive. However, newborns are not passive little bundles who don't notice the world around them.

Within the first half hour of life, infants will turn their head to watch a picture or drawing of a human face, but they will not turn their head to view an indistinguishable jumble of images.[7,8] Newborns also turn their head toward human voices, and they have definite taste preferences. Sugar water and mother's milk? Yes, please! Milk with a spoiled taste or smell to it? No, thanks!

Nearly all full-term newborns don't have to learn sucking, swallowing, or grasping. These *reflexes* (automatic, unlearned responses) are survival behaviors, and nearly every baby comes equipped with them. To help find the breast or bottle that supplies nourishment, newborns have a **rooting reflex,** a baby's tendency, when touched on the cheek, to open the mouth and search for the nipple.

But newborns don't just roll off the assembly line, any one interchangeable with another. Even in the first few hours of life, a baby's **temperament**—characteristic emotional excitability—is evident. In the weeks following birth, an easy baby displays predictable sleeping and eating patterns, appears relaxed, and is cheerful. During these same weeks, a difficult baby is unpredictable, intense, and irritable. And the slow-to-warm-up baby will avoid new situations, have relatively low activity levels, and take more time to adapt to something new.[9] Temperament appears to be tied to our genetic makeup.[10] Studies showing how identical twins have more similar temperaments than fraternal

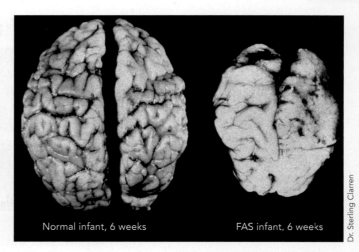

Normal infant, 6 weeks   FAS infant, 6 weeks

Dr. Sterling Clarren

▲ **Fetal Alcohol Syndrome** Symptoms of fetal alcohol syndrome (FAS) include distinctive facial misproportions such as a short, upturned nose; a sunken nasal bridge; and small eyelid openings. If his mother had stayed free of alcohol during her pregnancy, this child would not have been born with FAS. (From MayoClinic.com, 2006.)

LIFE MATTERS
We don't often think of medications as teratogens, but a few commonly used medications that should be avoided while pregnant are Accutane, ibuprofen, Motrin, cold and allergy decongestants, and Aleve.

teratogens Substances that cross the placental barrier and prevent the fetus from developing normally.

fetal alcohol syndrome (FAS) Physical and cognitive abnormalities that appear in children whose mothers consumed large amounts of alcohol while pregnant.

rooting reflex A baby's tendency, when touched on the cheek, to open the mouth and search for the nipple.

temperament A person's characteristic emotional excitability.

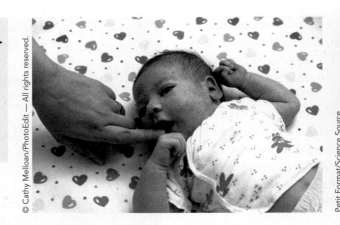

Reflexes in Newborns Stroking this baby's cheek initiates the rooting reflex as the baby searches for something to suck (left). The grasping reflex allows this newborn (right) to support its own weight. This reflex disappears by the baby's first birthday.

twins suggest that our biologically based temperament sets the stage for our personality.[11]

Temperament is also a relatively stable personality aspect. The most intense preschoolers grow up to be intense young adults.[12] Inhibited, fearful 2-year-olds generally become shy second graders.[13]

MAKE IT STICK!

1. What do we call a fertilized egg for the first 14 days of its existence?

   a. A zygote
   b. An embryo
   c. A fetus
   d. A placenta

2. What do we call the issue regarding the interaction between heredity and environment?

   a. Stability and change
   b. Continuity and stages
   c. Growth and birth
   d. Nature and nurture

3. What is the safe amount of alcohol a pregnant woman can drink without fear of harming her fetus?

   a. One beer per day
   b. None
   c. Two beers per day
   d. Three beers or glasses of wine per day

4. A label on a medication says, Should not be taken by pregnant women. This warning indicates that the medication could be a _____.

5. Temperament research shows that a person who is social, has a quick temper, and loves to take risks probably

   a. was an intense baby and child.
   b. did not respond to the rooting reflex.
   c. had an excess of genes as a newborn.
   d. was exposed to dangerous teratogen levels.

Physical Development in Infancy and Childhood

 12-2 How do genes and early experiences affect infant and child development?

Infancy is the first year of a child's life. From about 1 year to 3 years of age, a child is a toddler. Childhood includes the years between toddler and teenager. From infancy through childhood, we develop at an amazing pace on many fronts—physically, cognitively, emotionally, and socially. Let's look first at physical development during this early part of life.

The Developing Brain

During prenatal development, your body made nerve cells at the rate of 4000 per *second*. With your first breath of air, your brain cells were where they needed to be, but your nervous system was still immature. You could not walk, talk, or remember as you now do because your brain had not yet formed the neural networks that would let you perform these behaviors. In part, these neural networks, which continue developing even in adolescence, were a result of **maturation**—the biological growth processes that enable orderly changes in behavior. Experience has little effect on maturation. You rolled over, sat up, walked, and learned to run based largely on your genetic blueprint, and no amount of experience can change that. However, experience does affect *development*. Parents who talk and read to their children foster neural connections that help reading skills develop (see **Figure 12.2**). Those who abuse and neglect their children also deprive them of these complex neural connections and hinder development.

At birth   3 months   15 months

▲ **FIGURE 12.2**
Neural Development
These drawings show how the brain's neural networks grow increasingly more complex as a child matures. Complex activities such as problem solving and reasoning are among the last areas to mature.

maturation Biological growth processes that enable orderly changes in behavior.

From ages 3 to 6, the most rapid neurological growth appears to be in the part of the brain responsible for thinking rationally. Indeed, preschoolers often show amazing growth in their ability to behave and pay attention to a leader.[14]

To see how maturation affects memory, try to remember anything about your first birthday party, or try to remember wearing diapers. Any luck? If you're like most of us, the answer is *no*. We can't remember much before about the age of 3, and we remember little that happened during ages 3 through 5 because we did not have the neural connections in our brains that allow us to remember. Elizabeth Loftus[15] uses a computer example to explain this. In a way, trying to remember things that happened before age 5 (over a decade for you) is like trying to open the assignment you just wrote using word-processing software from the 1990s. Good luck with that!

So, do our memories function when we are very young? Yes, but in different ways:

- Most 1-year-olds will imitate the making of a rattle (putting a button in a box) 3 months after observing this act.[16]

- Most 3-year-olds recognize an out-of-focus picture more quickly if they saw a clear version of the picture 3 months earlier.[17]

- Most 10-year-olds say they recognize only one in five of the classmates they have not seen since preschool. But their physiological responses (measured as skin perspiration) are greater to former classmates, even to those they claim they don't recognize. The nervous system remembers what the conscious mind does not.[18]

As you can see, your memory was working when you were an infant and a young child, but it was working differently than it does now. The parts of the brain dealing with memory continue to develop well into the teen years.[19]

Motor Development

Physical skills and muscular coordination are products of the developing brain. The neural pathways and muscles necessary for crawling (or scooting on your bottom) mature before the pathways and muscles for walking. We all walk before we run because we are developmentally ready to walk before we are ready to run (see **Figure 12.3**).

Unfortunately, developmental charts that show "normal" ages for crawling, standing, and walking haunt some new parents. I've seen parents trying to force their child to crawl, ignoring the baby's tearful protests, as a "deadline for normal behavior" approached. Here's some good advice you can give if you see a parent prodding a child to catch up: Relax! Developmental charts provide age *ranges*. In this country, 25 percent of the babies walk at 11 months. Within a week of their first birthday, 50 percent are walking, and almost all of the remaining 50 percent will walk sometime shortly thereafter. The child's brain creates the readiness for crawling or walking, not the parents' prodding. The same holds true for all physical skills, including bladder and bowel control. Before a baby achieves the needed neural and muscular maturation, no amount of begging, bribing, or scolding will accomplish toilet training. Knowledge of this fact helped me potty-train my daughters (when they were ready, not when I was ready) in a few days instead of a prolonged period of several months.

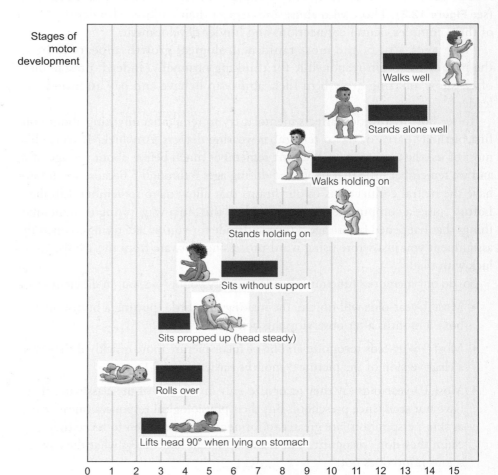

▲ FIGURE 12.3
Motor Development
Some infants reach each milestone sooner or later than others, but the order of the stages is the same for all infants. The colored bars show developmental norms—the ages at which infants master the motor skill. The left end of the bar indicates the age by which 50 percent have mastered the movement. The right end of the bar indicates the age by which 90 percent have mastered the movement.

MAKE IT STICK!

1. Which of the following is the best term for the biological growth processes that enable orderly changes in behavior?

   a. Temperament
   b. Nature
   c. Nurture
   d. Maturation

2. Which statement is accurate about the relationship between brain development and memory?

   a. Events occurring during infancy usually aren't remembered because of a lack of neural connections.
   b. The brain develops most of its brain cells after birth, so memories of infancy are rare.
   c. Brain development is finished at birth and does not have a dramatic effect on memory.
   d. Some remember infancy because they were born with more brain neurons than others.

3. Which of the following kinds of development will be affected *least* by early life experiences?

   a. Attachment development
   b. Cognitive development
   c. Motor development
   d. Social development

4. Which is more important in determining when a child walks: its brain or the urging of its parents?

Cognitive Development in Infancy and Childhood

 12-3 How does Jean Piaget's theory of cognitive development describe how children think at specific cognitive stages?

JEAN PIAGET [PEE-AH-ZHAY] (1896–1980) Pioneer in the study of developmental psychology who introduced a stage theory of cognitive development that led to a better understanding of children's thought processes.

Few people have had a greater impact on **developmental psychology** than Swiss psychologist **Jean Piaget** (pronounced pee-ah-ZHAY). In 1920, Piaget was working on intelligence tests to determine the age at which children were likely to answer questions correctly. However, Piaget became interested in the *incorrect* responses children gave, cleverly realizing there was a lot to learn from wrong answers. Children at a given age were making remarkably similar mistakes.

Over the next 50 years, Piaget[20] advanced the belief that the way children think and solve problems depends on their stage of cognitive development. **Cognition** refers to all mental activities associated with thinking, knowing, and remembering. Children know less than you and I know, but they also think *differently*. Trying to explain to a 3-year-old how you exchange pretend money for property will get you nowhere, but an 8-year-old can understand that Boardwalk costs $400 when you're playing Monopoly. Given your more advanced reasoning skills, that same 8-year-old will not stand much of a chance against you if you're playing a game of strategy.

Piaget wrote that all people, even infants, regularly face and adapt to environmental challenges. We do so by developing **schemas** (sometimes called *schemes*), which are concepts or mental frameworks that organize and interpret information. As a toddler, for example, your schema for getting food may have been to pull on the pant leg of the nearest adult or to start crying. By now, you have countless schemas, from how to start the car to which remote you need to which buttons you push to switch from Netflix to the Food Network. How did you develop all of these helpful mental plans? Piaget's answer would be that you used two different experiences:

developmental psychology A subfield of psychology that studies physical, cognitive, and social change throughout the life span.

cognition All mental processes associated with thinking, knowing, and remembering.

schemas Concepts or mental frameworks that organize and interpret information.

Two-year-old Jocelyn has learned the schema for *dog* from her picture books.

Jocelyn sees a cat and calls it a "dog." She is trying to assimilate this new animal into an existing schema. Her mother tells her, "No, it's a cat."

Jocelyn accommodates her schema for four-legged animals and continues to modify that schema to include different kinds of dogs and cats in the neighborhood.

FIGURE 12.4 ▲
Assimilation and Accommodation
These experiences allow children to make sense of their worlds either by interpreting new information with existing schemas or by changing a current schema.

assimilation Interpreting new experience in terms of existing schemas.

accommodation Adapting current schemas to incorporate new information.

- **Assimilation**—Interpreting your new experiences in terms of your existing schemas

- **Accommodation**—Adapting your current schemas to incorporate new information

Children assimilate and accommodate all the time. Consider a 2-year-old, whose simple schema for *doggie* is *four-legged animal*. This concept works wonderfully for all the dogs in the neighborhood but not for cats. The toddler must accommodate or modify her schema to account for four-legged animals that are not doggies (see **Figure 12.4**).

In addition to explaining how we form plans to organize and interpret information, Piaget proposed that we all pass through four separate stages of cognitive development on our journey from childhood to adulthood. **Table 12.1** outlines Piaget's sensorimotor, preoperational, concrete operational, and formal operational stages.

TABLE 12.1	Piaget's Stages of Cognitive Development	
Typical Age Range	**Description of Stage**	**Key Developmental Events**
Birth to nearly 2 years	***Sensorimotor*** Experiencing the world through senses and actions (looking, touching, mouthing, and grasping)	• Object permanence
About 2 to 6 or 7 years	***Preoperational*** Representing things with words and images but lacking logical reasoning	• Pretend play • Egocentrism • Language development
About 6 or 7 to 11 years	***Concrete operational*** Thinking logically about concrete events; grasping concrete analogies and performing arithmetical operations	• Conservation • Mathematical transformations
About 12 through adulthood	***Formal operational*** Abstract reasoning	• Abstract logic • Potential for mature moral reasoning

Sensorimotor Stage

According to Piaget, during the **sensorimotor stage** (from birth to about age 2), infants learn about the world through their sensory impressions and motor activities. Infants gain information by mouthing, grasping, looking, hearing, and touching—and this is how they develop their schemas.

Infants focus on things they can perceive through their senses. At first, the things they couldn't see or hear did not exist. But eventually, infants develop **object permanence,** the awareness that things continue to exist even when you cannot see or hear them.

Piaget assumed object permanence was not possible until around 8 months of age, but research indicates that he underestimated a young child's abilities. Piaget did not think infants could think or deal with abstract ideas, but other researchers have produced evidence of very early logical thinking. Consider the following:

- One-month-old babies were allowed to suck on one of two differently shaped pacifiers without seeing either (see **Figure 12.5**). Later, when the infants were shown the two pacifiers, they looked almost exclusively at the one they had *felt* in their mouth, indicating the memory necessary for object permanence.[21] This study was replicated with babies just 12 hours old with similar results.[22]

- At 5 months of age, babies stare longer or do double takes at impossible situations.[23,24] The example in **Figure 12.6** shows how researchers observed this behavior. Infants also show surprise when a puppet that usually jumps three times jumps only twice.[25] Piaget would not have predicted that such young children could show either numerical thinking skills or awareness of change.

sensorimotor stage In Piaget's theory, the stage (from birth to about 2 years of age) during which infants learn about the world through their sensory impressions and motor activities.

object permanence The awareness that things continue to exist even when you cannot see or hear them.

FIGURE 12.5
Early Memories
After sucking on one of these two pacifiers, babies looked longer at the pacifier they had felt in their mouth. This is evidence of early logical thinking. (Research from Meltzoff & Borton, 1979.)

1. Objects placed in case.

2. Screen comes up.

3. One object is removed in front of child.

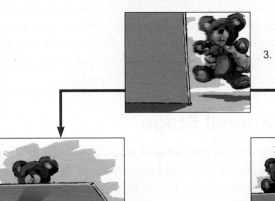

4a. Possible outcome: Screen drops, revealing one object.

4b. Impossible outcome: Screen drops, revealing two objects.

FIGURE 12.6
Early Object Permanence
When shown a numerically impossible outcome (there still being two objects after watching one being taken away), 5-month-old infants stare longer at the two objects, a finding that supports the development of object permanence far earlier than Jean Piaget assumed. (Research from Wynn, 1992.)

Preoperational Stage

preoperational stage
In Piaget's theory, the stage (from about 2 to 6 or 7 years of age) during which a child learns to use language but cannot yet think logically.

conservation The principle (which Piaget believed to be a part of concrete operational reasoning) that properties such as mass, volume, and number remain the same despite changes in the forms of objects.

egocentrism In Piaget's theory, the inability of the preoperational child to take another person's point of view or to understand that symbols can represent other objects.

Piaget defined the **preoperational stage** (from about age 2 to about age 6 or 7) as a time during which a child learns to use language but cannot yet think logically. If you show 5-year-olds two identical clear glass beakers, each with a cup of blue liquid in them, they'll know the beakers hold the same amount. However, if you then pour the contents of one beaker into a taller, narrower beaker, causing the water line to move up, the preoperational child will probably tell you the new beaker now holds more liquid. Although the different-sized beakers hold the same amount of liquid, 5-year-olds typically focus only on the height dimension. These children lack an understanding of **conservation,** the principle that properties such as mass, volume, and number remain the same even if the object's form changes. Without this understanding, 5-year-olds do not have the cognitive skills to mentally pour the tall beaker's contents back into the regular beaker (see **Figure 12.7**).

Preoperational children develop language skills, but their communication is often egocentric. **Egocentrism** is the inability to consider another's point of view. This means that preoperational children are likely to say whatever is on their mind without taking into account what others have said. Egocentrism shows up in the actions and statements of young children. For example, many years ago, my oldest daughter used to close her eyes when she didn't want anybody to see her. Ask a 4-year-old why the sun shines in the morning, and you might hear the answer, To wake me up.

Bianca Moscatelli/Worth Publishers

FIGURE 12.7 ▲
Conservation Problem
Conservation is the principle that properties such as mass, volume, and number remain the same even if the object's form changes. The two beakers in the third panel clearly have the same amount of liquid, but a 5-year-old would probably not understand this conservation problem.

We've learned that taking another's viewpoint, a form of symbolic thinking, appears earlier in the preoperational mind than Piaget thought. In one study, 3-year-olds were able to use a scale model of a real room to locate a hidden stuffed animal. If little Snoopy was hidden under a pillow in the scale model, 3-year-olds knew to look under the pillow in the real room 80 percent of the time. However, only 30 percent of 2½-year-olds knew where to look for little Snoopy in the real room.[26] Piaget probably would have been surprised that symbolic thinking could be shown at such an early age and also that 6 months made such a difference in children's ability to use the scale model of a room as a symbol.

Concrete Operational Stage

concrete operational stage
In Piaget's theory, the stage of cognitive development (from about 6 or 7 to 11 years of age) during which children gain the mental skills that let them think logically about concrete events.

Piaget believed that in the **concrete operational stage** (from about age 6 or 7 to about age 11) children gain the mental skills that let them think logically about concrete events. Concrete operational children comprehend that mass and volume stay the same despite changes in the forms of objects (a sign of understanding *conservation*). They know that change in shape does not affect quantity. Whether you roll a batch of dough into one big loaf of bread or divide it into a dozen rolls, a child at the concrete operational stage knows that you still have the same amount of dough.

In the concrete operational stage, Piaget said that children could also comprehend mathematical transformations. For example, they enjoy math-based jokes that used to be over their heads, like this one:

A king asked his baker to bring him a pie. When the baker brought a pie cut in six pieces, the king yelled at the baker, "Why didn't you bring me a pie cut in two pieces? I could never eat six!"

Obviously, that king can't conserve. Concrete operational children understand the joke (even if it's not that funny).

Formal Operational Stage

Concrete reasoning requires actual experience. In the **formal operational stage** (age 12 and over), children begin to think logically about abstract concepts and form strategies about things they may not have experienced. The ability to create and use the strategies necessary to play chess is a sign of formal operational thought. Think of the abstract reasoning necessary to understand chemical equations and the laws of physics. Concrete thinkers would struggle in these classes. Young adolescents, said Piaget, become capable of solving hypothetical problems. They can figure out the answer to *If this, then what* questions, such as the following: Whenever Emily goes to school, Meredith also goes to school. Emily went to school. What can you say about Meredith?

Every formal operational thinker knows that Meredith also went to school—but so do most second-graders,[27] who do not fit Piaget's expected age range for this stage. Once again, recent research differs from Piaget's expectations; the mental skills that form the basis for Piaget's stages appear earlier than he predicted.

Assessing Piaget

We've seen that Piaget's pioneering research underestimated children's abilities in virtually every stage of his theory. Further, most developmental psychologists now believe development is fairly *continuous,* rather than divided into the discrete stages Piaget proposed. And Piaget's work did not reflect the effects of culture on cognitive development. For example, if you were raised in a cultural environment that made minimal use of numbers (such as the Munduruku and Pirahã of the Amazon rain forest), your language might have number words only up to 2, with all numbers or quantities after that might simply be called *many.* This type of language difference appears to delay the development of quantity conservation.[28,29]

Nevertheless, Piaget's identification of cognitive milestones broke new ground. Stimulated by his work, thousands of psychologists ran experiments on how the mind develops and wrote countless articles on the development of children. Piaget taught us that we learn best when the lesson builds on what we already know (schemas). He showed that new reasoning abilities require the stepping stones of previous abilities. Furthermore, he taught us that children simply cannot reason using adult logic and that it is unrealistic to expect a 3-year-old to reason like a 7-year-old. Piaget provided a wonderful base on which other psychologists could build our current understanding of cognitive development.

formal operational stage
In Piaget's theory, the stage of cognitive development (beginning about age 12) during which people begin to think logically about abstract concepts and form strategies about things they may not have experienced.

LIFE MATTERS
When watching a child interact with their parent in line at the grocery store, it's easy to perceive the child as ungrateful or entitled and in need of stricter discipline. How might Piaget's theory of cognitive development change your perspective of the child's behavior?

MAKE IT STICK!

1. Which Piagetian stage is characterized by pretend play and egocentrism?

   a. Preoperational
   b. Sensorimotor
   c. Concrete operational
   d. Formal operational

2. Which Piagetian stage is characterized by the belief that mass and volume stay the same despite changes in the form of objects?

   a. Sensorimotor
   b. Concrete operational
   c. Formal operational
   d. Preoperational

3. What do we call adapting your current schemas to incorporate new information?

   a. Assimilation   c. Maturation
   b. Accommodation   d. Abstract logic

4. A child develops the idea that all teachers are female because the child encounters only female teachers. This idea is an example of

   a. a formal operation.
   b. preoperational thinking.
   c. a schema.
   d. conservation.

5. True or false? A 6-year-old who can't seem to understand anything other than her point of view is probably going through the formal operational stage.

Social Development in Infancy and Childhood

 12-4 What are the probable effects of attachment types and parenting styles?

stranger anxiety The fear of strangers that infants commonly display, beginning by about 8 months of age.

Stranger Anxiety
This 8-month-old seated with the man in the red suit is clearly experiencing stranger anxiety. ▼

Jim David/Shutterstock

Some neighbors recently called me to come over and watch their 9-month-old son take some wobbly steps as he was learning to walk. The excitement in their voices was clear: Baby Tommy was taking his first steps! When I arrived, Tommy's father was changing his son's diaper, so I sat for a moment waiting for the baby's grand entrance. His dad brought Tommy in, placed him in a standing position, and encouraged him to walk. However, much to the dismay of his parents, Tommy took one look at me and started crying loudly enough to make the dog get up and leave the room. The child then started grabbing at his father's legs, frantically trying to climb up to safety.

Now, I don't exactly think of myself as scary looking, but Tommy was frightened by what he saw. His reaction to me was normal for his age and was a classic sign of **stranger anxiety,** the fear of strangers that infants commonly display beginning around 8 months of age. Around this age, children have established schemas for familiar faces and often greet strangers with crying and distress. Tommy had not assimilated my face into any of his existing schemas.

Tommy's reaction shows how physical, cognitive, and social–emotional behaviors develop simultaneously. A few months later, I thought I should give Tommy another try. So, I invited Tommy's family to our house, and he was fine when he came in. Then Emily, my oldest daughter, made the mistake of reaching out her arms and asking, "May I hold you?" Tommy immediately tightened his grip on his mother and started saying, "No!" with plenty of volume. This time, Tommy was showing *attachment* to his mother. Let's take a closer look at attachment and its effects on development.

Attachment

Attachment is an emotional tie with another person, shown by seeking closeness to the caregiver and distress on separation. At least three elements contribute to the infant–parent bond that forms during attachment—body contact, familiarity, and responsiveness.

Body Contact
Which is more important to fostering attachment: being fed or being held? Are you more likely to become attached to the person who nourishes you or to the person who provides you *contact comfort*? For years, developmental psychologists thought this question was a no-brainer. Surely, providing nourishment is the way to an infant's heart. Then in the 1950s, psychologists Harry and Margaret Harlow tested this idea, using infant monkeys to assess whether food or contact comfort of something cuddly is more important for attachment.

In the experiment, the Harlows' infant monkeys could choose between two artificial mothers. One was foam rubber covered with soft terry cloth, and the other was a bare-wire cylinder. It was no surprise that if both "mothers" had a bottle attached for feeding, the baby monkeys preferred the soft, cuddly mother. But what if only the wire mother had the bottle? Which mother would the baby cling to when alarmed or spend most of its time with? The Harlows surprised other psychologists (and parents) when they revealed that the infant monkeys preferred contact with the cuddly mother even while feeding from the wire mother[30] (see **Figure 12.8**).

Attachment is not primarily a function of who provides the food. Human infants become attached to warm, soft parents who cuddle, rock, *and* feed. Early on, emotional communication between parent and infant takes place most often through touch. Snuggling soothes a baby, whereas tickling elicits smiles and laughter.[31]

Attachment provides an infant with a secure base from which to set out for wobbly explorations of the environment. Tommy needed the closeness of his mother, especially when he was stressed by the presence of someone he didn't know. The attachment children experience shows up when they become parents. Those who did not experience secure attachment are more likely to describe parenting as stressful and unsatisfying, while securely attached children are more likely to describe parenting as enjoyable and meaningful.[32]

Attachment appears to play a role in our adult lives in other ways as well. Adults who experienced secure attachment as children are more driven to achieve and less likely to express a fear of failure.[33] We still seek to maintain a secure base as we mature, although that base tends to become good friends and partners.[34] We have a greater chance of flourishing when we know a trusted friend or loved one will stand behind us, no matter what.

attachment The emotional tie with another person shown by seeking closeness to the caregiver and showing distress on separation.

FIGURE 12.8
Out to Lunch
The Harlows' monkeys preferred the soft, comfortable "mother" to the bare wire, wooden-headed "mother," even though the wire model provided nourishment. This discovery, that attachment is formed more through comfort than through nourishment, surprised many psychologists.

Harlow Primate Laboratory, University of Wisconsin

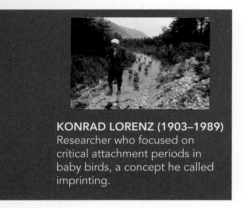

KONRAD LORENZ (1903–1989)
Researcher who focused on critical attachment periods in baby birds, a concept he called imprinting.

critical period The optimal period shortly after birth when an organism's exposure to certain experiences produces proper development.

imprinting The process by which certain animals form attachments during a critical period early in life.

Familiarity Body contact is one piece of the attachment puzzle; familiarity is another. My daughter and I were unfamiliar faces to Tommy, so he pulled back to the safety of his parents. For some species, the attachment bond forms during a **critical period**—an optimal period shortly after birth when an organism's exposure to certain experiences produces proper development. **Konrad Lorenz**[35] found that a newborn duckling, chick, or gosling will follow the first moving object it sees, which typically is the little creature's mother. This process, known as **imprinting,** is an adaptive response: Following and staying close to Mom provides safety and nourishment for these birds. Lorenz showed, however, that because of the critical period for attachment in baby birds, fledglings would also imprint on black boots with yellow stripes or on bouncing balls if either of those objects was the first thing they saw.[36] Ducklings that imprinted on the boots would follow those boots wherever they went, regardless of who was wearing them. Attachment in these animals is hard to reverse once established.

Do humans have a similar critical period for attachment? *No.* Humans do not imprint, and babies who are adopted days, weeks, or even months after birth can become every bit as attached to their new caregiver as any child does to its birth parents. Familiarity fosters contentment, but human attachment develops gradually.

Responsiveness The third element of the attachment bond is responsiveness. Responsive parents are aware of what their children are doing, and they respond appropriately. Unresponsive parents often ignore their babies, helping them only when they feel like it. Mary Ainsworth[37] found that responsiveness appears to affect whether a child is securely or insecurely attached. *Securely attached* children happily explore their environment when their primary caregiver is around. If that caregiver leaves, they appear distressed, and they go to their caregiver as soon as he or she returns. *Insecurely attached* children are often clingy and are less likely to explore and learn about the environment. When their caregiver leaves, they either cry loudly or show indifference to the caregiver's departure and return.

Dutch researcher Dymphna van den Boom[38] designed a study to assess the role of the environment in attachment. She took 100 temperamentally difficult infants and randomly assigned half to a group in which their mothers received training on how to be a responsive caregiver and half to a group where the mothers received no training. When the children reached their first birthday, van den Boom assessed their attachment to their mothers. A whopping 68 percent of the children whose mother received training were deemed securely attached. Only 28 percent of the children in the other group were securely attached. Responsiveness matters.

Effects of Attachment

Does what we learn in the cradle last to the grave? Said differently, does secure or insecure attachment have long-term effects, or do these terms simply describe some bonds and behaviors limited to our early childhood? Consider the following:

- *Secure attachment predicts social competence.* Children identified as securely attached between 12 and 18 months of age were more outgoing, more confident, and more persistent in solving challenging tasks when restudied as 2- and 3-year-olds.[39]

- *Deprivation of attachment is linked to negative outcomes.* Babies who grow up in institutions without a caregiver's regular attention do not form normal attachments and often appear withdrawn and frightened.[40] Physical and emotional abuse often disrupts attachment as well. While most abused children show great resilience and do not grow up to be violent criminals or abusive parents, most abusive parents were, in fact, battered or emotionally abused as children.[41]

- *A responsive environment helps most infants recover from attachment disruption.* Children who have been neglected but who are later adopted between 6 and 16 months of age at first have trouble sleeping, eating, and relating to their new parents.[42] However, by age 10, this same group of adopted children showed virtually no adverse effects from the early neglect.

The evidence is consistent and clear. Children who have a warm relationship with familiar, responsive caregivers reap the benefits of secure attachment. Most often, attachment is a direct result of the parenting children receive. As long as parents are responsive, does the way they parent—their parenting *style*—matter? Let's take a look.

Parenting Patterns

Most people your age eventually wind up raising a child. Assume for a moment that you are the parent of a 2-year-old. What kind of parent are you? Do you try to talk everything out? Are you strict or permissive? Do you follow through on the rules you set? How will your parenting style affect your child's development?

Diana Baumrind[43,44] was the first to describe three main parenting styles—authoritarian, permissive, and authoritative—and their characteristics (see **Figure 12.9**):

- **Authoritarian parenting** is marked by imposing rules and expecting obedience. These parents are low in warmth, and their version of discipline is strict and often physical. Communication is high from parent to child but low from child to parent. Maturity expectations are high.

authoritarian parenting
A style of parenting marked by imposing rules and expecting obedience.

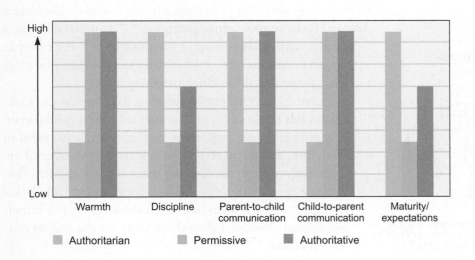

FIGURE 12.9
Parenting Styles
These three parenting styles differ greatly in the areas of warmth toward children, discipline, communication, and expectations. What kind of parent would you like to be?

Which Style?
Is this parent more likely to be authoritative or authoritarian?

CHEEVERWOOD   by Michael Fry

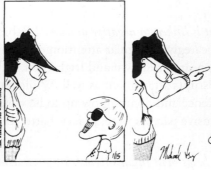

permissive parenting
A style of parenting marked by submitting to children's desires, making few demands, and using little punishment.

authoritative parenting
A style of parenting marked by making demands on the child, being responsive, setting and enforcing rules, and discussing the reasons behind the rules.

- **Permissive parenting** is marked by submitting to children's desires and using little punishment. These parents are high in warmth, but they rarely discipline their children. Communication is low from parent to child but high from child to parent. Expectations of maturity are low.

- **Authoritative parenting** is marked by making demands on the child, being responsive, setting and enforcing rules, and discussing the reasons behind the rules. These parents are high in warmth, and their version of discipline is moderate. Communication is high from parent to child *and* from child to parent. Maturity expectations are moderate.

A fourth style often added to Baumrind's work is called *neglectful parenting*. In this kind of parenting, parents provide for a child's physical needs but are often distant or disengaged emotionally. Neglectful parents are low in warmth and responsiveness and are less likely to hold their children responsible for their behaviors.

Does one form of parenting have a clear advantage over the other forms? According to Baumrind and others, authoritative parents often produce children high in self-esteem, self-reliance, and social competence.[45] These children are usually more successful, happy, and generous with others. What accounts for these findings? One factor may be that authoritative parents allow their children to develop a *sense of control* over their lives. People who believe they have some control over their destiny tend to be motivated and self-confident. Those without a sense of control are more likely to feel incompetent and helpless.[46]

Parenting style is not, however, a one-size-fits-all proposition. Bolder children often need more restrictive parenting, whereas fearful children often respond better to more gentle parenting.[47,48] Cultural differences and expectations also influence parenting style.[49] For example, parents in cultures that emphasize respect for elders are more likely to use the authoritarian parenting style.

Parenting is a challenging full-time job. Anyone can make a baby, but it takes a lot of character to make a good parent. Few gifts are more important than parents' investment of time, love, and warm responsiveness to their children. I am more likely to regret the time not spent with my children than the time spent with them. Perhaps former First Lady Jackie Kennedy summed it up best when she said, "If you bungle raising your children, I don't think whatever else you do matters very much."[50]

"DON'T YOU REALIZE, JASON, THAT WHEN YOU THROW FURNITURE OUT THE WINDOW AND TIE YOUR SISTER TO A TREE, YOU MAKE MOMMY AND DADDY VERY SAD?"

MAKE IT STICK!

1. Stranger anxiety typically starts to show in children of about what age?

   a. Birth
   b. 2 years
   c. Stranger anxiety actually does not exist.
   d. 8 months

2. Which of the following is true about children who are securely attached to their primary caregiver?

   a. They are more socially competent than insecurely attached children.
   b. Deprivation of attachment is linked to positive outcomes.
   c. A responsive environment does not help infants recover from attachment disruption.
   d. Securely attached children tend to lack confidence and lack persistence when solving problems.

3. What kind of parenting is characterized by meeting a child's physical needs but remaining distant emotionally?

   a. Authoritarian   c. Permissive
   b. Authoritative   d. Neglectful

4. Parents who want to increase the likelihood of their children developing secure attachments to them should pay most attention to

   a. the concrete operational stage.
   b. their own responsiveness.
   c. imprinting shortly after birth.
   d. sensorimotor stage schemas about temperament.

5. Which of the following best describes the most advantageous parenting style according to Diana Baumrind's research?

   a. Parents set rules and make sure children follow the rules without questioning or discussion.
   b. Parents encourage children to learn the rules themselves and don't set family rules or enforce them.
   c. Parents require children to follow rules but explain and discuss the rules as a family.
   d. Parents let the children set and enforce the rules of the family and work to be friends with their children.

Three Key Developmental Issues

 12-5 What are the three major issues developmental psychologists debate regarding infant and child development?

We have looked at some of the important research on physical, cognitive, social, and emotional development during infancy and childhood. We can view this research on development in terms of three important issues: continuity and stages, stability and change, and nature and nurture. Here's what the experts have to say about these issues.

Continuity and Stages

How is our development continuous, and how do we develop in stages? In some areas, such as attachment, development is a continuous process. Cognitive development is also more continuous than stagelike. But in other areas—such as motor development, where milestones are more easily viewed—we clearly pass through stages.

Stability and Change

What remains stable across our development, and how do we change? Clearly, we change physically, cognitively, and socially as we grow up. On the other end of the spectrum, temperament is relatively stable throughout the life span. Fortunately, change is possible for infants from neglectful backgrounds who move into more nurturing homes if the move takes place early enough in the child's life.

Nature and Nurture

How does the interaction of nature and nurture affect development? The interaction between heredity (nature) and environment (nurture) shapes a child's development. In the area of physical development, for example, environmental factors combine with a child's genetic tendencies to shape the fetus until the moment of birth. Two outcomes stemming from this interaction are evident: the relative health of a child whose mother avoided alcohol and nicotine during pregnancy, and the illnesses of children with FAS. In the area of cognitive development, children learn new behaviors based not only on developmental readiness but also on whether they are raised in a stimulating or a nonstimulating environment. And in the area of social development, children's interactions are influenced by both their inborn temperament and the supportive or neglectful environments in which they are raised.

We have evidence for both continuity and stages in a child's growth. Children's lives have both stability and the capacity for change. And both nature and nurture make us who we are.

MAKE IT STICK!

1.   Discussions on temperament typically fall under the category of which major developmental issue?

     a. Stability and change
     b. Nature and nurture
     c. Continuity and stages
     d. Assimilation and accommodation

2.   Which key developmental psychology issue is most relevant to criticism of Piaget's cognitive development theory?

     a. Stability and change
     b. Continuity and stages
     c. Nature and nurture
     d. Assimilation and accommodation

3.   Which key developmental psychology issue best addresses the question, Does basic personality develop over time, or do people keep the personality they had as children?

Module 12 Summary and Assessment
Prenatal and Childhood Development

 12-1 How do humans grow from single cells into newborns?

- The prenatal stage of development starts at conception and ends at birth.

- Fertilized eggs, called zygotes, divide rapidly, implant in the uterine wall, and at 14 days are called an embryo.

- At 9 weeks, the organism is called a fetus and is human in form.

- The fetus receives nutrients through the placenta, which shields it from most harmful substances (except teratogens).

 12-2 How do genes and early experiences affect infant and child development?

- Physical development occurs quickly during the infancy and childhood stages.

- At birth, the brain has not yet formed the neural networks that control complex behaviors (such as motor skills) and cognitions (such as memory).

- Motor skills develop with the neural network, guided by our genetic blueprint.

 12-3 How does Jean Piaget's theory of cognitive development describe how children think at specific cognitive stages?

- Piaget's theory includes four stages of cognitive development: sensorimotor (learning through sensory impressions and motor activities), preoperational (learning to use language but not yet able to think logically), concrete operational (gaining the schemas required for logical analysis of concrete events), and formal operational (thinking logically about abstract concepts and strategizing).

- Piaget's stages accurately describe the order of cognitive development, although he underestimated children's cognitive abilities in each stage. Cognitive development also is more continuous than Piaget thought.

 12-4 What are the probable effects of attachment types and parenting styles?

- Social development occurs in predictable patterns during infancy and childhood. For example, most children go through a period of stranger anxiety.

- Body contact, familiarity, and responsiveness influence attachment to parents, which in turn influences later characteristics such as social competence, ability to form other attachment, and effect of attachment disruption.

 12-5 What are the three major issues developmental psychologists debate regarding infant and child development?

- Developmental psychology research can be analyzed in terms of three issues: continuity and stages, stability and change, and nature and nurture.

- Some elements, such as attachment and cognitive development, develop in a more continuous process. But other factors, such as motor development, develop in more discrete stages.

- Many factors change as we develop and grow older, but some (like temperament) remain relatively unchanged as we age.

- The interaction of heredity (nature) with environment (nurture) shapes development.

Summative Assessment

1. Compared to a normal infant, the brain of a child suffering from fetal alcohol syndrome is

   a. about normal size.
   b. much smaller.
   c. much bigger.
   d. abnormally long.

2. Which of the following would most likely be considered a teratogen for a pregnant woman?

   a. Potatoes
   b. Vitamin D
   c. Vodka
   d. Hamburger

3. An infant who looks for a toy after it has been hidden is demonstrating

    a. object permanence.
    b. conservation.
    c. imprinting.
    d. attachment.

4. Which stage of Piaget's cognitive development theory is characterized by abstract reasoning?

    a. Formal operational
    b. Concrete operational
    c. Preoperational
    d. Hypothetical operational

5. Which of the following did the Harlows believe was most important in forming parental attachment?

    a. Regular feeding
    b. Potty training
    c. Anxiety reduction
    d. Body contact

6. Which style of parenting is characterized by meeting physical needs but not being emotionally responsive?

    a. Authoritarian
    b. Neglectful
    c. Permissive
    d. Authoritative

7. What do we call the major developmental issues that are most likely to address the importance of environment on development?

    a. Stability and change
    b. Continuity and stages
    c. Nature and nurture
    d. Attachment and anxiety

8. One of the more consistent criticisms of Piaget is that he consistently _____ the abilities of children.

    a. underestimated
    b. lost track of
    c. neglected
    d. overestimated

9. Tragically, fetal alcohol syndrome

    a. is preventable.
    b. is far more common in mothers living below poverty.
    c. results in lifelong struggles.
    d. All of these are true.

10. As we grow from childhood to adolescence, temperament is most likely to

    a. fluctuate dramatically.
    b. pretty much stay the way it was.
    c. change without much warning.
    d. become unpredictable.

KEY TERMS AND KEY PEOPLE

zygote, p. 178

genes, p. 178

embryo, p. 178

fetus, p. 178

teratogens, p. 179

fetal alcohol syndrome (FAS), p. 179

rooting reflex, p. 179

temperament, p. 179

maturation, p. 181

developmental psychology, p. 183

cognition, p. 183

schemas, p. 183

assimilation, p. 184

accommodation, p. 184

sensorimotor stage, p. 185

object permanence, p. 185

preoperational stage, p. 186

conservation, p. 186

egocentrism, p. 186

concrete operational stage, p. 186

formal operational stage, p. 187

stranger anxiety, p. 188

attachment, p. 189

critical period, p. 190

imprinting, p. 190

authoritarian parenting, p. 191

permissive parenting, p. 192

authoritative parenting, p. 192

Jean Piaget [pee-ah-ZHAY] (1896–1980), p. 183

Konrad Lorenz (1903–1989), p. 190

Adolescence

It's sometimes frustrating to be an adolescent; you're too old to act like a little kid, but you haven't yet reached full adult status. Despite the frustrations, it's a stage of life packed with significant changes. Better than that, it's *your* stage of life!

Just for a minute, think of yourself in the fourth grade. Think of your physical self, the things you liked to do, the sorts of thoughts that occupied your mental life, the activities you engaged in, and the friends you had. How have you changed between then and now? Just the thought might leave you chuckling, glad that you've left your former self behind. The changes that occur during adolescence are probably the most dramatic changes you'll ever go through, with the possible exception of the rapid changes that occurred very early in your life.

In a sense, everything about an introductory psychology course relates to you. Pick any module and you will find relevant material that helps you understand yourself and your world better. Yet no module is more relevant to you than this one. Adolescence is where you're at! The physical, cognitive, and social aspects we discuss in this module are psychology's best and most current efforts to explain this time of your life.

What Is Adolescence?

13-1 What is adolescence, and how does our culture affect it?

Imagine living in a hunting and gathering society that celebrated your thirteenth birthday with a ceremony proclaiming you an adult. Shortly thereafter, you would marry, start your family, and settle into your adult life-style. Your occupational choices would be quite limited. If you're female, you would likely devote yourself to child-rearing and domestic tasks. If you're male, your occupation might well be hunting. Societies like this still exist in some parts of the world. Had you been born into one, your adolescent experience would be brief and vastly

adolescence The transition period from childhood to adulthood, extending from puberty to independence.

different from what you are most likely experiencing now as a teen in the developed world. Even in the more rural 1800s, your transition from childhood to adult life would have happened more quickly. At that time, formal education for many young people ended with eighth grade, and young couples married, began farming, and started a family before they turned 20. Now, however, adolescence is becoming increasingly long and complex. **Adolescence** is the transition period from childhood to adulthood; it extends from puberty to independence.

Adolescence begins with sexual maturation, which is happening about 2 years earlier than it did 100 years ago (see **Figure 13.1**).[1] Adolescence is being prolonged on the other end, too. As more and more students continue their formal education to college and beyond, independent adult status is delayed longer and longer. Many young men and women are also waiting longer to marry and start families. Adolescents may depend at least partially on their parents for financial support well into their twenties and sometimes longer.

The fact that most teenagers reach physical maturity long before they are able to assume adult roles can—and does—create some tension and frustration, which you have most likely experienced. One day you may be eager to sample a more adult activity (say, a road trip to another town to visit friends), only to have your parents deny permission because they feel you're not quite ready for that much independence. Next thing you know, your harmless but exuberant roughhousing with a sibling or friend is interrupted with a parental admonishment to grow up and act your age. When you want to be an adult, the message is often to be patient and wait. When you want to act like a child, you hear that it's important to be responsible and mature.

This is not to imply that adolescence must be a time of stormy rebellion and confusion. Teenagers display tremendous accomplishments—excelling in school, on the job, as volunteers, at sports, and in other creative endeavors. The transition from child to adult is jarring for some families, who struggle mightily with issues surrounding the amount of independence and responsibility teenagers should have. But others seem to navigate these waters with a minimum of disturbance and disruption. For most families, the gradual growth in maturity and responsibility on the part of the teen is matched by a growing confidence on the part of the parents.

For most teenagers, the experience of adolescence is an exciting opportunity to explore the possibilities of adult life. In fact, four out of five teenagers agree with the statement, "I would choose my life the way it is right now."[2]

**FIGURE 13.1
Adolescence Is
Taking Longer**
Puberty is happening earlier, and marriage, financial independence, and the end of formal education are happening later. These events are stretching adolescence on both ends. (From Guttmacher Institute, 2006.)

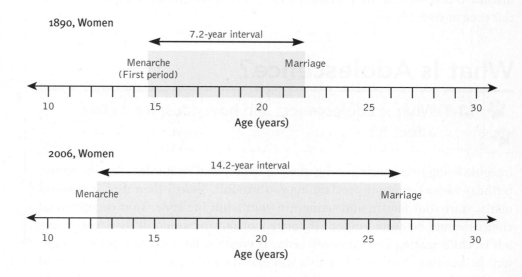

▶ **Adolescent Scenes**
Are these activities that you enjoy? Can you identify other typical adolescent activities?

MAKE IT STICK!

1. Which of the following aspects of adolescence is most likely to differ among cultures?

   a. Menarche
   b. The development of primary sex characteristics
   c. The effect of hormonal changes on secondary sex characteristics
   d. How the end of adolescence is defined

2. True or false? Adolescence is longer in more complex societies.

3. True or false? The path through adolescence resembles a stormy rebellion in most families.

Physical Development in Adolescence

 13-2 What major physical changes occur during adolescence?

puberty The period of sexual maturation, during which a person becomes capable of reproducing.

The most important physical development of adolescence is **puberty,** the period of sexual maturation during which a person becomes capable of reproducing. A flood of hormones, which lead to physical and emotional changes, triggers this amazing time of change. Puberty generally begins earlier in girls (about 11 years of age) than it does in boys (around 13 years). Although puberty begins years later in some individuals than in others, it generally starts earlier now than it used to.[3] One of the most obvious changes is a growth spurt. Sixth- or seventh-grade girls often tower

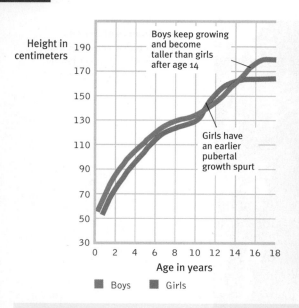

Marili Forastieri/Getty Images

▲ **FIGURE 13.2**
The Growth Spurt
Girls start the growth spurt earlier, but once boys catch up around age 14, they tend to grow taller than girls. (From Tanner, 1978.)

over their male classmates, but soon the boys catch up and outgrow the average female (see **Figure 13.2**).[4]

During the growth spurt, both primary and secondary sex characteristics develop (see **Figure 13.3**). The **primary sex characteristics** are the reproductive organs—the *testes* in males and the *ovaries* in females. The **secondary sex characteristics** are nonreproductive sexual characteristics, such as breast and hip development in girls and voice quality and facial hair in boys.

Two of the more obvious events of puberty are the beginning of menstruation (known as *menarche*) for females and the beginning of ejaculation for boys (which often happens during sleep as a *nocturnal emission*). Each is a memorable event that produces a variety of emotions in the young woman or young man. Teens who have been prepared to expect these events are more likely to view them as positive, rather than frightening or negative, experiences.[5,6,7]

primary sex characteristics
The reproductive organs—ovaries, testes, and external genitalia.

secondary sex characteristics
Nonreproductive sexual characteristics, such as breast and hip development in females and voice quality and facial hair in males.

FIGURE 13.3
The Wonder of Puberty
The release of hormones during puberty triggers amazing changes in the body. Some of those changes are illustrated here.

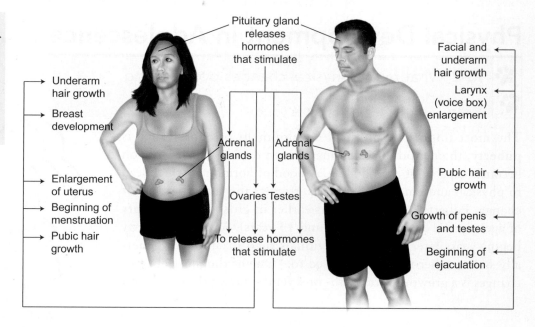

Sexuality is certainly a *biological* event, but *cognitive* and *cultural* factors also govern sexual behaviors. Our culture is saturated with sexual imagery. A typical hour of prime-time network television contains about 15 sexual references, most of which ignore the risks of unwanted pregnancy and sexually transmitted diseases.[8,9,10] Add to this the sexual content of popular music, movies, print media, and the internet, mix in the increased sex drive triggered by the hormones released during puberty, and you have a recipe for the dramatic increase in teen sexual activity in the United States over the course of the past century.[11] Teens receive a decidedly mixed message calling not only for abstinence but also for safe sex, protected by condom use. Rarely discussed are the tremendous emotional risks of committing oneself sexually to another person. Is it any wonder that making decisions is sometimes so difficult, especially when teens are still working to complete their development of decision-making skills (as we will see in the next section)? The good news is that in recent years, many teens seem to be handling this pressure better than they were a few years ago. The rate of teen pregnancy in the United States is declining because fewer teens are sexually active, and the ones who are do a better job of protecting themselves.[12,13]

Another potential source of conflict, anxiety, and misunderstanding is **sexual orientation,** one's attraction toward people of a particular gender. Heterosexuals (or straight people) are attracted to members of the opposite sex, whereas homosexuals (gay men and lesbian women) are attracted to members of the same sex. A number of scientific studies indicate that 1 percent of men and 4 percent of women are homosexual.[14,15,16] Most of the remaining men and women are heterosexual, with perhaps 1 percent bisexual (attracted to members of both sexes).

We do not know precisely what determines sexual orientation, but research suggests that some possibilities are unlikely. Studies have *not* been able to establish that homosexuality is related to parenting styles, a person's hatred or fear of the opposite sex, or a childhood history of being raised by or exploited by homosexual adults.[17–19] There have been studies suggesting that a variety of biological factors may impact sexual orientation. For example, several hundred animal species exhibit some same-sex behavior,[20] and researchers have changed the sexual orientation of rats by manipulating the mother's hormones during pregnancy.[21,22]

A final aspect of physical development in adolescence relates to continued maturation of the brain, a process that begins before birth. After puberty, the brain becomes more efficient as unused connections among nerve cells in the brain disappear.[23] The frontal lobes of the brain—responsible for planning, judgment, and controlling impulses—are the last to complete this development, a process that isn't fully completed until about 25 years of age.[24]

> **sexual orientation** Enduring sexual attraction toward people of the opposite sex (heterosexuality), one's own sex (homosexuality) or to both sexes (bisexuality).

MAKE IT STICK!

1. _____ is a girl's first menstruation.

2. True or false? Development of the testes is a secondary sexual characteristic.

3. Enduring sexual attraction toward members of one's own or the other gender is called sexual _____.

Cognitive Development in Adolescence

13-3 How does adolescent reasoning differ from that of younger children?

Reasoning

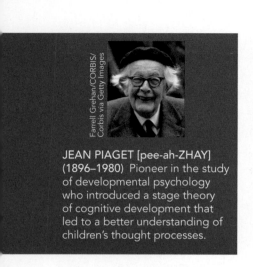

JEAN PIAGET [pee-ah-ZHAY] (1896–1980) Pioneer in the study of developmental psychology who introduced a stage theory of cognitive development that led to a better understanding of children's thought processes.

As we move through our childhood, we progress through a sequence of increasingly sophisticated cognitive abilities. By the time adolescence begins, we are approaching what developmental psychologist **Jean Piaget** (pronounced pee-ah-ZHAY) called the *formal operational stage,* when we may develop adult thinking and reasoning. Formal logic, abstract thinking, and hypothetical reasoning are now possible, and these changes represent *qualitative* growth in cognitive skills. Adolescents with these skills don't just think more, they think differently. Trying to teach a typical 6-year-old calculus would be futile because children at this age simply can't get it. Introducing these courses in high school is a different story. By adolescence, most young people will have the mental tools to take on these abstract concepts.

Of course, adolescents don't think with perfect clarity and logic all the time. According to David Elkind,[25] this is an age when one tends to focus on the self, often imagining that one's own feelings are unique. Falling in love for the first time may lead to the feeling that this experience is unlike anything anyone else has ever felt. And a first breakup can be so intense that it's nearly impossible to believe that others (even parents!) have had similar experiences.

This focus on the self makes some adolescents prone to impulsive behavior and risk taking (for example, think of the time you spent several hours on a video game instead of finishing a required school project, the teens who start smoking, or those who take risks on mountain bikes or skateboards). As we learned in the previous section, this may be partly biological, too. The brain's frontal lobes, largely responsible for long-term planning and impulse control, aren't fully mature until the mid-twenties.

Despite this focus on self, people of your age are fully capable of idealistic thinking and can quickly recognize and condemn the hypocrisy you now so easily detect in the adult world around you. You and your age mates tend to work hard for causes in which you believe. Plus, your newfound formal operational skills may also lead you to examine your own and others' religious beliefs on a much deeper level than your childhood understandings allowed.[26,27] This ability to think about your own thinking is called *metacognition,* an important skill that can help you process information and learn more effectively.

Growing Cognitive Capabilities
Teenagers are often eager to exercise the reasoning skills that mark their entry into Jean Piaget's formal operational stage. For some, this takes the form of involvement in society's important ethical debates. For example, students across the country demonstrated for increased gun control after the school shooting in Parkland, Florida, in 2018.

Morality

One special aspect of cognitive development is morality—a sense of right and wrong. Psychologist **Lawrence Kohlberg's** theory of moral reasoning demonstrates how our way of thinking about moral situations changes with our level of development.[28,29] In his research, Kohlberg posed moral dilemmas to his research participants. Here is one such dilemma Kohlberg used:

In Europe, a woman was near death from a very bad disease, a special kind of cancer. There was one drug that the doctors thought might save her. It was a form of radium that a druggist in the same town had recently discovered. The drug was expensive to make, but the druggist was charging 10 times what the drug cost him to make. He paid $200 for the radium and charged $2000 for a small dose of the drug. The sick woman's husband, Heinz, went to everyone he knew to borrow the money, but he could get together only about $1000, which was half of what it cost. He told the druggist that his wife was dying and asked him to sell it cheaper or let him pay later. But the druggist said, "No, I discovered the drug and I'm going to make money from it." Heinz got desperate and broke into the man's store to steal the drug for his wife.

This story has a very dated feel to it now, but you can see how Kohlberg used it to identify people's thought processes. He was not interested so much in whether a person decided Heinz was right or wrong. Rather, he wanted to capture the moral *reasoning* individuals used to make their decisions about this and other scenarios. From the answers he received, he developed a theory that organized moral development into three levels in which the focus shifts from concern with self (preconventional), to concern with fitting in (conventional), to concern with broader ethical principles (postconventional). We can think of these levels as three rungs on a moral ladder (see **Figure 13.4**):

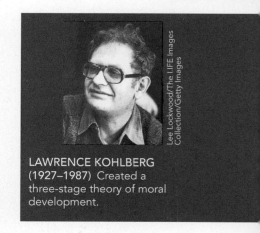

LAWRENCE KOHLBERG (1927–1987) Created a three-stage theory of moral development.

▲ **FIGURE 13.4**
Climbing Lawrence Kohlberg's Ladder of Moral Development
As moral reasoning progresses, the focus changes from concern with self (preconventional), to concern with fitting in (conventional), to concern with broader ethical principles (postconventional).

1. *Preconventional moral reasoning*—This primitive level of moral reasoning is characterized by a desire to avoid punishment or gain reward. Most children under the age of 9 show this type of moral reasoning, and some adults never progress beyond this level. Examples of statements that indicate preconventional reasoning include, Heinz was wrong to steal the drug because he might be put in jail, or Heinz was right to steal the drug because he would then have the companionship of his wife longer.

2. *Conventional moral reasoning*—The primary concern of conventional moral reasoning is to fit in and play the role of a good citizen. People at this level have a strong desire to follow the rules and laws of society. Conventional moral reasoning is typical of most adults, according to Kohlberg. It is generally apparent by early adolescence, when Piaget's formal operational thought kicks in. Examples of statements indicating conventional moral reasoning include, Heinz was wrong to steal because stealing breaks the law, or Heinz was right to take the drug because most people would do what they must to protect a family member.

3. *Postconventional moral reasoning*—Postconventional moral reasoning is characterized by references to universal ethical principles that represent the rights or obligations of all people. Most people do not reach this third level. Individuals at the postconventional level might say, Heinz was justified because everyone has a right to live, and he was simply trying to help his wife stay alive, or Heinz was wrong because everyone must respect the property of others, even the property of a selfish and greedy druggist.

Has Kohlberg's theory of moral reasoning survived the test of time and the scrutiny of other researchers? As is often the case, some evidence supports his theory, while some doesn't fit quite so well. Follow-up studies support the idea of a progression from preconventional to conventional thought in childhood.[30] The postconventional stage is not strongly supported. The evidence indicates that this stage is largely a product of the white male population Kohlberg sampled.[31,32] This sample came mostly from groups that value *individualism*. In North America and Western European countries, for example, individual goals tend to take precedence over group objectives (children are taught to stand on their own two feet and think for themselves). And in these countries, there is evidence of a progression to postconventional thinking. But in more *collectivist* cultures (like many in Asia), with a greater emphasis on shared group goals (children are taught to put the needs of the family and community ahead of the self), the notion that postconventional morality is superior to conventional morality receives less support. Similarly, North American women, who tend to be more communal than their male counterparts, also show less of Kohlberg's postconventional reasoning.

Kohlberg emphasized moral reasoning, but Jonathan Haidt[33–35] believes that *feelings* are more important than reasons. Haidt argues that we make up our minds in moral situations based on intuition—what our gut tells us—and then use reasoning to defend our gut reactions. Whether our moral choices are based more on reasoning or more on our head or our gut, they are important choices in our lives. Ten years from now, how do you think you will feel about the moral choices you are making now as a teenager?

1. Which best describes the stage that Jean Piaget stated most young people enter during adolescence?

   a. Reasoning that involves thinking about the effects our moral actions have on others
   b. The ability to think logically and form theories about abstract questions
   c. A search for both identity and intimacy through exploration
   d. The risk-taking stage because of crucial sexuality decisions

2. According to Lawrence Kohlberg, most adolescents would think it's wrong to drive through a red light because

   a. you might get caught and have to go to traffic court.
   b. we need to respect the rights of other drivers.
   c. we imagine what it's like to be in a car hit by the car that runs the red light.
   d. it's against the law and the rules of the road.

3. Kohlberg's stages may not apply in _____ cultures—cultures that place greater emphasis on shared group goals.

Social Development in Adolescence

 13-4 What behaviors support Erikson's idea that developing a sense of identity is the primary challenge of adolescence?

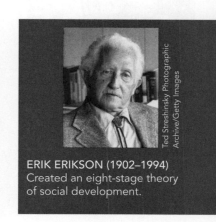

ERIK ERIKSON (1902–1994) Created an eight-stage theory of social development.

To be human is to be social. Even the shyest among us experiences some social interaction as a part of normal development. Social interaction lies at the heart of all communication, from daily negotiations between siblings to the gestures exchanged by drivers squabbling over who has the right of way at an intersection. Your friendships and romances, decisions about conformity and nonconformity, and concerns about popularity and separation from family all relate to social development.

Erik Erikson's theory of social development[36] illustrates how certain issues peak during different periods of life, including adolescence. He divided the life span into eight stages, ranging from infancy to late adulthood (see **Table 13.1**). Each stage has its own psychosocial developmental task. This task is a challenge, and the way the individual handles the task will lead to a more desirable or less desirable outcome. For example, in healthy situations, infants will develop more trust than mistrust, toddlers will develop more autonomy than shame or doubt, and preschoolers will show more initiative than guilt about their attempts to be independent. Let's take a closer look at what Erikson had to say about adolescence and young adulthood, the two stages you are closest to.

Developing Identity

During adolescence and into the early twenties, your primary task is to develop an **identity,** a strong, consistent sense of who and what you are. According to Erikson, the adolescent's task is to solidify this sense of self by testing and integrating various roles. As you try on different ways of thinking and behaving (What do I value in life? What are my priorities? Why did I act that way?), your goal is to generate an ever-stronger sense of self.

identity One's sense of self; according to Erikson, the adolescent's task is to solidify a sense of self by testing and integrating various roles.

Initiative versus guilt

Industry versus inferiority

Identity versus role confusion

TABLE 13.1 Erikson's Stages of Psychosocial Development

Stage (Approximate Age)	Issues	Description of Task
Infancy (0 to 1 year)	*Trust vs. mistrust*	If needs are dependably met, infants develop a sense of basic trust.
Toddlerhood (1 to 3 years)	*Autonomy vs. shame and doubt*	Toddlers learn to exercise their will and do things for themselves, or they doubt their abilities.
Preschooler (3 to 6 years)	*Initiative vs. guilt*	Preschoolers learn to initiate tasks and carry out plans, or they feel guilty about efforts to be independent.
Elementary school (6 years to puberty)	*Industry vs. inferiority*	Children learn the pleasure of applying themselves to tasks, or they feel inferior.
Adolescence (teen years into 20s)	*Identity vs. role confusion*	Teenagers work at refining a sense of self by testing roles and then integrating them to form a single identity, or they become confused about who they are.
Young adulthood (20s to early 40s)	*Intimacy vs. isolation*	Young adults struggle to form close relationships and to gain the capacity for intimate love, or they feel socially isolated.
Middle adulthood (40s to 60s)	*Generativity vs. stagnation*	Middle-aged people discover a sense of contributing to the world, usually through family and work, or they may feel a lack of purpose.
Late adulthood (late 60s and older)	*Integrity vs. despair*	When reflecting on his or her life, the older adult may feel a sense of satisfaction or failure.

The search for identity during adolescence has several characteristics:

- *Experimentation*—Adolescents often experiment in healthy ways: exploring and taking advantage of a variety of school opportunities, observing various adult role models, or imagining life in a variety of careers. (What would it be like to be a physician? An artist? What about a schoolteacher, a nurse, or a firefighter?) As adolescents sort out what is and isn't appealing, experimentation can become less healthy and productive, such as involvement with drugs or risky sexual behavior.

- *Rebellion*—Healthy development includes building some independence. Most parents have an image of what their children should become, and most children maintain the same core values as their parents. Nevertheless, the search for identity during adolescence may involve testing the limits parents set or adopting styles of fashion and grooming that adults may not accept or understand. But the drive for independence becomes unhealthy when rebelling against society's standards takes the form of criminal or self-destructive behavior. Healthy adolescents exercise their independence in ways that do not harm themselves or others.

- *"Self"-ishness*—Relationships during adolescence tend to be "self"-ish. Teens increasingly learn about their unique selves as they move in and out of friendship cliques and romances. Each new relationship is a chance to try different ways of interacting. Teen friendships are genuine and important, but they tend to be temporary. Some people do maintain lifelong friendships with high school friends, but most young adults find that these friendships become fond memories as they settle into career and family patterns a few years later. Of course, if you'd told me this when I was a teenager, I would have said you were nuts! My friends were the center of my life in high school, but as I finished my education and moved on to my career, most of these friendships gradually and naturally gave way to others that have lasted longer. It will be interesting to see if technology makes it easier for your generation to maintain high school relationships than it was for mine, which had no access to social media apps and had to make costly long-distance phone calls.

"Mom, you were young once ... right?"

- *Optimism and energy*—Most teenagers, armed with their new and more powerful cognitive skills, view the world with a fresh (and refreshing) perspective. They have trouble understanding why some children go to bed hungry and why adults tolerate pollution, discrimination, racism, or a thousand other injustices. Many adolescents are willing to tackle serious issues related to human rights, environmental concerns, political campaigns, and other causes. This willingness to contribute time and effort not only helps make the world a better place, but also helps teens develop a strong sense of their own priorities. (For more on the benefits of optimism, see Adolescence, Optimism, and Positive Psychology.)

Some adolescents realize a strong sense of identity with little or no struggle. A few may remain confused throughout their lives. Meeting this psychosocial challenge is especially difficult for those individuals who have struggled with the developmental tasks of previous stages. As you might imagine, achieving a sense of who you are is a lot easier if you're already trusting, autonomous, full of initiative, and industrious. Erikson felt that adolescents who had not achieved the developmental goals of their younger years could experience profound confusion about their place in the world. But even if developmental goals do not come easily, they are always within reach. Most of us hit some rough patches before the pieces settle into place in the late teens or twenties.

Who Am I?
As adolescents search for a strong sense of identity, they may experiment with a variety of different looks.

Adolescence, Optimism, and Positive Psychology

Erik Erikson teaches us that optimism is an important characteristic of adolescent identity. But how do you measure optimism? And does optimism really provide benefits? According to research done by positive psychologists, optimism truly is an important ingredient for happy, productive lives. Before we take a look at some of the benefits of optimism, answer this brief survey to see how you measure up on optimism.

Life Orientation Test: How Optimistic Are You?

Respond to each statement using the following scale:

0—strongly disagree; 1—disagree; 2—neutral; 3—agree; 4—strongly agree

1. In uncertain times, I usually expect the best.

2. If something can go wrong for me, it will.

3. I'm always optimistic about my future.

4. I hardly ever expect things to go my way.

5. I rarely count on good things happening to me.

6. Overall, I expect more good things to happen to me than bad.

To score yourself, first reverse the numbers you placed in answer to statements 2, 4, and 5. That is, for each of these items, change 0 to 4, 1 to 3, 3 to 1, and 4 to 0 (a 2 remains a 2). Leave the numbers in front of the rest of the statements unchanged. Then add up the numbers in front of all items to obtain a final score. Scores range from 0 to 24, with higher scores reflecting greater optimism. The average (mean) score is between 14 and 15.[37]

If you scored 15 or above on the test, you are above average in optimism. Among college students, those who are more optimistic are less likely to experience loneliness, stress, and depression.[38] They are also less likely to experience physical illness.[39] These psychological and physical benefits seem to persist throughout the life span. In fact, optimistic people live an average of 7.5 years longer than those who are less optimistic.[40]

Developing Intimacy

According to Erikson, young adults strive to achieve **intimacy**—the ability to form close, loving, and open relationships with other people; relationships that involve honest self-disclosure of feelings, ideas, and activities. Many people have their most intense, intimate relationship with a spouse, but not all marriages achieve this type of closeness. Intimacy is not necessarily sexual by nature, and it often occurs outside marriage with close, trusted friends and family members.

As noted earlier, Erikson realized that baggage from previous developmental stages would accumulate as we move from one stage to the next and that this baggage would affect our ability to negotiate current developmental challenges. Young adults facing the challenge of intimacy versus isolation cannot share themselves honestly and openly if they are still confused about their own sense of self.

Independence From Family

In Western cultures, separating from family to become more independent begins in childhood but picks up speed in adolescence.[41] Children move from a primary

Ron Levine/Getty Images

Intimacy ▲
Young adults strive to develop intimate relationships based on open, honest communication.

intimacy In Erikson's theory, the ability to form close, loving, open relationships; a primary task in early adulthood.

LIFE MATTERS
The Affordable Care Act now allows children up to the age of 26 to remain on their parents' health insurance. As you become an emerging adult, you can discover exactly who you are and what you want from life without the added expense of healthcare.

attachment to their parents to a primary attachment to their peers. You can observe this in any mall if you watch parents interacting with their preschool-age children and then watch parents interacting with their teenage children. Your first observation will probably be that not as many teenagers go to the mall with their parents! In fact, teens mostly hang out with other teens, and their relationships may be cliquish.[42] Because of this teenage tendency for cliques, some teenagers feel excluded; these teenagers are prone to depression and loneliness, and a few of them may even lash out violently.[43]

When parents and adolescents are together, they will probably display less warmth and emotional closeness than you'll see in families with younger children. **Figure 13.5** shows how this progression develops over time. As children become adolescents, arguments with parents tend to become both more frequent[44] and more intense.[45]

Some families suffer as this move toward independence separates parents and children, but a much greater number adjust with a minimum of turmoil. Most of the time, parents and teenagers get along quite well, with 97 percent of U.S. teenagers reporting that they get along either "fairly" or "very" well with their parents.[46] In another study, more than half of all middle-class teenagers in a worldwide survey said that family relationships were the "most important" guiding principle in their lives, and 80 percent rated family relationships as "important."[47] This is good because a growing number of children will remain at least partially dependent on their parents for financial support and housing until their mid-twenties, a phase called *emerging adulthood*, which is defined in the next module.[48-50]

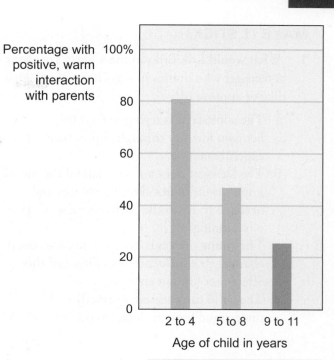

▲ **FIGURE 13.5**
Changes in Parent–Child Relationships Over Time
A large survey of Canadian families shows that there is less warmth, and presumably more distance, in parent–child interactions as children grow older. (From Statistics Canada, 1999.)

▲ **Independence**
Most adolescents achieve independence with relatively little friction in the family. Sometimes, however, things can become tense.

MAKE IT STICK!

1. What would Erik Erikson most likely say about a teenager who dresses in ways her parents don't like or approve of?

   a. The adolescent is trying to establish her own identity through appropriate experimentation.

   b. The teenager does not understand the moral implications of her clothing choices and needs to move to the postconventional stage of reasoning.

   c. The young person is experiencing hormonal changes that influence sexuality, and this affects her fashion choices.

   d. The child can't reason abstractly and understand how she looks to other people.

2. Erik Erikson's theory explains that many adolescents seem overly focused on themselves because

   a. they haven't yet developed the postconventional reasoning skills they need.

   b. they are going through hormonal changes that affect frontal lobe development.

   c. their hypothetical reasoning skills are just beginning to develop.

   d. they are searching for their sense of personal identity.

3. _____ _____ describes a period when children remain partially dependent on their parents for support into their twenties.

Three Key Developmental Issues

 13-5 How do developmental psychology's three major issues apply to adolescence?

Let's take a quick look at the three major developmental issues as we prepare to leave adolescence behind.

Continuity and Stages

Is our development more like the stage development of a tadpole turning into a frog or more like the continuous, gradual development of a sapling imperceptibly changing over many years into a towering oak tree? In adolescence and throughout the life span, there is support for both positions. The theorists who have played such a prominent role in developmental psychology have focused on the abrupt changes as individuals move through stages. Piaget identified these jumps for cognitive development, Kohlberg was concerned with changes in moral development, and Erikson examined transitions in social development. Other researchers turn their attention to the more gradual growth that occurs within stages, similar to the slow but steady increase in strength produced by a weight-training program. Development relies on both continuity and stages.

Stability and Change

The period of adolescence is affected by both stability and change. Temperament and values are most likely to stay constant; relationships and certain behaviors are more likely to change. Many successful and happy adults were troubled people at your age.

Nature and Nurture

This pervasive issue is as important in adolescence as in other developmental periods. We can see the role of nature in the genetically determined sequence of changes that spark sexual feelings and interests. But nurture's hand is also evident: Adolescents learn to make decisions about expressing sexuality from their families and society. The expression of sexuality is determined by a complex interaction of both nature and nurture.

The opportunities and challenges of modern adolescence are a reflection of a complex world. Life was simpler in the nineteenth century, when educational and career opportunities were more limited, but few of us would choose to return to those more limiting times. Navigating adolescence successfully can be difficult, and most who travel this road will hit a few potholes along the way. It can also be an exciting adventure as people learn new freedoms and master new skills.

MAKE IT STICK!

1. Which of the following factors is most likely to remain stable throughout adolescence?

a. Identity
b. Abstract thinking skills
c. Temperament
d. Risk-taking behaviors

2. True or false? Nature refers to the impact of genetics on development.

3. _____ is the idea that changes throughout life are slow and gradual.

Module 13 Summary and Assessment

Adolescence

 13-1 What is adolescence, and how does our culture affect it?

- Adolescence is the transition period from childhood to adulthood.
- Adolescence begins with sexual maturation.
- The end of adolescence is more variable because people become adults at different times depending on how their society defines adulthood.

 13-2 What major physical changes occur during adolescence?

- Puberty, triggered by hormones, is the period of sexual maturation during which a person becomes capable of reproducing.
- Primary sex characteristics are related to the reproductive organs.
- Secondary sex characteristics are nonreproductive, like beard development in boys and breast development in girls.

 13-3 How does adolescent reasoning differ from that of younger children?

- Adolescents reason in Jean Piaget's formal operational stage, during which adult thinking and reasoning skills develop.
- Lawrence Kohlberg described how moral reasoning develops as we mature. Adolescents usually think at the conventional moral reasoning stage.

 13-4 What behaviors support Erikson's idea that developing a sense of identity is the primary challenge of adolescence?

- The search for identity during adolescence has several characteristics: experimentation, rebellion, "self"-ishness, and optimism and energy.
- Adolescents change their primary attachment from their parents to their peers, which can cause turmoil, but most adolescents report positive relationships with their parents.

13-5 How do developmental psychology's three major issues apply to adolescence?

- Researchers describe distinct stages that depict development in adolescence, but continuous development also occurs.

- The period of adolescence is affected by both stability (values) and change (new friendships).

- The development of sexuality during adolescence is determined by a complex interaction between nature and nurture.

Summative Assessment

1. Adolescence ends when a person
   - a. turns 21 and achieves legal adult status.
   - b. turns 20 and leaves the teen years behind.
   - c. is fully independent.
   - d. has a child.

2. In the United States, adolescence
   - a. is getting longer.
   - b. is getting shorter.
   - c. lasts about as long as it did a century ago.
   - d. got longer for several decades but is now getting shorter again.

3. A physical change in adolescence is
   - a. the development of identity.
   - b. puberty.
   - c. an increase in the sophistication of moral reasoning.
   - d. the beginning of formal operational thinking.

4. By the time the changes of puberty are complete, the brain
   - a. is fully developed.
   - b. continues to generate many more connections in the brain.
   - c. begins to slowly shrink in size.
   - d. continues to develop for almost 10 additional years.

5. Erik Erikson is noted for describing _____ changes in adolescence.
   - a. physical
   - b. moral
   - c. social
   - d. cognitive

6. A collectivist culture would be most likely to
   - a. try to provide each child with his or her own bedroom.
   - b. allow children to try to solve their own problems independently.
   - c. consider the toys in the family to be owned by all the children together.
   - d. emphasize individual goals over the goals of a group.

7. Erik Erikson argued that the search for identity was most likely to be characterized by
   - a. optimism and energy.
   - b. postconventional reasoning.
   - c. formal operational thinking.
   - d. decisions based on feeling rather than reasoning.

8. Erik Erikson believed that intimate relationships are
   - a. always sexual.
   - b. always with one's spouse.
   - c. likely to interfere with other important life goals.
   - d. always close, open, and loving.

9. As you move from childhood to adolescence, it is common for
   - a. family relationships to become less important and peer relationships to become more important.
   - b. peer relationships to become less important and family relationships to become more important.
   - c. both family and peer relationships to increase in importance.
   - d. both family and peer relationships to decrease in importance.

10. During normal adolescent development, which is most likely to stay stable?
    - a. Food preferences
    - b. Friendships
    - c. Temperament
    - d. The ability to reason

KEY TERMS AND KEY PEOPLE

adolescence, p. 198

puberty, p. 199

primary sex characteristics, p. 200

secondary sex characteristics, p. 200

sexual orientation, p. 201

identity, p. 205

intimacy, p. 208

Jean Piaget [pee-ah-ZHAY] (1896–1980), p. 202

Lawrence Kohlberg (1927–1987), p. 202

Erik Erikson (1902–1994), p. 205

Adulthood and Aging

Module 14

From childhood and adolescence to adulthood and senior citizenship, aging brings about many transitions.

Learning Goals

14-1 Define the concept known as the *social clock*; describe how it relates to the transition from adolescence to adulthood.

14-2 Describe the physical changes that occur in middle and late adulthood.

14-3 Explain the cognitive changes that occur in middle and late adulthood.

14-4 Describe the likely effects of social changes (such as marriage, meaningful employment, and the aging process) on happiness and life satisfaction.

How many times have you been asked, What are you going to do after you graduate? You've given this some thought, right? Will you go to college or enter the work force? No doubt you're getting all kinds of advice. Perhaps you've even been told what type of job to take, where to go to college, what your major should be, or how you would benefit from sitting out a year just to take a break from learning. Making decisions about life after high school is a big milestone in your ongoing transition from adolescence to early adulthood, from being dependent on your parents to being dependent on yourself. In this module, we look at some other transitions that we all make as we move from early to middle to late adulthood (see **Table 14.1**).

TABLE 14.1 Periods of Adulthood

Period	Approximate Age Brackets
Early adulthood	20–35 years
Middle adulthood	36–64 years
Late adulthood	65 years and over

Early Adulthood Transitions and the Social Clock

14-1 What is the concept known as the social clock, and how does it relate to the transition from adolescence to adulthood?

As you continue your journey from adolescence to adulthood, you'll face many other important questions: When will you move out of your parents' house? Where

social clock The culturally preferred timing of social events such as marriage, parenthood, and retirement.

will you live? Will you marry? If so, when? And if you decide to raise children, how many? The **social clock,** the culturally preferred timing of age-related social events such as marriage, parenthood, and retirement, may influence your answers to these questions. For example, if you got your driver's license shortly after you turned 16 or 18 (depending on your state), you were "on time." However, if you were 34 and still didn't have your driver's license, you would be "off time" and people would be likely to ask, What's wrong with you? These social events or transitions can cause anxiety for those who feel they're not keeping up with their peers.

Social clocks have different settings in different cultures. For instance, in Jordan, 40 percent of all brides are in their teens, but in Hong Kong, only 3 percent of brides are this young.[1] The settings of a social clock can change within a culture, too. In the United States, for example, the "normal" time span for many life events, including marriage, has changed. Both men and women are marrying later in life than they did even 10 years ago.[2]

The transitions in early adulthood can be stressful, often because we make so many of them at once. Where you are 2 years from now will be different from where you were as a ninth grader. Yet your transition to adulthood will probably be less abrupt than it would have been a generation ago. Developmental psychologists have noticed that adolescents are easing more slowly into the self-sufficiency of true adulthood. A new developmental stage between age 18 and the mid-twenties (and longer), called **emerging adulthood,** is receiving a lot of attention from researchers.[3,4] Christopher Munsey[5] has summarized the five features of emerging adulthood:

emerging adulthood A period from the late teens to the mid-twenties (and sometimes later), bridging the gap between adolescent dependence and full independence and responsible adulthood.

- *Age of identity exploration*—The process of deciding who you are and what you would like to get out of school, love, and work.

- *Age of instability*—Marked by moving from place to place; the frequent moves usually end once a career or a family is in place.

- *Age of self-focus*—Deciding who to be with, where to go, and what to do without being concerned about parental restrictions (or the constraints of a family).

▲ **Culture Affects the Social Clock**
In developed countries, even great-grandmothers go for their diplomas, as did this 87-year-old Smith College graduate, and teenagers are discouraged from marriage and parenting. However, grandmothers don't often go to college in developing nations, such as Indonesia, and teenagers often marry and have children.

- *Age of feeling between*—Even though you're taking responsibility for your decisions, you still don't feel like an adult.

- *Age of possibilities*—Full of optimism, emerging adults believe they will live better than their parents and will find a soul mate.

Consider my friends Andrew and Jennifer, who are 25 years old and married. In changing careers and moving from one state to another, Andrew and Jennifer made an 8-month stopover at his parents' home to prepare for their new jobs and to save money for rent in their new city. Andrew and Jennifer would like to have children someday, but they don't yet feel settled enough to be parents. Andrew and Jennifer aren't unique. Amos, another friend of mine, is 34 and has a good job, but he still brings laundry to his parents' home on the weekends. He also relies on their financial assistance periodically to make ends meet. Andrew, Jennifer, and Amos are increasingly common examples of the changing social clock in Western cultures. They aren't adolescents, but they have not quite made the complete transition into adulthood.

Time to Grow Up?
Some emerging adults stretch out the transition time from adolescence to adulthood.

MAKE IT STICK!

1. Which of the following is most likely to be influenced by your culture's social clock?

   a. Going through menopause
   b. Giving birth to a first child
   c. Being diagnosed with Alzheimer's disease
   d. Declining fluid intelligence

2. According to this textbook, which of the following is not one of the five features of emerging adulthood?

   a. Impossibilities
   b. Identity exploration
   c. Instability
   d. Self-focus

3. True or false? Someone who, after graduating from college, moves back in with her parents to figure out what she wants to do with her life might be going through what's referred to as the dependent adulthood stage.

Physical Changes and Transitions

14-2 What are the physical changes that occur in middle and late adulthood?

You're not there yet, but you are less than a decade from reaching your performance peak for reaction time, sensory awareness, and cardiac output. Most of these physical abilities will top out sometime during your twenties. Olympic sprinters notice their times slowing as they age regardless of how hard they work out, as they start to lose races they used to win. For the rest of us, the early signs of physical decline are harder to detect.

Middle Adulthood's Physical Changes

The midlife years, from around age 36 to 64, are a time of noticeable physical changes, and these changes bring their own transitions. Twenty-five years ago, I was always told to go long during my family's annual Thanksgiving Day touch football game. Sprinting down the field, I would look over my shoulder for a high, arching pass that would score a touchdown if I managed to catch it. Now, though, my nieces, nephews, and daughters are the touchdown threats. Me? I hike the ball and pretty much just stand there while the quarterback throws the ball to someone who can, well, run.

Is This Middle Age?
Midlife identity crises are the exception, not the norm.

menopause When the menstrual cycle ends; also refers to the biological changes a woman experiences as her ability to reproduce declines.

Some cultures welcome the outward signs of growing older, believing that the older members of society deserve status and respect. This is not the case in the United States, where cheating the aging process is a billion-dollar business that just keeps growing. I can remember sitting in church as a child, trying to figure out how many people around me dyed their hair. If I played this game now, the count would be much higher. Fewer middle-aged adults, male or female, carry the heads of gray hair I saw as a child. And the camouflage doesn't stop with hair color. Some try to hide wrinkles with cream; others stretch their skin surgically with a face lift to appear younger.

A clear sign of aging in women is **menopause,** when the menstrual cycle ends, which is usually between the ages of 45 and 55. Contrary to popular belief, menopause *does not* make most women depressed or irrational. Most women do experience hot flashes as their body adjusts to the decreased amount of estrogen in their hormonal systems, but study after study has found that menopausal women are no more or no less depressed than women who are not experiencing this change.[6-8] Most women express "only relief" once their periods stop, with a mere 2 percent expressing "only regret."[9]

There is no male reproductive event equal to menopause. Men's testosterone levels drop, but not at the sharp rate at which estrogen levels decrease in women. Although sperm counts decline, men do not lose their fertility. And for men, as for women, the notion of a midlife crisis is more Hollywood than reality. Midlife crises are the exception, not the norm, and they usually coincide with a traumatic event, such as the death of a spouse or a close friend of a similar age.

Later Adulthood's Physical Changes

When I was a young boy, my grandmother would turn on every light in the room when she saw me reading. I'd tell her there was plenty of light; she'd tell me it was too dark. Now I know that we were both correct: The light was fine for me but not for her. How could this be so? The answer lies in the physical changes that affect our senses and our health as we age.

Our sight, smell, and hearing usually begin to decline significantly once we hit age 65 (see **Figure 14.1**). That decline began in early adulthood, but most people fail to notice the small sensory loss until they are older. Muscle strength and stamina also diminish in late adulthood, and our bodies take longer to heal after injury.

FIGURE 14.1
Declining Senses
Our ability to see, smell, and hear declines with age. (Data from Doty et al., 1984.)

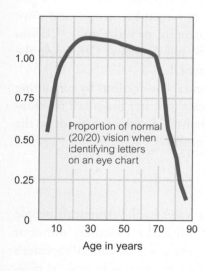

Proportion of normal (20/20) vision when identifying letters on an eye chart

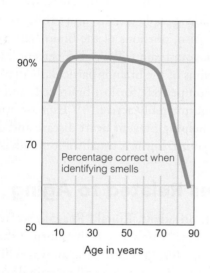

Percentage correct when identifying smells

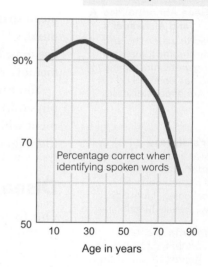

Percentage correct when identifying spoken words

So, why did Grandma turn on all the lights? Her 72-year-old corneas and lenses had become less transparent, letting in only about 30 percent of the light that entered my young eyes. To experience the same level of illumination I was experiencing, Grandma needed lights three times brighter.

▲ **Fountain of Youth?**
Exercise is important throughout the life span to maintain mental and physical health.

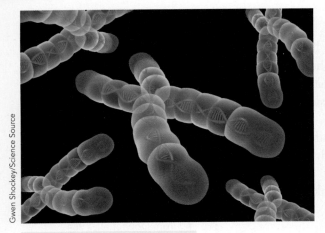

Gwen Shockey/Science Source

Gene Abnormalities and Alzheimer's ▲

Dead tissue on the end of some chromosomes can alter genetic functioning and has been linked to Alzheimer's disease.

Alzheimer's disease
A progressive and irreversible brain disorder characterized by gradual deterioration of memory, reasoning, language, and, finally, physical functioning.

senile dementia Mental disintegration that accompanies alcoholism, tumor, stroke, aging, and, most often, Alzheimer's disease.

Does health automatically take a downhill turn as you become advanced in years? The answer is *yes* and *no*. Your immune system will weaken as you age, increasing your susceptibility to disease. However, by the time you hit 65, you'll have built up antibodies to all the viruses you've ever had, making you less likely to catch a common cold.

Aging also slows travel on our neural pathways. Our chromosomes' protective tips, called *telomeres*, fray much like the end of a rope as a person gets older, especially if the person smokes (which shortens telomeres), is under stress, or is overweight. Without perfect telomeres, the chromosomal cells may die without an identical genetic replacement.[10,11] So, frayed telomeres in the chromosomal cells necessary for memory could mean that older people require more time to react, remember names, and solve puzzles.[12,13] Also, portions of the brain start to atrophy, or waste away.[14] If you live to be 80, your brain will weigh 5 percent less than it does now. Cell loss in the memory regions of the brain is particularly detrimental.

You can compensate for lost brain cells and neural connections by remaining physically and mentally active.[15,16] Exercise appears to foster brain cell development while helping prevent heart disease and obesity.[17] Exercise may not be the fountain of youth, but it is usually a fountain of health.

Diseases Related to Aging

Our fortieth president, Ronald Reagan, wrote a letter to the American people in 1994, stating, "I now begin the journey that will lead me into the sunset of my life." At age 83, President Reagan was telling the world he had **Alzheimer's disease,** a progressive and irreversible brain disorder characterized by gradual deterioration of memory, reasoning, language, and, ultimately, physical functioning.

Memory loss is caused by deteriorating neurons that produce a vital brain chemical (acetylcholine). Without this chemical, thinking and memory are greatly impaired. Almost 3 percent of the world's population develops Alzheimer's disease by age 75.

Certain drugs (for instance, Exelon and Namzaric) slow down the advance of Alzheimer's disease, but there is no known cure. Research is showing that challenged and active minds—that is, the minds of people who read a lot and continue to learn across the life span—are at lower risk for Alzheimer's onset.[18] Inactive and obese individuals are more likely to experience Alzheimer's disease.[19] Gene abnormalities and dead tissue on the ends of neurons (that prevent normal functioning) have been linked to Alzheimer's disease, and a simple blood test can now be used to at least partially determine the likelihood of developing the disease.[20]

Senile dementia is another form of mental decline (see **Figure 14.2**). Dementia can be caused by alcoholism, tumor, strokes, or anything else that results in a major loss of brain cells.

Not every older adult who forgets song titles or the location of that misplaced address book has senile dementia or Alzheimer's disease. Some memory loss is a normal part of aging. And the news about cognitive functioning isn't all bad, either. Look next at what happens to our thinking processes as we age.

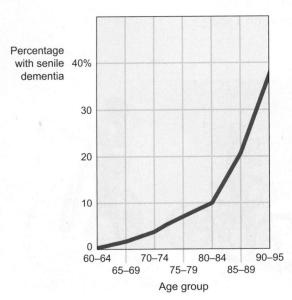

Percentage with senile dementia (y-axis: 0, 10, 20, 30, 40%)
Age group (x-axis: 60–64, 65–69, 70–74, 75–79, 80–84, 85–89, 90–95)

FIGURE 14.2 ▲
Senile Dementia and Age
The likelihood of senile dementia increases as we grow older. (Data from Jorm et al., 1987, based on 22 studies in industrialized nations.)

1. What is a common misconception about menopause?

   a. Menopause causes a decline in intelligence.
   b. Menopause is influenced by cultural social clocks.
   c. Menopause leads to senile dementia.
   d. Menopause leads to regret, confusion, and depression in most women.

2. Which of the following is a progressive and irreversible brain disorder that is characterized by gradual deterioration of memory and reasoning?

   a. Menopause   c. Alzheimer's
   b. Telomeres   d. Emerging adulthood

3. True or false? All older adults who forget song titles or where they put things have either senile dementia or Alzheimer's disease.

Cognitive Changes and Transitions

 14-3 What are the cognitive changes that occur in middle and late adulthood?

Most 65-year-olds cannot run as fast as most 20-year-olds. Do thinking skills slow just as much as physical skills? What do you think: Can't teach an old dog new tricks or Never too late to learn? Researchers have been taking a close look at how our thinking skills decrease as we age, and the findings show that the answer partly depends on what kind of memory and intelligence we are discussing.

Memory

When you're 50, what will you remember about your high school days? Will it be getting your driver's license? Your first job? Your longest Snapstreak? Some cell phone app (that likely no longer exists)? Graduation? When asked to remember the most important events in their lives, people in their fifties and older usually recall events from their teens or early twenties.[21] This is an important time of life!

People your age tend to do better on *recall* memory tasks—tasks that give us no clues to jog our memories—than people in virtually any other age group. One study found that young adults recalled people's names significantly better than did people in their seventies.[22] Another study asked British people to tell about where they were, whom they were with, and what they were doing when a popular prime minister resigned from office. Participants had to tell the story twice: once within hours of the resignation and the second time 11 months later. Among participants in their twenties, 90 percent told the same story they had related 11 months earlier. Interestingly, only 42 percent of those 50 and over told stories with the same details.[23] In the older group, recall of the event changed over time.

Research reveals a clear tendency for younger adults to have better recall, but what does it tell us about other kinds of memory? One study revealed that *recognition* remains stable from age 20 to 60.[24] Older adults had difficulty recalling a list of words, but they could recognize them in multiple-choice questions just as

"My advice is to learn all the tricks you can while you're young."

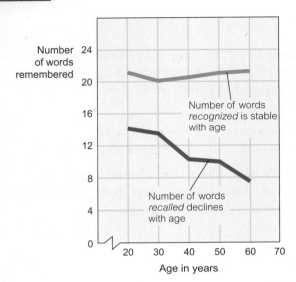

FIGURE 14.3
Better at Recognition
In late adulthood, the ability to recognize words does not decrease as rapidly as the ability to recall words. (Data from Schonfield & Robertson, 1966.)

fluid intelligence
The ability to reason speedily and abstractly.

crystallized intelligence
Accumulated knowledge and verbal skills.

FIGURE 14.4
Age and Intelligence Test Scores
Even after adjusting for educational background, verbal intelligence test scores (a measure of crystallized intelligence) remain steady with age. (Adapted from Kaufman et al., 1989.)

easily as people 40 years younger (see **Figure 14.3**). Older adults maintain the ability to remember meaningful materials (like anniversaries) yet lose the skills necessary to remember meaningless information (like a series of nonsense syllables).[25–27] As a teen, you are better at remembering to do something than your 70-year-old relatives.[28] Prospective memory, which is the ability to remember habitual tasks like taking medicine every day and time-oriented tasks like appointments, also declines in older adults.[29–31]

It's important to note that in all of these studies we are only talking about average tendencies. I know people in their seventies who have incredible memories for historical facts and events. On the flip side, I have teenage students who can't seem to remember the difference between Piaget and Kohlberg. I've seen 60-year-old retirees outperform college students on a memory test, but I also know of others in their sixties who can't out-remember eighth-graders. These individual differences also show up in measures of intelligence.

Intelligence

As with memory, the question of whether intelligence declines as we age depends on the kind of intelligence we're considering. **Fluid intelligence** is our ability to reason speedily and abstractly. We use fluid intelligence to solve novel logic problems like Sudoku puzzles. This kind of intelligence tends to *decrease* during late adulthood. **Crystallized intelligence,** our accumulated knowledge and verbal skills, tends to *increase* with age.[32,33] Intelligence test scores show this difference. Common IQ tests often measure verbal intelligence scores—a measure of crystallized intelligence—and these scores tend to remain stable with age. Nonverbal IQ tests (for example, the time it takes to put a puzzle together) measure fluid intelligence and decline over time (see **Figure 14.4**).

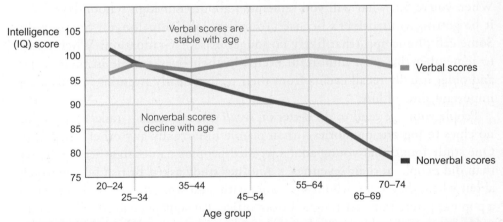

Nonverbal Intelligence

Verbal Intelligence

Perhaps increased crystallized intelligence is one of the reasons most chief executive officers of companies and international leaders are in the latter half of their life span. Similarly, literature, like William Shakespeare's *Julius Caesar,* often depicts sages as older people who dole out advice for everyone to follow. Professions that favor one type of intelligence over another also differ in their patterns of creativity. Historians and philosophers tend to produce their best work in their forties, fifties, and sixties, whereas mathematicians and scientists often do their most creative work in their twenties and thirties.[34,35]

MAKE IT STICK!

1. Which of the following intelligence-related tasks would probably be harder for *older* people than *younger* people?

   a. Remembering their anniversary
   b. Recalling the name of someone they made an appointment with last week
   c. Recognizing a picture of their kindergarten teacher
   d. Determining whether a picture of an object matches the label of the object

2. Which of the following tasks would probably be harder for *younger* people than *older* people?

   a. Listing 50 words that were just shown on flash cards
   b. Putting a jigsaw puzzle together
   c. Solving a crossword puzzle
   d. Figuring out the answer to a new logic problem

3. True or false? Crystalized intelligence tends to decrease in most 50- to 60-year-olds.

Social Changes and Transitions

14-4 What are the likely effects of significant life events (such as marriage, meaningful employment, and the aging process) on happiness and life satisfaction?

Many transitions of adulthood hinge on significant *life events,* rather than physical or cognitive changes. Family and work-related events often bring major life-style alterations. For instance, marriage brings both the happiness of a close relationship and the challenge of blending two lives together. Starting a new job creates new friends, expectations, and demands. The birth of a child starts a series of new responsibilities that last a lifetime. All of these life events involve social transitions. Next, we discuss two major parts of adulthood—work and love.

College Majors, Work, and Happiness

Deciding on a first career is an important and difficult decision. You may have a twinge of envy for a classmate who already knows she is going to be an engineer and who will declare a major in the first month of college. But you can take heart in knowing that your classmate is the exception, not the rule. Most first- or second-year college students

1. change their initial major field of study.

2. cannot accurately predict the careers they will have later in life.

3. change careers after entering the work force.

Challenge, Accomplishment, and Happiness
Happiness at work depends on whether you feel good about what you've accomplished at the end of the day and whether you felt challenged while doing it.

Keep in mind that postcollege employment is often unrelated to a college major.[36]

Many people think that a career should make someone feel self-fulfilled and satisfied with life. One study addressing the work–happiness connection compared women who were employed and those who were not employed (by choice). The researchers concluded that it's the *quality of the experience,* as a paid worker or as a stay-at-home mother, that most influences happiness. At the end of the day, happiness is about having work that is challenging, provides a sense of accomplishment, and fits your interests.[37,38]

Love and Marriage

Do opposites really attract? Yes, but only if we're talking about magnets. It doesn't really work for love. And love by any name—commitment, devotion, intimacy, or attachment—is vital to a happy adulthood. Love lasts longer and is most satisfying when marked by

- intimate self-disclosure (that is, sharing embarrassing moments or deep secrets).
- shared emotional support (like empathy when things go wrong) and material (monetary) support.
- similar interests (leisure activities) and values (political, moral, and religious).

For many, love translates into marriage: 90 percent of our population gets married at least once. Those marriages are more likely to last if both members are in their mid-twenties or older, have a stable income from good employment, dated a long time (at least a year) before getting married, and are well educated.[39] Out of every two marriages in the United States, one will end in divorce.[40] Three out of four who divorce will marry a second time.[41]

A Happy Union
Married men and women report greater happiness than unmarried, separated, or divorced individuals.

Despite the prevalence of divorce, the bond of marriage remains a popular living arrangement, just as it has in various human societies through the centuries. One reason the institution of marriage endures is because of the well-being it brings to the couple. Married men and married women report greater happiness than unmarried, separated, or divorced individuals.[42] Females in committed same-sex relationships also report greater well-being than individuals who remain alone.[43,44]

Must a marriage be free of conflict to last? *No.* In fact, few marriages avoid conflict, but one indicator of marital success is the way that couples interact. Stable marriages typically have a 5-to-1 ratio of positive to negative interactions. Marriages last when each partner compliments, hugs, and smiles at least five times more than he or she insults or criticizes.[45,46]

Love and marriage often result in the birth of children, an event that is usually met with great happiness. However, raising a child requires a serious investment of time, money, and emotion, which can exact a heavy toll on a couple's satisfaction with each other. As couples make the transition to being parents, they may disagree about the division of labor in the new family structure. Many women who work outside the home still do most of the child-raising and housekeeping.[47,48] Couples who make the effort to spread the workload more evenly can anticipate a double reward: a more satisfying and successful marriage and better parent–child relationships for both parents.[49]

The empty nest syndrome, when children move out of the house, is also a significant event. Yet you may be surprised to hear that an empty nest brings more happiness than sadness.[50–52] Middle-aged women with children at home report lower levels of happiness and less marital satisfaction than those with an empty nest. If the relationship with the children moving out is positive and close, parents are likely to experience a "postlaunch honeymoon."[53]

▲ **Sharing the Load**
Couples who balance household duties have a more satisfying marriage and better relationships with their children.

A Lifetime of Well-Being

Aging often brings a shrinking income, a deteriorating body, less energy, and the loss of friends and family to death, yet retired adults still have a strong sense of well-being.

In one study, researchers collected interview data from almost 170,000 people in 16 nations and found that older people are every bit as happy and satisfied with life as younger folks are[54] (see **Figure 14.5**). Another study showed that young people around the age of 25 are far more likely to report feeling worthless, sad, or nervous than are those in their seventies.[55] Is it any wonder that—with some of the biggest stressors of life behind them, like choosing a career and a partner for

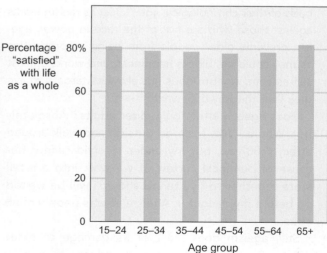

▲ **FIGURE 14.5**
Satisfaction Remains High
This multinational survey shows that age does not matter much when it comes to being satisfied with your life. (Data from Inglehart, 1990.)

marriage—the older set is satisfied with life as a whole? We can all take comfort in these findings as we look forward to our own aging future. (See Psychology in the Real World: Ageism.)

We also tend to mellow as we age.[56,57] Emotions are less extreme and more enduring later in life. Older people tend to experience life more evenly—the good things don't make them overly happy, and bad things don't drag them down. An older adult is less likely to feel on top of the world but also less likely to feel depressed.[58] This middle way appears to offer contentment, even if intense joy is rare.

As an older adult, well-being may also depend on how you reflect on your past. Will you be satisfied with what you've done, or will you look back with regret? Interestingly, most of the regrets retirees express run along the lines of I wish I had done that bike ride across Iowa or I'm sorry I didn't tell my father more often that I loved him. Most regrets seem to focus on things the person *didn't* do rather than on mistakes made while actively pursuing a goal.[59]

PSYCHOLOGY IN THE REAL WORLD

Ageism

Common beliefs about the aging process result in negative stereotypes—oversimplified and biased views of what people are like. . . . The stereotype would have us believe that old people are tired, cranky, passive, without energy, weak, and dependent on others.[60]

Does the preceding quote reflect your beliefs about elderly people? If so, your thoughts also reflect *ageism*, the tendency to categorize and judge people on the basis of their chronological age.[61] Just as racism works against those who are not of the race in power, ageism prevents older people from being as productive as they could be, blocks happiness, and works against self-esteem. Ageism does not allow its targets to live their lives the way they want.[62]

Does ageism affect only older adults? *Absolutely not.* Where I live, I can go outside and walk around after 11:00 P.M., but my under-18 child cannot because of our local curfew. If we walk into a retail store together to buy tennis shoes, I will be waited on before my daughter. Ageism affects people of all ages.

Still, ageism does most of its damage to older adults. By prejudging them, it reduces their self-steem and their ability to participate in society. It also fosters an attitude that accepts ageist policies, such as mandatory retirement. However, the tide seems to be turning. As Baby Boomers age and swell the numbers of retired Americans, stereotyping the elderly is becoming more difficult. The clichéd image of the rocking-chair grandparent is being replaced by mountain-climbing, marathon-running older people living life to the fullest.

As the number of retirees increases, society is finding it more difficult to ignore the needs of this segment of the population. The politician who endorses legislation that negatively affects the over-65 set stands to lose a sizable number of votes from a group that regularly makes its opinion known at the polls. Finally, advances by *gerontologists*, those who scientifically study old age, may help change the perception of older people as tired, cranky, and passive. This change in perception may also help all of us identify with older people as our future selves instead of elderly others.[63]

THINK ABOUT . . . Psychology in the Real World

1. What do we call the tendency to judge people based on age?

2. What is another word for those who scientifically study old age?

3. How does ageism affect you? Recall a time when you felt discriminated against due to your age.

Adding Life to Your Years

Some would say that *successful aging* is an oxymoron. Not so, says Harvard psychiatrist and world-renowned aging expert George Vaillant, whose research has shown that "you can add life to your years instead of just years to your life."[64]

Vaillant has been involved in the most comprehensive study on aging ever conducted for over 40 years. The original study began in the 1930s, with over 800 students at Harvard tracked from adolescence until old age or death. What leads to a healthier, longer life? The results have been both surprising and reassuring.

"I had expected that the longevity of your parents, the quality of your childhood, and your cholesterol levels would be very influential," says Vaillant. "So I was very surprised that these particular variables weren't more important than they were."[65]

Obsessing over things we can't control, such as genetic factors, is time poorly spent. Vaillant[66] recommends several tips to increase the likelihood of moving successfully from middle age to your eighties and nineties:

- Pursue education as far as your intelligence permits.

- Stop smoking if you've started.

- Maintain strong social relationships (including a stable marriage).

- Don't use alcohol to the point of shaming yourself or your family.

- Keep your weight down.

- Stay physically active: Walk, mow the grass, or play tennis.

- Use ingenuity to cope with stress (make lemonade out of lemons).

With regard to the last tip about stress, Vaillant emphasizes that stressful events were not a great predictor of long and healthy lives. According to Vaillant, "Some people had a lot of stress, but aged very well. But how you deal with that stress does matter quite a bit."[67]

Dying and Death

Few escape the sadness of having to cope with the death of relatives or friends. One spouse typically outlives the other, a grief suffered five times more often by women than by men. When the death is sudden and unexpected, grief and subsequent depression can be particularly hard to handle and may continue for years.[68]

Reactions to death vary from culture to culture. In some African cultures, death brings status to an elder, who joins the ancestors in watching over those still living in the village.[69] Some cultures encourage a stiff upper lip and hiding of grief; others, including many Muslim nations, expect outward and obvious expressions of grief by both men and women.[70] No matter what the culture, there are always individuals who grieve significantly more or significantly less than others.[71]

In the United States, attitudes toward death appear to be changing. There is a greater openness toward the inevitability of death and facing

Hospice Care
This nurse is checking in on a man with a terminal disease. The fresh flowers on the mantel help create a more pleasant atmosphere than that of a typical hospital.

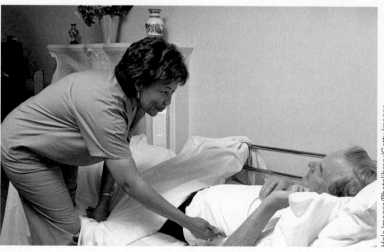

Hola Images/Photolibrary/Getty Images

it with dignity. Many patients with terminal illnesses are choosing *hospice care* instead of an impersonal and lingering hospital death. In hospice care, patients receive comforting medical attention (often in their own homes) but avoid advanced life-support measures (such as heart defibrillation or inserting a tracheal tube through the throat to breathe). Hospice care strives to make the dying person's remaining days as pleasant as possible while keeping family and friends informed and encouraging them to visit. Part of the hospice philosophy is helping the dying prepare for death while maintaining human dignity.

Although we know that everyone eventually dies, dealing with the death of a loved one can be very difficult. One popular misconception about grieving is that those who express strong grief immediately get rid of their grief more quickly. This simply is not true.[72] And there is no evidence to support the idea that we progress through predictable stages, like anger, denial, and acceptance.[73] Some people grieve briefly, while others grieve for months or years. Both counseling and the passage of time possess healing power.[74] Kathleen Berger[75] reminds us of the value of grief:

> No matter what rituals are followed or what pattern is evident in human reactions to death, the result may give the living a deeper appreciation of themselves as well as of the value of human relationships. . . . [T]he lessons of death may lead to a greater appreciation of life, especially of the value of intimate, caring relationships. (p. 25 of the epilogue)

What are the lessons of death from mourners? We should learn from the grieving, who say, I should have told him how much I loved him. Tending to our important human relationships, resolving differences, and expressing appreciation to those we love may help us avoid devastating regret later in life.

MAKE IT STICK!

1. Which of the following best describes the research findings related to work and happiness?

   a. Happiness leads to certain work decisions, not the other way around.

   b. Higher-paying careers lead to increased happiness levels.

   c. Work and happiness aren't strongly related; social relationships determine happiness.

   d. Interesting and challenging work is most likely to increase happiness levels.

2. What do we call it when a patient receives comforting medical attention (often in their own home) and avoids advanced life-support measures?

   a. Ageism   c. Hospice care
   b. Well-being   d. Empty nest syndrome

3. According to your textbook, love lasts longer and is more satisfying when marked by all of the following except

   a. one person controlling all the money.

   b. intimate self-disclosure.

   c. shared emotional support.

   d. similar interests (political, moral, and religious).

4. Which of the following is the worst predictor of happiness at work?

   a. Work that fits your interests

   b. Work that pays well

   c. Work that you find challenging (to a point)

   d. Work that provides a sense of accomplishment

Module 14 Summary and Assessment
Adulthood and Aging

 14-1 What is the concept known as the social clock, and how does it relate to the transition from adolescence to adulthood?

- The culturally preferred timing of social events, referred to as social clocks, differs across cultures and historical periods.

- Developmental psychologists refer to the stage between adolescence and adulthood as emerging adulthood, a period that includes identity exploration, instability, self-focus, a feeling of being between, and a feeling of possibility.

 14-2 What are the physical changes that occur in middle and late adulthood?

- We reach our physical peak (in reaction time, sensory awareness, and cardiac output) in our twenties, and these attributes begin to decline in our mid to late thirties.

- Some cultures value the signs of aging, but others resist them.

- Women experience menopause in middle adulthood, usually between the ages of 45 and 55. There is no male equivalent of menopause, although testosterone levels and sperm count drop somewhat as men age.

- In late adulthood, our eyesight weakens as our eyes let in less light. Our immune system also weakens, and the neural pathways in our brain slow.

 14-3 What are the cognitive changes that occur in middle and late adulthood?

- Our performance on memory recall tasks worsens as we age, but our performance on memory recognition tasks remains stable as we age (at least between the ages of 20 and 60).

- Fluid intelligence tends to decrease during late adulthood, while crystallized intelligence tends to increase with age.

 14-4 What are the likely effects of significant life events (such as marriage, meaningful employment, and the aging process) on happiness and life satisfaction?

- Research indicates any work that is challenging, provides a sense of accomplishment, and fits our interests will likely increase our general happiness.

- Romantic relationships last longer when they include high levels of self-disclosure, emotional support, and similar interests. Men and women in committed relationships report greater well-being than individuals who remain alone.

- Older people report happiness and life satisfaction levels similar to the levels reported by younger people.

- Reactions to death vary from culture to culture and vary widely among different people.

Summative Assessment

1. What do we call the period of the late teens to the mid-twenties that bridges the gap between adolescent dependence and responsible adulthood?

   a. Social clock
   b. Identity exploration
   c. Self-focus
   d. Emerging adulthood

2. What did Christopher Munsey call the time in a person's life when one is full of optimism and believes that he or she will find a soul mate?

   a. Age of possibilities
   b. Age of feeling between
   c. Age of self-focus
   d. Age of instability

3. What is another word for the biological changes a woman experiences as her ability to reproduce declines?

    a. Social clock

    b. Telomeres

    c. Menopause

    d. Alzheimer's disease

4. What is another term for our accumulated knowledge and verbal skills?

    a. Crystallized intelligence

    b. Fluid intelligence

    c. Dementia

    d. Alzheimer's disease

5. Which of the following helps love last longer?

    a. Holding back emotional support

    b. Keeping leisure activities separate from one another

    c. Sharing embarrassing moments

    d. Having different political and religious views

6. In general, which of the following is an accurate statement about older adults?

    a. Middle-aged women with children report being happier than same-aged women with no children.

    b. The empty nest syndrome often brings more happiness than sadness.

    c. Older people are not nearly as happy as younger people.

    d. Those older than 65 are more likely to experience extreme emotions; bad things really drag them down.

7. What do we call the tendency to judge people based on age?

    a. Well-being

    b. Ageism

    c. Gerontology

    d. Crystallized thinking

8. Which of the following is likely to benefit moving successfully from middle age to your eighties?

    a. Cutting strong social relationships

    b. Reducing physical activity

    c. Using ingenuity to cope with stress

    d. Eating and drinking as much as you want

9. What do we call the kind of care that strives to make a dying person's final days as pleasant as possible?

    a. Death-defying intervention

    b. Ageism

    c. Life satisfaction

    d. Hospice

10. Psychological research has conclusively _____ the theory that most people go through predictable stages of grieving, such as anger, denial, and acceptance.

    a. debunked

    b. supported

    c. ignored

    d. taken a neutral stance toward

KEY TERMS

social clock, p. 214

emerging adulthood, p. 214

menopause, p. 216

Alzheimer's disease, p. 218

senile dementia, p. 218

fluid intelligence, p. 220

crystallized intelligence, p. 220

Language Development

Our lives are awash in words. Words populate our songs, provide the basis for our conversations, and make TV shows understandable. This book is literally filled with them. How is it that language has become such an important part of our lives? Let's find out!

Learning Goals

15-1 Describe the building blocks of language.

15-2 Explain the evidence for each of the competing theories of language acquisition.

15-3 Summarize the stages of language development.

What if you couldn't share your thoughts and ideas with others? Our awesome ability to communicate is perhaps the most impressive of our *cognitive*, or mental, abilities. **Language** includes our spoken, written, or gestured words and the ways we combine them to communicate in a meaningful way. Without language, a tremendous amount of our technology would be useless—phones, computers, radios, music streaming services, and televisions are all, in essence, machines to help us communicate. The technological revolution enhanced our ability to use language, but communication was healthy long before the advent of high-tech tools. Books, newspapers, and letters all depend on language, as do the relationships we cherish with family and friends. Remove language and we sever our link to our past, forcing each generation to rethink, reinvent, and re-experience all the things our ancestors could have taught us.

language Our spoken, written, or gestured words and the ways we combine them to communicate meaning.

kali9/E+/Getty Images

sirtravelalot/Shutterstock

▲ **Lessons in Culture**
Language is one important way children learn about their culture. Human culture as we know it would not exist without language, which lets us transmit our ideas across barriers of time and space.

229

Building Blocks of Language

 15-1 What are the building blocks of language?

To build a house, you need materials and knowledge of the rules required to assemble the materials properly. A particular house might require concrete, wood, drywall, plumbing fixtures, and so forth. If you try to assemble these parts without following construction and engineering principles, the house probably won't survive the first windstorm. Language is similar—we build our language from basic elements and follow rules to determine how we can combine the pieces.

The most basic building block is the **phoneme,** the smallest distinctive unit of sound in a language. Make the sound represented by the letter *k*—that's a phoneme. So is the sound represented by the letter *b,* and the sound from the combination *th.* Each of our vowels has several phonemes (the sound of the *a* in *shape* is different from the sound of the *a* in *hat*). Hundreds of phonemes, including clicking sounds and tones, have been identified. The English language has about 40; the number of phonemes in other languages ranges from 20 to over 80. Notice that phonemes represent *spoken* sounds, not written symbols. (We will have more to say about written symbols later.)

As a young baby, you could produce all the phonemes of all the languages in the world—but only for a short time. The basic rule here is use 'em or lose 'em. By the time you reached your first birthday, you lost your remarkable ability to babble in multiple languages and instead settled into using the phonemes of your native tongue. If you are a Japanese speaker, you may find distinguishing the English *r* and *l* sounds challenging because these sounds are not part of the Japanese language. English speakers have trouble with German's breathy *ch* sound (found in *Ich,* the German word for *I*). German speakers may struggle with the English *th* and thus may pronounce *this* as *dis.*

Even sign languages (there are over 200 different sign languages) use building blocks similar to phonemes, but in this case the phonemes are hand shapes and movements. It may be difficult to learn signs if you haven't used them in childhood. People who learn sign language in China and then come to the United States and learn American Sign Language usually have an accent in the new language![1]

Phonemes don't have meaning in and of themselves—the *p* sound doesn't mean anything, nor does the *f* sound. But we can combine phonemes to form a **morpheme**—the smallest unit that carries meaning in a language. Sometimes a single phoneme can also be a morpheme, as in *I.* More often, several phonemes combine to form a morpheme like *water,* which has four phonemes: *w, a, t,* and *r* (the written *e* has no sound of its own in this word). Words often have more than one morpheme. *Waterfall,* for example, has two: *water,* the liquid that fills lakes and rivers, and *fall,* the idea that the water is going over an edge and cascading downward (see **Figure 15.1**). How many morphemes do you think there are in *watered*? If you said two, you're right. In this case, the second morpheme is the *-ed* suffix, indicating an event that happened in the past. Every time you add a prefix or suffix to a word (like *un-* in *unwind* or *-less* in *motionless*), you've added a morpheme. The important thing is that these two building blocks—phonemes

---

phoneme In language, the smallest distinctive sound unit.

morpheme In language, the smallest unit that carries meaning.

● Fun with language: How do you pronounce *ghoti*? (Turn the page after making your best guess.)

LIFE MATTERS

Using a mnemonic device is helpful when memorizing similar sounding terms. Morpheme has an "m" and morphemes are the smallest unit of meaningful language, which also starts with an "m."

FIGURE 15.1
Phonemes and Morphemes
The word *waterfall* has seven distinct sounds, or phonemes. There are two morphemes, one to represent that wet stuff and one to indicate that it's cascading over a ledge. ▼

7 phonemes

W A T E R F A L L

2 morphemes

and morphemes—allow almost infinite flexibility in language. In spoken English, we use our 40 phonemes to construct an estimated 100,000 morphemes. With those building blocks of meaning, we can generate hundreds of thousands of words. From here, the estimates almost seem silly, with literally trillions of possible unique sentences (see **Figure 15.2**). The level of complexity that can be generated from simple building blocks is the distinguishing feature of language.[2]

As you know, just stringing several words together does not create a sentence. To have a sentence, you must follow the rules of **grammar**—a system of rules that govern how we can combine phonemes, morphemes, and words to produce meaningful communication. Despite these elaborate rules, language can still be hopelessly, and sometimes humorously, unclear (see **Figure 15.3**). Consider the phrase, Don't threaten someone with a chainsaw. This sentence has perfect grammar, but you still can't tell which of the two possible meanings the speaker intended. Take a minute to identify what the two meanings are. If you can't, ask a friend to help you figure it out. Personally, I think either interpretation constitutes good advice!

The grammar we've been talking about is not the system of rules you learn in your English or writing classes. Those classes do teach some rules of English grammar, but you were able to put sentences together long before you ever entered a classroom. Written language is a separate topic because it's a system by which we use symbols (in a visual representation or code) to represent spoken sounds. Even people who live in remote areas of the world with no ability to read or write use complicated grammar in their everyday speech. Such grammar, for example, has specific rules for placing adjectives (Do we say *red rose* or *rose red*?) or for indicating the status or gender of someone you are addressing (for example, you wouldn't say, "Hey, dude!" to your school principal). Grammar is part of our spoken language, and how we learn it and everything else we call language has generated a lot of debate in psychology. You probably won't be surprised to find that the debate focuses on nature and nurture.

Trillions of sentences

Hundreds of thousands of words

100,000 morphemes

40 phonemes

26 letters

▲ **FIGURE 15.2**
Flexibility in Language
The phonemes and morphemes of the English language can be combined in countless ways to produce an almost infinite number of meaningful sentences, which we write using an alphabet of only 26 characters.

grammar The system of rules governing how we can combine phonemes, morphemes, and words to produce meaningful communication.

Snapshots

FIGURE 15.3
Grammar Isn't Everything
Despite being grammatically correct, this sentence is open to several interpretations: "The artist painted me on the front porch."

● Answer to the question at the start of this section: Consider how *gh* is pronounced in the word *enough*, how *o* is pronounced in the word *women*, and how *ti* is pronounced in the word *emotion*. That's right—*ghoti* is pronounced *fish*!

Language Acquisition

 15-2 What is the evidence for each of the competing theories of language acquisition?

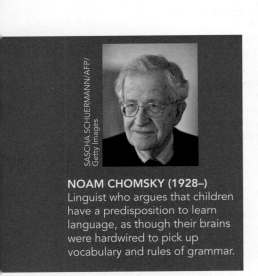

NOAM CHOMSKY (1928–)
Linguist who argues that children have a predisposition to learn language, as though their brains were hardwired to pick up vocabulary and rules of grammar.

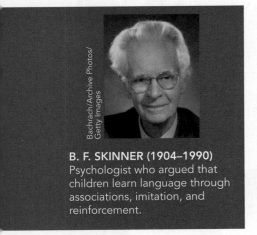

B. F. SKINNER (1904–1990)
Psychologist who argued that children learn language through associations, imitation, and reinforcement.

Linguist **Noam Chomsky** believes that our brains are wired to process vocabulary and rules of grammar virtually without effort.[3,4] According to this view, we have a predisposition to language—it's part of our heritage as a human species, just as flying is part of a bird's heritage. Even deaf children with no instruction in language will develop gestures to communicate and use grammatical rules to govern the use of the gestures.[5]

But is it part of our heritage to speak a *particular* language? If you are a native English speaker, imagine bending over the crib of your firstborn child, putting the baby to sleep for the night. The child looks up at you, smiles sleepily, and says, *Gute Nacht,* or *Bonne nuit.* Wouldn't you be amazed—perhaps even a little nervous? Babies from English-speaking homes are supposed to speak English, not some other language. Why? This is where nurture steps in. **B. F. Skinner,** famous for his studies of the effects of rewards on behavior, maintained that language learning is nothing special—we learn it just as we learn everything else. Thus, he said, we learn our language through *association* (linking certain sounds with certain people or objects), *imitation* (doing what we see others doing, including their manner of speaking), and receiving (or not receiving) *rewards* (hugs, smiles, and so on).[6]

Most psychologists today believe that Chomsky and Skinner were both partially right and both partially wrong. Chomsky's view that humans have a predisposition to learn language helps explain why all languages in the world have complicated sets of rules that children seem to master at amazingly young ages. Skinner's view that we learn language through association, imitation, and rewards helps explain why we speak the language we hear at home. As is the case in so much of psychology, language is neither simply nature nor simply nurture. It's both, interacting to give us a rich tool with which we communicate events, feelings, beliefs, and emotions to other humans.

There is no question regarding the importance of language acquisition, because language influences how we think. Bilingual individuals experience this all the time, and the impact can be pretty profound. For example, when Chinese-born students at a university in Canada were asked to describe themselves in Chinese, they responded with statements that would be typical of Chinese culture. However, when they described themselves in English, their descriptions were similar to those of native Canadians. It's almost like they became slightly different people when they switched languages![7]

Let's look now at how and when children master this wonderful tool we call language. (And also take a look at Thinking Like a Psychological Scientist: Animal Language to discover whether animals can learn human languages.)

MAKE IT STICK!

1. _____ argued that a child will repeat a parent's words to earn the parent's praise.

2. Which of the following statements best summarizes the language acquisition debate between behaviorists (like B. F. Skinner) and cognitive psychologists (like Noam Chomsky)?

   a. Behaviorists think language is acquired through rewards, and cognitive psychologists think the brain is wired to learn language.

   b. Language is acquired in stages according to behaviorists, but cognitive psychologists think it is acquired mostly in childhood.

   c. Cognitive psychologists emphasize how we model language use, and behaviorists look to brain research to explain language acquisition.

   d. Noam Chomsky thinks language is best learned as an adult, and B. F. Skinner thinks it's easiest to learn language as a child.

3. True or false? Most researchers now believe that nurture has much more to do with the acquisition of language than nature does.

THINKING LIKE A PSYCHOLOGICAL SCIENTIST

Animal Language

Do animals have language? I often sense that my Labradoodle is trying to tell me something, and he often appears to understand what I tell him. Sometimes he even obeys! With enough time and effort, could we expand our communication into a full-fledged language?

Psychologists have been trying to answer this question for more than a century, most often with chimpanzees. In the 1930s, Winthrop and Luella Kellogg raised an infant chimpanzee, Gua, in their home, along with their son, Donald. They wondered whether the chimpanzee might develop language abilities if they raised it as a human. The Kelloggs did learn some interesting things from their work with Gua, but—despite eating in a high chair and wearing clothes like little Donald's—the chimpanzee never did learn to talk.[8]

Maybe Gua didn't learn to talk because chimpanzees' vocal structure differs from that in humans. To get around this problem, later researchers, most notably Allen and Beatrix Gardner, launched a project to teach chimpanzees American Sign Language (ASL), used by deaf humans.[9] The Gardners' first student was the now-famous Washoe,

who soon acquired a vocabulary of 132 signs. Roger Fouts, who with Deborah Fouts would later become the leading spokesperson for chimpanzees, was one of the Gardners' assistants in the late 1960s, charged with making baby Washoe's life "as stimulating and linguistic" as possible. In 1970, Washoe—and the research program that grew up around her—became Roger Fouts's primary responsibility. He and Deborah Fouts set up a program in which many of the people caring for Washoe and other chimpanzees were themselves deaf and whose first language was ASL. Washoe continued to thrive, and by the late 1990s, she had increased her vocabulary to almost 200 signs, where it remained until her death in 2007.[10] She sometimes used amazing creativity to combine these signs to describe items. And perhaps most amazing of all, Washoe taught signs to her adopted son, Loulis, who picked up 55 signs while under her care. Here is a sample conversation between Loulis and his chimpanzee playmate, Dar:[11]

1. Loulis asked for a water balloon from Dar by holding his hand toward the balloon and signing, "Hurry, hurry."

(Continued)

THINKING LIKE A PSYCHOLOGICAL SCIENTIST (Continued)

2. When Dar moved away, Loulis signed, "Want."

3. When Dar moved away again, Loulis signed, "Hurry, hurry. Gimme."

4. Dar gave the balloon to Loulis, and the two chimpanzees separated.

Gary Stewart/Ap photos

▲ **Washoe**
Washoe could communicate with humans (and other chimpanzees) using a vocabulary of nearly 200 signs.

Nobody doubts that these accomplishments are remarkable. The key question is, do they constitute language? The answer depends on how you define *language*. Even with a loose definition, psychologists are skeptical that any chimpanzee's communication skills can come close to matching those of a young human. One trained chimpanzee used 16 signs to ask for an orange: "Give orange me give eat orange me eat orange give me eat orange give me you."[12] The idea comes across, but hardly with the type of efficiency one would hope for. A great deal of effort produces limited results with chimpanzees, whereas humans master language almost effortlessly. As amazing as these communicating chimpanzees are, their very limitations help illustrate how astounding human language ability is.

THINK ABOUT . . . Psychological Science

1. What method did Winthrop and Luella Kellogg use to determine whether or not the chimpanzee Gua was capable of learning language?

2. Why do you suppose Allen and Beatrix Gardner chose to teach their chimpanzees American Sign Language instead of spoken English?

3. How do you think true language differs from communication?

Language Stages

 15-3 What are the stages of language development?

Have you ever tried to learn a second language? If so, you're surely aware that language is immensely complicated. There's a lot of work involved, and even if you're diligent about it, progress is usually slow if you are a teenager or older. If you travel to an area where the language is spoken, you'll quickly realize that despite your efforts, you're nowhere near fluent. The few students who do become fluent usually still have an accent unlike that of native speakers. Why is it so much harder for you to learn the language in high school than it is for your 2-year-old cousin, who picks it up with no quizzes or vocabulary flashcards? It's because our predisposition to learn language easily only exists during the early years of our childhood. Just as we go through a maturational sequence of learning how to walk early in life, we also go through one for learning how to talk. Here are the steps involved:

1. *Babbling*—By 4 months of age, amazing human language skills are already becoming apparent. Babies are spontaneously producing phonemes and are sophisticated enough to be able to discriminate speech sounds made by others.[13,14] When babbling, children will produce phonemes they have never heard before, but within a few months they will begin to specialize in the

sounds used in the languages they hear spoken. By 10 months of age, an expert can identify the language spoken in a home by merely listening to the babbling baby.[15]

2. *One-word stage*—About the time of their first birthday, most babies begin to use their new ability to produce sounds to communicate meaning. They start with short, one-syllable words like *ma* or *da,* and they may produce them so unreliably that other members of the family argue over whether the children are communicating intentionally. Babies' skills rapidly improve, however, and soon there is a vocabulary of single words used to describe both things (*kitty*) and actions (*swing*). The pace at which children learn words accelerates rapidly, and by 18 months, the average child is learning a new word every day.

3. *Two-word stage*—By the time most children reach their second birthday, they have entered the two-word stage. Now they are building two-word sentences. Amazingly, the way they arrange these words shows an appreciation for the grammatical rules of their native language. English-speaking children put adjectives before nouns (*big house*), but Spanish speakers put the noun first (*casa grande*).

The two-word stage marks the end of the language stages. As **Table 15.1** indicates, after age 2, children build on the phonemes, morphemes, words, and grammatical rules they have already mastered to develop longer and more complex sentences.[16] Their vocabulary continues to grow, too. Throughout childhood, an average person learns 5000 words a year, most outside school.[17] That's more than 13 words a day! By the time they hit elementary school, children understand complex sentence structures. If you're average, by the time you graduate from high school, you will have a vocabulary of 60,000 words.[18]

TABLE 15.1 Stages of Language Development	
Age in Months (Approximate)	**Achievement**
4	Babbling of many speech sounds
12	One-word expressions
24	Two-word sentences
24+	Rapid development of complete sentences

As children develop their language skills, they drop interesting clues that support Chomsky's theory of language acquisition. One of the most interesting is *overgeneralization,* which occurs when children make mistakes by applying a grammatical rule they have learned too broadly. For example, English allows us to turn nouns into verbs. The object I use to play baseball is called a *bat,* and when I am standing at the plate I am *batting.* Once children master this principle, they sometimes apply it where they shouldn't (see **Figure 15.4**). A child who knows what a *broom* is may say he is *brooming,* rather than *sweeping,* the floor. The child has never been encouraged to use the word *brooming;* he has never even heard it before. Instead, he is overgeneralizing the internalized grammatical rule. Likewise, children will say that they *goed* to the store rather than *went* to the store. Beyond being kind of cute and amusing, this overgeneralization points to the brain's ability to easily soak up language rules.

Notice again that the natural, easy learning of language applies to *spoken* language. Spoken language appeared long before written language in human history. Our brains are equipped to handle it easily, but we have not yet developed mechanisms to handle

Wavebreakmedia/iStock/Getty Images

▲ **FIGURE 15.4
Overgeneralization**
This 4-year-old makes mistakes by applying rules to instances that are considered exceptions in English. For example, he might tell his grandpa about how he helped his mommy "broom the floor" before they "goed to the toy store." These mistakes show he has internalized the grammatical rules of the language.

Rachel Epstein/ PhotoEdit, Inc.

the written word as easily. We learn to speak without conscious effort as young children, yet we must go to school and work to master reading and writing. Even spoken language becomes more difficult after about age 10—when a critical developmental window seems to slam shut. In rare, tragic cases in which a child has been raised in isolation through the first decade of life, language development does not proceed normally. After this window of opportunity closes, those of us who easily developed a first language must struggle to learn a second one. Knowing this, linguists often argue that it makes more sense to introduce foreign languages in preschool than in middle or high school.

Your introductory psychology course barely scratches the surface when it comes to the wonders of human language, but one thing is certain: The course could not exist without it. The very fact that you can read about and discuss language proves its importance—which extends to every aspect of human interaction.

Beyond the Critical Period
We can learn language, and even more than one language, as a natural, automatic process when we are children because we are born with a predisposition to learn language. But there seems to be a catch—if we haven't learned language by the time we reach high school, the window of easy learning seems to slam shut and we have to work hard to master grammar and vocabulary. We should be offering foreign language in preschool!

MAKE IT STICK!

1. A young child usually enters the one-word stage at about

   a. 6 months of age.
   b. 12 months of age.
   c. 18 months of age.
   d. 24 months of age.

2. True or false? Babies babble using only the phonemes of their native language.

3. _____ is the spontaneous production of phonemes by babies.

Module 15 Summary and Assessment
Language Development

15-1 What are the building blocks of language?

- The basic building block of language is the phoneme, the smallest distinctive unit of sound in a spoken language.

- A morpheme is a single phoneme or a combination of phonemes and is the smallest unit that carries meaning in a language.

- Grammar is a system of rules that govern how we can combine phonemes, morphemes, and words to produce meaningful communication.

15-2 What is the evidence for each of the competing theories of language acquisition?

- Noam Chomsky believes that our brains are wired to process vocabulary and rules of grammar virtually without effort. Evidence for this is that all languages have complicated rules that young children are able to master.

- B. F. Skinner stated that we learn our language through association (linking certain sounds with certain objects), imitation (modeling how we see others speak), and rewards (hugs, smiles, and so on). The fact that we speak the language we hear at home is evidence of this theory.

15-3 What are the stages of language development?

- Language develops through a series of stages: babbling, the one-word stage, and the two-word stage.

Summative Assessment

1. Which of the following represents a single phoneme?

   a. The sound you make when you pronounce *bat*
   b. The sound you make when you pronounce *eat*
   c. The sound you make when you pronounce *shh*
   d. The sound you make when you pronounce *ten*

2. Young babies have the ability to produce

   a. all phonemes humans are capable of producing.
   b. only the phonemes of the language(s) spoken in their homes.
   c. only the phonemes of the language(s) spoken in their homes and other phonemes from similar languages.
   d. only the phonemes that are modeled for them by caregivers.

3. A morpheme

   a. always communicates meaning.
   b. determines the order of words in a sentence.
   c. is not likely to be produced by a baby after the babbling stage.
   d. represents a particular speech sound.

4. Noam Chomsky believes that

   a. learning language depends primarily on being reinforced for using words correctly.
   b. learning language involves making associations between words and objects.
   c. learning language gets easier as children get older.
   d. the brains of children are predisposed to make it easy to learn language.

5. Which language acquisition theorist best explains the fact that children grow up speaking the language of their parents instead of a foreign language?

   a. Chomsky
   b. Skinner
   c. Both Chomsky and Skinner provide good explanations for this.
   d. Neither Chomsky nor Skinner provides a good explanation for this.

6. Washoe, the chimpanzee,

   a. was able to learn only a few signs despite years of effort by her trainers.
   b. learned to use several thousand signs appropriately, but could not use them as flexibly and creatively as human children.
   c. learned thousands of symbols and used American Sign Language as effectively as human children.
   d. was able to teach dozens of signs to another chimpanzee.

7. The first language stage is the _____ stage.

   a. phoneme
   b. morpheme
   c. babbling
   d. one-word

8. Children enter the two-word stage of language when they are about

   a. 6 months old.
   b. 1 year old.
   c. 2 years old.
   d. 3 years old.

9. A person learns, on average, more than _____ words a day throughout childhood.

   a. 3
   b. 8
   c. 13
   d. 20

10. Which of the following is an example of overgeneralization?

   a. A child says, "Look at the three deers in the back yard."
   b. A child points at the family dog and says, "Meow, meow."
   c. A child points at her mother and says, "Daddy!"
   d. A child says, "My friend and I has two balls."

KEY TERMS AND KEY PEOPLE

language, p. 229	morpheme, p. 230	Noam Chomsky (1928–), p. 232
phoneme, p. 230	grammar, p. 231	B. F. Skinner (1904–1990), p. 232

Module 16 | Classical Conditioning

Does the name Pavlov ring a bell with you? This module, which includes the story of Ivan Pavlov and his salivating dogs, will teach you the meaning of that old and not-so-very-funny punch line.

If you ask a dozen friends what the word *learning* means, most of them will probably respond by talking about cognitive (mental) processes. One might say, "Learning is when you understand something." Another might reply, "Learning is comprehension of a topic." A third might argue, "You've learned something when it's been memorized." Surprisingly, many of the psychologists who pioneered the study of learning steered in another direction. To them, it was difficult to scientifically study these between-the-ears phenomena. Since learning is usually reflected in what a person does, these psychologists defined it as a relatively permanent change in behavior caused by experience. This emphasis on behavior is no longer as strong as it once was because psychologists have developed ways to scientifically study cognition, and this has led to a new definition: the process of gaining, through experience, relatively permanent information and behaviors. The next three modules explore three different ways that learning can occur: classical conditioning, operant conditioning, and observational learning.

Experiencing Classical Conditioning

 16-1 What is classical conditioning?

My freshman dorm in college was a cheaply built affair, and the college had cut costs on plumbing for the large, shared bathrooms on each floor. The cold water pipes were too small to supply enough water to both the showers and the toilets, which created a real problem if you were showering when someone flushed a toilet. The toilet would siphon off most of the cold water, and the shower temperature would momentarily turn hot enough to scald.

This reality led to a rule: When someone was about to flush a toilet while a dorm mate was in the shower, he was to yell, "Flush!" to warn the showerer. This was a good solution, once you learned to respond appropriately, but I had not made the connection the morning of my first shower. I heard the word "Flush!" as I languished half asleep in the water, but I did not associate it with myself and my shower. When I was struck by the painfully hot water I jumped out of the way, but my jump was a reflexive, automatic response to the hot water. I still had not made the connection.

Much learning depends on these connections or associations that are formed when two events are linked. This is why we often associate habitual behaviors, like always following the same route between classes or always turning off the TV as dinner is about to be served, with particular contexts or environments.[1] So, was I able to make the connection in my dorm? You bet I was.

After I experienced a hot water dousing a few more times, **learning** occurred. When a dorm mate yelled, "Flush!" I instantly jumped to the side, with time to spare before the water temperature spiked. I did not realize it at the time, but I had experienced **classical conditioning,** a type of learning by association where a stimulus gains the power to cause a response. I had come to associate a new **stimulus** (the word *flush*) with another stimulus (hot water). "Flush!" was now a reliable predictor that scalding water was coming, and I began to respond to the word in the same way I had responded to the hot water itself. After repeated pairings, the two stimuli were associated in my mind, and each now produced the same **response**—an immediate jump to the side. This change in behavior was proof that learning had occurred.

Classical conditioning is learning (as evidenced by my changed behavior) in which a stimulus (Flush!) gains the power to cause a response (jumping away) because it predicts another stimulus (scalding water) that already produces the response (jumping away). Whew, that's a mouthful—but at its center it's really not too complicated (see **Figure 16.1**). One stimulus begins to produce the same response as another stimulus because the learner has developed an association between the two.

Classical conditioning can help us understand a variety of behavioral and emotional responses.

learning The process of gaining, through experience, relatively permanent information and behaviors.

classical conditioning A type of learning in which a stimulus gains the power to cause a response.

stimulus Anything in the environment that one can respond to.

response Any behavior or action.

Two related events:

Stimulus 1: Calling the word "Flush!" before flushing the toilet warns that water in the shower will soon be scalding.

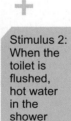

Stimulus 2: When the toilet is flushed, hot water in the shower gets much hotter.

Result after repetition:

Stimulus: We hear "Flush!"

Response: We jump, anticipating hot water.

FIGURE 16.1
An Example of Classical Conditioning
Classical conditioning is a type of learning in which a stimulus gains the power to cause a response. In this example, classical conditioning led me to respond to the word *flush* in the same way I responded to painfully hot water.

MAKE IT STICK!

1. Learning is the process of gaining, through experience, relatively permanent _____ and _____.

2. Which of the following is an example of classical conditioning?

   a. A cat learns to take the same path through the garden each day because it has found mice there before.

   b. A parrot learns to say, Hello after hearing its owner repeat the word hundreds of times.

   c. A dog learns to flinch when it sees lightning because lightning is usually followed by loud thunder.

   d. A child practices her multiplication tables until she can do them perfectly.

3. True or false? If a person jumps every time he hears the word "Flush!" the word is a response.

Components of Classical Conditioning

 16-2 How are the four main components of classical conditioning defined?

Classical conditioning is a straightforward, logical process. It is easier to understand after you have mastered a few key terms. Because we will use these terms over and over throughout our discussion of learning, it is a good idea to read through this section on the components of classical conditioning and the next section on the processes of classical conditioning a couple times. Pause at the end of each bulleted paragraph, reflect for a moment on the meaning of each term that has been introduced, and quiz yourself to make sure you've mastered the terms.

- **Unconditioned stimulus (US)**—The unconditioned stimulus is a stimulus that triggers a response reflexively and automatically, just as scalding water in a shower makes someone jump away. Hot shower water is an unconditioned stimulus for jumping away. Classical conditioning cannot happen without an unconditioned stimulus. The only behaviors and emotions that can be classically conditioned are those that can be reliably produced by a unconditioned stimulus.

- **Unconditioned response (UR)**—The unconditioned response is the automatic response to the unconditioned stimulus. If hot water is the unconditioned stimulus, jumping away is the unconditioned response. Again, notice that the relationship between the unconditioned stimulus and the unconditioned response is *reflexive and automatic,* not learned.

- **Conditioned stimulus (CS)**—The conditioned stimulus is a previously neutral stimulus that, through learning, gains the power to cause a (conditioned) response. On my first day in the dorm, the word *flush* was a neutral stimulus—I did not associate it with showers, and it did not make me jump away. Thousands of other sights and sounds around the dormitory were equally neutral stimuli for jumping away. The process of classical conditioning changed the word *flush* from a neutral stimulus to a conditioned stimulus. (This constitutes learning!) All those other neutral stimuli

unconditioned stimulus (US)
A stimulus that triggers a response reflexively and automatically.

unconditioned response (UR)
An automatic response to the unconditioned stimulus.

conditioned stimulus (CS)
A previously neutral stimulus that, through learning, gains the power to cause a response.

remained neutral. In basic classical conditioning, the neutral stimulus and the conditioned stimulus are always the same thing. The term *neutral stimulus* describes the stimulus *before* conditioning, and the term conditioned stimulus describes the stimulus *after* conditioning.

- **Conditioned response (CR)**—The conditioned response is the response to the conditioned stimulus. In basic classical conditioning, it is the same behavior that is identified as the unconditioned response. If I jump because of hot water (an unconditioned stimulus), my jumping is an unconditioned response. However, if I have learned to jump when someone yells, "Flush!" (a conditioned stimulus), my jumping is now a conditioned response.

> **conditioned response (CR)** The response to the conditioned stimulus.

MAKE IT STICK!

1. James blinks when air is puffed through a straw toward his eye. In this case, the air puff is a(n) _____ and the blink is a(n) _____.

2. Jamie blinks when she hears a tuning fork. In this case, the sound of the tuning fork is a(n) _____ and the blink is a(n) _____.

Classical Conditioning Processes

 16-3 What are the two basic processes in classical conditioning?

> Remember:
> - **Unconditioned** means automatic and reflexive
> - **Conditioned** means learned
> - A **stimulus** is something presented to the learner
> - A **response** is something the learner does

Now that you understand the four main components of classical conditioning, you need to know a little more about two basic processes in this type of learning: acquisition and extinction.

Acquisition

The most basic process in classical conditioning is **acquisition,** the process of developing a new, learned response. Acquisition occurs when a neutral stimulus is repeatedly paired with a US. Each pairing is called a *trial*.

> **acquisition** The process of developing a learned response.

In my dorm, I *acquired* the new conditioned response when a neutral stimulus—the word *flush*—was repeatedly paired with the unconditioned stimulus of hot water. Notice that we do not yet refer to the word *flush* as a conditioned stimulus because we have yet to demonstrate that the response, jumping away, was caused by anything other than the unconditioned stimulus (hot water).

To see if a conditioned response has actually been acquired, you could conduct a test trial. In this case, you would shout the word *flush* to a person (me!) in the shower without presenting scalding water (meaning you wouldn't flush the toilet). Then you would observe whether anything happened. If there is no response (no jumping away), it means the word is not yet a conditioned stimulus. However, if the person in the shower does jump away, this means "Flush!" has become a conditioned stimulus. The person jumps away because he heard the word, so the act of jumping away is a conditioned response (not an unconditioned response). "Flush!" has become a conditioned stimulus, and the jumping away has

extinction In classical conditioning, the diminishing of a learned response after repeated presentation of the conditioned stimulus alone.

become a conditioned response. You have shown that the acquisition process in classical conditioning has occurred. Once acquired, the conditioned response will be maintained only if the conditioned stimulus continues to be paired with the US on some trials.

Extinction

In classical conditioning, **extinction** is the gradual disappearance of a learned response. Extinction occurs as the conditioned stimulus loses its power to trigger a conditioned response. Recall that when we want someone to acquire a conditioned response, we repeatedly pair a neutral stimulus with the unconditioned stimulus. But if we want to reverse this learning, we must weaken the association between the two stimuli. We do this by repeatedly presenting the conditioned stimulus alone.

In the shower example, if prank-minded friends had repeatedly shouted, "Flush!" but the word was never followed by a hot-water dousing, the conditioned response to the word would eventually have weakened and died. This is because each prank "Flush!" alarm would weaken the association between *flush* and hot water. When a conditioned response has completely disappeared, we can say that it has been *extinguished*.

Figure 16.2 illustrates the processes of acquisition and extinction.

FIGURE 16.2
Two Basic Classical Conditioning Processes
Acquisition occurs as the CS and the US are repeatedly paired. Extinction happens if the CS alone is presented over time.

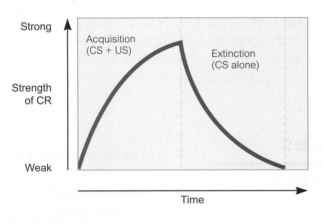

MAKE IT STICK!

1. How could you use a mild electric shock to classically condition a rat to flex its forepaw when a tone is sounded?

2. Extinction may occur when you present the _____ by itself repeatedly.

   a. unconditioned response
   b. unconditioned stimulus
   c. conditioned response
   d. conditioned stimulus

3. True or false? If a stimulus does not yet produce a conditioned response, it is called a neutral stimulus.

IVAN PAVLOV (1849–1936)
Russian physiologist and learning theorist famous for the discovery of classical conditioning, in which learning occurs through association.

Ivan Pavlov's Discovery

🐾 **16-4** How did Ivan Pavlov discover classical conditioning?

One of the most famous names in the history of psychology is **Ivan Pavlov.** Pavlov, a Russian physiologist, earned a Nobel Prize for his studies of digestion in 1904. As happens to many good scientists, however, some unexpected findings sparked his curiosity and led him in new directions. He landed squarely in the realm of behavioral psychology.

At the time, Pavlov was investigating the effects of salivation (drool) on the digestive process. In a surgical procedure of his own design, he inserted a small

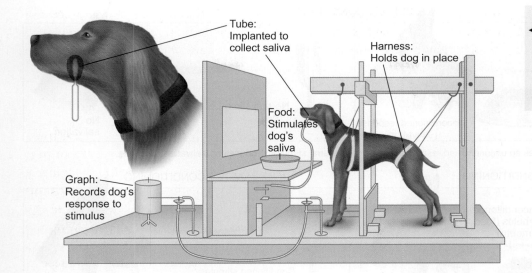

tube to divert and collect salivary secretions from dogs (see **Figure 16.3**). To stimulate the production of saliva, he then introduced meat into the dogs' mouths.

When Pavlov first began working with a dog, the procedure was just fine. Pavlov would restrain the animal in a harness and stimulate the production of saliva with the meat, but after Pavlov had worked with a dog for a while, problems began to crop up. The more familiar the dog became with the procedure, the less likely it was to wait for the food before salivating. Some dogs began to drool as they were being harnessed. Some even salivated when they heard the experimenter come toward the kennel around the same time each day. If you have a family dog, you may have noticed this learning by association yourself. As your dog's regular dinnertime draws near, does it begin to salivate in anticipation as you start to prepare the food? If so, you may find this behavior funny or interesting, but the premature drooling was disruptive for Pavlov.

Intrigued with his dogs' "misbehavior," Pavlov began to wonder if he could control the salivation response by manipulating other stimuli in the environment. Would it be possible to choose a stimulus, such as the sound of a tuning fork, and intentionally create a salivation response to that stimulus? As Pavlov began to investigate these new questions about the dogs' behavior, he identified the central features of classical conditioning.

Let's use Pavlov's basic demonstration of classical conditioning to review the concepts we have already discussed. His task was to teach a dog to salivate to the sound of a tuning fork. Think about the *components* of this experiment, and try to identify the neutral stimulus, unconditioned stimulus, unconditioned response, conditioned stimulus, and conditioned response. Then check your ideas by reading the summaries that follow and looking closely at **Figure 16.4**.

- The *unconditioned stimulus* (US) is the meat, because it automatically produces a salivation response without prior learning.

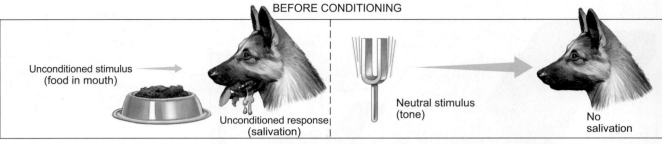

BEFORE CONDITIONING

Unconditioned stimulus (food in mouth) → Unconditioned response (salivation)

Neutral stimulus (tone) → No salivation

An unconditioned stimulus produces an unconditioned response.

A neutral stimulus produces no salivation response.

DURING CONDITIONING

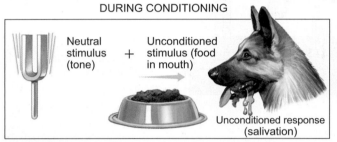

Neutral stimulus (tone) + Unconditioned stimulus (food in mouth) → Unconditioned response (salivation)

The unconditioned stimulus is repeatedly presented just after the neutral stimulus. The unconditioned stimulus continues to produce an unconditioned response.

AFTER CONDITIONING

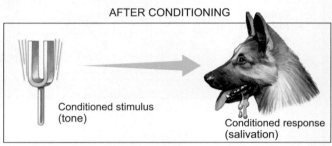

Conditioned stimulus (tone) → Conditioned response (salivation)

The neutral stimulus alone now produces a conditioned response, thereby becoming a conditioned stimulus.

FIGURE 16.4 ▲
Pavlov's Experiment
Pavlov demonstrated the processes of classical conditioning by using meat to train a dog to salivate to the sound of a tuning fork.

Science Source

Did You Flinch? ▲
If so, you've been classically conditioned! Try to identify the unconditioned stimulus, unconditioned response, conditioned stimulus, and conditioned response for this example of conditioning. Check your answers by turning the page.

- The *unconditioned response* (UR) is salivation, because salivation is the response to the unconditioned stimulus of meat. No learning has taken place yet. The ability of meat to make a hungry dog drool is reflexive, not learned.

- The neutral stimulus is the sound of the tuning fork before the dog has been conditioned. This stimulus is neutral because it does not produce a salivation response. Pavlov, of course, could have used many other stimuli—bells, whistles, or even lights or touches—as the neutral stimulus. None of these stimuli ordinarily produce salivation.

- The *conditioned stimulus* (CS) is the sound of the tuning fork after the dog has been conditioned, because that tone now produces the response of salivation. Notice that the tone serves as both the neutral stimulus and the conditioned stimulus at different times in the conditioning process.

- The *conditioned response* (CR) is salivation, because salivation is now the response to the sound of the tuning fork. Notice that salivation can be either the unconditioned response or the conditioned response, depending on what stimulus led to the salivation.

Now let's look at the processes in this classical conditioning experiment. To produce *acquisition*, Pavlov repeatedly sounded the tuning fork just before introducing meat into the dog's mouth. He knew acquisition had occurred because he tested for a learned response: He presented the sound of the tuning fork without the meat. If the dog salivated (and it did), the salivation was a conditioned response, proving that the sound of the tuning fork had become a CS.

To extinguish the classically conditioned response, Pavlov repeatedly sounded the tuning fork without the meat. The learned association between the sound of the tuning fork and the taste of meat gradually weakened under these circumstances, and as the link weakened, the dog produced less and less saliva. When the salivation response had disappeared, *extinction* had occurred.

Generalization and Discrimination

 16-5 What are generalization and discrimination?

Now that we've reviewed the components and processes of classical conditioning, we will look at two concepts that broaden our understanding of how we learn—generalization and discrimination.

Generalization occurs when an organism produces the same response to two similar stimuli. Assume for a moment that Pavlov somehow lost the tuning fork he had used with one of his dogs and was forced to substitute a different tuning fork, one with a slightly different tone. Let's also assume that Pavlov had progressed far enough so that the tone of the original tuning fork had become a conditioned stimulus that generated a strong conditioned response of salivation. What do you think would happen when Pavlov sounded the substitute tuning fork, producing a tone that had never been paired with meat? Pavlov discovered that the dog did respond by salivating and that the more similar the substitute tone was to the original tone, the stronger the salivation response was. **Figure 16.5** illustrates some generalization data Pavlov collected using touches to various body parts as stimuli.

Discrimination occurs when an organism produces different responses to two stimuli. Continuing with the example in the last paragraph, what would happen if Pavlov found his missing tuning fork and now had two (the original and the substitute)?

generalization Producing the same response to two similar stimuli.

discrimination The ability to distinguish between two signals or stimuli and produce different responses.

FIGURE 16.5
Generalization
Pavlov conditioned dogs to salivate when their thighs were stimulated by a slight vibration. This graph shows how much saliva was produced when other parts of the dogs' bodies were stimulated. The dogs salivated more when the stimulated spot was nearer to the point of original conditioning. If chemicals look too similar to food and drink packaging, a child may generalize and ingest dangerous products.

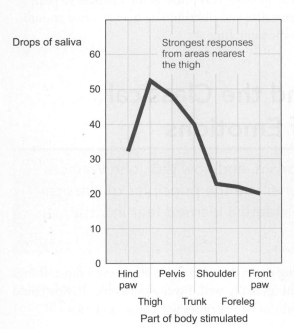

Steven Puetzer/Getty Images

Generalizing and Discriminating
A little girl who fears all buzzing insects is generalizing. If she fears bees but not flies, she is discriminating.

Thanks to generalization, both would be capable of producing salivation. Finally, what would happen if he paired the original tuning fork with the US of meat on some trials, but never paired the substitute tuning fork with the US? Assuming the dog could actually hear the difference between the tones made by the two tuning forks, the conditioned salivation response to the sound of the original tuning fork would be maintained (because this tone tells the dog that food is on the way), but the response to the sound of the substitute tuning fork would be extinguished (because that tone never leads to meat). Now the dog is no longer generalizing (from one tone to a similar tone). Instead, the dog is discriminating (between the two tones).

Generalization and discrimination appear often in the world around us. For example, I know of a little girl named Antonia who developed a classically conditioned fear of buzzing insects after a painful bee sting on the ear. The sting paired pain—an unconditioned stimulus that naturally produces fear—with the buzzing bee. Through this learned association, the buzzing bee became a conditioned stimulus for the conditioned response of fear. This fear then generalized to all buzzing insects, and for a while, Antonia feared everything that buzzed. With additional real-life experience, however, Antonia soon began to make appropriate discriminations. Her conditioned response of fear stayed strong for buzzing things that give painful stings (like bees and hornets), but it was extinguished for buzzing things that don't give these stings (like disgusting flies or annoying gnats).

Antonia's example involves classical conditioning, but generalization and discrimination can occur for other types of learning as well. I was fascinated when my son Eric was learning animals and their names as a 1-year-old. He used the word *bow-wow* to describe all dogs (a generalization), but he could also discriminate between dogs and other animals, like *meow-meows* and *moo-moos*.

MAKE IT STICK!

1. Which of the following is an example of generalization?

   a. A dog both salivates and wags its tail when provided with meat.

   b. A dog barks when a researcher enters the laboratory.

   c. A dog responds to a stroke on its left side the same way it responds to a stroke on its right side.

   d. A dog learns to stop salivating to the sound of a tuning fork.

2. Provide an example of discrimination.

3. True or false? It is possible for a person to both generalize and discriminate between two stimuli at the same time.

● Answers to the Did You Flinch? questions on page 244: The unconditioned stimulus is the explosion of the popped balloon. The unconditioned response is the flinch produced by the pop. The conditioned stimulus is the sight of the pin approaching the balloon. The conditioned response is the flinch produced by the sight of the pin approaching the balloon.

John Watson and the Classical Conditioning of Emotions

  16-6 What is behaviorism, and how did John Watson and Rosalie Rayner use the principles of classical conditioning to create a learned fear in Little Albert?

The beauty of classical conditioning is not that it explains all, or even most, things but rather that it explains some things really well. Psychologists like Pavlov could predict and control classically conditioned responses with great accuracy.

Therefore, classical conditioning was a core topic of introductory psychology textbooks early in the twentieth century. This type of learning relied on **behaviorism,** the view that psychology must restrict its efforts to studying observable behaviors, not mental processes. This school of psychology was led by U.S. psychologist **John B. Watson,** who believed you could control a learner's behavioral response by manipulating a stimulus in the environment. There was no need to consider what happened inside the learner's head. Indeed, we know that a dog has learned to sit if he does it when asked, that a musician has learned a new piece when she can play it, that a gymnast has learned a new routine when he can perform it, that a child has learned to walk when she can make it across the room on two legs, and that a student has learned psychology when he can do well on a test. In all these cases, learning is reflected in behavior.

With his passionate belief that psychology should study only stimulus–response relationships, Watson was not pleased with the growing acceptance of Freud's psychodynamic viewpoint, which relied heavily on the unconscious mind as a means to explain human behavior. Freudian psychoanalysts, for example, viewed phobias (disruptive, irrational fears) as a symbolic result of unconscious fears left over from childhood.

Watson, working with Rosalie Rayner at Johns Hopkins University in 1920, set out to demonstrate that such phobias could be explained by the principles of classical conditioning. In one of the most famous and controversial demonstrations in the history of psychology in the United States, he intentionally established a fear of rats in an 11-month-old boy who became known as Little Albert. Initially, Albert was not afraid of the tame white laboratory rat. (In the world of classical conditioning, the rat was a neutral stimulus.) Albert did not respond to rats with crying or any facial expressions signifying fear. Watson and Rayner were able to change this quite easily by sneaking up behind Albert when he was in the presence of the rat and banging a steel bar to make a startling noise. The noise was an unconditioned stimulus that produced an unconditioned response of fear (crying). Because the unconditioned stimulus was paired with the rat, the rat became a CS to produce the same fear response (see **Figure 16.6**).

behaviorism The theory that psychology should only study observable behaviors, not mental processes.

JOHN B. WATSON (1878–1958)
Founder of behaviorism, the theory that psychology should restrict its efforts to studying observable behaviors, not mental processes.

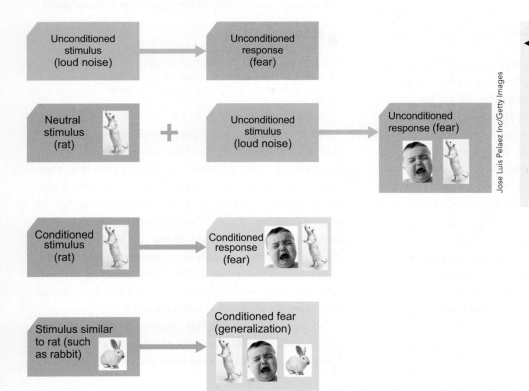

FIGURE 16.6
Conditioning Little Albert
By pairing the neutral stimulus of a white rat with the unconditioned stimulus of a loud noise, John Watson and Rosalie Rayner were easily able to classically condition fear. They also demonstrated generalization when Little Albert became afraid of other white furry animals.

Watson and Rayner demonstrated that Little Albert's fear was a predictable outcome of an environmental condition and, in this case at least, did not represent a repressed, unconscious conflict.

They also demonstrated generalization (Albert also showed fear of a furry white rabbit) and discrimination (he did not show fear of dissimilar toys). Albert's mother apparently began to have some doubts about the research and withdrew the boy before Watson and Rayner were able to extinguish Albert's newly established phobia. Perhaps the mother's doubts about this demonstration match your own—how can it be considered appropriate or ethical to intentionally produce a fear in an innocent young child who could not give his consent? (For more on Little Albert, see Thinking Like a Psychological Scientist: What Ever Happened to Little Albert?)

THINKING LIKE A PSYCHOLOGICAL SCIENTIST

What Ever Happened to Little Albert?

Research by Hall Beck and Sharman Levinson in 2009 shed new light on one of the longstanding mysteries of American psychology[2]—what ever happened to Little Albert, the 11-month-old boy in Watson and Rayner's experiments? In establishing how widespread curiosity about Little Albert has been, Hall and Levinson even cite a previous edition of this book, where we speculated that Little Albert might still be alive, an old man with a lingering fear of rats. We are used to thinking of experimental research done in the here and now, but Beck and Levinson demonstrated that research techniques can also be used to deepen our understanding of the history of psychology.

Beck and Levinson approached the Little Albert mystery by gathering information from a wide variety of sources. They looked for clues about the identity of Little Albert in Watson and Rayner's published articles, expense reports, letters, and films they made of their research. They also scoured journals to learn what had been uncovered by others interested in the puzzle. In order to better understand a date discrepancy, they surveyed librarians to verify when the journal publishing the Little Albert study was actually received. They hoped to find evidence of Albert by examining the patient records of the hospital home at Johns Hopkins University, where they knew he lived, but the records had all been destroyed. Instead they sought out data from the 1920 national census and state birth certificates. They identified three babies who fit their criteria for possibly being Little Albert.

Behaviorism
John Watson and Rosalie Rayner set out to prove that all behavior was the result of environmental factors by classically conditioning a fear of rats and other small, furry animals in an 11-month-old boy known as Little Albert.

All this digging led these researchers to believe that Albert was really Douglas Merritte, the child of Arvilla Irons, born on March 9, 1919. From this, they used the Internet to locate Gary Irons, Douglas's half-brother. He was able to provide a photograph of young Douglas. Experts compared the photograph with stills of Little Albert made by Watson during the original research and concluded that the photos could be of the same child. They decided, "...the available evidence strongly supports the hypothesis that Douglas Merritte is Little Albert."

So, what happened to this "Albert"? Sadly, 6-year-old Douglas Merritte died in 1925 of a brain disorder called hydrocephalus. (His mother lived until 1988.) Beck and

THINKING LIKE A PSYCHOLOGICAL SCIENTIST (Continued)

Levinson found no evidence that he suffered any negative effects from Watson and Rayner's research.

But, there's more to the story! Russell Powell and Nancy Digdon did not believe that the evidence identifying Douglas Merritte was all that strong. Watson had described Little Albert as "healthy from birth," not a correct description of a hydrocephalic baby. Powell and Digdon think the evidence points to another of the three babies who fit the criteria, William Martin. William's middle name was Albert, and this was the name his family called him.[3] Hmm! This baby lived to be 87 and died in 2007, only a few years too soon to be "discovered"—if indeed he was the real baby Albert. As was the case with Douglas Merritte, there is no evidence that William Martin suffered ill effects from his participation (except, perhaps, that he had a lifelong fear of dogs).

We may never know the identity of Little Albert with certainty, but half the fun is in the search. Given the current ethical guidelines for human research (see module 2)—developed because of questionable studies like this one—we can only hope there will be no more Little Alberts in the future.

THINK ABOUT . . . Psychological Science

1. What are some of the techniques that have been used to try to identify Little Albert?

2. Why is the Watson and Rayner research now considered unethical?

3. Is it ever appropriate to put children in scary situations for research purposes?

What can we conclude from Watson and Rayner's research? The main point is that whenever you associate an emotional response with a particular stimulus, classical conditioning is probably involved. Advertisers learned this point quickly and have used it to their advantage for years. Nestea® commercials, for example, repeatedly pair images of cool, refreshing swimming pools and Nestea® instant iced tea. The images of the pools function as an unconditioned stimulus to produce in viewers a feeling of being cool and refreshed. After being repeatedly paired with these images, the product name becomes a conditioned stimulus. Alone, it, too, produces a conditioned response of being cool and refreshed. Thus, when I walk in the grocery store and see a dozen brands of instant iced tea mix, I am more likely to select Nestea because just looking at that label makes me feel cool and refreshed.

Advertisers spend millions of dollars to create classically conditioned emotional desire, often for products of questionable value. Marlboro ads establish a rugged, macho image. Mountain Dew® ads establish a youthful image. Victoria's Secret ads establish a sexy image. All are attempts to use the principles of classical conditioning to sell more products.

You don't need a big advertising budget to find other examples of classically conditioned emotions. Say you are seeing a new person and things

LIFE MATTERS

How do you think advertising has impacted your life? What have you purchased recently and how did it make you feel? Making yourself aware of the emotional associations you feel towards products can help you become a more critical and responsible consumer.

Michelle Pedone/Getty Images

Advertising and Classical Conditioning

Ads for particular beverages, like some iced teas, might use classical conditioning to try to link a specific feeling with a product. In this case, they want the cool and refreshing response we naturally associate with a day by the pool to be linked to a particular brand of iced tea. Can you think of other products that use advertising to connect an emotional response to a product?

Classically Conditioned Emotion

Apple spends advertising dollars to associate its products, like the iPhone, with a particular emotional response. If you have an iPhone, you must be cool!

are going delightfully well. The budding relationship is an unconditioned stimulus for positive emotions. During the evening, you hear a new song on the radio. What happens? The song becomes "your song." Whenever you hear it, you feel better because it produces the same positive emotions that the relationship itself does. The song has become a CS, and classical conditioning is at work. In my life, a similar thing happens with running shoes. For me, running functions as an unconditioned stimulus for relaxation and stress relief. The more miles I put on a new pair of shoes, the more comforting they become. Eventually, all I have to do is put on the shoes (now a CS) to start feeling better. Maybe this is one reason I generally prefer my old, broken-in clothes to brand new ones. The old jeans are associated with a wealth of pleasant memories that bring me comfort as reliably as the tone of Pavlov's tuning fork made a dog drool.

Negative emotions can be conditioned, too. Some women who have been raped destroy the clothes they were wearing at the time of the attack. The act of rape is an extraordinarily powerful unconditioned stimulus for negative feelings—powerful enough to produce conditioning with a single pairing. The clothes, because they were associated with the crime, become a conditioned stimulus that elicits the same feelings. Even buildings can take on emotional baggage. Watch the facial expressions of students walking into your high school in the morning. Those who find school to be a generally pleasant experience will brighten up as soon as they walk through the door. Because it's a place associated with good things happening, the building itself can produce positive feelings. Unfortunately, the school building will have the opposite effect on other students. Their associations are mostly negative, and the building will be a CS for negative emotions. Similarly, places of worship, favorite restaurants, hospitals, and sites of automobile accidents can all trigger emotions—some positive, some negative, but all classically conditioned.

Classically Conditioned Comfort

Because of the many pleasant events that may be associated with wearing them, old clothes and shoes often become conditioned stimuli that produce a relaxed, comforting response. New clothes may be stylish, but they don't have this ability to help us unwind.

MAKE IT STICK!

1. In Watson's research with Little Albert, which of the following functioned initially as an unconditioned stimulus for fear?

   a. Crying
   b. A white rat
   c. A loud noise
   d. Rosalie Rayner

2. Why did Watson want to use behaviorism to explain phobias?

3. True or false? Advertisers use classical conditioning to establish a logical reason for people to buy their products.

Cognition and Biological Predispositions

 16-7 Why are the roles of cognition and biological predispositions important in learning?

Watson was influential in his day, but behaviorism no longer dominates psychology. A growing body of evidence indicates that all kinds of learning, including classical conditioning, can be understood only in light of **cognition**—mental processes like thinking and memory. To most of us, this is simply common sense. If you ask a group of friends to define *learning*, they will almost surely tell you that it is something that occurs in your head. *Learning is when you understand something* and *Learning occurs when you remember* are typical answers, and they both reflect the importance of cognition. Behaviorists like Watson were suspicious of using such explanations because they thought it was impossible to study cognitive processes in a truly scientific way. In contrast, contemporary psychologists believe it is impossible to understand classical conditioning without reference to cognitive processes.

cognition All mental processes associated with thinking, knowing, and remembering.

Cognition and Classical Conditioning

For several decades before the 1980s, original research in classical conditioning had largely come to a halt. From Pavlov on, a growing body of evidence seemed to support the idea that classical conditioning was purely behavioral and required only that a neutral stimulus be repeatedly paired with an unconditioned stimulus. This way of thinking became so well established that hardly anybody bothered to question it anymore. But **Robert Rescorla** and Allan Wagner began to think outside the box. They realized that certain aspects of classical conditioning situations simply could not be explained without reference to *cognition*—the dreaded mental processes the behaviorists were trying to avoid.

Rescorla and Wagner conducted clever experiments showing that a simple pairing of stimuli is not enough to ensure classical conditioning.[4] The key feature appears to be predictability. If a formerly neutral stimulus (Flush!) allows the learner to reliably predict that an unconditioned stimulus (hot water) is about to occur, the neutral stimulus will morph into a conditioned stimulus. If the unconditioned stimulus is not predictable, the neutral stimulus will stay neutral. If Pavlov's tuning fork tone had sometimes been followed by meat and sometimes not, it would not have become a conditioned stimulus, and the conditioned response of drooling would not have developed. The tone would not have *reliably predicted* the unconditioned stimulus (meat). Calculating whether an event is predictable is, of course, a cognitive process, a mental assessment that requires thinking.

ROBERT RESCORLA (1940–) Developed, along with colleague Allan Wagner, a theory that emphasized the importance of cognitive processes in classical conditioning.

Taste Aversion and the Role of Biology

The biological perspective has influenced our understanding of another aspect of classical conditioning. In 1966, **John Garcia** and Robert Koelling showed how classically conditioned taste aversion—an avoidance of certain tastes—could develop.[5] While doing radiation research on rats, Garcia and Koelling noticed that the rats began to avoid drinking from the water bottles in the radiation

JOHN GARCIA (1917–2012) Raised in poverty, Garcia was unable to attend school regularly as a child. He was in his late twenties before starting junior college, and he didn't receive his Ph.D. until he was almost 50. Despite these obstacles, Garcia was elected to the National Academy of Sciences and received the American Psychological Association's Distinguished Scientific Contribution Award for his work in conditioning.

Classically Conditioned Taste Aversion

Have you ever become sick after eating seafood? If so, you probably learned to avoid similar foods in the future. Why are taste aversions likely to develop?

chambers. Like Pavlov, these researchers became intrigued by this unexpected result of their research. In new trials, they discovered that it was possible to use a nausea-producing drug as an unconditioned stimulus to condition an aversion response to a particular taste. Paired with the drug that produced nausea, a particular food or drink became a conditioned stimulus that, without the nausea drug being present, also produced the feelings of nausea.

Originally, behaviorists thought the principles of classical conditioning would operate with any stimulus, for any species. This is not the case. Garcia's work on taste aversion shows that we are biologically predisposed to develop an aversion to the taste of the food we ate before becoming sick rather than, for example, to the place where we ate the food. I once became ill one evening after eating cheddar cheese soup, which had been one of my favorite foods. Sure enough, I now have no desire to smell or taste this soup. Note that of all the stimuli that were present the evening I became sick, *only* the smell and taste of the soup produced an aversion. I was with my wife that evening, but I did not develop an aversion to her—thank goodness!

This biological predisposition to develop taste aversions may protect us from revisiting foods that could be poisonous and may be part of our evolutionary heritage.

People who easily developed taste aversions were more likely to survive and have offspring. Those who snacked repeatedly on tainted food were less likely to live to reproduce. Other common fears—heights, thunderstorms, or snakes—may offer similar protection against threats that have existed since the beginning of human history.[6] Perhaps unfortunately, we are less likely to fear modern technological threats, like automobiles and unseen pollutants in the water supply. These significant threats to our well-being have not been around long enough to become part of the evolutionary baggage we will pass on to future generations.

Classical conditioning remains an important aspect of modern psychology. Research has moved us from a purely behavioral explanation of this type of learning to one that is more heavily influenced by cognitive and biological factors. Even so, classically conditioned behaviors and emotions are an important part of the world around us.

MAKE IT STICK!

1. Robert Rescorla believes cognition plays a key role in classical conditioning because

   a. emotions are always involved.
   b. a CS must have a predictive value.
   c. Watson's experiments proved that cognition was necessary.
   d. very primitive species cannot learn.

2. John Garcia's work with _____ in rats indicates that classical conditioning is influenced by biology.

3. We probably have biological predispositions to avoid certain foods because

   a. they enhance the predictive value of a stimulus.
   b. without them, our ancestors would have gained too much weight.
   c. without them, eating behavior would have been extinguished.
   d. without them, our ancestors would have been more likely to eat poisonous foods.

Module 16 Summary and Assessment

Classical Conditioning

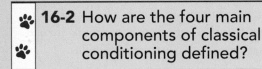 16-1 What is classical conditioning?

- Classical conditioning is a type of learning by association. This means that two stimuli appear together in such a consistent and reliable way that one stimulus gains the power to predict the response that the other stimulus already produces.

16-2 How are the four main components of classical conditioning defined?

- In a classically conditioned response, the unconditioned stimulus (US) triggers the unconditioned response (UR) automatically. The previously neutral conditioned stimulus (CS) is repeatedly paired with the unconditioned response, and eventually the CS triggers the conditioned response (CR).

16-3 What are the two basic processes in classical conditioning?

- The two basic processes in classical conditioning are (1) acquisition, developing a new, learned response; and (2) extinction, the diminishing of a learned response.

16-4 How did Ivan Pavlov discover classical conditioning?

- Pavlov discovered the basic principles of classical conditioning during his research on the digestive process. He found that he could classically condition dogs to salivate (conditioned response) to the sound of a tuning fork (conditioned stimulus) by pairing the tuning fork with meat (unconditioned stimulus), a stimulus that produced salivation automatically (unconditioned response).

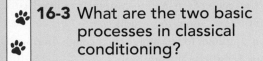 16-5 What are generalization and discrimination?

- Generalization is a process in which we make the same response (a high five, for example) to two similar stimuli (a touchdown in football and a volleyball kill).

Discrimination is a process in which we make different responses to two stimuli (high five for winning a state championship, tears for losing).

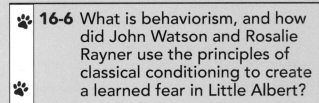 16-6 What is behaviorism, and how did John Watson and Rosalie Rayner use the principles of classical conditioning to create a learned fear in Little Albert?

- Watson established the perspective of behaviorism, the view that psychology should restrict its efforts to studying observable behaviors, not mental processes.

- Watson and Rayner extended the study of classical conditioning to emotional responses. In an ethically troubling set of experiments, they conditioned a child, Little Albert, to fear white rats by applying the principles of classical conditioning. Watson and Rayner demonstrated that whenever you associate an emotional response with a particular stimulus, classical conditioning is probably involved.

16-7 Why are the roles of cognition and biological predispositions important in learning?

- Researchers have demonstrated that even learning acquired through classical conditioning is affected by our thought processes.

- Robert Rescorla and Allan Wagner demonstrated that a learned association will not develop unless the CS predicts the unconditioned stimulus. This recognition is a mental process (cognition).

- Biological predispositions—our inborn tendencies—make us less likely to do things (like playing with snakes and spiders) that might threaten our lives. John Garcia and Robert Koelling showed how classically conditioned taste aversion could develop quickly, demonstrating that some species are more likely to learn some responses than to learn others based on their biological predispositions.

Summative Assessment

1. Learning is generally defined as a change in

   a. memory.   c. emotion.

   b. thinking.   d. behavior.

2. In classical conditioning,

   a. a response gains the power to cause a stimulus.

   b. a stimulus gains the power to cause a response.

   c. two similar stimuli cause the same response.

   d. two similar stimuli cause different responses.

3. A stimulus that produces a response reflexively and automatically is called a(n) _____ stimulus.

   a. conditioned   c. unconditioned

   b. extinguished   d. neutral

4. A conditioned stimulus always begins as a(n)

   a. conditioned response.

   b. unconditioned response.

   c. neutral stimulus.

   d. unconditioned stimulus.

5. Pairing a neutral stimulus with an unconditioned stimulus produces

   a. acquisition.   c. discrimination.

   b. extinction.   d. generalization.

6. Ivan Pavlov's original research interest involved

   a. how the brain works.   c. how children learn.

   b. memory.   d. digestion.

7. Which of the following is an example of discrimination?

   a. A college student in the shower jumps when someone yells, "Flush!" and when someone yells, "Flesh!"

   b. Pavlov's dog salivates to the tones produced by two different tuning forks.

   c. Little Albert shows fear in the presence of a rat but not in the presence of a rabbit.

   d. Antonia is afraid of spiders and wasps.

8. Which of the following demonstrates the importance of cognition in classical conditioning?

   a. A neutral stimulus will become a conditioned stimulus only if it predicts an unconditioned stimulus.

   b. A dog will learn to salivate to the sound of one tone, but not to the sound of a different tone.

   c. A teenager will learn not to eat shrimp if he gets sick from eating shrimp.

   d. A dog will learn to salivate to a tone similar to one that was trained as a conditioned stimulus.

9. Classical conditioning is probably involved if a(n)

   a. little girl learns to fear snakes after watching her older sister freak out when a snake crosses the sidewalk in front of her.

   b. young woman succeeds in mastering a difficult song on the guitar after months of practice.

   c. advertiser succeeds in getting customers to develop romantic associations to a product.

   d. person continues to buy a particular cough drop because he believes it works well.

10. What will happen if a dog that has been classically conditioned to salivate to a tone hears the tone 100 times without having it paired with meat?

    a. The salivation response will generalize.

    b. The salivation response will extinguish.

    c. Acquisition will occur.

    d. Taste aversion will occur.

KEY TERMS AND KEY PEOPLE

learning, p. 239

classical conditioning, p. 239

stimulus, p. 239

response, p. 239

unconditioned stimulus (US), p. 240

unconditioned response (UR), p. 240

conditioned stimulus (CS), p. 240

conditioned response (CR), p. 241

acquisition, p. 241

extinction, p. 242

generalization, p. 245

discrimination, p. 245

behaviorism, p. 247

cognition, p. 251

Ivan Pavlov (1849–1936), p. 242

John B. Watson (1878–1958), p. 247

Robert Rescorla (1940–), p. 251

John Garcia (1917–2012), p. 251

Operant Conditioning

What can you learn from a pigeon in a box? Plenty, as we shall see when we look at the work of B. F. Skinner and others who studied the principles of operant conditioning.

The Nature of Operant Conditioning

 17-1 What is operant conditioning?

A few years ago, I was in the grocery store on a busy preholiday afternoon. In front of me in the checkout line were a mother and her preschool-age daughter. When the girl spotted the candy bar display, she asked if she could have one. Mom, clearly tired and running out of patience on a hectic day, said, "No." The girl, a bit cranky herself, started to fuss, and the battle was on. It quickly escalated to a full-fledged tantrum on the girl's part and yelling on the mom's. A short while later, the mother apparently decided the girl was not about to settle down while they waited to pay for their groceries. With an exasperated "Here, just take it and be quiet," she tossed a candy bar toward the girl, who instantly went from tantrum mode to a bright smile as she tore into the treat.

You may be thinking, "Aha! That little girl certainly had her mother trained." In fact, both the mother's and the daughter's behaviors were affected by **operant conditioning,** a type of learning in which the frequency of a behavior depends on the consequence that follows that behavior. In operant conditioning, how often a behavior occurs (its frequency) depends on the event that follows the behavior (its consequence). By giving her daughter the candy bar, the mother was inadvertently using operant conditioning to teach her daughter to throw tantrums. At the same time, by stopping her tantrum, the daughter was unknowingly using operant conditioning to teach her mother to buy her candy (see **Figure 17.1**). You decide who was the more effective psychologist!

Operant conditioning is straightforward in its most basic form. Suppose your parents handed you a $100 bill each evening if you cleared your own dinner dishes

operant conditioning
A type of learning in which the frequency of a behavior depends on the consequence that follows that behavior.

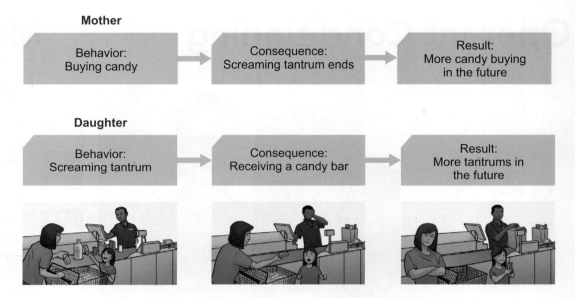

Mother

| Behavior: Buying candy | → | Consequence: Screaming tantrum ends | → | Result: More candy buying in the future |

Daughter

| Behavior: Screaming tantrum | → | Consequence: Receiving a candy bar | → | Result: More tantrums in the future |

FIGURE 17.1 ▲
Operant Conditioning for Better or for Worse
This child doesn't know it, but she is using operant conditioning to train her mother to buy candy. Her mother is unwittingly operantly conditioning the child to have tantrums.

from the table after completing your meal. Would this consequence influence your dish-clearing behavior? Most likely, you would begin to clear your dishes more regularly and more quickly than before. What if your parents somehow wired the television so that you received a painful electric shock every time you touched the power button on the set or the remote control? The shock is a consequence, too. Would it influence how often you touched the power button?

Wouldn't it be great if we could influence others—parents, siblings, friends, teachers, employers—to behave the way we want them to? The pair in the grocery store stumbled upon a powerful behavior-changing tool. Let's take a closer look at how operant conditioning techniques work.

MAKE IT STICK!

1. In operant conditioning, the frequency of a behavior is determined by the behavior's _____.

2. Which of the following is an example of operant conditioning?

   a. A boy who watches his brother ride a bicycle learns how to ride a bicycle.

   b. A girl practices spelling Mississippi until she learns to spell it perfectly.

   c. A baby learns to startle every time the doorbell rings.

   d. A dog that is given a piece of food after begging at the dinner table learns to beg more frequently.

EDWARD THORNDIKE (1874–1949) Author of the law of effect, the principle that forms the basis of operant conditioning.

The Law of Effect

 17-2 What is the law of effect?

Operant conditioning developed from research conducted by **Edward Thorndike,** an early U.S. psychologist. Thorndike's work led him to describe the *law of effect,* which simply states that behaviors with favorable consequences will occur more frequently and behaviors followed by unfavorable consequences will occur less frequently. Another U.S. psychologist, **B. F. Skinner,** built his life's work on this idea, developing the fundamental principles and techniques of operant conditioning (see Thinking Like a Psychological Scientist: B. F. Skinner). Two of the more important concepts used in operant conditioning are reinforcement and punishment.

- **Reinforcement** is any consequence that *increases* the future likelihood of a behavior.

- **Punishment** is any consequence that *decreases* the future likelihood of a behavior.

Keep in mind that the learner, not the teacher, casts the vote that determines whether a consequence will be a reinforcement or a punishment. When my two children were younger, they had different feelings about broccoli. Carl really liked broccoli, and if I had given him some after he took out the garbage, he would have been more likely to take out the garbage in the future. For him, broccoli was a *reinforcement*. But Eric did *not* like broccoli. If I had given Eric broccoli after he took out the garbage, he probably would never have done that chore again. Broccoli was a *punishment* for Eric. My feelings about broccoli (which I like, especially with cheese sauce) make no difference.

Parents and other authority figures don't always understand this aspect of consequences. A parent will sometimes yell at a child for misbehavior, thinking that yelling is a form of punishment. However, a child who is usually ignored may actually crave being yelled at because it's about the only parental attention the child gets. In this case, the law of effect predicts the behavior that preceded the parent's yelling—misbehavior that the parent was trying to prevent—will actually be *more* likely to happen again. Likewise, a school administrator might suspend a student for skipping class, not realizing that for a student who doesn't care for school, this punishment is not a punishment at all: It may even make future skipping more likely!

reinforcement Any consequence that increases the future likelihood of a behavior.

punishment Any consequence that decreases the future likelihood of a behavior.

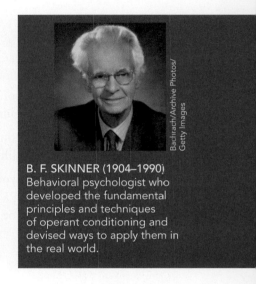

B. F. SKINNER (1904–1990) Behavioral psychologist who developed the fundamental principles and techniques of operant conditioning and devised ways to apply them in the real world.

▲ **Thorndike's Puzzle Box**
Thorndike constructed puzzle boxes such as this one to study how cats learned to escape. At first, a cat's ability to find the lever that had to be pressed to open the door depended on trial and error, but later the animal had a tendency to repeat the behaviors that had been successful before. This research led to the development of the law of effect.

▲ **Reinforcement and the Law of Effect**
Fishing crews in the Cayman Islands have cleaned their catch in this bay for years, thus providing an easy meal for the stingrays that live in the surrounding waters. The rays began to hang around, and then divers and swimmers began feeding them by hand and even petting them. Can you see how the law of effect has been at work in this situation?

How Do You Get What You Want? This little child enjoys sleeping with Mom and Dad. What behaviors on the child's part might have led to this reinforcement? Is it possible Mom and Dad are reinforcing behaviors they really don't want the child to engage in?

MAKE IT STICK!

1. _____ is any consequence that decreases the future likelihood of a behavior.

2. _____ is any consequence that increases the future likelihood of a behavior.

3. Your dog, Pavlov, loves your attention. Lately, Pavlov has been barking a lot, and every time he does, you yell, "Pavlov, be quiet!" Which of the following is true?

a. Pavlov will bark less in the future because you reinforced him.
b. Pavlov will bark less in the future because you punished him.
c. Pavlov will bark more in the future because you reinforced him.
d. Pavlov will bark more in the future because you punished him.

THINKING LIKE A PSYCHOLOGICAL SCIENTIST

B. F. Skinner

Few have done more than B. F. Skinner to advance the notion of psychology as a scientific discipline. In one study, almost 2000 psychologists ranked Skinner as the most eminent psychologist of the twentieth century.[1] Through his research and his writing, Skinner spent his career developing a behavioral technology that did not rely on references to unseen thought processes. His goal was to understand and control the actions of other organisms. His new behavioral technology was operant conditioning.

Skinner believed that all behaviors in all species are governed by the same principles. To identify these principles, Skinner studied simple behaviors, mostly of rats and pigeons. He and his assistants taught rats to press a lever with their paws and pigeons to peck a disk with their beaks. The rats and pigeons per-formed these acts in an invention that Skinner called an *operant chamber*, but that most others call a *Skinner box*. The Skinner box gives the experimenter an opportunity to control the environment and precisely record an animal's responses. Using this arrangement, Skinner identified principles of operant conditioning that he felt could be used to understand and control complicated behaviors in the real world.

Skinner, never content to limit himself to the laboratory, became a ceaseless advocate for his point of view. He was often the center of controversy because of many books and articles written by and about him. Skinner's public fame started when in a magazine article he detailed how he and his wife were using a climate-controlled "air crib" for their daughter (which some felt was too similar to a rat's or pigeon's operant chamber).[2]

(Continued)

THINKING LIKE A PSYCHOLOGICAL SCIENTIST (Continued)

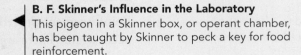

▶ B. F. Skinner's Influence in the Laboratory
This pigeon in a Skinner box, or operant chamber, has been taught by Skinner to peck a key for food reinforcement.

▶ The "Baby in a Box"
B. F. Skinner's daughter spent time in this specially designed environment. Some thought this was awful; others thought it was less of a problem than a standard baby crib with bars.

Freedom and Dignity, describing his belief that human freedom was an illusion. This sparked enough public discussion to land him on the covers of national news magazines.

Skinner loved the debate and was passionate about defending his positions and the science on which they were based. His final speech, delivered at the American Psychological Association convention only 8 days before he died of leukemia in 1990, was a spirited defense of behaviorism and critique of cognitive science, which he believed wasn't scientific at all.[4]

Skinner's viewpoints were extreme, but his work does have a number of successful, practical applications. As you will see throughout this module, operant conditioning principles affect our behavior at home, in school, in the world of sports, and at work.[5] Skinner may not have always won people's hearts and minds, but he did contribute importantly to our understanding of learned behavior and the development of psychology as a science.

Skinner stayed in the public eye for the rest of his career. In the late 1940s, he published *Walden Two*, a novel presenting his ideas for a perfect community based on principles of operant conditioning. In the book, Skinner criticized democracy, the nuclear family, the use of money, and religion. Nevertheless, he inspired a number of groups to start communities that avoided punishment and used reinforcement to encourage desirable behaviors. Some are still in existence, and I once had a class write Skinner to learn what he thought of them. He replied that his principles were applied most appropriately at Los Horcones in Sonora, Mexico.[3] In 1971, Skinner published *Beyond*

THINK ABOUT . . . Psychological Science

1. How did Skinner identify the principles of operant conditioning?

2. Why was Skinner's air crib controversial?

3. Explain why you would or wouldn't consider living in a community built on the ideas Skinner explained in *Walden Two*.

Reinforcement

 17-3 What are the different kinds of reinforcement?

Reinforcement procedures strengthen responses by making them more likely to occur again. There are two basic ways to reinforce a behavior: positive reinforcement and negative reinforcement (see **Figure 17.2**).

Positive reinforcement is anything that increases the likelihood of a behavior by following it with a desirable event or state. For example, if a student earns an A in psychology and his mother pays him $10 for that, then she has positively reinforced his behavior.

Negative reinforcement is anything that increases the likelihood of a behavior by following it with the removal of an undesirable event or state. Negative reinforcement is a tricky concept. Note that the behavior is a means of either escaping or avoiding an undesirable situation. Notice that the words *positive* and *negative* in this context do not mean "good" reinforcement and "bad" reinforcement, but rather are used in a mathematical sense. Here, *positive* simply means that something desirable is *added,* and *negative* means that something undesirable is *subtracted*—in fact, it may be helpful to think of the math symbols + and – when you see the words positive and negative. For example, Roshni's headache is undesirable. If taking ibuprofen provides relief from the headache, Roshni's behavior of taking ibuprofen has been negatively reinforced. Negative reinforcement, like all reinforcement, *strengthens* a behavior. So, Roshni becomes more likely to take ibuprofen to escape a headache in the future.

The concept of negative reinforcement can be confusing at first. Sometimes students think it is simply a more technical term for punishment, but this is not the case. Punishment, as you will see soon, weakens a behavior. Negative reinforcement always strengthens a behavior that removes an undesirable stimulus. Here are two more examples of negative reinforcement:

1. The girl in the grocery store at the beginning of this module used negative reinforcement to teach her mom to buy her candy. The mother found the tantrum undesirable, and she escaped it by buying her daughter the candy she wanted. The end of the tantrum negatively reinforced the mother's candy-buying behavior, which is likely to happen again in the future.

positive reinforcement In operant conditioning, anything that increases the likelihood of a behavior by following it with a desirable event or state.

negative reinforcement In operant conditioning, anything that increases the likelihood of a behavior by following it with the removal of an undesirable event or state.

FIGURE 17.2 Reinforcement Strengthens Behavior Positive and negative reinforcement work differently, but both types of reinforcement make a behavior more likely to happen again.

POSITIVE REINFORCEMENT
Behavior is followed by a desirable event or state.

$10 for an A makes it more likely a student will earn more As.

NEGATIVE REINFORCEMENT
Behavior ends an undesirable event or state.

Taking aspirin relieves headaches and makes it more likely that aspirin will be taken in the future.

2. Hitting the snooze button on my annoying alarm clock is negatively reinforcing because the behavior allows me to escape from the alarm. This strengthens the behavior and helps ensure that I will hit the snooze button in the future.

Immediate Versus Delayed Reinforcement

Which affects our learning more—immediate rewards or delayed rewards? If psychologists had designed the warning label on cigarette packs, it might say, Warning: If you smoke these cigarettes, your breath will smell awful for the rest of the day! Psychologists know that we are more likely to respond to immediate consequences (bad breath) than to delayed consequences (the long-term risk of lung or heart disease). In other words, *immediate reinforcement* is more effective than *delayed reinforcement*. This also helps explain why it is difficult to *quit* smoking cigarettes. The desirable consequence—the rush produced by the chemicals in tobacco—is immediate. The undesirable effects on the lungs and cardiovascular system are longer term. It's no surprise, then, that in addition to the physiological effects that drugs have on the brain, those that produce the most immediate reinforcement, like nicotine and cocaine, are the most addictive.[6] You can see the same relationship in those who overeat. The taste of fattening foods provides immediate positive reinforcement, but the effects of obesity are delayed.

Rats and pigeons, like people, prefer immediate reinforcement, and they seem to require it for learning. A rat, for example, will not learn to press a bar if the reinforcement (usually food) for that behavior is delayed by 30 seconds or more. Humans, however, have a great ability to adapt, and one of the things we learn as we develop is that delayed reinforcers are sometimes worth the wait. Paychecks may not be issued until the end of the month and grades aren't given until the end of the grading period, yet they still influence us. In fact, the ability to delay gratification is a real advantage. For example, children who prefer a big reward in the future over a smaller reward now—perhaps by saving their allowance for a desired toy rather than spending it each week on candy—are likely to become higher-achieving adolescents than children who prefer immediate gratification.[7] It is possible that the instant gratification provided by social media and other screen-based activities is making it difficult for people to develop an appreciation for the long-term rewards provided by more time consuming pursuits like nurturing face-to-face relationships and reading books.

Primary Versus Secondary Reinforcement

Primary and secondary reinforcement are similar in that they both affect the frequency of behaviors, but they differ in one important way. A **primary reinforcement** is something that is naturally rewarding, such as food (if you are hungry), warmth (if you are cold), and water (if you are thirsty). A **secondary reinforcement** is something you have *learned* is rewarding because it has been paired with a primary reinforcer (see **Figure 17.3**).

Money, for example, is a secondary reinforcer because you have learned you can use it to purchase various forms of primary reinforcement, such as pizza and clothes. But money itself is not naturally rewarding. If you give a $100 bill to a 4-month-old baby, she will probably put it in her mouth to see if it tastes good. (She's checking for a primary reinforcer!) When the baby discovers the money doesn't taste good, she will spit it out and show no further interest. Is this how you respond when given a $100 bill? Not likely! For you, that piece of paper has

primary reinforcement
Something that is naturally reinforcing, such as food (f you were hungry), warmth (if you were cold), and water (if you were thirsty).

secondary reinforcement
Something that you have learned to value, like money.

FIGURE 17.3 ▶
Primary and Secondary Reinforcements
Primary reinforcers, such as food, are naturally rewarding. Secondary reinforcers are rewarding because we have learned that they are associated with primary rewards.

PRIMARY REINFORCEMENT

Food is a primary reinforcer for a dog.

SECONDARY REINFORCEMENT

An owner's words can become secondary reinforcement when they're associated with petting and approval.

value—so much value that you would work hard to get more. And if you really are hungry, the money becomes even more valuable to you—in one experiment, participants were less likely to donate to charities if asked when they were hungry.[8]

Grades are a major influence on student behavior. Are they a primary or a secondary reinforcement? If you said secondary, you're right. You had to learn the value of grades. Without this learning, grades have no value. (Try training your dog by giving a B plus for sitting or heeling, instead of a primary reinforcement in the form of attention or a dog biscuit.) Some students never learn to associate much value with school grades, so grades have little effect on their behavior.

MAKE IT STICK!

1. Explain the distinction between positive and negative reinforcement.

2. Which of the following is an example of negative reinforcement?

   a. A husband gets a kiss on the cheek from his wife after he takes out the garbage.

   b. A third grader reads five books for a gold star award at school.

   c. A football player goes to the weight room every day to gain strength.

   d. A twisted ankle hurts less after taking Tylenol.

3. True or false? Both positive and negative reinforcement make a behavior more likely.

Punishment

 17-4 How does punishment influence behavior?

The Process of Punishment

We noted earlier in this module that punishment *weakens* a behavior, or makes it less likely to occur again in the future. Punishment can take either of two forms (see **Figure 17.4**):

- The first, positive punishment, occurs when the behavior leads to something undesirable. Positive punishment is anything that decreases the likelihood of a behavior by following it with an undesirable event or state. For example, if a toddler puts her hand on a painfully hot stove burner, the behavior of touching the burner is punished because it leads to an undesirable event: getting burned (Ouch!). Because stove touching has been punished, that behavior is less likely to happen in the future.

- The second form of punishment, negative punishment, occurs when the behavior ends something desirable. Negative punishment is anything that decreases the likelihood of a behavior by following it with the removal of a desirable event or state. Let's say a young boy pulls his sister's hair while watching television and his father takes away TV privileges for the rest of the day. The behavior of hair pulling has ended something desirable—watching television. The loss of privileges should make the boy's hair-pulling behavior less likely to occur in the future. Parking tickets are another example of punishment that removes something desirable. If I engage in the behavior of illegal parking and then have to pay some of my desirable money, I should be less likely to park illegally in the future.

This is exactly parallel to what we learned about positive and negative reinforcement. *Positive* and *negative* are again being used in the mathematical sense and do not imply that one type of punishment is good while the other one is bad. Positive punishment simply means that something undesirable is *added*. Negative punishment means that something desirable is *subtracted*.

POSITIVE PUNISHMENT

Behavior is followed by an undesirable event or state.

A toddler burned by a hot stove will be less likely to touch the stove again.

NEGATIVE PUNISHMENT

Behavior ends a desirable event or state.

A boy who loses his TV privileges for pulling his sister's hair will be less likely to pull her hair again.

FIGURE 17.4
Punishment Weakens Behavior
Here are two forms of punishment, positive and negative. In one, the punished behavior is followed by an undesirable event, which is *added*. In the other, the punished behavior is followed by the loss of a desirable event or state, which is *subtracted*. Although the types of punishment differ, each decreases the likelihood that the behavior will happen again.

Problems With Punishment

Many learning experts oppose the use of punishment, especially physical punishment, to control behavior.[9,10] They feel that punishment is likely to backfire in the long run for a variety of reasons. For starters, punishment does not end the desire to engage in a behavior. Children punished for using inappropriate language often continue to use the bad language—just not in the presence of the one who punished them for it. Likewise, adults punished for speeding may simply purchase a radar detector rather than drive moderately.

Punishment can also lead to fear and anxiety. Children or animals punished frequently may learn to engage in *avoidance* behaviors: Harshly punished children may run away from home, and harshly punished students may drop out of school. A final criticism of punishment is that when adult role models use aggression to solve their problems, children can learn to model that aggressive behavior as a problem-solving strategy. This may help explain why abusive parents tend to come from abusive families (although, impressively, most abused children do not go on to become abusive parents).[11]

So, despite all these problems, why is punishment used so often? One reason seems to be that when a punished individual stops misbehaving, even for just a few minutes, this consequence negatively reinforces the behavior it followed—which in this case is punishment. This consequence in turn makes the punishing behavior more likely to happen in the future. The result is a vicious cycle: Punishment leads to *temporary* suppression of misbehavior, which reinforces the punishment, which is then even more likely to be used when the suppressed misbehavior inevitably returns, which leads to another reinforcing, temporary suppression, and so on. For example, a teacher scolds a child who likes to talk in her first-grade classroom, and then the child quiets down for a few minutes—this negatively reinforces the teacher for scolding. However, the effects of the scolding do not last long, and the child begins talking again before you know it. The teacher, having been previously reinforced for scolding, will likely scold again. Thus, it goes round and round like a dog chasing its tail!

There is a role for punishment in learning, but it is a limited one. Swift, sure punishment can effectively control certain behaviors, especially if the punisher's goal is to protect a child from a dangerous situation.[12] For example, if a toddler has developed the bad habit of running into the street, a harsh reprimand or swat on the behind may be appropriate. A young child needs to develop some fear and avoidance of the street. But punishment is generally most effective when used least. Have you ever had a class where the teacher was constantly punishing the students by losing her temper and yelling at the class? How effective was the teacher's behavior after it occurred several times? Compare that scenario with a class's reaction to angry behavior on the part of a teacher who rarely yells and screams. If your memories are similar to mine, you'll see that the less often punishment happens, the more effective it is.

For all the reasons we've discussed here, most psychologists recommend *reinforcing an incompatible behavior* as an effective alternative to punishment. Rather than punishing a child for lying, for example, parents might consider reinforcing the child with praise for telling the truth. This will increase the amount of truth telling, and because a child cannot tell the truth and lie at the same time, the amount of lying must decrease. The basic philosophy here is to catch the child being good and reinforce accordingly. This approach will lead to a more

Pros and Cons of Punishment
Punishment, under the right circumstances, can decrease behavior, but it also has several undesirable side effects. It can produce fear and anxiety.

gradual change of behavior, but the change will be more permanent than the temporary suppression of behavior that follows punishment. Reinforcement also has two other benefits. First, it tends to lead to *approach* behaviors that draw people together (one reason kids are often so eager to see their mostly reinforcing grandparents) rather than feelings of fear and anxiety. Second, children who model positive reinforcement are more pleasant to be with than children who model aggressive behaviors.

MAKE IT STICK!

1. Positive punishment _____ the frequency of behavior. Negative punishment _____ the frequency of behavior.

2. What are two reasons psychologists usually oppose the use of spanking?

3. True or false? One of the advantages of punishment is that it usually permanently changes behavior.

Reinforcement Procedures

 17-5 How can you use operant conditioning to teach a new behavior or make an operantly conditioned behavior stop?

> **shaping** Reinforcement of behaviors that are increasingly similar to the desired one; the operant technique used to establish new behaviors.

Now that you know a little bit about how reinforcement and punishment work, we can begin to explore some other procedures that make operant conditioning so useful. In this section, we show how you can use shaping to establish new behaviors and how discrimination and generalization can fine-tune when behaviors will occur.

Shaping

The law of effect says that reinforcing a behavior makes the behavior more likely to occur in the future. But how can you apply operant conditioning to a behavior that hasn't yet occurred? To do this, Skinner developed a technique called **shaping,** reinforcement of behaviors that are increasingly similar to the one you want to occur. Shaping is the operant conditioning technique used to establish new behaviors. When you shape a behavior, you positively reinforce behaviors that move ever closer to the target behavior.

B. F. Skinner, for example, demonstrated how to train a pigeon to turn in clockwise circles. He started by providing a food reward every time the pigeon turned its head to the right. Pigeons turn their heads frequently, and the law of effect says that reinforcing this behavior will cause the pigeon to turn its head to the right more often. Now the trick was to gradually extend how far the pigeon must turn its head before Skinner gave it a food reward. After a series of increasingly longer turns, the pigeon finally turned all the way around. By breaking the circling behavior into a succession of gradual steps, Skinner easily shaped it.

Many other examples of shaping happen in everyday life. Remember when you learned to ride your bicycle without training wheels? Chances are, someone held

Shaping
When this child falls, as she surely will, Dad will praise her attempt. Parents who give such praise know that it is important to provide reinforcement following first attempts, even if they are failures, to encourage a child to ride ever farther.

Marc Romanelli/Getty Images

discrimination The ability to distinguish between two similar signals or stimuli and produce different responses.

extinction In operant conditioning, the loss of a behavior when no consequence follows it.

the seat, ran beside you until you were reasonably well balanced, and then let go. You probably managed to roll several feet on your own before falling, at which point you were rewarded with a hearty, Good job! It really wasn't that good a job—you only made it a few feet—but for a first attempt it deserved reinforcement. Gradually, as your riding skills improved, your trainer made you ride farther and farther before giving you a compliment. You were being shaped!

Discrimination and Extinction

Shaping is useful for training behaviors that otherwise probably wouldn't happen. Other issues that make operant conditioning useful include *discrimination* and *extinction*. **Discrimination** is the ability to distinguish among similar signals or stimuli. **Extinction** is the loss of a learned response when a consequence no longer follows it.

Life would be fairly chaotic if we made the same response to all stimuli that were similar. For safety reasons, students and teachers need to learn to *discriminate* between class bells and fire alarms—two kinds of fairly similar stimuli. We do this by learning the difference between the similar signals. What signal tells you it's time to leave the classroom at the end of the period? How does it differ from the fire alarm signal? And false-alarm fire drills—where students are sometimes called back to class before they've even left the building—need to be kept to a minimum to prevent the extinction of the evacuation response.

Discrimination
This trainer is teaching the dolphin to discriminate between different hand signals. Reinforcement—a fish treat—is provided only when the animal performs the proper behavior for that signal.

DOLPHIN INST./Science Source

Sometimes, however, *extinction* is a good thing. If the mom in the checkout line at the beginning of this module had managed to ignore her child's tantrums, those behaviors would eventually have died out on their own. Remember that without reinforcement, behaviors learned through operant conditioning will eventually disappear.

Without discrimination, we wouldn't know when to answer the phone and when to answer the door. We wouldn't know whether to say, Hi, Jill or Hi, Jane when a friend comes into view. Without extinction, we wouldn't stop repeating the same unsuccessful chess strategy or stop flirting with someone who doesn't respond to our interest. These operant conditioning concepts can help us understand why certain behaviors thrive and others die out. Your reading behavior has obviously not extinguished, so let's continue!

Cartoon Stock

"Will whoever has the doorbell ringtone please set your phone to vibrate?"

Signals Can Be Powerful
Can you explain why the speaker wants the dogs in the audience to avoid the doorbell ringtone?

🧠 Learning New Habits

If you could learn or develop one new habit, what would it be? Eating healthier? Exercising more? Keeping track of your stuff better? Positive psychologists are learning how to best change a behavior you'd like to improve. More specifically, they're learning how to grow the skills you need to create the habits you want in life.

Not surprisingly, learning a new habit involves self-control (often called *self-regulation* by psychologists). Self-control is the process of exerting control over your thoughts, feelings, and actions.[13] The less self-control you have, the harder it is to learn and develop a new habit. So, if self-control is not one of your strengths, does this mean you're out of luck when it comes to learning a new habit? *No.* It turns out that there is a fairly simple way to increase your self-control.

Joseph Forgas, Roy Baumeister, and Dianne Tice (2009) have learned that one of the better things you can do to gain the self-control you need to create a new habit is to practice self-control over *any* area of your life.[14] They explain what this means by using the results from two studies. In the first, participants were asked to exert self-control over spending money for several months. In the second, participants were taught an exercise routine and instructed to follow the routine every day for 2 months. The researchers found that while saving money increased in the first study and participants lost weight in the second, there were also unanticipated side benefits: The self-control used on finances and exercise showed up in *other* aspects of the participants' lives. Not only had they saved money or improved their health, but they also reported studying more, watching less television, and doing more household chores that they usually avoided. The narrowly focused self-control of the participants was like a muscle that was made stronger through regular use. It made it easier for these individuals to exert self-control more widely in other aspects of life.

So, if you want to build up the self-control skills you need to change bad habits or to learn new good habits, start by trying to control one thing that doesn't turn your world upside down. That is, start with something that only requires a little self-control. Tell yourself you're only going to check Facebook twice a day, and for no longer than 30 minutes ever. As psychologist Senia Maymin puts it, "Structure something concrete into your life. That's the best way to develop self-control."[15]

MAKE IT STICK!

1. Describe how you'd use shaping to teach a young child how to play catch with a Nerf ball.

2. We know to stop at a red light and go when the light turns green because of _____.

3. Extinction occurs when a behavior

   a. is punished.
   b. indicates discrimination has been learned.
   c. is shaped.
   d. is no longer followed by reinforcement.

Schedules of Reinforcement

 17-6 What are the advantages and disadvantages of different schedules of reinforcement?

What do buying food from a vending machine and playing the lottery have in common? They are both behaviors maintained by positive reinforcement. However, you're more likely to continue playing the lottery after having purchased a losing ticket than you are to put more money into a vending machine that has just failed to produce the desired potato chips. This is because the two examples illustrate different schedules of reinforcement—continuous reinforcement for the vending machine and partial reinforcement for the lottery.

Continuous Reinforcement

In **continuous reinforcement,** a reward follows every correct response, just as a vending machine is supposed to operate. The vending machine trains you to behave in a certain way—inserting your money in the machine—by continuously reinforcing your behavior. If you put the money in properly, you will be reinforced every time by receiving a bag of potato chips.

> **continuous reinforcement**
> In operant conditioning, a schedule of reinforcement in which a reward follows every correct response.

Continuous reinforcement is most useful for establishing new behaviors. Lots of reinforcement is often necessary when you are trying to teach someone to do something new, such as to speak a new language. One problem with behaviors that have been continuously reinforced, however, is that they are quite easy to extinguish. If the learner is used to being reinforced for each correct behavior and the reinforcement stops, extinction will occur rapidly. Think about how you behave when you put money in a vending machine and the machine doesn't dispense your product. Do you quickly put more money in? Probably not! When the goal is to establish behavior that is resistant to extinction, one of the partial reinforcement schedules works better.

Partial Reinforcement

In **partial reinforcement schedules,** a reward follows only some correct responses. When our behavior is reinforced *intermittently* (only some of the time), hope springs eternal and we are reluctant to give up. If a vending machine is a good example of continuous reinforcement, a lottery is a good example of partial reinforcement. People don't expect to win every time they buy a ticket. Therefore, they will continue to buy tickets even if they don't win. As lottery commissions know, partial reinforcement schedules produce behavior that is hard to extinguish.

There are four partial reinforcement schedules.[16] Two of the partial reinforcement schedules, called *interval schedules,* focus on the time that elapses between reinforcements. The other two partial reinforcement schedules, called *ratio schedules,* focus on the number of responses required before reinforcement occurs. Let's take a closer look at each of these four partial reinforcement schedules.

Fixed-Interval Schedule   A **fixed-interval** partial reinforcement schedule rewards only the first correct response after some defined period of time has passed. For example, a researcher might always reinforce the first time a rat presses a bar after 60 seconds have passed. After receiving a food pellet (a reinforcement) for that response, the rat has to wait 60 seconds before it will be reinforced for another correct response. The interval (60 seconds) is unchanging, and there is no way the rat can earn reinforcement until the end of that 60-second interval—thus the term *fixed-interval schedule.*

A rat experienced with a fixed-interval schedule learns not to respond during the first part of the fixed time interval, when there is no way to earn a reinforcement. Toward the end of the interval, the rat starts pressing the bar, checking to see if the time is up. The rate of checking increases as the end of the fixed interval approaches. The result is the response pattern you can see in the yellow line in **Figure 17.5**.

Do fixed-interval schedules happen in real life? You bet! Have you ever had a class with a quiz every Friday? If so, you were being reinforced (with a good grade) for your behavior (studying) on a fixed-interval (once a week) schedule. Did you study much for the quiz on Monday, Tuesday, or Wednesday? Many students don't. Instead, they pack the main part of their responding (studying) into the end of the interval (Thursday night), just as the rats did in Skinner's research on fixed-interval schedules.

Variable-Interval Schedule   A **variable-interval** partial reinforcement schedule rewards the first correct response after an unpredictable amount of time has passed. The amount of time changes after each reinforcement, so a bar-pressing rat has no way to know how long the interval will be. The rat must keep checking

partial reinforcement schedule   In operant conditioning, a schedule of reinforcement in which a reward follows only some correct responses.

fixed-interval schedule   In operant conditioning, a partial reinforcement schedule that rewards only the first correct response after some defined period.

variable-interval schedule   In operant conditioning, a partial reinforcement schedule that rewards the first correct response after an unpredictable amount of time.

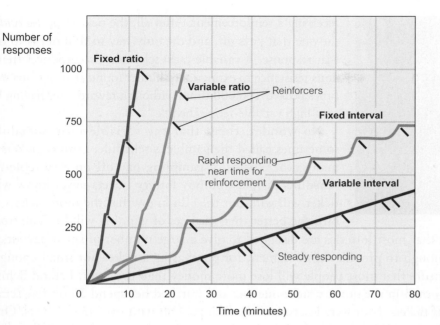

FIGURE 17.5
The Cumulative Record
Skinner used graphs like this one to track the responses of pigeons and rats. The horizontal axis of the graph measures time, and the vertical axis measures total responses. The small slash marks indicate points at which the animal received a reinforcement (such as a food pellet). The slopes of the lines connecting the slashes show the rate of responding—a steeper line indicates more responses per minute. Skinner's pigeons showed these four patterns of responding for the partial schedules of reinforcement. The ratio schedules produce a faster response rate (a steeper line) than the interval schedules. (Adapted from Skinner, 1961.)

by pressing the bar to see whether anything happens. When the variable interval is up, the next correct press on the bar earns the rat its food pellet.

Recall that on the fixed-interval schedule, the rat (or the student) can sit out the first part of the interval (that is, not respond) without risking the loss of a reward. Not so on a variable-interval schedule, where any given time interval might be short. Instead, the rat learns to respond at a moderate, steady rate, as the red line in Figure 17.5 shows. Faster responding doesn't result in many extra rewards, so response rate is not very important with a variable-interval schedule.

As many psychology teachers know, pop quizzes operate on a variable-interval schedule. When a quiz can occur at any time, it's best to study a little bit each day. If there is no quiz today, there may be one tomorrow. If there is a quiz today, there may be another one tomorrow. To earn the most reinforcement (good grades on your quizzes), you must be a steady studier.

Fixed-Ratio Schedule A **fixed-ratio** partial reinforcement schedule provides a reward only after a certain number of correct responses. The word *ratio* in the term refers to the ratio of reinforcements to responses, such as 1 reinforcement for every 20 correct responses. Fixed-ratio schedules do place a premium on speedy responding: The faster the rat makes the required number of responses, the faster it will be fed, which means more to eat for a hungry rat. A rat with some experience on the fixed-ratio schedule will run through the required number of responses rapidly. As you can see in the blue line in Figure 17.5, it will then take a short break. After "catching its breath," the rat will run through the next set of responses as rapidly as possible.

Coffee shops that run buy 10, get 1 free specials are using a fixed-ratio schedule of reinforcement. You may have found yourself buying 10 lattes quickly to qualify for your reinforcement—the free drink. After enjoying your free coffee, you may not buy again for a while. (You're probably a little sick of coffee after drinking several a day!) However, after catching your breath for a few days, you may be back to ordering double espressos again to earn the next free drink.

Variable-Ratio Schedule A **variable-ratio** partial reinforcement schedule rewards an unpredictable number of correct responses. The number of correct responses is unpredictable because it changes after each reinforcement. Rats on a variable-ratio schedule tend to respond fast and to continue responding after

fixed-ratio schedule
In operant conditioning, a partial reinforcement schedule that rewards a response only after some defined number of correct responses.

variable-ratio schedule In operant conditioning, a partial reinforcement schedule that rewards after an unpredictable number of correct responses.

Eric Raptosh Photography/Getty Images

receiving a reinforcement. After all, the next response *could* be the one that pays off, and the only way to find out is to make that response. A variable-ratio schedule also produces tremendous resistance to extinction. Skinner found that pigeons sometimes pecked 150,000 times without a reward after having been on a high variable-ratio schedule.[17]

No wonder, then, that the variable-ratio schedule is sometimes called the gambler's schedule. Lottery tickets and many other forms of gambling pay off on a variable-ratio schedule. People who buy lottery tickets never know which ticket will win, but they do know that the more tickets they buy, the better their chances of winning will be. The trouble is that most lotteries are designed to give a large number of small payouts, big enough to provide reinforcement for purchasing a ticket but small enough to ensure that most people will lose more money than they win. I stood behind a woman in the grocery store one day and watched her spend $5 on five scratch-off tickets. Four were losers, and the fifth paid off with two "free" tickets. One of these paid $2, and as she left she turned to her friend and said, "I won!" She had actually lost $3 ($5 minus her $2 win), yet her small win had reinforced her ticket-buying behavior. Do you think she was motivated to buy additional tickets the next time she was at the store?

Schedules of Reinforcement in Real Life
This gambler is being reinforced on a variable-ratio schedule. She does not know how many times she has to play to win. The variable-ratio schedule produces a high, steady response rate, much to the delight of the casino owners.

LIFE MATTERS
Thinking about purchasing a lottery ticket? The odds of winning the Mega Millions is 1 in 302.5 million. You are more likely to get into Harvard, get killed by a vending machine, or get elected as POTUS, and yet the average American spends $207 annually on lottery tickets.

MAKE IT STICK!

1. Reinforcing only some correct responses is called
   a. negative reinforcement.
   b. partial reinforcement.
   c. primary reinforcement.
   d. continuous reinforcement.

2. If you don't know when to expect text messages from your friends, checking to see if you've received a text is reinforced on a _____ schedule.
   a. variable-interval
   b. variable-ratio
   c. fixed-interval
   d. fixed-ratio

3. A fitness tracker that produces a starburst screen every time you complete 10,000 steps in a day utilizes _____ reinforcement.

4. True or false? A variable-interval schedule of reinforcement usually produces a consistent rate of responding.

New Understandings of Operant Conditioning

17-7 How do cognition and biology affect the operant conditioning process?

Cognition (our thought processes) affects all types of learning, including operant learning. Furthermore, our biology sets boundaries for how and what we can learn.

The Role of Cognition

With **latent learning,** the learning occurs but is not apparent until the learner has an incentive to demonstrate it. Latent learning is a good example of how our thinking—not just whether we are reinforced—affects our learning. In a now-classic experiment, researchers demonstrated how a **cognitive map,** or mental representation of a place, can influence learning.[18] In this experiment, researchers trained one group of rats to find its way through a maze by putting a food reward in a box at the end of the maze. As the number of trials increased, the rats in this group completed the maze faster and faster to find the food (see the blue line in **Figure 17.6**). The researchers also placed a second group of rats in the maze, but they did not reward them with food for finding the end of the maze. Rats in this second group wandered through the maze, exploring it, but their times did not improve during this first phase of the experiment. In the second phase of the experiment, the researchers put a food reward in the box at the maze's end for the second group of rats. Now the performance of the second group of rats rapidly improved until they made fewer errors than the first group. The rats in the second group had developed a cognitive map as they wandered through the maze in the first phase of the experiment. They had learned, but the learning occurred cognitively before it was expressed behaviorally.

The **overjustification effect** provides more support for cognition's role in operant conditioning. Rewarding an already enjoyable behavior *overjustifies* it and may actually *decrease* the frequency of that behavior. This is the direct opposite of the effect Skinner's principles would predict—an increase in the rewarded behavior. Unfortunately, overjustification sometimes happens in school. Activities like reading, which should be (and are) naturally reinforcing for most young children, can be overjustified if the school provides lots of special rewards, such as gold stars, grades, and special parties for meeting reading goals.

latent learning Learning that occurs but is not apparent until the learner has an incentive to demonstrate it.

cognitive map The mental representation of a place.

overjustification effect The effect of promising a reward for doing what one already likes to do; the reward may lessen and replace the person's original, natural motivation so that the behavior stops if the reward is eliminated.

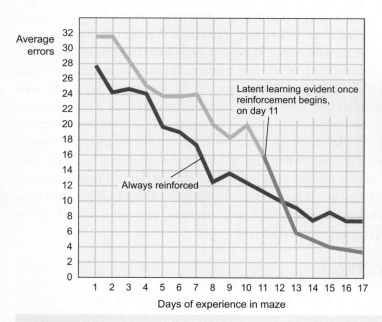

Will & Deni McIntyre/Science Source

▲ **FIGURE 17.6**
Learning Without Reward
If this rat is allowed to wander through the maze on several occasions, it will develop a cognitive map of the maze—an example of latent learning. But the rat will not demonstrate that learning until researchers add some positive reinforcement for showing the knowledge of the maze paths. (From Tolman & Honzik, 1930.)

LIONEL CIRONNEAU/AP Images

Matching the Species to the Behavior ▲
Operant conditioning works best when it focuses on behaviors that come naturally to a species, such as jumping-up behaviors in dogs.

The danger is that these rewards may begin to overwhelm the child's natural motivation to read and become the primary means of maintaining the behavior. When the rewards stop, the behavior stops as well. ("What, I don't get free pizza for reading 10 books?")

Even grades can lead to overjustification. One experiment divided fifth graders into two groups. The researchers told one group to read a passage and informed students in the group that they would be graded on how much they'd learned. They told the other group that they should read the passage but they wouldn't be graded, simply questioned to find out what they remembered. There was little difference in how much the two groups remembered, but the second group thought the passage was more interesting.[19] There seems to be a link between external environmental rewards and internal cognitive factors. If we ignore cognition, we won't get the whole picture about how operant conditioning works. (To see how cognition can influence personal habits for the better, see Learning New Habits.)

The Role of Biology

Why don't the principles of operant conditioning work equally well for all behaviors in all species?

Like cognition, biology clearly influences how we learn and what we learn, including what we learn through operant conditioning. Some species are *biologically predisposed* to learn some behaviors easily and other behaviors only with great difficulty.

Pigeons, for example, easily learn to flap their wings to avoid a mild electric shock and to peck at a disk for food. Operant conditioning principles would suggest that you could reverse these two behaviors and teach the birds to flap for food and peck to avoid shock. This turns out to be difficult, however, because it defies the biological tendencies of the species.[20] Wing flapping is a natural defense mechanism for pigeons and thus lends itself well to avoidance behaviors. Pecking is a response naturally associated with eating, so pigeons easily learn to peck for food.

Erik Isakson/Tetra Images/Alamy Stock Photo

Individualized Learning ▲
Many electronic instructional programs take advantage of operant conditioning principles. This girl will have her answers shaped by a program that breaks instruction down into a series of easy steps. She will receive positive reinforcement for each correct answer.

Operant conditioning offers practical and useful techniques for altering behavior in families, schools, and workplaces. When I was a child, my parents kept a checklist of chores I had to complete each week before receiving my allowance. This policy was based on operant conditioning principles. So is my school's Renaissance Program, which rewards students who earn high grades with gift certificates and special privileges. So was the system of bonuses that kept my son motivated during his brief career in telemarketing. Operant conditioning can indeed change the way people act, and like all science-based theories, it is alive and changing. New research has shed light on cognitive and biological factors that influence operant procedures, which helps us employ these principles even more effectively.

MAKE IT STICK!

1. Rewarding individuals for behavior they already enjoy may cause them to do the behavior less when the rewards stop. This is called the _____ effect.

2. Latent learning demonstrates the importance of _____ in operant conditioning.
   a. extinction
   b. biology
   c. punishment
   d. cognition

3. True or false? Biology helps determine what behaviors will be easiest for an animal to learn.

Module 17 Summary and Assessment
Operant Conditioning

🐾 17-1 What is operant conditioning?

- Operant conditioning is a type of learning in which the frequency of a behavior depends on the consequence that follows that behavior.

🐾 17-2 What is the law of effect?

- Edward Thorndike's law of effect states that behaviors with favorable consequences (reinforced behaviors) will occur more often, and behaviors followed by less favorable consequences (punished behaviors) will occur less often.

🐾 17-3 What are the different kinds of reinforcement?

- Behavior can be increased with positive or negative reinforcement.
- Immediate reinforcement is more effective than delayed reinforcement.
- Reinforcement can be primary (naturally rewarding) or secondary (learned).

🐾 17-4 How does punishment influence behavior?

- Behavior can be decreased with positive or negative punishment.
- Punishment can create problems when used to control behavior: Punishment does not end the desire to engage in a behavior, punishment can lead to fear and anxiety, and children may imitate aggressive forms of punishment (such as spanking).
- Punishment can be an effective way to stop dangerous behaviors if it is used immediately and only occasionally.

🐾 17-5 How can you use operant conditioning to teach a new behavior or make an operantly conditioned behavior stop?

- New behaviors can be shaped by reinforcing behaviors that are increasingly similar to the desired behavior.

- Discrimination occurs when the learner behaves differently toward similar stimuli.
- The extinction, or loss, of a learned behavior occurs when a consequence no longer follows it.

🐾 17-6 What are the advantages and disadvantages of different schedules of reinforcement?

- Continuous reinforcement, useful for establishing new responses, occurs when a reward follows every correct response.
- It is harder to extinguish behavior that has been maintained with a partial reinforcement schedule, in which a reward follows only some correct responses.
- Partial reinforcement can reward behaviors after time has passed (fixed interval and variable interval), or it can provide a reward only after a particular number of responses (fixed ratio and variable ratio).

🐾 17-7 How do cognition and biology affect the operant conditioning process?

- Latent learning and cognitive maps are examples of how our thinking—not just whether we are reinforced—affects our learning.
- The overjustification effect occurs when a reward replaces a person's original motivation so that a behavior stops if the reward is eliminated.
- Some species are biologically predisposed to learn some behaviors easily and other behaviors only with great difficulty.

Summative Assessment

1. In operant conditioning, behavior is determined by
   a. pairing a neutral stimulus with an unconditioned stimulus.
   b. consequences.
   c. the attitude of the learner.
   d. the event that precedes the behavior.

2. B. F. Skinner received his first public recognition when an article was published about his
   a. work with pigeons in the Skinner box.
   b. air crib for babies.
   c. extension of Pavlov's work to animals other than dogs.
   d. affair with a graduate student.

3. Two possible consequences in operant conditioning are
   a. cognitive and biological.
   b. interval and ratio.
   c. fixed and variable.
   d. reinforcement and punishment.

4. The law of effect indicates that
   a. reinforcement increases the future likelihood of a behavior.
   b. punishment increases the future likelihood of a behavior.
   c. positive consequences increase the future likelihood of a behavior.
   d. negative consequences increase the future likelihood of a behavior.

5. Which of the following is a secondary reinforcement?
   a. lemonade
   b. candy
   c. a gift certificate
   d. bread

6. Punishment can be
   a. positive but not negative.
   b. negative but not positive.
   c. neither positive nor negative.
   d. either positive or negative.

7. Which of the following is NOT a potential problem with punishment?
   a. Punishment is so effective that its results cannot be reversed.
   b. Punishment can model aggressive behavior for the learner.
   c. Punishment can cause the learner to avoid the teacher.
   d. The effects of punishment are temporary.

8. A mother has been teaching her child to make his bed. She does this by praising the child's first efforts, even though they are not very good. The mother is using the technique of
   a. shaping.
   b. extinction.
   c. discrimination.
   d. delayed reinforcement.

9. Which of the following represents reinforcement on a variable-interval schedule?
   a. Ahmad buys 10 raffle tickets, hoping to win the computer being given away for a local charity fundraiser.
   b. Rosie addresses envelopes for a local company. She is paid $20 for every 100 envelopes she completes.
   c. Charlie studies hard to prepare for his semester finals.
   d. Juan checks his phone repeatedly to see if an important email has arrived.

10. The overjustification effect is important because it illustrates the importance of _____ in operant conditioning.
    a. biology
    b. extinction
    c. cognition
    d. discrimination

KEY TERMS AND KEY PEOPLE

Observational Learning

Learning Goals

18-1 Define observational learning; explain the implications of Albert Bandura's experiments and how they can be explained by mirror neurons.

18-2 Describe how observational learning can lead to prosocial and antisocial behaviors.

18-3 Explain how violence in the media affects violent behaviors and attitudes in real life.

Believe it or not, the most famous experiment of observational learning was done with an inflatable Bobo doll, like the one in this illustration. In this module, you'll find out what Albert Bandura learned from this children's toy.

How much have you learned by watching others? Can you imagine what it would be like to drive a car if you had never seen another person do it? Even if you'd been able to read the owner's manual (which explains how the car works) and your state driver's manual (which explains the rules of the road), actually driving the car would be next to impossible. It's one thing to read about transmissions, windshield wipers, and passing lanes, but it's something else entirely to watch other people actually driving.

This is the stuff of *observational learning*, and thank goodness we are capable of it. Can a child learn from watching her older siblings? *You bet.* A Little Leaguer can learn from watching his favorite Major League player, a video gamer can learn from watching her expert-level friend, and a new employee can learn on the job from watching a more experienced colleague. Not only can we profit from our own experiences, we can also profit from the experiences of others. You may be surprised to learn that this is a type of learning shared with other species, including rats, birds, gorillas, and monkeys.[1,2] The expression monkey see, monkey do is true!

The Nature of Observational Learning

18-1 What is observational learning? What are the implications of Albert Bandura's experiments, and how can they be explained by mirror neurons?

Observational learning takes place by watching others. It differs from other kinds of learning in that another person—the **model**—actually practices or repeats behaviors, which the learner observes and mimics in a process called **modeling.** It's an amazing thing, isn't it, that we can learn by modeling our behavior after that of another person? This learning occurs in our brains as a cognitive process.

observational learning
Learning by observing others.

model The person observed in observational learning.

modeling The process of observing and imitating a specific behavior.

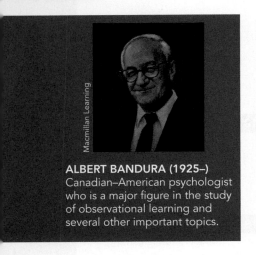

ALBERT BANDURA (1925–)
Canadian–American psychologist who is a major figure in the study of observational learning and several other important topics.

Albert Bandura's Experiments

Canadian–American psychologist **Albert Bandura** conducted groundbreaking experiments in observational learning in the 1960s.[3] In one experiment, the researchers arranged for a young child to play in a room, while an adult in another part of the room punched, kicked, and threw an inflatable Bobo doll (the kind that are several feet tall with a weighted base so they right themselves when knocked over). The adult's tirade lasted for about 10 minutes, and all the while the adult shouted things at Bobo like, Sock him in the nose! Hit him down! Kick him!

In the next step of the experiment, Bandura took the child to a playroom with many interesting toys. When the child was happily engaged with the toys, the researcher interrupted to say that the playing would have to stop because the cool toys were being saved "for the other children." The child, now frustrated, was then taken to yet another room and left alone with only a few less interesting toys— and Bobo.

Bandura was interested in seeing how the child would now behave. He found that children who had observed an adult's violent behavior with the Bobo doll exhibited more aggression than children who hadn't observed the violent adult model. Children who had observed an attack on the Bobo doll not only were more aggressive, but also mimicked the exact behaviors and words they had seen. Observational learning was at work.

In another variation of his research, Bandura studied the effect of consequences delivered to the *model*—in this case, the adult who demonstrated violent behavior for the child.[4] Would such consequences affect the *observer*—in this case, the child observing the aggressive adult? We know that consequences—good and bad— affect how and what we learn. But what happens when we observe another person experiencing those consequences? To test this, Bandura produced a film that

How Would You Treat Bobo? ▶
We learn by observing the behavior of others. Bandura's research showed that children imitated, with uncanny precision, the behaviors they saw modeled.

showed an adult model behaving and shouting aggressively ("Sockeroo!") toward the ever-present Bobo doll. For this film, however, the researchers could choose one of three endings:

1. Another adult rewards the violent adult model with praise and candy. One group of children saw this ending.

2. Another adult calls the model a bad person and spanks the model. A second group of children saw this ending.

3. The model receives neither a reward nor a punishment. A third group saw this neutral ending.

After viewing the video, each child in each group spent time in the playroom with the Bobo doll and other toys. Children who saw the violent model rewarded for aggression behaved most aggressively in the playroom, and those who saw the violent model spanked behaved least aggressively. This is referred to as **vicarious learning**—learning by seeing the consequences of another person's behavior. When the consequence is a reward, the observer is more likely to repeat the behavior (see **Figure 18.1**).

In variation after variation, Bandura's experiments showed the same results—we learn by watching others if the following four conditions are met:[5]

1. *Attention*—To learn, you must be aware of the behaviors of those around you. A student who is attentive during cooking class stands a good chance of actually learning how to make an omelet!

vicarious learning Learning by seeing the consequences of another person's behavior.

LEARNER OBSERVES BEHAVIOR BEING PUNISHED

Young Henry observes cookie jar.

Big sister Ella reaches for cookie from jar.

Mom tells Ella, "No!"

LEARNER DOES NOT REPEAT OBSERVED BEHAVIOR

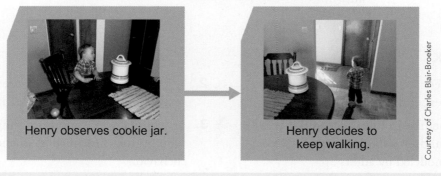

Henry observes cookie jar.

Henry decides to keep walking.

Courtesy of Charles Blair-Broeker

FIGURE 18.1
Vicarious Learning
Not only do we learn when we receive consequences for our behaviors, but we also learn when we observe others getting consequences for their behaviors.

Margot Granitsas/The Image Works

Modeling Mom ▲
Here, Mom is serving as the model for her daughter, who is modeling the use of chopsticks. She will be an expert in no time!

mirror neurons Brain cells located in the front of the brain that activate when a person performs certain actions or when the person observes another do so.

2. *Retention*—You must remember the behavior you witnessed. Will the attentive student be able to retain—from one week to the next—all those details so expertly modeled by the driver education teacher?

3. *Ability to reproduce the behavior*—I have watched my sons skateboard many times, but I do not possess the required skills to do the tricks. Despite all my watching, my minimal sense of balance means I can barely stand on the board, even if it isn't moving!

4. *Motivation*—We are more likely to feel motivated to learn if the model we've observed has been rewarded for the behavior and if we like the model. Nike and other corporations pay huge endorsement fees to star athletes because their advertising agencies believe likable megastars are effective models.

Mirror Neurons

Italian researchers discovered a biological explanation for observational learning in the early 1990s.[6] They had implanted electrodes in the *frontal lobe* of a monkey's brain to track the activity of cells that controlled when the monkey put food in his mouth. The researchers were amazed when they noticed the same cells showing the same activity when the monkey saw one of the researchers lick an ice cream cone. These brain cells are now known as **mirror neurons**—cells that activate *either* when an individual performs certain actions *or* when the individual observes someone else doing so. For example, in a monkey's brain, these neurons function the same way when they are watching another monkey grasp an object as they do when the monkey grasps the object on its own.[7,8]

It turns out that mirror neurons can help explain far more than such simple behaviors. Just as we can imitate the actions of another person, we can also imitate a person's emotional state (an ability known as empathy). Brain scans show that for both people and monkeys, the same mirror neurons are active when experiencing or observing an emotion.[9] Some now believe that "broken mirrors" (mirror neurons that don't function correctly) may explain the development of autism.[10,11]

MAKE IT STICK!

1. What was Albert Bandura trying to learn from his Bobo doll experiments?

   a. The best method to train aggressive behavior
   b. Whether children will repeat aggressive behaviors modeled by adults
   c. Whether children are naturally aggressive when they play with clown dolls
   d. The age at which children begin to imitate aggressive behavior

2. _____ neurons in the brain help explain how observational learning occurs.

3. True or false? Vicarious learning occurs when you see the consequences of another person's behavior.

Observational Learning in Everyday Life

 18-2 How can observational learning lead to prosocial and antisocial behaviors?

Children are capable of learning by observation almost from the beginning. Shortly after birth, babies will imitate an adult who sticks out his tongue and will imitate gestures within the first year.[12] This means that observations have a tremendous cumulative effect on behavior in both positive and negative ways. Children learn much that's appropriate from models, but—as demonstrated in the Bobo experiments—they also learn much that's inappropriate.

People are often unaware of the effect they have on others. Retired professional basketball star Charles Barkley repeatedly argued in the early 1990s that he was a basketball player, not a role model. (And in 2010, pop star Miley Cyrus argued similarly, declaring that fans shouldn't look to her for how to act.) It's easy to understand why he didn't want to be considered responsible for those mimicking his bad boy behaviors, but Barkley's position was not realistic. It is impossible to choose *not* to be a role model. If you're in the public eye as a professional athlete or entertainer, you are—by the nature of your position—a powerful role model. Even those of us who are not in the public eye will almost certainly influence others. If you have younger brothers or sisters, rest assured they look up to you and learn from you how to behave in a variety of situations, just as you may have learned from older siblings. If a new person is hired at your place of work, or if you're a senior on a sports team, *you* are a role model. Whether you realize it or not, others are watching and learning from you.

But even if you can't control whether or not others will see you as a role model, you have control over the *kind* of role model you will be. You can model **antisocial behaviors,** which are negative and destructive, like some students in my school whose "leadership" resulted in a rash of vandalism in the name of "pranks" during homecoming week. Or you can model **prosocial behaviors,** which are positive and constructive, like other students in my school whose behavior spearheads an annual drive to collect tens of thousands of pounds of food for our local food bank. In each case, the actions (modeling) of a few students snowballed into a bigger trend. Your choices do make a difference!

Antisocial Behavior Role Model
Outspoken music stars such as Miley Cyrus create controversy because the public cannot agree about whether the modeled behaviors are appropriate. Can you think of other stars who create such controversy?

Jeff Kravitz/FilmMagic, Inc/Getty Images

Ken Murray/Icon Sportswire via AP Images

Prosocial Behavior Role Model
People will imitate either prosocial or antisocial behavior. The same learning principles apply no matter what behavior is modeled. J. J. Watt of the Houston Texans modeled prosocial behavior in the aftermath of Hurricane Harvey in 2017.

antisocial behavior Negative, destructive, unhelpful behavior.

prosocial behavior Positive, constructive, helpful behavior.

MAKE IT STICK!

1. Briefly describe a situation when students in your school modeled antisocial behavior.

2. Briefly describe a situation when students in your school modeled prosocial behavior.

Observational Learning of Violence From the Media

18-3 How does violence in the media affect violent behaviors and attitudes?

Maica/Vetta/Getty Images

Real-Life Instant Replay to Follow?
There is a connection between violence in the media and violence in society. Research indicates that we learn aggression from what we observe.

If you're one of the 90 percent of U.S. teenagers who watch television every day,[13] by the time you graduate from high school, you will have spent more time watching television than you spent in school—an average of 4 hours a day for teenagers in the United States.[14,15] Not only does almost every home have a TV set, but most have more than one. And what about the content of all this TV programming? Much of it is undeniably violent. The average U.S. student has witnessed about 8000 murders and well over 100,000 violent acts by the end of elementary school (Huston et al., 1992). Only about half of these cases of violence portray pain or harm to the victim in a realistic way (Mediascope, 1995). The other cases show sanitized violence in which, for example, pointing and firing a gun is shown accurately, but the pain and suffering of the victim is not. In such cases, viewers may learn how to behave violently but not gain an adequate appreciation for the true consequences of violent behavior. Experts agree that this mixture fuels aggression in viewers.[16] Keep in mind that these statistics relate only to television. Movies, video games, print media, and the Internet provide even more exposure to violence.

The key question is whether all this observation of violence makes any difference in real life. Research indicates it does. Bandura's experiments, and more like them, indicate that we learn aggression from what we observe. The American Psychological Association Commission on Violence and Youth reached these conclusions after an extensive review of the available research:[17]

- Higher levels of viewing violence on television are associated with increased acceptance of aggressive attitudes and increased aggressive behavior.

- Children's exposure to violence in mass media, particularly at young ages, can have harmful lifelong consequences.

- Film and TV portrayals of women in victim roles and of ethnic minorities in aggressive and violent roles worsen the violence experienced by women and ethnic minorities.

- The viewing of TV programming and commercials affects our concept of reality and how we believe others live.

The commission also concluded that television *could* be an effective prosocial force by demonstrating behaviors that benefit others. The media are sources of observational learning. Society can, however, choose whether the media will function as a prosocial or antisocial learning model.

Notice that our discussion and the American Psychological Association commission have focused on the effects of television, a form of media that is being supplemented by the Internet, video games, music, and movies. All of these contribute additional doses of daily violence to our lives.

We take, we give. We learn, we teach. Others have served as role models for you, and you serve as role models for others. Give some thought to the lessons you are providing for others, and choose carefully the models you follow.

MAKE IT STICK!

1. Should parents be concerned about the amount of violence their children view?

   a. No, observational learning of aggression occurs with real-life models but not media models.

   b. Yes, violent movies are more likely to produce aggression than other forms of media.

   c. No, viewing movie violence is a safe way for children to express their aggression through fantasy.

   d. Yes, viewing violence in the media is associated with increased aggression.

2. Summarize the conclusions of the American Psychological Association Commission on Violence and Youth.

3. True or false? Exposure to media has the potential to create both positive and negative changes in viewers.

Module 18 Summary and Assessment
Observational Learning

 18-1 What is observational learning? What are the implications of Albert Bandura's experiments, and how can they be explained by mirror neurons?

- Observational learning is learning by observing others.

- Bandura's famous Bobo doll experiments showed that children learned violent behavior from adult models.

- A biological explanation for observational learning has recently been discovered in the form of mirror neurons, which are brain cells located in the front of the brain that activate when performing certain actions or when observing another do so.

18-2 How can observational learning lead to prosocial and antisocial behaviors?

- Observational learning works equally well for antisocial and prosocial behaviors. It can lead children to imitate negative, antisocial behaviors or be a force for the learning of positive, prosocial behaviors.

 18-3 How does violence in the media affect violent behaviors and attitudes?

- Watching violence in the media is correlated with acceptance of aggressive attitudes and increased aggression; this affects our ideas about how others live and what is normal.

- Media sources can also encourage prosocial behaviors through observational learning.

Summative Assessment

1. Learning by watching others is called

   a. imitative learning.

   b. operant conditioning.

   c. observational learning.

   d. classical conditioning.

2. You can learn new behaviors by watching a(n)

   a. instigator.

   b. model.

   c. actor.

   d. inflatable toy.

3. Groundbreaking research in observational learning was done by

   a. John Watson.

   b. B. F. Skinner.

   c. Robert Rescorla.

   d. Albert Bandura.

4. All of the following were important for the original research in observational learning EXCEPT a(n)

   a. peer of the learner.
   b. Bobo doll.
   c. child who observed videos.
   d. adult who interacted with toys.

5. When children observed adults interacting with inflatable Bobo dolls, they

   a. were not likely to imitate aggressive behaviors.
   b. were aggressive but didn't imitate exact behaviors and words of the adults.
   c. were aggressive and imitated some of the exact behaviors and words of the adults.
   d. imitated exact behaviors but not exact words.

6. Which of the following is true of vicarious learning?

   a. It only applies to aggressive behavior.
   b. In only applies to nonaggressive behavior.
   c. It is determined by the consequences of another person's behavior.
   d. It occurs by observation of media but not real-life events.

7. Mirror neurons

   a. are located in the brain of the model but not in the brain of the observer.
   b. are located in the brain of the observer but not in the brain of the model.
   c. provide a neurological explanation of why aggression modeled in the media is more significant than aggression modeled in real life.
   d. provide a neurological explanation of why observational learning occurs.

8. Which of the following is an example of prosocial behavior?

   a. A high school class collecting cans for a food drive
   b. A student studying to do her best job ever on a psychology test
   c. A star athlete dunking a basketball
   d. A politician harassing a student intern

9. Which of the following has NOT proven to be necessary for observational learning?

   a. Witnessing a behavior at least three times
   b. Remembering the modeled behavior
   c. The ability to reproduce the behavior
   d. Motivation to learn

10. All of the following are conclusions of the American Psychological Association Commission on Violence and Youth EXCEPT:

    a. higher levels of viewing violence on television are associated with increased aggressive attitudes.
    b. higher levels of viewing violence on television are associated with increased aggressive behaviors.
    c. exposure of children to media violence can have lifelong consequences.
    d. media violence and aggressive behavior by viewers are correlated, but this may not represent a cause-and-effect relationship.

KEY TERMS AND KEY PEOPLE

observational learning, p. 275

model, p. 275

modeling, p. 275

vicarious learning, p. 277

mirror neurons, p. 278

antisocial behavior, p. 279

prosocial behavior, p. 279

Albert Bandura (1925–), p. 276

DOMAIN 4

Sociocultural

Tracy Fillimonow/Shutterstock

Module 19 | Social Thinking and Social Influence

Learning Goals

19-1 Describe how attribution theory predicts the way we explain the behavior of others.

19-2 Explain how attitudes affect actions and how actions affect attitudes.

19-3 Describe what research says about conformity and obedience.

19-4 Explain how being around others affects our behavior, and how group membership affects our thinking and decision making.

19-5 Describe how personal control influences our behavior.

social psychology
The scientific study of how we think about, influence, and relate to one another.

What social factors influence whether you say "Yes" or "No" to a request you know is wrong? Let's find out.

Each November at my school, the student council sponsors a canned-food drive for our local food bank. The drive is set up as a voluntary competition among fourth-period classes, and about half of the teachers eagerly agree to let their classes participate. Are the teachers who agree to participate more sensitive to human needs? Are they simply more competitive or more outgoing? And what of the teachers who do not participate? Were they already busy on another philanthropy project? Do they think collecting cans of food will waste valuable class time and cause too much classroom disruption? Or are they simply "not as much fun" as other teachers? Why do these teachers act so *differently*, even when they are in the same situation? Personality psychologists might answer that last question by looking at the inner, enduring elements of the teachers' personalities. However, social psychologists would be more inclined to study the social influences that help explain why people act differently in the same situation and why the same person might act differently in different situations. **Social psychology** is the scientific study of how we think about, influence, and relate to one another.

Social Thinking

How do we form our beliefs and attitudes about the world around us? We often do this so automatically, without conscious thought, that we're not even aware of the process. Let's slow down this process to understand how it all happens so that we can work toward more fair and accurate attributions (that is, the way we explain events and behavior to ourselves) and attitudes.

Attributing Behavior to Personal Disposition or the Situation

🐾🐾 **19-1** How does attribution theory predict the way we explain the behavior of others?

When we meet people, we have a tendency to analyze and categorize them based on the behaviors we observe. By now, you have decided whether your psychology teacher is reserved or spirited, straitlaced or easygoing, serious or light-hearted, and you have probably assigned, or attributed, those traits to your teacher's internal *disposition* (for instance, his or her tendencies, nature, or temperament) rather than to the classroom *situation*. Have you ever considered how your teacher might act in a different situation, maybe at a party with friends or at home with family? According to **attribution theory,** we tend to explain the behavior of others as an aspect of either an internal disposition (an inner trait) or the situation.[1] And we often make the **fundamental attribution error,** the tendency to *attribute the behaviors of others* (that is, the reason somebody did something) to inner dispositions rather than to situations. Let's unpack those terms.

Say the person sitting next to you asks to borrow and copy your class notes. Almost automatically, you start to assign a cause, or a reason, to your classmate's request. If you think your neighbor is lazy and didn't listen, then you are making a *dispositional* attribution. If you remember your classmate was absent the day before, then you are making a *situational* attribution.

As we try to "figure someone out," we are more likely to lean in the dispositional direction and to underestimate the situation. I sometimes make the fundamental attribution error by mentally assigning the label *shy* to students who never say a word in class. I'm often surprised when I see them transformed into loudmouths at a basketball game against a rival, insulting the other team's players and singing "Three Blind Mice" when the referee makes a call against our team. These students behave very differently when in different situations. This means that I *underestimated* the effect of the situation and *overestimated* the effect of personal disposition. If you get cut off in traffic, are you more likely to think, "Stupid driver!" or, "That person must have a good reason for being in a hurry"? I don't know about you, but I'm more likely to make the dispositional attribution. It's hard to resist attribution errors.

In one study assessing attributions, participants talked to a woman who acted *either* warm and friendly *or* distant and critical. Half of the participants, group A, heard that the woman had been told to act one way or the other. The other half, group B, heard the woman's behavior was natural. In other words, group A was given a situational explanation of the woman's behavior, and group B was given a dispositional explanation. What effect did these explanations have on the two groups' assessment of this woman? None.

Canned-Food Drive
Given the opportunity to donate cans of food for the food bank, some people donate and some do not. Psychologists study why people act differently in similar situations.

attribution theory The theory that we tend to explain the behavior of others as an aspect of either an internal disposition (an inner trait) or the situation.

fundamental attribution error The tendency to attribute the behavior of others to internal dispositions rather than to situations.

Lazy Note-Taker or Absent From Class?
If you think your friend deserves to borrow your notes because he missed class, you've made a situational attribution for his need for notes. If you think he's lazy and didn't want to take notes, you've made a dispositional attribution.

White House Photo/Alamy

If the woman acted unfriendly, *both* group A and group B labeled her as innately unfriendly. They underestimated situational factors and overestimated dispositional factors.[2]

Actors complain of being typecast, meaning that after playing a certain role for a long time, perhaps a villain in a movie, they can no longer land other kinds of parts. The problem? Directors know that viewers make attributions to actors that are hard to overcome. Daniel Radcliffe has played the role of good guy Harry Potter in eight movies, and we might have a hard time believing he could play a criminal. Therefore, we might decide not to see a movie in which he played a villainous part. Could you watch comic geniuses like Steve Carell, Ellen DeGeneres, and Tina Fey act the parts of serial murderers and find them believable? We judge actors as having a certain disposition, and in so doing, we commit the fundamental attribution error.

What about you? Are you shy or outgoing? In answering that question, you might say you are shy in class but not around your friends. You might say that you talk less at a big party but you could talk for hours at an overnighter with three of your close friends. When we explain our own behavior, we tend to include the situation as part of our answer. But when we explain the behavior of others, we wear blinders, attributing their behavior to their permanent, personal qualities. Interestingly, we tend to attribute the bad things we do to situations and the good things we do to our dispositions.[3]

Another common dispositional phenomenon is the **self-serving bias,** which is a readiness to perceive oneself favorably. For instance, if you blame a bad test score on the test itself instead of your preparation, it's possible that your self-serving bias is showing. Be careful, as this bias may prevent you from looking at your grade critically in such a way as to do better on your next test. That is, there is nothing you can do about a poorly constructed test, but you can certainly control your preparation.

Every day, we try to make sense of what others do or say by making attributions. Did the person at the next locker not say, "Good morning," because she is unfriendly or because she's exhausted from staying up late studying for her biology exam? Does the college admissions counselor look at your transcript, see a low grade in chemistry, and think you don't care about science? Or does the same admissions person look at the rest of the term to see whether the courses you took were particularly challenging? Sit on a jury, and you may have to decide whether someone acted in self-defense or is aggressive by nature and should be put behind bars. The point is, these judgments or attributions matter, and whether we make the judgments based on the person or the situation also matters.[4] A wife says to her husband, "Must you always spend so much money?" In happy marriages, the husband will tend to attribute this statement to something situational, thinking something like "She must have had a bad day at the office." In an unhappy marriage, the husband is more likely to attribute the statement to disposition, perhaps thinking, "She's so stingy."[5]

Are there political implications for attributions? *Of course!* Several researchers have shown that political liberals tend to explain social problems, such as poverty and unemployment, as a result of the situation.[6–9] Conservatives are more likely to cite personal dispositions of the unemployed and poor. The liberal might ask, "If you could not get a good education, had to face discrimination, and lived in a

Disposition

If Ellen DeGeneres or any famous comedian were cast as a vicious criminal in a movie, we'd probably have a hard time believing in the character. Because of the fundamental attribution error, we would assume that the role the comedian plays in public reflects her personal qualities, not the characteristics of the situation.

self-serving bias A readiness to perceive oneself favorably.

LIFE MATTERS

As you strive to be a leader at school, understanding that others around you are more likely to interpret your behavior as a disposition can help you be mindful of your reactions to setbacks or adversity.

poor neighborhood, would you be any better off than the poorer people in your city?" The conservative's response is likely to be something like "The poor who work hard enough will pull themselves out of poverty. People pretty much get what they deserve." Social scientists are more likely to blame present and past situations, not disposition.

Culture also affects attribution. Several banks and investment firms around the world lost millions of dollars years ago when employees made unauthorized transactions. Why did these financial institutions lose money? In the United States, we tended to blame unethical individuals—a dispositional attribution. In Japan, newspapers blamed a lack of organizational controls or regulations—a situational attribution.[10] Research shows that people raised in Western countries like the United States tend to make attributions based on dispositions (and are more likely to commit the fundamental attribution error) far more often than those from East Asian cultures.[11]

It may be impossible to identify all attribution errors we make in a given week or day. What is possible, however, is to realize that our attributions about others—our judgments about whether their behavior is caused by situational or personal factors—carry lasting consequences (see **Figure 19.1**).

PEANUTS

Negative behavior
Someone cuts into the line in front of you.

Situational attribution
"That tired mother is so busy with her little boy, she didn't even notice me in the line."

Tolerant reaction

Dispositional attribution
"Who does that lady think she is? I bet she always cuts in front of people in lines."

Unfavorable reaction

▲ **FIGURE 19.1**
Negative Behavior: Cutting in Line
Whether you tolerate a negative behavior or respond unfavorably to it will depend partly on how you interpret the event.

MAKE IT STICK!

1. You hear someone cursing at a locker that won't open because the opening mechanism is jammed. You think, "Wow, what a bad temper!" Which of the following concepts best explains your initial judgment?

    a. self-serving bias

    b. underestimating disposition

    c. typecasting

    d. underestimating the situation

2. The tendency to attribute the behavior of others to internal disposition instead of situational factors is called the _____.

3. True or False: Research shows that liberal and moderate lawmakers are more likely to avoid the fundamental attribution error than conservative lawmakers.

4. What did your book call a "readiness to perceive oneself favorably"?

Attitudes and Actions

 19-2 How can attitudes affect actions? And how can actions affect attitudes?

A friend tells you Mr. Doane is mean and grades unfairly. Although you may never take a class with this teacher, your friend's assessment could affect your **attitude**—a belief and feeling that predisposes you to respond in a particular way to people, events, and objects. You may develop a feeling of dislike for this teacher and perhaps even respond in an unfriendly way if he ever requested anything from you. Attitudes have a powerful effect on behavior.

> **attitude** The belief and feeling that predisposes someone to respond in a particular way to objects, people, and events.

The Effects of Attitudes on Actions Several studies have shown that attitudes and behaviors are not always perfect matches.[12] The same students who say they're against cheating may later look at someone's paper for an answer. The white person who claims to treat all people equally may behave differently toward members of an ethnic group that is different from his. Why do we sometimes talk one way but act another? Do attitudes ever predict behavior?

Some studies show that our attitudes can predict behavior if the circumstances are right[13,14] (see **Figure 19.2**). Sometimes we *do* talk the talk *and* walk the walk—but most likely only in the following cases:

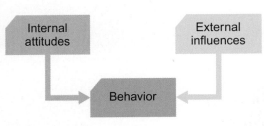

FIGURE 19.2
Behavioral Influences External influences and internal attitudes affect behavior.

1. *The outside influences on what we do are minimal.* Perhaps your friend Darius swore in seventh grade that he would never smoke. Several years later, most members of Darius's new peer group are smokers. Giving in to this increased outside pressure, Darius starts to light up. Had the outside influences remained minimal, his attitude toward smoking would have had a better chance of remaining the same as it was in the seventh grade.

2. *We are keenly aware of our attitudes.* When we are conscious of what we believe, our behavior is more likely to match our beliefs.[15] Darius might never have started smoking if something had made him more fully aware of his attitude toward smoking (for example, a writing assignment or the death of a loved one from lung cancer due to smoking).

3. *The attitudes are relevant to the behavior.* If you think exercise is essential for good health but you really dislike getting sweaty, then you may avoid working out even though you know it's good for you. Your attitude toward exercise

will guide your physical fitness program. Darius might never have started smoking if he valued (attitude) exercise (the relevant behavior) as a way to stay healthy and knew smoking would interfere with his ability to exercise.

The Effects of Actions on Attitudes
But behavior can also affect attitudes. The concepts of foot-in-the-door phenomenon, role-playing, and cognitive dissonance help us understand how behavior often precedes and fosters attitudes.

FOOT-IN-THE-DOOR PHENOMENON A student group at our school was trying to raise money for the Make-A-Wish Foundation. The highest amount our school had raised in previous years was $800. In planning the fundraiser, the students made a series of requests from the administration. First they asked, "If we raise $500, can we print the names of the top five donors in the daily bulletin?" The answer was "Yes." Then, "If we raise $1000, can we print the names of the top five donors and give them a free school lunch for a week?" The answer? "Yes."

Requests for rewards for increasing amounts of money continued until the students asked, "If we raise $10,000 [an unheard-of amount at my school], would you release school an hour early the last Friday of the fundraiser?" The administration approved the early dismissal, and the publicity machine for this event shifted into high gear.

Posters declaring this ultimate incentive were distributed to every classroom. At the end of two weeks, our school presented a check for more than $11,000 to the Make-A-Wish Foundation. Everybody (except the teachers) started the weekend an hour early. It's amazing what students will do for an extra hour off, isn't it?

One of the students who made the requests of the administration later admitted to having read about the **foot-in-the-door phenomenon** in psychology class. This phenomenon is the tendency for people who have first agreed to a small request to comply later with a larger request. One researcher found that if you want people to agree to something big, then you should start small and work your way up.[16] The escalating actions fuel the attitudes, and each successive act is easier to agree to. Would you put a large, ugly "Drive Carefully" sign in your front yard? One study found that only 17 percent of the people in a California neighborhood would agree to post such a sign. However, when this request was made two weeks after people had agreed to display a small, 3-inch-high "Be a Safe Driver" sign, a whopping 76 percent allowed the large, unsightly sign in their yard.[17] Putting the small sign in the yard first (the behavior) likely had an impact on the increased percentage of homeowners who thought it would be okay (the attitude) to put the larger (and uglier) sign in their yards.

So, were the students running the fund drive for the Make-A-Wish Foundation smart to start with the small requests? Would the principal have agreed to the hour off from school if it had been the first request? What do you think?

ROLE-PLAYING When you go to college, you'll be taking on a new **role.** We think of a role as a set of expectations in a social setting that defines how one ought to behave. At first, it may feel a little weird, as if you're "playing college" as you adjust to professors who don't take attendance and truly don't want to know when you use the restroom. You may at first feel strange about attending fewer classes each day, but before long, your actions will no longer seem so

Foot In or Out of the Door? Using their understanding of the foot-in-the-door phenomenon, these students were able to leave school an hour early.

Monkey Business Images/Shutterstock.com

foot-in-the-door phenomenon The tendency for people who have first agreed to a small request to comply later with a larger request.

role A set of expectations in a social setting that define how one ought to behave.

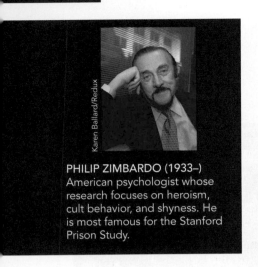

PHILIP ZIMBARDO (1933–)
American psychologist whose research focuses on heroism, cult behavior, and shyness. He is most famous for the Stanford Prison Study.

Karen Ballard/Redux

Role-Playing Prison Guards
Philip Zimbardo had to call off his prison study after the role-playing became too intense.

Philip G. Zimbardo, Inc.

cognitive dissonance theory The theory that we act to reduce the discomfort (dissonance) we feel when two of our thoughts (cognitions) are inconsistent.

FIGURE 19.3
Cognitive Dissonance in Action
When two thoughts are incompatible, we often reduce the discomfort (dissonance) by changing an attitude.

artificial. You'll not only *act* like a college student, you'll *feel* like one. What we do, we eventually become. Several studies have confirmed this effect, including the Zimbardo prison study.

Psychologist **Philip Zimbardo** randomly assigned a group of Stanford University students to play the part of either a guard or a prisoner in a simulated prison.[18] Although the study was designed to last much longer, it ended after only six days. Why? Zimbardo called it off because the students playing guards were displaying humiliating aggressiveness and cruelty toward the students playing the prisoner role. Both guards and prisoners had adopted uncharacteristic roles, and both were becoming the characters they were playing. Behavior can shape beliefs and attitudes.

COGNITIVE DISSONANCE A former student, J.J., who vocally supported politically liberal causes, fell head over heels for an officer in the Teenage Republicans club. At her request, J.J. joined the Teenage Republicans and started attending meetings. After joining, he began to feel a sort of tension between his liberal beliefs and his actions supporting the conservative club. Then J.J. noticed that his attitudes were changing from negative to positive toward the club's conservative projects. Why did J.J.'s attitudes change? According to **cognitive dissonance theory,** we act to reduce the discomfort (dissonance) we feel when our thoughts (cognitions) and actions are inconsistent. When his attitudes and actions clashed, J.J. reduced the resulting dissonance by changing his attitudes (see **Figure 19.3**).

Research regarding the ongoing war in Iraq provides an international example of cognitive dissonance. Before the war began in 2003, 80 percent of the people

J.J.'s attitude
"My political beliefs are liberal."

J.J.'s behavior
J.J. joins the Teenage Republicans because his girlfriend is an officer.

Cognitive dissonance
(awareness that attitude and behavior are inconsistent)

Dissonance resolved
"Maybe the conservatives have a point."

PSYCHOLOGY IN THE REAL WORLD

Harvesting Heroism

Psychologists note, however, that in atrocity-producing situations like Zimbardo's prison study, not everybody gives in to the power of the situation.[19,20] Zimbardo's recent work centers on the "hero in waiting" that he contends is in each one of us. That is, he believes we must get beyond our traditional notion of heroes as larger-than-life figures if we want to increase the number of heroic acts in our society.[21] The goal should be to create everyday heroes.

> Most people who do heroic deeds, ordinary people, typically do a single heroic deed only once because to be a hero you need an opportunity. . . . What I'm trying to do is promote the notion that any of us could be a hero if we are willing to act on behalf of other people in need or a moral cause, knowing that there is potential personal cost.[22]

This cost, says Zimbardo, could be ridicule or even personal harm. Zimbardo started the Heroic Imagination Project (or HIP, found at http://heroicimagination.org) with the aim to increase civil acts—in other words, to increase everyday heroism. Those involved in HIP learn three fundamental points:

1. You don't have to fight to be a hero; you can be a peace hero.

2. Heroic acts need not be extraordinary. Rather, they can be acts that are performed every day because our society needs and expects these acts.

3. Anyone can be a hero.

So, how do we foster everyday heroism? It starts with a commitment to the belief that everyone is a "hero in waiting" and that we all have the potential to act heroically when the situation demands it. Zimbar-

do identifies small acts (such as being willing to ask for help or complimenting others on things they've done well) as examples of nondramatic heroism. The next step, particularly with students your age, is to nurture heroic imaginations.[23]

1. Encourage people to recognize when others need help. Recognizing that things are odd, out of place, or not quite right can be the trigger that gets you to defuse danger before it explodes. For example, realizing someone is about to bully a classmate is necessary before you can take action to stop the bully.

2. Encourage and expect action over inaction. When parents, friends, or teachers discuss situations that might require intervention and indicate intervention as the expectation, the likelihood of everyday heroism increases. Don't just stand around watching a bully harm a classmate.

3. Teach or model ways for students or classmates to resolve conflicts. It's far more heroic to talk through a problem than to fight over it.

Zimbardo concludes that "what the world needs now is more heroes." He hopes that more of us will "learn to become wise and effective heroes who can change the world, one positive step at time."[24]

THINK ABOUT . . . Psychology in the Real World

1. What does it mean to be a "hero in waiting"?

2. What are the goals of the Heroic Imagination Project?

3. What can you do to prepare for a time when you need to act heroically?

in our country believed weapons of mass destruction (WMD) would be found in Iraq and that this justified an overthrow of its leader, Saddam Hussein.[25] At that time, only 38 percent of our population believed war was justified even if Saddam did not have WMD.[26] That is, 62 percent of Americans did not believe going to war with Iraq was justified if Saddam lacked such weapons. When no WMD were found, dissonance occurred. Because dissonance is uncomfortable, some people reduced their dissonance by changing the primary reason in their minds for going

Behaviors

Attitudes

FIGURE 19.4
Attitudes and Behaviors Go Hand in Hand
Helping someone, even after knocking him over, promotes respect. Respect promotes positive behavior.

to war, from getting rid of Iraq's WMD to liberating Iraqis from Saddam Hussein's regime. The number of Americans believing war was justified without WMD shot from 38 percent to 58 percent.[27] When hopes dimmed of bringing relatively quick and easy peace to the region, support for the war dropped below 40 percent.[28] Today, polls show that fewer than 20 percent think the war with Iraq has been worth the effort.[29]

So, we can see through the foot-in-the-door phenomenon, role-playing, and cognitive dissonance that attitudes can follow behaviors. We can apply this principle to our advantage. If we have an attitude we'd like to change, such as negative feelings toward people from different social groups, then we can start by changing our behavior toward those individuals. In clinical settings, cognitive behavior therapists use this principle for the benefit of their patients—for example, by encouraging patients with depression to talk more positively and to avoid putting themselves down.[30] Therapists hope that these more positive behaviors will help change their patients' attitudes about themselves.

Social psychologists study not only the interesting ways in which we are affected by our own attitudes and actions but also the ways in which we are affected by the attitudes and actions of those around us (see **Figure 19.4**).

Social Influence

Do other people influence us? *Of course!* Consider these scenarios:

- The person next to you in class yawns. Then the person in front of you yawns. Within seconds, you are fighting the urge to follow suit. Even more interesting is the fact that the better you are at understanding someone's emotions (your empathic skills), the greater your likelihood of yawning.[31]

- A group of five students stands outside the front door of a building. For no good reason, they start to look up. As long as the five are out there, almost everybody approaching the building looks up as they enter, even though there is nothing special to see.

- In the eight days following a murderous shooting spree in a Colorado high school, 49 states report copycat threats. Pennsylvania led the way with 60 threats.[32]

- Over a brief stretch of 18 days, a school with 1500 students reports 2 suicides, 7 attempted suicides, and 23 students contemplating suicide.[33]

- Defendants standing trial for Nazi war crimes, participants in the Holocaust that brought death to more than 6 million Jews, are asked why they took part in these murders. Many, including Adolf Eichmann, the Nazi director of deportation of Jews to concentration camps, respond by saying, "I was only following orders."[34]

There is no denying the titanic power of social influence on our actions and attitudes. Advertisers use it to sell products, and politicians use it to win votes. But in *tragic and violent* instances, such as the suicide clusters, school shootings, and genocide, what is the role of social influence? In search of answers, social psychologists have studied both conformity and obedience.

MAKE IT STICK!

1. Jayden wanted to convince her father to loan her $50 for a concert ticket. First, she asked for $30. After he agreed, she asked for the loan to be $40, which he also accepted. Then she got him to agree to the $50 loan she really wanted. Which technique did Jayden use?

   a. role-playing
   b. cognitive dissonance
   c. foot-in-the-door
   d. attitude modification

2. True or False: If you discover your behavior isn't consistent with your beliefs, you might experience cognitive dissonance?

3. Which of the following is *not true* about being a hero?

   a. You don't have to fight to be a hero; you can be a peace hero.
   b. Heroic acts can be acts that are performed every day because our society needs and expects these acts.
   c. Anyone can be a hero.
   d. We can increase the number of heroic acts that take place each day if we focus on the larger-than-life heroes we see in the news from time to time.

Conformity and Obedience

 19-3 What does research say about conformity and obedience?

Suppose you have a test scheduled for Friday in your psychology class. In preparation, you study hard in the evenings leading up to the test. Then on Thursday, a classmate asks that the test be moved to Monday. You sense a wave of support for this request as other class members voice their agreement. But you don't think it is such a good idea. You have a marching band trip planned for the weekend and you'll arrive home late Sunday night, exhausted from the travel and hectic schedule. A Monday morning exam is not what you need. The teacher says the test will be moved to Monday if *every* member of the class votes in favor of the move. When the vote is called for, every hand in the class goes up except yours. Your vote will make the difference. What will you do? Will you vote your beliefs or *conform* to the class's desire to delay?

Conformity is adjusting behavior or thinking to coincide with a group idea or standard. Under what conditions is conformity likely to occur? Social psychologists have been asking—and answering—that question since the mid-twentieth century. **Solomon Asch** conducted one of the more ingenious conformity studies.[35] To get a feel for how this experiment worked, you're going to have to use your imagination.

So, you're a college student, and you've signed up to participate in a study on perceptual judgment. Arriving at the experiment's location, you are assigned seat 6 (out of 7), and you sit down around a large table with six others. You're told you will be shown sets of cards, and your task is to identify which of the three lines on card B is identical to the one line on card A (see **Figure 19.5**). The first set is displayed. Clearly, the answer is line 2. One by one, every participant in the room agrees. The experimenter records your answers one at a time and then puts up the second set of cards. You think to yourself, "This is easy." Again, you all agree on the same lines. Then comes the third trial, which appears to be just as easy as the first two. You're ready to say, "Line 2," but to your surprise, the first person gives an answer you

conformity Adjusting behavior or thinking to coincide with a group standard.

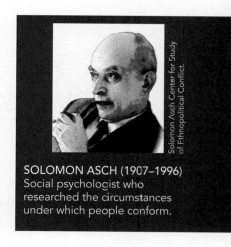

SOLOMON ASCH (1907–1996)
Social psychologist who researched the circumstances under which people conform.

Solomon Asch Center for Study of Ethnopolitical Conflict.

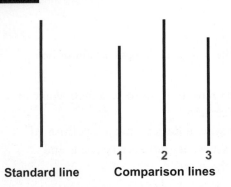

Standard line   **Comparison lines**

Susan Vandivert Olin for William Vandivert

FIGURE 19.5
Conformity
Which comparison line is closest in length to the standard line? What would you say if you were in a room with several others who all said line 1 was closest? Asch found that many people conformed, agreeing to the wrong answer. Not conforming led to considerable stress, as is evident here in the subject in the middle.

think is clearly wrong. Your amazement continues as all five people in front of you choose the wrong line! Now it's your turn, and you must give an answer. What you don't know is that everyone else in the room *is in on* the experiment. They've all been instructed to lie during the third trial. You, the person in seat 6, are the only participant. What will you say when it is your turn? Will you go along with the majority, or will you trust your judgment and remain true to yourself?

Asch found that if nobody else was in the room, then participants made mistakes on the third trial about 1 percent of the time. However, if the five other people gave a wrong answer before the participant replied, then participants gave the same wrong answer about 33 percent of the time. In essence, roughly one-third were willing to say that up was down to conform to the group.

An interesting follow-up to Asch's study assessed the role of judgment difficulty on conformity.[36] Picking the longest line out of three is pretty easy, especially when you can stare at it for several minutes. But what about picking a stranger out of a lineup when you have had only a brief look at the person you're supposed to identify? In one study, researchers showed participants two slides. The first showed the man they were to identify, and the second showed a four-man lineup. Participants viewed slide 1 for either 5 seconds (making the decision easy) or half a second (making the decision more difficult). Then they tried to select the correct person in slide 2. Also, half the group was told their judgments were unimportant (that this was simply some preliminary testing) or important (that norms for actual police procedure were being developed and the person making the most accurate identifications would receive $20). Researchers found that when judgments were easy and were deemed *un*important, fewer than 20 percent conformed to the judgments of the other participants. But more than 50 percent conformed to others' judgment when the task was labeled important and difficult. It appears that if being correct matters and we're unsure of our answer, then we are open to the opinions of others.

Other studies have shown that conformity tends to increase when

- you feel incompetent or insecure.

- you are in a group of three or more. (Groups larger than three show no additional conformity.)

- the rest of the group is unanimous.

- you are impressed by the status of the group.

- you have made no prior commitment to a response.

- you are being observed by others in the group.

- your culture strongly encourages respect for social standards (as in, if your culture encourages you to avoid standing out in a crowd, you're more likely to conform).

www.CartoonStock.com

g. di Chiarro

"But Mom. all the girls are doing it."

Our perception of whether social influence is good or bad is directly related to our beliefs. If social influence supports an ideal we oppose, then we might be inclined to complain about weak-minded conformists who can't think for themselves. But be careful of the double standard: What if social influence supports an ideal we favor? Do we suddenly think of conformists as forward thinking, responsive, and intellectual? Our view of conformity often reflects our values.

Use your imagination one more time. This time, you're going to become a participant in what may be social psychology's most famous and most controversial study.

What would you do in the following situation? You and another person show up to participate in a study. The experimenter, wearing a lab coat and carrying a clipboard, greets you and explains that this is a study of the effects of punishment on learning. You and the other participant, Mr. Wallace, draw slips of paper to see who will be the learner and who will be the teacher. Your slip says, "Teacher." As the teacher, you must punish Mr. Wallace with an electric shock every time he makes an error on the learning task.

You then help the experimenter strap Mr. Wallace into a chair in the learner's room and attach electrodes to his skin. The experimenter uses electrode paste, he explains, to avoid burns and blisters. The experimenter also says that the electric shocks to Mr. Wallace may cause extreme pain but they should not result in "permanent tissue damage."[37] You are given a sample of the shock Mr. Wallace will receive if he makes a mistake, and it hurts.

Next, you take your seat in the teacher's room. You can't see Mr. Wallace, but you can hear him and talk to him. In front of you is an eerie-looking machine that will send the shocks to Mr. Wallace following an incorrect answer. The machine has 30 switches, each with a label indicating the number of volts that will be delivered for increasing levels of shock. You are told to deliver a "slight" shock (15 volts) for the first mistake and then to increase the voltage each time Mr. Wallace makes an error. Above the 150-volt switch, it says, "Strong Shock." The message above the 375-volt switch reads, "Danger: Severe Shock." Above the last switch, 450 volts, it simply says, "XXX."

You are told to begin. Mr. Wallace makes a mistake, you flip the little black switch, and a buzzing sound fills the air. But Mr. Wallace continues to make mistakes. After you throw the tenth switch, Mr. Wallace shouts, "Get me out of here! I won't be in the experiment anymore! I refuse to go on!" You look at the experimenter, who says, "Please continue." You express concern, and the experimenter says, "The experiment requires you to continue." You protest, but the experimenter says, "It is absolutely essential that you continue."

What would you do? Would you stop? Continue? If you obey the experimenter, the learner will start yelling, obviously in agony with the increasingly painful shocks. In the experiment, the teacher continues, and at the 330-volt mark, the learner refuses to answer. He is now screaming in pain at the shocks he is receiving. Eventually, there is only silence from Mr. Wallace. The experimenter explains that silence is considered a wrong answer and the teacher should deliver the shocks all the way to the 450-volt switch.

Perhaps you've guessed by now that this experiment had nothing to do with learning. The "learner" was an actor with a script, and he never received a shock. The researcher, **Stanley Milgram,** wanted to know how far the "teachers" would go—how much shock they would deliver to another person because they had been told to do so.

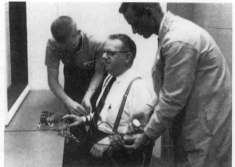

▲ **Mr. Wallace: Learner**
In Stanley Milgram's experiment on obedience, researchers attached electrodes to the "learner's" body. He was to be "shocked" every time he made a mistake.

▲ **Milgram's Teaching Machine**
Voltage appeared to range from 15 to 450 volts.

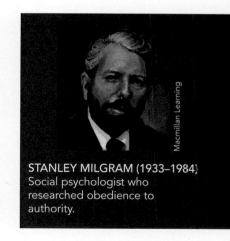

STANLEY MILGRAM (1933–1984)
Social psychologist who researched obedience to authority.

How far would you have gone as the teacher? Milgram asked dozens of psychiatrists and psychologists to predict the results of his experiment. They all agreed that there was only a remote possibility that anyone would go all the way to 450 volts. Only sadists, those fringe members of society who enjoy inflicting pain, would inflict such severe shocks on a learner.

All the experts were wrong. Milgram found that an incredible 63 percent of the participants (all men) obeyed instructions, flipping all 30 switches (see **Figure 19.6**). Follow-up studies showed that women complied at a similar rate.[38] Had the participants figured out that the learner was not really receiving shock? *No.* Videotapes showed the nervous teachers, biting their lips, trembling, and drenched in sweat.

FIGURE 19.6
Shocking Results
About two-thirds of Milgram's participants obeyed the experimenter to the fullest extent. (Data from Milgram, 1974.)

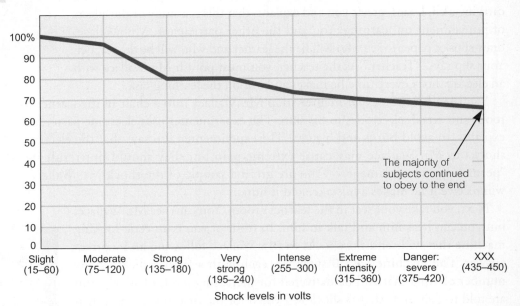

Percentage of subjects who obeyed experimenter

The majority of subjects continued to obey to the end

Shock levels in volts

obedience The tendency to comply with orders, implied or real, from someone perceived as an authority.

Milgram ran several versions of this experiment and found that the likelihood of **obedience** increased when the victim could not be seen, the authority figure giving the orders was close at hand, and the authority figure was part of a prestigious organization or institution. Obedience decreased if participants could observe a defiant role model.

Milgram's obedience experiment provoked a debate over research ethics. The American Psychological Association's *Ethical Principles of Psychologists and Code of Conduct,* developed after Milgram conducted his research, prohibits studies that stress participants as Milgram's did. Yes, the researchers debriefed the "teachers" after the experiment was over, and they all were able to see that Mr. Wallace had not been hurt. But 63 percent of those teachers had walked out of the laboratory thinking they had just shocked someone into silence. Milgram was concerned about the aftereffects on participants.[39] He identified 40 teachers who had seemed most agonized and arranged for them to be interviewed by a psychiatrist. None of them appeared to be suffering emotionally.

Experiments similar to Milgram's studies would not be allowed today, although a re-creation using virtual reality was recently conducted. Participants had to shock a virtual (and clearly nonhuman) woman on a TV screen. These participants responded similarly to those in the original study, experiencing the same racing heart and perspiration.[40]

What can we learn from Milgram's work? The lesson is not simply whether we should shock people to help them learn. Milgram, like most researchers, was not trying to re-create real-life behaviors in his laboratory. Rather, he was interested in the underlying thought processes that mold behaviors.

The lesson Milgram wanted us to carry away was that ordinary people can be corrupted by an evil situation. Despite the predictions of behavior experts, normal, everyday, well-adjusted men and women were willing to follow orders and severely punish another human being for making a mistake. Soldiers also may follow orders and shoot unarmed civilians. Ordinary students who plan and carry out cruel initiation practices into clubs or other groups, using "tradition" as a lame justification, embark on a similar path. Milgram said, in summarizing his findings, "The fundamental lesson of our study is that ordinary people, simply doing their jobs, and without any particular hostility on their part, can become agents in a terrible destructive process."[41] This is a vivid lesson in the power of the situation. Situational factors, such as the presence of an authority figure, have far more influence on our behavior than most of us realize.

MAKE IT STICK!

1. Which statement best summarizes Asch's conformity studies?

   a. When role-playing, authority figures can change our attitudes toward others.
   b. Over 30 percent of people will conform to an obviously wrong answer given by others in a group.
   c. Smart people do not conform to the beliefs of others, but less intelligent people do.
   d. About 63 percent of people will conform to the orders of an authority figure.

2. What question did Milgram attempt to answer in his obedience experiments?

   a. Are people more likely to conform to an obviously wrong answer if they are in a group?
   b. Will people obey an authority figure, even if it means hurting a stranger?
   c. Do people try harder, or less hard, on a difficult task if they are ordered to obey?
   d. Have studies proven that obedience is more or less powerful than conformity?

3. True or False: Psychologists correctly predicted the outcome of Milgram's obedience experiments.

4. Adjusting behavior or thinking to coincide with a group idea is called _____.

Group Influence

 19-4 How does being around others affect our behavior, and how does group membership affect our thinking and decision making?

Have you ever had a friend who was friendly enough when no one else was around but ignored you when other people were present? Does your behavior change when you're in a group of friends? When you're playing sports? When you're with your family? When you're around teachers or the principal? Social psychologists are interested in how we behave in small and large groups.

Our Behavior in the Presence of Others   A track coach once told me that the fastest times in both the short- and long-distance races were always turned in when lots of people are watching (rarely during practice). Research supports the track coach's statement. Our behavior changes noticeably (although not always for the better) in the presence of others.

social facilitation Improved performance on tasks in the presence of others.

Running Faster
Social facilitation theory predicts faster races with an audience present. ▼

David J. Phillip/AP Images

LIFE MATTERS
LeBron James makes roughly 64% of his attempted clutch shots, and while these may look to be a stroke of good luck, his success can be attributed to social facilitation. LeBron spends hours practicing these trick shots, and therefore, his performance is enhanced during buzzer-beating moments.

social loafing The tendency for people in a group to exert less effort when pooling their efforts toward attaining a common goal than when individually accountable.

SOCIAL FACILITATION AND SOCIAL INTERFERENCE The improved performance on tasks in the presence of others is called **social facilitation.** Some studies supporting social facilitation were done more than a century ago. One researcher discovered that cyclists scored faster times when racing one another than when simply racing the clock.[42] The same researcher asked a different set of participants to reel in a fishing line as fast as possible. These "fastest" times were bettered when the same people reeled in the same fishing line in the presence of another person reeling in line.

Both of these tasks are relatively easy. Later research has demonstrated that social facilitation is at its best with simple or well-learned tasks. Being watched increases our arousal. Arousal strengthens our ability to perform well-learned tasks, but it diminishes our performance on tasks we have not yet mastered. This was illustrated in a study of pool players.[43] Master pool players made 71 percent of their shots when alone but upped that score to 80 percent when four people observed them play. Not-so-good pool players made 36 percent of their shots with nobody watching but only 25 percent in the presence of others. Research supports the notion that being observed by others is a coin with two sides.[44,45] The other side of the coin is called *social interference*. Tasks we find difficult may seem impossible with an audience watching. But give us an audience for the things we do well—especially a supportive audience—and we're likely to do even better. Does this mean there's a home-field advantage in sports? To a degree, *Yes* (see **Table 19.1**). Social facilitation helps explain this advantage.

TABLE 19.1	Home-Field Advantage in Major Team Sports	
Sport	**Games Studied**	**Home Team Winning Percentage**
Baseball	23,034	53.5%
Football	2,592	57.3
Ice hockey	4,322	61.1
Basketball	13,596	64.4
Soccer	37,202	69.0

Source: From Courneya and Carron (1992).

SOCIAL LOAFING Have you ever been asked by a teacher to work on a group project? Suppose you're put in a group of five and your project will be given one grade. All group members will receive the same grade, regardless of how much work they put in. What usually happens in this situation? If your experience is anything like mine, a couple of people usually end up doing most of the work. Social psychologists call this **social loafing,** the tendency for individuals in a group to exert themselves less when pooling their efforts toward attaining a common goal than when individually accountable. In essence, individuals in a group have a tendency to think their lack of effort will not be noticed. Several studies have illustrated this tendency. In one, researchers blindfolded students, handed them a rope, and asked them to pull as hard as they possibly could.[46] When the blindfolded students thought three others were behind them pulling, their "best" pulling efforts dropped by almost 20 percent, compared with earlier measures of their individual ability.

Why does social loafing occur? Perhaps it's because people working in a group feel less accountable for the result. With less accountability comes less worry about what others think. Or perhaps social loafers think their efforts are simply not necessary.[47,48] Whether it's in the classroom or in business, when group members know they will receive an equal share of group benefits, slackers, in the form of social loafers, are likely to emerge.

DEINDIVIDUATION Social facilitation increases physiological arousal. Social loafing decreases the sense of responsibility. What happens when people are in a group and they become aroused *and* lose their sense of responsibility? Social psychologists might predict that the combination would increase the chances of **deindividuation**—the loss of self-awareness and self-restraint occurring in group situations that foster arousal and anonymity. Negative examples of deindividuation are easy to find, and they make the news when taken to an extreme. A few years back at the end of a National Football League season, Cleveland fans covered one end of the field with beer bottles when they thought a referee's call cost them the game. Sports fans often yell things during a game that they would never yell if they were alone in the stands and easily identified. Store lootings during riots are another example of deindividuation. The less restrained and self-conscious a person feels, the more likely deindividuation is to occur. It's easy to see how deindividuation can lead people to make very bad decisions. For instance, take the white supremacists who marched through the University of Virginia campus at night carrying torches and shouting "blood and soil," a phrase tied to Nazi ideology. The supremacists thought they would be able to protest without being recognized. However, social media was used to identify and report individuals to their employers, and many were either fired or suspended from work for their participation.[49] These supremacists lost their sense of self-awareness and chanted things they would never chant at work or in their classroom, no matter their beliefs. We are more responsive to group influence when we lose self-awareness.

Group Interaction Effects

The presence of others can affect us in good and bad ways. The same is true of group interactions. Let's take a closer look at group polarization and groupthink.

GROUP POLARIZATION When politically oriented clubs, such as the Young Democrats or Teenage Republicans (as they are called in my school), gather to discuss local and national political issues, what's most likely to happen to their attitudes? Do the liberals become more or less

▲ **Social Loafing?**
In small groups, some people do less work than others. Social loafing may happen because people feel less responsible or simply because they feel their help is not really needed.

Hero Images/Getty Images

deindividuation The loss of self-awareness and self-restraint occurring in group situations that foster arousal and anonymity.

Samuel Corum/Anadolu Agency/Getty Images

▲ **Deindividuation at Work?**
These white supremacist marchers thought they would be anonymous, but several were identified using social media.

group polarization
Enhancement of a group's already-existing attitudes through discussion within the group.

liberal as they talk with one another? Are the conservatives more or less likely to take more conservative stances on issues by the close of their meeting? **Group polarization,** the enhancement of a group's already-existing attitudes through discussion within the group, would predict that liberals will become more liberal and conservatives will become more conservative. Evidently, our attitudes tend to migrate to an extreme, like the poles of Earth, when we're around like-minded people. David Myers and George Bishop found just this effect.[50] Low-prejudice groups who discussed racial issues expressed even less prejudice after their discussion than they had before (see **Figure 19.7**). Similarly—and unfortunately—high-prejudice groups expressed higher levels of prejudice following their discussion of racial issues. Discussion among the like-minded tends to strengthen preexisting attitudes.

Other researchers studied terrorism as an example of group polarization.[51] Terrorism does not just suddenly erupt. The terrorist mentality builds as people with the same grievances gather and become more extreme in their views. In the absence of any moderating influences, terrorism reaches the point of kidnappings, murder, and suicide bombings. Fanatics grow more fanatical as group polarization takes hold.

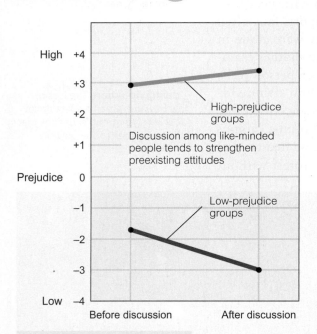

FIGURE 19.7
Group Polarization
When like-minded people discuss issues involving prejudice, their original views are likely to intensify. (Data from Myers & Bishop, 1970.)

groupthink The mode of thinking that occurs when the desire for harmony in a decision-making group overrides a realistic appraisal of the alternatives.

Groupthink Group polarization drives us to extremes, but groupthink tends to paralyze us. I watched this happen a couple of years ago, when our drill team was getting ready to perform at halftime at a state boys' basketball game. They decided to wear an article of clothing, a small crop top, that the administration had banned. The music came up, they danced their five-minute show in the crop tops, and then they left the court. When administrators later questioned the team members in an attempt to find out who was responsible for the decision to wear the banned clothing, they were amazed by the responses. Not one member of the dance group had spoken up against wearing the crop top, even though they all knew it was banned. Two had even written an advance apology to the principal, sliding it under his door after school an hour *before* the game. A senior on the squad later explained, "We didn't think anything would happen to us since it was our last performance. We had paid for the outfits and deserved to be able to wear them. And we all just wanted to get along for our last performance." What this senior did was explain that groupthink had taken place. **Groupthink** occurs when the desire for harmony in a decision-making group overrides a realistic appraisal of alternatives. We go along with a decision to get along with other people. In the case of the drill team, conformity, self-justification, overconfidence, and group polarization all fed into their groupthink decision to break the rules. (For more on groupthink, take a look at Psychology in the Real World: Groupthink.)

Before taking office, Barack Obama expressed a clear awareness of groupthink. He said, "One of the dangers in a White House, based on my reading of history, is that you get wrapped up in groupthink, and everybody agrees with everything, and there's no discussion and there are no dissenting views."[52] Did his own administration avoid groupthink? Historians looking back on his years in office will let us know.

PSYCHOLOGY IN THE REAL WORLD

Groupthink

Groupthink seems to have played a role in several national fiascos and tragedies. Groupthink may have contributed to the 1986 explosion of the U.S. space shuttle *Challenger*, which killed seven crew members, including social studies teacher Christa McAuliffe.[53] The National Aeronautics and Space Administration (NASA) management team had tremendous confidence in their ability to launch *Challenger* into space, but they had been frustrated by numerous delays of this high-profile launch. Just before the launch was to take place, engineers voiced their opposition, citing concerns that rocket seals would not hold in the below-freezing weather. The management team demanded proof, and they did not pass on the engineers' concerns to the NASA executive in charge of the launch. The executive, thinking everybody had approved the mission, gave the order to launch, and *Challenger* flew into the history books as a space disaster. The managers, who agreed to overlook the engineers' weather-related concerns, had given in to the lure of groupthink.

As you can see, resisting groupthink is sometimes vitally important. But *how* do you resist it? Irving Janis has three suggestions for group leaders:

1. Assign people to identify problems.
2. Be open to, and welcome, various opinions.
3. Invite experts to critique plans in various stages of development.[54]

When it comes to making important decisions, there is strength in numbers—but only if you carefully consider your reasons for casting your vote with the majority.

THINK ABOUT . . . Psychology in the Real World

1. How can you avoid groupthink when trying to guide a group of your friends to a decision?
2. Apply groupthink to a time you and a group of others made a bad decision.
3. Think of and explain a time when students or adults at your school made a decision that appeared to be a result of groupthink. What was the outcome of that decision?

MAKE IT STICK!

1. What does this textbook call the enhancement of a group's already-existing attitudes through discussion within the group?

    a. group polarization
    b. social loafing
    c. groupthink
    d. deindividuation

2. You're assigned to a group project with three friends. You and one of the others end up doing most of the work. What phenomenon explains the lack of work by the other two members in the group?

3. Statements such as "Let's all get along" and "Don't rock the boat" could lead a group of people to dismiss the critical thinking necessary to make a decision. This is called _____.

4. True or False: The loss of self-awareness and the loss of self-restraint are both characteristic of social loafing.

Our Power as Individuals

 19-5 How does personal control influence our behavior?

We have talked at length about social thinking and social influence, or the power of the group. What about personal control, or the power of the individual? We can see this power in self-fulfilling prophecies and minority influence.

Self-Fulfilling Prophecies

My grandfather used to say, "Whether you think you can or you can't, you're right." He didn't originate that quotation, but he was offering a perfect description of a **self-fulfilling prophecy:** We believe something to be true about others (or ourselves), and we act in ways that cause this belief to come true. In one study, researchers told men that a certain woman found them either attractive or unattractive. The researchers then recorded and analyzed conversations between the men and the woman, revealing a self-fulfilling prophecy. If the man thought the woman saw him as attractive, he was more charming and she was more likely to act as if she did think he was attractive.[55]

If self-fulfilling prophecies come true, could we foster relationships by idealizing our partners? *Apparently so.* Over time, people seem to accept their partner's idealized perceptions as reality.[56,57] So, if your partner thinks of you as thoughtful and smart, you may internalize this perception and behave more thoughtfully and competently. Perhaps we can adapt my grandfather's philosophy: If you think your partner is bright or dim, clever or slow, honest or untruthful, sensitive or insensitive, then you may turn out to be right.

Minority Influence

Throughout the history of our world, individuals have had tremendous influences on groups. Rosa Parks refused to give up her seat to a white man and move to the back of a bus, and she fueled a civil rights movement. Mahatma Gandhi refused to eat as a political protest, and India won independence from Britain. Both overcame the majority's resistance to change.

Social history is often made by individuals who risk harm or ridicule when standing up against and speaking out about something wrong. A few years back, when prisoners in Iraq were being mistreated, Navy dog handler William Kimbro

One Person Can Make a Difference
Rosa Parks refused to sit in the back of the bus, the section reserved for African-Americans. Her refusal triggered a boycott of buses, and eventually those rules changed. Parks's actions helped set the civil rights movement in motion.

Bettmann/Getty Images

refused to allow his attack dogs to be used in efforts to frighten and intimidate. Another soldier, Lieutenant David Sutton, knew prisoners were being abused and reported mistreatment to his commanding officer. The actions of two or three soldiers put an end to the abuse at this Iraqi prison.[58]

Minorities can sway majorities, but only if they stand firm. Social psychologists have found that minorities who waffle in their convictions have trouble persuading others; those who are unwavering are far more successful in their persuasive efforts.[59] The people steadfastly holding minority opinions may not win any popularity contests, but they may become influential. If you have the courage to voice your belief in a minority opinion, your influence on others may not be obvious at first. But by causing members of the majority to rethink their opinions, you may be planting the seeds of change.

MAKE IT STICK!

1. Rosa Parks's refusal to give up her seat sparked a boycott that ended discriminatory seating rules on buses and fueled the civil rights movement. Parks's courageous act illustrates how the actions of a _____ influence can affect _____ opinion.

2. True or False: One or two people can say or do something that causes a big organization, like the U.S. Army, to change a policy.

Module 19 Summary and Assessment
Social Thinking and Social Influence

 19-1 How does attribution theory predict the way we explain the behavior of others?

- According to attribution theory, we tend to explain the behavior of others as an aspect of either an internal disposition (an inner trait) or the situation.

- We often make the fundamental attribution error, the tendency to attribute the behaviors of others to inner dispositions rather than to situations.

 19-2 How can attitudes affect actions? And how can actions affect attitudes?

- Attitudes can predict behavior under certain conditions: if the outside influences on what we do are minimal, if we are keenly aware of our attitudes, or if the attitudes are relevant to the behavior.

- Our behavior can also affect our attitudes, as shown by the foot-in-the-door phenomenon, role-playing, and the concept of cognitive dissonance.

 19-3 What does research say about conformity and obedience?

- Solomon Asch's conformity studies indicated that about one-third of participants were willing to give incorrect answers to conform to the group.

- Stanley Milgram's obedience studies indicated that 63 percent of participants would obey all instructions, including those that seemed to injure other participants.

 19-4 How does being around others affect our behavior, and how does group membership affect our thinking and decision making?

- Arousal provided by being in the presence of others strengthens our ability to perform well-learned tasks, but it diminishes our performance on tasks we have not yet mastered.

- In the presence of others, social facilitation, social loafing, and deindividuation can occur.

- Group membership can lead to both group polarization and groupthink.

 19-5 How does personal control influence our behavior?

- A self-fulfilling prophecy occurs when we believe something to be true about others (or ourselves) and we act in ways that cause this belief to come true.

- Minorities can sway majorities by planting the seeds of change and causing the members of the majority to rethink opinions.

Summative Assessment

1. An actor being typecast for the same type of role over and over again is an example of which of the following?

   a. groupthink
   b. situational explanation
   c. fundamental attribution error
   d. self-serving bias

2. Alan is a new friend you met in biology class. One day he comes into class and passes you without responding to your "hello" and sits at his desk with his head down. If you interpret his behavior using *situational attribution*, you tell yourself,

   a. "He's ignoring me. I knew he was kind of stuck on himself."
   b. "He's sometimes a little weird. I'm going to forget him."
   c. "I thought he liked me. I guess we're not friends after all."
   d. "He must be having a bad day. I should ask him if he's okay."

3. What concept is occurring when we try to reduce the discomfort we feel when our thoughts and actions are inconsistent?

   a. cognitive dissonance
   b. fundamental attribution error
   c. social influences
   d. self-serving bias

4. What is happening when people who have at first agreed to a small request later agree to a larger request?

   a. role playing
   b. cognitive dissonance
   c. foot-in-the-door phenomenon
   d. the effects of attitudes on actions

5. As you are headed to the library, two of your best friends run into you ask you to join them for a movie. You tell them you have to study for a test tomorrow, but they are very persuasive and tease you about being a nerd. You agree to go to the movie even though you know you should be studying. What is this behavior an example of?

   a. fundamental attribution error
   b. conformity
   c. social facilitation
   d. obedience

6. Stanley Milgram conducted studies finding that ordinary people could be corrupted by an evil situation. These studies researched what phenomenon?

   a. obedience to authority
   b. conformity
   c. social facilitation
   d. group polarization

7. Discussion among like-minded people tends to strengthen preexisting attitudes. This is an example of which of the following?

   a. social loafing
   b. group polarization
   c. groupthink
   d. minority influence

8. Which of the following is an example of *groupthink*?

   a. welcoming various opinions
   b. inviting experts to critique plans
   c. keeping harmony among the team
   d. considering pros and cons of an issue

9. Tasks that are hard for us seem harder when we have others watching. Conversely, we are likely to do better with tasks that are easy for us when we have a supportive audience. This is an example of which of the following?

   a. group polarization
   b. social loafing
   c. social facilitation
   d. groupthink

10. Which of the following is an example of *conformity*?

   a. If being correct matters and we're feeling unsure, we are influenced by the opinion of others.
   b. We are likely to do what an authority figure tells us to do and are unlikely to be defiant.
   c. If we are asked to perform a task, we are likely to do better in the presence of others.
   d. When we are around like-minded people, our attitudes will migrate to the extreme.

KEY TERMS AND KEY PEOPLE

social psychology, p. 284

attribution theory, p. 285

fundamental attribution error, p. 285

self-serving bias, p. 286

attitude, p. 288

foot-in-the-door phenomenon, p. 289

role, p. 289

cognitive dissonance theory, p. 290

conformity, p. 293

obedience, p. 296

social facilitation, p. 298

social loafing, p. 298

deindividuation, p. 299

group polarization, p. 300

groupthink, p. 300

self-fulfilling prophecy, p. 302

Philip Zimbardo (1933–), p. 290

Solomon Asch (1907–1996), p. 293

Stanley Milgram (1933–1984), p. 295

Social Relations

Social networking makes it easy to connect with others, but good relationships with others depend on much more than the Internet.

Learning Goals

20-1 Identify factors that influence attractiveness.

20-2 Describe the differences between passionate and companionate love.

20-3 Identify factors that influence altruistic behavior.

20-4 Describe how stereotypes are formed and how can they lead to prejudice and discrimination.

20-5 Explain the biological and learning factors that lead to aggressive behavior.

20-6 Describe how shared goals help to resolve conflict between groups.

Liking, loving, helping, hating, fighting, and befriending: We exhibit a wide range of behaviors in the way we relate to one another, all of which we consider in this module. As with so many areas of psychology, a complex combination of biological and environmental factors affects our social relations.

Attraction

 20-1 What factors influence attractiveness?

Who are your friends, and how did they become your friends? Does a person have to look a certain way, dress in a certain style, or listen to the same kind of music to be your friend? *Social psychologists* consider these and other questions in their scientific study of how we think about, influence, and relate to one another. Researchers have found three key ingredients to attraction: proximity, physical attractiveness, and similarity.

Proximity

If you attend Springboro High School in Ohio, you don't stand much of a chance of becoming friends with the Broken Bow High School students in Nebraska. A friendship can't develop if it doesn't begin. Several studies have shown that the people we like, date, and even marry are typically the people living in our neighborhood, sitting next to us in class, or working in the same building. What's near becomes dear partly because of the **mere exposure effect,** in which repeated exposure to novel stimuli increases our liking of them. You can easily see how this works if you think of an album you found on Spotify because it had a hit song on track 1. Did you end up also liking the songs on tracks 2 and 3 after listening

mere exposure effect
The phenomenon that repeated exposure to novel stimuli increases one's liking of them.

Amir Mukhtar/Getty Images

Love at First Listen? ▲
Have you ever started to like a song only after listening to it several times? The mere exposure effect may explain why you like something you initially didn't care for.

LIFE MATTERS

For fans of *Stranger Things*, it's impossible not to adore Mike's unwavering affection for Eleven. However, is there a chance that his attraction began because of their close proximity, living in the same house together?

to the album several times, even though you didn't particularly like them at first? Did those songs even become favorites after you listened to them repeatedly? If so, you experienced the mere exposure effect.

The mere exposure effect works for human faces as well and promotes fondness for the people with whom we spend time.[1,2] Two researchers demonstrated the mere exposure effect by enrolling four women, all of whom were judged equally attractive, in a 200-student college class.[3–5] The first never attended class, the second went 5 times, the third 10 times, and the fourth attended 15 classes. After the course ended, students judged the woman who had attended most often as the most attractive and the woman who never attended as the least attractive.

Our ancestors benefited from the mere exposure effect. Familiar faces were less likely to be dangerous or threatening than unfamiliar faces. Some researchers believe we are born with a tendency to bond with those who are familiar to us and to be leery of those we don't know.[6]

The Internet is proving proximity, or the physical distance between potential romantic partners, need not be quite so limiting. Online dating has become a booming business. In 2013, about 5 percent of adults in the United States reported using online dating services. Five years later, the use of dating apps has exploded, and the percentage of adults using online services has tripled. A whopping 27 percent of U.S. citizens in the 18 to 24 age range have used online dating to meet someone. And about 1 in 20 say they met their significant other online.[7]

It remains to be seen whether proximity via keyboard really can measure up to the more traditional ways of meeting people. Interestingly, some researchers have found that romances and friendships formed online have a greater chance of lasting over two years than do relationships formed face to face.[8] Still, it's common knowledge that many in the online dating game often misrepresent themselves by lying about their age, occupation, and physical appearance.[9] Exercising caution when corresponding or chatting with someone you've never met is a must. My daughter, who uses online dating regularly, always meets in a public place and tells some key friends where she is going and who she is meeting. As her dad, I tell her you can't be too careful when meeting strangers. I think she's listening.

Physical Attractiveness

What most affects our first impression of others? Is it their wit? Charm? Politeness? Intelligence? Researchers have found that first impressions are based on something far shallower than brains or personality. Hundreds of studies indicate that *appearance* is the first filter we use to sort out the people we want to get to know from those we don't. We need look no further than the research on speed dating, which shows that first impressions and the desire to get to know someone better are strongly influenced by attractiveness.[10]

In another study, researchers matched students with blind dates. Before the date, all participants took a number of personality and intelligence tests, and the researchers rated them on attractiveness. After two hours of talking and dancing, all participants rated their dates. The researchers found that the only measure reliably predicting whether the two daters liked each other was attractiveness.[11] Other researchers found that women are more likely to say that the way a person looks does not affect them, but a woman's behavior is nevertheless affected by a man's looks.[12,13]

© Randy Glasbergen

"I prefer online dating. Deleting someone with one click is less exhausting than a long and painful breakup!"

As a country, we go to great economic lengths to look good. Spending on beauty supplies exceeds the combined amount of money spent on education and social services.[14] Why? We give attractive people the benefit of the doubt. We judge them as happier, healthier, and more successful than those who are less attractive, even when we know virtually nothing about these people.[15,16] Your feelings about your own attractiveness predict how much you'll date and how popular you'll feel.[17] The attractive people in the most successful movies are often portrayed as morally superior to the unattractive actors.[18] For instance, in the movie *Wonder Woman* (2017 version), Gal Gadot, Chris Pine, and Robin Wright are all good-looking heroes. The main villain in the movie, German General Ludendorff, always looks menacing and looks downright ugly by the end of the show. All this evidence tips the scale in favor of attractiveness, but there is more to the attractiveness story.

Fortunately, few of us think of ourselves as unattractive. And despite what observers think, attractiveness does not seem to predict happiness or feelings of self-esteem for the person behind that appealing face.[19,20] Very attractive people are often suspicious of praise for their work ("Are you saying that only because I'm good-looking?"), whereas less attractive individuals are more likely to see praise as sincere.[21]

We should also remember that standards for attractiveness for women and men come and go and vary from culture to culture. In the 1920s, ultrathin was in for white U.S. women. By the 1950s, attractiveness in women reflected the full-figured voluptuousness of Marilyn Monroe. In the late 1960s, the flat-chested

What's Attractive? Society's standards for female attractiveness change over time. Left to right: In the 1920s, thin was in; the 1950s favored a fuller figure. Today's look combines the skinny waistline of the 1920s with the buxomness of the 1950s, which can be difficult to attain.

H. ARMSTRONG ROBERTS/ClassicStock/Alamy Stock Photo

Bettmann/Getty Images

Sarah Edwards/WENN Ltd/Alamy Stock Photo

model Twiggy was in and busts were out. Today, attractive women are depicted as both lean and busty. Cultural standards have led to push-up bras and even breast-enlargement surgery in North America, but women in other cultures strap on leather clothing to give the appearance of a flat chest. I never had a student with a pierced nose the first five years that I taught, but women in India and Pakistan have been piercing their noses for centuries. Likewise, the most handsome men in the 1950s where not known for having six-pack abs, but today's males seeking to be attractive often feel the pressure to look thin and muscular. While the "man bun" hairstyle is a relatively recent phenomenon in the United States, paintings of Japanese warriors with topknots date from the sixteenth century. Standards for attractiveness vary from culture to culture and definitely change over time.

Similarity

OK, so you live close to someone, and each of you thinks the other is attractive. What predicts whether you will become friends? Do opposites really attract? In the movies, we're intrigued by stories in which people who are different from each other end up together. But in real life, the princess does not fall for some lowly smuggler. We are reluctant to include people *dissimilar* from us in our circle of friends.[22] Your friends are likely to share your interests, attitudes, age, intelligence level, and economic status, as well as your beliefs on religion, smoking, and race relations. Birds of a feather do flock together. And the more alike you and your friends are, the longer you are likely to stay together.[23]

Similarity, physical attractiveness, and proximity all contribute to attraction, but there are other components to this feeling. One of them is our tendency to like people who like us. We respond positively and warmly to those who like us, which typically increases their affection and friendliness for us. Expressing friendship toward another increases our attractiveness. If you want a friend, be a friend.

MAKE IT STICK!

1. What best summarizes the social effect of physical attractiveness?

   a. A person's physical attractiveness is not correlated with anything predictable.

   b. Physically attractive people are judged as happier and healthier.

   c. We judge physically attractive people more harshly than less physically attractive people.

   d. The social effect of physical attractiveness increases the mere exposure effect.

2. True or False: Opposites attract because individuals are less likely to be attracted to people similar to them or who live in close proximity.

3. True or False: Research shows that expressing friendship toward another person makes us seem more attractive to that person.

4. What have hundreds of studies identified as the typical "first filter" we use to determine who we want to get to know better?

BOL's EYE by Shaun Boland

Byron, the brutally honest bachelor

Oh, Byron... I love you more than the morning sunrise.

I love you almost as much as my X-Box.

www.bolseye.com

From "In the Eye of the Beholder: A Collection of Bol's Eye Cartoons by Shaun Boland - www.bolseye.com"

passionate love An aroused state of intense positive absorption in another, usually present at the beginning of a love relationship.

gradyreese/E+/Getty Images

Passionate Love ▲
After the highly charged passion fades and the feet get back on the ground, will there still be a loving relationship? Not likely, unless a deeper attachment has formed.

Romantic Love

🐾🐾 **20-2** What are the differences between passionate and companionate love?

The poet Walt Whitman once wrote, "I never could explain *why* I love anybody, or anything." It may be difficult to explain why we love, but we can identify at least two kinds of love: passionate and companionate.[24]

Passionate Love

At the beginning of a love relationship, we are likely to feel **passionate love,** an aroused state of intense positive absorption in another. Emotions hit us in two ways: physical arousal and perceptions (that is, our explanations to ourselves) of that arousal. But what if arousal from some other source coincides with meeting a new person? How do we interpret that arousal? Psychologists decided to find out, and they discovered that men who are revved up by running in place, being frightened, or listening to something funny tend to rate a new attractive acquaintance or a girlfriend as more attractive. Those who are aroused apparently attribute some of that arousal to the presence of someone they see as attractive.[25–27]

I've noticed that every year at least a few students who act together in the school plays end up going out. I know that proximity and similarity play a role in these relationships, but I've wondered if the arousal brought on by being in front of a large audience is sometimes transferred to another desirable person onstage.

In nearly all passionate romances, the fire goes out and heads come out of the clouds. For a select few, a more enduring companionate love may develop.

Companionate Love

In countries such as India, Niger, Chad, Japan, and Iraq, many young people learn that passionate love, while thrilling and exciting, is not a good basis for marriage. They expect their families to select a partner for them—a person with similar interests and background. Interestingly, in cultures where love is not rated as important or essential for marriage, the divorce rate is lower than in the United States.[28] Perhaps couples in these cultures strive for a more lasting **companionate love**—a deep, affectionate attachment for those with whom our lives are intertwined. This mature, steady love fosters friendship and commitment and is based more on affection than obsession. Couples sharing companionate love stand a better chance of an enduring relationship. In contrast, couples who fail to recognize the fleeting nature of passionate love may find their relationship in trouble when passions cool down.[29]

So, how do we develop and maintain a companionate relationship? Equity and self-disclosure are two important factors. **Equity** is a condition in which people contribute to and receive from a relationship at a similar rate. In these 50–50 relationships, couples share decision making and possessions, and they freely give and receive emotional support. In relationships where equity exists, the likelihood of a continuing companionate love is good.[30,31]

Self-disclosure is the revealing of intimate aspects of oneself to others. Intimate aspects of our lives include our likes, dislikes, fears, accomplishments, shameful moments, and goals. Self-disclosing promotes and deepens friendship. This was demonstrated in an experiment in which one group of pairs asked each other self-disclosing questions ("When did you last cry in front of another?") or small-talk questions ("What was your high school like?"). After 45 minutes, the self-disclosing pairs reported feeling closer to their partners than the small-talking pairs did.[32] Closeness is a key ingredient in companionate love, and it is more likely to be a reality in equitable relationships in which people feel they can share intimate and important details.

Processing your relationship in writing is another way to deepen a relationship. To demonstrate this, 86 dating couples agreed to have one partner spend 20 minutes for three consecutive days writing either about the day's events *or* about their deepest feelings and thoughts about their partner. Three months later, dating couples who had one partner write about thoughts and feelings were 50 percent more likely to be together than those who didn't.[33]

> **companionate love** A deep affectionate attachment we feel for those with whom our lives are intertwined.
>
> **equity** The condition in which people contribute to and receive from a relationship at a similar rate.
>
> **self-disclosure** Revealing intimate aspects of oneself to others.

Subbotina Anna/Shutterstock

▲ Companionate Love
Loving relationships built on more than passion are more likely to endure.

MAKE IT STICK!

1. Which of the following types of love is more likely to be enduring?

   a. common-law love
   b. romantic love
   c. companionate love
   d. equitable love

2. Which of the following factors in a relationship are likely to help establish and maintain a companionate love relationship?

   a. equity and self-disclosure
   b. proximity and similarity
   c. superordinate goals and passionate love
   d. the mere exposure effect and ingroup bias

3. True or False: Self-disclosure often promotes and deepens friendships?

LIFE MATTERS

Being vulnerable with another person can be terrifying, but the only way to truly develop a meaningful relationship is to allow someone in.

 20-3 What factors influence altruistic behavior?

Altruism

Acts of courage are not reported in the media at the same rate as acts of lawlessness, but the stories we do hear are heartwarming and impressive:

- Don Matthews stayed with a stranger to keep her alive during a mass shooting at a country music festival in Las Vegas that left 59 people dead and over 500 injured.[34]

- First grade teacher Vicky Soto hid her students in a closet and confronted a gunman when he entered her classroom. The gunman did not find the children, but he shot at and killed Ms. Soto.[35]

- New York firefighters charged to their deaths up the steps of the burning and doomed World Trade Center in search of the injured on September 11, 2001.

- James Harrison, a college student, directed and helped pull others out of a burning plane after it had skidded down a runway and burst into flames. He died making one last trip into the cabin looking for survivors.

Altruistic Behavior ▲
Victoria Soto, a first grade teacher, was shot to death when protecting her students at Sandy Hook Elementary. Her unselfish regard for the well being of those students was a perfect example of altruism.

altruism Unselfish regard for the welfare of others.

All these people showed uncommon courage, but they also exhibited **altruism,** unselfish regard for the welfare of others. Regard for the welfare of others and a concept known as the *bystander effect* became major social psychology concerns after a particularly hideous rape and murder took place in the early morning hours of March 13, 1964.

Kitty Genovese, a young woman living in Queens, New York, worked a night shift that kept her up well into the early morning hours most days. Just before 3:00 A.M. on the night of her death, a stalker surprised Genovese on her way home from work. Over the course of the next hour, Genovese valiantly tried to fight off her attacker. An initial *New York Times* report stated that at least 38 people in nearby apartments heard her scream, "Oh my God, he stabbed me!" and "Please help me!" (The number of bystanders, while later contested, was still substantial.) Lights came on, people looked out their windows, but none came to her rescue

or called the police while she was being assaulted. One person looking out a window yelled at and temporarily drove off the attacker, but the attacker returned after seeing the neighbor close his window and turn off his light.[36] Genovese was raped and died of multiple stab wounds just outside her own apartment. A neighbor finally called police at 3:50 A.M., and a friend was holding her as she died.[37]

Kitty Genovese and the Neighborhood in Which She Was Attacked ▲
Although many people heard her screams for help, nobody came to her rescue or called for help.

The failure of those who admitted to hearing and seeing Genovese's attack and murder stirred up an international outrage. How could her own neighbors hear her calls for help and not respond? Had they become desensitized to violence? Did they simply not care? How could all these bystanders be so apathetic to someone so desperately in need of help? Social psychologists sprang into action, searching for answers to these questions.

Two researchers, **John Darley** and **Bibb Latané,** approached the issues surrounding Genovese's death from a unique angle.[38] They suspected the lack of intervention was not due to the fact that the bystanders had cold, uncaring personalities. Instead, they thought the answers would be found in the influence of the *situation.* That is, are there situations in which people are more or less likely to help others?

Darley and Latané decided to test this idea by setting up a number of situations in which people appeared to need help. In one study, for example, a student acted as if he were having an epileptic seizure. In another study, a person lay down on a public sidewalk with his eyes closed. In each study, the underlying questions were the same: Would others come to the aid of the person who appeared to need assistance? Would participants help someone having a seizure and call for help, or check to see if a person lying on a sidewalk was okay? After staging hundreds of false "emergencies," Darley and Latané had their answers.

In the case of the epileptic seizure, Darley and Latané found that people usually helped if they thought they were alone. That is, if participants thought they were the only ones who could help, they did. But look at **Figure 20.1.** Fewer people helped if they thought others were also hearing the calls for help. Those who thought others were close by were more likely to act the way Kitty Genovese's neighbors did. This evidence provides support for the **bystander effect,** which is the tendency for any given onlooker to be less likely to give aid if other onlookers (bystanders) are present.

A decision-making process involving at least three steps appears to influence our likelihood of helping someone else. Would you help a stranger lying flat on his back in a public place? First, you would have to notice the situation. If you noticed it, then you would have to interpret it as an emergency. Finally, you would have to assume responsibility for helping (see **Figure 20.2**).

Altruism researchers have uncovered several additional situations and circumstances that increase the odds of helping someone in need. We are more likely to help if we

- are not in a hurry.
- believe the victim deserves help.
- are in a good mood.
- believe the victim is similar to us.
- are feeling guilty.
- are in a small town or rural area.
- just saw someone else being helpful.

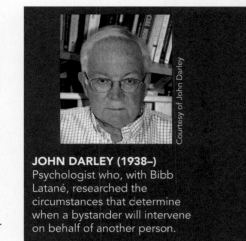

JOHN DARLEY (1938–)
Psychologist who, with Bibb Latané, researched the circumstances that determine when a bystander will intervene on behalf of another person.

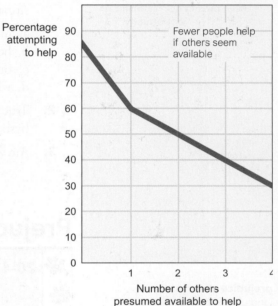

▲ **FIGURE 20.1**
When Do We Help?
People are less likely to help someone in need if they believe that other people are around who could also help. (Data from Darley & Latané, 1968.)

bystander effect The tendency for a person to be less likely to give aid if other people are present.

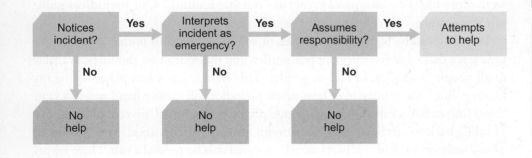

◄ **FIGURE 20.2**
How We Decide to Help
This flowchart shows the events and thought processes we seem to go through in deciding whether to intervene when someone needs help.

"Women and children first!"

Altruism Gone Awry ▲
The captain seems to have missed his "altruistic opportunity."

Harris, T. Russell/Cartoon Stock

Of all the items on that list, the most consistent finding is that happy people are helpful. No matter what it is that is making us happy, we are more eager to help and are more generous when we're in a good mood.[39]

Interestingly, this relationship between altruism and happiness can also be seen in people's generosity with money. What happens when we give our hard-earned cash away? Those who give activate reward centers in the brain and are happier than those who spend all their money on themselves.[40,41] You can see how a pretty positive cycle can develop here! Altruism can increase happiness, which in turn can lead to future altruistic acts.

MAKE IT STICK!

1. Research regarding the murder of Kitty Genovese revealed that a major factor determining whether people will help someone in an emergency situation is

   a. our past training in emergency situations (first-aid training and so on).
   b. how serious we perceive the situation to be.
   c. our religious beliefs.
   d. whether we think we are alone or with a large group of people.

2. True or False: The bystander effect describes the fact that any given bystander is more likely to help if other bystanders are present.

3. Are we more likely to help others if we are in a good mood or a bad mood?

Prejudice

🐾🐾 **20-4** How are stereotypes formed, and how can they lead to prejudice and discrimination?

prejudice An unjustifiable (and usually negative) attitude toward a group and its members.

stereotype A generalized (sometimes accurate but often overgeneralized) belief about a group of people.

discrimination In social relations, taking action against a group of people because of stereotyped beliefs and feelings of prejudice.

LIFE MATTERS
Stereotypes can be dangerous! Regardless of whether you believe the stereotype to be true or not, just its existence can negatively affect your decision making.

Prejudice is an unjustifiable (and usually negative) attitude toward a group and its members. Prejudice usually goes hand in hand with **stereotypes,** which are generalized beliefs about a group of people. Taking action against a group because of stereotyped beliefs and feelings of prejudice is **discrimination.** Prejudicial beliefs may focus on people's gender, race, age, religion, body size, or numerous other characteristics.

Prejudice filters what we see and influences how we think about it. One study from the 1970s asked participants to interpret a videotape of a black man shoving a white man.[42] Participants judged the shove to be an act of violence. However, when a different group of participants saw a white man shoving a black man, they were more likely to interpret this act as "horsing around." Our prejudices guide our perceptions.

Prejudice can be blatant and obvious or subtle and hard to notice. Most people now agree that schools, athletic opportunities, and transportation should be available to all people, regardless of race or gender. This change has taken place during my lifetime. But I was reminded of how subtle prejudice still exists when I was in a large city trying to hail a cab with a psychology professor from the University of Virginia. Heading back to our hotel after a wonderful meal, my friend stood on the corner of a busy intersection with his hand raised—a signal that he needed a cab. Three empty cabs passed him by, two of which slowed and then sped off. He looked at me and said, "You'd better try." I held up my hand, a cab stopped, and we climbed in.

What had just happened? A well-dressed, well-educated, middle-aged man stood on a corner and was ignored. I wasn't dressed nearly as well, but I was able to hail a cab almost instantly. "Has this happened to you before?" I asked. "It happens all the time," he replied. I'm of European-American descent. He is of African-American descent.

Similar forms of subtle prejudice are not hard to find. A study of drivers on the New Jersey Turnpike showed that African-Americans were only 13.5 percent of the drivers but they made up 35 percent of those pulled over by police. A survey asked college students if they felt excluded from school activities. Around 6 percent of the European-American students felt left out. Yet 24 percent of the Asian-Americans and 53 percent of the African-Americans felt excluded.[43]

In another study, over 1000 Los Angeles landlords received an e-mail from a researcher using a fictitious name to ask about an apartment vacancy. If the researcher signed off using the name "Patrick McDougall," a favorable response was received from the landlord 89 percent of the time. However, if the researcher signed the identical message as "Sayeed Al-Rahman," an encouraging reply was received only 66 percent of the time.[44]

Another researcher uncovered a disturbing form of prejudice when he asked participants to grade a poor essay.[45] Half the participants were told that a white student had written the essay and the other half that a black student had written it. Which paper do you think received the higher grade? If you guessed the one supposedly written by a white student, you guessed wrong. When participants thought a black student wrote the essay, they gave much higher grades and never handed out harsh criticism. The researcher proposed that this phenomenon might be the result of lower expectations for papers written by black students. If so, is this evidence of prejudice? *Yes,* and it's discrimination. Less constructive criticism and inflated praise can suppress learning and achievement.

Prejudice also promotes gender inequalities. The United Nations estimates that close to 1 billion adults worldwide cannot read or write and that two-thirds of these adults are women.[46,47] In the United States, those who take care of our children in day-care centers (usually women) are typically paid less than garbage collectors (usually men). The roots of gender prejudice can be seen in a study asking parents-to-be in the United States whether they would prefer a boy or a girl. Of those who expressed a preference, 67 percent wanted a son.[48]

So, how does prejudice begin? Let's look at both social and thought processes that carry some responsibility for the development of prejudice.

HighwayStarz/AGE Fotostock

▲ **Prejudice in Action**
Treating someone differently because of their race, is racial prejudice. Discrimination is acting on a prejudice and is often related to race, gender, or age.

Ingroup–Outgroup: We and They

Not long ago, a student told me he hated a high school five miles west of ours. The other school's soccer team had defeated our school's team, and this student played soccer. I asked, "You mean you hate the entire school?"

"No," he replied, "Just the kids who go there. All of them."

I was curious. "Why don't you like any of those kids?"

"They aren't us," he said. "They aren't like us at all."

Vicky Kasala/Getty Images

Ingroup or Outgroup? People with a common identity often form an ingroup that excludes others.

ingroup "Us"—people with whom we share a common identity.

outgroup "Them"—those perceived as different or apart from "us."

ingroup bias The tendency to favor our own group.

scapegoat theory The theory that prejudice offers an outlet for anger by providing someone to blame.

Like a lot of students, this young man believed his school was better than anyone else's, even in the same town. He had drawn a mental boundary around our school, creating an **ingroup,** an "us," or people with whom he shared a common identity. Creating an ingroup simultaneously creates a "them," an **outgroup,** or a group of people we perceive as different or apart from our ingroup.

The desire to tell our friends from our foes and to have our group dominate other groups programs us to be prejudiced against strangers.[49] We develop an **ingroup bias,** a tendency to favor members of our own group, often at the expense of those in the outgroup. In schools, students often form cliques that streamline judgment about others. Are you in a clique? The preps? Hipsters? Skaters? Indie, band, or drama kids? Jocks or alternative jocks? Geeks or freaks? Floaters? How does your clique prejudge those who aren't members?

When things don't go as planned, we often aim our anger at a target, someone or something we can blame for the problem. The soccer player who disliked students in the rival school didn't stop at the players on the other team. "The refs were terrible!" he explained. "And they never called penalties on the other team. We should have won, but we couldn't beat the refs." **Scapegoat theory** states that prejudice offers an outlet for anger by giving us someone to blame. Evidence for scapegoating is seen in studies where temporary frustration intensifies prejudice against another group.[50]

One result of putting others down is a boost in our own self-esteem or feelings of status. In one experiment, participants were made to feel insecure after experiencing failure. Self-esteem returned after the participants belittled and criticized another person or a rival school.[51,52] Perhaps this explains why my soccer-player student cheered when he learned that the rival school had lost at the state tournament.

Are You in a Clique? Are you a member of an ingroup? Band kid? Drama kid? Jock? Skater? What other cliques exist in your school?

strickke/iStock /Getty Images

Caiaimage/Trevor Adeline/Getty Images

A. Ramey/ PhotoEdit, Inc.

Tony Freeman/ PhotoEdit, Inc.

Thought Processes and Prejudice

Prejudice grows out of our tendency to form groups and from our urge to vent anger or blame others when times are hard. Prejudice is also a result of our mind's attempt to make the world around us easier to understand. Two ways in which we do this are through categorization and thinking through the lens of the just-world phenomenon.

Categorization It is easier for a cook to find recipes in a cookbook when they are grouped by categories, such as breakfast foods or pastas. Pharmacists keep track of the medicines they distribute by using categories such as painkillers and cough suppressants. Psychologists also categorize when they publish their findings, with brain research likely to end up in a journal of neurology and conformity data to appear in a social psychology journal. The cook, pharmacist, and psychologist categorize to simplify what they do. We all categorize in everyday life, too, especially when we assign people to groups. When we categorize, we don't have to think as hard as when we assess each person for who they really are. Categorization simplifies our thought processes.

How does categorization affect us? Studies have shown that categorization of people can lead to the development of the **other-race effect,** also called the *own-race bias*. This tendency shows up when we say that members of an ethnic group other than our own act alike, look alike, or have similar personality traits, while maintaining that members of our own ethnic group have great diversity.[53] Indeed, I've had several Asian-American students complain to me about white students who say, "You [Asian-Americans] all look alike to me" and "You're all good at math." The white students making these statements are exhibiting the other-race effect.

Unfortunately, we often stereotype those we've categorized. Stereotypes may or may not contain a hint of truth, but they are likely to bias our perceptions of others. One study asked participants to listen to the radio broadcast of a basketball game, to view a photo of a particular player, and to evaluate his performance. Those who saw a photo of a black athlete assessed the player's efforts more highly than those who viewed a photo of a white athlete.[54]

Categorization adversely affects our awareness of diversity. We know the strengths, weaknesses, and even the peculiarities of people in our own groups, but we are often ignorant of, or indifferent to, diversity in those we categorize. Overestimating the similarities of those not in our group simplifies our thought processes: By thinking others are the same, we don't have to spend time sorting one person out from another. The question is, does your personal categorization of someone negatively or positively impact your behavior toward him or her? For instance, if you see an African-American male you've never met, wearing a hoodie approaching you on a sidewalk, what are your default thoughts, and how do you act in the situation? Do you smile and make eye contact and say "hello," or do you look down and cross the street to avoid him? The answer rests in whether you categorize African-American males wearing hoodies positively or negatively. One of these responses likely represents the use of a negative stereotype, resulting in a prejudicial response.

Just-World Phenomenon The **just-world phenomenon** is the tendency to believe that the world is just or fair and that people get what they deserve and deserve what they get. This belief reflects what many of us were taught as children: that good is rewarded and evil is punished. This kind of false assumption promotes such thoughts as "Unsuccessful people are bad, and the poor get what they deserve." The flip-side thought is "Successful people are good, and the rich deserve their riches."

other-race effect The tendency to recall faces of one's own race more accurately than faces of other races.

just-world phenomenon The tendency to believe that people get what they deserve and deserve what they get.

The Just-World Phenomenon?
The way we judge the fairness of a situation may be directly related to our personal perspective.

THERE IS NO JUSTICE IN THE WORLD.

THERE IS SOME JUSTICE IN THE WORLD.

THE WORLD IS JUST.

MANKOFF

Bob Mankoff/www.cartoonstock.com

By thinking the world is fair, we justify our prejudices: Everything is as it should be. Just-world thinking wrongly suggests that ghettos are filled with people who are poor because they don't want to work; therefore, the poor deserve their poverty. In reality, poverty is closely tied to education (the more education, the better), family structure, race, and poverty-related policies that stoke poverty instead of arresting it.[55] Older people can't afford prescription drugs? Just-world thinking suggests that this is their own fault for not saving enough money for their retirement, while perhaps dismissing factors (like a catastrophically high medical bill from a car crash or prolonged cancer treatment) that contributed to the inability to pay for their medications.

MAKE IT STICK!

1. A letter to the editor claims, "Rich people have worked hard and deserve every dime they make." This letter writer's beliefs are an example of

   a. the just-world phenomenon.
   b. companionate attitudes.
   c. altruism.
   d. outgroup bias.

2. Which theory states that prejudice offers an outlet for anger by providing someone to blame?

3. True or False: Stereotypes are generalized beliefs about a group of people.

4. What is another phrase for the other-race effect?

Aggression

 20-5 What biological and learning factors lead to aggressive behavior?

We hear or read about the baseball player stealing second base, the volleyball player spiking the ball over the net, or the salesperson who won't take "no" for an answer. Are these individuals behaving aggressively? Not according to psychology's definition of **aggression,** which is any physical or verbal behavior intended to hurt or destroy. Deliberately passing nasty, false rumors around school about a classmate or a political opponent is acting aggressively. A person who swears at you for standing in front of his locker is also acting aggressively.

> **aggression** Any physical or verbal behavior intended to hurt or destroy.

Many people outside the United States see us as a country full of aggressive people. How else can we explain the fact that you are five times more likely to be murdered if you live in the United States than in Canada?[56,57] Are these critics right? Are people in the United States more aggressive than people in other countries? Psychologists have not yet found the answer to that question, but they are taking a hard look at biological and environmental factors—nature and nurture—for a better understanding of why people are aggressive.

Syda Productions/Shutterstock

Aggressive Behavior ↑ Such behavior can be physical or verbal.

The Biology of Aggression

What triggers aggressive behavior in bullies and criminals? Biological factors bear some of the blame. The biological influences include genes, the nervous system, and biochemistry.

Genetic and Neural Influences Evidence for genetic aggression is apparent in certain dog breeds that have been selectively bred to be aggressive watchdogs. Psychologists have bred genetically aggressive rats in laboratories. And in life outside the lab, studies show that genetically identical twins are more likely than fraternal (nonidentical) twins to report that both have violent tempers.[58,59]

Our nervous system is set up to make aggression possible if we are aggravated or provoked and if nothing is restraining us. Evidence suggests there is no one area in the brain controlling violence. Rather, we have a complex neural system that either stimulates or inhibits aggressive behavior, depending on the circumstances.[60] A part of the brain that seems to play a prominent role in aggression is the *amygdala* (pronounced uh-MIG-duh-la). One report of this connection comes from neurosurgeons trying to diagnose a woman's disorder. When they activated an electrode implanted next to her amygdala, the woman stood up, ordered someone to take her blood pressure ("Take it now!"), and started beating her doctor. Another interesting report comes from Dorothy Lewis and her colleagues, who studied the histories of 15 death row inmates and found that all 15 had suffered brain trauma through a severe head injury.[61] Although most neurologically impaired people are nonviolent, the research suggests that a neurological disorder may have contributed to the inmates' aggressive crimes.

Biochemistry Alcohol, neurotransmitters, and hormones can tip the balance of your neural system's aggression control system. The primary biochemical player appears to be testosterone—the most important of the male sex hormones. Consider the following:

- Violent criminals are usually young males with lower intelligence test scores, lower levels of serotonin (a brain chemical), and higher testosterone levels.[62,63]

- High testosterone levels have been associated with frustration, irritability, and impulsiveness, all of which can set the stage for aggression.[64]

- Testosterone-reducing drugs suppress aggressive behavior.[65]

- In teenage boys, high testosterone levels are correlated with hard drug use, delinquency, and bullying responses to frustration.[66–68]

We should note that all these studies represent data from correlational studies. Keep in mind that the existence of a correlation does not prove that a cause-and-effect relationship exists. Correlations tell us that certain variables *are* related but not *why* they are related. Still, correlations are useful in helping us make predictions. If testosterone levels in young males drop, then we can accurately predict that their aggressiveness will decrease. In fact, both testosterone levels and the likelihood of committing a crime decrease as males age. Aggressiveness decreases with age as well.

Alcohol appears to have both a biological and a psychological effect on aggression. Frustration is more likely to produce aggression in those who have been drinking alcohol.[69–71] People under the influence of alcohol commit 40 percent of all violent crimes and 75 percent of all spousal abuse.[72] Psychologically, aggressiveness also increases in those who *think* they've been drinking even when they haven't.[73] For other activities that researchers have found to increase aggressiveness, see Psychology in the Real World: Video Games and Violence.

Frightening Statistics
By the age of 18, most people will have seen tens of thousands of portrayals of murders in movies, in video games, and on television. The violent acts portrayed in media rarely show the suffering and pain that accompany murder and mayhem.

VILLEROT/BSIP SA/Alamy Stock Photo

PSYCHOLOGY IN THE REAL WORLD

Video Games and Violence

Take on the game identity of Ethan Winters in *Resident Evil 7*, and with a little practice you can stay alive for minutes on end, firing handguns, shotguns, and flamethrowers or using explosives and chainsaws (not to mention bacteria) into the Baker family and watch them slump, twitch, and bleed to death. What do we learn from video games? This question was debated with great intensity about 20 years ago after school murders in Paducah, Kentucky, and Littleton, Colorado, when authorities revealed that the assailants were particularly good at playing violent video games like *Doom*, *Mortal Kombat*, and *Duke Nukem*.

Video games appear to encourage aggressive thoughts and increase aggression. In one study, the most physically aggressive college males were the students who had spent the most time playing violent video games.[74] The same researchers found that those assigned to a nonviolent game (like *Sims 4*) became less hostile in follow-up tasks than those assigned to play games featuring blood, gore, and groaning victims. In another study, students became desensitized to real-life violence after exposure to violent video games.[75] Yet another researcher found that young adolescents who play a lot of violent video games get into more fights and arguments, are more hostile, and get worse grades compared to those who avoid games such as the latest *Fortnite* and *Grand Theft Auto 6*.[76]

There is still a lot to learn. Yes, thousands of students play violent video games and never physically harm one another. But there is little doubt that playing these games increases aggressive responses and lowers sensitivity to cruelty. Also, no data support

PBWPIX/Alamy Stock Photo

What Do Video Games Teach?
Research shows exposure to violent video games desensitizes people to real violence.

the idea that violent games serve as valuable "release valves" for feelings of fury and anger, as some say in defense of *Call of Duty* and others. In fact, playing these games seems to increase feelings of hostility.[77]

THINK ABOUT . . . Psychology in the Real World

1. How might video games promote aggressive thoughts and behaviors?

2. Why do you think young adolescents who play a lot of violent video games get into more fights and arguments, are more hostile, and get worse grades compared to those who avoid violent games?

3. What do video games teach us, and how would you test your theory?

Learning Aggression

Aggression in response to a threatening event may be a natural response. But we also learn aggression through having our aggressive behavior rewarded and by watching role models behave aggressively.

If a bully takes your lunch money today and gets away with it, she'll probably have lunch at your expense quite often in the future. When experience teaches us that being aggressive gets us what we want, the chances increase that we'll be aggressive in the future. Children can learn this by proxy: If they see another rewarded for being aggressive, they are more likely to imitate that model's behavior. Parents sometimes display the exact behavior they don't want when they discipline their children by beating them. The message children receive? One way to solve problems is through aggression.[78,79]

So, what does this mean for your generation and your younger brothers and sisters? If you're average, by the time you reach age 18, you will have spent more time watching television and viral videos on a computer or phone screen than you will have spent in school. The typical grade-school child sees more than 8000 murders and 100,000 violent acts before even reaching middle school or junior high.[80] Rarely do these violent acts show the victims' trauma that follows the offense.

Does watching violence, on television or at the movies, influence people to be aggressive? Correlational studies suggest that it does. Homicide rates in the United States and Canada doubled between 1956 and 1974, widely considered television's booming growth years. The same increase in homicide rates was seen in white South Africa after television was introduced in 1975.[81] After reviewing experimental data, the American Psychological Association made the following official statement: "There is absolutely no doubt that higher levels of viewing violence on television are correlated with increased acceptance of aggressive attitudes and increased aggressive behavior."[82] Elliot Aronson provides four reasons exposure to media violence might increase aggression:

1. *"If they can do it, so can I."* Previously learned inhibitions on being violent may be weakened by watching violent TV characters.[83]

2. *"Oh, so that's how you do it."* Watching violent acts on television may spur imitation.

3. *"I think it must be aggressive feelings I'm experiencing."* The experience of watching violence on television may make anger and aggressive responses more accessible to the viewer.

4. *"Ho-hum, another brutal beating; what's on the next channel?"* Watching violence on television may desensitize our reactions to mayhem and redluce our sympathy for victims. Living with violence becomes easier.

Do not forget, however, that watching violent crimes on television does not automatically turn a person into a villain. Likewise, lots of children grow up in violent situations but do not grow up to be aggressive. Having a parent who regularly uses severe physical punishment does not doom a child to the same actions. Like all behavior, aggression is an interaction between nurture (outside situational factors) and nature (inner personal factors).

MAKE IT STICK!

1. Aggression research finds that which of the following chemicals is associated with higher levels of aggression?

   a. dopamine   c. testosterone
   b. caffeine   d. serotonin

2. True or False: If a member of the marching band told other band members they were crummy musicians and bad marchers, this would not be considered aggressive behavior.

3. Which of the following is seen as a reason exposure to media violence might lead to aggression?

   a. Previously learned inhibitions on being violent may be strengthened by watching violent TV characters.

   b. Watching violent acts on television does not spur imitation.

   c. The experience of watching violence on television may make anger and aggressive responses less accessible to the viewer.

   d. Watching violence on television may desensitize our reactions to mayhem and reduce our sympathy for victims.

Cooperation

20-6 How do shared goals help resolve conflict between groups?

Friendly contact between different ethnic or racial groups can decrease prejudice.[84,85] But contact is not usually enough to break down the barriers between two different groups. One way to break down barriers is by using **superordinate goals,** which are shared goals that override differences among people and require cooperation. Muzafer Sherif[86] discovered the power behind superordinate goals in a study of 22 boys attending a summer camp.

> **superordinate goals** Shared goals that override differences among people and require their cooperation.

Sherif divided the boys into two groups. He assigned each group an area of the campsite, apart from the other. The groups then competed against each other in a series of events. The winners received prizes from camp counselors and contempt from the losers. Within days, the two groups were raiding each other's cabins, engaging in food fights over dinner, and when brought together, taunting each other.

L.G. Patterson/AP Images

Using superordinate goals, Sherif then turned the foes into friends. First, he created a water supply emergency. To obtain water, both groups had to pitch in and work together. A truck quit running, and all the boys had to push it to get it going. Soon, the taunting stopped, and the boys even pooled their money to pay for a recreational activity they could not otherwise afford. Competition and isolation had created enemies, but *cooperative contact* created friends.

Cooperation can lead people to melt the icy walls of noninclusive subgroups, creating a new, more inclusive group.[87] An "us" and "them" mentality turns into a "we" state of mind.

Superordinate Goals Cooperation is necessary to meet shared goals, especially if people need to overcome differences.

Cooperative learning, where students work together on projects, promotes interracial friendships in multicultural schools.[88,89] Cooperative learning also enhances student achievement.[90] These results are so positive that thousands of teachers around the country have brought interracial cooperative learning to their classrooms.[91] These experiences set the stage for "adult work life and for citizenship in a multicultural society."[92]

Perhaps there is a message on the value of cooperative contact at a time when we see increasing strife, fragmentation, and warlike activities on our planet. With increased international exchanges, maybe we'll discover that our similarities far outweigh our differences and that we share such basic goals as having a healthy family, a safe home, and food on the table.

MAKE IT STICK!

1. Muzafer Sherif found that one of the most effective ways to reduce prejudices between groups is to

   a. provide educational classes about each group's culture and history.

   b. reduce the mere exposure effect through increased self-disclosure.

   c. create a shared goal that requires the groups to cooperate to succeed.

   d. eliminate the bystander effect by requiring everyone in the group to speak.

2. What do we call shared goals that override differences among people and require their cooperation?

3. Research has shown that competition and isolation often lead to _____, while cooperative contact often creates _____.

Module 20 Summary and Assessment
Social Relations

 20-1 What factors influence attractiveness?

- Proximity is a major factor in attraction: The people we like, date, and even marry typically live near us.

- Appearance (physical attractiveness) is the first filter we use to sort the people we want to get to know from those we don't.

- Similarity is a major factor in attraction—we are likely to share our interests, attitudes, age, intelligence level, and economic status, as well as our beliefs on religion, smoking, and race relations, with our friends.

 20-2 What are the differences between passionate and companionate love?

- The aroused state of passionate love is more likely to occur at the beginning of a relationship and sometimes develops into companionate love.

- Equity and self-disclosure are two important factors in developing and maintaining companionate love.

 20-3 What factors influence altruistic behavior?

- Altruism research reveals specific situations and circumstances that increase the odds of helping someone in need, including our beliefs about the victim, our mood, our similarity to the victim, if we are experiencing feelings of guilt, if it is an urban or rural context, and if we observe others helping.

 20-4 How are stereotypes formed, and how can they lead to prejudice and discrimination?

- People readily form generalized beliefs about groups of people.

- Ingroup bias is the tendency to favor members of our group, often at the expense of those in the outgroup.

- Categorization simplifies thought processes, but these mental categories can also lead to the development of stereotypes and prejudice.

 20-5 What biological and learning factors lead to aggressive behavior?

- Biological influences on aggression include genetic influences, the nervous system, and biochemistry.

- People learn aggression by having their own aggressive behavior rewarded and by watching role models behave aggressively.

 20-6 How do shared goals help resolve conflict between groups?

- Superordinate goals require cooperation and override differences among people. Isolation can create enemies, but cooperative contact, through the use of superordinate goals, can create friends.

Summative Assessment

1. Liking something you didn't initially care for is an example of what?

   a. similarity
   b. the mere exposure effect
   c. companionate love
   d. attraction

2. Researchers have found that first impressions and the desire to get to know someone are based on what?

   a. appearance
   b. politeness
   c. intelligence
   d. charm

3. Altruism is defined as

    a. a condition in which people contribute to and receive from a relationship at a similar rate.

    b. the revealing of intimate aspects of oneself to others.

    c. an unselfish regard for the welfare of others.

    d. deep, affectionate attachment for those with whom our lives are intertwined.

4. In which situation are we most likely to give help to someone else as described by the bystander effect?

    a. A woman falls nearby in a crowded shopping mall.

    b. A child falls into the deep end at a public swimming pool.

    c. A car accident happens in the next lane on a busy street.

    d. A man riding a bike on a secluded trail crashes nearby.

5. An unjustifiable attitude toward a group and its members is called

    a. prejudice.

    b. stereotype.

    c. discrimination.

    d. categorization.

6. A generalized belief about a group of people is called

    a. prejudice.

    b. discrimination.

    c. categorization.

    d. a stereotype.

7. Taking action against a group of people because of stereotyped beliefs and feelings is called

    a. prejudice.

    b. scapegoat theory.

    c. discrimination.

    d. categorization.

8. Prejudice that offers an outlet for anger by providing someone to blame is called

    a. categorization.

    b. scapegoat theory.

    c. discrimination.

    d. a stereotype.

9. Which of the following statements is an example of just-world phenomenon?

    a. People get what they deserve.

    b. People of "that group" are the same.

    c. Strangers can't be trusted.

    d. I'm afraid of people who look different from me.

10. Which of the following is an example of a superordinate goal?

    a. Students write essays to win a college scholarship.

    b. Rival high school football teams play for the state championship.

    c. Adults and teens plan and build a neighborhood skate park.

    d. Dance teams across the city meet for an annual competition.

KEY TERMS AND KEY PEOPLE

mere exposure effect, p. 305

passionate love, p. 308

companionate love, p. 309

equity, p. 309

self-disclosure, p. 309

altruism, p. 310

bystander effect, p. 311

prejudice, p. 312

stereotype, p. 312

discrimination, p. 312

ingroup, p. 314

outgroup, p. 314

ingroup bias, p. 314

scapegoat theory, p. 314

other-race effect, p. 315

just-world phenomenon, p. 315

aggression, p. 316

superordinate goals, p. 320

John Darley (1938–), p. 311

Nature and Nurture in Psychology

So, is it environment or genetics that most affects who we become and how we behave? Let's take a closer look.

Learning Goals

21-1 Describe the elements of the genetic code.

21-2 Explain how twin studies and adoption studies are used to learn about the influences of nature and nurture.

21-3 Explain what research has revealed about the relationship between environmental influences and early brain development, parents, peers, and our culture.

Imagine for a moment that your adoring parents, who believe you are perfect, decide to clone you, creating a perfect genetic replica of you. Would the new baby, your identical twin, grow up to be exactly like you? What if the baby were exposed to a different prenatal environment—one polluted (or not) by drugs or viruses? What if your parents had to give this baby up for adoption or decided to move to a different part of the world? And how would this child be affected by growing up as a part of a different generation? (Remember that 18 years from now, when this new person is in high school, Jennifer Lawrence and Emma Watson will be over 45 years old, Dwayne "The Rock" Johnson will be pushing 65, and the classic or retro radio stations will be playing music by Taylor Swift and Jay-Z.)

These questions all illustrate one of psychology's big issues: How do our families, our friends, and the culture in which we live affect us? A whole field of study, **behavior genetics,** focuses on this key issue—studying the relative effects of genes and environment on our behavior. Psychologists call this the *nature–nurture issue.*

The influence of *nature* consists of the **genes**—the biochemical units of heredity that make up the chromosomes—passed along by your parents the moment you were conceived. The influence of *nurture* comes from the **environment**—every nongenetic influence, from prenatal nutrition to the people and things around us. Possible environmental factors are so numerous that it is impossible to keep them all in mind. Here are a few examples:

- being exposed to placental abnormalities, viruses, and drugs in the womb or not being exposed to these ill effects
- consuming lower-quality food and contaminated water or wholesome food and clean water

behavior genetics The school of thought that focuses on how much our genes and our environment influence our individual differences.

genes The biochemical units of heredity that make up chromosomes.

environment Every nongenetic influence, from prenatal nutrition to the people and things around us.

What Makes You You?
Are your personality and appearance more a result of genetics or your environment?

- growing up in a household with smokers or nonsmokers
- being raised in a monolingual (using one language) or a multilingual (using several languages) household
- identifying with a particular ethnic group
- learning how your culture expects boys or girls to think and act
- making countless life choices, such as on a career or partner
- deciding to live in an urban, a suburban, or a rural location

What roles do you think nature and nurture have played in making you who you are? In this module, we consider how genetics and the environment have worked together to make the person you see when you look in the mirror. We'll start with the nature side of the issue: genetics.

Genetics in Brief

 21-1 What are the elements of the genetic code?

chromosomes Threadlike structures made of DNA molecules that contain genes.

DNA (deoxyribonucleic acid) A complex molecule containing the genetic information that makes up chromosomes.

You (and every creature on this planet) have your own genetic code, a biological blueprint that is found in every cell nucleus and that contains the master plan for your entire body (see **Figure 21.1**). Inside each nucleus are 46 **chromosomes**, threadlike structures made of molecules that contain the genes. You received 23 chromosomes each from your mother and father, paired together at the moment of conception. Your chromosomes are composed of molecules called **DNA (deoxyribonucleic acid).** The smaller sections of DNA strands, the stairs on DNA's staircase, store your genetic code, your *genes*. Our genes not only set

FIGURE 21.1
Genes: Their Location and Composition
Every cell in your body has a nucleus. Note how *every* nucleus contains your chromosomes, which in turn contain your genes.

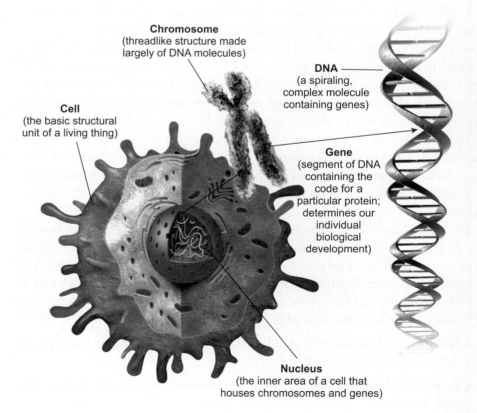

Chromosome
(threadlike structure made largely of DNA molecules)

DNA ———
(a spiraling, complex molecule containing genes)

Cell
(the basic structural unit of a living thing)

Gene
(segment of DNA containing the code for a particular protein; determines our individual biological development)

Nucleus
(the inner area of a cell that houses chromosomes and genes)

up our physical beings—making us humans, or dogs, or watermelons—but also influence our behaviors in many ways.

Genes are distinguished from one another by four-letter codes. Each letter in the code (A, T, C, or G) is called a *nucleotide.* Your largest chromosome has about 250 million nucleotides, and the smallest has 50 million.[1] Consider that all 46 chromosomes can be found in every cell nucleus you have: How many nucleotides must there be in every nucleus? Billions.

How many genes do you have? The fruit fly, with a circumference half that of an apple stem, has about 15,000 genes. So, humans must have a million or a billion, right? Imagine the astonishment of those mapping the human genome when they learned that humans have only about 25,000 genes.[2] You may be surprised to learn that *99.9 percent of your four-letter DNA sequences match that of every other human.*[3] Genetically, you are nearly identical to everyone else in the world. With so much identical genetic makeup, it is not surprising that people from all countries exhibit similar behaviors. Worldwide, we enjoy greeting loved ones whom we've missed. In countries around the globe, 3-month-old babies smile, which tends to elicit smiling, cooing, and cuddling from adults. And no matter where we live, we experience happiness when we make someone feel better and disappointment when someone breaks a promise. Does this mean you should look or act like everyone else in the world? *No.* Genes are responsible for *predisposing* our appearance and behavior, not for concretely determining either.

We are far more similar than we are different, but we do vary from one another. Scientists have found *snips,* or sites, throughout our DNA that naturally differ between two unrelated individuals, and other variations exist where they shouldn't. These DNA **mutations** are random errors in gene replication that lead to a change in an individual's genetic code. Mutation is the source of all genetic diversity. Some mutations are desirable—most of us would appreciate a mutation leading to superior eyesight, for example. Other mutations, like those that predispose someone to cancer, are undesirable and feared. Predispositions are passed through DNA to future generations.

Predisposition is an important concept, so let's look at this idea in a bit more detail. The presence of a predisposition for colon or breast cancer or some other disease does not necessarily doom someone to contract the disease. Predisposition merely means that the *possibility* of developing a disease exists. Whether that possibility will become reality often depends on environmental factors (poor diet, polluted air, stress). To choose a simple example, I may be predisposed to sunburn easily, but if I limit my exposure to the sun's rays, I won't have to put up with the pain of burned skin. Perhaps you can see why we refer to the nature *and* nurture issue, rather than nature *versus* nurture.

"So, how do you want to play this? Nature, nurture, or a bit of both?"

> **mutation** Random errors in gene replication that lead to a change in the individual's genetic code and are the source of all genetic diversity.

MAKE IT STICK!

1. Which of the following research questions would behavior geneticists be most interested in?

   a. How do humans perceive color?
   b. Which region of the brain controls voluntary movement?
   c. What is the most effective way to train an organism to respond in useful ways?
   d. Is personality more influenced by chromosomes or environment?

2. Which of the following most relates to the nature–nurture issue?

   a. parents and peers
   b. genes and environment
   c. culture and norms
   d. DNA and chromosomes

3. True or False: About 99.9 percent of President Trump's four-letter DNA sequences match those of former President Obama.

Nature and Individual Differences

Identical Twins
These teens developed from a single fertilized egg that divided into two identical copies.

 21-2 How are twin studies and adoption studies used to learn about the influences of nature and nurture?

Intertwined from the moment of conception until death, nature and nurture are the two parts of the complex equation that is you. Our genetic similarity is amazing, but there is still that fraction of a percent that, when combined with innumerable environmental factors, can make each of us enormously different from all others. Why do some people seem smarter than others? Why are some people always slower at understanding a joke? Why can some people sing beautifully, yet there are others whose mouths we would prefer stayed shut? *Behavior geneticists* study such questions using twin studies and adoption studies.

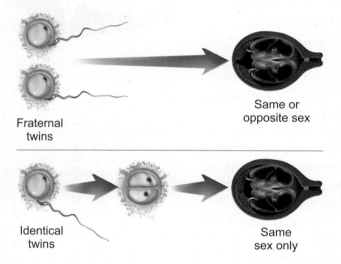

Fraternal twins

Same or opposite sex

Identical twins

Same sex only

FIGURE 21.2
Conception of Identical Versus Fraternal Twins
Identical twins develop from a single fertilized egg that divides into two identical copies. Fraternal twins develop from two different eggs, each fertilized by a different sperm cell.

identical twins Twins who develop from a single fertilized egg that splits in two, creating two genetically identical organisms.

fraternal twins Twins who develop from two different fertilized eggs; they are genetically no more similar than any other two siblings, but they share a fetal environment.

Twin Studies

Only in Hollywood movies do you find cloned humans living their lives in a genetically engineered environment so that some mad scientist can study what makes them tick. But nature has provided its own potential genetics-lab participants in the form of human twins. **Identical twins** are nature's human clones; they develop from a single fertilized egg that splits in two, creating two genetically identical organisms. **Fraternal twins** develop from two different fertilized eggs. They are no more genetically similar than any other two siblings, but they share a fetal environment (see **Figure 21.2**). So, do the genetically identical twins behave more similarly than their fraternal twin counterparts? This is a question that intrigues behavior geneticists, who study the **heritability** of various traits, or the degree to which our traits are inherited.

Here is a simplified example of how a behavior geneticist might set up a study of identical and fraternal twins to investigate the heritability of intelligence:

1. Collect and compare data on the intelligence levels of *identical twins* raised in the same home.

2. Collect and compare data on the intelligence levels of *fraternal twins* raised in the same home.

3. Compare the similarity in intelligence levels of the identical twins with the similarity in intelligence levels of the fraternal twins.

If the intelligence levels of the identical twins are significantly more similar than the intelligence levels of the fraternal twins, then we can infer that genetics, or nature, is at work. In other words, if our results show that the identical twins have IQs within 4 points of each other but the fraternal twins have IQs that are usually 12 points apart, we could safely assume that IQ is inherited (nature). As it turns out, researchers have indeed found a greater similarity in intelligence among identical twins when compared to fraternal twins.[4]

Genetic influences on personality traits appear to follow the same pattern. Studies in Sweden and Finland, using thousands of twin pairs, reveal that if one identical twin is outgoing, the other identical twin is likely to be outgoing—more so than in the case of fraternal twins. The same increased similarity can be found in the emotional stability of identical twins versus fraternal twins.[5]

One twin study[6] that looked at middle-aged twin divorce rates even suggests that genes influence the likelihood of divorce. The results showed that if one identical twin was divorced, then the odds of the other identical twin divorcing went up 5.5 times. However, if a fraternal twin divorced a spouse, the other fraternal twin was only 1.6 times more likely to wind up divorced.

But wait a minute! How can divorce be heritable? It's not even an option in some cultures, which forbid it. What we must remember is that *the behavior itself*—in this case, divorce—*is not inherited.* What *is* inherited are the genetic predispositions that may lead to the behavior. For instance, those with a greater predisposition to anger or conflict may be more likely to divorce than those who are not so predisposed.

As you can see, twin studies have helped us learn about the heritability of certain traits. Equally important is that they have taught us much about the influence of environment. Studies of reunited twins, those separated at birth and raised apart from each other, have helped demonstrate that *no* trait is completely inherited and that the behaviors of identical twins are not identical. Yet these genetic replicas, who sometimes grew up in dramatically different environments, have exhibited startling similarities in tastes and habits. Take identical twins Oskar Stohr and Jack Yufe. Oskar was raised by his grandmother in Germany as a Catholic and a Nazi, while Jack was raised by his father in the Caribbean as a Jew.[7] Despite the obvious differences in their environments, both enjoy spicy foods, are domineering toward women, and report flushing the toilet before using it. The similarities between the two did not stop there, but perhaps you are wondering the same thing critics of the separated twin studies wonder: Couldn't two strangers sit down at a table and over the course of a couple of hours discover many bizarre but coincidental similarities? Perhaps, but here is where scientific methods help us to understand the difference between coincidence and biological significance.

Using scientific measuring equipment, psychologists have studied separated identical twins and have found remarkable similarities in heart rates, brain waves, and intelligence levels.[8–10] Other studies have found statistically significant similarities in personalities, abilities, attitudes, and fears.[11–13] If a soccer match were held to determine whether nature or nurture has a greater effect on development, clearly the evidence from genetics and twin studies would be a goal scored for the nature team. But before we announce the winner, consider adoption studies.

heritability The degree to which traits are inherited.

Stephanie Diani/The New York Times/Redux

▲ **Fraternal (Nonidentical) Twins**
These teens are also twins, but they developed from two different eggs, which in turn were each fertilized by a different sperm cell.

Adoption Studies

Another way to assess the effects of nature and nurture is through adoption studies. Here the biological parents are providing the nature, and the adoptive parents are providing the nurture. By the time an adopted 1-week-old girl reaches the

Nature and Nurture ▲
In adoption studies, biological parents supply the nature, and adoptive parents supply the nurture.

age of 10, will her personality more closely resemble her biological parents' personalities or the personalities of the parents who raised her? What's your guess?

Study after study has yielded the same surprising result: Adopted children share more personality trait similarities with their biological parents than with their adoptive parents.[14] Score one more goal for nature.

But the match is far from over. Although our personality seems to be something we are mostly born with, there are many other powerful areas in which parenting can influence a child. What about values, attitudes, and manners? What about political and religious beliefs? For all of these areas, nurture scores a goal. Several adoption studies show that parenting plays a major role in belief system (for instance, values, religious faith, convictions) development and development of behaviors important to functioning as a good citizen in our diverse societies.[15–17] Adopted children score higher on intelligence tests and are more likely to be involved in charitable activities than their biological parents.[18] Good parenting remains important. Nurture is back in the game.

MAKE IT STICK!

1. In twin studies, behavior geneticists are looking for

   a. differences between fraternal twins because they are raised in the same home.
   b. whether being a twin affects emotional development and social behaviors.
   c. similarities between identical twins because they share the same genetic code.
   d. how many times identical and fraternal twins occur in different cultures.

2. If adopted children are more similar in political views to their adopted parents than to their biological parents, then

   a. random mutations may be responsible for the differences between adopted children and adoptive parents.
   b. the genetic code determining political views probably occurs randomly.
   c. political views probably are not genetically predisposed.
   d. specific genes probably predispose people to political views.

3. True or False: Study after study shows that the personalities of adopted children appear to be more like that of their biological parents than their adoptive parents.

Environment Matters

 21-3 What has research revealed about the relationship between environmental influences and early brain development, parents, peers, and our culture?

One of the more celebrated separated-twin cases illustrates how easy it is to lay credit or blame at the feet of a child's parents for any given behavior. In this case, two identical twin boys, separated at birth and raised apart, were reunited in their thirties. Both could be considered "neat freaks" in the way they kept their homes, dressed, and scrubbed their "hands regularly to a raw, red color." When asked to explain the origin of the neatness, the first twin credited his mother and growing up in an extremely ordered environment, where he learned to appreciate that everything should be kept in its proper place. The second twin also credited his mother, although for different reasons. Why the perfectionism? "The reason is quite simple. I'm reacting to my mother, who was an absolute slob."[19]

Parents are an important part of most people's early environment. With genetic influences accounting for roughly half the variation in our personality traits, parenting is a likely source to turn toward in accounting for the other 50 percent of those traits. It has been shown that parents influence their children's politics, faith, manners, and attitudes.[20] But how much credit do parents deserve for the child who wins a debate tournament, dances the role of Clara in the *Nutcracker Suite* ballet, or is elected president of the student council? How much blame should we heap on parents for the teenager who always shows up late to practice or rehearsal, takes up smoking, or has frequent scrapes with the law? If we listen to pop psychology, we hear all kinds of unfounded claims:

Parents Matter
The nurturing of parents and guardians plays an important role in the development of a child.

- Overprotective or overbearing parenting permanently underprepares a child for the real world.

- Parents who spank leave irreparable scars on a child's personality.

- Lenient parents who do not punish children severely create irresponsible children who will become troublemakers.

Is the mother or father who, even with the best intentions, occasionally pulls too hard in parenting's tug-of-war inflicting permanent psychological damage? Should we blame our parents for our failures in life and, subsequently, blame ourselves when our children fail? For answers to such questions, many researchers look to comparisons of nonidentical siblings raised together. Behavior geneticist Robert Plomin has found that "two children in the same family [are on average] as different from one another as are pairs of children selected randomly from the population."[21] Another well-respected researcher, Sandra Scarr, believes parents should receive less blame for children who do not turn out as hoped or expected and less credit for children who do.[22]

Certainly, environment matters, but growing up in the same household accounts for only a small portion (around 10 percent) of our personality differences. What other environmental factors might account for nurture's role in personality development? Let's look at three possible answers: early learning experiences, peer influence, and culture.

Early Learning and Brain Development

You've heard the phrase "Use it or lose it." Nowhere is this truer than with your brain, where experience nurtures nature. We do not remember everything we learn, but the brain processes we used in early learning do pave the way for later learning of more complex information. Consider the following neurological evidence:

- Rats housed for 60 days in an enriched (fun, stimulating) environment had brain weight increases of 7 to 10 percent more than rats housed in an impoverished (boring) environment.[23] The same study found a dramatic 20 percent increase in communication connections in the brain (see **Figure 21.3**).

- Premature babies who receive special handling (touch, massage) grow more rapidly, both physically and neurologically, than preemies who do not receive the same treatment.[24–26]

- Sixth graders from impoverished environments who were given stimulating care as infants had higher intelligence test scores than their classmates who did not receive such care.[27]

FIGURE 21.3
Experience Affects Brain Development
Mark Rosenzweig and David Krech reared rats either alone in an environment without playthings or with others in an environment enriched with playthings that were changed daily. In 14 of 16 repetitions of this basic experiment, the rats placed in the enriched environment developed significantly more cerebral cortex (relative to the rest of the brain's tissue) than did those in the impoverished environment. (From Rosenzweig et al., 1972.)

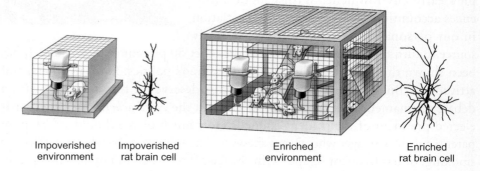

Impoverished environment — Impoverished rat brain cell — Enriched environment — Enriched rat brain cell

For our brains to meet their developmental potential, early experience is critical. The child born with perfect pitch will never have a chance to develop this gift if prevented from hearing music in early life. A child raised in abusive isolation will never learn to read, write, or speak like a normal adult.

As you get older, your brain's tissue will continue to change. The brain's pathways maintained through practice or experience will remain strong, and neglected pathways will fade with disuse. I recently found this out the hard way. Although I had learned to roller skate in sixth grade and had skated periodically after that, I had to relearn this skill after seven years without putting on my in-line skates. Similarly, you will find that the theorems and proofs you learned in geometry seem foreign to you later in life unless you pursue a mathematically oriented career. The examples are endless, but one thing is clear: Use those brain pathways, created by nurture and nature, or lose them.

 ## Nurturing Happiness

On many occasions, my grandmother said, "Nobody is born happy." She meant this both literally and figuratively. Literally, it's a good sign if a newborn baby has a loud, healthy cry upon birth. Figuratively, she was saying that you shouldn't wait for happiness to come to you. Rather, you should try to figure out things you can do to help make your life happier.

Science and positive psychologists agree with my grandmother: There are many simple things you can do to nurture happiness. Happiness and other positive emotions are increased when you

- express gratitude to others for things they have done to help you.

- challenge discouraging thoughts about the past.

- savor the good things in life (for example, a good grade on a test, sunsets, a tasty treat, or your favorite song) that we often take for granted.[28]

Martin Seligman has used what he calls the "good things in life" exercise as a savoring intervention to improve happiness. The exercise is designed to increase positive emotion about the recent past. To do this, he asks individuals to

1. record, every day for a week, three good things that happened.

2. also record why those good things occurred.

3. share those good things with a friend or family member.

Could nurturing happiness be just that simple? The answer is a clear *Yes*. After completing this exercise, Seligman found that participants compared to control groups, scored higher on tests to measure happiness and were also happier and less depressed at a three-month follow-up.

Seligman points out that positive psychology is not meant to imply that there is a negative psychology. Promoting happiness, positive emotions, and well-being is in part an attempt to promote a *balanced* psychology. He writes, "We are committed to a psychology that concerns itself with repairing weakness (for example, therapy) as well as nurturing strengths—a psychology that concerns itself with remedying deficits as well as promoting excellence."[29]

Peer and Parent Influence

The tango danced by nature and nurture continues from childhood into adolescence, where peer influence becomes powerfully real and tangible. One of the most reliable predictors of dropout rate and failure in school is social rejection by a peer group.[30] Why, despite the antismoking warnings on cigarette packages does smoking (and subsequent vaping) among teenagers periodically increase? Those inclined to pin blame on smoking parents are surprised to learn that parental concern over smoking is less of a factor than researchers originally believed. Rather, teens in peer groups in which members smoke are far more at risk to start this life-endangering habit than are those with nonsmoking peers.[31] Peer groups with smokers (1) offer easy access to cigarettes, (2) model pleasure from smoking, and (3) present the message that fitting in includes lighting up. Thousands of U.S. teens start their smoking addiction each day.

Peer group influence has been demonstrated in younger peer groups, too. Preschoolers who won't eat a particular food at home are more likely to eat that food when seated at a table with peers who like it.[32] Younger immigrant children living in an environment filled with nonimmigrant peers will quickly adopt the culture of the peer group, sometimes at the expense of the culture they share with their parents. Children pick up the accent and conversational style of their neighborhood peers.[33] Psychologist Howard Gardner clearly sees the importance of a peer group *and* parents in raising children:[34]

> Parents are more important when it comes to education, discipline, responsibility, orderliness, charitableness, and ways of interacting with authority figures.[35] Peers are more important for learning cooperation, for finding the road to popularity, and for inventing styles of interaction among people of the same age. Youngsters may find their peers more interesting, but they will look to their parents when contemplating their own futures. Moreover, parents [often] choose the neighborhoods and schools that supply the peers.

Peers Also Matter
None of these teens smoke, and research indicates that if they continue to hang out together it is unlikely that any of them ever will. Peers can greatly affect our behaviors.

Cultural Influences

Culture is an elusive, invisible, abstract concept that forms the basis for much of our understanding of life.[36] **Culture** is the shared attitudes, beliefs, norms, and behaviors of a group communicated from one generation to the next. **Norms** are the understood rules for accepted and expected behavior within a group. Culture influences our food selection, religious choices, family activities, and more.

culture The shared attitudes, beliefs, norms, and behaviors of a group communicated from one generation to the next.

norms Understood rules for accepted and expected behavior.

ton koene/Alamy Stock Photo

Cultural Effects
Our cultural backgrounds are a big part of the "nurture" that influences our behavior and attitudes.

Because of the cultural rules we all possess, we develop a set of expectations about the kinds of behaviors others should exhibit. If others behave according to expectation, we may think, "This person is good." When others behave in a way we do not consider "normal" or socially appropriate, we have negative reactions, such as frustration and anger. In such cases, we may think, "This person is bad," or, "This person is stupid." Sadly, we tend to make these snap judgments without a second thought, often toward people whose skin color, sexuality, or religion is different from our own.

We tend to believe that *our* culture's way of raising children is the *best* way. Be careful: Successful child rearing has been accomplished using many methods. There is tremendous diversity worldwide in the way children are brought up, and leaders and heroes have emerged from a wide range of cultures.

So, how do nature and nurture work together to make us who we are? While we have some clues, we don't yet fully know the answer to that question. Behavior genetics is still in its infancy. The ethical implications of genetic engineering and cloning are just beginning to emerge, and much reflection on the meaning of this research lies ahead.

MAKE IT STICK!

1. Which of the following behaviors are our peers most likely to influence?

   a. popularity at school
   b. exercise habits
   c. giving money to a charity
   d. keeping our room clean

2. A culture's _____ are its understood rules for accepted and expected behavior.

3. True or False: Your own personal happiness is likely to increase if you regularly express gratitude to others for the things they have done to help you.

Module 21 Summary and Assessment

Nature and Nurture in Psychology

 21-1 What are the elements of the genetic code?

- The human genetic code is made up of 46 chromosomes composed of DNA.

- Humans have about 25,000 sections of chromosomes, called genes, which predispose people for specific physical and behavioral traits.

 21-2 How are twin studies and adoption studies used to learn about the influences of nature and nurture?

- Studies with identical twins help researchers consider the effects of different environments on the traits and behavior of genetically identical people.

- Studies with fraternal twins allow researchers to consider the effects of similar environments on genetically different people.

- Studies reveal that adopted children share more personality trait similarities with their biological parents than with their adoptive parents. Adopted children are more similar to their adoptive parents in belief systems and the development of behaviors important to functioning in society.

 21-3 What has research revealed about the relationship between environmental influences and early brain development, parents, peers, and our culture?

- For our brains to meet their developmental potential, early experience is critical.

- Parents are important when it comes to education, discipline, responsibility, orderliness, charitableness, and ways of interacting with authority figures.

- Peers strongly influence how we learn cooperation, find the road to popularity, and learn the styles of interaction among people of the same age.

- Our culture and norms affect our thinking and behavior in profound ways.

Summative Assessment

1. What do we call a segment of DNA that determines our individual biological development?

   a. a cell
   b. a gene
   c. a chromosome
   d. a nucleus

2. Behavior geneticists would be most interested in which research question?

   a. How do humans perceive taste?
   b. Which region of the brain controls speech?
   c. Do chromosomes or environment influence personality more?
   d. What is the most effective way to train mice to push a lever?

3. What have studies with twins helped researchers learn more about?

   a. heritability
   b. chromosomes
   c. mutations
   d. adoption

4. Which of the following best describes the *nature–nurture* issue?

   a. identical and fraternal twins
   b. DNA and chromosomes
   c. norms and culture
   d. genes and environment

5. What would explain the idea that adopted children are more similar in political beliefs to their adopted parents than to their biological parents?

   a. DNA mutations
   b. genes
   c. nurture
   d. heritability

6. What do we call the shared attitudes, beliefs, and behaviors of a group that have been communicated over generations?

   a. culture
   b. nature
   c. norms
   d. development

7. What is the name for twins that are created as a result of a single fertilized egg dividing into two?

   a. inherited
   b. identical
   c. mutation
   d. fraternal

8. What do we call random errors in gene replication that lead to a change in an individual's genetic code?

   a. genetics
   b. DNA
   c. inheritance
   d. mutations

9. Why does your doctor ask about your family medical history?

   a. to know what might be contagious in your family
   b. to better understand what stress you're under
   c. to know what medical predispositions you may have
   d. to educate you on how to care for your family members

10. Multiple studies have shown results that adopted children share more personality traits with their biological parents than with their adoptive parents. How have researchers interpreted these findings?

    a. Genes have a strong influence on personality.
    b. Adoptive parents have a strong influence on personality.
    c. Mutations in genes have a strong influence on personality.
    d. Peers have a strong influence on personality.

KEY TERMS

behavior genetics, p. 323
genes, p. 323
environment, p. 323
chromosomes, p. 324

DNA (deoxyribonucleic acid), p. 324
mutation, p. 325
identical twins, p. 326

fraternal twins, p. 326
heritability, p. 326
culture, p. 331
norms, p. 331

The Psychology of Culture and Gender

Learning Goals

22-1 Define culture, and explain the factors that influence how cultures develop.

22-2 Describe the effects of individualist and collectivist cultures on sense of self, achievement motivation, and emotional perceptions.

22-3 Explain how culture influences personality, development, and parent–child attachment.

22-4 Describe the effects of ethnocentrism.

22-5 Define gender, and explain the factors that influence gender identity.

If asked, "What is your culture?" what would you say? Reading this module will help you answer this question.

Culture

22-1 What is culture, and what factors influence how cultures develop?

One of my daughters once brought home a note announcing Multicultural Day at her school. On the given day, she was to dress in clothes and bring food representing the country of her ancestors. Of course, the school was really advertising a *nationality* day. Nationality is not culture. Many nations, including the United States, have multiple, equally important, coexisting cultures. To say that your nation is your culture is to ignore the multiple cultures in a nation. Your passport does not always determine your culture.

Race is not culture either. First, two people of the same race can be either different or similar culturally. Second, the term *race* is becoming biologically mean-ingless because researchers have discovered that the genetic differences among people *within* a race are pretty much equal to those that distinguish people of two *different* races.[1] Your *race* is a set of characteristics (such as the amount of pigment in skin) programmed into your genetic code. Your *culture* is a set of behaviors and beliefs you learn from the people in your environment.

Race Is Not Culture ▶
Two people of the same race may have different cultures.

Tom Marvin/istockphoto

uriy/istockphoto

Ethnicity is a term that reflects the traits you have in common with some relatively large group of people with whom you share a history. Knowing a person's ethnicity or race does not provide meaningful information about how that person thinks and might behave. What do you know about me if I tell you that my name is Pat Dolan, I check the "black" box for race on government forms, and my ethnicity is African-American, Irish-American, and Cherokee? Could you predict my thoughts or behaviors? Surely not. What other clues might you pick up from knowing my culture? To answer that question, you must know more about culture.

Psychologist **David Matsumoto** defines **culture** as a system of subtle and obvious rules established by a group to ensure its survival.[2,3] These rules include the shared attitudes, beliefs, norms, and behaviors of a group that are passed from one generation to the next. Matsumoto sums up this definition by calling culture "the software of our minds."[4]

Culture is the basis for much of our understanding of life, influencing most of the daily decisions we make. It is reflected in the food we eat, the clothes we wear, the houses we live in, and the technology we use. The effects of cultural differences are also seen in our modes of transportation, family activities, and governments. Is culture also evident in religion and science? *Yes.* Although we never see culture itself, we see the manifestations of culture everywhere. How and why do so many cultural traditions develop? At least four factors influence culture development and diversity:[5]

- *Population density*—Societies with higher population densities require more rules for maintaining social order. For example, there are more traffic laws on the books in Los Angeles, with its four- and five-lane highways, than there are in my hometown of Broken Bow, Nebraska, which I think has about four or five stoplights. The laws in Los Angeles have become a part of the culture, reflecting a huge city's attempt to maintain order while letting people travel as they need to.

- *Climate*—Life-style adapts to climate. Weather affects the clothing people put on their backs and the food they put on the table. The life-style of a family living in a sparsely populated Iraqi village will be different from that of a family living in downtown Chicago. Each will need nourishment and protection from the forces of nature, but they will handle these needs in different ways.

DAVID MATSUMOTO (1959–)
Psychologist and cross-cultural psychology expert.

culture The shared attitudes, beliefs, norms, and behaviors of a group communicated from one generation to the next.

▲ **Climate Affects Culture**
Life-style and clothing, both of which reflect culture, are affected by climate.

- *Resources*—Working together to survive is essential in a land where resources are scarce. Teamwork is less likely to occur in places where resources are abundant. People in Afghanistan, where resources such as food and clothing are often harder to come by, tend to experience more close-knit local societies than their counterparts in France or England.

• *Technology*—Inventions such as computers and cell phones allow people to work alone, without any need for face-to-face interactions. The woman doing business from a personal computer in the basement of her Connecticut home will not have the face-to-face experiences of the woman working as a cashier at Walmart or Costco.

MAKE IT STICK!

1. Which of the following is best described as the traits you have in common with some relatively large group of people with whom you share a history?

   a. nationality
   b. ethnicity
   c. race
   d. multiculturalism

2. What is another word for what David Matsumoto describes as "the software of our minds"?

3. Teamwork is a necessity in areas of the world where resources are scarce. Groups of people who develop social rules that encourage cooperation are more likely to survive in these areas. This is an example of how resources can influence _____ development.

Individualism and Collectivism

22-2 What are the effects of individualist and collectivist cultures on sense of self, achievement motivation, and emotional perceptions?

ITSUO INOUYE/AP Images

▲ **Collectivist Societies**
People raised in a collectivist society are more likely to value the needs of a group over needs of the individual.

individualism Giving priority to personal goals over group goals and defining identity in terms of personal attributes rather than group identification.

collectivism Giving priority to the goals of the group (often the extended family or work group) and defining personal identity accordingly.

Do you see yourself as an independent person whose personal goals take precedence over the needs of others? Or do you see yourself connected to others, sacrificing your needs to satisfy the group? Your answer to those questions may reveal whether you were raised in a culture that values individualism or one that values collectivism. **Individualism** is a cultural style that places personal goals or needs ahead of group goals or needs. Individualists define their identity in terms of personal attributes rather than group identification. In an individualistic society, a personal achievement like winning a spelling bee is seen as something for the individual winner to savor. The winner is congratulated, given a trophy to keep, and perhaps a scholarship that belongs only to him or her. **Collectivism** is a cultural style that places group goals or needs ahead of personal goals or needs and defines personal identity accordingly. The spelling contest winner in a collectivist society is congratulated, but the winner's achievement is seen as more of a reflection of his or her teachers (and family) and a win for the school. Asians and Africans typically raise their children in a collectivist environment. Western Europeans and North Americans are usually raised as individualists.

Of course, not every culture can be classified as either individualist or collectivist. Therefore, it's more realistic to speak of an individualism–collectivism dimension, a scale on which you can indicate the degree to which your needs, wishes, and values reflect you or the groups to which you belong.[6] A teenager in Japan, a country with a tendency toward collectivism, would probably put group needs ahead of personal needs. Teens in the United States, a country with a strong tendency toward individualism, would probably place personal goals ahead of group goals. These different cultural viewpoints manifest themselves in a number of ways. One interesting study asked teenagers whether the phrase

"My parents will be disappointed in me" ever rings true as a concern. Japanese teens were three times more likely than their U.S. counterparts to indicate that this is a concern.[7] A comparison of individualism and collectivism can be seen in **Table 22.1**.

One advantage of using the individualism–collectivism dimension is that we can predict and interpret cultural differences without relying on an *impression* we have about a particular cultural group, perhaps based on something we've seen on television. Let's explore how this dimension affects cultural differences in our self-concept, motivations, and emotions.

TABLE 22.1 Comparing Individualism and Collectivism		
Concept	Individualism	Collectivism
Self	Independent (identity from individual traits)	Interdependent (identity from belonging)
Life task	Discover and express one's uniqueness	Maintain connections, fit in, perform role
What matters	Me—personal achievement and fulfillment, rights and liberties, self-esteem	Us—group goals and solidarity, social responsibilities and relationships, family duty
Relationships	Many, often temporary or casual, confrontation acceptable	Few, close and enduring, harmony valued
Understanding behavior	Behavior reflects one's personality and attitudes	Behavior reflects social norms and roles

Source: Adapted from Schoeneman (1994) and Triandis (1994).

Self-Concept

Your sense of self—who you are—is closely tied to how you understand the world and your relationships with others. The way we think about ourselves varies from culture to culture.

People raised in an individualist culture have an *independent* understanding of self. Most people from the United States have this independent sense of self. So, when asked to explain who you are, you are likely to discuss your individual preferences, abilities, and goals. You probably have a sense that you are *separate* from people relevant to your life. Indeed, I asked my two teenage daughters to explain who they are, and they said things like "I'm an AP U.S. History student," and "I play piano." For the record, there was also "I like pizza." These would be considered strange and inappropriate answers from teenagers raised in a collectivist culture. Those young people probably have an *interdependent* understanding of self. They see their primary task as fitting in and helping maintain cohesiveness among individuals in their group. They also have a sense that they are *connected* to other people. For people with this collectivist view of self, explaining who you are more likely includes a discussion of the roles you play within a group, and something about your family.[8]

Viewing your own abilities ("I play the piano") as the most important information you can offer about yourself is a characteristic of individualist cultures. Those of us who come from an independent culture also tend to explain other people's behavior in terms of their disposition ("He sure is cranky") and to ignore the effects of the situation ("He is recovering from surgery"). In contrast, members of collectivist cultures are more likely to believe their success in fitting in with their group ("I am respected by my family") is their most important characteristic and that behavior (such as responding angrily to a simple request) is guided by situational factors. Being raised in an individualist or collectivist culture influences more than our self-concepts. It also significantly affects what motivates our behavior and our emotional reactions.

Motivation and Emotion

How many times have your family and teachers urged you to excel—to be the best you can be or to strive to achieve your goals? *Achievement motivation* refers to this desire to excel, and it is very much a product of your cultural environment. Desire to achieve is rooted in the tangible personal rewards of achievement, which often means pulling ahead of other students. Individualist cultures, which view motivation as an internal push and achievement as an individual triumph, like achievement motivation. Collectivist cultures have different achievement goals, and they relate to enhancing the family's social standing. Desires to achieve emerge out of a sense of indebtedness to parents and are guided by the expectations of family members and other relevant people. Obligation to others or a sense of duty to the group drives this version of achievement.[9] For example, a researcher addressing why some students earn higher grades than others despite similar levels of intelligence would be wise to consider these cultural differences in achievement motivation as a possible factor.

But how can culture influence our emotional reactions? Consider this: How good are you at recognizing emotions? Can you tell when your friends are happy, angry, or embarrassed? Would you be able to recognize a more subtle emotion, combining compassion, love, and sadness? The Ifaluk of Micronesia can. They call this emotion *fago,* and they believe it promotes helping behavior. But a similar emotion, *ker,* combines happiness with excitement, and the Ifaluk view it as socially disruptive and dangerous.[10] The collectivist views of the Ifaluk likely colored their emotional expression and interpretation, just as our individualist views color ours. It's impossible to identify all the emotions that people around the world recognize, but isn't it interesting to consider that emotions exist that we've never been exposed to? Researchers have discovered that many emotions—including anger, fear, and happiness—are found in all cultures, but others, such as *ker,* are unique and identified only in particular cultures.[11]

Ted Horowitz/Alamy Stock Photo

Fago or Ker? ▲
This person is experiencing an emotion the Ifaluk of Micronesia might call *ker,* a combination of happiness and excitement they consider socially disruptive. Culture affects our display of emotion and our perception of it.

MAKE IT STICK!

1. A person who stays at home to care for his aging parents instead of accepting a scholarship to college may be expressing what aspect of culture?

   a. collectivism
   b. independent self-concept
   c. achievement motivation
   d. individualism

2. What kind of culture tends to highly value "be the best you can be" achievement motivation?

   a. collectivist
   b. individualist
   c. resource rich
   d. densely populated

3. True or False: Emotions such as anger, fear, and happiness are found in every culture.

Culture and Personality, Development, and Attachment

22-3 How does culture influence personality, development, and parent–child attachment?

We report results from hundreds of studies in this book. For example, we explore the circumstances under which people are likely to help others, the conditions that set the stage for obedience to an authority, and the situations leading to attachment between parent and child. Much of the research supporting these and other findings was conducted in the United States. Do the findings on helping, obedience, and attachment hold true in other parts of the world? **Cross-cultural research** tests hypotheses on many groups of people to understand whether principles apply across cultures. Psychologists who conduct research from this perspective travel great distances to study people in various settings. Cross-cultural researchers also run studies to obtain data from one cultural group and compare them with data obtained from another.[12]

Cross-cultural research often reveals that some psychological principles are *universal,* or true for people of all cultures. For example, all people use language to communicate. However, sometimes cross-cultural research indicates that psychological principles or behaviors are true only for people of a certain culture, making them **culture specific,** or *culture bound.* For example, in some cultures, it is customary to shake hands when greeting someone, while in others, people bow as a greeting gesture.

cross-cultural research Research that tests hypotheses on many groups of people to understand whether principles apply across cultures.

culture specific Principles that are true only for people of a certain culture.

Laura Natividad/Getty Images · RubberBall/Alamy Stock Photo · Nick Dolding/Getty Images · Joe Raedle/Getty Images

Universal or Culture Specific? Which of these behaviors would you find in all cultures? Which are culture bound?

Some behaviors can be viewed as both universal and culture specific. Suppose you are talking to a new student who has just moved to town. She looks down while you're speaking with her, avoiding eye contact. Eye contact is made once or twice, but is quickly broken off. Her behavior seems odd because you are used to looking people straight in the eye when you talk and having them look back at you. You wonder, "Is this person interested in our conversation?" or "Do I seem boring? What is up with her?" Perhaps you are so put off by this behavior that you avoid talking to this student in the future. At the same time, however, the other student is wondering, "Why are you staring at me? Don't you know it's rude to stare at someone while you're talking?" Obviously, the two of you come from different cultures: One culture says looking at someone while you talk is polite, and the other says not looking at someone while you talk is polite. Whether you gaze at the person while speaking is culture specific. However, the motivation behind looking or not looking at someone else, which is the desire to be polite to another while speaking, is more likely a universal principle.[13]

Cross-cultural researchers examine everything from language development to emotions and from child-rearing practices to psychological disorders. Let's see what they have to say about personality.

Culture and Personality

Many of the personality theorists from the previous century, including Sigmund Freud, Carl Jung, Abraham Maslow, and Carl Rogers, came from Western civilizations. All four saw personality as a relatively enduring set of behaviors and thought processes, stable over time and in different situations. But some cultures take a different view of personality. Cross-cultural research suggests that the concept of personality is culture bound, tied to the thinking of people in a particular culture.[14] In some parts of Africa, for example, people use a three-layer model to explain personality, which is different from the theories of Freud and Maslow. The three-layer model assumes that a person's personality will change according to the situation. At the core, the inner layer is spirituality. The second layer, around the core, is psychological strength. The outer layer is physical strength. Combine these layers, add a person's ancestral line, and you have another culture's take on what personality is. What's accepted as an explanation of personality in one culture may not hold true in another.

Western personality theorists also discuss the individual's **locus of control,** a person's perception of the source of control over fate or what happens in life.[15] Some people have an *external locus of control* (they believe outside forces determine what happens to them) and others have an *internal locus of control* (they believe they control or manage their own fate). Cross-cultural research indicates that culture affects locus of control. People in the United States and other Western nations are far more likely to have an internal locus of control than are their Asian and African counterparts.[16]

locus of control People's perception of the source of control over fate or what happens in life: People with an internal locus of control believe they control their fate through their behavior; people with an external locus of control believe their fate is controlled by external circumstances.

Developmental Psychology

Your development from the time you were conceived until this minute has involved physical, cognitive (ways of thinking), and social changes. Not only have you grown bigger and stronger, but you have also learned new ways of thinking and new ways of acting around friends, neighbors, and family. These broad statements are cultural universals, true of all children in all cultures. But how does the particular culture in which we're raised affect our development?

From a young age, we each learn and internalize the rules and patterns of behavior expected in our culture. Part of the socialization process includes learning what it means to be a boy or a girl, as we will explore in greater detail later in this module. But we also learn a wealth of other things, from how to greet an older person to how to play with friends. We learn these rules from sources such as parents, relatives, friends, television, the Internet, and schools. What we learn depends on where we live, and sometimes we adopt manners and ways specific to a smaller subculture. Perhaps you grew up in a culture where it is appropriate to pray before eating or to cover your head before leaving your home. Adopting these cultural rules helps us feel comfortable, knowing we are meeting the expectations of our group. These paths to comfort all disappear when we find ourselves in a situation with different cultural expectations. What if you grew up in Mexico City and then moved to Atlanta at age 15 to start high school? You would have to adapt to a new situation with new cultural norms. It might take you a while to figure out how to fit in and regain your feelings of being comfortable. When a family moves to a new country, the parents often worry that their children will forget "the old ways" and learn new and different manners or behaviors that will not meet with their parental approval. And often their concerns are justified; psychologists know that peer influence is powerful.

Let's turn now to what cross-cultural research can teach us about attachment.

Attachment

In the United States, we typically think of *secure attachment* (emotional tie) between infant and caregiver as the ideal bond. But not all cultures share this notion.

A survey of parents in other parts of the world shows that families from countries other than the United States do not necessarily value secure attachment. For example, German parents are more likely to see securely attached infants as "spoiled."[17] And traditionally raised Japanese infants often show a high degree of what U.S. researchers call "anxious unsure attachment" (where children act clingy and withdraw from others).[18] Japanese parents tend to prefer this type of attachment, believing that it fosters family loyalty.[19] Finally, there is the case of a forest-dwelling tribe, the Efe, who live in West Africa. Efe (sometimes still disparagingly referred to as "pygmies," a name the Efe do not like) parents often spend time away from their infants. They leave the children in the care of a variety of people. Even when in the care of parents, the children can always be seen or heard by around 10 others. Efe children show no emotional deficits despite having multiple caregivers.[20]

Peter Titmuss/Alamy

We need to be aware of the effect of cultural differences on attachment. The attachment pattern we consider "best" in our culture, whether we were born in Japan, Africa, or the United States, may not be best for all people. Different cultures have different values, and their preferred ways of raising children often reflect these values.

Cross-cultural psychology is particularly relevant to the study of development. As David Matsumoto explains, examining the socialization and development processes of other cultures helps us see who we are and how we developed into the people we are today.[21]

▲ **Learning New Rules**
Moving from one part of the world to another often means adapting to a culture that is different from the one you grew up with.

MAKE IT STICK!

1. After receiving the highest score on a test, Reesa said, "I studied hard and made sure I got a lot of sleep the night before." Reesa's explanation demonstrates that she has a(n)

    a. collectivist sense of her achievement.
    b. culture-specific idea about intelligence.
    c. external locus of control.
    d. internal locus of control.

2. According to the research presented, which statement about parent–child attachment styles is most accurate?

    a. Attachment is universal: Cultures around the world value the same things about the attachment between parents and children.

    b. Attachment is individualist: Cultures that value the individual over the group value parent–child attachment more.

    c. Attachment is culture specific: Different cultures think differently about what is the best kind of parent–child attachment.

    d. Attachment is collectivist: Cultures that value the group over the individual value parent–child attachment more.

3. True or False: Psychological principles or behaviors that are true only for people of a certain culture can be called culture specific.

Ethnocentrism

 22-4 What are the effects of ethnocentrism?

You turn on the television and start flipping channels. On one channel, the pope is addressing a large group of people outside the Vatican. On another channel, a parade celebrates Columbus Day. A third channel shows actors imitating past presidents, making these famous leaders look rather foolish. How do you react to these programs? Do you stop and listen to the pope or skip quickly to the next channel? Do you call a brother or sister over to watch the parade, or do you comment on how celebrations of Columbus Day are an insult to the Native Americans who lived in the lands Columbus "discovered"? Are you amused or offended by the fun poked at our past presidents? **Ethnocentrism,** the tendency to view the world through our own cultural filters, will surely affect your reactions. Ethnocentrism is not necessarily a bad or a good thing—it is just a reflection of the way we view the world. We all look at the world through cultural filters.

Our ethnocentrism shows up in the spoken and unspoken rules we live by and expect of others. When someone behaves in a way we do not consider socially appropriate or "normal," we often react negatively. Those who celebrate a holiday such as Christmas may avoid (perhaps not sit with at lunch) those who don't celebrate the holiday, perhaps even making jokes at their expense. As you might predict, we seem to see some of the strongest negative reactions to people coming from countries whose culture reflects a combination (language, religion, clothing choice) of differences that the majority of people in the community do not share. We may find refugees who have moved to the United States from war-torn parts of the world "peculiar" because of their dress, their mannerisms, and the way they speak, so we avoid them. In the United States it is common for people to take baths or shower every day, so citizens born here may be quickly offended when someone from another country unknowingly violates this cultural rule.

If people behave according to our cultural expectations, we say, "You all are good." But when others behave in ways we do not expect, or that are contrary to our beliefs, then we are more likely to think of these people as bad or weird. The problem is, our ethnocentrism makes us susceptible to making split-second judgments based on very little information about others that may not be fair or even true. (For more on becoming aware of your own ethnocentrism, see Psychology in the Real World: Acknowledging Ethnocentrism.)

Cultural conflicts will not disappear simply because we are aware of and study them, but we are better equipped to understand cultural differences when they occur if we have studied the importance of culture. Studying culture builds respect for, and appreciation of, all the cultural differences we will encounter in our everyday lives. Psychologists today are indeed more sensitive to culture's effect on experimental results and build measures into their studies that help ensure meaningful results. Cross-cultural psychologists hope to continue their work toward discovering both universal and culture-specific results in an ongoing effort to broaden our view of the field of psychology.

ethnocentrism The tendency to view the world through your own cultural filters.

MAKE IT STICK!

1. A hand gesture that means something in one culture but something different in another culture is an example of a _____ kind of behavior.

   a. culture-specific
   b. individualist
   c. universal
   d. locus-of-control

2. Accepting that we are all ethnocentric and that our cultural filters can distort reality is called _____ ethnocentrism.

PSYCHOLOGY IN THE REAL WORLD

Acknowledging Ethnocentrism

Although we are all ethnocentric to some degree, many of us are not aware of our ethnocentric tendencies. If you are unaware of your cultural filters, you are likely to develop *inflexible ethnocentrism*, which inevitably leads to problems in our multicultural world. Your inability to see beyond your cultural filters may create a wall between you and those who have different cultural viewpoints. Inflexibility discourages us from learning about other cultures in our states, cities, and schools. To counter these tendencies, David Matsumoto suggests trying to establish a *flexible ethnocentrism* when interacting with others.[22] Flexible ethnocentrism has the following goals:[23]

1. Accept that we are all ethnocentric and that our cultural filters vary.

2. Realize that our cultural filters can distort reality so that we see things only in a certain way.

3. Recognize and appreciate that people of different cultural backgrounds produce their own distortions of reality.

4. Learn to deal with our emotions and our judgments of morality and personality as a result of ethnocentrism.

How do you achieve that fourth goal? First, if you believe a negative initial reaction to someone may be caused by your own limiting ethnocentrism, try to put your emotional reactions on hold. Next, try to learn the other person's viewpoints. Finally, do not assume

mediaphotos/iStock/Getty Images

▲ **Flexible Ethnocentrism**
Moving beyond your initial emotional reaction is an important step in understanding people from cultures different from your own.

that you need to abandon your cultural filters to avoid inaccurate perceptions of others. Increasing your knowledge of other cultures allows you to *add* to your own filters, helping you see things from many perspectives.

THINK ABOUT . . . Psychology in the Real World

1. What are some of the things you can do to alter the emotions that might arise as a result of ethnocentrism?

2. Why is flexible ethnocentrism better than inflexible ethnocentrism?

3. How might you be able to tell whether someone is using flexible or inflexible ethnocentrism?

Culture and Gender

22-5 What is gender, and what factors influence our gender identity?

Now let's take a look at gender, another fundamental way in which we differ. The moment you were conceived, your sex was genetically determined. Whether you were going to be a boy or a girl was set by a single chromosome, as just 1 out of 46 chromosomes determines being male or female. Girls receive an *X chromosome* from their father to pair with the X chromosome from their mother. Boys receive a *Y chromosome* from their father to pair with the X from their mother.

When errors in the number of chromosomes occur, such as having an extra X chromosome (XXY) or missing the second X chromosome (X0), the simple genetic distinction between girls and boys can become much more complicated.

gender Our definition of male and female, based on socially and culturally influenced characteristics, as well as biology.

gender role A set of expected behaviors for males or for females.

gender identity Our sense of being male or female.

transgender a broad term describing people whose gender identity or behavior differs from that associated with their birth-designated sex.[34]

For example, some genetic XY males are androgen insensitive, making them resistant to male hormones, which can cause them to develop as female. If a chromosomally and genitally female is exposed in the womb to the level of testosterone meant for an XY male, she could develop male genitalia before and after birth.

Genetically speaking, girls and boys are far more similar than they are different. Of course, biological differences between the sexes do appear throughout the journey from birth to adulthood. Girls typically enter puberty two years earlier than boys and women outlive men by five years. Boys have more muscle and are, on the average, several inches taller than girls by the time they are done growing. Females are twice as likely to be diagnosed with depression. Boys are far more likely to be diagnosed with ADHD (attention deficit/hyperactivity disorder). Such biological differences exist, but not all differences between boys and girls are due to genetics. **Gender** is our definition of male and female, based on socially and culturally influenced characteristics as well as biology.

Whereas a person's sex is determined genetically, his or her **gender role** is largely a result of culture. Gender role is a set of expected behaviors for males or for females. Your sense of being either a male or a female is your **gender identity,** and your gender role arises from it. **Transgender** is a broad term for people whose gender identity or behavior doesn't conform to the sex assigned at conception.[24] So, how much of your gender role is due to society's expectations, and how much is influenced by biology? We can begin to explore the answer to this question by looking at gender roles inside and outside the home and at an example of a biological influence.

When I was born, my aunt and uncle gave me a shirt that said "Little Slugger" on the front. The same aunt and uncle gave my sister a little doll and a pink shirt that said "Princess." Clearly, gender expectations are expressed by friends and relatives at a very early age, based on whether the doctor announces, "It's a boy!" or "It's a girl!" upon birth. I'm no longer a "little slugger," but in my home, if wood needs to be chopped and stacked for the fireplace, I chop and stack it. I enjoy cooking, but when my girls were young, most of our family dinners were prepared by my wife. We also tried to share child-care duties equally, but I rarely bought our children clothing or took them to the doctor when they were sick. On this small, household scale, we all often behave in ways society says are appropriate, based on accepted gender roles. Is there a biological influence? Well, yes. I have more muscle mass, am stronger, and can chop wood more quickly and efficiently. So, our genetics did not determine who would cook or chop, but it influenced the culture we grew up in, which socialized us to believe that these roles are primarily male or female oriented.

Outside the home, gender roles play out on a much larger scale. Politically, over 80 percent of the world's nationally elected governing leaders are male.[25] Of the 195 countries in the world, only two countries, Rwanda and Bolivia, have a congress or parliament that is over 50 percent female.[26] Women have had an uphill climb when it comes to political power. When the twentieth century began in 1901, New Zealand was the only country on the planet where women could cast ballots in national elections. Women were not allowed to vote in the United States—let alone hold office—until 1920. Holding office in the U.S. Congress started out as a "males only" club. After the 2010 election, 17 of the 100 U.S. senators were women, and that number grew to 21 after the 2016 elections. This number denotes progress since 1920 but also shows how far our country is from electoral equality of the sexes.

Biological males tend to be more physically aggressive than biological females.[27] The aggression center in all human brains, the *amygdala,* is activated by the hormone

502nd Air Base Wing/Public Affairs/U.S. Air Force photo by Ismael Ortega

Fewer Barriers ▲
Roles for women are not as limited as they were when your parents were born.

testosterone, which is found in greater concentration in biological males. Does this biological difference show up in behavior? *Yes.* For instance, hunting is an aggressive act, and over 90 percent of the hunting permits issued in my state go to men. Fighting war is primarily a male activity.[28] Culture plays a role here, too. It's not that women can't physically pull a trigger, but culturally, men get the message that loading and firing a gun, whether for killing game or fighting in a war, is acceptable and in some cases encouraged. Perhaps the tendency to be more aggressive in the first place is a big reason why men outnumber women in the U.S. Army by about six to one.[29]

Socially, girls are more likely to play in a small group or with a single friend, while boys are often involved in a large group with a competitive (or aggressive) focus.[30] Females in their mid- to late teens are more likely to spend time on Facebook than same-aged males, taking more time to connect socially.[31] Men are more likely to use conversations to solve problems, while women tend to explore relationships in similar conversational settings.[32]

Let's take a moment to note, however, that whether in the workplace or in Congress, gender roles are forever evolving. The year I started high school (1976, for those keeping track), fewer than 20 percent of medical school graduates were women. Today, virtually half of med school grads are women. As you can see from **Figure 22.1**, the number of psychologists who are women has increased significantly this century, and it continues to increase. What's considered acceptable or even expected of males and females shifts over time. Power and status, whether you are former president of the United States, chancellor of Germany, the CEO of YouTube, or managing director of the International Monetary Fund, are more important these days than brute strength, and illustrate how both men and women are viewed as fully "capable of effectively carrying out organizational roles at all levels."[33]

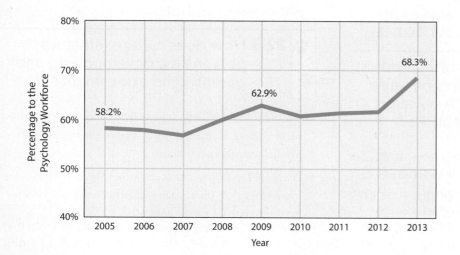

FIGURE 22.1
Women in Psychology
The number of women in the workforce with psychology-related jobs continues to rise. (Data from 2005–2013 ACS files from U.S. Census Bureau.)

Culture and Gender Learning to appreciate the ways we are different helps us understand and respect other people's behaviors, attitudes, and traditions.

So, the answer to the question of whether it's biology or culture (nature or nurture) that influences who we are is to be found by combining the two. Nature creates the biological differences (for example, the way testosterone affects the brain's aggression center), while cultural expectations amplify such differences. Our tendency is to fill the role, both in terms of our culture and our gender, that society supports. That said, we are human beings, not robots. Cultural influences like peer pressure or examples in the media can sometimes push us toward behaving inappropriately, but we are built to make choices. The decisions you make today will influence your environment tomorrow. Hopefully, your culture will help you make the right decisions.

MAKE IT STICK!

1. The name of the brain's aggression center is the _____, and it is activated by the hormone _____.

2. Men are more likely to use conversations to _____, while women tend to use conversations to _____.

3. True or False: There are more men than women in the U.S. Army, but there are more women than men in psychology-related fields.

Module 22 Summary and Assessment
The Psychology of Culture and Gender

 22-1 What is culture, and what factors influence how cultures develop?

- Culture is the shared attitudes, beliefs, norms, and behaviors of a group communicated from one generation to the next.

- At least four factors influence culture development and diversity: population density, climate, natural resources, and technology.

 22-2 What are the effects of individualist and collectivist cultures on sense of self, achievement motivation, and emotional perceptions?

- Individualist cultures place personal goals or needs ahead of group goals or needs, which gives people an independent sense of self. Collectivist cultures place group goals or needs ahead of personal goals or needs, which gives people an interdependent sense of self.

- Achievement motivation refers to this desire to excel and is a product of cultural environment. Individualist cultures view achievement as an individual triumph, and collectivist cultures view achievement in relation to enhancing a family's social standing.

- Culture affects our display of emotion and our perception of it in collectivist and individualist cultures.

 22-3 How does culture influence personality, development, and parent–child attachment?

- Cross-cultural research suggests that the concept of personality is culture bound, or tied to the thinking of people in a particular culture.

- People in the United States and other Western nations are more likely than their Asian and African counterparts to have an internal locus of control.

- The socialization process involves learning and internalizing the rules and patterns of behavior (cultural norms) expected in our culture.

- Culture influences the type of attachment that is valued and develops between parents and children.

 22-4 What are the effects of ethnocentrism?

- Ethnocentrism is the tendency to view the world through our own cultural filters. When someone behaves in a way we do not consider socially appropriate or "normal," we react negatively.

- Studying culture builds respect for, and appreciation of, all the cultural differences we will encounter in our everyday lives.

 22-5 What is gender, and what factors influence our gender identity?

- Gender is our definition of male and female, based on socially and culturally influenced characteristics, as well as biology.

- While sex is determined genetically, our gender roles are a result of culture. Biology and culture are both important in defining our gender identities.

- Gender roles change over time and across cultures.

Summative Assessment

1. What type of culture raises people more likely to value the needs of the group?

   a. collectivist
   b. individualist
   c. behaviorist
   d. impressionist

2. What has *cross-cultural* research found?

   a. All behaviors are culture bound.
   b. All behaviors are universal.
   c. Some behaviors are culture specific.
   d. No behaviors are universal.

3. What do we call the tendency to view the world from our own cultural lens?

   a. individualism
   b. collectivism
   c. mannerism
   d. ethnocentrism

4. What determines your sex at conception?

   a. a nucleotide
   b. an X or a Y chromosome from your mother
   c. an X or a Y chromosome from your father
   d. genes

5. What do we call the identification of male and female, based on socially and culturally influenced characteristics?

   a. attachment
   b. gender
   c. sex
   d. amygdala

6. What do we call the way we behave in society based on what society says is appropriate for our sex?

   a. gender role
   b. ethnocentricity
   c. gender identity
   d. culture

7. What biological pair influences aggressive behavior?

   a. chromosomes and DNA
   b. amygdala and testosterone
   c. nucleotides and chromosomes
   d. nature and nurture

8. What do we call the set of behaviors and beliefs learned from the people in our environment?

   a. culture
   b. ethnicity
   c. climate
   d. race

9. Which of the following is NOT a factor that influences culture development and diversity, as studied by Dr. David Matsumoto?

   a. population density
   b. climate
   c. resources
   d. individualism

10. Of the 195 countries in the world, how many have governing bodies (for example, a congress or a parliament) that are over 50 percent female?

    a. 120
    b. 95
    c. 40
    d. 2

KEY TERMS AND KEY PEOPLE

culture, p. 335

individualism, p. 336

collectivism, p. 336

cross-cultural research, p. 339

culture specific, p. 339

locus of control, p. 340

ethnocentrism, p. 342

gender, p. 344

gender role, p. 344

gender identity, p. 344

transgender, p. 344

David Matsumoto (1959–), p. 335

DOMAIN **5**

Cognition

Lucky Business/Shutterstock.com

Information Processing

H-O-M-E-S
Huron
Ontario
Michigan
Erie
Superior

SPRING FORWARD
FALL BACK

$5 \times (3 + 6)^2 \div (3 + 2)$

P-E-M-D-A-S
Parentheses
Exponents
Multiplication
Division
Addition
Subtraction

RIGHTY TIGHTY
LEFTY LOOSEY

M. SVTESKI

I bet you've seen memory tricks like these. The technical term for them is *mnemonic devices.* As you will see in this module, they are an excellent strategy for encoding information into our memory. Because the information is so effectively encoded, retrieval of the memory is easy. This module is filled with practical information for improving your memory.

Learning Goals

23-1 Summarize the factors that allow for effective encoding of information into memory.

23-2 Explain the differences between sensory, short-term/working memory, and long-term memory.

23-3 Summarize the factors that influence what we can remember and what we forget.

Information processing enables memory, a cognitive skill so important that it's impossible to imagine life without it. Before leaving for school in the morning, I need to remember to let the dog out. I also need to remember to put the student papers I read last night into my briefcase and take some ground beef out of the freezer for tonight's dinner. As I sit here working, I can remember details from my recently completed weekend. On Friday evening, I had great fun playing pickleball with friends. My wife and I went to see a pretty good movie on Saturday. The football game I saw on television was close enough to hold my attention all the way to the end.

We rely on memory all the time, and not just for the details of our daily lives. I need to remember who I am and what I stand for. I need to remember the norms our society has developed—the "proper" rules for behavior: what to do with my trash, how to order a meal in a restaurant, which side of the hall to walk on, and a thousand other guidelines that let us coexist in a complex society. I also need to remember how to cook, how to reconcile my credit card statement, how to wash my clothes, and how to program the alarm on my cell phone. And though I am not consciously aware of it, I even need to remember the meanings of words in my language and the processes necessary for walking or standing upright.

In this module, we focus on memory, using an updated version of a classic information-processing model.[1] There are certainly differences between how a human brain works and how a computer works, but they both process information in three basic steps (see **Figure 23.1**):

1. **Encoding,** or getting information into the memory system
2. **Storage,** or retaining information in memory over time
3. **Retrieval,** or getting information out of memory storage

encoding The process of getting information into the memory system.

storage The retention of encoded information in memory over time.

retrieval The process of getting information out of memory storage.

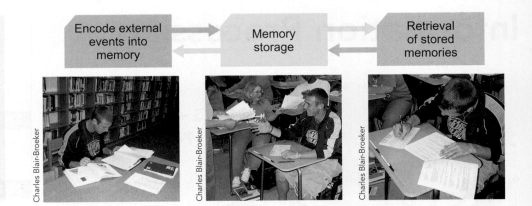

We can look at how these three steps work for computers as they process information.

First, nothing happens unless you can *encode* information, or get it into the computer. There are various options for doing this, but two common devices for encoding information are keyboards and Internet connections. Once encoded, the information must be retained in *storage*. Computers offer several kinds of storage, some more permanent than others. Temporary storage takes place in the active memory of the computer that keeps the various applications open on your screen. You know how temporary this memory is if you've ever briefly lost power while working on a project. More-permanent storage is available on the computer's drive. This storage can even survive the computer's "loss of consciousness" when it's turned off. Cloud storage is even more permanent—your work is still there even if the computer you did it on gets run over by a truck! But all this encoding and storage would be useless if you couldn't *retrieve* information from storage. If you're careful about setting up folders and subfolders, this can be a snap. If you're not careful, you can lose documents. You may know that you've stored your English paper, but if you can't recall what you named it or the folder in which you placed it, then you won't be able to retrieve it easily.

Humans also encode information. Instead of an Internet connection or keyboard, we use our senses to gather information. Then we must store the information, either temporarily or permanently. Finally, we must gain access to the memories we have permanently stored. Let's take a more detailed look at these three steps in the human system.

Encoding

23-1 What are the factors that allow us to effectively encode information into our memory system?

Encoding is the process in which you move information—the raw material, the stuff that you will remember—into your memory system. Good students are invariably good encoders of information. Fortunately, we can control several factors that influence how well we encode information. In this section, we examine the following:

- The role of effort in encoding
- The effect of the order of the information on encoding, known as the serial position effect

- The significance of how you space out the rehearsal of the information to be encoded
- The huge contribution of the meaning of information to be encoded
- The effectiveness of encoding visual images
- The use of mnemonic devices, or memory tricks
- The importance of organizing information to be encoded

Have you ever noticed that committing items to memory sometimes takes a heck of a lot of work? That brings us to our first topic, the distinction between automatic and effortful processing of information.

Automatic Processing and Effortful Processing

Automatic processing is the unconscious process of encoding certain information without effort. Have you ever had the frustrating experience of taking a test and being able to remember exactly *where* in your textbook the information is but not being able to remember the more important bit of *what* the information is? That's because we encode place information automatically (probably because it provides an evolutionary advantage—it's important to remember where threats in the environment came from, for example). We also tend to encode information about time (you can remember what time your friend called) and frequency (how many times your brother interrupted you with questions while you were studying) automatically.

Well-learned information can be processed automatically. (Compare how easily you can process information in a video game that you have played hundreds of times with how difficult it was to keep track of everything going on the first few times you played.) Unfortunately, when you're trying to learn the content of this textbook, you don't usually automatically capture *what* is written there. To master that information, you must engage in **effortful processing,** encoding that requires attention and conscious effort (see **Figure 23.2**). Research indicates that some processing strategies are more effective than others, and the most important one seems to be **rehearsal,** the conscious and focused repetition of information.

Hermann Ebbinghaus taught us much of what we know about the importance of rehearsal (which is another word for practice). Ebbinghaus, a nineteenth-century German philosopher, wanted data to support his ideas about memory. To obtain those data, he spent a considerable amount of time memorizing lists of three-letter nonsense syllables. If this sounds like nonsense to you, keep in mind that Ebbinghaus wanted

> **automatic processing**
> The unconscious and effortless process of encoding information such as space, time, and frequency.
>
> **effortful processing** Encoding that requires attention and conscious effort.
>
> **rehearsal** The conscious repetition of information.

> **LIFE MATTERS**
> We are not effective at multi-tasking or switch-tasking. 21% of teen drivers involved in fatal accidents were distracted by their cell phones. Paying attention to the road and texting a friend both require effort. Keep yourself and other drivers safe by putting the phone down while driving.

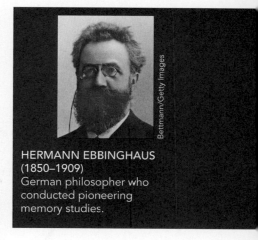

HERMANN EBBINGHAUS (1850–1909)
German philosopher who conducted pioneering memory studies.

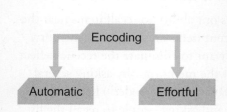

> **FIGURE 23.2**
> **Automatic Processing and Effortful Processing**
> Thanks to automatic processing, this student may be able to remember where in his textbook he found the information he needs to study with no effort. But he will have to pay attention and use effortful processing to encode the information he's trying to learn from the book.

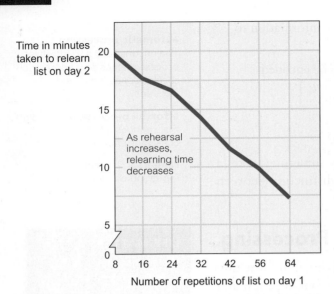

FIGURE 23.3
Rehearsal and Retention
Hermann Ebbinghaus discovered that the more times he rehearsed a list on the first day, the less time it took to be able to repeat the list with no errors on the second day. (Data from Baddeley, 1982.)

to memorize only unfamiliar items. His major conclusion? The more you rehearse, the more you retain (see **Figure 23.3**). Focused practice, indeed, does make perfect. In the years since Ebbinghaus conducted his research, psychological scientists have learned much more about rehearsal. One of the most important findings is that rehearsal that involves testing yourself over the material is particularly effective.[2–4] So, here's your first tip for becoming a good encoder: *The more time you invest in actively rehearsing and testing yourself over information, the more effective your memory will be.*

Another effective processing strategy is overlearning—continuing to rehearse information even after you have memorized it. Students who play musical instruments know they should continue to practice pieces that they can already play without error. And gymnasts know that they must continue to rehearse mistake-free routines to give their best performances in competition. Overlearning is just as important for course-related information. So, here's your second tip: *Continue to rehearse academic information even after you think you have it mastered.* This is one of the best ways to make sure the information is available under stressful test conditions.

Without question, then, rehearsal is important. It's not the only factor that influences encoding, however. Let's turn our attention to the serial position effect and see how the order of presented information affects encoding.

Serial Position Effect

serial position effect The tendency to recall the first and last items in a list more easily.

How many times have you taken a test in which you had to remember a list of items? Probably a lot. At such times, the **serial position effect**—the tendency to recall the first and last items on the list more easily—comes into play. Chances are good that you struggled most with recalling the middle items (see **Figure 23.4**). You may also have experienced the serial position effect if you were introduced to a dozen new people at a party. By the end of the evening, which ones were you most likely to remember? It's probably the folks you met first and last. Each of these conditions has its own term:

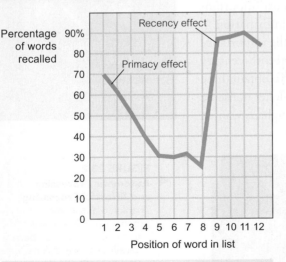

- The *primacy effect* enhances our ability to recall items near the beginning of a list. We have more opportunities to rehearse those first items. Memory researchers who want to minimize the primacy effect may present the list of items quickly, thus eliminating the opportunity to rehearse between items.

- The *recency effect* enhances our ability to recall items near the end of a list. The most recent items are freshest in memory. Memory researchers who want to eliminate the recency effect will delay recall or distract the memorizer by asking several unrelated questions ("What is your zip code?") between presenting the final items and asking people to recall the list.[5]

FIGURE 23.4
The Serial Position Effect
People given a list of items and later asked to recall the items had little trouble remembering the first few items (the primacy effect) and the last few items (the recency effect). The hardest items to recall are those in the middle. (Data from Craik & Watkins, 1973.)

Here is your third tip: *Devote extra rehearsal time to the middle of lists you must memorize.* However, it's not just the amount of rehearsal that's important. Our next topic shows that how you divide up the rehearsal matters, too.

Spacing of Rehearsal

The effectiveness of rehearsal depends on when you do it. More than 300 experiments on the spacing of rehearsal show *distributed rehearsal*—or spread-out sessions—works better than *massed rehearsal,* rehearsal packed together into fewer, longer sessions (cramming).[6] Consider the way performers practice. Do actors or musicians mass all their rehearsals for the week into a single, daylong session? No, because as the performers tire, additional rehearsal becomes less valuable. So, here's your fourth tip: *If you cram all your studying into one long session the night before an exam, then you will not encode the information as effectively as you would if you spaced your study time fairly evenly throughout the unit.* Even if you somehow manage to put in as many hours, you won't learn as much per hour. The research about distributed rehearsal is one of the most powerful arguments for the use of comprehensive final exams—reviewing the material from a course throughout the term enhances *lifelong* retention of the material.[7] And, speaking of final exams, there is evidence that if you continually quiz yourself on the material you are studying, the effectiveness of those distributed study sessions increases significantly.[8] By self-testing, you make sure you are actively involved with the material.

Now let's turn to one of the most important encoding factors. Once, when I was a high school junior, my English teacher made our class memorize a section of Chaucer's *Canterbury Tales* in its original Middle English. I had a horrible time with this task because I didn't know how most of these Middle English words translated into modern English. As we're about to learn, meaning matters.

Encoding Meaning

Rehearsal is central to encoding, but what's also important is how meaningful the information is. You might well think of rehearsal and how meaningful the information is as the twin pillars of encoding. If you're interested in cutting down the amount of time you spend in rehearsal (and what student isn't?), then your most effective option is to make the material meaningful, a process known as **semantic encoding.**

Research shows that when we encode according to meaning, we remember more effectively than when we encode either sounds *(acoustic encoding)* or images *(visual encoding)*. In one experiment, researchers flashed words to participants and then followed with questions that led to semantic, acoustic, or visual processing of information (see **Figure 23.5**). For example, to make participants process acoustically, the researchers might ask whether the flashed word rhymed with another word. To promote semantic encoding, researchers would ask whether the flashed word would make sense in a particular sentence. The participants remembered better when they had encoded the material semantically.[9] We now know that each of these types of encoding uses a different part of the brain.[10]

An excellent way to enhance meaning is to use dual coding. This method relies on having the learner formulate ways to make information visual. This could involve creating a timeline, diagram, graphic organizer, or cartoon. Creating an image makes information more meaningful.

Ebbinghaus himself estimated that it was *10 times* harder to learn nonsense syllables than meaningful material. This is why it is wise to search for meaning. So, here is your fifth tip: *One good way to add meaning to material is to use the*

semantic encoding Encoding of meaning.

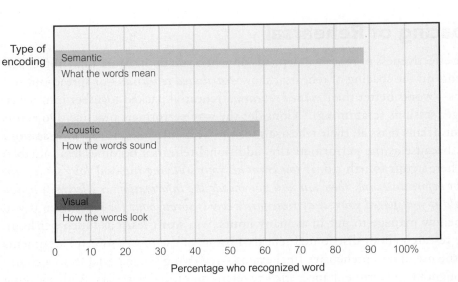

FIGURE 23.5
The Advantage of Semantic Encoding
This graph shows the results of a study in which researchers flashed words and caused people to process the words according to their meaning (semantic encoding), sound (acoustic encoding), or image (visual encoding). They found that people were most likely to remember the words if they had considered their meaning. (Data from Craik & Tulving, 1975.)

Type of encoding

Semantic
What the words mean

Acoustic
How the words sound

Visual
How the words look

0   10   20   30   40   50   60   70   80   90   100%
Percentage who recognized word

Image Source/Alamy Stock Photo

Practice Makes Perfect!
Whether in sports, music, or academics, more rehearsal leads to better performance.

LIFE MATTERS
Do you wait until the last minute to study for a test? Distributed practice is much more effective than cramming, but if you must cram, do it the night before an exam rather than the day of. REM is an important process in embedding long-term memories, and you will be more likely to remember information after a night's rest.

self-reference effect by relating it to your own life. Physics students in my school spend a day each spring at the amusement park. The principles of physics that make the rides both exciting and safe are somehow more meaningful—and memorable—when you're twisting through space on the roller coaster. Of course, you don't have to go to the amusement park to take advantage of this. If you can think about and imagine such connections, then any material will be encoded and remembered more effectively.[11] This is especially true in Western cultures like the United States, where there is a strong emphasis on the importance of the individual.[12] And meaningful connections are particularly easy to find in a psychology course because the subject matter—behavior and mental processes—relates to *you.*

When it comes to encoding, the old expression that a picture is worth a thousand words holds a great deal of truth. Can you picture the Rocky Mountains? The White House? Jennifer Lawrence? Let's look at the relationship between images and encoding.

Encoding Imagery

Encoding visual images is relatively easy. Visual images tend to stick in our minds, as you well know if you've ever struggled to rid your mind of the image of an unpleasant event. If you've seen photos or videos of the 9/11 collapse of the World Trade Center towers, the raising of the flag over Iwo Jima in World War II, or Neil Armstrong walking on the surface of the moon in 1969, you know how memorable these iconic images are. Images of positive personal events especially tend to stick in our minds. Do you have positive images of your elementary school days? For many of us, these happy snapshots overwhelm the less-pleasant aspects of grade school. The third-grade make-your-own-sundae party remains, but the day you suffered through class with a stomach ache does not. This tendency to encode images of the high points while letting the tedious or less joyous moments pass causes us to recall events—like elementary school—more positively than we actually felt about them at the time. Just think, this *rosy retrospection*[13] will probably apply one day to your high school memories! The tests, relationship hassles, and scheduling difficulties will likely be overwhelmed by more pleasant images.

Do you like tricks? Mnemonic devices can influence the encoding of information, too.

Mnemonic Devices

Which way do you set your clock for daylight saving time? To come up with the right answer, I remember "spring forward". When using a screwdriver, it's righty-tighty, lefty-loosey. I do well naming the Great Lakes, too, because of the acronym HOMES—Huron, Ontario, Michigan, Erie, and Superior. These are examples of **mnemonic devices** (pronounced nih-MON-ik), a formal term for memory tricks. If you recall that we encode visual images fairly easily, then you'll understand why so many of these memory tricks rely heavily on imagery. The method of loci and the peg-word system are two of the best-known image-based mnemonic devices.

Have you ever heard a speaker preface major points of a talk with phrases like "In the first place, I'd like to discuss . . ." or "In the second place, let's shift our attention to . . ."? Where are these "places" the speaker is referring to? They are in the imagination, and they relate to an old speaker's technique for remembering major points in the days before teleprompters. This mnemonic device is called the *method of loci:* You associate items you want to remember with imaginary places. Suppose I want to remember to remind my classes of an upcoming assignment for a day when I'll miss class because of a teacher's conference. To use the method of loci, I might imagine my living room, with student papers strewn all over my couch, waiting to be corrected. I could "see" myself trying to enter the room and tripping over a suitcase sitting by the door. Later, in school, I would return to this scene in my mind. The couch would remind me of the assignment, and the suitcase would remind me of the trip.

Another mnemonic device that depends on imagery is the *peg-word system,* in which you associate words you want to remember with a list of peg words you have already memorized. To use this memory trick, you would learn a set of peg words— words or phrases on which you can hang the items you want

► **The Power of Images** These images of historic events are memorable. Once you've seen them, you're not likely to forget them.

mnemonic [nih-MON-ik] device A memory trick or technique.

The Mnemonic Plague.

One is a bun. Two is a shoe. Three is a tree. Four is a door. Five is a hive.

Six is a pile of sticks. Seven is heaven. Eight is a gate. Nine is a line. Ten is a hen.

to remember (see **Figure 23.6**). The more striking and unusual the image, the less likely you are to forget the item. For example, assume that the first item I want to remember is carrots, and my peg for Item 1 is *bun.* To come up with a vivid image linking carrots and buns, I could imagine a steaming hot carrot in a hot dog bun and see myself adding ketchup, mustard, onions, and relish before taking a big, delicious bite. Then I'd associate my second item with the peg *shoe,* and so on. You are right if you're thinking this is a lot of effort, but memories encoded with the peg-word system can last a long time. When I use it to teach a 10-item list to my students, they can usually recall the list perfectly more than a month later. So, here's your sixth encoding tip: *Memory tricks like the method of loci and the peg-word system can create vivid images that you won't easily forget.*

Have you ever wasted time because you could not find your keys, your homework assignment, or your flip-flops? Just as getting organized is important in day-to-day life, it's important for encoding information, too.

Organizing Information

I happened to stumble upon a NASCAR race on television the other day and was amazed by the efficiency of the pit crews. They were able to accomplish more in a few seconds than my local mechanic can do in an hour. Many factors help explain this, not the least of which is organization. Each member of the pit crew plays a meaningful role in a highly organized structure designed to produce maximum efficiency.

chunking Organizing information into meaningful units.

Here's your seventh tip for becoming a successful encoder: *You can encode more efficiently if you take a few moments to organize your information first.* Organizing information into meaningful units is called **chunking.** You can encode many more letters if they are organized into meaningful words and sentences than you can if they are just randomly grouped (see **Figure 23.7**).

Organizing information into a *hierarchy* is another effective encoding technique. Hierarchies are organizational systems that focus on the relationships between pieces of information. The most familiar example of a hierarchical organization is an outline, which you've probably done for papers or other assignments. By indenting subpoints beneath main points, you get a sense of how each piece of information relates to the rest of the information. Chemistry's periodic table of elements is another example of hierarchical organization. It is so central to the field that it hangs on the wall of every chemistry classroom and is

| ROW 1 | RNN TYW KTYU ACDF OAHNSOO RTA UO UCR OYO |
| ROW 2 | ASK NOT WHAT YOUR COUNTRY CAN DO FOR YOU |

FIGURE 23.7
Effectiveness of Chunking
Give yourself 10 seconds to learn the letters in row 1. How well did you do? Now try row 2. Did you do any better? The identical letters appear in both rows, but they are easier to encode if they are chunked, or organized into meaningful units—in this case, into words and then into a meaningful sentence.

printed inside the cover of every chemistry textbook. Each row and column provides specific meaning to help the user know how the elements relate to one another.

One way to think of encoding is to consider whether your strategy is *shallow* or *deep*. Deep encoding involves processing information in a way that is rich and multifaceted. Adding emotion, imagery, personal connections, and organization are all ways to encode more deeply. The more deeply you encode, the more effectively you encode, so strive to create as much depth as you can when you are faced with memory tasks. Avoid shallow encoding as you review and master the tips on becoming a better encoder. The list is summarized next.

Tips for Becoming a Better Encoder

The goal of positive psychology is to achieve optimal human functioning. A good memory helps you function better and make fewer mistakes in virtually every aspect of day-to-day life. It's important to realize that almost everyone can improve memory skills by applying the principles of encoding that we have discussed in this module.

Here, in one place, are the seven encoding tips that have been presented in this module. Think about each one in relation to your own study skills. Are there a couple you can focus on to improve your memory and become a better student?

1. *Rehearse*—The more time you invest in rehearsing, and especially testing yourself over information you're trying to learn, the more effective your memory is going to be.

2. *Overlearn*—Continue to rehearse academic information even after you think you have it mastered.

3. *Overcome the serial position effect*—Devote extra rehearsal time to the middle of lists you must memorize.

4. *Benefit from the spacing effect*—If you cram all your studying into one long session the night before an exam, you will not encode the information as effectively as you would if you spaced your study time fairly evenly throughout the unit.

5. *Take advantage of the self-reference effect*—One good way to add meaning to material is to relate it to your own life.

6. *Use mnemonic devices*—Memory tricks like the method of loci and the pegword system can create vivid images that you won't easily forget.

7. *Chunk material or arrange it in a hierarchy*—You can encode more efficiently if you take a few moments to organize your information first.

MAKE IT STICK!

1. The _____ effect enhances encoding by making information personally relevant.

2. True or False: Frequent short study sessions are more effective than a few lengthy study sessions.

3. The ability to remember the first and last items on a list more readily than the ones in the middle is called the _____ effect.
   a. mnemonic device   c. serial position
   b. semantic encoding   d. distributed rehearsal

4. Associating items you need to remember with imaginary places is called the _____.

5. Which of the following does NOT enhance deep encoding?
   a. Imagery
   b. Repetition
   c. Self-referencing
   d. Mnemonic devices

Storage

 23-2 What distinguishes sensory, short-term/working, and long-term memories?

Storage is the retention of information, the very core of memory. Humans have three distinct storage systems, each with a different degree of permanence. We will deal with them in order from least permanent to most permanent: sensory memory, short-term/working memory, and long-term memory. Next, we will look at how your brain stores long-term memories and then explore explicit and implicit memories.

Sensory Memory

Our senses are constantly bombarded with sensory input. Consider how many objects are in view right now. If you're in a classroom, there are undoubtedly displays on the wall, scenes visible through windows (if you're lucky enough to have windows in your room), and people to look at. Each of those people offers much to see—facial features, hairstyle, items of clothing, jewelry, and so forth. And that's just visual input. What can you hear right now? Is anyone talking? Is there machinery operating? Is there music in your environment? Even a quiet environment might include the rustling of papers or the gentle sound of someone breathing. Add to this the smells, tastes, touches, and internal feedback on balance and position that you receive from your body, and it becomes obvious that we gather more information at any instant than we can possibly cope with or hope to use. **Sensory memory** is the brief, initial encoding of sensory information in the memory system.

> **sensory memory** Brief, initial coding of sensory information in the memory system.

We can hold visual information in sensory memory for less than half a second, just long enough to make a decision about its importance. We do this while it is in the *iconic store*.[14] (Think of the little pictures that constitute computer icons to remember that *iconic* is visual.) It is the iconic store that helps us hold one image in our visual field until another image replaces it. We hold auditory, or sound, information in sensory memory for perhaps 3 or 4 seconds, in the *echoic store*.[15,16] (Think of the word *echo* to remember that *echoic* is acoustic.) Have you ever been spacing out in class and had a teacher ask, with an irritated tone, "What did I just say?" Did you notice that you can generally retrieve that information, even though you truly weren't paying attention? Thank your echoic store for this ability.

Short-Term/Working Memory

Your **short-term/working memory** is more permanent than sensory memory. This part of your memory system contains information you are consciously aware of before it is either stored more permanently or forgotten. Short-term memory is referred to as working memory to emphasize the active auditory processing and visual processing that occur there.[17] In this way, it is similar to the active memory on your computer that allows you to manipulate and use several applications at once.

> **short-term/working memory** The part of your memory system that contains information you are consciously aware of before it is stored more permanently or forgotten.

Sensory memory is brief but huge. Short-term memory is far more limited because our consciousness itself is limited—we can attend to only a few things at one time. How many? George Miller established that short-term memory can maintain roughly seven chunks of information, or—as his classic research article put it in the title—"The Magical Number Seven, Plus or Minus Two."[18] In other words, most people can handle somewhere between five and nine chunks of information at one time. When my co-author spells his name for other people, he can run it all together: E-r-n-s-t. With a five-letter name, people have no problem maintaining the whole thing in their short-term memory at once. When I spell my name for others, however, I can't just run the letters together. *Blair-Broeker* contains 13 characters, including the hyphen, and that is enough to overwhelm short-term memory. I have to pause at least a couple times as I spell it if there is to be any hope of the other person getting it down correctly. Newer research indicates that the magical number may in fact be closer to four items in most cases.[19,20] The point is that we can only work with a relatively small amount of information at any one time. Notice that the capacity of short-term/working memory is a limited number of *chunks,* but you can hold chunks almost as easily as individual items. Holding five words in short-term memory, for example, means that you are likely holding more than five syllables and a lot more than five letters. Chunking is an effective technique not only for encoding but also for increasing the capacity of short-term memory.

What about the duration of short-term memory—how *long* can we retain information in this portion of our memory? About as long as you keep rehearsing it. If you meet a new and interesting person at a party, you will retain the person's name as long as you keep repeating it to yourself. But what if you become distracted? How long will the name stay? To answer this question, researchers presented participants with short, three-consonant groups of letters to remember. They then distracted the participants by giving them an arithmetic task that prevented rehearsal. As the results show (see **Figure 23.8**), short-term memory is indeed short term. Even though people had to remember only three consonants, these items disappeared from memory in less than 20 seconds when rehearsal was prevented.[21]

Short-term memory, with its limited capacity and short duration, is like a stovetop on which you're preparing your dinner. Having only four burners limits the number of dishes and volume of food you can cook. You also must pay active attention to the food you're preparing if you're going to avoid ruining the meal or burning down the house. All the rest of the food stored in your cupboards, refrigerator, and freezer—the food you don't need to pay attention to—represents our next topic: long-term memory.

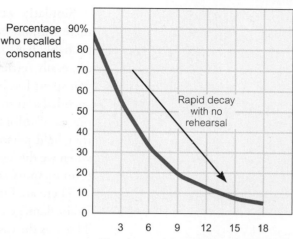

▲ FIGURE 23.8
How Long Does Short-Term Memory Last?
As this graph shows, when people are not allowed to rehearse, short-term memory decays rapidly. Within a few seconds, most people are unable to recall three consonants. By the time 20 seconds have passed, nearly everybody has lost their memory of the three consonants. (Data from Peterson & Peterson, 1959.)

Long-Term Memory

Long-term memory is the relatively permanent and limitless storehouse of the memory system. It can hold memories without conscious effort. Remember the computer analogy here. Short-term memory is like the active memory on your computer that allows you to deal with the various projects on your screen. Constant power (attention) is necessary to maintain short-term memory. What happens to your work if the power blinks off? It's gone! As a result, most of us have learned to save our work frequently (or rely on software that does it automatically). This means we make a more permanent copy of the project on the computer's hard drive or in the Cloud—methods that will retain the information even when the machine is turned off.

long-term memory The relatively permanent and limitless storehouse of the memory system.

Similarly, we can file information in our long-term memory and have it stay there without paying attention to it. It's available (we hope) when we want it. You probably have not been thinking about these bits of information, but I'll bet you can easily retrieve your zip code, the name of your English teacher, details of how you spent last New Year's Eve, and countless other facts and events that you have encoded and stored in long-term memory. Note that you effectively encoded these pieces of information either because you rehearsed them frequently or because they held personal meaning for you—two of the factors we identified as crucial when we discussed encoding. And now they are permanent residents in your long-term memory storehouse.

There are huge individual differences in the capabilities of long-term memory. Brain damage can destroy a person's ability to store memories for the long term. This was the case with a patient known as H.M. (identified as one Henry Molaison after his 2008 death), whose memory was damaged as an unfortunate side effect of brain surgery. He was able to retrieve long-term memories that were in place at the time of the surgery but could not store memories of any event after it. A researcher who worked with him for over 40 years after his memory was damaged said, "I've known H.M. since 1962, and he still doesn't know who I am."[22]

On the other end of the scale is the case of a Russian journalist known as S, later identified as Solomon Shereshevsky, who could effortlessly recall tiny details of events that had occurred years earlier. For example, he could recall strings of up to 70 digits that he had heard presented just one time. Once learned, he could perfectly recall the numbers even years later, along with details like the clothes worn by the individual who presented the numbers.[23] Perhaps even more amazing is the case of Akira Haraguchi, who recited from memory the first 100,000 digits of pi correctly on October 3 and 4, 2006.[24] Some people also seem to have a remarkable ability to recall their personal history, as you can see in Thinking Like a Psychological Scientist: What Were You Doing on November 4, 2008?

Long-term memory is as expansive as short-term/working memory is limited. What is its duration? Nobody knows for sure, but it's clear that humans can maintain memories for about a century. (Are you willing to trust your computer's hard drive to last that long?) Short-term memory can generally hold four to seven chunks. What's the capacity of long-term memory? Again, nobody knows. Like a sponge with unlimited capacity, your long-term memory can always absorb more, even on days when you feel you can't possibly take in even one more piece of information.

One especially interesting kind of long-term memory is **flashbulb memory,** a vivid memory of an emotionally significant moment or event. I have lots of these: driving home in my first car (a used powder blue 1965 Mustang GT); the sunshine briefly breaking through in the middle of our outdoor wedding; and being left in the hallway as they wheeled my wife in for an emergency cesarean section on the night our son Carl was born. Sometimes flashbulb memories center on a shared event. People in their 60s and older probably recall with amazing (but not necessarily accurate) detail what they were doing when they heard the news of the assassination of President John F. Kennedy. People alive at the time probably have flashbulb memories of the explosion of the space shuttle *Challenger* or of the September 11, 2001, terrorist attacks on the World Trade Center. For many, vivid memories of Hurricane Harvey will last a lifetime.

flashbulb memory A vivid, clear memory of an emotionally significant moment or event.

ROBERT J. ERWIN/Science Source

Clark's Nutcracker
Do you ever have trouble remembering where you left your psychology book or your wallet? Compare your memory to that of the Clark's nutcracker. It can remember up to 6000 places where it has stored seeds for the winter (Shettleworth, 1993).

THINKING LIKE A PSYCHOLOGICAL SCIENTIST

What Were You Doing on November 4, 2008?

What if you couldn't forget? What if every detail of every day of your life was accurately stored in your memory? For example, what if you could accurately recall that Barack Obama was elected president on November 4, 2008, and what the weather was like on that day (and the day before and the day after)? And you could also recall what you were wearing that day, and what you ate for dinner, and a conversation you had with your mom about a neighbor's birthday, and the silly joke your math teacher told during second period, and how much you paid for the shoes you bought in the afternoon? What if, in fact, you could correctly answer any question put to you about anything you experienced that day (or any other day)?

Amazingly, there are such people, and they have recently captured the attention of researchers interested in their *highly superior autobiographical memory* (HSAM).[25] James McGaugh, Larry Cahill, and their colleagues at the University of California at Irvine were intrigued when McGaugh received an out-of-the-blue e-mail from a woman named Jill Price:

> I am thirty-four years old and since I was eleven I have had this unbelievable ability to recall my past, but not just recollections. My first memories are of being a toddler in the crib (circa 1967). . . . [However,] I can take a date, between 1974 and today, and tell you what day it falls on, what I was doing that day. . . . [If] anything of

great importance (. . . The *Challenger* Explosion, Tuesday, January 28, 1986) occurred on that day I can describe that to you as well.[26]

McGaugh and Cahill were skeptical but agreed to meet with Ms. Price. Years of testing convinced them they were dealing with a form of memory that had never been identified before. Even people like the Russian journalist described earlier lacked the comprehensive, day-to-day recall that Ms. Price has repeatedly and reliably demonstrated. She has no special skill at memorizing poems or baseball statistics or the elements of the periodic table, but the details of her life, even the seemingly trivial ones, have remained with her for decades.

And she is not the only one. McGaugh and Cahill have now identified over 50 people with highly superior autobiographical memory, including actress Marilu Henner.[27] This form of memory is obviously not common, but we really do not know yet how many people possess it. They do not seem to be above average in intelligence, nor do they excel at other aspects of memory—only at accurately remembering details of their personal lives. More importantly, we don't know how the brains of these extraordinary individuals accomplish it. They have identified some ways in which their brains are different, and there are some trait differences between the super-rememberers and control groups, but they really don't know if the differences are the causes of their memory skills or the result of them.[28]

Dan Tuffs/Getty Images

Chris Pizzello/AP Images

Highly Superior Autobiographical Memory School administrator Jill Price and actress Marilu Henner live very different lives, but they have one remarkable thing in common: Each can remember virtually every detail of every day of her adult life. Studying them and other individuals with this type of super memory may increase our understanding of how memory works.

(Continued)

THINKING LIKE A PSYCHOLOGICAL SCIENTIST (Continued)

McGaugh, Cahill, and their colleagues are memory experts. Now, because of an unexpected e-mail message, they are exploring the hows and whys of a previously unknown phenomenon. We do not know what they will find, but we do know that the path they have started down is a fascinating—and memorable—example of the process of scientific discovery.

THINK ABOUT . . . Psychological Science

1. What is superior autobiographical memory?

2. How could you verify that someone who claimed to have superior autobiographical memory was telling the truth?

3. Would you want to have superior autobiographical memory? What are some of the benefits and drawbacks?

Memory and the Brain

How, exactly, does the brain go about storing long-term memories? This mystery has occupied scientists for decades, but in the past several years, researchers have uncovered some important clues. We now know that our brain does not function like a tape recorder, holding permanent, accurate records of every experience, ready to be played back if the right button is pushed. Current memory research indicates that memories are constructed from myriad bits and pieces of information.[29,30] Our brain *builds* our memories, just as you would assemble a jigsaw puzzle. When pieces are missing, we invent new ones to fill in the spaces. Because of this, some of our memories are accurate and others are way off.

Another important clue to how memories are stored is that each memory appears to activate a particular specific pattern of firing in brain cells—neurons. The key to the process lies in the synapses that form the connecting points between the neurons. As the sequence of neurons that represents a particular memory fires repeatedly, the synapses between these neurons become more efficient, a process known as **long-term potentiation** (see **Figure 23.9**). Learning and memory stimulate the neurons to release chemicals (primarily the neurotransmitter serotonin) at the synapses, making it easier for the neurons to fire again in the future.[31,32] The tracks formed in your brain are almost like a trail blazed through deep snow from a cabin to the woodpile. With each repeated trip, the trail becomes easier to follow.

The concept of long-term potentiation helps explain several other memory phenomena. A variety of things, including a blow to the head, can disrupt neural function and the formation of new memories. This is why football players who have suffered concussions may have trouble remembering the play during which the injury occurred.[33] Drugs can also enhance or disrupt memories by

long-term potentiation
An increase in a synapse's firing efficiency that occurs when the sequence of neurons that represents a particular memory fires repeatedly; believed to be the neural basis of learning and memory.

FIGURE 23.9
Growing a Memory
These two electron microscope images show one way that long-term potentiation makes a synapse more efficient. The left image, before long-term potentiation, shows only one receptor site (gray shows the receiving neuron). The right image shows two receptor sites. This dual target increases the likelihood that a message from the sending neuron will make it across the synapse to the receiving neuron. The growth of the second site is an indication that something may have been learned and remembered.

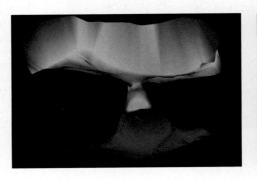
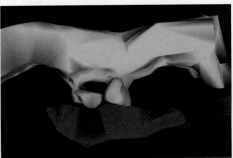

From N. Toni, et al., Nature, 402, Nov. 25, 1999. Dominique Muller

interacting with the neurotransmitters necessary for long-term potentiation. Alcohol is one such drug, which accounts for the alcohol-induced memory blackout that often accompanies a night of heavy drinking.[34]

Stress hormones also affect memory. Do you think they disrupt or enhance the ability to form long-term memories? Here's a hint: Stress is often the body's response to danger. It is important that we retain details of dangerous situations so that we can protect ourselves in the future. It's not surprising, then, that stress enhances memories. The hormones tell your body that something significant is happening, and they trigger biological changes that stimulate the formation of memories. People given a drug to block the effect of hormones in a stressful situation tend to remember fewer details of an upsetting story than their counterparts who did not receive the drug.[35] The part of the brain that processes stress-induced emotion activates the region responsible for forming memories and enhances its ability to function.[36,37]

▶ **Stress and Memory**
Stressful events, such as this car accident, stimulate the release of stress hormones that enhance the formation of memories. These drivers are not likely to forget this day. Such memories may help encourage defensive driving in the future.

Explicit and Implicit Memories

Let's examine one last aspect of long-term memory. There are many types of memories, but one major division separates explicit memory from implicit memory (see **Figure 23.10**). **Explicit memory** is what we normally think of when we think of memory: the recall of facts and experiences. At what temperature does water freeze? Where did you eat dinner last night? What is your mother's middle name? Answering

explicit memory The memory of facts and experiences.

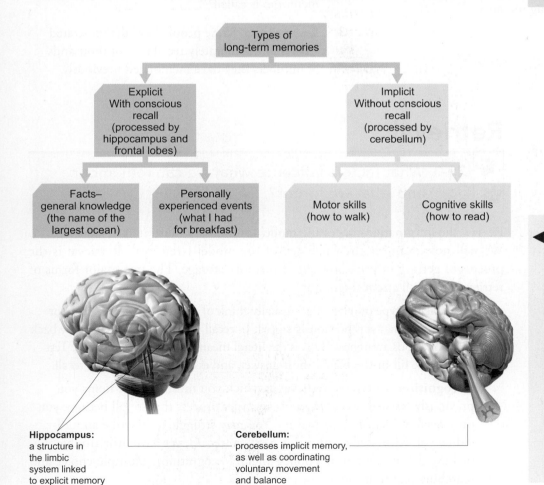

Hippocampus:
a structure in the limbic system linked to explicit memory

Cerebellum:
processes implicit memory, as well as coordinating voluntary movement and balance

◀ **FIGURE 23.10**
Explicitly or Implicitly Remembered?
Long-term memories can be classified as either explicit or implicit. These two types of memories are processed by different parts of the brain. Explicit memories of facts and experiences are processed through the hippocampus, a part of the limbic system deep in the center of the brain. Implicit memories for procedures and skills, however, are processed by the cerebellum, a structure at the bottom rear of the brain.

implicit memory The memory of skills and procedures.

all these questions requires a conscious effort to retrieve and state information. **Implicit memory** is the recall of skills and procedures, like walking. It requires no such conscious effort. You don't have to think about how to ride a bicycle before pedaling off. Nor do you have to think about how to read or how to button your shirt. Your ability to perform all these tasks depends on memory, but it is implicit, not explicit.

Explicit memory and implicit memory appear to be entirely different systems, controlled by different brain parts. Explicit memories are processed through the *hippocampus,* a small structure located in the central region of the brain, and the prefrontal cortex, the most forward part of the frontal lobes.[38,39] Implicit memories are processed through other parts, including the *cerebellum,* the rounded structure at the bottom rear of the brain (see Figure 23.10). Odd things can happen because of this split. A man who experienced damage to the hippocampus, for example, would be unable to form new explicit memories, but his ability to form implicit memories would remain intact. What would happen if he went to play golf on the same course each day? He would have no explicit memory of the course—it would seem like a new place every time. His scores, however, would gradually improve over time because his implicit memories would allow him to get better at golf as he continued to practice.

MAKE IT STICK!

1. What memory storage system holds the information you are thinking about right now?

   a. short-term/working memory
   b. sensory memory
   c. long-term memory
   d. flashbulb memory

2. An increase in a synapse's firing efficiency that seems to represent how the brain forms memories is called _____.

3. True or False: Some people have demonstrated an ability to accurately recall tens of thousands of numbers they have memorized previously.

Retrieval

 23-3 What factors influence what we can remember and what we forget?

Review the information processing model for memory illustrated in **Figure 23.11**. We will now examine the final step of the model—retrieval. Retrieval is the process of getting information out of memory storage. The two major forms of retrieval are recall and recognition:

recall The type of retrieval in which you must search for information that you previously stored, as on a fill-in-the-blank test.

recognition The type of retrieval in which you must identify items you learned earlier, as on a multiple-choice test.

- **Recall** is the type of retrieval we usually think of as memory—searching for information that was previously stored. In recall, we are calling a memory back into conscious awareness. This is the literal meaning of the word *re-call.* Test makers use fill-in-the-blank, short-answer, and essay questions to tap recall.

- **Recognition** is a type of retrieval in which you must identify items you previously learned. Recognition is an easier process than recall because you only need to identify information. You may struggle to describe an individual you witnessed committing a crime (recall), yet have little trouble picking the person out of a police lineup (recognition). Multiple-choice and matching questions often test recognition.

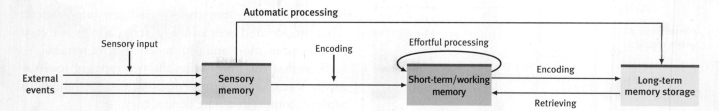

FIGURE 23.11
Information Processing Model
This figure provides a nice visual review of the information-processing model. Automatic processing can take place without effort. When effort is required, it occurs in short-term/working memory, the part of the system that involves conscious awareness. From short-term/working memory, information can be moved into and back out of long-term memory.

How do we get to the memories we need to retrieve? We follow pathways, often multiple pathways, that lead to the memory. When I need to contact a friend, I can do so by hopping in the car and driving to her house. If I'm less rushed, I can walk over. I can also text her, call her on the phone, find her on Facebook, or send a message via a mutual friend who I know will see her before I do. The point is, I have lots of ways to reach her. Likewise, there are many pathways I can follow to retrieve a memory. I can connect to a memory of, say, Mount Rushmore by remembering a family trip, by thinking of a TV show I might have seen, or by seeing a photo in a magazine. In each case, my memory of Mount Rushmore is primed, or triggered, by a memory retrieval cue (see **Figure 23.12**).

Memories weave a web of neural pathways inside the brain, and retrieval cues send us down one pathway or another in our search for memories. Have you ever noticed that the more you know about a subject, the easier it is to learn even more about it? Learning and retrieval build on each other. For example, if you know only one or two isolated facts about how the U.S. federal government works, you don't have much of a framework upon which to hang new information, but if you already know about the Constitution, the three branches, the role of the civil service, significant Supreme Court decisions, and close presidential elections, it

Courtesy Randal Ernst

Courtesy Charles Blair-Broeker

High School Days
Here is how my co-author and I looked when we were your age. Our present students might have difficulty identifying us, but our high school classmates would probably have no trouble.

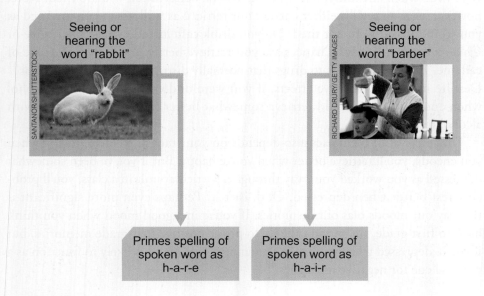

SANTANOR/SHUTTERSTOCK

RICHARD DRURY/GETTY IMAGES

FIGURE 23.12
A Hare-Raising Experience
If you show people a picture, you can activate certain associations in their memory pathways—a process known as priming. When you later ask them to spell a word that can be spelled in two ways (*hare* or *hair*), their response may reflect the content of the picture. Thus, a picture of a rabbit is likely to activate the spelling h-a-r-e. A picture of a barber at work is likely to activate the spelling h-a-i-r. (Adapted from Bower, 1986.)

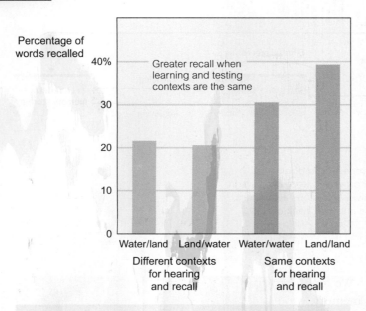

Percentage of words recalled

Greater recall when learning and testing contexts are the same

Water/land Land/water Water/water Land/land

Different contexts for hearing and recall

Same contexts for hearing and recall

FIGURE 23.13
Context and Memory
As this rather odd experiment demonstrated, retrieval is best when it occurs in the same environment where encoding took place. In this case, the context was either under 10 feet of water (while scuba diving) or sitting on the shore. (Adapted from Godden & Baddeley, 1975.)

context effect The enhanced ability to retrieve information when you are in an environment similar to the one in which you encoded the information.

state-dependent memory The enhanced ability to retrieve information when you are in the same physical and emotional state you were in when you encoded the information.

becomes relatively easy to integrate new information. This interrelated web of association allows for easy priming of memory and thus more effective retrieval.

Now that you know what the two types of retrieval are, let's turn to two factors that influence our ability to retrieve: context and state dependency.

Context

Context is the environment in which you encode or retrieve information. When you are in an environment similar to the one in which you encoded the information, you may experience the **context effect**—an enhanced ability to retrieve information more effectively. This happened when my wife and I visited a little town in Oregon where her family vacationed many years before. When we arrived, her memories began flooding back, and she was able to direct me to several landmarks around town. Returning to the context where she had encoded the memories primed the retrieval of those memories years later. One rather quirky experiment carried this idea even further. The researchers divided scuba divers into groups and read each group a list of words. One group heard the list onshore; the other group heard the list underwater (see **Figure 23.13**). Later, those who heard the words onshore recalled more of the words when they were onshore, and those who heard the list underwater recalled the words better underwater.[40] Any environment provides countless cues that can later function to prime the retrieval of memories.

State Dependency

Our ability to retrieve memories also depends on the physical or emotional state we were in at the time we encoded an event. **State-dependent memory** is the enhanced ability to retrieve information when you are in the same physical and emotional state as you were when you encoded the information. Strangely, if you were tired when encoding, retrieval will also be better when you are tired. Note, however, that you will neither encode nor retrieve as well when you are tired as you would if you were not tired. Do you drink caffeinated drinks, like coffee or Coke, when you study? Chances are you retrieve better under the influence of caffeine. This even extends to drugs that normally disrupt learning, like alcohol.[41] Despite its overall negative effects, if you were under the influence of alcohol when encoding, you would retrieve somewhat better (although not well!) with alcohol in your system.

The retrieval of memories also depends on your mood. If you're happy when you encode, you'll retrieve better when you're happy. But if you've been somewhat depressed as you worked your way through a particular unit in a class, you'll probably test better when depressed. Odd, isn't it? Perhaps even more significant is the way our moods bias our memories. If you're in a good mood when you think back to first grade, the mood is likely to prime positive first-grade memories, but if you're depressed when you try to remember, your mood is likely to function as a retrieval cue for negative memories.[42]

Lose your memories, and you've lost your sense of self. Without the past, both joy and sadness would be fleeting, and our world would be shallow indeed. We would have no way to connect events, and we would be unable to learn anything. Our waking hours are a constant progression of encoding important information into memory, storing countless pieces of information on both a short-term and a long-term basis, and retrieving needed information from long-term storage. If you remember nothing else about this topic, remember the remarkable, amazing role memory plays in our daily lives.

MAKE IT STICK!

1. How can context and state contribute to the retrieval of memories?

2. True or False: A multiple-choice test is based on recall retrieval.

3. Memories can be triggered or _____ by other memories or stimuli that lead you down the neural pathway to a memory.

Module 23 Summary and Assessment

Information Processing

 23-1 What are the factors that allow us to effectively encode information into our memory system?

- Automatic processing is the unconscious process of encoding certain information without effort. Effortful processing is encoding that requires attention and conscious effort.

- The serial position effect is the tendency to recall the first and last items on a list more easily. Distributed rehearsal works better than massed rehearsal.

- Semantic encoding is the process of making material meaningful. Visual images are often automatically encoded and remembered well. Mnemonic devices are memory tricks like the method of loci and the peg-word system. Chunking and organizing information into a hierarchy are effective encoding techniques.

 23-2 What distinguishes sensory, short-term/working, and long-term memories?

- Sensory memory is the brief, initial encoding of iconic (visual) and echoic (sound) information in the memory system. Short-term/working memory contains information

you are consciously aware of before it is stored more permanently or forgotten. Long-term memory is the relatively permanent and limitless storehouse of the memory system. Memories are stored in the brain through long-term potentiation.

- Stress hormones tell your body that something significant is happening, triggering biological changes that enhance memories. Explicit memories—recall of facts and experiences—are processed through the hippocampus. Implicit memories—recall of skills and procedures—are processed through the cerebellum.

 23-3 What factors influence what we can remember and what we forget?

- Identifying whether something matches information in our long-term memory (recognition) is easier than recalling information.

- The other major factor that influences what we remember is context: It is easier to remember information if we are in an environment similar to the environment the information was encoded in (context effect) or if we are in the same emotional and physical state we were in when we encoded the information (state-dependent memory).

Summative Assessment

1. Which of the following sequences is in the correct order?

   a. sensory memory, encoding, short-term/working memory, retrieval

   b. short-term/working memory, sensory memory, encoding, retrieval

   c. short-term/working memory, encoding, sensory memory, retrieval

   d. encoding, sensory memory, short-term/working memory, retrieval

2. Which of the following is an example of automatic processing?

   a. encoding your new password to your Twitter account

   b. encoding of where a particular photograph appears on the page of this textbook

   c. encoding of the three steps of the information-processing model

   d. encoding the names of your co-workers when you begin a new job

3. Hermann Ebbinghaus's research established the importance of

   a. mnemonic devices.   c. semantic encoding.

   b. the serial position effect.   d. rehearsal.

4. The self-reference effect is a tool used to improve

   a. semantic encoding.   c. chunking.

   b. distributed rehearsal.   d. mnemonic devices.

5. Which of the following is associated with sensory memory?

   a. the hippocampus   c. the echoic store

   b. long-term potentiation   d. recall

6. Short-term/working memory

   a. holds a lot of information and lasts a long time.

   b. holds a lot of information but only lasts a short time.

   c. doesn't hold much information but lasts a long time.

   d. doesn't hold much information and only lasts a short time.

7. A vivid memory of meeting the person who later becomes your spouse is an example of

   a. working memory.

   b. the serial position effect.

   c. a flashbulb memory.

   d. the iconic store.

8. An example of an implicit memory is remembering

   a. details of a trip to your grandparents' house last summer.

   b. how to walk.

   c. your cell phone number.

   d. how to change Wi-Fi networks on your cell phone.

9. What best explains the finding that if you always drink coffee while studying, you will probably do better on tests if you also drink coffee?

   a. state-dependent memory

   b. long-term potentiation

   c. implicit memory

   d. flashbulb memory

10. The cerebellum is involved in _____ memory.

    a. flashbulb   c. implicit

    b. iconic   d. explicit

KEY TERMS AND KEY PEOPLE

Forgetting and Memory Construction

Um, OK, where are my keys? And I can't finish this project without my calculator. Have you seen my coffee cup? Sure, I'll contribute a dollar to the food drive . . . if I can find my billfold, that is. Aw, forget it. Let's just move on to the new module.

Learning Goals

24-1 Explain how encoding failure can lead to forgetting.

24-2 Explain how storage failure can lead to forgetting.

24-3 Explain how retrieval failure can lead to forgetting.

24-4 Describe how memory construction can contribute to inaccurate memories.

"I forgot." When was the last time you used this simple, two-word phrase? Did it relate to a forgotten assignment? A chore you should have done? A friend's birthday? We all suffer from memory lapses fairly regularly. In this module, we'll see what psychology has learned about forgetting.

We process information into our memory through three stages: **encoding** (getting information into memory), **storage** (retaining that information), and **retrieval** (getting the information back out after it's been stored). When we say, "I forgot," we could be describing a failure at any of these three stages: lack of encoding *or* ineffective storage *or* inability to retrieve what has been adequately stored. Forgetting is complicated!

The types of forgetting described in this module are experienced by all people and are not considered disorders. Most of the disorders relate to forms of amnesia, an inability to form (anterograde) or retrieve (retrograde) memories. Amnesia can be caused by many things and can be either temporary or permanent in nature. Amnesia is one of the symptoms of Alzheimer's disease, a progressive brain disease usually diagnosed in people who are in their 60s or older.

encoding The process of getting information into the memory system.

storage The retention of encoded information in memory over time.

retrieval The process of getting information out of memory storage.

Forgetting as Encoding Failure

 24-1 How does encoding failure lead to forgetting?

The cafeteria in the school where I taught for 36 years is in the basement. Its roof is held up by a series of pillars. By the time students reached my class as juniors and seniors, they had been in that room hundreds of times, both for lunch

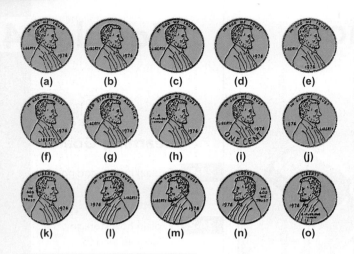

FIGURE 24.1
How Can You Remember What You Haven't Encoded?
Can you pick out the real deal? (See answer on page 372) Most of us can't because we've never bothered to encode this information. The penny spends just as well whether we can identify the correct version or not. (Data from Nickerson & Adams, 1979.)

and for study halls. When I quizzed them on the number of pillars in the cafeteria, however, only about a quarter of them could correctly recall that there are 11 of them. Students guessed as few as 2 or as many as 20. How can it be that these bright young people did so poorly remembering something they had seen so often? Despite numerous exposures to the 11 pillars, few students encoded this information into memory because it was unimportant to them. As long as there were enough pillars to hold up the roof (an issue of trust for almost everyone), they didn't care how many there were.

We all fail to encode information in our environment, as you will see if you try this simple quiz. On the back of a U.S. penny, you will find the value listed as one cent.

- What is the similar value statement on the back of a dime? How about on a quarter?

- Which way does Lincoln face on the penny—to his left or to his right? (After you answer this question, try your luck at identifying the real penny in **Figure 24.1**.)

- Finally, which way does Washington face on the quarter?

Think of how many hundreds of times you have seen and used these coins. Yet unless you have an interest in coin collecting, you may not be able to answer any of these questions. (You can find the answers when you turn the page.) You probably haven't *forgotten* the answers. Rather, you never bothered to encode this information because you weren't paying active attention and don't need to know these details to be able to spend the coins.

Encoding failure may contribute to the increasing forgetfulness some older people experience. As we age, the parts of the brain active during encoding respond more slowly.[1] Older people may forget where they left their eyeglasses or what time to take their medication because they did not succeed in encoding the information.

MAKE IT STICK!

1. Which of the following instances of forgetting is mostly likely caused by encoding failure?

   a. not remembering the name of your third-grade teacher

   b. not remembering how many windows there are on the front side of your school building

   c. not remembering the birthday of your best friend

   d. not remembering the main character of *To Kill a Mockingbird* after studying the book in class

2. True or False: Most Americans can accurately identify details about U.S. coins even though they're not sure about their answers.

Forgetting as Storage Failure

 24-2 How does storage failure lead to forgetting?

I've long been fascinated by the compost pile that we keep behind our house. A never-ending stream of grass clippings, leaves, weeds, eggshells, grapefruit rinds, coffee grounds, and other organic rubbish makes its way into the pile, only to rapidly decompose to a small fraction of its original bulk. Are memories like that, decaying like the material in the compost pile?

This idea of decay is consistent with the results obtained by **Hermann Ebbinghaus,** famous for his pioneering studies of memory.[2] His "forgetting curve" (see **Figure 24.2**) indicates that most forgetting happens rapidly and then levels off. Most memory loss occurs in the first few days (just as the most decomposition occurs early in the compost pile) and then slows considerably. More recent research has looked at the process of forgetting far beyond the 30 days Ebbinghaus examined[3] (see **Figure 24.3**). The researcher was interested in how well people remembered the vocabulary they had learned in Spanish class decades earlier. He found that most vocabulary was lost in three years, but that after that initial loss the forgetting curve leveled off. Words people remembered after three years were likely to remain in their memories a half-century later. The term **permastore memory** is used to describe these long-term memories that are especially resistant to forgetting and are likely to last a lifetime.

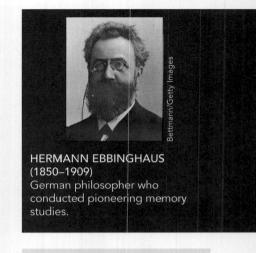

HERMANN EBBINGHAUS (1850–1909) German philosopher who conducted pioneering memory studies.

permastore memory Long-term memories that are especially resistant to forgetting and that are likely to last a lifetime.

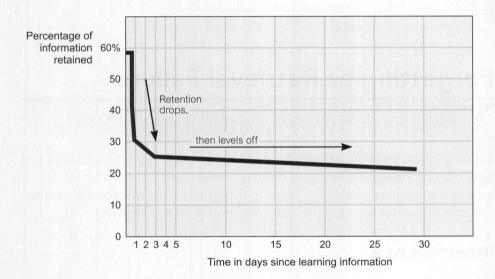

Percentage of information retained

Retention drops, then levels off

Time in days since learning information

FIGURE 24.2 The Forgetting Curve Hermann Ebbinghaus demonstrated more than a century ago that most forgetting occurs soon after learning. After a steep initial drop, we retain most of the remaining information. (Adapted from Ebbinghaus, 1885.)

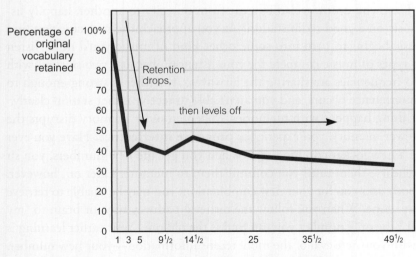

Percentage of original vocabulary retained

Retention drops, then levels off

Time in years after completion of Spanish course

FIGURE 24.3 Permastore Memory This graph shows how well people retained Spanish vocabulary they had learned in school a half-century earlier. Note that although the timeline differs, this forgetting curve has the same shape as the one in Figure 24.2, which Ebbinghaus identified. (Adapted from Bahrick, 1984.)

● Answer to the penny exercise in Figure 24.1: Penny (a) is the real penny.

● Answers to the questions in the list about coins on page 370: A dime reads "one dime," a quarter reads "quarter dollar," Lincoln faces to his left, and Washington faces to his right.

We still don't know enough about how long-term memories are stored in the brain to understand whether they actually decay with time. The work on permastore memory seems to indicate that some memories do not decay. It will be interesting to see whether future research demonstrates a change in the physical storage of the memories that decay. What we do know for sure is that we sometimes forget because we are unable to retrieve memories that are still stored.

MAKE IT STICK!

1. High school Spanish vocabulary is likely to be remembered for a half-century or more if a person still remembers it after

    a. 6 months.
    b. 30 days.
    c. 3 years.
    d. 10 years.

2. True or False: All memories eventually decay.

Forgetting as Retrieval Failure

 24-3 How does retrieval failure lead to forgetting?

Retrieval failure probably accounts for most of our forgetting. You've encoded and stored the information. It's in there, but you can't get it out. Sometimes this is true because the memory you're after is being disrupted by *interference*. Other times you may have a reason to not remember, creating *motivated forgetting*.

Interference

Interference
Have you ever had trouble figuring out which remote was for which device? Have you ever struggled to find an on–off button or a volume control because these functions are in different places on different remotes? Life would be simpler if we only had one remote or at least one layout for the buttons. Interference—both proactive and retroactive—causes us to struggle as we switch from one to another. ▼

Interference is a retrieval problem that occurs when one memory gets in the way of another. Have you ever traveled in a car from one city to another, happily listening to music on a good radio station? As you approach the new city, you find that the music begins to turn into some other kind of music you'd never listen to. The two types of music compete for your attention because two stations with similar radio frequencies are sharing the airwaves. If neither is strong enough to dominate, interference occurs, and you aren't able to receive either station clearly.

A similar thing happens with memories. When an older memory disrupts the recall of a newer memory, you experience **proactive interference.** Have you ever had to learn a new locker combination? When you get the new numbers, you sit down and rehearse them until you commit them to memory. Later on, however, when somebody asks you for your new combination, you may be unable to retrieve it by memory alone. When you follow the retrieval pathway in your brain to "my combination," the only number you can find is the old one. Your earlier learning is interfering with your retrieval of the more recent information—your new number. Here are some other examples of proactive interference:

Kelly Sillaste/Getty Images

proactive interference An older memory disrupting the recall of a newer memory.

- Remembering an old Internet password proactively interferes with remembering a newer password

- Calling out to your current girlfriend by using your *former* girlfriend's name (This actually happened to me when I was in high school—not a pleasant experience!)

- Remembering the word for something in the first foreign language you studied but not being able to recall the word for that item in the most recent foreign language you studied

You can also suffer from **retroactive interference,** which occurs when a more recent memory disrupts the recall of an older memory. I can remember the land-line phone number I had for more than 20 years as an adult. I rehearsed it so well and so long that I find it impossible to retrieve earlier phone numbers that I had for shorter periods of time. When I was in college, I easily retrieved my dorm phone number, but I no longer have any idea what it was. My newer phone number retroactively interferes with it. There are lots of examples of this phenomenon, too:

- Your memory of your class schedule for this year has overwhelmed the schedule you followed last year.

- Your memory of current sports champions (World Series, Super Bowl, NCAA basketball, and so forth) will probably displace memories of champions from previous years.

- You can remember the sequence of buttons necessary to activate your current electronic devices (cell phone, DVD player, and so on), but you probably can't remember how to operate the ones you had five years ago.

Interference isn't the only thing that interferes with the retrieval of memories. Sometimes we are motivated to not retrieve.

Motivated Forgetting

Sometimes, you have a reason to forget. The act of forgetting can provide protection from anxiety or from potentially distressing information. If you're trying to exercise more, those two days you were a couch potato last week might just slip your mind. If you're trying to cut calories, that candy bar your friend shared with you between classes may not make it into your daily calorie count. To remember these things would be to admit that you hadn't quite lived up to your goals. That's motivation to forget them.

Does scientific evidence support the idea of motivated forgetting? *Yes.* In one experiment, students took a study skills course in which they were asked to recall their previous study habits. They remembered studying less than they actually had, which allowed them to think the study skills course was more effective.[4]

There is less scientific support for **Sigmund Freud's** famous attempt to understand motivated forgetting through **repression,** the process of moving anxiety-producing memories to the unconscious mind. This, he thought, may be how we protect ourselves from painful memories, although the memories continue to lurk beneath the level of consciousness and can haunt us in a variety of ways. One goal of therapy, Freud thought, is to bring these buried memories to the surface so that they can be fully understood.

Many of Freud's ideas about the unconscious mind have worked their way into popular culture. Movies and novels often illustrate how repression is supposed to work. Despite the reality that there is little experimental evidence to support this theory, 90 percent of college students still believe that the process of repression protects people by pushing painful memories to the unconscious.[5] Actually, stressful incidents tend to stimulate the release of stress hormones that *enhance* the

retroactive interference A more recent memory disrupting the recall of an older memory.

repression In Sigmund Freud's psychoanalytic theory, the process of moving anxiety-producing memories to the unconscious mind.

Slavica/E+/Getty Images

▶ **Repression**
Sigmund Freud argued and some psychotherapists still believe that we block from consciousness—or repress—memories that could cause us anxiety. Research evidence is mixed on this issue, making the concept of repression controversial.

Macmillan Learning

SIGMUND FREUD (1856–1939)
Founder of psychoanalysis, a controversial theory about the workings of the unconscious mind.

encoding and storage of memories.[6] So, although we seem readily able to forget minor details when motivated, we are, unfortunately, more—not less—likely to remember painful events.[7]

MAKE IT STICK!

1. Sigmund Freud believed that _____ led to motivated forgetting.

2. Sara, a seventh grader, tries to remember the name of her first-grade teacher but can only remember her fifth-grade teacher's name. This is an example of

    a. proactive interference.
    b. the misinformation effect.

   c. motivated forgetting.
   d. retroactive interference.

3. Provide examples from your own life of proactive and retroactive interference. Explain what makes each answer proactive or retroactive.

Memory Construction

 24-4 How does memory construction contribute to inaccurate memories?

Many people believe that memories are like cell phone videos. As long as you can find the right video to replay, you can access the recorded memory. Not so. Retrieving a memory is more like building a jigsaw puzzle (see **Figure 24.4**). That's because of the way we store memories. When you commit an event to memory, your brain stores the memory in tiny pieces. Some pieces are invariably lost, so when you try to reassemble the puzzle, there are holes. Like a creative carpenter, your brain builds new pieces to fill those gaps. The new pieces may or may not represent what was there originally, but once they take their place in the assembled puzzle, you have no way of determining whether they are real or fictional.

Shall we try it? You will need a piece of paper and a pencil. When you're all set, give yourself 30 seconds to commit to memory as many of the following words and phrases as possible. Don't continue reading until you've spent your 30 seconds memorizing:

textbook, all-nighter, quiz, flashcards, review, lecture, vocabulary, GPA, outline, essay, notes, term, exam, due date, grading scale, assignment, unit test, memorize, class project, handouts, tutor, chapter guide

Now, in whatever order you can, and without referring to the original list, see how many of the words you can write on your paper. Take as long as you like. Then go back and check your list against the original. Chances are you will have remembered quite a few of the items. You are also likely to have left off some items—that was a lot to learn in 30 seconds. Now, without looking at the list, answer these four questions:

1. Was the word *lecture* on the list?

2. Was the word *grading scale* on the list?

3. Was the word *study* on the list?

4. Was the word *school* on the list?

FIGURE 24.4
How Does Memory Work?
Memory is less like a DVD or a computer hard drive than like a jigsaw puzzle with missing pieces. Your brain "manufactures" new pieces to fill the holes and construct a complete memory.

Study and *school* were not on the original list, but people often "remember" them anyway. If you said *study* and *school* were on the original list, you might be thinking that I fooled you. After all, these two words seem to belong on this list. That's just the point. As you struggled with the difficult memory task and the follow-up questions, you began to speculate on items that reasonably belonged on the list. Now you have a problem—which items were really there at first, and which were imagined? Your memory was constructed out of some things that were real and some that were not. Distinguishing between the real and the imagined words will now be difficult.

Psychologist **Elizabeth Loftus** of the University of California, Irvine, was the first to demonstrate in the laboratory this tendency to construct memories.[8] She and her colleague John Palmer showed participants a film of a car accident (see **Figure 24.5**). They varied the wording in their questions, asking one group, "About how fast were the cars going when they *smashed* into each other?" and the other, "About how fast were the cars going when they *hit* each other?" This seemingly minor difference was enough to produce significantly greater speed estimates by the "smashed" group. The researchers were able to alter memory simply by the way they phrased the question, and the participants were never aware of the manipulation.

ELIZABETH LOFTUS (1944–)
Psychologist at University of California, Irvine, whose research established the constructed nature of memory.

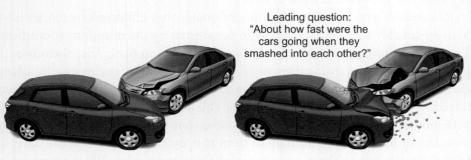

Leading question: "About how fast were the cars going when they smashed into each other?"

Depiction of actual accident   Memory construction

FIGURE 24.5
The Nature of Memory
What we remember depends partly on the wording of the questions we are asked. People who were asked questions about cars "smashing" remembered a worse collision than those who were asked questions about cars "hitting" each other. (Information from Loftus, 1979.)

Loftus and Palmer demonstrated another important aspect of memory a week later, when they asked participants whether they recalled seeing broken glass at the scene of the accident. The "smashed" group was more than twice as likely as the "hit" group to recall broken glass. There was no broken glass. The question led participants to construct memories of broken glass because this is a reasonable outcome of an accident, especially one in which the cars had smashed into each other. Incorporating misleading information into a memory, as occurred here, is known as the **misinformation effect.**

Hundreds of experiments have verified the tendency to construct memories. Misinformation can cause a hammer to be recalled as a screwdriver and breakfast cereal to be recalled as eggs, among a myriad of similar transformations.[9] And the more time that passes before the misleading information is provided, the greater the misinformation effect will be.[10] Even asking students to imagine that something happened, like breaking a window with their hand, led a quarter of the questioned students to later recall the event as real.[11] This may be because imagining an event activates the same parts of the brain that would be activated by the event itself.[12]

Think for a minute about how important this finding is. If memory can be altered by the way questions are asked, this has major implications for courtroom testimony. A skillful attorney can actually change a witness's memory by carefully wording the questions, and the witness will probably be unaware of

misinformation effect
Incorporating misleading information into a memory of an event.

the manipulation. When you realize that eyewitness testimony is one of the most damning kinds of evidence in a criminal trial, you can see that everyone involved—particularly the jury—should be aware of the basic processes that control memory and forgetting. Inaccurately constructed memories help us understand why 200 convicts in one study were later found innocent by DNA testing. Seventy-nine percent of them had been convicted partially because of inaccurate eyewitness identification.[13] Psychology becomes especially relevant when it can help prevent the miscarriage of justice.

The media spotlight has been shining on two related areas of interest in recent years: children's testimony in alleged cases of child abuse and recovered memories of abuse. Let's look at what researchers have learned about these two important topics.

Children's Recall

Child abuse occurs with alarming regularity, and people who abuse children must be identified and prosecuted as the criminals they are. Yet as important as it is to punish abusers, we must also protect innocent adults from being falsely accused of crimes they did not commit—a situation that also happens regularly. When people are charged with child abuse, their innocence or guilt may be determined by the testimony of young children. Is such testimony reliable? Are children's memories accurate? Let's look at some evidence.

Researchers who have set out to intentionally alter children's memories have been remarkably successful, especially in demonstrating the misinformation effect. Two of the leading researchers in this area were able to plant false memories in preschoolers by interviewing them once a week for 10 weeks and repeatedly asking questions like "Can you remember going to the hospital with a mousetrap on your finger?"[14] Eventually, a large number of the children constructed stories that ended with mousetraps and hospital visits. The stories were false but convincing, and they were almost impossible to distinguish from true memories. Children can develop false memories even without repetition of the misinformation. When preschoolers overheard a false remark that a magician's rabbit had escaped, over three-fourths of them actually remembered having seen the rabbit when later asked.[15]

Researchers have established two general principles about children's memory (see **Figure 24.6**). First, children's memories grow more accurate with age. Compared with older children and adults, preschool-age children are more susceptible to suggestion—and therefore less accurate—90 percent of the time.[16] For example, studies report that younger children are more likely than older children to falsely report that someone had licked their knee or that something yucky had been put in their mouth.

The second and more important principle is that there are ways to minimize these false memories in children. The key is to eliminate the suggestibility and misinformation that can lead children, in their effort to please the adults asking questions, to construct false memories. One surprising example of suggestibility involved the anatomically correct dolls (dolls with realistic sexual organs) that investigators often use when asking children about possible abuse. The problem is that these unusual dolls, *in and of themselves,* may suggest to children that they should talk about genital contact. In one study, researchers asked 3-year-olds to use anatomically correct dolls to illustrate how they had

FIGURE 24.6
The Accuracy of Children's Recall
This adult is likely to obtain less accurate information from the child on the left because that child is younger. Older children recall events more accurately than younger children do. Children's memories are also more accurate if the adult uses words the child can understand and refrains from using leading or suggestive questions.

been touched during a doctor's examination. Although none of these children had been touched in their genital area, more than half of them reported such contact, apparently because these details on the dolls suggested to the children that such a response was desired.[17]

Knowing that young children are prone to constructing false memories, investigators should develop techniques to minimize the misinformation effect. Studies show that children's testimony is most likely to be accurate when the interviewing adult does the following:[18,19]

- Phrases questions using words the child can understand (Goodman, 2006)

- Has had no contact with the child before the investigation

- Uses neutral language and does not ask leading or suggestive questions

Even children younger than 5 years can provide accurate information if these rules are followed.[20] But if interviewers violate these rules, children may construct false memories. When that happens, it will be almost impossible to undo the damage and determine what parts of the memories are real. In most cases, children who construct these memories are sincerely trying to do what is right—there is no intentional lying involved.

▲ **Eager to Please**
Children crave the approval of adults. This desire to please makes it more likely that children will remember things the way they think an adult wants them to.

asiseeit/E+/Getty Images

Recovered Memories

Perhaps you know something about recovered memories from watching talk shows on daytime television. This issue has received a great deal of attention in such forums. Celebrities such as Roseanne Barr have claimed that, as adults, they recovered long-repressed memories of childhood abuse. They argue that the trauma of abuse caused the memories to be repressed—buried in the unconscious mind— only to be recovered when triggered by some event years later.

One indisputable fact is that childhood physical and sexual abuse occurs, with devastating effects on the victims. Beyond this, things become murkier. Many sincere, legitimate therapists are convinced that some of their patients have experienced such repression and that they have helped them recover these memories through therapy. Other psychologists are skeptical, however, and worry that well-meaning therapists are leading suggestible people into constructing false memories. Can research on memory help shed light on the truth? Let's break it down into two specific questions:

1. *Can repression of memories occur?* In other words, can a memory of a traumatic event be lost from consciousness? To find out, one researcher located more than 100 adult women who were documented victims of sexual abuse as children.[21] When interviewed, most women did recall the abusive event, but more than a third of them were not able to. Sometimes they recalled other abusive events or were confused about the event in question. Although the victims may have been too young to remember, this research at least leaves the door open—repression of traumatic events may be possible. And if it is possible to repress the memories into unconsciousness, it may also be possible to recover them.

2. *Can recovered memories be false?* Some therapists, unfortunately, use techniques that seem to increase the likelihood of false memories. As reports of childhood abuse became more common in the 1980s and 1990s, some therapists believed it was important to frame questions in a way that tapped into the possibility of repression. Patients were told that "denial"

PETE DASILVA/AP Images

Recovered Memories in the Courts

In 1990, Eileen Franklin was the major witness against her father, George, when he was tried for the murder of an 8-year-old girl. Eileen claimed to have recovered a previously repressed memory of George hitting the victim on the head with a rock, and he was convicted mostly because of this testimony. Seven years later the conviction was overturned after Elizabeth Loftus testified about the constructive nature of memory. The murder remains unsolved.

and "repression" could happen easily. One popular book suggested, "If you are unable to remember any specific instances . . . but still have a feeling that something abusive happened to you, it probably did."[22] The techniques used to "uncover" memories include hypnosis (creating a state of suggestibility and asking the patient about possible past experiences), imagery (having the patient imagine and try to re-create possible past experiences), and dream analysis (exploring the patient's dreams for hidden hints of possible past experiences). In each of these techniques, therapists make suggestions to their patients. We now know this can lead people to unwittingly construct false memories. The authority and prestige of the therapist make these suggestions even more powerful.

These two conflicting lines of evidence leave the recovered-memory debate mired in an unsatisfying and potentially dangerous lack of clarity. Memories may be created, lost, and recovered, which seems to suggest that therapy could be used as a tool to identify previously undiscovered cases of child abuse. However, recovered memories are often inaccurate, and memories relating to events that occurred before the age of 3 (before most people's brains have matured enough to be physically capable of long-term storage) are especially likely to be inaccurate. If a therapist suggests childhood abuse as a possible source of adult difficulties, this suggestion may function as misinformation that produces false memories.

Victims of child abuse have suffered tremendously, yet adults falsely accused of abuse based on the "evidence" of recovered memories have suffered, too. Families have been torn apart because of unprovable allegations of childhood abuse that may or may not be true. Perhaps psychological science will one day identify a more reliable way to sort out the false memories. For now, we clearly need to be cautious and avoid jumping to conclusions about recovered memories.

Maybe it is the mysteries of memory that make it so fascinating. Our memories have tremendous power to keep the past alive. They can also deceive us (see **Figure 24.7**). Even experts suffer from falsely constructed memories. Famous child psychologist Jean Piaget remembered in detail an attempt to kidnap him in a park when he was a child. He had for years been grateful for his nursemaid's efforts to successfully foil the kidnapping. But as an adult, he learned that this vivid memory was false. He had constructed it from a story told by his nursemaid, who later admitted she had lied about the kidnapping attempt. We are accustomed to dealing with fact or fiction, yet memory seems to be fact and fiction, with no clear way to distinguish between the two. Should we trust our memories? *Yes,* but we should also be aware that they are not always reliable.

**FIGURE 24.7
Don't Always Trust Your Memory!**
Why aren't memories more accurate? Many factors contribute to the complicated process of memory. When you consider all that can go wrong, maybe the remarkable thing is that our memories are as accurate as they are.

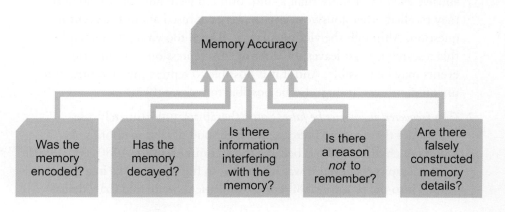

Memory Accuracy

Was the memory encoded? | Has the memory decayed? | Is there information interfering with the memory? | Is there a reason *not* to remember? | Are there falsely constructed memory details?

MAKE IT STICK!

1. Which of the following is the best analogy for memory?

    a. a cell phone video

    b. an encyclopedia

    c. a newspaper

    d. a jigsaw puzzle

2. Why are young children more likely than older children to have false memories?

3. Incorporating wrong ideas learned from others into a memory is known as the _____ effect.

Module 24 Summary and Assessment
Forgetting and Memory Construction

 24-1 How does encoding failure lead to forgetting?

- Some information cannot be retrieved because it was not perceived as important enough to be encoded.

 24-2 How does storage failure lead to forgetting?

- Some memories decay over time.
- Hermann Ebbinghaus's research indicated that most forgetting happens rapidly after initial learning and then levels off (the forgetting curve).

 24-3 How does retrieval failure lead to forgetting?

- Retrieval failure—caused by interference or motivated forgetting—probably accounts for most forgetting.
- Interference occurs when information you learned in the past interferes with the recall of information you learned more recently (proactive interference) or when information you learned recently interferes with the recall of information you learned in the past (retroactive interference).
- Motivated forgetting occurs when forgetting provides protection from anxiety or from potentially distressing information.

 24-4 How does memory construction contribute to inaccurate memories?

- Elizabeth Loftus demonstrated the tendency to construct memories, often falsely, because of the misinformation effect.
- Constructed memories and the misinformation effect have important implications for courtroom testimony, especially regarding the accuracy of eyewitness testimony.
- Studies indicate that children may be especially prone to constructed memories and the misinformation effect.
- Reports of recovered memories (adult memories, often of physical and sexual abuse suffered as children) are controversial, and memory researchers continue to try to uncover the truth about this phenomenon.

Summative Assessment

1. For a few minutes, Carlos couldn't remember the name of his math teacher from last year. Then, it popped back into his head. What is the most likely explanation for Carlos forgetting the name?

    a. encoding failure   c. permastore failure

    b. storage failure   d. retrieval failure

2. Georjeanna couldn't tell her friend what color the house on the corner was, even though she had walked by it dozens of times. What is the most likely explanation for Georjeanna forgetting the color of the house?

    a. encoding failure   c. permastore failure

    b. storage failure   d. retrieval failure

3. Sejal couldn't remember what she had for dinner two birthdays ago. All she could remember was what she ate for her most recent birthday dinner. Sejal experienced

 a. encoding failure.
 b. storage failure.
 c. proactive interference.
 d. retroactive interference.

4. Ebbinghaus demonstrated that most forgetting occurs within a few _____ after learning.

 a. days
 b. weeks
 c. months
 d. years

5. Permastore memory

 a. refers to the impact of very old memories on new memories.
 b. relates to encoding, but not to storage or retrieval.
 c. is an effective studying technique.
 d. refers to memories that are especially resistant to forgetting.

6. Repression is a concept popularized by

 a. Ebbinghaus.
 b. Freud.
 c. Loftus.
 d. Ernst.

7. Motivated forgetting is most likely to explain why we

 a. forget to include a candy bar in our calorie count when on a diet.
 b. can't remember information we studied for a history quiz.
 c. usually don't do well in classes we don't like.
 d. can't remember details of some things we've seen repeatedly, like the details on a dollar bill.

8. Interference relates to

 a. encoding.
 b. storage.
 c. permastorage.
 d. retrieval.

9. Which of the following has NOT been shown to enhance the accuracy of the results of adult interviews with children?

 a. using words the child can understand
 b. using anatomically correct dolls
 c. having no contact between the adult and the child before the interview
 d. using neutral language that doesn't suggest a particular answer

10. When therapists use hypnosis, imagination techniques, and dream analysis to help patients recover repressed memories,

 a. the accuracy of the recovered memories increases.
 b. the accuracy of the recovered memories increases for adults but decreases for children.
 c. the accuracy of the recovered memories increases for children but decreases for adults.
 d. any recovered memories are likely to be false.

KEY TERMS AND KEY PEOPLE

encoding, p. 369

storage, p. 369

retrieval, p. 369

permastore memory, p. 371

proactive interference, p. 372

retroactive interference, p. 373

repression, p. 373

misinformation effect, p. 375

Hermann Ebbinghaus (1850–1909), p. 371

Sigmund Freud (1856–1939), p. 373

Elizabeth Loftus (1944–), p. 375

Thinking

I know there is very little resemblance between Auguste Rodin's famous sculpture titled *The Thinker* and me, but it turns out that thinking is something humans are very good at. We make our share of thinking mistakes, but our survival as a species is largely dependent on how well we conceptualize and solve problems.

Learning Goals

25-1 Describe how and why we form concepts.

25-2 Explain the roles of algorithms, heuristics, and insight in problem solving.

25-3 Explain how fixation, confirmation bias, the use of heuristics, overconfidence, and framing can influence the quality of our decisions.

What is it that makes us human? Are there characteristics that separate us from other species, characteristics uniquely human that only we can claim? How about our thinking abilities? Indeed, in **cognitive abilities**—the mental activities associated with thinking, knowing, and remembering—humans have no equals. Consider that you spend your entire waking day in thought, from deciding what clothes to put on in the morning ("Does this shirt match my pants? It's cold—maybe I need a sweatshirt."), to making the judgments necessary for safe driving, to ironing out differences of opinion with friends.

We organize and process vast amounts of information with ease. The processing of sensory information—of depth and color, for example, and the monitoring of balance, body temperature, and other internal systems—often takes place subconsciously, without our being actively aware that it's occurring. On the conscious level, we turn our attention to solving countless problems in the course of a day. We exercise judgment regularly. We do make mistakes sometimes, but most of the time our thinking is remarkably accurate. Let's look at some components of thinking, a topic so central to psychology and being human that it has found a place in the title of this book.

> **cognitive abilities** All mental activities associated with thinking, knowing, and remembering.

Concepts

 25-1 How and why do we form concepts?

Psychologists define a **concept** as a mental group based on shared similarities. This definition differs from the more general definition of *concept* as an *idea* that we hear in everyday speech. Psychologists use the more precise definition of concept when they study the conceptual categories we form when we use our brain's built-in capacity to group objects, events, and people that share some similar characteristics. Your

> **concept** A mental grouping based on shared similarity.

Cartoon Stock

"YOU LOOK LIKE YOU HAVE A LOT ON YOUR MIND, JIM!"

prototype A typical best example incorporating the major features of a concept.

When Is a Chair Not a Chair?
We are quicker to recognize the item on the left as a chair because it more closely resembles our prototype than does the beanbag chair on the right. ▼

Purestock/Getty Images

Bambu Productions/Iconica/Getty Images

kitchen is more efficient with its various items sorted—silverware in one place, measuring cups in another. Your brain also sorts information into conceptual categories. You have a concept for trees, another for bicycles, yet another for balls. These mental categories let you make instant judgments about new objects you've never seen before. When you come across a new tree, you know as quickly as you perceive it that it belongs in the concept category of tree.[1] You know this because it is similar (a bark-covered, wooden cylinder with branches and needles or, in the right season, leaves) to other trees you have seen. Effortlessly grouping objects into concepts certainly beats wondering, "Gee, what the heck is that tall thing with the green top?"

Encountering new information for which you have no matching concepts is awkward. I can remember being invited to a friend's room during my first year in college. Steve had been given a beanbag chair. They had just been invented, and I had never seen one before. He said, "How do you like my new chair?" I actually argued that it wasn't a chair. My concept of chair included many kinds of chairs, but not beanbags. This glaring inability to classify the new object was memorable because we typically categorize almost effortlessly.

One of the ways we decide whether something belongs in a concept is by matching it with our **prototype,** a typical best example that incorporates the major features of a concept.[2] The closer the new object is to our prototype, the faster and more easily we can categorize it. We are quicker to recognize an oak tree as a tree than we are to assign a tiny Japanese bonsai tree to this category. Both qualify as trees, but the oak is much closer to our prototype—it is somehow more treelike than a bonsai (to us, at least; the Japanese bonsai grower might pause at the sight of a giant California sequoia). I struggled to identify my friend's beanbag as a chair because it was much further from my chair prototype than the desk chair and old armchair that furnished my dorm room. Some prototype biases are more serious. For example, we may not recognize an illness as quickly if the symptoms don't match our prototype for that disease.[3] This can be a fatal error for people who don't realize they are having a heart attack because their symptoms don't match their prototype for this condition.

We develop *concept hierarchies* to keep mental information organized. Consider our hierarchy for organizing food in our culture. We begin by learning basic concepts like bread and cake. From there, we identify more specific concepts that fit under each of the basic ones—bread includes white bread, French bread, and banana bread, and cake includes angel food cake, sheet cake, and cupcakes. Bread and cake, in turn, fit into the larger category of baked goods. Similarly, we can break the basic concepts of cheese and milk into more specific concepts (cheddar, skim) or lump them into a broader concept (dairy products). This organizational hierarchy, which we begin to build as we learn the basic concepts (bread, cake, cheese, and milk) as young children, helps us process information about food quickly and efficiently. Grocery stores organize their products to take advantage of our understanding of broad categories, such as frozen food and canned goods. We develop similar hierarchies to deal with concepts as diverse as tools, vehicles, and recreation (see **Figure 25.1**). Our brains have a strong tendency to keep information neat and tidy. Most of us organize our computer files in a similar fashion, with folders representing a few broad categories (school, music, pictures, and so on) each containing more folders with ever more specific topics. When you organize your computer's folders and files, you are creating a hierarchy. (I wonder why the one on my computer is less organized than the one in my head.)

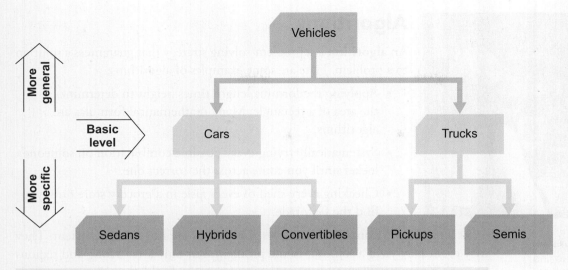

FIGURE 25.1
A Concept Hierarchy
Children use concept hierarchies to organize the world around them and learn about it. First, they master basic concepts (cars and trucks). Then, as their thinking becomes more sophisticated, they connect those basic concepts to both more general concepts (vehicles) and to more specific ones (hybrids).

MAKE IT STICK!

1. True or False: Concepts are useful for organizing information, but using them is time consuming and slows down cognitive processes.

2. Which of the following is a prototype for the concept "bird"?

   a. ostrich   c. penguin
   b. emu   d. robin

3. A concept _____ organizes information into more general, basic, and specific levels.

Problem Solving

25-2 What roles do algorithms, heuristics, and insight play in the solution of problems?

Are there enough problems in your life? *Probably so.* Problems exist when something blocks you from achieving a desired outcome. If you need to get to school but are caught in traffic, that's a problem. If you want a B in your psychology class but are 30 points short, that's a problem. Problems can range from trivial (deciding which playlist to queue up) to serious (figuring out what path will allow you to achieve your career goals after graduating). We all have several strategies we apply when problems arise in our lives. Many of these strategies fall into the broad categories of algorithms and heuristics.

Animals Are Problems Solvers, Too
Humans aren't the only ones who can solve problems. Many species of animals have demonstrated remarkable abilities to generate solutions when something blocks them from achieving a desired outcome. Two examples from the history of psychology are shown here. The photograph on the left shows a cat in a puzzle box designed by Edward Thorndike. Cats were able to complete a sequence of steps to open the door and gain access to food. On the right is Sultan, a chimpanzee studied by Wolfgang Köhler. Sultan, in a flash of insight, figured out he could stack the boxes and climb on them to reach a banana suspended from the top of his cage.

Nina Leen/Pix Inc./The LIFE Picture Collection/Getty Images

American Philosophical Society

Algorithms

An **algorithm** is a problem-solving strategy that guarantees a solution to a problem. Here are some examples of algorithms:

- Applying the formula length times height to determine the area of a rectangle. Many mathematical formulas are algorithms.

- Systematically trying every possible combination on someone's locker until you come across the correct one.

- Checking every shelf of every aisle in a grocery store until you find the Gatorade.

Algorithms and Heuristics
If your problem is to find a particular sports book as a gift for your younger brother, would you be better off systematically checking every book on every shelf— an algorithm—or starting in the sports section—a heuristic? If you're like me, you may even try another heuristic—asking for help.

As you can tell from these examples, algorithms are not always efficient. They may eventually yield a solution to the problem, but only after a long and tedious process. Knowing this, computer programmers may build algorithms into their software. The computers do the tedious work, and we benefit from the solutions.

Heuristics

A **heuristic** is a rule-of-thumb problem-solving strategy that makes a solution more likely but does not guarantee one. Here are some examples of heuristics:

- Using spelling rules such as *i* before *e* except after *c*.

- Checking the canned-goods section of a grocery store to find a particular brand of baked beans.

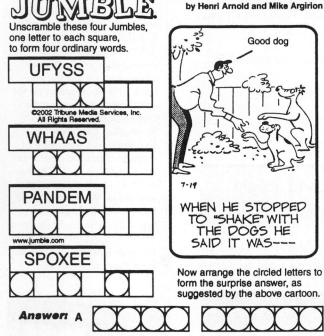

Heuristics are shortcuts. When they work, we are likely to reuse them the next time we need to save time and increase our mental efficiency in a similar situation. Unlike algorithms, however, there is no guarantee that a heuristic will produce a correct solution.

Insight

Have you ever spent time trying to figure out where you left your psychology book when—all of a sudden—it dawns on you that you left it on the counter by the refrigerator? Nice, right? These wonderfully rewarding moments are examples of **insight,** the sudden realization (Aha!) of a solution to a problem. Typically, the answer is just there, with no prior sense that it's about to appear.[4] Cartoons often express a moment of insight as a light bulb over a character's head. Insight is fun, satisfying, and one of the reasons most of us enjoy working on word jumbles and other types of mental puzzles—we experience a pleasing excitement when that answer pops

FIGURE 25.2
Insight
Enjoy the "Aha!" as the solutions to these jumbled words pop into your head (turn the page for the answers).

into our head (see **Figure 25.2**). Researchers have discovered that the brain areas involved in insight are different from those involved in other kinds of problem solving.[5] Chimpanzees appear to share the ability to form insights with humans. In one classic study,[6] a chimp suddenly realized he could stack several boxes to form a platform from which he could reach bananas that had been suspended from the ceiling (see photo on page 383).

MAKE IT STICK!

1. A(n) _____ for finding which key on a big key ring will start a car is to begin by eliminating all the keys that do not look like car keys.

2. A(n) _____ for finding which key on a big key ring will start a car is to systematically try each key in order until you find the one that fits.

3. Which of the following is an example of solving a problem by insight?
   a. Asking your friends to learn how they succeeded in a class with a difficult teacher.
   b. Unpacking your whole backpack to find a pen that you know for sure is in there.
   c. Trying several strategies to get your car unstuck from a snowbank.
   d. Suddenly realizing the perfect gift to get your mom for her birthday.

Problems Solving Problems

25-3 How can fixation, confirmation bias, and the use of heuristics, overconfidence, and framing influence the quality of our decisions?

> **algorithm** A problem-solving strategy that guarantees the solution to a problem.
>
> **heuristic** A rule-of-thumb problem-solving strategy that makes finding a solution more likely and efficient but does not guarantee a solution.
>
> **insight** The sudden realization (Aha!) of the solution to a problem.

Have you ever had trouble estimating how long a school project will take? Have you ever struggled to find a substitute for a broken shoelace? A variety of normal tendencies can hinder our ability to solve such problems effectively. Many of them give us tunnel vision, preventing us from searching for alternatives that might offer terrific solutions. In this section, we look at five of these tendencies: fixation, confirmation bias, inappropriate use of heuristics, overconfidence, and framing. Knowing about these pitfalls will help you avoid them and become a more effective problem solver.

Fixation

We have a tendency, known as a **mental set,** to approach a particular problem in a particular way. Mental sets are often helpful because they are efficient and may lead to a rapid solution. Chess players, for example, may have a particular move they like to open with because they have learned it usually leads to a win. Mechanics often use a particular approach when diagnosing and repairing engine problems. Technical support team members learn mental sets to help them help customers with computer problems. They ask questions designed to focus on specific problems, usually beginning with basic, but sometimes overlooked, issues. ("Is the computer plugged in?")

> **mental set** The tendency to approach a particular problem in a particular way.
>
> **fixation** A mental set applied so rigidly that it hinders the solution of a problem.

Sometimes, however, a mental set can get in the way. Instead of becoming an efficient problem-solving strategy, it becomes a **fixation**—a mental set applied so rigidly that it hinders the solution to a problem. Have you heard the expression "thinking outside the box"? It implies breaking away from routine, conventional ways of thinking—away from your mental set. Even though these old ways of thinking may have worked in the past, something new and different may now be required. Henry Ford was able to see that cars could be mass-produced by having workers specialize in a single task as an assembly line brought each vehicle past them. By thinking outside the box, he was able to manufacture cars far more cheaply than he could have if a small team of individuals had built one car at a

FIGURE 25.3
The Luchins Water Jar Problem
Can you measure out the amount of water in the right-hand column, using any of the three jars (A, B, and C) with volumes as shown in the middle column? A solution appears as Figure 25.6 on the next page. (Data from Luchins, 1946.)

Problem	Given jugs of these sizes			Measure out this much water
	A	B	C	
1	21	127	3	100
2	14	46	5	22
3	18	43	10	5
4	7	42	6	23
5	20	57	4	29
6	23	49	3	20
7	15	39	3	18

functional fixedness The tendency to think of things only in terms of their usual functions.

● Answers to Jumble puzzle in Figure 25.2: Fussy, awash, dampen, expose; A paws pause.

LIFE MATTERS

Charles Darwin said, "It's not the strongest of the species that survives, nor the most intelligent that survives. It is the one most adaptable to change." Those who are able to overcome functional fixedness,and other cognitive biases, are more likely to thrive personally and professionally.

time from the ground up. Ford revolutionized manufacturing by breaking free from old traditions. Can you break free from your own fixations? Find out by trying your hand at the puzzles in **Figures 25.3** and **25.4**. (Their solutions are in **Figures 25.6** and **25.7**.)

A special kind of fixation is known as **functional fixedness,** the tendency to think of things only in terms of their usual functions. What if you need to remove a screw, but you don't have access to a screwdriver? If you have trouble thinking of other things that can be used to perform this function, you are suffering from functional fixedness. However, if you are mentally flexible enough to realize that a coin, a butter knife, the edge of a credit card, or a paper clip (among many other items) can all be used as a substitute screwdriver, then you are good at overcoming functional fixedness. If there's no molasses for the cookies, a clever baker substitutes honey. If there's no bracket for a loose tailpipe, a clever mechanic substitutes a coat hanger. If there's no toilet paper in the supplies box, a clever camper substitutes a leaf (a solution employed long ago by a friend of mine, who, unfortunately, had never learned to identify poison ivy). Finding new uses for duct tape has produced a cult following. Ready for a functional fixedness challenge? See **Figure 25.5** (and **Figure 25.8** for the solution).

FIGURE 25.4 ▲
The Nine-Dot Problem
Make a copy of this figure on a piece of scratch paper (*not* in this book, please!) and try to connect all nine dots with four straight lines without lifting your pen or pencil from the paper or retracing a line. A solution appears in Figure 25.7 on the next page.

FIGURE 25.5 ▲
The Candle-Mounting Problem
Can you think of a way to use these materials to mount the candle on a bulletin board? A solution appears in Figure 25.8 on the next page. (Data from Duncker, 1945.)

(Problem 1)

(Problem 6)

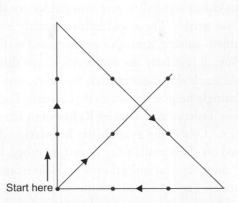

Start here

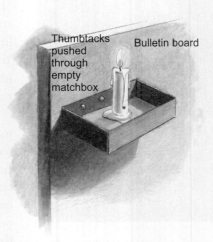

Thumbtacks
pushed
through
empty
matchbox

Bulletin board

▲ **FIGURE 25.6**
Solution to the Luchins Water Jar Problem
Problems 1 through 7 can all be solved by filling Jar B, then pouring off enough water to fill Jar A once and Jar C twice (desired volume = B – A – 2C). However, Problem 6 can be solved with a simpler formula (A – C), and so can Problem 7 (A + C). Many people miss these easy solutions because the mental set from the first several problems becomes fixated. Did your thinking stay flexible? (Data from Luchins, 1946.)

▲ **FIGURE 25.7**
Solution to the Nine-Dot Problem
This problem literally requires you to "think outside the box." Only by leaving the square created by the outer dots can you solve the problem.

▲ **FIGURE 25.8**
Solution to the Candle-Mounting Problem
If you could not imagine using the box as anything other than a container to hold matches, functional fixedness impaired your problem-solving ability. (Data from Duncker, 1945.)

> **confirmation bias** The tendency to focus on information that supports preconceptions.

Confirmation Bias

Confirmation bias is our tendency to focus on information that supports our preconceptions. I had a student drop by one day because she was concerned about her grade in my class. She felt she must be doing better than the grade indicated. I sometimes make mistakes in calculating a student's grade, but in this case, the problem was hers. She was recalling accurately the quizzes on which she had done well, but she had forgotten several on which she had performed poorly at the beginning of the quarter. She knew she was a bright, capable student. This preconception made her more likely to notice (and remember) the quiz scores that confirmed this idea than the ones that refuted it. As a result, her own estimate of what her grade should be was inflated.

Confirmation bias can seriously affect juries in criminal trials. As testimony unfolds, each member of the jury begins to develop a hypothetical story to explain what happened. One juror may speculate, for example, that the defendant acted out of fear. From this point on, the juror will be more likely to notice testimony that supports this particular story and will be less likely to consider nonconfirming testimony. Once the testimony is complete and deliberations begin, the assembled jury is often surprised to learn that various members have generated (and confirmed) several different stories during the trial.[7,8]

moodboard/Brand X Pictures/Getty Images

▲ **Confirmation Bias**
As testimony unfolds, each member of this jury will develop a personal story to explain the crime and will then focus more on the evidence that supports that personal story. When the jury meets later to deliberate, the jurors may be surprised to discover how individual their stories are and how different pieces of evidence and testimony stood out as a result.

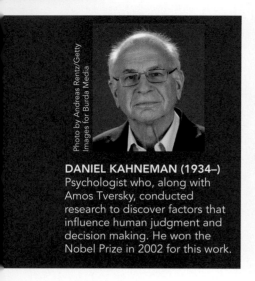

DANIEL KAHNEMAN (1934–)
Psychologist who, along with Amos Tversky, conducted research to discover factors that influence human judgment and decision making. He won the Nobel Prize in 2002 for this work.

availability heuristic
Estimating the likelihood of events based on their availability in memory.

Availability Heuristic ▲
Available images can distort our thinking. Many people buy lottery tickets regularly because images such as this one lead them to believe winning big is more likely than it actually is.

overconfidence Confidence that is greater than accuracy.

Counterproductive Heuristics

"Look before you leap." "A stitch in time saves nine." "Don't judge a book by its cover." No doubt you've been hearing expressions such as these since you were little. Such statements are designed to lead you to better decisions and judgment. Your elders wanted to give you guidelines that would help you survive and thrive in the world. These guidelines qualify as *heuristics,* the quick rule-of-thumb problem-solving strategies we discussed earlier.

We all regularly use heuristics to get through the countless decisions we must make each day. Sometimes, however, our brain can fall into the trap of using seemingly helpful heuristics that actually lead us to inaccurate or harmful decisions. Amos Tversky and **Daniel Kahneman** identified several counterproductive heuristics.[9] One is the **availability heuristic,** which estimates the likelihood of events based on their availability in our memory. Information that is readily available in our memory can indeed be a good indicator that an event is likely. When I hear thunder, I am quick to assume that rain will follow because I have many instances available in my memory when thunder signaled rain. Sometimes, however, the information available in memory is not such a good indicator.

The lottery commission in my state of Iowa intentionally uses the availability heuristic to influence people's judgment of their likelihood of winning. The commission does this by running ads and commercials featuring the gleeful winners. Often these winners are holding huge million-dollar cardboard checks and talking about the wonderful ways in which the money will improve their lives. These images are readily available in viewers' memories when they next think about playing the lottery. ("Big winners must be common because we see them on TV all the time!") Unfortunately, the commission does not show an equal number of dramatic images of those in a much more common category—lottery losers. As a result, many people greatly overestimate their chances of winning, which encourages them to play more than they otherwise would have. In these cases, the availability heuristic has clouded people's judgment.

Kahneman's work with Tversky on how such cognitive factors influence judgment led to a Nobel Prize in 2002. It helps us explain how media coverage of plane crashes or shark attacks can lead us to overestimate the frequency with which these events occur. In circumstances like this, our reasoning is based more on our emotions and less on statistical probability.[10]

Overconfidence

Every student is familiar with the sinking feeling of getting a test back where you haven't done as well as you thought you had. People often overestimate the likelihood that they are correct. **Overconfidence** occurs when our confidence is greater than our accuracy. One study asked participants to estimate answers to factual questions by completing such statements as "I feel 98 percent certain that the population of New Zealand is more than _____ but less than _____." Did the instruction to be 98 percent certain produce answers that were correct 98 percent of the time? Not even close. People were able to "trap" the correct answer—3.7 million people—only two-thirds of the time. The gap between certainty (98 percent) and accuracy (66 percent) was nicely concealed by overconfidence.[11] Even when participants are 100 percent certain of their answers, they are right only 85 percent of the time.[12]

It's not just experiments that produce overconfidence. Decisions tainted by overconfidence work their way into everyday life regularly. A friend of mine, the late psychologist Charles Brewer, often reminded people that "everything takes longer than it takes" to help dampen the frustration borne of overconfident planning. One study showed that students typically took twice as many days to complete a project as they originally predicted.[13] I can relate. The writing I'm doing on this module tonight is taking much longer than I anticipated.

Why do so many of us appear programmed to make false, overconfident judgments so regularly? It may be a way to protect our well-being. Overconfidence is associated with happiness and making tough decisions more easily.[14,15] The overconfidence allows us to think everything will work out, and belief in our own judgment can keep us from fretting and stewing about things.

Framing

Framing is the way we word or present an issue, and it can profoundly affect judgment. Framing the same issue in two different ways can produce two different results. Consider these two statements:

1. Condoms have a 95 percent success rate in preventing the spread of HIV, the virus that causes AIDS.

2. Condoms have a 5 percent failure rate in preventing the spread of HIV, the virus that causes AIDS.

The two statements are equally true, yet 90 percent of college students who read only the first statement rated condoms as effective. Only 40 percent did so after reading the second statement.[16]

Can you imagine what would happen if ground beef were marketed as 20 percent fat instead of 80 percent lean? What if a surgeon bragged about a 2 percent death rate, rather than a 98 percent success rate? Framing makes a difference.

We can all make better decisions. Part of making that happen is to be aware of how fixation, confirmation bias, the use of heuristics, overconfidence, and framing can get in the way. You can work hard to identify and minimize these factors in your own life. The next time an exasperated parent or teacher exhorts you to think! you can honestly reply that you are thinking. To be human is to think. We hope this module has provided you with some ideas not for thinking more but for thinking better.

> **framing** How an issue is worded or presented, which can influence decisions and judgments.

MAKE IT STICK!

1. Some people overestimate the odds of shark attacks because when shark attacks do occur, they are widely publicized. This illustrates a counterproductive aspect of

   a. the prototype effect.
   b. framing.
   c. the availability heuristic.
   d. confirmation bias.

2. Attending a political debate and only remembering statements from the candidates you agree with is an example of

   a. confirmation bias.
   b. framing.
   c. overconfidence.
   d. the availability heuristic.

3. True or False: Overconfidence can lead you to underestimate the time you need to complete a school project.

4. If I don't realize that the edge of my school ID card can be used to scrape frost from my windshield, I am experiencing _____.

Module 25 Summary and Assessment

Thinking

 25-1 How and why do we form concepts?

- Our mind uses concepts to organize the world into mental categories. These mental categories—including prototypes and concept hierarchies—usually help us think quickly and efficiently.

- Concept hierarchies keep mental information organized.

 25-2 What roles do algorithms, heuristics, and insight play in the solution of problems?

- An algorithm is a problem-solving strategy that guarantees a solution to a problem.

- A heuristic is a rule-of-thumb problem-solving strategy that makes a solution more likely but does not guarantee a solution.

- Insight is the sudden realization of a solution to a problem.

 25-3 How can fixation, confirmation bias, and the use of heuristics, overconfidence, and framing influence the quality of our decisions?

- A mental set is a tendency to approach a particular problem in a particular way.

- Confirmation bias is a tendency to focus on information that supports preconceptions.

- The availability heuristic estimates the likelihood of events based on their availability in memory. This can either enhance or hinder problem solving.

- Overconfidence occurs when confidence in an answer is greater than accuracy.

- Framing is the way an issue is presented or worded; it affects what solutions are thought of and produced.

Summative Assessment

1. Which of the following is a basic category?

   a. kidney beans
   b. cheese
   c. soy milk
   d. gluten-free products

2. Which of the following is a heuristic?

   a. retracing your steps to find where you left your phone
   b. looking in every cupboard to find a pan you know is in the kitchen
   c. trying every unused piece in every space to fit in the last 20 pieces in a jigsaw puzzle
   d. going through the football team roster to identify all of the linebackers on the team

3. Which of the following represents insight?

   a. suddenly realizing what you are going to use as the topic of your English essay
   b. carefully revising your college application
   c. having a good idea of what your friend is really thinking
   d. creating a computer program to calculate the area of geometric shapes

4. When trying to unscramble the letters SPOXEE into a common word, Stefano remembered that many words begin with the letters EX. Once he remembered this, it was relatively easy to figure out that the solution is EXPOSE. Stefano made use of

   a. an algorithm.
   b. a concept hierarchy.
   c. insight.
   d. a heuristic.

5. Even though it wasn't working, Mary continued to use the checkers strategy that served her well as a child when she played the game with her new friend. The fact that she didn't change her strategy shows

   a. confirmation bias.
   b. framing.
   c. overconfidence.
   d. fixation.

6. When he couldn't find a fly swatter, Li Wei used a rolled-up magazine to swat an annoying fly in his bedroom. In this way, he overcame

   a. the availability heuristic.
   b. a mental set.
   c. functional fixedness.
   d. confirmation bias.

7. Elizabeth was pretty sure the Senate candidate she supported would win easily because her friends on Facebook, where she got most of her news, kept posting links to articles that talked about her candidate's accomplishments. Her friends never posted links to critical articles. Because of _____, she was very surprised when the candidate lost.

a. overconfidence
b. confirmation bias
c. framing
d. a mental set

8. A movie advertisement reporting that 95% of viewers gave the movie a thumbs-up rating is likely to be more effective than an advertising that 5% of viewers gave the movie a thumbs-down rating because of

a. framing.
b. the availability heuristic.
c. insight.
d. confirmation bias.

9. After they take a test one day, a teacher asks students to estimate what percentage of the questions they got right. The class estimated that they got 84% of the questions right, but when the tests were graded, it turned out the class actually got 71% right on the test. This indicates

a. fixation.
b. a mental set.
c. overconfidence.
d. the availability heuristic.

10. Tom avoids going downtown because he has read several news stories about muggings that occurred downtown. Official police reports indicate that you are actually more likely to get mugged in the suburbs. The fact that Tom won't go downtown indicates he is being influenced by

a. the availability heuristic.
b. concept hierarchies.
c. functional fixedness.
d. insight.

KEY TERMS AND KEY PEOPLE

cognitive abilities, p. 381

concept, p. 381

prototype, p. 382

algorithm, p. 384

heuristic, p. 384

insight, p. 384

mental set, p. 385

fixation, p. 385

functional fixedness, p. 386

confirmation bias, p. 387

availability heuristic, p. 388

overconfidence, p. 388

framing, p. 389

Daniel Kahneman (1934–), p. 388

Module 26

Intelligence and Intelligence Testing

Learning Goals

26-1 Summarize the debate concerning how many kinds of intelligence there are.

26-2 Describe how intelligence tests have been developed and how they have changed since they were first introduced.

26-3 Define what aptitude and achievement tests measure, and explain how these intelligence tests are evaluated.

26-4 Explain what causes the differences in IQ among different groups of people.

We all have brains, but we aren't all equally smart. As you will see, we aren't even smart enough to figure out exactly what being smart means, or how to measure it.

Think of some of the intelligent people you know. Do they share the same ways of thinking? Would your friends all agree that these people are intelligent, or would some disagree? Questions such as these have challenged psychologists for more than a century. Here are the basic issues:

- What is intelligence?
- Where does intelligence come from?
- Can we use tests to reliably and validly measure intelligence?
- Are there ethnic or gender differences in intelligence test scores, and if so, what do the differences mean?

Ariel Skelley/Getty Images

These important questions about intelligence have significance for society. Even though we can't fully answer some of these questions, the use of intelligence tests has grown dramatically since they were first introduced. You and most other high school students have probably taken intelligence tests many times as you worked your way through the school system. The results of those tests, along with other standardized test scores, have regularly been used to make decisions about students' future education. Let's see what we can learn about intelligence and the tests designed to measure it. Then, perhaps you will be in a better position to reap their benefits and avoid their pitfalls.

Do Your Scores Add Up? ▶

Most schools use a program of standardized testing, including intelligence tests, to track the performance of students and identify problems that can be solved. Have you ever seen the scores in your guidance folder? You have a right to know what's in there, and this module will help you understand what you'll find if you choose to check it out.

The Nature of Intelligence

 26-1 How many kinds of intelligence are there?

intelligence The ability to learn from experience, solve problems, and use knowledge to adapt to new situations.

What is intelligence? This is an easy question, right? Everyone knows what intelligence is. To be intelligent is to be smart, bright, with it, quick, and on top of things. Psychologists consider **intelligence** to be the ability to learn from experience, solve problems, and use knowledge to adapt to new situations. They disagree, however, about what this general definition actually entails. For example, we speak of intelligence as though it were one thing, but it may be more accurate to speak of *multiple intelligences.*

Howard Gardner

One leading intelligence theorist, **Howard Gardner,** argues that there are at least eight independent kinds of intelligence, as illustrated in **Figure 26.1.**[1,2] Traditionally, schools have tended to emphasize reading, writing, and

LIFE MATTERS

In high school, it may seem like verbal-linguistic and logical-mathematical intelligence is the only path to success, but that's simply not true. According to the National Association of Colleges and Employers, the most sought-after skills are problem-solving skills, the ability to work with a team, communication skills, leadership, and a strong work ethic. (NACE, 2017)

	Intelligence	Examples
	Verbal–Linguistic	Reading comprehension Writing
	Logical–Mathematical	Solving math and logic problems
	Bodily–Kinesthetic	Balance Strength Endurance
	Visual–Spatial	Judging distance Map reading Geometry
	Musical–Rhythmic	Appreciating and creating music Music theory
	Interpersonal	Listening Cooperation Sensitivity to others
	Intrapersonal	Knowledge of self
	Naturalistic	Appreciating nature Ability to work with plants and animals

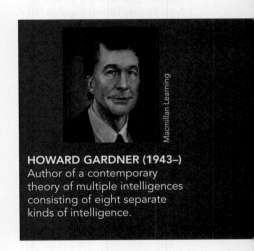

HOWARD GARDNER (1943–)
Author of a contemporary theory of multiple intelligences consisting of eight separate kinds of intelligence.

FIGURE 26.1
Howard Gardner's Multiple Intelligences
Gardner's theory proposes that each person has these eight independent kinds of intelligence. Being high in one kind of intelligence says little about your level in the other kinds of intelligence. (From Gardner, 1999.)

arithmetic, which, in Gardner's model, are represented by *verbal-linguistic* and *logical–mathematical* intelligence. Gardner sees them as two different intelligences, which may explain why some students are good in math classes but not English classes, or vice versa. Schools may not place an equal value on other kinds of intelligence, such as an actor's *intrapersonal* abilities, a woodworker's *bodily–kinesthetic* skills, or a wildlife biologist's *naturalistic* intelligence.

Some critics argue that Gardner's intelligences lack empirical support, and that some move well beyond what is normally considered to be intelligence, which is usually classified as mental ability. By adding things like musical ability and bodily–kinesthetic ability, these critics say he is broadening the concept of intelligence to include areas that used to be considered skills or talents.

Robert Sternberg

Psychologist **Robert Sternberg** has a different way of organizing multiple intelligences. His theory defines three separate types of intelligence[3–5] (see **Figure 26.2**):

ROBERT STERNBERG (1949–)
Author of a contemporary theory of multiple intelligences consisting of analytical, creative, and practical intelligence.

Courtesy of Dr. Sternberg

FIGURE 26.2
Robert Sternberg's Three-Type Theory of Intelligence
Sternberg believes people have the three types of intelligence pictured here. (From Sternberg, 1999.)

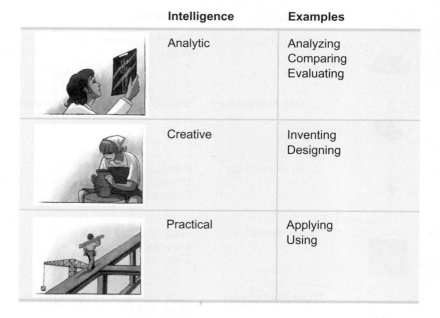

	Intelligence	Examples
	Analytic	Analyzing Comparing Evaluating
	Creative	Inventing Designing
	Practical	Applying Using

● I once heard Robert Sternberg tell a joke to illustrate practical intelligence: Two men were walking through the Northwoods when a large, mean-looking bear appeared on the other side of a clearing. One of the men sat down, opened his backpack, and took out his tennis shoes. When he started to change his heavy hiking boots for the lighter shoes, his friend said, "What are you doing? You can't possibly outrun that bear." The friend replied, "I don't have to outrun the bear; I only have to outrun you!" Now that's practical intelligence.

- *Analytic intelligence*—This is the kind of intelligence most often stressed in schools. It helps people do things like analyze, compare, and evaluate, and it closely matches most people's traditional view of intelligence. If you study published reports of various makes and models of cars to determine which would be the best purchase, then you have used analytic intelligence.

- *Creative intelligence*—Individuals high in creative intelligence can do things like create, invent, and design—they come up with new ideas and adapt to new situations. If you develop clever budgeting or saving strategies to be able to buy a new gaming system, then you have used creative intelligence.

- *Practical intelligence*—Practical intelligence is the sort of common sense that helps you complete the various tasks you face. It allows you to apply, use, and do. If you successfully negotiate a great deal at the local car dealership, then you have used practical intelligence.

Traditional intelligence tests focus on analytic intelligence. They do a reasonably good job of predicting school grades, but they don't do a good job of predicting occupational success. There is a practical intelligence test that predicts managerial success more successfully than traditional intelligence tests do—it focuses on tasks like keeping workers motivated and writing effective memos.[6,7] Sternberg and his colleagues are also working on new, more comprehensive college admissions tests to better predict college success.[8,9]

"Hi—Where do I go to take the intelligence test?"

Emotional Intelligence

Yet another theory of intelligence, popularized in a book[10] by Daniel Goleman, distinguishes between academic intelligence and **emotional intelligence**—the ability to perceive, express, understand, and regulate emotions.[11,12] People with high emotional intelligence are more in touch with their feelings. They can face setbacks without losing their motivation or optimism, and they can manage their emotions in a way that allows them to get along well with others. Academic skills seem different from the social skills that flow from emotional intelligence. Perhaps this is why academically bright people are not much better than average folks when it comes to success in occupations, marriages, child-rearing, and maintaining mental health.[13] Psychologist John Mayer and his colleagues have now developed tests to measure emotional intelligence, just as more traditional intelligence tests measure our more traditional concept of intelligence.

As you can see, psychologists have not yet reached a consensus about what, exactly, intelligence is. It's a complicated concept, and it won't be settled until more research is done. One question that has not been fully answered is whether some underlying factor fuels all types of intelligences (whatever they may be), much as AAA batteries can power up everything from flashlights to video game controllers. More than a half-century ago, Charles Spearman proposed just such a factor, called **general intelligence**, or *g*, which he believed underlies all multiple intelligences. Spearman was impressed by the tendency of people who excelled in one area to also excel in others. Gardner, Sternberg, and others who emphasize multiple intelligences are more impressed by the different and separate nature of their various proposed factors. All these theories give us wonderful glimpses of what intelligence may really entail.

emotional intelligence
The ability to perceive, express, understand, and regulate emotions.

general intelligence (g)
The factor that Charles Spearman believed underlies all multiple intelligences.

How Many Intelligences?
Howard Gardner of Harvard University and Robert Sternberg of Oklahoma State University are two of the leading cognitive psychologists in the United States today. Each of them believes it is accurate to speak of multiple intelligences, but they disagree on how many kinds of intelligence there are.

Intelligence Testing

 26-2 How have intelligence tests developed and changed since they were first introduced?

Have you ever taken an intelligence test? Chances are that you have, but—if you're like many of my students—you didn't realize it. Most schools in the United States have a standardized testing program for their students, and some of these tests are indeed intelligence tests. Intelligence tests are widely used to increase the chances that elementary students with intellectual problems will receive the help they need, but there is much misunderstanding about what the tests can—and cannot—tell us. Let's continue our own quest for understanding by looking at the history of intelligence tests.

Alfred Binet and the First Intelligence Test

Testing has been around for a long time, but we can trace the roots of modern, standardized intelligence tests back to early twentieth-century France. That's when **Alfred Binet** developed the test that would lead to today's intelligence tests. Back then, France had new laws requiring education for all children. In the face of such overwhelming numbers of French children entering school, teachers needed an efficient way to place them in the proper classes. The French government was also concerned that some teachers would be biased in their placement of students. Wouldn't it be better to give each child an efficient and fair test? Government officials asked Binet and a colleague, Théodore Simon, to develop a test that could spot any student likely to struggle in an age-grouped classroom.

Binet and Simon started by assuming that children's intellectual abilities grow year by year. Thus, a typical 7-year-old should be able to answer harder questions than a typical 6-year-old, a typical 8-year-old should answer harder questions than a typical 7-year-old, and so on. However, not every member of each age group is typical—some 7-year-olds can successfully answer

ALFRED BINET (1857–1911)
Developer of the first test to classify children's abilities using the concept of mental age.

questions that are usually appropriate for 8- or even 9-year-olds. Other 7-year-olds may struggle with questions most 6- or even 5-year-olds can easily answer.

Binet and Simon used these assumptions to measure **mental age (MA),** a shorthand description of the difficulty level of the questions a child can answer. Thus, a child who can answer 8-year-old questions has a mental age of 8, no matter what the child's *chronological age* (actual age) is. Binet and Simon predicted that children who fell significantly behind their age-mates in mental age were the ones who would struggle in an age-grouped classroom. Even at this early time, Binet was concerned that his test, developed for such noble purposes, would be used to label some children as "backward" and to limit their opportunities.[14]

Gregg Vignal/Alamy

▲ **Mental Age**
Everyone in this group is 5 years old and will start school soon. They are not all the same, however. Some of them have more advanced mental abilities than others. Alfred Binet designed his tests to tap this quality—children's mental age—as contrasted with their chronological age (5 years, for these children).

Lewis Terman and the IQ Formula

Binet believed that intelligence is determined mostly by environment and that slow children could be provided remedial exercises to help them increase their mental abilities. Some of those who followed him, however, were convinced that intelligence was largely determined by genetics. This meant they were less interested in providing remedial programs for less capable students.

Stanford University's **Lewis Terman** was one psychologist who disagreed with Binet and believed that intelligence was reasonably fixed. Terman revised the original Binet and Simon test for use with U.S. children. The revision was called the *Stanford-Binet intelligence test,* and a modern version is still in wide use today. Terman, in collaboration with William Stern, devised a way to express an individual's performance on the test with a single, easy-to-interpret number. The **intelligence quotient (IQ)** is the number that results from dividing mental age (MA) by chronological age (CA) and multiplying by 100. This formula was as famous in psychology as Albert Einstein's $E = mc$ was in physics—and it became widely known by the public. IQ was calculated as follows:

$$IQ = MA/CA \times 100$$

This means a child whose mental age (MA) and chronological age (CA) matched (in other words, a child with average mental development) would have an IQ score of 100. Children whose mental age had advanced beyond their chronological age would have an IQ score above 100. For example, a 10-year-old child who could answer questions suited to the average 11-year-old would have an IQ of 11/10 × 100, or 110. Similarly, a child who lagged behind agemates in mental development would slip below 100. An 8-year-old who could answer only 6-year-old questions would have an IQ of 6/8 × 100, or 75. This simple measuring stick proved handy and easy to apply.

Modern intelligence tests all use this same basic technique—comparing a person's actual age with that person's level of mental development. This is done by using sample groups to standardize the test and establish scoring norms. Scores are adjusted so that 100 represents average intelligence for the person's age group. The original formula, however, is no longer used. And the term *IQ* is now shorthand for *intelligence test score.* One problem with the formula is the assumption that mental abilities increase a little every year; this statement holds true only for children. If a 12-year-old boy attempts to learn calculus and finds it too difficult, it makes sense for him to wait a few years and try again—his mental abilities will continue to grow during his teen years. But if a 20-year-old man finds calculus too

Courtesy Stanford University Archives

LEWIS TERMAN (1877–1956)
Adapted Binet's tests for use in the United States as an intelligence test that reported intelligence as a calculated IQ score.

mental age (MA) The chronological age that corresponds to the difficulty level of the questions a child can answer.

intelligence quotient (IQ) The number that results from dividing mental age by chronological age and multiplying by 100.

difficult, waiting probably won't increase his chances of becoming a math whiz—material that is too hard at 20 will probably remain so. This leveling-off process caused problems when people became interested in giving IQ tests to adults as well as children. An average 20-year-old woman would have an IQ of 100, calculated by dividing 20 (MA) by 20 (CA) and multiplying by 100. By age 40, however, the formula would drop her IQ to 50 because her chronological age has doubled but the mental age has stayed the same.

Beyond the problem of adjusting for adult scores, the notion of an IQ formula is perhaps too simplistic. It reduces the complex concept of intelligence to a single number without considering other characteristics that can influence its interpretation. As public interest focused on the new IQ scores, people began to draw inappropriate conclusions: "Your IQ is 103? Hah—mine is 104. I'm smarter than you are!" These conclusions were particularly destructive when averages from one ethnic group were compared to those from another because it made it seem like some groups were genetically inferior to other groups (read more about this in the Group Differences in Intelligence Test Scores section beginning on page 404). Unfortunately, Terman's personal beliefs about racial and ethnic groups fostered such comments.

Unlike Binet, Terman assumed intelligence was largely fixed by heredity—he lined up on the nature side of the nature–nurture debate. He also worked hard to promote the wide use of IQ testing, and his goal was to discourage the spread of what he called feeble-mindedness (intellectual weakness) through "indiscriminate breeding."[15] Terman and others shared the belief that measured differences in IQ among various ethnic and national groups were largely inborn, and these beliefs partially accounted for the restrictive U.S. policies of the 1920s that set low immigration quotas for people who did not come from northern Europe. Policymakers never considered cultural and personal factors that might have accounted for the differences. Terman later acknowledged that such factors were significant, but his early belief that people could and should be categorized by the IQ averages of their native country shows how easily values and beliefs can influence science.

David Wechsler

In the 1930s, **David Wechsler** began work on a battery of intelligence tests that have become the most widely used individual intelligence tests in the United States. The *Wechsler intelligence scales* introduced several innovations, including the following:

- *Different tests for different age groups*—Rather than trying to test all people with the same instrument, Wechsler developed three tests for different age groups: the Wechsler Adult Intelligence Scale (WAIS), the Wechsler Intelligence Scale for Children (WISC), and the Wechsler Preschool and Primary Scale of Intelligence (WPPSI).

- *Separate scores for verbal and nonverbal abilities*—In addition to providing an overall intelligence score, the Wechsler tests divide intelligence into verbal and performance categories. The verbal intelligence section tests vocabulary, math, and similar skills. The performance section tests abilities on tasks such as the assembly of objects.

- *Subtests*—The Wechsler tests are really a battery of about a dozen subtests, some of which tap verbal abilities and others performance abilities. Each subtest is scored separately, so people using the results can more easily determine the test-taker's strengths and weaknesses.

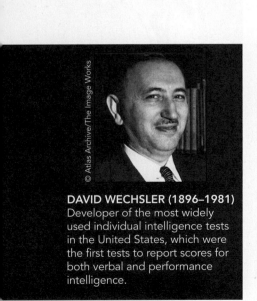

DAVID WECHSLER (1896–1981)
Developer of the most widely used individual intelligence tests in the United States, which were the first tests to report scores for both verbal and performance intelligence.

© Atlas Archive/The Image Works

Both the Stanford-Binet (**Figure 26.3**) and the Wechsler tests are individual intelligence tests, which means that a trained examiner gives the test to one person at a time. The tests are periodically revised to remain current and competitive with one another. It is a little like the competition between Coke and Pepsi—just as these two major brands of cola account for most of the market, these two tests account for most of the individual intelligence tests given in the United States. (For more on extreme scores for these tests, see Psychology in the Real World: Extremes of Intelligence—The Ends of the Normal Curve.)

Taking an Intelligence Test
In individual intelligence tests, such as the Wechsler tests, the tester works one-on-one with the person taking the test. This child is working on the block design subtest of the Wechsler Intelligence Scale for Children. The tester has set up the equipment and will time the child as one measure of performance.

Group Tests

Although the Stanford-Binet and Wechsler tests are the most widely given individual intelligence tests, most people have never taken either of them. The tests given so regularly in public school districts are *group intelligence tests*. These tests were originally developed by the U.S. Army in the early 1900s to help evaluate the massive number of recruits during World War I. The Army uses these tests because they are efficient. Many people can take them at one time, using nothing more than a test booklet and an answer sheet. The person supervising the test needs no extensive training, which is required for people who give the individual tests. Scoring is equally easy, with the help of an answer key or a computer program.

It is this tremendous efficiency that makes group tests appealing to schools, too. Schools cannot afford to hire trained testers to give individual tests to each student, but most school budgets can cover group tests administered in a classroom under the supervision of teachers. The answer sheets can be sent to the test supplier for economical computer scoring. And there are lots of choices available, including the Cognitive Abilities Test, the Differential Aptitude Test, and the Otis-Lennon School Ability Test. If the Stanford-Binet and Wechsler individual tests are comparable to Coke and Pepsi, the various group tests more closely resemble the wide array of makes of automobiles. The U.S. Army sticks with its original vehicle—the Army Alpha Test—to evaluate recruits.

However, there is a trade-off with group tests. Their economic efficiency comes at the cost of test reliability. We cannot count on the results of these tests to the same extent that we can count on the results of individual tests. School districts compromise by using both kinds of tests. Every child takes a group test every year or two through the elementary school years. If the results fall within the normal range, the results are filed away and nothing further is done. However, if the test indicates a potential problem because of a low score, most districts follow up by having the school psychologist administer the more expensive (but more reliable) individual test, usually the Wechsler or the Stanford-Binet. If that test also indicates special needs, school officials may recommend special programming for that child.

FIGURE 26.3
The Stanford-Binet Intelligence Test
Here, a young boy takes the Stanford-Binet intelligence test one-on-one with a tester.

But a question remains: What makes one test more reliable than another? To answer that question, we need to look at test construction.

PSYCHOLOGY IN THE REAL WORLD

Extremes of Intelligence—The Ends of the Normal Curve

Most people score near the middle of the range of human intelligence, but what about those who are far below or far above the middle? If you look at **Figure 26.4**, you will see that intelligence test scores show a normal distribution, or bell-shaped curve. In any *normal distribution*, whether of intelligence test scores or some measure of friendliness, most scores pile up near the middle—the farther you move from the middle, the fewer people are represented.

About 3 percent of the population has an intelligence test score below 70.[16] People with an intelli-

gence score below 70 have an intellectual disability (formerly referred to as *mental retardation*) if the low score is coupled with difficulty living independently. This difficulty may involve understanding language, telling time, or using money (conceptual skills), getting along with others or following laws and rules (social skills), or maintaining good health and holding down a job (practical skills). Within the category of intellectual disability, individuals are further classified as having mild, moderate, severe, or profound disability (see **Table 26.1**). Notice that

FIGURE 26.4
Intelligence and the Normal Distribution
This graph shows how often various intelligence test scores occur in the general population. The average score is 100, and about two-thirds of the population score within 15 points of this average. The further from average you get, the fewer people achieve that score. It is rare to have scores below 55 or above 145.

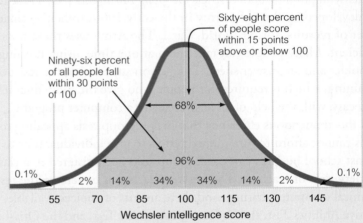

TABLE 26.1	Degrees of Intellectual Disability		
Level	**Typical Intelligence Scores**	**Percentage of Persons With Disability**	**Adaptation to Demands of Life**
Mild	50–69	85%	May learn academic skills up to sixth-grade level. Adults may, with assistance, achieve self-supporting social and vocational skills.
Moderate	35–49	10%	May progress to second-grade level academically. Adults may contribute to their own support with employment in sheltered workshops.
Severe	20–34	3–4%	May learn to talk and to perform simple work tasks under close supervision but are generally unable to profit from vocational training.
Profound	Below 20	1–2%	Require constant aid and supervision.

Source: Adapted from the *Diagnostic and Statistical Manual of Mental Disorders*, Fifth Edition, Text Revision. Copyright 2013 American Psychiatric Association.

PSYCHOLOGY IN THE REAL WORLD (Continued)

most individuals with intellectual disability are in the mild category and that most people with mild disability can, with proper training, lead largely independent lives. People with moderate disability often thrive living in group homes and doing productive work in sheltered workshops. Independence is limited or impossible for people with severe and profound disability.

What causes intellectual disability? Hundreds of factors can contribute, including genetics (Down syndrome is caused by an extra chromosome) and problems during pregnancy (excessive use of drugs or alcohol can have an effect) or childbirth. Environmental problems, such as malnutrition during childhood, can also produce disability. Normal intelligence is determined by a combination of nature and nurture. The same is true for intellectual disability, especially when it is mild.[17]

On the opposite end of the normal curve are those who score above average on intelligence tests. There is no universally agreed-upon definition for *genius*, but psychologists have extensively studied high-scoring individuals. Lewis Terman in 1921 began

▲ **Chess Champ**
At the age of 10, Fabiano Caruana was already a candidate for grandmaster of chess, a distinction he later received as a mere 14-year-old. Here, he won 14 matches out of the 15 he had been playing simultaneously. His rare intellectual skills would probably be reflected in a high intelligence test score indicating genius.

the most famous of these studies, tracking 1500 California schoolchildren with scores higher than 135. Stereotypes about exceptionally bright children being "nerdy," deficient in social skills, or unhealthy proved untrue as their lives played out over seven decades. These high-scoring children were healthy and well adjusted in school, and as adults they generally succeeded in such challenging professions as law and medicine (Holahan & Sears, 1995). Several more recent studies have confirmed that students who do well on intelligence tests in school are successful in many other ways as well.[18–20]

Intelligence tests are important tools that help psychologists measure a quality we all share. Fascinating people populate the entire range of intelligence.

▲ **Nothing Gets Her Down**
Evie Alge's Down syndrome may be her least interesting attribute. She's shown here, in Washington D.C., advocating for legislation that will improve her life!

THINK ABOUT . . . Psychology in the Real World

1. What do studies of gifted children show about their lives as adults?

2. Why is it important to consider difficulty living independently as well as intelligence test scores when determining whether someone has an intellectual disability?

3. Why do you think they have replaced the term *mental retardation* with the term *intellectual disability*?

MAKE IT STICK!

1. Alfred Binet developed the first intelligence test to identify

   a. whether young people should apply for college or trade school.
   b. proper grade placement.
   c. individuals who needed remedial work in specific areas.
   d. individuals to ultimately serve in the French government.

2. Which of the following is a disadvantage of group intelligence tests?

   a. They are less reliable than individual tests.
   b. They are more biased than individual tests.
   c. They can only measure IQ, not general intelligence.
   d. They can only measure single and not multiple intelligences.

3. The IQ formula was designed to show that people of average intelligence have an IQ score of _____.

4. Group intelligence tests were developed by

   a. for-profit corporations.
   b. the public schools.
   c. the government.
   d. the military.

Test Construction

 26-3 What do aptitude and achievement tests measure? How are these intelligence tests evaluated?

Probably no generation in the history of the world has been tested as much as yours. Can you remember when you took your first test? *Probably not.* If you were born in a hospital, as my sons were, chances are good that you were tested within the first minute of your life. Newborns are given the Apgar test to determine their overall physical condition and whether medical intervention is necessary. My older son, Carl (who has grown up fine and healthy, I'm happy to say), "failed" this early test—because he was not breathing! After your Apgar, the tests came fast and furiously, as people checked your hearing and vision, watched you swim to determine whether you could go in the deep end of the pool, assessed your readiness for kindergarten, judged your intelligence, measured what you had achieved in the classroom, and put you behind the wheel of a car to watch you drive. And your tests aren't over yet—you can still look forward to high school exit exams, college entrance exams, graduate school admissions exams, and various professional tests, like the bar exam required of lawyers or the certificate exams to become a master electrician. Is it any wonder we all become tired of being tested? Since we can't avoid them, let's try to understand the general principles behind test design and applications.

Tests and More Tests
It's hard to get through a day without being tested for something.

Spencer Grant/ PhotoEdit, Inc.

LStockStudio/Shutterstock

RichLegg/Getty Images

Achievement and Aptitude Tests

One major way of characterizing tests is to distinguish between those that assess achievement and those that gauge aptitude. **Achievement tests** attempt to *measure* what the test-taker has accomplished. The classroom tests you take regularly measure how much you've achieved in your various units of study. Standardized achievement tests that you and other students around the country take are attempts to determine what each of you has accomplished in relation to your classmates. These standardized achievement tests also help schools know how their students are doing in comparison with state and national groups.

Aptitude tests attempt to *predict* the test-taker's future performance. College entrance exams like the ACT (American College Test) and the SAT Reasoning Test are both aptitude tests, because college admissions officials use them to provide a glimpse into an applicant's likelihood of success. Intelligence tests are also considered aptitude tests because they attempt to assess the test-taker's ability to learn.

achievement tests Tests that attempt to measure what the test-taker has accomplished.

aptitude tests Tests that attempt to predict the test-taker's future performance.

Reliability and Validity

Have you ever taken a test with questions you thought were unfair? Almost every student has. Knowing this, testing experts have worked hard to eliminate problems, especially from standardized tests used to make decisions about individuals' futures. Good tests—those that are well designed—are both reliable and valid.

Test Reliability In tests, **reliability** is the extent to which a test yields consistent results. If a test is reliable, then the results will be the same, no matter who gives the test. Just as a reliable friend is one you can count on, so is a reliable test. Here are some ways that test designers assess whether a test is reliable:

- *Does it have test–retest reliability?* If so, a person who retakes a test will get almost the same score the second time as the first. For example, if you take an intelligence test twice in three months, your score should be roughly the same each time, even if the questions are different.

- *Does it have split-half reliability?* If so, your score on the even-numbered items should be about the same as your score on the odd-numbered items. For example, if I give you a 100-question multiple-choice test, you should have about the same number of correct answers on the odd-numbered questions as you do on the even-numbered questions.

- *Does it have scorer (or inter-rater) reliability?* If so, two people should be able to score the same test and show the same result. My co-author and I, given two identical copies of your exam, should give you the same grade.

Test Validity **Validity** is the extent to which a test measures or predicts what it is supposed to. What if I designed a test to measure your intelligence by checking your hat size? I could do this fairly reliably—I would have consistent answers every time I checked the size tag on the inside of your hat. Would you be satisfied with my conclusion about your intelligence? Maybe—if you have a really big head! But most people would object, saying that this is a bad test. And they'd be right. This is not a *valid* test of intelligence because people with big heads are not necessarily more intelligent than people with small heads. This test does not measure what it is supposed to measure. Reliability alone does not guarantee a good test.

One of the best indicators of test validity is a test's ability to make accurate predictions. College admissions tests are considered somewhat valid because they do a reasonably good job of predicting how well a student will do in the first year

▲ **Ever Taken an Unfair Test?** Psychologists avoid unfair tests by making sure they are both reliable and valid.

reliability The extent to which a test yields consistent results, regardless of who gives the test or when or where it is given.

validity The extent to which a test measures or predicts what it is supposed to test.

of college. It is generally true that students who do well on the tests are those who also do well in college. There are enough exceptions, however, that the use of college admissions tests remains controversial.

Notice that you cannot determine whether a test is valid *unless you know its purpose.* A test can be valid for some purposes but not for others. Intelligence tests, for example, have more validity for predicting how well children will do in elementary school than they do for predicting occupational success for adults. It's interesting that the purpose for which Binet developed the first test—predicting school success—is still the one that is most valid.

MAKE IT STICK!

1. A test that determines whether a person is likely to be successful in law school is an

    a. analytic intelligence test.
    b. achievement test.
    c. individual intelligence test.
    d. aptitude test.

2. True or False: A thermometer that consistently measures one degree too warm is reliable.

3. True or False: At the end of an elementary student's first keyboarding class, he might be required to take a test to measure how many words per minute he can type. This is an example of an achievement test.

Group Differences in Intelligence Test Scores

 26-4 What causes the differences in IQ among different groups of people?

Can tests be biased? Can they put certain individuals at a disadvantage because of their gender, race, or cultural background? Psychologists who design tests are concerned about these questions because some groups tend to outscore others on some tests. Males do better than females on tests of math problem solving.[21] Israeli Jews do better than Israeli Arabs on intelligence tests.[22] Israeli Arabs, like black Americans, are a minority group within a larger, dominant culture. In the United States, as in Israel, the minority group's scores are often lower. In 1994, a group of more than 50 researchers looked at a series of studies and concluded that the average score for black Americans was roughly 15 points lower than for white Americans.[23] Some evidence indicates that this IQ gap has closed to about 10 points among children tested more recently.[24,25] But the bigger question is why this gap appears. Group differences like the three cited here deserve close study so that we don't leap to inappropriate conclusions about the people involved.

It is interesting to note that 80 years ago, the average intelligence test score was only 76 points by today's standards. This historic increase, known as the Flynn effect because of James Flynn's research on the phenomenon,[26,27] has been observed worldwide in rising performance in 20 countries.[28] Few would suggest that today's group of test-takers are inherently more intelligent than were their great-grandparents.

So, are the tests biased? Are they testing intelligence or something else? We know that different groups in the United States have different experiences as participants in U.S. society. Do members of disadvantaged minority groups have the same kinds of experiences that the mostly white middle-class Americans who designed these tests have? *Probably not.* So, to the extent that these tests require a knowledge of mainstream U.S. culture, the tests are not valid intelligence tests. In that sense, the tests are biased. Lower scores on the part of some groups reflect the fact that those groups have not had the same kind of "preparation." Notice that we are talking about group differences here and that scores among the individuals within each group vary tremendously. Some black American children score higher than almost all white American children, and some white American children score lower than almost all black American children. We cannot predict how any individual child will do based on the group the child comes from—just as we cannot predict how long any individual person will live, even though we know that women, in general, live longer than men.

> **Group Differences in Intelligence Test Scores**
> On some intelligence tests, different groups have different average scores. The question is, Why? Most psychologists believe that environmental factors, not heredity, account for these group differences.

So, does heredity also play a role in racial differences on intelligence test scores? Let's look at what psychologists have discovered about the extent to which intelligence is inherited. This area, as much as any, illustrates the importance of the nature–nurture debate. Is intelligence determined by *nature*—the inborn influence of heredity—or is it determined by *nurture*—the influence of the environment we are raised in? The answer has profound significance for our society. If certain racial groups are likely to be less intelligent because of the genes they were born with, an argument could be made that they are less qualified to hold positions of responsibility. But if environmental factors cause the lower intelligence scores, no such argument can be made because the differences will disappear if opportunities become more equal. So, which is it—nature or nurture?

The answer is that both nature *and* nurture shape an individual's intelligence. How do we know this? We have been shown this by studies that used a number of techniques to untangle the threads linking environment and heredity to intelligence. Studies of identical twins, for example, are useful because identical twins share the same heredity (see **Figure 26.5**). Any differences between them cannot be genetic and must be environmental. Fraternal twins

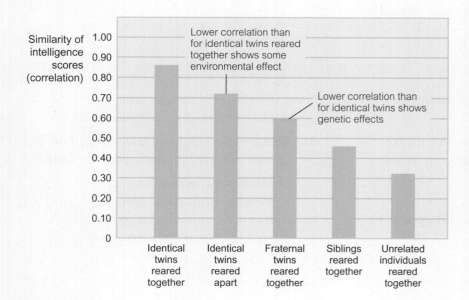

> **FIGURE 26.5**
> **Twins and Intelligence**
> Twin studies show that intelligence test scores for twins are more similar than scores for either siblings who grow up together or unrelated individuals who grow up together. Environmental effects are apparent in the studies of identical twins reared apart. Heredity's role is apparent in studies of fraternal twins raised together. (Data from McGue et al., 1993.)

© John McPherson/Distributed by Universal Uclick via CartoonStock.com

www.CartoonStock.com

After taking daily supplements of Smarties™, Glenn discovers that they actually do increase one's IQ.

are no more genetically similar than any other brothers and sisters are. They are less similar in intelligence test scores than identical twins but more similar than nontwin siblings. Why? It's because twins—whether fraternal or identical—share a more similar environment, being exposed to a variety of experiences together, than other siblings. Adoption studies are also useful. If an adopted child is more similar to the biological parents than the adoptive parents, there is support for the effect of heredity.

When we roll together the results of the studies of twins—those raised together and those raised apart, identical or fraternal—and of adopted children, it becomes clear that heredity plays a big role in our intelligence. But it also becomes clear that environment plays a role significant enough to explain why group differences exist. Racial minority groups are likely to be at an economic disadvantage, which could have an impact on diet and nutrition, access to medical care, quality of schools, and family resources, among other things. Genetics researchers have established that individual differences in intelligence *within* a race are much greater than differences in intelligence *between* racial groups.[29,30] Racists have tried to find conclusive support in the research to establish that some groups are superior to others because of their genes, but the research doesn't exist. Just as you can't judge a book by its cover, you can't judge a human by color. After all, 99.9 percent of your genes are an exact match to those of every other human.[31] Similar problems arise when you try to analyze gender differences. Again, there is more variability within each gender group than between them, but males and females do show some differences in mental abilities. Girls, for example, show more verbal fluency,[32] and boys score higher when solving math problems.[33] Some part of these gender differences may be biological, but differing social expectations for boys and girls certainly have an effect as well.

The answers intelligence tests were supposed to provide have never come quite as easily as some had hoped. The tests can provide a good estimate of a person's intellectual potential. However, the unanswered questions about intelligence and the tests that attempt to measure it remain more interesting than the questions on the tests themselves.

MAKE IT STICK!

1. True or False: Nature refers to the impact that heredity has on intelligence.

2. Intelligence researchers believe that the IQ differences among racial groups can be best explained by

   a. genetic differences.
   b. the difference between mental age and chronological age.

   c. the effects of environment.
   d. low reliability for intelligence tests.

3. Which of the following, on average, show the greatest similarity in intelligence test scores?

   a. identical twins raised together
   b. identical twins raised apart
   c. fraternal twins raised together
   d. nontwin siblings raised together

Module 26 Summary and Assessment

Intelligence and Intelligence Testing

 26-1 How many kinds of intelligence are there?

- Some psychologists consider intelligence to be one thing, and others conceive of multiple intelligences.

- Howard Gardner argues that there are at least eight independent kinds of intelligence.

- Robert Sternberg defines three separate types: analytic, creative, and practical intelligence.

- Daniel Goleman distinguishes between academic intelligence and emotional intelligence—the ability to perceive, express, understand, and regulate emotions.

- Charles Spearman proposed a factor called general intelligence, or *g,* which he believed underlies all multiple intelligences.

 26-2 How have intelligence tests developed and changed since they were first introduced?

- Alfred Binet and Théodore Simon developed the first intelligence test to help French educators place students in classes appropriate for their intelligence levels.

- Lewis Terman revised the original Binet and Simon test into the Stanford-Binet intelligence test. This test established the intelligence quotient (IQ) as the number that results from dividing mental age (MA) by chronological age (CA) and multiplying by 100.

- David Wechsler developed a battery of intelligence tests that have become the most widely used individual intelligence

tests in the United States. The Wechsler intelligence scales include several innovations, including different tests for different age groups, separate scores for verbal and nonverbal abilities, and subtests for strengths and weaknesses.

- Many other intelligence tests are designed to be administered to groups.

 26-3 What do aptitude and achievement tests measure? How are these intelligence tests evaluated?

- Achievement tests attempt to measure what the test-taker has accomplished.

- Aptitude tests attempt to predict the test-taker's future performance.

- Reliability is the extent to which a test yields consistent results.

- Validity is the extent to which a test measures or predicts what it is supposed to test.

  26-4 What causes the differences in IQ among different groups of people?

- There are group differences in IQ scores.

- Because different groups have different experiences, to the extent that intelligence tests require a knowledge of mainstream U.S. culture, the tests may be considered biased.

- Both nature and nurture shape an individual's intelligence.

Summative Assessment

1. Which of the following would be part of visual–spatial intelligence?

    a. being able to read a complicated text
    b. being able to judge how much space there is between your car and the car in front of you
    c. being able to understand how your best friend is really feeling
    d. knowing how far apart you should plant corn seeds in your garden

2. Practical intelligence would include being able to

    a. calculate the correct answer to a complex algebraic formula.
    b. find the best bargain on a new cell phone.

    c. write and perform a rap for your best friend's birthday.
    d. invent a new way to prop open a closet door that always closes unexpectedly.

3. The IQ formula is no longer used because

    a. experts don't believe its assumptions apply anymore.
    b. IQ tests are rarely given anymore.
    c. it doesn't work well for calculating the IQ of adults.
    d. the Flynn effect means that the formula is no longer useful.

4. Which of the following is an innovation David Wechsler made in intelligence tests?

    a. He developed a formula to calculate an IQ score.
    b. He compared mental age to chronological age.

c. He developed the first group tests.

d. He divided intelligence into verbal and nonverbal abilities.

5. An early intelligence test used in France over a hundred years ago was developed by

a. Charles Spearman.

b. David Wechsler.

c. Lewis Terman.

d. Alfred Binet.

6. A 10-year-old child took the original Stanford-Binet intelligence test. The child was able to answer questions typically answered by 12-year-olds. According to the IQ formula, the child's IQ is

a. 90.

b. 100.

c. 110.

d. 120.

7. The determination of intellectual disability is made by considering intelligence test scores and

a. overall physical health.

b. the level of emotional intelligence.

c. the ability to live independently.

d. whether the disability is caused by nature or nurture.

8. A child takes an IQ test and gets a score of 120. A month later, the same child takes the same test and gets a score of 90. From this decrease in scores, you can conclude that the test is not a _____ test.

a. good achievement

b. good aptitude

c. valid

d. reliable

9. Emotional intelligence does NOT involve

a. controlling emotion.

b. expressing emotion appropriately.

c. understanding one's own emotional responses.

d. explaining emotions to others.

10. A thermometer always measures two degrees hotter than the actual temperature. This thermometer is

a. both reliable and valid.

b. neither reliable nor valid.

c. reliable but not valid.

d. valid but not reliable.

KEY TERMS AND KEY PEOPLE

intelligence, p. 393	achievement tests, p. 403	Robert Sternberg (1949–), p. 394
emotional intelligence, p. 395	aptitude tests, p. 403	Alfred Binet (1857–1911), p. 396
general intelligence (*g*), p. 395	reliability, p. 403	Lewis Terman (1877–1956), p. 397
mental age (MA), p. 397	validity, p. 403	David Wechsler (1896–1981), p. 398
intelligence quotient (IQ), p. 397	Howard Gardner (1943–), p. 393	

Individual Variations

Antonio Guillem/Shutterstock.com

Module 27 | Motivation

Learning Goals

27-1 Describe how early psychologists explained human motivation, and identify the limitations of their theories.

27-2 Explain how the concepts of optimum level of arousal and homeostasis apply to motivation.

27-3 Describe how we are motivated by external and internal factors.

27-4 Explain how Maslow's hierarchy of needs and Murray's achievement motivation theory describe motivation.

27-5 Describe the physiological and environmental factors that control hunger.

motivation A need or desire that energizes and directs behavior toward a goal.

Motivation ▶
Motivational speakers often urge us to take some kind of action. Have you been motivated to act by anyone at a school assembly?

The motivation to eat—or not to eat—can be both biological and cognitive. Let's see what psychologists have to say about what motivates us to do what we do.

"It always seems impossible until it's done."

These are the words (attributed to the late Nelson Mandela) our most recent motivational speaker ended with at an all-school assembly.

Ever have a motivational speaker at your school? Perhaps an assembly where your teacher escorts your class to the gym? If yours are like ours, a speaker entertains us while leading up to a message intended to motivate us to take action. At our last assembly, the speaker encouraged us to stop bullying. He talked about why students bully others and why we should try to stop it.

For more than a century, psychologists have searched for the roots of behavior, attempting to understand why we do what we do. This quest to understand **motivation** (from the Latin *movere,* meaning "to move") has led psychology in several directions. In this module, we will examine biological, cognitive, and clinical explanations for motivation and explore how some of these ideas can help us motivate others and ourselves. Finally, we will look at our hunger motivation and how it goes awry in those with eating disorders.

Historical Explanations

 27-1 How did early psychologists explain human motivation, and what were the limitations of these theories?

The study of motivation is far from new to psychologists. Some of the earliest questions asked by psychological researchers involved trying to figure out why we do what we do. The earliest researchers in the field of motivation gathered information on instincts and drives.

> **instinct** A complex, inherited behavior that is rigidly patterned throughout a species.

Instincts

An **instinct** is an inherited complex behavior that is rigidly patterned throughout a species. Examples include the migration patterns of birds that fly south for the winter and the human infant's instinct to suck.

In the first published psychology textbook, William James listed 37 human instincts, including the "mental instincts" of jealousy, curiosity, and cleanliness.[1] Thus, instinct theory was the original psychological explanation of motivation. Many theorists back then found James's list inadequate, so they kept adding instincts, such as the desire to dominate and the desire to make things. Eventually, the number of proposed instincts swelled to a mind-boggling 10,000, making the study of instincts, shall we say, cumbersome.[2] Further, instinct theorists fell into a trap, using instincts both to label and to explain a behavior. For instance, they might say that studying behavior would be explained by the studying instinct. And what's the studying instinct? Well, it's studying behavior. Given this circular reasoning, interest in explaining behavior through instincts understandably dropped off.

Thirst Quenching
The young woman and the cat have the same motive, but they inherited different ways to meet this need. The cat's behavior pattern is fixed, and it drinks only by curling its tongue backward as it laps water out of a container. With a more advanced nervous system, humans can learn a variety of ways to quench their thirst.

Drives

Still searching for a way to explain motivation, psychologists looked hopefully at the study of *drives* (physiological needs). Consider the hunger drive, for example. Ever miss breakfast because you got up late? By 10:00 A.M., you're starving. Skipping your Honey Nut Cheerios creates an internal physiological *need* for food, which leads to hunger, a psychological *drive*. The drive to eat and the need for food disappear after you eat lunch. **Drive-reduction theory** is the idea that a physiological need (such as food or water) creates a state of tension (a drive) that motivates an organism to satisfy that need (see **Figure 27.1**). Eating and drinking are drive-reducing behaviors: Eating reduces the hunger drive, and drinking reduces the thirst drive.

> **drive-reduction theory** The idea that a physiological need creates a state of tension (a drive) that motivates an organism to satisfy the need.

FIGURE 27.1
Drive-Reduction Theory
This theory states that need creates the tension (drive) necessary for you to be motivated enough to satisfy or reduce the need.

Like instinct theory, drive-reduction theory had a great deal of difficulty explaining particular activities and did not produce the explanations of motivation many had desired. For instance, what drive is reduced when a first-time skydiver pays $150 for the privilege of leaping headfirst out of a plane? Again, the search for an explanation of motivation's origins shifted, this time to the biological, cognitive, and clinical arenas.

MAKE IT STICK!

1. True or false: The instinct theory of motivation became a less popular way to explain behavior because humans are not animals and do not have instincts.

2. Which motivation theory best fits this description of behavior: "When we are cold, we are motivated to stand next to the fire to warm up"?

   a. drive-reduction theory
   b. James's motivation theory

   c. instinct theory
   d. mental motivation theory

3. What is a one-word synonym for physiological need?

Arousal and Homeostasis

 27-2 How do the concepts of optimum level of arousal and homeostasis apply to motivation?

As we saw in the previous section, drives and instincts are often explained at a psychological level. Some psychologists believed that the key to understanding motivation would be found in biological processes. One group searched for the answer in our level of psychological arousal, and another group looked closely at how we regulate our body chemistry.

Arousal Theories

It's Friday night, and you're sitting in a Burger King with three friends who have registered to take the same college entrance exam the next morning. You know that all three have about the same level of intelligence and knowledge base, but they seem to have different approaches to the test-taking process:

- *Friend A:* "You know, I don't really care about the test. I'm going to a trade school because I want to become a better welder. I'm only taking the test because my parents want me to. Can I have some of your fries?"

- *Friend B:* "I want to do well, but if I screw up on this test, it's not going to permanently ruin my life. I'll give it my best shot. Where's the ketchup?"

- *Friend C:* "It's all on the line tomorrow. If I don't get a good score, it will change my life forever. I'm so nervous, I can't eat—take my fries."

Each of these three people has a different level of *arousal;* the brain of each has activated different levels of alertness. So, which of them will stand the best chance of acing the exam? One arousal theory, the Yerkes–Dodson law, would predict the best performance by Friend B. The **Yerkes–Dodson law** is the theory that a degree of psychological arousal helps performance, but only to a point. The optimum level of arousal depends on the difficulty of the task. Too much or too little arousal can decrease

"What do you think . . . should we get started on that motivation research or not?"

Yerkes–Dodson law
The theory that a degree of psychological arousal helps performance, but only to a point.

performance, as shown in **Figure 27.2**. Using this reasoning, Friend A's level of arousal would be too low to ace the exam and Friend C may be too overstimulated to do well.

Arousal theorists think that each of us has an optimal level of stimulation we like to maintain. When you're stressed out (overstimulated), how do you relax? If your optimal level of stimulation is low, perhaps you'll go for a quiet walk or talk casually with a friend. If your optimal stimulation level is high, you might crank up your favorite music or enjoy a vigorous workout. Arousal theorists explain the motivation behind our behaviors as our attempts to maintain this optimal level of stimulation. And this explanation, they would say, tells us why skydivers (who presumably have a high optimal stimulation level) pay good money to leap headfirst through half a mile of space!

We are also biologically driven to learn. There are areas of the brain that make us feel good after we've learned something. We hunger for information once our biological needs are met.[3] A similar idea is the basis of the next biological motivation theory, which focuses on maintaining a balanced internal state.

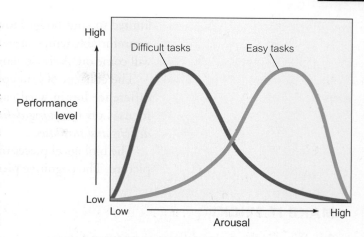

FIGURE 27.2
Arousal and Performance
The Yerkes–Dodson law describes the relationship between performance and arousal. In general, arousal will increase performance up to a point, after which further arousal impairs performance. However, optimal arousal changes according to the difficulty of the task. For a simple task, higher arousal leads to optimal performance. Lower arousal is best for difficult tasks. (From Hembree, 1988.)

Homeostasis

What is your average body temperature? Most of us maintain a fairly constant 98.6 degrees Fahrenheit. But if you ride a bike, dance, or play basketball, your temperature will rise until perspiration and other body mechanisms kick in to bring your temperature back down to normal. This return to normal is a product of **homeostasis,** the body's tendency to maintain a balanced or constant internal state. Balancing our internal states means regulating such things as hormone levels, water levels in our cells, and blood sugar level. Any change in the normal level, up or down, will be corrected, bringing us back to the comfort zone (see **Figure 27.3**). Is this concept

homeostasis A tendency to maintain a balanced or constant internal state.

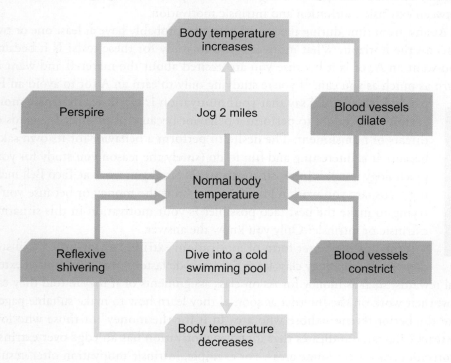

FIGURE 27.3
An Example of Homeostatic Regulation
When body temperature increases or decreases, body mechanisms like those illustrated here kick into gear, returning your temperature to normal.

limited to your body? How about the shopping mall? The thermostat there is set at a comfortable temperature, and if the temperature drops below that setting, the heat will come on. A rise in temperature will activate the air conditioner.

The concept of homeostasis sounds like drive-reduction theory, doesn't it? The difference lies in what each emphasizes. Remember that drive-reduction theory focuses on *removing deficits.* Homeostatic regulation focuses on *avoiding both deficits and surpluses.*

The biological pieces to motivation's puzzle help us see parts of motivation's big picture. The cognitive pieces make the picture clearer.

MAKE IT STICK!

1. What is the major difference between drive-reduction theory and homeostasis theory?

   a. Homeostasis is an older theory than drive-reduction theory.

   b. Drive-reduction theory describes instincts, while homeostasis describes mostly drives.

   c. Drive-reduction theory focuses on removing deficits, but homeostasis focuses on avoiding both deficits and surpluses.

   d. Drive-reduction theory is mostly environmental, while homeostasis is biological.

2. Optimal level of arousal for peak performance is supported by the _____.

3. True or false: Arousal theorists think that each of us has an optimal level of stimulation we like to maintain.

Cognitive Explanations

🐾 27-3 Are we more motivated by external or internal factors?

extrinsic motivation A desire to perform a behavior because of promised rewards or threats of punishment.

intrinsic motivation A desire to perform a behavior for its own sake and to be effective.

Cognitive theories examine the role thoughts play in motivating behavior. Let's look at one key example of a cognitive theory of motivation—the difference between extrinsic motivation and intrinsic motivation.

At any given time during the school year, you probably have at least one or two tests on the horizon. What motivates you to study for these tests? Is it because you want an A, or is it because you are excited about the material and want to learn as much as you can? If you're studying only to earn an A (or to avoid an F), psychologists would say that your motivation is extrinsic. **Extrinsic motivation** is the desire to perform a behavior because of promised rewards or threats of punishment. The desire to perform a behavior for its own sake, because it is interesting and fun to do (surely the reason you study for your psychology tests), is **intrinsic motivation**. So, if you work at Taco Bell making tacos, are you working because you want the money or because you're trying to make the best taco possible? Is your motivation in this situation extrinsic or intrinsic? Only you know the answer.

Which is the better form of motivation: extrinsic or intrinsic? Will students in a technology class learn how to code faster if they're promised external rewards, such as money for As on class assignments or if they're told they can post their work on the Internet as soon as they learn how to make suitable pages? Are the better teachers those who are "in it for the money" or those who love to teach? Research indicates that intrinsic motivation has an edge over extrinsic motivation, at least in some areas. For example, intrinsic motivation often results

Pier Marco Tacca/Anadolu Agency/Getty Images

Paid to Perform ▲
This athlete is receiving an extrinsic reward for playing volleyball. Would she likely play even harder if her rewards were intrinsic?

in high achievement, whereas extrinsic motivation does not.[4] The most creative scientists, artists, teachers, actors, directors, and writers are those working from intrinsic motivation.[5] Does this mean that those most exemplary in their field are oblivious to the extrinsic rewards of success? *No,* but rather than being the focus of their efforts, the money and fame seem more like a pleasant surprise.

Intrinsic and extrinsic motivations surely work together for some of our activities. Sometimes, of course, external rewards can help us achieve a goal. The marching band kids who wash cars every summer weekend to pay for a trip to a New Year's Day parade are extrinsically motivated to earn some extra money.

A primary concern about external rewards, however, is that behaviors maintained by extrinsic motivation alone may not be effectively sustained once the rewards are removed. That is, will grades go down if a parent stops giving money rewards for anything above a C? Evidence suggests removal of an extrinsic motivator may result in behavior levels even lower than before the rewards occur.[6] There is also evidence to suggest that external incentives (such as money) can actually decrease one's intrinsic motivation to do something. This is called the overjustification effect.[7] Finally, suddenly introducing external rewards can disrupt the intrinsic pleasure found in certain activities. If your little sister loves to shoot baskets but you start giving her a piece of candy for every shot she puts in the hoop, she may start playing basketball for the candy instead of the pure joy of the activity. Be careful of those external rewards.

Learning to Lead

To be an effective leader—with friends, with family, or on the job—you will have to know how to motivate others. Motivating others is a four-step process:

1. *Cultivate intrinsic motivation.* We know that intrinsic motivation produces greater achievement. You can cultivate intrinsic motivation by providing appropriately challenging tasks that foster curiosity. The other side of this coin is avoiding manipulative extrinsic rewards that control behavior ("I'll give you $10 for every A"). Extrinsic rewards can be effective if they *inform* ("Look at this great report card! Let's go out to dinner to celebrate!") rather than *control.* Praising effort more than ability also helps.[8]

2. *Attend to individual motives.* Not everybody moves to the beat of the same drummer. If you know this, you will try to discover what motivates each individual in your group. You can challenge those who value *accomplishment* to achieve excellence in a variety of settings. You can pay extra attention to those who require *recognition.* And you can provide competitive opportunities for those who value *power.*

3. *Set specific challenging goals.* Several studies show that setting specific challenging goals motivates higher achievement.[9–11] Clear objectives promote effort, direct attention, and stimulate creative strategies. Help others define their goals while providing consistent feedback on progress.[12]

4. *Choose an appropriate leadership style.* Figuring out which leadership style is best for you or for the situation can be a challenge, but the results are worth it. Consider two general styles. Task leadership is goal oriented. Leaders using this style set standards, organize work, and focus attention on goals. Social leadership emphasizes group efforts, builds teamwork, resolves conflict, and offers support. Those working with social leaders may buy into the process, feeling more motivated to achieve if they are in on the decision making.

Keep these steps in mind or refer to them the next time you're in a leadership position and need to motivate others.

Clinical Explanations

27-4 How do Maslow's hierarchy of needs and Murray's achievement motivation theory describe motivation?

Clinical psychologists, those who assess and treat people with psychological disorders, have shed additional light on our understanding of motivation. Here, we consider two clinical explanations of motivation: Abraham Maslow's famous hierarchy of needs and Henry Murray and David McClelland's views on achievement motivation.

Survival Needs Are Not Always Most Important
The actions of these hunger strikers would not have been predicted by the hierarchy of needs.

Hierarchy of Needs

If you're sleepy, with your body craving a nap, you may not feel like reading *Lord of the Flies.* Similarly, if you're stranded on foot in an unfamiliar city late at night and concerned for your safety, you probably won't be thinking about the next time you're going to see your best friend. Some of your needs are clearly more basic than others. The need for sleep will take precedence over the need to learn, just as the need for safety will take precedence over the need for companionship.

Recognizing that some needs take priority over others, **Abraham Maslow** designed his famous **hierarchy of needs**[13] (see **Figure 27.4**). The idea behind this pyramid structure is that we must satisfy physiological needs (air, water, food, sleep) before safety needs and psychological needs can motivate us. One of the higher needs, according to Maslow, is **self-actualization,** the need to realize full and unique potential.

Maslow's hierarchy has been widely applied in business and industry. That is, if the need for self-esteem (fourth level up on the pyramid) includes working on important projects, then the wise employer should take steps to ensure that the social needs of the third level have already been met. The notion is that employees need to feel accepted before they are ready to work on projects that would bring self-esteem. Above the esteem level, people are said to realize their own potential by self-actualizing. And at the top of the pyramid, the self-transcendence level, people go beyond the self to strive for purpose and meaning.[14]

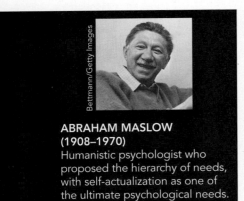

ABRAHAM MASLOW (1908–1970)
Humanistic psychologist who proposed the hierarchy of needs, with self-actualization as one of the ultimate psychological needs.

Self-transcendence needs
Need to find meaning and identity beyond the self

Self-actualization needs
Need to live up to our fullest and unique potential

Esteem needs
Need for self-esteem, achievement, competence, and independence; need for recognition and respect from others

Belongingness and love needs
Need to love and be loved, to belong and be accepted; need to avoid loneliness and separation

Safety needs
Need to feel that the world is organized and predictable; need to feel safe

Physiological needs
Need to satisfy hunger and thirst

FIGURE 27.4
Abraham Maslow's Hierarchy of Needs
Maslow's theory proposes that we must satisfy our basic physiological needs before we can try to meet higher-level safety and psychological needs. (From Maslow, 1970.)

hierarchy of needs Maslow's pyramid of human needs, beginning at the base with physiological needs that must be satisfied before higher-level safety needs and then psychological needs become active.

self-actualization According to Maslow, an ultimate psychological need that arises after basic physical and psychological needs are met and self-esteem is achieved; the motivation to realize our full and unique potential.

achievement motivation A desire for significant accomplishment; for mastery of things, people, or ideas; and for attaining a high standard.

The hierarchy of needs has been in nearly every introductory psychology textbook for 50 years, but we should be careful about putting too much empirical stock in the theory, as critics have found fault with Maslow's research methods. His sample size was too small, he selected his own participants for study, and he defined his terms ambiguously. Moreover, many people behave in ways that don't conform to Maslow's hierarchy. For instance, how does the hierarchy account for the political prisoner who goes on a hunger strike? Putting a political principle above the need for food does not fit into Maslow's most famous work. The hierarchy of needs does not cover all situations.

Achievement Motivation

Clinical psychologists often find themselves treating people who struggle to succeed in life. Why do some succeed against all odds, whereas others fail despite having been given every opportunity? What motivates you to stay in high school when 19 percent of your peers across the country are dropping out of school? Why do some students persist in their quest for a college degree when so many give up after a term or two? And why do some camp out overnight in line to buy tickets to a concert you couldn't pay others to attend? The answer may partly be **achievement motivation** (see Psychology in the Real World: Motivating Ourselves). According to **Henry Murray,** such motivation includes a desire for

- significant accomplishment.
- mastery of ideas, things, or people.
- attaining a high standard.[15]

Appreciating differences in achievement motivation is one thing; comparing those differences is quite another. Without physiological indicators, how might we measure achievement motivation? David McClelland and his colleagues

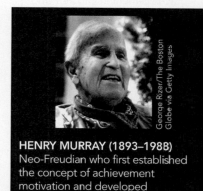

HENRY MURRAY (1893–1988)
Neo-Freudian who first established the concept of achievement motivation and developed important personality testing tools.

FIGURE 27.5 ▲
What's Going on Here?
Motivation researchers use people's responses to ambiguous photos like this to assess achievement motivation. They ask research participants to invent stories about the people in the photo, and then the researchers analyze the stories, watching for achievement themes.

grit Passionate dedication to an ambitious goal.

"Maybe they didn't try hard enough."

Storybook Achievers ▲
The main character in children's stories often works hard to overcome obstacles. Does this theme help establish an expectation of achievement in children who hear these stories?

devised a way.[16] Look at the photo of the young girl in **Figure 27.5**. If you had to write a story about what was going on in that photo, what would you say? McClelland assumed that people tell stories that reflect their own achievement motivation. So, if people told stories about heroic acts, pride in accomplishment, or pursuit of a goal, McClelland labeled them as having an achievement theme. And he gave people who consistently wrote stories with achievement themes high scores for achievement motivation.

People high in achievement motivation persist in the face of difficulty. Is it any surprise that a study of gifted artists, scholars, and athletes showed that all had impressive, self-disciplined motivation to meet their goals?[17] What distinguishes these outstanding high achievers is not their raw talent. Rather, their daily practice regimen eclipses that of less-accomplished colleagues. Achievement is much more than ability: Those with a passion to perfect and the discipline to prepare are often the best in their fields. High achievers often display **grit,** which is described as passionate dedication to an ambitious goal. Evidence of grit, or self-discipline, in high school seniors better predicts which of them will succeed in college than grades, SAT or ACT scores, or graduation honors.[18] As my Grandpa Ledbetter used to say, "I think you'll get a lot luckier at baseball, Randy, if you practice a bit more!"

Persisting despite difficulties brings rewards to the not-so-rich-and-famous, too: People who were underachievers in high school tend to have more difficulty later in life holding on to a job compared with their high-achieving counterparts.[19]

Now that you have a general understanding of how psychologists explain our motivational processes, let's look at a key motivator: hunger. Hunger has physiological components, but key psychological factors also contribute to our motivation to eat, as evidenced by the devastating effects of eating disorders.

▲ **Motivate Yourself!**
Celebrate those good grades or that healthy heart and know that your hard work is paying off. If your grades or your fitness aren't so great, don't write yourself off. Such feats take dedication and discipline. Setting reasonable daily and long-term goals will help.

PSYCHOLOGY IN THE REAL WORLD

Motivating Ourselves

Who are your heroes? Do they hold public office, help keep our communities safe, or help you learn? Perhaps they're exceptionally good at running, acting, or singing. Somewhere along the line, our heroes and role models became motivated to succeed. Judging from their lives, their achievement motivation must be high. Did you ever wonder where such motivation to succeed comes from? Or whether you could increase your own level of motivation? If so, you'll be happy to know that the experts say, "Yes!" Here are three ways you can further develop your self-motivation:

1. *Associate your high achievement with positive emotions.* If you score high on a test, don't attribute it to luck. Celebrate! You did well because you are bright.

2. *Connect your achievement with your efforts.* A bad grade may simply mean you need to spend more time studying than you're used to. The best athletes and actors have had to work hard, even though they make it look effortless when we watch them perform.

3. *Raise your expectations.* Your goals should be high enough so that you are challenged, but not so unreasonably high that you become discouraged.

THINK ABOUT . . . Psychology in the Real World

1. Explain what you can do to increase your own level of motivation.

2. Why is self-motivation important?

MAKE IT STICK!

1. Which of the following behaviors would Abraham Maslow's hierarchy of needs have the most trouble explaining?

   a. stealing a loaf of bread
   b. risking physical harm by protesting for civil rights
   c. working on a difficult school project to increase self-esteem
   d. voluntarily taking a difficult college course

2. Henry Murray and the achievement motivation theorists found that high-achieving artists, scholars, and athletes often had greater _____ than people who didn't achieve as much.

3. True or false: Maslow's hierarchy of needs does not cover all situations.

Hunger: A Closer Look

 27-5 What physiological and environmental factors control hunger?

Ever been asked to describe an embarrassing moment from your past? I don't have to think that long to come up with several examples, one of which includes my first college date. It was Friday morning, the second week of college. The plan was to meet at the snack bar after English class, where we could have a Coke and work through that early what-do-I-say awkwardness. If things progressed, perhaps we would go out to a meal and a movie.

Peanuts

Keep in mind that this was long before the age of Internet dating, so we got together to discuss biographical information. No sooner did we sit down than my stomach let out a growl so loud that people in both booths across from us turned quickly to look. In the hopes of distracting this girl from Des Moines, I started naming movies I'd like to see. But it happened again! Not quite as loud, perhaps, but twice the duration. These empty-stomach pangs, which I was powerless to control, did not make a good impression. I did go out for a meal and a movie that night, but it was with my roommate, Chad.

Inopportune stomach rumblings are a fact of life and generally indicate hunger. However, other factors—some physiological, some environmental—also tell us when to eat.

Physiology of Hunger

For a physiological understanding of hunger, we turn first to some key substances in your body and then to your brain's control of these substances.

- *Glucose*—This form of sugar circulates throughout your body. Run low on glucose, and you will feel hungry. Glucose is a major source of energy for your body.

- *Insulin*—This hormone allows your cells to use glucose for energy or convert it to fat. When levels of insulin go up, glucose levels go down.

- *Leptin*—This protein is produced by bloated fat cells, which send out a "stop eating" message. Artificially increased leptin levels in mice stimulate activity and reduce eating. Obese mice receiving leptin injections lose weight.[20] The leptin receptors in obese humans may be insensitive to leptin, however, and studies are under way to determine whether some drug treatment might help activate those receptors.[21]

- *Orexin*—This hunger-triggering hormone is produced by the hypothalamus. When glucose levels drop, orexin levels rise and we feel hungry.

FIGURE 27.6
The Hypothalamus
The hypothalamus (colored orange in this picture) contains important hunger controls. Depending on the information it receives through substances in your blood, your hypothalamus can send messages that encourage you to eat or stop eating. ▼

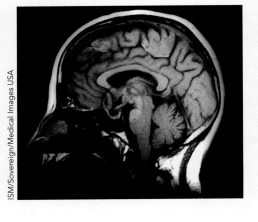

What do all these substances have in common besides hunger? Your brain controls each substance in some way. Your *hypothalamus,* a key structure in your brain, actively regulates your appetite in many ways (see **Figure 27.6**). For example, the hypothalamus monitors leptin levels to estimate available fat. We've learned a lot from medical records of people who had tumors near the base of the brain (the location of the hypothalamus) and subsequently became overweight.[22] We've also learned a lot from rats. Damage to parts of the hypothalamus that restrain eating will produce excessive eating in rats. Stimulate those areas instead, and a rat will starve to death.

Research studies involving rats have also indicated the importance of carbohydrates in your diet. These starchy foods help boost levels of the neurotransmitter *serotonin* in your brain, which helps calm you when stressed. Rats will eat more Oreo cookies (high in carbs) when stressed than when unstressed.[23]

One interesting theory views the hypothalamus as a "weight thermostat." This thermostat is genetically engineered to maintain a **set point,** which is the weight a full-grown active person hovers around when not trying to gain or lose weight.[24] When a body falls below this set-point weight, increased hunger and a lowered metabolic rate may act to restore lost weight. (As a teen, your body doesn't yet have a set point because you're still growing and still gaining weight as a part of normal development.) Regardless of how much the person eats in a given day (and calorie intake does vary), the scale will pretty much register the same weight. Set-point theory relies on three underlying concepts:

1. We have a **basal metabolic rate,** the body's resting rate at which we burn calories for energy.

2. We start out with a specific number of fat cells, which can expand in size and increase in number.

3. We have hormones that work together to keep our weight where it's designed to be.

The metabolism of a normal-weight person who overeats will speed up, preventing weight gain. But an overweight person's metabolism reacts differently. When overweight people diet, their bodies react to the reduced intake of calories as if they are starving. Their metabolism slows down to conserve energy, converting more glucose to fat in preparation for the apparent "famine." Set-point theory may help explain why so many people who lose weight by dieting gain the weight back: They are returning to their set point.

Environment and Hunger

Certainly, our body chemistry and the thermostat-like action of the hypothalamus fuel our drive to eat. But physiology is not the only hunger catalyst. We should also consider external incentives and culture.

External Incentives The sight, sound, and smell of food—all external incentives—seem to affect some people more than others (whose eating habits appear to be triggered more by internal factors). This difference is so striking that researchers have labeled the first group "externals" and the other group "internals." In one study, researchers had internals and externals fast for 18 hours. They then took the two groups into a laboratory where steak was cooking. Compared with the internals, the externals experienced a greater increase in blood insulin levels in hopeful anticipation of incoming food energy.[25] External stimuli affect the hunger-related physiological states in many individuals.

Culture Like external incentives, culture shapes our attitudes toward eating. White Americans often see obesity as a weakness or a sign of laziness. African-Americans and Latinos tend to be less concerned about weight and generally more accepting of those

Hunger in the Brain
Damage to the part of the hypothalamus responsible for controlling eating leads to a threefold increase in weight in rats, providing evidence for the brain's control of hunger mechanisms.

Reproduced with permission of The Jackson Laboratory

set point The point at which an individual's "weight thermostat" is supposedly set; when the body falls below this weight, an increase in hunger and a lowered metabolic rate may act to restore the lost weight.

basal metabolic rate The body's resting rate at which we burn calories for energy.

Eating and Attitudes
Our culture affects what we eat, how much, and when.

World Religions Photo Library/Alamy

who are overweight.[26,27] Culture also affects taste. We tend to shun foods to which we have not been exposed, but we don't think twice about eating the familiar foods we've seen all our lives on the dinner table. I've never eaten horse, dog, or rat meat, but people in other parts of the world readily accept these foods and even prefer them to foods I consider a great treat, such as salmon. Repeated exposure to new foods increases our willingness to give them a try.[28,29]

The situation in which we are eating also affects our appetite. For example, researchers have found that we consume more when eating with others than when eating alone.[30]

Eating Disorders

> **anorexia nervosa** An eating disorder in which normal-weight people (usually adolescent females) have a distorted self-perception of being "fat," put themselves on self-starvation regimens, and become dangerously underweight (15 percent or more below normal).

> **bulimia nervosa** An eating disorder characterized by episodes of overeating—usually of high-calorie foods—followed by vomiting, use of laxatives, fasting, or excessive exercise.

A member of my daughter's ballet class looked like a normal 15-year-old at the beginning of the year—5 feet, 5 inches tall, and weighing 120 pounds. As the year went by, however, this young woman became increasingly thin, even as she continued to make remarks to other members of the class about how "fat" she was. Some wondered if she was ill. Obsessed with losing weight, she hit 90 pounds before finally undergoing treatment for **anorexia nervosa,** an eating disorder in which a normal-weight person (usually adolescent females, but also women, men, and boys) has a distorted self-perception of being overweight. People with anorexia put themselves on self-starvation regimens and become dangerously underweight (15 percent or more below normal).

Despite the attention the press has given to eating disorders lately, they aren't confined to the present time. Years ago, I remember hearing stories of how cheerleaders and drill-team members (all girls) at other schools had to "weigh in" every Monday morning as a means of monitoring weight. Rumors also flew that many of these girls were bulimic, which meant they had **bulimia nervosa,** an eating disorder characterized by overeating (usually high-calorie foods) followed by vomiting (purging), laxative use, fasting, or excessive exercise. Binge–purge eaters fear gaining weight, are preoccupied with food, and often suffer from depression, anxiety, or both.[31] Individuals with anorexia often display bulimic characteristics as well.

Srdjanns74/ iStock/Getty Images

Recipe for Eating Disorders
Excessive concern over weight may lead to anorexia nervosa or bulimia nervosa.

What causes these eating disorders? For some, there may be a genetic link. Twin studies show that identical twins are more likely to have the same eating disorder than fraternal twins are.[32,33] Without question, however, the genetic factors interact with a cultural pressure to be thin. These pressures are particularly strong in weight-conscious cultures. Mothers who are unusually concerned about their own weight and about the weight and appearance of their daughters are more likely to have a child with an eating disorder.[34] Anorexia usually starts as a diet, and bulimia often has its origins in a diet broken by gorging. Furthermore, those who idealize thinness are more prone to eating disorders. These thinness worshipers, not surprisingly, are also more likely to have great dissatisfaction with the way their own bodies look.[35]

Our society bombards us with pictures of the "perfect" body in commercials and advertisements, an image unobtainable by nearly everyone. Our weight-obsessed culture worsens the situation, sending the message that fat equals weakness. Susan Wooley and Orland Wooley sum up culture's effect: "An increasingly stringent cultural standard of thinness for women has been accompanied by a steadily increasing incidence of serious eating disorders in women."[36] Fortunately, research suggests that interactive prevention programs work to help increase acceptance of body appearance.[37]

The common thread running through these discussions of biological, cognitive, and clinical explanations is the notion of *motives*. The same thread that weaves its way through hunger and eating disorders continues through discussions of terrorism, leadership, and other motivated behaviors. Though hidden, like the processor in a computer, motives energize and direct behavior, whether the goal is for good or bad. Understanding motives helps us predict and control all kinds of behaviors.

The Advertising Archives

▲ **The Perfect Form?**
Because pictures of what are considered perfect body types surround them, many people feel imperfect by comparison.

MAKE IT STICK!

1. Which of the following factors best explains why people who lose weight on a diet often gain it back eventually?

   a. bulimia nervosa   c. hierarchy of needs
   b. instinct   d. set point

2. True or false: The sight, sound, and smell of food are considered internal incentives.

3. What do we call the body's resting rate at which we burn calories for energy?

Module 27 Summary and Assessment
Motivation

 27-1 How did early psychologists explain human motivation, and what were the limitations of these theories?

- After William James's efforts to identify human instincts, other instinct theorists listed thousands of instincts to explain human motivation.

- Drive-reduction theorists thought that all human behaviors were motivated by physiological needs. We act to reduce these physiological needs.

- Both instinct theory and drive-reduction theory have difficulty explaining the motivations behind many specific examples of human behavior (such as risk taking).

 27-2 How do the concepts of optimum level of arousal and homeostasis apply to motivation?

- Arousal theory predicts that everyone has an optimum level of arousal.

- We are also motivated to maintain a balanced internal physiological state (homeostasis).

27-3 Are we more motivated by external or internal factors?

- Intrinsic motivation is associated with higher achievement levels.

- Introducing extrinsic motivators can reduce intrinsic motivation, and behaviors motivated by extrinsic factors are not sustained if the extrinsic motivator is removed.

 27-4 How do Maslow's hierarchy of needs and Murray's achievement motivation theory describe motivation?

- Abraham Maslow's hierarchy of needs explains that humans are motivated to achieve the next level on a hierarchy that begins with physiological needs and ends with higher-level needs such as self-actualization and self-transcendence.

- Henry Murray's achievement motivation theory states that humans are motivated by desires for significant accomplishment, mastery, and attaining high standards.

 27-5 What physiological and environmental factors control hunger?

- The hypothalamus in the brain controls levels of sugar, hormones, and proteins in the body to regulate hunger.

- The brain works to maintain a set point—a target weight—through metabolic rate, expansion or contraction of the number of fat cells, and hormone levels.

- Culture affects our attitudes toward body size and different kinds of foods.

- Eating disorders like anorexia nervosa and bulimia nervosa both involve preoccupations with body weight and dangerous eating habits.

Summative Assessment

1. Drive-reduction theory describes which of the following?
   a. After eating a bag of popcorn, you become very thirsty and drink water.
   b. You select a vacation that will allow you to experience a different climate.
   c. Birds migrate south to a warmer environment during the cold winter.
   d. A cat hisses when a dog tries to approach it.

2. What term do we use to describe the brain when it has been activated to alertness?
   a. homeostasis
   b. arousal
   c. motivation
   d. intrinsic

3. Which situation would result in better performance on the final test in your science class as predicted by the Yerkes–Dodson law?
   a. your teacher reminding you as you enter the room for the test that you need a good grade on the test to pass the class
   b. staying up until 3:00 A.M. to read the five chapters from your book being covered on the test
   c. reviewing your notes on the drive to school the morning of the test because you spent your time focusing on the geometry test the day before
   d. studying your class and lab notes with a classmate the day before the test, making sure you get enough sleep the night before the test, and having breakfast the day of the test

4. What do we call regulation that focuses on avoiding both deficits and surpluses?
   a. homeostasis
   b. drive-reduction theory
   c. arousal
   d. Yerkes–Dodson law

5. Which of the following is an example of intrinsic motivation?
   a. getting money from your parents for good report card grades
   b. getting a coupon for free pizza for good attendance
   c. challenging yourself to get a better grade on a test
   d. getting extra credit in P.E. for the time spent practicing free throws

6. What do we call a desire to perform a behavior because of promised rewards or threats of punishment?

    a. internal factors

    b. extrinsic motivation

    c. homeostasis

    d. instincts

7. Which of the following is a trait that distinguishes high achievers?

    a. self-discipline

    b. raw talent

    c. extrinsic motivation

    d. drives

8. Which of the following is a major source of energy for your body?

    a. insulin

    b. orexin

    c. leptin

    d. glucose

9. Which of the following is NOT an underlying concept of set-point theory?

    a. We have a resting rate at which we burn calories for energy.

    b. We start out with a specific number of fat cells.

    c. External stimuli affect hunger-related physiology.

    d. Hormones work together to keep a set point for weight.

10. Which of the following characterizes eating disorders, such as anorexia nervosa?

    a. external pressure to eat more fruits and vegetables

    b. a distorted self-perception of being overweight

    c. the desire to regularly exercise

    d. not eating "fast food" and sugary drinks

KEY TERMS AND KEY PEOPLE

motivation, p. 410	intrinsic motivation, p. 414	basal metabolic rate, p. 421
instinct, p. 411	hierarchy of needs, p. 416	anorexia nervosa, p. 422
drive-reduction theory, p. 411	self-actualization, p. 416	bulimia nervosa, p. 422
Yerkes–Dodson law, p. 412	achievement motivation, p. 417	Abraham Maslow (1908–1970), p. 416
homeostasis, p. 413	grit, p. 418	
extrinsic motivation, p. 414	set point, p. 421	Henry Murray (1893–1988), p. 417

Module 28 | Emotion

Learning Goals

28-1 Explain how historical approaches to emotion differ from modern theories of emotion.

28-2 Describe the physiological changes that occur during a fear reaction, and the parts of the nervous system that are involved in these changes.

28-3 Explain how gender and culture affect the ability to express and interpret nonverbal communications of emotion.

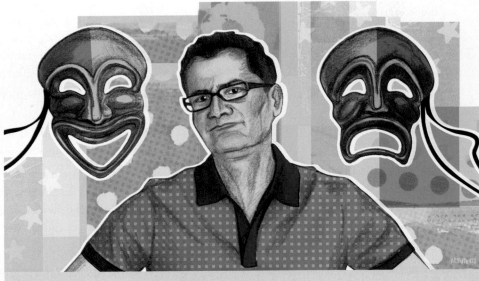

Whether we feel happy, sad, or fearful, emotions play a big part in our lives.

Did You Make It? ►
The student on the right saw her name on the cast list for the new play. The two students on the left did not. All are experiencing emotion.

emotions Whole-organism responses, involving physiological arousal, expressive behaviors, and conscious experience.

Every school year, I see lists of names posted by the theater, band room, athletic office, and other locations around the school. Have you ever searched a list looking for your name? The cast list for a play? The honor roll? An election? Chair placements in the band? Did your name appear where you'd hoped—or where you'd feared? Perhaps it was left off altogether.

Having posted a few lists myself for student council elections, I've witnessed students jumping and screaming with happiness, excitement, and surprise. I've seen others, clearly disappointed and with tears in their eyes, force a smile and walk bravely away. Still others did little to disguise their anger.

Spencer Grant/ PhotoEdit

The **emotions** these students were having were full-body responses, involving physical arousal, expressive behaviors, and conscious experiences. Let's see how this might work. Imagine that you and a good friend check the National Honor Society list to see whether either of you has been chosen. A smile breaks across your friend's face as she sees her name. She pumps her fist above her head and gives a little whoop of joy. Then, checking the list again, she notices your name is missing. Reining in her emotions, she starts providing explanations, such as "I was lucky to have made it" or "Maybe your name was left off by mistake." Her shift from personal happiness to shared sadness with you contains the three ingredients of emotion:

- *Physiological activation*—Increased heart rate as she reads the good news; decreased heart rate as she consoles you.

- *Expressive behaviors*—Smiling and pumping her fist after seeing her name; losing the smile and putting an arm around your shoulder when she notices your name is missing.
- *Conscious experience*—Interpreting what it means to be selected as a member; understanding what it means to you to be left out.

Compared with other species, from dolphins to deer to ducks, humans appear to be the most emotional.[1] This rich source of human behavior has intrigued psychologists for more than a century and has sparked some emotional debates. Those debates revolve around two controversies, both addressing the order in which each ingredient is stirred into the recipe for emotions:

1. Which comes first, physiological arousal or the subjective experience of an emotion? Do you feel happy because your heart is pounding, or is your heart pounding because you feel happy?
2. Can we react emotionally before appraising a situation, or does thinking always precede emotion? Did you feel joy at seeing your name on the list before you thought about what that meant, or did you interpret the situation and then feel joy?

To answer these questions, psychologists have been proposing theories and designing experiments to test them for more than a hundred years.

"I don't sing because I am happy. I am happy because I sing."

▲ **Which Comes First?**
Is it the physiological arousal or the emotional experience? This issue has been widely debated in psychology.

Theories of Emotion

 28-1 How do historical approaches to emotion differ from modern theories of emotion?

As is often the case when several perspectives exist on a given topic, the theories of emotion are complementary: Each theory of emotion provides some insight into why or how we experience emotions.

Historical Approaches

Ask the person with the locker next to yours why she is smiling, and she might say, "Because I'm happy." Why did you slam your locker door? "Because I'm angry." Why are you trembling? "Because I'm afraid." Common sense explains any of these emotions as a result of a *stimulus*. For instance, a fire alarm might lead to a conscious feeling (fear) and a physiological response (shaking, increased heart rate). In other words, the fire alarm sounds, you experience fear, and your heart starts to race. Early theories on emotion do not agree with this commonsense approach.

In the 1890s, psychologist **William James** and physiologist **Carl Lange** both proposed theories that challenged the commonsense sequence of emotions. The **James–Lange theory** says that we experience emotion because we are aware of our bodily response to an emotion-producing stimulus. So, the fire alarm sounds, you start shaking, you become aware of the shaking, and then feel afraid.

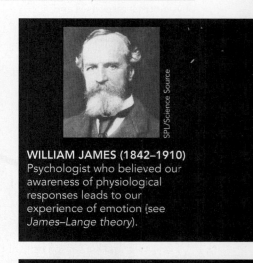

WILLIAM JAMES (1842–1910)
Psychologist who believed our awareness of physiological responses leads to our experience of emotion (see *James–Lange theory*).

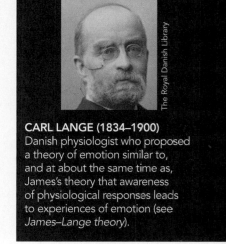

CARL LANGE (1834–1900)
Danish physiologist who proposed a theory of emotion similar to, and at about the same time as, James's theory that awareness of physiological responses leads to experiences of emotion (see *James–Lange theory*).

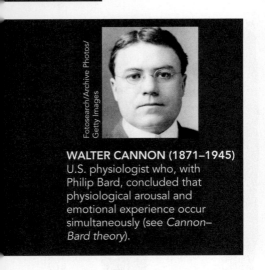

WALTER CANNON (1871–1945)
U.S. physiologist who, with Philip Bard, concluded that physiological arousal and emotional experience occur simultaneously (see *Cannon–Bard theory*).

James–Lange theory The theory that we experience emotion because we are aware of our bodily response to an emotion-arousing stimulus.

Cannon–Bard theory The theory that an emotion-arousing stimulus simultaneously triggers physiological responses and the subjective experience of emotion.

Walter Cannon disagreed with the James–Lange view of emotion. Cannon noted that the heart races whether we're frightened, angry, or exhilarated.[2] How, then, can the same physiological reaction trigger such different emotional interpretations? And how do we explain circumstances where we have such reactions without any emotion-provoking stimuli? Chopping onions, for example, produces the bodily response usually associated with sadness, but chopping onions does not cause sadness. After elaboration by Philip Bard, this view became known as the **Cannon–Bard theory** of emotion.[3] It proposed that an emotion-arousing stimulus *simultaneously triggers* physiological responses and the subjective experience of emotions.

Each of these older theories helps us understand emotion. We do feel emotions, to some degree, by observing changes in our bodies, as the James–Lange theory maintains. But the Cannon–Bard theory was also correct in asserting the important role that the brain and the nervous system play in our conscious feelings (see **Figure 28.1**). Modern psychophysiological explanations tie the importance of hormone levels to emotions. Higher levels of testosterone, for example, are linked to aggression. But does aggression cause testosterone levels to increase, do higher levels of testosterone cause aggression, or does some third factor cause both of them? To answer such questions, psychologists have examined the way our thoughts influence our emotions.

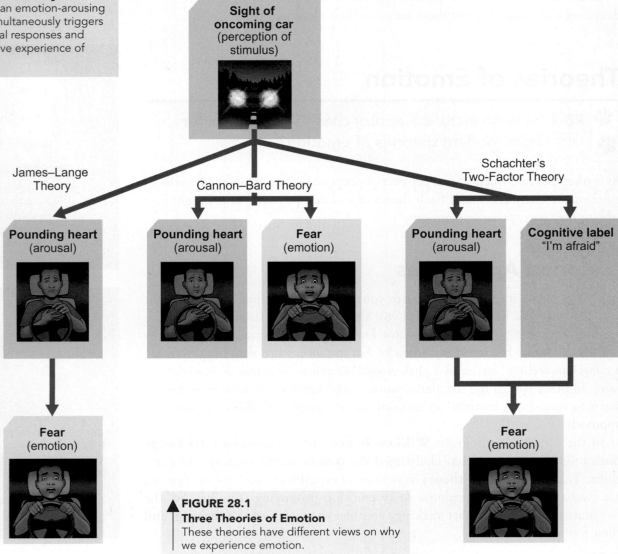

▲ **FIGURE 28.1**
Three Theories of Emotion
These theories have different views on why we experience emotion.

Cognition and Emotion

Which comes first—our thoughts about a situation (our *cognitive appraisal*) or our experience of the emotion? This chicken-and-egg dilemma characterizes the second of the two controversies in the study of emotion. Let's look at some contemporary cognitive approaches to emotion: the two-factor theory and two different theories that attempt to explain the sequence of events in emotions.

Stanley Schachter (pronounced SHACK-ter) and Jerome Singer developed one of the leading cognitive theories of emotion.[4] Their **two-factor theory** of emotion proposes that to experience emotion we must be physically aroused and must cognitively identify the arousal. The first factor, *physiological arousal,* can be brought about by anything from a loud stimulus to a drug. The second factor is a *cognitive label* of the physiological arousal. The bottom line to this theory is that we distinguish emotions by how we label or name the arousal we feel. If you're aroused and you believe the appropriate emotion is fear, then you'll feel afraid. If you think anger is the appropriate emotion, then you'll instead explain your arousal as anger. According to two-factor theorists, our physical experiences of emotions are so similar that we must cognitively figure out and label our reactions to experience an emotion. So, the fire alarm sounds (that's the first factor), you start shaking, and you label or name the arousal (that's the second factor) as fear.

Do all cognitive psychologists agree with this viewpoint? *Certainly not.* **Robert Zajonc** (pronounced ZI-yence) argued that emotion and cognition are sometimes separate.[5] Zajonc also suggested that our interpretations of situations are sometimes slower than our emotional reactions. In other words, before we know what we think about a situation, we know how we feel about it. Keeping the fire alarm example, the alarm sounds, it startles you and makes you start shaking without conscious appraisal. It's only after this automatic physiological response that we label the alarm as a threat and feel afraid.

Complex research supports Zajonc's argument. We have pathways in our brain that carry or transmit messages from one part of our nervous system to another. Certain pathways skip the cortical (thinking) parts of the brain and take a more direct path to the amygdala, an emotion control center in the brain (see **Figure 28.2**). Some researchers, such as Joseph LeDoux and Jorge Armony, believe these shortcuts explain why our

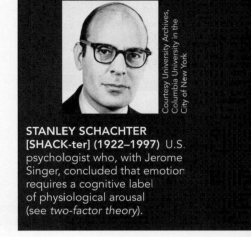

two-factor theory The theory that to experience emotion we must be physically aroused and must cognitively label the arousal.

STANLEY SCHACHTER [SHACK-ter] (1922–1997) U.S. psychologist who, with Jerome Singer, concluded that emotion requires a cognitive label of physiological arousal (see *two-factor theory*).

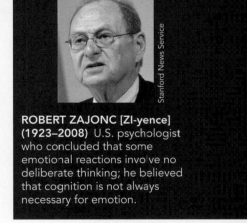

ROBERT ZAJONC [ZI-yence] (1923–2008) U.S. psychologist who concluded that some emotional reactions involve no deliberate thinking; he believed that cognition is not always necessary for emotion.

Prefrontal cortex

Sensory cortex

Thalamus

Fear stimulus

Amygdala

Fear response

(a) The thinking high road

Thalamus

Fear stimulus

Amygdala

Fear response

(b) The speedy low road

FIGURE 28.2
First Run, Then Think!
Your brain has shortcuts that allow you to react almost instantly to a frightening situation instead of thinking about what you should do and why you should do it.

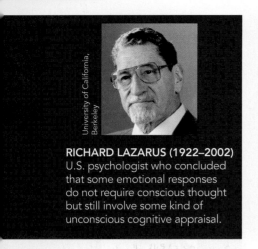

RICHARD LAZARUS (1922–2002)
U.S. psychologist who concluded that some emotional responses do not require conscious thought but still involve some kind of unconscious cognitive appraisal.

feelings are more likely to control our thoughts than our thoughts are to control our feelings, particularly when we're surprised.[6] For example, imagine that you are raking leaves on a fall afternoon. You notice some leaves rustling, and you jump back, not knowing whether the rustling was caused by the wind or by a snake in the grass. After your immediate fear response, the thinking part of your brain takes over, and you take steps to determine whether danger is present ("It's a snake! Run!").

Zajonc believed that emotions are basic to human existence and that they developed before cognition in the history of our species. For these reasons, cognition need not always take place prior to emotion. Of course, not all emotion researchers agree with Zajonc.

Richard Lazarus agreed that our brains can process information outside our *conscious* awareness and that some emotional responses do not require conscious thought.[7,8] However, Lazarus contended that there must be at least a minimal amount of *unconscious* thinking, even for emotions we feel instantaneously. How else would we know what we're reacting to? The initial appraisal of the rustling leaves produces the emotion of fear and an accompanying jump away, based on a snap assessment that the situation may be harmful. A secondary, conscious appraisal involves deciding what to do after the immediate, initial response.

In brief, Schachter, Singer, and Lazarus would maintain that complex feelings like love or moods like depression are profoundly influenced by expectation, interpretations, and memory. Zajonc and LeDoux's research suggests that simple dislikes and likes, as well as fears, need not involve conscious thought (see **Figure 28.3**). Changes in our thinking will likely not affect these latter emotional responses. That is, you've heard that fire alarm every year at school. Your memory of it will not keep you from being startled when that alarm goes off unexpectedly.

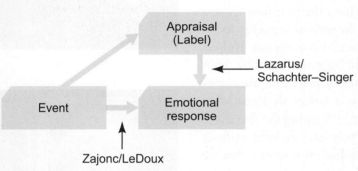

FIGURE 28.3
Two Paths to Emotional Responses
According to Robert Zajonc, some emotional responses are immediate and do not require conscious appraisal. However, for Richard Lazarus and Stanley Schachter, emotional responses are also determined by the appraisal and labeling of events.

Most of the emotions we face daily are much more complex than a primitive fear of snakes, and they require more sophisticated cognitive appraisals. Being the first one in your family *not* to make the National Honor Society might produce immediate disappointment that, after further analysis, leads to the complex emotion of shame. A note of consolation from a friend who did make it can produce a slow, warming feeling of happiness if you choose to see the effort as heartfelt and if you have a history of warm exchanges with that friend. Our more complex emotions, such as love, happiness, shame, and guilt, are rooted in our conscious interpretations, appraisals, and memories of earlier experiences. *How* we think about situations also affects these emotions. Thinking positively about situations makes us feel better; thinking negatively makes us feel worse. Further, research shows that the more positive emotion we experience in life, the more likely we are to cope with life's challenges. A leader in this field, Barbara Fredrickson, has developed the "broaden-and-build" theory of emotion, which evaluates the impact that positive emotions, thinking positively, and thinking negatively have on our well-being.[9]

 ## Broadening and Building Better Health Through Positive Emotion

The study of emotion has intrigued psychologists for over a hundred years, and the work of psychologist Barbara Fredrickson and others brings that endeavor into the twenty-first century. Fredrickson has proposed the broaden-and-build theory of positive emotions.[10–12] Existing theories deal with how emotions prepare us psychologically and physically to act. That is, if we see a snake, we feel afraid and we escape. If we get angry, we have the urge to fight. What Fredrickson rightly points out is that positive emotions have never fit very well into these existing frameworks.

Enter the broaden-and-build theory. Fredrickson's research has shown that just like negative emotions (for example, fear), positive emotions are also important for survival, but in different and more advanced ways. "Positive emotions expand cognition, behavioral tendencies, and increase your options when it comes to using your resources."[13]

Put more simply, experiencing positive emotions increases our intellectual, physical, social, and psychological resources (see **Figure 28.4**).

Intellectual Resources
Develop problem-solving skills
Learn new information

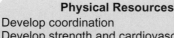

Physical Resources
Develop coordination
Develop strength and cardiovascular health

Social Resources
Solidify bonds
Make new bonds

Psychological Resources
Develop resilience and optimism
Develop sense of identity and goal orientation

FIGURE 28.4
Broaden and Build
Research shows that experiencing positive emotions increases our intellectual, physical, social, and psychological resources. (From Fredrickson, 2006b.)

Fredrickson's research involves inducing negative, positive, or neutral emotions in her research participants. What she has found is that in addition to reporting greater happiness, those who experience positive emotions get along better with others, learn nearly all coursework more easily, overcome problems faster, spend less time absent due to illness, have better relationships, make more friends, and volunteer to help others more often than those experiencing negative or neutral emotion. Fredrickson calls this "broadening and building your mind-set." She contends that negative emotions tend to do the opposite by closing us down and making us less likely to increase our resources.

Fredrickson[14] suggests that we can maximize the benefits of positive emotions by

1. working at ways to remember times when we felt safe, relaxed, and joyful.

2. sincerely expressing gratitude, thanks, and appreciation to those who have helped us.

3. keeping track of when we have felt optimistic, hopeful, and encouraged by the possibility of a good outcome.

4. logging what makes us laugh or amuses us.

Seeking that which inspires us increases positive emotion, as does savoring a bright orange sunset, a favorite poem, or a beautiful song. However, we must make the choice to seek the sunset, read the poem, or play the song in order to tap into this positive emotion that can broaden and build our mind-set. Fredrickson's research indicates that consciously choosing the "upward spiral" of increasing positive emotions will lead to our best future, and ultimately to a better world.

Although there are competing theories about our understanding of emotion, there is little debate about how your body reacts to certain emotions, such as fear. It's time to take an in-depth look at what we know about fear.

MAKE IT STICK!

1. True or false: The broaden-and-build theory of emotion states that how we experience emotion is a combination of the emotion we think we're experiencing and the biological changes happening in our body.

2. Because research indicated that some emotional responses did not require conscious thought, Richard Lazarus concluded that

   a. biological responses happen and we are only aware of them later.

   b. emotional responses are produced by a combination of consciously labeling them and biological responses.

   c. cognition strongly influences how we respond emotionally.

   d. we must interpret events unconsciously and react emotionally.

3. True or false: The two-factor theory of emotions states that first we give something a cognitive label, and then we have a physiological reaction.

Fear: A Closer Look

> 🐾🐾 **28-2** What physiological changes occur during a fear reaction, and what parts of the nervous system are involved in the changes?

FIGHT OR FLIGHT

Sympathetic Nervous System Arousal?
Evidently this man is not a fighter.

autonomic [aw-tuh-NAHM-ik] nervous system The division of the peripheral nervous system that controls the glands and muscles of the internal organs; its subdivisions are the sympathetic (arousing) division and the parasympathetic (calming) division.

Your body undergoes changes as you experience emotions like fear. Some are obvious: A fire alarm goes off, and your stomach seems to turn inside out, your muscles tense, and your mouth may even go dry. But your body is also busy in other not-so-obvious ways, preparing you for this alarming situation. Your blood is flowing from organs with momentarily nonessential functions and coursing toward other body parts you may need in this emergency. For instance, your digestion slows, but bloodflow increases to the muscles you'd need to run away. Your pupils dilate, or increase in size, allowing more light into your eyes and improving your vision. Your liver dumps sugar into your bloodstream for energy, and perspiration appears to cool your churned-up body. All these involuntary activities underscore your body's incredible and wonderful response to a dangerous situation. Perhaps most wondrous of all, you did not have to think about or consciously activate this system of defenses.

Your response to dangerous situations is coordinated by a two-pronged arrangement called your **autonomic nervous system (ANS),** the part of the nervous system that controls the glands and the muscles of the internal organs. Your autonomic nervous system has two divisions: one that arouses and one that calms (see **Figure 28.5**). The arousing side, the *sympathetic division,* accelerates your heart rate, increases respiration (breathing level), and increases the secretion of hormones that help prepare your body for fight or flight. The calming side, the *parasympathetic division,* slows your breathing, heart rate, and secretion of stress hormones (see **Figure 28.6**).

Measuring ANS responses to questions is sometimes used in a misguided effort to detect whether someone is telling the truth (see Psychology in the Real World: Detecting Lies).

In addition to ANS activity, your brain has structures, such as the amygdala, that appear to play a key role in associating certain situations with fear.[15] Individuals with a damaged amygdala have shown decreased fear in situations where they should have been fearful.[16]

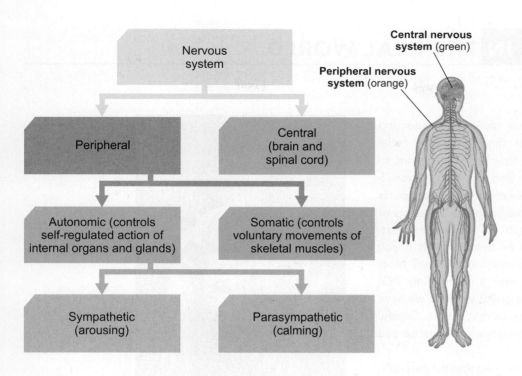

Nervous system

Peripheral

Central (brain and spinal cord)

Autonomic (controls self-regulated action of internal organs and glands)

Somatic (controls voluntary movements of skeletal muscles)

Sympathetic (arousing)

Parasympathetic (calming)

Central nervous system (green)

Peripheral nervous system (orange)

FIGURE 28.5
The Main Divisions of the Human Nervous System
Your nervous system has two main divisions (peripheral and central). Your body's reaction to fear is best explained using the autonomic branch of the peripheral nervous system.

FIGURE 28.6
Autonomic Nervous System and Physiological Arousal
The sympathetic (left) and the parasympathetic (right) branches of the autonomic nervous system (ANS) work to keep your body in balance. If one branch arouses or activates a system, the other starts to calm or inhibit the same system.

Sympathetic division (arousing)		Parasympathetic division (calming)
Pupils dilate	EYES	Pupils contract
Decreases	SALIVATION	Increases
Perspires	SKIN	Dries
Increases	RESPIRATION	Decreases
Accelerates	HEART	Slows
Inhibits	DIGESTION	Activates
Secrete stress hormones	ADRENAL GLANDS	Decrease secretion of stress hormones

MAKE IT STICK!

1. Which two parts of the nervous system are most involved in the fight-or-flight response?

   a. the central nervous system and parasympathetic nervous system

   b. the autonomic nervous system and frontal lobe

   c. the sympathetic nervous system and autonomic nervous system

   d. the two factors of two-factor theory

2. True or false: Research shows that innocent people examined by polygraph machines can be found guilty.

3. True or false: The parasympathetic division of your nervous system is responsible for slowing your breathing and heart rate.

PSYCHOLOGY IN THE REAL WORLD

Detecting Lies

Even though our brains are skilled at detecting emotions, we have a hard time detecting facial expressions that give away liars.[17] Still, we want to know who is telling the truth and who isn't, especially when a crime has been committed. News reports often provide details of crime suspects agreeing or refusing to take a polygraph or lie-detector test. Would you agree to take a lie-detector test if you were wrongly accused of committing a crime? Most of us answer this question with a resounding, "Of course!" After all, if we're not guilty, what do we have to hide, right? Well, it's not quite that simple. Careful review of the research on polygraphs may cause you to rethink your answer.

A polygraph machine monitors changes in heart rate, respiration, and perspiration to determine whether a person is feeling emotional stress about a particular question. The underlying assumption is that a person will show stronger autonomic nervous system (ANS) responses when lying than when telling the truth.

Unfortunately, polygraphs measure *all* stress reactions, including those from honest people who are upset by a question and not lying in their answer. Controlled studies of polygraph interpretations have produced some disturbing results. In one study,[18]

Tek Image/SPL/Science Source

▲ **A Typical Polygraph Setup**
Research casts doubt on this machine's ability to reliably predict who tells the truth and who doesn't.

professional polygraph interpreters judged 37 percent of the innocent people they tested guilty. In the same study, these experts correctly identified the guilty

The Expression of Emotion

  28-3 How do gender and culture affect the ability to express and interpret nonverbal communications of emotion?

Researchers have been able to study emotional response through a variety of physiological measures. However, these results cannot tell us everything. If we measure the heart rate, breathing, and perspiration levels of people watching a scary, anger-provoking, or sexually arousing movie, we can't tell by looking at the data who's afraid, mad, or aroused. The biological signatures of different emotions appear to be similar.[23] But if we look deeper than a beating heart and sweat—that is, if we measure brain activity—we do see differences. Research has shown that different emotions activate different parts of the brain while using different brain circuits.[24] Emotions like fear and anger appear to register on the right side of the brain, for example, while enthusiastic people typically show more activity on the left side of the brain.[25]

PSYCHOLOGY IN THE REAL WORLD (Continued)

parties only 76 percent of the time, meaning nearly one-fourth of the real liars fooled the machine (see **Figure 28.7**). Hundreds of other studies on the validity of polygraph tests yield similar results.[19]

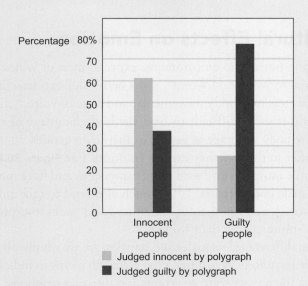

FIGURE 28.7
How Accurate?
One research study (Kleinmuntz & Szucko, 1984) showed that expert interpretations of polygraph tests judged more than one-third of the innocent people taking the tests to be guilty. In addition, almost one-fourth of the guilty were judged innocent by the test.

A more effective polygraph test asks questions about details that would be known only by those committing the crime.[20] Even this test, however, relies on the same underlying assumption: Strong ANS responses indicate lying. This means that we must exercise extreme caution in how we use polygraph test results.

Researchers today are going deeper than the skin's surface. Much deeper. Are different parts of the brain activated when someone tells a lie? The answer appears to be *Yes*. The EEG (electroencephalograph) recordings and fMRI (functional MRI) brain scans of liars show very different activity compared to those telling the truth.[21] Millions of dollars are being spent on this technology to assess its appropriate uses by law enforcement agencies.[22] Look for brain activity measures as a way to help convict the guilty (while protecting the innocent) in the near future.

THINK ABOUT . . . Psychology in the Real World

1. What are some of the things polygraph machines measure?

2. Why are polygraph results considered unreliable?

3. Should polygraph results be used in criminal cases? Why or why not?

Measuring physiological changes through the use of sophisticated electronic equipment is not the only means of recognizing emotions, however. We communicate emotions all the time without saying a word.

Nonverbal Communication

Has this ever happened to you? A teacher calls on you to answer a question, and you kind-of-sort-of know the answer. While you stumble your way through your reply, your teacher stops nodding in agreement, turns with arms crossed and brow furrowed, and looks at the floor. Meanwhile, the student next to you shoots her arm up in the air, apparently ready to answer after you're through trying. Both your classmate and the teacher clearly communicated their feelings, even though they said nothing. You knew exactly what they were thinking because they communicated with you *nonverbally*.

Nonverbal communication, or *body language*, is a frequent messenger of our emotions to others. Our facial expressions, tone of voice, and hand gestures often give us away. We tend to look at a person's mouth to detect happiness but at the eyes for anger and

Reading Between the Lines
Research shows that women are better than men at reading nonverbal emotional cues.

George Rudy/Shutterstock

fear. When we talk about someone "wearing his heart on his sleeve," we mean that person readily communicates emotions nonverbally. With either a quickly averted glance or an extended gaze, we can communicate everything from submission to dominance, disinterest to intimacy.[26]

How we communicate and interpret emotions seems to depend on whether we are male or female and on what our culture has taught us about appropriate public behavior.

Gender and Cultural Effects on Emotion

Who is better at reading the nonverbal emotions we express: men or women? Studies regularly give the nod to women.[27] Women show better skills at detecting emotion in people's facial expressions, body movements, and tone of voice.[28] But both males and females find it more difficult to read the body language of the opposite sex than to read the body language of people of their own gender.[29]

Men and women also differ in the way they express emotions (see **Figure 28.8**). North American women smile more, gesture with more expression, and have more expressive faces than their male counterparts.[30,31] Women also tend to talk more about their emotions.[32] North American men, on the other hand, seem to express only one emotion—anger—more openly than women.[33]

How can we explain these differences? As males and females, are we simply physiologically different or do we learn to behave differently? Research seems to indicate that at least two factors affect the way we learn to express and interpret emotions:

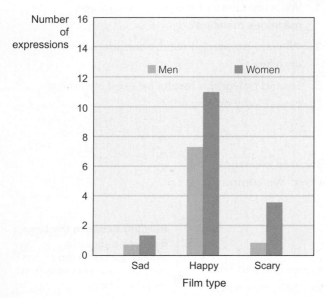

- *Power* is the first factor in interpreting nonverbal communications. In any relationship, from boss–employee to teacher–student, one person always has more power than the other. The person with *less* power will be more motivated to read the nonverbal emotional cues, and will probably read them better, than the person in charge.[34] In one study, Sara Snodgrass randomly assigned males and females to be either the leader or the follower in two-person teams.[35] She found that the followers were more sensitive than the leaders to nonverbal signals regardless of whether the leader was male or female.

- *Culture* is the second factor in interpreting nonverbal communication. People raised in expressive families, or in cultures that value being emotionally expressive, are likely to be more expressive regardless of whether they are male or female.[36]

FIGURE 28.8
Females and Males Express Emotions Differently
Although females and males report about the same amount of experienced emotion, females *show* more emotion while watching emotional films. (From Kring & Gordon, 1998.)

Culture also influences how we express emotions and how we interpret the emotions of others. Consider the meeting, years ago, between a U.S. secretary of state and Iraqi Foreign Minister Tariq Aziz. Saddam Hussein, Iraq's president at the time, sent Aziz to represent him at this meeting, which followed Iraq's invasion of Kuwait.[37] The U.S. secretary of state told Aziz, "If you do not move out of Kuwait, we will attack you." The message was clear and direct, and the secretary's body language was calm and subdued. Aziz reported to Saddam Hussein that the U.S. was just talking and would not attack. He misread the secretary's nonverbal communication, and thousands died in the war that followed.

What went wrong at this meeting? The answer lies in how the secretary of state delivered his message, with the restraint customary for a U.S. diplomat. Hussein's representative viewed the communication through the cultural window of his Iraqi heritage, which expects expression to be more emotional. To him, a truly angry person would have gestured, shouted, and stomped his foot. Aziz was not aware of the **display rules** for U.S. diplomats—the cultural rules governing how and when a person may express emotion.[38]

Even the display rules for something as simple as when it's appropriate to smile can vary from one culture to the next. Germans, who smile less often than people from the U.S., often think Americans are hiding their true feelings behind false smiles. Japanese observers of U.S. behavior might disagree, stating that people from the U.S. don't smile often enough. In Japan, it is rude to display disappointment or distrust publicly, so the Japanese smile even more than Americans.[39]

Cultures also disagree about the meaning behind gestures. Former presidents Richard Nixon and George H. W. Bush both got themselves into hot water by giving the "OK" sign in countries (Brazil, Germany, Russia) where this gesture is considered rude. The hand sign given by University of Texas football fans (index and pinkie fingers up, two middle fingers down) would seriously insult a man in Italy, where that gesture means his wife has been unfaithful.

And what about facial expressions? Are they read differently across cultures? Several studies[40-43] have attempted to find the answer by showing photographs of different facial expressions to people around the world and asking participants to guess the emotion. How would you do on such a test? Take a minute or two to see if you can label the emotions in the facial expressions in **Figure 28.9**.

> **display rules** The cultural rules governing how and when a person may express emotion.

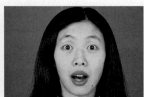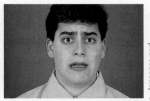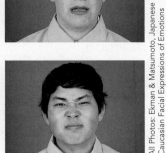

All Photos: Ekman & Matsumoto, Japanese and Caucasian Facial Expressions of Emotions

> ◀ **FIGURE 28.9**
> **Facial Expressions and Culture**
> Are facial expressions culturally specific or culturally universal? Can you tell which face shows surprise? Happiness? Sadness? Fear? Disgust? Anger? Find the answers below. (From Matsumoto & Ekman, 1989.)

How did you do? Chances are, regardless of your cultural background, you did fairly well. Researchers have found that certain basic expressions and the display rules governing how to read them are consistent across cultures. Physiological measures of emotion also show consistency across cultures.[44] As in many other areas of study in psychology, we see that although there are significant cultural and gender differences, there is a core of similarity among all humanity across the globe.

● Answers to the questions in Figure 28.9: From left to right and top to bottom, the emotions displayed in these photos are happiness, surprise, fear, sadness, anger, and disgust.

MAKE IT STICK!

1. True or false: You learn in a class that women have historically had less power in many relationships in society. This historical fact may help explain why women are often better at reading nonverbal behavior than men.

2. The _____ of a culture might most affect how a person behaves when angry.

3. Power is the first factor in interpreting nonverbal communications. According to this textbook, what's the second?

Module 28 Summary and Assessment

Emotion

 28-1 How do historical approaches to emotion differ from modern theories of emotion?

- According to the James–Lange theory, we experience emotion because we are aware of our bodily response to an emotion-producing stimulus.

- The Cannon–Bard theory of emotion proposed that an emotion-arousing stimulus simultaneously triggers physiological responses and subjective experience of emotions.

- Schachter's two-factor theory proposes that the experience of emotion is produced by a combination of physical arousal and how we cognitively identify the arousal.

- Zajonc's brain research indicates that our interpretations (cognitive labels) sometimes come after our emotional experience.

- Lazarus agrees with Zajonc that some emotional responses do not require conscious thought but argues that emotional responses are influenced by unconscious thinking.

 28-2 What physiological changes occur during a fear reaction, and what parts of the nervous system are involved in the changes?

- The sympathetic division of the autonomic nervous system is activated during a fear response, accelerating heart rate, increasing respiration, and increasing hormone levels that help prepare the body for fight or flight.

- The parasympathetic division of the autonomic nervous system slows the body after the fear response is finished.

 28-3 How do gender and culture affect the ability to express and interpret nonverbal communications of emotion?

- Research indicates that women are better at understanding nonverbal expressions of emotions and that North American women are more expressive nonverbally than men. Both males and females have a more difficult time understanding nonverbal cues from the opposite sex.

- Power and culture affect how people express and interpret the emotions of others.

- Display rules, rules governing how and when a person displays emotion, differ between cultures.

- Facial expressions for basic emotions are consistent across cultures.

Summative Assessment

1. Which of the following was a conclusion drawn by early researchers of emotions?

   a. We experience emotion because we are aware of our bodily responses to an emotion-producing stimulus.

   b. Interpretations of situation are sometimes slower than our emotional reactions.

   c. To experience emotion, we must be physically aroused and must cognitively identify the arousal.

   d. Some emotional responses do not require conscious thought but still involve some kind of unconscious cognitive appraisal.

2. Chopping onions may make your eyes tear up, but the tears do not make you sad. Why not?

   a. Physical responses are only caused by an emotion-arousing stimulus.
   b. Emotion is triggered by an emotion-arousing stimulus.
   c. You decided not to be sad.
   d. If you produce tears long enough, you will eventually feel sad.

3. Some researchers believe our feelings are more likely to control our thoughts than our thoughts are to control our feelings. What evidence is used to explain this?

   a. We are conscious of a stimulus before we react to it.
   b. Nervous system pathways pass through the cortical parts of the brain.
   c. Some nervous system pathways bypass the cortical parts of the brain.
   d. The amygdala processes a stimulus before you react.

4. What do researchers Schachter, Singer, and Lazarus believe complex feelings like love are influenced by?

   a. expectation, interpretation, and memory
   b. stimulus, response, and cognition
   c. memory, unconscious thinking, and response
   d. awareness, response, and stimulus

5. Sincerely expressing gratitude, thanks, and appreciation to those who have helped us is an example of what?

   a. the broaden-and-build theory
   b. the Cannon–Bard theory
   c. the two-factor theory
   d. the James–Lange theory

6. What is the role of the autonomic nervous system?

   a. to respond to dangerous situations
   b. to measure if someone is telling the truth
   c. to think carefully about a problem
   d. to decrease fear responses

7. The autonomic nervous system contains what two main divisions?

   a. peripheral and central
   b. somatic and autonomic
   c. sympathetic and parasympathetic
   d. central and somatic

8. Which of the following explains why polygraph machines are unreliable in detecting lies?

   a. They measure stress reactions only in people who lie.
   b. They measure all stress reactions, even from people who tell the truth.
   c. They are able to distinguish people who lie from people who tell the truth.
   d. They are impossible to fool if you're lying.

9. Observing and interpreting someone's body language is called

   a. observation.
   b. emotion response.
   c. expression.
   d. nonverbal communication.

10. Which two factors attempt to explain why women and men differ in the way they express emotions?

   a. power and culture
   b. gender and bias
   c. body language and arousal
   d. physical responses and cognition

KEY TERMS AND KEY PEOPLE

emotions, p. 426

James–Lange theory, p. 427

Cannon–Bard theory, p. 428

two-factor theory, p. 429

autonomic [aw-tuh-NAHM-ik] nervous system, p. 432

display rules, p. 437

William James (1842–1910), p. 427

Carl Lange (1834–1900), p. 427

Walter Cannon (1871–1945), p. 428

Stanley Schachter [SHACK-ter] (1922–1997), p. 429

Robert Zajonc [ZI-yence] (1923–2008), p. 429

Richard Lazarus (1922–2002), p. 430

Module 29 | Psychodynamic and Humanistic Perspectives on Personality

personality An individual's characteristic pattern of thinking, feeling, and acting.

Can we predict or explain a person's personality based on his or her description of an inkblot? Some psychologists think so. Let's see how psychologists try to understand personality.

What is personality? I hear students use this word all the time. LaDonna likes how Ron looks but admits sadly, "It's true; he doesn't have much of a personality." And for those who do have personality, they have been labeled everything from "rotten" to "winning." These everyday notions of personality are fine for discussing friends between classes or at lunch, but psychologists use the term more carefully.

Psychologists define **personality** as an individual's characteristic pattern of thinking, feeling, and acting. In this module, we consider the psychodynamic and humanistic perspectives, two different viewpoints on how personality develops and how it can be assessed.

The Psychodynamic Perspective on Personality

 29-1 How does the psychodynamic perspective explain personality?

After going out for 3 months and then breaking up, Pete says, "I know I'm in *denial*, but I think we'll get back together." Mei refuses to talk about a past relationship, saying she doesn't remember much about it. "I've *repressed* that whole thing." In a class full of ill-mannered students, the teacher might say, "You've all *regressed* to eighth grade." These three commonly used terms— *denial, repression,* and *regression*—can all be traced back to **Sigmund Freud,** an Austrian physician who proposed psychology's first and most famous theory of personality. Freud believed that an individual's personality—the person's characteristic thoughts, feelings, and behaviors—emerges from tensions generated by unconscious motives and unresolved childhood conflicts (many of them sexual). To uncover these conflicts and help patients resolve them, Freud used an approach he called **psychoanalysis,** a therapeutic technique that attempts to provide insight into thoughts and actions by exposing and interpreting the underlying unconscious motives and conflicts.

SIGMUND FREUD (1856–1939)
Founder of psychoanalysis, a controversial theory about the workings of the unconscious mind.

Over the last three-quarters of the twentieth century, a more moderate **psychodynamic perspective** on personality emerged. The contemporary psychodynamic perspective incorporates some aspects of Freudian theory (such as the importance of unconscious thought processes), but psychodynamic therapists are less likely than Freud was to see unresolved childhood conflicts as a source of personality development.

Yet, because of Freud's continuing popularity in pop psychology, in movies, and on television, you are more likely to be familiar with Freud's outdated terminology than with almost any other set of terms we introduce in this book. Freudian theory's popularity and controversial nature have led to hundreds of jokes in magazines and newspapers, several of which you'll see in this module. Let's outline Freud's original ideas so that you know how the buzz got started.

Freud's Office
Freud wanted his patients to relax in a reclining position, facing away from him, while he conducted his version of psychotherapy— psychoanalysis.

Freud's View of the Mind

Freud's theory of psychoanalysis grew from his early observations that some of his patients had problems that didn't seem to have a clear physical cause. Freud became intrigued by a neurologist in France who was treating patients using hypnosis. (Hypnosis is a social interaction in which one person—the hypnotist—makes forceful suggestions to another person that certain events or responses will occur.) Amid the unethical treatment of patients at the asylum, Freud was amazed to find that some patients' physical symptoms disappeared after the hypnotic experience.

Freud experimented with hypnosis, but he found that some patients could not be hypnotized. As an alternative to hypnosis, Freud asked his patients to relax and say whatever came to mind, regardless of how trivial or embarrassing the statement seemed. Freud viewed this technique, which he called **free association,** as a window into the unconscious mind.

Freud compared the human mind to a big iceberg consisting of three regions: the conscious, preconscious, and unconscious (see **Figure 29.1**). Just as most of an iceberg is below sea level and unseen, Freud felt that most of the mind is hidden from view. The *conscious* mind, the thoughts and feelings we're aware of, is comparable to the visible part of the iceberg above sea level. Just below the water line

psychoanalysis Freud's theory of personality; also, a therapeutic technique that attempts to provide insight into thoughts and actions by exposing and interpreting the underlying unconscious motives and conflicts.

psychodynamic perspective A view of personality that retains some aspects of Freudian theory (such as the importance of unconscious thought processes) but is less likely to see unresolved childhood conflicts as a source of personality development.

free association A method of exploring the unconscious in which the person relaxes and says whatever comes to mind, no matter how trivial or embarrassing.

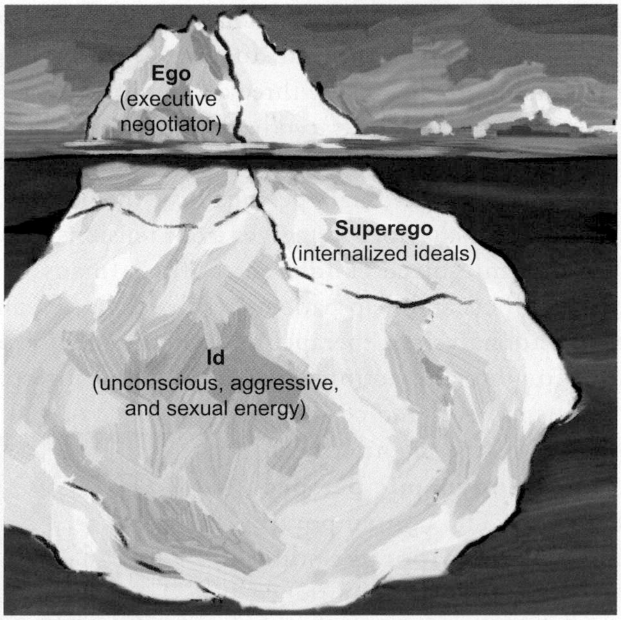

Conscious mind

Preconscious mind

Unconscious mind

FIGURE 29.1
The Mind According to Freud
Freud thought only a small part of the mind or personality, the thoughts and feelings we attend to, was "visible." Freud represented the part of the mind we're aware of using a "tip of the iceberg" comparison. (Adapted from Freud, 1933, p. 111.)

preconscious According to Freud, a region of the mind holding information that is not conscious but is retrievable into conscious awareness.

unconscious According to Freud, a region of the mind that is a reservoir of mostly unacceptable thoughts, wishes, feelings, and memories.

is the **preconscious,** a region of the mind holding information that is not conscious but is retrievable into conscious awareness. Finally, at the deepest level is the **unconscious,** a region of the mind holding mostly unacceptable thoughts, wishes, feelings, and memories. If he could help patients open the door to this unconscious region, Freud believed, they could recover painful childhood memories and healing could occur.

According to Freud, treating someone with a psychological disorder meant delving into their unconscious, revealing the nature of that person's inner conflicts, and releasing tensions. Through free association and dream analysis, Freud tried to catch glimpses of the unconscious. He also searched for evidence in people's habits and in their slips of the tongue. These "Freudian slips," as they are often called today, are supposed to reflect what people would *like* to say. Freud illustrated this concept with an example of a money-strapped patient who did not want any large pills: "Please do not give me any bills, because I cannot swallow them."

Freud's view of personality also had three parts. All three fit into the iceberg: the id, the superego, and the ego.

The Id, Ego, and Superego

Freud believed that personality grows out of a basic human conflict. Each of us is born with aggressive, pleasure-seeking biological impulses. But we live in a society, and—as we grow up—we internalize social roadblocks that restrain these impulses. The way each of us resolves the conflict between social restraints and pleasure-seeking impulses shapes our individual personality. Three forces interact during this conflict:

id The part of personality that, according to Freud, consists of unconscious psychic energy and strives to satisfy basic sexual and aggressive drives; operates on the pleasure principle, demanding immediate gratification.

- The **id,** present at birth, consists of unconscious psychic energy and strives to satisfy basic sexual and aggressive drives. Operating from the *pleasure principle,* the id demands immediate gratification. For instance, a newborn cries for whatever it needs, whenever it needs it, regardless of what anybody else wants or needs.

- The **superego** consists of the internalized ideals and provides standards for judgment (the conscience) and for future aspirations. The superego develops as the child interacts with parents, peers, and society. It is the voice of conscience that focuses on what we *should* do, not what we'd like to do. The superego wants perfection, and those with a weak superego are likely to give in to their urges and impulses without regard to rules. On the other hand, an overly strong superego often produces someone who is virtuous yet guilt ridden.

- The **ego** is the largely conscious "executive" part of the personality that negotiates among the demands of the id, the superego, and reality. The ego makes decisions after "listening" to both the demands of the id and the restraining rules of the superego. Operating from the *reality principle,* the ego satisfies the id's desires in ways that will realistically bring pleasure rather than pain. The ego, Freud thought, represented good sense and reason.

Let's examine an example of how these forces work together. It's Saturday night, and you're at a friend's party. Your curfew is 11:00 P.M., but you're having a great time. According to Freud, your id impulses would lead you to blow off the curfew and stay at the party because it's fun (pleasure!). Your superego would urge you to leave the party in time to get home by 11:00 P.M. (follow the rules!). Your ego would take information from the situation (that is, you're having fun, but it's getting late) and work toward a solution, such as calling home to ask if you can stay out another hour.

Freud believed that the id, ego, and superego could help us understand the mind. Freud thought that a healthy personality is one that could successfully express pleasure-seeking impulses while avoiding punishment or guilt. This task is not an easy one, however, and to achieve it, the ego must sometimes resort to defensive tactics.

Defense Mechanisms

Anxiety, wrote Freud, is the price we pay for living in a civilized society. The conflict between the id's wishes and the superego's social rules produces this anxiety. However, the ego has an arsenal of unconscious **defense mechanisms,** protective methods of reducing anxiety by unconsciously distorting reality. You have probably heard of several of these defense mechanisms. We consider seven (see **Table 29.1**):

superego The part of personality that, according to Freud, represents internalized ideals and provides standards for judgment (the conscience) and for future aspirations.

ego The largely conscious "executive" part of personality that, according to Freud, negotiates among the demands of the id, the superego, and reality; operates on the reality principle, satisfying the id's desires in ways that will realistically bring pleasure rather than pain.

ScienceCartoonsPlus.com

▲ **Id, Ego, and Superego**
Which speed limit sign represents immaturity? Which represents too much caution?

defense mechanisms In psychoanalytic theory, the ego's protective methods of reducing anxiety by unconsciously distorting reality.

TABLE 29.1	Seven Defense Mechanisms
Defense Mechanism	**Means of Protection**
Repression	Banishing provoking thoughts (that could reemerge dreams)
Regression	Moving back to a previous psychosexual stage
Denial	Refusing to admit that something unpleasant has happened
Reaction formation	Making unacceptable impulses look like opposites
Projection	Attributing threatening impulses to others
Rationalization	Self-explaining things in a way that hides the behavior's actual reason
Displacement	Diverting aggressive feelings to an acceptable object

1. *Repression* banishes anxiety-arousing thoughts, feelings, and memories from consciousness. According to Freud, the most frequently repressed thoughts are of an unacceptably erotic nature. Freud believed repression was the basis for all the other anxiety-reducing defense mechanisms. The aim of psychoanalysis was to draw repressed, unresolved childhood conflicts back into consciousness to allow resolution and healing.

2. *Regression* allows an anxious person to retreat to a more comfortable, earlier stage of life. The 6-year-old who, after a new baby is born into the family, wants to sit in Mom's lap while she reads to him may be regressing to a more comfortable time.

3. *Denial* lets an anxious person refuse to admit that something unpleasant is happening. Thoughts of invincibility, such as "I won't get hooked on cigarettes; it can't happen to me," represent denial. The drinker who consumes a six-pack a day but claims not to have a drinking problem is also using the defense mechanism of denial.

4. *Reaction formation* reverses an unacceptable impulse, causing an anxious person to express the opposite of (or overcompensate for) the anxiety-provoking unconscious feeling. To keep the "I hate him" thoughts from entering consciousness, the ego generates an "I love him" feeling. If you're interested in someone who is already going out with another person and you find yourself feeling a curious dislike (instead of fondness) for the unobtainable person, then Freud would say you're experiencing reaction formation.

5. *Projection* disguises threatening feelings of guilty anxiety by attributing the problem to others. "I don't trust him" (the defensive, conscious thought) really means, "I don't trust myself" (the original, unconscious thought). The thief thinks everyone else is a thief.

6. *Rationalization* displaces real, anxiety-provoking explanations and replaces them with more comforting justifications for actions. Rationalization makes mistakes seem reasonable and often sounds like an excuse. The smoker insists she smokes "just to look older" or "only when I go out with friends." After becoming addicted to cigarettes, she might say, "It's no big deal; I can quit whenever I want."

7. *Displacement* shifts an unacceptable impulse toward a more acceptable or less threatening object or person. The classic example is the company owner who becomes upset and yells at the manager, who yells at the clerk, who goes home and yells at the kids, who end up kicking the dog. All except the dog have been displacing.

According to Freud, all of these defense mechanisms help us feel better be relieving the anxiety associated with stress.

Freud's Psychosexual Stages

psychosexual stages
Childhood stages of development (oral, anal, phallic, latency, and genital) during which, according to Freud, the id's pleasure-seeking energies focus on different parts of the body.

Freud's analyses of his patients led him to conclude that personality forms during the first 5 or 6 years of life. He believed that his patients' problems originated in conflicts that had not been resolved during childhood. In Freud's view, the patient had become "stuck," or *fixated,* in one of the **psychosexual stages** of development. These childhood stages of development include the oral, anal, phallic, latency, and genital stages, during which the id's pleasure-seeking energies focus on different parts of the body (see **Table 29.2**):

TABLE 29.2	Freud's Psychosexual Stages
Stage	**Focus**
Oral (1–18 months)	Pleasure centers on the mouth—sucking, biting, chewing
Anal (18–36 months)	Pleasure focuses on bowel and bladder function; coping with demands for control
Phallic (3–6 years)	Pleasure zone is the genitals; coping with incestuous sexual feelings
Latency (6 years to puberty)	Dormant sexual feelings
Genital (puberty on)	Maturation of sexual interests

1. The *oral stage* lasts through the first 18 months of life. Pleasure comes from chewing, biting, and sucking. Weaning, the transition from breast feeding to eating other food, can be a conflict in this stage.

2. The *anal stage* lasts from 18 months to 3 years of age. Gratification comes from bowel and bladder function. Potty training can be a conflict in this stage.

3. The *phallic stage* lasts from ages 3 to 6. The pleasure zone shifts to the genitals. Freud believed boys felt love for their mothers and hatred, fear, or jealousy for their fathers. Viewing Dad as a rival for Mom's love, the boy fears punishment from his father during the phallic stage. Freud called this collection of feelings the *Oedipus* (ED-uh-pus) *complex,* named after the Greek tragedy in which Oedipus (spoiler alert!) unwittingly kills his father and marries his mother (and pokes his eyes out after realizing what he has done). Freud did not believe in a parallel process for girls, although other psychoanalysts have written about an Electra complex, in which girls love Dad and fear Mom.

Stage Theory
Freud's beliefs on development set the stage for future research-based theories on child development.

4. During the *latency stage,* which lasts from 6 years of age to puberty, children repress their feelings for the rival parent. Instead of fearing the same-sex parent, girls and boys start to "buddy up" to Mom and Dad, respectively. The result is girls learn to do girl-like things and boys learn boy-like behaviors. Freud called this the *identification process.* This process offers one explanation of *gender identity,* which is our sense of what it means to be either a man or a woman.

5. The *genital stage* starts at puberty, as the person begins experiencing sexual feelings toward others.

Freud thought that unresolved conflicts in any of the psychosexual stages could cause problems later in life. The adult who has not worked through the conflict associated with a given stage may be fixated to that stage. For instance, a child who has a bad experience during potty training may develop an anal fixation. This conflict may manifest itself, wrote Freud, in the adult who likes everything neat, perfect, and in its proper place. (Now you know where the label "anal-retentive" comes from!)

Imagno/Hulton Archive/Getty Images

Arriving Late and Hitting an Iceberg

Sigmund Freud used the iceberg metaphor (see Figure 29.1) to illustrate parts of the personality that can't easily be seen—that exist beneath surface level. Today's psychologists are more likely to talk about icebergs in the context of **resilience** than the id and the ego. Let's look at a scenario that might involve a different kind of iceberg.

You decide to see a movie with your friend Chris.

The plan: Leave from Chris's place an hour before the show, grab a burger, park near the theater, and get seated in time to enjoy the previews. However, you end up running late because of a flat tire. You text Chris 30 minutes before the show: "Flat tire, on my way." Driving up, you jump out of the car and race to the house. As you ring the doorbell, an angry, red-faced Chris opens the door and yells, "You're always late. You always make me late. Just—forget it," and then slams the door. The depth of Chris's anger surprises you. What's going on?

Chris likely had an "iceberg belief" along the lines of "You should respect others enough not to keep them waiting." Iceberg beliefs are defined as deeply embedded assumptions about how the world should operate; they are beliefs or core values about ourselves and others.[1] Given Chris's iceberg belief, he felt disrespected.

Psychologists often refer to resilience as the ability to grow and thrive in the face of challenges, or in other words, to bounce back from adversity.[2] Ever notice how some people recover quickly after a bad event, like missing a penalty kick in soccer, getting dumped, or being made late for a movie? These folks are more resilient than others. Unfortunately, not everybody is naturally resilient. The good news is that everyone can learn the skills that foster resiliency.

One of these skills is "detecting icebergs." Here are some examples of iceberg beliefs:

- I am smart.
- All people should be treated equally.
- Teachers should grade all students fairly.
- You should respect others enough not to keep them waiting.

Resiliency experts explain that these deep values and beliefs often drive our emotions and reactions to adversity. When your reaction seems out of proportion to the problem and begins to undermine your performance or effectiveness, you may have an iceberg belief that needs re-examining. Is this iceberg belief useful and accurate, or is it actually keeping you from seeing helpful information?

Chris's iceberg belief was about respect. Because he thought you disrespected him by being late, he blew up. His anger kept him from hearing about the flat tire. A more resilient thought would have been, "Yes, I'm upset. I might miss the movie, but there must be a good reason why my friend is late."

Iceberg beliefs can be useful or misleading. When you suspect that your reaction to a problem is stronger than it should be, stop to think about it. Ask yourself if there's an iceberg belief driving your reaction and whether it's useful and promotes accurate thinking. If it's not useful, be flexible enough in your thinking to seek alternative explanations for the adversity.[3] You just might save yourself a lot of grief.

resilience The ability to grow and thrive in the face of challenges and to bounce back from adversity.

inferiority complex According to Adler, a condition that comes from being unable to compensate for normal inferiority feelings.

collective unconscious Jung's concept of a shared, inherited reservoir of memory traces from our ancestors.

MAKE IT STICK!

1. Sigmund Freud thought that personality was most influenced by

   a. defense mechanisms.   c. repression.
   b. the unconscious mind.   d. free association.

2. According to Freud, a traumatic childhood memory might be

   a. encoded into the neural network of the hippocampus.

   b. the reason for a larger "iceberg" of id, ego, and superego.
   c. repressed into the unconscious mind.
   d. the basis of the ego.

3. Which defense mechanism allows an anxious person to retreat to a more comfortable, earlier stage of life?

The Neo-Freudians

 29-2 How did later psychodynamic theorists assess personality, and what were the new concepts added to psychodynamic theory by the neo-Freudians?

Freud attracted many followers. Those who agreed with the basic ideas of psychoanalysis but disagreed with specific parts of Freud's theory were known as *neo-Freudians*. Three of these pioneering psychoanalysts were Alfred Adler, Carl Jung, and Karen Horney.

Alfred Adler Agreeing with Freud's views on the importance of childhood experiences, **Alfred Adler** differed in that he thought social tensions (not sexual tensions) were crucial in the development of personality. Adler believed that psychological problems in personalities centered on feelings of inferiority. Furthermore, if we start to organize our thoughts based on our perceived shortcomings or mistakes, we might develop an **inferiority complex.** (This is the origin of another famous label you've probably already heard.) For example, a younger sibling who sees his older sister excelling in her field may compare himself negatively if he feels he's not living up to his parents' expectations.

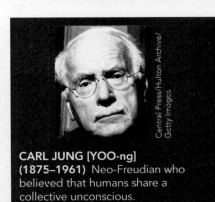

ALFRED ADLER (1870–1937) Neo-Freudian who thought social tensions were more important than sexual tensions in the development of personality.

Carl Jung Unlike Adler, **Carl Jung** (pronounced YOO-ng) discounted social factors, but he broke with Freud over the importance of the role of the unconscious in personality development. Jung kicked the idea up a notch, saying we not only have an individual unconscious, but also—as a species—have a **collective unconscious.** This is a shared, inherited reservoir of memory traces from our ancestors. Jung thought the collective unconscious included information hardwired from birth on things we all know. He saw evidence of the collective unconsciousness in the *archetypes* (pronounced AR-kuh-types), or universal symbols, found in stories, myths, and art. For instance, the shadow archetype is the darker, evil side of human nature. Supposedly, we hide this archetype from the world and ourselves.

Contemporary psychologists reject the notion of inherited memory. However, many believe that our shared evolutionary history has contributed to some

CARL JUNG [YOO-ng] (1875–1961) Neo-Freudian who believed that humans share a collective unconscious.

KAREN HORNEY [HORN-eye] (1885–1952) Neo-Freudian who found psychoanalysis negatively biased toward women and believed cultural variables are the foundation of personality development.

LIFE MATTERS

George Lucas, the creator of *Star Wars*, was heavily influenced by the book, *The Hero with a Thousand Faces*, which included Carl Jung's concept of the collective unconscious (specifically the archetype of the shadow). May the Force be with you—thanks to Carl Jung.

projective test A personality test, such as the Rorschach or TAT, that provides ambiguous stimuli to trigger projection of inner thoughts and feelings.

The Thematic Apperception Test (TAT) Some psychologists believe that patients who tell stories about ambiguous pictures are projecting feelings they have about themselves.

universal behavior tendencies (like hiding our worst secrets from others) or dispositions (evil).

Karen Horney Trained as a psychoanalyst, **Karen Horney** (pronounced HORN-eye) broke from Freud in several ways. She pointed out that Freud's theory was male dominated and that his explanation of female development was inadequate. She also stated that social variables, not biological variables, are the foundation of personality development. She felt that social expectations, not anatomy, created the psychological differences between males and females. Basic anxiety, wrote Horney, is the helplessness and isolation people feel in a potentially hostile world, brought on by the competitiveness of today's society.[4] Horney and the other neo-Freudians started the movement toward revising Freud's psychoanalysis into the psychodynamic perspective that is primarily used today.

Assessing Personality From a Psychodynamic Perspective

Before providing therapy for a personality disorder, psychologists need to assess personality characteristics. Techniques for assessing personality characteristics differ from one perspective to another because the tests are tailored to a particular theory of personality. Psychoanalytic and psychodynamic therapists want assessments that reach into and reveal elements of the unconscious. True-false tests are of no interest, as they would only tap into surface elements of the conscious. Instead, Freud turned to assessment techniques such as dream analysis, which he called the "royal road to the unconscious." Later psychodynamic theorists became interested in **projective tests,** personality tests that provide ambiguous stimuli to trigger projection of inner thoughts and feelings. Projective tests are designed to provide insight into the test-taker's unconscious motives, and therapists use several kinds of such tests. Two particularly well-known projective tests are the Thematic Apperception Test (TAT) and the Rorschach inkblot test.

- The **Thematic Apperception Test (TAT)** is a projective test in which people express their inner feelings and interests through the stories they make up about ambiguous scenes. The images are deliberately ambiguous—you can't really tell what's happening. If you were taking a TAT, you might be shown a picture of two men in a room, one seated and looking out a window and the other standing with his back turned to the camera. The person administering the test would ask you to tell stories about the image, describing what is going on in the picture, as well as what happened before and after the scene.

- The **Rorschach** (pronounced ROAR-shock) **inkblot test,** designed by Hermann Rorschach, is the most widely used projective test. It is a set of 10 inkblots that a therapist uses to attempt to identify people's inner feelings by analyzing their interpretations of the inkblot. If you were taking this test, you would be asked to look at an inkblot and describe what you see. If you see a bat on a part of the inkblot where most people see a bat, your response would be considered "normal." But if you see a gun where most people see a bat, you might be revealing an aggressive personality.

Are there problems with tests like the Rorschach? *Yes.* Research has shown that people functioning normally run the risk of being diagnosed as pathological by those administering this inkblot assessment.[5] And even though researchers equipped with computer-aided scoring programs have expressed confidence that the situation will improve,[6] there is a fair chance that two or more raters will score the same inkblot responses in different ways. This means that the test is not reliable. No one has developed any single, universally accepted scoring system for this test. Furthermore, the Rorschach is not the emotional X-ray some hoped it would be. The scientific community now agrees that the Rorschach does not accurately predict personality characteristics.[7]

Some clinicians use the Rorschach to break the ice at the start of a therapy session; others use it as part of a series of personality tests and look for trends among all the results. But critics maintain there is "no scientific basis for justifying the use of the Rorschach scales in psychological assessments."[8]

▲ **The Rorschach**
A therapist attempts to understand this girl's personality and her emotional well-being by analyzing her interpretations of the inkblot.

Freeograph/Shutterstock

Thematic Apperception Test (TAT) A projective test in which people express their inner feelings and interests through the stories they make up about ambiguous scenes.

Rorschach inkblot test The most widely used projective test; a set of 10 inkblots designed to identify people's inner feelings by analyzing their interpretations of the blots.

MAKE IT STICK!

1. The neo-Freudians generally agreed with Freud's basic theory of the unconscious but disagreed with Freud's emphasis on

   a. the importance of social tensions.
   b. archetypal symbols of the collective unconscious.
   c. the importance of sexual tensions and sexual anxiety.
   d. personality development in females.

2. True or false: The main purpose of a projective test is to reveal unconscious thoughts and tensions.

3. Jung is to collective unconscious as Adler is to

   a. ego.   c. Thematic Apperception Test.
   b. archetypes.   d. inferiority complex.

Evaluating the Psychodynamic Perspective

 29-3 How have contemporary researchers evaluated the validity of the psychodynamic perspective on personality?

No discussion of Freud's work would be complete without an update and critique. Indeed, most contemporary psychodynamic theorists do not believe Freud's assertion that sex is the basis of personality.[9] Nor do they classify patients as "oral" or "anal." They do agree with Freud that much of our mental life is unconscious; that we struggle with inner conflicts among values, wishes, and fears; and that childhood experiences shape our personalities.[10]

Freud's personality theory was comprehensive, unlike any personality theory before. It influenced psychology, literature, religion, and even medicine. Still, we need to be aware of some of the weaknesses of this perspective:

- Freud's work was based on individual case studies of troubled upper-class Austrian white women who lived 100 years ago. Are their experiences applicable to a population of, say, today's middle-class Japanese men, or single-parent households? Were the results even applicable to most Austrian women outside Freud's study a century ago? *Probably not.*

- Development is a lifelong process; it is not fixed in childhood.

- Boys' gender identity does not result from an Oedipus complex around the time of kindergarten. Gender identity is achieved even without a same-sex parent around the house.[11]

- Freud underestimated peer influence on personality development, and he overestimated parental influence.

- The neural network of children under age 3 is insufficiently developed to sustain the kind of emotional trauma Freud described.

- Freud asked his patients leading questions that may have led to false recall of events that never happened.[12,13] These same concerns exist today over reports of "repressed memories" of childhood sexual abuse. Evidence suggests therapists may inadvertently implant false memories of abuse in the way they ask clients questions.[14,15]

- Freud's personal biases (primarily sexist beliefs) are evident in his focus on male development.

- Freud's theory is not scientific. It's difficult to submit concepts such as the Oedipus complex or the id to the rigors of scientific testing. Testability is essential in sciences such as psychology, and much of Freud's work was not really testable.

Freud left a lasting legacy, even if most of the references to concepts such as psychoanalysis are now outside psychology.[16] Our language is filled with psychoanalytic terms, from *repression* to *inferiority complex*. Freud's ideas have been steadily declining in importance in the academic world and with most psychologists for years, but some therapists, talk show hosts, and the public still love the concepts.[17]

MAKE IT STICK!

1. True or false: Freud's theory is considered unscientific by most psychologists.

2. Which Freudian conclusion do most contemporary psychodynamic theorists support?

   a. Development is fixed in childhood.
   b. Much of our mental life is unconscious.
   c. Gender identity can be achieved only when a child has a same-sex parent in the home.
   d. A focus on male personality development is the right approach.

The Humanistic Perspective on Personality

 29-4 How did the humanistic psychologists view personality and how our personality changes and grows?

In contrast to Freud's focus on unconscious thought and troubled people, **humanistic psychology** focuses on conscious experiences, the individual's freedom to choose, and the individual's capacity for personal growth. This movement began gaining credibility and momentum in the United States in the 1960s. Humanistic psychologists wanted a psychology that

1. emphasized conscious experience.

2. focused on free will and creative abilities.

3. studied all factors (not just observable behaviors) relevant to the human condition.[18]

Humanistic psychologists thought psychology in the 1960s was ignoring human strengths and virtues. Freud studied the motives of "sick" people, those who came to him with psychological problems. Humanists, such as Abraham Maslow and Carl Rogers, thought we should also study "healthy" people. They believed human personality was shaped more by our unique capacity to determine our future than by our unconscious conflicts or past learning.

Abraham Maslow and Self-Actualization

Studying psychologically healthy people, **Abraham Maslow** constructed a *hierarchy of needs* to help explain personality and personal growth[19] (see **Figure 29.2**). Maslow believed we must satisfy our basic physiological needs for food, water, and air before attempting to meet the security and safety needs of the second level of the hierarchy and the love and belongingness of the third level. Then, after meeting our needs for self-esteem, we could strive to achieve our full and unique potential as humans and obtain **self-actualization,** one of the higher levels of his hierarchy. The self-actualized person works toward a life that is challenging, productive, and meaningful.

Searching for examples of self-actualized people, Maslow studied paragons of society, like Eleanor Roosevelt and Abraham Lincoln. He found that those who live productive and rich lives are

- self-aware and self-accepting.

- open and spontaneous.

- loving and caring.

- not paralyzed by others' opinions.

- focused on a particular task they often see as a mission.

- involved in a few deep relationships, not many superficial ones.

- likely to have been moved by personal peak experiences that surpass ordinary consciousness.

humanistic psychology
A perspective that focuses on the study of conscious experience, the individual's freedom to choose, and the individual's capacity for personal growth.

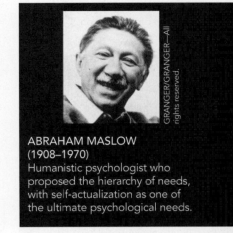

ABRAHAM MASLOW (1908–1970) Humanistic psychologist who proposed the hierarchy of needs, with self-actualization as one of the ultimate psychological needs.

FIGURE 29.2
Abraham Maslow's Hierarchy of Needs
Maslow's theory proposes that we must satisfy our basic physiological needs before we can try to meet higher-level safety and psychological needs. (From Maslow, 1970.)

Self-transcendence needs
Need to find meaning and identity beyond the self

Self-actualization needs
Need to live up to our fullest and unique potential

Esteem needs
Need for self-esteem, achievement, competence, and independence; need for recognition and respect from others

Belongingness and love needs
Need to love and be loved, to belong and be accepted; need to avoid loneliness and separation

Safety needs
Need to feel that the world is organized and predictable; need to feel safe

Physiological needs
Need to satisfy hunger and thirst

[handwritten: Comfortable being unpopular, not necessarily choosing to be]

self-actualization According to Maslow, an ultimate psychological need that arises after basic physical and psychological needs are met and self-esteem is achieved; the motivation to realize our full and unique potential.

unconditional positive regard According to Rogers, an attitude of total acceptance toward another person.

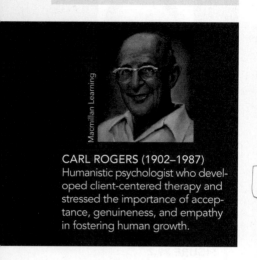

CARL ROGERS (1902–1987)
Humanistic psychologist who developed client-centered therapy and stressed the importance of acceptance, genuineness, and empathy in fostering human growth.

These mature adult qualities, wrote Maslow, are found in those who have "acquired enough courage to be unpopular," discovered their calling, and learned enough in life to be compassionate. These individuals have also outgrown any mixed feelings toward their parents and are "secretly uneasy about the cruelty, meanness, and mob spirit so often found in young people."[20]

Carl Rogers and the Person-Centered Approach

Humanistic psychologist **Carl Rogers** agreed with Maslow that people are good and strive for self-actualization. Rogers viewed people much like seeds that thrive when they have the right mixture of conditions.[21] Just as seeds flourish when given water, soil, and sun, Rogers said, people will flourish when given acceptance, genuineness, and empathy.

[handwritten: critiquing others?]

How do we nurture proper human growth in others? By being *accepting*—ideally, through **unconditional positive regard**, or an attitude of total acceptance toward another person. This attitude values others even though we are aware of their faults and failings. Rogers thought that family members and close friends who express unconditional positive regard for us provide us with great relief. We can let go, confess our most troubling thoughts, and not have to explain ourselves.

We also nurture growth by being *genuine*, according to Rogers. Genuine people freely express their feelings and aren't afraid to disclose details about themselves.

Finally, we nurture growth by being *empathic*. Empathy involves sharing thoughts and understanding and reflecting the other person's feelings. The key to empathy is listening with understanding. When the listener shows understanding, the person sharing feelings has an easier time being open and honest. Rogers wrote, "Listening, of this very special kind, is one of the most potent forces for change that I know."[22]

Acceptance, genuineness, and empathy help build a strong relationship between parent and child, teacher and student, manager and employee, or any two people. Rogers believed these three qualities—unconditional positive regard, genuineness, and empathy—are particularly important in the relationship between a client (a term Rogers thought had less baggage than "patient") and a therapist.

Assessing Personality and the Self From a Humanistic Perspective

If Rogers, Maslow, or any humanistic psychologist wanted to assess your personality, he or she probably would ask you to answer questions that would help evaluate your self-concept. Your **self-concept** includes all your thoughts and feelings about yourself in answer to the question "Who am I?" Rogers, for example, often asked clients to describe themselves first as they actually were and then as they would ideally like to be. He believed that the closer the actual self was to the ideal self, the more positive the person's self-concept. Assessing personal growth during therapy was a matter of measuring the difference between ratings of ideal self and actual self (see **Figure 29.3**).

For some humanistic psychologists, any kind of structured personality test is simply too impersonal and detached from the real person. For them, only a series of lengthy interviews and personal conversations can allow us to understand an individual's unique experiences and personality.

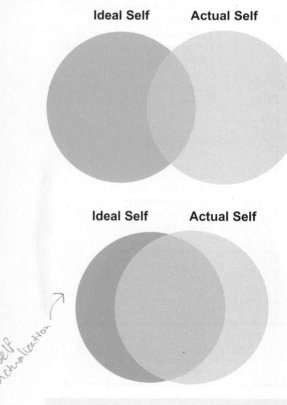

Ideal Self   Actual Self

Ideal Self   Actual Self

[handwritten: self actualization]

FIGURE 29.3 Self-Concept
Humanistic psychologists believed that the way you describe yourself ("actual self") and the way you'd like to describe yourself ("ideal self") should overlap. They thought the more they overlap, the better you feel about yourself.

MAKE IT STICK!

1. What is one of the more important differences between the humanistic and psychodynamic personality theories?

   a. Psychodynamic theory is historical and humanistic theory is current.

   b. Freud is much better known than Abraham Maslow.

   c. Humanists focus on "healthy" personalities, and the psychodynamic theorists focus on "ailing" or "sick" personalities.

   d. Psychodynamic theory is based on scientific method, but humanistic psychology is based only on stories.

2. Which personality theorist would most likely agree with the statement "Patients need to know that we respect them, no matter what choices they make"?

   a. Karen Horney

   b. Sigmund Freud

   c. Alfred Adler

   d. Carl Rogers

3. True or false: Rogers believed that defense mechanisms, genuineness, and dream interpretation are particularly important in the relationship between a client and a therapist.

Evaluating the Humanistic Perspective

 29-5 How have contemporary research findings evaluated the validity of the humanistic perspective on personality?

Carl Rogers once said, "Humanistic psychology has not had a significant effect on mainstream psychology. We are perceived as having relatively little importance."[23] Was Rogers correct?

Society has benefited from humanistic psychology. Therapy practices, child-rearing techniques, and workplace management can all attest to a positive humanistic influence.

But there have been unintentional negative effects as well. Some people have mistakenly interpreted unconditional positive regard for children as meaning that we should never offer constructive criticism to a child—or worse, never tell a child no. Critics also point out that many humanistic terms are vague and hard to define precisely so that other researchers can test them. Maslow, for example, stated that the self-actualized person is *spontaneous, loving,* and *productive.* How do we define these terms to allow Maslow's assumptions to be tested scientifically? Without such tests, how do we know whether these terms simply reflect Maslow's personal values?

Whatever its effect on mainstream psychology, humanistic psychology laid the foundation for the positive psychology movement that began in the 1990s. As a result, many researchers are studying the human strengths and virtues (like bravery, gratitude, and kindness) of healthy people, rather than just the disorders of those who are not psychologically healthy. Martin Seligman, the leader of this new movement, has called research "the protector and shield" of positive psychology.[24] His point is that most humanistic psychology proponents were not connected with university research labs. Without the research to back up its ideas, humanistic psychology faded.

self-concept All our thoughts and feelings about ourselves in answer to the question "Who am I?"

Too Impersonal?
Most humanistic psychologists believe that written personality tests are not an adequate way to assess personality. They prefer conversations and interviews that reveal the individual's uniqueness.

Tek Image/SPL/Science Source

"He flunked everything except 'Self-Esteem.'"

Baloo/Jantoo.com/CartoonStock Ltd

MAKE IT STICK!

1. Some parents have mistakenly interpreted unconditional positive regard as meaning they should never offer _____ to a child.

2. Humanistic psychology helped pave the way for _____.

3. True or false: Humanistic psychology lacked the research support it needed to be more widely accepted.

Module 29 Summary and Assessment

Psychodynamic and Humanistic Perspectives on Personality

🐾 29-1 How does the psychodynamic perspective explain personality?

- Sigmund Freud's psychoanalytic theory was the first comprehensive personality theory. Freud believed that an individual's personality emerges from tensions generated by unconscious motives and unresolved childhood conflicts. Personality results from the interaction of three forces: id, ego, and superego.

- Freud used various techniques, like free association, to reveal unacceptable thoughts, wishes, feelings, and memories held in the unconscious mind. Freud explained many of our thoughts and behaviors as defense mechanisms, protective methods of reducing anxiety by unconsciously distorting reality.

- The Freudian perspective held that personality forms during the first 5 or 6 years of life and is influenced by development through five psychosexual stages.

🐾 29-2 How did later psychodynamic theorists assess personality, and what were the new concepts added to psychodynamic theory by the neo-Freudians?

- Neo-Freudians such as Alfred Adler, Carl Jung, and Karen Horney agreed with the basic ideas of psychoanalysis, but each introduced new ideas by modifying some part of Freud's theory.

- Later psychodynamic theorists used projective tests (like the TAT and the Rorschach inkblot test) to reveal unconscious thoughts and associations.

🐾 29-3 How have contemporary researchers evaluated the validity of the psychodynamic perspective on personality?

- The modern psychodynamic perspective on personality incorporates some aspects of Freudian theory, such as the connection between personality and unconscious thought processes.

- Freud's theory was not scientific and was based on interpretations of reports from a nonrepresentative group of patients. Several of Freud's original claims (for example, the Oedipus complex creating gender identity in boys) have been disproved by more recent psychological research.

🐾 29-4 How did the humanistic psychologists view personality and how our personality changes and grows?

- Humanistic psychology is based on the optimistic view that all of us are striving to improve our personalities and become the best people we can be. It emphasizes freedom and our ability to choose our own directions in life.

- Abraham Maslow constructed a hierarchy of needs to help explain personality and personal growth of psychologically healthy people toward self-actualization.

- Carl Rogers believed that people need unconditional positive regard, as well as a genuine and empathic environment, to overcome obstacles and develop in healthy ways.

- Humanistic psychologists assess personality through questions that reveal an individual's ideal and actual self-concepts.

🐾 29-5 How have contemporary research findings evaluated the validity of the humanistic perspective on personality?

- The rise of humanistic psychology influenced therapy practices, child-rearing techniques, and workplace management theories.

- The theory is often misinterpreted, however, and it is difficult to establish through research because many humanistic terms are vague and hard to define.

- Humanistic psychology laid the foundation for the positive psychology movement, which has the advantage of being research based.

Summative Assessment

1. What do we call an individual's characteristic pattern of thinking, feeling, and acting?

   a. preconscious
   b. psychoanalysis
   c. personality
   d. psychodynamic

2. What did Sigmund Freud call his therapeutic approach?

   a. preconscious
   b. psychoanalysis
   c. personality
   d. psychodynamic

3. Freud believed he could help patients heal by opening the door to

   a. the conscious mind.
   b. the preconscious mind.
   c. the unconscious mind.
   d. the human mind.

4. Which of the following anxiety-provoking behaviors can be explained by the defense mechanism of rationalization?

   a. A thief who mistrusts others thinks everyone else is a thief.
   b. A person who overeats says it's okay because he will diet tomorrow.
   c. A smoker refuses to admit she might become addicted to cigarettes.
   d. A boss becomes upset and yells at an employee, who later yells at his wife.

5. According to neo-Freudian Alfred Adler, what do we call our organization of thoughts based on our perceived shortcomings or mistakes?

   a. the collective unconscious
   b. personality development
   c. psychodynamic theory
   d. an inferiority complex

6. What did neo-Freudian Karen Horney believe was the foundation of personality development?

   a. helplessness and isolation
   b. differences between males and females
   c. cultural variables and social expectations
   d. the collective unconscious

7. Which of the following defines humanistic psychology?

   a. focus on the study of conscious experience, the individual's freedom to choose, and the individual's capacity for personal growth
   b. an ultimate psychological need that arises after basic physical and psychological needs are met and self-esteem is achieved
   c. the need to love and be loved, to belong and be accepted, and to avoid loneliness and separation
   d. a condition that comes from being unable to compensate for normal inferiority feelings

8. Which of the following defines self-actualization?

   a. focus on the study of conscious experience, the individual's freedom to choose, and the individual's capacity for personal growth
   b. an ultimate psychological need that arises after basic physical and psychological needs are met and self-esteem is achieved
   c. the need to love and be loved, to belong and be accepted, and to avoid loneliness and separation
   d. a condition that comes from being unable to compensate for normal inferiority feelings

9. What did Abraham Maslow call his theory that proposes we must satisfy our basic psychological needs before we can try to meet higher-level safety and psychological needs?

   a. humanistic psychology
   b. the psychodynamic perspective
   c. the hierarchy of needs
   d. the psychosexual stages

10. Humanistic psychologists believe that the way you describe yourself and the way you'd like to describe yourself should overlap. What is this called?

   a. self-concept
   b. unconditional positive regard
   c. self-actualization
   d. the hierarchy of needs

KEY TERMS AND KEY PEOPLE

personality, p. 440

psychoanalysis, p. 441

psychodynamic perspective, p. 441

free association, p. 441

preconscious, p. 442

unconscious, p. 442

id, p. 442

superego, p. 443

ego, p. 443

defense mechanisms, p. 443

psychosexual stages, p. 444

resilience, p. 446

inferiority complex, p. 447

collective unconscious, p. 447

projective test, p. 448

Thematic Apperception Test (TAT), p. 448

Rorschach inkblot test, p. 448

humanistic psychology, p. 451

self-actualization, p. 451

unconditional positive regard, p. 452

self-concept, p. 452

Sigmund Freud (1856–1939), p. 441

Alfred Adler (1870–1937), p. 447

Carl Jung [YOO-ng] (1875–1961), p. 447

Karen Horney [HORN-eye] (1885–1952), p. 448

Abraham Maslow (1908–1970), p. 451

Carl Rogers (1902–1987), p. 452

Trait and Social-Cognitive Perspectives on Personality

Are you open? Outgoing? Agreeable? Psychologists study the traits we often use to describe others and ourselves.

Remember the last time a friend asked for your opinion of another person? Perhaps you said that person was generous, friendly, and sweet, or maybe you described someone who was self-centered, cranky, and mean. Terms like these describe **traits,** aspects of personality that are relatively consistent. Some psychologists who study **personality**—an individual's characteristic pattern of thinking, feeling, and acting—find traits a useful tool for describing different personality types. Psychologists taking this *trait perspective* tend to consider our consistent patterns of behavior, those that we're born with and that stay fairly constant across situations.

Other psychologists believe that understanding personality involves considering how people are affected by a particular situation, by what they have learned, by how they think, and by how they interact socially. Psychologists who take this **social-cognitive perspective** would consider how the same person could be generous in one situation and self-centered in another, or friendly and sweet on one day and cranky and mean the next.

In this module, we take a closer look at these two perspectives on personality.

The Trait Perspective

 30-1 Are there different personality types? If so, how do trait theorists suggest that we describe and measure them?

Think of the last car you rode in, perhaps on your way to or from school. What kind of car was it? What about the color? Was it a compact, small, medium, or large car? Note how we are using descriptive techniques to classify the cars as

traits Aspects of personality that are relatively consistent.

personality An individual's characteristic pattern of thinking, feeling, and acting.

social-cognitive perspective A perspective stating that understanding personality involves considering how people are affected by a particular situation, by what they have learned, by how they think, and by how they interact socially.

Personality Types ▲
How would the ancient Greeks have classified this personality type?

HASLOO / iStock/Getty Images

distinct *types*. Can we use similar techniques to classify personalities? People have been attempting to do so for millennia.

Thousands of years ago, the ancient Greeks classified personalities using four types: sanguine (cheerful), melancholic (depressed), choleric (irritable), and phlegmatic (unemotional). And how did the ancient Greeks explain whether you were cheerful or irritable? They spoke of your body fluids, or "humors." If melancholic humor filled your body, for example, you had a depressive personality.

Psychologists still use descriptive techniques to classify personality, but they now attempt to identify characteristic and consistent patterns of behavior using valid and reliable assessment techniques. (Don't confuse these techniques with the tests you find online and in teen magazines. Unfortunately, most of those "personality assessments" are no more valid or reliable than the ancient Greeks' descriptions of "humors.")

MAKE IT STICK!

1. What do we call aspects of personality that are pretty consistent?

2. What do we call an individual's characteristic pattern of thinking, feeling, and acting?

3. True or false: Psychologists use descriptive techniques to classify personality.

Identifying Traits

 30-2 How did psychologists Gordon Allport, Raymond Cattell, and Hans Eysenck identify traits?

One early attempt to classify personality made assumptions based on a person's body type. In this view, overweight people were viewed as jolly and thin people as highly strung.[1] Personality researchers realized, however, that these oversimplified classification systems tend to eliminate each person's individuality. Three researchers—Gordon Allport, Raymond Cattell, and Hans Eysenck—offered broader alternatives to account for these trait variations.

Gordon Allport's Trait Theory After graduating from college, **Gordon Allport** traveled to Vienna to visit Sigmund Freud, the Austrian physician famous for his theory of psychoanalysis. Their meeting profoundly affected the trait theory Allport developed years later.

At the time, Freud was developing his theory of the unconscious, a hidden reservoir of unacceptable thoughts and feelings. He viewed personality as the result of a long history of interactions between the unconscious and conscious minds of a person. Freud often studied people with psychological conflicts, and he searched for answers in childhood experiences.

Allport disagreed with Freud in many ways. First, Allport played down the role of the unconscious in healthy people. Unlike Freud, Allport believed personality should be studied only in normal adults, not in those suffering from a psychological problem. Furthermore, wrote Allport, current experiences have a far greater effect on an adult than the early childhood experiences upon which Freud dwelled.

Allport also resisted the idea of a "personality law," or some one-size-fits-all approach to explaining personality that would apply to everyone. Instead, he strongly believed that individual personalities are unique. This belief, which manifested itself

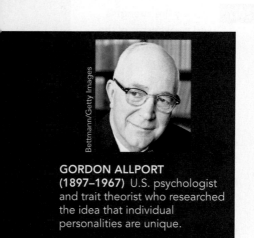

GORDON ALLPORT
(1897–1967) U.S. psychologist and trait theorist who researched the idea that individual personalities are unique.

Bettmann/Getty Images

in his trait theory, led psychology in two directions. First, Allport identified several kinds of traits, which paved the way for other personality researchers and brought respectability to the study of personality.[2] The second direction was more problematic: Allport's emphasis on individual uniqueness made it difficult to produce general ideas that could be tested by others. Allport classified traits into three main categories. The first category he called cardinal traits, which he saw as the most important. Examples included self-sacrifice and ambition. The second category he called central traits. These "building block" traits were consistent over time (as were cardinal traits). Examples included friendliness, happiness, and honesty. The third category he called secondary traits. Allport maintained that secondary traits were harder to detect because they were less consistent and not as obvious as cardinal and central traits. Examples of secondary traits included irritability, shyness, and anxiety. By the time he was done, Allport had listed more than *18,000 ways* to describe people.[3] That number was simply unmanageable. Would it be possible to condense all the possible traits into a manageable few? The answer was *Yes,* according to Raymond Cattell.

Raymond Cattell's Factor Analysis English psychologist **Raymond Cattell's** (pronounced kuh-TELL) contribution to the trait perspective flowed from his interest in knowing whether some traits predicted others. For instance, if you identify yourself as timid, are you more likely to report feeling suspicious? If you say you are kind, would you be more likely to tell the truth? Cattell used statistical techniques, especially *factor analysis,* to compute the relationships among traits until he came up with 16 core personality dimensions, or factors[4] (see **Figure 30.1**).

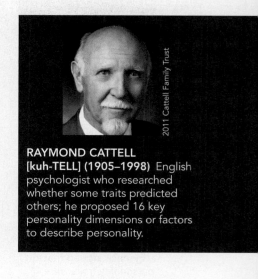

RAYMOND CATTELL [kuh-TELL] (1905–1998) English psychologist who researched whether some traits predicted others; he proposed 16 key personality dimensions or factors to describe personality.

2011 Cattell Family Trust

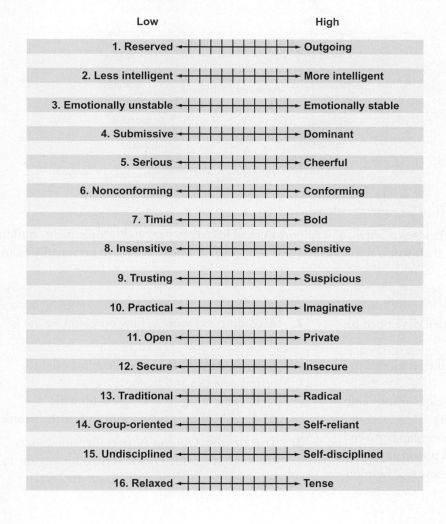

Low		High
1. Reserved		Outgoing
2. Less intelligent		More intelligent
3. Emotionally unstable		Emotionally stable
4. Submissive		Dominant
5. Serious		Cheerful
6. Nonconforming		Conforming
7. Timid		Bold
8. Insensitive		Sensitive
9. Trusting		Suspicious
10. Practical		Imaginative
11. Open		Private
12. Secure		Insecure
13. Traditional		Radical
14. Group-oriented		Self-reliant
15. Undisciplined		Self-disciplined
16. Relaxed		Tense

FIGURE 30.1 Raymond Cattell's 16 Personality Dimensions or Factors Cattell identified 16 core personality dimensions, or factors, each of which has a continuum with a "low" end and a "high" end. For instance, on the tension dimension, you could rate anywhere between "relaxed" and "tense." (Adapted from Cattell, 1963.)

HANS EYSENCK
[EYE-zink] (1916–1997)
German psychologist who
researched the genetically
influenced dimensions
of personality, including
extraversion and introversion.

Each factor can be measured using a questionnaire and plotted on a continuum.[5] Take, for instance, social boldness: How would you rate yourself on a scale of 1 to 10 on the timid–bold continuum, where 1 equals timid and 10 equals bold? Such ratings produce a profile for the individual being assessed.

How many factors are there to personality? Cattell insisted personality should be assessed using 16 factors, or traits.[6] However, Hans Eysenck thought 16 traits were too many (see Figure 30.1).

Hans Eysenck's Biological Dimensions

German psychologist **Hans Eysenck** (pronounced EYE-zink) searched for personality dimensions in biology, and his model of genetically influenced dimensions has broad research support. Like Cattell, Eysenck used statistical analysis to come up with his dimensions. Two of his findings are the extraversion–introversion dimension and the emotional stability–instability dimension.

Extraverts, according to Eysenck, are outgoing and sociable; *introverts* keep to themselves and are quiet. Emotionally stable people are generally relaxed and calm, whereas emotionally unstable people are anxious and tend to worry. Analyzing data from a questionnaire he developed, Eysenck found he could predict personality traits along these biologically inherited dimensions[7] (see **Figure 30.2**).

FIGURE 30.2
Hans Eysenck's
Personality Factors
Eysenck argued that
personality traits were
inherited. Notice how
Eysenck's four quadrants
align with the four
personality types of the
ancient Greeks. (From
Eysenck & Eysenck, 1963.)

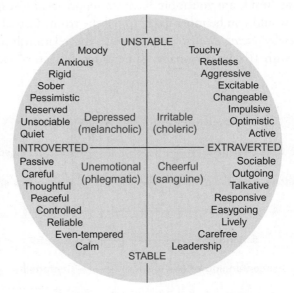

Eysenck, Cattell, and Allport were all leaders in personality assessment. Building on their work, researchers have now identified a new core set of personality factors.

MAKE IT STICK!

1. Which best describes how Cattell developed his list of 16 personality traits?

   a. factor analysis to compute the relationships among traits

   b. analysis of patients' unconscious minds and projective tests of personality

   c. experiments to study the relationship between environmental situations and personality factors

   d. focus on individual uniqueness like Gordon Allport

2. According to Eysenck, how outgoing we are is most determined by

   a. what situations we have been exposed to.

   b. our genetics and biology.

   c. the parenting style we grew up with.

   d. the role of the unconscious in healthy people.

3. True or false: Gordon Allport identified over 18,000 traits, which made it hard for anyone to learn and apply these traits to others.

The Big Five Traits

 30-3 What are the dimensions of the Big Five trait theory?

Clearly, there is some debate over the number of basic personality traits. How many traits would it take to adequately describe your best friend? Would three be enough to paint this picture? Would 16 cause you to start repeating yourself? In the mid-1980s, researchers decided that an adequate description of personality relied on five essential factors now usually referred to as the Big Five.[8,9] Try it for yourself. Can you give an adequate description of your best friend using the five dimensions in **Figure 30.3**? Findings from around the world show that most people tend to mention these five traits when describing one another.[10,11]

The Big Five Personality Factors

(*Memory tip*: Picturing a CANOE will help you recall these.)

Trait Dimension	Endpoints of the Dimension		
Conscientiousness	Organized	↔	Disorganized
	Careful	↔	Careless
	Disciplined	↔	Impulsive
Agreeableness	Soft-hearted	↔	Ruthless
	Trusting	↔	Suspicious
	Helpful	↔	Uncooperative
Neuroticism (emotional stability vs. instability)	Calm	↔	Anxious
	Secure	↔	Insecure
	Self-satisfied	↔	Self-pitying
Openness	Imaginative	↔	Practical
	Preference for variety	↔	Preference for routine
	Independent	↔	Conforming
Extraversion	Sociable	↔	Retiring
	Fun-loving	↔	Sober
	Affectionate	↔	Reserved

FIGURE 30.3
The Big Five Personality Factors
Most personality theorists tend to agree that human personality can be described using these factors or traits. (Adapted from McCrae & Costa, 1996.)

The Big Five traits—conscientiousness, agreeableness, neuroticism, openness, and extraversion (memory trick: Use the first letter of each trait to spell *canoe* or *ocean*)—appear to be stable in adults. This means that it's unlikely an agreeable 30-year-old will suddenly become suspicious and uncooperative at age 60. In fact, agreeableness and conscientiousness tend to increase as you get older.[12]

Genetic predispositions influence personality traits.[13] *Predisposition* merely means that a biological tendency to develop a trait exists. Whether the trait actually will develop may depend on environmental factors (such as stress or upbringing). So, if you are genetically predisposed to instability (that is, being uncertain in your decision making or unreliable), this trait might not reveal itself if you live a stress-free life where you don't have to meet deadlines or make important decisions. The Big Five traits also predict other personal attributes. For example, marital satisfaction typically suffers for those scoring low on agreeableness, stability, and openness.[14,15]

Do the Big Five represent all we need to know about personality traits? Some argue the Big Five should be expanded to include dimensions such as positive and negative emotion or femininity and masculinity. Further assessment of traits may someday expand the Big Five, but for now, the Big Five do a good job of describing personality's essential factors.

MAKE IT STICK!

1. Which of the Big Five personality traits would most influence whether a person feels comfortable telling a joke in front of a group of strangers?

   a. extraversion
   c. openness
   b. neuroticism
   d. conscientiousness

2. Which statement is a key research finding about the Big Five personality traits?

   a. The traits match up with those of historical personality trait theories.
   b. The traits affect the preconscious mind.
   c. The traits interact in important ways in different social situations.
   d. The traits appear to be stable in adults.

3. True or false: A married man who scores low on tests of agreeableness, openness, and stability is likely to report more satisfaction in his marriage.

Testing for Traits

 30-4 How do trait theorists assess personality?

Some personality researchers use projective tests to assess personality by asking people to respond to ambiguous pictures like inkblots—images where the meaning is not clear. Trait researchers prefer **personality inventories,** questionnaires on which people respond to items designed to gauge a range of feelings and behaviors. These two approaches differ in important ways. *Projective tests* ask the person being tested to "project" unconscious motives onto an ambiguous image in a free-flowing, narrative style. In contrast, personality inventories are *objective tests.* Test-takers provide answers to questions, which are usually in the form of true-false or multiple-choice. The administration of objective tests has been standardized (made consistent) to help ensure that results from all test-takers are compared to the same standard.

Objective tests have shown greater **validity**—the extent to which a test measures or predicts what it is supposed to test—than projective assessments. If you are a clinical psychologist trying to assess anxiety or depression in a patient, the objective test is more likely than the projective test to measure these conditions accurately. Objective tests also offer greater **reliability,** which is the extent to which a test yields consistent results, regardless of who gives the test or when or where it is being given.[16] Finally, the two types of tests differ in the training required to score them. Scoring or interpreting projective tests requires years of extensive training and practice, but scoring objective tests is simple and uncomplicated.

The best-known personality inventory has more than 500 questions. It's called the **Minnesota Multiphasic Personality Inventory** (mercifully abbreviated as the **MMPI**), and it is the most widely researched and clinically used of all personality tests. The MMPI was originally developed to identify emotional disorders (still considered its most appropriate use), but this test is now used for many other screening purposes. The second version of the test, the MMPI-2, was standardized on a more diverse sample of people than the original MMPI. The original MMPI was standardized using mostly Midwestern Protestant white married couples, but the test was used to diagnose people of all ethnicities and religions. This was a problem because what's standard for one culture may not be standard for another. There is also a third version of the test, the MMPI-A, which was designed specifically for teenagers.

The MMPI-2 assesses test-takers on 10 clinical scales used to diagnose psychological disorders (see **Figure 30.4**). An additional 15 content scales measure all kinds of attributes, including anger, attitude toward work, and whether a person is trying to fake mental illness.

personality inventories Questionnaires (often with true-false or agree-disagree items) on which people respond to items designed to gauge a range of feelings and behaviors; used to assess selected personality traits.

validity The extent to which a test measures or predicts what it is supposed to test.

reliability The extent to which a test yields consistent results, regardless of who gives the test or when or where it is given.

Minnesota Multiphasic Personality Inventory (MMPI) The most widely researched and clinically used of all personality tests; originally developed to identify emotional disorders (still considered its most appropriate use), this test is now used for many other screening purposes.

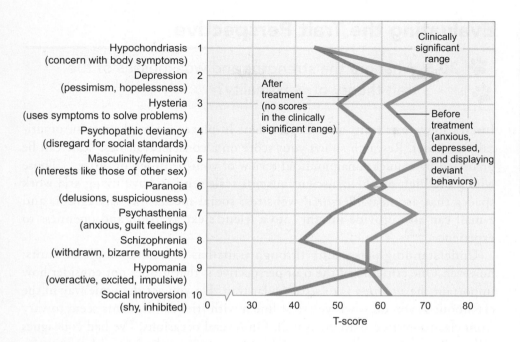

Hypochondriasis 1
(concern with body symptoms)

Depression 2
(pessimism, hopelessness)

Hysteria 3
(uses symptoms to solve problems)

Psychopathic deviancy 4
(disregard for social standards)

Masculinity/femininity 5
(interests like those of other sex)

Paranoia 6
(delusions, suspiciousness)

Psychasthenia 7
(anxious, guilt feelings)

Schizophrenia 8
(withdrawn, bizarre thoughts)

Hypomania 9
(overactive, excited, impulsive)

Social introversion 10
(shy, inhibited)

T-score

FIGURE 30.4
A Minnesota Multiphasic Personality Inventory Profile
These are the scores of a young man suffering depression and anxiety—before and after treatment for his disorders. An average T-score is 50, and scores over 65 suggest a psychological disorder.

Therapists are not the only people administering the MMPI-2. Many school admissions officers and personnel departments use the MMPI-2 to assess potential students or employees. Unfortunately, these agencies may be using the test in ways that were not intended.[17] For example, insurance agencies have been known to require someone making an insurance claim to take the MMPI to help determine whether to pay the person making the claim or to fight it.[18]

Is it possible to beat the MMPI-2, presenting yourself as something you are not? *You bet.* Although objective tests have greater validity than projective tests, they aren't always valid. It may be difficult to fake mental illness on the MMPI-2, but it is possible to fake near-perfection on some other scales by answering in socially desirable ways. If you were applying for a job and your potential employer gave you a test asking how often you become angry, what would you say? A person with an anger problem who wants a job might say, "Sometimes," or, "Almost never," to look more favorable to the boss.

This anger example hints at a potential problem with self-report data: How honest are we when assessing ourselves? Can you accurately say how helpful you are? Some researchers suggest peer reports are more likely than self-reports to provide valid and reliable information.[19,20] What if you say you're not helpful but all your friends and relatives rate you high in helpfulness? Chances are you *are* helpful.

MAKE IT STICK!

1. Which statement reveals an important difference between objective and projective tests?

   a. Objective tests are more personal and reveal deeper issues than projective tests.

   b. Objective tests reveal issues that are more important to patients.

   c. Objective tests show greater validity and reliability than projective tests.

   d. Objective tests are valid, but only projective tests are reliable.

2. A personality test that shows the same results each time you take it but whose results do not match your personality has high _____ but low _____.

   a. objectivity; projectivity

   b. optimism; pessimism

   c. reliability; validity

   d. validity; reliability

3. True or false: The MMPI-2 is not always used as its developers intended.

Evaluating the Trait Perspective

 30-5 What are the strengths and weaknesses of the trait theory of personality?

Interestingly, our traits are often evident in places we might not automatically consider. Research shows your score on a conscientiousness scale can be predicted by a quick, unannounced review of your bedroom or office.[21] Those who score high on the conscientiousness scale tend to have living and work spaces that are neat. Personal websites, social media like Instagram, and e-mail can also provide insight into a friend's extraversion and openness to experience.[22,23]

Understanding personality through traits has at least a couple of faults, however. One criticism of the trait perspective is that it does not consider how important the *situation* is to a particular trait. Do you act the same way in the classroom as you do when you're at lunch with friends? Students seem to vary from classroom to classroom as well. On several occasions, I've had colleagues tell me how quiet or how outgoing a student is, only to see the opposite behavior in my class. Trait behavior seems to be related to where we are and whom we're with.[24]

Trait theories have another glaring weakness: their inability to explain *why* we behave the way we do. Traits may describe us well, but they limit themselves to statements of *how* we behave. Felicia is calm and secure, so we label her as high in emotional stability. Trait theories do not explain why Felicia is calm and secure.

Will the Big Five ever change? Some theorists are suggesting the possibility of adding dimensions to the Big Five.[25] Perhaps in the future we'll have a Big Eight that includes the likes of positive and negative emotion, femininity and masculinity, and religiousness. Time, and research, will tell.

Trait theories also do not consider the effects of our thoughts on our behavior. The social-cognitive perspective, however, has a lot to say about how thoughts and situations affect personality.

MAKE IT STICK!

1. Which statement is the most valid criticism of the trait theory of personality?

   a. Trait theory does not help explain why we behave in the ways we do.
   b. Trait theory is based on patient reports, not objective scientific research.
   c. Trait theory does not state a particular number of traits.
   d. Trait theory is based on psychologists' interpretations of projective tests.

2. One problem with trait theory is that it often fails to account for the power of the _____ when addressing an individual's motivation.

3. True or false: Trait theories take into account the effects of our thoughts on behavior.

The Social-Cognitive Perspective

 30-6 How do social-cognitive theorists explain the development of our personality and the relationship among personality, the environment, and behavior?

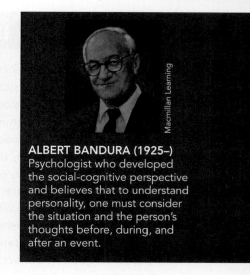

ALBERT BANDURA (1925–)
Psychologist who developed the social-cognitive perspective and believes that to understand personality, one must consider the situation and the person's thoughts before, during, and after an event.

The social-cognitive perspective is an interactive theory that combines research on social behavior, cognition, and learning. Some call this theory the *cognitive social learning theory* or the *cognitive-behavioral approach,* but we stick with the *social-cognitive perspective,* the name used by **Albert Bandura.**[26] Bandura and other social-cognitive theorists contend that we learn by observing and modeling the behaviors of others or by having certain behaviors reinforced or rewarded. Proponents of the social-cognitive perspective believe that to understand personality, we need to consider the situation the person is in, how that person thinks, and how that person interacts socially. (The desire to understand personality—especially our own—can unfortunately lead us astray, as seen in Psychology in the Real World: Planets, Palms, and Personalities.)

PSYCHOLOGY IN THE REAL WORLD

Planets, Palms, and Personalities

After sending an e-mail with the word *horoscope* in the subject line, I noticed some "sponsored links" beside the responses from my friends that included all kinds of find-your-fate websites. For only $4.95 per month, I could get my dreams analyzed, find out where I am on the "love meter," and have my fortune told. All things considered, this was a cheap price to pay to discover everything about myself and what I should do with my life. One of the links said it would get this "100 percent reliable information" by consulting the position of the stars and planets, and the phase of the moon, after I revealed my birth date. Another encouraged me to send a scan of my palm and a handwriting sample to find out what kind of person I am and how long I will live. Is there anything to these methods? Do these techniques reveal who you are? Psychologists have seriously considered these questions and so far have found no scientific support for psychics' claims.

I'll admit, the other day I read my Capricorn horoscope and agreed with what it said. But that same day I also read Sagittarius, Libra, and Leo and thought those descriptions applied equally well to me! This is not surprising, because few people can pick out their horoscope when all 12 are presented without labels.[27,28] Similar studies have shown that handwriting analysis

"experts" do no better than chance in predicting people's occupations from their handwriting samples.[29,30]

With such a bad track record, how do astrologers and palm readers stay in business? One former palm reader, research psychologist Ray Hyman, provides some insight into their apparently successful techniques.[31] The "seer" often starts by offering generally true statements few of us would disagree with, such as the following:

- "You worry about things more than you let on."
- "I sense you are nursing a grudge against someone; you really ought to let that go."
- "You are adaptable to social situations and your interests are wide ranging."

Any of those sound like you? I was in a class once where we were all given a "personality test" that would provide us with a personal character analysis. The next day, we were all handed our individual analyses, then asked how much we agreed with what had been said. Almost all of us said the character analysis closely described our personalities, and some were amazed at the accuracy. Imagine our surprise when the instructor revealed that we had all received the same analysis, taken at random from an astrology magazine!

PSYCHOLOGY IN THE REAL WORLD (Continued)

"Seers" also pay close attention to your body language, clothing, and physical features. Therapeutic shoes may indicate physical discomfort. Haircut or clothing could indicate music preference. Facial expressions can indicate mood. Expensive jewelry? Wealth. After sizing you up, the seer may then say something like "I can tell you're dealing with a problem and that you are not sure what to do about it." This sympathy technique builds trust. If the person seeking insight gives a positive nod in response, the seer will reassert the statement more strongly. Seers are also good at deflecting negative responses. If the statement seems inaccurate, you will just have to work harder to make sense of the "vision" or message.

The bottom line is that we should all be wary of those who use these techniques. Reading your horoscope and chuckling at the generalized statements is one thing, but planning your life around them is definitely not a good idea.

THINK ABOUT . . . Psychology in the Real World

1. What are some of the techniques palm readers use to stay in business?

2. What are two different reasons why people might read their horoscope?

3. What would you say to a friend who was telling you he was going to have his palm read before deciding whether to go to college?

Interacting With Our Environment: Three Influences

A colleague who taught down the hall from me was, by most accounts, a tranquil person. Students described him as "calm" and "gentle." One Saturday afternoon, my daughter's recreational league basketball team played against the team coached by my serene colleague, and I witnessed a completely different person. He looked sternly at his players as they warmed up. He yelled constantly at the teen referee during the game. After the game, he huddled with his players and, in a loud voice, told each what she had done wrong during the game—even though they had won by eight points. What would explain the difference in behavior between teacher and coach?

Social-cognitive theorists would likely explain that my colleague's behavior differences were caused by **reciprocal determinism,** the mutual influences between personality and environmental factors.[32,33] Reciprocal determinism includes the interaction of three factors:

> **reciprocal determinism**
> The mutual influences between personality and environmental factors.

1. Your thoughts or cognitions

2. Your environment

3. Your behaviors

Each factor interacts with the others (see **Figure 30.5**), according to social-cognitive theorists, in determining your personality. To understand the teacher/coach's changing personality, we would then need to consider the following questions:

- *How does his behavior change in different situations?* Does he act the same way at home as he does on the basketball court, or is his home behavior more like his classroom behavior? Would he have been calmer if the referee had been an adult?

- *How does he perceive each situation?* Is he more confident in the classroom, and thus more in control? Is coaching so overwhelming that he loses track of his emotions? Did he sense weakness in the 14-year-old referee and alter his approach to the game?

Behavior
(learning to swim
and dive)

**Cognition, or
Thoughts**
(liking to take risks)

Environment
(friends who dive
off the high dive)

JAN HALASKA/Science Source

**FIGURE 30.5
Reciprocal Determinism**
Albert Bandura's social-cognitive perspective suggests that personalities are shaped by the interaction of environment, behaviors, and thoughts (cognitions).

- *How do the elements of the situation affect his behavior?* Do parents breathe down his neck, demanding a victory? Had this same referee called a poor game the week before?

We can't expect to know a person's personality by observing that individual in one situation or at one point in time. All behavior is the result of the interplay between external (environment) and internal (thoughts, perceptions) factors.

Personal Control

Do you feel as though your environment controls you, or do you believe you are in control of your environment? Social-cognitive psychologists who study personal control believe that the way you answer this question can provide clues to your personality. Psychologists who study personality from this perspective are especially interested in two questions:

1. How do feelings of control predict achievement and behavior?
2. How does explanatory style (how you explain the things that happen to you) affect our well-being?

Locus of Control Consider the following statements:

- There's no reason to vote in an election—your vote doesn't really count.
- When you try to get a job, it's not *what* you know that matters but *whom* you know.
- One person can make a difference in the way elected representatives think.
- If you want to be a success, depend on hard work, not luck.

Which two are closest to what you believe? For a social-cognitive psychologist, these four statements are clues to your *locus of control*. (*Locus* is from a Latin word meaning "place.") The first two reflect what Julian Rotter called an **external locus of control,** the perception that chance, or forces outside yourself and beyond your control, determines your fate. If you feel more comfortable with the second two statements, you probably have an **internal locus of control,** the perception that you control your own fate. Dozens of studies have compared how an external or internal locus of control correlates with behavior and achievement. Look at these results.

LIFE MATTERS

It's easy to confuse external locus of control with external motivation. For example, you may study for an exam in order to get a good grade (external motivation). However, you may feel that your teacher is unfair so no matter how hard you study you won't do well (external locus of control).

external locus of control
The perception that chance, or forces beyond your control, determines your fate.

internal locus of control
The perception that you control your own fate.

Monkey Business Images/Shutterstock

Internal Versus External Control
People with an internal locus of control are healthier, cope better with stress, and are less likely to be depressed than people with an external locus of control.

learned helplessness
The hopeless feeling when an animal or human can't avoid repeated bad events.

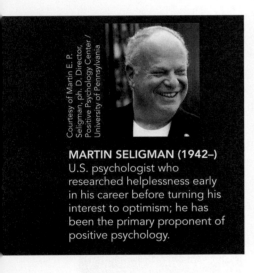
Courtesy of Martin E. P. Seligman, ph. D. Director, Positive Psychology Center / University of Pennsylvania

MARTIN SELIGMAN (1942–)
U.S. psychologist who researched helplessness early in his career before turning his interest to optimism; he has been the primary proponent of positive psychology.

When compared with people with an external locus of control, those with an internal locus of control

- are less depressed.[34]
- are more likely to be healthy.[35]
- achieve more in school and act more independently.[36,37]
- cope better with stress, including serious stressors like marital problems.[38]

This is good news for people with an internal locus of control, but not for those with an external locus of control. If you have an external locus of control, is it possible to change? Researchers today are working on that very question, which we explore in our next section.

Learned Helplessness and Learned Optimism Researcher Ellen Langer once said, "Perceived control is basic to human functioning."[39] Indeed, depressed people often feel a lack of control.[40,41] People or animals who feel hopeless when they can't avoid repeated bad events tend to develop **learned helplessness.** In a landmark study, **Martin Seligman** demonstrated the development of learned helplessness in dogs that had no control over negative events.[42] The researchers placed one group of dogs in individual cages divided by a low barrier. These dogs received an electric shock, but they could jump over the barrier to the other side of the cage to escape the shock. A second group of dogs, in similar cages, received the same shocks, but they were restrained in harnesses that prevented escape. After several trials in which shocks were administered but escape was impossible, the researchers removed the harnesses. Sadly, the dogs in this second group did not even attempt to escape from the shocks, even though they could now easily jump over the barrier to the other side of the cage. Instead, most cowered on the cage floor. The dogs had developed a sense that they had no control over their environment. They had learned helplessness (see **Figure 30.6**).

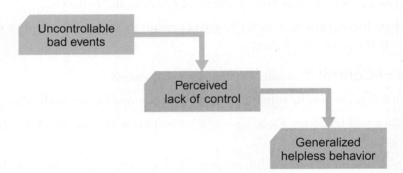

▲ **FIGURE 30.6**
Learned Helplessness
People and animals are likely to learn helplessness when they repeatedly experience bad events over which they have no control.

People learn helplessness, too. Depression and hopelessness emerge in people who face traumatic events over which they have no control. However, several studies show that morale and health can be boosted by giving people control where they had none before, such as control of the television in a prison or control over the arrangement of personal belongings in a nursing home.[43,44] And according to one study, those living in a stable democracy, where empowerment and personal freedom are more likely, report higher levels of happiness.[45,46]

After demonstrating learned helplessness, Seligman wondered if optimism could also be learned. His interests led him to found **positive psychology,** a movement that studies optimal human functioning and the factors that allow individuals and communities to thrive. Could an optimistic attitude be one of those factors? Let's see what Seligman and others have discovered.

> **positive psychology**
> A movement in psychology that focuses on the study of optimal human functioning and the factors that allow individuals and communities to thrive.

Learned Helplessness's Other Side— Some Dogs Never Gave Up

A few years back, I had the chance to talk with Martin Seligman, one of positive psychology's founders. At one point, a tone of sadness crept into his voice. "When I talk to teachers, the first question I usually get is about learned helplessness, how we taught dogs to give up in a seemingly helpless situation. The fact is, I was always more interested in the dogs that never quit." Indeed, some of the dogs, no matter what the conditions, never quit trying to avoid or escape the shocks delivered during the learned helplessness experiments. Interest in these animals played a key role in Seligman's shift away from the study of helplessness.

Seligman wrote *Learned Optimism* in 1991, which laid the groundwork for his research on human strengths, well-being, and flourishing. Seven years later, in the biggest landslide in the American Psychological Association's hundred-year history, Seligman was elected president of the APA.

Martin Seligman's 1998 APA presidential address kick-started the positive psychology movement, which focuses on the study of optimal human functioning and the factors that allow individuals and communities to thrive. In that address, Seligman reminded psychologists of the field's three distinct missions in the years before World War II:[47]

1. Curing mental illness

2. Making life more productive and fulfilling

3. Identifying and nurturing high talent

According to Seligman, by the end of the twentieth century, psychology had lost track of the second and third missions. Seligman and many others have called for a return to the other two "distinct missions" of psychology. He suggests moving from a preoccupation with *repairing* the worst things in life to *building* on positive qualities. Seligman writes,

> The field of positive psychology . . . is about positive individual traits: the capacity for love and vocation, courage, interpersonal skill, perseverance, forgiveness, originality, future mindedness, spirituality, high talent, and wisdom. At the group level, it is about civic virtues and the institutions that move individuals toward better citizenship: responsibility, nurturance, altruism, moderation, tolerance, and work ethic.[48]

Some say the topics addressed by positive psychologists resemble the topics humanistic psychologists discussed 40 years ago. A major difference between the two is that Seligman sees *research* as positive psychology's "protector and shield," guarding against the unscientific self-help techniques that grew out of humanistic psychology's great promise. Positive psychologists often encourage people to discover and build on their "signature strengths," which can be assessed by taking one of several online tests endorsed by Seligman and other positive psychologists (see, for example, the tests at www.authentichappiness.org).

Seligman has also researched how we explain the good and bad things that happen to us every day. Each of us has, to some degree, an optimistic or pessimistic *explanatory style.* If you have an optimistic style and something goes wrong, you are more likely to explain the problem as temporary, not your fault, and something that will not spread beyond present circumstances. In contrast, those with a pessimistic explanatory style tend to blame themselves, make the event a catastrophe, and see the problem as something beyond their control. Researchers have found a link between pessimistic style and an external locus of control. Pessimists also are more likely than optimists to receive bad grades, experience depression, and have a shorter life span because of poorer health.[49,50]

Fortunately, Seligman has found that pessimists can work to overcome this deficit in their outlook. One successful method is disputing pessimistic thoughts.[51] Arguing with ourselves about pessimistic beliefs can help us to perform better in stressful situations. For instance, if just before giving a speech you've rehearsed for days, you think, "I'm not ready for this!" Seligman would suggest you quickly take stock of your preparation method and push back by saying, "That's not true. I am ready because I've rehearsed, I have my notecards, and my PowerPoint slides are ready to go." That is to say, the negative thoughts are unfounded. Coming to terms with this can help us distance ourselves from pessimism's destructiveness. Checking for evidence that disproves pessimistic beliefs also helps us consider alternative explanations for bad events. That is, if you fail a test, look for reasons to disprove the thought "I'm stupid." Perhaps you'd earn a better grade if you were able to get more sleep, had studied better, or went in after school to ask the teacher for help. Finally, it's important not to generalize too much from a bad situation. After a bad test score, don't think, "I'm a stupid idiot, and I'll never do well." Instead, think, "I didn't do well on this particular test because I didn't study hard enough." Note the alternative explanation provided in the second answer, which gives the test-taker a more hopeful approach. (Study harder and do better next time.)

Optimist or Pessimist?
Some may go a bit too far, but being able to overlook your faults can help you cope better with everyday stress.

PEANUTS

There are advantages to adjusting your thinking from pessimistic to optimistic, but can you have too much optimism? *Yes.* One researcher notes that an unrealistic optimism is a common bias among optimistic thinkers.[52–54] Optimism in its worst form may lead to a false sense of invincibility. For instance, optimistic sexually active college women are less likely to think unprotected sex will lead to a sexually transmitted infection than their pessimistic sexually active counterparts.[55] The result? Optimistic sexually active college females contract more STIs than pessimists. And perhaps too much optimism is a factor for those who enter into and maintain ill-fated relationships, even though they are well aware of the U.S.' one-in-every-two divorce rate. Aristotle's observation—"Nothing in excess"—applies to optimism as well as to pessimism.

Assessing Behavior in Situations

Social-cognitive theorists believe that there are better ways to assess a person's personality than the trait theorists' multiple-choice personality inventory.[56] They prefer experiments that study how differing situations affect people's attitudes and behavior. Do you want to know whether children will be more aggressive with their peers after observing televised boxing? Or whether children will help one another more after watching a *Sesame Street* program on helpfulness? Social-cognitive psychologists say that the way to know such things is to run an experiment: Vary the situation and look for personality consistencies across similar situations.

In another kind of assessment, social-cognitive psychologists look at a person's past behavior patterns to predict the person's future behavior.[57,58] If the person and the situation remain the same, the best predictor of future behaviors is previous actions. The classmate most likely to drink beer at a party is the classmate who drank beer at the last party. The teacher most likely to turn back papers the day after picking them up is the teacher who handed them back the next day on the last set of papers. Schools that train teachers know that student teaching is a way of putting prospective teachers in real teaching situations to gather data for predicting how they will perform in the future. Similarly, if you live in a city of 50,000 or more people, your community probably has an assessment center for evaluating firefighters and police officers.[59] An assessment simulating actual conditions—of teaching, policing, or some other set of behaviors—is second only to assessing behavior under the demands of the real task.

MAKE IT STICK!

1. A person with an external locus of control who gets an F in math is likely to say,

   a. "I wish I liked math more."
   b. "Teachers just don't like me, so I never pass those kinds of classes."
   c. "If I had studied harder, I bet I would have passed."
   d. "Next time I take a class like that, I'll know how to do better on the tests."

2. True or false: Martin Seligman has shown that pessimists can learn to think more optimistically.

3. People who feel hopeless when they can't avoid repeated bad events tend to develop _____.

Evaluating the Social-Cognitive Perspective

 30-7 What are the strengths and weaknesses of the social-cognitive theory of personality?

The social-cognitive approach draws upon cognition and learning research for its conclusions.[60] Its objective, scientific approach to understanding personality makes it an attractive perspective. It has also sensitized researchers to the importance of considering the situation in the assessment of personality.

But wait a minute. Are we merely a product of what we learn? Are we stimulus–response creatures who act a certain way, based on the rewards and punishments we receive? Even if situations do guide our behavior, what role does emotion play? What effects do our unseen motives, such as revenge or greed, have on our behavior? Furthermore, are there consistent traits, such as shyness or openness, that become lost in social-cognitive explanations of behavior?

While the experts continue to seek answers to personality's questions, one fact appears indisputable: We can view personality from several perspectives, and each perspective fills in a piece of the puzzle that is personality. The trait and social-cognitive perspectives on personality have strengths and weaknesses, but each helps us understand human behavior. Like so many other parts of psychology—and human life—personality is best understood if we view it from multiple perspectives.

MAKE IT STICK!

1. Which of the following is LEAST likely to be addressed in a social-cognitive study on personality?

   a. the emotional state of the person
   b. the power of the situation
   c. what the person is thinking while in a situation
   d. how a person behaves

2. The main difference between the trait and social-cognitive theories of personality is that the latter

   a. is based on statistical analysis, rather than personal stories and self-reports.
   b. is a historical theory, and trait theory is a more current perspective.
   c. is negative about human nature, and trait theory is more optimistic.
   d. focuses on the interaction among personality traits, thinking, and the environment.

3. True or false: Personality is best understood if we view it from multiple perspectives.

Module 30 Summary and Assessment
Trait and Social-Cognitive Perspectives on Personality

 30-1 Are there different personality types? If so, how do trait theorists suggest that we describe and measure them?

- Trait theory psychologists think there are different types (or dimensions) of personality that can be described and measured.

- Trait theorists use descriptive techniques to classify personality, identifying characteristic and consistent patterns of behavior.

 30-2 How did psychologists Gordon Allport, Raymond Cattell, and Hans Eysenck identify traits?

- Allport resisted the idea of a "personality law" that would apply to everyone, believing that individual personalities are unique. However, he identified several kinds of traits, which paved the way for other trait theory researchers.

- Cattell used factor analysis to compute the relationships among traits until he came up with 16 core personality dimensions, or factors.

- Eysenck used factor analysis to determine dimensions of personality, including the extraversion–introversion dimension and the emotional stability–instability dimension.

 30-3 What are the dimensions of the Big Five trait theory?

- Current theorists describe at least five distinct dimensions of personality (the Big Five) and assess these dimensions using objective personality inventories. These five dimensions (conscientiousness, agreeableness, neuroticism, openness, and extraversion) appear to be stable in adults.

- Genetic predispositions influence personality traits.

- The Big Five traits also predict other personal attributes, such as marital satisfaction.

 30-4 How do trait theorists assess personality?

- Trait theorists assess personality through objective personality inventories.

- The Minnesota Multiphasic Personality Inventory (MMPI) uses 10 clinical scales to diagnose psychological disorders and 15 content scales to measure all kinds of attributes, including anger, attitude toward work, and whether a person could be trying to fake mental illness.

 30-5 What are the strengths and weaknesses of the trait theory of personality?

- Trait theory describes elements of personality in detail but does not address how important situations are to particular traits or try to explain why we behave the way we do.

 30-6 How do social-cognitive theorists explain the development of our personality and the relationship among personality, the environment, and behavior?

- Social-cognitive theorists describe how our personality and behaviors result from interactions among the ways we think, our environment, and our behaviors. To truly describe personality, we need to consider not just personality traits but also how our environment affects the ways we think and vice versa.

- Albert Bandura and other social-cognitive theorists believe we learn by observing and modeling the behaviors of others or by having certain behaviors reinforced or rewarded.

- Martin Seligman described learned helplessness, the feeling of hopelessness we experience when our actions have no effect on the bad events happening to us.

- Social-cognitive theorists use experiments to study how different situations affect people's attitudes and behavior.

 30-7 What are the strengths and weaknesses of the social-cognitive theory of personality?

- The social-cognitive approach sensitized researchers to the importance of the situation in the assessment of personality, but the approach does not consider how emotions may affect behavior and may underemphasize the effect of enduring personality traits.

Summative Assessment

1. Which of the following are two important conclusions identified by Gordon Allport?

    a. There are four personality types, and whichever one fits you is a humor that fills your body.
    b. Personality should be studied only in normal adults, and individual personalities are unique.
    c. Some traits predict others, and personality should be assessed using 16 core dimensions.
    d. Personality is the result of interactions between the unconscious and conscious minds and is a result of childhood experiences.

2. What was Raymond Cattell's breakthrough in personality research?

    a. Personality is the result of interactions between the unconscious and conscious minds and is a result of childhood experiences.
    b. There are more than 18,000 ways to describe a person's unique personality.
    c. There are 16 core personality dimensions, each on a continuum of "low" to "high."
    d. Personality traits are inherited and fall into one of four quadrants.

3. In what way were Eysenck, Cattell, and Allport breakthrough leaders in the area of personality research?

 a. They researched people suffering from psychological problems.

 b. They focused on early childhood experiences to diagnose problems.

 c. They categorized people into one of four personality categories.

 d. They were all leaders in personality assessment to identify individual traits.

4. Which trait dimension of the Big Five Personality Factors would be low for a person who remains calm during stressful events?

 a. openness
 b. conscientiousness
 c. extraversion
 d. neuroticism

5. What can best help a clinical psychologist diagnose anxiety in a patient?

 a. The patient takes an objective test.
 b. The patient takes a projective test.
 c. The patient tells stories from pictures.
 d. The patient writes about their feelings.

6. In order to understand personality, what do proponents of the social-cognitive perspective believe?

 a. Consideration needs to be taken for the situation the person is in.

 b. How people see themselves should be considered.

 c. What your friends and relatives describe as your strengths should be considered.

 d. How you tell a story based on a picture you are given should be considered.

7. What do psychologists call the mutual influences between personality and environmental factors?

 a. personality dimensions
 b. the cognitive-behavioral approach
 c. reciprocal determination
 d. biological dimensions

8. Which of the following does NOT influence reciprocal determination?

 a. your thoughts or cognitions
 b. your environment
 c. your behaviors
 d. your childhood

9. What do we call the movement that focuses on the study of optimal human functioning and the factors that allow individuals and communities to thrive?

 a. optimistic explanatory style
 b. internal locus of control
 c. positive psychology
 d. trait theory of personality

10. Which of the following is an example of optimistic explanatory style?

 a. I failed that test because I didn't study. I will do better next time.

 b. I failed that test because the teacher doesn't like me.

 c. I failed that test because I am not smart enough. I'll never get this.

 d. I failed that test because I'm bad at math just like my mom.

KEY TERMS AND KEY PEOPLE

traits, p. 457

personality, p. 457

social-cognitive perspective, p. 457

personality inventories, p. 462

validity, p. 462

reliability, p. 462

Minnesota Multiphasic Personality Inventory (MMPI), p. 462

reciprocal determinism, p. 466

external locus of control, p. 467

internal locus of control, p. 467

learned helplessness, p. 468

positive psychology, p. 469

Gordon Allport (1897–1967), p. 458

Raymond Cattell [kuh-TELL] (1905–1998), p. 459

Hans Eysenck [EYE-zink] (1916–1997), p. 460

Albert Bandura (1925–), p. 465

Martin Seligman (1942–), p. 468

Introduction to Psychological Disorders

Psychologists specializing in psychological disorders try to unlock the secrets behind harmful thoughts, feelings, and behaviors. Let's take a closer look at attempts to understand and classify disorders.

Observing people's strange-seeming behaviors, we may wonder what is going on inside their heads. Consider the following behaviors and then decide whether you think they are evidence of a psychological disorder:

1. A man walks up to a window, through which no one can see him, carrying a chair. He puts down the chair, opens the window, takes off his clothes, and seats himself on the chair. Why? He says he feels the need for an "air bath."

2. Every morning, a woman who lives in a New York City suburb asks her husband to bring in the morning newspaper, which the carrier throws just inside their fence. She does this because she is terribly afraid of encountering a venomous snake. Her husband, concerned about her behavior, repeatedly tells her that no venomous snakes have been seen in their area for over 30 years. Nevertheless, she is afraid to leave the house.

3. A teenage boy packs a blanket and some water. Ignoring near-freezing temperatures, he climbs a nearby mountain, spreads the blanket on the ground, sits cross-legged on it, closes his eyes, and remains there throughout the night. In the morning, he runs home and tells his father he has seen a vision.

4. A teenage girl misses school for 3 days. She periodically breaks into tears. She finds it nearly impossible to get out of bed in the morning, although she cannot sleep for more than an hour or two at a time. She has no appetite and becomes nauseated if people urge her to eat.

Marilyn Angel Wynn/Getty Images

Most people would say these behaviors are out of the ordinary—perhaps even puzzling or disturbing. But are they so abnormal that we can attribute them to a psychological disorder? Before attempting to answer that question, we must first decide what *psychological disorder* means. Let's see how psychologists define this term.

Defining Disorder

 31-1 How do psychologists define what kind of behavior is diagnosed as a psychological disorder?

psychological disorder
A harmful dysfunction in which thoughts, feelings, or behaviors are maladaptive, unjustifiable, disturbing, and atypical.

Psychologists define a **psychological disorder** as a harmful dysfunction in which thoughts, feelings, or behaviors are maladaptive, unjustifiable, disturbing, and atypical.[1,2] Consider each of these terms:

- *Maladaptive: destructive to oneself or others.* The behavior of the woman whose fear of snakes prevented her from leaving her home is maladaptive. In some cases, fear of venomous snakes is a wise and practical response: If bitten, you could die from their deadly venom. But the woman's extreme fear is destructive to her because it keeps her from leading a normal life. As you can see, maladaptive behaviors are sometimes—although not always—an exaggeration of normal, acceptable behavior. The behavior of the teenage girl may also be maladaptive. She is showing some classic symptoms of depression—an inability to sleep, eat, or function normally. And what about the teenage boy who sat on a blanket all night in near-freezing temperatures? This behavior seems self-destructive, too. Finally, what can we say about the man who sat naked to take an air bath? His behavior may seem strange, but he wasn't doing anything that could be considered destructive to himself or others (since no one else could see him naked), so we can't classify his behavior as maladaptive.

- *Unjustifiable: without a rational basis.* Here again, the behavior of the woman with the extreme fear of snakes qualifies as unjustifiable. It is not rational to refuse to leave your home to avoid a snakebite in an urban area that has no venomous snakes. But the teenage girl with symptoms of depression? What if I tell you that her entire family died three days ago, when her home was destroyed by fire? Suddenly, her inability to sleep, eat, or function seems understandable: These behaviors have a rational basis. And the young man who sat on the blanket all night? What if I tell you that he was a young member of the Santee Sioux nation, living in South Dakota in 1920, and a vision quest was part of his spirituality? In this case, too, the behavior seems quite rational, at least to other members of his culture and others with knowledge of it. But surely, you say, the man taking the air bath was performing an act with no rational base. Not so.

HANS DERYK/AP Images

Disordered?
This rabid sports fan may behave in an atypical way, but psychologists would not label him disordered because his behavior is not maladaptive, unjustifiable, or disturbing (except to the other team's players).

That man was Benjamin Franklin, signer of the Constitution and one of our country's greatest philosophers and thinkers. His "air bath" was an accepted practice in his day and, in that context, was justifiable. It is important to consider context when determining whether a behavior is rational or not.

- *Disturbing: troublesome to other people.* This criterion is fairly easy to score for all four individuals. The woman's fear of snakes disturbs at least her husband, who worries about her. The young girl's reaction to her loss probably disturbs people concerned about her. The young American Indian's vision quest probably pleased his parents and other relatives. Benjamin Franklin's air bath, which was unobserved by others, did not disturb anyone.

- *Atypical: so different that it violates a norm.* Notice that this definition has two parts, and they are equally important: The behavior is not like other people's behaviors (so different), and it violates a *norm*—a rule for accepted and expected behavior in a particular culture. In terms of defining psychological disorders, it doesn't matter if my behavior is unlike yours if we live in *different* cultures; it only matters whether people in *my* culture think my behavior is abnormal. So, look again at the four examples. The woman who can't leave her suburban home because of her fear of nonexistent snakes is definitely behaving differently from almost all people in her culture. The grief-stricken girl is behaving in a way that most people in her culture would consider within the typical range for someone who had recently suffered such a loss. The young man who had a vision is behaving in a way that Santee culture would consider acceptable and typical for males his age. And Benjamin Franklin was bathing in a way that we may consider strange three centuries later but that his eighteenth-century friends would have found unexceptional.

So, how many of these people meet the four criteria for having a psychological disorder? Only one: the woman with the extreme fear of snakes. As these examples illustrate, a behavior may be maladaptive or unjustifiable or disturbing or atypical. However, to be judged part of a psychological disorder, it has to meet all four of these criteria. (If you have trouble remembering these four points, try my memory trick: Form a "word"—*MUDA*—from the first letter of each point [maladaptive, unjustifiable, disturbing, and atypical].)

Now that we have some agreement on what we mean by *psychological disorder,* we can look at how psychologists attempt to understand and classify these disorders.

"I'm always like this, and my family was wondering if you could prescribe a mild depressant."

▲ **Too Happy?**
In reality, few would cite happiness as a psychological disorder in need of treatment.

MAKE IT STICK!

1. Cutting oneself when stressed would be likely categorized as _____ by a psychologist.

2. True or false: Atypical behavior is behavior that violates one or more norms.

3. Behavior that does not have a rational basis is called what?

Understanding Disorders

 31-2 Historically, what were considered the causes of psychological disorders, and what are the current perspectives?

Understanding Disorders
Philippe Pinel, here depicted unchaining inmates at a Paris asylum, and other reformers promoted the humane treatment of those with mental disorders.

Perspectives on psychological disorders have changed through the centuries. Written records of attempts to understand abnormal behavior go back at least 4000 years.[3] Ancient Babylonians viewed disorders as the result of demonic possession and attempted to treat them with prayer and magic. Ancient Hebrews saw psychological disorders as punishment for sin, and they, too, looked to religion for a cure. Socrates and other ancient Greek philosophers blamed faulty thought processes for psychological disorders and believed in the healing power of words. All three cultures used humane treatment methods.[4]

Unfortunately, not all approaches to treatment have been humane. Fifteenth-century Europeans suspected that people showing symptoms of psychological disorders were possessed by demons, and they often tortured or executed the sufferers to oust these bad spirits. By the eighteenth century, conditions had improved (at least the executions had stopped), but people with mental illnesses were often chained and locked up in filthy institutions or displayed like zoo animals. Humane treatment was rare—at least until French physician **Philippe Pinel** and other reformers worked to eliminate this institutionalized brutality. Pinel and others helped change Europe's view of psychological disorders. Dorothea Dix worked for similar goals in North America.

PHILIPPE PINEL (1745–1826)
French physician who worked to reform the treatment of people with mental disorders.

medical model The concept that mental diseases have physical causes that can be diagnosed, treated, and in most cases, cured.

The Medical Model

Pinel saw psychological disorders as sickness, not demonic possession. Pinel favored talking to patients, treating them gently, and providing clean living conditions. Still, the question lingered: If psychological disorders resulted from sickness, what caused the sickness?

This question was particularly pointed in the 1800s, because medical researchers had recently discovered the brain-damaging and mind-altering syphilis germ. If the dementia that accompanies syphilis had a physical cause, might it be that *all* mental disorders could be traced to diseases of the body? This question led to the **medical model** of mental illness—the concept that mental diseases have physical causes that can be diagnosed, treated, and in most cases, cured. The reforms started by Pinel and others like him, combined with the new medical model, replaced the ugliness of asylums and torture with the humaneness of hospitals and therapy.

The medical model is alive and well today. Contemporary research has uncovered physical causes, both genetic and biochemical, for symptoms of some of the more troubling psychological disorders, including *schizophrenia,* a group of severe disorders characterized by disturbed thinking, perceiving, feeling, and acting. This new level of understanding has led to new medical treatments, often involving drug therapy. But the medical model has not always led to the miracle cures some health workers hoped for. In its quest to find physiological explanations for mental diseases, the medical model focuses almost exclusively on nature and almost never on nurture. By failing to consider environment or culture, the medical model overlooks the influence of such factors as stress, upbringing, and personal history. Another approach, the bio-psycho-social model, offers a more inclusive view of the causes of psychological disorders.

The Bio-Psycho-Social Model

Psychologists who use the **bio-psycho-social model** (see **Figure 31.1**) study how biological, psychological, and social factors combine and interact to produce psychological disorders. The bio-psycho-social approach studies both nature *and* nurture, and it focuses on their interaction.

bio-psycho-social model
A contemporary perspective that assumes biological, psychological, and social factors combine and interact to produce psychological disorders.

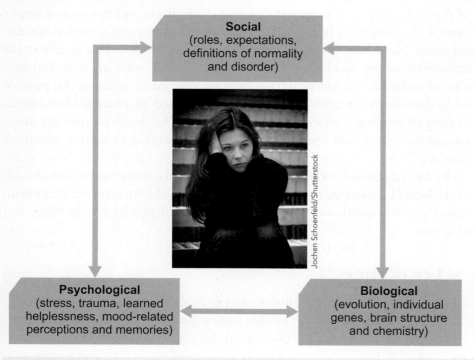

FIGURE 31.1
The Bio-Psycho-Social Model
Most psychologists today believe that biological, psychological, and social factors interact to produce mental disorders.

The bio-psycho-social model agrees with the medical model that there is a biological component to psychological disorders, but it views it as one leg of a three-legged stool. The biological component includes your genetic *predisposition,* or hereditary susceptibility to a disorder. Genetic predisposition may help explain why some young people endure breakups with a boyfriend or girlfriend without becoming too depressed, but others become so sad that they can't go to school. The second group of students may have a greater genetic predisposition to depression than the first group.

The psychological component of the bio-psycho-social model includes our thoughts or thinking patterns. In the breakup example, these two groups of students may differ in the way they explain the breakup to themselves. The first group, for example, may explain things in terms of the situation. ("I'll really miss being with her [or him], but we're going to be 200 miles apart this summer. It wouldn't have worked") Perhaps the second group explains bad events by defining them as examples of permanent faults. ("I'm stupid and ugly, and I always say the wrong thing. It's all my fault") If so, they are more likely to feel bad about the breakup. How you think about an event can shape your feelings and your actions.

Finally, there is the social component of the bio-psycho-social model. Perhaps the students in the two groups had different expectations about the relationships. If the first group of students saw the breakup as the end of a casual dating arrangement, it might not seem so serious. But if the second group of students saw the breakup as the end of a long-term and permanent bond, they might react more intensely.

Social and cultural beliefs can affect even the behaviors and beliefs characterizing psychological disorders. Most people your age have heard of *anorexia nervosa,* an eating disorder in which a person becomes significantly underweight but continues to diet or restrict their eating. This disease appears to be a largely Western phenomenon: In countries where food is scarce, no term for this disease exists. Now, have you ever heard of *susto? Probably not.* Few people in the United States have ever been diagnosed with, or even heard of, *susto.* But residents of certain Latin American countries are very much aware of this psychological disorder. They know that *susto* is characterized by a fear of black magic, resulting in extreme restlessness and severe anxiety. As these examples illustrate, cultures have their own unique sources of stress, leading to their own unique disorders.[5,6]

The bio-psycho-social model reminds us that to understand and classify psychological disorders, we need to account for the interaction of physiological, psychological, and sociocultural forces, all of which help shape our behaviors.

MAKE IT STICK!

1. True or false: Philippe Pinel worked to establish the bio-psycho-social model as the proper way to view mental illness, replacing theories about demonic possession and punishment for sin.

2. The psychological component of the _____ model of psychological disorders emphasizes the effect of how people think and interpret events on psychological disorders.

3. What is another word for hereditary susceptibility to a disorder?

Classifying Disorders

 31-3 How do psychologists categorize the different psychological disorders?

All sciences classify information to create a sense of order within the discipline. Chemists classify elements to keep track of atomic weight and the number of electrons orbiting the nucleus. Biologists classify living things into categories, telling us, for example, whether animals are hatched or born live, cold-blooded or warm-blooded. Clinical psychologists (psychologists trained to diagnose and treat emotional disturbance, behavior problems, and diseases of the brain) and psychiatrists (physicians who treat psychological

Wisdom and Knowledge

- Curiosity
- Love of learning
- Judgment and open-mindedness (critical thinking)
- Creativity
- Perspective (wisdom)

Courage (Overcoming Opposition)

- Bravery (valor)
- Industry and perseverance
- Integrity and honesty
- Zest (vitality and enthusiasm)

Humanity

- Love
- Kindness
- Social intelligence

Justice

- Citizenship and teamwork
- Fairness and equity
- Leadership

Temperance

- Modesty and humility
- Self-control
- Prudence and caution
- Forgiveness and mercy

Transcendence

- Appreciation of beauty and excellence
- Gratitude
- Hope (optimism)
- Playfulness and humor
- Spirituality and purpose

MAKE IT STICK!

1. True or false: A criticism of the DSM is that it is biased in favor of the medical model of psychological disorders. *true*
2. What is the focus of the "un-DSM"? *positive psychology*
3. True or false: Terminology in the DSM never changes, meaning once a disorder gets a certain name, it keeps that name. *false*

Labeling Disorders

 31-4 What are the potential dangers of diagnostic labels, and what are the benefits?

In the presidential election of 1972, Republican President Richard Nixon was running for reelection. Senator George McGovern of South Dakota won the top spot on the opposing Democratic Party's ticket, and he chose Thomas Eagleton as his running mate. The McGovern–Eagleton ticket was doing relatively well in national polls until rumors surfaced about Eagleton's mental health.

In a flurry of activity, the media reported that Eagleton had suffered "nervous exhaustion" in the previous decade and had twice received *electroconvulsive*

Anonymous/AP Images

Labeling Disorders ▲
Nominated by the Democratic Party to run for U.S. president in 1972, George McGovern chose Thomas Eagleton (left) as his vice-presidential nominee. Eagleton left the ticket amid rumors about his mental health.

shock therapy (ECT). The stigma attached to the disorder and to ECT was so grave that McGovern asked Eagleton to drop out of the race. McGovern's candidacy never rallied, and he lost every state except Massachusetts in that election.

Research suggests we view people differently after they have been labeled.[12] Studies have shown a clear bias against those labeled with a psychological disorder. Think about this: If you owned an apartment complex, would you rent a room to someone who had been in a mental institution? One study put this very question to 180 people in Toronto, Ontario, using phone numbers from ads listing furnished rooms for rent.[13] Check out these results:

- If the caller merely asked if the room was available, the answer was usually *Yes.*

- If the caller said she was about to be released from a mental hospital, three out of four people told her the room was not available.

- If the caller had someone else call back after she had been turned down, asking if the room was available, the answer was usually *Yes.*

- If the caller said she was calling to rent the room for her brother, who was about to get out of jail, three out of four people told her the room was not available.

WENN Ltd/Alamy

Coping Strategies ▲
Many performers develop strategies to cope with anxiety. Sia, who has been diagnosed with bipolar disorder, depression, and anxiety, often wears a wig covering her face.

The stigma against released prisoners and mental health patients appears to produce the same results.

The power of labeling is clear in other research as well. In one controversial study, eight *healthy* people from Stanford University went to a local mental hospital to check themselves in.[14] All eight gave false names and occupations, and they acted as they normally would—with one exception: Each complained to the interviewer of hearing voices that said *thud, hollow,* or *empty.* Hospital personnel diagnosed all eight as mentally ill and admitted them to the hospital. Once admitted to the hospital, the eight people exhibited no further symptoms.

We should not be surprised that these eight were admitted. After all, if you complained of a headache and sore throat, you'd probably be allowed to stay home from school, even if you really felt fine. What is surprising is that *after* these eight were admitted, clinicians "discovered" the causes of the psychological disorders after analyzing their quite normal life histories. For example, one of the eight was said to be reacting with mixed emotions about his parents. For the others, the clinicians perceived abnormal behavior in ordinary acts, such as taking notes, which were often mistakenly labeled as symptoms. Although the eight patients did not report hearing voices again or having similar symptoms, they had average hospital stays of 19 days, meaning it took nearly 3 weeks to be deemed eligible for release.

So, how much do labels influence our perceptions? *Apparently, quite a bit.* In another study, researchers asked participants to judge a videotaped interview and rate the person in the video.[15,16] All participants saw the same video, but

PSYCHOLOGY IN THE REAL WORLD

Psychological Disorder Rates

No known culture is free of depression or schizophrenia.[17–20] In 2016, 15.4 percent of people in the United States received mental health care.[21] This includes people who were admitted to mental hospitals and those who were troubled (but not disabled) who received outpatient care from clinics and other mental health organizations. Most of us will eventually have some experience with the mental health care system, either personally or indirectly by way of close friends or relatives.

Poverty seems to be connected with disorder rates. People below the poverty line are twice as likely as their wealthier counterparts to have a serious psychological disorder.[22] But this is a correlation, so we cannot assume anything about cause and effect. Does poverty cause the disorder? Does the disorder cause poverty? Or are both caused by something else? The answer varies from disorder to disorder. Schizophrenia, a series of disorders in which a person loses touch with reality, is likely to lead to job loss and poverty. But the stressful and demoralizing conditions of poverty may also contribute to disorders such as substance abuse in men and depression in women which are common among people in the U.S. today.[23] A recent report issued by the U.S. National Institute of Mental Health estimates that nearly 20 percent of Americans

TABLE 31.2 Percentage of Americans Reporting Selected Psychological Disorders in the Past Year	
Psychological Disorder	**Percentage**
Depressive disorders or bipolar disorder	9.3
Phobia of specific object or situation	8.7
Social anxiety disorder	6.8
Attention-deficit/ hyperactivity disorder (ADHD)	4.1
Posttraumatic stress disorder (PTSD)	3.5
Generalized anxiety disorder	3.1
Schizophrenia	1.1
Obsessive-compulsive disorder	1.0

Data from: National Institute of Mental Health, 2015.

currently experience some kind of emotional or mental disorder (see **Table 31.2**).

THINK ABOUT . . . Psychology in the Real World

1. What is something we know about culture and the existence of depression?
2. How might poverty contribute to depression?
3. Why is it difficult to assess poverty's role in the onset of depression?

they did not receive the same information *before* viewing and rating the person. Some participants were therapists who believed they were viewing patients. Others were observers who thought they were seeing job applicants. Those who thought they were evaluating a psychiatric patient saw the interviewee as a "passive-dependent type," "frightened of his own impulses," or something similar. Those who thought the person was interviewing for a job saw none of these qualities. The context given to the participants (psychiatric patient or job applicant) appeared to make the difference in what participants saw. Yes, labels can be helpful, but they also hold the potential to shape our thoughts and lead us astray.

Perhaps the media should shoulder some blame for the way we view those with psychological disorders. One 1980s report found that TV programs portrayed 70 percent of the people with psychological disorders as criminals or violent.[24] This percentage is way out of line with real life, in which 90 percent of the people with psychological disorders are *not* dangerous. Anxious, withdrawn, or depressed? *Yes,* that's common. Dangerous? *Unlikely.* If those released from mental hospitals don't use alcohol or other drugs, they are no more likely to become violent than their friends and neighbors.[25] Former U.S. surgeon general David Satcher reinforced this point clearly when he wrote that "there is very little risk of violence or harm to a stranger from casual contact with an individual who has a mental disorder."[26] (See Psychology in the Real World: Psychological Disorder Rates for information on the frequency of various disorders.)

So, are labels good or bad? Helpful or harmful? *It depends.* Labels describe abnormal behavior; they don't explain it. If I tell you my friend has bipolar disorder, you can read the list of symptoms in the DSM-5 and know how he behaves. But you won't have a clue about how or why he developed this disorder. And as we've seen, those who diagnose psychological disorders must be aware of the dangers and drawbacks of labeling, including their effect on our perceptions. The misdiagnosis of eight healthy people shows us just how easily misdiagnosis can occur.[27]

But we must also remember the benefits of labeling. As we noted earlier in this module, classifications are helpful in giving us thumbnail sketches that let us understand and communicate quickly. A lead author of the current classification system points out that psychiatric diagnosis helps mental health professionals communicate with one another about psychological disorders, understand some of the processes at work, and guide people toward better outcomes in their treatment.[28]

Have we made any progress since 1972, when the stigma of receiving treatment for a psychological disorder drove Thomas Eagleton out of a presidential campaign? The answer, it is to be hoped, is *Yes.* Seeking treatment for psychological disorders such as depression is now more likely to be seen as a strength than a weakness. Many celebrities, including Lady Gaga and Dwayne "The Rock" Johnson, have acknowledged the benefit of seeking and receiving treatment for depression.

Certainly, there are factors that increase the likelihood of mental illness, and the World Health Organization has identified many of these.[29,30] But just as there are circumstances that increase the chances of a mental disorder developing, so, too, are there protective factors that serve to buffer us against such illness (see **Table 31.3**). Exercise, resilience in coping with adversity, and social support from family and friends are just a few of these. And the good news is that many of these protective factors are within our control to increase or improve.

Getting Help ▲
Many celebrities have sought treatment to overcome depression, often described as the "common cold" of mental illness.

Many have endured the bewilderment of psychological disorder and also flourished in some ways, including Leonardo da Vinci, Isaac Newton, and the Nobel Prize–winning economist John Nash (the subject of the Oscar-winning movie *A Beautiful Mind*). Nash was fortunate in that he was able to overcome his symptoms, even though they didn't go away entirely, and behave in ways that were not maladaptive, unjustifiable, disturbing, and atypical. For others, hope rests with increased understanding of disorders and improved psychological treatments.

TABLE 31.3 Risk and Protective Factors for Mental Disorders

Research has identified factors, summarized in this table, that are associated with more or less risk of developing mental disorders. These factors are correlated with the development of mental disorders—we don't know if the relationships are cause-and-effect.

Risk Factors	Protective Factors
Academic failure	Aerobic exercise
Birth complications	Community offering empowerment, opportunity, and security
Caring for chronically ill patients or patients with dementia	Economic independence
Child abuse and neglect	Feelings of security
Chronic insomnia	Feelings of mastery and control
Chronic pain	Effective parenting
Family disorganization or conflict	Literacy
Low birth weight	Positive attachment and early bonding
Low socioeconomic status	Positive parent-child relationships
Medical illness	
Neurochemical imbalance	Problem-solving skills
Parental mental illness	Resilient coping with stress and adversity
Parental substance abuse	
Personal loss and bereavement	Self-esteem
Poor work skills and habits	Social and work skills
Reading disabilities	Social support from family and friends
Sensory disabilities	
Social incompetence	
Stressful life events	
Substance abuse	
Trauma experiences	

Source: World Health Organization (2004a, 2004b).

MAKE IT STICK!

1. True or false: Diagnostic labels tell us how an individual developed a psychological disorder.

2. True or false: When diagnosing a patient, the context provided to the therapist will never make a difference in the diagnosis.

3. True or false: Research shows that landlords are about as likely to rent an apartment to a person with mental illness as they are to released convicts.

Module 31 Summary and Assessment
Introduction to Psychological Disorders

 31-1 How do psychologists define what kind of behavior is diagnosed as a psychological disorder?

- A psychological disorder is a harmful dysfunction in which thoughts, feelings, or behaviors are maladaptive, unjustifiable, disturbing, and atypical.

- Maladaptive behaviors are destructive to oneself or others. Unjustifiable behaviors are actions without rational basis. Disturbing behaviors are troublesome to other people. And atypical behaviors are so different that they violate social norms.

 31-2 Historically, what were considered the causes of psychological disorders, and what are the current perspectives?

- Perspectives on psychological disorders have changed through the centuries. In the past, many "treatments" for psychological disorders were inhumane.

- French physician Philippe Pinel and other reformers worked to improve the treatment of people with psychological disorders. Pinel's work led to the medical model of mental illness. Use of the medical model has led to successful treatments for many psychological disorders, often involving drug therapy. However, the medical model does not emphasize environmental explanations, overlooking the influence of such factors as stress, upbringing, and personal history.

- The bio-psycho-social approach to psychological disorders studies both nature and nurture and focuses on their interaction. The biological component of the model includes genetic predisposition, or hereditary susceptibility to a disorder. The psychological component of the model includes thoughts or thinking patterns. The social component acknowledges that social and cultural beliefs can affect even the behaviors and beliefs characterizing psychological disorders.

 31-3 How do psychologists categorize the different psychological disorders?

- Clinical psychologists and psychiatrists classify psychological disorders according to their symptoms. This allows them to describe the disorder, predict its future course, treat the disorder appropriately, and provide a springboard for research.

- The American Psychiatric Association developed the *Diagnostic and Statistical Manual of Mental Disorders* (DSM), a classification system for psychological disorders.

 31-4 What are the potential dangers of diagnostic labels, and what are the benefits?

- Research indicates that people who suffer from mental disorders are stigmatized and discriminated against. Studies show that labels tend to alter how we perceive others and labels tend to stick with people even when behaviors are no longer disordered.

- Diagnostic labels from the DSM have disadvantages, but they also help psychologists communicate about psychological disorders, help psychologists understand some processes at work, and can enable better treatment outcomes.

Summative Assessment

1. A psychological disorder is a harmful dysfunction in which thoughts, feelings, or behaviors are maladaptive, disturbing, atypical and

   a. unusual.
   b. unhappy.
   c. unified.
   d. unjustifiable.

2. What do we call behaviors that are destructive to oneself or others?

   a. predestined
   b. maladaptive
   c. disturbing
   d. predispositioned

3. Which of the following would be most likely categorized as disturbing by a psychologist?

  a. speaking in nonsense words in public in a loud voice
  b. feeling compelled to hurt another when tired
  c. refusing to read newspapers or watch the news on television
  d. believing that aliens are responsible for starting life on Earth

4. Which of the following would most likely be explained as a product of the medical model?

  a. using drugs to treat a disorder
  b. discussing stressors with a therapist
  c. reviewing environmental causes of a disorder
  d. examining how a person was raised

5. Which of the following is most likely a goal of the DSM's authors?

  a. Identify labels for psychological disorders in various cultures at various historical periods.
  b. List human strengths and weaknesses to guide therapists' advice for patients trying to improve their lives.
  c. Gather all statistics involving psychological disorders to advise government health agencies on policy matters.
  d. Categorize psychological disorders and describe them specifically enough to guide future research.

6. The study from Stanford University of healthy individuals who admitted themselves to a mental hospital showed that psychological labels

  a. do not help increase the reliability of diagnoses.
  b. cause excessive stress, which can lead to heart disease.

  c. influence how psychologists interpret normal behaviors of patients.
  d. benefit patients because they enable them to be admitted to effective treatment programs.

7. Clinical psychologists classify psychological disorders according to their symptoms. This allows them to describe the disorder, predict its future course, treat the disorder appropriately, and

  a. provide a springboard for research.
  b. charge more money for their services.
  c. certify their credentials.
  d. avoid labeling.

8. Which approach to psychological disorders studies both nature and nurture and focuses on their interaction?

  a. medical
  b. social-predispositional
  c. a. bio-psycho-social
  d. DSM

9. Research indicates that most people who suffer from mental disorders are

  a. stigmatized and discriminated against.
  b. routinely given the best housing.
  c. easily able to shed the disorder label.
  d. faking their illness in order to get sympathy.

10. What do some psychologists call the "un-DSM"?

  a. bravery, courage, and zest
  b. the bio-psycho-social model
  c. the categories and descriptions of disorders
  d. a listing and explanation of character strengths

KEY TERMS AND KEY PEOPLE

psychological disorder, p. 476
medical model, p. 478

bio-psycho-social model, p. 479
DSM-5, p. 481

Philippe Pinel (1745–1826), p. 478

Module 32

Anxiety Disorders, Obsessive-Compulsive Disorder, Post-Traumatic Stress Disorder, Depression, and Bipolar Disorder

Learning Goals

32-1 Describe the anxiety disorders and their causes.

32-2 Describe obsessive-compulsive disorder and its causes.

32-3 Describe post-traumatic stress disorder and its causes.

32-4 Describe major depressive disorder and its causes.

32-5 Describe bipolar disorder.

Are you scared of snakes? Spiders? Maybe for you it's heights or crowds. Almost all of us feel anxious under some circumstances, and we also experience a variety of moods in our daily lives. When these normal reactions make it difficult to function, we have anxiety or mood disorders. They are among the most common psychological disorders of all.

This module covers some of the most common categories of psychological disorders. There is little doubt that you know individuals who struggle mightily with problems related to anxiety and mood. If you are "normal," you have probably struggled occasionally with such problems yourself.

An odd and sometimes troubling aspect of psychological disorders is that it's easy to see the symptoms—almost all the symptoms—in yourself. The symptoms of psychological disorders usually fall along a continuum. They can be mild, serious, or anything between. Typically, there is a "gray area" where it's difficult to decide whether there is a significant problem. This is different from many medical conditions that are more likely to be either present or absent, with nothing between. It doesn't make sense to talk about a woman being kind of pregnant, but it is surely possible to be sort of anxious.

So, I'm going to give you the warning I was given years ago: Don't overreact if you begin to discover in yourself the symptoms we discuss in this module. That's typical, and there's even a name for it—"psychology student's disease." The point to remember is that we all have some of these symptoms some of the time.

They don't suggest a psychological disorder unless they meet four important criteria: symptoms must be *maladaptive* (disrupting normal functioning), *unjustifiable, disturbing,* and *atypical.* For most people most of the time, these symptoms do not meet these criteria. However, if you become concerned that you might be one of the many people affected by the psychological disorders we discuss in this module, you owe it to yourself to have it checked out. Talk to your parents, your physician, or your guidance counselor for a referral to a mental health professional who can either lay your concerns to rest or help you resolve a problem if it does exist.

Now let's take a look at the some specific disorders. These psychological disorders, like all others, are diagnosed according to the criteria established in the American Psychiatric Association's *Diagnostic and Statistical Manual of Mental Disorders,* fifth edition[1] (DSM-5). This guide identifies the symptoms that must be present for a diagnosis to be made.

Anxiety Disorders

 32-1 What are the anxiety disorders, and what causes them?

When psychologists speak of **anxiety,** they are referring to a vague feeling of apprehension and nervousness. You've probably experienced anxiety in relation to specific events—big tests, school projects, or important medical tests, for example. You may also have experienced a more general anxiety, such as feeling ill at ease about the changes that college or a new job might bring or concern about how troubling world events will play out. These are normal types of feelings. Anxiety disorders differ from these feelings in that anxiety—or efforts to control it—begins to take control and dominate life. When this happens, quality of life suffers,[2] and unhappiness increases.[3] We will discuss three specific anxiety disorders and then turn our attention to possible causes:

> ▲ **Anxiety**
> We all experience anxiety in our lives, often as a response to stressful events. Anxiety is not a disorder unless it begins to create significant difficulties in a person's life.

- **Generalized anxiety disorder,** marked by disruptive levels of persistent, unexplained feelings of apprehension and tenseness

- **Panic disorder,** marked by sudden bouts of intense, unexplained panic

- **Phobia,** marked by disruptive, irrational fears of objects, activities, or situations

Generalized Anxiety Disorder and Panic Disorder

Until pharmaceutical companies began advertising drugs to combat *generalized anxiety disorder,* many people had never heard of this condition. It doesn't have the dramatic symptoms of many other psychological disorders and until recently had escaped public attention. The drug company advertisements probably leave many people uneasy because most of us have physical and psychological symptoms on occasion that characterize this disorder. However, the symptoms are more lasting

anxiety A vague feeling of apprehension or nervousness.

generalized anxiety disorder An anxiety disorder characterized by disruptive levels of persistent, unexplained feelings of apprehension and tenseness.

panic disorder An anxiety disorder characterized by sudden bouts of intense, unexplained anxiety, often associated with physical symptoms like choking sensations or shortness of breath.

phobia An anxiety disorder characterized by disruptive, irrational fears of objects, activities, or situations.

Willie B. Thomas/istockphoto

for those who suffer generalized anxiety disorder and are often not attached to any specific event. **Table 32.1** lists these symptoms. Individuals with generalized anxiety disorder must experience at least three of them.

TABLE 32.1 Symptoms of Generalized Anxiety Disorder
Restlessness
Feeling on edge
Difficulty concentrating or mind going blank
Irritability
Muscle tension
Sleep disturbance

Source: Adapted from American Psychiatric Association (2000).

Sometimes the anxiety is accompanied by *panic attacks*—episodes of unexplained terror and fear that something bad is going to happen. The panic attacks, which may last several minutes, usually involve such physical symptoms as choking sensations or shortness of breath. Have you ever experienced panic? I can recall an episode when I was about 12 years old. My parents were out and I had watched a frightening show on television. Although I had no reason to do so, I became temporarily convinced that something horrible had happened to my parents. They were fine, of course, but the panic I experienced was so intense that I still remember it clearly almost 50 years later.

We may all feel panic at some point in our lives, but imagine having these attacks several times each day or having them without being able to explain why. You're sitting in class, trying to take notes, and the waves of fear start to wash over you for no apparent reason. Your ability to concentrate is destroyed; all your energy is directed toward trying to regain control. Such is the life of a person with *panic disorder*.

Phobias

Almost everyone has heard the word *phobia,* which many people use to mean fear. ("I have a phobia about taking tests.") To psychologists, however, a phobia is more than just a normal fear—it is a fear that is both irrational and disruptive. If you were being stalked on a dark street late at night, your fear of the stalker would not be irrational. Note that irrational fear alone is not enough to define what is technically known as *specific phobia*—the fear must also be disruptive. Most of us have irrational, nondisruptive fears—of harmless snakes or closed-in spaces, for example. My own particular irrational fear is the step from a ladder to a roof. Despite knowing that I can make the step safely, I hate it. I hate it to the extent that I have never been on the roof of the house in which I have lived for more than 30 years. If I were a roofer or a fireman, this fear would be disruptive. But I'm a teacher, and I seldom need to climb onto my roof. On those rare occasions when this becomes necessary, I simply have one of my sons do it or call someone else to do the job. My fear is intense and irrational, but it's not disruptive.

Why are phobias considered anxiety disorders? Because they focus general feelings of anxiety onto a feared object, activity, or situation (see **Figure 32.1**).

I'm scared of heights.

Relax... That's a depth.

www.CartoonStock.com

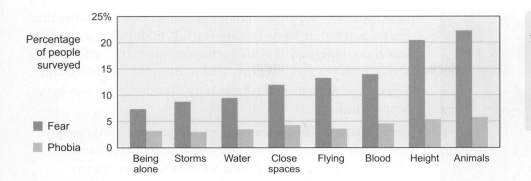

Most phobias involve fear of a particular object, and their names are formed by combining the Greek word for the object with *phobia,* which is the Greek word for "fear." Fear of spiders, for example, is called arachnophobia. Broader phobias also occur.

*Social anxiety disorder (*also known as *social phobia)* produces fear in social situations. For example, some people have extreme difficulty speaking in public, even to the extent of being unable to respond to questions from a clerk in a store. Others cannot eat in the presence of others or use public restrooms. As you might imagine, social phobias can seriously impair a person's ability to lead a normal life.

Agoraphobia is fear of situations the person views as difficult to escape from if anxiety or panic begin to build. Many people with this disorder become trapped in their own homes or in similar safe zones. I once had dinner with a woman from my town who was recovering from agoraphobia. She was a middle-aged widow who lived by herself and could not leave her home without experiencing intense fear. She described to me the difficulty of ordinary tasks like grocery shopping, which was to her similar to a military commando raid. Only with intense planning and determination could she leave her car, quickly collect the two or three items she needed most, and make it through checkout before dashing back to her car. Often she began to feel panicky during her few minutes in the store, and sometimes she had to abandon her grocery shopping, only to face another trial the next day. Over the course of the last 15 years, which had included some therapy, she had largely conquered her agoraphobia. She was happy to say she had even been able to take a European vacation a few years ago.

Arachnophobia
Movie characters often portray irrational fears. Here, Ron Weasley appears to be afraid of spiders.

Causes of Anxiety Disorders

Anxiety disorders could be caused by nature (the effect of our inherited biology) or nurture (the influence of our environment). As is almost always the case, both factors are important.

Biological Factors Anxiety disorders, like so many other areas that psychologists study, illustrate the interaction between our biology and our environment. The following are some biological factors that contribute to anxiety disorders:

- *Heredity*—Some of us inherit a *predisposition,* or likelihood, for developing anxiety disorders. Evidence for this comes from studies of identical twins, who are genetically the same. Even when raised in different families, identical twins sometimes have similar phobias.[4,5] The influence of

Eugenio Marongiu/Cultura/Getty Images

Heredity and Fear ▲
We don't appear to inherit specific fears, but we do inherit a predisposition to develop fears. This is why identical twins are more likely than other siblings to share the same fears, even if they are not raised together.

Nature or Nurture?
The baby may be biologically predisposed to fear heights, but she may also learn this fear by watching her mother. ▼

Owen Franken/Getty Images

heredity is also apparent in monkey studies demonstrating that fearful parents are likely to have fearful children.[6] The specific fear is not inherited, but the predisposition to be fearful is. The search is on for the genes that lead to this predisposition, and 17 genes with connections to anxiety disorder symptoms have been identified.[7]

- *Brain function*—Brain-scanning techniques show that people with anxiety disorders have brains that literally function differently than those of people who do not have anxiety disorders. An emotion center, the *amygdala,* shows differences for people with phobias.[8–10] It's possible that their intense fear is caused by the activity in the amygdala. Because brain function is involved, anxiety disorders often respond to treatment with medication.

- *Evolution*—We are likely to fear situations that posed danger to the earliest humans. Dangerous animals, heights, and storms were threats, and people who didn't have a healthy dose of fear were less likely to survive. Those who did survive passed on to us—their descendants—their tendency to fear these dangers. Many of us share these fears to this day, even though our modern world has made these threats less dangerous than they once were. For example, preschool children can find a snake in a picture more quickly than they can find a flower or a frog.[11] We are primed to find snakes more quickly because they are more likely to cause us harm. Unfortunately, we don't have a similar inherited tendency to fear threats that have developed more recently. Cars, for example, kill far more people in the modern world than snakebites do, yet more people fear snakes than fear cars.

Learning Factors Learning gone awry can also produce anxiety disorders. Sometimes we learn to respond well in stressful situations, but if we learn maladaptive responses (responses that cause problems rather than solving them), they can blossom into anxiety disorders. These factors can contribute:

- *Classical conditioning*—Ivan Pavlov became famous for his studies in which dogs learned to associate the sound of a tuning fork with the taste of meat, salivating equally to both. Humans can also learn to associate fear with certain places or things. John B. Watson and Rosalie Rayner demonstrated this in their famous research with "Little Albert," an infant who learned to fear white rats.[12] Watson and Rayner established the fear by pairing the sight of a rat with loud, frightening noises. Few of us would deliberately teach a child fear, but the child might learn to associate fear and dogs if exposed to a menacing growl or bite when young. Unpredictable and uncontrollable bad events can contribute to the conditioning of anxiety.[13,14]

- *Observational learning*—Children can also learn fears at their parents' knees. If a child sees a parent or older sibling responding with fear to thunderstorms, bees, or high places, the child may begin to experience the same fear. Even young monkeys learned to fear snakes when given the opportunity to watch other monkeys avoid situations in which a snake was present.[15]

- *Operant conditioning*—We also learn to associate emotions with actions, depending on the results that follow those actions. A person with a fear of heights can reduce the fear by avoiding heights. That release from anxiety is a form of reinforcement that makes it more likely that the person will avoid heights in the future. We tend to repeat responses that have good results and avoid those that have bad results.

Preventing Anxiety Disorders

Stress is a constant in life—everybody experiences difficult events—but the response to stress is not the same for everyone. Why is it that some people struggle in the face of adversity, while others seem to survive or even thrive? Far more people experience trauma than develop post-traumatic stress disorder.[16] Most combat veterans and even most victims of political torture do not develop PTSD. What determines who does and who doesn't?

Those who make it through the aftermath of trauma largely unscathed possess a quality known as *survivor resiliency*.[17,18] Some go beyond resiliency and experience *post-traumatic growth*. Their suffering has led to inner strength, increased appreciation, and better relationships. A primary goal of positive psychology is to increase the percentage of people who can weather the storms of trauma more effectively. The key seems to be to prepare people in advance with cognitive and behavioral strategies that allow them to cope with stress more effectively.

Is this possible? It is increasingly looking like the answer is *Yes*. Work done by Martin Seligman and his colleagues to develop positive education in school systems has resulted in programs that teach teachers how to develop resiliency skills in students.[19] These programs have shown lasting reductions in anxiety and depression among the students who are taught the new skills.

Perhaps the most ambitious initiative of all began in 2009 with the start of the U.S. Army's Comprehensive Soldier and Family Fitness (CSF2) program.[20] Under this program, Seligman's team at the University of Pennsylvania is preparing thousands of army master resiliency trainers. These master trainers teach appropriate resiliency skills to army leaders in every battalion and brigade. All new recruits learn resiliency skills as a part of their basic training. The family members of soldiers and civilian workers in the military are trained as well. All these individuals are, or are close to, people at high risk for PTSD, especially when soldiers are deployed in combat. The goal is to increase resiliency to prevent psychological disorders and help everyone live healthier, happier lives. And the lessons learned are now being applied to new groups, including first responders and athletes.[21]

No one has an anxiety-free life, but when the anxiety begins to take control (as in the case of a generalized anxiety disorder), to refocus as fear (as in the case of a phobia), anxiety has crossed the line and has become a psychological disorder.

MAKE IT STICK!

1. All of a sudden, Roberto started sweating, his heart started racing, and he felt like he couldn't breathe. Which of the following fits Roberto's symptoms best?

   a. panic disorder
   b. social anxiety disorder
   c. agoraphobia
   d. specific phobia

2. Baghya fears flying and feels relieved whenever she can avoid traveling by air. This is an example of how phobias can be influenced by

   a. observational learning.
   b. reinforcement.
   c. heredity.
   d. evolution.

3. True or false: Children can learn phobias through observation, but there is little evidence that reinforcement contributes to phobias.

Obsessive-Compulsive Disorder (OCD)

 32-2 What is obsessive-compulsive disorder, and what causes it?

obsessive-compulsive disorder (OCD) An anxiety disorder characterized by unwanted, repetitive thoughts and/or actions.

The two major symptoms of **obsessive-compulsive disorder** are, as you might imagine, obsessions and compulsions. *Obsessions* are repetitive thoughts, and *compulsions* are repetitive actions, and either one alone is enough to merit a diagnosis. Almost everyone experiences both obsession-like thoughts and compulsion-like behaviors on a harmless level. In my classroom, I notice a lot of faraway stares as homecoming and prom weekends approach. I know many of these students can't stop thinking about the upcoming event (at least that was the case for me when I was a student!). Other times we may hear a song and then be unable to get it out of our head.

We all have compulsion-like behaviors, too. One day I watched a student walk down the hall tapping the eraser of his pencil on every locker. Somehow, he missed the last locker in the row and managed to make it about 10 yards down the hall before having to return to tap that last locker. You could almost feel his discomfort until the task was completed. You may have done something similar as a child. Remember that old rhyme about "step on a crack and break your mother's back"? Were you able to step on sidewalk cracks easily after learning that rhyme, or did you compulsively avoid them?

Obsessive-compulsive tendencies can be helpful sometimes. Most good athletes are obsessed with winning and compulsive about training. And most good students are a bit obsessed with grades and a bit compulsive about studying. These tendencies help us develop important routines, such as fastening our safety belts when we get into a car or brushing our teeth regularly.

Obsessions and compulsions—even the normally helpful tendencies discussed above—can begin to take control with some people, and this is when helpful tendencies become OCD. One common obsession focuses on germs and develops with a compulsion in the form of repetitive hand washing. Individuals may wash their hands hundreds of times each day. Often, they engage in a hand-washing ritual that may take many minutes to complete, much like a surgeon scrubbing up before an operation. As long as such people have the opportunity to engage in their rituals, their anxiety remains under control. If they are somehow prevented from engaging in their ritual behavior, then anxiety and panic rapidly build. The thoughts and behaviors consume vast quantities of the sufferer's time, making it impossible to live a normal life.

Other common patterns of OCD involve dressing rituals, where a person may take hours to shower and dress each morning because he has hundreds of required steps that must be followed. Another common pattern is checking and rechecking a lock or an electrical switch. The person might return to the car 10 times in a row to make sure the lights are off and the door is locked. **Table 32.2** lists some common obsessions and compulsions of children and adolescents with this disorder.

Don't Touch Me
The title of Howie Mandel's 2009 memoir clearly illustrates the comedian and TV host's germ phobia.

Jeffrey Mayer/WireImage/Getty Images

TABLE 32.2 Common Obsessions and Compulsions Among Children and Adolescents With Obsessive-Compulsive Disorder	
Thought or Behavior	**Percentage Reporting Symptom**
• **Obsessions (repetitive thoughts)**	
Concern with dirt, germs, or toxins	40
Something terrible happening (fire, death, illness)	24
Symmetry, order, or exactness	17
• **Compulsions (repetitive behaviors)**	
Excessive hand washing, bathing, tooth brushing, or grooming	85
Repeating rituals (in/out of a door, up/down from a chair)	51
Checking doors, locks, appliances, car brakes, homework	46

Source: Adapted from Rapoport (1989).

Causes of Obsessive-Compulsive Disorder

You'll notice a pattern here. The cause of most psychological disorders is a mixture of nature and nurture; of biological and environmental factors. It was true for anxiety disorders and it's true for OCD as well.

On the nature side, heredity and evolutionary factors play a role. In terms of brain function, there is a difference in how active certain brain regions are. As **Figure 32.2** illustrates, brain scans show a higher degree of activity in a part of the frontal lobes of people with OCD.[22] Because the frontal lobes are involved with decision making, the bright red and yellow shown in that area of the brain of the person with OCD may indicate a source of the problem.

Learning can nurture obsessive-compulsive tendencies, too. For example, a person with an obsessive-compulsive hand-washing ritual can reduce anxiety by washing. Realizing this reduction in anxiety makes it more likely the action will be repeated.

FIGURE 32.2
The Brain and Obsessive-Compulsive Disorder
Brain scans have been used to show that people with obsessive-compulsive disorder (OCD) have more activity in decision-making areas at the front of the brain than do people without OCD. The brain scans of those with OCD indicated increased activity in a part of the brain known as the anterior cingulate cortex.

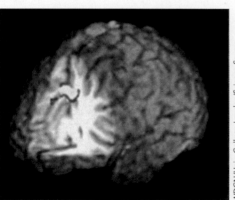

WDCN/Univ. College London/Science Source

MAKE IT STICK!

1. True or false: Obsessive-compulsive disorder produces increased activity in the rear of the brain.

2. A person with a(n) _____ might wash his or her hands 100 times each day.

3. True or false: It is possible for both obsessive and compulsive tendencies to be useful at some level.

Post-Traumatic Stress Disorder (PTSD)

 32-3 What is post-traumatic stress disorder, and what causes it?

post-traumatic stress disorder (PTSD) An anxiety disorder characterized by reliving a severely upsetting event in unwanted, recurring memories and dreams.

What do military combat veterans, victims of sexual assault, hurricane survivors, abused children, and rescue workers who have to clean up gruesome accident sites have in common? They, along with others who are exposed to stressful situations, are all at increased risk for **post-traumatic stress disorder.** Intense stress is the trigger, and symptoms include nightmares, persistent fear, difficulty relating normally to others, hypervigilance, self-destructive behavior, and troubling memories of or flashbacks to the traumatic event.[23]

The September 11, 2001, attacks on the World Trade Center and the Pentagon were events with the potential to produce many cases of PTSD, with one study showing that 20 percent of the people living near the World Trade Center experienced symptoms like nightmares.[24] Those who were indoors at the time of the attack were twice as likely to experience symptoms compared to those who were outside.[25]

Children may be particularly vulnerable because witnessing or experiencing trauma may instill a sense of hopelessness about the future and may impair their ability to trust. The negative consequences of bad experiences can produce increased anxiety and other symptoms for many years. PTSD can have a particularly devastating impact on combat veterans. One in four U.S. veterans from the conflicts in Iraq and Afghanistan were diagnosed with a psychological disorder in one study, and the most frequent of these was PTSD.[26]

Christophe Calais/Corbis via Getty Images

Combat and Stress ▲
One goal of positive psychology is to prevent psychological problems related to the stress of combat. Helping soldiers and their families become more resilient may result in fewer problems to treat when the soldiers return from war.

Not everyone who experiences extreme stress develops PTSD. For example, 7.6 percent of Afghanistan combat veterans were diagnosed with the disorder.[27] This is certainly tragic, but this also means that over 90 percent of the combat veterans were not diagnosed. How can two soldiers experience stressful situations and only one suffer from post-traumatic stress? One factor is the intensity of the stress. Individuals who are in more stressful situations are more likely to be diagnosed.[28] There are also biological factors involved. We know that genes play a role because twins are more likely to be alike in cognitive factors associated with PTSD than are brothers and sisters who are not twins.[29] Women are twice as likely as men to develop PTSD.[30] Finally, the limbic system, heavily involved in emotion, can be more active in individuals with PTSD.[31] (For encouraging news on reducing the incidence of PTSD in soldiers and others, see Preventing Anxiety Disorders.)

LIFE MATTERS
Boston University found that the SKA2 gene in the prefrontal cortex is linked with PTSD. Further research could help screen soldiers for potential risks. If you discovered that you had an increased likelihood of suffering from PTSD, how would that impact your decision to enlist in the military?

MAKE IT STICK!

1. True or false: Women are almost twice as likely as men to develop PTSD.

2. An emotional center in the brain called the _____ system is likely to be more active in people with PTSD.

Major Depressive Disorder

 32-4 What is major depressive disorder, and what causes it?

Major depressive disorder is the official DSM-5 classification for serious depression. Like other psychological disorders you've read about in this module, major depressive disorder is a serious magnification of our normal reactions.

It is a rare individual who never feels depressed. Can any of us say that we never feel down, sad, or drained of energy? Depression is a normal response to the loss of many of the important things in life, including the death of loved ones, the end of important relationships, the loss of a job, or even graduation from the comfortable familiarity of high school.[32] We can even become depressed over distant events, such as famines or outbreaks of violence in far corners of the world. From an evolutionary perspective, depression probably exists to give us time to slow down and reflect on why a bad thing has occurred. This allows us to perhaps avoid similar losses in the future.[33]

Major depressive disorder, the technical name for serious depression, is one of the most common disabilities in the world, affecting almost 5 percent of the population.[34,35] Females are diagnosed with major depressive disorder 2 to 3 times more often than males.[36] Almost a third of American high school students have experienced symptoms strong enough to stop doing usual activities for 2 weeks.[37] Among college students, 44 percent in one survey said that they had been depressed enough that it was difficult to function at least once in the past year.[38] DSM-5 says that depression has crossed the line from a normal reaction to major depressive disorder when five of the following nine symptoms have been present for two or more weeks. (Note that one of the first two symptoms must be included in those five.)[39]

> **major depressive disorder**
> A mood disorder in which a person, for no apparent reason, experiences at least 2 weeks of depressed moods, diminished interest in activities, and other symptoms, such as feelings of worthlessness.

- Depressed mood most of the day, nearly every day (in children and adolescents, an irritated mood satisfies this requirement)

- Little interest or pleasure in almost all activities

- Significant changes in weight or appetite

- Sleeping more or less than usual

- Agitated or decreased level of activity

- Fatigue or loss of energy

- Feelings of worthlessness or inappropriate guilt

- Diminished ability to think or concentrate

- Recurrent thoughts of death or suicide

These symptoms must also produce distress or impaired functioning to qualify as indicators of major depressive disorder. There may be no apparent trigger for major depressive disorder. Persistent depressive disorder may be diagnosed if the symptoms are milder and last longer (at least a year for children or adolescents and at least 2 years for adults).

Major depressive disorder feels like an inescapable weight affecting every aspect of life, and it can even lead to suicide (see Psychology in the Real World: Suicide on pages 503–505).

SMG/ZUMA Press/Newscom

▲ **Depression**
Anguished depression can be a normal response to tragic events, such as the Douglas High School shooting in Parkland, Florida. Specific criteria must be met before a diagnosis of major depressive disorder is made.

Causes of Major Depressive Disorder

No single explanation sheds light on all depression. Again, biology and environment interact. Stress also seems to play a role, providing a trigger that sparks depression when other factors are present.

Biological Factors Our physical and psychological future is not written in our genes, but genetics does set limits on some of our choices. For depression, both heredity and brain function appear to be important biological factors.

- *Heredity*—Many disorders run in families, and mood disorders are no exception. We can see the influence of heredity in twin studies. Genetically, fraternal twins (who develop from two fertilized egg cells) differ from each other as much as any other two siblings. If one fraternal twin has major depressive disorder, the other twin has a 20 percent chance of developing depression. The odds are significantly higher for identical twins (who have identical genes because they develop from a single fertilized egg cell). If one identical twin has major depressive disorder, the second twin's chances rise to about 50 percent. The trend is even more pronounced for bipolar disorder, with the second identical twin having a 70 percent chance of developing bipolar disorder if the first twin has it. Note, however, that genes do not guarantee the disorder will be present. For major depressive disorder, 50 percent of identical twins do *not* develop the condition if their twin has the disorder. If it were genes alone that caused depression, this number would be 100 percent because identical twins share the same genes. For bipolar disorder, 30 percent do not develop it if the other twin has it.[40]

- *Brain function*—Depressed people have depressed brains (see **Figure 32.3**). Positive emission tomography (PET) scan studies indicate that the brain is less active during major depression, especially in frontal lobe regions that are normally active during positive emotions.[41] It is also true that certain neurotransmitters—the chemical messengers that allow individual neurons in the brain to communicate with one another—appear to be out of balance in the case of depression. The two neurotransmitters that are most involved are serotonin and norepinephrine, which are lacking during times of depression. The levels of these neurotransmitters may ultimately be controlled by genes. People who experience major stress are much more likely to develop depression if there is a problem with a gene that controls serotonin levels.[42] Prozac and other antidepressant medications help restore the proper levels of these neurotransmitters.

FIGURE 32.3
Bipolar Disorder and Brain Scans
These PET scans show that mood and brain activity are correlated. The yellow and red areas of the middle scan indicate that the brain is more active during the manic phase of bipolar disorder.

All Images: Courtesy of Drs. Lewis Baxter and Michael E. Phelps, UCLA School of Medicine

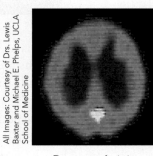

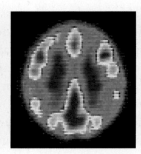

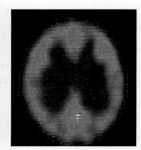

Depressed state
(May 17)   **Manic state**
(May 18)   **Depressed state**
(May 27)

Social-Cognitive Factors Psychologists operating from the biological and cognitive perspectives have made tremendous progress in explaining behavior and mental processes in recent years. In addition to the biological influences described in the previous paragraphs, researchers have identified a number of important social and cognitive influences. Psychologists look closely at the interplay among the way we think, the situations we find ourselves in, and the way we feel. These social and cognitive factors actually affect brain chemistry and are affected by it. Complicated? *Yes,* but depression is complex, and it would be unrealistic to expect simple explanations for these conditions. Consider a few social-cognitive influences:

JAIME PUEBLA/AP Images

- *Learned helplessness*—People develop a sense of helplessness when subjected to unpleasant events over which they have little or no control. As they acquire this feeling of helplessness, they give up and no longer try to improve their situation because they learned in the past that efforts to improve the situation will not work. This alone can produce depression. Learned helplessness may be one reason women suffer higher rates of depression than men do. Compared with men, women are more likely to be abused, stressed, and overwhelmed.[43,44]

- *Attributions*—When things go wrong, we try to explain them. Your *explanatory style* is determined by the nature of the explanations, or attributions, that you make. These attributions can vary from person to person. It turns out that depressed people are likely to make attributions with the following characteristics (see **Figure 32.4**):

- *Stable*—The bad situation will last a long time.

- *Internal*—This happened because of my actions, not because of the actions of someone else and not because of the circumstances.

- *Global*—My explanation applies to many areas of my life.

> **Learned Helplessness**
> When people find themselves in unpleasant situations over which they have little control (like this woman doing tedious, poorly paid factory work), learned helplessness can set in. This, in turn, is associated with depression.

WHY WERE YOU FIRED?

	Stable	Internal	Global
Associated With Depression	"I am a bad person."	"It was all my fault."	"I mess everything up."
	Not Stable	External	Specific
Not Associated With Depression	"I say things I don't mean when I'm tired."	"Yesterday was a really bad day."	"I make mistakes when I rush."

FIGURE 32.4
Attributions and Depression
How we explain events—such as losing a job—is associated with depression. People with depression are likely to explain events with stable, internal, and global statements.

If I fail a history test and explain this by saying, "I'm stupid," I've met all these conditions. This attribution is stable (stupidity doesn't come and go; it stays with me), internal (stupidity is a personal characteristic), and global (being stupid affects most of the things I do). One theory says that these attributions lead to a sense of hopelessness that produces depression.[45,46]

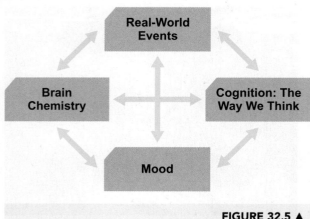

FIGURE 32.5
What Determines Mood?
Mood flows from a complex interaction of biological and social-cognitive factors. These factors influence one another and are influenced by external events and internal moods. Attempts to improve mood can focus on controlling the environment, prescribing medications to change brain chemistry, or changing the way the person thinks.

Notice that this sense of hopelessness is less likely if attributions change. If I say I failed a history test because I was sick that day, even though being sick is internal and global, my explanation is not stable (I haven't said I'll *always* be sick). Thus, I'm less likely to feel hopeless and depressed. If I say I failed the history test because I have a bad teacher, my attribution is not internal—I haven't taken personal responsibility. Again, I avoid depression. Teaching people to change their attributions can be an effective way of treating depression.

All these factors, biological and social-cognitive, can interact to form a vicious cycle of depression (see **Figure 32.5**). A person's heredity might predispose depression by allowing the balance of neurotransmitters to operate in a range associated with mood disorders or by "programming" the brain to function differently. The environment might be stressful and full of situations over which a person has little control. This might produce learned helplessness and discouragement, which—combined with attributions that are stable, global, and internal—pave the way to mood disorders. It is possible that the mood disorders, environmental conditions, or the way a person thinks can produce further alterations of brain chemistry and function, making negative thinking and emotions even more likely in the future. These factors, working together, become a psychological trap.

MAKE IT STICK!

1. _____ is a neurotransmitter associated with depression.

2. Depressed people are likely to make attributions that are stable, internal, and _____.

3. True or false: Depression is usually a response to loss.

4. Which of the following is NOT considered a symptom of major depressive disorder?

    a. Loss of energy
    b. Inability to concentrate
    c. Panic attacks
    d. Depressed mood

5. Psychologists studying the development of mood disorders who look for the effects of the way we think, the situations we find ourselves in, and the way we feel are searching for _____ factors that may influence the development of a mood disorder.

Bipolar Disorder

 32-5 What is bipolar disorder?

bipolar disorder A mood disorder (formerly called *manic depressive disorder*) in which the person alternates between the hopelessness of depression and the overexcited and unreasonably optimistic state of mania.

People with **bipolar disorder** (previously known as *manic depressive disorder*) alternate between the hopelessness of depression and the overexcited and unreasonably optimistic state of mania. This disorder is less common than major depressive disorder, but it has a more devastating effect on people's ability to function. Twice as many workdays are lost each year to bipolar disorder as to major depression.[47]

Mania is a period of abnormally high emotion and activity. Has anyone ever said to you, "Don't be so manic"? People often use that statement when they simply mean "Calm down—don't get so excited." Life would be dull if we could never feel

Wheatfield with Reaper, 1889 (oil on canvas)/Gogh, Vincent van (1853-90)/
Van Gogh Museum, Amsterdam, The Netherlands/Bridgeman Images

Snark/Art Resource, NY

▲ **Vincent van Gogh**
It is difficult to diagnose mental illness in historical figures, but van Gogh quite possibly suffered from bipolar disorder. His life alternated between periods of blazing creativity—sometimes he finished more than a painting a day—and periods of deep depression. He completed suicide in 1890.

elated or excited or wildly enthusiastic. But what if you felt intense mania for days or even weeks and just couldn't calm down? Some people do, and it's not pleasant.

It's good to be optimistic, but the manic phases of someone with bipolar disorder are well beyond normal. During mania, the person may go long periods without sleeping and may experience racing thoughts, be easily distracted, and set impossible goals.

These depressed and manic phases are like emotional hills and valleys. Moods generally follow cyclical patterns—most people find that they swing through some periods when they feel a little down and others when they feel great. And, mania is sometimes associated with bursts of creative energy.[48,49] Many well-known creative people, from Mark Twain to Vincent van Gogh, are believed to have suffered from bipolar disorder.

PSYCHOLOGY IN THE REAL WORLD

Suicide

When I was a junior in high school, back in the late 1960s, a fellow student didn't appear for class one day shortly after breaking up with a longtime girlfriend. As the day wore on, rumors that he had completed suicide began to travel through the student body. The rumors proved to be true, but nobody ever dealt with the issue openly. Teachers, counselors, administrators, and parents seemed united in their desire not to talk about something they found disturbing and unexplainable. Students were left to sort out their questions and feelings on their own, and the school never even issued an official acknowledgment of what had happened.

There were also student suicides and suicide attempts in the school where I taught. Seeing this important issue brought into the open has been gratifying. In recent years, the administration put into place a crisis response plan to help both students and faculty members cope with the emotional effect of the loss or injury of a student. Instead of pretending that nothing has happened, the school issues announcements, runs articles in the school newspaper, and ensures that counselors are available to help friends and classmates with their grief and questions. Bringing the topic of suicide into the light of day may save others from this tragic fate.

PSYCHOLOGY IN THE REAL WORLD (Continued)

Ian Shaw/Alamy

▲ Symptoms of Depression
One symptom of depression is the diminished ability to think or concentrate. This student has difficulty concentrating on her schoolwork.

One surprising fact about suicide is that people who are deeply depressed rarely kill themselves until after the depression starts to lift. This is confusing to friends, because the suicide occurs just as the person seems to be getting better. Ironically, this lifting of depression gives the person the energy to execute a plan developed when depression was so overwhelming that it effectively stopped action.[50] Similarly, suicide risk increases during the manic phase of bipolar disorder.[51]

For adolescents, to have occasional passing thoughts of suicide is neither unusual nor a cause for concern. But becoming obsessed with thoughts of suicide or starting to develop plans for completing suicide is. It's quite likely that a suicide or suicide attempt of someone you know will touch your life, if it has not

already done so. If you have a friend who appears deeply depressed, is preoccupied with death, begins to give away prized possessions, or talks openly about suicide, take the signs seriously. Encourage the person to seek help immediately—one option is to call the National Suicide Prevention Hotline, available toll-free 24 hours a day at 1-800-273-8255. The Lifeline is free, confidential, and always available. Another option is to text the word "help" to the Crisis Text Line at 271271. Consult with a parent, teacher, counselor, physician, or religious leader to help support you. If you begin to feel suicidal, seek help. The dark mood will lift, and better days do lie ahead.

Over 800,000 people (more than the population of North Dakota) worldwide complete suicide each year.[52] The rate of suicide is three to five times greater for people who experience anxiety or mood disorders.[53,54] Consider these differences in suicide rates for different groups:

- In general, Western countries have a higher rate of suicide than non-Western countries, but there is great variation even among Western countries. The rate in England is about half the U.S. rate, and the rate in Finland is about double.[55]

- In most parts of the world, men are more likely than women to complete suicide. Women, however, are at least twice as likely to attempt suicide. Men succeed more often because their method of choice is firearms, which are more lethal than the drug overdoses preferred by women.[56]

- White Americans and Native Americans have a higher suicide rate than other racial groups.[57]

- Suicide rates increase with age. The highest rate of suicide is among older men (see **Figure 32.6**).

FIGURE 32.6
Suicide, Gender, and Age
Suicide is more common among men than women at all ages. Elderly males have the highest rate of suicide. (From Statistical Abstracts, 2008.) ▶

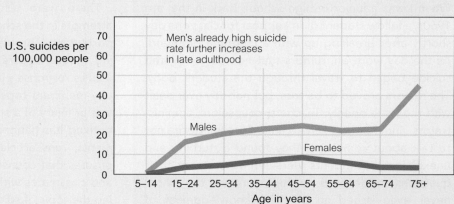

U.S. suicides per 100,000 people

Men's already high suicide rate further increases in late adulthood

Males

Females

Age in years

PSYCHOLOGY IN THE REAL WORLD (Continued)

- Suicide rates have been increasing over time. For 15- to 25-year-olds, the suicide rate doubled between 1960 and 1990.[58]

- There is a strong link between drug and alcohol use and suicide. The risk of suicide is 100 times greater among those dependent upon alcohol.[59]

Sometimes people intentionally hurt themselves by cutting, burning, or in other ways, but do not complete or attempt suicide. This is called *nonsuicidal self-injury* (NSSI). This is most common among adolescent females[60] and may be related to bullying and stress.[61,62] People with NSSI should seek help. Most sufferers do not complete suicide, but it is associated with increased risk for suicide attempts.[63–65]

THINK ABOUT . . . Psychology in the Real World

1. What are three factors that are associated with greater risk of suicide?

2. What should someone do if their friend starts to talk about suicide?

3. In the long term, what kind of societal changes do you think would result in a lower suicide rate?

MAKE IT STICK!

1. True or false: The depressed phase of bipolar disorder has a negative effect on people's lives, but the manic phase is mostly positive.

2. True or false: Bipolar disorder used to be known as manic depressive disorder.

3. Alvin came out of a period of intense depression, but now goes days without sleeping, has racing thoughts, and sets impossible goals for himself. He may be experiencing

   a. an anxiety disorder with mood swings.
   b. the manic phase of bipolar disorder.
   c. post-traumatic stress disorder.
   d. the major phase of his major depressive episode.

According to some estimates, roughly one-quarter of us will experience a disorder described in this module at some point in our lives.[66] Researchers have begun to unravel the complicated mix of nature and nurture that contributes to their prevalence. As they continue to make progress, more effective treatment options will become available to help those who suffer from these widespread conditions.

Module 32 Summary and Assessment

Anxiety Disorders, Obsessive-Compulsive Disorder, Post-Traumatic Stress Disorder, Depression, and Bipolar Disorder

 32-1 What are the anxiety disorders, and what causes them?

- Generalized anxiety disorder is marked by disruptive levels of persistent, unexplained feelings of apprehension and tenseness.

- Panic disorder is marked by sudden bouts of intense, unexplained panic.

- Phobia is marked by disruptive, irrational fears of objects, activities, or situations.

- Several biological factors may contribute to anxiety disorders, including heredity and brain function as well as evolution and natural selection.

- People may learn maladaptive responses that can blossom into anxiety disorders. These include associating fear with certain places or things (conditioning), learning fear or anxiety responses by watching others experience them (observational learning), and learning to associate emotions with actions and the results that follow those actions (reinforcement or punishment).

 32-2 What is obsessive-compulsive disorder, and what causes it?

- Obsessive-compulsive disorder is marked by unwanted repetitive thoughts and actions. Obsessions are repetitive thoughts. Compulsions are repetitive actions.

- Obsessive-compulsive disorder is influenced by a combination of biological and environmental factors.

 32-3 What is post-traumatic stress disorder, and what causes it?

- Post-traumatic stress disorder is characterized by reliving a severely upsetting event in unwanted recurring memories and dreams.

- Post-traumatic stress disorder is influenced by the intensity of stress experienced, genetics, gender, and the brain.

 32-4 What is major depressive disorder, and what causes it?

- Major depressive disorder is diagnosed when five of the following nine symptoms (including one of the first two) are present for two or more weeks: depressed mood most of the day, little interest in activities, changes in appetite, changes in sleep, changes in activity level, fatigue, feelings of worthlessness, inability to concentrate, and recurrent thoughts of suicide.

- Several biological factors may contribute to major depressive disorder, including heredity and brain function.

- Researchers have identified a number of important social and cognitive influences on the development of major depressive disorders, including the way we think (attributions) and the situations in which we find ourselves (as with learned helplessness).

 32-5 What is bipolar disorder?

- People with bipolar disorder alternate between the hopelessness of depression and the overexcited and unreasonably optimistic state of mania.

Summative Assessment

1. Which of the following is NOT a symptom of anxiety?

   a. restlessness
   b. excitement about upcoming events
   c. irritability
   d. feeling on edge

2. Phobias are disruptive, _____ fears.

   a. irrational
   b. unconscious
   c. observable
   d. justified

3. A person with agoraphobia experiences fear

   a. when near farmland.
   b. of anything made of wool.
   c. of situations that would be difficult to escape from.
   d. in the presence of any animal with horns.

4. Which of the following is true of obsessions and compulsions?

   a. Both are always considered disorders.
   b. Obsessions are always disorders, but compulsions may or may not be disorders.
   c. Compulsions are always disorders, but obsessions may or may not be disorders.
   d. They are not considered abnormal unless they disrupt a person's life.

5. Which of the following is true regarding biological causes of anxiety disorders?

   a. Specific genes that cause anxiety disorders have been discovered.
   b. People with anxiety disorders may show more activity in the frontal lobes of the brain.
   c. People with anxiety disorders may show reduced activity in the amygdala.
   d. We are rapidly evolving to develop anxiety about modern threats like cars.

6. Which of the following is NOT a symptom of major depressive disorder?

   a. changes in weight or appetite
   b. diminished ability to concentrate
   c. sleep changes
   d. periods of mania

7. Bipolar disorder involves

   a. swinging between depression and unreasonable and disruptive optimism.
   b. depression that is even deeper than major depressive disorder.
   c. a delayed reaction to highly stressful situations.
   d. episodes of unexplained terror.

8. The highest rate of suicide occurs among

   a. adolescent females.
   b. adolescent males.
   c. middle-age females.
   d. elderly males.

9. If one identical twin is diagnosed with major depressive disorder,

   a. there is little increased likelihood that the other twin will develop depression.
   b. there is about a 50–50 chance that the other twin will develop depression.
   c. it is almost certain that the other twin will develop depression.
   d. there is a high chance that the other twin will develop depression if the twins are female, but a low chance if the twins are male.

10. Vicky was unable to get a date for the Valentine's Day dance. She concluded that "nobody will ever love me." Which of the following is true?

    a. She has an unstable, external, and specific explanatory style, and this is associated with depression.
    b. She has an unstable, external, and specific explanatory style, and this is not associated with depression.
    c. She has a stable, internal, and global explanatory style, and this is associated with depression.
    d. She has a stable, internal, and global explanatory style, and this is not associated with depression.

KEY TERMS

anxiety, p. 491
generalized anxiety disorder, p. 491
panic disorder, p. 491
phobia, p. 491

obsessive-compulsive disorder (OCD), p. 496
post-traumatic stress disorder (PTSD), p. 498

major depressive disorder, p. 499
bipolar disorder, p. 502

Module 33 | Dissociative Disorders, Schizophrenia, and Personality Disorders

Is it possible to be two different people? Can you really split from reality? Serious psychological disorders are the topic of this module.

Consider Gene Saunders. Gene was a manager at a manufacturing company. Work had become a struggle, with missed production goals, criticism from his supervisor, and disappointment when an expected promotion didn't come through. The stress at work led to additional problems at home, including a violent argument with his teenage son. Two days after the argument, Gene disappeared. A year and a half later, police in a town hundreds of miles away picked up a drifter who had been working as a short-order cook. The drifter's name was Burt Tate, and although Burt knew what town he was in, he had no knowledge of his life before arriving in town. There were no physical or drug problems that would account for the memory loss. You guessed it—Gene and Burt are the same person.[1]

Consider Emilio. His twelfth hospitalization occurred when he was 40 because his mother, with whom he lived, feared him. He dressed in a ragged old coat and bedroom slippers, with several medals around his neck. Much of what he said was simply nonsense. When interviewed, he claimed he had been "eating wires and lighting fires." He alternated from being angry toward his mother to childlike giggling, and he heard nonexistent voices. Emilio had been unable to hold a job since his first hospitalization at age 16.[2,3]

Consider Mary. She was 26 years old when referred for hospitalization by her therapist because she had urges to cut herself with a razor. For more than 10 years, Mary struggled with issues related to religion and philosophy. Her academic performance in college dropped when she began experimenting with a variety of drugs. When Mary entered therapy, she became both hostile and demanding, sometimes insisting on two therapy sessions a day. She did not exhibit stability in her moods or relationships.[4]

Gene, Emilio, and Mary suffer from psychological disorders we discuss in this module. These disorders are not nearly as common as *anxiety disorders* (such as phobias) and *major depressive disorder*, but they represent an sample of the variety of disturbances that can plague people. Keep in mind that in this text we do not come even close to examining all disorders—the American Psychiatric Association's *Diagnostic and Statistical Manual of Mental Disorders*, fifth edition (DSM-5), lists more almost 300 specific mental disorders. Several of the people you read about in this module have lost some aspect of their sense of self like Gene (dissociative disorders); others have lost contact with reality like Emilio (schizophrenia); and still others have developed lasting and counterproductive patterns of behavior like Mary (personality disorders).

dissociative disorders
Disorders in which the sense of self has become separated (dissociated) from previous memories, thoughts, or feelings.

Memory and Your Sense of Self
We often joke about forgetfulness, but the dissociative disorders all involve serious disruption of memory.

Dissociative Disorders

 33-1 What are the symptoms and causes of dissociative disorders?

Dissociate is the opposite of *associate* (to make connections). If a person has a **dissociative disorder,** his sense of self has become separated (dissociated) from his memories, thoughts, or feelings. Dissociative disorders are quite rare and usually represent a response to overwhelming stress. Two specific forms are dissociative amnesia and dissociative identity disorder (see **Figure 33.1**).

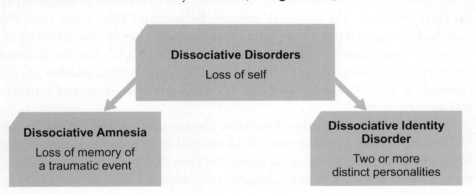

Dissociative Disorders
Loss of self

Dissociative Amnesia
Loss of memory of a traumatic event

Dissociative Identity Disorder
Two or more distinct personalities

FIGURE 33.1
Dissociative Disorders
Two dissociative disorders are dissociative amnesia and dissociative identity disorder.

Dissociative Amnesia

Can you remember the meaning of the word *amnesia?* Amnesia is memory loss, and any number of factors, including drug use, can cause it. Drinking too much alcohol, for example, can lead to a blackout of all memories of the drinking episode. Head injury, fatigue, and physical disorders such as Alzheimer's disease can also cause amnesia. To qualify as **dissociative amnesia,** however, the memory loss is usually a reaction to a traumatic event. Serious personal threats are the most common causes of dissociative amnesia. Combat soldiers may report losing their memory for hours or days.[5] Survivors of natural disasters, such as floods or wildfires, sometimes experience similar losses.[6]

In one case of dissociative amnesia, an 18-year-old man lost his memory of sailing with friends off the coast of Florida. A storm had come up, and only he had the foresight to put on a life jacket and tie himself to the boat. His friends

Trauma and Amnesia
People under extreme stress, such as these soldiers in combat in Afghanistan, may experience dissociative amnesia.

dissociative amnesia
A dissociative disorder characterized by loss of memory in reaction to a traumatic event.

dissociative fugue
A dissociative disorder characterized by loss of identity and travel to a new location.

dissociative identity disorder
A rare and controversial dissociative disorder in which an individual exhibits two or more distinct and alternating personalities.

were swept overboard in the high waves. Psychologists determined that, because of the emotional trauma, the young man lost all memory of the tragic storm and the several days he spent hoping to be rescued.[7]

Dissociative fugue is an extended form of dissociative amnesia characterized by loss of identity and travel to a new location. (The word *fugue* comes from the same root as *fugitive*.) A dissociative fugue state can be short, lasting only a few hours, or long, lasting months or even years. The person may develop a new identity, form new friendships, or even enter a new line of work. The case of Gene Saunders at the beginning of this module represents dissociative fugue. His stressful work and home situations led to his disappearance, and even he was not aware of the history behind his transformation into Burt Tate.

Dissociative Identity Disorder

Have you ever felt like a different person? Have you ever said, "I have no idea why I did that"? Magnified to an extreme, these feelings are central features of **dissociative identity disorder** (formerly known as *multiple personality disorder*)—a rare and controversial disorder in which an individual exhibits two or more distinct and alternating personalities. These subpersonalities reportedly can differ in age, gender identity, and self-perception of physical characteristics. Some researchers have even reported changes in brain function or handedness as a patient switches from one personality to another. Sometimes subpersonalities seem to be aware of one another, and sometimes they do not.[8–10]

Diagnosed cases of dissociative identity disorder increased dramatically in the final decades of the twentieth century. Before the 1970s, fewer than 100 cases had ever been reported in professional journals. Then, in the 1980s alone, reports of more than 20,000 diagnosed cases of dissociative identity disorder appeared, almost all of them in North America.[11] The average number of subpersonalities also increased—from 3 to 12.[12] In some cases, dozens of personalities were reported.

Psychologists debate whether dissociative identity disorder really exists. Are clinicians simply more knowledgeable about and willing to make the diagnosis? Are better diagnostic rules reducing the number of cases that in the past were misdiagnosed as other disorders, such as schizophrenia? Skeptics believe the power of suggestion has been at work here. Clinicians, who now have read a great deal about these fascinating cases, may unintentionally suggest multiple personalities to their clients.[13] Questions such as "Have you ever felt another part of you is in control?" may lead the patient (who has also read about the disorder or seen depictions in the media) to construct subpersonalities in an effort to please the therapist by responding to perceived expectations. This, of course, is also unintentional.

Sybil Dorsett's famous case of dissociative identity disorder was the subject of a book, *Sybil,* and a made-for-TV movie of the same name in 1976 (remade in 2007). However, after the death of Sybil's psychiatrist, a different picture emerged. After reading her recently released records, some experts have come to believe that Sybil's multiple personalities were the result of her therapist's suggestions.[14] By giving names to Sybil's emotional states and asking her to take on these roles as part of the therapeutic process, the psychiatrist could have led Sybil to believe that she possessed multiple personalities. (Other problems that originate in the mind can have physical results, as discussed in Psychology in the Real World: Mind and Body in Psychological Disorders.)

John Springer Collection/CORBIS/Corbis via Getty Images

The Everett Collection

The Media and Mental Disorders

The controversy about dissociative identity disorder has been partially fueled by the public's interest in the disorder. Two classic films—*The Three Faces of Eve* (left) and *Sybil* (right)—have showcased "multiple personality." Some are concerned that these kinds of films and other media attention lead to false diagnoses of this disorder.

PSYCHOLOGY IN THE REAL WORLD

Mind and Body in Psychological Disorders

The relationship between mind and body has fascinated psychologists since this science was born. Psychological disorders are a good place to look for this interaction, because such disorders almost always have both psychological and physical components. This is most dramatic in **somatic symptom disorder**, in which the symptoms take a bodily form without apparent physical cause and the reasons behind many visits to the doctor are "medically unexplained."[15] (*Somatic* comes from a Greek word for "body.")

You're probably already familiar with one of these disorders—**illness anxiety disorder**, formerly called hypochondriasis and commonly referred to as *hypochondria*, which is characterized by imagined symptoms of illness (see **Figure 33.2**). People with illness anxiety disorder actually experience symptoms of physical illness, such as headaches and fleeting joint pains, but medical exams reveal nothing physically wrong with their bodies. The disorder is, quite literally, all in the mind. However, people with illness anxiety disorder suffer because they *believe* they are sick. All of us occasionally have anxiety about our physical condition, worrying that we may be sick but then turning out to be fine. Athletes, who must be tuned in to their bodies, may experience these worries frequently—but not usually to the extent seen in this mind–body disorder. Let's be clear about one more thing: *Pretending* to be sick to avoid responsibility or

Mind-Body Problems

Illness Anxiety Disorder

Imagined illness

Psychophysiological Disorders

Medical condition produced by psychological factors

Conversion Disorder

Anxiety producing a loss of physical function

FIGURE 33.2
Somatic Symptom and Related Disorders
Somatic symptom and related disorders include illness anxiety disorder, conversion disorder, and psychophysiological disorders.

PSYCHOLOGY IN THE REAL WORLD (Continued)

to gain attention does not qualify as illness anxiety disorder or somatic symptom disorder (although DSM-5 does have a category known as malingering to cover this situation).

Another related disorder, *conversion disorder* (formerly called *hysteria*), takes its name from its main symptom—the change, or conversion, of a psychological factor (typically anxiety) into an actual loss of physical function. A person with conversion disorder might suddenly experience blindness, laryngitis, or paralysis that has no physical cause. Have you ever been so frightened you momentarily lost the ability to move, or so stunned you momentarily lost the ability to speak? Then you've experienced, on a minor, short-term level, the core requirement of conversion disorder—loss of function for psychological reasons. Although some disorders, such as major depression, appear to be increasing in modern times, conversion disorder has become quite rare.

The symptoms of illness anxiety disorder and conversion disorder have no real physical basis, but sometimes psychological factors can lead to or aggravate real medical conditions. Stress, for example, contributes to asthma, ulcers, headaches, and high blood pressure. Such conditions, called *psychophysiological* or *psychosomatic disorders*, involve a more complete interaction of mind and body. With these disorders, it's not mind *or* body—it's mind *and* body interacting to produce trouble.

> **somatic symptom and related disorders**
> Psychological disorders in which the symptoms take a bodily form without apparent physical cause.
>
> **illness anxiety disorder** A disorder characterized by imagined symptoms of illness.

THINK ABOUT . . . Psychology in the Real World

1. What characterizes illness anxiety disorder?
2. What's the nature of conversion disorder?
3. Hypothesize how the mind and body interact when it comes to somatic symptom and related disorders.

MAKE IT STICK!

1. True or false: Dissociative amnesia is often caused by drug use or head injuries.

2. What extended form of dissociative amnesia is characterized by loss of identity and relocating?

3. True or false: Psychologists debate whether dissociative identity disorder really exists.

Schizophrenia

 33-2 What are the symptoms and causes of schizophrenia?

Schizophrenia is perhaps the most frightening and most misunderstood psychological disorder. Here are some facts to help dispel the myths:

schizophrenia A disorder characterized by disorganized and delusional thinking, disturbed perceptions, and inappropriate emotions and behaviors.

- **Schizophrenia** is characterized by disorganized and delusional thinking, disturbed perceptions, and inappropriate emotions and behaviors.

- Schizophrenia is not "split personality." *Schiz* does come from a word that means "split," but the split represents a break from reality, not a division of personality. (There is no psychological disorder called *split personality*. Dissociative identity disorder, discussed earlier in this module, comes closest.)

- Schizophrenia occurs in about 1 percent of the world's population.[16] Schizophrenia typically develops in late adolescence or early adulthood and strikes men at a slightly greater rate than it strikes women.[17,18]

Symptoms of Schizophrenia

A variety of symptoms characterize schizophrenia (see **Figure 33.3**). No one will experience them all, but everyone with the disorder will experience some of them. Common symptoms include delusions, hallucinations, and inappropriate emotions or behaviors.

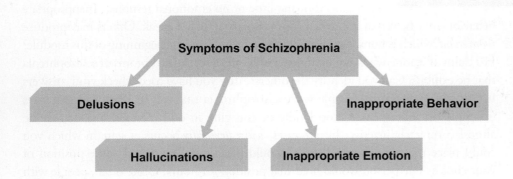

FIGURE 33.3
Symptoms of Schizophrenia
It would be unusual for a person with schizophrenia to experience all of these symptoms, but some of them will be present.

Delusions A **delusion** is an irrationally held false belief. We all believe false things sometimes, but the delusions of schizophrenia are more extensive, more complex, and often longer term. It may be that these delusions develop initially because individuals with schizophrenia have trouble focusing their attention on appropriate environmental stimuli. Instead, their attention may be captured by insignificant things, or they may not notice important ones.[19] Delusions fall into several broad categories:

- *Delusions of grandeur* are false beliefs that you are more important than you really are. People with schizophrenia may actually believe they are someone else, such as a famous political leader (Abraham Lincoln, for example) or religious figure (Jesus).

- *Delusions of persecution* are false beliefs that people are out to get you. A person may believe that she is being followed or that the CIA is engaging in an elaborate plot to capture her.

- *Delusions of sin or guilt* are false beliefs of being responsible for some misfortune. For instance, a person might believe he is responsible for a plane crash because he failed to brush his teeth one morning.

- *Delusions of influence* are false beliefs of being controlled by outside forces: "The devil made me do it."

delusions False beliefs that are symptoms of schizophrenia and other serious psychological disorders.

Hallucinations A **hallucination** is a false perception, in other words, a false sensory experience. The hallucinations people with schizophrenia most often experience are *auditory.* Many report hearing voices, and sometimes the voices are troubling or tell them what to do. If the hallucination is *visual,* then the person sees nonexistent objects or distorted images of items or people. *Tactile* hallucinations occur when people feel skin stimulation, such as a tingling or burning or touch that is not real. Hallucinations can also distort *taste* and *smell.* Note the difference: Delusions are beliefs with no logical basis; hallucinations are perceptions with

hallucinations False perceptions that are symptoms of schizophrenia and other serious psychological disorders.

Hallucinations ▲
John Nash, the Nobel Prize–winning mathematician featured in the 2001 movie *A Beautiful Mind,* suffered many classic symptoms of schizophrenia, including disturbing hallucinations. In this photo, Nash (played by Russell Crowe) is seeing, hearing, and feeling things that are not there.

no outside stimulation. But hallucinations often provide "evidence" for delusions—it's quite logical to believe someone is plotting to kill you if you can taste poison in your food. Life becomes unimaginably difficult if we can't trust the input from our own senses.

Inappropriate Emotions or Behaviors Many specific symptoms fit into the broad category of inappropriate emotions or behaviors. Schizophrenia can produce wildly inappropriate emotions. A patient might laugh uncontrollably when sadness is the more appropriate response. Another sufferer might have flat emotions, showing little or no emotional response. Inappropriate behaviors may be verbal or physical. Some people may not speak. Others may produce *word salad,* which is nonsense talk. (Remember Emilio at the beginning of this module? His claim of "eating wires and lighting fires" is one of several symptoms of schizophrenia that he exhibits. Can you identify the others? After you have tried, check your answers in the next paragraph.) People with schizophrenia may act in inappropriate ways (examples include speaking too loudly or engaging in odd mannerisms) or may be almost completely inactive. In rare cases, *waxy flexibility* occurs, a state in which you could place the person's arm, as you would place a doll's arm, in some position of your choice. The person would hold that position for hours. Quite often, people with schizophrenia withdraw from the affairs of the real world. This withdrawal further limits their knowledge of current events and their social skills.

Emilio exhibits several symptoms of schizophrenia. We've already established that he is speaking in *word salad.* His bizarre dress is *inappropriate behavior.* His mood swings are *inappropriate emotion.* Finally, the voices he hears are *auditory hallucinations.*

Causes of Schizophrenia

Complex disorders have complicated causes, and there is probably no psychological disorder more complex than schizophrenia. As is often the case, biological factors and psychological factors seem to interact to produce schizophrenia.

Biological Factors The biological approach to schizophrenia has received so much research support in recent years that some experts say we are wrong to call it a psychological disorder. Rather, it is a brain disorder that produces changes in a person's mind. Let's examine the biological factors in more detail.

- *Genetics*—The risk of schizophrenia increases substantially if relatives have the disorder (see **Figure 33.4**). Although roughly 1 percent of the general population has schizophrenia, the risk rises to about 10 percent if a parent or sibling has the disorder. These odds are even higher—almost 50 percent—if the relative with schizophrenia is an identical twin.[20] This evidence shows that, while genetics is an important factor, no single gene or set of genes guarantees schizophrenia will develop. If there were, the risk for an identical twin whose co-twin had the disorder would be 100 percent, because identical twins have identical genes. Instead, genetics seems to produce a *predisposition* for schizophrenia—an increased likelihood that the disorder will develop. The search is on for the specific genes that might combine to alter the brain in a way that produces schizophrenia.[21-23] Other factors, as you will see, determine whether the increased likelihood will lead to a full-fledged disorder. A similar situation

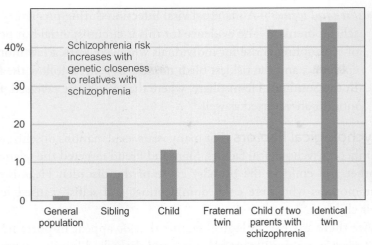

Lifetime risk, per 100 people, of developing schizophrenia for relatives of a person with schizophrenia

Schizophrenia risk increases with genetic closeness to relatives with schizophrenia

Relationship to person with schizophrenia

©AP Images

▲ **FIGURE 33.4**
Genetics and Schizophrenia: The Genain Quadruplets
Nora, Iris, Myra, and Hester Genain are identical quadruplets who all developed schizophrenia. If they had been randomly selected, the probability of this would be 1 in 100 million. We can assume that no single gene or set of genes is directly responsible for schizophrenia, however. If such a direct cause existed, the figure for identical twins, who are genetically identical, would be 100 percent. Because two of the sisters have more serious forms of schizophrenia, it is likely that both heredity and environment—nature and nurture—are involved. (Adapted from Gottesman, 2001.)

exists for various kinds of heart disease. Genetics may put a person at risk, but factors such as exercise, diet, and smoking play a critical role in determining whether the disease will develop.

- *Brain structure*—The brain structure of people with schizophrenia differs markedly from normal brain structure (see **Figure 33.5**). Brain scans show that schizophrenia is often associated with smaller amounts of brain tissue and larger, fluid-filled spaces around that tissue.[24] Particular brain structures may be affected by schizophrenia. For example, the thalamus, responsible for the routing of incoming sensory information, is smaller when schizophrenia is present and may hinder the person's ability to focus attention.[25]

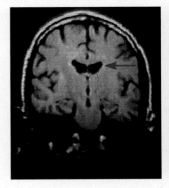

From Suddath, Richard L., et al. (1990). Anatomical abnormalities in the brains of monozygotic twins discordant for schizophrenia. *The New England Journal of Medicine, 322,* 12. 1990 by the Massachusetts Medical Society. Photo courtesy of Daniel R. Weinberger, M.D., NIH-NIMH/NSC.

- *Brain function*—Positron emission tomography (PET) scans, which show the parts of the brain that are active during particular tasks, reveal that the brain of a person with schizophrenia operates differently than does the brain of someone without the disorder. One difference appears in the frontal lobes—the center of our most advanced thinking abilities—which show less activity when schizophrenia is present.[26,27] Brain chemistry also differs for a person with schizophrenia. Researchers have discovered as many as six times the normal number of receptor sites for the neurotransmitter *dopamine* when they examined the brains of people with schizophrenia after death.[28] This abnormally high number of receptors may explain the delusions and hallucinations associated with schizophrenia. Medication that blocks these receptor sites reduces such symptoms. Researchers are working on medications for another neurotransmitter, glutamate, in an attempt to diminish other symptoms of schizophrenia.[29]

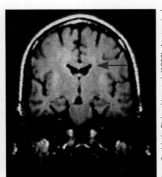

▲ **FIGURE 33.5**
Schizophrenia and Brain Structure
These two brain scans are from identical twins, one who has schizophrenia and one who does not. Note that the open space (actually, a cavity in the brain filled with fluid) is larger for the twin with schizophrenia (Suddath et al., 1990). Because identical twins have identical genes, this difference must have been caused by some environmental factor, such as a virus.

- *Prenatal viruses*—A maternal viral infection during pregnancy may cause schizophrenia.[30] The evidence for this is circumstantial but persuasive. Rates of schizophrenia rise for individuals who were born a few months after a flu epidemic, and the riskiest birth months in general follow the flu season.[31,32] In the Southern Hemisphere, where the seasons are reversed, the high-risk months are reversed as well.[33]

Psychological Factors For many years, explanations of schizophrenia focused mainly on psychological factors. Sigmund Freud targeted the relationship between mother and child as the primary cause of the disorder. He mistakenly thought that mothers who were cold, domineering, and selfish caused schizophrenia in their children.[34]

Are there any psychological factors that *do* appear important? The two areas that seem most significant are stress and disturbed family communication patterns. Recall that the major genetic contribution to schizophrenia seems to be a predisposition—a tendency to develop the disorder. Stress may be the trigger that sets off the series of events that converts schizophrenia from a possibility into a reality. Disturbed family communications are also correlated with the development of schizophrenia, but at this point, it's impossible to tell whether they are a *cause* of schizophrenia or a *result* of the disorder. One study did find that young people who developed schizophrenia were more likely to be socially withdrawn and to exhibit odd behavior before becoming schizophrenic.[35]

The bizarre world of schizophrenia has puzzled and fascinated students of human behavior for centuries. We are making progress both in understanding and in effectively treating this devastating disorder. It seems to result from a complex interaction of biological and psychological factors. To be effective, treatment must address both of these components.

MAKE IT STICK!

1. Delusions of _____ involve false beliefs that people are out to get you.

2. Roughly _____ percent of the general population has schizophrenia.

3. Nonsense talk, a symptom of schizophrenia, is also called _____.

Personality Disorders

 33-3 What kinds of personality disorders are there?

personality disorders
Psychological disorders characterized by rigid and lasting behavior patterns that disrupt social functioning.

Personality disorders are lasting, rigid behavior patterns that disrupt social functioning. The DSM-5 lists 10 personality disorders related to anxiety, odd or eccentric behaviors, and dramatic or impulsive behaviors (see **Figure 33.6**). The specific personality disorders are often difficult to diagnose because there is a lot of overlap among them. The behavior patterns are usually evident by adolescence and obvious to others, but the person with the personality disorder often does not recognize the problem exists, which can make treatment difficult. Let's take a look at personality disorders and a sample of the specific disorders included in each cluster.

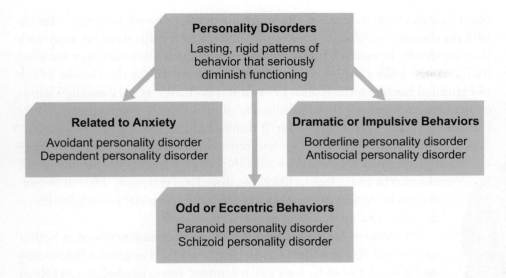

FIGURE 33.6
Clusters of Personality Disorders
The main clusters of personality disorders relate to anxiety, odd or eccentric behaviors, and dramatic or impulsive behaviors.

Personality Disorders Related to Anxiety

Individuals with *avoidant personality disorder* are so sensitive about being rejected that personal relationships become difficult. Those with *dependent personality disorder* behave in clingy, submissive ways and display a strong need to have others take care of them. Juanita, for example, is a 28-year-old with dependent personality disorder. She still lives with her mother and feels unable to live in her own apartment because she has trouble making decisions about day-to-day life. She needs constant reassurance from her mother and is afraid to disagree with her because she wants to avoid criticism, making her entirely dependent on her mother.

Personality Disorders With Odd or Eccentric Behaviors

Individuals with *paranoid personality disorder* show deep distrust of other people. This suspiciousness gets in the way of personal relationships. Those with *schizoid personality disorder* are detached from social relationships. They are true hermits, preferring the life of a loner and avoiding intimate interactions with others at all costs. Henry is such a person. He does his shopping online because he doesn't like having to talk to clerks in stores. He has always lived on his own and does not attend any family holiday celebrations despite repeated invitations from relatives. He does not own a telephone.

Personality Disorders With Dramatic or Impulsive Behaviors

Those with *borderline personality disorder* exhibit, above all else, instability—of emotions, self-image, behavior, and relationships. Mary, whose story is one of the cases that opens this module, is an example of a person with borderline personality disorder. Her academic struggles in college, inability to resolve religious and philosophical issues, unrealistic demands, and self-cutting all add up to a life filled with instability.

People with **antisocial personality disorder** (sometimes called psychopathic or sociopathic personality disorder) show a lack of conscience for wrongdoing and a lack of respect for the rights of other people. Antisocial personality disorder is the most dramatic and troubling of all personality disorders. Because of this lack of conscience, people with this disorder are willing to engage in wide-ranging criminal behaviors about which they show no remorse. This disorder is more likely to

antisocial personality disorder A personality disorder in which the person (usually a man) shows a lack of conscience for wrongdoing and a lack of respect for the rights of others.

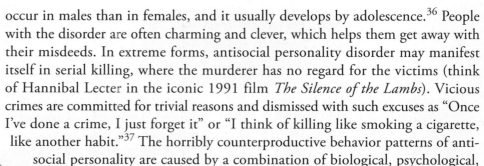

Murderous Minds
Researchers have found reduced activation in a murderer's frontal lobes. This may result in a lack of judgment and less ability to control impulsive or aggressive tendencies. ▼

Frontal lobes

occur in males than in females, and it usually develops by adolescence.[36] People with the disorder are often charming and clever, which helps them get away with their misdeeds. In extreme forms, antisocial personality disorder may manifest itself in serial killing, where the murderer has no regard for the victims (think of Hannibal Lecter in the iconic 1991 film *The Silence of the Lambs*). Vicious crimes are committed for trivial reasons and dismissed with such excuses as "Once I've done a crime, I just forget it" or "I think of killing like smoking a cigarette, like another habit."[37] The horribly counterproductive behavior patterns of antisocial personality are caused by a combination of biological, psychological, and social factors. Once in place, the disorder is extremely difficult to treat effectively. As you can imagine, people with antisocial personality disorder often end up in jail instead of in treatment

Dissociative disorders, schizophrenia, and personality disorders help us understand that abnormal functioning is as varied as normal functioning and that the reasons for it are just as complex. Just as psychology can help us understand and promote productive behavior and mental processes, it can also help us comprehend the fascinating and sometimes frightening world of mental disorders. This is the first step on the road to effective treatment.

MAKE IT STICK!

1. True or false: Personality disorders usually involve patterns of behavior that are obvious to others by the time an individual is a teenager.

2. What do psychologists call lasting, rigid behavior patterns that disrupt social functioning?

3. True or false: People diagnosed with borderline personality disorder exhibit instability— of emotions, self-image, behavior, and relationships.

Module 33 Summary and Assessment
Dissociative Disorders, Schizophrenia, and Personality Disorders

 33-1 What are the symptoms and causes of dissociative disorders?

- Dissociative amnesia is memory loss caused by a reaction to a traumatic event.

- Dissociative fugue is an extended form of dissociative amnesia characterized by loss of identity and travel to a new location.

- Dissociative identity disorder (formerly known as multiple personality disorder) is a rare and controversial disorder in which an individual exhibits two or more distinct and alternating personalities.

- Dissociative disorders are usually a response to overwhelming stress. They cause individuals to lose their sense of self and separate (dissociate) from their memories, thoughts, or feelings.

 33-2 What are the symptoms and causes of schizophrenia?

- Schizophrenia includes symptoms of delusions, hallucinations, and inappropriate emotions or behaviors.

- The risk of schizophrenia increases substantially if biological relatives have the disorder, indicating a genetic predisposition for the development of schizophrenia. Brain structure, brain function, and maternal viral infection during pregnancy may also contribute to schizophrenia.

- The psychological factors of stress and disturbed family communication patterns may be triggers for the underlying biological factors that cause a person to manifest schizophrenic symptoms.

Summative Assessment

1. Psychologists skeptical about the increase in the number of people diagnosed with dissociative identity disorder believe the increase is likely due to
   a. better diagnostic criteria.
   b. an increase in severe child abuse.
   c. genetic factors that may trigger the disorder.
   d. therapists who "cause" the disorder through suggestion.

2. Individuals with a deep distrust of others might be diagnosed with _____ personality disorder.
   a. paranoid
   b. avoidant
   c. borderline
   d. antisocial

3. According to the DSM-5, how many kinds of personality disorders are there?
   a. 10
   b. 100
   c. 200
   d. 300

4. Which of the following is characterized by memory loss caused by a reaction to a traumatic event?
   a. dissociative fugue
   b. dissociative amnesia
   c. dissociative identity disorder
   d. dissociative paranoia

5. A person who becomes paralyzed because of a stressful situation might be diagnosed with
   a. somatic symptom disorder.
   b. borderline personality disorder.

33-3 What kinds of personality disorders are there?

- Personality disorders are lasting, rigid behavior patterns that disrupt social functioning.

- Personality disorders are divided into three clusters related to anxiety, to odd or eccentric behaviors, and to dramatic or impulsive behaviors.

- Antisocial personality disorder involves a lack of conscience and a lack of respect for the rights of other people.

   c. conversion disorder.
   d. dissociative amnesia.

6. What kind of disorders are usually a response to overwhelming stress?
   a. antisocial
   b. schizophrenic
   c. predispositional
   d. dissociative

7. What is the disorder characterized by disorganized and delusional thinking, disturbed perceptions, and inappropriate emotions and behaviors called?
   a. schizophrenia
   b. amnesia
   c. multiple personality
   d. impulsive disorder

8. Which of the following is NOT considered a biological factor related to schizophrenia?
   a. genetics
   b. blood type
   c. brain function
   d. brain structure

9. What do we call a disorder where the person's sense of self has become separated from memories, thoughts, or feelings?
   a. illness anxiety disorder
   b. anxiety
   c. mood
   d. dissociative

10. What kind of personality disorder involves a lack of conscience and a lack of respect for the rights of other people?
    a. antisocial
    b. dissociative identity
    c. dependent
    d. schizophrenia

KEY TERMS

dissociative disorders, p. 509
dissociative amnesia, p. 509
dissociative fugue, p. 510
dissociative identity disorder, p. 510

somatic symptom and related disorders, p. 511
illness anxiety disorder, p. 511
schizophrenia, p. 512

delusions, p. 513
hallucinations, p. 513
personality disorders, p. 516
antisocial personality disorder, p. 517

DOMAIN 7

Applications of Psychological Science

VGstockstudio/Shutterstock

Psychological Therapies

Psychotherapy comes in many forms. One of the earliest therapists, Sigmund Freud, had patients lie down during therapy sessions. Is this approach common? How many different approaches are there? Let's take a look.

Learning Goals

34-1 Define psychotherapy, and explain Sigmund Freud's psychoanalytic theory.

34-2 Explain how humanistic therapists try to help people with emotional problems.

34-3 Explain how behavior therapists apply the principles of classical conditioning and operant conditioning in their practice.

34-4 Describe the basis of cognitive therapy and cognitive-behavioral therapy.

34-5 Summarize the advantages of group therapy, and explain when group therapy is most often used.

When you think of *therapy*, what do you envision? Perhaps you see someone lying on a couch, reflecting on childhood memories while a therapist listens and takes notes. **Sigmund Freud** devised this once-innovative mode of healing over 100 years ago, and for many people, this image represents a prototype for therapy. Although traditional Freudian-style therapy is still popular in movies and cartoons, only a few key remnants of his methods can be found in therapists' offices today.

Have you ever wondered whether therapy of any kind really works? Psychologists concerned with this question have developed many approaches in their attempt to help people cope with psychological problems. As a result, therapists can select from a variety of techniques to find the one best suited to resolving a particular problem.

Therapy sometimes involves prescription medications and even medical procedures in severe cases, but more often, it involves nonmedical options, which are the focus of this module. Psychological therapy, or **psychotherapy,** is an interaction between a trained therapist and someone who is seeking to overcome psychological difficulties or achieve personal growth.[1,2] All told, there are around 250 types of psychotherapy.[3] But each centers on one or more of four major approaches: psychoanalytic, humanistic, behavioral, and cognitive. Depending on the person's problems, a therapist may use techniques from various forms of therapy in an **eclectic approach.**

We begin our explanation of psychotherapy by considering the four individual perspectives and then exploring how families and groups may benefit from going through therapy together. Let's start with the first comprehensive approach to therapy, Freud's psychoanalysis.

psychotherapy
An interaction between a trained therapist and someone who is seeking to overcome psychological difficulties or achieve personal growth.

eclectic approach
An approach to psychotherapy that, depending on the person's problems, uses techniques from various forms of therapy.

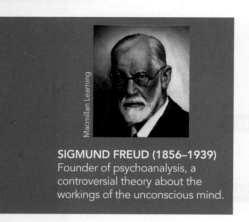

SIGMUND FREUD (1856–1939)
Founder of psychoanalysis, a controversial theory about the workings of the unconscious mind.

psychoanalysis Freud's theory of personality; also, a therapeutic technique that attempts to provide insight into thoughts and actions by exposing and interpreting the underlying unconscious motives and conflicts.

Psychoanalysis

 34-1 What is psychotherapy in general, and what is Sigmund Freud's psychoanalytic theory in particular?

Few therapists practice psychotherapy the way Freud did at the turn of the century, but his influence is easy to spot in the treatment methods of several current therapies. Let's take a closer look at Freud's **psychoanalysis** so that we can better understand its broad influence.

Psychoanalytic Assumptions

Freud liked to compare personality to an iceberg composed of three primary elements: the pleasure-seeking *id,* the reality-oriented *ego,* and the *superego,* a set of internalized ideals (the conscience). Just as most of an iceberg floats beneath the water and is invisible, so the greater portion of personality is impossible to see (as shown in Figure 29.1 in Module 29). The waterline separating the visible parts of personality from the invisible parts, Freud said, is the boundary between the conscious and the unconscious regions of our mind. We are conscious of the portion of personality above the waterline but not of the portion below.

The iceberg represents the structure of personality. But how does personality develop? According to Freud, personality forms during our early childhood, when we pass through a series of stages, such as the oral stage (0 to 18 months) and the anal stage (18 to 36 months). Each stage is a time of potential conflicts, and failure to adequately resolve these conflicts, Freud believed, could result in problems in later adult years. For instance, the child who does not resolve conflicts at the oral stage might wind up as a smoker. Relief from these psychological problems is possible, Freud believed, if the analyst helps patients bring the repressed, unconscious conflicts and impulses of childhood to the surface, or into the conscious mind. Freud thought that *insight* into the origin of the psychological disorder would allow the person to work through previously buried feelings. Wellness and health, according to this theory, result from the release of the energy previously (and unconsciously) devoted to resolving these conflicts.

Psychoanalytic Methods

Psychoanalysis aims to dig up the past to clarify the present. Analysts dig with several different therapeutic tools, and one of the most useful is *free association.* How does free association work? First, the analyst asks the patient to relax, perhaps reclining on a couch, with the head slightly elevated. The analyst, seated nearby, may ask the patient to think of a childhood memory as a starting point and to talk about whatever comes to mind—perhaps a favorite game, childhood friends, or dreams.

That may sound easy, but what if you were the patient and you thought of something embarrassing? Would you hesitate before talking about it? Would you leave something out of your story, change the subject, or joke your way out of the situation?

A psychoanalyst would probably classify all of these free association interruptions as **resistance,** or the blocking from consciousness of anxiety-laden material. It is the analyst's job to make patients aware of these sensitive areas and to offer **interpretation,** ideas on the meaning behind dreams, resistances, and other significant behaviors to promote insight. Why did you stop in the middle of a story about your father? Is there an unresolved childhood conflict buried in your memory? Analysts dig for these conflicts and the meaning underneath them.

Jacob Lund/Alamy

Freud believed dreams were a rich source of information about unconscious conflicts. He called them the "royal road to the unconscious." Dream analysis is a key element of the psychoanalytic process, and Freud was particularly interested in the *latent content,* or censored meaning, of dreams. This was why Freud spent so much time trying to figure out what his patients' dreams *really* meant. Did that dream about being trapped in a room really mean that the patient felt stuck in a bad relationship? Freud believed dreams were actually symbolic of some other issue.

Freud theorized that patients transfer strong emotions (such as love or hatred) linked with other relationships to the analyst, a process he called **transference.** Freud felt that patients could gain insight into current and past relationships by exploring these transferred feelings for their analyst and dealing with the long-repressed issues they represent. That is, Freud thought that a patient who says "I hate my father" could gain insight into these feelings of hate if he redirected them to his psychoanalyst.

Freud's ideas have influenced therapy, but contemporary critics of psychoanalysis note several critically important problems with Freud's methods:

- The foundation of psychoanalysis rested on Freud's belief in *repressed memories.* However, many psychologists doubt that we repress important memories. This topic has sparked intense debate.

- Traditional psychoanalysis is expensive, requires several sessions a week, and can last for years. Psychoanalytic therapists say that this process takes so long because inner conflicts take time to understand and overcome.[4] With sessions typically costing more than $100 per visit, this kind of therapy is available only to the wealthy.

- Refuting psychoanalytic interpretation gets you nowhere. If you disagree with the interpretation, your analyst might say, "Ah, more resistance. You confirm my interpretation." And if you agree, well, you might hear something like "Excellent, no more resistance. You confirm my interpretation." The analyst does not lose many of these arguments, and most psychologists find this kind of thinking unproductive.

The Psychodynamic Perspective

Although few therapists practice strict psychoanalysis today, Freud's innovative techniques for healing have broadly influenced the work of many of them. These therapists make *psychodynamic assumptions* (that is, assumptions related to psychoanalysis). They try to understand a person's problems by looking at childhood experiences, unconscious drives, and unresolved conflicts. But those working from a

▲ **Costs of Therapy**
Traditional psychoanalytic therapy typically costs more than $100 per session and continues for months, even years. Insurance companies will not cover so many sessions, and few people can afford it on their own.

resistance In psychoanalysis, the blocking from consciousness of anxiety-laden material.

interpretation In psychoanalysis, the analyst's noting of ideas on the meaning behind dreams, resistances, and other significant behaviors to promote insight.

transference In psychoanalysis, the patient's transfer of strong emotions (such as love or hatred) linked with other relationships to the analyst.

PSYCHOLOGY IN THE REAL WORLD

Are Alternative Therapies Effective?

You may have noticed that we haven't yet discussed many of the therapy techniques you see advertised in the media. Have you heard of aromatherapists, reflexologists, or anger-release therapists? Princess Diana of England sought psychological relief from representatives of all three.[5] The world is filled with would-be healers making claims that do not stand up to scientific research. Here, at least as much as anywhere else, you will need to apply your critical thinking skills to assess such claims. Testimonials and popular interest aside, what does the evidence say about alternative therapies? Let's take a closer look at one of them: light-exposure therapy.

Light-Exposure Therapy

Some call it the wintertime blahs. Others call it the cold weather blues. Therapists recognize this legitimate form of depression as *seasonal affective disorder* (SAD). Whatever you call it, the feelings accompanying this condition seem to result from the decreased amount of sunlight during the winter months.

About 20 years ago, therapists working for the National Institute of Mental Health came up with a treatment idea. What if SAD patients received a daily dose of bright light? Would the extra light nudge their natural body rhythms back into a normal pattern? Clinical studies indeed reported that light brought re-

lief from the winter blues. Now you can buy or rent light boxes to increase your exposure to light and brighten your winter days. But wait a minute. Doesn't this sound like yet another example of an *expectation effect* ("I feel better because I thought I would feel better")? In this case, additional research has shown that there is more to light-exposure therapy than meets the eye.

One of these studies exposed SAD patients to either bright light treatments or to a phony placebo treatment (a "negative ion generator"). Investigators displayed equal enthusiasm about each treatment. After four weeks, 61 percent of the participants

psychodynamic perspective today are more likely to request weekly meetings for only a few months, in contrast to Freud's recommendation of several meetings weekly for many years.

Freud's techniques have also influenced *interpersonal psychotherapy.* Therapists using this 12- to 16-session method try to foster insight into the origins of a problem, but they focus on what's going on in the patient's life *now,* rather than trying to untie the knots of a long-ago childhood conflict. Interpersonal therapy asks how current relationships can be mended and social skills improved. This attempt to find relief for symptoms caused by today's conflicts has proved effective against depression.[6]

To see how psychoanalytic, psychodynamic, and interpersonal therapies differ, consider the case of Serena, a college senior who is two months away from graduating. She has been going out with the same person for two squabble-free years, but recently, they've been having regular disagreements. Serena has developed trouble sleeping, and she reports feeling easily irritated and depressed. How would therapists from the three approaches treat Serena?

PSYCHOLOGY IN THE REAL WORLD (Continued)

receiving bright light in the morning had improved tremendously, but only 32 percent of those receiving "negative ion" treatment had improved.[7] Alfred Lewy and his colleagues reported a biological link between morning light exposure and levels of melatonin, a hormone that plays a role in body rhythm regulation. It turns out that increased exposure to light was indeed a bright idea for treating people with SAD.[8]

Note that applying scientific reasoning and critical thinking while considering new claims does not necessarily mean you will debunk the claim, but it does mean you will know with more confidence whether the claim has merit. A group of researchers recently analyzed data from over 34,000 participants and concluded that SAD is more of a myth than reality! What's the truth on SAD? Keep an eye out for future studies the will help, um, shed light on seasonal affective disorder.[9]

People who seek therapy usually feel better after getting help. People who could use professional therapy but do not seek it may recover anyway. This ability to spontaneously recover shows that humans are resourceful and that we have a capacity to care for one another. Still, we know that those who receive therapeutic help are more likely to get well than those who do not. Effective therapists possess empathy for their clients, show care and concern, listen respectfully, and reassure. They help give hope to those who have lost it while providing a perspective on life that is fresh and believable.

▲ **Seasonal Affective Disorder**
Those with seasonal affective disorder have shown improvement when exposed to bright lights.

THINK ABOUT . . . Psychology in the Real World

1. What evidence supports light-exposure therapy?

2. Why are some therapists skeptical of light-exposure therapy?

3. If you could design a study to examine the prevalence of seasonal affective disorder, how would you do it?

- A psychoanalyst would want to delve completely into Serena's childhood over the course of many visits. The analyst might ask her about her dreams or watch to see whether she transfers her feelings for her significant other to the analyst.

- A psychodynamic therapist would also be interested in Serena's childhood and how that may be affecting her relationships, but this therapist would meet with Serena in far fewer sessions and would focus more on her current issues.

- An interpersonal therapist would also seek insight but would encourage Serena to think almost exclusively about her current symptoms and problems. Thus, attention might focus on how she can assess the relationship, resolve disputes with her significant other, and better express her emotions.

Before moving on to the next perspective, take a look at the wider world of psychological therapy in Psychology in the Real World: Are Alternative Therapies Effective?

Humanistic Therapies

 34-2 How do humanistic therapists try to help people with emotional problems?

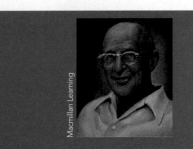

CARL ROGERS (1902–1987)
Humanistic psychologist who developed client-centered therapy and stressed the importance of acceptance, genuineness, and empathy in fostering human growth.

client-centered therapy
A humanistic therapy, developed by Rogers, in which the therapist uses techniques such as active listening within a genuine, accepting, empathic environment to facilitate the client's growth.

active listening Empathic listening in which the listener echoes, restates, and clarifies.

To a humanistic therapist, the potential for self-fulfillment already exists in each of us. Humanistic therapy aims to promote self-fulfillment by increasing self-acceptance and self-awareness. The humanistic approach to therapy differs from the psychoanalytic approach by

- fostering growth instead of relieving illness; thus, these therapists refer to people in therapy as "clients," not "patients."
- focusing on the present and future instead of the past.
- emphasizing conscious thoughts instead of unconscious thoughts.

Humanistic therapists typically use *nondirective* methods: Therapists listen without interpreting and do not direct clients to any particular insight. **Carl Rogers** developed the most famous form of humanistic therapy. His **client-centered therapy** uses active listening within a genuine, accepting, and empathic environment to facilitate the client's growth. Rogers believed that for client-centered therapy to be successful, therapists must provide a supportive environment that includes **active listening,** where the therapist echoes, restates, and then clarifies the client's thoughts and feelings:

- *Echoing feelings*—The therapist mirrors the feelings of the client with statements like "That must really be frustrating."
- *Restating*—The therapist uses the words of the client to summarize the conversation.
- *Clarifying*—The therapist encourages the client to say more by asking questions like "Could you give me an example of what you're saying?"

The following excerpt is an example of an interaction between a Rogerian therapist and a client. See if you can spot where the therapist echoes, restates, and clarifies feelings:[10]

> **Client:** I really feel bad today . . . just terrible.
> **Therapist:** You're feeling pretty bad.
> **Client:** Yeah, I'm angry and that's made me feel bad, especially when I can't do anything about it. I just have to live with it and shut up.
> **Therapist:** You're very angry and feel like there's nothing you can safely do with your feelings.

Client: Uh-huh. I mean . . . if I yell at my wife, she gets hurt. If I don't say anything to her, I feel tense.

Therapist: You're between a rock and a hard place—no matter what you do, you'll wind up feeling bad.

Client: I mean she chews ice all day and all night. I feel stupid saying this. It's petty, I know. But when I sit there and try to concentrate I hear all these slurping and crunching noises. I can't stand it . . . and I yell. She feels hurt—I feel bad—like I shouldn't have said anything.

Therapist: So, when you finally say something you feel bad afterward.

Client: Yeah, I can't say anything to her without getting mad and saying more than I should. And then I cause more trouble than it's worth.

The therapist is accepting and understanding while becoming this client's psychological mirror. The goal is for the client to be able to see himself more clearly at the conclusion of therapy.

Can therapy be *completely* nondirective? That is, should a therapist stick to echoing and restating statements by the patient to be successful? Rogers said *No,* adding that nondirectivity was not the key element of therapy. Rather, the client should feel *unconditional positive regard,* a feeling of being accepted that does not depend on any specific behaviors. This feeling will follow, Rogers believed, from the therapist's nonjudgmental, accepting environment. Unconditional positive regard allows clients to feel valued and to accept themselves.

If you want to become a more active listener in your relationships, look back at the three suggestions Rogers made to achieve this result. Active listening is not reserved only for therapists. Think of your best friends. Chances are, you like them because they are good listeners.

> **Carl Rogers**
> The psychologist (far right) is actively listening to a client during this client-centered group therapy session.

Michael Rougier/The LIFE Picture Collection/Getty Images

MAKE IT STICK!

1. What would humanistic therapists say is essential for productive therapy?

2. True or False: Humanistic therapist Carl Rogers would most likely agree that most psychological problems are caused by transference.

Behavior Therapies

  34-3 How do behavior therapists apply the principles of classical conditioning and operant conditioning?

Say you have a fear of dogs. A psychoanalyst might try to trace this fear to some unresolved childhood conflict. A humanistic therapist might offer you unconditional positive regard while helping you get in touch with your feelings. Behavior therapists would reject both of these approaches and instead attempt to replace your fearful thoughts and related behaviors with constructive, relaxing thoughts

behavior therapy Therapy that applies learning principles to the elimination of unwanted behaviors.

and actions. **Behavior therapy** applies learning principles to the elimination of unwanted behaviors. Both classical conditioning and operant conditioning principles have contributed to the behavior therapy methods.

Classical Conditioning Techniques

Classical conditioning is a type of learning in which we associate two things that occur together. Classical conditioning pioneer John B. Watson showed that we can learn to associate most emotions with behaviors, such as fear with public speaking. If we can learn such fears, can we "unlearn" them? In some cases, *Yes,* through the process of *counterconditioning,* a behavior therapy technique that teaches us to associate new responses to places or things that have in the past triggered unwanted behaviors. Two popular counterconditioning techniques are systematic desensitization and aversive conditioning.

Orientations ▲
The psychoanalytic (Freudian) therapist may ask questions about childhood, whereas the behavior therapist asks about current actions and activities.

systematic desensitization
A type of counterconditioning that associates a pleasant, relaxed state with gradually increasing anxiety-triggering stimuli.

Systematic Desensitization Think of something that makes you feel anxious. Perhaps it's a difficult test you have to take, the opening night of a show you're in, or the first minute of an athletic contest you've suited up for. Now, imagine the most relaxing place for you on Earth. Is it a secluded beach on a beautiful, sunny day? A quiet valley in the mountains? A hillside close to a pond? Now, can you think of the anxious situation and the relaxing situation at the same time? If you're like most people, you won't be able to. You might be able to alternate between the two settings quickly, but you won't be able to imagine both simultaneously. The most widely used behavior therapy is based on just this idea: You can't feel relaxed and anxious at the same time. **Systematic desensitization** is a type of counterconditioning that associates a pleasant, relaxed state with gradually increasing anxiety-triggering stimuli.[11-13] If you can repeatedly relax when faced with increasingly higher levels of the anxiety-producing stimulus, you can gradually overcome your problem. This technique is commonly used to treat phobias, so we can apply it to a common fear: flying in an airplane.

A behavior therapist using systematic desensitization may start by having you write down a hierarchy of anxiety-triggering flying situations. Your fear-of-flying hierarchy would include a range of situations from least to most anxiety provoking. What flying-related event would cause you the worst anxiety? How about being seated in an airplane while it takes off? If so, this would be the bottom item on your list. What flying-related event would cause you only a little anxiety? Perhaps looking at an airplane from a mile away? This would be the top item on your list.

After establishing your hierarchy, you would be trained to relax using *progressive relaxation.* With this technique, you learn to relax different sets of muscle groups until you approach a near-complete state of relaxation. While you are in that state, your therapist tells you to close your eyes and to imagine the first (least troublesome) item on your hierarchy. If imagining this scene causes you to feel anxious, you signal by raising an index finger. The therapist then instructs you to quit thinking about the situation and to practice deep relaxation again. You repeat these steps until imagining the scene does not cause anxiety. At that point, you move to the second situation on your hierarchy—perhaps looking at a photo of a plane (see **Figure 34.1**). After several therapy sessions, thoughts and photos are replaced by experience, beginning with somewhat easy tasks like watching planes land a mile away and leading gradually to boarding an airplane. Eventually, you become a confident flyer. Conquering the fear of the actual event increases self-confidence.[14,15]

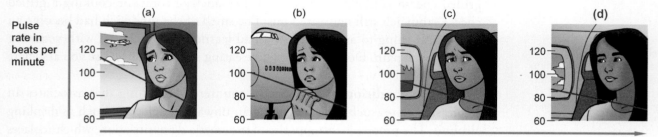

Pulse rate in beats per minute

(a) (b) (c) (d)

Time

▲ **FIGURE 34.1**
Systematic Desensitization
Systematic desensitization helps people overcome fears, such as a fear of flying. Patients work through a hierarchy of anxiety-producing events associated with flying and learn to relax at each level of the hierarchy. For instance, once the photo of an airplane no longer produces anxiety (a), the person with the fear may go to an airport and look at a real airplane from far away (b). Eventually, the patient works up to touching the plane, boarding the plane (c), and ideally, becoming a confident flyer (d).

Sometimes an anxiety-arousing situation is too embarrassing, challenging, or expensive to be re-created. A breakthrough in systematic desensitization occurred with the introduction of **virtual reality exposure therapy.**[16] Virtual reality is more vivid than your imagination. You wear a headset projecting a three-dimensional virtual world into your visual field. Virtual reality exposure therapy has effectively helped people cope with fears of flying, public speaking, heights, post-traumatic stress, and animals.[17–23] These results are encouraging. With today's sophisticated animation technology, it seems likely that avatars (true-to-life computer representations of people seeking help) will be increasingly common in such treatments, helping more people work through their fears.[24]

Systematic desensitization has been combined with modeling to help some patients overcome disruptive fears. For instance, someone with a fear of dogs could watch another person playing with and petting a dog. Gradually, the person learns to model the coach's behavior and touches and handles the dog.[25]

virtual reality exposure therapy An anxiety treatment that progressively exposes people to simulations of their greatest fears, such as airplane flying, spiders, or public speaking.

Qi qi-Imaginechina/AP Photo

William Britten /E+/Getty Images

◄ **A 3-D Virtual World**
The vivid images displayed in this virtual reality headset should help desensitize this person to his fear of heights.

Whether using desensitization or modeling, behavior therapists do not spend a lot of time looking for the cause of the problem, trying to find out when you first experienced it, or considering your level of self-awareness. They believe that it is overcoming the maladaptive behavior that helps you feel better about yourself.

Aversive Conditioning During my second year of college, I suffered a two-day stomach illness. The last food I ate before becoming sick was a grilled cheese sandwich. Weeks later, the smell of someone cooking a grilled cheese sandwich still nauseated me. The smell of the sandwich had become an unpleasant thing to avoid because I had learned to associate it with vomiting and stomach pain. Do you have trouble eating some food because you associate it with illness?

Aversive conditioning is a type of counterconditioning that associates an unpleasant state (such as nausea) with an unwanted behavior (such as drinking alcohol). The process is the opposite of systematic desensitization, which replaces a negative (fearful) response with a positive (relaxed) response. Aversive conditioning replaces a *positive* response to a harmful experience (like drinking alcohol) with a *negative* (aversive) response. Aversive conditioning has been used to treat nail biting and the sexual deviancy of child molesters. We will use the treatment of alcohol abuse to show how this form of therapy works.

In treating a dependence on alcohol with aversive conditioning, therapists give people their drink of choice but with a little twist. Added to the drink is a tasteless, odorless drug that produces severe nausea. The goal is to link drinking with violent nausea so that the person develops an aversion to the smell and taste of the drink. The formerly positive reaction to drinking becomes negative (see **Figure 34.2**).

Does this treatment for alcoholism last? In one study, 63 percent of the people treated with aversive conditioning were still abstaining from alcohol one year later.[26] These people had received several booster treatments during that year. Unfortunately, however, only 33 percent of them were successfully abstaining from alcohol after three years.

Therapists recognize the limitations of aversive treatment. They often combine it with another form of treatment to produce the best results.

> **aversive conditioning**
> A type of counterconditioning that associates an unpleasant state (such as nausea) with an unwanted behavior (such as drinking alcohol).

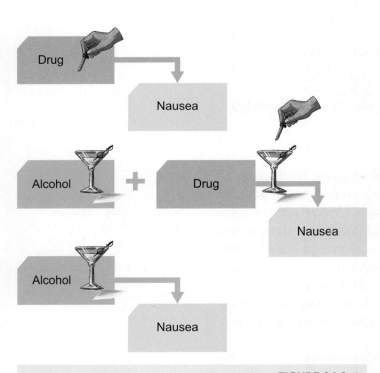

FIGURE 34.2
Unwanted Reactions
In an example of aversive conditioning, people with a dependence on alcohol agree to have a substance put in their drink that makes them vomit. In theory, these people associate the vomiting with drinking and become less inclined to drink substances containing alcohol.

Operant Conditioning Techniques

Our voluntary behaviors are greatly influenced by their consequences. Therapists have applied this basic principle of *operant conditioning* to help people solve problems at home, at school, and in other settings. This simple principle—reward desired behaviors and withhold rewards or punish unwanted behaviors—has even helped those with disorders learn to function in normal settings. People with schizophrenia, for example, have been taught to act more rationally and behave more appropriately with others. Individuals with intellectual disabilities have learned basic self-care. In both cases, therapists shaped behavior by reinforcing small steps in the right direction.

Operant conditioning techniques also give hope to parents of children with autism. These children are typically unresponsive to others, lack communication skills, and often engage in unusually repetitive behaviors. In one study, 19 uncommunicative, withdrawn 3-year-olds with autism took part in an intensive 2-year study. Parents worked 40 hours per week reinforcing appropriate or desired behavior while ignoring or punishing self-abusive and aggressive behaviors.[27] By first grade, only 1 out of 40 children with autism *who did not* undergo treatment showed improvement. However, 9 of the 19 receiving treatment became successfully functioning first graders with normal intelligence. Once again, therapy provides hope.

One operant conditioning technique has been used in institutions to encourage getting out of bed on time, dressing, cleaning a room, and cooperating with others. A **token economy** attempts to modify behavior by giving rewards for desired behaviors with some kind of small item. Patients (or in some cases, inmates) earn the tokens by behaving appropriately and then exchange them for simple rewards, like candy, or privileges, like watching television. Token economies have been successfully used with various populations (people with schizophrenia, delinquent teens, and other groups) and in various settings, including day-care centers, schools, hospitals, and my own home!

Critics point to two problems with behavior modification, one practical and the other ethical. First, what happens after a person is no longer reinforced for proper behavior? People who leave an institution will not receive tokens for getting out of bed on time, after all. Behavior modification therapists are aware of this problem, and they attempt to gradually shift patients from tokens and other external rewards and move them toward more internal rewards, such as satisfaction from receiving others' approval.

The second criticism asks the question of whether behavior modification is ethical. Is it right to deprive someone of a television program or dessert to obtain a desired behavior? Or is this process too controlling? Proponents insist that they are working to eliminate or modify destructive behaviors and that an improved life outweighs the temporary loss of privileges. The debate continues.

LIFE MATTERS

Although behavioral therapies for autistic children have yielded results in making them more typical, there is a great deal of criticism in removing common autistic behaviors (like flapping or spinning). Feeling that you are not accepted for who you are creates shame. Autistic advocates envision a world where their differences will be appreciated and valued rather than removed to fit into society.

token economy An operant conditioning procedure that attempts to modify behavior by rewarding desired behaviors with some small item.

MAKE IT STICK!

1. Which of the following psychological problems would most likely respond well to systematic desensitization therapy?

   a. hearing voices that aren't there
   b. feeling depressed and suicidal
   c. acting violently and aggressively toward others
   d. feeling anxiety about flying on an airplane

2. A parent who gives her child a gold star every time the child reads a book is using which form of behavior therapy?

   a. token economy
   b. positive conditioning
   c. systematic desensitization
   d. unconditional positive regard

3. True or False: Aversive conditioning is a type of counterconditioning.

Cognitive Therapies

 34-4 What is the basis of cognitive therapy and cognitive-behavioral therapy?

A revolution has taken place in psychology in the last half-century as psychologists have refocused their interest on thought processes—*cognition*—as well as behavior. This revolution is apparent in therapy, where almost half of all clinical psychologists working in university settings refer to themselves as having some sort of cognitive orientation[28] (see **Figure 34.3**). These therapists believe our thinking affects how we feel. Cognitive explanations of illnesses like depression include the idea that self-blame ("I lost my job because I'm worthless") and overgeneralization ("I'm worthless at everything") set the stage for feeling depressed. Cognitive therapists assume that our thoughts filter the events in our lives and influence our emotional reactions to them. **Cognitive therapies** teach people new, more adaptive ways of thinking and acting.

The best psychological therapies for depression, especially major depression, appear to be cognitively based. A depressed friend might interpret your friendship as pity, your suggestions as criticism, and your questions as blame. These negative thoughts fuel depression, sustaining and worsening negative moods. In addition, whereas most of us tend to judge ourselves favorably, this *self-serving bias* is absent during depression. When something good happens, people with depression do not give themselves credit. The person might, for example, explain away an award for being helpful in class as the result of an external circumstance: "They probably drew my name out of a hat." People with depression are good at blaming themselves squarely for any failure. What was the reason for the failing grade on the U.S. history test? "I'm stupid." (Not "I didn't study hard enough" or "the test covered material the teacher hadn't gone over in class.")

Cognitive therapists teach clients to think constructively instead of destructively (see **Figure 34.4**). They try to help depressed people take more responsibility for things that go well and to encourage them to give less permanent and devastating explanations for failure. One researcher and her colleagues showed depressed adults the advantages of optimistic *explanatory styles*.[29] The researchers trained these adults to reform their negative thinking patterns and asked them to record each day's good events and the role they played in each event. Depression in these newly trained positive thinkers dropped significantly, compared with levels of depression in people waiting for treatment to become available (see **Figure 34.5**). Furthermore, research shows that previously depressed college students and young children who have been trained to dispute self-defeating or negative thoughts are 50 percent less likely to develop depression in the future.[30,31] Clearly, thoughts matter.

Cognitive-behavioral therapy combines cognitive therapy (changing self-defeating thoughts) with behavior therapy (changing inappropriate behaviors).

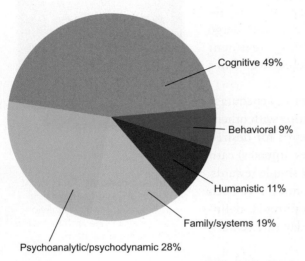

Cognitive 49%

Behavioral 9%

Humanistic 11%

Family/systems 19%

Psychoanalytic/psychodynamic 28%

FIGURE 34.3
Psychologists' Orientations
Almost half of all psychologists working in university settings who conduct therapy say they have some sort of cognitive orientation.
(From Mayne et al., 1994.)

cognitive therapy Therapy that teaches people new, more adaptive ways of thinking and acting.

cognitive-behavioral therapy Integrative therapy that combines changing self-defeating thinking with changing inappropriate behaviors.

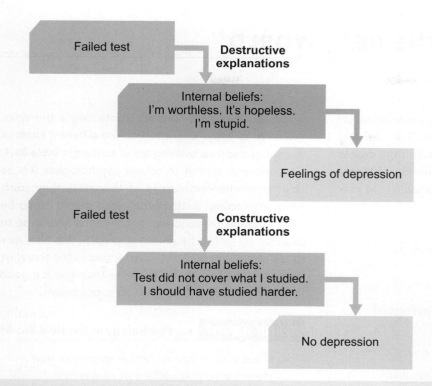

FIGURE 34.4
Constructive Interpretations
Cognitive therapists help people explain bad events constructively instead of destructively.

With this therapy, people become aware of their irrationally negative thoughts and are taught to think more realistically and to practice behaviors that are incompatible with the problem.[32] Let's work through an example of cognitive-behavioral therapy.

Obsessive-compulsive disorder (OCD) is characterized by unwanted repetitive thoughts (obsessions), actions (compulsions), or both. In one study, therapists had people with this disorder view a positive emission tomography (PET) scan that showed abnormal activity in their brain when a compulsive urge, like the desire to repeatedly wash hands, was present.[33] Next, the therapists taught these people to relabel their compulsions, instead telling themselves, "I'm having a compulsive urge," and attributing the urge to their brain's abnormal activity. Finally, these people learned to engage in a pleasant alternative behavior, like gardening or taking a walk, instead of acting on the urge to wash their hands. The goal was to "unstick" the brain by focusing attention on something else and using a different part of the brain. After two or three months of weekly therapy sessions and practice at home, most participants showed normal brain activity on their PET scans and a decrease in obsessive-compulsive disorder symptoms. Several additional studies show that cognitive-behavioral therapy is especially effective in treating depression and anxiety.[34–36] (For information about other symptoms that may signal a need for professional help, see Psychology in the Real World: Seeking Help.)

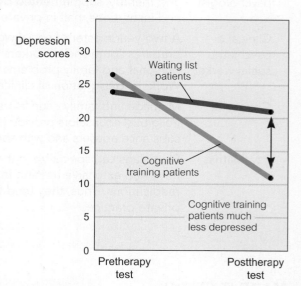

FIGURE 34.5
Optimistic Outlook
Participants who learn optimistic ways of explaining negative events stand a good chance of seeing depression levels decline. (From Rabin et al., 1986.)

PSYCHOLOGY IN THE REAL WORLD

Seeking Help

Chances are that you or someone you know will need psychological services at some point. The ups and downs of a hectic world are inevitable, but the downs are sometimes a little more than we can handle alone. The following are common signs of trouble that may require professional help:

- Thoughts of suicide
- Self-destructive behavior, such as abuse of alcohol or another drug
- Disruptive fears
- Deep and lasting depression or feelings of hopelessness
- Sudden mood shifts
- Compulsive rituals, such as hand washing

Knowing you need some help to make it through a rough time in your life is a sign of strength, not weakness. If you do consider contacting a therapist, you need to know where to go. The different kinds of therapists and their training are described in **Table 34.1**. Counselors at school or school psychologists will be able to recommend names of therapists they trust. After contacting a therapist, you should describe your situation or concerns and ask the therapist to describe his or her treatment approach. It is also wise to ask about the therapist's credentials (is the therapist licensed?) and fees. If you think the therapist is a good fit for you, consider setting up an appointment.

THINK ABOUT . . . Psychology in the Real World

1. What should you ask a therapist after you describe your situations or concerns?
2. Why is it important to ask questions of a potential therapist?

TABLE 34.1   Therapists and Their Training

Type	Description
Clinical psychologist	Most are psychologists with a Ph.D. or Psy.D. and expertise in research, assessment, and therapy, supplemented by a supervised internship. About half work in agencies and institutions, half in private practice.
Clinical or psychiatric social worker	A two-year master of social work graduate program plus postgraduate supervision prepares some social workers to offer psychotherapy, mostly to people with everyday personal and family problems. About half have earned the National Association of Social Workers' designation of clinical social worker.
Counselor	Marriage and family counselors specialize in problems arising from family relations. Pastoral (religious) counselors provide counseling to countless people. Abuse counselors work with substance abusers and with spouse and child abusers and their victims.
Psychiatrist	Physicians can specialize in the treatment of psychological disorders. Not all psychiatrists have had extensive training in psychotherapy, but as M.D.s they can prescribe medications. Thus, they tend to see those with the most serious problems. Many have a private practice.

MAKE IT STICK!

1. The way we think about life events is central to the _____ approach to therapy.

2. True or False: Combining a cognitive approach with behavioral techniques never leads to improvement in self-defeating thoughts and inappropriate behaviors.

3. What is the term or phrase we use to describe the tendency to judge ourselves favorably?

Family and Group Therapies

 34-5 What are the advantages of group therapy, and when is group therapy most often used?

Most therapies we've examined so far can occur either individually, one on one with a therapist, or in small groups of 6 to 10 people. Cognitive, behavior, and humanistic therapists lead group therapy sessions that typically run up to 90 minutes per week. Group therapy participants discuss and react to one another's issues. Families in conflict are often recommended for group therapy.

THE SEVEN DWARFS AFTER THERAPY

Compared with one-on-one therapy, group therapy has some advantages:

- Therapists can help more people in less time.

- Therapy sessions typically cost less.

- The social context of the therapy allows people to discover that others have problems similar to their own. Simply learning that others share the same troublesome feelings can bring great relief.

- Group meetings foster a sense of community. Bereaved, addicted, or divorced people often have a longing for the connectedness found in a group.[37]

▲ **Helpful Group Therapy?** Nobody really wants to be called Dopey or Grumpy, do they?

Families sometimes need outside help when the group's need to connect emotionally conflicts with one individual's need to be more independent. **Family therapy,** which treats the family as a system, is a special kind of group therapy. A child who rebels inappropriately adds to and is affected by family tension. Family therapy views an individual's unwanted behaviors as influenced by or directed at other members of the family. Family therapists help the members of the family discover the roles they play inside their family's social unit. They try to guide the family toward positive relationships and improved communication. Opening the communication pathways within a family helps its members learn new ways of resolving and preventing conflicts.[38,39]

family therapy Therapy that views an individual's unwanted behaviors as influenced by or directed at other members of the family and attempts to guide the family toward positive relationships and improved communication.

Perhaps it comes as no surprise that the number of support groups for those experiencing difficulty continues to rise. Alcoholics Anonymous (AA) reports having more than 2 million members in 114,000 functioning groups worldwide. AA's 12-step program has helped those dependent on alcohol get sober when compared to other alcohol treatment programs.[40,41] Those seeking the comfort of a support group often enjoy the emotional boost achieved by being around and interacting with others.[42] See **Table 34.2** for a comparison of the types of therapy we have discussed.

▲ **Family Therapy** When a family receives therapy, relationships and communication typically improve.

TABLE 34.2 Comparison of a Sample of Major Psychotherapies

Therapy	Assumed Problem	Therapy Aims	Method
Psychodynamic	Unconscious forces and childhood experiences	Reduced anxiety through self-insight	Analysis and interpretation
Humanistic	Barriers to self-understanding and self-acceptance	Personal growth through self-insight	Active listening and unconditional positive regard
Behavioral	Maladaptive behaviors	Extinction and relearning	Counterconditioning, exposure, desensitization, aversive conditioning, and operant conditioning
Cognitive	Negative, self-defeating thinking	Healthier thinking and self-talk	Reveal and reverse self-blaming
Family and group	Stressful relationships	Relationship healing	Understanding family social system; exploring roles; improved communication

---

MAKE IT STICK!

1. True or False: Group therapy gets to the real root of psychological problems, but individual therapy takes less time.

2. Ethan has been skipping classes, hanging out with a rough crowd, and getting into serious trouble at school when he does attend. The school guidance counselor has heard that there may be some trouble at home. She has arranged for the school psychologist to meet with Ethan, his sisters and brothers, and his parents. She has set up a _____ therapy session.

3. True or False: One good thing about group therapy is that it allows people to discover that many others have similar, if not the same, problems to work through.

Module 34 Summary and Assessment

Psychological Therapies

34-1 What is psychotherapy in general, and what is Sigmund Freud's psychoanalytic theory in particular?

- Psychotherapy is an interaction between a trained therapist and someone who is seeking to overcome psychological difficulties or achieve personal growth.

- Psychoanalysis is a theory of personality and a therapeutic technique that attributes thoughts and actions to unconscious motives and conflicts. According to psychoanalysis, psychological problems can be resolved if the analyst helps the patient bring the repressed, unconscious conflicts and impulses of childhood into the conscious mind.

- Psychoanalytic theory is criticized because of its assumption of repression, its expense to patients, and the irrefutable nature of its conclusions. Current therapists modify traditional psychoanalytic theory, using psychodynamic assumptions to understand unconscious drives and conflicts.

34-2 How do humanistic therapists try to help people with emotional problems?

- Humanistic therapy aims to promote self-fulfillment by increasing self-acceptance and self-awareness.

- Carl Rogers developed the most famous form of humanistic therapy. His client-centered therapy uses active listening within a genuine, accepting, and empathic environment to facilitate the client's growth.

- During active listening, the therapist echoes, restates, and then clarifies the client's thoughts and feelings.

 34-3 How do behavior therapists apply the principles of classical conditioning and operant conditioning?

- Behavior therapy applies classical conditioning learning principles to the elimination of unwanted behaviors through such methods as systematic desensitization and aversive conditioning.

- Therapists apply the basic principles of operant conditioning (reward desired behaviors and withhold rewards or punish unwanted behaviors) to help people solve problems. A token economy is one such technique, which provides rewards (some kind of token) for desired behaviors.

Summative Assessment

1. Sigmund Freud was the founder of what controversial theory?

   a. psychoanalytic therapy
   b. light-exposure therapy
   c. client-centered therapy
   d. behavior therapy

2. What type of therapy uses a method that involves weekly sessions over a few months and focuses on what's going on in the patient's life now?

   a. psychoanalytic
   b. psychodynamic
   c. interpersonal
   d. eclectic

3. What is the key to client-centered therapy?

   a. light exposure
   b. active listening
   c. free association
   d. transference

 34-4 What is the basis of cognitive therapy and cognitive-behavioral therapy?

- Cognitive therapy teaches people new, more adaptive ways of thinking and acting.

- Cognitive therapists teach clients to think constructively instead of destructively. Negative thoughts can fuel psychological issues, such as depression, and sustain and worsen negative moods. Changing destructive thinking patterns into productive ones, like optimistic explanatory styles, can be beneficial to patients.

- Cognitive-behavioral therapy combines cognitive therapy (changing self-defeating thoughts) with behavior therapy (changing inappropriate behaviors).

 34-5 What are the advantages of group therapy, and when is group therapy most often used?

- Many therapies can be conducted individually or in group sessions.

- Group therapies can help more people in less time, cost less, and foster a sense of community.

- Family therapy can be of benefit because it views an individual's unwanted behaviors as influenced by or directed at other members of the family.

4. What does Carl Rogers call a feeling of being accepted that does not depend on any specific behaviors?

   a. psychodynamic assumptions
   b. latent content
   c. repressed memories
   d. unconditional positive regard

5. What type of therapy applies learning principles to the elimination of unwanted behaviors?

   a. behavior therapy
   b. psychotherapy
   c. interpersonal therapy
   d. humanistic therapy

6. What type of therapy gradually helps you overcome an anxiety-producing stimulus?

   a. operant conditioning
   b. systematic desensitization
   c. aversive conditioning
   d. cognitive therapy

7. What type of therapy can help desensitize people to fears?

   a. token economy
   b. cognitive therapy
   c. virtual reality therapy
   d. aversive conditioning

8. What is the process behind aversive conditioning?

   a. replacing a positive response to a harmful experience with a negative response
   b. replacing a negative response to a fearful experience with a positive response

   c. overcoming a maladaptive behavior to feel better about yourself
   d. rewarding desired behaviors and withholding rewards or punishing unwanted behaviors

9. What do cognitive therapists believe?

   a. Our thinking affects how we feel.
   b. We need to be rewarded for our behaviors.
   c. Desensitization helps us to overcome fears.
   d. Our childhood traumas affect us today.

10. What type of therapy helps people become aware of irrationally negative thoughts and behaviors?

   a. cognitive-behavioral therapy
   b. aversive conditioning
   c. virtual-reality therapy
   d. systematic desensitization

KEY TERMS AND KEY PEOPLE

psychotherapy, p. 521

eclectic approach, p. 521

psychoanalysis, p. 522

resistance, p. 523

interpretation, p. 523

transference, p. 523

client-centered therapy, p. 526

active listening, p. 526

behavior therapy, p. 528

systematic desensitization, p. 528

virtual reality exposure therapy, p. 529

aversive conditioning, p. 530

token economy, p. 531

cognitive therapy, p. 532

cognitive-behavioral therapy, p. 532

family therapy, p. 535

Sigmund Freud (1856–1939), p. 521

Carl Rogers (1902–1987), p. 526

Biomedical Therapies

Medications are available for many psychological disorders, but in deciding to use them, one must consider the side effects as well as the potential benefits.

Learning Goals

35-1 Describe the uses and effectiveness of antipsychotic, antianxiety, and antidepressant drugs.

35-2 Explain what "shock therapy" is, including what it is used for as well as its effectiveness.

35-3 Summarize why lobotomies were performed and why they are no longer used.

Many films have explored **biomedical therapies**—the treatment of psychological disorders by changing the brain's functioning with prescribed drugs, electroconvulsive therapy, or surgery. Two of them are classics that have won multiple Academy Awards, including Best Picture. In 1975, *One Flew Over the Cuckoo's Nest* illustrated the horror of inappropriately using shock treatments and brain surgery as a way of punishing hospitalized mental patients rather than treating them. In 2001, *A Beautiful Mind*, based on the true story of Nobel Prize–winning mathematician John Nash's descent into and apparent recovery from schizophrenia, brought the issue of involuntary drug treatment to the forefront. These films and numerous other movies and television shows illustrate the issues and controversies that swirl around biomedical therapies.

> **biomedical therapy**
> The treatment of psychological disorders by changing the brain's functioning with prescribed drugs, electroconvulsive therapy, or surgery.

The Everett Collection

The Everett Collection

> **Dramatic Illustrations**
> *One Flew Over the Cuckoo's Nest* (left) and *A Beautiful Mind* (right) both provide a historical perspective on how therapists have used biomedical treatments for mental disorders. They raise controversial issues related to these treatments.

Biomedical approaches have received a lot of media attention, some portraying them accurately and some not. This has led to a degree of fear and uncertainty. Here we set the record straight concerning the three major biomedical approaches: drugs, electric shock, and surgery.

FIGURE 35.1
Treatment or Torture?
Benjamin Rush developed this chair 200 years ago, believing that the restraint and restricted sensation it provided would help patients regain their self-control. Although this apparatus may look inhumane to us today, it was Rush who founded a movement to reform mental health care and treat mental patients with kindness. ▼

Drug Therapies

 35-1 What do antipsychotic, antianxiety, and antidepressant drugs do, and how effective are they?

Until the 1950s, few options existed for treating serious psychological disorders such as schizophrenia. People with these disorders were usually hospitalized, but even in this environment, the number of tools available for treatment was limited. Some hospitals were run well, with staff members who genuinely cared about the patients. Less-competent institutions served largely as warehouses, hiding away a segment of the population for whom little could be done. Patients often spent their days whiling away the hours in bare wards with no structured activities to occupy their time. Treatment—particularly in the 1800s and early 1900s—often subjected patients to mechanical devices that today strike us as little more than means of torture (see **Figure 35.1**). Restraints such as straitjackets, bed straps, and padded isolation rooms prevented violent patients from harming themselves or others. It was a bleak picture of long-term hospitalization in a mental health system that rarely produced improvement.

That picture changed dramatically with the development of effective drug therapies in the middle of the twentieth century. Suddenly, therapists had a way to help patients overcome the most devastating symptoms of their illness and "break through" to a more stable hold on reality. Moreover, these drugs made it possible to release patients from the large, warehouselike hospitals that everyone agreed constituted a horrible environment in which to get well. Patient populations at the hospitals dropped rapidly. Releasing hospitalized mental patients to their communities is called **deinstitutionalization,** a mouthful of a word but one that accurately describes what occurred. By the end of the last century, there were only one-fifth as many hospitalized patients as there were in 1950.[1]

In theory, deinstitutionalization was a wonderful advance. In practice, it did not work out quite as well as expected. If released patients lack resources and the support of family or friends, they often end up on the streets. This happened repeatedly as people were increasingly treated with drugs and released from state, county, and private mental hospitals. Once they were released, they often stopped taking their medication because of negative side effects and other reasons. The country's homeless population has increased as the population of hospitalized mental patients has decreased. Research shows that about one-quarter of the homeless population has a serious psychological disorder, compared to about 6 percent of all people in the U.S.[2] In other cases, individuals who would have been admitted to hospitals now end up in prison; up to a third of inmates have a serious psychological disorder.[3] The vast majority of these people are not violent; their untreated disorders simply make it impossible for them to cope with modern life.

Hospital or Warehouse? ▲
Before the advent of effective biomedical treatment, mental hospitals often did little more than house patients in bleak, crowded wards. How easy would it be to get well in an environment like this?

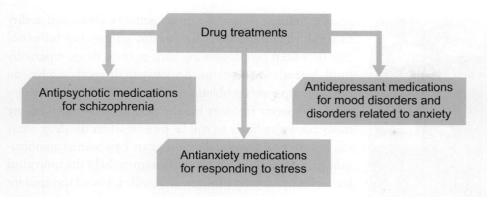

The drugs that enabled deinstitutionalization fall into three broad categories (see **Figure 35.2**): antipsychotic, antianxiety, and antidepressant. Like all drugs, they produce both main effects and side effects, some of which are undesirable. Establishing the correct dosage can be tricky because not everyone responds the same way. A decision to prescribe these drugs must therefore be made carefully, with attention to the details of the individual case.

Antipsychotic Drugs

Antipsychotic drugs are used primarily to treat *schizophrenia,* a serious psychological disorder that usually involves distorted thinking and perception in the form of delusions and hallucinations. Antipsychotic medications reduce the severity and number of delusions and hallucinations.[4] They also help people with schizophrenia focus their attention on significant aspects of their environment rather than irrelevant aspects. For example, antipsychotic drugs help patients who find it impossible to stop focusing endlessly on the color of a wall or the sound of a clock. This makes many patients feel more connected to the real world.

Antipsychotic drugs work by blocking the activity of the neurotransmitter dopamine, the brain chemical that, in high levels, is associated with schizophrenia. The first dopamine-lowering drug, and the one most responsible for starting the move toward deinstitutionalization, was Thorazine, which is still on the market. It has a host of negative side effects, including dry mouth, blurred vision, and constipation. Its most serious side effect is a permanent condition of muscle tremors known as *tardive dyskinesia,* which most often develops in patients who have taken large doses of the drug over a long period of time. This condition is similar to Parkinson's disease, which also is associated with low levels of dopamine.[5]

Note that no antipsychotic drug is a feel-good drug—these powerful substances do not produce the euphoric "high" that many people associate with drug use. The negative side effects are unpleasant enough that many people resist taking them, which contributes to the homelessness and prison problem of deinstitutionalized patients. Individuals no longer under the supervision of hospital staff may not be motivated enough to continue their medication. Then the symptoms of their disease return, and they have even more difficulty succeeding in the outside world.

Antianxiety Drugs

Antianxiety drugs are most often prescribed to treat people with anxiety disorders or people suffering from stress. Often, people taking antianxiety drugs have recently experienced significant stress in their lives—divorce, loss of a job, the death of a loved one, and so forth. These drugs work, in part, by boosting a neurotransmitter (GABA) that helps the brain reduce the anxiety associated with such stressful situations. This

deinstitutionalization The release of patients from mental hospitals into the community.

antipsychotic drugs A category of medications used primarily to treat schizophrenia.

antianxiety drugs A category of medications used to treat people undergoing significant stress; they can be helpful in treating people with anxiety disorders.

AFP/Newscom

relief of tension—plus the drugs' sedative effect and ability to produce euphoria—is a powerful reinforcing influence that may keep people coming back to these drugs repeatedly until dependency develops. Antianxiety drugs themselves do not solve a person's problems. Rather, they provide temporary relief. Whatever stressors led the person to take antianxiety medications are likely to still be present when the drug wears off. For all these reasons, these drugs are best used in combination with other forms of psychotherapy to help the individual learn effective coping strategies that will eliminate the need for the drug.

Examples of antianxiety drugs are Valium, Librium, and Xanax. They should not be taken with other central nervous system depressants, such as alcohol, because the interaction of the two types of substances can produce a potentially lethal overdose. Since psychological and physiological dependence may develop, antidepressants, instead of antianxiety drugs, are now frequently used to treat anxiety disorders.

Unavoidable Stress
Antianxiety drugs may be helpful for individuals suffering from unusual levels of unavoidable stress, like these victims of the Japanese tsunami in 2011. The drugs provide temporary relief, but they do not solve the problem that led to the stress in the first place.

antidepressant drugs
A category of medications used primarily to boost serotonin levels in the brain; they can be helpful in treating major depression.

Antidepressant Drugs

As the name so clearly indicates, **antidepressant drugs** are useful for treating major depression. In recent years, they have also been used for obsessive-compulsive disorder, post-traumatic stress disorder, and other anxiety disorders.[6] There are several groups of antidepressants, classified by the way they work, but all of them affect neurotransmitter chemicals in the brain, particularly serotonin. Low levels of serotonin are associated with depression, and these drugs boost the mood-lifting effect of serotonin in the brain.

This category includes Prozac, Zoloft, Lexapro, and Celexa, all of which are classified as *selective serotonin reuptake inhibitors (SSRIs)*. This scary-sounding phrase simply describes what the drugs do, which is block the *reuptake,* or reabsorption, of serotonin after it has been released into the synapse—the gap separating two nerve cells (neurons) (see **Figure 35.3**). This blocking action causes the

Message is sent across synaptic gap.

Message is received; excess neurotransmitter molecules are reabsorbed by sending neuron.

Prozac partially blocks normal reuptake of the neurotransmitter serotonin; excess serotonin in synapse enhances its mood-lifting effect.

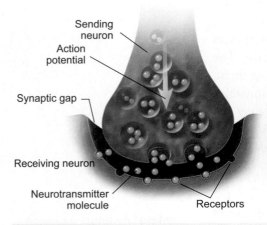

Sending neuron
Action potential
Synaptic gap
Receiving neuron
Neurotransmitter molecule
Receptors

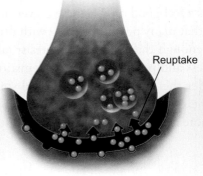

Reuptake

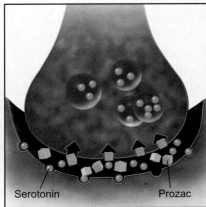

Serotonin   Prozac

▲ **FIGURE 35.3**
Prozac and the Brain
Prozac, an example of a selective serotonin reuptake inhibitor used to treat depression, acts to keep the neurotransmitter serotonin active longer than it otherwise would be. Higher levels of serotonin are associated with lower levels of depression.

serotonin to remain active in the synapse longer than it otherwise would. The use of antidepressants has skyrocketed in recent years, and they are taken by millions of people around the world. Almost one out of 20 men and one out of 10 women in the U.S. have taken an antidepressant in the last month.[7] Some veterinarians even prescribe Prozac for dogs to cure them of emotional problems perceived by their owners! Given their widespread use and the potential for negative side effects (such as weight gain and dizzy spells), it's important to remember that there are other effective ways to treat depression. Cognitive therapy, for example (described in Module 34), can be used instead of or in addition to drug therapy.

For reasons not yet fully understood, antidepressant medications must be taken for about a month before becoming fully effective. This *therapeutic lag* can be frustrating for the patient, especially if the first prescribed dose is too low to be effective or if the first prescribed drug produces undesirable side effects. In such cases, several more weeks must elapse before the effectiveness of a different dose or a new drug can be determined. During this time, other factors can increase or decrease the patient's depression, clouding the effects of the drug. Once the proper dose of the proper drug has been determined, however, a person can usually stay on it for long periods with no further adjustment.

Some newer drugs, like ketamine, operate on different neurotransmitters and may avoid therapeutic lag by providing relief more rapidly. However, serious side effects may occur, such as hallucinations, and the relief may only last a week.[8–11] Researchers are working to identify drugs that will maximize effectiveness with the fewest side effects.

Judging the overall effectiveness of antidepressants is particularly difficult because depression is a *cyclical* disorder (see **Figure 35.4**). This means that depression goes through cycles—just as normal moods do—lifting and deepening over time. Can you see how this cyclical path makes it difficult to judge whether a medication is working? Say that a person with depression begins taking a drug like Prozac. Before any judgment can be made, the one-month therapeutic lag must pass. What if the depression lifts after that month? Can you reliably say that the drug worked? *Not really*, because you still don't know whether the improvement was a result of the drug or of the cyclical nature of the disorder.

Other research confuses matters even further. One study combined the effects of almost two dozen carefully conducted studies. These studies compared the drug treatment results of one group given an antidepressant and another group given a *placebo*—a pill that has no chemical effect. People given the placebo reported almost as much improvement as people given the antidepressant medication.[12] In other words, people's belief that they would feel better after being given a pill had almost as much effect on mood as did the real serotonin-enhancing drug. More recent research indicates that the placebo effect could account for as much as 75 percent of the overall impact of the drug.[13–15]

Additional research will help determine whether the improvement prompted by antidepressants is more the result of the chemical effects of these drugs or the result of the expectations they produce. Such drugs sometimes have remarkably positive effects on people who might otherwise be seriously impaired, but they are not a miracle cure that instantly rids sufferers of their depression. Some negative media reports about the effects of the drugs—for example, that they produce suicidal behavior in a percentage of users—also require careful evaluation and have led to warning labels about the potential dangers of these drugs when used with adolescents. Remember, however, that users of antidepressant drugs are taking these substances precisely

HOW DO ANTIDEPRESSANTS WORK?

1. They affect brain neurotransmitters.
2. They don't work. People's moods improve on their own because of the cyclical nature of depression.
3. They work because users expect them to work (the placebo effect).

▲ **FIGURE 35.4**
A Mystery
Researchers have yet to nail down exactly how antidepressants work. Their effect may be a combination of the factors listed here or of other factors not yet identified.

because they are searching for relief from depression. It should come as no surprise that a percentage of these users are suicidal—not because of the drug but because of the severity of their disorder. This idea is supported by studies involving hundreds of thousands of depressed people who were shown to be *less* likely to commit suicide if antidepressants were prescribed.[16–18]

One other mood-stabilizing drug deserves mention before we leave the antidepressants behind. It has been known since the 1940s that bipolar disorder, which produces wild mood swings from depression to mania (marked by excessive optimism and energy), responds well to compounds of *lithium.* Despite science's lack of understanding of exactly how lithium works, 70 percent of people with bipolar disorder show improvement when they take this drug.[19]

Drug therapies are changing rapidly, as new drugs are developed and older drugs are tested for multiple purposes. Our understanding of neurochemistry is growing daily, and as knowledge continues to accumulate, drug treatments should become more effective and the number of negative side effects should diminish.

MAKE IT STICK!

1. Because the stressors that contribute to anxiety disorders will still be present after taking antianxiety drugs, patients may be encouraged to

   a. never take antianxiety drugs.
   b. combine antianxiety drugs with psychotherapy or counseling.
   c. combine antianxiety drugs with electroconvulsive therapy.
   d. take a combination of antianxiety and antipsychotic drugs.

2. Antidepressant medications act by influencing levels of the neurotransmitter

   a. serotonin.   c. dopamine.
   b. GABA.   d. ACh.

3. True or False: It may take several weeks before the effects of antidepressant drugs are felt.

4. The development of drug therapies for psychological disorders led to the release of many hospitalized patients, a trend known as

   _____.

Electroconvulsive Therapy

 35-2 What is "shock therapy," and is it effective?

electroconvulsive therapy (ECT) Therapy for major depression in which a brief electric current is sent through the brain of an anesthetized patient.

"Shock treatments." The very phrase is frightening, raising images of electrocution, pain, jerky convulsions, and Frankenstein-like laboratory experiments. Why would a doctor administer **electroconvulsive therapy (ECT),** a brief electric current that is sent through the brain of an anesthetized patient until a convulsion is produced?

This form of therapy began in Europe in the first half of the twentieth century. A depressed patient who also had diabetes experienced a convulsion after being given the wrong dose of insulin. Remarkably, when he recovered from the convulsion, his depression had lifted. This led to experiments in which nondiabetic depressed patients were given enough of a drug to "shock" them into a convulsion. The results were encouraging, but the drugs were difficult to manage. Too small a dose would fail to produce a convulsion, and too large a dose would lead to death by overdose. By the late 1930s, researchers found that they could trigger convulsions far more reliably and safely with electricity than with chemicals. To do this, they placed electrodes on the patient's right and left temples and passed a current directly through the brain.

Although effective in treating depression, ECT was frightening to observe in its early days. Patients felt no pain when the shock was administered because they instantly lost consciousness. However, the resulting convulsion caused every muscle in the body to contract, sometimes with enough force to break bones. At a minimum, patients would be sore following the procedure. The modern version of ECT is far more humane (see **Figure 35.5**). Medical personnel administer muscle relaxants in advance to greatly dampen the convulsion—often the only visible indication of convulsion is a minor twitch of the extremities. A sedative puts the patient to sleep, avoiding the rapid loss of consciousness that many found unpleasant.

ECT is almost always used to treat major depression, often when antidepressant drugs have failed. When a series of shocks is given (usually three a week for two to four weeks), 80 percent of people—even those who had not responded favorably to antidepressant drugs—show improvement.[20] ECT works more quickly than drugs and is effective even with deep depression, so it is sometimes used to treat suicidal patients.

ECT's most serious side effect is disruption of memory, especially for the approximate time the treatment was administered, but researchers have been unable to identify any brain damage resulting from the procedure. The newest version of the procedure uses briefer electrical pulses and often administers them only to one side of the brain. This seems to cause less memory loss.[21]

If you're wondering just how administering electric shocks to the brain could alleviate depression, you are not alone. One possibility is that the shocks stimulate new neurons and synapses in certain parts of the brain.[22,23] Our lack of understanding

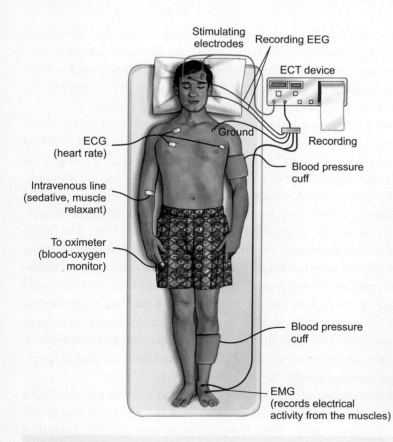

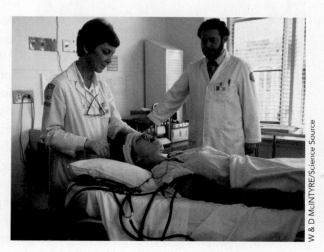

▲ **FIGURE 35.5**
Electroconvulsive Therapy
ECT is an effective treatment for depression. Patients receiving this treatment are carefully monitored throughout the procedure. Physicians administer drugs and use a rubber bite block to eliminate injuries caused by convulsions and to relax the patient.

about how ECT works, combined with its potential for serious side effects, such as memory loss, fuel continuing controversy about this treatment. To those who have been helped, however, the reason it works is less important than the fact that it does.

Research is under way to discover related, less traumatic procedures. One promising technique, *repetitive transcranial magnetic stimulation (rTMS)*, uses magnetic fields instead of electricity and usually does not produce convulsions. In recent studies, people who received a series of rTMS treatments showed significantly more improvement than a control group did.[24–27]

MAKE IT STICK!

1. True or False: Electroconvulsive therapy is less effective than antidepressant drugs in the treatment of depression.

2. True or False: Electroconvulsive therapy has

largely been replaced by repetitive transcranial magnetic stimulation.

3. Electroconvulsive therapy is usually used to treat major _____.

Psychosurgery

 35-3 Why were lobotomies performed, and why are they no longer used?

lobotomy A now-rare form of psychosurgery once used to try to calm uncontrollably emotional or violent patients; the procedure cut the nerves that connect the frontal lobes of the brain to the deeper emotional centers.

If the specter of therapy by shocking the brain is frightening, the thought of curing it by cutting it is downright terrifying. The most famous example of psychosurgery is a now-rare procedure called a **lobotomy** that was once used to calm uncontrollably emotional or violent patients. The procedure cut the nerves that connect the frontal lobes of the brain to the deeper emotional centers.

The lobotomy has a fascinating history, and it touched the lives of tens of thousands of patients in the U.S. until drug treatments replaced it in the 1950s.[28] When Egas Moniz first introduced this surgery in Portugal, it was greeted with such enthusiasm that he received a Nobel Prize for his work. Moniz theorized that serious disorders such as schizophrenia occurred because the brain's deep emotional centers overwhelmed the person's ability to use the rational functions of the frontal lobe. The "solution" was to disconnect the frontal lobe from the emotional centers. How? By inserting an ice pick–like tool next to the eye of an unconscious patient, driving it through the thin bone of the eye socket, and swinging the pick to cut the connections at the base of the frontal lobe. This procedure could be done in minutes without even opening the skull. Two U.S. physicians, Walter Freeman and James Watts, brought the procedure to the U.S. and toured from hospital to hospital performing literally thousands of lobotomies.

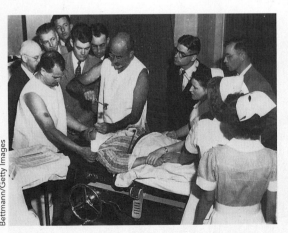

Bettmann/Getty Images

Lobotomy ▲
In this 1949 photograph, Walter Freeman demonstrates the procedure for a lobotomy. Freeman and his colleague James Watts performed thousands of such operations in the 1940s.

Moniz and his followers intended lobotomies to be used only on uncontrollable and violent patients with schizophrenia. Remember that the procedure was developed before the antipsychotic drugs, when few treatments were available. It worked well in isolated cases, but the initial rush of confidence in the procedure meant that most cases were not thoroughly evaluated for appropriateness and few were adequately followed up after the surgery. It would be an overstatement to say that lobotomized patients were "vegetables," but too often the procedure reduced them to an unmotivated and immature state in which they vacantly stared into space for long periods of time.

Public reaction to lobotomies was so negative that researchers have been reluctant to explore other, less drastic surgical procedures. In a relatively small number of cases, precisely guided surgical lesions are used to destroy small areas of brain tissue in an effort to control seizures or disrupt severe obsessive-compulsive patterns that have not responded to other kinds of treatment.[29] Given the permanent nature of surgery and the sorry history of lobotomies in the U.S. and around the world, these new procedures are used only as a last resort.

A variety of therapies are available for treating psychological disorders. In this module, we have focused on biologically based medical approaches. Researchers have made tremendous strides in learning what treatments are effective, and they now guide patients toward the right treatment—or combination of treatments—to reduce their suffering. As former American Psychological Association president Martin Seligman says, "At least 14 disorders, previously intractable, have yielded their secrets to science and can now be either cured or considerably relieved."[30] We can surely say that the future is indeed much brighter than the past for the treatment of mental disorders.

MAKE IT STICK!

1. Lobotomies were originally intended as a treatment for

    a. schizophrenia.   c. anxiety disorders.

    b. depression.   d. bipolar disorder.

2. True or False: To perform a lobotomy, the surgeon would enter the brain through the eye socket.

Module 35 Summary and Assessment

Biomedical Therapies

  35-1 What do antipsychotic, antianxiety, and antidepressant drugs do, and how effective are they?

- Antipsychotic drugs work by blocking the activity of the neurotransmitter dopamine and are used primarily to treat schizophrenia.

- Antianxiety drugs boost the neurotransmitter GABA and are most often prescribed to treat people with anxiety disorders or people suffering from stress.

- Antidepressant drugs increase the neurotransmitter serotonin and are useful for treating major depression.

- The development of these drugs enabled many people with serious mental illnesses to be deinstitutionalized and improved the quality of life for millions of people.

 35-2 What is "shock therapy," and is it effective?

- Electroconvulsive therapy (ECT) consists of a brief electric current sent through the brain of an anesthetized patient until a convulsion is produced.

- ECT is often an immediately effective treatment for major depression. It may be used when antidepressant drugs have failed.

 35-3 Why were lobotomies performed, and why are they no longer used?

- A lobotomy is a surgical procedure in which the nerves that connect the frontal lobes of the brain to the deeper emotional centers are cut.

- This surgery was developed when few treatments were available and often calmed uncontrollably emotional or violent patients. However, it was overused, often reduced people to an unmotivated and immature state, and fell out of favor with the development of antipsychotic drugs.

Summative Assessment

1. Which of the following is NOT considered a biomedical therapy?

   a. repetitive transcranial magnetic stimulation therapy
   b. cognitive therapy
   c. electroconvulsive therapy
   d. drug therapies

2. The factor most responsible for deinstitutionalization after the 1950s was

   a. a new edition of DSM that reclassified several categories of disorders.
   b. the growth in the use of lobotomies.
   c. a change in federal law.
   d. the development of effective drugs.

3. Antipsychotic drugs are most effective when used to treat

   a. depression.
   b. anxiety disorders.
   c. schizophrenia.
   d. post-traumatic stress disorder.

4. Tardive dyskinesia is

   a. a new treatment for substance abuse disorders.
   b. a serious side effect of antipsychotic medications.
   c. a technique that involves using magnets to stimulate the brain.
   d. the term that describes the amount of time it often takes before antidepressant medications take effect.

5. The major side effect of electroconvulsive therapy is

   a. muscle tremor.   c. weight gain.
   b. hallucinations.   d. memory loss.

6. One advantage of electroconvulsive therapy over drugs is

   a. ECT is much less expensive.
   b. we understand how ECT works but how the drugs work is a mystery.
   c. ECT may work more quickly than drugs.
   d. ECT can be used to treat a greater number of disorders than drugs can.

7. Antipsychotic medications

   a. boost the effect of dopamine.
   b. block the effect of dopamine.
   c. boost the effect of serotonin.
   d. block the effect of serotonin.

8. Prozac is an _____ medication.

   a. antipsychotic   c. antidepressant
   b. antianxiety   d. anticonvulsive

9. The original purpose of a lobotomy was to

   a. destroy memories of traumatic events.
   b. stimulate the growth of new neurons and synapses.
   c. sedate the patient.
   d. disconnect the emotional parts of the brain from the rational parts of the brain.

10. Repetitive transcranial magnetic stimulation is being developed as a possible replacement for

   a. lobotomies.
   b. antipsychotic medication.
   c. electroconvulsive therapy.
   d. antianxiety medication.

KEY TERMS

biomedical therapy, p. 539

deinstitutionalization, p. 540

antipsychotic drugs, p. 541

antianxiety drugs, p. 541

antidepressant drugs, p. 542

electroconvulsive therapy (ECT), p. 544

lobotomy, p. 546

Effects of Stress

Sometimes stress gets the better of us. How does stress affect you? Let's find out.

Learning Goals

36-1 Define stress, and explain how our bodies react to it.

36-2 Identify the effects of perceived control, optimism, and pessimism on stress reactions.

36-3 Explain the effects of stress on cancer and heart disease.

"Worry affects the circulation, the heart, the glands, the whole nervous system."

—Dr. Charles Mayo (1865–1939)

Although the situation was not funny, I must admit that I chuckled. For the second consecutive year, Debbie (a former student of mine) had been cast as a female lead in the school musical. And for the second straight year, Debbie lost her voice the Monday before the show opened. Students in the cast and teachers in the hallways wondered, "How could this happen two years in a row?" Was Debbie's condition "all in her head"—that is, with no physiological cause? Was she bluffing in some odd attempt for sympathy? Was she simply "stressed out" and in need of rest? According to the show's director, no other lead in the previous 10 years had experienced this problem.

Well, the show went on, and Debbie sang "Oklahoma" and all her other songs beautifully all three nights, just as she had the year before. Debbie's reaction to her upcoming onstage performance differed from that of several other actors who were nervously anticipating the show. She never developed any cold symptoms, for example, but she did lose and regain her voice. Why did this happen?

This puzzle is just one example of the effects of stress on health, the topic of this module. The relationship between stress and health, like so many others that psychologists study, involves both the mind and the body. We begin with a close look at how psychologists define *stress*.

Stress

 36-1 What is stress, and how do our bodies react to it?

Suppose it's Friday morning, and tonight—after months of wanting to go out with someone—you finally will have that big date, a date that has made it hard to concentrate at times during the week. You've decided what you're going to wear, and

A Stress Reaction? Blemishes that appear at inopportune times are often reactions to stress.

stress The process by which we perceive and respond to certain events, called stressors, that we appraise as threatening or challenging.

health psychology A subfield of psychology that focuses on how stress affects well-being and health.

you and your date have decided where you're going to eat and what movie you'll see. Brushing your teeth, you look in the mirror and discover the start of a rather large pimple on the right side of your nose. A perfect situation just became less perfect. Welcome to **stress**—the process by which we perceive and respond to events, called *stressors*, that we appraise as threatening or challenging.

Where is the stress in this situation? Is it the date, the pimple, or both? Most psychologists would say that neither the date nor the pimple is stress. Rather, the date is a *stressor*, an event you could appraise as threatening or challenging. The pimple is a *stress reaction*, although it may become a stressor as well. Remember, stress is a process of perceiving and responding. Our appraisal of an event as potentially threatening or challenging can make a huge difference in what we experience and in how effectively we respond.

The subfield of **health psychology** focuses on how stress affects our well-being and our health. Health psychologists ask questions such as the following:

- How are stress and illness related?
- How do our perceptions of stress affect our health?
- Can we control our reactions to stress?
- What behaviors and attitudes help prevent health problems?

Given that three out of four people say they often experience stress daily, understanding our responses to stress and their effects on our health is of great importance.[1]

Responding to Stress

Stress is inevitable, but unhealthy responses to it are not. When faced with a stressor, such as a dead cell phone when you need to call your friend, how do you respond? Is the dead cell phone a threat? ("My friend will think I don't care! He'll hate me.") Or is it a challenge? ("I can handle this. Let's see, what are my options?") Your appraisal of the situation is crucial. If you see the stressor as a threat, you'll be more likely to panic and freeze up, making it more difficult to solve your problem. If, instead, you view the stressor as a challenge, your response will be focused, and you'll be more likely to overcome the obstacle (see **Figure 36.1**). Your perception of the stressor directly

FIGURE 36.1 | Assessing Stress Your appraisal of a stressful event greatly influences how you will respond to it emotionally and physically.

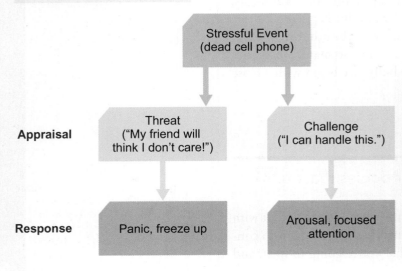

Stressful Event (dead cell phone)

Appraisal

Threat ("My friend will think I don't care!")

Challenge ("I can handle this.")

Response

Panic, freeze up

Arousal, focused attention

affects your emotional responses. The top athletes, the best teachers, and the most effective leaders seem to thrive when faced with what they perceive as a challenge.

Our emotional responses to stressors vary, but our physical responses share some important similarities. Imagine the following scenario. You were supposed to finish reading *Julius Caesar* for English class yesterday, but you forgot your book at school. This morning, your teacher started class by saying, "For today's short-answer quiz, please take out a blank sheet of paper." Surprised by the announcement and unprepared to succeed, you experienced a unified mind–body stress response. Physiologist **Walter Cannon** found that a number of situations—from emotion-arousing incidents like a pop quiz to physically stressful conditions like extreme cold—trigger the release of stress hormones into the nervous system.[2] Your nervous system, as part of its stress response, increases your heart rate, dulls your sensation of pain, and sends more blood to your larger muscles, preparing you either to take action against the challenge (fight) or to flee from it (flight).

Everyday Hassles
Depending on your response to stressors, your health may suffer from the combined effects of daily hassles.

Cannon's work on the fight-flight-freeze response paved the way for another scientist, whose highly respected research greatly expanded our understanding of stress.

Hans Selye (pronounced SELL-yay) discovered a predictable recurring response to all stressors that can be likened to a motion detector that turns on a light regardless of the motion detected. This response to stressors is so general in nature that Selye called it the **general adaptation syndrome (GAS)**.[3,4]

According to Selye, the general adaptation syndrome has three phases (see **Figure 36.2**). Phase 1 is an *alarm reaction,* which happens when your nervous

WALTER CANNON (1871–1945) U.S. physiologist who, with Philip Bard, concluded that physiological arousal and emotional experience occur simultaneously (see *Cannon–Bard theory*).

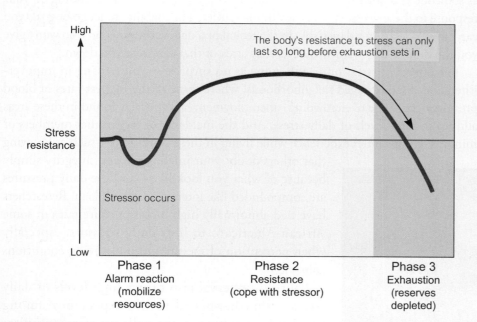

High

Stress resistance

The body's resistance to stress can only last so long before exhaustion sets in

Stressor occurs

Low

| Phase 1 | Phase 2 | Phase 3 |
| Alarm reaction (mobilize resources) | Resistance (cope with stressor) | Exhaustion (reserves depleted) |

▲ **FIGURE 36.2**
Selye's General Adaptation Syndrome (GAS)
Following a traumatic event, the body enters an initial alarm phase. Over time, the body's resistance to stress decreases.

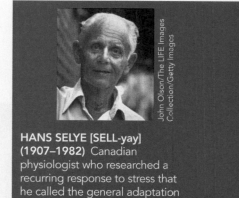

HANS SELYE [SELL-yay] (1907–1982) Canadian physiologist who researched a recurring response to stress that he called the general adaptation syndrome (GAS).

general adaptation syndrome (GAS) Selye's concept of the body's adaptive response to stress in three phases—alarm, resistance, and exhaustion.

system is activated following an emotional or physical trauma (as explained in Cannon's fight-or-flight research). With your heart pumping faster and all other resources at the ready, your body mobilizes itself to meet the challenges of Phase 2, *resistance.* The outpourings of stress-related hormones keep your respiration, temperature, and blood pressure high. However, your body is not built to sustain this kind of resistance indefinitely. With extended exposure to the traumatic event, your body's reserves become depleted, and Phase 3, *exhaustion,* becomes likely. Exhaustion brings greater susceptibility to illness and, under extreme circumstances, death. Selye's bottom line: Although our bodies are built to handle temporary stress, prolonged stress will produce physical deterioration. Evidence supporting Selye's bottom line includes brain scans of those who have lived through extended combat conditions or child abuse. The flood of stress hormones accompanying these traumatic events appears to correspond with the shrinking of a brain structure called the *hippocampus.* This brain structure is vital for memory recall, and those experiencing the trauma may experience memory difficulties.[5,6]

This isn't to say that stress always has a negative physical effect. For example, sudden, temporary stress can kick your immune system into gear, helping you heal faster and fight off infection.[7]

Stressful Events

Researchers investigating the relationship between stress and health have been interested in three types of stressors: daily stress, significant life changes, and catastrophes.

Daily Stress Your locker jams. Your lab partner fails to complete his part of the lab. The lunch line is so long you'll probably have all of five minutes to eat by the time you collect your food. According to several researchers, the most significant sources of stress may be the everyday hassles we regularly face.[8–10] Ever lose your keys when you were already late? Can't locate your concert ticket? Wear the same shirt to school as someone you don't like? Combine these hassles over time, and depending on your response to these stressors, your health may suffer. The inability to let go of goals you can't meet—getting a dance solo in the recital or a date with someone who won't give you the time of day—is also an everyday stressor that can wear you down.[11]

The effects of stress on health come as no surprise to those living in impoverished and disadvantaged neighborhoods, where some of the highest rates of blood pressure occur. The overcrowding, unemployment, and poverty found in these areas add up to high levels of daily stress. Add the incidents of racism that members of minority groups often experience while living in these conditions—such as knowing that others doubt your intelligence and integrity simply because of what you look like—and the daily pressures are compounded like interest on a bank loan. Researchers have tied abnormally high blood pressure rates in some African-Americans to life's daily stressors, especially when perception of racism and poor living conditions coincide.[12,13]

Political upheaval also brings high levels of daily stress. What happened to life expectancy among Russian men following the collapse of communism in the 1990s and uncertainty about jobs, food, and the future became the norm? It fell by five years, and suicide, divorce, and murder rates all rose.[14]

Reaction to War
With prolonged exposure to warlike conditions, this family's resistance to the stressors of famine and war may lead to exhaustion and increase the likelihood of illness. ▼

SERGEI GRITS/AP Images

The persistent daily hassles that are part of daily work life can produce the state of physical, emotional, and mental exhaustion called *burnout*.[15] When you hear people say they're "burned out" on something, it typically means they've had enough. Police officers worn down by high-stress situations, parents worn down by persistent parenting hassles, and teachers worn down by the during- and after-school demands of teaching are all candidates for burnout. The results of burnout include the following:

- Depression (from the emotional exhaustion)
- Decreased performance or productivity (from the physical exhaustion)
- Cynicism (from the mental exhaustion)

"Your mother and I are feeling overwhelmed, so you'll have to bring yourselves up."

▲ **Overwhelmed Parents**
In fact, it's not a laughing matter: The demands of making ends meet while raising a family can lead to burnout in parents.

Significant Changes Significant personal changes in your life are the second kind of life event stressor. The death of a loved one, leaving home to live on your own, and divorce are examples of stressors related to life transitions.

There are at least two ways to study the health effects of significant life changes. The first is to compare the lives of those who suffer the same illness, such as a stroke, to determine whether they shared similar life changes that would predict the illness. The second and more time-consuming method involves tracking people over time, noting whether a life change precedes an illness. Two such long-term studies found a greater vulnerability to disease in people who had recently been fired, widowed, or divorced.[16,17] Another study found that the likelihood of death in widowed people doubles in the week after their partner's death.[18] So, while people experience many different life changes, researchers hypothesize that increased stress contributes to contracting a disease at much greater rates than similarly aged people who do not have a significant life change.

LIFE MATTERS
Do you feel trepidation over what to do after high school? If this or other difficult transitions are causing you stress, remember that school counselors are available to help.

Catastrophes Hurricanes, terror attacks, and earthquakes are all large-scale, relatively unpredictable life-threatening events. Do these catastrophic stressors affect health? If the September 11, 2001, terrorist attacks, the hurricanes Katrina, Harvey, Maria, and Florence, and the earthquakes from Iran to Mexico are any indication, the answer is *Yes*. Around 65 percent of all people surveyed in the U.S. indicated difficulty sleeping in the weeks after the 9/11 attacks.[19] According to the Centers for Disease Control and Prevention (CDC), 44 percent of hurricane-related deaths are related to stress.[20] Four months after massive Hurricane Katrina hit New Orleans, the suicide rate in that city tripled.[21] In the 24 hours after an earthquake hit Los Angeles in 1994, the number of sudden-death heart attacks reported was five times the normal rate, but only 13 percent of these deaths were deemed a result of running, lifting debris, or some other form of physical exertion. What accounted for the remainder of the increase? The likely answer is stress.[22]

▼ **Catastrophes**
Catastrophes, such as 2017's Hurricane Maria in Puerto Rico, shown here, are deadly with both the flooding and stress they bring.

Catastrophes often mean prolonged exposure to stress. A comprehensive review of studies addressing the psychological effects of disasters showed a 17 percent increase in the likelihood of depression and other disorders.[23] The stress of catastrophes puts us at psychological and physical risk.

MAKE IT STICK!

1. Which of the following questions would most likely interest a health psychologist?

   a. What types of parenting styles lead to the healthiest children?
   b. Which kinds of rewards are the most effective in healthy rats learning mazes?
   c. How do hypochondriacs respond to clinical therapy treatments?
   d. Does deep breathing after encountering a stressor lessen a stress reaction?

2. What are the three phases in Hans Selye's general adaptation syndrome?

3. True or False: Physical, emotional, and mental exhaustion help define burnout.

Effects of Perceived Control

 36-2 What are the effects of perceived control, optimism, and pessimism on stress reactions?

The negative effect of every stressor in our lives—running out of gas, failing an exam, feeling obligated to buy a holiday gift for someone who unexpectedly gave you one at the last minute—is magnified if we think of the stressor negatively and as something beyond our control. Let's look at how a sense of control and optimism is linked to stress effects.

Several lines of research demonstrate the importance of perceived control on health. One study showed that uncontrollable stress (along with a bacterial infection) produces the harshest stomach ulcers in humans.[24] Another study by Judith Rodin compared nursing home patients who perceived little control over their activities with similar patients who were able to control some of their daily routines. Rodin found that patients perceiving less control declined in health more rapidly and died sooner than those with more control.[25] Other research found lowered immunity to disease among rats exposed to uncontrolled stress.[26] When two rats simultaneously received the same amount of mild electrical shock, the rat that could turn off the shock stayed just as healthy as a rat receiving no shock. These "empowered" rats were healthier than shocked rats that had no control over the shocking mechanism.

Optimism also seems to offer some protection against the effects of stress. How would you respond to the statement "In uncertain times, I usually expect the best"? If you agree, you may have an optimistic approach to life. Compared with their pessimistic counterparts (those with a negative approach to life), students identified as optimists have stronger immune systems and are less likely to become ill or fatigued during the last month of the term. Optimists also recover more quickly from heart surgery than pessimists, miss fewer days of work due to illness, and when stressed, register lower blood pressure readings.[27,28] One study of

2400 Finnish men revealed that those with a hopeless, bleak outlook on life were twice as likely to die during a 10-year span than were those labeled optimists.[29]

So, why are optimism and a perceived sense of control good predictors of better health? And why do pessimism and perceived loss of control predict poor health? The answer, once again, involves the interplay between mind (your perceptions or appraisals) and body (your physiology).

Both pessimism and perceived loss of control lead to the production and release of *stress hormones*. Ridding yourself of these hormones uses up your body's reserves of disease-fighting white blood cells. This weakens and thereby hinders your immune system's ability to ward off diseases it would otherwise defeat. Surgical wounds in both humans and animals, for example, heal more slowly under stressful conditions. In one ingenious study showing this effect, researchers made a small, precise puncture wound in the skin of volunteer dental students. Puncture wounds made during summer vacation healed significantly faster than wounds made three days before major exams.[30] Another study by Sheldon Cohen and his colleagues revealed that when given a cold virus, research participants who reported high life stress scores were more likely to go on to develop a cold[31] (see **Figure 36.3**). Later research showed that the cold virus was similarly best resisted by the happiest and most relaxed participants.[32,33] Stressed-out individuals have weaker disease-fighting mechanisms than those who are relatively free of stress. So, if you catch a cold, you'd better chill.

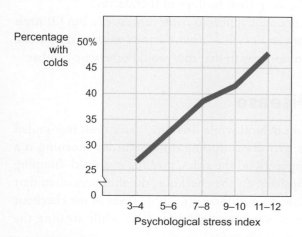

▲ **FIGURE 36.3**
Stress and Illness
When given a cold virus, people who went on to develop a cold had the highest life stress scores. (From Cohen et al., 1991.)

MAKE IT STICK!

1. True or False: Appraising a life event optimistically as a challenge rather than a threat is a poor predictor of better health.

2. A patient in a hospital shows significant improvement when she is given control over her pain medication. This example demonstrates the importance of

   a. good patient–doctor communication.
   b. perceived control over a stressor.
   c. high-quality pain control medication.
   d. being in a good hospital when in pain.

3. True or False: Students identified as optimists have stronger immune systems and are less likely to become ill or fatigued than students identified as pessimists.

Stress and Disease

 36-3 What are the effects of stress on cancer and heart disease?

It's well documented that stress makes minor illnesses, such as colds, more likely. Stress also plays a role in significant diseases.

Cancer and Stress

Because of conflicting research, the relationship between stress and cancer is not entirely clear. Some researchers have looked for—but not found—a connection between stress and cancer.[34,35] For example, World War II concentration camp survivors underwent prolonged horrific stress, but they have not shown higher than normal cancer rates.

Other researchers have found evidence of a stress–cancer connection. In one study, people with a history of workplace stress were five times more likely to develop colon cancer than were those without workplace stress.[36] Cancer patients who verbalize their feelings (presumably releasing stress) have a slightly higher survival rate than cancer patients who keep their feelings to themselves.[37–39]

Two things are clear: (1) Stress does not appear to *create* cancer cells, but (2) stress weakens the body's ability to fight cancer cells.[40] That is, stress-weakened immune systems are more likely to allow tumor growth that they would otherwise combat.

Type A A term for competitive, hard-driving, impatient, verbally aggressive, and anger-prone people.

Type B A term for easygoing, relaxed people.

Stress and Heart Disease

Although I've never been hit from behind while driving, I *have* been rear-ended in a grocery store. Where I live, grocery shopping on a Saturday morning is a bad idea. Saturday morning shoppers flood the aisles, pushing oversized shopping carts from the produce to the Popsicles. At the checkout, the shoppers often dart from one line to the next, looking to minimize wait time. I was in the checkout line when one of these speed shoppers rear-ended me while stealing the spot behind me from a slower shopper.

These impatient, competitive, hard-driving, verbally aggressive, and anger-prone people have what Meyer Friedman and Ray Rosenman call **Type A** personalities. These two researchers contrasted these hard-driving types with **Type B** personalities, those who are more easygoing and relaxed. The origin of these two classifications is intriguing, and their importance in understanding the link between stress and heart attack is significant. Let's look at the way Friedman and Rosenman arrived at their conclusions.

In the mid-1950s, Friedman and his associates initially studied the eating habits of married white couples living in the San Francisco area, and they discovered an interesting fact: The women ate just as much fat and cholesterol as their husbands did, but the men were more likely to experience heart disease. Friedman ruled out sex differences (for example, female sex hormones) as a reason for this effect after finding that African-American women with similar diets were just as prone to heart disease as the men. Perplexed, Friedman could not figure out what caused the coronary differences. Then one woman in the study announced,

ScienceCartoonsPlus.com

"TYPICAL 'TYPE A' BEHAVIOR."

Stressful! ↑
There are probably few "Type B" conductors.

If you really want to know what is going to give our husbands heart attacks, I'll tell you. It's stress . . . the stress they have to face in their businesses, day in, day out. Why, when my husband comes home at night, it takes at least one martini just to unclench his jaws.[41]

The woman making the statement did not work outside her home, nor did most of the white women in the study. But most of the African-American women did hold jobs. Could work stress, or stress in general, be the answer?

To test the stress–heart disease link, Friedman measured blood-clotting speed and cholesterol level (both associated with heart attack risk) in tax accountants in the months leading up to their busiest time of the year, the April 15 tax-filing deadline. In January and February, the readings were normal. However, during the incredibly intense days leading up to the deadline, with the accountants scrambling to meet their clients' deadlines and working long hours, the clotting and cholesterol readings skyrocketed to dangerous levels. In May, the readings were back to normal. Stress *did* predict risk of heart attack.

In the nine-year study that followed, Friedman and Rosenman tracked 3000 healthy men between the ages of 35 and 59, labeling each man as either Type A or Type B, based on a 15-minute interview. By the end of the study, 257 men had suffered heart attacks, and 69 percent of them were Type A. None of the "pure" Type Bs, the most easygoing, had heart attacks. (See Psychology in the Real World: Managing Anger for more on effective ways to control anger.) That said, scientists have questioned Friedman and Rosenman's data. Being that their sample was mostly middle-aged white men, would the results have been the same if they'd used a more diverse sample? There were also possible confounding factors (socialization, socioeconomic status, biological predisposition) that were not controlled. If they'd controlled for these factors, would their findings have been different? Regardless, interest in their personality type classifications remains relatively high.

Yes, the scientific world clamored for more information regarding Type A and Type B individuals. Which aspects (if any) of the Type A personality—hard-driving, verbally aggressive, anger-prone, competitive—were most toxic? The winners (or losers, depending on how you look at it) turned out to be anger and one other negative emotion—depression.[42,43] Consider these findings:

- Those experiencing instant anger over minor annoyances, especially those with aggressive–reactive personalities, are the most prone to heart attacks.[44]

- Young and middle-aged adults who get angry over little things are more likely to have heart attacks than those who let the small stuff slide.[45]

- A review of 57 studies shows that depression significantly increases the risk of death by heart attack.[46]

- Cynical and hostile college students are five times more likely to die of heart attacks in middle age than are their trusting, gentler classmates.[47]

It is clear that stress has a significant effect on our health, but it is also true that *how* we respond to stress matters. While the root causes of many stressors lie beyond our control, we can all seek ways to turn unhealthy stress responses into something more positive and productive.

Philip Scott Andrews/AP Images

Occupational Hazards?
Some jobs are more stressful on your heart than others, which may increase the likelihood of heart disease.

LIFE MATTERS

Do you crave sugar, fatty foods or both when you are stressed out? Sugar and high calorie, fatty foods serve as a comfort, masking the negative effects of stress, but the relief these foods have on stress is short lived. Make a healthier choice by eating an apple, meditating, or going for a walk.

PSYCHOLOGY IN THE REAL WORLD

Managing Anger

Treatment for depression is readily available from clinical psychologists and physicians, but is there any treatment for anger? Is anger something people, particularly those who are Type A, should seek to overcome? In both cases, the answer is *Yes*. Psychologists suggest two ways of handling anger that are better than merely "blowing off steam," which actually tends to amplify hostile feelings.[48,49] First, although it sounds simple, if you feel angry give yourself time to calm down. I was told as a young boy to "count to 10" before doing anything when I was angry with my brother. The physiological storm that anger stirs up in your body will drop below hurricane level when given time to calm down. Second, try to vent the anger by exercising, confiding in a friend, or writing in a journal. Finally, for more long-term benefits, consider taking up yoga or meditating on a regular basis. Both activities have been shown to decrease the likelihood of angry episodes.[50] These behaviors will let you sift through your feelings without stifling them and will help you avoid explosive reactions later.[51] Also, avoid sulking, which simply allows rehearsal of the reasons for being angry.

Actively trying to control anger instead of letting it control you is effort well spent. Keep in mind the words of Charles Spielberger and Perry London, who perhaps put it best when they warned that rage "seems to lash back and strike us in the heart muscle."[52]

THINK ABOUT . . . Psychology in the Real World

1. If you are angry at someone, why is it a good idea to give yourself time to calm down before speaking to that person?

2. What are things you can do to help yourself calm down when you are angry?

3. What will you do to calm yourself the next time you get angry? What is your plan?

MAKE IT STICK!

1. Research indicates that high levels of stress

   a. create immune-boosting hormones that fight cancerous tumors.
   b. always cause cancer.
   c. negatively affect the body's ability to fight cancer.
   d. result from cancer patients verbalizing their feelings about the disease.

2. When Reesa's boss accidentally misplaced the 200-page report Reesa had been working on for weeks, Reesa laughed and said, "No problem. Everyone loses something occasionally." Based on this example, which personality type would you say fits Reesa best?

   a. Type A
   b. verbalizing type
   c. Type B
   d. anger-prone type

3. True or False: Those experiencing instant anger over minor annoyances, especially those with aggressive–reactive personalities, are the most prone to heart attacks.

Module 36 Summary and Assessment

Effects of Stress

 36-1 What is stress, and how do our bodies react to it?

- Stress is the process by which we perceive and respond to threatening or challenging events, called stressors.

- Walter Cannon found that stressors trigger the fight, flight, or freeze response.

- Hans Selye identified the general adaptation syndrome (GAS), which describes the three phases of the body's response to stressors.

- Psychologists divide stressors into three categories: daily stress (everyday hassles like becoming stuck in traffic), significant changes (important changes in life like leaving to live at college), and catastrophes (large-scale, life-threatening events).

 36-2 What are the effects of perceived control, optimism, and pessimism on stress reactions?

- Uncontrollable stress is more physically damaging than stress we perceive as controllable.

- Optimism shields people from some damaging effects of stressors.

- Pessimism can add to the negative effect of stress.

 36-3 What are the effects of stress on cancer and heart disease?

- Stress does not cause cancer or heart disease, but stress reactions affect the body's ability to fight these illnesses.

- People with Type A personalities (anger-prone, aggressive, and competitive) are more likely to experience heart disease than those classified as Type B (easygoing and relaxed).

Summative Assessment

1. What do psychologists call the process by which we perceive and respond to certain events that we appraise as threatening or challenging?

   a. stress
   b. health
   c. response
   d. appraisal

2. What is the Cannon–Bard theory?

   a. a recurring response to stress while participating in sport
   b. the body's resistance to stress in times of peace
   c. physical arousal and emotional experience occurring simultaneously
   d. your health suffering from the combined effects of daily stress

3. Which of the following most likely influences how we respond to a stressful event?

   a. our physical response to the event
   b. our appraisal of the event
   c. our cynicism about the event
   d. our resistance to the event

4. What did Hans Selye call the results of his research on a recurring response to a stressor?

   a. health psychology
   b. stress reaction
   c. perceived control
   d. general adaptation syndrome

5. What will prolonged stress do to the body?

   a. cause physical deterioration
   b. result in fight or flight
   c. make a person more resilient
   d. develop coping skills

6. Saying to yourself, "In uncertain times, I usually expect the best" is an example of

   a. depression.
   b. optimism.
   c. stress.
   d. resistance.

7. Pessimism and perceived loss of control lead to

   a. production of stress hormones.
   b. optimism.
   c. catastrophes.
   d. general adaptation syndrome.

8. People who are optimists tend to be

   a. depressed.
   b. chronically ill.
   c. healthier.
   d. stressed.

9. Which of the following is NOT an example of the effects of prolonged production of stress hormones?

   a. heart disease
   b. cancer risk
   c. depression
   d. strong immune system

10. The general adaptation syndrome includes the

   a. alarm reaction, resistance, and exhaustion.
   b. alarm reaction, acceptance, and reflection.
   c. alarm reaction, acceptance, and exhaustion.
   d. alarm reaction, resistance, and reflection.

KEY TERMS AND KEY PEOPLE

stress, p. 550

health psychology, p. 550

general adaptation syndrome (GAS), p. 551

Type A, p. 556

Type B, p. 556

Walter Cannon (1871–1945), p. 551

Hans Selye [SELL-yay] (1907–1982), p. 551

Promoting Wellness

We all know there are physical benefits to exercising, but what are the mental benefits? How does exercise contribute to "feeling better"? Psychologists have a lot to say about wellness.

Learning Goals

37-1 Summarize the research findings related to wellness and exercise, social ties, and spirituality.

37-2 Explain the relationship between wellness and flow experiences, happiness, and optimistic explanatory styles.

37-3 Identify the challenges associated with trying to quit smoking or to lose weight.

Before Jonas Salk created the polio vaccination in 1954, polio terrorized the U.S. Thousands were crippled, including President Franklin Delano Roosevelt, and thousands more died. In 1984, research psychologist **Martin Seligman** had a life-changing conversation with the famous Dr. Salk.

Seligman and Salk were together at a conference where immunologists and psychologists were discussing how both fields contribute to making life better. Salk told Seligman,

> If I were a young scientist today, I would still do immunization. But instead of immunizing kids physically, I'd do it your way. I'd immunize them psychologically. I'd see if these psychologically immunized kids could then fight off mental illness better. Physical illness too.[1]

Given the tenfold increase in the rate of clinical depression since the years just before World War II, an "immunization" against this particular mental illness would, indeed, make life better.[2] Depression makes you feel miserable. It also hurts your productivity at school and work, and it puts your physical health in jeopardy. We could avoid much pain, sickness, and lost work time if we could stay well and never start down depression's dark path.

In this module, we explore the concept of **wellness,** which is the result of a healthy life-style and healthy attitudes. We also examine ways to promote psychological and physical well-being and to overcome behaviors that lead to illness.

Martin E.P. Seligman, Ph.D. Fox Leadership Professor of Psychology, University of Pennsylvania

MARTIN SELIGMAN (1942–) U.S. psychologist who researched helplessness early in his career before turning his interest to optimism; he has been the primary proponent of positive psychology.

Mental and Physical Health Studies show that aerobic exercise is good for both your muscles and your mind.

skynesher/E+/Getty Images

wellness The common result of a healthy life-style and healthy attitudes.

Healthy Life-Styles

 37-1 What are the research findings related to wellness and exercise, social ties, and spirituality?

Several roads lead to a healthy life-style. Let's take a closer look at three of these roads, starting with exercise.

Exercise

In 2002, President George W. Bush asked all people in the U.S. to exercise at least 30 minutes each day. Later, First Lady Michelle Obama initiated the Let's Move! campaign to help promote healthy life-styles in children.[3] Their motives included improving the health of U.S. citizens. Both had probably seen the research showing that people who regularly exercise are more likely to stay healthy and miss work less often due to illness. Time will tell if these White House initiatives increase the health of the U.S. population and lower health care bills.

Do you exercise regularly? If so, you are part of a growing minority in the U.S. The physical benefits of aerobic exercise, such as increased lung and heart fitness, are well documented. Are there psychological benefits as well? The answer appears to be a resounding *Yes*.

Many studies show that exercise is an effective nonmedical means of reducing anxiety and depression.[4,5] Lisa McCann worked with a group of mildly depressed college women, randomly assigning the women to one of three groups:

- Group A participated in an aerobic exercise program.
- Group B worked through a series of relaxation exercises.
- Group C received no treatment.

Ten weeks after the treatment programs began, those in the aerobic exercise group showed the greatest decrease in depression[6] (see **Figure 37.1**). This dramatic finding illustrates that exercise can help reduce or prevent depression, the common cold of mental illness.

Physical fitness also leads to greater self-confidence and self-discipline.[7] Exercise lowers blood pressure while increasing our ability to deal with stress.[8] Unfortunately, many of us bypass daily exercise because we think we need to run 5 miles a day to make a difference. Not true. Moderate exercise, such as a 10-minute walk, can increase energy levels and lower tension.[9,10]

So, we know exercise boosts mood. But *how* does aerobic exercise make us feel better? Several factors contribute:

- Exercise increases the output of the mood-boosting chemicals your nervous system produces.[11,12]
- Exercise enhances your cognitive abilities, such as memory, to some degree.[13]
- Exercise lowers your blood pressure.[14]
- Exercise has positive side effects, such as better sleep, that provide an emotional benefit.

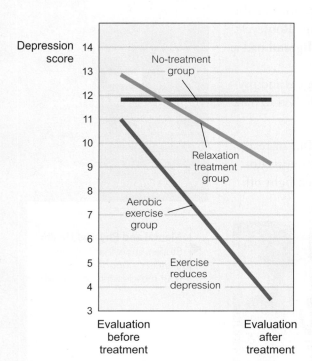

FIGURE 37.1
Exercise for Mental Health
Feelings of depression decreased dramatically when exercise was included as a part of treatment. (Adapted from McCann & Holmes, 1984.)

Regular exercise cuts heart attack risk in half and increases longevity by as much as two years.[15,16] Exercise, if done regularly in later life, also reduces the likelihood of Alzheimer's disease.[17] So, after finishing your homework, why not pump up your bike tires or lace up those running shoes?

Jumping the Hurdles That Prevent Exercise

You'll rarely hear someone say, "I'm glad I'm not in shape," or, "I wish I were in worse physical shape than I am now." Indeed, regardless of age, most of us wish we were in better shape. The exercise required to establish and maintain physical fitness has the added benefit of reducing stress, reducing symptoms of depression, stimulating brain cell growth, and making us feel better. Not exercising speeds up the aging process.[18]

Unfortunately, many who wish that they exercised regularly often find reasons to keep their sneakers in the closet. Finding the time and the motivation to exercise can be a challenge. Positive psychology researchers have identified a number of ways to increase the likelihood you'll get into an exercise groove.[19]

1. *Include others.* Positive psychologist Chris Peterson said it most simply and best: Other people matter. Exercise with someone you enjoy and who will encourage you to get out there even when you don't feel like it.

2. *Get your sleep.* Overcoming a lack of pre-exercise energy is a huge obstacle. Turn off the television (or computer) and get your sleep.

3. *Keep track of progress.* Keep track of what you do and when you did it by using a personal or public blog, a wall calendar, a phone app, a wristband activity tracker, or some other record-keeping device. What you measure winds up becoming more valued.

4. *Improve your mood before exercise.* Happy moods increase our activity levels.[20] Listen to some of your favorite upbeat music or call a fun friend for an update before hitting the gym.

5. *Match the challenge with your skills.* Avoid setting your immediate sights on a 20-minute jog if you have yet to run for 10 consecutive minutes. Instead, consider initially aiming for two 10-minute jogs if 20 minutes is your goal.

6. *Peak your endings.* Research shows that we often remember something by how much we liked the ending.[21] Structure workouts so that you finish by doing something you really enjoy.

7. *Use your strengths.* If you haven't yet done so, take an online test that helps determine your strengths. (The Brief Strengths Test can be found at www.authentichappiness.org.) Use your strengths to help work up a sweat. So, if a love of learning is one of your top strengths, explore machines at a gym that you've never tried. If bravery is in your top five, call upon this strength to contact people who can help you get started, even if you've never met them (for example, a neighbor who is in good shape or a trainer at a fitness club).

The answer to the question of whether we should or should not exercise is obvious; what's tougher is how to find the motivation we need to get our hearts pumping. If you or someone you know is having trouble getting started, perhaps the above list will help. It's never too late to commit to be fit.

Family and Friends

The second of the three roads to a healthier life-style involves cultivating good relationships with family and friends. That sounds simple, but sometimes it is easier said than done.

What, if anything, has caused you emotional strain in the past 24 hours? Think about that for a moment. The most common answer, according to a good news–bad news research finding, is "family."[22] This is understandable. Each day, families juggle time, energy, and resources in an attempt to satisfy each person's needs for food, transportation, and belonging in today's increasingly busy world. The results often include stress, which can be toxic to our bodies. It can lead to heart disease, suppress the immune system, and contribute to high blood pressure.

However, the good news is that the family juggling act also brings happy moments. When the same researchers asked *what had prompted pleasure* in the previous 24 hours, the answer again, by an even larger margin, was "family." The close relationships found in families and with some good friends are most often sources of happiness. Family and friends offer social support, making us feel liked and wanted. This social support provides the cognitive rewards of happiness and contentment. Several studies have also linked social support to health and wellness:

- People with more social ties (family, friends, and support groups) are less likely to die prematurely.[23]

- Heart attack victims living alone are twice as likely to have another heart attack within six months as are those living with a family member.[24]

- An amazing study followed children with high IQ scores for 70 years. Regardless of economic status, the children who grew up with parents who did not divorce outlived the children of divorce by an average of 4 years.[25] Do intact families provide more social support for children? *Probably*.

Married people tend to live longer than those who are unmarried, but a marriage filled with conflict is not good for the health of either spouse.[26,27] Marriage itself is not the predictor of health, but a healthy, happy marriage predicts fewer heart attacks, less obesity, and lower cholesterol rates.[28]

One of the more compelling and ingenious attempts to examine the relationship between a healthy social environment and the functioning of immune systems involved a study of 276 participants. Each participant agreed to allow drops of a cold germ–laden liquid to be dripped into their healthy noses. What these researchers found is nothing to sneeze at: Those with the most social ties were less likely to catch a cold and also produced less mucus. (How they measured the mucus, I'm not quite sure.) The study's results showed that social support aids in resisting the common cold.[29,30]

Close friends and relationships create social ties that appear to be beneficial in a number of ways. The opportunity to confide in others, for example, lowers blood pressure, slows the heart rate, and decreases the level of stress hormones in your body.[31]

MBI/Alamy

Joy and Strife
Our family members sometimes bring us stress, but they also bring us support and happiness.

So, do all these findings mean that your health is destined to fail if you have a messed-up family and no trustworthy friends? *Not necessarily.* We all have access to a wide range of support groups if we know where to look for them. Group membership can provide the sense of belonging that is so beneficial to emotional and psychological health. Many local schools and religious organizations sponsor support groups, and your school counselor should be able to point you in the right direction if you're interested in exploring the possibilities.

Stress is unavoidable, but the help and encouragement of family, friends, and support groups provide a buffer against the ill effects of stress. Another buffer for many is the *faith factor.*

The Faith Factor

Do religion and spirituality relate to health? One poll showed that 80 percent of all people in the U.S. believe they do.[32] But is it possible to assess this relationship scientifically? Several researchers have tried, and they found a *correlation* between being religiously active and having longevity.[33] This means the researchers found that certain factors tend to occur together, but they did not do follow-up experiments that would show cause and effect. In this study, they found that people from a variety of religious backgrounds who attended religious services regularly tended to live longer than those who attended infrequently. Another study followed 21,204 people for eight years.[34] These researchers found that people who did not attend religious services were 1.87 times more likely to have died than those who attended services weekly (see **Figure 37.2**). Put another way, the life expectancy of a 20-year-old in this study would be 83 years for the most frequent attendees and 75 years for nonattendees. This eight-year difference certainly ranks up there with the positive effects of exercise and nonsmoking.

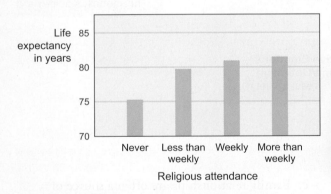

▲ **FIGURE 37.2**
The Faith Factor?
People who frequently attend religious services tend to live longer than those who do not attend. (From Hummer et al., 1999.)

Does this mean that your life expectancy will go up if you start attending religious services frequently? *Not exactly.* We cannot say that religious involvement guarantees wellness and longevity. What we can say is that at least three factors associated with the religiously active seem to contribute to better health (see **Figure 37.3**):

1. The beliefs of the religiously active often promote healthier life-styles. Religiously active people claim to smoke and drink less and get more sleep than those who, say, stay up all night partying.[35]

2. Attending religious services is a communal, not a solo, experience. Faith communities provide social support.[36] When members of one of the 350,000-plus faith communities in North America fall down, the other members are there to pick them up.

3. Religiously active people often experience less anxiety and stress because of a worldview promoting optimism, gratitude, and hope for the future. Optimists have stronger immune systems than pessimists. Religiously active people have stronger immune systems and have fewer hospital stays than religiously inactive people.[37,38]

The relationship between spirituality and health has not escaped the notice of the nation's medical schools. In 1994, only 3 out of 126 U.S. medical schools offered courses in spirituality and health. Ten years later, over 75 percent of them did, and today, it's over 90 percent.[39,40] The ongoing research in this area, a direct result of renewed interest in studying the relationship between health and faith, may yield new and helpful information in the coming years.

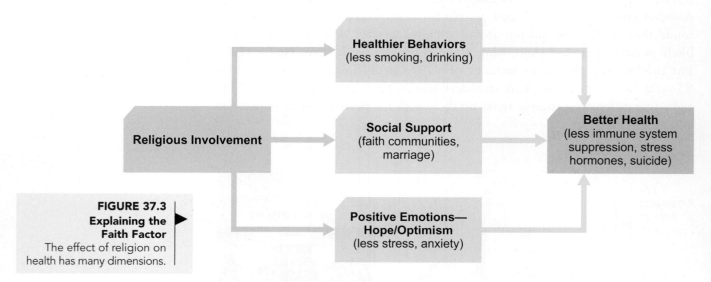

FIGURE 37.3
Explaining the Faith Factor
The effect of religion on health has many dimensions.

MAKE IT STICK!

1. _____ is the common result of a healthy life-style and healthy attitudes.

2. Which of the following statements best describes the relationship between social ties and wellness?

   a. Family relationships have less effect on wellness rates than relationships with friends.

   b. Relationships with family and friends are often a source of stress, and social ties are positively correlated with heart disease.

   c. Family relationships are often a source of stress, but the social support that families offer is important to wellness.

   d. No relationships with family and friends cause higher rates of social ties and wellness.

3. True or False: Heart attack victims living alone are twice as likely as those living with a family member to have another heart attack within six months.

Positive Experiences and Well-Being

37-2 What is the relationship between wellness and flow experiences, happiness, and optimistic explanatory styles?

Experience success in the classroom, on the ball field, or with a gaming controller in your hand, and you feel some degree of happiness. When we're happy, we're more likely to forgive the friend who borrowed a calculator and didn't give it back, to help those who do not understand an assignment, or to tolerate the driver who cuts us off in traffic. Wouldn't it be great if we could "bank" these positive experiences after they occur, building up a reserve that would help get us through rough times? And could this reserve then "inoculate" or help prevent us from becoming depressed during difficult times, as Jonas Salk had hoped? The answer is a solid *Yes.*

Years after his conversation with Salk, Martin Seligman and many others began promoting the subfield of psychology called **positive psychology** by studying emotions, feelings, and the positive experiences that foster well-being and allow us to thrive. Ed Diener explains *well-being* as a "concept that includes life satisfaction, feelings of fulfillment, pleasant emotions, and a low level of unpleasant emotions."[41] Experiences (including both thoughts and feelings) that produce pleasant emotions lead a person to judge life as satisfying, fulfilling, and "going well." For example, if a goal of yours is to earn an A in your psychology class and you earn a 97 percent on a test, seeing that grade will be a positive experience that promotes your well-being. Why are positive experiences important? Research shows that the more positive experiences you have, the more likely you are to

- have better relationships with others.
- contribute more to your community.
- excel in academics and sports.
- provide leadership.
- propose new ideas in such areas as science and business.
- help others.
- be less of a drain on psychological and physical health systems.[42,43]

But note that, as of this writing, most research linking well-being and positive experiences is *correlational.* We don't know which is the cause and which is the effect. Do the positive experiences cause all these wonderful characteristics to exist in the people who have them? Or do people who already have these wonderful characteristics tend to have experiences that are more positive? One thing is clear: Our potential for well-being consists of the goals that are important to us and the degree to which we are achieving those goals.

Researchers in positive psychology have found at least three kinds of experiences that have powerful effects on the individual. Flow, happiness, and optimism all contribute to our sense of well-being.

> **positive psychology**
> A movement in psychology that focuses on the study of optimal human functioning and the factors that allow individuals and communities to thrive.

> **In the Flow**
> A challenge-requiring skill, clear goals, and feedback can become a flow activity.

Peter Hvizdak/The Image Works

flow A state of optimal experience that involves a challenge, requires skill, has clear goals, and provides feedback.

Flow

Flow, defined by Mihaly Csikszentmihalyi (pronounced chick-SENT-me-hi), is a state of optimal experience.[44] Activities we perform for the satisfaction of doing them, and not for extrinsic rewards, put us in a state of flow. Reading a book we can't put down, playing a game of three-on-three basketball in the driveway with friends, or acting in the school play can all be flow experiences. People in flow situations report losing track of time and being hard to distract. They also lose any sort of self-consciousness about their appearance or other people's opinions of them. Let's take a closer look at flow, using the basketball example.

For flow to occur, we need a challenge-requiring skill. A challenging activity requiring highly developed skills that you have cultivated leads to flow. An activity that is not challenging and requires little or no skill leads to apathy (see **Figure 37.4**). Playing basketball (a challenge for me) meets this requirement; watching television does not. Clear goals (trying to put the ball in the hoop, keeping someone else from scoring, winning the game) and feedback (each basket counts for 1 point, first team to 11 wins) are also flow necessities.

Flow can happen in all areas of life, including the workplace. You may have a job where you are so bored that you count the minutes until it's time to leave. Perhaps you work there only for the money. Such a job is sheer drudgery, a direct contrast to flow. In what kind of job might you experience flow every day? Teaching? Acting? Writing? You may want to keep that question in mind as you think about employment after graduation or select your major in college.

Flow is a subjective experience that contributes to another kind of positive experience: happiness.

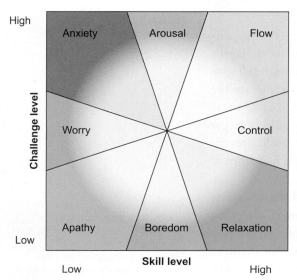

FIGURE 37.4
Achieving Flow
This figure shows the relationship between challenges and skills in achieving flow. For a person to experience flow, the activity needs to be higher than average in both challenge and skill. (Adapted with permission from Csikszentmihalyi, 1998.)

Happiness

You walk into school, and the first person you talk to says, "Nice haircut—looks sharp," bringing a smile to your face. Next, you go to class and find that the project you worked on for two weeks received a better grade than you'd anticipated. Finally, you solve a math problem that is giving most of your classmates a struggle. If you then begin helping your classmates solve that problem, a psychologist would not be surprised. Research shows that when we're happy, we're more likely to help others.[45,46] Happy people also make decisions more easily.[47] They cooperate more.[48] And they live longer, complain less, and recover more quickly from injury.[49]

Of course, not everyone responds to "Nice haircut" in the same way. I'll bet you know someone who would say, "What? Didn't you like my hair before?" How can the same event lead to happiness in some and gloom or distress in others? Part of the answer may lie in several qualities and tendencies that happy people possess (see **Table 37.1**). Compared with their less happy counterparts, happy people tend to be more outgoing, interact more with others, have a larger circle of friends, and participate in more rewarding activities. Having more friends often provides more social support and more opportunities for affection. Happy people also have a higher sense of personal control over their lives and exhibit higher levels of hope when facing challenges. Hope, according to Rick Snyder, is a better predictor of how well a student will do in college than the standardized tests students take to get in. Optimistic attitudes, as you will see next, provide health bonuses as well.[50,51]

TABLE 37.1	Happiness	
Researchers Have Found These Factors in Happy People	**Happiness Does *Not* Seem Greatly Related to These Factors**
High self-esteem (in Western countries)	Age
An optimistic, outgoing, and agreeable personality	Gender (women are more often depressed but also more often joyful)
Close friendships or a satisfying marriage	Education levels
Work and leisure that engage their skills	Parenthood (having children or not)
A meaningful religious faith	Physical attractiveness
Sufficient sleep and exercise	

Source: Summarized from DeNeve and Cooper (1998), Myers (1993, 2000), and Myers and Diener (1995, 1996).

Optimism

You've probably heard phrases like "Optimists see the glass as half full; pessimists see it as half empty." But what is the difference between an optimist and a pessimist? *Optimism* is the belief that bad events

- are temporary.
- are not your fault.
- are not indicative of how things usually are.

Pessimism is the opposite of optimism—the tendency to expect the worst. Let's look more closely at these contrasting attitudes, using the common situation of being let down by a friend. Imagine that the weekend is approaching and you're making plans for Friday night. Your friend Chris says, "I'll text you when we get where we're going." You wait for the text, but it never comes. How would you explain this to yourself? Would you assume Chris blew you off and didn't want to do anything with you? Or would you suppose something came up that kept your friend from texting? More specifically, which of the following phrases would best describe your reaction?

1. "I didn't get a text because Chris really doesn't like me."
2. "Maybe Chris wanted to text but had a dead cell phone."
3. "I wonder what came up that kept Chris from texting?"
4. "Chris doesn't really want to hang out with me Friday or any day."

The way you answered that question may give some clues to whether you are optimistic or pessimistic. Our habits for thinking about causes of good or bad events determine whether we have an optimistic or pessimistic **explanatory style.** People with an optimistic explanatory style are more likely to think of reasons 2 and 3, which provide temporary explanations that do not create a personal reason or fault for Chris's failure to call. Those with a pessimistic explanatory style would be likely to choose options 1 and 4, which place the blame on themselves and are permanent in nature.

Why is this optimism–pessimism thing important to wellness? In addition to spending less time in hospitals, healing faster, and living longer, optimists are far less likely to become depressed.[52–54]

explanatory style Habits we have for thinking about the good or bad causes of events.

Still Waiting
What do you think is this person's explanatory style?

I think HE is messing with us

www.cartoonstock.com

Fortunately, if you lean more to the pessimistic side and want to avoid some of the side effects of the negative explanatory style, there are steps you can take to think more positively about both good and bad events.

Techniques for Overcoming Pessimism

Too much optimism can result in an inappropriate lack of responsibility, but pessimism—expecting the worst or explaining bad events in the worst way—can lead to sadness, passivity, and depression. Developing a positive explanatory approach can help most people overcome pessimism.

Studies conducted under the supervision of Martin Seligman showed that changing from a negative to a positive explanatory style is possible and is especially beneficial for people at risk for depression. Most of these studies dealt with children identified as prone to depression.[55] Those who went through a program to change their thinking style were far less likely to show depressive symptoms later in life than those who did not go through the program.

There are at least two techniques for overcoming pessimism—distraction and disputation.[56,57] The first technique, *distraction*, attempts to delay the pessimistic thought until a more appropriate time. Distraction is especially useful when a situation requires immediate action and negative thoughts could prove disastrous. Soldiers approaching an enemy outpost, for example, must somehow distract themselves from such thoughts as "I could be killed," thoughts that could cause hesitation and possibly death.

Disputation, the second technique, is arguing with oneself about pessimistic beliefs. A longer-lasting technique than distraction, disputing pessimistic thoughts changes reactions from dejection to optimism. We can dispute pessimism in at least four ways:

- *Distancing*—Realizing that negative thoughts are usually unfounded helps distance us from pessimism's destructiveness. We do not tolerate insults about ourselves from others. Why accept them from ourselves? Do not think after a bad test score, "I'm a stupid idiot." Instead, think, "I didn't do well on *this* test."

- *Checking for evidence*—Evidence from other times and places can disprove a pessimistic belief. You may have received a bad math score this time, but that doesn't make you a failure at math. What about your score on a previous test, a homework assignment, or some other standardized test?

- *Considering alternatives*—Bad events often have multiple explanations, but pessimists usually focus on the most harmful and defeating. Instead of thinking, "I'm stupid, and I'll always stink at math" (a personal and permanent thought if there ever was one), think of explanations that pinpoint nonpersonal, specific, and changeable causes for the event. Your math score was bad, but did you study enough? Did you study effectively? Did other tests scheduled for the same day divide your attention?

- *Minimizing catastrophic thinking*—Finally, what if the negative thought is correct? If math is not your strength, realizing that this is not the end of the world can ease the pain brought by this belief. It may be that math is not your strong suit, but you have other gifts.[58]

LIFE MATTERS

Humor can temporarily reduce depression and can improve happiness. To heighten your mood, make a list of the three funniest things that happened to you this week or think about a humorous solution to a stressful problem.

Overcoming Illness-Related Behaviors

 37-3 What makes it difficult to quit smoking or lose weight?

Some behaviors increase our chances of becoming ill. Two of these behaviors are smoking and being significantly overweight. Note the following discussion on smoking does not take vaping into account, given that the research on vaping and health is still emerging.

Smoking

If a bus crashed, killing all 50 passengers aboard, this would be tragic. Imagine 25 of those buses crashing every day for a year and you have roughly the same number of annual deaths caused by smoking in the U.S. alone! With this kind of death rate, you'd think the public outcry to ban the sale of cigarettes would echo around the globe. Sadly, the World Health Organization predicts that 10 million people will soon be dying annually from smoking, meaning that a billion people (that's billion, not million) could die from smoking this century.[59,60] Smoking is a killer.

If you start smoking in your teens and never quit, you have a 50 percent chance of dying a premature and agonizing death from your addictive habit. This is an especially dangerous time for you, because almost all smokers start as adolescents, often to try to look older or to gain acceptance from peers[61] (see **Figure 37.5**). If your parents, siblings, and friends smoke, the chances are higher that you'll light up as well. Students who drop out, receive poor grades, or feel less control over their futures are also at a high risk.[62,63] But for those of you who haven't started smoking by the time you graduate from high school, the odds are tremendously low that you'll ever start this habit. And if your best friends and parents are nonsmokers, those odds drop to almost zero.[64]

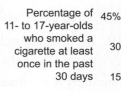

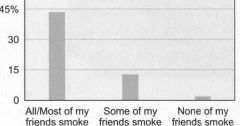

FIGURE 37.5
Peer Pressure
You are less likely to start a bad habit like smoking if your friends don't smoke.

We know smoking is bad for the lungs and heart, but smokers suffer other health risks:

- Smokers have high rates of depression and divorce.[65,66]
- Smokers lose 12 minutes off their life for every cigarette.[67]
- Smokers are three times more likely than nonsmokers to drink alcohol.[68]
- Smokers are 17 times more likely than nonsmokers to smoke marijuana illegally.[69]
- Smoking harms nearly every organ in your body.[70]

So, why don't teenage smokers throw out their cigarettes when they learn these facts? In part, it's because nicotine is incredibly addictive. One in three people who try cigarettes becomes hooked.[71] The craving for nicotine sets in quickly; even attempts to quit within the first weeks of smoking often fail.[72] Also, the withdrawal symptoms that accompany attempts to quit are horrible: Insomnia, anxiety, craving, and irritability are a few of the symptoms, all of which can be relieved by just a few puffs.

In contrast, the addictive qualities of nicotine are numerous and rewarding. Nicotine calms anxiety, boosts awareness, suppresses appetite, and reduces sensitivity to pain. These effects of nicotine surely compound the difficulty smokers face when attempting to kick the habit, even when they know death looms as a long-term smoking result.

Almost half of all smokers try to quit each year. For those who try to quit, the success rate is about 14 percent. If you have friends or relatives who would like to quit, you might want to pass along these 10 guidelines, published by the U.S. Agency for Health Care Policy and Research, as a way to improve their odds:

1. Set a quit date.
2. Inform family and friends.
3. Get rid of all cigarettes.
4. Review things you learned from previous attempts to quit and anticipate challenges.
5. Use a nicotine patch or gum.
6. Be abstinent—not one puff.
7. Avoid alcohol (which leads to relapse).
8. If other smokers live or work with you, quit together.
9. Avoid places where others are likely to smoke.
10. Exercise; research shows higher success rates in quitters assigned to regular physical activity.[73,74]

Smoking is an illness-related behavior you can control from the outset: Never try smoking, and you'll never be a smoker. We have less control over body weight, the next topic. We must also note that vaping is on the rise, and research is taking place to determine its risk. Our advice? Stay away from vaping too.

Obesity

Obesity rates are on the rise. More than one-third of all adults in the U.S. are obese, a percentage that has doubled in my lifetime.[75] Australia, France, and Canada are not far behind. Some have called the worldwide obesity increase a "global epidemic," not least because of the related rise in serious diseases such as diabetes.[76]

© Paul J. Milette/Palm Beach Post/ZUMA Press

Kick Butts!
Some communities plan special days to encourage smokers to kick the habit.

LIFE MATTERS
According to the 2018 Surgeon General Report, 5.6 million American kids that are currently under the age of 18 will die due to a smoking-related disease. No one starts smoking with the intent of becoming addicted, and yet only 1 out of 3 young smokers are able to quit. Stay away from nicotine... whether from a cigarette or from vaping.

Obesity's health risks are not as clear-cut as those connected to smoking. Still, people who are obese, with a **body mass index (BMI)** of 30 or more, face an increased risk of diabetes, high blood pressure, heart disease, arthritis, sleep disorders, and certain types of cancer, according to the National Institutes of Health.[77] In addition to the physical health risks, obesity carries significant mental health risks. Obesity affects how we think about ourselves and how others think about us and treat us. Seriously overweight people are often stereotyped as sloppy, slow, and lazy.[78,79] Researchers observed this type of discrimination in a study in which professional actors pretended to interview for a job.[80] The researchers videotaped the actors in two different situations, giving the same answers to the same questions and using the same voice intonation and gestures (see **Figure 37.6**).

The only difference between the two videotapes was the apparent weight of the job applicant. In one tape, the actors were their normal, average-weight selves. In the other, makeup and padding were added to make the actors look 30 pounds heavier. The researchers then assigned participants to view one of the two tapes and rate their willingness to hire the person. Those evaluating the "obese" applicant routinely rated the heavy person as *less worthy* of hiring. Discrimination against obese people rivals race and gender discrimination, and it occurs at every employment step from hiring and compensation to promotion and dismissal.[81,82] This discrimination is unfair, given the physiology of fat.

Weight Control

Have you ever wondered, "How does so-and-so eat that much but never gain any weight?" Do you have friends or relatives who always seem to be on some sort of diet but never make much progress in their attempts to lose weight? Are the people who buy the plus-size clothes merely gluttons who can't control the urge to eat? Let's unravel the mystery that is weight control.

The thin look has not always been "in," as it is today. Look at the paintings reflecting European high society centuries ago, and you'll see that being round, even rotund, was viewed as desirable. Obesity is still valued in countries where huge supermarkets are not found. In areas where famine strikes regularly, obesity often signifies wealth and social status.[83]

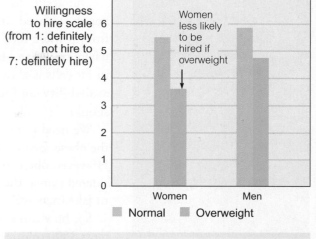

FIGURE 37.6
Discrimination
Overweight individuals, especially women, are less likely to be hired than are normal-weight individuals. (From Pingitore et al., 1994.)

body mass index (BMI) An individual's weight in kilograms (pounds multiplied by 0.45) divided by squared height in meters (inches divided by 39.4). The U.S. government guidelines encourage a BMI under 25. The World Health Organization and many countries define obesity as a BMI of 30 or higher.

Desired Look
Today's advertisements promote unrealistic body images.

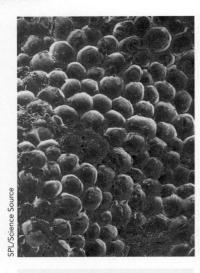

Human Fat Cells ▲
Fat cells like these divide after reaching a certain size. Dieting reduces the size of each fat cell, but dieting cannot reduce the overall *number* of fat cells.

set point The point at which an individual's "weight thermostat" is supposedly set; when the body falls below this weight, an increase in hunger and a lowered metabolic rate may act to restore the lost weight.

Our ability to store energy in fat cells reflects the feast-or-famine life-style our ancestors faced thousands of years ago. Fat is the perfect fuel reserve. We draw from it when food is scarce. But now that most people in the U.S. live in a world where sweets and fatty foods are abundant, our genetic program for storing energy in fat cells is about as outdated as 1980s software. With today's increased food availability, an increasing number of folks are carrying more weight than they should.

We need to make sure we draw a line between the moderately overweight and the obese. Being a little overweight does not pose near the health risks of obesity.[84] However, obese 40-year-olds die an average of three years earlier than those considered slim at the same age.[85] Sadly, once the pounds are on, most find it difficult to take them off.

So, how can we lose our excess pounds? The energy equivalent of a pound of fat is 3500 calories. But cutting 3500 calories from our food intake won't drop our weight by 1 pound. To understand why weight loss is not that simple, you have to know a bit more about fat cells, set point, and metabolism.

The average adult has about 30 billion fat cells. As we take in more calories than we need, these cells enlarge. Once fat cells reach a certain size, they divide and create more cells. Does dieting reduce the number of fat cells? *No.* Dieting only reduces the *size* of these cells, all of which remain ready to grow again once we resume a higher-calorie regimen.[86,87]

A second reason that reducing your diet by 3500 calories does not automatically cause you to drop a pound relates to your **set point**—a "weight thermostat" set to keep your body weight within a certain range. If your weight drops below your set-point range, your body thinks, "Famine!" and attempts to conserve energy by increasing your hunger and slowing your metabolism—the rate at which you burn calories. To make things worse, when your diet ends and you start eating normally, your body remains in this energy-conservation mode. The amount of food that formerly *maintained* your normal weight may now actually *increase* your weight.

Metabolic rates vary from person to person. You and a friend who is your height and weight may eat the same amount of food, but one of you may put on pounds, while the other does not, even though you both maintain the same activity level. If your resting metabolism is slower than your friend's, you'll be the one who burns fewer calories, making you prone to weight gain (see Psychology in the Real World: Losing Weight).

The roots of your metabolic rate are genetic. Genes may also determine how quickly your brain receives a "full" signal once you start eating and the efficiency with which you convert extra calories to fat. Will there someday be a pill that blocks the chemical "time-to-eat" messages in your nervous system? For some overweight people, such a pill may be the only way to overcome the physiology of obesity. Ultimately, it is better to accept a few pounds than to slip into a continual state of guilt over weight that leads to diets and bingeing.

The goal of wellness is important and worthy. The good news is that wellness can be strengthened through healthy attitudes and a healthy life-style. One could easily argue that we'd be better off in our schools (and communities) if we were just as concerned about wellness as we are about standardized math scores. So, challenge yourself, your peers, and your family to make physical and psychological well-being part of the daily routine. You'll never regret increasing the wellness in yourself and in those you love and respect.

PSYCHOLOGY IN THE REAL WORLD

Losing Weight

Your physiological deck may be stacked against weight loss. Still, if you (or a friend) are looking to shed a few pounds, here are some hints that may prove helpful:

- *Reduce exposure to tempting food cues.* Keep the chips and ice cream out of the house, and don't go near sweet shops. Never, ever go to the supermarket when you're hungry.

- *Boost your metabolism.* Exercise speeds up your metabolism and lowers your set point. Walking, jogging, and swimming empty fat cells, build muscle, and make you feel better.

- *Be patient, realistic, and moderate.* Extreme thinness is riskier than moderate heaviness.[88] The National Institutes of Health says that a reasonable amount of time to lose 10 percent of your body weight is six months.

- *Permanently change the food you eat.* You can modify both your hunger and your metabolism by eating foods with more fiber and color (the natural kind) and less fat, salt, and sugar, as well as by eating more fruits and vegetables. The sugar in fruits stimulates less hunger-producing insulin than the refined sugar in soft drinks, candy, and Lucky Charms.

- *Control your portions.* Eat slowly to give your body a chance to send "I'm full" signals to your brain. Don't stuff yourself, and don't feel obliged to finish the oversized portions you'll receive in many restaurants.

- *Don't skip breakfast and lunch to eat a big dinner.* This eating pattern slows metabolism and is common among overweight people.

RODNEY KICKED OFF HIS NEW FITNESS REGIME BY BUYING A HEAVIER REMOTE CONTROL ...THIS WAS NOT ENOUGH!

www.cartoonstock.com

▲ **Couch Potato?**
Watching television will not boost your metabolism.

- *Set attainable goals.* You guarantee defeat if you set your target weight unrealistically low. Realistic goals, like exercising three times per week, can build a sense of persistence.

THINK ABOUT . . . Psychology in the Real World

1. What does it mean to say that your "physiological deck may be stacked against you" with regard to controlling your weight?

2. Someone says to you, "I want to lose weight." What three hints or tips would you give this person?

3. Looking at your responses to question number 2, explain why you chose those three hints or tips.

MAKE IT STICK!

1. What is the term used to describe an individual's "weight thermostat"?

2. People who do not start smoking by the time they graduate high school
   a. are unlikely to ever start smoking.
   b. don't have the genetic predisposition for smoking.
   c. are at high risk for starting smoking during college.
   d. probably have parents who smoke.

3. True or False: Research shows that people evaluating "obese" job applicants routinely rated the heavy person as less worthy of hiring due to appearance.

Module 37 Summary and Assessment

Promoting Wellness

 37-1 What are the research findings related to wellness and exercise, social ties, and spirituality?

- Exercise is an effective nonmedical way to reduce anxiety and depression and has many specific positive benefits, including improving mood, enhancing cognitive abilities, lowering blood pressure, and improving sleep. Physical fitness leads to greater self-confidence and self-discipline.

- Social ties are important to overall wellness.

- Spirituality is positively correlated with aspects of wellness such as longevity.

 37-2 What is the relationship between wellness and flow experiences, happiness, and optimistic explanatory styles?

- Flow experiences contribute to happiness and wellness.

- Happy people tend to be more outgoing, interact more with others, have a larger circle of friends, participate in more rewarding activities, have a higher sense of personal control over their lives, and exhibit higher levels of hope when facing challenges.

- People with optimistic explanatory styles are more physically healthy, live longer, and are far less likely to become depressed than people with pessimistic explanatory styles.

 37-3 What makes it difficult to quit smoking or lose weight?

- Smoking is an addictive habit correlated with depression, divorce, premature death, alcoholism, and other drug abuse. One in three people who try cigarettes becomes hooked, and withdrawal symptoms such as insomnia, anxiety, craving, and irritability make quitting difficult.

- Our metabolic rate, the rate at which we burn calories, is genetically predisposed.

- The set point influences our metabolic rate, making weight loss more difficult.

Summative Assessment

1. According to research, which of the following treatments has shown the greatest decrease in depression?

   a. aerobic exercise
   b. relaxation exercise
   c. no treatment
   d. sleep therapy

2. Which of the following does NOT provide a buffer against the effects of stress?

   a. exercise
   b. family and friends
   c. optimism
   d. smoking

3. What do we call the study of emotions, feelings, and experiences that foster well-being and allow us to thrive?

   a. faith
   b. positive psychology
   c. well-being
   d. achieving flow

4. Which of the following describes the state of flow?

   a. activities we perform for the satisfaction of doing them
   b. experiences that foster well-being and allow us to thrive
   c. the tendency to be more outgoing and interact with others
   d. the belief that bad events are temporary

5. What do we call our habits for thinking about the causes of good or bad events?

   a. explanatory style
   b. pessimism
   c. optimism
   d. flow

6. Which of the following helps overcome pessimistic thinking?

   a. maximizing catastrophic thinking
   b. ignoring alternatives
   c. checking for evidence
   d. set point

7. Which of the following would improve the odds that a person could quit smoking?

   a. avoiding alcohol
   b. keeping cigarettes in a drawer
   c. going to places where others smoke to face temptation
   d. staying away from nicotine patches

8. A person with a BMI of _____ is considered obese.

   a. 15
   b. 5
   c. 30
   d. −10

9. Which of the following best describes your set point?

   a. menu guide
   b. calorie counter
   c. body mass index
   d. weight thermostat

10. Which of the following would NOT help you lose weight?

   a. Set an attainable target weight.
   b. Skip breakfast and lunch so that you can eat a big dinner.
   c. Be patient and realistic about your progress.
   d. Reduce exposure to tempting food cues.

KEY TERMS AND KEY PEOPLE

wellness, p. 561

positive psychology, p. 567

flow, p. 568

explanatory style, p. 569

body mass index (BMI), p. 573

set point, p. 574

Martin Seligman (1942–), p. 561

Careers in Psychology

Learning Goals

A-1 Identify some of the different kinds of jobs that psychologists do.

Ever ponder pursuing a career in psychology? There are many options.

The most popular college major in the country is business. The fourth most popular major is psychology. More than 118,000 college students graduate annually with a degree in psychology.[1] Figure A.1 shows the number of psychology undergraduate and graduate degrees issued just a couple of years ago.

Types of Psychologists

 A-1 What are some of the different kinds of jobs that psychologists do?

Why is a psychology major so popular? Yes, psychology is incredibly interesting, but psychology can also prepare you for a number of jobs after you graduate. **Table A.1** shows the top 10 occupations for people who graduate with a bachelor's degree in psychology, the degree that college undergraduates typically earn after four years of study.

To be a *psychologist*, however, you will need a graduate degree beyond a bachelor's. Most psychology graduate students take five to seven years to earn a doctoral degree in one of psychology's subfields. The most common kind of psychologist is a *clinical psychologist* (also called a *clinician*). These psychologists use their skills as therapists, assessment specialists, and researchers to promote

TABLE A.1   Top 10 U.S. Occupations That Employ People With a Psychology Degree

1. Top- and mid-level managers, executives, administrators
2. Sales occupations, including retail
3. Social workers
4. Other management-related occupations
5. Personnel, training, labor relations specialists
6. Other administrative occupations
7. Insurance, securities, real estate, business services
8. Other marketing and sales occupations
9. Registered nurses, pharmacists, therapists, physician assistants
10. Accountants, auditors, other financial specialists

Source: Fogg et al. (2004).

psychological health in groups and individuals. They may work to help someone overcome a phobia or to help make life better for someone with a psychological disorder such as schizophrenia. Clinicians often open up private practices, but they also work in medical systems, schools, counseling centers, government agencies, and mental health service organizations. Clinical psychologists must also pass tests to ensure competence (in conducting therapy) in the states where they practice.

When most people think of a psychologist, they picture a therapist in a chair with notebook in hand and the patient or client talking about life's problems while reclining on a couch in the therapist's office. Contrary to popular belief, not all psychologists make a living diagnosing and treating patients for psychological problems. While clinical psychologists and *counseling psychologists* do represent the largest number of professional psychologists, psychology is made up of a number of subfields (see **Figure A.1**). Psychologists work in many different locations beyond clinical settings where therapy is conducted.

**FIGURE A.1
Psychologists at Work**
Number of psychology master's and doctoral degrees awarded by year: 2004–2013 (Data from APA Center for Workplace Studies, 2015.)

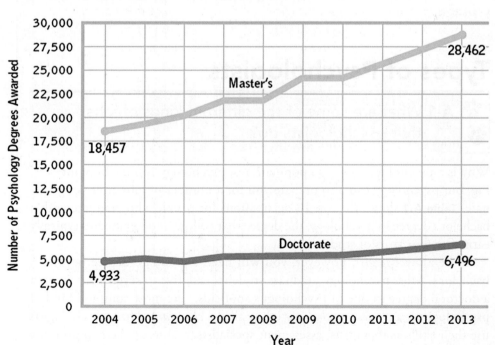

Academic Psychologists

Many of those earning a doctorate in psychology become *academic psychologists*. These psychologists work in colleges and universities conducting **basic research** in a number of subfields. To appreciate some of their interests, consider these examples of academic psychologists and the kinds of questions they might attempt to answer:

basic research Pure science that aims to increase the scientific knowledge base.

- *Neuropsychologists* (also called *biological psychologists* or *biopsychologists*) explore how the structures of the brain work to produce behaviors. Using the most advanced technology, such as magnetic resonance imaging (MRI), functional MRI (fMRI), and single-photon-emission computed tomography (SPECT), neuropsychologists often study a disorder, such as bipolar disorder, attempting to diagnose, treat, and explain how this disorder disrupts normal neurological functioning. A biological psychologist might ask "How does the brain scan of someone with bipolar disorder who is in a depressed state differ from the brain scan of the same person while in a manic state?" The answers to this and similar questions help neuropsychologists search for new and improved disorder treatments. Neuropsychologists work most often in university or college settings, where they teach classes and conduct research.

Chad Studholme

▲ **Neuroimaging**
Images like these help neuropsychologists study brain activity in people with disorders such as bipolar disorder. The top photos use MRI technology, the second row shows SPECT technology, and the third shows how the two are combined and recolored to demonstrate the differences between them.

- *Social psychologists* explore how our behaviors, feelings, and beliefs are influenced by our interactions with others. Social psychologists study topics such as conformity, attitudes, leadership, prejudice, and group behavior. They provide some of the most interesting research findings you will read in any introductory psychology textbook. A social psychologist might ask "Under what circumstances do young adults feel compelled to light up a cigarette, even when they know it is unhealthy?" To answer this question, social psychologists might show one group of teens a video of famous people smoking at a party and then a second group of teens a video of the same celebrities at a party *not* smoking. Following the viewing of the video clips, the teens' attitudes toward smoking would be assessed. Social psychologists work in a number of settings, including businesses that conduct marketing research, consulting firms, government agencies, and universities, where they teach classes and conduct research.

- *Developmental psychologists* study the growth or development that takes place from womb to tomb. It is common for developmental psychologists to study several aspects of development (for example, growth patterns or memory skills) or to provide input on educational issues, child-care policies, or geriatric matters. A developmental psychologist might ask "How does attending day care affect readiness for kindergarten?" To answer this question, a developmental psychologist might give a letter recognition test to 5-year-olds who attended day care and 5-year-olds who did not. Comparing the two groups to see who had more correct answers could help parents decide whether they should put their children in day care or not. The developmental psychologists who specialize in research can be found working in university settings. Other developmental psychologists might work for government agencies, day-care facilities, hospitals, or senior centers.

Psychology: A Science and a Profession
Psychologists experiment with, observe, test, and treat behavior. Here we see psychologists testing a child, recording children's behavior, and doing face-to-face therapy.

- *Cognitive psychologists* study thought processes in an effort to add to psychology's reservoir of knowledge. The thought processes they study include an array of topics: intelligence, anger, problem solving, attention, decision making, language, happiness, perception, memory, forgetting, and more. A cognitive psychologist might ask "How do old memories interfere with new memories?" The work of cognitive psychologists explains why it can be difficult to remember a new password for Facebook. You have used the old password so many times that the memory of it interferes with the way your brain accesses the new password. Most cognitive psychologists work in educational settings, but some find jobs as industrial consultants or in other business settings.

- *Experimental* or *research psychologists* focus on doing research and can be specialists in any of psychology's subfields. They can ask any question pertinent to psychological science: "Do personality traits change from childhood to old age?" "How does neural activity during sleep promote learning in rats?" "Can regular exercise reduce the effects of stress?" Most experimental psychologists work in a college or university setting, but many work for government agencies or for businesses that base their production or marketing decisions on scientific research.

Cognitive Psychologists
Business leaders often consult cognitive psychologists to determine the best way to operate their businesses. These psychologists explain the human factors involved in effectively running businesses.

Psychologists Who Solve Problems

Other psychologists are more interested in **applied research**—solving specific practical problems rather than expanding the scientific knowledge base of psychology. To appreciate this approach, consider the following examples of psychologists who lean toward the applied side and the types of questions they might attempt to answer:

applied research Scientific study that aims to solve practical problems.

- *Forensic psychologists* apply both law and psychology to legal issues. Perhaps you've seen a forensic psychologist or two on one of the many TV shows that re-create crimes. Indeed, forensic psychologists analyze crime scenes and evidence to help law officials solve crimes. However, they also use their scientific training to help settle insurance claims and custody disputes. A forensic psychologist might ask "Is it in a child's best interest to testify in a custody case?" To answer this question, a forensic psychologist might look at past cases in which young children took the stand to testify and research how giving the testimony affected the children. Did the children become more withdrawn after testifying? Did they experience depression? Did their school marks suffer? Or did they seem unaffected in school and in life? You'll find forensic psychologists working in correctional facilities, law-enforcement agencies, mental health agencies, and academic settings (including law schools).

▲ **Forensic psychologists**
Forensic psychologists, like the one played by Aisha Tyler on *Criminal Minds*, help police conduct criminal investigations.

- *Sports psychologists* explore the psychological issues revolving around the improvement of athletic performance. Golfers who have trouble putting, basketball players who miss most of their free throws, and football players who suddenly cannot kick the ball between the goalposts might consider consulting a sports psychologist to help improve their concentration or focus. The sports psychologists on the U.S. Olympic team often take athletes through a "positive visualization" of their events to help prepare them for the high-stress situations they'll be in once the Olympic Games start. A sports psychologist might ask "What kind of visual imaging should an athlete do before competing to increase the chances of success?" The sports psychologist might suggest that a golfer visualize standing over the golf ball, putter in hand, and then picture making a backswing, tapping the ball, and watching the ball go into the cup. Many sports psychologists are hired by professional and college sports teams, but some open private practices.

- *Educational psychologists* study how humans learn and often look for ways to improve the learning process. They study the psychological processes associated with learning, develop strategies to improve learning, and explore the relationship between learning and social or physical environment. An educational psychologist might ask "How do we help fifth-grade students who are reading at a third-grade level catch up with their peers?" The educational psychologist might then assign and help the fifth-graders work through reading exercises that, if successfully completed, would increase the chances of reading at the proper age and grade level. The educational psychologists might also be hired to design and implement the employee-training program new hires have to complete to work for a fast-food chain like Taco Bell or Subway. Employment locations include psychology departments in university settings, school systems, private practice, and government agencies.

- *Human factors psychologists* explore how people and machines interact at home and in the workplace to minimize frustration and maximize safety and productivity. For instance, a human factors psychologist might examine computer software and then make suggestions about how to make the software programs simpler to learn, install, or run. Human factors psychologists also study workplace *ergonomics,* which aims to reduce discomfort and fatigue while maximizing productivity. A human factors psychologist might ask "How should computer keyboards be positioned to keep hands and fingers from getting tired after prolonged use?" These psychologists work in the business world and are often hired by government and military agencies.

- *Industrial-organizational (I/O) psychologists* use psychological concepts to help entire businesses and organizations operate better and more efficiently. An I/O psychologist might help hire the right people for a given job, suggest ways to promote job satisfaction, or study consumer behavior so that businesses can make decisions about the products they want to sell. An I/O psychologist might ask "What's the best way to change the overall work environment to maximize productivity?" For instance, the work of I/O psychologists has suggested that multitasking actually decreases workplace productivity.[2] You will find I/O psychologists in government, industry, business, and academic settings, although some run their own consulting firms.

- *School psychologists* work to improve the development of children in an elementary, middle, or high school setting. Most often, they are involved in the testing or assessment of children in educational settings. After analyzing testing results, a school psychologist meets with parents, educators, and specialists to develop an appropriate intervention if necessary. Helping children deal with the emotional, social, and cognitive problems they experience at school or at home is common practice for school psychologists. A school psychologist might ask "What kind of an individual educational plan does this student need to maximize potential learning?" To help develop this plan, the school psychologist would look at the results of the data gathered on a student—perhaps a third-grader having difficulty with math—and set up the mentoring sessions that would help the child learn how to multiply and divide. You will find school psychologists in child guidance centers; public or private elementary, middle, or high school systems; and in federal or government agencies.

Psychologists Apply Research ▶
The sports psychologist and the school psychologist in these pictures apply knowledge learned from basic research to do their jobs.

Ross Kinnaird/Getty Images

pressmaster/Deposit Photos

- *Consumer psychologists* use research to help figure out why some people buy a product and others do not. They want to know what influences consumer responses. The goal is to be able to describe and predict consumer practices, beliefs, and emotions. A consumer psychologist might ask "What kind of a slogan or advertisement will help sell this new iPhone?" The consumer psychologist would conduct tests to see whether iPhone ads featuring the singer Drake were more likely to grab attention than iPhone ads featuring royalty like the Duke and Duchess of Sussex (Prince Harry and Meghan Markle). Consumer psychologists, like many psychologists, most often work in business and academic settings.

Better Deal?
Would you be more likely to watch an advertisement featuring a famous musical artist or a royal couple?

- *Rehabilitation psychologists* help those who have suffered an accident or illness that has resulted in the loss of optimal cognitive or physical skills. Head injury or stroke victims often require the assistance of rehabilitation psychologists to relearn language or the motor activity involved in tasks like eating or drinking. A rehabilitation psychologist might ask "What part of the brain has been injured?" to predict the relearning that will likely be necessary. For instance, knowing that the injured part of the stroke victim's brain was responsible for communication, the rehabilitation psychologist would create a recovery program in which the stroke patient would practice basic speaking skills. Rehabilitation psychologists most often work in medical rehabilitation settings.

- *Health psychologists* research ways to prevent disease and promote health. These psychologists are likely to design and evaluate programs to help people lose weight, stop smoking, or improve sleep. Health psychologists look at the factors that lead to health problems and suggest the interventions necessary to make life better. Another common health psychologists' practice is meeting with government officials to advocate and develop public health policy. A health psychologist might ask "What are the benefits of banning smoking from public places like restaurants and bars?" Health psychologists are employed at hospitals, public health agencies, rehabilitation centers, and universities. If a health psychologist has clinical training, working in a private practice is also likely.

- *Social workers* are individuals with an undergraduate or master's degree in psychology or social work who want to improve the lives of others. Usually, social workers are not psychologists. (That is, they do not have doctoral degrees.) Social workers may help resolve family problems, work to find adequate housing for those who need it, or assist those facing disability, substance abuse, or unemployment. A social worker might ask "How does improving the home environment help a person function best?" Perhaps the answer to that question begins with trying to make sure the family regularly eats dinner together. Social workers are most often employed by government agencies, schools, and residential care facilities.

There are many more types of psychologists working in the field. **Table A.2** lists many of the American Psychological Association's (APA's) 55 divisions, each of which may have a number of specialized subfields. Although many psychologists help people work through depression, overcome fears, or analyze character, the range of other available roles is wide.

TABLE A.2   Selected APA Divisions by Number and Name
1. Society for General Psychology
2. Society for the Teaching of Psychology
3. Experimental Psychology
5. Evaluation, Measurement, and Statistics
6. Behavioral Neuroscience and Comparative Psychology
7. Developmental Psychology
8. Society for Personality and Social Psychology
12. Society of Clinical Psychology
14. Society for Industrial and Organizational Psychology
15. Educational Psychology
19. Society for Military Psychology
20. Adult Development and Aging
21. Applied Experimental and Engineering Psychology
22. Rehabilitation Psychology
23. Society for Consumer Psychology
29. Psychotherapy
30. Society of Psychological Hypnosis
33. Intellectual and Developmental Disabilities
34. Population and Environmental Psychology
35. Society for the Psychology of Women
36. Psychology of Religion
38. Health Psychology
40. Clinical Neuropsychology
43. Family Psychology
45. Society for the Psychological Study of Ethnic Minority Issues
46. Media Psychology
47. Exercise and Sport Psychology
48. Society for the Study of Peace, Conflict, and Violence: Peace Psychology Division
50. Addictions

Source: American Psychological Association.

MAKE IT STICK!

1. Which of the following issues is a clinical psychologist most likely to deal with?

   a. what neurons are involved in emotional reactions

   b. a phobia about flying

   c. how children's thinking develops as they age

   d. what teaching methods are most effective

2. What is one goal all applied research psychologists share?

   a. to conduct basic research that expands the knowledge base of psychology

   b. to help people with mental illnesses

   c. to use the scientific method to diagnose and treat psychological disorders

   d. to use existing psychological research to solve specific, practical problems

Appendix A Summary and Assessment
Careers in Psychology

A-1 What are some of the different kinds of jobs that psychologists do?

- The most common psychological career is clinical psychology. Clinical psychologists use their skills to promote psychological health in groups and individuals. Clinical psychologists work in private practices, medical systems, schools, counseling centers, government agencies, and mental health service organizations.

- Academic psychologists work in colleges and universities conducting basic research. Neuropsychologists (or biopsychologists) explore how the structures of the brain work to produce behaviors. Social psychologists explore how our behaviors and mental processes are influenced by our interactions with others. Developmental psychologists study growth or development that takes place over the life span. Cognitive psychologists study mental processes. Experimental psychologists specialize in doing research in any of psychology's subfields.

- Applied researchers work to solve specific practical problems rather than to expand the scientific knowledge base of psychology. Forensic psychologists apply the law and psychological research methods to legal issues. Sports psychologists explore the psychological issues involved in improving athletic performance. Educational psychologists study how humans learn and look for ways to improve the learning process. Human factors psychologists explore how people and machines interact to minimize frustration and maximize safety and productivity. Industrial/organizational (I/O) psychologists use psychological concepts to help businesses and organizations operate better and more efficiently. School psychologists work to improve the development of children in school settings. Consumer psychologists use research to figure out why people buy products. Rehabilitation psychologists help those who have lost optimal cognitive or physical skills because of medical conditions. Health psychologists research ways to prevent disease and promote health. Social workers have an undergraduate or master's degree in psychology or social work and want to improve the lives of others.

KEY TERMS

basic research, p. A-3   applied research, p. A-4

Answers to Summative Assessment Questions

Appendix B

Module 2
1. a
2. c
3. b
4. d
5. a
6. a
7. b
8. c
9. a
10. d

Module 3
1. d
2. b
3. d
4. c
5. c
6. d
7. b
8. a
9. c
10. d

Module 4
1. a
2. d
3. c
4. c
5. c
6. c
7. b
8. a
9. d
10. d

Module 5
1. c
2. b
3. d
4. d
5. a
6. a
7. d
8. c

9. b
10. b

Module 6
1. a
2. d
3. d
4. c
5. b
6. c
7. a
8. a
9. d
10. b

Module 7
1. a
2. d
3. a
4. c
5. c
6. d
7. b
8. a
9. c
10. d

Module 8
1. b
2. d
3. d
4. c
5. a
6. b
7. b
8. d
9. b
10. a

Module 9
1. a
2. c
3. b
4. a
5. d

6. d
7. b
8. c
9. c
10. d

Module 10
1. c
2. d
3. a
4. c
5. b
6. b
7. d
8. c
9. a
10. b

Module 11
1. b
2. d
3. c
4. b
5. a
6. c
7. b
8. d
9. a
10. b

Module 12
1. b
2. c
3. a
4. a
5. d
6. b
7. c
8. a
9. d
10. b

Module 13
1. c
2. a

3. b
4. d
5. c
6. c
7. a
8. d
9. a
10. c

Module 14
1. d
2. a
3. c
4. a
5. c
6. b
7. b
8. c
9. d
10. a

Module 15
1. c
2. a
3. a
4. d
5. b
6. d
7. c
8. c
9. c
10. a

Module 16
1. d
2. b
3. c
4. c
5. a
6. d
7. c
8. a
9. c
10. b

Module 17
1. b
2. b
3. d
4. c
5. c
6. d
7. a
8. a
9. d
10. c

Module 18
1. c
2. b
3. d
4. a
5. c
6. c
7. d
8. a
9. a
10. d

Module 19
1. c
2. d
3. a
4. c
5. b
6. a
7. b
8. c
9. c
10. a

Module 20
1. b
2. a
3. c
4. d
5. a
6. d
7. c
8. b
9. a
10. c

Module 21
1. b
2. c

3. a
4. d
5. c
6. a
7. b
8. d
9. c
10. a

Module 22
1. a
2. c
3. d
4. c
5. b
6. a
7. b
8. a
9. d
10. d

Module 23
1. d
2. b
3. d
4. a
5. c
6. d
7. c
8. b
9. a
10. c

Module 24
1. d
2. a
3. d
4. a
5. d
6. b
7. a
8. d
9. b
10. d

Module 25
1. b
2. a
3. a
4. d
5. d

6. c
7. b
8. a
9. c
10. a

Module 26
1. b
2. b
3. c
4. d
5. d
6. d
7. c
8. d
9. d
10. c

Module 27
1. a
2. b
3. d
4. a
5. c
6. b
7. a
8. d
9. c
10. b

Module 28
1. a
2. b
3. c
4. a
5. a
6. a
7. c
8. b
9. d
10. a

Module 29
1. c
2. b
3. c
4. b
5. d
6. c
7. a
8. b

9. c
10. a

Module 30
1. b
2. c
3. d
4. d
5. a
6. a
7. c
8. d
9. c
10. a

Module 31
1. d
2. b
3. b
4. a
5. d
6. c
7. a
8. c
9. a
10. d

Module 32
1. b
2. a
3. c
4. d
5. b
6. d
7. a
8. d
9. b
10. c

Module 33
1. d
2. a
3. a
4. b
5. c
6. d
7. a
8. b
9. d
10. a

Module 34
1. a
2. c
3. b
4. d
5. a
6. b
7. c
8. a
9. a
10. a

Module 35
1. b
2. d

3. c
4. b
5. d
6. c
7. b
8. c
9. d
10. c

Module 36
1. a
2. c
3. b
4. d
5. a

6. b
7. a
8. c
9. d
10. a

Module 37
1. a
2. d
3. b
4. a
5. a
6. c
7. a
8. c

9. d
10. b

Appendix A
1. b
2. d

Glossary

English	Español
A	

absolute threshold The minimum amount of stimulation needed to detect a particular stimulus. (p. 93)

umbral absoluto Intensidad mínima requerida para detectar un estímulo. (pág. 93)

accommodation Adapting current schemas to incorporate new information. (p. 184)

acomodación Acción de adaptar el entendimiento que se posee (esquemas) con el propósito de incorporar nueva información. (pág. 184)

achievement motivation A desire for significant accomplishment; for mastery of things, people, or ideas; and for attaining a high standard. (p. 417)

motivación de logro Deseo de lograr algo importante, con respecto a cosas, personas o ideas; deseo de lograr un alto estándar. (pág. 417)

achievement tests Tests that attempt to measure what the test-taker has accomplished. (p. 403)

pruebas de rendimiento Pruebas destinadas a medir los logros de la persona que las toma. (pág. 403)

acquisition The process of developing a learned response. (p. 241)

adquisición Proceso mediante el cual se adquiere una respuesta aprendida. (pág. 241)

action potential A neural impulse; a brief electrical charge that travels down the axon of a neuron. (p. 63)

potencial de acción Impulso nervioso; corriente eléctrica breve que pasa por el axón de una neurona. (pág. 63)

Adler, Alfred (1870–1937) Neo-Freudian who thought social tensions were more important than sexual tensions in the development of personality. (p. 447)

Adler, Alfred (1870–1937) Neofreudiano que sostenía que las tensiones sociales son más importantes para el desarrollo de la personalidad que las tensiones sexuales. (pág. 447)

active listening Empathic listening in which the listener echoes, restates, and clarifies. (p. 526)

escuchar activamente Escuchar compenetradamente, haciendo eco, repitiendo y clarificando lo que dice otra persona. (pág. 526)

adolescence The transition period from childhood to adulthood, extending from puberty to independence. (p. 198)

adolescencia Etapa de transición de la niñez a la edad adulta, que se extiende desde la pubertad hasta la independencia del individuo. (pág. 198)

aggression Any physical or verbal behavior intended to hurt or destroy. (p. 316)

agresión Comportamiento físico o verbal que tiene la intención de causar daño o destruir. (pág. 316)

agonist A drug that boosts the effect of a neurotransmitter. (p. 68)

agonista Medicamento que aumenta el efecto de un neurotransmisor. (pág. 68)

algorithm A problem-solving strategy that guarantees the solution to a problem. (p. 384)

algoritmo Estrategia de resolución de problemas que garantiza la solución correcta. (pág. 384)

all-or-none principle The principle stating that if a neuron fires, then it always fires at the same intensity; all action potentials have the same strength. (p. 64)

principio de todo o nada Principio que sostiene que si una neurona transmite un impulso, siempre lo hace con la misma intensidad; todos los potenciales de acción tienen la misma potencia. (pág. 64)

Allport, Gordon (1897–1967) U.S. psychologist and trait theorist who researched the idea that individual personalities are unique. (p. 458)

Allport, Gordon (1897–1967) Psicólogo y teórico de rasgos de la personalidad, nacido en los Estados Unidos, que realizó investigaciones basadas en la idea de que cada personalidad es única. (pág. 458)

altruism Unselfish regard for the welfare of others. (p. 310)

altruismo Consideración desinteresada por el bienestar de los demás. (pág. 310)

Alzheimer's disease A progressive and irreversible brain disorder characterized by gradual deterioration of memory, reasoning, language, and, finally, physical functioning. (p. 218)

enfermedad de Alzheimer Trastorno progresivo e irreversible del cerebro, que se caracteriza por el deterioro gradual de la memoria, el razonamiento, el lenguaje y, por último, el funcionamiento físico. (pág. 218)

amphetamines Drugs that stimulate neural activity, speeding up body functions. (p. 157)

anfetaminas Medicamentos que estimulan la actividad nerviosa acelerando las funciones del organismo. (pág. 157)

amygdala [uh-MIG-duh-la] An almond-shaped neural cluster in the limbic system that controls emotional responses, such as fear and anger (p. 82)

amígdala Conjunto de fibras nerviosas con forma de almendra que se hallan en el sistema límbico e intervienen en emociones tales como el miedo y el enojo. (pág. 82)

anorexia nervosa An eating disorder in which normal-weight people (usually adolescent females) have a distorted self-perception of being "fat," put themselves on self-starvation regimens, and become dangerously underweight (15 percent or more below normal). (p. 422)

anorexia nerviosa Trastorno alimenticio en el cual las personas de peso normal (generalmente muchachas adolescentes) padecen de delirios que les hacen pensar que pesan demasiado, se someten a dietas de hambre y llegan a la delgadez extrema y peligrosa (bajando de peso un 15 por ciento o más). (pág. 422)

antagonist A drug that blocks the effect of a neurotransmitter. (p. 68)

antagonista Medicamento que bloquea el efecto de un neurotransmisor. (pág. 68)

antianxiety drugs A category of medications used to treat people undergoing significant stress; they can be helpful in treating people with anxiety disorders. (p. 541)

medicamentos antiansiedad Categoría de medicamentos que se emplean para tratar a personas que padecen de trastornos de ansiedad o estrés. (pág. 541)

antidepressant drugs A category of medications used primarily to boost serotonin levels in the brain; they can be helpful in treating major depression. (p. 542)

medicamentos antidepresivos Categoría de medicamentos que se emplean principalmente para tratar la depresión grave. (pág. 542)

antipsychotic drugs A category of medications used primarily to treat schizophrenia. (p. 541)

medicamentos antipsicóticos Categoría de medicamentos que se emplean principalmente para tratar la esquizofrenia. (pág. 541)

antisocial behavior Negative, destructive, unhelpful behavior. (p. 279)

comportamiento antisocial Conducta negativa, destructiva y poco servicial. (pág. 279)

antisocial personality disorder A personality disorder in which the person (usually a man) shows a lack of conscience for wrongdoing and a lack of respect for the rights of others. (p. 517)

trastorno antisocial de la personalidad Trastorno de personalidad en el cual un individuo (generalmente un hombre) no es consciente de que causa daño y no respeta los derechos de los demás. (pág. 517)

anxiety A vague feeling of apprehension or nervousness. (p. 491)

ansiedad Sensación vaga de aprensión o nerviosismo. (pág. 491)

applied research Scientific study that aims to solve practical problems. (pp. 10, A-4)

investigación aplicada Estudio científico que tiene el propósito de resolver problemas prácticos. (págs. 10, A-4)

aptitude tests Tests that attempt to predict the test-taker's future performance. (p. 403)

pruebas de aptitud Pruebas cuyo propósito es predecir el desempeño futuro de una persona. (pág. 403)

Asch, Solomon (1907–1996) Social psychologist who researched the circumstances under which people conform. (p. 293)

Asch, Solomon (1907–1996) Psicólogo social que estudió las circunstancias bajo las cuales las personas demuestran conformismo. (pág. 293)

assimilation Interpreting new experience in terms of existing schemas. (p. 184)

asimilación Interpretación que realiza una persona de una experiencia nueva basándose en esquemas ya existentes. (pág. 184)

attachment The emotional tie with another person shown by seeking closeness to the caregiver and showing distress on separation. (p. 189)

apego Lazo emocional con otra persona que se demuestra al buscar cercanía con la misma y que crea angustia al romperse. (pág. 189)

attitude The belief and feeling that predisposes someone to respond in a particular way to objects, people, and events. (p. 288)

actitud Creencia y sentimiento que predispone a un individuo a responder de una manera en particular a objetos, personas y sucesos. (pág. 288)

attribution theory The theory that we tend to explain the behavior of others as an aspect of either an internal disposition (an inner trait) or the situation. (p. 285)

teoría de atribución Teoría según la cual tendemos a dar una explicación casual del comportamiento de una persona, generalmente atribuyéndolo a la situación o la disposición de esa persona. (pág. 285)

auditory nerve The nerve that carries sound information from the ears to the temporal lobes of the brain. (p. 106)

nervio auditivo Nervio que transmite la información sonora de los oídos al lóbulo temporal del cerebro. (pág. 106)

authoritarian parenting A style of parenting marked by imposing rules and expecting obedience. (p. 191)

crianza autoritaria Estilo de crianza en el que se imponen reglas y se exige obediencia. (pág. 191)

authoritative parenting A style of parenting marked by making demands on the child, being responsive, setting and enforcing rules, and discussing the reasons behind the rules. (p. 192)

crianza disciplinada Estilo de crianza en el cual los padres exigen cosas al niño, son receptivos, imponen reglas y las hacen cumplir conversando con el niño acerca de las razones por las que imponen dichas reglas. (pág. 192)

automatic processing The unconscious and effortless process of encoding information such as space, time, and frequency. (p. 351)

procesamiento automático Codificación inconsciente de cierta información, tal como el espacio, el tiempo y la frecuencia, que se lleva a cabo sin esfuerzo. (pág. 351)

autonomic [aw-tuh-NAHM-ik] nervous system The division of the peripheral nervous system that controls the glands and muscles of the internal organs; its subdivisions are the sympathetic (arousing) division and the parasympathetic (calming) division. (pp. 71, 432)

sistema nervioso autónomo División del sistema nervioso periférico que controla las glándulas y los músculos de los órganos (tales como el corazón). Sus subdivisiones son la división simpática (estimulación) y la división parasimpática (relajación). (págs. 71, 432)

availability heuristic Estimating the likelihood of events based on their availability in memory. (p. 388)

heurística de la disponibilidad Estimación de la probabilidad de que ocurra un suceso, que se basa en la disponibilidad de dicho suceso en la memoria. (pág. 388)

aversive conditioning A type of counterconditioning that associates an unpleasant state (such as nausea) with an unwanted behavior (such as drinking alcohol). (p. 530)

condicionamiento aversivo Tipo de condicionamiento en el que se asocia un estado desagradable (tal como las náuseas) con un comportamiento inapropiado (tal como la ingestión de alcohol). (pág. 530)

axon The extension of a neuron through which neural impulses are sent. (p. 63)

axón Prolongación de una neurona por la que se transmiten los impulsos nerviosos. (pág. 63)

axon terminal The end point of a neuron, where neurotransmitters are stored. (p. 63)

terminal del axón Extremo de una neurona, en donde se almacenan los neurotransmisores. (pág. 63)

B

Bandura, Albert (1925–) Canadian–American psychologist who is a major figure in the study of observational learning. He developed the social-cognitive perspective and believes that to understand personality, one must consider the situation and the person's thoughts before, during, and after an event. (pp. 276, 465)

Bandura, Albert (1925–) Psicólogo canadiense estadounidense quien es figura principal en el estudio del aprendizaje observacional. Desarrolló la teoría cognitivo social de la personalidad, enfatizando que se debería considerar la situación y los pensamientos del individuo antes, durante y después de un acontecimiento. (págs. 276, 465)

Bartoshuk, Linda (1938–) Renowned researcher on the role of genetics and the treatment of disorders in the chemical senses of taste and smell. (p. 108)

Bartoshuk, Linda (1938–) Renombrada por investigar el papel de la genetica y el tratamiento de trastornos químicos en los sentidos del gusto y olfato. (pág. 108)

basal metabolic rate The body's resting rate at which we burn calories for energy. (p. 421)

índice de metabolismo basal Índice del consumo de energía del cuerpo durante el descanso. (pág. 421)

basic research Pure science that aims to increase the scientific knowledge base. (pp. 10, A-3)

investigación básica Ciencia pura cuya mira es aumentar la base de los conocimientos científicos. (págs. 10, A-3)

behavior genetics The school of thought that focuses on how much our genes and our environment influence our individual differences. (pp. 22, 323)

genética del comportamiento Corriente de pensamiento que se concentra en lo mucho que nuestros genes y el medio ambiente influyen nuestras diferencias individuales. (págs. 22, 323)

behavior therapy Therapy that applies learning principles to the elimination of unwanted behaviors. (p. 528)

terapia conductual Terapia que aplica principios de apredizaje a la eliminación de comportamientos no deseados. (pág. 528)

behaviorism The theory that psychology should only study observable behaviors, not mental processes. (pp. 15, 247)

conductismo Perspectiva según la cual la psicología debe limitarse a estudiar la conducta observable y no los procesos mentales. (págs. 15, 247)

Binet, Alfred (1857–1911) Developer of the first test to classify children's abilities using the concept of mental age. (p. 396)

Binet, Alfred (1857–1911) Creador de la primera prueba para clasificar la capacidad de los niños empleando el concepto de la edad mental. (pág. 396)

binocular cues Depth cues that require the use of both eyes. (p. 118)

señales binoculares Señales de profundidad visual que requieren el usar ambos ojos. (pág. 118)

biological perspective School of thought that focuses on the physical structures and substances underlying a particular behavior, thought, or emotion. (p. 20)

perspectiva biológica Corriente de pensamiento que se concentra en las estructuras físicas y en las sustancias que influencian un comportamiento, pensamiento o sentimiento en particular. (pág. 20)

biological rhythms Periodic physiological fluctuations. (p. 134)

ritmos biológicos Fluctuaciones fisiológicas periódicas. (pág. 134)

biomedical therapy The treatment of psychological disorders by changing the brain's functioning with prescribed drugs, electroconvulsive therapy, or surgery. (p. 539)

terapia biomédica Tratamiento de trastornos psicológicos que supone cambiar el funcionamiento del cerebro con medicamentos recetados, terapia electroconvulsiva o cirugía. (pág. 539)

bio-psycho-social model A contemporary perspective that assumes biological, psychological, and social factors combine and interact to produce psychological disorders. (p. 479)

modelo biopsicosocial Perspectiva contemporánea que supone que los trastornos psicológicos se producen por la combinación e interacción de factores biológicos, psicológicos y sociales. (pág. 479)

bipolar disorder A mood disorder (formerly called *manic depressive disorder*) in which the person alternates between the hopelessness of depression and the overexcited and unreasonably optimistic state of mania. (p. 502)

trastorno bipolar Trastorno anímico (anteriormente se denominaba enfermedad maníaco depresiva) en el que el individuo oscila entre la desesperanza de la depresión y la excitación extrema y el estado irracional optimista de la manía. (pág. 502)

blind spot The point at which the optic nerve travels through the retina to exit the eye; the lack of rods and cones at this point creates a small blind spot. (p. 101)

punto ciego Punto en el cual el nervio óptico pasa por la retina para salir del ojo. La falta de bastoncillos y conos receptores en este lugar produce un pequeño punto ciego. (pág. 101)

body mass index (BMI) An individual's weight in kilograms (pounds multiplied by 0.45) divided by squared height in meters (inches divided by 39.4). The U.S. government guidelines encourage a BMI under 25. The World Health Organization and many countries define obesity as a BMI of 30 or higher. (p. 573)

índice de masa corporal (IMC) Peso de una persona en kilogramos (número de libras multiplicado por 0.45) dividido por el cuadrado de su estatura en metros (número de pulgadas dividido por 39.4). La guía del gobierno estadounidense recomienda un IMC menos de 25. La Organización Mundial de la Salud y muchos países definen la obesidad como un IMC de 30 o más. (pág. 573)

bottom-up processing Information processing that analyzes the raw stimuli entering through the many sensory systems. (p. 92)

procesamiento del fondo hacia arriba Procesamiento de la información en bruto que entra por los diversos sistemas sensoriales. (pág. 92)

brainstem The oldest part and central core of the brain; it begins where the spinal cord swells as it enters the skull and is responsible for automatic survival functions. (p. 80)

tronco cerebral Parte central y más antigua del cerebro, que comienza en donde la médula espinal se ensancha para entrar en el cráneo. Controla las funciones automáticas de la sobrevivencia. (pág. 80)

Broca's area A brain area of the left frontal lobe that directs the muscle movements involved in speech. (p. 86)

área de Broca Parte del lóbulo frontal izquierdo del cerebro, que dirige los movimientos musculares relacionados con el habla. (pág. 86)

bulimia nervosa An eating disorder characterized by episodes of overeating—usually of high-calorie foods—followed by vomiting, use of laxatives, fasting, or excessive exercise. (p. 422)

bulimia nerviosa Trastorno de alimentación que se caracteriza por episodios de ingestión excesiva de alimentos, generalmente de alto contenido calórico, seguidos de vómito, uso de laxantes, ayuno o ejercicios físicos excesivos. (pág. 422)

bystander effect The tendency for a person to be less likely to give aid if other people are present. (p. 311)

comportamiento de transeúnte Tendencia de un transeúnte a ser menos capaz de prestar ayuda si están presentes otros transeúntes. (pág. 311)

C

caffeine Stimulant found in coffee, chocolate, tea, and some soft drinks. (p. 154)

cafeína Estimulante que se halla en el café, el chocolate, el té y algunas bebidas gaseosas. (pág. 154)

Cannon, Walter (1871–1945) U.S. physiologist who, with Philip Bard, concluded that physiological arousal and emotional experience occur simultaneously (see *Cannon–Bard theory*). (pp. 428, 551)

Cannon, Walter (1871–1945) Psicólogo estadounidense que, junto con Philip Bard, concluyó que la estimulación fisiológica y la experiencia emocional ocurren simultáneamente (véase la teoría de Cannon-Bard). (págs. 428, 551)

Cannon–Bard theory The theory that an emotion-arousing stimulus simultaneously triggers physiological responses and the subjective experience of emotion. (p. 428)

teoría de Cannon-Bard Teoría según la cual un estímulo que evoca emociones provoca simultáneamente reacciones fisiológicas y la experiencia subjetiva de la emoción. (pág. 428)

case study A research technique in which one person is studied in depth in the hope of revealing universal principles. (pp. 29, 77)

estudio de caso Técnica de investigación en la cual se estudia a un individuo a fondo con la esperanza de descubrir principios universales. (págs. 29, 77)

Cattell, Raymond [kuh-TELL] (1905–1998) English psychologist who researched whether some traits predicted others; he proposed 16 key personality dimensions or factors to describe personality. (p. 459)

Cattell, Raymond (1905–1998) Psicólogo inglés que estudió la posibilidad de que unos rasgos predijeran otros. Propuso 16 dimensiones clave o factores para describir la personalidad. (pág. 459)

central nervous system (CNS) The brain and the spinal cord. (p. 70)

sistema nervioso central El cerebro y la médula espinal. (pág. 70)

cerebellum [sehr-uh-BELL-um] The "little brain" attached to the rear of the brainstem; it helps coordinate voluntary movements and balance. (p. 81)

cerebelo Es el "pequeño cerebro" y está unido a la parte posterior del tronco cerebral; permite coordinar los movimientos voluntarios y el equilibrio. (pág. 81)

cerebral [seh-REE-bruhl] cortex The intricate fabric of interconnected neurons that form the body's ultimate control and information-processing center. (p. 83)

corteza cerebral Estructura compleja de células nerviosas conectadas entre sí, que forman los hemisferios cerebrales; principal centro de control y procesamiento de información del organismo. (pág. 83)

Chomsky, Noam (1928–) Linguist who argues that children have a predisposition to learn language, as though their brains were hardwired to pick up vocabulary and rules of grammar. (p. 232)

Chomsky, Noam (1928–) Lingüista que sostuvo que los niños están predispuestos a aprender el lenguaje, como si su cerebro tuviera un sistema integrado que les permitiera absorber vocabulario y reglas gramaticales. (pág. 232)

chromosomes Threadlike structures made of DNA molecules that contain genes. (p. 324)

cromosomas Estructuras filamentosas compuestas de moléculas de ADN que contienen los genes. (pág. 324)

chunking Organizing information into meaningful units. (p. 356)

agrupamiento de pensamientos Información ordenada en unidades coherentes. (pág. 356)

circadian [ser-KAY-dee-un] rhythms Biological rhythms (for example, of temperature and wakefulness) that occur approximately every 24 hours. (p. 134)

ritmos circadianos Ritmos biológicos (por ejemplo, de temperatura y estado de vigilia) que ocurren aproximadamente cada 24 horas. (pág. 134)

Clark, Kenneth (1914–2005) and Mamie Phipps Clark (1917–1983) Researchers whose work was used in the *Brown v. Board of Education* case that overturned segregation in schools. (p. 17)

Clark, Kenneth (1914–2005) y Mamie Phipps Clark (1917–1983) Investigadores cuyo trabajo fue usado en el caso Brown vs. Junta de Educación que puso fin a la segregación racial en las escuelas. (pág. 17)

classical conditioning A type of learning in which a stimulus gains the power to cause a response. (p. 239)	**condicionamiento clásico** Tipo de aprendizaje en el cual un estímulo adquiere el poder de producir una respuesta. (pág. 239)
client-centered therapy A humanistic therapy, developed by Rogers, in which the therapist uses techniques such as active listening within a genuine, accepting, empathic environment to facilitate the client's growth. (p. 526)	**terapia centrada en el cliente** Tipo de psicoterapia humanista creada por Rogers, en la cual el terapeuta emplea técnicas tales como escuchar activamente dentro de un entorno genuino, con aceptación y empatía, para facilitar el crecimiento personal del cliente. (pág. 526)
cocaine Stimulant derived from the leaves of the coca plant. (p. 156)	**cocaína** Estimulante que proviene de las hojas de la planta de coca. (pág. 156)
cochlea [KOHK-lee-uh] The major organ of hearing; a snail-shaped, bony, fluid-filled structure in the inner ear where sound waves are changed to neural impulses. (p. 106)	**cóclea** Órgano principal del oído. Estructura con forma de caracol, ósea y rellena de fluido que se halla en el oído interno en donde las ondas sonoras se convierten en impulsos nerviosos. (pág. 106)
cognition All mental processes associated with thinking, knowing, and remembering. (pp. 183, 251)	**cognición** Todos los procesos mentales asociados con el pensamiento, el saber y el recordar. (págs. 183, 251)
cognitive abilities All mental activities associated with thinking, knowing, and remembering. (p. 381)	**habilidades cognitivas** Todas las actividades mentales asociadas con el pensamiento, el conocimiento y la memoria. (pág. 381)
cognitive dissonance theory The theory that we act to reduce the discomfort (dissonance) we feel when two of our thoughts (cognitions) are inconsistent. (p. 290)	**teoría de la disonancia cognitiva** Teoría que dice que actuamos con el propósito de reducir la incomodidad (disonancia) que sentimos cuando tenemos dos pensamientos (cogniciones) contradictorios. (pág. 290)
cognitive map The mental representation of a place. (p. 271)	**mapa cognitivo** Representación mental de un lugar. (pág. 271)
cognitive perspective School of thought that focuses on how people think—how we take in, process, store, and retrieve information. (p. 20)	**perspectiva cognitiva** Corriente de pensamiento que se concentra en la forma en que absorbemos, procesamos, almacenamos y recuperamos información. (pág. 20)
cognitive therapy Therapy that teaches people new, more adaptive ways of thinking and acting. (p. 532)	**terapia cognitiva** Terapia que enseña la gente nuevas y más adaptables formas de pensar y actuar. (pág. 532)
cognitive-behavioral therapy Integrative therapy that combines changing self-defeating thinking with changing inappropriate behaviors. (p. 532)	**terapia cognitiva-conductual** Terapia integrativa que combina el cambio de creencias contraproducentes con el cambio de comportamientos inapropiados. (pág. 532)
collective unconscious Jung's concept of a shared, inherited reservoir of memory traces from our ancestors. (p. 447)	**inconsciente colectivo** Concepto de Carl Jung que dice que una reserva compartida y heredada de los recuerdos proviene de la historia de nuestros antepasados. (pág. 447)
collectivism Giving priority to the goals of the group (often the extended family or work group) and defining personal identity accordingly. (p. 336)	**colectivismo** Dando prioridad a los objetivos del grupo (a veces la familia extendida o el grupo de trabajo) y definiendo la identidad personal en acuerdo con él. (pág. 336)
companionate love A deep affectionate attachment we feel for those with whom our lives are intertwined. (p. 309)	**amor entre personas relacionadas** Apego profundo y cariñoso que sentimos por aquellos con quienes se comparte la vida. (pág. 309)
computed axial tomography (CT or CAT) A series of X-ray photographs taken from different angles and combined by computer into a composite representation of a slice through the body. (p. 78)	**tomografía axial computarizada (TC o TAC)** Serie de imágenes radiográficas obtenidas desde ángulos diferentes y combinadas digitalmente para reconstruir un corte transversal del cuerpo. (pág. 78)
concept A mental grouping based on shared similarity. (p. 381)	**concepto** Agrupación mental basada en semejanzas compartidas. (pág. 381)
concrete operational stage In Piaget's theory, the stage of cognitive development (from about 6 or 7 to 11 years of age) during which children gain the mental skills that let them think logically about concrete events. (p. 186)	**período operacional concreto** Según la teoría de Piaget, nivel del desarrollo cognitivo (desde aproximadamente los seis o siete años hasta los once años) durante el cual los niños adquieren la capacidad mental que les permite pensar lógicamente en situaciones concretas. (pág. 186)
conditioned response (CR) The response to the conditioned stimulus. (p. 241)	**respuesta condicionada** La respuesta al estímulo condicionado. (pág. 241)
conditioned stimulus (CS) A previously neutral stimulus that, through learning, gains the power to cause a response. (p. 240)	**estímulo condicionado** Estímulo previamente neutral que, mediante el aprendizaje, ha adquirido el poder de provocar una respuesta condicionada. (pág. 240)
cones Visual receptor cells located in the retina that can detect sharp details and color. (p. 101)	**conos** Células receptoras de la vista ubicadas en la retina que detectan los detalles bien definidos y el color. (pág. 101)
confirmation bias The tendency to focus on information that supports preconceptions. (pp. 28, 387)	**sesgo confirmatorio** Tendencia a concentrarse en la información que confirma las ideas preconcebidas que uno tiene. (págs. 28, 387)

conformity Adjusting behavior or thinking to coincide with a group standard. (p. 293)

conformidad Acomodación del comportamiento o el pensamiento para coincidir con el estándar de un grupo. (pág. 293)

confounding variable In an experiment, a variable other than the independent variable that could produce a change in the dependent variable. (p. 37)

variable de confusión En un experimento, la variable distinta a la variable independiente que podría influir un cambio sobre la variable dependiente. (pág. 37)

consciousness Awareness of yourself and your environment. (pp. 133, 165)

consciencia Conocimiento de uno mismo y su ambiente. (págs. 133, 165)

conservation The principle (which Piaget believed to be a part of concrete operational reasoning) that properties such as mass, volume, and number remain the same despite changes in the forms of objects. (p. 186)

conservación Principio (que Piaget consideraba parte del razonamiento operacional concreto) que sostiene que las propiedades tales como la masa, el volumen y el número se mantienen iguales a pesar de los cambios que ocurren en la forma de los objetos. (pág. 186)

context effect The enhanced ability to retrieve information when you are in an environment similar to the one in which you encoded the information. (p. 366)

efecto del contexto Capacidad de recordar información más fácilmente cuando se está en un ambiente similar al ambiente donde se estaba cuando se adquirió dicha información. (pág. 366)

continuous reinforcement In operant conditioning, a schedule of reinforcement in which a reward follows every correct response. (p. 267)

refuerzo continuo Según el condicionamiento operante, programa de refuerzo en el cual se da una recompensa después de cada respuesta correcta. (pág. 267)

control group The participants in an experiment who are not exposed to the independent variable. (p. 36)

grupo control Participantes de un experimento que no están expuestos a la variable independiente. (pág. 36)

convergence A binocular depth cue related to the tension in the eye muscles when the eyes track inward to focus on objects close to the viewer. (p. 119)

convergencia Señal de profundidad binocular relacionada con la tensión de los músculos del ojo cuando los ojos se mueven hacia adentro para enfocarse en objetos que están cerca de la cara. (pág. 119)

cornea The clear, curved bulge on the front of the eye that bends light rays to begin focusing them. (p. 99)

córnea Bulto transparente en la parte anterior del globo ocular que refracta los rayos de luz y comienza a enfocarlos. (pág. 99)

corpus callosum [KOR-pus kah-LOW-sum] The large band of neural tissue that connects the two brain hemispheres and allows them to communicate with each other. (p. 84)

cuerpo calloso Franja gruesa de fibras nerviosas que conecta los dos hemisferios cerebrales y transmite mensajes entre los mismos. (pág. 84)

correlation coefficient A statistical measure of the strength of the relationship between two variables. (p. 55)

coeficiente de correlación Medida estadística de la fuerza de la relación entre dos variables. (pág. 55)

correlational study A research project strategy that investigates the degree to which two variables are related to each other. (p. 30)

estudio de correlación Proyecto de investigación que permite descubrir hasta qué punto dos variables están relacionadas entre sí. (pág. 30)

critical period The optimal period shortly after birth when an organism's exposure to certain experiences produces proper development. (p. 190)

período crítico Etapa óptima inmediatamente después de nacer, en la cual la presencia de ciertos estímulos o experiencias produce un desarrollo apropiado del organismo. (pág. 190)

critical thinking Thinking that does not blindly accept arguments and conclusions. (p. 28)

pensamiento crítico Forma de pensar en la que no se aceptan razones y conclusiones ciegamente. (pág. 28)

cross-cultural research Research that tests hypotheses on many groups of people to understand whether principles apply across cultures. (p. 339)

estudio transcultural Investigación que prueba hipótesis en varios grupos de personas para averiguar si los principios se aplican a distintas culturas. (pág. 339)

cross-sectional study A research technique that compares individuals from different age groups at one time. (p. 33)

estudio transversal Método de investigación en el cual se comparan individuos de distintas edades al mismo tiempo. (pág. 33)

crystallized intelligence Accumulated knowledge and verbal skills. (p. 220)

inteligencia cristalizada Conocimiento acumulado y capacidad verbal de una persona. (pág. 220)

culture The shared attitudes, beliefs, norms, and behaviors of a group communicated from one generation to the next. (pp. 331, 335)

cultura Actitudes, creencias, normas y comportamientos de un grupo que se transmiten de una generación a la próxima. (págs. 331, 335)

culture specific Principles that are true only for people of a certain culture. (p. 339)

específico de una cultura Principios que son válidos solamente entre las personas de una cultura en particular. (pág. 339)

D

Darley, John (1938–) Psychologist who, with Bibb Latané, researched the circumstances that determine when a bystander will intervene on behalf of another person. (p. 311)

Darley, John (1938–) Psicólogo que, junto con Bibb Latané, estudió las circunstancias que determinan cuándo un transeúnte intervendrá a favor de otra persona. (pág. 311)

defense mechanisms In psychoanalytic theory, the ego's protective methods of reducing anxiety by unconsciously distorting reality. (p. 443)

mecanismos de defensa Según la teoría psicoanalítica, estrategias de protección del ego para reducir la ansiedad, en las que se distorsiona inconscientemente la realidad. (pág. 443)

deindividuation The loss of self-awareness and self-restraint occurring in group situations that foster arousal and anonymity. (p. 299)

desindividuación Pérdida de la consciencia de uno mismo y de las inhibiciones, que ocurre cuando se está en un grupo en el que se fomenta la excitación y el anonimato. (pág. 299)

deinstitutionalization The release of patients from mental hospitals into the community. (p. 540)

desinstitucionalización Dar de alta a pacientes de hospitales psiquiátricos permitiéndoles reingresar a la comunidad. (pág. 540)

delusions False beliefs that are symptoms of schizophrenia and other serious psychological disorders. (p. 513)

delirios Creencias falsas que son síntomas de esquizofrenia y otros trastornos psicológicos graves. (pág. 513)

Dement, William (1928–) Sleep researcher who coined the term *rapid eye movement (REM)*. (p. 135)

Dement, William (1928–) Investigador que estudió el sueño y creó el término sueño de movimientos oculares rápidos (MOR). (pág. 135)

dendrite The branching extensions of a neuron that receive information and conduct impulses toward the cell body (soma). (p. 63)

dendrita Prolongación ramificada de la neurona que recibe mensajes y envía impulsos hacia el cuerpo neuronal (soma). (pág. 63)

dependence State of physiological or psychological need (or combined need) to take more of a drug after continued use. (p. 149)

dependencia Necesidad fisiológica o psicológica (o necesidad combinada) de aumentar el consumo de una sustancia después del uso prolongado. (pág. 149)

dependent variable (DV) The variable that should show the effect of the independent variable. (p. 36)

variable dependiente (VD) La variable sobre la que influye la variable independiente. (pág. 36)

depressants Drugs (such as alcohol and sedatives) that reduce neural activity and slow body functions. (p. 151)

depresivos Sustancias (tales como el alcohol y los sedantes) que reducen la actividad nerviosa y hacen más lentas las funciones del organismo. (pág. 151)

depth perception The ability to see in three dimensions and to judge distance. (p. 117)

percepción de profundidad Capacidad de ver en tres dimensiones y juzgar la distancia. (pág. 117)

developmental psychology A subfield of psychology that studies physical, cognitive, and social change throughout the life span. (p. 183)

psicología del desarrollo Rama de la psicología que estudia los cambios físicos, cognitivos y sociales durante toda la vida. (pág. 183)

difference threshold (just noticeable difference) The minimum amount of difference needed to detect that two stimuli are not the same. (p. 94)

umbral diferencial (diferencia que apenas se nota) Cantidad mínima necesaria para detectar que dos estímulos no son lo mismo. (pág. 94)

discrimination In social relations, taking action against a group of people because of stereotyped beliefs and feelings of prejudice. (p. 245)

discriminación En las relaciones sociales, tomar acción en contra un grupo de personas debido a las creencias estereotipadas y los sentimientos prejuiciosos. (pág. 245)

discrimination In operant conditioning, the ability to distinguish between two similar signals or stimuli and produce different responses. (p. 266)

discriminación Según el condicionamiento operante, capacidad de distinguir entre dos señales o estímulos similares y formar distintas respuestas. (pág. 266)

discrimination In classical conditioning, the ability to distinguish between two signals or stimuli and produce different responses. (p. 312)

discriminación Según el condicionamiento clásico, capacidad de distinguir entre dos señales o estímulos y formar distintas respuestas. (pág. 312)

display rules The cultural rules governing how and when a person may express emotion. (p. 437)

reglas de expresión Reglas culturales que dictan cómo y cuándo puede una persona expresar sus emociones. (pág. 437)

dissociative amnesia A dissociative disorder characterized by loss of memory in reaction to a traumatic event. (p. 509)

amnesia disociativa Trastorno disociativo que se caracteriza por la pérdida de la memoria como reacción a un suceso traumático. (pág. 509)

dissociative disorders Disorders in which the sense of self has become separated (dissociated) from previous memories, thoughts, or feelings. (p. 509)

trastornos disociativos Trastornos en los cuales la identidad de una persona se separa (se disocia) de recuerdos, pensamientos y sentimientos previos. (pág. 509)

dissociative fugue A dissociative disorder characterized by loss of identity and travel to a new location. (p. 510)

fuga disociativa Trastorno disociativo en el que la persona pierde su identidad y viaja para establecerse en otro lugar. (pág. 510)

dissociative identity disorder A rare and controversial dissociative disorder in which an individual exhibits two or more distinct and alternating personalities. (p. 510)

trastorno de identidad disociativo Trastorno disociativo poco común y controvertido, en el cual una persona experimenta dos o más personalidades claramente definidas que se alternan entre sí. (pág. 510)

divided consciousness theory Theory that during hypnosis our consciousness splits so that one aspect of consciousness is not aware of the role other parts are playing. (p. 168)

teoría de la consciencia dividida Teoría que sostiene que, durante la hipnosis, nuestra consciencia (o conocimiento de nosotros mismos y de los demás) se divide y una parte de ésta no tiene conocimiento del papel que cumplen las otras partes. (pág. 168)

DNA (deoxyribonucleic acid) A complex molecule containing the genetic information that makes up chromosomes. (p. 324)

ADN (ácido desoxirribonucleico) Molécula compleja que contiene la información genética que forma los cromosomas. (pág. 324)

double-blind procedure A research procedure in which both the data collectors and the research participants do not know the expected outcome of the experiment. (p. 39)

procedimiento doble ciego Procedimiento experimental en el que tanto los participantes y los recolectores de datos no saben el resultado esperado del experimento. (pág. 39)

drive-reduction theory The idea that a physiological need creates a state of tension (a drive) that motivates an organism to satisfy the need. (p. 411)

teoría de reducción de impulsos Idea de que una necesidad fisiológica produce la activación de un estado de tensión (impulso) que motiva a un organismo a satisfacer dicha necesidad. (pág. 411)

DSM-5 The American Psychiatric Association's *Diagnostic and Statistical Manual of Mental Disorders,* fifth edition; a widely used system for classifying psychological disorders. (p. 481)

DSM-5 Manual diagnóstico y estadístico de los trastornos mentales editado por la Asociación Estadounidense de Psiquiatría, quinta edición; sistema de clasificación de los trastornos mentales de uso generalizado. (pág. 481)

dual processing The principle that information is often processed on separate conscious and unconscious tracks at the same time. (p. 166)

procesamiento doble El principio que a menudo, la información es procesada distintamente en pistas concientes e inconcientes al mismo tiempo. (pág. 166)

E

Ebbinghaus, Hermann (1850–1909) German philosopher who conducted pioneering memory studies. (pp. 351, 371)

Ebbinghaus, Hermann (1850–1909) Filósofo alemán que fue pionero en el estudio de la memoria. (págs. 351, 371)

eclectic approach An approach to psychotherapy that, depending on the person's problems, uses techniques from various forms of therapy. (p. 521)

perspectiva ecléctica Enfoque psicoterapéutico que, dependiendo los problemas de la persona, utiliza técnicas de distintas formas de terapia. (pág. 521)

ecstasy Also called MDMA, a hallucinogenic stimulant that produces lowered inhibitions, pleasant feelings, and greater acceptance of others. (p. 157)

éxtasis También llamado MDMA, es un estimulante alucinógeno que reduce las inhibiciones, produce sensaciones agradables y hace aceptar más a los demás. (pág. 157)

effortful processing Encoding that requires attention and conscious effort. (p. 351)

procesamiento esforzado Codificación que requiere atención y esfuerzo continuo. (pág. 351)

ego The largely conscious "executive" part of personality that, according to Freud, negotiates among the demands of the id, the superego, and reality; operates on the reality principle, satisfying the id's desires in ways that will realistically bring pleasure rather than pain. (p. 443)

ego Parte "ejecutiva" de la personalidad y mayormente consciente que, según Freud, actúa como mediadora entre las exigencias del ello, el superyó y la realidad. El ego funciona a partir del principio de la realidad y busca satisfacer los deseos del ello (o id) de maneras que, siendo realistas, brindarán placer en vez de dolor. (pág. 443)

egocentrism In Piaget's theory, the inability of the preoperational child to take another person's point of view or to understand that symbols can represent other objects. (p. 186)

egocentrismo Según la teoría de Piaget, incapacidad del niño preoperacional de tomar el punto de vista de otra persona o de entender que los símbolos pueden representar otros objetos. (pág. 186)

electroconvulsive therapy (ECT) Therapy for major depression in which a brief electric current is sent through the brain of an anesthetized patient. (p. 544)

terapia electroconvulsiva Terapia para el tratamiento de la depresión grave. Consiste en el suministro de breves descargas eléctricas al cerebro del paciente, mientras éste está bajo anestesia. (pág. 544)

electroencephalogram (EEG) An amplified recording of the waves of electrical activity that sweep across the brain's surface; these waves, measured by electrodes placed on the scalp, are helpful in evaluating brain function. (p. 79)

electroencefalograma Registro amplificado de las ondas de actividad eléctrica provenientes de la superficie del cerebro. Estas ondas se miden con electrodos colocados sobre el cuero cabelludo y permiten evaluar el funcionamiento del cerebro. (pág. 79)

electroencephalograph (EEG) Machine that amplifies and records waves of electrical activity as they sweep across the brain's surface; electrodes placed on the scalp measure these waves. (p. 138)

electroencefalógrafo Instrumento que amplifica y registra las ondas de actividad eléctrica provenientes de la superficie del cerebro. Estas ondas se miden con electrodos colocados sobre el cuero cabelludo. (pág. 138)

embryo A developing human organism from about 2 weeks after fertilization through the end of the eighth week. (p. 178)

embrión Organismo humano en desarrollo, desde aproximadamente la segunda semana después de la fecundación hasta el final de la octava semana. (pág. 178)

emerging adulthood A period from the late teens to the mid-twenties (and sometimes later), bridging the gap between adolescent dependence and full independence and responsible adulthood. (p. 214)

adultez emergente Un período de adolescencia a mediados de los veinte años (y a veces hasta más tarde) que llena el vacío entre la dependencia adolescente y la independencia completa y la adultez responsable. (pág. 214)

emotional intelligence The ability to perceive, express, understand, and regulate emotions. (p. 395)

inteligencia emocional Capacidad de percibir, expresar, entender y regular las emociones. (pág. 395)

emotions Whole-organism responses, involving physiological arousal, expressive behaviors, and conscious experience. (p. 426)

emociones Respuestas de todo el organismo que presentan estimulación fisiológica, comportamientos expresivos y experiencia consciente. (pág. 426)

encoding The process of getting information into the memory system. (pp. 349, 369)

codificación Proceso de obtener información en el sistema de la memoria. (págs. 349, 369)

endocrine [EN-duh-krin] system One of the body's two communication systems; a set of glands that produce hormones, chemical messengers that circulate in the blood. (p. 72)

sistema endocrino Uno de los dos sistemas de comunicación del cuerpo; conjunto de glándulas que producen hormonas, los mensajeros químicos que circulan en sangre. (pág. 72)

environment Every nongenetic influence, from prenatal nutrition to the people and things around us. (p. 323)

ambiente Toda influencia que no es genética, desde la alimentación prenatal hasta las personas y las cosas que nos rodean. (pág. 323)

equity The condition in which people contribute to and receive from a relationship at a similar rate. (p. 309)

equidad Condición dentro de una relación en la cual las personas reciben en proporción a lo que dan. (pág. 309)

Erikson, Erik (1902–1994) Created an eight-stage theory of social development. (p. 205)

Erikson, Erik (1902–1994) Fundador de la teoría de las ocho etapas del desarrollo psicosocial. (pág. 205)

ethnocentrism The tendency to view the world through your own cultural filters. (p. 342)

etnocentrismo Tendencia a ver el mundo a partir de las experiencias personales y a través de los "filtros culturales" que uno tiene. (pág. 342)

evolutionary psychology School of thought that focuses on the principles of natural selection to study the roots of behavior and mental processes. (p. 22)

psicología evolutiva Corriente de pensamiento que se centra el los principios de la selección natural para estudiar las raíces del comportamiento y los procesos mentales. (pág. 22)

excitatory effect A neurotransmitter effect that makes it more likely that the receiving neuron will generate an action potential, or fire. (p. 65)

efecto excitador Efecto de un neurotransmisor que aumenta la probabilidad de que la neurona receptora genere un potencial de acción (impulso). (pág. 65)

experiment A research method in which the researcher manipulates and controls certain variables to observe the effect on other variables. (p. 34)

experimento Método de investigación en la cual el investigador manipula y controla ciertos factores para observar su efecto en otras variables. (pág. 34)

experimental group The participants in an experiment who are exposed to the independent variable. (p. 36)

grupo experimental Sujetos de un experimento que están expuestos al tratamiento, o sea, a la variable independiente. (pág. 36)

explanatory style Habits we have for thinking about the good or bad causes of events. (p. 569)

estilo explicativo Costumbres que se adquieren al pensar en las buenas o las malas causas de los sucesos. (pág. 569)

explicit memory The memory of facts and experiences. (p. 363)

memoria explícita Memoria de hechos y experiencias. (pág. 363)

external locus of control The perception that chance, or forces beyond your control, determines your fate. (p. 467)

locus de control externo Impresión de que nuestro destino está controlado por el azar o por fuerzas que están más allá de nuestro control. (pág. 467)

extinction In classical conditioning, the diminishing of a learned response after repeated presentation of the conditioned stimulus alone. (p. 242)

extinction/extinción En el condicionamiento clásico, disminución de un comportamiento aprendido después de la presentación repetida de sólo el estímulo condicionado. (pág. 242)

extinction In operant conditioning, the loss of a behavior when no consequence follows it. (p. 266)

extinction/extinción En el condicionamiento operante, pérdida de un comportamiento cuando no está seguido de una consecuencia. (pág. 266)

extrasensory perception (ESP) The controversial claim that perception can occur apart from sensory input. (p. 126)

percepción extrasensorial Idea polémica que propone la posibilidad de que la percepción ocurra por una vía distinta de la estimulación de los sentidos. (pág. 126)

extrinsic motivation A desire to perform a behavior because of promised rewards or threats of punishment. (p. 414)

motivación extrínseca Deseo de llevar a cabo un comportamiento porque promete recompensas o existe la amenaza de un castigo. (pág. 414)

Eysenck, Hans [EYE-zink] (1916–1997) German psychologist who researched the genetically influenced dimensions of personality, including extraversion and introversion. (p. 460)

Eysenck, Hans [EYE-zink] (1916–1997) Psicólogo alemán que investigó las dimensiones de la personalidad que tienen influencia genética, incluidas la extraversión y la introversión. (pág. 460)

F

family therapy Therapy that views an individual's unwanted behaviors as influenced by or directed at other members of the family and attempts to guide the family toward positive relationships and improved communication. (p. 535)

terapia de familia Terapia que trata a la familia como a un sistema. Considera que los comportamientos inapropiados de un individuo son influenciados por otros miembros de la familia o dirigidos hacia ellos; guía a los miembros de la familia para que logren tener relaciones positivas y mejorar la comunicación. (pág. 535)

fetal alcohol syndrome (FAS) Physical and cognitive abnormalities that appear in children whose mothers consumed large amounts of alcohol while pregnant. (p. 179)

síndrome de alcoholismo fetal Anormalidades físicas y cognitivas que aparecen en los niños cuyas madres consumen grandes cantidades de alcohol durante el embarazo. (pág. 179)

fetus A developing human organism from 9 weeks after conception to birth. (p. 178)

feto Organismo humano en desarrollo, desde la novena semana después de la concepción hasta el nacimiento. (pág. 178)

figure–ground The organization of the visual field into objects (figures) that stand out from their surroundings (ground). (p. 115)

figura y fondo Disposición del campo visual en donde los objetos (las figuras) resaltan en su entorno (el fondo). (pág. 115)

fixation A mental set applied so rigidly that it hinders the solution of a problem. (p. 385)

fijación Predisposición mental que dificulta la solución a un problema. (pág. 385)

fixed-interval schedule In operant conditioning, a partial reinforcement schedule that rewards only the first correct response after some defined period. (p. 268)

programa de intervalo fijo En el condicionamiento operante, programa de refuerzo parcial en el cual se suministra una recompensa solamente para la primera respuesta correcta, después de haber transcurrido un determinado período de tiempo. (pág. 268)

fixed-ratio schedule In operant conditioning, a partial reinforcement schedule that rewards a response only after some defined number of correct responses. (p. 269)

programa de proporción fija En el condicionamiento operante, programa de refuerzo parcial en el cual se suministra una recompensa solamente después de que haya ocurrido un número definido de respuestas correctas. (pág. 269)

flashbulb memory A vivid, clear memory of an emotionally significant moment or event. (p. 360)

memoria episódica Recuerdo vívido y claro de un momento o suceso emocionalmente significativo. (pág. 360)

flow A state of optimal experience that involves a challenge, requires skill, has clear goals, and provides feedback. (p. 568)

fluidez Estado óptimo de experiencia; para que ocurra la fluidez, las experiencias deben significar un desafío que requiera destreza, metas claras y la producción de respuestas. (pág. 568)

fluid intelligence The ability to reason speedily and abstractly. (p. 220)

inteligencia fluida Capacidad de una persona de razonar de manera rápida y abstracta. (pág. 220)

foot-in-the-door phenomenon The tendency for people who have first agreed to a small request to comply later with a larger request. (p. 289)

fenómeno del pie en la puerta Tendencia de las personas que accedieron a un pedido menor de acceder luego a un pedido de mayores proporciones. (pág. 289)

formal operational stage In Piaget's theory, the stage of cognitive development (beginning about age 12) during which people begin to think logically about abstract concepts and form strategies about things they may not have experienced. (p. 187)

período operacional formal Según la teoría de Piaget, etapa del desarrollo cognitivo (normalmente desde los doce años) durante la cual las personas comienzan a pensar de manera lógica en conceptos abstractos y a formar estrategias. (pág. 187)

framing How an issue is worded or presented, which can influence decisions and judgments. (p. 389)

encuadre Forma en que se presenta una cuestión; el encuadre puede influenciar las decisiones y las opiniones. (pág. 389)

fraternal twins Twins who develop from two different fertilized eggs; they are genetically no more similar than any other two siblings, but they share a fetal environment. (p. 326)

gemelos bivitelinos Hermanos gemelos que se forman de dos óvulos distintos. En términos genéticos, su relación no es más cercana que la que existe con los demás hermanos y hermanas, excepto que comparten el ambiente fetal. (pág. 326)

free association A method of exploring the unconscious in which the person relaxes and says whatever comes to mind, no matter how trivial or embarrassing. (p. 441)

asociación libre En el psicoanálisis, método para explorar el inconsciente durante el cual la persona se siente tranquila y dice todo lo que le viene a la mente, sin importarle lo trivial o incómodo que sea lo que dice. (pág. 441)

frequency distribution A list of scores ordered from highest to lowest. (p. 47)

distribución de frecuencias Lista de puntajes ordenados de mayor a menor. (pág. 47)

Freud, Sigmund (1856–1939) Founder of psychoanalysis, a controversial theory about the workings of the unconscious mind. (pp. 14, 373, 441, 521)

Freud, Sigmund (1856–1939) Fundador del psicoanálisis, una teoría controvertida acerca del funcionamiento de la parte inconsciente de la mente. (págs. 14, 373, 441, 521)

frontal lobes The portion of the cerebral cortex lying just behind the forehead that is involved in planning and judgment; it includes the motor cortex. (p. 84)

lóbulos frontales Porción de la corteza cerebral que se halla inmediatamente detrás de la frente; incluye la corteza motora y se relaciona con la planificación y la formación de opiniones. (pág. 84)

functional fixedness The tendency to think of things only in terms of their usual functions. (p. 386)

fijeza funcional Tendencia a pensar en las cosas solamente en términos de sus funciones acostumbradas; impedimento en la resolución de problemas. (pág. 386)

functionalism Theory that emphasized the functions of consciousness or the ways consciousness helps people adapt to their environment. (p. 13)

funcionalismo Teoría que enfatizaba las funciones de la consciencia y las formas en que ésta permitía a las personas adaptarse a su ambiente. (pág. 13)

fundamental attribution error The tendency to attribute the behavior of others to internal dispositions rather than to situations. (p. 285)

error fundamental de la atribución Tendencia a atribuir el comportamiento de otros a las disposiciones internas en lugar de a las situaciones. (pág. 285)

G

Garcia, John (1917–2012) Raised in poverty, Garcia was unable to attend school regularly as a child. He was in his late twenties before starting junior college, and he didn't receive his Ph.D. until he was almost 50. Despite these obstacles, Garcia was elected to the National Academy of Sciences and received the American Psychological Association's Distinguished Scientific Contribution Award for his work in conditioning. (p. 251)

García, John (1917–2012) García se crió en la pobreza y cuando era niño no logró asistir a la escuela con regularidad. Fue cerca de los treinta años que inició sus estudios superiores y no obtuvo su doctorado hasta casi alcanzar los 50 años. A pesar de esos obstáculos, García fue elegido para la Academia Nacional de Ciencias de Estados Unidos y recibió el premio de la Asociación Estadounidense de Psicología por su trabajo sobre el condicionamiento. (pág. 251)

Gardner, Howard (1943–) Author of a contemporary theory of multiple intelligences consisting of eight separate kinds of intelligence. (p. 393)

Gardner, Howard (1943–) Autor de una teoría contemporánea de inteligencias múltiples que distingue entre ocho tipos distintos de inteligencia. (pág. 393)

gender Our definition of male and female, based on socially and culturally influenced characteristics, as well as biology. (p. 344)

género Nuestra definición de hombre y mujer, basada en características influenciadas socialmente y culturalmente, así como la biología. (pág. 344)

gender identity Our sense of being male or female. (p. 344)

identidad de género Nuestro sentido de ser hombre o mujer. (pág. 344)

gender role A set of expected behaviors for males or for females. (p. 344)

papel de género Conjunto de creencias existentes sobre los comportamientos de los hombres y de las mujeres. (pág. 344)

general intelligence (g) The factor that Charles Spearman believed underlies all multiple intelligences. (p. 395)

inteligencia general (g) Segun Charles Spearman, el factor que subyace todas las inteligencias múltiples. (pág. 395)

generalization Producing the same response to two similar stimuli. (p. 245)

generalización Proceso en el cual un organismo genera la misma respuesta a dos estímulos similares. (pág. 245)

general adaptation syndrome (GAS) Selye's concept of the body's adaptive response to stress in three phases—alarm, resistance, and exhaustion. (p. 551)

síndrome de adaptación general Concepto de Selye según el cual el cuerpo responde al estrés pasando por tres fases: la inquietud, la resistencia y el agotamiento. (pág. 551)

generalized anxiety disorder An anxiety disorder characterized by disruptive levels of persistent, unexplained feelings of apprehension and tenseness. (p. 491)

trastorno de ansiedad generalizado Trastorno que se caracteriza por sentimientos persistentes e inexplicables de aprensión y tensión que alcanzan niveles perjudiciales. (pág. 491)

genes The biochemical units of heredity that make up chromosomes. (pp. 178, 323)

genes Unidades bioquímicas de la herencia que forman cromosomas. (págs. 178, 323)

gestalt The whole, or the organizational patterns that we tend to perceive; the Gestalt psychologists emphasized that the whole is greater than the sum of its parts. (p. 114)

gestalt Se dice del "todo", o patrones de organización, que tendemos a percibir. Los psicólogos que ejercían la psicología Gestalt enfatizaban la idea de que el todo es más grande que la suma de las partes que lo componen. (pág. 114)

Gestalt [gih-SHTALT] psychology Psychological perspective that emphasized our tendency to integrate pieces of information into meaningful wholes. (p. 13)

psicología Gestalt Perspectiva psicológica que enfatiza nuestra tendencia a integrar datos para formar totalidades significativas. (pág. 13)

grammar The system of rules governing how we can combine phonemes, morphemes, and words to produce meaningful communication. (p. 231)

gramática Sistema de reglas que dicta cómo combinar morfemas y palabras y ordenarlos en oraciones para comunicarnos con los demás. (pág. 231)

grit Passionate dedication to an ambitious goal. (p. 418)

grit Pasión y dedicación para llegar a una meta ambiciosa. (pág. 418)

group polarization Enhancement of a group's already-existing attitudes through discussion within the group. (p. 300)

polarización grupal Potenciación de las actitudes predominantes de un grupo, cuando los miembros de éste se hallan enfrascados en una conversación. (pág. 300)

grouping The perceptual tendency to organize stimuli into understandable units. (p. 116)

agrupamiento Tendencia de percepción que clasifica los estímulos en grupos que tienen sentido. (pág. 116)

groupthink The mode of thinking that occurs when the desire for harmony in a decision-making group overrides a realistic appraisal of the alternatives. (p. 300)

pensamiento grupal Modo de pensar que ocurre en un grupo que debe tomar decisiones, cuando el deseo de mantener la armonía, anula una evaluación realista de las alternativas. (pág. 300)

H

hair cells The receptor cells for hearing; these are located in the cochlea and are responsible for changing sound vibrations into neural impulses. (p. 106)

células ciliares Células receptoras sensibles al sonido, que se hallan en la cóclea y se encargan de convertir las vibraciones del sonido en impulsos nerviosos. (pág. 106)

hallucinations False perceptions that are symptoms of schizophrenia and other serious psychological disorders. (p. 513)

alucinaciones Percepciones falsas que son síntomas de la esquizofrenia y otros trastornos psicológicos graves. (pág. 513)

hallucinogens Psychedelic (mind-manifesting) drugs, such as LSD, that distort perceptions and evoke sensory images in the absence of sensory input. (p. 158)

alucinógenos Drogas psicodélicas, tales como el ácido lisérgico y dietilamina, que distorsionan las percepciones y provocan imágenes sensoriales sin la presencia de estimulación sensorial. (pág. 158)

health psychology A subfield of psychology that focuses on how stress affects well-being and health. (p. 550)

psicología de la salud Extensión de la psicología que se centra en cómo el estrés afecta el bienestar y la salud. (pág. 550)

heritability The degree to which traits are inherited. (p. 326)

heredabilidad Proporción de la variación entre individuos que es posible atribuir a la herencia. (pág. 326)

heuristic A rule-of-thumb problem-solving strategy that makes finding a solution more likely and efficient but does not guarantee a solution. (p. 384)

heurística Regla práctica en la estrategia de resolución de problemas que hace que una solución sea más probable y eficaz, pero que no garantiza soluciones. (pág. 384)

hierarchy of needs Maslow's pyramid of human needs, beginning at the base with physiological needs that must be satisfied before higher-level safety needs and then psychological needs become active. (p. 416)

jerarquía de necesidades Pirámide de Maslow de las necesidades humanas, en cuya base están las necesidades fisiológicas, y luego siguen las necesidades de seguridad personal y, por último, las necesidades psicológicas. Las necesidades de nivel más elevado no se activan hasta que las de niveles más bajos estén satisfechas. (pág. 416)

Hilgard, Ernest (1904–2001) Pioneering hypnosis researcher and an advocate of the divided consciousness theory of hypnosis. (p. 168)

Hilgard, Ernest (1904–2001) Investigador pionero en el campo de la hipnosis y defensor de la teoría de la consciencia dividida. (pág. 168)

hippocampus A neural center located in the limbic system that wraps around the back of the thalamus; it helps process new memories for permanent storage. (p. 82)

hipocampo Centro nervioso ubicado en el sistema límbico; participa en el procesamiento de recuerdos nuevos para su almacenamiento permanente. (pág. 82)

homeostasis A tendency to maintain a balanced or constant internal state. (p. 413)

homeóstasis Tendencia a mantener un estado interno equilibrado y constante. (pág. 413)

hormone A chemical messenger produced by the endocrine glands and circulated in the blood. (p. 72)

hormona Mensajero químico producido por las glándulas endocrinas que circula en la sangre. (pág. 72)

Horney, Karen [HORN-eye] (1885–1952) Neo-Freudian who found psychoanalysis negatively biased toward women and believed cultural variables are the foundation of personality development. (p. 448)

Horney, Karen (1885–1952) Neofreudiana que consideraba que el psicoanálisis estaba prejuiciado en contra de la mujer y creía que las variables culturales eran la base del desarrollo de la personalidad. (pág. 448)

humanistic psychology A perspective that focuses on the study of conscious experience, the individual's freedom to choose, and the individual's capacity for personal growth. (pp. 15, 451)

psicología humanista Perspectiva que enfatiza el estudio de la experiencia consciente, la libertad de decisión del individuo y la capacidad de crecimiento personal. (págs. 15, 451)

hypnosis Social interaction in which a hypnotist makes suggestions about perceptions, feelings, thoughts, or behaviors and those suggestions are followed. (p. 167)

hipnosis Interacción social en la cual un hipnotizador hace sugerencias relacionadas con percepciones, sentimientos, pensamientos o comportamientos y después esas sugerencias son seguidas. (pág. 167)

hypothalamus [hi-po-THAL-uh-muss] A neural structure lying below the thalamus; it helps regulate many of the body's maintenance activities, such as eating, drinking, and body temperature, and is linked to emotion. (p. 82)

hipotálamo Estructura nerviosa ubicada debajo del tálamo; dirige actividades de mantenimiento tales como la ingestión de alimentos y de líquidos y la temperatura del cuerpo, y está ligado a las emociones. (pág. 82)

hypothesis A testable prediction about the outcome of research. (p. 34)

hipótesis Predicción comprobable sobre el resultado de una investigación. (pág. 34)

I

id The part of personality that, according to Freud, consists of unconscious psychic energy and strives to satisfy basic sexual and aggressive drives; operates on the pleasure principle, demanding immediate gratification. (p. 442)

ello Según Freud, parte de la personalidad compuesta por energía psíquica e inconsciente que busca satisfacer los impulsos sexuales y agresivos básicos. Funciona de acuerdo con el principio del placer y requiere satisfacción inmediata. (pág. 442)

identical twins Twins who develop from a single fertilized egg that splits in two, creating two genetically identical organisms. (p. 326)

gemelos univitelinos Gemelos que se forman de un sólo óvulo fecundado, el cual se divide en dos y crea dos organismos idénticos. (pág. 326)

identity One's sense of self; according to Erikson, the adolescent's task is to solidify a sense of self by testing and integrating various roles. (p. 205)

identidad Sentido de uno mismo; de acuerdo con Erikson, la tarea del adolescente es solidificar el sentido de sí mismo probando e integrando una variedad de roles. (pág. 205)

illness anxiety disorder A disorder characterized by imagined symptoms of illness. (p. 511)

trastorno hipocondríaco Trastorno caracterizado por síntomas de enfermedad imaginarios. (pág. 511)

implicit memory The memory of skills and procedures. (p. 364)

memoria implícita Memoria de habilidades y procedimientos. (pág. 364)

imprinting The process by which certain animals form attachments during a critical period early in life. (p. 190)	**impronta** Proceso mediante el cual ciertos animales forman apegos durante un período crítico que ocurre a muy temprana edad. (pág. 190)
independent variable (IV) The variable that the researcher will actively manipulate and, if the hypothesis is correct, that will cause a change in the dependent variable. (p. 36)	**variable independiente (IV)** Variable de un experimento que el investigador manipula activamente y, si la hipótesis es correcta, producirá un cambio en la variable dependiente. (pág. 36)
individualism Giving priority to personal goals over group goals and defining identity in terms of personal attributes rather than group identification. (p. 336)	**individualismo** Dar prioridad a metas personales más que a las metas del grupo y definiendo la identidad de acuerdo con las cualidades personales en vez que la identificación del grupo. (pág. 336)
inferential statistics Statistics that can be used to make a decision or reach a conclusion about data. (p. 56)	**estadística inferencial** Estadística que se puede emplear para tomar una decisión o llegar a una conclusión basada en los datos. (pág. 56)
inferiority complex According to Adler, a condition that comes from being unable to compensate for normal inferiority feelings. (p. 447)	**complejo de inferioridad** De acuerdo con Alfred Adler, estado que resulta de la incapacidad de compensar por sentimientos normales de inferioridad. (pág. 447)
infradian [in-FRAY-dee-un] rhythms Biological rhythms that occur once a month or once a season. (p. 134)	**ritmos infradianos** Ritmos biológicos que ocurren una vez al mes o una vez por estación. (pág. 134)
ingroup "Us"—people with whom we share a common identity. (p. 314)	**grupo propio** "Nosotros", o sea, las personas con las que uno comparte una identidad en común. (pág. 314)
ingroup bias The tendency to favor our own group. (p. 314)	**estereotipo de grupo propio** Tendencia a favorecer al grupo al que uno pertenece. (pág. 314)
inhibitory effect A neurotransmitter effect that makes it less likely that a receiving neuron will generate an action potential, or fire. (p. 65)	**efecto inhibitorio** Efecto de un neurotransmisor que hace menos probable que la neurona receptora genere un potencial de acción (impulso). (pág. 65)
insight The sudden realization (Aha!) of the solution to a problem. (p. 384)	**agudeza** Entendimiento repentino (¡Ajá!) de cómo se resuelve un problema. (pág. 384)
insomnia Recurring problems in falling asleep or staying asleep. (p. 144)	**insomnio** Dificultad recurrente para conciliar el sueño o para mantenerse dormido. (pág. 144)
instinct A complex, inherited behavior that is rigidly patterned throughout a species. (p. 411)	**instinto** Comportamiento complejo y heredado que está rigurosamente estampada a través de una especie. (pág. 411)
intelligence The ability to learn from experience, solve problems, and use knowledge to adapt to new situations. (p. 393)	**inteligencia** Capacidad de aprender de la experiencia, resolver problemas y emplear conocimientos para adaptarse a situaciones nuevas. (pág. 393)
intelligence quotient (IQ) The number that results from dividing mental age by chronological age and multiplying by 100. (p. 397)	**coeficiente intelectual (CI)** Número derivado de la fórmula de Terman y Stern, que se emplea para calcular el nivel de inteligencia de una persona: edad mental (EM) dividida por la edad cronológica (EC) multiplicada por 100. (pág. 397)
internal locus of control The perception that you control your own fate. (p. 467)	**locus de control interno** Impresión de que controlamos nuestro propio destino. (pág. 467)
interneurons Nerve cells in the brain and spinal cord responsible for processing information. (p. 67)	**interneuronas** Células nerviosas del cerebro y la médula espinal que se encargan de procesar información. (pág. 67)
interpretation In psychoanalysis, the analyst's noting of ideas on the meaning behind dreams, resistances, and other significant behaviors to promote insight. (p. 523)	**interpretación** En el psicoanálisis, observación que hace el analista de supuestos significados de sueños, resistencias y otros comportamientos significativos, con el propósito de facilitar el entendimiento. (pág. 523)
intimacy In Erikson's theory, the ability to form close, loving, open relationships; a primary task in early adulthood. (p. 208)	**intimidad** Según la teoría de Erikson, capacidad de formar relaciones cercanas, afectivas y abiertas; tarea primaria del comienzo de la vida adulta. (pág. 208)
intrinsic motivation A desire to perform a behavior for its own sake and to be effective. (p. 414)	**motivación intrínseca** Deseo de llevar a cabo un comportamiento por el sólo hecho de hacerlo y de tener el resultado esperado. (pág. 414)
iris A ring of muscle tissue that forms the colored portion of the eye and regulates the size of the pupil. (p. 99)	**iris** Aro de tejido muscular que forma la parte coloreada del ojo y regula el tamaño de la pupila. (pág. 99)

J

James, William (1842–1910) First American psychologist and author of the first psychology textbook. He believed our awareness of physiological responses lead to our experience of emotion (see *James–Lange theory*). (pp. 13, 427)	**James, William (1842–1910)** Primer psicólogo estadounidense y escritor del primer libro de texto de psicología, que pensaba que nuestra consciencia de las reacciones fisiológicas nos lleva a sentir las emociones (véase la teoría de James-Lange). (págs. 13, 427)

James–Lange theory The theory that we experience emotion because we are aware of our bodily response to an emotion-arousing stimulus. (p. 428)

teoría de James-Lange Teoría según la cual nuestra experiencia de una emoción es la consciencia que tenemos de nuestras reacciones fisiológicas ante un estímulo que evoca emociones. (pág. 428)

Jung, Carl [YOO-ng] (1875–1961) Neo-Freudian who believed that humans share a collective unconscious. (p. 447)

Jung, Carl (1875–1961) Neofreudiano que pensaba que los seres humanos comparten un inconsciente colectivo. (pág. 447)

just-world phenomenon The tendency to believe that people get what they deserve and deserve what they get. (p. 315)

fenómeno de un mundo justo Tendencia a suponer que las personas reciben lo que merecen y merecen lo que reciben. (pág. 315)

K

Kahneman, Daniel (1934–) Psychologist who, along with Amos Tversky, conducted research to discover factors that influence human judgment and decision making. He won the Nobel Prize in 2002 for this work. (p. 388)

Kahneman, Daniel (1934–) Psicólogo que, junto con Amos Tversky, realizó estudios para descubrir los factores que influyen en las opiniones y la toma de decisiones de los seres humanos. Su trabajo lo llevó a obtener el premio Nobel en 2002. (pág. 388)

kinesthetic sense The system for sensing the position and movement of individual body parts. (p. 110)

sentido cinético Sistema que permite sentir la posición y el movimiento de las partes del cuerpo. (pág. 110)

Kohlberg, Lawrence (1927–1987) Created a three-stage theory of moral development. (p. 202)

Kohlberg, Lawrence (1927–1987) Creó una teoría que divide al desarrollo moral en tres etapas. (pág. 202)

L

Lange, Carl (1834–1900) Danish physiologist who proposed a theory of emotion similar to, and at about the same time as, James's theory that awareness of physiological responses leads to experiences of emotion (see *James–Lange theory*). (p. 427)

Lange, Carl (1834–1900) Fisiólogo danés que propuso, casi simultáneamente, una teoría de las emociones similar a la de William James, que propone que nuestra consciencia de las respuestas fisiológicas nos lleva a experimentar las emociones (véase la teoría de James-Lange). (pág. 427)

language Our spoken, written, or gestured words and the ways we combine them to communicate meaning. (p. 229)

lenguaje Palabras habladas, escritas o gesticuladas y las formas en las que las combinamos para comunicar significados. (pág. 229)

latent learning Learning that occurs but is not apparent until the learner has an incentive to demonstrate it. (p. 271)

aprendizaje latente Aprendizaje que ocurre pero no es aparente hasta que la persona tiene un incentivo para manifestarlo. (pág. 271)

Lazarus, Richard (1922–2002) U.S. psychologist who concluded that some emotional responses do not require conscious thought but still involve some kind of unconscious cognitive appraisal. (p. 430)

Lazarus, Richard (1922–2002) Psicólogo estadounidense que concluyó que algunas respuestas emocionales no requieren pensamientos conscientes pero aún involucran una forma de evaluación cognitiva inconsciente. (pág. 430)

learned helplessness The hopeless feeling when an animal or human can't avoid repeated bad events. (p. 468)

impotencia aprendida Desesperanza y resignación pasiva que aprende un animal o ser humano cuando es incapaz de evitar una sucesión de episodios desagradables. (pág. 468)

learning The process of gaining, through experience, relatively permanent information and behaviors. (p. 239)

aprendizaje Proceso de adquirir a través de la experiencia, informaciones y comportamientos que son relativamente permanentes. (pág. 239)

lens A transparent structure behind the pupil in the eye that changes shape to focus images on the retina. (p. 99)

cristalino del ojo Estructura transparente ubicada detrás de la pupila del ojo que cambia de forma para enfocar las imágenes en la retina. (pág. 99)

limbic system A ring of structures at the border of the brainstem and cerebral cortex; it helps regulate important functions such as memory, fear, aggression, hunger, and thirst, and it includes the hypothalamus, the hippocampus, and the amygdala. (p. 82)

sistema límbico Aro de estructuras ubicadas en el borde del tronco cerebral y la corteza cerebral; contribuye a la regulación de funciones importantes tales como la memoria, el miedo, la agresión, el hambre y la sed. Incluye el hipotálamo, el hipocampo y la amígdala. (pág. 82)

lobotomy A now-rare form of psychosurgery once used to try to calm uncontrollably emotional or violent patients; the procedure cut the nerves that connect the frontal lobes of the brain to the deeper emotional centers. (p. 546)

lobotomía Tipo de psicocirugía, actualmente rara, que se empleaba para calmar a pacientes emocionalmente incontrolables o violentos. El procedimiento consiste en cortar los nervios que conectan los lóbulos frontales del cerebro con los centros emocionales más profundos. (pág. 546)

locus of control People's perception of the source of control over fate or what happens in life: People with an internal locus of control believe they control their fate through their behavior; people with an external locus of control believe their fate is controlled by external circumstances. (p. 340)

locus de control Impresión que tiene una persona acerca de la fuente de control de su destino o lo que pasa en su vida. Las personas que tienen un locus de control interno creen que controlan su destino a través de su comportamiento. Las personas que tienen un locus de control externo creen su destino es controlado por circunstancias externas. (pág. 340)

Loftus, Elizabeth (1944–) Psychologist at University of California, Irvine, whose research established the constructed nature of memory. (p. 375)

Loftus, Elizabeth (1944–) Psicóloga de la Universidad de California, Irvine, cuya investigación demostró la naturaleza estructurada de la memoria. (pág. 375)

longitudinal fissure The long crevice that divides the cerebral cortex into the left and right hemispheres. (p. 83)	**cisura interhemisférica** Surco largo que se extiende desde la parte anterior hasta la parte posterior de la corteza cerebral y separa el hemisferio derecho del izquierdo. (pág. 83)
longitudinal study A research technique that follows the same group of individuals over a long period. (p. 33)	**estudio longitudinal** Técnica de investigación en la cual se estudia el mismo grupo de individuos durante un largo período de tiempo. (pág. 33)
long-term memory The relatively permanent and limitless storehouse of the memory system. (p. 359)	**memoria remota** Centro de almacenamiento relativamente permanente e ilimitado del sistema de la memoria. (pág. 359)
long-term potentiation An increase in a synapse's firing efficiency that occurs when the sequence of neurons that represents a particular memory fires repeatedly; believed to be the neural basis of learning and memory. (p. 362)	**potenciación a largo plazo** Aumento en la eficacia de una sinapsis para transmitir impulsos. Se considera la base nerviosa del aprendizaje y la memoria. (pág. 362)
Lorenz, Konrad (1903–1989) Researcher who focused on critical attachment periods in baby birds, a concept he called imprinting. (p. 190)	**Lorenz, Konrad (1903–1989)** Investigador que estudió las etapas críticas de apego en los pichones de aves, concepto que denominó impronta. (pág. 190)
LSD (lysergic acid diethylamide) Powerful hallucinogenic drug; also known as acid. (p. 158)	**ácido lisérgico y dietilamina** Poderosa droga alucinógena; también se conoce como ácido. (pág. 158)

M

magnetic resonance imaging (MRI) and functional magnetic resonance imaging (fMRI) Techniques using magnetic fields and radio waves to produce computer-generated images that distinguish among substances; this allows us to see structures within the brain (MRI) and track blood flow to determine what parts of the brain are more active (fMRI). (p. 79)	**imagen por resonancia magnética (IRM) e imagen por resonancia magnética funcional (IRMf)** Técnicas en que se utilizan los campos magnéticos y las ondas de radio para producir imágenes procesadas por computadora que pueden distinguir diferentes sustancias; permiten observar las estructuras del cerebro (IRM) y el flujo sanguíneo para determinar qué áreas del cerebro están más activas (IRMf). (pág. 79)
major depressive disorder A mood disorder in which a person, for no apparent reason, experiences at least 2 weeks of depressed moods, diminished interest in activities, and other symptoms, such as feelings of worthlessness. (p. 499)	**trastorno de depresión grave** Trastorno del estado de ánimo en el que un individuo, sin razón aparente, experimenta por lo menos dos semanas de depresión, disminución de interés en actividades y síntomas tales como la sensación de que su vida no tiene valor. (pág. 499)
marijuana Leaves, stems, resin, and flowers from the hemp plant; when smoked, lowers inhibitions and produces feelings of relaxation and mild euphoria. (p. 159)	**marihuana** Hojas, tallos, resina y flores de la planta de cáñamo que, al fumarse, reduce las inhibiciones y produce sensaciones de tranquilidad y euforia leve. (pág. 159)
Maslow, Abraham (1908–1970) Humanistic psychologist who proposed the *hierarchy of needs*, with *self-actualization* as one of the ultimate psychological needs. (pp. 15, 416, 451)	**Maslow, Abraham (1908–1970)** Psicólogo humanista que propuso una jerarquía de necesidades, en donde la realización personal es la máxima necesidad psicológica. (págs. 15, 416, 451)
Matsumoto, David (1959–) Psychologist and cross-cultural psychology expert. (p. 335)	**Matsumoto, David (1959–)** Psicólogo y experto internacional en el estudio de la psicología transcultural. (pág. 335)
maturation Biological growth processes that enable orderly changes in behavior. (p. 181)	**maduración** Procesos de crecimiento biológico que permiten cambios ordenados en el comportamiento y son relativamente independientes de la experiencia. (pág. 181)
mean The mathematical average of a distribution, obtained by adding the scores and then dividing by the number of scores. (p. 49)	**media** Promedio aritmético de una distribución, que se obtiene sumando los puntajes y luego dividiéndolos por el número de puntajes. (pág. 49)
median The middle score in a ranked distribution; half the scores are above it, and half are below it. (p. 50)	**mediana** Puntaje que está en el medio de una distribución clasificada; la mitad de los puntajes está por encima de la mediana y la otra mitad, por debajo. (pág. 50)
medical model The concept that mental diseases have physical causes that can be diagnosed, treated, and in most cases, cured. (p. 478)	**modelo médico** Concepto que afirma que las enfermedades tienen causas físicas que pueden ser diagnosticadas, tratadas y en la mayoría de los casos, curadas. (pág. 478)
medulla [muh-DUL-uh] Located at the base of the brainstem, it controls basic life-support functions like heartbeat and breathing. (p. 80)	**médula** Base del tronco cerebral; controla las funciones vitales, tales como el latido del corazón y la respiración. (pág. 80)
melatonin Hormone that helps regulate daily biological rhythms. (p. 137)	**melatonina** Hormona que contribuye a la regulación de los ritmos biológicos diarios. (pág. 137)
menopause When the menstrual cycle ends; also refers to the biological changes a woman experiences as her ability to reproduce declines. (p. 216)	**menopausia** Período de la vida en que cesa naturalmente la menstruación; también se refiere a los cambios biológicos que experimenta una mujer a medida que disminuye su capacidad de reproducción. (pág. 216)

mental age (MA) The chronological age that corresponds to the difficulty level of the questions a child can answer. (p. 397)

edad mental Edad cronológica que corresponde con el nivel de dificultad de las preguntas que un niño es capaz de contestar. (pág. 397)

mental set The tendency to approach a particular problem in a particular way. (p. 385)

predisposición mental Tendencia a resolver problemas de una forma en particular. (pág. 385)

mere exposure effect The phenomenon that repeated exposure to novel stimuli increases one's liking of them. (p. 305)

efecto de mera exposición Fenómeno en el cual la exposición repetida a estímulos novedosos aumenta el agrado que se siente ante dichos estímulos. (pág. 305)

Milgram, Stanley (1933–1984) Social psychologist who researched obedience to authority. (p. 295)

Milgram, Stanley (1933–1984) Psicólogo social que investigó la obediencia a la autoridad. (pág. 295)

Minnesota Multiphasic Personality Inventory (MMPI) The most widely researched and clinically used of all personality tests; originally developed to identify emotional disorders (still considered its most appropriate use), this test is now used for many other screening purposes. (p. 462)

Inventario Multifásico de la Personalidad de Minnesota Prueba de la personalidad que es, entre todas, la más ampliamente estudiada y empleada clínicamente. Se elaboró originalmente para identificar trastornos emocionales, y aún hoy este uso se considera el más apropiado. Actualmente también se emplea para muchos otros propósitos de examinación. (pág. 462)

mirror neurons Brain cells located in the front of the brain that activate when a person performs certain actions or when the person observes another do so. (p. 278)

neuronas espejo Células cerebrales localizadas en la parte delantera del cerebro que se activan al ejectuar ciertas acciones o al observar la misma actividad ejecutada por otro individuo. (pág. 278)

misinformation effect Incorporating misleading information into a memory of an event. (p. 375)

efecto de información errónea Incorporación de información engañosa en la memoria de un acontecimiento. (pág. 375)

mnemonic [nih-MON-ik] device A memory trick or technique. (p. 355)

recurso nemotécnico Técnica para auxiliar a la memoria. (pág. 355)

mode The most frequently occurring score or scores in a distribution. (p. 49)

moda Puntaje que ocurre más frecuentemente en una distribución. (pág. 49)

model The person observed in observational learning. (p. 275)

modelo Persona que se observa en el aprendizaje por observación. (pág. 275)

modeling The process of observing and imitating a specific behavior. (p. 275)

modelar Proceso de observar e imitar un comportamiento en particular. (pág. 275)

monocular cues Depth cues that require the use of only one eye. (p. 118)

claves monoculares Señales de profundidad que requieren el uso de un solo ojo. (pág. 118)

morpheme In language, the smallest unit that carries meaning. (p. 230)

morfema En el lenguaje, unidad más pequeña con significado. (pág. 230)

motivation A need or desire that energizes and directs behavior toward a goal. (p. 410)

motivación Necesidad o deseo que vigoriza y dirige el comportamiento. (pág. 410)

motor cortex A strip of brain tissue at the rear of the frontal lobes that controls voluntary movements. (p. 84)

corteza motora Parte del cerebro en la parte posterior de los lóbulos frontales, que controla los movimientos voluntarios. (pág. 84)

Murray, Henry (1893–1988) Neo-Freudian who first established the concept of achievement motivation and developed important personality testing tools. (p. 417)

Murray, Henry (1893–1988) Neofreudiano, fue el primero en establecer el concepto de motivación de logro; también creó importantes mecanismos para evaluar la personalidad. (pág. 417)

mutation Random errors in gene replication that lead to a change in the individual's genetic code and are the source of all genetic diversity. (p. 325)

mutación Errores en la duplicación de los genes, que se producen al azar y resultan en un cambio en el código genético de un individuo y son la fuente de toda la diversidad genética. (pág. 325)

N

narcolepsy Sleep disorder characterized by uncontrollable sleep attacks; the sufferer may lapse directly into REM sleep, often at inopportune times. (p. 145)

narcolepsia Trastorno caracterizado por ataques incontrolables de sueño. El individuo entra directamente en el sueño REM, generalmente en momentos inoportunos. (pág. 145)

naturalistic observation Observing and recording behavior in naturally occurring situations without manipulating or controlling the situation. (p. 29)

observación naturalista Observación y registro de comportamientos en situaciones que ocurren naturalmente, sin tratar de manipular y controlar dichas situaciones. (pág. 29)

negative reinforcement In operant conditioning, anything that increases the likelihood of a behavior by following it with the removal of an undesirable event or state. (p. 260)

Refuerzo negativo En el condicionamiento operante, cualquier cosa que aumenta la probabilidad que se produzca un comportamiento por seguirlo con la eliminación de un suceso o estado desagradable. (pág. 260)

neuron A nerve cell; the basic building block of the nervous system. (p. 62)

neurona Célula nerviosa; unidad básica del sistema nervioso. (pág. 62)

neurotransmitter A chemical messenger that travels across the synapse from one neuron to the next and influences whether a neuron will generate an action potential. (p. 65)

neurotransmisor Mensajero químico que, al ser liberado por una neurona, atraviesa la sinapsis (espacio entre dos neuronas) y entra en los receptores de las neuronas receptoras, formando el siguiente eslabón en la cadena de comunicación del sistema nervioso. (pág. 65)

nicotine Stimulant found in tobacco. (p. 155)

nicotina Estimulante del comportamiento que se halla en el tabaco. (pág. 155)

night terrors Sleep-related problem characterized by high arousal and an appearance of being terrified; unlike nightmares, they occur during NREM 3 sleep, occur within 2 or 3 hours of falling asleep, and are seldom remembered. (p. 145)

terrores nocturnos Trastorno del sueño caracterizado por excitación fisiológica intensa y expresión de miedo extremo en la cara del sujeto. A diferencia de las pesadillas, los terrores nocturnos ocurren durante la fase 3 del sueño NMOR en las primeras dos o tres horas de estar dormido y raramente son recordados. (pág. 145)

normal distribution A frequency distribution that is shaped like a symmetrical bell. (p. 53)

distribución normal Una distribución de frecuencias que tiene forma de una campana simétrica. (pág. 53)

norms Understood rules for accepted and expected behavior. (p. 331)

normas Reglas establecidas para el comportamiento aceptado y esperado. (pág. 331)

O

obedience The tendency to comply with orders, implied or real, from someone perceived as an authority. (p. 296)

obediencia Tendencia a hacer caso a las órdenes, ya sea implícitas o explícitas, de alguien a quien se percibe como autoridad. (pág. 296)

object permanence The awareness that things continue to exist even when you cannot see or hear them. (p. 185)

permanencia del objeto Consciencia de que las cosas continúan existiendo aún cuando no se las ve ni se las escucha. (pág. 185)

observational learning Learning by observing others. (p. 275)

aprendizaje observacional Aprendizaje que ocurre por la observación a otras personas. (pág. 275)

obsessive-compulsive disorder (OCD) An anxiety disorder characterized by unwanted, repetitive thoughts and/or actions. (p. 496)

trastorno obsesivocompulsivo Trastorno de ansiedad que se caracteriza por pensamientos y acciones indeseadas y repetitivas. (pág. 496)

occipital [ahk-SIP-uh-tuhl] lobes The portion of the cerebral cortex lying at the back of the head; it includes the primary visual processing areas of the brain. (p. 84)

lóbulos occipitales Porción de la corteza cerebral ubicada en la parte posterior de la cabeza; incluye las áreas de procesamiento de la visión. (pág. 84)

operant conditioning A type of learning in which the frequency of a behavior depends on the consequence that follows that behavior. (p. 255)

condicionamiento operante Tipo de aprendizaje en el que la frecuencia de un comportamiento depende de las consecuencias que éste provoca. (pág. 255)

operational definition An explanation of the exact procedures used to make a variable specific and measurable for research purposes. (p. 34)

definición operacional Especificación de los procedimientos exactos que se deben llevar a cabo para que una variable sea específica y se pueda medir durante un experimento. (pág. 34)

opponent-process theory A theory of color vision that says color is processed by cones organized in opponent pairs (red–green, yellow–blue, and black–white); light that stimulates one half of the pair inhibits the other half. (p. 103)

teoría de los colores opuestos Teoría de la visión del color según la cual el color se procesa en pares de opuestos (rojo-verde, amarillo-azul y negro-blanco). Cuando la luz estimula la mitad de un par, inhibe la otra mitad. (pág. 103)

optic nerve The nerve that carries visual information from the eye to the occipital lobes of the brain. (p. 101)

nervio óptico Nervio que lleva información visual desde el ojo hasta los lóbulos occipitales del cerebro. (pág. 101)

other-race effect The tendency to recall faces of one's own race more accurately than faces of other races. (p. 315)

effecto de otras razas Tendencia a recordar la caras de su propia raza con mejor precisión que las caras de otras razas. (pág. 315)

outgroup "Them"—those perceived as different or apart from "us." (p. 314)

grupo ajeno "Ellos", o sea, las personas a las que percibimos como distintas o separadas de "nosotros". (pág. 314)

overconfidence Confidence that is greater than accuracy. (p. 388)

exceso de confianza Cuando la confianza es más que la precisión. (pág. 388)

overjustification effect The effect of promising a reward for doing what one already likes to do; the reward may lessen and replace the person's original, natural motivation so that the behavior stops if the reward is eliminated. (pp. 271, 415)

efecto de justificación excesiva Efecto de prometer una recompensa por algo que a uno de antemano le gusta hacer. La recompensa podría disminuir y reemplazar la motivación original y natural de la persona, por lo que el comportamiento se interrumpe si la recompensa se elimina. (págs. 271, 415)

P

panic disorder An anxiety disorder characterized by sudden bouts of intense, unexplained anxiety, often associated with physical symptoms like choking sensations or shortness of breath. (p. 491)

trastorno del pánico Trastorno de ansiedad que se caracteriza por ataques repentinos de pánico intenso e inexplicable y con frequencia asociada con síntomas físicos como la sensación de ahogo o la falta de aliento. (pág. 491)

parasympathetic division The part of the autonomic nervous system that calms the body. (p. 72)

división parasimpática Parte del sistema nervioso autónomo que calma el cuerpo. (pág. 72)

parietal [puh-RYE-uh-tuhl] lobes The portion of the cerebral cortex lying at the top of the head and toward the rear; it includes the somatosensory cortex and general association areas used for processing information. (p. 84)

lóbulos parietales Porción de la corteza cerebral ubicada en la parte superior de la cabeza y hacia atrás; incluye la corteza somatosensorial y las áreas de asociación general que participan en el procesamiento de información. (pág. 84)

partial reinforcement schedule In operant conditioning, a schedule of reinforcement in which a reward follows only some correct responses. (p. 268)

programa de refuerzo parcial En el condicionamiento operante, programa de refuerzo que premia sólo algunas respuestas correctas. (pág. 268)

participant bias A tendency for research participants to behave in a certain way because they know they are being observed or they believe they know what the researcher wants. (p. 29)

parcialidad de participante Tendencia de los participantes de un experimento a responder de cierta manera porque saben que se los está observando o creen saber lo que tiene en mente el investigador. (pág. 29)

passionate love An aroused state of intense positive absorption in another, usually present at the beginning of a love relationship. (p. 308)

amor apasionado Estado de entusiasmo y concentración positiva e intensa en otra persona, que generalmente se presenta al comienzo de una relación amorosa. (pág. 308)

Pavlov, Ivan (1849–1936) Russian physiologist and learning theorist famous for the discovery of classical conditioning, in which learning occurs through association. (pp. 15, 242)

Pavlov, Ivan (1849–1936) Fisiólogo ruso que se hizo famoso por su descubrimiento del condicionamiento clásico en donde el aprendizaje ocurre a través de la asociación. (págs. 15, 242)

percentage A comparative statistic that compares a score to a perfect score of 100 points. (p. 54)

porcentaje Estadística comparativa en la que se compara un puntaje con un puntaje perfecto, suponiendo que el puntaje perfecto es de 100 puntos. (pág. 54)

percentile rank A comparative statistic that compares a score to other scores in an imaginary group of 100 individuals. (p. 54)

categoría de porcentil Estadística comparativa en la que se compara un puntaje con otros, suponiendo que hay cien puntajes en total. (pág. 54)

perception The process of organizing and interpreting incoming sensory information. (pp. 92, 114)

percepción Proceso de organización e interpretación de información sensorial. (págs. 92, 114)

perceptual constancy Perceiving the size, shape, and lightness of an object as unchanging even as the image of the object on the retina of the eye changes. (p. 123)

constancia perceptiva Percepción de que el tamaño, la forma y el peso de un objeto no cambian, aún cuando cambie la imagen de dicho objeto en la retina. (pág. 123)

perceptual set A mental predisposition to perceive something one way and not another. (p. 125)

predisposición perceptiva Predisposición mental a percibir algo de una manera y no de otra. (pág. 125)

peripheral nervous system (PNS) The sensory and motor nerves that connect the brain and the spinal cord to the rest of the body. (p. 71)

sistema nervioso periférico Nervios sensoriales y motores que conectan el sistema nervioso central con el resto del cuerpo. (pág. 71)

permastore memory Long-term memories that are especially resistant to forgetting and that are likely to last a lifetime. (p. 371)

memoria permanente Recuerdos de la memoria remota que son especialmente resistentes al olvido y se conservan generalmente toda la vida. (pág. 371)

permissive parenting A style of parenting marked by submitting to children's desires, making few demands, and using little punishment. (p. 192)

crianza permisiva Estilo de crianza en el cual los padres se someten a los deseos de los niños, tienen pocas exigencias y emplean pocos castigos. (pág. 192)

personality An individual's characteristic pattern of thinking, feeling, and acting. (pp. 440, 457)

personalidad Patrones de pensamiento, sentimiento y comportamiento característicos de un individuo. (págs. 440, 457)

personality disorders Psychological disorders characterized by rigid and lasting behavior patterns that disrupt social functioning. (p. 516)

trastorno de personalidad Trastornos psicológicos caracterizados por patrones de comportamiento inflexibles y duraderos que perturban el funcionamiento social. (pág. 516)

personality inventories Questionnaires (often with true-false or agree-disagree items) on which people respond to items designed to gauge a range of feelings and behaviors; used to assess selected personality traits. (p. 462)

inventarios de personalidad Cuestionarios (que generalmente se responden con las opciones verdadero-falso o de acuerdo–en desacuerdo) en los que se responde a preguntas diseñadas para medir una amplia variedad de sentimientos y comportamientos; se emplean para evaluar rasgos de la personalidad escogidos. (pág. 462)

phobia An anxiety disorder characterized by disruptive, irrational fears of objects, activities, or situations. (p. 491)

fobia Un trastorno de ansiedad caracterizado por el temor perturbador e irracional a objetos, actividades o situaciones. (pág. 491)

phoneme In language, the smallest distinctive sound unit. (p. 230)

fonema En el lenguaje hablado, unidad más pequeña en la que se distingue un sonido. (pág. 230)

Piaget, Jean [pee-ah-ZHAY] (1896–1980) Pioneer in the study of developmental psychology who introduced a stage theory of cognitive development that led to a better understanding of children's thought processes. (pp. 16, 183, 202)

Piaget, Jean (1896–1980) Pionero en el estudio de la psicología del desarrollo; propuso una teoría de las etapas del desarrollo cognitivo que condujo a un mejor entendimiento de los procesos del pensamiento de los niños. (págs. 16, 183, 202)

Pinel, Philippe (1745–1826) French physician who worked to reform the treatment of people with mental disorders. (p. 478)

pitch A sound's highness or lowness, which depends on the frequency of the sound wave. (p. 104)

pituitary gland The endocrine system's master gland; in conjunction with an adjacent brain area, controls the other endocrine glands. (p. 72)

placebo An inactive substance or condition used to control for confounding variables. (pp. 39, 172)

plasticity The brain's ability to change, especially during childhood, by reorganizing after damage or experience. (p. 85)

population The entire group of people about whom you would like to know something. (p. 32)

positive psychology A movement in psychology that focuses on the study of optimal human functioning and the factors that allow individuals and communities to thrive. (pp. 22, 469, 567)

positive reinforcement In operant conditioning, anything that increases the likelihood of a behavior by following it with a desirable event or state. (p. 260)

positron emission tomography (PET) scan A visual display of brain activity. (p. 79)

posthypnotic suggestion Hypnotic suggestion that the person will carry out after the hypnosis session has ended. (p. 170)

post-traumatic stress disorder (PTSD) An anxiety disorder characterized by reliving a severely upsetting event in unwanted, recurring memories and dreams. (p. 498)

preconscious According to Freud, a region of the mind holding information that is not conscious but is retrievable into conscious awareness. (p. 442)

prejudice An unjustifiable (and usually negative) attitude toward a group and its members. (p. 312)

preoperational stage In Piaget's theory, the stage (from about 2 to 6 or 7 years of age) during which a child learns to use language but cannot yet think logically. (p. 186)

primary reinforcement Something that is naturally reinforcing, such as food (if you were hungry), warmth (if you were cold), and water (if you were thirsty). (p. 261)

primary sex characteristics The reproductive organs—ovaries, testes, and external genitalia. (p. 200)

proactive interference An older memory disrupting the recall of a newer memory. (p. 372)

projective test A personality test, such as the Rorschach or TAT, that provides ambiguous stimuli to trigger projection of inner thoughts and feelings. (p. 448)

prosocial behavior Positive, constructive, helpful behavior. (p. 279)

prototype A typical best example incorporating the major features of a concept. (p. 382)

pseudoscientific claim Any assertion that appears scientific but is not based on science. (p. 134)

Pinel, Philippe (1745–1826) Médico francés que se dedicó a reformar el tratamiento de las personas con trastornos mentales. (pág. 478)

tono Intensidad de un sonido, que depende de la frecuencia de una onda sonora. (pág. 104)

glándula pituitaria "Glándula maestra" del sistema endocrino. Su importancia es tal que, junto con el cerebro, controla las demás glándulas endocrinas. (pág. 72)

placebo Sustancia o condición inactiva que se utiliza para control de los variables confundentes. (págs. 39, 172)

plasticidad La capacidad del cerebro para cambiar, especialmente durante la infancia, por reorganizarse después de una lesión o experiencia. (pág. 85)

población Todos los casos de un grupo, entre los cuales se pueden extraer muestras para un estudio. (pág. 32)

psicología positiva Movimiento en la psicología que se concentra en el estudio del funcionamiento óptimo del ser humano y en los factores que permiten la prosperidad de individuos y comunidades. (págs. 22, 469, 567)

refuerzo positivo En el condicionamiento operante, cualquier cosa que aumenta la probabilidad de que se produzca un comportamiento cuando se proporciona un suceso o estado deseable. (pág. 260)

tomografía por emisión de positrones Muestra visual de la actividad cerebral. (pág. 79)

sugestión poshipnótica Sugestión hecha durante una sesión de hipnosis, para que el sujeto la cumpla cuando ya no esté hipnotizado. (pág. 170)

trastorno de estrés postraumático Trastorno en el que se repite la experiencia de un suceso muy perturbador en recuerdos y sueños recurrentes. (pág. 498)

preconsciente Según Freud, la región de la mente en donde existe información que no es consciente pero que puede ser recordada conscientemente. (pág. 442)

prejuicio Actitud injustificable (y frecuentemente negativa) hacia un grupo y sus miembros. (pág. 312)

etapa preoperacional Según la teoría de Piaget, etapa (aproximadamente desde los dos hasta los siete años) durante la cual el niño aprende a emplear el lenguaje pero aún no comprende las operaciones mentales de lógica concreta. (pág. 186)

refuerzo primario Algo que refuerza naturalmente, tal como la comida (si se tiene hambre), el calor (si se tiene frío) y el agua (si se tiene sed). (pág. 261)

características sexuales primarias Estructuras del cuerpo (ovarios, testículos y órganos sexuales externos) que posibilitan la reproducción. (pág. 200)

interferencia proactiva Cuando una memoria vieja interrumpe el recuerdo de una memoria más reciente. (pág. 372)

pruebas de proyección Pruebas de la personalidad, tales como la Rorschach o la prueba de apercepción temática, que proveen estímulos ambiguos para provocar la proyección de los pensamientos y los sentimientos de una persona. (pág. 448)

comportamiento prosocial Comportamiento positivo, constructivo y útil. (pág. 279)

prototipo Ejemplo que incorpora más típicamente y de mejor manera las características principales de un concepto. (pág. 382)

planteamiento pseudocientífico Cualquier afirmación que aparece científica pero no se base en la ciencia. (pág. 134)

psychoactive drug Chemical substance that alters perceptions, mood, or behavior. (p. 149)

droga psicoactiva Sustancia química que altera las percepciones y el estado de ánimo. (pág. 149)

psychoanalysis Freud's theory of personality; also, a therapeutic technique that attempts to provide insight into thoughts and actions by exposing and interpreting the underlying unconscious motives and conflicts. (pp. 14, 441, 522)

psicoanálisis Teoría de la personalidad de Freud; también, técnica terapéutica que intenta proporcionar a un individuo un entendimiento de sus pensamientos y acciones exponiendo e interpretando los motivos y conflictos inconscientes subyacentes. (págs. 14, 441, 522)

psychodynamic perspective A view of personality that retains some aspects of Freudian theory (such as the importance of unconscious thought processes) but is less likely to see unresolved childhood conflicts as a source of personality development. (p. 441)

perspectiva psicodinámica Concepto de la personalidad que retiene algunas de las características de la teoría freudiana (tales como la importancia de los procesos inconscientes del pensamiento), pero que es menos capaz de ver los conflictos irresueltos de la niñez como fuente del desarrollo de la personalidad. (pág. 441)

psychological disorder A harmful dysfunction in which thoughts, feelings, or behaviors are maladaptive, unjustifiable, disturbing, and atypical. (p. 476)

trastorno psicológico Disfunción dañina en la cual los pensamientos, sentimientos o comportamientos se juzgan como inadaptados, injustificados, perturbadores y atípicos. (pág. 476)

psychology Scientific study of behavior and mental processes. (p. 10)

psicología Estudio científico del comportamiento y los procesos mentales. (pág. 10)

psychosexual stages Childhood stages of development (oral, anal, phallic, latency, and genital) during which, according to Freud, the id's pleasure-seeking energies focus on different parts of the body. (p. 444)

etapas psicosexuales Etapas del desarrollo de la niñez (oral, anal, fálica, latente y genital) durante las cuales, según Freud, las energías de búsqueda de placer del ello se concentran en las distintas zonas erógenas. (pág. 444)

psychotherapy An interaction between a trained therapist and someone who is seeking to overcome psychological difficulties or achieve personal growth. (p. 521)

psicoterapia Interacción entre un terapeuta calificado y alguien que está tratando de superar las dificultades psicológicas o lograr crecimiento personal. (pág. 521)

puberty The period of sexual maturation, during which a person becomes capable of reproducing. (p. 199)

pubertad Etapa de maduración sexual durante la cual una persona se vuelve capaz de reproducirse. (pág. 199)

punishment Any consequence that decreases the future likelihood of a behavior. (p. 257)

castigo Todo tipo de consecuencia que disminuye la futura probabilidad de que se produzca un comportamiento. (pág. 257)

pupil The adjustable opening in the center of the iris, which controls the amount of light entering the eye. (p. 99)

pupila Apertura ajustable del centro del iris; controla la cantidad de luz que entra al ojo. (pág. 99)

R

random assignment A procedure for creating groups that allows the researcher to control for individual differences among research participants. (p. 37)

asignación aleatoria Asignación al azar de participantes a grupos de control y experimentales, para minimizar diferencias preexistentes entre los asignados a distintos grupos. (pág. 37)

random sample A sample that fairly represents a population because each member of the population has an equal chance of being included. (p. 32)

muestra aleatoria Muestra que representa correctamente a una población porque cada uno de los miembros tiene igual probabilidad de ser incluido. (pág. 32)

range The difference between the highest and lowest scores in a distribution. (p. 51)

intervalo Diferencia entre el puntaje más alto y el más bajo de una distribución. (pág. 51)

rapid eye movement (REM) sleep Recurring sleep stage during which vivid dreams commonly occur. (p. 140)

sueño de movimientos oculares rápidos (MOR) Fase del sueño recurrente en el que generalmente ocurren los sueños vívidos. (pág. 140)

recall The type of retrieval in which you must search for information that you previously stored, as on a fill-in-the-blank test. (p. 364)

recordación Medida de la memoria que consiste en recuperar información aprendida anteriormente, tal como en las pruebas de rellenar espacios en blanco. (pág. 364)

receptor cells Specialized cells in every sensory system of the body that can turn other kinds of energy into action potentials (neural impulses) that the brain can process. (pp. 66, 100)

células receptoras Células que se encuentran en todo sistema sensorial y transforman (transducen) otros tipos de engergía en impulsos que el cerebro es capaz de procesar. (págs. 66, 100)

reciprocal determinism The mutual influences between personality and environmental factors. (p. 466)

determinismo recíproco Influencias de la interacción entre factores de la personalidad y del ambiente. (pág. 466)

recognition The type of retrieval in which you must identify items you learned earlier, as on a multiple-choice test. (p. 364)

reconocimiento Medida de la memoria que consiste en identificar cosas que se aprendieron anteriormente, tal como en una prueba de escogencia múltiple. (pág. 364)

rehearsal The conscious repetition of information. (p. 351)

ensayo Repetición consciente de información. (pág. 351)

reinforcement Any consequence that increases the future likelihood of a behavior. (p. 257)	**refuerzo** Todo tipo de consecuencia que aumenta la probabilidad de que se produzca un comportamiento en el futuro. (pág. 257)
reliability The extent to which a test yields consistent results, regardless of who gives the test or when or where it is given. (pp. 403, 462)	**fiabilidad** Medida en la que una prueba produce resultados uniformes, sin importar quién la administra o dónde se la da. (págs. 403, 462)
replicate To repeat the essence of a research study to see whether the results can be reliably reproduced. (p. 40)	**replicar** Repetir un estudio científico para observar si los resultados pueden ser reproducidos de forma fiable. (pág. 40)
repression In Sigmund Freud's psychoanalytic theory, the process of moving anxiety-producing memories to the unconscious mind. (p. 373)	**represión** Según la teoría psicoanalítica de Sigmund Freud, proceso en el que se pasan al inconsciente los recuerdos que producen ansiedad. (pág. 373)
Rescorla, Robert (1940–) Developed, along with colleague Allan Wagner, a theory that emphasized the importance of cognitive processes in classical conditioning. (p. 251)	**Rescorla, Robert (1940–)** Investigador que desarrolló, junto con su colega Allan Wagner, una nueva teoría que enfatizaba la importancia de los procesos cognitivos en el condicionamiento clásico. (pág. 251)
resilience The ability to grow and thrive in the face of challenges and to bounce back from adversity. (p. 446)	**elasticidad** Capacidad de crecer y prosperar a pesar de los desafíos y reponerse después de la adversidad. (pág. 446)
resistance In psychoanalysis, the blocking from consciousness of anxiety-laden material. (p. 523)	**resistencia** Según el psicoanálisis, bloqueo de la consciencia de recuerdos que producen ansiedad. (pág. 523)
response Any behavior or action. (p. 239)	**respuesta** Todo tipo de comportamiento o acción. (pág. 239)
resting potential The state of a neuron when it is at rest and capable of generating an action potential. (p. 64)	**potencial de reposo** Estado de descanso de una neurona cuando es capaz de generar un potencial de acción. (pág. 64)
reticular formation A nerve network in the brainstem that plays an important role in controlling wakefulness and arousal. (p. 80)	**formación reticular** Red de fibras nerviosas en el bulbo raquídeo, que cumple un papel importante en la regulación de la vigilia y la estimulación. (pág. 80)
retina The light-sensitive surface at the back of the eyeball. (p. 100)	**retina** Superficie sensible a la luz que está ubicada en la parte posterior del globo ocular. (pág. 100)
retinal disparity A binocular depth cue resulting from slightly different images produced by the retina of the left eye and the retina of the right eye. (p. 118)	**disparidad retiniana** Clave de profundidad binocular que resulta de la producción de imágenes ligeramente distintas por la separación de las retinas del ojo izquierdo y el derecho. (pág. 118)
retrieval The process of getting information out of memory storage. (pp. 349, 369)	**recuperación** Proceso mediante el cual se recuerda información almacenada en la memoria. (págs. 349, 369)
retroactive interference A more recent memory disrupting the recall of an older memory. (p. 373)	**interferencia retroactiva** Cuando un recuerdo más reciente perturba el recuerdo de una memoria mas vieja. (pág. 373)
rods Visual receptor cells located in the retina that can detect only black, white, and gray. (p. 100)	**bastoncillos** Células receptoras de la visión ubicadas en la retina que detectan sólo el negro, el blanco y el gris. (pág. 100)
Rogers, Carl (1902–1987) Humanistic psychologist who developed *client-centered therapy* and stressed the importance of acceptance, genuineness, and empathy in fostering human growth. (pp. 15, 452, 526)	**Rogers, Carl (1902–1987)** Psicólogo humanista que elaboró la terapia centrada en el cliente y enfatizó la importancia de la aceptación, la autenticidad y la empatía para fomentar el crecimiento personal del ser humano. (págs. 15, 452, 526)
role A set of expectations in a social setting that define how one ought to behave. (p. 289)	**rol** Conjunto de expectativas en un entorno social que definen cómo se debe actuar. (pág. 289)
rooting reflex A baby's tendency, when touched on the cheek, to open the mouth and search for the nipple. (p. 179)	**reflejo de búsqueda** Tendencia de los bebés, cuando se les toca la mejilla, a abrir la boca y buscar el pezón. (pág. 179)
Rorschach inkblot test The most widely used projective test; a set of 10 inkblots designed to identify people's inner feelings by analyzing their interpretations of the blots. (p. 448)	**prueba de Rorschach** Conjunto de diez manchas de tinta diseñado por Hermann Rorschach. Es la prueba de proyección empleada con más frecuencia y tiene el propósito de identificar los sentimientos de las personas mediante el análisis de sus interpretaciones de las manchas. (pág. 448)

S

scapegoat theory The theory that prejudice offers an outlet for anger by providing someone to blame. (p. 314)	**teoría de chivo expiatorio** Teoría según la cual el prejuicio representa una vía de escape al enojo porque proporciona a alguien a quién culpar. (pág. 314)

Schachter, Stanley [SHACK-ter] **(1922–1997)** U.S. psychologist who, with Jerome Singer, concluded that emotion requires a cognitive label of physiological arousal (see *two-factor theory*). (p. 429)

Schachter, Stanley (1922–1997) Psicólogo estadounidense que, junto con Jerome Singer, concluyó que las emociones requieren una identificación cognitiva de estimulación fisiológica (véase la teoría de las emociones de dos factores). (pág. 429)

schemas Concepts or mental frameworks that organize and interpret information. (p. 183)

esquemas Conceptos de marcos mentales que ordenan e interpretan información. (pág. 183)

schizophrenia A disorder characterized by disorganized and delusional thinking, disturbed perceptions, and inappropriate emotions and behaviors. (p. 512)

esquizofrenia Conjunto de trastornos graves caracterizados por pensamientos desordenados y delirantes, percepciones perturbadas y emociones y acciones inapropiadas. (pág. 512)

scientific method A method of learning about the world through the application of critical thinking and tools such as observation, experimentation, and statistical analysis. (p. 26)

método científico Método de aprendizaje del mundo que nos rodea mediante la aplicación del pensamiento crítico y mecanismos tales como la observación, la experimentación y el análisis estadístico. (pág. 26)

secondary reinforcement Something that you have learned to value, like money. (p. 261)

refuerzo secundario Se dice de algo que se ha aprendido a valorar, por ejemplo, el dinero. (pág. 261)

secondary sex characteristics Nonreproductive sexual characteristics, such as breast and hip development in females and voice quality and facial hair in males. (p. 200)

características sexuales secundarias Características sexuales que no están directamente relacionadas con la reproducción, tales como los senos y las caderas en la mujer, el tono de voz en el hombre y el vello del cuerpo. (pág. 200)

selective attention Focusing conscious awareness on a particular stimulus to the exclusion of others. (p. 96)

atención selectiva Capacidad de enfocar la consciencia en un estímulo en particular excluyendo a los demás. (pág. 96)

self-actualization According to Maslow, an ultimate psychological need that arises after basic physical and psychological needs are met and self-esteem is achieved; the motivation to realize our full and unique potential. (pp. 416, 451)

autorrealización Según Abraham Maslow, necesidad psicológica más importante que surge después de satisfacer las necesidades físicas y psicológicas y de lograr la autoestima; motivación de realizar el potencial personal. (págs. 416, 451)

self-concept All our thoughts and feelings about ourselves in answer to the question "Who am I?" (p. 452)

concepto de uno mismo Todo lo que pensamos y sentimos acerca de nosotros mismos cuando respondemos a la pregunta: "¿Quién soy?" (pág. 452)

self-disclosure Revealing intimate aspects of oneself to others. (p. 309)

revelación de uno mismo Revelación a los demás de cosas que uno considera íntimas. (pág. 309)

self-fulfilling prophecy When we believe something to be true about others (or ourselves) and we act in ways that cause this belief to come true. (p. 302)

predicción que acarrea su propio cumplimiento Cuando creemos que algo es verdadero acerca de otras personas (o de nosotros mismos) y actuamos de una manera que causa que esta creecia parezca o se haga verdad. (pág. 302)

self-serving bias A readiness to perceive oneself favorably. (p. 286)

sesgo de autoservicio Disposición a percibirse favorablemente. (pág. 286)

Seligman, Martin (1942–) U.S. psychologist who researched helplessness early in his career before turning his interest to optimism; he has been the primary proponent of positive psychology. (pp. 468, 561)

Seligman, Martin (1942–) Psicólogo estadounidense que investigó la incapacidad al principio de su carrera antes de interesarse en el optimismo; ha sido el defensor principal de la psicología positiva. (págs. 468, 561)

Selye, Hans [SELL-yay] **(1907–1982)** Canadian physiologist who researched a recurring response to stress that he called the general adaptation syndrome (GAS). (p. 551)

Selye, Hans (1907–1982) Psicólogo que investigó las respuestas recurrentes al estrés y que él denominó síndrome de adaptación general. (pág. 551)

semantic encoding Encoding of meaning. (p. 353)

codificación semántica Codificación del significado. (pág. 353)

senile dementia Mental disintegration that accompanies alcoholism, tumor, stroke, aging, and, most often, Alzheimer's disease. (p. 218)

demencia senil Desintegración mental que acompaña al alcoholismo, un tumor, un derrame cerebral, la edad y, más a menudo, la enfermedad de Alzheimer. (pág. 218)

sensation The process by which sensory systems (eyes, ears, and other sensory organs) and the nervous system receive stimuli from our environment. (p. 92)

sensación Proceso mediante el cual los sistemas sensoriales (ojos, oídos y otros órganos sensoriales) y el sistema nervioso reciben estímulos del ambiente. (pág. 92)

sensorimotor stage In Piaget's theory, the stage (from birth to about 2 years of age) during which infants learn about the world through their sensory impressions and motor activities. (p. 185)

etapa sensorio motriz Según la teoría de Piaget, etapa (desde el nacimiento hasta aproximadamente los dos años) durante la cual los niños conocen el mundo mayormente en términos de sus impresiones sensoriales y sus actividades motoras. (pág. 185)

sensory adaptation Diminished sensitivity to constant and unchanging stimulation. (p. 96)

adaptación sensorial Disminución en la sensibilidad que resulta de la estimulación constante. (pág. 96)

sensory memory Brief, initial coding of sensory information in the memory system. (p. 358)

memoria sensorial Etapa inicial y breve de codificación de información sensorial en el sistema de la memoria. (pág. 358)

sensory nerves Nerves that carry information from the sense receptors to the spinal cord and brain. (p. 67)

nervios sensoriales Nervios que transmiten información al sistema nervioso central. (pág. 67)

serial position effect The tendency to recall the first and last items in a list more easily. (p. 352)

efecto de posición serial Tendencia a recordar los elementos del comienzo y el fin de una lista con mayor facilidad. (pág. 352)

set point The point at which an individual's "weight thermostat" is supposedly set; when the body falls below this weight, an increase in hunger and a lowered metabolic rate may act to restore the lost weight. (pp. 421, 574)

punto fijo Punto en el que se supone que está puesto el "medidor de peso" de un individuo. Cuando el cuerpo baja de ese peso, es posible que aumente el hambre y disminuya el metabolismo para recuperar el peso perdido. (págs. 421, 574)

sexual orientation Enduring sexual attraction toward people of the opposite sex (heterosexuality), one's own sex (homosexuality) or to both sexes (bisexuality). (p. 201)

orientación sexual Experimentar una atracción sexual perdurable hacia personas del sexo opuesto (heterosexualidad), del mismo sexo (homosexualidad) o de ambos sexos (bisexualidad). (pág. 201)

shaping Reinforcement of behaviors that are increasingly similar to the desired one; the operant technique used to establish new behaviors. (p. 265)

modelamiento Refuerzo de comportamientos que son cada vez más similares al que uno desea que ocurra. Es la técnica del condicionamiento operante que se emplea para establecer nuevos comportamientos. (pág. 265)

short-term/working memory The part of your memory system that contains information you are consciously aware of before it is stored more permanently or forgotten. (p. 358)

memoria inmediata Memoria consciente y activada que retiene brevemente unos siete trozos de información antes de que ésta sea almacenada más permanentemente o se olvide. (pág. 358)

signal detection theory A theory that predicts how and when we detect the presence of a faint stimulus (signal) amid background stimulation (noise). (p. 94)

teoría de la detección de señales Conjunto de fórmulas y principios que predicen cuándo detectaremos la presencia de un estímulo leve ("señal") entre la estimulación de fondo ("ruido"). (pág. 94)

skewed Distorted; not evenly distributed around the mean. (p. 50)

asimétrico Distorsionado; que no está distribuido uniformemente alrededor de la media. (pág. 50)

Skinner, B. F. (1904–1990) American behavioral psychologist who developed the fundamental principles and techniques of operant conditioning and devised ways to apply them in the real world. He argued that children learn language through associations, imitation, and reinforcement. (pp. 15, 232, 257)

Skinner, B. F. (1904–1990) Psicólogo estadounidense que desarrolló los principios fundamentales y las técnicas del condicionamiento operante y creó maneras de aplicarlos en situaciones reales. Sostuvo que los niños aprenden el lenguaje a través de las asociaciones, la imitación y el reforzamiento. (págs. 15, 232, 257)

sleep apnea Sleep disorder characterized by temporary cessations of breathing during sleep and consequent momentary reawakenings. (p. 144)

apnea del sueño Trastorno del sueño en el que se interrumpe temporalmente la respiración, lo cual hace que la persona se despierte por momentos. (pág. 144)

social clock The culturally preferred timing of social events such as marriage, parenthood, and retirement. (p. 214)

reloj social Momento apropiado, según la preferencia cultural, para eventos sociales tales como el matrimonio, la crianza de los hijos y el retiro laboral. (pág. 214)

social facilitation Improved performance on tasks in the presence of others. (p. 298)

facilitación social Mejorar en la ejecución de tareas ante la presencia de otras personas. (pág. 298)

social influence theory Theory that powerful social influences can produce a state of hypnosis. (p. 168)

teoría de influencia social Teoría que propone que las influencias sociales de gran impacto son capaces de producir un estado hipnótico. (pág. 168)

social loafing The tendency for people in a group to exert less effort when pooling their efforts toward attaining a common goal than when individually accountable. (p. 298)

disminución de productividad en un grupo Tendencia de las personas de un grupo a esforzarse menos cuando aportan su esfuerzo para el logro de una meta común, que cuando son responsables de manera independiente. (pág. 298)

social psychology The scientific study of how we think about, influence, and relate to one another. (p. 284)

psicología social Estudio científico que observa cómo nos relacionamos con los demás, los influenciamos y pensamos en ellos. (pág. 284)

social-cognitive perspective A perspective stating that understanding personality involves considering how people are affected by a particular situation, by what they have learned, by how they think, and by how they interact socially. (p. 457)

perspectiva cognitivo-social Perspectiva según la cual el entendimiento de la personalidad se basa en considerar cómo las personas se ven afectadas por una situación, por lo que han aprendido, por lo que piensan y por la forma en que interactúan socialmente. (pág. 457)

social-cultural perspective School of thought that focuses on how thinking or behavior changes in different situations or as a result of cultural influences. (p. 20)

perspectiva sociocultural Corriente de pensamiento que se centra en cómo el pensamiento o comportamiento cambia en distintas situaciones o como resultado de las influencias culturales. (pág. 20)

somatic nervous system The division of the peripheral nervous system that controls the body's skeletal muscles. (p. 71)

sistema nervioso somático Subdivisión del sistema nervioso periférico que controla los músculos esqueléticos del cuerpo. (pág. 71)

somatic symptom and related disorders Psychological disorders in which the symptoms take a bodily form without apparent physical cause. (p. 511)

trastorno somatoforo y otros trastornos relacionados Trastornos psicológicos cuyos síntomas físicos no presentan una causa física aparente. (pág. 511)

somatosensory cortex A strip of brain tissue at the front of the parietal lobes that registers and processes body sensations. (p. 85)

corteza somatosensorial Parte cerebral ubicada delante de los lóbulos parietales que registra y procesa las sensaciones del cuerpo. (pág. 85)

somnambulism Sleepwalking, which usually starts in the deeper stages of NREM sleep; the sleepwalker can walk and talk and is able to see but rarely has any memory of the event. (p. 145)

sonambulismo Caminar dormido, lo cual generalmente comienza en las etapas de sueño NREM más profundo. La persona sonámbula es capaz de caminar, de hablar y también de ver, pero pocas veces recuerda esos episodios. (pág. 145)

standard deviation A computed measure of how much scores vary around the mean score of a distribution. (p. 51)

desviación estándar Medida calculada de cuántos puntajes varían alrededor del puntaje de la media. (pág. 51)

state-dependent memory The enhanced ability to retrieve information when you are in the same physical and emotional state you were in when you encoded the information. (p. 366)

memoria dependiente del estado Capacidad potenciada de recuperar información cuando uno está en el mismo estado físico y emocional que estaba cuando se codificó esa información. (pág. 366)

statistical significance A statistical statement of how likely it is that a result occurred by chance alone. (p. 57)

significación estadística Afirmación estadística que indica la probabilidad de que un resultado ocurra solamente por pura casualidad. (pág. 57)

stereotype A generalized (sometimes accurate but often overgeneralized) belief about a group of people. (p. 312)

estereotipo Creencia generalizadora (a veces acertada, pero a menudo demasiado generalizadora) acerca de un grupo de personas. (pág. 312)

Sternberg, Robert (1949–) Author of a contemporary theory of multiple intelligences consisting of analytical, creative, and practical intelligence. (p. 394)

Sternberg, Robert (1949–) Autor de una teoría contemporánea de inteligencias múltiples que distingue entre la inteligencia analítica, la creativa y la práctica. (pág. 394)

stimulants Drugs (such as caffeine, nicotine, and the more powerful amphetamines and cocaine) that excite neural activity and speed up body functions. (p. 154)

estimulantes Drogas (tales como la cafeína, la nicotina y otras más potentes como las anfetaminas y la cocaína) que estimulan la actividad nerviosa y aceleran las funciones del cuerpo. (pág. 154)

stimulus Anything in the environment that one can respond to. (p. 239)

estímulo Cualquier cosa del ambiente a lo que uno es capaz de responder. (pág. 239)

storage The retention of encoded information in memory over time. (pp. 349, 369)

almacenamiento Retención de información codificada a lo largo del tiempo. (págs. 349, 369)

stranger anxiety The fear of strangers that infants commonly display, beginning by about 8 months of age. (p. 188)

ansiedad ante los extraños Miedo a personas desconocidas que se presenta comúnmente en los bebés y que comienza aproximadamente a los ocho meses de vida. (pág. 188)

stress The process by which we perceive and respond to certain events, called stressors, that we appraise as threatening or challenging. (p. 550)

estrés Proceso mediante el cual percibimos y respondemos a ciertos sucesos estresantes, que calificamos como amenazantes o desafiantes. (pág. 550)

structuralism Theory that the structure of conscious experience could be understood by analyzing the basic elements of thoughts and sensations. (p. 12)

estructuralismo Teoría que la estructura de la experiencia consciente puede ser entendida mediante el análisis de los elementos básicos de los pensamientos y las sensaciones. (pág. 12)

superego The part of personality that, according to Freud, represents internalized ideals and provides standards for judgment (the conscience) and for future aspirations. (p. 443)

superyó Según Freud, componente de la personalidad que representa ideales internalizados y proporciona parámetros de juicio (el consciente) y de aspiraciones futuras. (pág. 443)

superordinate goals Shared goals that override differences among people and require their cooperation. (p. 320)

metas superiores Metas compartidas que anulan las diferencias entre individuos y requieren de su colaboración. (pág. 320)

survey method A research technique that questions a sample of people to collect information about their attitudes or behaviors. (p. 32)

método de estudio o encuesta Técnica de investigación diseñada para descubrir actitudes o comportamientos. Muestras de personas ofrecen sus comunicados voluntariamente mediante cuestionarios o entrevistas. (pág. 32)

sympathetic division The part of the autonomic nervous system that arouses the body to deal with perceived threats. (p. 72)

división simpática Parte del sistema nervioso autónomo que estimula al cuerpo para responder a situaciones que se perciben como amenazas. (pág. 72)

synapse [SIN-aps] The tiny, fluid-filled gap between the axon terminal of one neuron and the dendrite of another. (p. 65)

sinapsis El pequeño espacio lleno de líquido entre el extremo del axón de una neurona y la dendrita de otra. (pág. 65)

systematic desensitization A type of counterconditioning that associates a pleasant, relaxed state with gradually increasing anxiety-triggering stimuli. (p. 528)

desensibilización sistemática Tipo de contracondicionamiento en el cual se asocia un estado tranquilo y agradable con estímulos que provocan ansiedad y que se aplican de manera gradual y en aumento. (pág. 528)

T

temperament A person's characteristic emotional excitability. (p. 179)

temperamento Reacción e intensidad emocional características de un individuo. (pág. 179)

temporal lobes The portion of the cerebral cortex lying roughly above the ears; it includes the auditory (hearing) areas of the brain. (p. 84)

lóbulos temporales Porción de la corteza cerebral ubicada más o menos encima de las orejas; incluye las áreas auditivas (del oído). (pág. 84)

teratogens Substances that cross the placental barrier and prevent the fetus from developing normally. (p. 179)

teratógenos Sustancias que penetran la barrera placentaria e impiden el desarrollo normal del feto. (pág. 179)

Terman, Lewis (1877–1956) Adapted Binet's tests for use in the United States as an intelligence test that reported intelligence as a calculated IQ score. (p. 397)

Terman, Lewis (1877–1956) Adaptó las pruebas de Binet para su uso en los Estados Unidos en una prueba de inteligencia que reportó la inteligencia con un puntaje calculado de coeficiente intelectual (CI). (pág. 397)

thalamus [THAL-uh-muss] The brain's sensory switchboard, located on top of the brainstem; it directs messages to the sensory receiving areas in the cortex. (p. 81)

tálamo Tablero de control sensorial del cerebro, ubicado encima del tronco cerebral; dirige mensajes a las áreas de la corteza cerebral que reciben mensajes sensoriales. (pág. 81)

Thematic Apperception Test (TAT) A projective test in which people express their inner feelings and interests through the stories they make up about ambiguous scenes. (p. 448)

Prueba de apercepción temática Prueba de proyección en la cual las personas expresan sus sentimientos e intereses a través de cuentos que inventan basándose en escenas ambiguas. (pág. 448)

Thorndike, Edward (1874–1949) Author of the law of effect, the principle that forms the basis of operant conditioning. (p. 256)

Thorndike, Edward (1874–1949) Creador de la ley del efecto, principio que forma la base del condicionamiento operante. (pág. 256)

Titchener, Edward. B. (1867–1927) Founder of structuralism. (p. 12)

Titchener, Edward. B. (1867–1927) Fundador del estructuralismo. (pág. 12)

token economy An operant conditioning procedure that attempts to modify behavior by rewarding desired behaviors with some small item. (p. 531)

economía de fichas Procedimiento del condicionamiento operante que intenta modificar el comportamiento dando recompensas por los comportamientos deseables. (pág. 531)

tolerance Reduced responsiveness to a drug, prompting the user to take larger doses to achieve the same pleasurable effects previously obtained by smaller doses. (p. 150)

tolerancia Receptividad reducida a una sustancia, que da lugar a que la persona aumente la dosis para sentir los efectos que anteriormente obtenía con dosis más pequeñas. (pág. 150)

top-down processing Information processing that draws on expectations and experiences to interpret incoming sensory information. (p. 92)

procesamiento de arriba hacia abajo Procesamiento de información que enfatiza nuestras expectativas y experiencias cuando interpretamos la información sensorial que recibimos. (pág. 92)

traits Aspects of personality that are relatively consistent. (p. 457)

rasgo Aspectos de la personalidad que son relativamente uniforme. (pág. 457)

transgender a broad term describing people whose gender identity or behavior differs from that associated with their birth-designated sex. (p. 344)

transgénero término general que describe a personas cuya identidad de género o comportamiento es diferente del sexo que se les asignó al nacer. (pág. 344)

transference In psychoanalysis, the patient's transfer of strong emotions (such as love or hatred) linked with other relationships to the analyst. (p. 523)

transferencia En el psicoanálisis, transferencia del paciente al analista de emociones (tales como amor u odio) que están ligadas a otras relaciones. (pág. 523)

trichromatic theory A theory of color vision that says cones are sensitive to red, green, or blue light—the three colors that combine to create millions of color combinations. (p. 102)

teoría tricromática Teoría de la visión del color que plantea que los conos están "calibrados" para detectar la luz roja, verde o azul. En estos tipos de conos existen varios niveles de estimulación que nos permiten identificar millones de combinaciones de colores distintas. (pág. 102)

two-factor theory The theory that to experience emotion we must be physically aroused and must cognitively label the arousal. (p. 429)

teoría de las emociones de dos factores Teoría que propone que para experimentar emociones debe existir estimulación física e identificarse el estímulo a nivel cognitivo. (pág. 429)

Type A A term for competitive, hard-driving, impatient, verbally aggressive, and anger-prone people. (p. 556)

tipo A Término que se refiere a los individuos competidores, luchadores, impacientes, agresivos verbalmente y propensos al enojo. (pág. 556)

Type B A term for easygoing, relaxed people. (p. 556)

tipo B Término que se refiere a los individuos de trato fácil y tranquilos. (pág. 556)

U

ultradian [ul-TRAY-dee-un] rhythms Biological rhythms that occur more than once each day. (p. 134)

ritmos ultradianos Ritmos biológicos que ocurren más de una vez al día. (pág. 134)

unconditional positive regard According to Rogers, an attitude of total acceptance toward another person. (p. 452)

estima positiva incondicional Según la teoría de Carl Rogers, actitud de aceptación total hacia otra persona. (pág. 452)

unconditioned response (UR) An automatic response to the unconditioned stimulus. (p. 240)

respuesta incondicionada En el condicionamiento clásico, respuesta automática al estímulo no condicionado. (pág. 240)

unconditioned stimulus (US) A stimulus that triggers a response reflexively and automatically. (p. 240)

estímulo incondicionado En el condicionamiento clásico, estímulo que provoca una respuesta automática y reflexivamente. (pág. 240)

unconscious According to Freud, a region of the mind that is a reservoir of mostly unacceptable thoughts, wishes, feelings, and memories. (p. 442)

inconsciente Según Freud, región de la mente que actúa como reserva de pensamientos, deseos, sentimientos y recuerdos mayormente inaceptables. (pág. 442)

V

validity The extent to which a test measures or predicts what it is supposed to test. (pp. 403, 462)

validez Punto hasta el cual una prueba mide o predice lo que se supone provar. (págs. 403, 462)

variable-interval schedule In operant conditioning, a partial reinforcement schedule that rewards the first correct response after an unpredictable amount of time. (p. 268)

programa de intervalos variables En el condicionamiento operante, programa de refuerzo parcial que administra recompensas por la primera respuesta correcta después de una cantidad de tiempo impredecible. (pág. 268)

variable-ratio schedule In operant conditioning, a partial reinforcement schedule that rewards after an unpredictable number of correct responses. (p. 269)

programa de proporción variable En el condicionamiento operante, programa de refuerzo parcial que administra recompensas por un número impredecible de respuestas correctas. (pág. 269)

vestibular sense The system for sensing body orientation and balance, which is located in the semicircular canals of the inner ear. (p. 111)

sentido vestibular Sistema que percibe la orientación y el equilibrio del cuerpo y está ubicado en los canales semicirculares del oído interno. (pág. 111)

vicarious learning Learning by seeing the consequences of another person's behavior. (p. 277)

aprendizaje vicario Aprendizaje por observar las consecuencias del comportamiento de otra persona. (pág. 277)

virtual reality exposure therapy An anxiety treatment that progressively exposes people to simulations of their greatest fears, such as airplane flying, spiders, or public speaking. (p. 529)

terapia de exposición mediante realidad virtual Un tratamiento para la ansiedad que progresivamente expone a las personas a simulaciones de sus temores más grandes, como volar en avión, las arañas o hablar en público. (pág. 529)

visual cliff A laboratory device for testing depth perception in infants and young animals. (p. 117)

precipicio visual Aparato de laboratorio que examina la percepción de profundidad de los bebés recién nacidos y de los animales jóvenes. (pág. 117)

W

Watson, John B. (1878–1958) Founder of behaviorism, the theory that psychology should restrict its efforts to studying observable behaviors, not mental processes. (pp. 15, 247)

Watson, John B. (1878–1958) Fundador del conductismo, perspectiva según la cual la psicología debe limitarse a estudiar los comportamientos observables y no los procesos mentales. (págs. 15, 247)

Wechsler, David (1896–1981) Developer of the most widely used individual intelligence tests in the United States, which were the first tests to report scores for both verbal and performance intelligence. (p. 398)

Wechsler, David (1896–1981) Creador de las pruebas individuales de inteligencia que más se administran en los Estados Unidos. Fueron las primeras pruebas en tener puntajes tanto para la inteligencia verbal como para la de desempeño. (pág. 398)

wellness The common result of a healthy life-style and healthy attitudes. (p. 561)

bienestar Resultado de un estilo de vida y actitudes saludables. (pág. 561)

Wernicke's [VER-nik-ees] area A brain area of the left temporal lobe involved in language comprehension and expression. (p. 87)

área de Wernicke Parte del cerebro ubicada en el lóbulo temporal izquierdo que participa en la comprensión y la expresión del lenguaje. (pág. 87)

withdrawal Discomfort and distress that follow when a person who is dependent on a drug discontinues the use of that drug. (p. 149)

síntomas de abstinencia Malestar y angustia que ocurren a una persona que depende de una droga adictiva cuando deja de consumirla. (pág. 149)

Wundt, Wilhelm [VOONT] (1832–1920) Founder of modern psychology; he opened the first psychology laboratory (p. 11)

Wundt, Wilhelm (1832–1920) Fundador de la psicología moderna; abrió el primer laboratorio de psicología. (pág. 11)

Y

Yerkes–Dodson law The theory that a degree of psychological arousal helps performance, but only to a point. (p. 412)

ley de Yerkes-Dodson Teoría según la cual un grado de estimulación psicológica facilita el rendimiento, pero sólo hasta cierto punto. (pág. 412)

Z

Zajonc, Robert [ZI-yence] (1923–2008) U.S. psychologist who concluded that some emotional reactions involve no deliberate thinking; he believed that cognition is not always necessary for emotion. (p. 429)	**Zajonc, Robert (1923–2008)** Psicólogo estadounidense que concluyó que algunas reacciones emocionales no requieren un pensamiento intencionado y que la cognición no siempre es necesaria para la emocion. (pág. 429)
Zimbardo, Philip (1933–) American psychologist whose research focuses on heroism, cult behavior, and shyness. He is most famous for the Stanford Prison Study. (p. 290)	**Zimbardo, Philip (1933–)** Psicólogo estadounidense cuyas investigaciónes se centran en el heroísmo, los comportamientos de los cultos y la timidez. Es más famoso por el estudio de la prisión de Stanford. (pág. 290)
zygote A fertilized egg. (p. 178)	**cigoto** Óvulo fecundado. (pág. 178)

References

Domain 1

Module 2

1. **Watson, J. B.** (1913). Psychology as the behaviorist views it. *Psychological Review, 20,* 158–177.

2. **Schultz, D., & Schultz, S.** (2016). *A history of modern psychology* (11th ed.). Boston, MA: Cengage Learning.

3. **Seligman, M. E. P., & Csikszentmihalyi, M.** (2000). Positive psychology: An introduction. *American Psychologist, 55,* 5–14.

4. **Tversky, B.** (2008, June/July). Glimpses of Chinese psychology: Reflections on the APS trip to China. *Observer,* 13–14. Retrieved from http://www.psychologicalscience.org/index.php/publications/observer/

5. **Myers, D.G.** (2014). Myers' Psychology for AP* (2ⁿᵈ Ed.). New York, NY: Worth.

6. **Shankland, R., & Rosset, E.** (2016). Review of Brief School-Based Positive Psychological Interventions: a Taster for Teachers and Educators. *Educational Psychology Review,* 1–30.

7. **Shoshani, A., & Steinmetz, S.** (2014). Positive psychology at school: A school-based intervention to promote adolescents' mental health and well-being. *Journal of Happiness Studies, 15*(6), 1289–1311.

8. **White, M. A., & Murray, A. S.** (2015). Building a positive institution. In Evidence-Based Approaches in Positive Education (pp. 1–26). Springer Netherlands.

Module 3

1. **Holahan, C. K., & Sears, R. R.** (1995). *The gifted group in later maturity.* Stanford, CA: Stanford University Press.

2. **Diener, E., Emmons, R. A., Larsen, R. J., & Griffen, S.** (1985). The Satisfaction With Life Scale. *Journal of Personality Assessment, 49,* 71–75.

3. **Kirsch, I., & Sapirstein, G.** (1998). Listening to Prozac but hearing placebo: A meta-analysis of antidepressant medication. *Prevention and Treatment, 1.* Retrieved from http://www.apa.org/pubs/journals/index.aspx

4. **Plous, S., & Herzog, H. A.** (2000). Poll shows researchers favor lab animal protection. *Science, 290,* 711.

Domain 2

Module 6

1. **Macmillan, M., & Lena, M. L.** (2010). Rehabilitating Phineas Gage. *Neuropsychological Rehabilitation, 17,* 1–18.

2. **Greene, J. D., Morrison, I., & Seligman, M. E. P.** (2016). *Positive Neuroscience.* New York, NY: Oxford University Press.

3. **Bower, J. M., & Parsons, L. M.** (2003, August). Rethinking the "lesser brain." *Scientific American,* pp. 50–57.

4. **de Courten-Myers, G. M.** (2005, February 4). Personal correspondence (estimating total brain neurons, extrapolating from her carefully estimated 20 to 23 billion cortical neurons).

5. **Miller, G.** (2005). The dark side of glia. *Science, 308,* 778–781.

6. **Thiel, A., Hadedank, B., Herholz, K., Kessler, J., Winhuisen, L., Haupt, W. F., & Heiss, W.-D.** (2006). From the left to the right: How the brain compensates progressive loss of language function. *Brain and Language, 98,* 57–65.

7. **Doidge, N.** (2007). *The brain that changes itself.* New York, NY: Viking.

8. **Gazzaniga, M. S.** (1983). Right hemisphere language following brain bisection: A 20-year perspective. *American Psychologist, 38,* 525–537.

9. **Gazzaniga, M. S.** (1988). *Mind matters: How mind and brain interact to create our conscious lives.* Boston, MA: Houghton Mifflin.

10. **Gazzaniga, M. S.** (1983). Right hemisphere language following brain bisection: A 20-year perspective. *American Psychologist, 38,* 525–537.

11. **Gazzaniga, M. S.** (1988). *Mind matters: How mind and brain interact to create our conscious lives.* Boston, MA: Houghton Mifflin.

12. **Lilienfeld, S. O., Lynn, S. J., Ruscio, J., & Beyerstein, B. L.** (2010). *Fifty great myths of popular psychology: Shattering widespread misconceptions about human behavior.* Malden, MA: Wiley-Blackwell.

Module 7

1. **Galanter, E.** (1962). Contemporary psychophysics. In R. Brown (Ed.), *New directions in psychology.* New York, NY: Holt, Rinehart & Winston.

2. **Krosnick, J. A., Betz, A. L., Jussim, L. J., & Lynn, A. R.** (1992). Subliminal conditioning of attitudes. *Personality and Social Psychology Bulletin, 18,* 152–162.

3. **Greenwald, A. G., Spangenberg, E. R., Pratkanis, A. R., & Eskenazi, J.** (1991). Double-blind tests of subliminal self-help audiotapes. *Psychological Science, 2,* 119–122.

4. **Winerman, L.** (2006, January). Screening surveyed. *Monitor on Psychology,* pp. 28–29.

5. **Neitz, J., Carroll, J., & Neitz, M.** (2001). Color vision: Almost reason enough for having eyes. *Optics & Photonics News, 12,* 26–33.

6. **Boynton, R. M.** (1979). *Human color vision.* New York, NY: Holt, Rinehart & Winston.

7. **DeValois, R. L., & DeValois, K. K.** (1975). Neural coding of color. In E. C. Carterette & M. P. Friedman (Eds.), *Handbook of perception: Seeing* (Vol. 5, pp. 117–166). New York, NY: Academic Press.

8. **Corey, D. P., García-Añoveros, J., Holt, J. R., Kwan, K. Y., Lin, S.-Y., Vollrath, M. A., . . . Zhang, D.-S.** (2004). TRPA1 is a candidate for the mechanosensitive transduction channel of vertebrate hair cells. *Nature.* Retrieved from http://www.nature.com

9. **Brown, E. L., & Deffenbacher, K.** (1979). *Perception and the senses.* New York, NY: Oxford University Press.

10. **Middlebrooks, J. C., & Green, D. M.** (1991). Sound localization by human listeners. *Annual Review of Psychology, 42,* 135–159.

11. **McBurney, D. H., & Gent, J. F.** (1979). On the nature of taste qualities. *Psychological Bulletin, 86,* 151–167.

12. **Smith, D. V., & Margolskee, R. F.** (2001, March). Making sense of taste. *Scientific American,* pp. 32–39.

13. **Bartoshuk, L. M., Duffy, V. B., & Miller, I. J.** (1994). PTC/PROP taste: Anatomy, psychophysics, and sex effects. *Physiology and Behavior, 56,* 1165–1171.

14. **Bushdid, C., Magnasco, M. O., Vosshall, L. B., & Keller, A.** (2014). Humans can discriminate more than 1 trillion olfactory stimuli. *Science, 343,* 1370–1372.

15. **Melzack, R., & Wall, P. D.** (1965). Pain mechanisms: A new theory. *Science, 150,* 971–979.

16. **Wall, P.** (2000). *Pain: The science of suffering.* New York, NY: Columbia University Press.

17. **Winer, G. A., Cottrell, J. E., Gregg, V. R., Fournier, J. S., & Bica, L. A.** (2002). Fundamentally misunderstanding visual perception: Adults' belief in visual emissions. *American Psychologist, 57,* 417–424.

Module 8

1. **Rock, I., & Palmer, S.** (1990, December). The legacy of Gestalt psychology. *Scientific American,* pp. 84–90.

2. **Gibson, E. J., & Walk, R. D.** (1960, April). The "visual cliff." *Scientific American,* pp. 64–71.

3. **Yonus, A., & Granrud, C. E.** (2006). Infants' perception of depth from cast shadows. *Perception and Psychophysics, 68,* 154–160.

4. **Campos, J. J., Bertenthal, B. I., & Kermoian, R.** (1992). Early experience and emotional development: The emergence of wariness and heights. *Psychological Science, 3,* 61–64.

5. **Stewart, D.** (2000, February). Driving the wrong way. *The Psychologist,* pp. 64–65.

6. **Boring, E. G.** (1930). A new ambiguous figure. *American Journal of Psychology, 42,* 444–445.

7. **Robinson, T. N., Borzekowski, D. L. G., Matheson, D. M., & Kraemer, H. C.** (2007). Effects of fast food branding on young children's taste preferences. *Archives of Pediatric and Adolescent Medicine, 161,* 792–797.

8. **AP** (2007). AP-Ipsos poll of 1,031 U.S. adults taken October 16–18, 2007, and distributed via Associated Press.

9. **Blackmore, S. J.** (1997). Probability misjudgment and belief in the paranormal: A newspaper survey. *British Journal of Psychology, 88,* 683–689.

10. **Gallup, G. H., Jr., & Newport, F.** (1991, Winter). Belief in paranormal phenomena among adult Americans. *Skeptical Inquirer,* pp. 137–146.

11. **Nishizawa, S.** (1996). *The religiousness and subjective well-being of Japanese students.* Paper presented at the 26th International Congress of Psychology, Montreal, Canada.

12. **Nisbet, M.** (1998, May/June). Psychic telephone networks profit on yearning, gullibility. *Skeptical Inquirer,* pp. 5–6.

13. **Turpin, A.** (2005, April 3). The science of psi. *FT Weekend,* pp. W1, W2.

14. **Emery, G.** (2004). Psychic predictions 2004. Committee for the Scientific Investigation of Claims of the Paranormal. Retrieved from http://www.csicop.org

15. **Hoffman, D. D.** (1998). *Visual intelligence: How we create what we see.* New York, NY: Norton.

Module 9

1. **Massimini, M., Ferrarelli, F., Huber, R., Esser, S. K., Singh, H., & Tononi, G.** (2005). Breakdown of cortical effective connectivity during sleep. *Science, 309,* 2228–2232.

2. **Hines, T. M.** (1998). Comprehensive review of biorhythm theory. *Psychological Reports, 83,* 19–64.

3. **Dement, W. C.** (1999). *The promise of sleep.* New York, NY: Delacorte Press.

4. **Maas, J. B., & Robbins, R. S.** (2010). *Sleep for success: Everything you must know about sleep but are too tired to ask.* Bloomington, IN: AuthorHouse. Questionnaire also available from http://completewellbeing.com/article/sleep-well/

5. **Mason, H.** (2005, January 25). Who dreams, perchance to sleep? Gallup Poll News Service. Retrieved from http://www.gallup.com

6. **Massimini, M., Ferrarelli, F., Huber, R., Esser, S. K., Singh, H., & Tononi, G.** (2005). Breakdown of cortical effective connectivity during sleep. *Science, 309,* 2228–2232.

7. **Haimov, I., & Lavie, P.** (1996). Melatonin—A soporific hormone. *Current Directions in Psychological Science, 5,* 106–111.

8. **Webb, W. B.** (1992). *Sleep: The gentle tyrant.* Bolton, MA: Anker.

9. **Wagner, U., Gais, S., Haider, H., Verleger, R., & Born, J.** (2004). Sleep inspires insight. *Nature, 427,* 352–355.

10. **Ellenbogen, J. M., Hu, P. T., Payne, J. D., Titone, D., & Walker, M. P.** (2007). Human relational memory requires time and sleep. *Proceedings of the National Academy of Sciences, 104,* 7723–7728.

11. **Moorcroft, W. H.** (2003). *Understanding sleep and dreaming.* New York, NY: Kluwer/Plenum.

12. **Freud, S.** (1900). The interpretation of dreams. In J. Strachey (Ed.), *The standard edition of the complete works of Sigmund Freud* (Vol. 8). London, United Kingdom: Hogarth Press.

13. **McGrath, M. J., & Cohen, D. G.** (1978). REM sleep facilitation of adaptive waking behavior: A review of the literature. *Psychological Bulletin, 85,* 24–57.

14. **Palumbo, S. R.** (1978). *Dreaming and memory: A new information-processing model.* New York, NY: Basic Books.

15. **Domhoff, G. W.** (2002). *The scientific study of dreams: Neural networks, cognitive development, and content analysis.* Washington, DC: American Psychological Association.

16. **Saul, S.** (2007, March 15). F.D.A. warns of sleeping pills' strange effects. *New York Times.* Retrieved from http://www.nytimes.com

17. **Dement, W. C.** (1978). *Some must watch while some must sleep.* New York, NY: Norton.

18. **Taheri, S.** (2004). The genetics of sleep disorders. *Minerva Medica, 95*(3), 203–212.

19. **Taheri, S., Lin, L., Austin, D., Young, T., & Mignot, E.** (2002). Short sleep duration is associated with reduced leptin, elevated ghrelin, and increased body mass index. *PLoS Medicine, 1*(3), e62. Retrieved from http://www.plosmedicine.org

Module 10

1. **World Health Organization.** (2008b). *Mental health and substance abuse: Facts and figures.* Geneva, Switzerland: Author. Retrieved from http://www.who.int/en/

2. **Hoeft, F., Watson, C. L., Kesler, S. R., Bettinger, K. E., & Reiss, A. L.** (2008). Gender differences in the mesocorticolimbic system during computer game-play. *Journal of Psychiatric Research, 42,* 253–258.

3. **Feldman, R. S., Meyer, J. S., & Quenzer, L. F.** (1997). *Principles of neuropsychopharmacology.* Sunderland, MA: Sinauer.

4. **Julien, R. M.** (2007). A primer of drug action: A concise, nontechnical guide to the actions, uses, and side effects of psychoactive drugs. *Acta Psychiatrica Scandinavica, 76,* 465–479.

5. **Denton, K., & Krebs, D.** (1990). From the scene to the crime: The effect of alcohol and social context on moral judgment. *Journal of Personality and Social Psychology, 59,* 242–248.

6. **MacDonald, T. K., Zanna, M. P., & Fong, G. T.** (1995). Decision making in altered states: Effects of alcohol on attitudes toward drinking and driving. *Journal of Personality and Social Psychology, 68,* 973–985.

7. **Cooper, M. L.** (2006). Does drinking promote risky sexual behavior? A complex answer to a simple question. *Current Directions in Psychological Science, 15,* 19–23.

8. **Vaillant, G. E.** (2008). *Spiritual evolution: A scientific defense of faith.* New York, NY: Doubleday Broadway.

9. **Peterson, C., & Seligman, M. E. P.** (2004). *Character strengths and virtues: A handbook and classification.* New York, NY: Oxford University Press.

10. **Humphreys, K., & Moos, R. H.** (1996). Reduced substance abuse-related health care costs among voluntary participants in Alcoholics Anonymous. *Journal of Studies on Alcohol, 58,* 231–238.

11. **Julien, R. M.** (2007). A primer of drug action: A concise, nontechnical guide to the actions, uses, and side effects of psychoactive drugs. *Acta Psychiatrica Scandinavica, 76,* 465–479.

12. **Starbucks** (2010). Brewed coffee nutrition facts per serving. Retrieved from http://www.starbucks.com

13. **Julien, R. M.** (2007). A primer of drug action: A concise, nontechnical guide to the actions, uses, and side effects of psychoactive drugs. *Acta Psychiatrica Scandinavica, 76,* 465–479.

14. **World Health Organization.** (2008b). *Mental health and substance abuse: Facts and figures.* Geneva, Switzerland: Author. Retrieved from http://www.who.int/en/

15. **Rose, J. S., Chassin, L., Presson, C. C., & Sherman, S. J.** (1999). Peer influences on adolescent cigarette smoking: A prospective sibling analysis. *Merrill-Palmer Quarterly, 45,* 62–84.

16. **Jones, J. M.** (2007, July 25). Latest Gallup update shows cigarette smoking near historical lows. Gallup Poll News Service. Retrieved from http://www.poll.gallup.com

17. **Julien, R. M.** (2007). A primer of drug action: A concise, nontechnical guide to the actions, uses, and side effects of psychoactive drugs. *Acta Psychiatrica Scandinavica, 76,* 465–479.

18. **Julien, R. M.** (2007). A primer of drug action: A concise, nontechnical guide to the actions, uses, and side effects of psychoactive drugs. *Acta Psychiatrica Scandinavica, 76,* 465–479.

19. **Julien, R. M.** (2007). A primer of drug action: A concise, nontechnical guide to the actions, uses, and side effects of psychoactive drugs. *Acta Psychiatrica Scandinavica, 76,* 465–479.

20. **Laws, K. R., & Kokkalis, J.** (2007). Ecstasy (MDMA) and memory function: A meta-analytic update. *Human Psychopharmacology: Clinical and Experimental, 22,* 381–388.

21. **McCann, U. D.** (1999). Cognitive performance in 3,4-methylene-dioxymethamphetamine (MDMA, "Ecstasy") users. *Psychopharmacology, 143,* 417–425.

22. **Morgan, M. J.** (1999). Recreational use of "Ecstasy" (MDMA) is associated with elevated impulsivity. *Neuropsychopharmacology, 19,* 252–264.

23. **Hoffman, A.** (1994). Notes and documents concerning the discovery of LSD. *Agents and Actions, 43,* 79–81.

24. **Brody, J. E.** (2017). https://www.nytimes.com/2017/09/04/well/opioids-arent-the-only-pain-drugs-to-fear.html?emc=eta1

25. **Centers for Disease Control and Prevention. (2017).** https://www.cdc.gov/media/releases/2017/p0706-opioid.html

26. **Tarm, M., & Forliti, A.** (2016). https://apnews.com/3c35f1efbd3a4ae1adc3a3d787864475

27. **Hall, W.** (2006). The mental health risks of adolescent cannabis use. *PLoS Medicine, 3*(2), e39.

28. **Murray, R. M., Morrison, P. D., Henquet, C., & Di Forti, M.** (2007). Cannabis, the mind and society: The hash realities. *Nature Reviews: Neuroscience, 8,* 885–895.

29. **Wu, T. C., Tashkin, D. P., Djahed, B., & Rose, J. E.** (1988). Pulmonary hazards of smoking marijuana as compared with tobacco. *New England Journal of Medicine, 318,* 347–351.

30. **Landfield, P., Cadwallader, L. B., & Vinsant, S.** (1988). Quantitative changes in hippocampal structure following long-term exposure to delta-9-tetrahydrocannabinol: Possible mediation by glucocorticoid systems. *Brain Research, 443,* 47–62.

31. **Messinis, L., Kyprianidou, A., Malefaki, S., & Papathanasopoulos, P.** (2006). Neuropsychological deficits in long-term frequent cannabis users. *Neurology, 66,* 737–739.

32. **Childers, S. R., & Breivogel, C. S.** (1998). Cannabis and endogenous cannabinoid systems. *Drug and Alcohol Dependence, 51,* 173–187.

33. **Ladd, E. C.** (1998, August/September). The tobacco bill and American public opinion. *Public Perspective,* pp. 5–19.

34. **Newcomb, M. D., & Harlow, L. L.** (1986). Life events and substance use among adolescents: Mediating effects of perceived loss of control and meaninglessness in life. *Journal of Personality and Social Psychology, 51,* 564–577.

35. **Noble, E. P.** (1993). The D2 dopamine receptor gene: A review of association studies in alcoholism. *Behavior Genetics, 23,* 119–129.

36. **Johnston, L. D., O'Malley, P. M., Bachman, J. G., & Schulenberg, J. E.** (2009). *Monitoring the Future national results on adolescent drug use: Overview of key findings, 2008* (NIH Publication No. 09-7401). Bethesda, MD: National Institute on Drug Abuse.

Module 11

1. **Simons, D. J., & Ambinder, M. S.** (2005). Change blindness: Theory and consequences. *Current Directions in Psychological Science, 14,* 44–48.

2. **Lynn, S. J., Rhue, J. W., & Weekes, J. R.** (1990). Hypnotic involuntariness: A social cognitive analysis. *Psychological Review, 97,* 169–184, 294.

3. **Spanos, N. P., & Coe, W. C.** (1992). A social-psychological approach to hypnosis. In E. Fromm & M. R. Nash (Eds.), *Contemporary hypnosis research* (pp. 102–130). New York, NY: Guilford Press.

4. **Hilgard, E. R.** (1986). *Divided consciousness: Multiple controls in human thought and action.* New York, NY: Wiley.

5. **Hilgard, E. R.** (1992). Dissociation and theories of hypnosis. In E. Fromm & M. R. Nash (Eds.), *Contemporary hypnosis research.* New York, NY: Guilford Press.

6. **Kihlstrom, J. F., & McConkey, K. M.** (1990). William James and hypnosis: A centennial reflection. *Psychological Science, 1,* 174–177.

7. **Barnier, A. J., & McConkey, K. M.** (2004). Defining and identifying the highly hypnotizable person. In M. Heap, R. J. Brown, & D. A. Oakley (Eds.), *High hypnotisability: Theoretical, experimental, and clinical issues.* London, United Kingdom: Brunner-Routledge.

8. **Bowers, K. S.** (1976). *Hypnosis for the seriously curious.* New York, NY: Norton.

9. **Orne, M. T., & Evans, F. J.** (1965). Social control in the psychological experiment: Antisocial behavior and hypnosis. *Journal of Personality and Social Psychology, 1,* 189–200.

10. **Bowers, K. S., & LeBaron, S.** (1986). Hypnosis and hypnotizability: Implications for clinical intervention. *Hospital and Community Psychiatry, 37,* 457–467.

11. **Furnham, A.** (1993). A comparison between psychology and nonpsychology students' misperceptions of the subject. *Journal of Social Behavior and Personality, 8,* 311–322.

12. **McConkey, K. M.** (1992). The effects of hypnotic procedures on remembering: The experimental findings and their implications for forensic hypnosis. In E. Fromm & M. R. Nash (Eds.), *Contemporary hypnosis research.* New York, NY: Guilford Press.

13. **Druckman, D., & Bjork, R. A. (Eds.).** (1994). *Learning, remembering, believing: Enhancing human performance.* Washington, DC: National Academy Press.

14. **Gibson, H. B.** (1995, April). Recovered memories. *Psychologist,* pp. 153–154.

15. **McConkey, K. M.** (1995). Hypnosis, memory, and the ethics of uncertainty. *Australian Psychologist, 30,* 1–10.

16. **Bowers, K. S.** (1984). Hypnosis. In N. Endler & J. M. Hunt (Eds.), *Personality and behavioral disorders* (2nd ed.). New York, NY: Wiley.

17. **Spanos, N. P.** (1991). Hypnosis, hypnotizability, and hypnotherapy. In C. R. Snyder & D. R. Forsyth (Eds.), *Handbook of social and clinical psychology: The health perspective* (Vol. 162, pp. 644–663). New York, NY: Pergamon Press.

18. **True, R. M.** (1949). Experimental control in hypnotic age regression states. *Science, 110,* 583–584.

19. **Orne, M. T.** (1982, April 28). Affidavit to People v. Shirley, submitted to State of Pennsylvania.

20. **Druckman, D., & Bjork, R. A. (Eds.).** (1994). *Learning, remembering, believing: Enhancing human performance.* Washington, DC: National Academy Press.

21. **Patterson, D. R.** (2004). Treating pain with hypnosis. *Current Directions in Psychological Science, 13,* 252–255.

22. **Hilgard, E. R.** (1980). Consciousness in contemporary psychology. *Annual Review of Psychology, 31,* 1–26.

23. **Long, P.** (1986, January). Medical mesmerism. *Psychology Today,* pp. 28–29.

24. **Nestoriuc, Y., Rief, W., & Martin, A.** (2008). Meta-analysis of biofeedback for tension-type headache: Efficacy, specificity, and treatment moderators. *Journal of Consulting and Clinical Psychology, 76,* 379–396.

25. **Stetter, F., & Kupper, S.** (2002). Autogenic training: A meta-analysis of clinical outcome studies. *Applied Psychophysiology and Biofeedback, 27,* 45–98.

26. **Friedman, M., & Ulmer, D.** (1984). *Treating Type A behavior— and your heart.* New York, NY: Knopf.

27. **Davidson, R. J., Kabat-Zinn, J., Schumacher, J., Rosenkranz, M., Muller, D., Santorelli, S. F., . . . Sheridan, J. F.** (2003). Alterations in brain and immune function produced by mindfulness meditation. *Psychosomatic Medicine, 65,* 564–570.

28. **Alexander, C. N., Langer, E. J., Newman, R. I., Chandler, H. M., & Davies, J. L.** (1989). Transcendental meditation, mindfulness, and longevity: An experimental study with the elderly. *Journal of Personality and Social Psychology, 57,* 950–964.

Domain 3

Module 12

1. **Grobstein, C.** (1979, June). External human fertilization. *Scientific American,* pp. 57–67.

2. **Hall, S. S.** (2004, May). The good egg. *Discover,* pp. 30–39.

3. **Guinness Book of World Records** (retrieved 2/18/18). http://www.guinnessworldrecords.com/world-records/67461-most-premature-baby

4. **Slotkin, T. A.** (1998). Fetal nicotine or cocaine exposure: Which one is worse? *Journal of Pharmacological and Experimental Therapeutics, 285,* 931–945.

5. **Braun, S.** (1996). New experiments underscore warnings on maternal drinking. *Science, 273,* 738–739.

6. **Bee, H.** (1997). *The developing child* (8th ed.). New York, NY: Longman.

7. **Johnson, M. H., Dziurawiec, S., Ellis, H., & Morton, J.** (1991). Newborns' preferential tracking of face-like stimuli and its subsequent decline. *Cognition, 40,* 1–19.

8. **Mondloch, C. J., Lewis, T. L., Budreau, D. R., Maurer, D., Dannemiller, J. L., Stephens, B. R., & Kleiner-Gathercoal, K. A.** (1999). Face perception during early infancy. *Psychological Science, 10,* 419–422.

9. **Chess, S., & Thomas, A.** (1987). *Know your child: An authoritative guide for today's parents.* New York, NY: Basic Books.

10. **Rothbart, M. K.** (2007). Temperament, development, and personality. *Current Directions in Psychological Science, 16,* 207–212.

11. **Fox, N. A., Hane, A. E., & Pine, D. S.** (2007). Plasticity for affective neurocircuitry. *Current Directions in Psychological Science, 16,* 1–5.

12. **Larsen, R. J., & Diener, E.** (1987). Affect intensity as an individual difference characteristic: A review. *Journal of Research in Personality, 21,* 1–39.

13. **Kagan, J., Arcus, D., Snidman, N., Feng, W. Y., Hendler, J., & Greene, S.** (1994). Reactivity in infants: A cross-national comparison. *Developmental Psychology, 30,* 342–345.

14. **Garon, N., Bryson, S., & Smith, I.** (2008). Executive function of preschoolers: A review using an integrative framework. *Psychological Bulletin, 134,* 31–60.

15. **Loftus, E. F.** (1996). Memory distortion and false memory creation. *Bulletin of the American Academy of Psychiatry and the Law, 24,* 281–295.

16. **Mandler, J. M., & McDonough, L.** (1995). Long-term recall of event sequences in infancy. *Journal of Experimental Child Psychology, 59,* 457–474.

17. **Drummey, A. B., & Newcombe, N.** (1995). Remembering versus knowing the past: Children's explicit and implicit memories for pictures. *Journal of Experimental Child Psychology, 59,* 549–565.

18. **Newcombe, N., & Fox, N. A.** (1994). Infantile amnesia: Through a glass darkly. *Child Development, 65,* 31–40.

19. **Bauer, P. J.** (2007). Recall in infancy: A neurodevelopmental account. *Current Directions in Psychological Science, 16,* 142–146.

20. **Piaget, J.** (1930). *The child's conception of physical causality.* London, United Kingdom: Routledge & Kegan Paul.

21. **Meltzoff, A. N., & Borton, R. W.** (1979). Intermodal matching by human neonates. *Nature, 282,* 403–404.

22. **Kaye, K. L., & Bower, T. G. R.** (1994). Learning and intermodal transfer of information in newborns. *Psychological Science, 5,* 286–288.

23. **Wynn, K.** (1992). Addition and subtraction by human infants. *Nature, 358,* 749–759.

24. **Wynn, K.** (2000). Findings of addition and subtraction in infants are robust and consistent: Reply to Wakeley, Rivera, and Langer. *Child Development, 71,* 1535–1536.

25. **Wynn, K.** (1998). Psychological foundations of number: Numerical competence in human infants. *Trends in Cognitive Science, 2,* 296–303.

26. **DeLoache, J. S., & Brown, A. L.** (1987, October–December). Differences in the memory-based searching of delayed and normally developing young children. *Intelligence, 11*(4), 277–289.

27. **Ennis, R. H.** (1982). Children's ability to handle Piaget's propositional logic: A conceptual critique. In S. Modgil & C. Modgil (Eds.), *Jean Piaget: Consensus and controversy* (pp. 101– 130). New York, NY: Praeger.

28. **Dasen, P. R.** (1994). Culture and cognitive development from a Piagetian perspective. In W. J. Lonner & R. S. Malpass (Eds.), *Psychology and culture* (pp. 145–149). Needham Heights, MA: Allyn & Bacon.

29. **Everett., C.** (2017). https://theconversation.com/anumeric-people-what-happens-when-a-language-has-no-words-for-numbers-75828

30. **Harlow, H. F., Harlow, M. K., & Suomi, S. J.** (1971). From thought to therapy: Lessons from a primate laboratory. *American Scientist, 59,* 538–549.

31. **Hertenstein, M. J., Keltner, D., App, B., Bulleit, B., & Jaskolka, A.** (2006). Touch communicates distinct emotions. *Emotion, 6,* 528–533.

32. **Rholes, W. S., Simpson, J. A., & Friedman, M.** (2006). Avoidant attachment and the experience of parenting. *Personality and Social Psychology Bulletin, 32,* 275–285.

33. **Elliot, A. J., & Reis, H. T.** (2003). Attachment and exploration in adulthood. *Journal of Personality and Social Psychology, 85,* 317–331.

34. **Cassidy, J., & Shaver, P. R.** (1999). *Handbook of attachment.* New York, NY: Guilford Press.

35. **Lorenz, K.** (1937). The companion in the bird's world. *Auk, 54,* 245–273.

36. **Johnson, M. H.** (1992). Imprinting and the development of face recognition: From chick to man. *Current Directions in Psychological Science, 1,* 52–55.

37. **Ainsworth, M. D. S.** (1979). Infant-mother attachment. *American Psychologist, 34,* 932–937.

38. **Hazan, C., & Shaver, P. R.** (1994). Deeper into attachment theory. *Psychological Inquiry, 5,* 68–79.

39. **Sroufe, L. A., Fox, N. E., & Pancake, V. R.** (1983). Attachment and dependency in developmental perspective. *Child Development, 54,* 1615–1627.

40. **Blakeslee, S.** (1995, August 29). In brain's early growth, timetable may be crucial. *New York Times,* pp. C1, C3.

41. **Kempe, R. S., & Kempe, C. C.** (1978). *Child abuse.* Cambridge, MA: Harvard University Press.

42. **Yarrow, L. J., Goodwin, M. S., Manheimer, H., & Milowe, I. D.** (1973). Infancy experience and cognitive and personality development at ten years. In L. J. Stone, H. T. Smith, & L. B. Murphy (Eds.), *The competent infant* (pp. 1274–1281). New York, NY: Basic Books.

43. **Baumrind, D.** (1971). Current patterns of parental authority. *Developmental Psychology Monograph, 4*(1, Part 2).

44. **Baumrind, D.** (1996). The discipline controversy revisited. *Family Relations, 45,* 405–414.

45. **Buri, J. R., Louiselle, P. A., Misukanis, T. M., & Mueller, R. A.** (1988). Effects of parental authoritarianism and authoritativeness on self-esteem. *Personality and Social Psychology Bulletin, 14,* 271–282.

46. **Rohner, R. P.** (1994). Patterns of parenting: The warmth dimension in worldwide perspective. In W. J. Lonner & R. Malpass (Eds.), *Psychology and culture* (pp. 113–120). Boston, MA: Allyn & Bacon.

47. **Bates, J. P., Pettit, G., Dodge, K., & Ridge, B.** (1998). Interaction of temperamental resistance to control and restrictive parenting in the development of externalizing behavior. *Developmental Psychology, 34,* 982–995.

48. **Kochanska, G., & Thompson, R. A.** (1997). The emergence and development of conscience in toddlerhood and early childhood. In J. E. Grusec & R. A. Thompson (Eds.), *Parenting and children's internalization of values* (pp. 53–77). New York, NY: Wiley.

49. **Wachs, T. D.** (1999). Celebrating complexity: Conceptualization and assessment of the environment. In S. Friedman & T. D. Wachs (Eds.), *Measuring environment across the life span: Emerging methods and concepts* (pp. 357–392). Washington, DC: American Psychological Association.

50. **Lewis, J. J.** (2002). *Women's voices: Quotations by women. Jacqueline Kennedy Onassis.* Retrieved from http://womens history.about.com/library/qu/blquonas.htm

Module 13

1. **Guttmacher Institute** (2000). *Fulfilling the promise: Public policy and U.S. family planning clinics.* New York, NY: Guttmacher Institute.

2. **Lyons, L.** (2004, February 3). Growing up lonely: Examining teen alienation. *Gallup Poll Tuesday Briefing.* Retrieved from http://www.gallup.com

3. **Herman-Giddens, M. E., Wang, L., & Koch, G.** (2001). Secondary sexual characteristics in boys: Estimates from the National Health and Nutrition Examination Survey III, 1988–1994. *Archives of Pediatrics and Adolescent Medicine, 155,* 1022–1028.

4. **Tanner, J. M.** (1978). *Fetus into man: Physical growth from conception to maturity.* Cambridge, MA: Harvard University Press.

5. **Fuller, M. J., & Downs, A. C.** (1990). *Spermarche is a salient biological marker in men's development.* Poster presented at the American Psychological Society convention.

6. **Greif, E. B., & Ulman, K. J.** (1982). The psychological impact of menarche on early adolescent females: A review of the literature. *Child Development, 53,* 1413–1430.

7. **Woods, N. F., Dery, G. K., & Most, A.** (1983). Recollections of menarche, current menstrual attitudes, and premenstrual symptoms. In S. Golub (Ed.), *Menarche: The transition from girl to woman* (pp. 285–293). Lexington, MA: Lexington Books.

8. **Brown, J. D., Steele, J. R., & Walsh-Childers, K.** (2002). *Sexual teens, sexual media: Investigating media's influence on adolescent sexuality.* Mahwah, NJ: Erlbaum.

9. **Kunkel, D.** (2001, February 4). *Sex on TV.* Menlo Park, CA: Henry J. Kaiser Family Foundation. Retrieved from http://www.kff.org

10. **Sapolsky, B. S., & Tabarlet, J. O.** (1991). Sex in primetime television: 1979 versus 1989. *Journal of Broadcasting and Electronic Media, 35,* 505–516.

11. **Smith, T. W.** (1998, December). American sexual behavior: Trends, socio-demographic differences, and risk behavior (GSS Topical Report No. 25). Chicago, IL: National Opinion Research Center.

12. **CDC** (2016, accessed January 21). *Reproductive health: Teen pregnancy.* Centers for Disease Control and Prevention.

13. **Twenge, J. M., Sherman, R. A., & Wells, B. E.** (2016). Sexual inactivity during young adulthood is more common among US millennials and iGen: Age, period, and cohort effects on having no sexual partners after age 18. *Archives of Sexual Behavior, 6,* 1–8.

14. **Laumann, E. O., Gagnon, J. H., Michael, R. T., & Michaels, S.** (1994). *The social organization of sexuality: Sexual practices in the United States.* Chicago, IL: University of Chicago Press.

15. **Mosher, W. D., Chandra, A., & Jones, J.** (2005, September 15). Sexual behavior and selected health measures: Men and women 15–44 years of age, United States, 2002. *Advance Data From Vital and Health Statistics* (No. 362). Hyattsville, MD: National Center for Health Statistics, Centers for Disease Control and Prevention, U.S. Department of Health and Human Services.

16. **Smith, T. W.** (1998, December). American sexual behavior: Trends, socio-demographic differences, and risk behavior (GSS Topical Report No. 25). Chicago, IL: National Opinion Research Center.

17. **Bailey, J. M., Bobrow, D., Wolfe, M., & Mikach, S.** (1995). Sexual orientation of adult sons of gay fathers. *Developmental Psychology, 31,* 124–129.

18. **Golombok, S., & Tasker, F.** (1996). Do parents influence the sexual orientation of their children? Findings from a longitudinal study of lesbian families. *Developmental Psychology, 32,* 3–11.

19. **Storms, M. D.** (1983). *Development of sexual orientation.* Washington, DC: Office of Social and Ethical Responsibility, American Psychological Association.

20. **Bagemihl, B.** (1999). *Biological exuberance: Animal homosexuality and natural diversity.* New York, NY: St. Martin's Press.

21. **Dorner, G.** (1976). *Hormones and brain differentiation.* Amsterdam, Netherlands: Elsevier Scientific.

22. **Dorner, G.** (1988). Neuroendocrine response to estrogen and brain differentiation in heterosexuals, homosexuals, and transsexuals. *Archives of Sexual Behavior, 17,* 57–75.

23. **Blakemore, S.-J.** (2008). Development of the social brain during adolescence. *Quarterly Journal of Experimental Psychology, 61,* 40–49.

24. **Beckman, M.** (2004). Crime, culpability, and the adolescent brain. *Science, 305,* 596–599.

25. **Elkind, D.** (1978). *The child's reality: Three developmental themes.* Hillsdale, NJ: Erlbaum.

26. **Elkind, D.** (1970). The origins of religion in the child. *Review of Religious Research, 12,* 35–42.

27. **Worthington, E. L., Jr.** (1989). Religious faith across the life span: Implications for counseling and research. *Counseling Psychologist, 17,* 555–612.

28. **Kohlberg, L.** (1981). *The philosophy of moral development: Essays on moral development* (Vol. 1). San Francisco, CA: Harper & Row.

29. **Kohlberg, L.** (1984). *The psychology of moral development: Essays on moral development* (Vol. 2). San Francisco, CA: Harper & Row.

30. **Gibbs, J. C., Basinger, K. S., Grime, R. L., & Snarey, J. R.** (2007). Moral judgment development across cultures: Revisiting Kohlberg's universality claims. *Developmental Review, 27,* 443–500.

31. **Eckensberger, L. H.** (1994). Moral development and its measurement across cultures. In W. J. Lonner & R. Malpass (Eds.), *Psychology and culture.* Boston, MA: Allyn & Bacon.

32. **Miller, J. G., & Bersoff, D. M.** (1995). Development in the context of everyday family relationships: Culture, interpersonal morality, and adaptation. In M. Killen & D. Hart (Eds.), *Morality in everyday life: A developmental perspective.* New York, NY: Cambridge University Press.

33. **Haidt, J.** (2002). The moral emotions. In R. J. Davidson, K. Scherer, & H. H. Goldsmith (Eds.), *Handbook of affective sciences.* New York, NY: Oxford University Press.

34. **Haidt, J.** (2007). The new synthesis in moral psychology. *Science, 316,* 998–1001.

35. **Haidt, J.** (2008). Morality. *Perspectives in Psychological Science, 3,* 65–72.

36. **Erikson, E. H.** (1963). *Childhood and society.* New York, NY: Norton.

37. **Scheier, M. F., Carver, C. S., & Bridges, M. W.** (1994). Distinguishing optimism from neuroticism (and trait anxiety, self-mastery, and self-esteem): A reevaluation of the Life Orientation Test. *Journal of Personality and Social Psychology, 67,* 1063–1078.

38. **Aspinwall, L. G., & Taylor, S. E.** (1992). Modeling cognitive adaptation: A longitudinal investigation of the impact of individual differences and coping on college adjustment and performance. *Journal of Personality and Social Psychology, 63,* 989–1003.

39. **Scheier, M. F., & Carver, C. S.** (1985). Optimism, coping, and health: Assessment and implications of generalized outcome expectancies. *Health Psychology, 4,* 219–247.

40. **Levy, B. R., Slade, M. D., Kunkel, S. R., & Kasl, S. V.** (2002). Longevity increased by positive self-perceptions of aging. *Journal of Personality and Social Psychology, 83,* 261–270.

41. **Shanahan, L., McHale, S. M., Osgood, D. W., & Crouter, A. C.** (2007). Conflict frequency with mothers and fathers from middle childhood to late adolescence: Within-and between-families comparisons. *Developmental Psychology, 43,* 539–550.

42. **Aronson, E.** (2001, April 13). Newsworthy violence. E-mail to SPSP discussion list, drawing from *Nobody Left to Hate.* New York, NY: Freeman, 2000.

43. **Steinberg, L., & Morris, A. S.** (2001). Adolescent development. *Annual Review of Psychology, 52,* 83–110.

44. **Tesser, A., Forehand, R., Brody, G., & Long, N.** (1989). Conflict: The role of calm and angry parent–child discussion in adolescent development. *Journal of Social and Clinical Psychology, 8,* 317–330.

45. **Laursen, B., Coy, K. C., & Collins, W. A.** (1998). Reconsidering changes in parent–child conflict across adolescence: A meta-analysis. *Child Development, 69,* 817–832.

46. **Gallup International Institute.** (1996, February). Parents, grandparents OK with teens. *Youthviews,* p. 3.

47. **Stepp, L. S.** (1996, July 2). Universal goals: Family, achievement and dreams. *International Herald Tribune,* p. 2.

48. **Arnett, J. J.** (2006). Emerging adulthood: Understanding the new way of coming of age. In J. J. Arnett & J. L. Tanner (Eds.), *Emerging adults in America: Coming of age in the 21st century.* Washington, DC: American Psychological Association.

49. **Arnett, J. J.** (2007). Socialization in emerging adulthood: From the family to the wider world, from socialization to self-socialization. In J. E. Grusec & P. D. Hastings (Eds.), *Handbook of socialization: Theory and research* (pp. 208–230). New York, NY: Guilford Press.

50. **Reitzle, M.** (2006). The connections between adulthood transitions and the self-perception of being adult in the changing contexts of East and West Germany. *European Psychologist, 11,* 25–38.

Module 14

1. **United Nations.** (1992). *1991 demographic yearbook.* New York, NY: Author.

2. **Arnett, J. J.** (2004). *Emerging adulthood: The winding road from the late teens through the twenties.* New York, NY: Oxford University Press.

3. **Arnett, J. J.** (2004). *Emerging adulthood: The winding road from the late teens through the twenties.* New York, NY: Oxford University Press.

4. **Arnett, J. J.** (2007). Socialization in emerging adulthood: From the family to the wider world, from socialization to self-socialization. In J. E. Grusec & P. D. Hastings (Eds.), *Handbook of socialization: Theory and research* (pp. 208–230). New York, NY: Guilford Press.

5. **Munsey, C.** (2006). Emerging adults: The in-between age. *Monitor on Psychology, 7*(6), 68. Retrieved from http://www.apa.org/monitor/jun06/emerging.html

6. **Busch, C. M., Zonderman, A. B., & Costa, P. T.** (1994). Menopausal transition and psychological distress in a nationally representative sample: Is menopause associated with psychological distress? *Journal of Aging and Health, 6,* 209–228.

7. **Matthews, K. A.** (1992). Myths and realities of the menopause. *Psychosomatic Medicine, 54,* 1–9.

8. **McKinlay, J. B., McKinlay, S. M., & Brambilla, D. J.** (1987). Health status and utilization behavior associated with menopause. *American Journal of Epidemiology, 125,* 110–121.

9. **MacArthur Foundation Research Network on Successful Midlife Development.** (1999). *Report of latest findings.* Vero Beach, FL: MacArthur Foundation.

10. **Blackburn, E. H., Greider, C. W., & Szostak, J. W.** (2007). Telomeres and telomerase: The path from

maize, *Tetrahymena* and yeast to human cancer and aging. *Nature Medicine, 12*(10), vii–xii.

11. **Zhang, P., Dilley, C., & Mattson, M. P.** (2007). DNA damage responses in neural cells: Focus on the telomere. *Neuroscience, 145,* 1439–1448.

12. **Bashore, T. R., Ridderinkhof, K. R., & van der Molen, M. W.** (1997). The decline of cognitive processing speed in old age. *Current Directions in Psychological Science, 6,* 163–169.

13. **Verhaeghen, P., & Salthouse, T. A.** (1997). Meta-analyses of age–cognition relations in adulthood: Estimates of linear and nonlinear age effects and structural models. *Psychological Bulletin, 122,* 231–249.

14. **Schacter, D. L.** (1996). *Searching for memory: The brain, the mind, and the past.* New York, NY: Basic Books.

15. **Jarvik, L. F.** (1975). Thoughts on the psychobiology of aging. *American Psychologist, 30,* 576–583.

16. **Pfeiffer, E.** (1977). Sexual behavior in old age. In E. W. Busse & E. Pfeiffer (Eds.), *Behavior and adaptation in late life* (2nd ed., pp. 130–141). Boston, MA: Little, Brown.

17. **Kempermann, G., & Gage, F. H.** (1999, May). New nerve cells for the adult brain. *Scientific American,* pp. 48–53.

18. **Wilson, R. S., & Bennett, D. A.** (2003). Cognitive activity and risk of Alzheimer's disease. *Current Directions in Psychological Science, 12,* 87–91.

19. **Marx, J.** (2005). Preventing Alzheimer's: A lifelong commitment? *Science, 309,* 864–866.

20. **Grady, D.** (2007, December 26). Finding Alzheimer's before a mind fails. *New York Times.* Retrieved from http://www.nytimes.com

21. **Conway, M. A., Wang, Q., Hanyu, K., & Haque, S.** (2005). A cross-cultural investigation of autobiographical memory. On the universality and cultural variation of the reminiscence bump. *Journal of Cross-Cultural Psychology, 36,* 739–749.

22. **Crook, T. H., & West, R. L.** (1990). Name recall performance across the adult life-span. *British Journal of Psychology, 81,* 335–340.

23. **Cohen, G., Conway, M. A., & Maylor, E. A.** (1994, September). Flashbulb memories in older adults. *Psychology and Aging, 9*(3), 454–463.

24. **Schonfield, D., & Robertson, B. A.** (1966). Memory storage and aging. *Canadian Journal of Psychology, 20,* 228–236.

25. **Graf, P.** (1990). Life-span changes in implicit and explicit memory. *Bulletin of the Psychonomic Society, 28,* 353–358.

26. **Labouvie-Vief, G., & Schell, D. A.** (1982). Learning and memory in later life. In B. B. Wolman (Ed.), *Handbook of developmental psychology* (pp. 828–846). Englewood Cliffs, NJ: Prentice Hall.

27. **Perlmutter, M.** (1983). Learning and memory through adulthood. In M. W. Riley, B. B. Hess, & K. Bond (Eds.), *Aging in society: Selected reviews of recent research.* Hillsdale, NJ: Erlbaum.

28. **Zimmerman, T. D., & Meier, B.** (2006). The rise and decline of prospective memory performance across the lifespan. *Quarterly Journal of Experimental Psychology, 59,* 2040–2046.

29. **Einstein, G. O., & McDaniel, M. A.** (1990). Normal aging and prospective memory. *Journal of Experimental Psychology: Learning, Memory, and Cognition, 16,* 717–726.

30. **Einstein, G. O., McDaniel, M. A., Richardson, S. L., Guynn, M. J., & Cunfer, A. R.** (1995). Aging and prospective memory: Examining the influences of self-initiated retrieval processes. *Journal of Experimental Psychology: Learning, Memory, and Cognition, 21,* 996–1007.

31. **Einstein, G. O., McDaniel, M. A., Smith, R. E., & Shaw, P.** (1998). Habitual prospective memory and aging: Remembering intentions and forgetting actions. *Psychological Science, 9,* 284–288.

32. **Cattell, R. B.** (1963). Theory of fluid and crystallized intelligence: A critical experiment. *Journal of Educational Psychology, 54,* 1–22.

33. **Horn, J. L.** (1982). The aging of human abilities. In J. Wolman (Ed.), *Handbook of developmental psychology* (pp. 847–870). Englewood Cliffs, NJ: Prentice Hall.

34. **Simonton, D. K.** (1988). Age and outstanding achievement: What do we know after a century of research? *Psychological Bulletin, 104,* 251–267.

35. **Simonton, D. K.** (1990). Creativity in the later years: Optimistic prospects for achievement. *Gerontologist, 30,* 626–631.

36. **Rothstein, W. G.** (1980). The significance of occupations in work careers: An empirical and theoretical review. *Journal of Vocational Behavior, 17,* 328–343.

37. **Baruch, G. K., & Barnett, R.** (1986). Role quality, multiple role involvement, and psychological well-being in midlife women. *Journal of Personality and Social Psychology, 51,* 578–585.

38. **Wrzesniewski, A., & Tosti, J.** (2005). Career as a calling. In J. H. Greenhaus & G. A. Callanan (Eds.), *Encyclopedia of career development* (pp. 71–75). Thousand Oaks, CA: Sage.

39. **Myers, D. G.** (2000). *The American paradox: Spiritual hunger in an age of plenty.* New Haven, CT: Yale University Press.

40. **Bureau of the Census.** (2007). *Statistical abstract of the United States 2007.* Washington, DC: U.S. Government Printing Office.

41. **Vemer, E., Coleman, M., Ganong, L. H., & Cooper, H.** (1989). Marital satisfaction in remarriage: A meta-analysis. *Journal of Marriage and the Family, 51,* 713–725.

42. **Inglehart, R.** (1990). *Culture shift in advanced industrial society.* Princeton, NJ: Princeton University Press.

43. **Peplau, L. A., & Fingerhut, A. W.** (2007). The close relationships of lesbians and gay men. *Annual Review of Psychology, 58,* 405–424.

44. **Wayment, H. A., & Peplau, L. A.** (1995). Social support and well-being among lesbian and heterosexual women: A structural modeling approach. *Personality and Social Psychology Bulletin, 21,* 1189–1199.

45. **Fredrickson, B. L., & Losada, M. F.** (2005). Positive affect and the complex dynamics of human flourishing. *American Psychologist, 60*(7), 678–686.

46. **Gottman, J., with Silver, N.** (1994). *Why marriages succeed or fail.* New York, NY: Simon & Schuster.

47. **Belsky, J., Lang, M., & Huston, T. L.** (1986). Sex typing and division of labor as determinants of marital change across the transition to parenthood. *Journal of Personality and Social Psychology, 50,* 517–522.

48. **Hackel, L. S., & Ruble, D. N.** (1992). Changes in the marital relationship after the first baby is born: Predicting the impact of expectancy disconfirmation. *Journal of Personality and Social Psychology, 62,* 944–957.

49. **Erel, O., & Burman, B.** (1995). Interrelatedness of marital relations and parent–child relations: A meta-analytic review. *Psychological Bulletin, 118,* 108–132.

50. **Adelmann, P. K., Antonucci, T. C., Crohan, S. F., & Coleman, L. M.** (1989). Empty nest, cohort, and employment in the well-being of midlife women. *Sex Roles, 20,* 173–189.

51. **Gilbert, D. T.** (2006). *Stumbling on happiness.* New York, NY: Knopf.

52. **Glenn, N. D.** (1975). Psychological well-being in the postparental stage: Some evidence from national surveys. *Journal of Marriage and the Family, 37,* 105–110.

53. **White, L., & Edwards, J.** (1990). Emptying the nest and parental well-being: An analysis of national panel data. *American Sociological Review, 55,* 235–242.

54. **Inglehart, R.** (1990). *Culture shift in advanced industrial society.* Princeton, NJ: Princeton University Press.

55. **Mroczek, D. K., & Kolarz, D. M.** (1998). The effect of age on positive and negative affect: A developmental perspective on happiness. *Journal of Personality and Social Psychology, 75,* 1333–1349.

56. **Costa, P. T., Jr., Zonderman, A. B., McCrae, R. R., Cornoni-Huntley, J., Locke, B. Z., & Barbano, H. E.** (1987). Longitudinal analyses of psychological well-being in a national sample: Stability of mean levels. *Journal of Gerontology, 42,* 50–55.

57. **Diener, E., Emmons, R. A., & Sandvik, E.** (1986). *The dual nature of happiness: Independence of positive and negative moods.* Unpublished manuscript, University of Illinois.

58. **Blanchflower, D. G., & Oswald, A. J.** (2008). Hypertension and happiness across nations. *Journal of Health Economics, 27,* 218–233.

59. **Schaie, K. W., & Willis, S. L.** (1996). Psychometric intelligence and aging. In F. Blanchard-Fields & T. M. Hess (Eds.), *Perspectives on cognitive change in adulthood and aging* (pp. 293–322). New York, NY: McGraw-Hill.

60. **Berger, K. S.** (2012). *The developing person through the life span* (8th ed.). New York, NY: Worth.

61. **Butler, R. N., Lewis, M., & Sunderland, T.** (1991). *Aging and mental health: Positive psychosocial and biomedical holdings* (4th ed.). New York, NY: Merrill.

62. **Blaikie, A.** (1999). Ageing: Old visions, new times? *Lancet, 354*(Suppl. 4), 5103.

63. **Gilovich, T., & Medvec, V. H.** (1995). The experience of regret: What, when and why. *Psychological Review, 102,* 379–395.

64. **Cromie, W. J.** (2001, June 7). How to be happy and well rather than sad and sick. *Harvard Gazette.* Retrieved from http://www.news.harvard.edu/gazette/2001/06.07/01-happywell.html

65. **Healthy Aging Health Center** (2002). The secrets of aging well. Retrieved from http://www.webmd.com/healthy-aging/ features/secrets-of-aging-well

66. **Vaillant, G. E.** (2002). *Aging well: Surprising guideposts to a happier life from the landmark Harvard study of adult development.* Boston, MA: Little, Brown.

67. **Healthy Aging Health Center** (2002). The secrets of aging well. Retrieved from http://www.webmd.com/healthy-aging/ features/secrets-of-aging-well

68. **Lehman, D. R., Wortman, C. B., & Williams, A. F.** (1987). Long-term effects of losing a spouse or child in a motor vehicle crash. *Journal of Personality and Social Psychology, 52,* 218–231.

69. **Opoku, K. A.** (1989). African perspectives on death and dying. In A. Berger, P. Badham, A. H. Kutscher, J. Berger, M. Perry, & J. Beloff (Eds.), *Perspectives on death and dying* (pp. 14–23). Philadelphia, PA: Charles Press.

70. **Nobles, A. Y., & Sciarra, D. T.** (2000). Cultural determinants in the treatment of Arab Americans: A primer for mainstream therapists. *American Journal of Orthopsychiatry, 70*(2), 182–191.

71. **Ott, C. H., Lueger, R. J., Kelber, S. T., & Prigerson, H. G.** (2007). Spousal bereavement in older adults: Common, resilient, and chronic grief with defining characteristics. *Journal of Nervous and Mental Disease, 195,* 332–341.

72. **Wortman, C. B., & Silver, R. C.** (1989). The myths of coping with loss. *Journal of Consulting and Clinical Psychology, 57,* 349–357.

73. **Nolen-Hoeksema, S., & Larson, J.** (1999). *Coping with loss.* Mahwah, NJ: Erlbaum.

74. **Brown, S. L., Brown, R. M., House, J. S., & Smith, D. M.** (2008). Coping with spousal loss: Potential buffering effects of self-reported helping behavior. *Personality and Social Psychology Bulletin, 34,* 849–861.

75. **Berger, K. S.** (2012). *The developing person through the life span* (8th ed.). New York, NY: Worth.

Module 15

1. **Radetsky, P.** (1994, August). Silence, signs, and wonder. *Discover,* pp. 60–68.

2. **Hauser, M. D., Chomsky, N., & Fitch, W. T.** (2002). The faculty of language: What is it, who has it, and how did it evolve? *Science, 298,* 1569–1579.

3. **Chomsky, N.** (1959). Review of B. F. Skinner's *Verbal behavior. Language, 35,* 26–58.

4. **Chomsky, N.** (1987). *Language in psychological setting* (Sophia Linguistic Working Papers in Linguistics No. 22). Tokyo, Japan: Sophia University.

5. **Sandler, W., Meir, I., Padden, C., & Aronoff, M.** (2005). The emergence of grammar: Systematic structure in a new language. *Proceedings of the National Academy of Sciences, 102,* 2261–2265.

6. **Skinner, B. F.** (1957). *Verbal behavior.* Englewood Cliffs, NJ: Prentice Hall.

7. **Ross, M., Xun, W. Q. E., & Wilson, A. E.** (2002). Language and the bicultural self. *Personality and Social Psychology Bulletin, 28,* 1040–1050.

8. **Kellogg, W. N., & Kellogg, L.** (1933). *The ape and the child.* New York, NY: McGraw-Hill.

9. **Gardner, R. A., & Gardner, B. I.** (1969). Teaching sign language to a chimpanzee. *Science, 165,* 664–672.

10. **Sanz, C., Blicher, A., Dalke, K., Gratton-Farbi, L., McClure-Richards, T., & Fouts, R.** (1998, Winter–Spring). Enrichment object use: Five chimpanzees' use of temporary and semipermanent enrichment objects. *Friends of Washoe, 19*(1/2), 9–14.

11. **Fouts, R.** (with Mills, S. T.) (2003). *Next of kin: My conversations with chimpanzees.* New York, NY: Quill.

12. **Jolly, A.** (1985). *The evolution of primate behavior* (2nd ed.). New York, NY: Macmillan.

13. **Kuhl, P. K., Ramirez, R. R., Bosseler, A., Lin, J. L., & Imada, T.** (2014). Infants' brain responses to speech suggest analysis by synthesis. *PNAS, 111,* 11238–11245.

14. **Meltzoff, A. N., Kuhl, P. K., Movellan, J., & Sejnowski, T. J.** (2009). Foundations for a new science of learning. *Science, 325,* 284–288.

15. **de Boysson-Bardies, B., Halle, P., Sagart, L., & Durand, C.** (1989). A cross-linguistic investigation of vowel formats in babbling. *Journal of Child Language, 16,* 1–17.

16. **Fromkin, V., & Rodman, R.** (1983). *An introduction to language* (3rd ed.). New York, NY: Holt, Rinehart & Winston.

17. **Miller, G. A., & Gildea, P. M.** (1987, September). How children learn words. *Scientific American,* pp. 94–99.

18. **Bloom, P.** (2000). *How children learn the meaning of words.* Cambridge, MA: MIT Press.

Module 16

1. **Wood, W., & Neal, D. T.** (2007, October). A new look at habits and the habit-goal interface. *Psychological Review, 114,* 843–863.

2. **Beck, H. P., Levinson, S., & Irons, G.** (2009). Finding Little Albert: A journey to John B. Watson's infant laboratory. *American Psychologist, 64*(7), 605–614.

3. **Bartlett, T.** (2014). https://www.chronicle.com/interactives/littlealbert

4. **Rescorla, R. A., & Wagner, A. R.** (1972). A theory of Pavlovian conditioning: Variations in the effectiveness of reinforcement and nonreinforcement. In A. H. Black & W. F. Perokasy (Eds.), *Classical conditioning II: Current theory* (pp. 64–99). New York, NY: Appleton-Century-Crofts.

5. **Garcia, J., & Koelling, R. A.** (1966). Relation of cue to consequence in avoidance learning. *Psychonomic Science, 4,* 123–124.

6. **Cook, E. W., III, Hodes, R. L., & Lang, P. J.** (1986). Preparedness and phobia: Effects of stimulus content on human visceral conditioning. *Journal of Abnormal Psychology, 95,* 195–207.

Module 17

1. **Haggbloom, S. J., Warnick, R., Warnick, J. E., Jones, V. K., Yarbrough, G. L., Russell, T. M., . . . Monte, E.** (2002). The 100 most eminent psychologists of the 20th century. *Review of General Psychology, 6,* 139–152.

2. **Skinner, B. F.** (1945, October). Baby in a box. *Ladies' Home Journal, 62,* 30–31, 135–136, 138.

3. **Skinner, B. F.** (1988). Personal communication.

4. **Skinner, B. F.** (1990). Address to the American Psychological Association convention, Boston, MA.

5. **Flora, S. R.** (2004). *The power of reinforcement.* Albany, NY: SUNY Press.

6. **Marlatt, G. A.** (1991, August). Substance abuse: Etiology, prevention, and treatment issues. Master lecture, American Psychological Association convention, San Francisco, CA.

7. **Mischel, W., Shoda, Y., & Rodriguez, M. L.** (1989). Delay of gratification in children. *Science, 244,* 933–938.

8. **Briers, B., Pandelaere, M., Dewitte, S., & Warlop, L.** (2006). Hungry for money: The desire for caloric resources increases the desire for financial resources and vice versa. *Psychological Science, 17,* 939–943.

9. **Gershoff, E. T.** (2002). Parental corporal punishment and associated child behaviors and experiences: A meta-analytic and theoretical review. *Psychological Bulletin, 128,* 539–579.

10. **Marshall, M. J.** (2002). *Why spanking doesn't work.* Springville, UT: Bonneville Books.

11. **Straus, M. A., & Gelles, R. J.** (1980). *Behind closed doors: Violence in the American family.* New York, NY: Anchor/Doubleday.

12. **Larzelere, R. E., & Kuhn, B. R.** (2005). Comparing child outcomes of physical punishment and alternative disciplinary tactics: A meta-analysis. *Clinical Child and Family Psychology Review, 8,* 1–37.

13. **Maymin, S.** (2007, February 1). Create new habits: Self-regulation. *Positive Psychology News Daily.* Retrieved from http://positivepsychologynews.com/news/senia-maymin/2007020165

14. **Forgas, J. P., Baumeister, R. F., & Tice, D. M.** (2009). *Psychology of self-regulation: Cognitive, affective, and motivational processes.* Sydney, Australia: Psychology Press.

15. **Maymin, S.** (2007, February 1). Create new habits: Self-regulation. *Positive Psychology News Daily.* Retrieved from http://positivepsychologynews.com/news/senia-maymin/2007020165

16. **Skinner, B. F.** (1961, November). Teaching machines. *Scientific American,* pp. 91–102.

17. **Skinner, B. F.** (1953). *Science and human behavior.* New York, NY: Free Press.

18. **Tolman, E. C., & Honzik, C. H.** (1930). Introduction and removal of reward, and maze performance in rats. *University of California Publications in Psychology, 4,* 257–275.

19. **Grolnick, W. S., & Ryan, R. M.** (1987). Autonomy in children's learning: An experimental and individual difference investigation. *Journal of Personality and Social Psychology, 52,* 890–898.

20. **Foree, D. D., & LoLordo, V. M.** (1973). Attention in the pigeon: Differential effects of food-getting versus shock-avoidance procedures. *Journal of Comparative and Physiological Psychology, 85,* 551–558.

Module 18

1. **Byrne, R. W., & Russon, A. E.** (1998). Learning by imitation: A hierarchical approach. *Behavioral and Brain Sciences, 21,* 667–721.

2. **Dugatkin, L. A.** (2002, Winter). Watching culture shape even guppy love. *Cerebrum,* pp. 51–66.

3. **Bandura, A., Ross, D., & Ross, S. A.** (1961). Transmission of aggression through imitation of aggressive models. *Journal of Abnormal and Social Psychology, 63,* 575–582.

4. **Bandura, A.** (1965). Influence of a model's reinforcement contingencies on the acquisition of imitative responses. *Journal of Personality and Social Psychology, 1,* 589–595.

5. **Bandura, A.** (1977). *Social learning theory* (original work published in 1971). Englewood Cliffs, NJ: Prentice Hall.

6. **Blakeslee, S.** (2006, January 10). Cells that read minds. *New York Times.* Retrieved from http://www.nytimes.com

7. **Rizzolatti, G., Fadiga, L., Fogassi, L., & Gallese, V.** (2002). From mirror neurons to imitation: Facts and speculations. In A. N. Miltzoff & W. Prinz (Eds.), *The imitative mind: Development, evolution, and brain bases* (pp. 247–265). Cambridge, United Kingdom: Cambridge University Press.

8. **Rizzolatti, G., Fogassi, L., & Gallese, V.** (2006, November). Mirrors in the mind. *Scientific American,* pp. 54–61.

9. **Iacoboni, M.** (2008). *Mirroring people: The new science of how we connect with others.* New York, NY: Farrar, Straus & Giroux.

10. **Ramachandran, V. S., & Oberman, L. M.** (2006, November). Broken mirrors: A theory of autism. *Scientific American,* pp. 63–69.

11. **Williams, J. H. G., Waister, G. D., Gilchrist, A., Perrett, D. I., Murray, A. D., & Whiten, A.** (2006). Neural mechanisms of imitation and "mirror neuron" functioning in autistic spectrum disorder. *Neuropsychologia, 44,* 610–621.

12. **Jones, J. M.** (2007, July 25). Latest Gallup update shows cigarette smoking near historical lows. Gallup Poll News Service. Retrieved from http://www.poll.gallup.com

13. **Gallup, G. H., Jr.** (2002, April 30). Education and youth. *Gallup Poll Tuesday Briefing.* Retrieved from http://www.gallup.com/poll/tb/educaYouth/20020430.asp

14. **Elliot, A.** (1996, January 18). Personal communication between Nielsen Media Research director of communications and David Myers, via e-mail.

15. **Robinson, J. P., & Martin, S.** (2009). Changes in American Daily Life: 1965–2005. *Social Indicators Research, 93,* 47–56.

16. **Bushman, B. J., Gollwitzer, M., & Cruz, C.** (2015). There is broad consensus: Media researchers agree that violent media increase aggression in children, and pediatricians and parents concur. *Psychology of Popular Media Culture, 4,* 200–214.

17. **American Psychological Association Commission on Violence and Youth.** (1993). *Violence and youth: Psychology's response—Summary report of the American Psychological Association Commission on Violence and Youth* (Vol. 1). Washington, DC: American Psychological Association.

Domain 4

Module 19

1. **Heider, F.** (1958). *The psychology of interpersonal relations.* New York, NY: Wiley.

2. **Napolitan, D. A., & Goethals, G. R.** (1979). The attribution of friendliness. *Journal of Experimental Social Psychology, 15,* 105–113.

3. **Malle, B. F., Knobe, J. M., & Nelson, S. E.** (2007). Actor-observer asymmetries in explanations of behavior: New answers to an old question. *Journal of Personality and Social Psychology, 93,* 491–514.

4. **Fincham, F. D., & Bradbury, T. N.** (1993). Marital satisfaction, depression, and attributions: A longitudinal analysis. *Journal of Personality and Social Psychology, 64,* 442–452.

5. **Fletcher, G. J. O., Fitness, J., & Blampied, N. M.** (1990). The link between attributions and happiness in close relationships: The roles of depression and explanatory style. *Journal of Social and Clinical Psychology, 9,* 243–255.

6. **Furnham, A.** (1982). Explanations for unemployment in Britain. *European Journal of Social Psychology, 12,* 335–352.

7. **Pandey, J., Sinha, Y., Prakash, A., & Tripathi, R. C.** (1982). Right-left political ideologies and attribution of the causes of poverty. *European Journal of Social Psychology, 12,* 327–331.

8. **Wagstaff, G.** (1982). Attitudes to rape: The "just world" strikes again? *Bulletin of the British Psychological Society, 13,* 275–283.

9. **Zucker, G. S., & Weiner, B.** (1993). Conservatism and perceptions of poverty: An attributional analysis. *Journal of Applied Social Psychology, 23,* 925–943.

10. **Menon, T., Morris, M. W., Chiu, C.-Y., & Hong, Y.-Y.** (1999). Culture and the construal of agency: Attribution to individual versus group dispositions. *Journal of Personality and Social Psychology, 76,* 701–717.

11. **Masuda, T., & Kitayama, S.** (2005). Perceiver-induced constraint and attitude attribution in Japan and the U.S.: A case for the cultural dependence of the correspondence bias. *Journal of Experimental Social Psychology, 40,* 409–416.

12. **Wicker, A. W.** (1971). An examination of the "other variables" explanation of attitude-behavior inconsistency. *Journal of Personality and Social Psychology, 19,* 18–30.

13. **Kraus, S. J.** (1991). Attitudes and the prediction of behavior (Doctoral dissertation). Harvard University, Cambridge, MA.

14. **Wallace, D. S., Lord, C. G., & Bond, C. F., Jr.** (1996). Which behaviors do attitudes predict? Review and meta-analysis of 60 years' research. Unpublished manuscript. Ohio University, Athens, OH.

15. **Fazio, R. H.** (1990). Multiple processes by which attitudes guide behavior: The MODE model as an integrative framework. In M. P. Zanna (Ed.), *Advances in experimental social psychology* (Vol. 23). San Diego, CA: Academic Press.

16. **Cialdini, R. B.** (1993). *Influence: Science and practice* (3rd ed.). New York, NY: HarperCollins.

17. **Freedman, J. L., & Fraser, S. C.** (1966). Compliance without pressure: The foot-in-the-door technique. *Journal of Personality and Social Psychology, 4,* 195–202.

18. **Zimbardo, P. G.** (1972, April). Pathology of imprisonment. *Transaction/Society,* pp. 4–8.

19. **Franco, Z., & Zimbardo, P. G.** (2007, Fall/Winter). The banality of heroism. *Greater Good.* Retrieved from http://greatergood.berkeley.edu/greatergood/archive/2006fallwinter/francozimbardo.html

20. **Haslam, S. A., & Reicher, S.** (2007). Beyond the banality of evil: Three dynamics of an interactionist social psychology of tyranny. *Personality and Social Psychology Bulletin, 33,* 615–622.

21. **Zimbardo, P. G.** (2010b). Understanding heroism. Retrieved from http://heroicimagination.org/wp-content/uploads/2010/10/Understanding-Heroism.pdf

22. **Donati, R.** (2010). Community hero: Dr. Philip Zimbardo: Psychologist. Article and video posted at the My Hero website (myhero.com). Retrieved from http://myhero.com/go/hero.asp?hero=Philip_Zimbardo

23. **Donati, R.** (2010). Community hero: Dr. Philip Zimbardo: Psychologist. Article and video posted at the My Hero website (myhero.com). Retrieved from http://myhero.com/go/hero.asp?hero=Philip_Zimbardo

24. **Zimbardo, P. G.** (2010a). Heroic Imagination Project. Retrieved from http://heroicimagination.org

25. **Duffy, M.** (2003, June 9). Weapons of mass disappearance. *Time,* pp. 28–33.

26. **Gallup Organization.** (2003, July 8). American public opinion about Iraq. Gallup Poll News Service. Retrieved from http://www.gallup.com

27. **Gallup Organization.** (2003, July 8). American public opinion about Iraq. Gallup Poll News Service. Retrieved from http://www.gallup.com

28. **Gallup Organization.** (2006, July 13). American public opinion about Iraq. Gallup Poll News Service. Retrieved from http://www.gallup.com

29. **Dutton, S., De Pinto, J., Salvanto, A., & Backus, F.** (2014). https://www.cbsnews.com/news/most-americans-say-iraq-war-wasnt-worth-the-costs-poll/

30. **Seligman, M. E. P.** (2002). *Authentic happiness: Using the new positive psychology to realize your potential for lasting fulfillment.* New York, NY: Free Press.

31. **Morrison, C.** (2007). *What does contagious yawning tell us about the mind?* Unpublished manuscript. University of Leeds, Leeds, United Kingdom.

32. **Cooper, K. J.** (1999, May 1). This time, copycat wave is broader. *Washington Post.* Retrieved from http://www.washingtonpost.com

33. **Cooper, K. J.** (1999, May 1). This time, copycat wave is broader. *Washington Post.* Retrieved from http://www.washingtonpost.com

34. **Goldensohn, L.** (2004). *The Nuremberg interviews: An American psychiatrist's conversations with the defendants and witnesses.* New York, NY: Alfred A. Knopf.

35. **Asch, S. E.** (1955). Opinions and social pressure. *Scientific American, 193,* 31–35.

36. **Baron, R. S., Vandello, J. A., & Brunsman, B.** (1996). The forgotten variable in conformity research: Impact of task importance on social influence. *Journal of Personality and Social Psychology, 71,* 915–927.

37. **Milgram, S.** (1974). *Obedience to authority.* New York, NY: Harper & Row.

38. **Blass, T.** (1999). The Milgram paradigm after 35 years: Some things we now know about obedience to authority. *Journal of Applied Social Psychology, 29,* 955–978.

39. **Blass, T.** (1996). Stanley Milgram: A life of inventiveness and controversy. In G. A. Kimble, C. A. Boneau, & M. Wertheimer (Eds.), *Portraits of pioneers in psychology* (Vol. 2). Washington, DC: American Psychological Association.

40. **Slater, M., Antley, A., Davison, A., Swapp, D., Guger, C., Barker, C., . . . Sanchez-Vives, M. V.** (2006). A virtual reprise of the Stanley Milgram obedience experiments. *PLoS ONE, 1*(1), e39. doi:10.1371/journal.pone.0000039

41. **Milgram, S.** (1974). *Obedience to authority.* New York, NY: Harper & Row.

42. **Triplett, N.** (1898). The dynamogenic factors in pacemaking and competition. *American Journal of Psychology, 9,* 507–533.

43. **Michaels, J. W., Bloomel, J. M., Brocato, R. M., Linkous, R. A., & Rowe, J. S.** (1982). Social facilitation and inhibition in a natural setting. *Replications in Social Psychology, 2,* 21–24.

44. **Guerin, B.** (1986). Mere presence effects in humans: A review. *Journal of Personality and Social Psychology, 22,* 38–77.

45. **Zajonc, R. B.** (1965). Social facilitation. *Science, 149,* 269–274.

46. **Ingham, A. G., Levinger, G., Graves, J., & Peckham, V.** (1974). The Ringelmann effect: Studies of group size and group performance. *Journal of Experimental Social Psychology, 10,* 371–384.

47. **Harkins, S. G., & Szymanski, K.** (1989). Social loafing and group evaluation. *Journal of Personality and Social Psychology, 56,* 934–941.

48. **Kerr, N. L., & Bruun, S. E.** (1983). Dispensability of member effort and group motivation losses: Free-rider effects. *Journal of Personality and Social Psychology, 44,* 78–94.

49. **Selk, A.** (2017). https://www.washingtonpost.com/news/the-intersect/wp/2017/08/14/a-twitter-campaign-is-outing-people-who-marched-with-white-nationalists-in-charlottesville/?utm_term=.3f67fc526f95

50. **Myers, D. G., & Bishop, G. D.** (1970). Discussion effects on racial attitudes. *Science, 169,* 778–779.

51. **McCauley, C. R., & Segal, M. E.** (1987). Social psychology of terrorist groups. In C. Hendrick (Ed.), *Group processes and intergroup relations.* Beverly Hills, CA: Sage.

52. **Esser, J. K., & Lindoerfer, J. S.** (1989). Groupthink and the space shuttle *Challenger* accident: Toward a quantitative case analysis. *Journal of Behavioral Decision Making, 2,* 167–177.

53. **Janis, I. L.** (1982). *Groupthink: Psychological studies of policy decisions and fiascoes.* Boston, MA: Houghton Mifflin.

54. **Lee, C. E., & Martin, J.** (2008, December 1). Obama warns against White House "groupthink." *Politico.* Retrieved from http://www.politico.com/news/stories/1208/16076.html

55. **Ridge, R. D., & Reber, J. S.** (1998). *Women's responses to men's flirtations in a professional setting: Implications for sexual harassment.* Paper presented at the annual meeting of the American Psychological Society, Washington, DC.

56. **Murray, S. L., & Holmes, J. G.** (2000). The (mental) ties that bind: Cognitive structures that predict relationship resilience. *Journal of Personality and Social Psychology, 77,* 1228–1244.

57. **Murray, S. L., Holmes, J. G., & Griffin, D.** (1996). The benefits of positive illusions: Idealization and the construction of satisfaction in close relationships. *Journal of Personality and Social Psychology, 70,* 79–98.

58. **O'Conner, A.** (2004, May 14). Pressure to go along with abuse is strong, but some soldiers find strength to refuse. *New York Times.* Retrieved from http://www.nytimes.com

59. **Moscovici, S.** (1985). Social influence and conformity. In G. Lindzey & E. Aronson (Eds.), *The handbook of social psychology* (3rd ed.). Hillsdale, NJ: Erlbaum.

Module 20

1. **Moreland, R. L., & Zajonc, R. B.** (1982). Exposure effects in person perception: Familiarity, similarity, and attraction. *Journal of Experimental Social Psychology, 18,* 395–415.

2. **Nuttin, J. M., Jr.** (1987). Affective consequences of mere ownership: The name letter effect in twelve European languages. *European Journal of Social Psychology, 17,* 381–402.

3. **Bornstein, R. F.** (1989). Exposure and affect: Overview and meta-analysis of research, 1968–1987. *Psychological Bulletin, 106,* 265–289.

4. **Bornstein, R. F.** (1999). Source amnesia, misattribution, and the power of unconscious perceptions and memories. *Psychoanalytic Psychology, 16,* 155–178.

5. **Moreland, R. L., & Beach, S. R.** (1992). Exposure effects in the classroom: The development of affinity

among students. *Journal of Experimental Social Psychology, 28*, 255–276.

6. **Zajonc, R. B.** (1998). Emotions. In D. Gilbert, S. T. Fiske, & G. Lindzey (Eds.), *Handbook of social psychology* (4th ed., pp. 591–634). New York, NY: McGraw-Hill.

7. **Cullen & Masters** (2008). http://www.pewresearch.org/fact-tank/2016/02/29/5-facts-about-online-dating/

8. **McKenna, K. Y. A., Green, A. S., & Gleason, M. E. J.** (2002). What's the big attraction? Relationship formation on the Internet. *Journal of Social Issues, 58*, 9–31.

9. **Bargh, J. A., & McKenna, K. Y. A.** (2004). The Internet and social life. *Annual Review of Psychology, 55*, 573–590.

10. **Finkel, E. J., & Eastwick, P. W.** (2008). Speed-dating. *Current Directions in Psychological Science, 17*, 193–197.

11. **Walster (Hatfield), E., Aronson, V., Abrahams, D., & Rottman, L.** (1966). Importance of physical attractiveness in dating behavior. *Journal of Personality and Social Psychology, 4*, 508–516.

12. **Feingold, A.** (1990). Gender differences in effects of physical attractiveness on romantic attraction: A comparison across five research paradigms. *Journal of Personality and Social Psychology, 59*, 981–993.

13. **Sprecher, S.** (1989). The importance to males and females of physical attractiveness, earning potential, and expressiveness in initial attraction. *Sex Roles, 21*, 591–607.

14. **ASAPS.** (2008). Cosmetic procedures in 2007. American Society for Aesthetic Plastic Surgery. Retrieved from http://www.surgery.org

15. **Eagly, A. H., Ashmore, R. D., Makhijani, M. G., & Kennedy, L. C.** (1991). What is beautiful is good, but . . . : A meta-analytic review of research on the physical attractiveness stereotype. *Psychological Bulletin, 110*, 109–128.

16. **Feingold, A.** (1992). Good-looking people are not what we think. *Psychological Bulletin, 111*, 304–341.

17. **Hatfield, E., & Sprecher, S.** (1986). *Mirror, mirror . . . The importance of looks in everyday life.* Albany, NY: State University of New York Press.

18. **Smith, S. M., McIntosh, W. D., & Bazzini, D. G.** (1999). Are the beautiful good in Hollywood? An investigation of the beauty-and-goodness stereotype on film. *Basic and Applied Social Psychology, 21*, 69–80.

19. **Diener, E., Wolsic, B., & Fujita, F.** (1995). Physical attractiveness and subjective well-being. *Journal of Personality and Social Psychology, 69*, 120–129.

20. **Major, B., Carrington, P. I., & Carnevale, P. J. D.** (1984). Physical attractiveness and self-esteem: Attribution for praise from an other-sex evaluator. *Personality and Social Psychology Bulletin, 10*, 43–50.

21. **Berscheid, E.** (1981). An overview of the psychological effects of physical attractiveness and some comments upon the psychological effects of knowledge of the effects of physical attractiveness. In G. W. Lucker, K. Ribbens, & J. A. McNamara (Eds.), *Psychological aspects of facial form* (Craniofacial growth series, pp. 1–23). Ann Arbor: Center for Human Growth and Development, University of Michigan.

22. **Rosenbaum, M.** (1986). The repulsion hypothesis: On the nondevelopment of relationships. *Journal of Personality and Social Psychology, 51*, 1156–1166.

23. **Byrne, D.** (1971). *The attraction paradigm.* New York, NY: Academic Press.

24. **Hatfield, E.** (1988). Passionate and companionate love. In R. J. Sternberg & M. L. Barnes (Eds.), *The psychology of love* (pp. 191–217). New Haven, CT: Yale University Press.

25. **Carducci, B. J., Cosby, P. C., & Ward, D. D.** (1978). Sexual arousal and interpersonal evaluations. *Journal of Experimental Social Psychology, 14*, 449–457.

26. **Dermer, M., & Pyszczynski, T. A.** (1978). Effects of erotica upon men's loving and liking responses for women they love. *Journal of Personality and Social Psychology, 36*, 1302–1309.

27. **White, G. L., & Kight, T. D.** (1984). Misattribution of arousal and attraction: Effects of salience of explanations for arousal. *Journal of Experimental Social Psychology, 20*, 55–64.

28. **Levine, R., Sato, S., Hashimoto, T., & Verma, J.** (1995). Love and marriage in eleven cultures. *Journal of Cross-Cultural Psychology, 26*, 554–571.

29. **Berscheid, E., Gangestad, S. W., & Kulakowski, D.** (1984). Emotion in close relationships: Implications for relationship counseling. In S. D. Brown & R. W. Lent (Eds.), *Handbook of counseling psychology* (pp. 435–476). New York, NY: Wiley.

30. **Gray-Little, B., & Burks, N.** (1983). Power and satisfaction in marriage: A review and critique. *Psychological Bulletin, 93*, 513–538.

31. **Van Yperen, N. W., & Buunk, B. P.** (1990). A longitudinal study of equity and satisfaction in intimate relationships. *European Journal of Social Psychology, 20*, 287–309.

32. **Aron, A., Melinat, E., Aron, E. N., Vallone, R. D., & Bator, R. J.** (1997). The experimental generation of interpersonal closeness: A procedure and some preliminary findings. *Personality and Social Psychology Bulletin, 23*, 363–377.

33. **Slatcher, R. B., & Pennebaker, J. W.** (2006). How do I love thee? Let me count the words: The social effects of expressive writing. *Psychological Science, 17*, 660–664.

34. **Ellefson, L.** (2017). https://www.msn.com/en-us/news/us/husband-reunites-with-las-vegas-shooting-hero-who-saved-his-wife/ar-BBFyjlT

35. **Vera, A.** (2018). https://www.cnn.com/2018/02/15/us/football-coach-florida-school-shooting-trnd/index.html

36. **McFadden, R. D.** (2016). https://www.nytimes.com/2016/04/05/nyregion/winston-moseley-81-killer-of-kitty-genovese-dies-in-prison.html

37. **Taylor, E.** (2016). https://www.npr.org/2016/06/02/480442769/the-witness-looks-back-at-those-accused-of-ignoring-a-murder

38. **Darley, J. M., & Latané, B.** (1968). Bystander intervention in emergencies: Diffusion of responsibility. *Journal of Personality and Social Psychology, 8*, 377–383.

39. **Carlson, M., Charlin, V., & Miller, N.** (1988). Positive mood and helping behavior: A test of six hypotheses. *Journal of Personality and Social Psychology, 55*, 211–229.

40. **Dunn, E. W., Aknin, L. B., & Norton, M. I.** (2008). Spending money on others promotes happiness. *Science, 319*, 1687–1688.

41. **Harbaugh, W. T., Mayr, U., & Burghart, D. R.** (2007). Neural responses to taxation and voluntary giving reveal motives for charitable donations. *Science, 316*, 1622–1625.

42. **Duncan, B. L.** (1976). Differential social perception and attribution of intergroup violence: Testing the lower limits of stereotyping of blacks. *Journal of Personality and Social Psychology, 34*, 590–598.

43. **Hurtado, S., Dey, E. L., & Trevino, J. G.** (1994). *Exclusion or self-segregation? Interaction across racial/ethnic groups on college campuses.* Paper presented at the American Educational Research Association annual meeting, New Orleans, LA.

44. **Carpusor, A., & Loges, W. E.** (2006). Rental discrimination and ethnicity in names. *Journal of Applied Social Psychology, 36*, 934–952.

45. **Harber, K. D.** (1998). Feedback to minorities: Evidence of a positive bias. *Journal of Personality and Social Psychology, 74*, 622–628.

46. **United Nations** (1991). *The world's women 1970–1990: Trends and statistics.* New York, NY: Author.

47. **United Nations** (1993). *1992 demographic yearbook.* New York, NY: Author.

48. **Lyons, L.** (2003, September 23). Oh, boy: Americans still prefer sons. *Gallup Poll Tuesday Briefing.* Retrieved from http://www.gallup.com

49. **Whitley, B. E., Jr.** (1999). Right-wing authoritarianism, social dominance orientation, and prejudice. *Journal of Personality and Social Psychology, 77*, 126–134.

50. **Koltz, C.** (1983, December). Scapegoating. *Psychology Today*, pp. 68–69.

51. **Cialdini, R. B., & Richardson, K. D.** (1980). Two indirect tactics of image management: Basking and blasting. *Journal of Personality and Social Psychology, 39*, 406–415.

52. **Crocker, J., Thompson, L. L., McGraw, K. M., & Ingerman, C.** (1987). Downward comparison, prejudice, and evaluation of others: Effects of self-esteem and threat. *Journal of Personality and Social Psychology, 52*, 907–916.

53. **Kelly, D. J., Quinn, P. C., Slater, A. M., Lee, K., Ge, I., & Pascalis, O.** (2007). The other-race effect develops during infancy: Evidence of perceptual narrowing. *Psychological Science, 18*, 1084–1089.

54. **Stone, J., Perry, Z. W., & Darley, J. M.** (1997). "White men can't jump": Evidence for the perceptual confirmation of racial stereotypes following a basketball game. *Basic and Applied Social Psychology, 19*(3), 291–306.

55. **Haveman, R.** (2013). https://www.irp.wisc.edu/newsevents/workshops/teachingpoverty101/participants/Presentations/Haveman-CausesofPoverty1.pdf

56. **Federal Bureau of Investigation** (2009). Crime in the United States, 2008. Murder. *Uniform Crime Reports.* Retrieved from http://www.fbi.gov/about-us/cjis/ucr/crime-in-the-u.s/2008

57. **Statistics Canada** (2009). Homicide in Canada, 2008. Retrieved from http://www.statcan.gc.ca/daily-quotidien/091028/ dq091028a-eng.htm

58. **Miles, D. R., & Carey, G.** (1997). Genetic and environmental architecture of human aggression. *Journal of Personality and Social Psychology, 72*, 207–217.

59. **Rowe, D. C., Almeida, D. M., & Jacobson, K. C.** (1999). School context and genetic influences on aggression in adolescence. *Psychological Science, 10*, 277–280.

60. **Moyer, K. E.** (1983). The physiology of motivation: Aggression as a model. In C. J. Scheier & A. M. Rogers (Eds.), *G. Stanley Hall Lecture Series* (Vol. 3, pp. 123–139). Washington, DC: American Psychological Association.

61. **Lewis, D. O., Pincus, J. H., Feldman, M., Jackson, L., & Bard, B.** (1986). Psychiatric neurological, and psychoeducational characteristics of 15 death row inmates in the United States. *American Journal of Psychiatry, 143*, 838–845.

62. **Dabbs, J. M., Jr.** (1992). Testosterone measurements in social and clinical psychology. *Journal of Social and Clinical Psychology, 11*, 302–321.

63. **Dabbs, J. M., Jr., Ruback, R. B., & Chance, S. E.** (2001). Testosterone and ruthless homicide. *Personality and Individual Differences, 31*, 599–603.

64. **Harris, R. J.** (1994). The impact of sexually explicit media. In J. Brant & D. Zillmann (Eds.), *Media effects: Advances in theory and research* (pp. 247–272). Hillsdale, NJ: Erlbaum.

65. **Pendick, D.** (1994, January/February). The mind of violence. *Brain Work: The Neuroscience Newsletter*, pp. 1–3, 5.

66. **Berman, M., Gladue, B., & Taylor, S.** (1993). The effects of hormones, Type A behavior pattern, and provocation on aggression in men. *Motivation and Emotion, 17*, 125–138.

67. **Dabbs, J. M., Jr., & Morris, R.** (1990). Testosterone, social class, and antisocial behavior in a sample of 4,462 men. *Psychological Science, 1,* 209–211.

68. **Olweus, D., Mattsson, A., Schalling, D., & Low, H.** (1988). Circulating testosterone levels and aggression in adolescent males: A causal analysis. *Psychosomatic Medicine, 50,* 261–272.

69. **Bushman, B. J.** (1993). Human aggression while under the influence of alcohol and other drugs: An integrative research review. *Current Directions in Psychological Science, 2,* 148–152.

70. **Ito, T. A., Miller, N., & Pollock, V. E.** (1996). Alcohol and aggression: A meta-analysis on the moderating effects of inhibitory cues, triggering events, and self-focused attention. *Psychological Bulletin, 120,* 60–82.

71. **Taylor, S. P., & Chermack, S. T.** (1993). Alcohol, drugs and human physical aggression. *Journal of Studies on Alcohol,* Suppl. 11, 78–88.

72. **Greenfeld, L. A.** (1998). *Alcohol and crime: An analysis of national data on the prevalence of alcohol involvement in crime* (Document NCJ-168632). Washington, DC: Bureau of Justice Statistics. Retrieved from http://www.ojp.usdoj.gov/bjs

73. **White, H. R., Brick, J., & Hansell, S.** (1993). A longitudinal investigation of alcohol use and aggression in adolescence. *Journal of Studies on Alcohol,* Suppl. 11, 62–77.

74. **Anderson, C. A., & Dill, K. E.** (2000). Video games and aggressive thoughts, feelings, and behavior in the laboratory and in life. *Journal of Personality and Social Psychology, 78,* 772–790.

75. **Carnagey, N. L, Anderson, C. A., & Bushman, B. J.** (2006). The effect of video game violence on physiological desensitization to real-life violence. *Journal of Experimental Social Psychology, 43*(3), 489–496.

76. **Gentile, D. A., Saleem, M., & Anderson, C. A.** (2007). Public policy and the effects of media violence on children. *Social Issues and Policy Review, 1,* 15–61.

77. **Ballard, M. E., & Wiest, J. R.** (1998). *Mortal Kombat:* The effects of violent videogame play on males' hostility and cardiovascular responding. *Journal of Applied Social Psychology, 26,* 717–730.

78. **Patterson, G. R., Chamberlain, P., & Reid, J. B.** (1982). A comparative evaluation of parent training procedures. *Behavior Therapy, 13,* 638–650.

79. **Patterson, G. R., Reid, J. B., & Dishion, T. J.** (1992). *Antisocial boys.* Eugene, OR: Castalia.

80. **Huston, A. C., Donnerstein, E., Fairchild, H., Feshbach, N. D., Katz, P. A., & Murray, J. P.** (1992). *Big world, small screen: The role of television in American society.* Lincoln: University of Nebraska Press.

81. **Centerwall, B. S.** (1989). Exposure to television as a risk factor for violence. *American Journal of Epidemiology, 129,* 643–652.

82. **American Psychological Association Commission on Violence and Youth.** (1993). *Violence and youth: Psychology's response—Summary report of the American Psychological Association Commission on Violence and Youth* (Vol. 1). Washington, DC: American Psychological Association.

83. **Aronson, E.** (1999). *The social animal* (8th ed.). New York, NY: Worth.

84. **Pettigrew, T. F.** (1969). Racially separate or together? *Journal of Social Issues, 25,* 43–69.

85. **Pettigrew, T. F.** (1997). Generalized intergroup contact effects on prejudice. *Personality and Social Psychology Bulletin, 23,* 173–185.

86. **Sherif, M.** (1966). *In common predicament: Social psychology of intergroup conflict and cooperation.* Boston, MA: Houghton Mifflin.

87. **Dovidio, J. F., & Gaertner, S. L.** (1999). Reducing prejudice: Combating intergroup biases. *Current Directions in Psychological Science, 8,* 101–105.

88. **Johnson, D. W., & Johnson, R. T.** (1989). *Cooperation and competition: Theory and research.* Edina, MN: Interaction Books.

89. **Johnson, D. W., & Johnson, R. T.** (1994). Constructive conflict in the schools. *Journal of Social Issues, 50*(1), 117–137.

90. **Slavin, R. E.** (1989). Cooperative learning and student achievement. In R. E. Slavin (Ed.), *School and classroom organization* (pp. 45–57). Hillsdale, NJ: Erlbaum.

91. **Kohn, A.** (1987, October). It's hard to get left out of a pair. *Psychology Today,* pp. 53–57.

92. **Carnegie Council on Adolescent Development.** (1989, June). *Turning points: Preparing American youth for the 21st century* (The report of the Task Force on Education of Young Adolescents). New York, NY: Carnegie Corporation.

Module 21

1. **Wade, N.** (1999, September 23). Largest chromosome has 250 million nucleotides while the smallest has 50 million. *New York Times.* Retrieved from http://www.nytimes.com

2. **Pennisi, E.** (2005, July 1). Why do humans have so few genes? *Science, 309,* 80. Retrieved from http://www.sciencemag.org/cgi/content/full/309/5731/80

3. **Plomin, R., & Crabbe, J.** (2000). DNA. *Psychological Bulletin, 126,* 806–828.

4. **Lykken, D.** (1999). *Happiness.* New York, NY: Golden Books.

5. **Brody, N.** (1994). Heritability of traits. *Psychological Inquiry, 5*(2), 117–119. Retrieved from http://www.leaonline.com/doi/abs/10.1207/s15327965pli0502_3

6. **McGue, M., & Lykken, D. T.** (1992). Genetic influence on risk of divorce. *Psychological Science, 3,* 368–373.

7. **Woo, E.** (2015). http://www.latimes.com/local/obituaries/la-me-jack-yufe-20151111-story.html

8. **Holden, C.** (1980a). Identical twins reared apart. *Science, 207,* 1323–1325.

9. **Holden, C.** (1980b, November). Twins reunited. *Science, 80,* 55–59.

10. **Wright, W.** (1998). *Born that way: Genes, behavior, personality.* New York, NY: Knopf.

11. **Bouchard, T. J., Lykken, D. T., McGue, M., Segal, N. L., & Tellegren, A.** (1990). Sources of human psychological differences. The Minnesota study of twins reared apart. *Science, 250,* 223–228.

12. **DiLalla, D. L., Carey, G., Gottesman, I. I., & Bouchard, T. J., Jr.** (1996). Heritability of MMPI personality indicators of psychopathology in twins reared apart. *Journal of Abnormal Psychology, 105,* 491–499.

13. **Segal, N. L.** (1999). *Entwined lives: Twins and what they tell us about human behavior.* New York, NY: Dutton.

14. **Plomin, R., & Daniels, D.** (1987). Why are children in the same family so different from one another? *Behavioral and Brain Sciences, 10,* 1–60.

15. **Brodzinsky, D. M., & Schechter, M. D. (Eds.).** (1990). *The psychology of adoption.* New York, NY: Oxford University Press.

16. **Kelley, J., & De Graaf, N. D.** (1997). National context, parental socialization, and religious belief: Results from 15 nations. *American Sociological Review, 62,* 639–659.

17. **Rohan, M. J., & Zanna, M. P.** (1996). Value transmission in families. In C. Seligman, J. M. Olson, & M. P. Zanna (Eds.), *The psychology of values: The Ontario Symposium* (Vol. 8). Mahwah, NJ: Erlbaum.

18. **Sharma, A. R., McGue, M. K., & Benson, P. L.** (1998). The psychological adjustment of United States adopted adolescents and their nonadopted siblings. *Child Development, 69,* 791–802.

19. **Neubauer, P. B., & Neubauer, A.** (1990). *Nature's thumbprint: The new genetics of personality.* Reading, MA: Addison-Wesley.

20. **Reifman, A., & Cleveland, H. H.** (2007, March/April). *Shared environment: A quantitative review.* Paper presented to the Society for Research in Child Development, Boston, MA.

21. **Plomin, R., & Daniels, D.** (1987). Why are children in the same family so different from one another? *Behavioral and Brain Sciences, 10,* 1–60.

22. **Scarr, S.** (1993, May/June). Quoted in Nature's thumbprint: So long, superparents. *Psychology Today,* p. 16

23. **Rosenzweig, M. R., Bennett, E. L., & Diamond, M. C.** (1972). Brain changes in response to experience. *Scientific American, 226,* 22–29.

24. **Drummond, T.** (1998, July 27). Touch early and often. *Time, 152*(4). Retrieved from http://www.time.com/time/magazine/article/0,9171,988794,00.html

25. **Field, T., Hernandez-Reif, M., Feijo, L, & Freedman, J.** (2006). Prenatal, perinatal and neonatal stimulation: A survey of neonatal nurseries. *Infant Behavior and Development, 29,* 24–31.

26. **Field, T., Diego, M., & Hernandez-Reif, M.** (2007). Massage therapy research. *Developmental Review, 27,* 75–89.

27. **Ramey, S. L., & Ramey, C. T.** (1992). Early educational intervention with disadvantaged children—To what effect? *Applied and Preventive Psychology, 1,* 131–140.

28. **Seligman, M. E. P., Steen, T., Park, N., & Peterson, C.** (2005). Positive psychology progress: Empirical validation of interventions. *American Psychologist, 60,* 410–421.

29. **Seligman, M. E. P.** (2008, March). Address to Geelong Grammar School faculty, Corio, Victoria, Australia.

30. **Rubin, K. H., Coplan, R. J., Nelson, L. J., Cheah, C. S. L., & Lagrace-Seguin, D. G.** (1999). Peer relationships in childhood. In M. H. Bornstein & M. E. Lamb (Eds.), *Developmental psychology: An advanced textbook* (4th ed., pp. 451–502). Mahwah, NJ: Erlbaum.

31. **Rose, J. S., Chassin, L., Presson, C. C., & Sherman, S. J.** (1999). Peer influences on adolescent cigarette smoking: A prospective sibling analysis. *Merrill-Palmer Quarterly, 45,* 62–84.

32. **Harris, J. R.** (1998). *The nurture assumption.* New York, NY: Free Press.

33. **Harris, J. R.** (2007, August 8). Do pals matter more than parents? *The Times.* Retrieved from http://www.timesonline.co.uk

34. **Gardner, H.** (1998, November 5). Do parents count? *New York Review of Books.* Retrieved from http://www.nybooks.com

35. **Vandell, D. L.** (2000). Parents, peer groups, and other socializing influences. *Developmental Psychology, 36,* 699–710.

36. **Ernst, R. M., Matsumoto, D., Freeman, J., & Weseley, A.** (2000). *An introduction to cross-cultural psychology: A five-day unit plan prepared for APA teachers of psychology in secondary schools (TOPSS).* Washington, DC: American Psychological Association.

Module 22

1. **Keith, K. D.** (2011). Introduction to cross-cultural psychology. In K. D. Keith (Ed.), Cross-cultural psychology: Contemporary themes and perspectives (pp. 3-19). Chichester, UK: Wiley-Blackwell.

2. **Matsumoto, D.** (1999). *People: Psychology from a cultural perspective* (2nd ed.). Pacific Grove, CA: Brooks/Cole.

3. **Matsumoto, D., & Juang, L.** (2007). *Culture and psychology* (4th ed.). Belmont, CA: Wadsworth.

4. **Ernst, R. M., Matsumoto, D., Freeman, J., & Weseley, A.** (2000). *An introduction to cross-cultural psychology: A five-day unit plan prepared for APA teachers of psychology in secondary schools (TOPSS).* Washington, DC: American Psychological Association.

5. **Matsumoto, D.** (1993). Ethnic differences in affect intensity, emotion judgments, display rule attitudes, and self-reported emotional expression in an American sample. *Motivation and Emotion, 17*(2), 107–123.

6. **Matsumoto, D.** (1999). *People: Psychology from a cultural perspective* (2nd ed.). Pacific Grove, CA: Brooks/Cole.

7. **Atkinson, R.** (1988). *The teenage world: Adolescent self-image in ten countries.* New York, NY: Plenum Press.

8. **Ernst, R. M., Matsumoto, D., Freeman, J., & Weseley, A.** (2000). *An introduction to cross-cultural psychology: A five-day unit plan prepared for APA teachers of psychology in secondary schools (TOPSS).* Washington, DC: American Psychological Association.

9. **Yang, K. S.** (1982). Causal attributions of academic success and failure and their affective consequences. *Chinese Journal of Psychology* [Taiwan], *24,* 65–83. (Only the abstract is in English.)

10. **Lutz, C.** (1988). *Unnatural emotions: Everyday sentiments on a Micronesian atoll and their challenge to Western theory.* Chicago, IL: University of Chicago Press.

11. **Russell, J. A.** (1991). Culture and the categorization of emotions. *Psychological Bulletin, 110,* 426–450.

12. **Ernst, R. M., Matsumoto, D., Freeman, J., & Weseley, A.** (2000). *An introduction to cross-cultural psychology: A five-day unit plan prepared for APA teachers of psychology in secondary schools (TOPSS).* Washington, DC: American Psychological Association.

13. **Matsumoto, D.** (1994). *Cultural influences on research methods and statistics.* Pacific Grove, CA: Brooks/Cole.

14. **Berry, J. W., Poorting, Y. H., Segall, M. H., & Dasen, P. R.** (1992). *Cross-cultural psychology: Research and applications.* New York, NY: Cambridge University Press.

15. **Rotter, J. B.** (1954). *Social learning and clinical psychology.* Englewood Cliffs, NJ: Prentice Hall.

16. **Dyal, J. A.** (1984). Cross-cultural research with the locus of control construct. In H. M. Lefcourt (Ed.), *Research with the locus of control construct* (Vol. 3, pp. 209–306). New York, NY: Academic Press.

17. **Grossmann, K., Grossmann, K. E., Spangler, G., Suess, G., & Unzner, L.** (1985). Maternal sensitivity and newborns' orientation responses as related to quality of attachment in northern Germany. In I. Bretherton & E. Waters (Eds.). *Growing points of attachment theory and research. Monographs of the Society of Research in Child Development, 50*(1/2, Serial No. 209), 233–256.

18. **Cherry, K.** (2018). https://www.verywell.com/what-is-attachment-theory-2795337

19. **Miyake, K., Chen, S.-J., & Campos, J. J.** (1985). Infant temperament, mother's mode of interaction, and attachment in Japan: An interim report. In I. Bretherton & E. Waters (Eds.), *Growing points of attachment theory and research: Monographs of the Society of Research in Child Development, 50*(1/2, Serial No. 209), 276–297.

20. **Tronick, E. Z., Morelli, G. A., & Ivey, P. K.** (1992). The Efe forager infant and toddlers pattern of social relationships: Multiple and simultaneous. *Developmental Psychology, 28,* 568–577.

21. **Matsumoto, D.** (1994). *Cultural influences on research methods and statistics.* Pacific Grove, CA: Brooks/Cole.

22. **Matsumoto, D.** (1999). *People: Psychology from a cultural perspective* (2nd ed.). Pacific Grove, CA: Brooks/Cole.

23. **Ernst, R. M., Matsumoto, D., Freeman, J., & Weseley, A.** (2000). *An introduction to cross-cultural psychology: A five-day unit plan prepared for APA teachers of psychology in secondary schools (TOPSS).* Washington, DC: American Psychological Association.

24. **APA** (retrieved 12/18/2017). http://www.apa.org/topics/lgbt/transgender.aspx

25. **IPU** (2009). Women in national parliaments: Situation as of 30 April 2009. International Parliamentary Union. Retrieved from http://www.ipu.org

26. **IDEA** (accessed July 2017). *Gender Quotas Around the World.* http://www.quotaproject.org/

27. **Bettencourt, B. A., & Kernahan, C.** (1997). A meta-analysis of aggression in the presence of violent cues: Effects of gender differences and aversive provocation. *Aggressive Behavior, 23,* 447–457.

28. **Wood, W., & Eagly, A.** (2007). Social structural origins of sex differences in human mating. In S. W. Gagestad & J. A. Simpson (Eds.), *The evolution of mind: Fundamental questions and controversies* (pp. 383–390). New York, NY: Guilford Press.

29. **U.S. Army** (2009). http://labs.time.com/story/women-in-military/

30. **Rose, A. J., & Rudolph, K. D.** (2006). A review of sex differences in peer relationship processes: Potential trade-offs for the emotional and behavioral development of girls and boys. *Psychological Bulletin, 132,* 98–131.

31. **Pryor, J. H., Hurtado, S., Sharkness, J., & Korn, W. S.** (2007). *The American freshman: National norms for fall 2007.* Los Angeles, CA: UCLA Higher Education Research Institute.

32. **Tannen, D.** (1990). *You just don't understand: Women and men in conversation.* New York, NY: Morrow.

33. **Wood, W., & Eagly, A.** (2002). A cross-cultural analysis of the behavior of women and men: Implications for the origins of sex differences. *Psychological Bulletin, 128,* 699–727.

Domain 5

Module 23

1. **Atkinson, R. C., & Schiffrin, R. M.** (1968). Human memory: A control system and its control processes. In K. Spence (Ed.), *The psychology of learning and motivation* (Vol. 2). New York, NY: Academic Press.

2. **Brown, P. C., Roediger, H. L., III, & McDaniel, M. A.** (2014). *Make it stick: The science of successful learning.* Cambridge, MA: Harvard University Press.

3. **Pan, S. C., Pashler, H., Potter, Z. E., & Rickard, T. C.** (2015). Testing enhances learning across a range of episodic memory abilities. *Journal of Memory and Language, 83,* 53–61.

4. **Trumbo, M. C., Leiting, K. A., McDaniel, M. A., & Hodge, G. K.** (2016). Effects of reinforcement on test-enhanced learning in a large, diverse introductory college psychology course. *Journal of Experimental Psychology: Applied, 22,* 148–160.

5. **Craik, F. I. M., & Watkins, M. J.** (1973). The role of rehearsal in short-term memory. *Journal of Verbal Learning and Verbal Behavior, 12,* 599–607.

6. **Cepeda, N. J., Pashler, H., Vul, E., Wixted, J. T., & Rohrer, D.** (2006). Distributed practice in verbal recall tasks: A review and quantitative synthesis. *Psychological Bulletin, 132,* 354–380.

7. **Bahrick, H. P., Bahrick, L. E., Bahrick, A. S., & Bahrick, P. E.** (1993). Maintenance of foreign language vocabulary and the spacing effect. *Psychological Science, 4,* 316–321.

8. **Roediger, H. L., & Karpicke, J. D.** (2006). Test-enhanced learning: Taking memory tests improves long-term retention. *Psychological Science, 17,* 249–255.

9. **Craik, F. I. M., & Tulving, E.** (1975). Depth of processing and the retention of words in episodic memory. *Journal of Experimental Psychology: General, 104,* 268–294.

10. **Poldrack, R. A., & Wagner, A. D.** (2004). What can neuroimaging tell us about the mind? *Current Directions in Psychological Science, 13,* 177–181.

11. **Symons, C. S., & Johnson, B. T.** (1997). The self-reference effect in memory: A meta-analysis. *Psychological Bulletin, 121*(3), 371–394.

12. **Wagar, B. M., & Cohen, D.** (2003). Culture, memory, and the self: An analysis of the personal and collective self in long-term memory. *Journal of Experimental and Social Psychology, 39,* 458–475.

13. **Mitchell, T. R., Thompson, L., Peterson, E., & Cronk, R.** (1997). Temporal adjustments in the evaluation of events: The "rosy view." *Journal of Experimental Social Psychology, 33,* 421–448.

14. **Sperling, G.** (1960). The information available in brief visual presentations. *Psychological Monographs, 74*(11, Whole No. 498), 1–29.

15. **Cowan, N.** (1988). Evolving conceptions of memory storage, selective attention, and their mutual constraints within the human information-processing system. *Psychological Bulletin, 104,* 163–191.

16. **Lu, Z. L., Williamson, S. J., & Kaufman, L.** (1992). Behavioral lifetime of human auditory sensory memory predicted by physiological measures. *Science, 258,* 1668–1670.

17. **Baddeley, A. D.** (2002, June). Is working memory still working? *European Psychologist, 7,* 85–97.

18. **Miller, G. A.** (1956). The magical number seven, plus or minus two: Some limits on our capacity for processing information. *Psychological Review, 63,* 81–97.

19. **Cowan, N.** (2001). The magical number 4 in short-term memory: A reconsideration of mental storage capacity. *Behavioral and Brain Sciences, 24,* 87–185.

20. **Jonides, J., Lewis, R. L., Nee, D. E., Lustig, C. A., Berman, M. G., & Moore, K. S.** (2008). The mind and brain of short-term memory. *Annual Review of Psychology, 59,* 193–224.

21. **Peterson, L. R., & Peterson, M. J.** (1959). Short-term retention of individual verbal items. *Journal of Experimental Psychology, 58,* 193–198.

22. **Adelson, R.** (2005, September). Lessons from H.M. *Monitor on Psychology, 36*(8), 59.

23. **Luria, A. M.** (1968). In L. Solotaroff (Trans.), *The mind of a mnemonist.* New York, NY: Basic Books.

24. **Associated Press** (2006, October 4). Man recites pi to 100,000 places.

25. **Parker, E. S., Cahill, L., & McGaugh, J. L.** (2006). A case of unusual autobiographical remembering. *Neurocase, 12,* 35–49.

26. **Parker, E. S., Cahill, L., & McGaugh, J. L.** (2006). A case of unusual autobiographical remembering. *Neurocase, 12,* 35–49.

27. **McRobbie, L. R.** (2017). https://www.theguardian.com/science/2017/feb/08/total-recall-the-people-who-never-forget

28. **McRobbie, L. R.** (2017). https://www.theguardian.com/science/2017/feb/08/total-recall-the-people-who-never-forget

29. **Gonsalves, B., Reber, P. J., Gitelman, D. R., Parrish, T. B., Mesulam, M.-M., & Paller, K. A.** (2004). Neural evidence that vivid imagining can lead to false remembering. *Psychological Science, 15,* 655–659.

30. **Schooler, J. W., Gerhard, D., & Loftus, E. F.** (1986). Qualities of the unreal. *Journal of Experimental Psychology: Learning, Memory, and Cognition, 12,* 171–181.

31. **Kandel, E. R., & Schwartz, J. H.** (1982). Molecular biology of learning: Modulation of transmitter release. *Science, 218,* 433–443.

32. **Whitlock, J. R., Heynen, A. L., Shuler, M. G., & Bear, M. F.** (2006). Learning induces long-term potentiation in the hippocampus. *Science, 313,* 1093–1097.

33. **Yarnell, P. R., & Lynch, S.** (1970). Retrograde memory immediately after concussion. *Lancet, 1,* 863–864.

34. **Weingartner, H., Rudorfer, M. V., Buchsbaum, M. S., & Linnoila, M.** (1983). Effects of serotonin on memory impairments produced by ethanol. *Science, 221,* 472–473.

35. **Cahill, L.** (1994). (Beta)-adrenergic activation and memory for emotional events. *Nature, 371,* 702–704.

36. **Buchanan, T. W.** (2007). Retrieval of emotional memories. *Psychological Bulletin, 133,* 761–779.

37. **Kensinger, E. A.** (2007). Negative emotion enhances memory accuracy: Behavioral and neuroimaging evidence. *Current Directions in Psychological Science, 16,* 213–218.

38. **de Chastelaine, M., Mattson, J. T., Wang, T. H., Donley, B. E., & Rugg, M. D.** (2016). The neural correlates of recollection and retrieval monitoring: Relationships with age and recollection performance. *NeuroImage, 138,* 164–175.

39. **Michalka, S. W., Kong, L., Rosen, M. L., Shinn-Cunningham, B., & Somers, D. C.** (2015). Short-term memory for space and time flexibly recruit complementary sensory-biased frontal lobe attention networks. *Neuron, 87,* 882–892.

40. **Godden, D. R., & Baddeley, A. D.** (1975). Context-dependent memory in two natural environments: On land and underwater. *British Journal of Psychology, 66,* 325–331.

41. **Lowe, G.** (1987). Combined effects of alcohol and caffeine on human state-dependent learning. *Medical Science Research: Psychology and Psychiatry, 15,* 25–26.

42. **Eich, E.** (1995). Searching for mood dependent memory. *Psychological Science, 6,* 67–75.

Module 24

1. **Grady, C. L., McIntosh, A. R., Horwitz, B., Maisog, J. M., Ungeleider, L. G., Mentis, M. J., . . . Haxby, J. V.** (1995). Age-related reductions in human recognition memory due to impaired encoding. *Science, 269,* 218–221.

2. **Ebbinghaus, H.** (1885). *Über das Gedächtnis.* Leipzig: Duncker & Humblot. Cited in R. Klatzky (1980), *Human memory: Structures and processes.* San Francisco, CA: Freeman.

3. **Bahrick, H. P.** (1984). Semantic memory content in permastore: 50 years of memory for Spanish learned in school. *Journal of Experimental Psychology: General, 111,* 1–29.

4. **Conway, M., & Ross, M.** (1984). Getting what you want by revising what you had. *Journal of Personality and Social Psychology, 47*(4), 738–748.

5. **Kihlstrom, J. F.** (1990). The psychological unconscious. In L. A. Pervin (Ed.), *Handbook of personality: Theory and research* (pp. 445–464). New York, NY: Guilford Press.

6. **Cahill, L.** (1994). (Beta)-adrenergic activation and memory for emotional events. *Nature, 371,* 702–704.

7. **Payne, B. K., & Corrigan, E.** (2007). Emotional constraints on intentional forgetting. *Journal of Experimental Social Psychology, 43,* 780–786.

8. **Loftus, E. F., & Palmer, J. C.** (1974, October). Reconstruction of automobile destruction: An example of the interaction between language and memory. *Journal of Verbal Learning and Verbal Behavior, 13*(5), 585–589.

9. **Loftus, E. F., Levidow, B., & Duensing, S.** (1992). Who remembers best? Individual differences in memory for events that occurred in a science museum. *Applied Cognitive Psychology, 6,* 93–107.

10. **Loftus, E. F.** (1992). When a lie becomes memory's truth: Memory distortion after exposure to misinformation. *Current Directions in Psychological Science, 1,* 121–123.

11. **Mazzoni, G., & Memon, A.** (2003). Imagination can create false autobiographical memories. *Psychological Science, 14,* 186–188.

12. **Gonsalves, B., Reber, P. J., Gitelman, D. R., Parrish, T. B., Mesulam, M.-M., & Paller, K. A.** (2004). Neural evidence that vivid imagining can lead to false remembering. *Psychological Science, 15,* 655–659.

13. **Garrett, B. L.** (2008). Judging innocence. *Columbia Law Review, 108,* 55–142.

14. **Ceci, S. J., & Bruck, M.** (1993). Child witnesses: Translating research into policy. *Social Policy Report (Society for Research in Child Development), 7*(3), 1–30.

15. **Principe, G. F., Kanaya, T., Ceci, S. J., & Singh, M.** (2006). Believing is seeing: How rumors can engender false memories in preschoolers. *Psychological Science, 17,* 243–248.

16. **Bruck, M., & Ceci, S. J.** (1999). The suggestibility of children's memory. *Annual Review of Psychology, 50,* 419–439.

17. **Ceci, S. J., & Bruck, M.** (1993). Child witnesses: Translating research into policy. *Social Policy Report (Society for Research in Child Development), 7*(3), 1–30.

18. **Howe, M. L.** (1997). Children's memory for traumatic experiences. *Learning and Individual Differences, 9,* 153–174.

19. **Pipe, M. E.** (1996). Children's eyewitness memory. *New Zealand Journal of Psychology, 25,* 36–43.

20. **Pipe, M. E., Lamb, M. E., Orbach, Y., & Esplin, P. W.** (2004). Recent research on children's testimony about experienced and witnessed events. *Developmental Review, 24,* 440–468.

21. **Williams, L. M.** (1995, October). Recovered Memories of Abuse in Women with Documented Child Sexual Victimization Histories. *Journal of Traumatic Stress, 8*(4), pp. 649–673. Retrieved from https://link.springer.com/article/10.1007/BF02102893

22. **Bass, E., & Davis, L.** (1988). *The courage to heal.* New York, NY: Harper & Row.

Module 25

1. **Grill-Spector, K., & Kanwisher, N.** (2005). Visual recognition: As soon as you know it is there, you know what it is. *Psychological Science, 16,* 152–160.

2. **Rosch, E.** (1978). Principles of categorization. In E. Rosch & B. L. Lloyd (Eds.), *Cognition and categorization* (pp. 27–48). Hillsdale, NJ: Erlbaum.

3. **Bishop, G. D.** (1991). Understanding the understanding of illness: Lay disease representations. In J. A. Skelton & R. T. Croyle (Eds.), *Mental representation in health and illness* (pp. 32–59). New York, NY: Springer-Verlag.

4. **Knoblich, G., & Oellinger, M.** (2006, October/November). The eureka moment. *Scientific American Mind,* pp. 38–43.

5. **Sandkühler, S., & Bhattacharya, J.** (2008). Deconstructing insight: EEG correlates of insightful problem solving. *PLoS ONE, 3,* e1459. Retrieved from http://www.plosone.org

6. **Kohler, W.** (1925; reprinted 1957). *The mentality of apes.* London: Pelican.

7. **Kuhn, D., Weinstock, M., & Flaton, R.** (1994). How well do jurors reason? Competence dimensions of individual variation in a juror reasoning task. *Psychological Science, 5,* 289–296.

8. **Pennington, N., & Hastie, R.** (1993). The story model for juror decision making. In R. Hastie (Ed.), *Inside the juror: The psychology of juror decision making* (pp. 192–221). New York, NY: Cambridge University Press.

9. **Tversky, A., & Kahneman, D.** (1974). Judgment under uncertainty: Heuristics and biases. *Science, 185,* 1124–1131.

10. **Slovic, P.** (2007). "If I look at the mass I will never act": Psychic numbing and genocide. *Judgment and Decision Making, 2,* 79–95.

11. **Kahneman, D., & Tversky, A.** (1979). Intuitive prediction: Biases and corrective procedures. *Management Science, 12,* 313–327.

12. **Fischhoff, B., Slovic, P., & Lichtenstein, S.** (1977). Knowing with certainty: The appropriateness of extreme confidence. *Journal of Experimental Psychology: Human Perception and Performance, 3,* 552–564.

13. **Buehler, R., Griffin, D., & Ross, M.** (1994). Exploring the "planning fallacy": Why people underestimate their task completion times. *Journal of Personality and Social Psychology, 67,* 366–381.

14. **Baumeister, R. F.** (1989). The optimal margin of illusion. *Journal of Social and Clinical Psychology, 8,* 176–189.

15. **Taylor, S. E.** (1989). *Positive illusions.* New York, NY: Basic Books.

16. **Linville, P. W., Fischer, G. W., & Fischhoff, B.** (1992). AIDS risk perceptions and decision biases. In J. B. Pryor & G. D. Reeder (Eds.), *The social psychology of HIV infection* (pp. 5–38). Hillsdale, NJ: Erlbaum.

Module 26

1. **Gardner, H.** (1983). *Frames of mind: The theory of multiple intelligences.* New York, NY: Basic Books.

2. **Gardner, H.** (2006). *The development and education of the mind: The selected works of Howard Gardner.* New York, NY: Routledge.

3. **Sternberg, R. J.** (1985). *Beyond IQ: A triarchic theory of human intelligence.* New York, NY: Cambridge University Press.

4. **Sternberg, R. J.** (1999). The theory of successful intelligence. *Review of General Psychology, 3,* 292–316.

5. **Sternberg, R. J.** (2003). Our research program validating the triarchic theory of successful intelligence: Reply to Gottfredson. *Intelligence, 31,* 399–413.

6. **Sternberg, R. J., & Wagner, R. K.** (1993). The g-ocentric view of intelligence and job performance is wrong. *Current Directions in Psychological Science, 2,* 1–5.

7. **Sternberg, R. J., Wagner, R. K., Williams, W. M., & Horvath, J. A.** (1995). Testing common sense. *American Psychologist, 50,* 912–927.

8. **Sternberg, R. J.** (2006). The Rainbow Project: Enhance the SAT through assessments of analytical, practical, and creative skills. *Intelligence, 34,* 321–350.

9. **Sternberg, R. J.** (2007, July 6). Finding students who are wise, practical, and creative. *The Chronicle Review.* Retrieved from http://www.chronicle.com

10. **Goleman, D.** (1995). *Emotional intelligence.* New York: Bantam.

11. **Mayer, J. D., Caruso, D. R., & Salovey, P.** (2016). The ability model of emotional intelligence: Principles and updates. *Emotion Review, 8*(4), 290–300.

12. **Mayer, J. D., Caruso, D. R., & Salovey, P.** (2016). The ability model of emotional intelligence: Principles and updates. *Emotion Review, 8*(4), 290–300.

13. **Epstein, S., & Meier, P.** (1989). Constructive thinking: A broad coping variable with specific components. *Journal of Personality and Social Psychology, 57,* 332–350.

14. **Gould, S. J.** (1981). *The mismeasure of man.* New York, NY: Norton.

15. **Terman, L. M.** (1916). *The measurement of intelligence.* Boston, MA: Houghton Mifflin.

16. **Schalock, R. L., Borthwick-Duffy, S., Bradley, V. J., Buntinx, W. H. E., Coulter, D. L., Craig, E. M.** (2010). *Intellectual disability: Definition, classification, and systems of supports* (11th edition). Washington, DC: American Association on Intellectual and Developmental Disabilities.

17. **Reichenberg, A., Cederlof, M., McMillan, A., Trzaskowski, M., Kapara, O., Fruchter, E., . . . Plomin, R.** (2016). Discontinuity in the genetic and environmental causes of the intellectual disability spectrum. *PNAS, 113,* 1098–1103.

18. **Friedman, H. S., & Martin, L. R.** (2012). *The longevity project.* New York: Penguin (Plume).

19. **Koenen, K. C., Moffitt, T. E., Roberts, A. L., Martin, L. T., Kubzansky, L., Harrington, H., . . . Caspi, A.** (2009). Childhood IQ and adult mental disorders: A test of the cognitive reserve hypothesis. *American Journal of Psychiatry, 166,* 50–57.

20. **Lubinski, D.** (2016). From Terman to today: A century of findings on intellectual precocity. *Review of Educational Research, 86,* 900–944.

21. **Hedges, L. V., & Nowell, A.** (1995). Sex differences in mental test scores, variability, and numbers of high-scoring individuals. *Science, 269,* 41–45.

22. **Zeidner, M.** (1990). Perceptions of ethnic group modal intelligence: Reflections of cultural stereotypes or intelligence test scores? *Journal of Cross-Cultural Psychology, 21,* 214–231.

23. **Arvey, R. D., et al.** (1994, December 13). Mainstream science on intelligence. *Wall Street Journal,* A18.

24. **Dickens, W. T., & Flynn, J. R.** (2006). Black Americans reduce the racial IQ gap: Evidence from standardization samples. *Psychological Science, 17,* 913–920.

25. **Neisser, U., Boodoo, G., Bouchard, T. J., Jr., Boykin, A. W., Brody, N., Ceci, S. J., . . . Urbina, S.** (1996). Intelligence: Knowns and unknowns. *American Psychologist, 51,* 77–101.

26. **Flynn, J. R.** (1987). Massive IQ gains in 14 nations: What IQ tests really measure. *Psychological Bulletin, 101,* 171–191.

27. **Flynn, J. R.** (2012). *Are we getting smarter? Rising IQ in the twenty-first century.* Cambridge: Cambridge University Press.

28. **Daley, T. C., Whaley, S. E., Sigman, M. D., Espinosa, M. P., & Neumann, C.** (2003). IQ on the rise: The Flynn effect in rural Kenyan children. *Psychological Science, 14,* 215–219.

29. **Cavalli-Sforza, L., Menozzi, P., & Piazza, A.** (1994). *The history and geography of human genes.* Princeton, NJ: Princeton University Press.

30. **Lewontin, R.** (1982). *Human diversity.* New York, NY: Scientific American Library.

31. **Plomin, R., & Crabbe, J.** (2000). DNA. *Psychological Bulletin, 126,* 806–828.

32. **Halpern, D. F.** (1997). Sex differences in intelligence: Implications for education. *American Psychologist, 52,* 1091–1102.

33. **Hedges, L. V., & Nowell, A.** (1995). Sex differences in mental test scores, variability, and numbers of high-scoring individuals. *Science, 269,* 41–45.

Domain 6

Module 27

1. **James, W.** (1890). *The principles of psychology* (Vol. 2). New York, NY: Holt.

2. **Bernard, L. L.** (1924). *Instinct.* New York, NY: Holt, Rinehart & Winston.

3. **Biederman, I., & Vessel, E. A.** (2006). Perceptual pleasure and the brain. *American Scientist, 94,* 247–253.

4. **Spence, J. T., & Helmreich, R. L.** (1983). *Achievement and achievement motives: Psychological and sociological approaches.* New York, NY: Freeman.

5. **Amabile, T. M.** (1996). *The context of creativity.* Boulder, CO: Westview.

6. **Lepper, M. R., Greene, D., & Nisbett, R. E.** (1973). Undermining children's intrinsic interest with extrinsic rewards: A test of the "overjustification" hypothesis. *Journal of Personality and Social Psychology, 28,* 129–137.

7. **Deci, E.L.** (1995). Why we do what we do: The dynamics of personal autonomy. New York: G. P. Putnam's Sons.

8. **Mueller, C. M., & Dweck, C. S.** (1998). Praise for intelligence can undermine children's motivation and performance. *Journal of Personality and Social Psychology, 75,* 33–52.

9. **Locke, E. A., & Latham, G. P.** (1990). Work motivation and satisfaction: Light at the end of the tunnel. *Psychological Science, 1,* 240–246.

10. **Mento, A. J., Steel, R. P., & Karren, R. J.** (1987). A meta-analytic study of the effects of goal setting on task performance: 1966–1984. *Organizational Behavior and Human Decision Processes, 39,* 52–83.

11. **Tubbs, M. E.** (1986). Goal setting: A meta-analytic examination of the empirical evidence. *Journal of Applied Psychology, 71,* 474–483.

12. **Fishbach, A., Dhar, R., & Zhang, Y.** (2006). Subgoals as substitutes or complements: The role of goal accessibility. *Journal of Personality and Social Psychology, 91,* 232–242.

13. **Maslow, A. H.** (1970). *Motivation and personality* (2nd ed.). New York, NY: Harper & Row.

14. **Koltko-Rivera, M. E.** (2006). Rediscovering the later version of Maslow's hierarchy of needs: Self-transcendence and opportunities for theory, research, and unification. *Review of General Psychology, 10,* 302–317.

15. **Murray, H.** (1938). *Explorations in personality.* New York, NY: Oxford University Press.

16. **McClelland, D. C., Atkinson, J. W., Clark, R. A., & Lowell, E. L.** (1953). *The achievement motive.* New York, NY: Appleton-Century-Crofts.

17. **Bloom, B. S. (Ed.).** (1985). *Developing talent in young people.* New York, NY: Ballantine.

18. **Duckworth, A. L., & Seligman, M. E. P.** (2005). Discipline outdoes talent: Self-discipline predicts academic performance in adolescents. *Psychological Science, 12,* 939–944.

19. **McCall, R. B.** (1994). Academic underachievers. *Current Directions in Psychological Science, 3,* 15–19.

20. **Halaas, J. L., Gajiwala, K. S., Maffei, M., Cohen, S. L., Chait, B. T., Rabinowitz, D., . . . Friedman, J. M.** (1995). Weight-reducing effects of the plasma protein encoded by the obese gene. *Science, 269,* 543–546.

21. **Considine, R. V., Sinha, M. K., Heiman, M. L., Kriauciunas, A., Stephens, T. W., Nyce, M. R., . . . Caro, J. F.** (1996). Serum immunoreactive-leptin concentrations in normal-weight and obese humans. *New England Journal of Medicine, 334,* 292–295.

22. **Miller, N. E.** (1995). Clinical-experimental interactions in the development of neuroscience: A primer for nonspecialists and lessons for young scientists. *American Psychologist, 50,* 901–911.

23. **Artiga, A. I., Viana, J. B., Maldonado, C. R., Chandler-Laney, P. C., Oswald, K. D., & Boggiano, M. M.** (2007). Body composition and endocrine status of long-term stress-induced binge-eating rats. *Physiology and Behavior, 91,* 424–431.

24. **Lissner, L., Odel, P. M., D'Agostino, R. B., Stokes, J., Kreger, B. E., Belanger, A. J., & Brownell, K. D.** (1991). Variability of body weight and health outcomes in the Framingham population. *New England Journal of Medicine, 324,* 1839–1844.

25. **Rodin, J.** (1984, December). A sense of control [Interview]. *Psychology Today,* pp. 38–45.

26. **Crandall, C. S.** (1988). Social contagion of binge eating. *Journal of Personality and Social Psychology, 55,* 588–598.

27. **Hebl, M. R., & Heatherton, T. F.** (1998). The stigma of obesity in women: The difference is black and white. *Personality and Social Psychology Bulletin, 24,* 417–426.

28. **Pliner, P.** (1982). The effects of mere exposure on liking for edible substances. *Appetite: Journal for Intake Research, 3,* 283–290.

29. **Pliner, P., Pelchat, M., & Grabski, M.** (1993). Reduction of neophobia in humans by exposure to novel foods. *Appetite: Journal for Intake Research, 20,* 111–123.

30. **Hetherington, M. M., Anderson, A. S., Norton, G. N. M., & Newson, L.** (2006). Situational effects on meal intake: A comparison of eating alone and eating with others. *Physiology and Behavior, 88,* 498–505.

31. **Hinz, L. D., & Williamson, D. A.** (1987). Bulimia and depression: A review of the affective variant hypothesis. *Psychological Bulletin, 102,* 150–158.

32. **Fichter, M. M., & Noegel, R.** (1990). Concordance for bulimia nervosa in twins. *International Journal of Eating Disorders, 9,* 255–263.

33. **Kaplan, A.** (2004). Exploring the gene-environment nexus in anorexia, bulimia. *Psychiatric Times, 21.* Retrieved from http://www.psychiatrictimes.com/p040801b.html

34. **Pike, K. M., & Rodin, J.** (1991). Mothers, daughters, and disordered eating. *Journal of Abnormal Psychology, 100,* 198–204.

35. **Stice, E.** (2002). Risk and maintenance factors for eating pathology: A meta-analytic review. *Psychological Bulletin, 128,* 825–848.

36. **Wooley, S., & Wooley, O.** (1983). Should obesity be treated at all? *Psychiatric Annals, 13*(11), 884–885, 888.

37. **Stice, E., Shaw, H., & Marti, C. N.** (2007). A meta-analytic review of eating disorder prevention programs: Encouraging findings. *Annual Review of Clinical Psychology, 3,* 233–257.

Module 28

1. **Hebb, D. O.** (1980). *Essay on mind.* Hillsdale, NJ: Erlbaum.

2. **Cannon, W. B.** (1929). *Bodily changes in pain, hunger, fear, and rage.* New York, NY: Branford.

3. **Bard, P.** (1934). On emotional experience after decortication with some remarks on theoretical views. *Psychological Review, 41,* 309–329.

4. **Schachter, S., & Singer, J. E.** (1962). Cognitive, social, and physiological determinants of emotional state. *Psychological Review, 69,* 379–399.

5. **Zajonc, R. B.** (1984). On the primacy of affect. *American Psychologist, 39,* 117–123.

6. **LeDoux, J., & Armony, J.** (1999). Can neurobiology tell us anything about human feelings? In D. Dahneman, E. Diener, & N. Schwartz (Eds.), *Well-being: The foundations of hedonic psychology* (pp. 489–499). New York, NY: Sage.

7. **Lazarus, R. S.** (1991). Progress on a cognitive-motivational-relational theory of emotion. *American Psychologist, 46,* 352–367.

8. **Lazarus, R. S.** (1998). *Fifty years of the research and theory of R. S. Lazarus: An analysis of historical and perennial issues.* Mahwah, NJ: Erlbaum.

9. **Fredrickson, B. L.** (2009). *Positivity: Groundbreaking research reveals how to embrace the hidden strength of positive emotions, overcome negativity, and thrive.* New York, NY: Crown.

10. **Fredrickson, B. L.** (2001). The role of positive emotions in positive psychology: The broaden-and-build theory of positive emotions. *American Psychologist, 56,* 218–226.

11. **Fredrickson, B. L.** (2006a). The broaden-and-build theory of positive emotions. In M. Csikszentmihalyi & I. S. Csikszentmihalyi (Eds.), *A life worth living: Contributions to positive psychology* (pp. 85–103). New York, NY: Oxford University Press.

12. **Fredrickson, B. L., Cohn, M. A., Coffey, K. A., Pek, J., & Finkel, S. M.** (2008). Open hearts build lives: Positive emotions, induced through loving-kindness meditation, build consequential personal resources. *Journal of Personality and Social Psychology, 95*(5), 1045–1062.

13. **Fredrickson, B. L.** (2009). *Positivity: Groundbreaking research reveals how to embrace the hidden strength of positive emotions, overcome negativity, and thrive.* New York, NY: Crown.

14. **Fredrickson, B. L.** (2009). *Positivity: Groundbreaking research reveals how to embrace the hidden strength of positive emotions, overcome negativity, and thrive.* New York, NY: Crown.

15. Reijmers, L. G., Perkins, B. L., Matsuo, N., & Mayford, M. (2007). Localization of stable neural correlate of associative memory. *Science, 317,* 1230–1233.

16. Schacter, D. L. (1996). *Searching for memory: The brain, the mind, and the past.* New York, NY: Basic Books.

17. Porter, S., & ten Brinke, L. (2008). Reading between the lies: Identifying concealed and falsified emotions in universal facial expressions. *Psychological Science, 19,* 508–514.

18. Kleinmuntz, B., & Szucko, J. J. (1984). A field study of the fallibility of polygraph lie detection. *Nature, 308,* 449–450.

19. Ben-Shakhar, G., & Furedy, J. J. (1990). *Theories and applications in the detection of deception: A psychophysiological and international perspective.* New York, NY: Springer-Verlag.

20. Bashore, T. R., & Rapp, P. E. (1993). Are there alternatives to traditional polygraph procedures? *Psychological Bulletin, 113*(1), 3–22.

21. Langleben, D. D., Dattilio, F. M., & Gutheil, T. G. (2006). True lies: Delusions and lie-detection technology. *Journal of Psychiatry and Law, 34,* 351–370.

22. Dingfelder, S. (2007, December). $10 million project aims to integrate law and neuroscience. *Monitor on Psychology,* p. 11.

23. Barrett, L. F. (2006). Are emotions natural kinds? *Perspectives on Psychological Science, 1,* 28–58, 370.

24. Panksepp, J. (2007). Neurologizing the psychology of affects: How appraisal-based constructivism and basic emotion theory can coexist. *Perspectives on Psychological Science, 2,* 281–295.

25. Drake, R. A., & Myers, L. R. (2006). Visual attention, emotion, and action tendency: Feeling active or passive. *Cognition and Emotion, 20,* 608–622.

26. Kleinke, C. L. (1986). Gaze and eye contact: A research review. *Psychological Bulletin, 100,* 78–100.

27. Hall, J. A. (1987). On explaining gender differences: The case of nonverbal communication. In P. Shaver & C. Hendrick (Eds.), *Review of Personality and Social Psychology, 7,* 177–200.

28. Blum, D. (1998, September). Face it! *Psychology Today.* Retrieved from https://www.psychologytoday.com/us/articles/199809/face-it

29. Buck, R. (1984). *The communication of emotion.* New York: Guilford Press.

30. DePaulo, B. M., Blank, A. K., Swaim, G. W., & Hairfield, J. G. (1992). Expressiveness and expressive control. *Personality and Social Psychology Bulletin, 18,* 276–285.

31. Kring, A. M., & Gordon, A. H. (1998). Sex differences in emotion: Expression, experience, and physiology. *Journal of Personality and Social Psychology, 74,* 686–703.

32. Grossman, M., & Wood, W. (1993). Sex differences in intensity of emotional experience: A social role interpretation. *Journal of Personality and Social Psychology, 65,* 1010–1022.

33. Coats, E. J., & Feldman, R. S. (1996). Gender differences in non-verbal correlates of social status. *Personality and Social Psychology Bulletin, 22,* 1014–1022.

34. Fiske, Susan. (1993). Controlling Other People: The Impact of Power on Stereotyping. *The American Psychologist, 48,* 621–628.

35. Snodgrass, S. E. (1992). Further effects of role versus gender on interpersonal sensitivity. *Journal of Personality and Social Psychology, 62,* 154–158.

36. Kring, A. M., & Gordon, A. H. (1998). Sex differences in emotion: Expression, experience, and physiology. *Journal of Personality and Social Psychology, 74,* 686–703.

37. Triandis, H. C. (1994). *Culture and social behavior.* New York, NY: McGraw-Hill.

38. Ekman, P., Friesen, W. V., O'Sullivan, M., Chan, A., Diacoyanni-Tarlatzis, I., Heider, K., . . . Tzavaras, A. (1987). Universals and cultural differences in the judgments of facial expressions of emotion. *Journal of Personality and Social Psychology, 53,* 712–717.

39. Hall, E. T., & Hall, M. R. (1990). *Understanding cultural differences.* Yarmouth, ME: Intercultural Press.

40. Ekman, P. (1994). Strong evidence for universals in facial expressions: A reply to Russell's mistaken critique. *Psychological Bulletin, 115,* 268–287.

41. Ekman, P., & Friesen, W. V. (1975). *Unmasking the face.* Englewood Cliffs, NJ: Prentice Hall.

42. Izard, C. E. (1977). *Human emotions.* New York, NY: Plenum Press.

43. Izard, C. E. (1994). Innate and universal facial expressions: Evidence from developmental and cross-cultural research. *Psychological Bulletin, 115,* 288–299.

44. Matsumoto, D., Yoo, S. H., Fontaine, J., Anguas-Wong, A. M., Arriola, M., Ataca, B., . . . Grossi, E. (2008). Mapping expressive differences around the world: The relationship between emotional display rules and individualism versus collectivism. *Journal of Cross-Cultural Psychology, 39,* 55–74.

Module 29

1. Reivich, K. J. (2010). Master resilience training (binder 1): Guidelines for teaching resilience to U.S. Army soldiers. Philadelphia, PA: The Trustees of the University of Pennsylvania.

2. Reivich, K. J., Gillham, J. E., Chaplin, T. M., & Seligman, M. E. P. (2005). From helplessness to optimism: The role of resilience in treating and preventing depression in youth. In S. Goldstein & R. B. Brooks (Eds.), *Handbook of resilience in children* (pp. 223–237). New York, NY: Kluwer Academic/ Plenum.

3. Reivich, K. J. (2009). Proceedings on the training of trainers at the Penn Resiliency Program for teachers, Philadelphia, PA.

4. Horney, K. (1950). *Neurosis and human growth: The struggle toward self-realization.* New York, NY: Norton.

5. Wood, J. M., Nezworski, M. T., Garb, H. N., & Lilienfeld, S. O. (2006, Spring). The controversy over Exner's Comprehensive System for the Rorschach. *Independent Practitioner.*

6. Exner, J. E. (2003). *The Rorschach: A comprehensive system* (4th ed.). Hoboken, NJ: Wiley.

7. Sechrest, L., Stickle, T. R., & Stewart, M. (1998). The role of assessment in clinical psychology. In A. Bellack, M. Hersen (Series eds.), & C. R. Reynolds (Vol. ed.), *Comprehensive clinical psychology: Assessment* (Vol. 4, pp. 1–32). New York, NY: Pergamon Press.

8. Hunsley, J., & Bailey, J. M. (1999). The clinical utility of the Rorschach: Unfulfilled promises and an uncertain future. *Psychological Assessment, 11*(3), 266–277.

9. Westen, D. (1996, January). *Is Freud really dead? Teaching psychodynamic theory to introductory psychology.* Presentation to the Annual Institute on the Teaching of Psychology, St. Petersburg Beach, FL.

10. Erdelyi, M. H. (2006). The unified theory of repression. *Behavioral and Brain Sciences, 29,* 499–551.

11. Frieze, I. H., Parsons, J. E., Johnson, P. B., Ruble, D. N., & Zellman, G. L. (1978). *Women and sex roles: A social psychological perspective.* New York, NY: Norton.

12. Boag, S. (2006). Freudian repression, the common view, and pathological science. *Review of General Psychology, 10,* 74–86.

13. Powell, R. A., & Boer, D. P. (1994). Did Freud mislead patients to confabulate memories of abuse? *Psychological Reports, 74,* 1283–1298.

14. Erdelyi, M. H. (2006). The unified theory of repression. *Behavioral and Brain Sciences, 29,* 499–551.

15. Ofshe, R. J., & Watters, E. (1994). *Making monsters: False memory, psychotherapy, and sexual hysteria.* New York, NY: Scribners.

16. Cohen, P. (2007, November 15). Freud is widely taught at universities, except in the psychology department. *New York Times.* Retrieved from http://www.nytimes.com

17. Seligman, M. E. P. (1994). *What you can change and what you can't.* New York, NY: Knopf.

18. Schultz, D., & Schultz, S. (2008). *A history of modern psychology* (9th ed.). Belmont, CA: Thomson.

19. Maslow, A. H. (1970). *Motivation and personality* (2nd ed.). New York, NY: Harper & Row.

20. Schultz, D., & Schultz, S. (2008). *A history of modern psychology* (9th ed.). Belmont, CA: Thomson.

21. Rogers, C. R. (1980). *A way of being.* Boston, MA: Houghton Mifflin.

22. Schultz, D., & Schultz, S. (2008). *A history of modern psychology* (9th ed.). Belmont, CA: Thomson.

23. Cunningham, S. (1985, May). Humanists celebrate gains, goals. *APA Monitor,* pp. 16, 18.

24. Seligman, M. E. P. (2001, April 22). Personal communication.

Module 30

1. Sheldon, W. H. (1954). *Atlas of man: A guide for somatotyping the adult male of all ages.* New York, NY: Harper & Row.

2. Schultz, D., & Schultz, S. (2008). *A history of modern psychology* (9th ed.). Belmont, CA: Thomson.

3. Allport, G. W., & Odbert, H. S. (1936). Trait-names: A psycholexical study. *Psychological Monographs, 47*(1).

4. Wiggins, J. S. (1984). Cattell's system from the perspective of mainstream personality theory. *Multivariate Behavioral Research, 19,* 176–190.

5. Cattell, R. B. (1963). Theory of fluid and crystallized intelligence: A critical experiment. *Journal of Educational Psychology, 54,* 1–22.

6. Cattell, R. B., & Krug, S. E. (1986). The number of factors in the 16PF: A review of the evidence with special emphasis on methodological problems. *Educational and Psychological Measurement, 46,* 509–522.

7. Eysenck, S. B. G., & Eysenck, H. J. (1963). The validity of questionnaire and rating assessments of extraversion and neuroticism, and their factorial stability. *British Journal of Psychology, 54,* 51–62.

8. Jang, K. L., McCrae, R. R., Angleitner, A., Riemann, R., & Livesley, W. J. (1998). Heritability of facet-level traits in a cross-cultural twin sample: Support for a hierarchical model of personality. *Journal of Personality and Social Psychology, 74,* 1556–1565.

9. Wiggins, J. S. (1996). *The five-factor model of personality: Theoretical perspectives.* New York, NY: Guilford Press.

10. Costa, P. T., Jr., & McCrae, R. R. (2006). Trait and factor theories. In J. C. Thomas, D. L. Segal, & M. Hersen (Eds.), *Comprehensive handbook of personality and psychopathology, Vol. 1: Personality and everyday functioning* (pp. 96–114). Hoboken, NJ: Wiley.

11. Schmitt, D. P., Allik, J., McCrae, R. R., Benet-Martinez, V., et al. (2007). The geographic distribution of Big Five personality traits: Patterns and profiles of human self-description across 56 nations. *Journal of Cross-Cultural Psychology, 38,* 173–212.

12. Srivastava, S., John, O. P., Gosling, S. D., & Potter, J. (2003). Development of personality in early and middle adulthood: Set like plaster or persistent change? *Journal of Personality and Social Psychology, 84,* 1041–1053.

13. Loehlin, J. C., McCrae, R. R., & Costa, P. T., Jr. (1998). Heritabilities of common and measure-specific components of the Big Five personality factors. *Journal of Research in Personality, 32,* 431–453.

14. Botwin, M. D., Buss, D. M., & Shackelford, T. K. (1997). Personality and mate preferences: Five factors in mate selection and marital satisfaction. *Journal of Personality, 65,* 107–136.

15. Donnellan, M. B., Conger, R. D., & Bryant, C. M. (2004). The Big Five and enduring marriages. *Journal of Research in Personality, 38,* 481–504.

16. **Dawes, R. M.** (1994). *House of cards: Psychology and psychotherapy built on myth.* New York, NY: Free Press.

17. **Matarazzo, J. D.** (1983). Computerized psychological testing. *Science, 221,* 323.

18. **Senior, G., & Douglas, L.** (2001). Misconceptions and misuse of the MMPI-2 in assessing personal injury claimants. *NeuroRehabilitation, 16,* 203–213.

19. **Funder, D. C.** (1991). Global traits: A neo-Allportian approach to personality. *Psychological Science, 2,* 31–39.

20. **Funder, D. C.** (1995). On the accuracy of personality judgment: A realistic approach. *Psychological Review, 102,* 652–670.

21. **Gosling, S. D., Ko, S. J., Mannarelli, T., & Morris, M. E.** (2002). A room with a cue: Personality judgments based on offices and bedrooms. *Journal of Personality and Social Psychology, 82,* 379–398.

22. **Gill, A. J., Oberlander, J., & Austin, E.** (2006). Rating e-mail personality at zero acquaintance. *Personality and Individual Differences, 40,* 497–507.

23. **Gosling, S. D., Gladdis, S., & Vazire, S.** (2007). *Personality impressions based on Facebook profiles.* Paper presented at the Society for Personality and Social Psychology meeting.

24. **Mischel, W.** (2004). Toward an integrative science of the person. *Annual Review of Psychology, 55,* 1–22.

25. **Ashton, M. C., Lee, K., & Goldberg, L. R.** (2004). A hierarchical analysis of 1,710 English personality-descriptive adjectives. *Journal of Personality and Social Psychology, 87,* 707–721.

26. **Bandura, A.** (1986). *Social foundations of thought and action: A social-cognitive theory.* Englewood Cliffs, NJ: Prentice Hall.

27. **Carson, S.** (1985). A double-blind test of astrology. *Nature, 318,* 419–425.

28. **Kelly, I. W.** (1997). Modern astrology: A critique. *Psychological Reports, 81,* 1035–1066.

29. **Beyerstein, B., & Beyerstein, D. (Eds.).** (1992). *The write stuff: Evaluations of graphology.* Buffalo, NY: Prometheus Books.

30. **Dean, G. A., Kelly, I. W., Saklofske, D. H., & Furnham, A.** (1992). Graphology and human judgment. In B. Beyerstein & D. Beyerstein (Eds.), *The write stuff: Evaluations of graphology* (pp. 342–396). Buffalo, NY: Prometheus Books.

31. **Hyman, R.** (1981). Cold reading: How to convince strangers that you know all about them. In K. Frazier (Ed.), *Paranormal borderlands of science.* Buffalo, NY: Prometheus Books.

32. **Bandura, A.** (1986). *Social foundations of thought and action: A social-cognitive theory.* Englewood Cliffs, NJ: Prentice Hall.

33. **Bandura, A.** (2006). Toward a psychology of human agency. *Perspectives on Psychological Science, 1,* 164–180.

34. **Presson, P. K., & Benassi, V. A.** (1996). Locus of control orientation and depressive symptomatology: A meta-analysis. *Journal of Social Behavior and Personality, 11,* 201–212.

35. **Lachman, M. E., & Weaver, S. L.** (1998). The sense of control as a moderator of social class differences in health and well-being. *Journal of Personality and Social Psychology, 74,* 763–773.

36. **Lefcourt, H. M.** (1982). *Locus of control: Current trends in theory and research.* Hillsdale, NJ: Erlbaum.

37. **Ng, W. W. H., Sorensen, K. L., & Elby, L. T.** (2006). Locus of control at work: A meta-analysis. *Journal of Organizational Behavior, 27,* 1057–1087.

38. **Miller, P. C., Lefcourt, H. M., Holmes, J. G., Ware, E. E., & Saleh, W. E.** (1986). Marital locus of control and marital problem solving. *Journal of Personality and Social Psychology, 51,* 161–169.

39. **Langer, E. J.** (1983). *The psychology of control.* Beverly Hills, CA: Sage.

40. **Seligman, M. E. P.** (1975). *Helplessness: On depression, development, and death.* San Francisco, CA: Freeman.

41. **Seligman, M. E. P.** (1991). *Learned optimism.* New York, NY: Knopf.

42. **Seligman, M. E. P.** (1975). *Helplessness: On depression, development, and death.* San Francisco, CA: Freeman.

43. **Rodin, J.** (1986). Aging and health: Effects of the sense of control. *Science, 223,* 1271–1276.

44. **Ruback, R. B., Carr, T. S., & Hopper, C. H.** (1986). Perceived control in prison: Its relation to reported crowding, stress, and symptoms. *Journal of Applied Social Psychology, 16,* 375–386.

45. **Inglehart, R.** (1990). *Culture shift in advanced industrial society.* Princeton, NJ: Princeton University Press.

46. **Inglehart, R.** (2009). Cultural changes and democracy in Latin America. In F. Hagopian (Ed.), *Contemporary Catholicism, religious pluralism, and democracy in Latin America* (pp. 67–95). South Bend, IN: Notre Dame University Press.

47. **Seligman, M. E. P.** (1999). The President's address (annual report). *American Psychologist, 54,* 559–562.

48. **Seligman, M. E. P., & Csikszentmihalyi, M.** (2000). Positive psychology: An introduction. *American Psychologist, 55,* 5–14.

49. **Seligman, M. E. P.** (1994). *What you can change and what you can't.* New York, NY: Knopf.

50. **Seligman, M. E. P.** (2002). *Authentic happiness: Using the new positive psychology to realize your potential for lasting fulfillment.* New York, NY: Free Press.

51. **Reivich, K. J.** (2010). Master resilience training (binder 1): Guidelines for teaching resilience to U.S. Army soldiers. Philadelphia, PA: The Trustees of the University of Pennsylvania.

52. **Weinstein, N. D.** (1980). Unrealistic optimism about future life events. *Journal of Personality and Social Psychology, 39,* 806–820.

53. **Weinstein, N. D.** (1982). Unrealistic optimism about susceptibility to health problems. *Journal of Behavioral Medicine, 5,* 441–460.

54. **Weinstein, N. D.** (1996, October 4). 1996 optimistic bias bibliography. Formerly distributed via Internet.

55. **Burger, J. M., & Burns, L.** (1988). The illusion of unique invulnerability and the use of effective contraception. *Personality and Social Psychology Bulletin, 14,* 264–270.

56. **Mischel, W.** (1981). Current issues and challenges in personality. In L. T. Benjamin, Jr. (Ed.), *The G. Stanley Hall Lecture Series* (Vol. 1, pp. 85–99). Washington, DC: American Psychological Association.

57. **Ouellette, J. A., & Wood, W.** (1998). Habit and intention in everyday life: The multiple processes by which past behavior predicts future behavior. *Psychological Bulletin, 124,* 54–74.

58. **Schmidt, F. L., & Hunter, J. E.** (1998). The validity and utility of selection methods in personnel psychology: Practical and theoretical implications of 85 years of research findings. *Psychological Bulletin, 124,* 262–274.

59. **Lowry, P. E.** (1997). The assessment center process: New directions. *Journal of Social Behavior and Personality, 12,* 53–62.

60. **Mischel, W.** (1993). Toward a cognitive social learning reconceptualization of personality. *Psychological Review, 102,* 252–253.

Module 31

1. **Wakefield, J. C.** (1997). Normal inability versus pathological disability: Why Ossorio's definition of mental disorder is not sufficient. *Clinical Psychology Science and Practice, 4,* 249–258.

2. **Wakefield, J. C.** (2006). What makes a mental disorder mental? *Philosophy, Psychiatry, and Psychology, 13,* 123–131.

3. **Brems, C., Thevenin, D. M., & Routh, D. K.** (1991). The history of clinical psychology. In C. E. Walker (Ed.), *Clinical psychology: Historical and research foundations* (pp. 3–35). New York, NY: Plenum Press.

4. **Schultz, D., & Schultz, S.** (2008). *A history of modern psychology* (9th ed.). Belmont, CA: Thomson.

5. **Beardsley, L. M.** (1994). Medical diagnosis and treatment across cultures. In W. J. Lonner & R. Malpass (Eds.), *Psychology and culture* (pp. 279–284). Boston, MA: Allyn & Bacon.

6. **Castillo, R. J.** (1997). *Culture and mental illness: A client-centered approach.* Pacific Grove, CA: Brooks/Cole.

7. **Riskind, J. H., Beck, A. T., Berchick, R. J., Brown, G., & Steer, R. A.** (1987). Reliability of DSM-III diagnosis for major depression and generalized anxiety disorder using the structured clinical interview for DSM-III. *Archives of General Psychiatry, 44,* 817–820.

8. **Kessler, R. C., & Zhao, S.** (1999). The prevalence of mental illness. In A. V. Horwitz & T. L. Scheid (Eds.), *Sociology of mental health and illness* (pp. 58–78). Cambridge, United Kingdom: Cambridge University Press.

9. **Peterson, C., & Seligman, M. E. P.** (2004). *Character strengths and virtues: A handbook and classification.* New York, NY: Oxford University Press.

10. **Peterson, C., & Seligman, M. E. P.** (2004). *Character strengths and virtues: A handbook and classification.* New York, NY: Oxford University Press.

11. **Peterson, C.** (2005). Personal correspondence.

12. **Farina, A., & Fisher, J. D.** (1982). Beliefs about mental disorders: Findings and implications. In G. Weary & H. L. Mirels (Eds.), *Integrations of clinical and social psychology* (pp. 37–64). New York, NY: Oxford University Press.

13. **Page, S.** (1977). Effects of the mental illness label in attempts to obtain accommodation. *Canadian Journal of Behavioral Science, 9,* 84–90.

14. **Rosenhan, D. L.** (1973). On being sane in insane places. *Science, 179,* 250–258.

15. **Langer, E. J., & Abelson, R. P.** (1974). A patient by any other name . . . : Clinician group differences in labeling bias. *Journal of Consulting and Clinical Psychology, 42,* 4–9.

16. **Langer, E. J., & Imber, L.** (1980). The role of mindlessness in the perception of deviance. *Journal of Personality and Social Psychology, 39,* 360–367.

17. **Baumeister, H., & Härter, M.** (2007). Prevalence of mental disorders based on general population surveys. *Social Psychiatry and Psychiatric Epidemiology, 42,* 537–546.

18. **Draguns, J. G.** (1990a). Applications of cross-cultural psychology in the field of mental health. In R. W. Brislin (Ed.), *Applied cross-cultural psychology* (pp. 302–324). Newbury Park, CA: Sage.

19. **Draguns, J. G.** (1990b). Normal and abnormal behavior in cross-cultural perspective: Specifying the nature of their relationship. *Nebraska Symposium on Motivation 1989, 37,* 235–277.

20. **Draguns, J. G.** (1997). Abnormal behavior patterns across cultures: Implications for counseling and psychotherapy. *International Journal of Intercultural Relations, 21,* 213–248.

21. **Substance Abuse and Mental Health Services Administration.** (2016). National survey on drug use and health. Retrieved from https://www.nimh.nih.gov/health/statistics/mental-illness.shtml

22. **Centers for Disease Control and Prevention** (1992, September 16). Serious mental illness and disability in the adult household population: United States, 1989. *Advance Data From Vital and Health Statistics* (No. 218). Hyattsville, MD: National Center for Health Statistics, Centers for Disease Control and Prevention, U.S. Department of Health and Human Services.

23. **Dohrenwend, B., Pevav, I., Shrout, P. E., Schwartz, S., Naveh, G., Link, B. G., . . . & Stueve, A.** (1992). Socioeconomic status and psychiatric disorders: The causation-selection issue. *Science, 255,* 946–952.

24. **Gerbner, G.** (1985). Growing up with television: The cultivation perspective. In J. Bryant & D. Zillman (Eds.), *Media effects: Advances in theory and research* (pp. 17–41). Hillsdale, NJ: Erlbaum.

25. **Steadman, H. J., Mulvey, E. P., Monahan, J., Robbins, P. C., Appelbaum, P. S., Grisso, T., ... & Silver, E.** (1998). Violence by people discharged from acute psychiatric inpatient facilities and by others in the same neighborhoods. *Archives of General Psychiatry, 55,* 393–401.

26. **Satcher, D.** (1999). Mental health: A report of the surgeon general. Retrieved from http://www.surgeongeneral.gov/library/mentalhealth/chapter1/sec1.html

27. **Rosenhan, D. L.** (1973). On being sane in insane places. *Science, 179,* 250–258.

28. **Spitzer, R. L., Gibbon, M., Skodol, A. E., Williams, J. B. W., & First, M. B.** (1989). *DSM-III-R casebook.* Washington, DC: American Psychiatric Press.

29. **World Health Organization.** (2004a). *Prevention of mental disorders: Effective interventions and policy options. Summary report.* Geneva, Switzerland: Author.

30. **World Health Organization.** (2004b). Prevalence, severity, and unmet need for treatment of mental disorders in the World Health Organization World Mental Health Surveys. *Journal of the American Medical Association, 291,* 2581–2590.

Module 32

1. **American Psychiatric Association.** (2013). *Diagnostic and statistical manual of mental disorders* (5th ed.). Arlington, VA: American Psychiatric Publishing.

2. **Olatunji, B. O., Cisler, J. M., & Tolin, D. F.** (2007). Quality of life in the anxiety disorders: A meta-analytic review. *Clinical Psychology Review, 27,* 572–581.

3. **Kashdan, T. B., & Steger, M. F.** (2006). Expanding the topography of social anxiety: An experience-sampling assessment of positive emotions, positive events, and emotion suppression. *Psychological Science, 17,* 120–128.

4. **Carey, G.** (1990). Genes, fears, phobias, and phobic disorders. *Journal of Counseling and Development, 68,* 628–632.

5. **Eckert, E. D., Heston, L. L., & Bouchard, T. J., Jr.** (1981). MZ twins reared apart: Preliminary findings of psychiatric disturbances and traits. In L. Gedda, P. Paris, & W. D. Nance (Eds.), *Twin research: Intelligence, personality, and development* (Vol. 3, Pt. B). New York, NY: Alan Liss.

6. **Suomi, S. J.** (1986). Anxiety-like disorders in young nonhuman primates. In R. Gettleman (Ed.), *Anxiety disorders of childhood.* New York, NY: Guilford Press.

7. **Hovatta, I., Tennant, R. S., Helton, R., Marr, R. A., Singer, O., Redwine, J. M., ... & Barlow, C.** (2005). Glyoxalase 1 and glutathione reductase 1 regulate anxiety in mice. *Nature, 438,* 662–666.

8. **Etkin, A., & Wager, T. D.** (2007). Functional neuroimaging of anxiety: A meta-analysis of emotional processing in PTSD, social anxiety disorder, and specific phobia. *American Journal of Psychiatry, 164,* 1476–1488.

9. **Kolassa, I.-T., & Elbert, T.** (2007). Structural and functional neuroplasticity in relation to traumatic stress. *Current Directions in Psychological Science, 16,* 321–325.

10. **Maren, S.** (2007). The threatened brain. *Science, 317,* 1043–1044.

11. **LoBue, V., & DeLoache, J. S.** (2008). Detecting the snake in the grass: Attention to fear-relevant stimuli by adults and young children. *Psychological Science, 19,* 284–289.

12. **Watson, J. B., & Rayner, R.** (1920). Conditioned emotional reactions. *Journal of Experimental Psychology, 3,* 1–14.

13. **Field, A. P.** (2006). Is conditioning a useful framework for understanding the development and treatment of phobias? *Clinical Psychology Review, 26,* 857–875.

14. **Mineka, S., & Zinbarg, R.** (2006). A contemporary learning theory perspective on the etiology of anxiety disorders: It's not what you thought it was. *American Psychologist, 61,* 10–26.

15. **Mineka, S.** (1985). The frightful complexity of the origins of fears. In F. R. Brush & J. B. Overmier (Eds.), *Affect, conditioning and cognition: Essays on the determinants of behavior.* Hillsdale, NJ: Erlbaum.

16. **Ozer, E. J., & Weiss, D. S.** (2004). Who develops posttraumatic stress disorder? *Current Directions in Psychological Science, 13,* 169–172.

17. **Bonanno, G. A.** (2004). Loss, trauma, and human resilience: Have we underestimated the human capacity to thrive after extremely aversive events? *American Psychologist, 59,* 20–28.

18. **Bonanno, G. A.** (2005). Adult resilience to potential trauma. *Current Directions in Psychological Science, 14,* 135–137.

19. **Seligman, M. E. P., Ernst, R. M., Gillham, J., Reivich, K., & Linkins, M.** (2009). Positive education: Positive psychology and classroom interventions. *Oxford Review of Education, 35,* 293–311.

20. **Casey, G. W., Jr.** (2011). Comprehensive soldier fitness: A vision for psychological resilience in the U.S. Army. *American Psychologist, 66,* 1–3.

21. **Ernst, R. E.** Personal correspondence, 2/13/18.

22. **Ursu, S., Stenger, V. A., Shear, M. K., Jones, M. R., & Carter, C. S.** (2003). Overactive action monitoring in obsessive-compulsive disorder: Evidence from functional magnetic resonance imaging. *Psychological Science, 14,* 347–353.

23. **American Psychiatric Association.** (2013). *Diagnostic and statistical manual of mental disorders* (5th ed.). Arlington, VA: American Psychiatric Publishing.

24. **Susser, E. S., Herman, D. B., & Aaron, B.** (2002, August). Combating the terror of terrorism. *Scientific American,* pp. 70–77.

25. **Bonanno, G. A., Galea, S., Bucciarelli, A., & Vlahov, D.** (2006). Psychological resilience after disaster. *Psychological Science, 17,* 181–186.

26. **Seal, K. H., Bertenthal, D., Miner, C. R., Sen, S., & Marmar, C.** (2007). Bringing the war back home: Mental health disorders among 103,788 U.S. veterans returning from Iraq and Afghanistan seen at Department of Veterans Affairs facilities. *Archives of Internal Medicine, 167,* 467–482.

27. **McNally, R. J.** (2012). Are we winning the war against posttraumatic stress disorder? *Science, 336,* 872–874.

28. **King, D. W., King, L. A., Park, C. L., Lee, L. O., Pless Kaiser, A., Spiro, A., ... Keane, T. M.** (2015). Positive adjustment among American repatriated prisoners of the Vietnam War: Modeling the long-term effects of captivity. *Clinical Psychological Science, 3,* 861–876.

29. **Gilbertson, M. W., Paulus, L. A., Williston, S. K., Gurvits, T. V., Lasko, N. B., Pitman, R. K., & Orr, S. P.** (2006). Neurocognitive function in monozygotic twins discordant for combat exposure: Relationship to posttraumatic stress disorder. *Journal of Abnormal Psychology, 115,* 484–495.

30. **Olff, M., Langeland, W., Draijer, N., & Gersons, B.P. R.** (2007). Gender differences in posttraumatic stress disorder. *Psychological Bulletin, 135,* 183–204.

31. **Ozer, E. J., & Weiss, D. S.** (2004). Who develops posttraumatic stress disorder? *Current Directions in Psychological Science, 13,* 169–172.

32. **Wakefield, J. C., Schmitz, M. F., First, M. B., & Horwitz, A. V.** (2007). Extending the bereavement exclusion for major depression to other losses: Evidence from the National Comorbidity Survey. *Archives of General Psychiatry, 64,* 433–440.

33. **Watkins, E. R.** (2008). Constructive and unconstructive repetitive thought. *Psychological Bulletin, 134,* 163–206.

34. **WHO** (2017b). *Depression.* World Health Organization. Retrieved from who.int/mediacentre/factsheets/fs369/en

35. **Thornicroft, G., Chatterji, S., Evans-Lacko, S., Gruber, M., Sampson, N., Aguilar-Gaxiola, S., ... Bruffaerts, R.** (2017). Undertreatment of people with major depressive disorder in 21 countries. *British Journal of Psychiatry, 210,* 119–124.

36. **American Psychiatric Association.** (2013). *Diagnostic and statistical manual of mental disorders* (5th ed.). Arlington, VA: American Psychiatric Publishing.

37. **CDC.** (2008). National Youth Risk Behavior Survey overview. Centers for Disease Control and Prevention (www.cdc.gov).

38. **American College Health Association** (2006). American College Health Association National College Health Assessment. Baltimore, MD: Author. Retrieved from http://acha-ncha.org

39. **American Psychiatric Association.** (2013). *Diagnostic and statistical manual of mental disorders* (5th ed.). Arlington, VA: American Psychiatric Publishing.

40. **Tsuang, M. T., & Faraone, S. V.** (1990). *The genetics of mood disorders.* Baltimore, MD: Johns Hopkins University Press.

41. **Davidson, R. J., Pizzagalli, D., Nitschke, J. B., & Putnam, K.** (2002). Depression: Perspectives from affective neuroscience. *Annual Review of Psychology, 53,* 545–574.

42. **Moffitt, T. E., Caspi, A., & Rutter, M.** (2006). Measured gene-environment interactions in psychopathology: Concepts, research strategies, and implications for research, intervention, and public understanding of genetics. *Perspectives on Psychological Science, 1,* 5–27.

43. **Hankin, B. L., & Abramson, L. Y.** (2001). Development of gender differences in depression: An elaborated cognitive vulnerability-transactional stress theory. *Psychological Bulletin, 127,* 773–796.

44. **Mazure, C., Keita, G., & Blehar, M.** (2002). *Summit on women and depression: Proceedings and recommendations.* Washington, DC: American Psychological Association. Retrieved from http://www.apa.org/pi/wpo/women&depression.pdf

45. **Abramson, L. Y., Metalsky, G. I., & Alloy, L. B.** (1989). Hopelessness depression: A theory-based subtype. *Psychological Review, 96,* 358–372.

46. **Panzarella, C., Alloy, L. B., & Whitehouse, W. G.** (2006). Expanded hopelessness theory of depression: On the mechanisms by which social support protects against depression. *Cognitive Theory and Research, 30,* 307–333.

47. **Kessler, R. C., Akiskal, H. S., Ames, M., Birnbaum, H., Greenberg, P., Hirschfeld, R. M. A., ... & Wang, P. S.** (2006). Prevalence and effects of mood disorders on work performance in a nationally representative sample of U.S. workers. *American Journal of Psychiatry, 163,* 1561–1568.

48. **Jamison, K. R.** (1993). *Touched with fire: Manic-depressive illness and the artistic temperament.* New York, NY: Free Press.

49. **Jamison, K. R.** (1995, February). Manic-depressive illness and creativity. *Scientific American,* pp. 62–67.

50. **Chu, C., Podlogar, M. C., Hagan, C. R., Buchman-Schmitt, J. M., Silva, C., Chiurliza, B., ... Joiner, T. E.** (2016). The interactive effects of the capability for suicide and major depressive episodes on suicidal behavior in a military sample. *Cognitive Therapy and Research, 40,* 22–30.

51. **Schaffer, A., Isometsa, E. T., Tondo, L., Moreno, D., Turecki, G., Reis, C., ... Ha, K.** (2015). International society for bipolar disorders task force on suicide: Meta-analyses and meta-regression of correlates of suicide attempts and suicide deaths in bipolar disorder. *Bipolar Disorders, 17,* 1–16.

52. **WHO.** (2014b). *Global status report on alcohol and health 2014.* World Health Organization (who.int/substance_abuse/publications/global_alcohol_report/msb_gsr_2014_1.pdf).

53. **Bostwick, J. M., & Pankratz, V. S.** (2000). Affective disorders and suicide risk: A re-examination. *American Journal of Psychiatry, 157,* 1925–1932.

54. **Kanwar, A., Malik, S., Prokop, L. J., Sim, L. A., Feldstein, D., Wang, Z., & Murad, M. H.** (2013). The association between anxiety disorders and suicidal behaviors: A systematic review and meta-analysis. *Depression and Anxiety, 30,* 917–929.

55. **WHO.** (2011). Country reports and charts available. Geneva: World Health Organization. Retrieved from int/mental_health/prevention/suicide/country_reports/en/index.html

56. **WHO.** (2011). Country reports and charts available. Geneva: World Health Organization. Retrieved from int/mental_health/prevention/suicide/country_reports/en/index.html

57. **CDC** (2012, May 11). *Suicide rates among persons ages 10 years and older, by race/ethnicity and sex, United States, 2005–2009.* National Suicide Statistics at a Glance, Centers for Disease Control and Prevention (cdc.gov).

58. **Eckersley, R., & Dear, K.** (2002). Correlates of youth suicide. *Social Science and Medicine, 55,* 1891–1935.

59. **Murphy, G. E., & Wetzel, R. D.** (1990). The lifetime risk of suicide in alcoholism. *Archives of General Psychiatry, 47,* 383–392.

60. **CDC** (2009). *Self-harm, all injury causes, nonfatal injuries and rates per 100,000.* National Center for Injury Prevention and Control. Retrieved from webappa.cdc.gov/cgibin/broker.exe

61. **Liu, R. T., Cheek, S. M., & Nestor, B. A.** (2016). Nonsuicidal self-injury and life stress: A systematic meta-analysis and theoretical elaboration. *Clinical Psychology Review, 47,* 1–14.

62. **van Geel, M., Goemans, A., & Vedder, P.** (2015). A meta-analysis on the relation between peer victimization and adolescent non-suicidal self-injury. *Psychiatry Research, 230*(2), 364–368.

63. **Hawton, K., Bergen, H., Cooper, J., Turnbull, P., Waters, K., Ness, J., & Kapur, N.** (2015). Suicide following self-harm: Findings from the Multicentre Study of Self-harm in England, 2000–2012. *Journal of Affective Disorders, 175,* 147–151.

64. **Runeson, B., Haglund, Lichtenstein, P., & Tidemalm, C.** (2016). Suicide risk after nonfatal self-harm: A national cohort study, 2000–2008. *Journal of Clinical Psychiatry, 77,* 240–256.

65. **Willoughby, T., Heffer, T., & Hamza, C. A.** (2015). The link between nonsuicidal self-injury and acquired capability for suicide: A longitudinal study. *Journal of Abnormal Psychology, 124,* 1110–1115.

66. **Robins, L., & Regier, D.** (Eds.). (1991). *Psychiatric disorders in America.* New York, NY: Free Press.

Module 33

1. **Spitzer, R. L., Gibbon, M., Skodol, A. E., Williams, J. B. W., & First, M. B.** (1989). *DSM-III-R casebook.* Washington, DC: American Psychiatric Press.

2. **Spitzer, R. L., Gibbon, M., Skodol, A. E., Williams, J. B. W., & First, M. B.** (1989). *DSM-III-R casebook.* Washington, DC: American Psychiatric Press.

3. **Spitzer, R. L., Gibbon, M., Skodol, A. E., Williams, J. B. W., & First, M. B.** (2002). *DSM-IV-TR casebook: A learning companion to the Diagnostic and Statistical Manual of Mental Disorders, Fourth Edition, Text Revision.* Washington, DC: American Psychiatric Press.

4. **Spitzer, R. L., Gibbon, M., Skodol, A. E., Williams, J. B. W., & First, M. B.** (1989). *DSM-III-R casebook.* Washington, DC: American Psychiatric Press.

5. **van der Hart, O., Brown, P., & Graafland, M.** (1999). Trauma-induced dissociative amnesia in World War I combat soldiers. *Australian and New Zealand Journal of Psychiatry, 33,* 37–46.

6. **Kihlstrom, J. F., Tataryn, D. J., & Hoyt, I. P.** (1993). Dissociative disorders. In P. B. Sucker & H. E. Adams (Eds.), *Comprehensive handbook of psychopathology* (2nd ed., pp. 203–234). New York, NY: Plenum Press.

7. **Spitzer, R. L., Gibbon, M., Skodol, A. E., Williams, J. B. W., & First, M. B.** (1989). *DSM-III-R casebook.* Washington, DC: American Psychiatric Press.

8. **Elzinga, B. M., Ardon, A. M., Heijnis, M. K., De Ruiter, M. B., Van Dyck, R., & Veltman, D. J.** (2007). Neural correlates of enhanced working-memory performance in dissociative disorder: A functional MRI study. *Psychological Medicine, 37,* 235–245.

9. **Putnam, F. W.** (1991). Recent research on multiple personality disorder. *Psychiatric Clinics of North America, 14,* 489–502.

10. **Henninger, P.** (1992). Conditional handedness: Handedness changes in multiple personality disordered subject reflect shift in hemispheric dominance. *Consciousness and Cognition, 1,* 265–287.

11. **McHugh, P. R.** (1995). Resolved: Multiple personality disorder is an individually and socially created artifact. *Journal of the American Academy of Child and Adolescent Psychiatry, 34,* 957–959.

12. **Goff, D. C., & Simms, C. A.** (1993). Has multiple personality disorder remained consistent over time? *Journal of Nervous and Mental Disease, 181,* 595–600.

13. **Kihlstrom, J. F.** (2005). Dissociative disorders. *Annual Review of Clinical Psychology, 1,* 227–253.

14. **Nathan, D.** (2011). *Sybil exposed: The extraordinary story behind the famous multiple personality case.* New York: Simon & Schuster.

15. **Johnson, S. K.** (2008). *Medically unexplained illness: Gender and biopsychosocial implications.* Washington, DC: American Psychological Association.

16. **WHO** (2017a). *Mental disorders.* World Health Organization. Retrieved from who.int/mediacentre/factsheets/fs396/en

17. **Aleman, A., Kahn, R. S., & Selten, J. P.** (2003). Sex differences in the risk of schizophrenia: Evidence from meta-analysis. *Archives of General Psychiatry, 60,* 565–571.

18. **Picchioni, M. M., & Murray, R. M.** (2007). Schizophrenia. *British Medical Journal, 335,* 91–95.

19. **Reichenberg, A., & Harvey, P. D.** (2007). Neuropsychological impairments in schizophrenia: Integration of performance-based and brain imaging findings. *Psychological Bulletin, 133,* 833–858.

20. **Plomin, R., Fulker, D. W., Corley, R., & DeFries, J. C.** (1997). Nature, nurture, and cognitive development from 1 to 16 years: A parent-offspring adoption study. *Psychological Science, 8,* 442–447.

21. **Marx, J.** (2007). Evidence linking *DISC1* gene to mental illness builds. *Science, 318,* 1062–1063.

22. **Millar, J. K., Pickard, B. S., Mackie, S., James, R., Christie, S., Buchanan, S. R., . . . Porteous, D. J.** (2005). DISC1 and PDE4B are interacting genetic factors in schizophrenia that regulate cAMP signaling. *Science, 310,* 1187–1191.

23. **Williams, H. J., Owen, M. J., & O'Donovan, M. C.** (2007). Is *COMT* a susceptibility gene for schizophrenia? *Schizophrenia Bulletin, 33,* 635–641.

24. **Wright, I. C., Rabe-Hesketh, S., Woodruff, P. W. R., David, A. S., Murray, R. M., & Bullmore, E. T.** (2000). Meta-analysis of regional brain volumes in schizophrenia. *American Journal of Psychiatry, 157,* 16–25.

25. **Andreasen, N. C., Arndt, S., Swayze, V., II, Cizadlo, T., & Flaum, M.** (1994). Thalamic abnormalities in schizophrenia visualized through magnetic resonance image averaging. *Science, 266,* 294–298.

26. **Morey, R. A., Inan, S., Mitchell, T. V., Perkins, D. O., Lieberman, J. A., & Belger, A.** (2005). Imaging frontostriatal function in ultra-high-risk, early, and chronic schizophrenia during executive processing. *Archives of General Psychiatry, 62,* 254–262.

27. **Resnick, S. M.** (1992). Positron emission tomography in psychiatric illness. *Current Directions in Psychological Science, 1,* 92–98.

28. **Seeman, P., Guan, H. C., & Van Tol, H. H. M.** (1993). Dopamine D4 receptors elevated in schizophrenia. *Nature, 365,* 441–445.

29. **Javitt, D. C, & Coyle, J. T.** (2004, January). Decoding schizophrenia. *Scientific American,* pp. 48–55.

30. **Patterson, P. H.** (2007). Maternal effects on schizophrenia risk. *Science, 318,* 576–577.

31. **Mednick, S. A., Huttunen, M. O., & Machon, R. A.** (1994). Prenatal influenza infections and adult schizophrenia. *Schizophrenia Bulletin, 20,* 263–267.

32. **Torrey, E. F., Miller, J., Rawlings, R., & Yolken, R. H.** (1997). Seasonality of births in schizophrenia and bipolar disorder: A review of the literature. *Schizophrenia Research, 28,* 1–38.

33. **McGrath, J. J., & Welham, J. L.** (1999). Season of birth and schizophrenia: A systematic review and meta-analysis of data from the Southern Hemisphere. *Schizophrenia Research, 35,* 237–242.

34. **Fromm-Reichmann, F.** (1948). Notes on the development of treatment of schizophrenia by psychoanalytic therapy. *Psychiatry, 11,* 263–273.

35. **Johnstone, E. C., Ebmeier, K. P., Miller, P., Owens, D. G. C., & Lawrie, S. M.** (2005). Predicting schizophrenia: Findings from the Edinburgh High-Risk Study. *British Journal of Psychiatry, 186,* 18–25.

36. **Cale, E. M., & Lilienfeld, S. O.** (2002). Sex differences in psychopathy and antisocial personality disorder: A review and integration. *Clinical Psychology Review, 22,* 1179–1207.

37. **Darrach, B., & Norris, J.** (1984, August). An American tragedy. *Life,* pp. 58–74.

Domain 7

Module 34

1. **Frank, J. D.** (1982). Therapeutic components shared by all psychotherapies. In J. H. Harvey & M. M. Parks (Eds.), *The Master Lecture Series: Psychotherapy research and behavior change* (Vol. 1, pp. 73–122). Washington, DC: American Psychological Association.

2. **Myers, D. G.** (2011). *Myers' psychology for AP.* New York, NY: Worth.

3. **Parloff, M. B.** (1987, February). Psychotherapy: An import from Japan. *Psychology Today,* pp. 74–75.

4. **PINE Psychoanalytic Center.** (2018). http://www.pineanalysis.org/content/frequently-asked-questions#faq9

5. **Smith, S. B.** (1999). *Diana in search of herself: Portrait of a troubled princess.* New York, NY: Times Books.

6. **Weissman, M. M.** (1999). Interpersonal psychotherapy and the health care scene. In D. S. Janowsky (Ed.), *Psychotherapy indications and outcomes* (pp. 213–231). Washington, DC: American Psychiatric Press.

7. **Eastman, C. L., Young, M. A., Fogg, L. F., Liu, L., & Meaden, P. M.** (1998). Bright light treatment of winter depression: A placebo-controlled trial. *Archives of General Psychiatry, 55,* 883–889.

8. **Lewy, A. J., Bauer, V. K., Cutler, N. L., Sack, R. L., Ahmed, S., Thomas, K. H., . . . & Jackson, J. M. L.** (1998). Morning vs evening light treatment of patients with winter depression. *Archives of General Psychiatry, 55,* 890–896.

9. **Traffanstedt, M K., Mehta, S., & LoBello, S. G.** (2016). http://journals.sagepub.com/doi/abs/10.1177/2167702615615867

10. **Duke, M., & Nowicki, S., Jr.** (1979). *Abnormal psychology: Perspectives on being different.* Pacific Grove, CA: Brooks/Cole.

11. **Jones, M. C.** (1924). A laboratory study of fear: The case of Peter. *Journal of Genetic Psychology, 31,* 308–315.

12. **Wolpe, J.** (1958). *Psychotherapy by reciprocal inhibition.* Stanford, CA: Stanford University Press.

13. **Wolpe, J., & Plaud, J. J.** (1997). Pavlov's contribution to behavior therapy: The obvious and the not so obvious. *American Psychologist, 52,* 966–972.

14. **Foa, E. B., & Kozak, M. J.** (1986). Emotional processing of fear: Exposure to corrective information. *Psychological Bulletin, 99,* 20–35.

15. **Williams, S. L.** (1987, August). *Self-efficacy and mastery-oriented treatment for severe phobias.* Paper presented to the American Psychological Association convention, Atlanta, GA.

16. **Gregg, L., & Tarrier, N.** (2007). Virtual reality in mental health: A review of the literature. *Social Psychiatry and Psychiatric Epidemiology, 42,* 343–354.

17. **North, M. M., North, S. M., & Coble, J. R.** (1998). Virtual reality therapy: An effective treatment for phobias. In G. Riva, B. K. Wiederhold, & E. Molinari (Eds.), *Virtual environments in clinical psychology and neuroscience: Methods and techniques in advanced patient-therapist interaction* (pp. 112–119). Amsterdam, Netherlands: IOS Press.

18. **Powers, M. B., & Emmelkamp, P. M. G.** (2008). Virtual reality exposure therapy for anxiety disorders: A meta-analysis. *Journal of Anxiety Disorders, 22,* 561–569.

19. **Page, S., & Coxon, M.** (2016). Virtual Reality Exposure Therapy for Anxiety Disorders: Small Samples and No Controls? *National Center for Biotechnology Information.* Retrieved from https://www.ncbi.nlm.nih.gov/pmc/articles/PMC4786550/

20. **Rothbaum, B. O.** (2006). Virtual reality exposure therapy. In B. O. Rothbaum (Ed.), *Pathological anxiety: Emotional processing in etiology and treatment* (pp. 227–244). New York, NY: Guilford.

21. **Rothbaum, B. O., Hodges, L., Kooper, R., Opdyke, D., Williford, J., & North, M. M.** (1995). Effectiveness of computer-generated (virtual reality) graded exposure in the treatment of acrophobia. *American Journal of Psychiatry, 152,* 626–628.

22. **Rothbaum, B. O., Hodges, L., & Kooper, R.** (1997). Virtual reality exposure therapy. *Journal of Psychotherapy Practice and Research, 6,* 219–226.

23. **Vincelli, F., & Molinari, E.** (1998). Virtual reality and imaginative techniques in clinical psychology. In G. Riva, B. K. Wiederhold, & E. Molinari (Eds.), *Virtual environments in clinical psychology and neuroscience: Methods and techniques in advanced patient-therapist interaction* (pp. 67–72). Amsterdam, Netherlands: IOS Press.

24. **Gorini, A.** (2007). Virtual worlds, real healing. *Science, 318,* 1549.

25. **Bandura, A., Blanchard, E. B., & Ritter, B.** (1969). Relative efficacy of desensitization and modeling approaches for inducing behavioral, affective, and attitudinal changes. *Journal of Personality and Social Psychology, 13,* 173–199.

26. **Wiens, A. N., & Menustik, C. E.** (1983). Treatment outcome and patient characteristics in an aversion therapy program for alcoholism. *American Psychologist, 38,* 1089–1096.

27. **Lovaas, O. I.** (1987). Behavioral treatment and normal educational and intellectual functioning in young autistic children. *Journal of Consulting and Clinical Psychology, 55,* 3–9.

28. **Mayne, T. J., Norcross, J. C., & Sayette, M. A.** (1994). Admission requirements, acceptance rates, and financial assistance in clinical psychology programs. *American Psychologist, 49,* 806–811.

29. **Rabin, A. S., Kaslow, N. J., & Rehm, L. P.** (1986, August). *Aggregate outcome and follow-up results following self-control therapy for depression.* Paper presented at the American Psychological Association convention, Washington, DC.

30. **Seligman, M. E. P.** (2002). *Authentic happiness: Using the new positive psychology to realize your potential for lasting fulfillment.* New York, NY: Free Press.

31. **Seligman, M. E. P., Ernst, R. M., Gillham, J., Reivich, K., & Linkins, M.** (2009). Positive education: Positive psychology and classroom interventions. *Oxford Review of Education, 35,* 293–311.

32. **Moses, E. B., & Barlow, D. H.** (2006). A new unified treatment approach for emotional disorders based on emotion science. *Current Directions in Psychological Science, 15,* 146–150.

33. **Schwartz, J. M., Stoessel, P. W., Baxter, L. R., Jr., Martin, K. M., & Phelps, M. E.** (1996). Systematic changes in cerebral glucose metabolic rate after successful behavior modification treatment of obsessive-compulsive disorder. *Archives of General Psychiatry, 53,* 109–113.

34. **Covin, R., Oimet, A. J., Seeds, P. M., & Dozois, D. J. A.** (2008). A meta-analysis of CBT for pathological worry among clients with GAD. *Journal of Anxiety Disorders, 22,* 108–116.

35. **Mitte, K.** (2005). Meta-analysis of cognitive-behavioral treatments for generalized anxiety disorder: A comparison with pharmacotherapy. *Psychological Bulletin, 131,* 785–795.

36. **Norton, P. J., & Price, E. C.** (2007). A meta-analytic review of adult cognitive-behavioral treatment outcome across the anxiety disorders. *Journal of Nervous and Mental Disease, 195,* 521–531.

37. **Yalom, I. D.** (1985). *The theory and practice of group psychotherapy* (3rd ed.). New York, NY: Basic Books.

38. **Hazelrigg, M. D., Cooper, H. M., & Borduin, C. M.** (1987). Evaluating the effectiveness of family therapies: An integrative review and analysis. *Psychological Bulletin, 101,* 428–442.

39. **Shadish, W. R., Montgomery, L. M., Wilson, P., Wilson, M. R., Bright, I., & Okwumabua, T.** (1993). Effects of family and marital psychotherapies: A meta-analysis. *Journal of Consulting and Clinical Psychology, 61,* 992–1002.

40. **Ferri, M., Amato, L., & Davoli, M.** (2006). Alcoholics Anonymous and other 12-step programmes for alcohol dependence. *Cochrane Database of Systematic Reviews,* (3), CD005032.

41. **Moos, R. H., & Moos, B. S.** (2005). Sixteen-year changes and stable remission among treated and untreated individuals with alcohol use disorders. *Drug and Alcohol Dependence, 80,* 337–347.

42. **Gallup, G. H., Jr.** (1994, October). Millions finding care and support in small groups. *Emerging Trends,* pp. 2–5.

Module 35

1. **Bureau of the Census.** (2004). *Statistical abstract of the United States 2002.* Washington, DC: U.S. Government Printing Office.

2. **National Coalition for the Homeless** (2009). http://www.nationalhomeless.org/factsheets/Mental_Illness.pdf

3. **National Alliance on Mental Illness** (retrieved 2/27/2018). https://www.nami.org/Learn-More/Mental-Health-Public-Policy/Jailing-People-with-Mental-Illness

4. **Lehman, A. F., Steinwachs, D. M., Dixon, L. B., Goldman, H. H., Osher, F., Postrado, L., . . . & Zito, J.** (1998). Translating research into practice: The Schizophrenia Patient Outcomes Research Team (PORT) treatment recommendations. *Schizophrenia Bulletin, 24,* 1–10.

5. **Kaplan, H. I., & Saddock, B. J. (Eds.).** (1989). *Comprehensive textbook of psychiatry* (Vol. 5). Baltimore, MD: Williams & Wilkins.

6. **Wetherell, J. L., Petkus, A. J., White, K. S., Nguyen, H., Kornblith, S., Andreescu, C., . . . Lenze, E. J.** (2013). Antidepressant medication augmented with cognitive-behavioral therapy for generalized anxiety disorder in older adults. *American Journal of Psychiatry, 170,* 782–789.

7. **Winerman, L.** (2017). By the numbers: Antidepressant use on the rise. Retrieved from http://www.apa.org/monitor/2017/11/numbers.aspx

8. **Grimm, S., & Scheidegger, M.** (2013, May/June). A trip out of depression. *Scientific American Mind,* pp. 67–71.

9. **McGirr, A., Berlim, M. T., Bond, D. J., Fleck, M. P., Yatham, L. N., & Lam, R. W.** (2015). A systematic review and meta-analysis of randomized, double-blind, placebo-controlled trials of ketamine in the rapid treatment of major depressive episodes. *Psychological Medicine, 45,* 693–704.

10. **Naughton, M., Clarke, G., O'Leary, O. F, Cryan, J. F., & Dinan, T. G.** (2014). A review of ketamine in affective disorders: Current evidence of clinical efficacy, limitations of use and pre-clinical evidence on proposed mechanisms of action. *Journal of Affective Disorders, 156,* 24–35.

11. **Kishimoto, T., Chawla, J. M., Hagi, K., Zarate, C. A. J., Kane, J. M., Bauer, M., & Correll, C. U.** (2016). Single-dose infusion ketamine and non-ketamine N-methyl-D-aspartate receptor antagonists for unipolar and bipolar depression: A meta-analysis of efficacy, safety and time trajectories. *Psychological Medicine, 46,* 1459–1472.

12. **Kirsch, I., & Sapirstein, G.** (1998). Listening to Prozac but hearing placebo: A meta-analysis of antidepressant medication. *Prevention and Treatment, 1.* Retrieved from http://www .apa.org/pubs/journals/index.aspx

13. **Fournier, J. C., DeRubeis, R. J., Hollon, S. D., Dimidjian, S., Amsterdam, J. D., Shelton, R. C., & Fawcett, J.** (2010). Antidepressant drug effects and depression severity: A patient-level meta-analysis. *Journal of the American Medical Association, 303,* 47–53.

14. **Kirsch, I., Deacon, B. J., Huedo-Medina, T. B., Scoboria, A., Moore, T. J., & Johnson, B. T.** (2008). Initial severity and antidepressant benefits: A meta-analysis of data submitted to the Food and Drug Administration. *Public Library of Science Medicine, 5,* e45.

15. **Olfson, M., & Marcus, S. C.** (2009). National patterns in antidepressant medication treatment. *Archives of General Psychiatry, 66,* 848–856.

16. **Gibbons, R. D., Brown, C. H., Hur, K., Marcus, S. M., Bhaumik, D. K., & Mann, J. J.** (2007). Relationship between antidepressants and suicide attempts: An analysis of the Veterans Health Administration data sets. *American Journal of Psychiatry, 164,* 1044–1049.

17. **Simon, G. E., & Savarino, J.** (2007). Suicide attempts among patients starting depression treatment with medications or psychotherapy. *American Journal of Psychiatry, 164,* 1029–1034.

18. **Søndergård, L., Kvist, K., Andersen, P. K., & Kessing, L. V.** (2006). Do antidepressants prevent suicide? *International Clinical Psychopharmacology, 21,* 211–218.

19. **Solomon, D. A., Keitner, G. I., Miller, I. W., Shea, M. T., & Keller, M. B.** (1995). Course of illness and maintenance treatments for patients with bipolar disorder. *Journal of Clinical Psychiatry, 56,* 5–13.

20. **Pagnin, D., de Queiroz, V., Pini, S., & Cassano, G. B.** (2004). Efficacy of ECT in depression: A meta-analytic review. *Journal of ECT, 20,* 13–20.

21. **HMHL** (2007, February). Electroconvulsive therapy. *Harvard Mental Health Letter,* Harvard Medical School, pp. 1–4.

22. **Joshi, S. H., Espinoza, R. T., Pirnia, T., Shi, J., Wang, Y., Ayers, B., . . . Narr, K. L.** (2016). Structural plasticity of the hippocampus and amygdala induced by electroconvulsive therapy in major depression. *Biological Psychiatry, 79,* 282–292.

23. **Rotheneichner, P., Lange, S., O'Sullivan, A., Marschallinger, J., Zaunmair, P., Geretsegger, C., . . . Couillard-Despres, S.** (2014). Hippocampal neurogenesis and antidepressive therapy: Shocking relations. *Neural Plasticity, 2014,* 723915.

24. **George, M. S., & Belmaker, R. H. (Eds.).** (2007). *Transcranial magnetic stimulation in clinical psychiatry.* Washington, DC: American Psychiatric Publishing.

25. **Gross, M., Nakamura, L., Pascual-Leone, A., & Fregni, F.** (2007). Has repetitive transcranial magnetic stimulation (rTMS) treatment for depression improved? A systematic review and meta-analysis comparing the recent vs. the earlier rTMS studies. *Acta Psychiatrica Scandinavica, 116,* 165–173.

26. **Klein, E., Kreinin, I., Chistyakov, A., Koren, D., Mecz, L., Marmur, S., . . . & Feinsod, M.** (1999). Therapeutic efficacy of right prefrontal slow repetitive transcranial magnetic stimulation in major depression. *Archives of General Psychiatry, 56,* 315–320.

27. **O'Reardon, J. P., Solvason, H. B., Janicak, P. G., Sampson, S., Isenberg, K. E., Nahas, Z., . . . & Sackeim, H. A.** (2007). Efficacy and safety of transcranial magnetic stimulation in the acute treatment of major depression: A multisite randomized controlled trial. *Biological Psychiatry, 62,* 1208–1216.

28. **Valenstein, E. S.** (1986). *Great and desperate cures: The rise and decline of psychosurgery.* New York, NY: Basic Books.

29. **Sachdev, P., & Sachdev, J.** (1997). Sixty years of psychosurgery: Its present status and its future. *Australian and New Zealand Journal of Psychiatry, 31,* 457–464.

30. **Seligman, M. E. P., & Csikszentmihalyi, M.** (2000). Positive psychology: An introduction. *American Psychologist, 55,* 5–14.

Module 36

1. **Carroll, J.** (2008, January 2). Time pressures, stress common for Americans. Gallup Poll News Service. Retrieved from http://www.gallup.com

2. **Cannon, W. B.** (1929). *Bodily changes in pain, hunger, fear, and rage.* New York, NY: Branford.

3. **Selye, H.** (1936). A syndrome produced by diverse nocuous agents. *Nature, 138,* 32.

4. **Selye, H.** (1976). *The stress of life.* New York, NY: McGraw-Hill.

5. **Sapolsky, R.** (1999, March). Stress and your shrinking brain. *Discover,* pp. 116–120.

6. **Sapolsky, R.** (2003, September). Taming stress. *Scientific American,* pp. 87–95.

7. **Segerstrom, S. C.** (2007). Stress, energy, and immunity. *Current Directions in Psychological Science, 16,* 326–330.

8. **Kohn, P. M., & Macdonald, J. E.** (1992). The survey of recent life experiences: A decontaminated hassles scale for adults. *Journal of Behavioral Medicine, 15,* 221–236.

9. **Lazarus, R. S.** (1990). Theory-based stress measurement. *Psychological Inquiry, 1,* 3–13.

10. **Ruffin, C. L.** (1993). Stress and health—Little hassles vs. major life events. *Australian Psychologist, 28,* 201–208.

11. **Miller, G. E., & Wrosch, C.** (2007). You've gotta know when to fold 'em. *Psychological Science, 18,* 773–777.

12. **Clark, R., Anderson, N. B., Clark, V. R., & Williams, D. R.** (1999). Racism as a stressor for African Americans: A biopsychosocial model. *American Psychologist, 54,* 805–816.

13. **Mays, V. M., Cochran, S. D., & Barnes, N. W.** (2007). Race, race-based discrimination, and health outcomes among African Americans. *Annual Review of Psychology, 58,* 201–225.

14. **Holden, N., Cooper, C., & Carr, J.** (1998). *Dealing with the new Russia: Management cultures in collision.* Chichester, United Kingdom: Wiley.

15. **Maslach, C.** (1982). *Burnout: The cost of caring.* Englewood Cliffs, NJ: Prentice Hall.

16. **Dohrenwend, B., Pearlin, L., Clayton, P., Hamburg, B., Dohrenwend, B. P., Riley, M., & Rose, R.** (1982). Report on stress and life events. In G. R. Elliott & C. Eisdorfer (Eds.), *Stress and human health: Analysis and implications of research: A study by the Institute of Medicine/National Academy of Sciences.* New York, NY: Springer.

17. **Strully, K. W.** (2009). Job loss and health in the U.S. labor market. *Demography, 46,* 221–246.

18. **Kaprio, J., Koskenvuo, M., & Rita, H.** (1987). Mortality after bereavement: A prospective study of 95,647 widowed persons. *American Journal of Public Health, 77,* 283–287.

19. **Wahlberg, D.** (2001, October). We're more depressed, patriotic, poll finds. *Grand Rapids Press,* p. A15.

20. **Centers for Disease Control and Prevention.** (2006). Mortality associated with Hurricane Katrina— Florida and Alabama, August–October 2005. *Morbidity and Mortality Weekly Report, 55*(09), 239– 242. Retrieved from http://www.cdc.gov/mmwr/preview/mmwrhtml/mm5509a5.htm

21. **Saulny, S.** (2006, June 21). A legacy of the storm: Depression and suicide. *New York Times.* Retrieved from http://www.nytimes.com

22. **Muller, J. E., & Verrier, R. L.** (1996). Triggering of sudden death—Lessons from an earthquake. *New England Journal of Medicine, 334,* 460–461.

23. **Rubonis, A. V., & Bickman, L.** (1991). Psychological impairment in the wake of disaster: The disaster–psychopathology relationship. *Psychological Bulletin, 109,* 384–399.

24. **Overmier, J. B., & Murison, R.** (1997). Animal models reveal the "psych" in the psychosomatics of peptic ulcers. *Current Directions in Psychological Science, 6,* 180–184.

25. **Rodin, J.** (1986). Aging and health: Effects of the sense of control. *Science, 223,* 1271–1276.

26. **Weiss, J. M.** (1977). Psychological and behavioral influences on gastrointestinal lesions in animal models. In J. D. Maser & M. E. P. Seligman (Eds.), *Psychopathology: Experimental models* (pp. 232–269). San Francisco, CA: Freeman.

27. **Segerstrom, S. C., Taylor, S. E., Kemeny, M. E., & Fahey, J. L.** (1998). Optimism is associated with mood, coping, and immune change in response to stress. *Journal of Personality and Social Psychology, 74,* 1646–1655.

28. **Seligman, M. E. P.** (1991). *Learned optimism.* New York, NY: Knopf.

29. **Everson, S. A., Goldberg, D. E., Kaplan, G. A., Cohen, R. D., Pukkala, E., Tuomilehto, J., & Salonen, J. T.** (1996). Hopelessness and risk of mortality and incidence of myocardial infarction and cancer. *Psychosomatic Medicine, 58,* 113–121.

30. **Kiecolt-Glaser, J. K., Page, G. G., Marucha, P. T., MacCallum, R. C., & Glaser, R.** (1998). Psychological influences on surgical recovery: Perspectives from psychoneuroimmunology. *American Psychologist, 53,* 1209–1218.

31. **Cohen, S., Tyrrell, D. A. J., & Smith, A. P.** (1991). Psychological stress and susceptibility to the common cold. *New England Journal of Medicine, 325,* 606–612.

32. **Cohen, S., Doyle, W. J., Turner, R., Alper, C. M., & Skoner, D. P.** (2003). Sociability and susceptibility to the common cold. *Psychological Science, 14,* 389–395.

33. **Cohen, S., Alper, C. M., Doyle, W. J., Treanor, J. J., & Turner, R. B.** (2006). Positive emotional style predicts resistance to illness after experimental exposure to rhinovirus or influenza A virus. *Psychosomatic Medicine, 68,* 809–815.

34. **Edelman, S., & Kidman, A. D.** (1997). Mind and cancer: Is there a relationship? A review of the evidence. *Australian Psychologist, 32,* 1–7.

35. **Fox, B. H.** (1998). Psychosocial factors in cancer incidence and prognosis. In J. C. Holland (Ed.), *Psychooncology* (pp. 110–124). New York, NY: Oxford University Press.

36. **Courtney, J. G., Longnecker, M. P., Theorell, T., & de Verdier, M. G.** (1993). Stressful life events and the risk of colorectal cancer. *Epidemiology, 4,* 407–414.

37. **McKenna, M. C., Zevon, M. A., Corn, B., & Rounds, J.** (1999). Psychosocial factors and the development of breast cancer: A meta-analysis. *Health Psychology, 18,* 520–531.

38. **O'Leary, A.** (1990). Stress, emotion, and human immune function. *Psychological Bulletin, 108,* 363–382.

39. **Temoshok, L.** (1992). *The Type C connection: The behavioral links to cancer and your health.* New York, NY: Random House.

40. **Antoni, M. H., & Lutgendorf, S.** (2007). Psychosocial factors and disease progression in cancer. *Current Directions in Psychological Science, 16,* 42–46.

41. **Friedman, M., & Ulmer, D.** (1984). *Treating Type A behavior— and your heart.* New York, NY: Knopf.

42. **Miller, T. Q., Smith, T. W., Turner, C. W., Guijarro, M. L., & Hallet, A. J.** (1996). A meta-analytic review of research on hostility and physical health. *Psychological Bulletin, 119,* 322–348.

43. **Williams, R.** (1993). *Anger kills.* New York, NY: Times Books.

44. **Smith, T. W., & Ruiz, J. M.** (2002). Psychosocial influences on the development and course of coronary heart disease: Current status and implications for research and practice. *Journal of Consulting and Clinical Psychology, 70,* 548–568.

45. **Kupper, N., & Denollet, J.** (2007). Type D personality as a prognostic factor in heart disease: Assessment and mediating mechanisms. *Journal of Personality Assessment, 89,* 265–276.

46. **Wulsin, L. R., Vaillant, G. E., & Wells, V. E.** (1999). A systematic review of the mortality of depression. *Psychosomatic Medicine, 61,* 6–17.

47. **Williams, R.** (1989). *The trusting heart: Great news about Type A behavior.* New York, NY: Random House.

48. **Geen, R. G., & Quanty, M. B.** (1977). The catharsis of aggression: An evaluation of a hypothesis. In L. Berkowitz (Ed.), *Advances in experimental social psychology* (Vol. 10, pp. 1–37). New York, NY: Academic Press.

49. **Hokanson, J. E., & Edelman, R.** (1966). Effects of three social responses on vascular processes. *Journal of Personality and Social Psychology, 3,* 442–447.

50. **Fredrickson, B. L.** (2009). *Positivity: Groundbreaking research reveals how to embrace the hidden strength of positive emotions, overcome negativity, and thrive.* New York, NY: Crown.

51. **Baumeister, R. F., Stillwell, A., & Wotman, S. R.** (1990). Victim and perpetrator accounts of interpersonal conflict: Autobiographical narratives about anger. *Journal of Personality and Social Psychology, 59,* 994–1005.

52. **Spielberger, C., & London, P.** (1982). Rage boomerangs. *American Health, 1,* 52–56.

Module 37

1. **Seligman, M. E. P.** (1995). The effectiveness of psychotherapy: The *Consumer Reports* study. *American Psychologist, 50,* 945–974.

2. **Seligman, M. E. P.** (1994). *What you can change and what you can't.* New York, NY: Knopf.

3. **Obama, M.** (2010, August 2). A food bill we need. *Washington Post.* Retrieved from http://www.washingtonpost.com/wp-dyn/content/article/2010/08/01/AR2010080103291.html

4. **McMurray, C.** (2004, January 13). U.S., Canada, Britain: Who's getting in shape? *Gallup Poll Tuesday Briefing*. Retrieved from http://www.gallup.com

5. **Stathopoulou, G., Powers, M. B., Berry, A. C., Smiths, J. A. J., & Otto, M. W.** (2006). Exercise interventions for mental health: A quantitative and qualitative review. *Clinical Psychology: Science and Practice, 13*, 179–193.

6. **McCann, I. L., & Holmes, D. S.** (1984). Influence of aerobic exercise on depression. *Journal of Personality and Social Psychology, 46*, 1142–1147.

7. **Stephens, T.** (1988). Physical activity and mental health in the United States and Canada: Evidence from four population surveys. *Preventive Medicine, 17*, 35–47.

8. **Ford, E. S.** (2002). Does exercise reduce inflammation? Physical activity and C-reactive protein among U.S. adults. *Epidemiology, 13*, 561–569.

9. **Thayer, R. E.** (1987). Energy, tiredness, and tension effects of a sugar snack versus moderate exercise. *Journal of Personality and Social Psychology, 52*, 119–125.

10. **Thayer, R. E.** (1993). Mood and behavior (smoking and sugar snacking) following moderate exercise: A partial test of self-regulation theory. *Personality and Individual Differences, 14*, 97–104.

11. **Jacobs, B. L.** (1994). Serotonin, motor activity, and depression-related disorders. *American Scientist, 82*, 456–463.

12. **Hunsberger, J. G., Newton, S. S., Bennett, A. H., Duman, C. H., Russell, D. S., Salton, S. R., & Duman, R. S.** (2007). Antidepressant actions of the exercise-regulated gene VGF. *Nature Medicine, 13*, 1476–1482

13. **Etnier, J. L., Salazar, W., Landers, D. M., Petruzzello, S. J., Han, M., & Nowell, P.** (1997). The influence of physical fitness and exercise upon cognitive functioning: A meta-analysis. *Journal of Sport and Exercise Psychology, 19*, 249–277.

14. **Perkins, K. A., Dubbert, P. M., Martin, J. E., Faulstich, M. E., & Harris, J. K.** (1986). Cardiovascular reactivity to psychological stress in aerobically trained versus untrained mild hypertensives and normotensives. *Health Psychology, 5*, 407–421.

15. **Powell, K. E., Thompson, P. D., Caspersen, C. J., & Kendrick, J. S.** (1987). Physical activity and the incidence of coronary heart disease. *Annual Review of Public Health, 8*, 253–287.

16. **Paffenbarger, R. S., Jr., Hyde, R. T., Wing, A. L., & Hsieh, C. C.** (1986). Physical activity, all-cause mortality, and longevity of college alumni. *New England Journal of Medicine, 314*, 605–612.

17. **Kramer, A. F., & Erickson, K. I.** (2007). Capitalizing on cortical plasticity: Influence of physical activity on cognition and brain function. *Trends in Cognitive Sciences, 11*, 342–348.

18. **Ratey, J., & Hagerman, E.** (2008). *Spark: The revolutionary new science of exercise and the brain.* New York, NY: Little, Brown.

19. **Salvas, M.-J.** (2008, June 24). Top ten stimuli to exercise your body. Retrieved from http://positivepsychologynews.com/ news/marie-josee-salvas/20080624811

20. **Lyubomirsky, S.** (2008). *The how of happiness: A scientific approach to getting the life you want.* New York, NY: Penguin Books.

21. **Schwartz, B.** (2004). *The paradox of choice: Why more is less.* New York, NY: Ecco.

22. **Warr, P., & Payne, R.** (1982). Experiences of strain and pleasure among British adults. *Social Science and Medicine, 16*, 1691–1697.

23. **Cohen, S.** (1988). Psychosocial models of the role of social support in the etiology of physical disease. *Health Psychology, 7*, 269–297.

24. **Case, R. B., Moss, A. J., Case, N., McDermott, M., & Eberly, S.** (1992). Living alone after myocardial infarction: Impact on prognosis. *Journal of the American Medical Association, 267*, 515–519.

25. **Schwartz, J. E., Friedman, H. S., Tucker, J. S., Tomlinson-Keasey, C., Wingard, D. L., & Criqui, M. H.** (1995). Sociodemographic and psychosocial factors in childhood as predictors of adult mortality. *American Journal of Public Health, 85*, 1237–1245.

26. **Kaplan, R. M., & Kronick, R. G.** (2006). Marital status and longevity in the United States population. *Journal of Epidemiology and Community Health, 60*, 760–765.

27. **De Vogli, R., Chandola, T., & Marmot, M. G.** (2007). Negative aspects of close relationships and heart disease. *Archives of Internal Medicine, 167*, 1951–1957.

28. **Nielsen, K. M., Faergeman, O., Larsen, M. L., & Fold-spang, A.** (2006). Danish singles have a twofold risk of acute coronary syndrome: Data from a cohort of 128,290 persons. *Journal of Epidemiology and Community Health, 60*, 721–728.

29. **Cohen, S.** (2004). Social relationships and health. *American Psychologist, 59*, 676–684.

30. **Cohen, S., Doyle, W. J., Skoner, D. P., Rabin, B. S., & Gwaltney, J. M., Jr.** (1997). Social ties and susceptibility to the common cold. *Journal of the American Medical Association, 277*, 1940–1944.

31. **Graham, J. E., Christian, L. M., & Kiecolt-Glaser, J. K.** (2006). Marriage, health, and immune function. In S. R. H. Beach, M. Z. Wamboldt, N. J. Kaslow, R. E. Heyman, M. B. First, L. G. Underwood, & D. Reiss (Eds.), *Relational processes and DSM-V: Neuroscience, assessment, prevention, and treatment* (pp. 75–94). Washington, DC: American Psychiatric Association.

32. **Matthews, D. A., & Larson, D. B.** (1997). *The faith factor: An annotated bibliography of clinical research on spiritual subjects* (Vols. 1–4). Rockville, MD: National Institute for Healthcare Research and Georgetown University Press.

33. **McCullough, M. E., & Laurenceau, J. P.** (2005). Religiousness and the trajectory of self-rated health across adulthood. *Personality and Social Psychology Bulletin, 31*, 560–573.

34. **Hummer, R. A., Rogers, R. G., Nam, C. B., & Ellison, C. G.** (1999). Religious involvement and U.S. adult mortality. *Demography, 36*, 273–285.

35. **Park, C. L.** (2007). Religiousness/spirituality and health: A meaning systems perspective. *Journal of Behavioral Medicine, 30*, 319–328.

36. **Ai, A. L., Park, C. L., Huang, B., Rodgers, W., & Tice, T. N.** (2007). Psychosocial mediation of religious coping styles: A study of short-term psychological distress following cardiac surgery. *Personality and Social Psychology Bulletin, 33*, 867–882.

37. **Koenig, H. G., Cohen, H. J., George, L. K., Hays, J. C., Larson, D. B., & Blazer, D. G.** (1997). Attendance at religious services, interleukin-6, and other biological indicators of immune function in older adults. *International Journal of Psychiatry in Medicine, 23*, 233–250.

38. **Koenig, H. G., & Larson, D. B.** (1998). Use of hospital services, religious attendance, and religious affiliation. *Southern Medical Journal, 91*, 925–932.

39. **Koenig, H. G.** (2002, October 9). Personal communication from the director of the Center for the Study of Religion/Spirituality and Health, Duke University.

40. **Puchalski, C.** (2005, March 12). Personal correspondence from the director, George Washington Institute for Spirituality and Health.

41. **Diener, E.** (2002). Personal correspondence.

42. **Cohn, M. A., Fredrickson, B. L., Brown, S. L., Mikels, J. A., & Conway, A. M.** (2009). Happiness unpacked: Positive emotions increase life satisfaction by building resilience. *Emotion, 9*, 361–368.

43. **Fineburg, A.** (2000, October). *Positive psychology: A unit plan to teach positive psychology.* Paper presented at the second annual Positive Psychology Summit, Washington, DC.

44. **Csikszentmihalyi, M.** (1990). *Flow: The psychology of optimal experience.* New York, NY: Harper & Row.

45. **Diener, E.** (2000, January). Paper presented at Akumal II Conference, Akumal, Mexico.

46. **Diener, E., & Tov, W.** (2007). Subjective well-being and peace. *Journal of Social Issues, 63*, 421–440.

47. **Isen, A. M., & Means, B.** (1983). The influence of positive affect on decision-making strategy. *Social Cognition, 2*, 28–31.

48. **Forgas, J. P.** (1998). On feeling good and getting your way: Mood effects on negotiator cognition and bargaining strategies. *Journal of Personality and Social Psychology, 74*, 565–577.

49. **Diener, E., & Biswas-Diener, R.** (2008). *Happiness: Unlocking the mysteries of psychological wealth.* Malden, MA: Wiley-Blackwell.

50. **Snyder, C. R.** (1994). *The psychology of hope.* New York, NY: Free Press.

51. **Snyder, C. R., & Lopez, S. J.** (2007). *Positive psychology: The scientific and practical explorations of human strengths.* Thousand Oaks, CA: Sage.

52. **Sapolsky, R.** (2005). The influence of social hierarchy on primate health. *Science, 308*, 648–652.

53. **Seligman, M. E. P.** (1991). *Learned optimism.* New York, NY: Knopf.

54. **Seligman, M. E. P.** (1994). *What you can change and what you can't.* New York, NY: Knopf.

55. **Seligman, M. E. P.** (1995). The effectiveness of psychotherapy: The *Consumer Reports* study. *American Psychologist, 50*, 945–974.

56. **Reivich, K. J., Seligman, M. E. P., & McBride, S.** (2011). Master resilience training in the U.S. Army. *American Psychologist, 66*, 25–34.

57. **Seligman, M. E. P.** (1998, January). Building human strength: Psychology's forgotten mission. *APA Monitor.* Retrieved from http://www.apa.org

58. **Fineburg, A.** (2000, October). *Positive psychology: A unit plan to teach positive psychology.* Paper presented at the second annual Positive Psychology Summit, Washington, DC.

59. **World Health Organization** (2005). *Comprehensive report on smoking: Summary report.* Geneva, Switzerland: Author. Retrieved from http://www.who.int/en/

60. **World Health Organization** (2008e). *WHO report on the global tobacco epidemic, 2008.* Geneva, Switzerland: Author. Retrieved from http://www.who.int/en/

61. **Cin, S. D., Gibson, B., Zanna, M. P., Shumate, R., & Fong, G. T.** (2007). Smoking in movies, implicit associations of smoking with the self, and intentions to smoke. *Psychological Science, 18*, 559–563.

62. **Chassin, L., Presson, C. C., Sherman, S. J., & McGrew, J.** (1987). The changing smoking environment for middle and high school students: 1980–1983. *Journal of Behavioral Medicine, 10*, 581–593.

63. **Schulenberg, J., Bachman, J. G., O'Malley, P. M., & Johnston, L. D.** (1994, March). High school educational success and subsequent substance use: A panel analysis following adolescents into young adulthood. *Journal of Health and Social Behavior, 35*(1), 45–62.

64. **Moss, A. J., Allen, K. F., Giovino, G. A., & Mills, S. L.** (1992, December 2). Recent trends in adolescent smoking, smoking-update correlates, and expectation about the future. *Advance Data From Vital and Health Statistics* (No. 221). Hyattsville, MD: National Center for Health Statistics, Centers for Disease Control and

Prevention, U.S. Department of Health and Human Services.

65. **Doherty, E. W., & Doherty, W. J.** (1998). Smoke gets in your eyes: Cigarette smoking and divorce in a national sample of American adults. *Families, Systems, and Health, 16,* 393–400.

66. **Vita, A. J., Terry, R. B., Hubert, H. B., & Fries, J. F.** (1998). Aging, health risks, and cumulative disability. *New England Journal of Medicine, 338,* 1035–1041.

67. **Discover.** (1996, May). A fistful of risks, pp. 82–83.

68. **National Institute on Alcohol Abuse and Alcoholism** (1998, January). *Alcohol alerts: Alcohol and tobacco.* Rockville, MD: Author.

69. **National Center for Health Statistics** (1992, May). *Health, United States, 1991* (Publication No. PHS 92-1232). Hyattsville, MD: Department of Health and Human Services, Table 27.

70. **World Health Organization** (2005). *Comprehensive report on smoking: Summary report.* Geneva, Switzerland: Author. Retrieved from http://www.who.int/en/

71. **Heishman, S. J., Kozlowski, L. T., & Henningfield, J. E.** (1997). Nicotine addiction: Implications for public health policy. *Journal of Social Issues, 53,* 13–33.

72. **DiFranza, J. R.** (2008, May). Hooked from the first cigarette. *Scientific American,* pp. 82–87.

73. **Wetter, D. W., Fiore, M. C., Gritz, E. R., Lando, H. A., Stitzer, M. L., Hasselblad, V., & Baker, T. B.** (1998). Smoking cessation clinical practice guideline: Findings and implications for psychologists (The Agency for Health Care Policy and Research). *American Psychologist, 53,* 657–669.

74. **Bock, B. C., Marcus, B. H., King, T. E., Borrelli, B., & Roberts, M. R.** (1999). Exercise effects on withdrawal and mood among women attempting smoking cessation. *Addictive Behavior, 24,* 399–410.

75. **Centers for Disease Control and Prevention** (2007, November). *Obesity among adults in the United States—No change since 2003– 2004* (NCHS Data Brief). Retrieved from http://www.cdc.gov/nchs/data/databriefs/db01.pdf

76. **Yach, D., Struckler, D., & Brownell, K. D.** (2006). Epidemiologic and economic consequences of the global epidemics of obesity and diabetes. *Nature Medicine, 12,* 62–66.

77. **National Institutes of Health** (1998). Executive summary. *Clinical guidelines on the identification, evaluation, and treatment of overweight and obesity in adults* (NIH Publication No. 98-4083). Bethesda, MD: Obesity Evaluation Initiative, National Heart, Lung, and Blood Institute.

78. **Crandall, C. S.** (1994). Prejudice against fat people: Ideology and self-interest. *Journal of Personality and Social Psychology, 66,* 882–894.

79. **Ryckman, R. M., Robbins, M. A., Kaczor, L. M., & Gold, J. A.** (1989). Male and female raters' stereotyping of male and female physiques. *Personality and Social Psychology Bulletin, 15,* 244–251.

80. **Pingitore, R., Dugoni, B. L., Tindale, R. S., & Spring, B.** (1994). Bias against overweight job applicants in a simulated employment interview. *Journal of Applied Psychology, 79,* 909–917.

81. **Roehling, M. V.** (2000). Weight-based discrimination in employment: Psychological and legal aspects. *Personnel Psychology 52*(4), 969–1016.

82. **Roehling, M. V., Roehling, P. V., & Pichler, S.** (2007). The relationship between body weight and perceived weight-related employment discrimination: The role of sex and race. *Journal of Vocational Behavior, 71,* 300–318.

83. **Furnham, A., & Baguma, P.** (1994). Cross-cultural differences in the evaluation of male and female body shapes. *International Journal of Eating Disorders, 15,* 81–89.

84. **Gibbs, W. W.** (2005, June). Obesity: An overblown epidemic? *Scientific American,* pp. 70–77.

85. **Peeters, A., Barendregt, J. J., Willekens, F., Mackenbach, J. P., & Mamum, A. A.** (2003). Obesity in adulthood and its consequences for life expectancy: A life-table analysis. *Annals of Internal Medicine, 138,* 24–32.

86. **Sjostrom, L.** (1980). Fat cells and body weight. In A. J. Stunkard (Ed.), *Obesity* (pp. 72–100). Philadelphia, PA: Saunders.

87. **Spalding, K. L., Arner, E., Westermark, P. O., Bernard, S., Buchholz, B. A., Bergmann, O., . . . & Arner, P.** (2008). Dynamics of fat cell turnover in humans. *Nature, 453,* 783–787.

88. **Ernsberger, P., & Koletsky, R. J.** (1999). Biomedical rationale for a wellness approach to obesity: An alternative to a focus on weight loss. *Journal of Social Issues, 55,* 221–260.

Appendix A

1. **U.S. National Center for Education Statistics.** (2016). Table 261. Bachelor's degrees conferred by degree-granting institutions, by discipline division: Selected years, 1970–71 through 2005–06. *Digest of Education Statistics* (NCES 2008-022). Retrieved from https://nces.ed.gov/fastfacts/display.asp?id=37

2. **Gogan, C.** (2005). Multitasking— Are you at risk? *Canadian Union of Public Employees (CUPW) Newsletter.* Retrieved from http://www.cupe2950.ca/newsletter/2005/November2005.pdf

Name Index

Subject Index